Business Law: Text and Cases / *Second Edition*

Business Law
Text and Cases/Second Edition

Rate A. Howell
The Ohio State University

John R. Allison
University of Texas, Austin

N. T. Henley
Georgia State University

The Dryden Press
Hinsdale, Illinois

Acquisitions Editor: Feeny Lipscomb
Developmental Editor: Anne Boynton-Trigg
Project Editor: Bernice Gordon
Art Director: William Seabright
Production Manager: Peter Coveney

Text and cover design by Harry Voigt
Copy editing by Laurette Hupman

Copyright © 1981 by the Dryden Press
A division of Holt, Rinehart and Winston, Publishers
All rights reserved
Library of Congress Catalog Card Number: 80-65801
ISBN: 0-03-058111-7
Printed in the United States of America
 23-032-9876543

To our wives,
Carolyn, Diana, and Margo,
and to our children.

Preface

Business Law: Text and Cases was first published in January 1978, and within two years had become one of the leading texts in its field. This edition, therefore, retains the basic format and approach of its predecessor.

Several significant changes, nonetheless, have been made. First, chapters have been added covering the areas of wills, trusts and estates; consumer protection; and environmental protection. Second, many recent cases have been substituted for older ones in all areas—especially so in Part I, Legal Environment, and Part II, Contracts. (All cases from the first edition, however, that are models of clarity and of especially high reader-interest have been retained.)

Additionally, in response to users' suggestions, a greatly increased number of questions and problems at the end of each chapter are now based on actual court cases. This provides the instructor with a considerably greater resource for class-discussion questions (and, of course, the Instructors Manual furnishes him or her with the relevant points of the court's decision in each case.)

Lastly, the updating of text material in certain areas—and its expansion in others—merits special mention. The chapter on bankruptcy, for example, has been completely rewritten to reflect the changes brought about by enactment of The Bankruptcy Reform Act of 1978, and the chapters on constitutional law and torts have been particularly broadened. By contrast, a number of peripheral matters in the chapters on commercial paper and government regulation have been eliminated—again at the suggestion of users of the first edition.

Despite these changes, the primary strengths of the first edition have been completely retained. The authors continue to recognize the fact that both the environmental and traditional approaches to the subject of business law possess their separate and unique merits. Thus this edition continues to be traditional in the sense that the major portion is devoted to an in-depth treatment of such subjects as contracts, sales, and corporation law. At the same time, materials relating to the legal environment of business—such as the lawmaking processes, the roles and functions of the courts, and the subjects of constitutional law and torts—once again are more thoroughly covered in Part I than is true of most other texts.

The blending of the two approaches, environmental and legal, is retained in the more traditional areas of the text as well, with the continuing attempt to avoid the vice of "rule stating." In other words, rather than merely presenting one rule of law after another, the authors have expounded upon the reasons underlying the rules, and frequently provide illustrations of their applicability in the "real world."

The style of presentation of the actual cases from the appellate courts continues to eliminate three problems that often plague instructors when inadequately edited legal materials are placed in the hands of nonlaw students. First, the facts of each case are stated in the authors' own words, rather than in the often confusing language of the court itself. Second, the editing of the court opinions is not overly severe. Matters relating to extraneous issues have, of course, been deleted, but sufficient portions of the courts' opinions are left intact to permit analysis of the legal reasoning that was employed. Third, arcane legal jargon, sometimes found in the decisions, has in most cases been deleted or parenthetically explained.

Acknowledgments

As is always true with a work such as this, the authors owe an immeasureable debt to many persons, without whose help it would never have seen the light of day.

In this regard, we should perhaps first mention the many students who have passed through our hands in the last few years. Their fresh outlook, successes—and even problems—have continued to provide a welcome source of motivation.

We also thank our colleagues at other schools who have submitted wide-ranging suggestions, based on their experience with the first edition. And we similarly appreciate the comments of our reviewers:

C. George Alvey	Alvin A. Kabot
County College of Morris	*Hunter College*
Robert Bean	Michael A. Mass
De Anza College	*American University*
N. Jay Brantley	Charles E. Moran
Indiana State University	*West Valley College*
Gene T. Chambers	John Rogers
Florida Technological University	*San Jose State University*
Myron L. Erickson	William V. Schuster
University of Missouri	*Sacramento, California*
Susan Grady	Raymond A. Catanzano
University of Massachusetts, Amherst	*Nassau Community College*

We are also grateful, once again, to the National Conference of Commissioners on Uniform State Laws and the American Law Institute for their permission to publish the Uniform Commercial Code and the Uniform Partnership Act.

Lastly, Professor Howell extends special thanks to Mrs. Gay Crumpler, circulation librarian of The Ohio State University Law Library, who has continued to provide research help with her customary enthusiasm. Professor Allison expresses appreciation to his wife, Margo, for her constant assistance, support, and understanding, and to his colleagues at the University of Texas for freely sharing their ideas, expertise, and words of encouragement.

January, 1981

Rate A. Howell
Columbus, Ohio

John R. Allison
Austin, Texas

N. T. Henley
Atlanta, Georgia

Contents

Part II / Principles of Contract Law

Part III / Commercial Transactions

Part IV / Agency

Part V / Business Organizations

Part VII / Secured Transactions and Bankruptcy

Part VIII / Introduction to Government Regulation

Part I

The Legal Environment of Business

The general mass, if they consider the law at all, regard it as they regard some monster in the zoo. It is odd, it is extraordinary; but there it is, they have known it all their lives, they suppose that there must be some good reason for it, and accept it as inevitable and natural.
A. P. Herbert, *Uncommon Law*, 1936*

Nature and Sources of Law

1

While the law is not nearly as odd or extraordinary as many persons believe, it is undeniably "there"—an integral part of the environment that has been a source of great interest, even fascination, for centuries.

Considering the pervasiveness of the law, this is hardly surprising. Almost all human activity is affected by it in one manner or another, and this alone is adequate explanation for such widespread interest. Certainly, anyone contemplating a business transaction of any magnitude today realizes that he or she must consider not only the physical and financial effort it will entail but—to some extent, at least—the legal ramifications as well. And beyond the practical effect law has on individual conduct in specific situations, it possesses additional characteristics that make its study uniquely rewarding.

First, while the law is by no means an occult language understood only by lawyers, it clearly is a subject that is *academically stimulating*. For students to get any real benefit from a course in law, they must at the very least learn to recognize

---

*Reprinted by permission of Lady Herbert.

precise legal issues, understand the reasoning of the courts as set forth in their decisions, and subject this reasoning to critical analysis. These activities involve varying degrees of mental exercise; and while this is not always pleasurable, it fosters a degree of mental discipline that is not easily acquired elsewhere.

Second, students should have the opportunity to consider the law as a *societal institution*—to see how it has affected conduct and thought and how it has been influenced by them. Whatever the law is, it certainly is not static, and it certainly does not exist in a vacuum.

This approach, which emphasizes the impact of social and economic changes on the law, gives the subject a liberal arts flavor. When viewed in this light, the law and its processes become rewarding to anyone having even a passing interest in economics, sociology, and political science.

A Glimpse of Things to Come

There is always some disagreement as to the proper objectives of introductory business law courses. It is not surprising that teachers, lawyers, and businessmen, for example, hold varying views about which aspects of the law will provide the most lasting benefits to students. Upon closer examination, however, most of these differences are minor, relating only to which topics should receive the most emphasis. There is general agreement as to the substantive matters that ought to be presented, in both the environmental and traditional arenas.[1]

Certain environmental matters—such as the workings of the judicial processes, the nature of statutory and common law, and the sweeping subject of constitutional law—are so basic to an understanding of our legal system as to require extended treatment. Accordingly, in Part I, separate chapters are devoted to each of these topics and to others of comparable significance. Before proceeding to these matters, however, the remainder of this chapter will deal with more preliminary aspects of the law—including its nature, sources, purposes, and classifications.

What Is Law?

Ever since the law began to take form, scholars have spent impressive amounts of time and thought analyzing its purposes and defining what it is and what it ought to be—in short, fitting it into a philosophical scheme of one form or another. While space does not permit inclusion of even the major essays in which these philosophers defend their respective views, their conclusions provide us with useful observations about the nature of law. Consider, for example, the following:

> We have been told by Plato that law is a form of social control, an instrument of the good life, the way to the discovery of reality, the true reality of the social structure; by Aristotle that it is a rule of conduct, a contract, an

---

[1]The reader should refer to the preface for a fuller description of the environmental approach alluded to here.

ideal of reason, a rule of decision, a form of order; by Cicero that it is the agreement of reason and nature, the distinction between the just and the unjust, a command or prohibition; by Aquinas that it is an ordinance of reason for the common good, made by him who has care of the community, and promulgated [thereby]; by Bacon that certainty is the prime necessity of law; by Hobbes that law is the command of the sovereign; by Spinoza that it is a plan of life; by Leibniz that its character is determined by the structure of society; by Locke that it is a norm established by the commonwealth; by Hume that it is a body of precepts; by Kant that it is a harmonizing of wills by means of universal rules in the interests of freedom; by Fichte that it is a relation between human beings; by Hegel that it is an unfolding or realizing of the idea of right.[2]

While these early writers substantially agree as to the general *purpose* of law—the insuring of an orderliness to all human activity—their *definitions* of the term vary considerably. Today there is still no definition of *law* that has universal approval, even in legal circles—a fact that is no doubt attributable to its inherent breadth.[3]

Two Current Views

At the risk of oversimplification, it can be said that two major approaches to the law exist today. The *traditional approach* views the law as consisting of the rules that are in effect within a state or nation at a given time. This is very likely what practicing attorneys have in mind when they speak about the law, and it is a perfectly respectable view. Witness the following definition adopted by the American Law Institute: "[Law] is the body of principles, standards and rules which the courts . . . apply in the decision of controversies brought before them."[4]

The *environmental approach* sees the law in a broader light: the *processes by which the rules and principles are formulated* (rather than the rules and principles themselves) comprise the major element of law. Because law is necessitated solely by human activity, environmentalists contend that the ever-changing problems resulting from this activity and *the ways in which the law attempts to solve them* must receive primary emphasis if one is to gain a proper insight into the subject.

The following definition expresses this view: "*Law is a dynamic process, a system of regularized, institutionalized procedures for the orderly decision of social*

---

[2]Huntington Cairns, *Legal Philosophy from Plato to Hegel* (Baltimore: Johns Hopkins University Press, 1949).

[3]Consider, for example, just these few widely varying matters with which the law must deal: (1) the standards of care required of a surgeon in the operating room, (2) the determination of whether an "exclusive-dealing" provision in a motion picture distributor's contracts constitutes an unfair method of competition under federal law, and (3) the propriety of witnesses' testimony when it is challenged as constituting "hearsay" under the rules of evidence.

[4]*Restatement, Conflict of Laws 2d, § 4.* American Law Institute Publishers. Copyright 1971. Reprinted with the permission of The American Law Institute.

questions, including the settlement of disputes."[5] Since Part I of this text is concerned primarily with the environmental aspects of law, we shall adopt that definition for our purposes.

Law and Order

Implicit in Plato's observation that law is "a form of social control" is the possibility that there may be other forms—as, indeed, there are.[6] In any society, there is an ordering of things. If priorities between competing groups or individuals are not established by law, history demonstrates that they will be established by bare political or economic power—or, in extreme situations, by sheer physical force. When force is involved, it may derive from a central authority (as was true in Nazi Germany in the 1930s) or from group or individual action. An example of group action occurred in this country in the late 1800s around Virginia City, Montana Territory. Because of the remoteness of the area, federal authorities were powerless to enforce U.S. statutes, and widespread lawlessness ensued. Finally, vigilante committees were formed, whose members summarily hung some of the more notorious—albeit colorful—outlaws in 1877. The principle of the rule of law, with its emphasis on broad considerations of fairness and the orderly settling of disputes, is generally felt to be so superior to the alternatives that today it is the concept upon which the governments of all civilized nations are based.

The Nature of Legal Rules

Legal rules come in all shapes and sizes. While it is easy to think of them as narrow orders and regulations, particularly when referring to particular cases, most rules are actually expressed in general principles. We shall therefore define *legal rules* as general standards of human conduct, established and enforced by government officials. In addition to emphasizing the broad aspect of the law, this definition makes it clear that the rules must derive from the state. Thus, although the rules or standards that result from religious beliefs or membership in social and professional organizations affect one's conduct in given situations, they still fall outside the definition of law.

Requisites of a Legal System

In order for a legal system to function properly, particularly within a democratic government such as ours, it must command the respect of the great majority of

---

[5]James L. Houghteling, Jr., *The Dynamics of Law* (New York: Harcourt Brace Jovanovich, 1963).

[6]The term *control* should be interpreted broadly here, to avoid laying undue emphasis upon the negative, or restrictive, aspect of law. To be sure, every legal system does contain criminal statutes that absolutely prohibit certain kinds of activity, as well as other rules that impose duties upon individuals in particular situations. But most of the rules and principles that comprise the Anglo-American system of law are devoted to the creation and preservation of rights and liberties of the individual.

people governed by it. In order to do so, the legal rules which comprise it must, as a practical matter, possess certain characteristics. They must be (1) relatively certain, (2) relatively flexible, (3) known or knowable, and (4) apparently reasonable.

In the following chapters we will consider these requirements more fully and determine the extent to which our legal system satisfies them. For the moment, we will give brief descriptions of each of the four.

Certainty

One essential element of a stable society is reasonable certainty about its laws, not only at a given moment but over long periods of time. Many of our activities, particularly business activities, are based on the assumption that legal principles will remain stable into the foreseeable future. If this were not so, chaos would result. For example, no television network would enter into a contract with a professional football league, under which it was to pay millions of dollars for the right to televise league games, if it were not reasonably sure that the law would compel the league to live up to its contractual obligations or to pay damages if it did not. No lawyer would advise a client on a contemplated course of action without similar assurances.

Because of these considerations, the courts (and to a lesser extent the legislatures) are generally reluctant to overturn principles that have been part of the law for any appreciable length of time.[7]

Flexibility

In any nation, particularly a highly industrialized one such as the United States, societal changes occur with accelerating (almost dismaying) rapidity. Each change presents new legal problems that must be resolved without undue delay. This necessity was recognized by Justice Cardozo when he wrote that "the law, like the traveler, must be ready for the morrow."[8]

Some problems are simply the result of scientific and technological advances. Prior to Orville and Wilbur Wright's day, for example, it was a well-established principle that landowners had unlimited rights to the airspace above their property, any invasion of which constituted a *trespass*—a wrongful entry. But when the courts became convinced that the flying machine was here to stay, the utter

---

[7]This is not to say, of course, that the law is static. In the area of products liability, for example, the liability of manufacturers for injuries caused by defective products is much more extensive than it was twenty-five years ago. But even this enlargement of liability, and of similar changes in other areas, resulted from a series of modifications of existing principles rather than from an abrupt reversal of them.

[8]Benjamin N. Cardozo, *The Growth of the Law* (New Haven: Yale University Press, 1924), pp. 19–20.

impracticality of this view became apparent and owners' rights were subsequently limited to a "reasonable use" of their airspace.

Other novel problems result from changing methods of doing business or from shifting attitudes and moral views. Recent examples of the former are the proliferating use of the business franchise and of the general credit card. Attitudinal changes involve such questions as the proper ends of government, the propriety of Sunday sales, and the circumstances in which abortions should be permitted.

Some of these problems, of course, require solutions that are more political than legal in nature. This is particularly true where large numbers of the citizenry are faced with a common problem, such as the inability of many elderly persons to pay for proper health care, and where the alleviation of the problem may well be thought to constitute a legitimate function of either the state or federal government. The passage by Congress of the so-called Medicare Act of 1964 is an example of an attempted solution at the federal level of this particular problem.

Regardless of political considerations, however, the fact remains that there are many problems (particularly those involving disputes between individuals) which can be settled only through the judicial processes—that is, by one of the parties instituting legal action against the other. The duty to arrive at a final solution in all such cases falls squarely upon the courts, no matter how novel or varied the issues.

Knowability

One of the basic assumptions underlying a democracy—and, in fact, almost every form of government—is that the great majority of its citizens are going to obey its laws voluntarily. It hardly need be said that obeyance requires a certain knowledge of the rules, or at least a reasonable means of acquiring this knowledge, on the part of the governed. No one, not even a lawyer, "knows" all the law or all the rules that comprise a single branch of law; that could never be required. But it is necessary for persons who need legal advice to have access to experts on the rules—lawyers. It is equally necessary that the law be in such form that lawyers can determine their clients' positions with reasonable certainty in order to recommend the most advantageous courses of action.

Reasonableness

Most citizens abide by the law. Many do so even when they are not in sympathy with a particular rule, out of a sense of responsibility, a feeling that it is their civic duty, like it or not; others, no doubt, do so simply through fear of getting caught if they don't. But by and large the rules have to appear reasonable to the great majority of the people if they are going to be obeyed for long. The so-called Prohibition Amendment, which met with such wholesale violation that it was repealed in 1933, is the classic example of a rule lacking widespread acceptance. Closely allied with the idea of reasonableness is the requirement that the rules reflect, and adapt to, changing views of morality and justice.

Law and Morals

Although the terms *law* and *morals* are not synonymous, legal standards and moral standards parallel one another more closely than many people believe. For example, criminal statutes prohibit certain kinds of conduct that are clearly "morally wrong" —murder, theft, arson, and the like. And other rules of law impose civil liability for similar kinds of conduct which, though not crimes, are also generally felt to be wrongful in nature—such as negligence, breach of contract, and fraud. To illustrate: S, in negotiating the sale of a race horse to B, tells B that the horse has run an eighth of a mile in fifteen seconds on several occasions within the past month. In fact, the animal has never been clocked under eighteen seconds, and S knows this. B, believing the statement to be true, purchases the horse. In such a case S's intentional misstatement constitutes the tort of *fraud,* and B—assuming he can prove these facts in a legal action brought against S—has the right to set aside the transaction, returning the horse and recovering the price he has paid.

Why, then, are the terms *law* and *morals* not precisely synonymous? First, there are some situations where moral standards *are* higher than those imposed by law. For example, a person who has promised to keep an offer open for a stated period of time generally has the legal right to withdraw the offer before the given time has elapsed (for reasons appearing in a later chapter). Yet many persons who make such offers feel morally compelled to keep their offers open as promised, even though the law does not require this. Second, many rules of law or court decisions are based upon statutory or practical requirements that have little or no relationship to moral considerations. For example, in the area of minors' contracts, we will see later that most courts feel, on balance, that it is sound public policy to permit minors to disaffirm (cancel) their contracts until they reach the age of majority, even though the contracts were otherwise perfectly valid and even though the persons with whom they dealt did not overreach or take advantage of them in any way.

Law and Justice

The relationship between law and justice is similar to that between law and morals. Most results of the application of legal rules are "just"—fair and reasonable. Where this is not so to any degree, the rules are usually changed. Yet it must be recognized that results occasionally "aren't fair." Without attempting to defend the law in all such instances, some cautions should nevertheless be voiced.

First, there is never complete agreement as to what is just; there are always some decisions that are just to some people but not to others. And even if there were unanimity of opinion—a perfect justice, so to speak—the fact-patterns presented by some cases are such that it is simply impossible to attain this end.[9]

---

[9]*Fact-pattern* refers to the proven acts of each party that have led up to a particular controversy, together with the circumstances surrounding such acts. Facts of a case are usually determined by the jury but occasionally by the court—the judge.

In some situations, for example, a legal controversy may arise between two honest persons who dealt with one another in good faith, as sometimes occurs in the area of "mutual mistake." Take this case: P contracts to sell land to G for $40,000, both parties mistakenly believing that a General Motors plant will be built on adjoining land. When G learns that the plant will not be built, he refuses to go through with the deal. If a court rules that the mistake frees G of his contractual obligations, the result might be quite unjust as far as P is concerned. And if it rules otherwise, the decision might seem quite unfair to G. Yet a decision must be made, one way or the other.

Second, in some instances it is fairly clear who is right and who is wrong, but the situation has progressed to the point where it is impossible, either physically or legally, to put the "good" person back into the original position. These "bad check" cases will illustrate: A buys a TV set from Z, giving Z her personal check in payment. If the check bounces, it is clear that Z should be allowed to recover the set. But what if the TV has been destroyed by fire while in A's hands? Here the most the law can do is give Z a *judgment* against A—an order requiring A to pay a sum of money to Z equal to the amount of the check, which A may or may not be financially able to do. Or suppose that A had resold the TV to X before Z learned that the check had bounced. Would it not be unfair to permit Z to retake the set from X, an innocent third party?

Because of these considerations, and others to be discussed later, the most the law can seek to accomplish is *substantial* justice in the greatest possible number of cases that come before it.

The Law— Processes and Products

As we have already indicated, one of the major objectives of Part I is the examination of the *processes by which law is created*. The major processes are (1) formulation of rules by the courts, (2) enactment of statutes by legislative bodies, and (3) interpretation of statutes by the courts. We will examine these processes in some depth in subsequent chapters. In the meantime, however, certain basic characteristics of each should be recognized.

Formulation of Rules

There are some areas of law where the creation of basic principles has been left essentially to the courts—the judges—as they settle individual cases coming before them. One of the best examples is in our contract law, where, over the years, the courts have decided such matters as what constitutes an offer, an acceptance, a substantial breach of contract, and the like. The product of this process—the rules resulting from it—is ordinarily called "common law." This type of law, and the unique manner in which it has adjusted to changing social and economic conditions, will be discussed further in Chapter 3.

Enactment of Statutes

There are other areas of law, however, where the legislative bodies—state legislatures or Congress—have prescribed the rules by the enactment of statutes. The corporation laws of each state and such federal laws as the Civil Rights Act of 1964 are examples of statutes. Law that is promulgated in this fashion is *statutory law;* and—unlike common law—is set forth in the state and federal codes. The processes by which statutory law is created will be examined in Chapter 4.

Interpretation

Once a statute is passed, a further process, that of *judicial interpretation,* is invariably required. While the meaning of the typical statute is clear in general, cases are always arising that involve novel or narrow situations which do, indeed, present arguable points as to what the legislature really intended by passing the act in question. Only when the courts settle such specific controversies does the precise legal meaning of a statute become known.

Take, for example, this situation. A state statute prohibits the building of any structure over 100 feet in length outside municipalities without approval of the county commissioners. A farmer erects a 150-foot turkey shed without such permission, and legal action is brought by the county, asking for its removal. Is the shed a "structure" within the statute, and thus subject to removal? Or did the legislature mean "building," which could conceivably lead to a different result? Some vexatious problems of this sort, and the processes by which the courts search for the slippery thing called "legislative intention," are treated in Chapter 4.

While the judicial processes are our primary concern, the products resulting from these processes—the rules themselves—cannot escape attention. At the outset, particularly, it is useful to recognize some of the more common classifications of law.

Some Classifications of Law

Subject-matter Classification

One way of classifying all the law in the United States is on the basis of the *subject matter* to which it relates. Fifteen or twenty branches or subjects are of particular importance, among them:

Administrative law	Evidence
Agency	Partnerships
Commercial paper	Personal property
Constitutional law	Real property
Contracts	Sales
Corporation law	Taxation
Criminal law	Torts
Domestic relations	Wills and estates

Two observations can be made about this classification.

1. The subjects of agency, contracts, and torts are essentially *common law in nature,* while the subjects of corporation law, criminal law, sales, and taxation are *governed by statute.* Most of the remaining subjects, particularly evidence and property, are mixed in nature.

2. Several of these subjects obviously have a much closer relationship to the world of business than the others; these are the topics that fall within the usual business law or legal environment courses of a business school curriculum. Agency, contracts, corporation law, and sales are typical examples.

Federal and State Law

Another way of categorizing all law in this country is on the basis of the governmental unit from which it arises. On this basis, all law may be said to be either *federal law* or *state law.* While there are some very important areas of federal law, as we shall see later, the great bulk of our law is state (or "local") law. Virtually all the subjects in the preceding list, for example, are within the jurisdiction of the individual states. Thus it is correct to say that there are fifty bodies of contract law in the United States, fifty bodies of corporation law, and so on. But this is not as bewildering as it appears, because the rules that comprise a given branch of law in each state substantially parallel those that exist in the other states—particularly in regard to common-law subjects.

Common and Statutory Law

The term *common law* has, unfortunately, several different meanings. Sometimes it is used to refer to the law that was formulated and applied by *courts of law* in England, as distinguished from the rules that were applied by the *equity courts* of that country. In this text, however, it refers to the rules and principles existing in any state *that result from judicial decisions* in those areas of law where the legislatures have not seen fit to enact legislation. This type of law, to be examined further in Chapter 3, is frequently referred to as judge-made law, unwritten law, or case law.

The term *statutory law,* by contrast, is generally used to refer to the state and federal *statutes* in effect at a given time—that is, rules which have been formally adopted by legislative bodies rather than by the courts. When *statutory law* is used in contrast to *common law,* it also embraces state and federal constitutions, municipal ordinances, and even treaties. Statutory law is frequently referred to as "written law," in the sense that once a statute or constitutional provision is adopted, its exact wording is set forth in the final text as passed—though the precise meaning, we should recall, is still subject to interpretation by the courts. (The subjects of statutory law and judicial interpretation are covered in Chapter 4.)[10]

Civil and Criminal Law

Civil Law: When we talk about the civil laws of this country, we are referring to the rules which spell out the rights and duties that exist *between individuals.* For example, if one person refuses to live up to the terms of a binding agreement, the other party, under the law of contracts, has the right to recover damages—a sum of money equivalent to the loss sustained as a result of the breach of contract. The vast majority of our law falls within the "civil rules" category, and we will thus devote most of our attention to it hereafter.

Criminal Law: Criminal law, on the other hand, is comprised of those statutes by which a state (or the federal government) prohibits specified kinds of activity, and which provide for the imposition of *fines or imprisonment* upon persons convicted of violating them. While any incursion into the vast area of the criminal law is outside the scope of this text, three observations are in order.

1. In enacting criminal statutes, a state is saying that there are certain activities so inherently inimical to the public good that they must be flatly prohibited. Such statutes, then, simply provide the very minimum standards of conduct to which all persons must adhere. There are other standards of conduct above this level which the law also requires in certain situations, but one who fails to meet these higher standards is normally liable only in a civil action to the person who suffers a loss as a consequence of this wrong. To illustrate: X acts in a negligent (careless) manner and injures Y while doing so. While Y is entitled to recover damages from X in a civil suit because of the wrong that has occurred, the wrong is not of such a nature that the state could bring a criminal action against X.[11]

2. In addition to the nature of the liability that is imposed, criminal suits also differ from civil suits in another significant respect. In a criminal action (which is always brought by the state) it is necessary that the state's case be proved "beyond a reasonable doubt," whereas in civil actions the plaintiff—the person bringing the suit—need prove his or her allegations only by "a preponderance of the evidence." Because the defendant—the accused—in almost every case is able to raise some doubts regarding questions of fact (for example, whether the defendant actually

---

[10]Today, with but one or two exceptions too narrow to worry about, all federal law is statutory; in other words, there is no general federal common law. State law, on the other hand, is comprised of both common and statutory rules of law, with the latter making up the lion's share.

[11]Some wrongful acts are of a dual nature, subjecting the wrongdoer to both criminal and civil penalties. For example, if X steals Y's car, the state could bring a criminal action against X, and Y could also bring a civil action to recover damages arising from the theft.

acted as the plaintiff alleges), the doubts produced by evidence in a criminal action will sometimes be sufficient to cause the jury to return a verdict for the defendant —while the same evidence in a civil suit might be sufficient to support a jury verdict in favor of the plaintiff.[12]

3. Except for the most serious crime of treason, crimes are either *felonies* or *misdemeanors,* depending upon the severity of the penalty which the statute prescribes. The definition of *felony* differs somewhat from state to state, but it is usually defined as any crime where the punishment is either death or imprisonment, as in the cases of murder, arson, or rape. *Misdemeanors* are all crimes carrying lesser penalties.

Public and Private Law

Some branches of law deal more directly with the relationship that exists between the government and the individual than do others. On the basis of the degree to which this relationship is involved, law is occasionally classified as public law or private law.

When an area of law is directly concerned with the government-individual relationship, it falls within the *public law* designation. Subjects that are most clearly of this nature are criminal law, constitutional law, and administrative law. Since *criminal laws* consist of acts that are prohibited by a government itself, the violation of which is a "wrong against the state," such laws more directly affect the government-individual relationship than do any of the other laws. To the extent that our federal Constitution contains provisions substantially guaranteeing that certain rights of the individual cannot be invaded by federal and state government activities, the subject of *constitutional law* falls within the same category. *Administrative law*—comprised of the principles that govern the procedures and activities of government boards and commissions—is of similar nature, in that such agencies are also concerned with the enforcement of certain state and federal statutes (and regulations promulgated thereunder) against individual citizens.

Other areas of law, which are primarily concerned with the creation and enforcement of rights of one individual versus another, fall within the *private law* category. While a state is indeed concerned that all its laws be properly enforced, even when individuals' rights alone are being adjudicated, the concern in these areas is distinctly secondary to the interests of the litigants themselves.

Legal Misconceptions

Before proceeding to the more substantive areas of law, we will reflect briefly on some widely held misconceptions about our legal system.

---

[12]This type of problem, particularly the role of the jury in civil suits, is examined in some detail in the next chapter.

The Myth of the One Right Answer

It is widely believed that in any given fact-pattern there is one "correct" legal answer to the problem it presents. This is true in a good many situations but certainly not as often as many persons believe. The chief reasons for divergent legal opinions are quite explainable.

1. Many rules are expressed in rather general terms so as to fit varying situations. Consequently, they afford the courts considerable latitude in deciding how they should be applied to specific situations.

2. The ultimate legal processes are in the hands of people, the judges, whose application of rules is always subject, to some extent, to their individual economic and political philosophies and personal moral beliefs. The law, therefore, is not an exact science and never will be.[13]

3. The nature of most legal problems is such that something can be said in behalf of both litigants. The ordinary controversy does not present a clear-cut case of a "good" person suing a "bad" one. In some cases, each party has acted in good faith; in others, each is guilty of some degree of wrong. Additionally, there are some "legal collision" situations, where one general principle of law may lead to one result while a second will lead to a different result. In such instances each principle will probably have to undergo some modification when applied to particular cases, with results that are not always harmonious.

The Myth of the Expensive Lawyer

The belief is sometimes expressed, usually with great feeling, that a person who is represented by top-flight counsel is virtually "above the law." While it is undeniably true that a person who employs a competent lawyer will, in general, experience fewer legal problems than one who does not, this certainly does not mean that such a person can flout our legal rules without penalty. The average attorney is competent enough that, when the rules support his or her client, that person will fare well under the law—and when the rules do not, the client will be ordered to conform to them, no matter how skilled the counsel may be.

The Myth of Judicial Eccentricity

The feeling is sometimes expressed that the law is not based on common sense—that its rules are so esoteric and arbitrary, and the judges and lawyers so preoccupied with them, that the results that obtain are not in keeping with reality or with what a reasonable person would expect. This indictment, in very large measure, is false.

---

[13]It is sometimes said that the law is a "social science." While some view this term with a jaundiced eye, in that it seemingly ascribes to the principles of the social studies a precision and certainty equal to those of the physical sciences, the label is perhaps acceptable to the extent that the rules of law do apply to, and are concerned with, all human activities.

Cases invariably present practical problems for the courts, and the courts keep the practical considerations in mind in choosing the rules that apply.

Take, for example, this situation. C, a contractor, agrees to build a house according to certain specifications for O, the owner, for $50,000. When the house is completed, by which time O has paid $36,000, O discovers that the family room is four inches shorter than the plans specified. O refuses to make further payments for this reason, whereupon C brings suit to recover the balance of $14,000.

Now, as far as contract law is concerned, the principle is well established that a person who breaches his or her contract is not permitted to recover anything from the other party. The question here is: Should that rule be applicable to this specific situation, where its application would completely free O of liability? The practical person would reply, "Certainly not—the defect is far too trivial to impose such a drastic penalty on C as the loss of $14,000." The law reaches the same conclusion. (For an idea of the rules that determine the precise sum that O must now pay C, the reader will have to wait until we reach Part II.)

The foregoing does not mean, of course, that the law is perfect or that startling or unfair decisions never occur. They do. But by and large the unreasonable result occurs with much less frequency than reports in the news media would indicate; and even in such cases, the possibility usually exists that an appellate court will subsequently repair much of the damage.

The Case of the Errant Bee

In order for students to gain an adequate understanding of reported cases, they must have some familiarity with court procedures and jurisdiction. For this reason, major emphasis on cases will begin in the following chapter. Because there are practical advantages, however, in being introduced to real-life situations as early as possible, the case below is presented at this point.

Only three prefatory comments seem necessary in view of the simple fact-pattern:

1. This is a "negligence" action; the plaintiff is contending that the defendant's bus driver was operating the bus carelessly at the time of the accident—that is, with less care than a "reasonable, prudent person" would have exercised under the circumstances.

2. In a negligence action, the question of whether the defendant's actions did or did not constitute negligence is usually for the jury to decide. However, if the evidence is overwhelmingly convincing one way or the other, the court—the judge—may rule *as a matter of law* that the defendant's conduct was (or was not) negligent, thereby withdrawing that issue from the consideration of the jury. Generally, a finding of negligence as a matter of law can be made only when the court feels that the evidence is so strong that "reasonable minds could not differ"— that is, a jury of disinterested persons could not return a verdict to the contrary.

3. If a court does rule that the defendant is (or is not) guilty of negligence as a matter of law, the correctness of this ruling can always be reviewed by an appellate

court. If this court finds that the ruling was in error, the case will be returned to the trial court with instructions for a jury trial on the issue.

With these thoughts in mind, let us examine the nature of Vicki Schultz's complaint against the Cheney School District.

Schultz v. Cheney School District
Supreme Court of Washington, 371 P.2d 59 (1962)

Vicki Schultz, plaintiff, a passenger on defendant's school bus, was injured when the driver lost control of the bus after being stung by a bee. In the trial court—the Superior Court of Spokane County, Washington—plaintiff alleged that the actions of defendant's driver constituted negligence. Defendant disagreed, contending that the accident was "unavoidable."

At the trial, plaintiff asked the court to rule that the driver's conduct in this situation constituted negligence as a matter of law. The trial court refused to do so, and left the question of negligence to the jury.

Also, during the trial, the defendant asked the court to instruct the jury as to the circumstances under which an accident might be unavoidable. The court did so. (While the instruction does not appear in the record, an unavoidable accident is usually defined as one which occurred "without fault on the part of either party.")

The jury returned a verdict for defendant. Plaintiff then appealed to the Supreme Court of Washington, claiming that the above rulings of the trial court were erroneous.

Rosellini, Justice: . . . The evidence showed that the plaintiff fell or was thrown from her seat in the defendant's school bus when it was driven off the highway into a ditch. This occurred because the attention of the driver was diverted momentarily from the road when a bee flew in the window and stung him on the neck. He ducked his head and tried with his left hand to extricate the bee from under his collar. While he was thus engaged the bus veered to the left and onto the shoulder of the road, a distance of about 75 feet.

At this point the driver raised his head and perceived what had happened. He endeavored to turn the bus back onto the road, but because of the soft condition of the shoulder, he was unable to do so and the bus went down into a shallow ditch, tilting first to the left and then to the right before it could be stopped. It was this motion of the bus that caused plaintiff to fall into the aisle.

There was no contention that the driver was operating the bus in a negligent manner before the bee stung him. But the plaintiff urged in the trial court, and now urges here, that the evidence showed that he was negligent as a matter of law in failing to keep the bus under control after that incident. The testimony was that only a few seconds passed between the moment of the bee sting and the moment the driver discovered that the bus had veered across the highway. He testified that the sting startled him and that the bee continued to buzz under his collar after it had stung him.

We think the trial court correctly decided that it was for the jury to determine whether his action in lowering his head and endeavoring with one hand to remove the bee was instinctive, or whether reasonable care required him to maintain control of the bus in spite of this painful distraction. *It is not a question that can be decided as a matter of law.* [Emphasis added.]

The defendant, by its answer, denied negligence and affirmatively alleged that the accident was unavoidable. Error is assigned to the giving of an instruction defining "unavoidable accident." [The phrase *error is assigned* simply means that the appellant is *claiming* that this was an error.]

The plaintiff does not quarrel with the instruction as a correct statement of the law, but contends first that it was inapplicable in this case because the defendant was negligent as a matter of law, and second that such an instruction should never be given because it is misleading and superfluous.

For the reason previously stated in this opinion there is no merit to the first of these contentions. As to the second, it is well established in this jurisdiction [here, meaning "this state"] that an instruction on unavoidable accident is proper when the evidence shows or justifies an inference that an unavoidable accident has occurred, as that term has been defined.

The argument that the instruction is superfluous and misleading has been thoroughly considered in *Cooper v. Pay-N-Save Drugs, Inc.*, 371 P.2d 43. After analyzing the authorities, this court announced the following rule:

". . . It is proper to give the instruction if there is affirmative evidence that an unavoidable accident has occurred; stated negatively, it is error to give the instruction if there is no evidence of an unavoidable accident or if the only issue possible under the facts is that of negligence and contributory negligence" [on plaintiff's part].

In this case, the defendant was not negligent as a matter of law. It affirmatively alleged and introduced evidence that the accident was unavoidable. The jury could find the defendant liable if it found that the accident was the result of the driver's negligence, or it could find, as it did, that the driver lost control of his vehicle momentarily because of his instinctive reaction to the sudden and unexpected attack of the bee, and that his acts under the circumstances were not negligent. Implicit in this finding is a determination that the accident was unavoidable in the exercise of due care. The instruction was proper under the evidence.

The judgment is affirmed. [Justices Finley, Donworth, and Ott concur.]

Foster, Justice (dissenting): For the reasons stated by the Supreme Court of California in *Butigan v. Yellow Cab Co.*, 49 Cal.2d 652; the instruction on unavoidable accident should be banished from the law. I therefore dissent.

Comment: 1. Since this is our first case, a few comments about the mechanics of case reporting are in order.

a. The opinion, written by Judge Rosellini, is that of the appellate court—in this instance, the highest court in the state of Washington.

b. The elipsis points (. . .) appearing in an opinion indicate portions that have been deleted by the author. Deletions are made to eliminate redundancy or to exclude issues that are not relevant to points that the case has been selected to illustrate. Except for deletions and bracketed author comments, the statements of the higher court are presented *verbatim*.

c. In most cases appearing hereafter, the authors have chosen—for the sake of brevity—not to indicate whether any judges of the appellate court dissented from the majority opinion. Thus one cannot assume that all, or even most, of the following decisions were unanimous. Generally, dissenting opinions are included only where they present extraordinarily persuasive arguments or new matter. In the instant (immediate) case, the brief dissent appears only to indicate to the student that there are such things.

d. When a general principle of law is stated in a decision, the court will frequently *cite* (refer to) earlier cases in which that principle has been established. Here, for example, the court has referred to *Cooper v. Pay-N-Save Drugs, Inc.*, for such a purpose. To facilitate the reading of opinions, the authors have generally omitted such references without indicating that this has been done. A major exception to this policy exists where the cited case is relied upon heavily by the court to support its decision, as is true here. (The item "371 P.2d 43" indicates where the complete report of the cited case can be found. This will be explained in more detail in the next chapter.)

2. In regard to substantive matters presented by this case, the following can be noted.

a. Had the jury found the driver to be negligent, the school district would have been liable to plaintiff under *agency law*. While that subject is essentially outside the scope of this chapter, one of its principles imposes liability on an employer for the torts (wrongs) committed by employees if they were "carrying on the employer's business" at the time. (This specific question will be considered somewhat further in Chapter 30.)

b. If the jury had found the driver to be negligent and the school district had paid the amount of the judgment to plaintiff, another question would arise. In such event, could the school district bring action against the driver to recover the amount so paid (assuming that the loss was not covered by insurance)? The answer, legally, is yes, since the driver was the actual wrongdoer in this situation. (In practice, however, employers frequently forego such actions, particularly if the employee's financial position is such that he or she clearly would be unable to pay any judgment that might be obtained.)

3. A word of caution. It is imperative for readers to acquire the ability *to determine the precise issue of a case,* so they will not leap to unwarranted general conclusions. Could we say, for example, that the instant case establishes the principle that automobile drivers are never liable for accidents occasioned by bee stings? Not at all. There are some situations where the driver may very well be liable. If, for example, a motorist knows that he has such a visitor in his car and persists in driving a substantial time thereafter without attempting to remove it, it is entirely possible that a jury would conclude that his conduct was negligent if an accident subsequently ensued.

In the instant case, then, the issue in the trial court was whether the driver's conduct constituted negligence in the particular fact-pattern that existed. In the appellate court, the issue was even more narrow—whether the trial court was correct in refusing to rule that defendant was guilty of negligence as a matter of law. The answer, as we know now, was yes. (The rule of thumb to guide the courts in making such a decision will be set forth in the next chapter, and the general subject of negligence will receive fuller attention in Chapter 7.)

Questions and Problems

1. In the case of *Roe v. Wade,* 410 U.S. 113 (1973), the U.S. Supreme Court was asked to rule on the constitutionality of a Texas statute that made it a crime for anyone within the state to have an abortion, except where the abortion was done "upon medical advice for the purpose of saving the mother's life." Leaving aside the constitutional question, which will be briefly noted in Chapter 5, do you think that this is a proper subject for the law of a state to control, or attempt to control? Why or why not?

2. While there is no univeral agreement as to what law is when viewed in the abstract, there seems to be substantial agreement among philosophers as to what the *primary purpose* of law is.

    a. How would you describe this purpose?
    b. Identify the specific passage or clause in each of the philosophers' quoted observations that substantiates your conclusion.

3. Briefly summarize the main factors that require a nation's legal rules to be flexible and somewhat changing.

4. If X and Y make a contract and X later refuses to go through with the deal, having no reason to do so, we say that X's conduct is a *wrong* but it is not a *crime*. Why is it not a crime?

5. For some years the Washington Interscholastic Activities Association had a rule that prohibited girls from participating on high school football teams in the state. When this rule was challenged by parents of two girls who wanted to go out for football, the Supreme Court of Washington had to decide whether the rule violated the state constitution. (*Darrin v. Gould,* 540 P.2d 882, 1975). Leaving aside the precise legal question that was posed, do you think that such a rule is a good one? Discuss.

6. What is the main advantage that results from legal rules being *essentially certain* in nature? Explain.

7. Mrs. P sues the D Church to recover damages for injuries sustained when she tripped on a loose stair tread on church premises. For many years prior to this suit, the courts of the state had followed the rule that nonprofit organizations, such as churches, shall not be liable in such situations even where the injury is the result of their own carelessness. If the court hearing the case of *Mrs. P v. The D Church* is now asked to *overrule* that principle:

    a. Which of the four basic requirements (or characteristics) of an effective legal system would cause the court the most difficulty in granting Mrs. P's request for a change in the law?
    b. Which of the other basic requirements might cause the court to be sympathetic to arguments that the law ought to be changed?

8. What is the explanation for the fact that today, late in the twentieth century, a significant portion of the law of most states is still judge-made (or "common") law?

Under our constitutional system, courts stand against any winds that blow as havens of refuge for those who might otherwise suffer because they are helpless, weak, outnumbered, or because they are non-conforming victims of prejudice and public excitement.

Justice Hugo Black, *Chambers v. Florida*, 309 U.S. 227 (1940)

Court Systems, Jurisdiction, and Functions 2

Legal rules and principles take on vitality and meaning only when they are applied to real-life controversies between real persons, when the *rules* are applied to *facts*—when, for example, a particular plaintiff is successful (or unsuccessful) in his attempt to recover a piece of land or a sum of money from a particular defendant or to have the defendant ordered to do any of a number of other things. But the fitting of rules to facts—the settling of legal controversies—does not occur automatically. This process, which we call the *process of adjudication,* has to be in somebody's hands—the "somebody" being state and federal courts that hear the thousands of cases arising every year.

The primary reason, then, for looking at the courts and the work they do is to gain some familiarity with this important legal process. There is, however, another reason for doing so. In the following chapters many actual cases will be presented. The reader will be given the facts of a particular controversy, the ruling of the trial court, and the ruling of the higher court in reviewing the judgment of the trial court. Some basic familiarity with court systems and processes is essential if these decisions are to be meaningful.

21

In this chapter we will take a brief look at the state and federal court systems, some problems of jurisdiction arising thereunder, and the functions of the trial and appellate courts.

Court Systems

As a result of our federal system of government, we live under two distinct, and essentially separate, sovereign types of government—the state governments and the federal government. Each has its own laws and its own court system. For this reason, it is necessary to examine both systems in order to acquire an adequate knowledge of the court structures within which controversies are settled.

The Typical State System   *State Courts*

While court systems vary somewhat from state to state, most state courts fall into three general categories. In ascending order, they are (1) courts of limited jurisdiction, (2) general trial courts, and (3) appellate courts (which frequently exist at two levels).

Courts of Limited Jurisdiction: In every state some trial courts have *limited jurisdiction;* that is, they are limited as to the kinds of cases they can hear.[1] The common ones are justice of the peace courts, municipal courts, traffic courts, probate courts, and domestic relations courts. While such courts actually decide a majority of the cases that come to trial, we are going to substantially eliminate them from further consideration because they are not courts of general jurisdiction. Many of them deal with minor matters, such as the handling of small claims and traffic violations. Others (such as the probate courts) deal with much more substantial matters in terms of the amount of money involved; but even these courts are limited to cases of very specialized subject matter.

General Trial Courts: The most important cases involving state law, and the ones we will be most concerned with hereafter, commence in the *general trial courts.* These are courts of "general jurisdiction"; they are empowered to hear all cases except those expressly assigned by statute to the "minor" courts discussed above. Virtually all important cases involving contract law, criminal law, and corporation law, for example, originate in the general trial courts.[2] In some states these courts are called "district courts," in others "common pleas courts," and in still others "superior courts" (the latter being something of a misnomer). Whatever the specific name, such a court normally exists in every county of every state.

---

[1]Here *jurisdiction* means the legal power to act.

[2]These courts may occasionally be referred to hereafter simply as *state trial courts,* to distinguish them from federal trial courts. When this is done, reference is being made to the trial courts of *general jurisdiction* rather than to the minor trial courts.

Appellate Courts: All states have one or more *appellate courts,* which hear appeals from judgments entered by the courts below. In many states there is only one such court, usually called the "supreme court"; but in the more populous states there is a layer of appellate courts interposed between the trial courts and the supreme court. Ohio, for example, has ten intermediate appellate courts, each of which hears appeals on a geographical basis. That is, appeals from judgments of common pleas courts in one section of the state go to a particular intermediate court, while appeals in another cluster of counties go to a different intermediate court. Each of these courts, called "courts of appeal," has three judges.

The Federal Court System   Federal Courts

At the risk of oversimplification, we can say that federal courts fall within three main categories similar to those of the state courts: (1) specialized courts, (2) general trial courts (district courts), and (3) appellate courts (which are also found at two levels).

Specialized U.S. Courts: Some federal courts have limited jurisdiction, such as the court of customs and patent appeals and the court of claims. While these courts frequently deal with important matters, we will eliminate them from further consideration (as we did the similar state courts) because of their specialized nature.

General Trial Courts: The basic courts having general jurisdiction within the federal system are the *U.S. district courts,* sometimes called federal trial courts. Most federal cases originate in these courts.

There are eighty-eight U.S. district courts across the country, plus an additional five for the territories and possessions. Most states east of the Mississippi have two such courts within their boundaries, while those to the west usually have only one. (Major exceptions are California and Texas, each of which has four.)

Where there are two or more district courts within a single state, the jurisdiction of each is limited geographically. Thus in Ohio there is a U.S. District Court for Northern Ohio (with principal offices in Cleveland) and a U.S. District Court for Southern Ohio (with principal offices in Columbus). As is frequently the case, these district courts in turn are split into divisions. The Western Division of the U.S. District Court for Southern Ohio, for example, has offices in Dayton and Cincinnati, in addition to Columbus, and the court thus "sits" in all three cities. In any event, every square foot of land in this country is—geographically speaking —within the jurisdiction of a U.S. district court.

The Appellate Courts: Above the district courts are two levels of *federal appellate courts*—the U.S. courts of appeal—and, above them, the U.S. Supreme Court. There are twelve U.S. courts of appeal, each having jurisdiction to hear appeals from the district courts located in the states within its boundaries. For example, the 9th U.S. Court of Appeals in San Francisco hears appeals from district courts within the states of Montana, Idaho, Nevada, Arizona, California, Oregon, Washington, and Hawaii. Appeals from judgments of the courts of appeal—like appeals from some judgments of the state supreme courts—can be taken to the U.S. Supreme Court. However, that court actually hears only a small percentage of such appeals. This results from the fact that, with few exceptions, review by the highest court is not a matter of right. Rather, parties who seek a review do so by petitioning the Supreme Court for a *writ of certiorari,* and the Court has almost absolute discretion in deciding which cases are sufficiently important to warrant the granting of certiorari. In most instances certiorari is denied; in a typical year, for example, the Court hears only about 155 of the approximately 5,500 appeals that are made.[3]

Some Observations

If we eliminate the specialized state and federal courts, the typical state court system and the federal system can be diagrammed as follows (with the dotted lines indicating courts of appeal that exist in only some of the states):

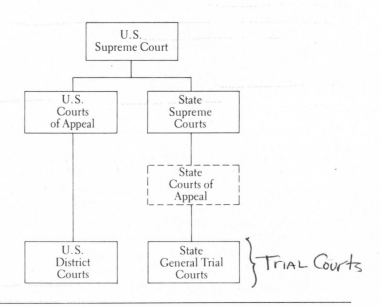

Several general comments can be made about this diagram.

1. The courts represented by the lowest box in each system are trial courts; all those above are appellate courts.

---

[3]A writ of certiorari is an order of a higher court requiring a lower court to forward to it the record and proceedings of a particular case.

2. Trial courts must settle questions of both *fact* and *law*, while appellate courts rule on questions of law only. (More will be said of this later.)

3. While a majority of the decisions of the trial courts are not appealed, a good many are—and hereafter we will be concerned primarily with the *decisions of the appellate courts.* There are several basic reasons for this. First, state trial courts usually enter a judgment without writing a formal opinion as to their reasoning; and, even if there is such an opinion, it is normally not "reported." Appellate courts, on the other hand, normally do write opinions which are reported, and access to them is available to anyone wishing to look up the rulings of law involved. Second, appellate courts have more time to adequately research the law than do trial judges—and more opportunity to delineate the legal issues in their opinions for the benefit of lawyers and others who may read them. And, third, if the appellate court disagrees with the result reached by the trial court, the appellate's decision is, of course, controlling.

4. Once a case is initiated within a given court system, it will normally stay within that system until a final judgment is reached. Thus, if a case is properly commenced in a state court of general jurisdiction, any appeal from the trial court's judgment must be made to the next higher state court rather than to a federal appellate court. And if a case reaches the highest court in the state, its judgment is final. In other words, on matters of state law, the state supreme courts are indeed supreme.[4] There is one notable exception, however. Once the highest court in a state has spoken, the "loser" in some instances can raise a *federal question* by claiming that the final ruling of that state court deprives him or her of a right guaranteed under the U.S. Constitution—such as the taking of property "without due process of law." On this basis, the person can ask the U.S. Supreme Court to review the state court's judgment.

5. Supreme courts in those states having an intermediate level of appellate courts —state courts of appeal—generally have wide discretion, somewhat akin to that of the U.S. Supreme court, in determining which appeals they will hear. The supreme courts of other states have little discretion in this matter.

6. With regard to the "title" of an appealed case, the state and federal courts follow somewhat different rules. In most state courts, the original plaintiff's name appears first—just as it did in the trial court. Suppose, for example, that Pink (plaintiff) sues Doe (defendant) in a state trial court, where the case is obviously *Pink v. Doe.* If the judgment of the trial court is appealed, the rule followed by most state courts is that the title of the case remains *Pink v. Doe* in the appellate courts, no matter which party is the *appellant* (the one bringing the appeal). In the federal courts, on the other hand, the appellant's name appears first. Under this rule, if Doe (defendant) loses in a U.S. district court and appeals to a U.S. court of appeals, the title of the case will be *Doe v. Pink* in the higher court. For this

---

[4]The normal terminology is being used here. In a few states, however, the "supreme court" label is given to an intermediate appellate court, with the highest court in the state bearing some other name. The court of last resort in the state of New York, for example, is the Court of Appeals of New York.

reason, when one sees a case in a federal appellate court so entitled, one cannot safely assume that Doe was the party who originated the action in the trial court. That determination must be made by referring to the facts of the case as set forth in the decision of the appellate court.

The "Style" of Case Reporting: As has been noted, the decisions of the appellate courts are published in chronologically numbered volumes. Most states have a dual system of reporting. When a state supreme court renders a decision, its opinion is printed in full both in "official reports," which are authorized by the state, and in a "regional reporter" published by the West Publishing Company, called the National Reporter System. Under the West system, the reports of state courts are grouped on a geographical basis under these headings: Atlantic (A.), Southeastern (S.E.), Northeastern (N.E.), Northwestern (N.W.), Southern (S.), Southwestern (S.W.), and Pacific (P.). For example, decisions of the courts of Iowa, Michigan, Minnesota, Nebraska, North Dakota, South Dakota, and Wisconsin appear in the Northwestern reports.

The volume and page numbers that appear after the title of a case comprise its "citation." Thus a case entitled *Schupak v. McDonald's System, Inc.,* 200 Neb. 485, 264 N.W.2d 827, will be found in volume 200 of the official Nebraska reports at page 485, and in volume 264 of the second series of the National Reporter System for states in the Northwestern area at page 827. (Only the citations of the West system are given for cases in this text, since a number of states have dispensed with the publication of their official reports.)

Problems of Jurisdiction

In order for a court to settle a particular controversy, it is necessary for it to have jurisdiction over the case.[5] This means that it must have jurisdiction of both the *subject matter* involved in the suit and, normally, of the *person* against whom the suit is being brought. If a trial court should enter a judgment in a case where it lacks either of these kinds of jurisdiction, its judgment is void—of no effect whatever.

Subject-matter Jurisdiction

As we have already seen, some courts in both the state and federal systems are sharply limited as to the kinds of cases they can hear. Within a state system, for example, probate courts are normally empowered to hear only those cases involving decedents' estates and guardianship proceedings; they clearly have no authority to hear ordinary breach of contract cases. Other courts, those of general jurisdiction, have much broader powers; they can hear all types of cases except the relatively few that by statute must originate in the specialized courts. Within a given court

---

[5]As earlier, *jurisdiction* means the legal power to act, especially to hear and decide controversies.

system, then, the subject-matter jurisdiction of the several courts is essentially clear.

Occasionally, however, cases will arise that present a more difficult problem, involving the lines of demarcation between the jurisdiction of the *state* courts and the *federal* courts. This occurs because while most cases must begin only in the state courts or only in the federal courts, some cases can be commenced in either court system. A brief look at jurisdictional rules is thus necessary.

Subject Matter: State versus Federal Jurisdiction

The primary rule is that all cases must commence in state courts. The exceptions are those cases which present a federal question and those in which diversity of citizenship exists. Since most controversies do not involve such matters, the great majority of cases originate in the state courts. Nevertheless, the rule does make it mandatory to understand the terms *federal question* and *diversity of citizenship* in order to have some idea of the kinds of cases the federal courts can hear.

Federal Questions: A federal question exists in any suit where the plaintiff's case—"cause of action"—is based in whole or in part upon a *federal statute* or upon a provision of the *U.S. Constitution* or a *U.S. treaty.* Once it is shown that a federal question is involved in a particular case, the federal courts usually have jurisdiction regardless of the amount in controversy (i.e., the amount the plaintiff is seeking or the value of the right the plaintiff is asserting). In a few situations, however, the federal courts have jurisdiction over "federal question cases" only if the amount in controversy exceeds $10,000.[6] This situation exists because the basic federal statute giving the federal courts jurisdiction over federal question cases imposes a general requirement that the amount in controversy exceed $10,000. However, in many specific federal statutes (such as the antitrust laws and civil rights laws) Congress has provided that the federal courts will have jurisdiction over cases arising under those statutes regardless of the amount in controversy. The great bulk of federal question cases stem from statutes like this.[*]

It should be noted further that federal and state courts often have *concurrent jurisdiction* over cases that present a federal question. In other words, a plaintiff who is entitled to bring a case in the federal courts under the rules discussed above usually has the option of commencing the action in a state court if he or she wishes to do so.[7]   As a matter of practice, however, in those situations where concurrent jurisdiction exists, suits are normally brought in the federal courts. And, if such a suit *is* commenced in a state court, the defendant then has the "right of removal"—the right to have the case transferred to the federal courts.

---

[6]Where this is required, those cases involving $10,000 or less must be filed in a state court.

[7]The option does not exist if a statute or constitutional provision confers exclusive jurisdiction on the federal courts. Bankruptcy proceedings and federal criminal actions, for example, must always be brought in the federal courts.

[*]Editor's note: subsequent to first printing of this edition, Congress eliminated the $10,000 requirement in *all* federal question cases.

Diversity of Citizenship: Under one section of the U.S. Constitution, the federal courts are authorized to hear cases in which the plaintiff and defendant *are citizens of different states,* even though no federal question is involved. By virtue of federal legislation that implements this section, however, a second requirement must be met: the amount in controversy must exceed $10,000 in all cases. (Suits between citizens of different states involving lesser amounts, therefore, can be initiated only in the state courts.)

At first glance, it may seem illogical that diversity cases are permitted to be brought in the federal courts, since no questions of federal law are presented by such cases. There is reason for this extension of federal jurisdiction, however, and it is succinctly stated as follows: "Diversity jurisdiction was created to alleviate fears that an out-of-state litigant might be subject to local bias in the courts of the state where his adversary resided, and to afford suitors the opportunity, at their option, to assert their rights in the federal rather than the state courts."[8]

Regardless of whether the fears of local bias are the motivation, it is true that a substantial percentage of the 60,000-odd cases that are filed in the federal courts each year are, in fact, based solely on "diversity" grounds. It is also true that in some cases—particularly those in which several parties are involved—the question of whether diversity exists is so complex as to be outside the scope of this text. Nevertheless, the following examples will illustrate the basic rules as they apply to the most common kinds of cases.

Example 1. X, a citizen of Michigan, seeks to enforce a $15,000 promissory note against Y, a citizen of Wisconsin residing in Madison. X's suit can be brought in the U.S. District Court for Western Wisconsin, if he so desires.

Example 2. P, a citizen of Ohio, is injured in Indianapolis when her car is negligently struck by a car driven by D, a citizen of Indiana residing in Indianapolis. If P files suit against D in the U.S. District Court for Southern Indiana, asking (in good faith) for damages in excess of $10,000, that court has jurisdiction of the case.[9]

Example 3. W and X, citizens of Nebraska, seek to recover $50,000 in damages from Y, a citizen of Nebraska, and Z, a citizen of Wyoming, the case arising out of an alleged breach of contract. Here diversity is lacking, since there are citizens of Nebraska on both sides of the case; this suit could not, therefore, be heard by a federal court.

Jurisdiction of the Person

A court does not have the power to hear a case simply because its subject matter, the general nature of the proceeding, falls within its jurisdiction. A second type of jurisdiction—jurisdiction over *the person of the defendant* (or, in some cases, property of the defendant)—must also be present. In other words, while subject-matter rules determine the court system that may hear a case, jurisdiction of person

---

[8]36 C.J.S., Federal Courts, § 55, Copyright 1960 by West Publishing Co.

[9]Here, again, jurisdiction of the federal courts is not exclusive. Thus these suits could have been brought in the *state courts* of Wisconsin and Indiana, respectively, if the plaintiffs had desired to do so.

rules determine the particular trial court within that system where the case must be commenced. In this regard, a distinction between *actions in personam* and *actions in rem* is to be noted.

Actions in Personam: The great majority of civil suits are actions *in personam*—that is, actions in which the plaintiff is seeking to hold the defendant liable on a personal obligation. Three of the most common examples are the following:

1. P sues D to recover damages (that is, a sum of money) arising out of a *breach of contract* on D's part.

2. P sues D to recover a *debt* that is owed by D.

3. P sues to recover damages for *personal injuries* that D has wrongly inflicted upon him.

Whenever a plaintiff brings an action *in personam* in a particular court, he or she must demonstrate to the court that it has "jurisdiction of the defendant's person." Under the laws of most states, this can be done only by showing (1) that the *defendant's residence* is within the territorial jurisdiction of the court, and that the summons was either served personally on the defendant or left with an adult at the defendant's place of residence, or (2) if the defendant's residence is elsewhere, that he or she was *personally served* with the summons while within the court's territorial jurisdiction. Since the second of these is difficult to accomplish, the result, in practice, is that the plaintiff must normally commence suit in a court of the state where the defendant lives, wherever that may be.[10]

Actions in Rem: In some actions the plaintiff is seeking merely to enforce a right against certain *property* that is owned by the defendant, or in which the defendant claims an interest. Such suits are *actions in rem,* and can be brought in any court within whose territorial jurisdiction the property—the "res" or thing—is located.

The typical case is the mortgage foreclosure action, which can be illustrated as follows. X, a Kentucky resident, owns an apartment building in Ohio with a $35,000 mortgage on it held by an Ohio bank. If X defaults on the mortgage payments, the bank can bring a mortgage foreclosure action *in Ohio* in the common pleas court of the county where the building is located. (Under the laws of most states relating to such actions, the bank need only publish notices of the suit in a newspaper in order to bring X's interest in the property within the jurisdiction

---

[10]Because of the difficulty and expense involved in suing an out-of-state resident, all states have adopted "long-arm statutes" of one kind or another, which permit some types of actions to be brought against out-of-state residents in the *plaintiff's* home state. One typical statute, for example, provides in essence that any nonresident who "engages in business" in the state is thereby giving his consent to be sued in that state by any person who has a claim against him arising out of the transaction of such business. In such an action the plaintiff need only have the service of process (the complaint and summons) be made on the secretary of state in the plaintiff's state in order to acquire jurisdiction on the nonresident defendant. Additionally, all states have similar statutes providing that nonresidents who operate motor vehicles within their borders are thereby appointing a designated state official, such as the secretary of state or director of the department of motor vehicles, to be their agent for the purpose of being sued if they are involved in an accident while in the state.

of the court, in which case service upon X is said to be made "by publication," as distinguished from "personal service.")

The following case presents a fact-pattern that is fairly typical in this area, since it involves an action *in personam* brought in a trial court in one state against a nonresident defendant who challenged that court's jurisdiction over him. In another respect the case is unique, however, in that the question of the jurisdiction of the trial court in California was litigated all the way to the U.S. Supreme Court. In any event, that court reached its decision on the basis of general constitutional principles (i.e., would due process of law be afforded the defendant if suit were allowed in California?), since there was no California long-arm statute that was applicable to the dispute.

Kulko v. Superior Court of California
U.S. Supreme Court 98 S.Ct. 1690 (1978)

Ezra and Sharon Kulko were married in 1959 in California, while he was on a three-day stopover en route from a military base in Texas to a tour of duty in Korea. At the time of the marriage both parties were residents of New York. After the marriage Mrs. Kulko returned to New York, and Ezra joined her there after his army duty was over. In 1961 a son was born in New York, and in 1962 a daughter was born, also in New York.

In March of 1972 the Kulkos separated, and a separation agreement was entered into in New York. It provided that the children would remain with their father during the school year but would spend Christmas, Easter and summer vacation with their mother. In addition, Kulko was to pay his wife $3,000 a year in child support for the three periods when the children were with her. After the agreement was signed Mrs. Kulko moved to California.

Thereafter Mrs. Kulko flew to Haiti and got a divorce, with the divorce decree incorporating the terms of the separation agreement. She then returned to California, where she remarried and took the name of Horn. In 1973 Mrs. Horn, with Kulko's consent, had their daughter Ilsa join her permanently in California. In 1975 their son, Darwin, joined his mother and sister in California, without Kulko's knowledge.

Mrs. Horn then brought this action *in a California court* against Kulko, asking that court to modify the Haiti divorce decree by awarding her full custody of the children, and by increasing Kulko's child support payments. When Kulko received a summons in New York he made a special appearance in the California court, contending that the California courts had no jurisdiction over him. (A "special appearance" means that a lawyer representing Kulko appeared in the California court for the sole purpose of challenging that court's jurisdiction.) The California trial court ruled that it *did* have jurisdiction, and the California Supreme Court agreed. Kulko then appealed that ruling to the U.S. Supreme Court.

Marshall, Justice: . . . The Due Process Clause of the Fourteenth Amendment operates as a limitation on the jurisdiction of state courts to enter judgments affecting rights or interests of nonresidents. *It has long been the rule that a valid judgment imposing a personal obligation or duty in favor of the plaintiff may be entered only by a court having jurisdiction over the person of the defendant.* (Emphasis added). The existence of personal jurisdiction, in turn, depends upon the presence of reasonable notice to the defendant that an action has been brought . . . and a sufficient connection between the defendant the forum State as to make it fair to require defense of the action in the forum.* . . .

The parties are in agreement that the constitutional standard for determining whether the State may enter a binding judgment against appellant here (Kulko) is that set forth in this Court's opinion in *International Shoe Co. v. Washington,* 326 U.S. 316: that a defendant "have certain minimum contacts with [the forum state] such that the maintenance of the suit does not offend 'traditional notions of fair play and substantial justice.' " . . . (Additionally) an essential criterion in all cases is whether the "quality and nature" of defendant's activity is such that it is "reasonable" and "fair" to require him to conduct his defense in that state.

Like any standard that requires a determination of "reasonableness," the "minimum contacts" test of *International Shoe* is not susceptible of mechanical application; rather, the facts of each case must be weighed to determine whether the requisite "affiliating circumstances" are present. . . .

(The court then noted that the California Supreme Court did not—and could not—base its claim of jurisdiction on the mere fact that Kulko was in California for the three-day stopover en route to Korea years ago, or the mere fact that his marriage occurred in that state. The court then turned to California's stated claim to jurisdiction.)

The "purposeful act" that the California Supreme Court believed did warrant the exercise of personal jurisdiction over appellant in California was his "actively and fully consenting to Ilsa living in California for the school year . . . and . . . sending her to California for that purpose." We cannot accept the proposition that appellant's acquiescence in Ilsa's desire to live with her mother conferred jurisdiction over appellant in the California courts in this action. A father who agrees, in the interests of family harmony and his children's preferences, to allow them to spend more time in California than was required under a separation agreement can hardly be said to have "purposefully availed himself" of the "benefits and protection" of California's laws.

Nor can we agree with the assertion of the court below that the exercise of *in personam* jurisdiction here was warranted by the financial benefit appellant derived from his daughter's presence in California for nine months of the year. This argument rests on the premise that, while appellant's liability for support payments remained unchanged, his yearly expenses for supporting the child in New York decreased. But this circumstance, even if true, does not support California's assertion of jurisdiction here. Any diminution in appellant's household costs resulted, not from the child's presence in California, but rather from her absence from appellant's home. Moreover, an action by appellee Horn could now be brought, and could have been brought when Ilsa first moved to California, in the State of New York; a New York court would clearly have personal jurisdiction over appellant and, if a judgment were entered by a New York court increasing appellant's child support obligations, it could properly be enforced against him in both New York and California. . . .

Finally, basic considerations of fairness point decisively in favor of appellant's State of domicile (New York) as the proper forum for adjudication of this case, whatever the merits of appellee's underlying claim. It is appellant who has remained in the State of the marital domicile, whereas it is appellee who has moved across the continent. . . . As noted above, appellant did no more than acquiesce in the stated preference of one of his children to live with her mother in California. This single act is surely not one that a reasonable parent would expect to result in the substantial financial burden and personal strain of litigating

---

*"Forum state" means the state in which suit is being brought.

a child-support suit in a forum 3,000 miles away, and we therefore see no basis on which it can be said that appellant could have anticipated being "haled before a (California) court." . . .

Reversed.

"Conflict of Laws" Questions: In any case brought in either a state or federal court and based solely upon state law, there is always the possibility that one of the parties will claim that the law of one state is applicable, while the other party will contend that the law of a different state is controlling. (This is especially true, as one might imagine, in the diversity cases initiated in the federal courts.)

The following example illustrates the nature of the problem. S, a citizen of Ohio, makes a contract in Indiana with T, a citizen of Illinois, with the contract calling for performance by T to be rendered in Texas. If T thereafter refuses to carry out his part of the bargain and is sued by S in a federal court in Illinois, it may well be that the court will have to decide whether the entire dispute is to be settled by the law of just one of the four states or whether certain points of dispute will be governed by the law of one state and other issues by the law of a second state.

In general, the courts of each state have been free to formulate their own rules by which "choice of law" questions are to be settled within their respective jurisdictions. The rules that have been devised in each state therefore comprise that state's "conflict of laws" rules. And, fortunately, it can be said that the rules adopted by the several states in this area of law are essentially—though not entirely—uniform. In regard to the application of contract law, for example, it is generally held that the *validity* of a contract is to be determined by the law of the state in which the contract was made, while questions having to do with *performance* of the contract are governed by the law of the state in which performance is to take place. And, in the area of tort law, many states adhere to the traditional rule that the law of the state in which the tort occurred is controlling. Thus if A should sue B in a negligence action in Delaware to recover damages resulting from B's allegedly negligent driving in New Jersey, determination of B's negligence would be on the basis of New Jersey law under this rule.

Law, Equity, and Remedies

In the remainder of this chapter we will examine the major steps in the process of adjudication, paying particular attention to the roles played by the trial and appellate courts in that process. We will see that in all legal controversies the plaintiff is asking for a "remedy"—an order addressed to the defendant, requiring that person to do (or not to do) a particular act. A remedy, then, is "the means by which a plaintiff's right is enforced, or the violation of a right is prevented, redressed, or compensated."[11] All remedies are either "legal" or "equitable" in nature, a fact that can be explained only by a brief history.

---

[11] *Black's Law Dictionary,* Revised Fourth Edition, Copyright 1968 by West Publishing Co.

Courts of Law

After the Norman conquest of England some nine hundred years ago, a nationwide system of courts was established. This was accomplished when the first Norman kings designated individuals throughout the country to be their personal representatives in the settling of certain kinds of legal controversies.

These early courts, which were called royal courts or king's courts, were sharply limited as to the kinds of remedies they could grant. Essentially, they could grant relief only in cases where the plaintiff was asking for (1) money damages, (2) the possession of real estate, or (3) the possession of personal property.

In settling the disputes within their limited jurisdiction, the courts made up their own rules as they went along, based largely on the customs and moral standards then prevailing, plus their own ideas of what kinds of conduct were "just" in particular situations. The formulation of rules in this manner, a process that continues today in some branches of law, gave birth to the common law. The courts ultimately became *courts of law,* and the three basic remedies they could grant were *remedies at law.*

Courts of Equity

While this system introduced a uniformity to the settling of disputes, controversies began to arise when plaintiffs sought remedies other than those that the courts of law could grant. Rebuffed by these courts, they frequently petitioned the king for relief. Most of the petitions were ruled on by the king's secretary, the chancellor, who granted relief when he thought the plaintiff's claim was a fair one. Out of the rulings of successive chancellors arose a new body of "chancery" rules and remedies for cases outside the jurisdiction of the courts of law.

Finally, a system of chancery courts, known as *courts of equity,* evolved. Thus it was that two systems of courts (each with different judges) and two bodies of rules—law and equity—existed concurrently. A plaintiff wanting a legal remedy brought an "action at law" in a court of law; a plaintiff wanting some other relief brought an "action in equity" in an equity court.

The two primary remedies that a court of equity could grant were the *injunction* and the *decree of specific performance.*

The Injunction: If a plaintiff brought an action in a king's court asking that the defendant be ordered to refrain from doing a particular act, his request was invariably denied. For example: If P asked the court to order D to stop grazing cattle on land belonging to P, the court could only grant damages for the past injury done to the land; it did not have the power to prevent such trespasses in the future. In such a case, P's only hope was that the chancellor, whose power to grant relief was not so circumscribed, would feel that his request was justified and would order the defendant to stop performing the wrongful act—an order that today is called the *injunction.* (In later years, as courts of equity became established, actions for injunctive relief were commenced directly in those courts.)

The Decree of Specific Performance: The foregoing is also applicable to cases in which a plaintiff was asking for a *decree of specific performance*—an order commanding the defendant to live up to the terms of a contract made with the plaintiff. Courts of law could not do this; all they could do was order the defendant to pay the plaintiff a sum of money (damages) to compensate the plaintiff for losses suffered as a result of the breach of contract. Courts of equity, on the other hand, were empowered to issue a decree of specific performance when they felt that awarding damages would be an inadequate remedy—that is, in those exceptional situations where a sum of money would not, in their opinion, adequately recompense the plaintiff for the loss of services promised by the defendant or for the property the defendant had contracted to convey. (As will be seen in Part II, the awarding of damages is the normal remedy in breach of contract suits. Only in exceptional cases, involving highly unique services or property, is specific performance granted.)[12]

The Present Scene

While the distinction between legal and equitable remedies persists today, there has been a "fusion" of law and equity courts in virtually all states. This means that courts of law and equity, as such, have been eliminated. Instead, the basic trial courts in the state and federal systems are empowered to hear both legal and equitable actions.

Today, the basic distinctions between the two kinds of actions are these:

1. Whether an action is one at law or in equity depends solely upon the *nature of the remedy* that the plaintiff is seeking.

2. There is *no jury* in an equitable action. Questions of both fact and law are decided by the court—the trial judge.

3. Proceedings in equitable actions are *less formal* than those at law, particularly in regard to the order in which witnesses' testimony can be presented and the determination of admissibility of their evidence.

Resolution of Disputes

Out-of-Court Settlements

Most disputes are settled without resort to the courts. In many instances the sums involved are too small to justify taking legal action, and in others the parties may come to a satisfactory compromise. And, even where substantial amounts are involved, one of the parties may choose to forego a legal remedy simply to preserve the other's goodwill.

---

[12]Other common equitable actions, in addition to those asking for injunctions and decrees of specific performance, are (1) divorce actions, (2) mortgage foreclosure suits, and (3) actions for an accounting, brought by one member of a partnership against another.

Arbitration Agreements

Another method of settling a dispute is through an *arbitration agreement,* a procedure that is being used increasingly today. In these agreements, the parties to a dispute agree that it will be submitted to one or more arbitrators of their choice and that the arbitrator's decision will be binding.

Compared to litigation, voluntary arbitration has several advantages: (1) disputes can be settled more quickly, (2) arbitrators can be chosen who have special expertise in the particular business practices that are the subject of the controversy, (3) the proceedings are relatively informal, and (4) the cost is ordinarily less than if the cases go to court.

Generally, there are two kinds of arbitration agreements: agreements to submit and submission agreements. *Agreements to submit* are usually part of a larger contract (such as a collective bargaining agreement) and provide that future disputes arising out of the contract will be submitted to arbitration. *Submission agreements* are agreements to submit existing disputes to arbitration.

While the legal validity of arbitration agreements used to be subject to considerable doubt, most of this has been resolved. A federal statute, for example, now makes such written agreements involving interstate commerce "valid, irrevocable, and enforceable, save on such grounds as exist at law or in equity for the revocation of any contract." Many states also have arbitration statutes; but because these vary in detail, the relevant statute of a state should be examined before any agreement of arbitration is entered into.

Settlement by Litigation

Despite out-of-court settlements and the settlement of disputes through arbitration proceedings, thousands of cases *are* initiated in the courts every year. It is only through the adjudication of these controversies by the courts that the implementation of the rules of law really takes place.

While the trial and appellate courts are both concerned with the same general goal, the orderly settling of legal disputes, their basic responsibilities differ to a significant degree. As was noted earlier, the trial courts must decide disputed questions of fact and then select the rules of law applicable thereto.[13] The appellate courts, by contrast, are concerned exclusively with settling questions of law. They decide whether the rulings of the trial court, about which the appellant is complaining, were correct. With these observations before us, we will now examine the processes by which the two levels of courts perform their duties.

Pretrial proceedings consist of two stages, the *pleading stage* and the *discovery stage.* We will look at each of these steps briefly.

The Trial Courts: Pretrial Proceedings

---

[13]While the rulings of the trial courts are appealable, the importance of their work can hardly be overstated. It is on their determination of the facts that the precise legal issues are framed, and most of their decisions are final. (That is, a majority of the judgments of the trial courts are not, in fact, appealed.)

The Pleading Stage

The typical suit is commenced by the plaintiff, through an attorney, filing a *complaint* (or petition) with the court having jurisdiction of the case. At the same time, the plaintiff asks the court to issue a summons to the defendant, notifying that person that a complaint is on file.[14] The defendant then has a prescribed period of time in which to file a response of some sort, normally an *answer,* to the complaint. After that has been done, the plaintiff can file a *reply* to the answer. The complaint, answer, and reply make up the *pleadings* of a case, the main purpose of which is to permit the court and the parties to ascertain the actual points in issue.

The complaint: The complaint briefly sets forth the plaintiff's version of the facts and ends with a "prayer" (request) for a certain remedy based on those facts. Its primary purpose is to notify the defendant that a claim is being asserted against him or her based on certain *allegations* of fact.

The answer: The defendant usually responds to the complaint by filing an *answer* (or, in circumstances to be noted later, a "motion to dismiss"). In the typical case the defendant will disagree with one or more allegations of fact set forth in the complaint, and the answer will indicate the specific points of disagreement. For example, three allegations in a complaint growing out of an automobile accident may be (1) that the defendant was the driver of a car that collided with the plaintiff's on a certain date, (2) that defendant's car was to the left of the center line at the time of impact, and (3) that defendant was driving negligently at the time. Depending upon the particular circumstances, the defendant might deny the first allegation (on which the others are obviously based), claiming that he was merely a passenger in the car, which was being driven by someone else. Or the defendant might admit allegations (1) and (2) but deny allegation (3), claiming that he was directed to drive left of center by a police officer who was investigating a prior accident at the scene. In either event, the answer would raise *questions of fact,* which would have to be settled at the trial.

The answer also permits the defendant to raise *affirmative defenses*—legal points that will absolve the defendant of liability even if his or her version of the facts is proven wrong. For example, the defendant in the above case may deny that he was driving negligently, and, in addition, may allege that plaintiff was himself guilty of *contributory negligence;* if this is true, it will free defendant of liability under the law of most states even if it is later established in the trial court that he was driving in a negligent manner at the time of the accident.

Motion to Dismiss: If a defendant contends that he or she is not legally liable even if the plaintiff's allegations of fact are true, defendant will file a *motion to dismiss*

---

[14]In the usual actions, actions *in personam,* the officer delivering the summons (such as a deputy sheriff) must either serve the summons on the defendant personally or leave it with some adult at the defendant's residence.

instead of an answer. Technically this is called a "motion to dismiss for the reason that the complaint states no cause of action"—i.e., the complaint fails to state a legally-recognizable claim. For example, if P brings suit against D to recover damages from D, her next door neighbor, alleging that D cut down two of his (D's) oak trees without P's consent, D will file such a motion. In this case, since D had a perfect right to cut down any trees he wished on his own property, the motion to dismiss will be "sustained" by the court and the suit will be ended at this point. (A trial court's ruling on such a motion, however, may always be appealed to a higher court. If such court rules that a motion to dismiss should have been overruled rather than sustained, then the case will be sent back to the trial court for further proceedings.)[15]

Two further points should be noted.

1. By filing a motion to dismiss on the ground that no cause of action is stated, the defendant does not admit that the plaintiff's version of the facts is correct. Rather, he is simply saying that even if the facts are as stated, plaintiff has no basis under the law for bringing the suit. Thus, if the motion is overruled, the defendant is permitted to raise questions of fact during the trial.

2. Such motions always raise a question of law: Assuming that the facts are as alleged in the complaint, does plaintiff have a cause of action? If the trial judge says no, the motion is granted and that ends matters, as far as proceedings in the trial court are concerned. On the other hand, if the trial judge rules that the complaint *does* state a cause of action, the motion is overruled and the defendant must file an answer. The case then continues in the trial court.

The reply. If the defendant raises new matter—i.e., additional facts—in his answer, then the plaintiff must file a reply. In this pleading plaintiff will either deny or admit the new facts alleged in the answer. (If, after all the pleadings are in, neither the facts nor inferences that can be drawn from them are in dispute, the court may enter a *summary judgment* in favor of one party or the other, depending upon the law applicable to such facts. Ordinarily, however, these conditions do not exist and the case procedes to trial.)

The Discovery Stage

In early years, cases moved directly from the pleading stage to the trial stage. This meant that each party, going into the trial, had little information as to the specific evidence that the other party would rely on in presenting his case. Trial proceedings, as a result, often became what was commonly described as a "cat and mouse" game, with the parties often bringing in evidence that surprised their opponents.

The undesirability of these proceedings was finally perceived by lawyers and

---

[15]The terminology used in referring to this particular type of "motion to dismiss" follows the rules of civil procedure that have, in recent years, been adopted by many states. The earlier name for this same pleading device—the "demurrer"—continues to be used in a number of states, however. In such states, what has been said here in regard to the motion to dismiss applies with equal force to the demurrer.

judges, with the result that the Federal Rules of Civil Procedure, adopted in 1938, provided—through "discovery proceedings"—means by which the facts of a particular case would be fully disclosed before it came on for trial. The most common discovery tools recognized by these rules, which have now been essentially adopted by the states, are *depositions, interrogatories,* and *requests for production of documents.*

A deposition is testimony of a witness that is taken outside of court. Such testimony is given under oath, and both parties to the case must be notified so that they can be present when the testimony is given, and thus have the opportunity to cross-examine the witness.

Interrogatories are written questions submitted by one party to the other, which he or she must answer under oath. Use of this device is a primary way by which the questioning party may gain access to evidence that otherwise would be solely in the possession of his adversary.

A demand for documents permits a party to gain access to those kinds of evidence—such as business records, letters, and hospital bills—which are in the possession of the other party. Under modern rules of civil procedure the party seeking the documents has the right to possess them for the purposes of inspection and reproduction.

The Trial Courts: Trial Proceedings

The Trial Stage

Unless a controversy is settled by a judgment on the pleadings (such as the granting of a motion to dismiss), or unless the parties settle out of court, a case will eventually come on for trial. There a jury may be impaneled, evidence presented, a verdict returned, and a judgment entered in favor of one of the parties.

Impaneling a Jury. In any civil action in which the plaintiff is asking for a remedy at law, questions of fact are often resolved by a jury. However, a jury can be "waived" (dispensed with) if this is agreeable to both parties. In such instances the court decides questions of both fact and law. While waiver of a jury is increasingly common in civil actions today, there are still many actions where at least one of the parties demands a jury trial. The remainder of this discussion thus assumes the presence of a jury.

The names of prospective jurors are drawn from a list of these who have been selected for possible duty during the term. Each prospective juror is questioned by the attorneys in an effort to make sure that the jury will be as impartial as possible. If questioning indicates that a particular person would probably not be capable of such impartiality, he or she can be *challenged for cause.* Prospective jurors can be challenged, for example, if it is shown that they have a close friendship with one of the parties or the party's attorney, a financial interest in the case, or a bias resulting from any other aspect of the action. Any prospective juror disqualified for cause is excused, and another takes his or her place and is questioned in like fashion.

When there are no more challenges for cause, the attorney for each party has a limited number of *peremptory challenges*. Such challenges permit the attorney to have a juror removed arbitrarily, without assigning a reason for doing so. Once the number of prospective jurors who have survived both kinds of challenges reaches the number required by law to hear the case, they are sworn in and the case proceeds. (Traditionally the number of jurors has been twelve, but in recent years many states have reduced the number to eight, or even fewer, in civil actions.)

Order of Presentation of Proof: After the opening statements, the case is presented by the plaintiff, who has the "burden of proof" (the duty to prove the facts alleged in the complaint). The plaintiff attempts to meet this burden by calling witnesses whose testimony supports his or her version of the facts.

After each of the plaintiff's witnesses is examined by the plaintiff's attorney ("direct examination") the defendant's attorney can "cross-examine" the witness for the purpose of discrediting the person's testimony on as many points as possible. For example, a cross-examination might divulge (1) that pertinent facts in the direct examination were omitted, (2) that a witness's powers of observation were poor, or (3) that the witness stood to benefit financially if the plaintiff won a judgment.

The Rules of Evidence: Before proceeding to the next steps in the trial of a case, a brief mention of *evidence* is necessary. As a practical matter, one of the most crucial steps in a lawsuit is the establishment of the facts—a final determination as to what actually happened. An early English judge said, "Without a known fact, it is impossible to know the law on that fact."[16] And unless a litigant can convince the jury that his or her version of the facts is correct, the case may very well collapse at the outset.

Because the findings of fact play such an important role in the outcome of a case, it is imperative that the jury determine the facts on the basis of the most reliable testimony possible—testimony that is relevant, unbiased, and based on direct observations of the witnesses. *The primary purpose of the rules of evidence is to exclude testimony that lacks these characteristics.* (With an exception to be noted later, the jury's findings of fact are conclusive. This means that an appellate court, in determining the propriety of a rule of law applied by a lower court, must normally accept the jury's version of the facts as being correct.)

While the rules of evidence are so numerous and so complex as to preclude any balanced survey of the subject here, it is possible to examine briefly three of the most common kinds of testimony that the rules ordinarily remove from the jury's consideration—assuming that timely objection to such testimony is made by counsel during the trial proceedings. That is, if improper testimony is elicited from a witness by the attorney for one of the parties, and the opposing counsel does *not*

---

[16]C. J. Vaughan, *Bushel's Case,* Jones (T.), 1670.

make a formal challenge by "objecting" to it at that time, such testimony is normally permitted to become part of the record.

Irrelevant testimony. If a witness is asked a question that can have no possible bearing on the facts in issue, the opposing counsel may enter an objection on the basis that the answer would be "irrelevant." In a personal injury suit, for example, such matters as the defendant's religious beliefs, or the fact that he was convicted of a charge of negligent driving several years earlier, would have no bearing on the instant case. Objections to such testimony would be "sustained" by the court.

Hearsay. It is essential that the jury have before it direct evidence—testimony based on the witnesses' own personal knowledge and observation. A witness is not, therefore, normally permitted to testify as to what someone else told him or her about the facts in issue—evidence that is called hearsay.[17] One of the main reasons hearsay is excluded is that the primary source of the testimony is not available for cross-examination by the other party, and the reliability of the testimony cannot, therefore, be established.

Opinion. Sometimes a witness is asked for, or volunteers, information about a matter he or she believes to be true but of which the person actually has no personal knowledge. Such testimony, calling for the *opinion* of the witness, is normally excluded. For example, a witness could testify that the defendant's car was weaving back and forth on a highway, but if he further testified—on the basis of that observation alone—that the defendant was "obviously drunk," a motion to strike that part of the testimony would be sustained. Not only does the witness lack personal knowledge as to the *cause* of the defendant's erratic behavior, but the statement also constitutes a "conclusion of fact"—an inference that the jury, rather than a witness, is to draw from the evidence presented.

Opinion testimony is not always excluded. On technical matters that lie outside the knowledge of ordinary jurors it is frequently necessary that qualified experts be permitted to state their opinions as an aid to the jury's determination of the probable facts. Thus a physician may give an opinion as to the cause of a death or an engineer as to the cause of a bridge collapsing.

A word about "presumptions." Experience has shown that the existence of some facts is, in the ordinary course of events, so likely to be attended by other facts that a jury, upon proof of the former, can justifiably assume that such other facts also exist, even though direct proof is lacking. For example, it is common knowledge that a very high percentage of U.S. mail actually reaches the addressee; hence, once it is proven that X in fact mailed a letter to Y, the jury can reasonably infer (or presume) that the letter was actually delivered to Y's address (in the absence of convincing evidence to the contrary). Thus it is not always necessary that each and every fact in issue be established by the introduction of direct evidence.

---

[17]There are several exceptions to the hearsay rule, as there are to all the general exclusionary rules of evidence. As one example, a witness can testify as to another party's age, as this information is usually reliable. (Of course, if the precise age of a party is a material issue in a case, this testimony can be rebutted by the introduction of other evidence.)

Motion for a Directed Verdict: After all the plaintiff's evidence has been presented, it is likely that the defendant's attorney will make a *motion for a directed verdict.* By doing so, the attorney is contending that plaintiff has failed to prove his case—that is, either plaintiff has failed to introduce evidence tending to prove one or more allegations of fact necessary to the case or the evidence on such points was too weak to present a jury question. Normally the plaintiff's evidence is not this defective, and the motion is denied. The defendant's attorney then presents his or her witnesses, and each is cross-examined by the plaintiff's attorney.

After all the evidence is in, both parties may make motions for a directed verdict, each claiming that the evidence he or she has presented is so conclusive that the court should find the facts in his or her favor *as a matter of law.* Normally the evidence is not that conclusive; the motions are thus denied and the questions of fact left to the jury.

A jury question. In determining whether the evidence justifies the granting of a motion for a directed verdict, one rule of thumb is usually followed. If the court is of the opinion, from the evidence presented, that "reasonable minds could not differ" as to the facts, then—and only then—the court can grant a motion for a directed verdict. Otherwise, as is normally the case, the question must be left to the jury.

Instructions: When a case is submitted to the jury, the court instructs it about the law applicable to the various findings of fact which it might make. For example, the judge might tell the jury: "If you find that defendant flatly told plaintiff he was not going to perform his contract with plaintiff, then this is a breach of contract for which defendant will be liable in damages; but if you find that defendant's statement was more in the nature of a request for additional time within which to perform, indicating a willingness to perform as contracted in the event the request was rejected, this will not constitute a breach of contract on defendant's part."

In the following case, the plaintiff requested the trial court to rule that the defendant was guilty of negligence as a matter of law, and the court refused to do so. The question for the higher court was whether this refusal was correct. In ruling on the question, the higher court's decision indicates more fully how the rule of thumb is applied to real-life situations—and what great importance the surrounding circumstances are in determining whether the ruling of the trial court was correct.

In November of 1943, at the Los Angeles Municipal Airport, a plane owned and operated by Douglas Aircraft collided with a government-owned plane. The United States brought this action against Douglas and its pilot, Scott, to recover $10,589 damages, claiming defendants were guilty of negligence. Defendants denied the charge of negligence, and, as an affirmative defense, contended that the plaintiff and its agents were guilty of contributory negligence. Judgment was for defendants, for reasons appearing below, and plaintiff appealed.

United States v. Douglas Aircraft Company
Circuit Court of Appeals, Ninth Circuit, 169 F.2d 755 (1948)

The Los Angeles airport consisted of two main runways, which were three hundred feet wide, running parallel to each other but separated by a clear plot of ground. These main runways were designated 25-R and 25-L, and were bisected by a narrower runway, runway 22, which cut across them diagonally.

On November 11 a P-51 plane owned by the government completed a test flight and landed on runway 25-L. The plane coasted down the runway to the intersection with the diagonal runway, where the pilot, Pitcairn, turned left and parked on the right side of runway 22. (Before landing, Pitcairn had requested the control tower to send a tractor to meet him at this point and tow the plane to the parking area.)

Shortly thereafter, an S.B.D. plane owned by Douglas landed on runway 25-R and coasted down to diagonal runway 22. Its pilot, Scott, after getting permission from the control tower, entered runway 22 and taxied toward the parked P-51.

Since, due to the shape of the plane, Scott was not in a position to see clearly ahead, he zigzagged the plane at 15° angles as he taxied in an effort to improve his forward vision. While taxiing in this manner, the Douglas plane collided with the parked P-51. The United States thereafter brought this action.

At the trial, the above facts were proven. In addition, Scott testified that he looked down the diagonal runway, though perhaps not "all the way down," and that he knew he could see all the way down to the end of it. Also, according to the record, it was a clear day but there was some haze; the hills in back of the parked plane were brown or sand color; and the P-51 itself was painted a brown camouflaged, army color. It was further established that the runway was painted several colors, that the grass alongside it was brown, and that Scott did not see the parked plane until he hit it.

Just after the collision, according to Scott, Pitcairn said, "I'm glad you cut the switch." Scott replied, "I am sorry, I didn't see you." Pitcairn replied, "I am sorry. I had no business being here. I have been here for about ten minutes. I called for a truck and they haven't come after me yet." There was conflicting evidence as to whether it was customary for the traffic tower to notify pilots of obstructions on the field. No notice was given Scott as to the parked plane.

After the evidence was in, plaintiff asked the court to rule that (1) defendants were guilty of negligence as a matter of law and (2) plaintiff was not guilty of negligence as a matter of law. The court rejected these motions and submitted both issues to the jury. (Additionally, over plaintiff's objection, the court instructed the jury as to the circumstances in which it might find the accident to be "unavoidable"—i.e., without fault on anyone's part.) The jury returned a general verdict for defendants, judgment was entered, and the United States appealed.

Stephens, Chief Justice: . . . 1. Plaintiff-appellant made a motion for a directed verdict upon the ground that the defendant-appellee pilot was negligent *as a matter of law* in failing to see the parked plane before the collision, [and contends now that the trial court erred in failing to grant its motion.] Defendant-appellees [on the other hand] contend that Scott exercised due care under the circumstances and that the collision was caused by the negligence of appellant's agents: the pilot of the parked plane, and the employees in the control tower. It is argued that the record shows that Scott did all that could be expected of him.

In *Brinegar v. Green,* 117 F.2d 316, the court set forth a test often used: *"The determi-*

nation of the existence of negligence where the evidence is conflicting or the undisputed facts are such that fair-minded men may draw different conclusions from them is a question of fact for the jury and not one of law for the court." [Emphasis added.] Measured by this test, we think the question of negligence was properly left to the jury.

Appellant argues that looking and not seeing something in plain sight constitutes negligence as a matter of law. It is not, however, clear that such a situation existed. We cannot say, as a matter of law, that Scott violated the duties of a reasonable man in the circumstances. . . .

2. Appellant made a motion for an instructed verdict to the effect that it was *not guilty of contributory negligence,* which was overruled, and appellant claims error. Appellee argues that there was ample evidence to sustain a finding of contributory negligence on the part of appellant. In *Snipes v. Southern Rd. Co.,* 166 F.1, affirming language by the Supreme Court in *Richmond & Danville Rd. Co. v. Powers,* 149 U.S. 43, the court states: "It is well settled that, where there is uncertainty as to the existence of either negligence or contributory negligence, *the question is not one of law, but of fact, and to be settled by a jury; and this whether the uncertainty arises from a conflict in the testimony, or because, the facts being undisputed, fair-minded men will honestly draw different conclusions from them."* [Emphasis added.]

Pitcairn's conduct plus his statement substantiating possible lack of care could lead reasonable men to draw different conclusions and thus became a question of fact for the jury. The evidence in regard to the parked plane's position, its right to be where it was parked, and the custom and practice of the Air Traffic Tower and its duties, is in conflict. The Air Traffic Tower agency of plaintiff had authority and control over traffic, and would appear to be in the best position to take precautions for the removal of parked planes as hazards to traffic or to warn and advise appellee's pilot of the parked plane's position. Whether or not the action or non-action of the traffic tower in any instance was customary, its operation may constitute negligence. Since more than one reasonable deduction can be drawn from the evidence, the issue is for the jury.

In *Zibbell v. Southern Pacific Co.,* 116 P. 513, the court rejected an argument that the court should instruct the jury that plaintiff was contributorily negligent as a matter of law: " 'It is only where no fact is left in doubt, and no deduction or inference other than negligence can be drawn by the jury from the evidence, that the court can say as a matter of law, that contributory negligence is established. Even where the facts are undisputed, if reasonable minds might draw different conclusions upon the question of negligence, the question is one of fact for the jury.' " . . .

3. The court instructed the jury upon the subject of *unavoidable or inevitable accident.* The appellant claims error because, he asserts, there is no evidence in the case from which it can be determined that the accident was unavoidable or inevitable.

The circumstances, other than the collision itself, are practically without dispute. It was a clear day with haze. The pilot of the parked plane had landed at a proper place and took the precaution to pull over to the side of the landing strip, if not entirely off it. His plane was camouflaged and could well have blended almost imperceptively with the brown background. It was ten minutes from the time the pilot requested a tractor in sending a machine to pull him to the hangar before the collision, but there was considerable activity upon the field by other planes. Scott, the Douglas test pilot, landed at a proper place, looked up the landing strip, and noticing no obstruction taxied forward but with the customary caution of S-ing or zigzagging his plane. These facts may well have convinced the jury that the accident happened notwithstanding all concerned used due and proper care throughout [and the instruction on unavoidable accident was therefore proper].

It is apparent from what we have already said that we do not agree with plaintiff-appellant's contentions that the court erred in denying its motion for a directed verdict or for a new trial, or that the evidence is insufficient to sustain or support the verdict.

Affirmed.

Comment: 1. As indicated earlier, a defendant in a negligence action is not liable (a) if the jury finds that he or she was, in fact, exercising reasonable care at the time of the accident—that is, was *not* negligent; or, in most states, (b) if the jury finds him or her to be negligent but finds that the plaintiff was also negligent—that is, *contributorily negligent.*

2. In this case, the jury simply returned a *general verdict* for the defendant. Thus it is not possible to know whether it found the facts as in (a) or (b). Either way, the result would be the same—a verdict for defendant.

After the Verdict: After the jury has returned its verdict, the court enters a judgment in conformity with it. Thereafter, as we have seen, the party against whom the judgment was entered may move for a new trial, alleging that certain errors occurred. If this motion is overruled by the trial court, the loser can then appeal the judgment to a higher court.

There is also one other possibility. After a verdict has been returned, the losing party may ask the court to disregard the verdict and enter a judgment in his or her favor; this is done by making a motion for *judgment notwithstanding the verdict.* If the court feels that reasonable people could have reached a verdict *only* in favor of the party who has made the motion, rather than the verdict which was actually returned, it will grant the motion. (Such a motion is granted only in exceptional circumstances, and the correctness of such a ruling can be appealed by the party against whom the judgment is entered.)

The Appellate Courts

An Overview

The work of the higher courts in ruling on appeals differs considerably from that of the trial courts.[18] In the first place, appellate courts are concerned only with *questions of law*—that is, whether the rulings of the trial court, of which the appellant complains, were legally correct. Secondly, intermediate appellate courts normally are comprised of three or more judges, while the highest court in a state usually has five or seven justices. This obviously brings to bear *more judicial experience* on the points in issue than can be afforded by the single trial judge.

---

[18]All appellate courts have *some* "original jurisdiction"; that is, certain exceptional cases can be properly commenced in them. However, we are not here concerned with the work of the appellate courts in such situations.

Thirdly, since only questions of law are in issue, there is *no reintroduction of evidence and thus no jury*. The questions of law are settled on the basis of the record in the lower court, together with consideration of the opposing parties' briefs (written arguments) and oral arguments as to the correctness of the rulings in question. As a result, unlike the rulings of the trial court, which must be made during "the heat of battle," the decisions of the appellate courts can be made in a detached and unhurried manner.

Questions of Law

A great number of "questions of law" will be brought out by the cases in the remainder of this text. For now, suffice it to say that some of the most common of them arise where the appellant is claiming that errors were made by the trial court in (1) admitting or excluding testimony, (2) ruling on motions, particularly on motions for a directed verdict, (3) stating the law in instructions to the jury, and (4) interpreting state or federal statutes.

Effect of Error

If the appellate court is of the opinion that an alleged error did occur and that it conceivably could have affected the outcome of the case, the lower court's judgment will be reversed (set aside), and normally the case will be *remanded* (sent back) to the trial court for a new trial. The reason for the remanding is that most errors are of such a nature that the higher court cannot be positive the verdict (and/or judgment) would have gone for the other party had the error not occurred. For example, if it were determined that the trial court erred in admitting hearsay testimony of one witness, it is *possible* that the verdict and judgment would still have been entered for the same party who won in the lower court even if the testimony had been excluded.

Some judgments, however, are reversed outright, with no further proceedings being necessary. This is particularly true where the rule of law that the trial court has applied to the established facts is simply contrary to the law then existing in that state. In such a situation the appellate court will apply the correct rule of law and enter final judgment accordingly.

Setting Aside a Verdict

In most cases each party is able to introduce *some* evidence tending to prove that his or her version of the facts is correct, and it is for the jury (or the court, in the absence of a jury) to determine which testimony is the more convincing. As we have seen, the appellate courts are normally bound by the jury's verdict; that is, they must accept the jury's decision on the *facts*—with one major exception.

To guard against the possibility that a jury will make a finding of fact that is totally unwarranted, an appellant can always contend that one or more findings of fact were "unsupported by the evidence." This presents a *question of law* for the appellate court, and the court can reverse the judgment if it agrees with the appellant's contention. If a jury makes a finding of fact that is unsupported by *any* evidence, the verdict obviously can be set aside by the appellate court. Similarly, if a jury inadvertently makes a finding of fact that is contrary to a "stipulated fact" (a matter that both parties admitted to be true during the trial), the verdict can be set aside. These instances, however, are quite exceptional.

Much more common are situations where one of the parties introduces substantial evidence tending to prove the existence of a certain fact, while the other party introduces less, or weaker, evidence to the contrary. If the jury chooses to base its verdict on the lesser or weaker evidence, the party whose evidence was ignored will very likely ask the appellate court to set aside the verdict on the general ground that it is contrary to the evidence.

In such situations, there is some diversity among the states as to the rules that should be applied in determining whether the verdict should be set aside. Some states, for example, permit the verdict to stand as long as there is "any credible (believable) evidence" to support it; other states permit the verdict to stand if it is supported by "substantial evidence," by "any substantial evidence," or by evidence that is "not inherently improbable" or "not inherently unbelievable." Since most states have adopted one or the other of these rules, a verdict supported by any credible evidence will probably not be set aside even if the evidence is "vague, weak, or unsatisfactory," and even if there is substantial evidence to the contrary.

Some states follow rules that make it easier to set aside verdicts. For example, in some jurisdictions a verdict can be set aside if it is not supported by the "weight of the evidence," or by a "preponderance of the evidence." Even under these rules, however, the setting aside of a verdict is still somewhat exceptional because of what is meant by *weight* and *preponderance*. Testimony of just one witness can constitute the weight or preponderance of the evidence, if the testimony is unbiased, positive, and persuasive—even though others testify to the contrary. For example, statements like the following frequently appear in court decisions: "The 'preponderance' of the evidence is not determined by the number of witnesses, but by the greater *weight of the evidence,* which does not necessarily mean the greater number of witnesses, but [rather upon the witnesses'] opportunity for knowledge, information possessed, and [their] manner of testifying . . . "[19]

The following case presents a typical situation in which the appellant is contending that a verdict against him was not supported by the evidence. Specifically, the defendant-appellant is seeking to set aside a finding by the jury that it was he, rather than a third party, who offered plaintiff a ride in defendant's automobile; the Supreme Court of Montana, in upholding the verdict, cites several generally accepted rules by which the propriety of a verdict is to be tested.

---

[19]*Garver v. Garver,* 121 P. 165 (1912).

D. A. (Jim) Batchoff was injured in November of 1940 when he was thrown from a car in which he was being driven from Billings to Butte, Montana. The car was owned by Craney, the defendant, and was being driven by Baily Stortz, a friend of the defendant.

Batchoff brought this action against Craney to recover damages, alleging (1) that Stortz was guilty of gross negligence in the operation of the vehicle, and (2) that Stortz was an agent of defendant Craney while making the drive to Butte. Defendant contended, on the other hand, that Stortz was acting as an agent of U.S. Senator Burton K. Wheeler at the time of the accident.

At the trial, plaintiff testified that he was at the Northern Pacific depot in Billings on the morning of November 2, waiting for the train to Butte, when he ran into the defendant, who said, "Oh, hell, Jim, stay here and miss this train. Senator and Mrs. Wheeler and Baily Stortz [Wheeler's secretary] are getting off of this train. . . . I am going to leave my automobile with Baily to drive it back to Butte and you can ride along with him." (Defendant himself was remaining in Billings.)

Later in the day plaintiff and Stortz set out for Butte in defendant's car, with Stortz driving. Plaintiff further testified that Stortz drove the car from 70 to 75 miles per hour; that he complained of the excessive speed but, instead of slowing down, the speed was increased to 85 miles per hour; there were wet spots in the road; the car hit a wet spot, skidded around several times; a door of the car swung open and plaintiff was thrown from the car into a borrow pit and the car followed and struck him, rendering him unconscious and causing the injuries complained of.

The jury accepted plaintiff's version of the facts and returned a verdict in his favor for $10,000. On appeal, the primary contention of the defendant was that the jury's verdict was unsupported by the evidence, and ought to be set aside for this reason.

In support of this contention, defendant argued that the jury should not have believed plaintiff's testimony that defendant offered plaintiff the ride, in view of the fact that defendant's witnesses testified that defendant had in fact *loaned his car to Senator Wheeler* for the day, and in view of the fact that plaintiff, in an earlier proceeding before the State Industrial Accident Board, *had testified that it was Stortz, rather than the defendant, who had offered him the ride.*

(We shall now see, in the opinion below, how the Montana Supreme Court went about the job of determining whether the defendant-appellant's allegation of error was well founded.)

Batchoff v. Craney
Supreme Court of Montana, 172 P.2d 308 (1946)

Angstmann, Justice: . . . Defendant produced witnesses who testified that he lent his car to Senator Wheeler for his use in and around Billings, and that Stortz was acting as agent of Senator Wheeler in returning the car to Butte when the accident occurred. In other words, the evidence was in sharp conflict if it can be said that the testimony of plaintiff is worthy of belief. *Whether his testimony was worthy of belief was for the jury to determine.* [Emphasis added.]

Thus in *Wallace v. Wallace,* 279 P. 374, this court said,

A jury may believe the testimony of one witness and disbelieve that of another, or any numbers of others, and the determination of the jury in this regard is final; having spoken, this court must assume that the facts are as stated by the witnesses, believed by the jury, and claimed by the prevailing party. The preponderance of the evidence may be established by a single witness as against a greater number of witnesses who testify to the contrary.

It follows that wherever there is a conflict in the evidence, this court may only review the testimony for the purpose of determining whether or not there is *any substantial evidence in the record to support the verdict of the jury, and must accept the evidence there found as true, unless that evidence is so inherently impossible or improbable as not to be entitled to belief; and, where a verdict is based upon substantial evidence which, from any point of view, could have been accepted by the jury as credible, it is binding upon this court, although it may appear inherently weak.* [Emphasis added.]

[The court then ruled, in regard to the statements made by plaintiff before the Industrial Accident Board, that such statements could not be used as substantive evidence by the jury. At the most, the court said, such statements could cause the jury to question plaintiff's testimony in the trial court, and if it chose to accept his testimony despite the contradictory statements made earlier, it could do so. On this aspect of the case, the court quoted an opinion in *State v. Peterson,* 59 P.2d 61, as follows:]

A witness false in one part of his testimony is to be distrusted in others, and a witness may be impeached [by showing] . . . that he has made at other times statements inconsistent with his present testimony; but while proof of . . . inconsistent statements at other times . . . may discredit the witness, such proof goes only to the credibility of the witness, of which the jury remains the sole judge, as well as the weight to be given thereto.

It follows that, although the jury may reject the false testimony and assume, regarding the rest of it, an attitude of distrust, the jurors may render a verdict based upon the testimony of such witness if after examination they find it worthy of belief.

[In the instant case] there is nothing inherently incredible or improbable in plaintiff's version of what happened. . . .

Judgment affirmed.

Comment: When the owner of an automobile permits another person to drive it, and the driver injures a third party as a result of operating it negligently, the owner is *not necessarily* liable to the injured party. Under the law of Montana and many other states, the injured party must ordinarily prove that the driver was an *agent* of the owner of the automobile at the time of the accident in order to recover a judgment against the owner.

That is why, in the instant case, defendant Craney would have escaped liability if the jury had accepted the testimony of his witnesses to the effect that Craney had actually loaned his car to Senator Wheeler for the day (and that Stortz, without Craney's knowledge, offered plaintiff the ride). In such a situation, Stortz would have been Wheeler's agent, rather than Craney's. As we know now, the jury rejected this version of the facts in returning a verdict for plaintiff.

A good many criticisms are made of the manner in which controversies are settled under our present legal system. Many of these have to do with the general nature of the "adversary system," the role of the jury, and the selection and performance of judges.

Analysis of the Adjudicative Processes

The Adversary System

Most legal disputes are settled through *adversary proceedings,* where the parties meet face to face (legally speaking) with each permitted to contest the allegations of fact and points of law raised by the other. The attorney for each party determines how to prove that his or her client's version of the facts is correct, and each researches the law to find legal principles upon which to base the client's case. The parties themselves thus frame the issues, and the judge simply rules on the issues that are presented.

It is sometimes said that the adversary system puts an undue premium on the relative effectiveness of the competing attorneys and too greatly limits the trial judge's role in the outcome of the case. Overall, these criticisms are probably not as valid as they seem.

In the first place, the skill of the competing lawyers is usually equal enough for each party to be able to introduce the evidence and to present rules of law in support of his or her position. Additionally, the rules of procedure and evidence, and the normal desire of the trial judge to see that each party has a fair opportunity to "have a say," place certain limits on the practical advantage that one party might have in a case where his or her counsel is markedly more able than the other litigant's counsel.

The Role of the Jury

Many weaknesses, real or imagined, are attributed to the jury's role in the adjudicative processes, including the following: (1) that jurors cannot understand the complex issues that are presented; (2) that jurors are too likely to be influenced by the personalities of the attorneys rather than by objective considerations; and (3) that, given the rules of law applying to the various alternative findings that they may return, juries frequently ignore (or overemphasize) evidence in order to bring in a verdict in favor of a party for whom they have sympathy or against a party for whom they have animosity.

Supporters of the jury system, on the other hand, feel that most of these criticisms are not, in general, supported by the facts. First, in many cases there are only one or two controlling issues, and these are quite understandable to the average person. Second, verdicts can be set aside if they are clearly based on "passion or prejudice," in addition to the other grounds mentioned earlier. Third, there is substantial evidence that most jurors take their duties seriously and try to perform them conscientiously.

Performance of the Judges

The overall performance of a legal system obviously depends to a great extent upon the character and competence of its judges. For this reason, particularly, it is distressing to note that the judges of this country have, as a class, come in for rather heavy criticism over the years. While some of this criticism may be unjustified, there is considerable evidence that the performance of a significant percentage of our judges (though certainly not a majority) can be characterized as barely adequate, or worse.

Three factors are chiefly responsible. First, judges' salaries are often lower than the income that can be earned in private practice by topnotch attorneys. Second, in the United States, persons who aspire to a career in the judiciary are not required to take special training and/or go through an apprenticeship of a year or two on an appeals court, as is the case in many countries. And, third, the judges of our state courts have traditionally been elected. This has frequently resulted in the nomination of candidates by the political parties on the basis of their party service and loyalty, rather than on ability and experience. And, once elected, incumbent judges have not easily been dislodged even when their performance is mediocre or worse.

In recent years, in an effort to alleviate the shortcomings resulting from the election of judges, over 30 states and the District of Columbia have adopted some form of "merit plan" selection of judges. While these plans vary to some extent, they all are based on the idea that when a judicial vacancy occurs, a judicial nominating commission develops a list of three to five persons whom they feel to be the best qualified persons for the job. (These commissions are nonpartisan in nature, and are usually comprised equally of lawyers and nonlawyers.) The list of names is submitted to the governor, who selects one person to fill the vacancy. Thereafter, appointees must indicate before their terms of office expire whether they wish to stand for another term. If so, the appointee runs unopposed in the next general election, with the voters simply indicating whether they are satisfied with the performance rendered during the first term of office. If the appointee loses on this vote, the appointive process then begins anew.

Questions and Problems

1. Gatch was an employee of a radio station (Arrow Broadcasting) who brought suit against Hennepin Broadcasting to recover $8,000 damages, alleging that Hennepin interfered with his contract with Arrow, and that this interference constituted a wrong under Minnesota law. (Gatch was a Minnesota resident, and Hennepin was a Minnesota corporation.) When Gatch filed this suit in a Minnesota state court, Hennepin asked that it be removed to the federal courts, claiming that a *federal question* was presented in view of the fact that Hennepin was subject to the rules and regulations of the Federal Communications Commission. Do you agree that this fact raises a federal question? Why or why not? (*Gatch v. Hennepin Broadcasting,* 349 F.Supp. 1180, 1972.)

2. Rate, a Georgia lawyer, is owed $18,250 in legal fees by Jackson, a Florida resident. Although Rate could have brought suit to recover the debt in a federal court in Florida on

grounds of diversity of citizenship, he chose, instead, to file his suit in a Florida court in the county in which Jackson lives. If Jackson now asks that the suit be transferred to the federal courts, will his request have to be granted? Explain.

3. While walking across Gomez's property one evening, North is injured when he falls into an unguarded excavation. When North brings a negligence action against Gomez in the proper state court to recover damages, that court applies the rule that a trespasser cannot hold a landowner liable even if he is guilty of negligence, and dismissed the action. North appeals the decision to the state supreme court, which affirms the rule of nonliability. In this case, is the ruling of the state supreme court final? (I.e., if North were to appeal to the U.S. Supreme court, would it refuse to consider the case?) Why or why not?

4. California has a "long arm" statute which provides, in essence, that any out-of-state resident who drives an automobile within the state is thereby giving his consent to be sued in the California courts if he is involved in an accident while in the state. (The statute further provides that the employer of the driver, if any, may also be sued in the California courts.)

With this statute in effect, Hall (a California resident) was struck by a car driven in California by a Nevada resident. The driver, an employee of the State of Nevada, was in California on official state business, and was driving a car owned by the State of Nevada at the time of the accident. Hall thereafter sued the driver and the State of Nevada in a California court to recover damages.

At the trial, the State of Nevada contended that there were several constitutional reasons why it could not be sued in such an action. The gist of the state's argument was that the state courts of one state (here, California) did not have jurisdiction over it. (I.e., Nevada contended that the courts of one state do not have the power to determine the liability of a sister state.) Basing your answer on the limited exposure to the subject of jurisdiction that we have experienced so far, do you think Nevada's argument is a good one? Discuss. (*Nevada v. Hall,* 99 S.Ct. 1182, 1979.)

5. In regard to some cases that present federal questions, the state and federal courts are said to have "concurrent jurisdiction." What is meant by this?

6. Evashevski Building Associates (EBA), makes a contract with Kinnick in Des Moines, Iowa, under which it is to build an apartment complex in Omaha, Nebraska, for $1,500,000. Later, EBA refuses to do the work, whereupon Kinnick sues it for damages for breach of contract. At the trial, EBA contends that the contract was invalid under Nebraska law (although admittedly valid under Iowa law.) Is EBA correct in its contention that the validity of the contract is governed by Nebraska law, in view of the fact that the building was to have been constructed in that state? Why or why not?

7. In *United States v. Douglas Aircraft,* page 41, the trial court refused to rule that the defendants were guilty of negligence as a matter of law; it also refused to rule that the plaintiff was not guilty of contributory negligence as a matter of law. What specific circumstances of the case caused the appellate court to decide that each of these rulings was correct? (I.e., why did the appellate court agree that both issues presented jury questions?)

8. Normally, the findings of fact made by a jury are binding upon an appellate court. What is the major exception to this rule, and how can the exception be explained?

I have heard that lawyers in one of the Western states, when they cite a decided case as a precedent in support of an argument, never say, as the Louisiana lawyers say, that the precedent "fits like a glove," or is "on all fours" . . . [with] the case being argued. They say that the precedent is a "goose case." The expression arose from the perplexity of a so-called "case lawyer," who was unprepared to advise his client whether he was liable in damages because his geese had trespassed on his neighbor's lawn. The lawyer said he had found several cases where the owners were held liable because their horses, cows, sheep, goats, or dogs had committed acts of trespass; but he could not find a "goose case." The distinction which he observed was that his "goose case" was not "on all fours."
Justice O'Neill, dissenting, *Taylor v. Allen*, 151 La. 82 (1921)

3

Common Law

While the lawyer in the above quote should be chided for his reluctance to form an opinion until he found a "goose case," his basic technique, at least, is quite proper. Whenever a controversy presents an issue that is not governed by statutory law, the attorneys for both parties—and the judge—look to earlier cases in an effort to determine whether a principle of law has been laid down that is applicable to the present controversy.

In Chapter 1 we indicated that there are three basic processes by which law is made: (1) the establishment of precedents by the courts, (2) the enactment of statutes by the legislatures and by Congress, and (3) the interpretation of statutes by the courts. In this chapter we will examine the first of these processes; the others will be discussed in the next chapter.

In our discussion of the early king's courts, we observed that they largely made up the law on a case-by-case basis. If a plaintiff asked for damages for breach of contract in a situation where the defendant denied that a contract ever existed, the court had to spell out the nature of a contract in reaching a conclusion. Similarly, if a defendant admitted making the contract in question but sought to escape liability for reasons of illness or military service, the court had to decide what kinds of defenses were legally recognizable.

Over a period of time, then, as more and more cases were settled, a rudimentary body of contract law came into being. Thereafter, when other cases arose involving contractual matters, the courts quite naturally looked to the earlier cases to see what principles of law had been established. The same procedure was followed in many other branches of law, and the legal rules that arose in this manner constituted the *common law.*

In fashioning common-law principles, the early courts laid great stress on the customs, morals, and forms of conduct that were generally prevailing in the community. Additionally, where such factors were not well established or where they led to questionable results, the judges' personal feelings as to what kinds of conduct were just and fair undoubtedly entered the picture.

Most of the common-law rules that had developed in England were, quite logically, adopted by early courts in the U.S. Gradually, however, the legislatures of the states began to pass increasing numbers of statutes, with the result that today most branches of the law are statutory in nature. For example, all states now have comprehensive statutes governing the areas of corporation law, criminal law, tax law, municipal corporations, and motor vehicles. Some of these statutes have been based largely on the common-law principles that were in effect earlier. Others, however, have been passed to create a body of rules that did not exist previously or to expressly overrule common-law principles.

Despite the ever-increasing amount of statutory law in this country, several branches of law are still essentially common law in nature, particularly *contracts, torts,* and *agency.* In these areas, where the legislatures have not seen fit to enact comprehensive statutes, the courts still settle controversies on the basis of judge-made or case law—the rules formulated by the courts in deciding earlier cases over the years.

The Doctrine of *Stare Decisis*

The heart of the common-law process lies in the inclination of the courts to follow established precedents. Here the doctrine of *stare decisis* reigns supreme. *Stare decisis* means, literally, "to stand by decisions." Thus, when a controversy involves a given fact-pattern, the attorneys for both parties search for earlier cases involving similar fact-patterns in an effort to determine whether applicable principles of law have been established. If this research produces a number of similar cases (or even one) within the state where a rule has been applied by the appellate courts, the trial court will ordinarily feel constrained to follow the same rule in settling the current controversy.

The basic strength of the doctrine of *stare decisis* is that it brings relative certainty to the law. As a principle is applied to more and more cases presenting the same (or substantially similar) issues, attorneys can be increasingly confident that the rule will be followed in the future and can advise their clients on this basis. And, to a somewhat lesser extent, the well-established principles become increasingly known to the general populace. In the case below, the Supreme Court of Ohio was called upon to decide whether a rule adopted in a case in 1885 should continue to be followed in that state.

Hall v. Rosen

Supreme Court of Ohio
383 N.E.2d 725 (1977)

In February of 1969 Patricia Hall, seven months pregnant, married Jerry Ross. At the time of the marriage Ross knew of her obvious pregnancy, and also knew that he was not the unborn child's father. Mrs. Ross subsequently gave birth to a daughter, Lisa Renee.

In 1970 the Rosses were divorced, at which time she assumed her maiden name. Three years later she brought this action for child support against John Rosen, Lisa's biological (natural) father.

The trial court dismissed the suit without a trial, basing its action on a case decided by the Ohio Supreme Court in 1885, *Miller v. Anderson,* 3 N.E. 605. In that case the court held that "the natural father of a child *can not be held for its support* . . . if the mother, after the child was begotten, and during pregnancy, contracts a marriage with another man who marries her with full knowledge of her condition." [Emphasis added.] In such a situation, the court continued, "the man so marrying consents to stand in *loco parentis* [in the place of a parent] of such child," and is "conclusively presumed" to be the father of the child.

Ms. Hall appealed this decision to a court of appeals, which held that the rule of *Miller v. Anderson* had been impliedly overruled by the Ohio Supreme Court in a case decided in 1972. Accordingly, the court of appeals reversed the judgment and remanded the case to the trial court for further proceedings. Rosen appealed to the Ohio Supreme Court.

Locher, Justice: . . . Pivotal to the resolution of the case is the question of whether the rule of law formulated in *Miller v. Anderson* should continue to be the law in Ohio. [The court here held that the court of appeals misinterpreted its decision in the 1972 case, and it then explained why the case of *Miller v. Anderson* continued to be the law, in these words:]

The rule of law espoused in *Miller v. Anderson* constitutes a landmark adhered to by a plethora of subsequent decisions [in this state]. At its genesis is the common-law presumption of legitimacy. . . .

It has long been recognized, and the judicial policy of *stare decisis* has derived therefrom, that the law should provide a degree of certainty upon which individuals may rely in the conduct of their affairs. The doctrine of *stare decisis* is the judicial recognition of this need to promote the certainty, stability and predictability of the law. . . .

The statement of law formulated in *Miller v. Anderson* has been accepted not once, but in numerous decisions, the most recent in 1976. On this issue the law has been clear. The rights and liabilities of the individuals have been clearly set out. There has existed a degree of certainty and predictability upon which individuals may rely in the course of their lives. Reliance having been placed in these defined rights and liabilities, they should not now be swept away by mere judicial fiat or pretensions of improvement founded in speculation. . . .

[The court then conceded that the rule of a prior case should not continue to be followed if it were no longer a reasonable one. However, the court defended both the reason and logic of the rule of *Miller v. Anderson* in these words:] Behind the principle that a biological father may not be sued for support if another man marries the mother knowing her to be pregnant, is the concept that by marriage the husband is held to adopt the child at birth into his family, and the law holds him liable for its support as one standing in *loco parentis*. . . . Thus, the husband has voluntarily assumed the burden of supporting the child. Preventing suit against the biological father . . . is consistent with the husband's assent to become the child's father, thereby altering the status, rights and responsibilities of others. . . .

Rejection of the long-accepted policy proclaimed by *Miller v. Anderson* should be undertaken only with a comprehension of the inherent evils to be aroused by such a course . . . [For example,] the creation of an invitation to bring support actions against biological fathers, perhaps many years after the fact, portends the possibility of "father-shopping," i.e., seeking support from the most successful of possible candidates. These actions would . . . raise the possibility of disrupting other established families by moral disparagement and suddenly increased financial responsibilites. Invitation of these evils is not a sagacious one. We believe the basic principles of law formulated in *Miller v. Anderson* are of continued utility and validity.

Judgment of the court of appeals is reversed [and the trial court's order of dismissal reinstated.]

Comment: In the interest of accuracy it is to be noted that the natural father *is* held liable for child support in a number of states in similar circumstances—a fact given considerable weight by three members of the Ohio Supreme Court in a dissenting opinion.

Choice of Precedent

The application of *stare decisis* raises little difficulty where the facts of the earlier cases are virtually identical to those of the case under discussion—"goose cases," so to speak—and where one rule has been uniformly followed, as in the case of *Hall v. Rosen.* In many situations, however, while a number of prior cases have involved similar fact-patterns, the courts have applied different rules to each. In other words, they have distinguished some cases from others, feeling that the fact-patterns of the cases were sufficiently dissimilar to justify the varying decisions.

This is unquestionably one of the problems arising under the doctrine of *stare decisis:* the decided cases frequently are so similar on the facts that it is an extremely close question as to how far distinctions can honestly be made by the courts. Critics claim that this is a weakness of the doctrine, in that it produces a degree of uncertainty in the law. But it also constitutes an element of strength, for it affords the courts some latitude in choosing which rule of law will bring about the most desirable result in a specific controversy.

The following case clearly indicates the nature of the problem. It is also significant in two other respects. First, the reasoning of the majority of the Court of Appeals of New York has been widely (though not universally) followed in other states in negligence cases brought against manufacturers. Second, the issue presented by it permits some observations about the impact of changing social and economic considerations on the law's evolution.

The case raises the question of whether a plaintiff can, on the negligence theory, recover damages from a careless manufacturer where the plaintiff did not purchase the defective goods directly from the manufacturer. Prior to 1900, and for some years thereafter, the general rule in New York and many other states was that the plaintiff could not, that the only recourse was to bring an action against the person from whom the goods were purchased.

This rule of nonliability was partly based on both social and economic considerations. From a social standpoint, cases involving this question were relatively few because manufacturing was in its infancy in this country. Thus the refusal to award damages did not affect large numbers of people. From an economic standpoint, the courts were reluctant to adopt a rule of liability that might impose serious economic hardship on young and financially struggling manufacturers.

By the time this case was heard, both these conditions had changed to some extent. And, perhaps for other reasons as well, the New York courts had begun to recognize certain exceptions to the general rule, dating as far back as the *Winchester* case in 1853. With these observations in mind, let us see how Justice Cardozo and his colleagues viewed the cases that arose between 1853 and 1916 in determining which rules should be applicable to MacPherson's action against the Buick Motor Company.

MacPherson v. Buick Motor Co.

Court of Appeals of New York, 111 N.E. 1050 (1916)

The Buick Motor Company, defendant, manufactured an automobile and sold it to a retail dealer. MacPherson, plaintiff, purchased it from the dealer and was subsequently injured when the car collapsed. The collapse was due to the "crumbling" of the wooden spokes of one of the car's wheels while MacPherson was driving it. He brought this action against Buick, contending that it had manufactured the car negligently.

Defendant denied the claim of negligence on the ground that the defective wheel was made by another manufacturer, the Imperial Wheel Company, from whom defendant had purchased it. Additionally, defendant contended that it had no liability to plaintiff even if it were negligent, for the reason that no contractual relationship existed between it and plaintiff.

There was evidence tending to prove that the wood in the wheel was defective, that a reasonable inspection by Buick would have disclosed the defect, and that Buick omitted any inspection of the purchased wheels. The trial court instructed the jury that if it believed this evidence, and if it felt that Buick's care was less than that which a manufacturer should reasonably have exercised, then Buick was guilty of negligence. The court further instructed the jury that, in such event, Buick would be liable to plaintiff despite the fact there was no privity of contract (relationship) between it and plaintiff.

Under these instructions, the jury returned a verdict for plaintiff. An intermediate court, the Appellate Division of the Supreme Court, affirmed the judgment of the trial court, and Buick appealed to the highest court in New York State.

Cardozo, Justice: ... The question to be determined is whether the defendant owed a duty of care and vigilance to any one but the immediate purchaser....

[Cardozo at this point examined five earlier negligence cases, in each of which the defendant sought to escape liability on the ground that the plaintiff was a "remote party"— that is, that plaintiff did not deal directly with the defendant. In the first of these, *Thomas v. Winchester,* liability was imposed, because of the unusual danger that resulted from the negligence. In the remaining cases, the question was whether the "Thomas rule" was applicable. The court discussed the five cases as follows:]

The foundations of this branch of the law, at least in this state, were laid in *Thomas v. Winchester,* 6 N.Y. 397 (1853). A poison was falsely labeled. The sale was made to a druggist, who in turn sold it to a customer. The customer recovered damages from the seller who affixed the label. *"The defendant's negligence," it was said, "put human life in imminent danger."* [Emphasis added.] A poison falsely labeled is likely to injure any one who gets it. Because the danger is to be foreseen, there is a duty to avoid the injury. Cases were cited by way of illustration in which manufacturers were not subject to any duty irrespective of contract. The distinction was said to be that the manufacturers' conduct (in those cases), though negligent, was not likely to result in injury to any one except the purchaser. We are not required to say whether the chance of injury was always as remote as the distinction assumes. The principle of the distinction is for present purposes the important thing.

Thomas v. Winchester became quickly a landmark of the law. *In the application of its principle there may at times have been uncertainty or even error. There has never in this state been doubt or disavowal of the principle itself.* [Emphasis added.] The chief cases are well known, yet to recall some of them will be helpful. *Loop v. Litchfield,* 42 N.Y. 351 (1870), is the earliest. It was the case of a defect in a small balance wheel used on a circular saw. The manufacturer pointed out the defect to the buyer, who wished a cheap article and was ready to assume the risk. The risk can hardly have been an imminent one, for the wheel lasted five years before it broke. In the meanwhile the buyer had made a lease of the machinery. It was held that the manufacturer was not answerable to the lessee. *Loop v. Litchfield* was followed in *Losee v. Clute,* 51 N.Y. 494, the case of the explosion of a steam boiler (in which a manufacturer was again held not to be answerable to a remote plaintiff). That decision has been criticized *(Thompson on Negligence, 233; Shearman & Redfield on Negligence, 117);* but it must be confined to its special facts. It was put upon the ground that the risk of injury was too remote. The buyer in that case had not only accepted the boiler, but had tested it. The manfacturer knew that his own test was not the final one. The finality of the test has a bearing on the measure of diligence owing to persons other than the purchaser.

These early cases suggest a narrow construction of the [Thomas] rule. Later cases, however, evince a more liberal spirit. First in importance is *Devlin v. Smith,* 89 N.Y. 470. The defendant, a contractor, built a scaffold for a painter. The painter's servants were injured. The contractor was held liable. He knew that the scaffold, if improperly constructed, was a most dangerous trap. He knew that it was used by the workmen. He was building it for that very purpose. Building it for their use, he owed them a duty, irrespective of his contract with their master, to build it with care.

From *Devlin v. Smith* we pass over intermediate cases and turn to the latest case in this court in which *Thomas v. Winchester* was followed. That case is *Statler v. Ray Mfg. Co.,* 195 N.Y. 478. The defendant manufactured a large coffee urn. It was installed in a restaurant. When heated, the urn exploded and injured the plaintiff. We held that the manufacturer was liable. We said that the urn "was of such a character inherently that, when applied to the purposes for which it was designed, it was liable to become a source of great danger to many people if not carefully and properly constructed."

It may be that Devlin v. Smith *and* Statler v. Ray Mfg. Co. *have extended the rule of* Thomas v. Winchester. *If so, this court is committed to the extension.* [Emphasis added.] The defendant argues that things imminently dangerous to life are poisons, explosives, deadly weapons—things whose normal function it is to injure or destroy. But whatever the rule in *Thomas v. Winchester* may once have been, it has no longer that restricted meaning. A scaffold is not inherently a destructive instrument. It becomes destructive only if imperfectly constructed. A large coffee urn may have within itself, if negligently made, the potency of danger, yet no one thinks of it as an implement whose normal function is destruction. . . . We have mentioned only cases in this court. But the rule has received a like extension in our courts of intermediate appeal. . . . We are not required at this time either to approve or to disapprove the application of the rule that was made in each of these cases. It is enough that they help to characterize the trend of judicial thought. . . .

We hold then, that the principle of Thomas v. Winchester *is not limited to poisons, explosives, and things of like nature, implements of destruction. If the nature of a thing is such that it is reasonably certain to place life and limb in peril when negligently made, it is then a thing of danger.* [Emphasis added.] Its nature gives warning of the consequences to be expected. If to the element of danger there is added knowledge that the thing will be used by persons other than the purchaser, and used without new tests, then, irrespective of contract, the manufacturer of this thing of danger is under a duty to make it carefully. That is as far as we are required to go for the decision of this case. There must be knowledge of a danger, not merely possible, but probable. It is possible to use almost anything in a way that will make it dangerous if defective. That is not enough to charge the manufacturer with a duty independent of his contract. Whether a given thing is dangerous may be sometimes a question for the court and sometimes a question for the jury. There must also be knowledge that in the usual course of events the danger will be shared by others than the buyer. Such knowledge may often be inferred from the nature of the transaction. But it is possible that even knowledge of the danger and of the use will not always be enough. The proximity or remoteness of the relation is a factor to be considered. We are dealing now with the liability of the manufacturer of the finished product, who puts it on the market to be used without inspection by his customers. *If he is negligent, where danger is to be foreseen, a liability will follow.* [Emphasis added.]

We are not required, at this time, to say that it is legitimate to go back to the manufacturer of the finished product and hold the manufacturer of the component parts. . . . We leave that question open. We shall have to deal with it when it arises. . . .

From this survey of the decisions, there thus emerges a definition of the duty of a manufacturer which enables us to measure this defendant's liability. Beyond all question, the nature of an automobile gives warning of probable danger if its construction is defective. This automobile was designed to go 50 miles an hour. Unless its wheels were sound and strong, injury was almost certain. It was as much a thing of danger as a defective engine for a railroad. The defendant knew the danger. It knew also that the car would be used by persons other than the buyer. This was apparent from its size; there were seats for three persons. It was apparent also from the fact that the buyer was a dealer in cars, who bought to resell. The maker of this car supplied it for the use of purchasers from the dealer just as plainly as the contractor in *Devlin v. Smith* supplied the scaffold for use by the servants of the owner. The dealer was indeed the one person of whom it might be said with some approach to certainty that by him the car would not be used. Yet the defendant would have us say that he was the one person whom it was under a legal duty to protect. The law does not lead us to so inconsequent a conclusion. *Precedents drawn from the days of travel by stagecoach do not fit the conditions of travel today. The principle that the danger must be imminent does not change, but the things subject to the principle do change.* [Emphasis added.] They are whatever the needs of life in a developing civilization require them to be. . . .

Judgment affirmed.

Additional Precedent Problems

A second problem, quite different from that of the *MacPherson* case, is presented when there are few or no cases within the state involving the precise issue currently being raised. In such instances, the court has relatively free choice in deciding what rule of law should be applicable. If a particular precedent has been widely established in other states in similar cases, the court will no doubt seriously consider its adoption, but it is under no obligation to do so.

A third possibility is that of a "split of authority"—where some states have adopted one rule and others a contrary rule. Such situations exist in several areas of contract law, one illustration of which involves the right of a minor to disaffirm (cancel) a contract and recover payments made to the other party. For example: M, a minor, purchases a car from X for $1,000. Six months later, while he is still under the age of eighteen, M offers to return the car to X and demands the return of his $1,000. X refuses, citing the fact that the car has depreciated $400 while in M's hands. In such a case, many states hold the minor liable for the depreciation, permitting M to recover only $600. However, many other states do *not* charge the minor with the depreciation, and in those jurisdictions he is entitled to recover the full $1,000 regardless of the condition of the car. In such a situation, an appellate court of a state which has not previously been faced with the issue is at liberty to decide which rule to adopt, or even to reject both views in favor of another.

A fourth possibility, considerably more unlikely than the others, is that little or no authority exists in any state on the issue at hand. Here the court may be asked to draw analogies from existing principles applicable to somewhat different situations, or it may simply prefer to fashion a rule of law based on its own ideas of justice and fair-dealing.

Overruling a Precedent

One possible danger inherent in a slavish adherence to the doctrine of *stare decisis* is the possibility that a "bad" rule will become so embedded in the law that it will bring about undesirable results for many years to come.[1] (A rule could be bad either because it produced a result that was of doubtful wisdom at the outset or because it was based upon conditions that had changed in later years.)

While the danger does exist, it is not very great. In the first place, most of the decisions in precedent-setting cases are, in fact, supported by some degree of logic. The courts that settle these issues, like others, normally search for a rule that brings about a reasonable result—one that is not clearly bad. And, especially in recent years, appellate courts have felt increasingly free to modify or discard earlier rules if they feel that changes in social views or economic conditions require them to do so.

The case that follows presents a situation where the original reasons for the rule no longer exist, and the court is called upon to decide whether this is a sufficient ground for reversal of the precedent. While it cannot be said that all courts will (or should) abandon a precedent in the light of changing economic conditions, the Supreme Court of Pennsylvania advances powerful arguments as to why this ought to be done—at least where the evidence of such a change is substantial.

Flagiello v. Pennsylvania Hospital
Supreme Court of Pennsylvania, 208 A.2d 193 (1965)

Mrs. Flagiello, a patient in the Pennsylvania Hospital in Philadelphia, fell and broke an ankle while being moved by two of its employees. She brought this action against the hospital to recover damages, alleging that the employees were guilty of negligence. The defendant hospital moved for a judgment on the pleadings, contending that under the case law of Pennsylvania, it was well established that a charitable institution was not responsible for the wrongs of its employees. The trial court sustained this motion and entered judgment for defendant. Plaintiff appealed to the Supreme Court of Pennsylvania.

Musmanno, Justice: ... The hospital has not denied that its negligence caused Mrs. Flagiello's injuries. It merely announces that it is an eleemosynary institution, and, therefore, owed no duty of care to its patient. It declares in effect that it can do wrong and still not be liable in damages to the person it has wronged. It thus urges a momentous exception to the generic proposition that in law there is no wrong without a remedy. From the earliest days of organized society it became apparent to man that society could never become a success unless the collectivity of mankind guaranteed to every member of society a remedy for a palpable wrong inflicted on him by another member of that society. In 1844 Justice Storrs of the Supreme Court of Connecticut crystallized into epigrammatic language that wise concept, as follows: "An injury is a wrong; and for the redress of every wrong there is a remedy; a wrong is a violation of one's right; and for the vindication of every right there is a remedy." *Parker v. Griswold,* 17 Conn. 288.

[The court addressed itself to several specific arguments advanced by the defendant to support its contention that charitable institutions were not, and should not be, subject to the general rule stated above. One of these arguments was that, on economic grounds alone,

---

[1]This possibility is perhaps the kind of thing that Justice Frankfurter had in mind when he quoted T. H. Huxley's statement that "a theory survives long after its brains are knocked out." *Massachusetts Bonding and Insurance Co. v. U.S.,* 352 U.S. 128 (1956).

the imposition of liabilty on charitable institutions would be financially ruinous to them. The court rejected this argument, noting first that, as a general rule, a defendant is never permitted to escape liability as to valid claims solely on the ground that an entry of a judgment against him would be financially burdensome to him, or might even force him into bankruptcy. The court also noted that the rule of immunity as to charitable institutions originated in this country at a time when most of their patients paid nothing for the services they received, and that the rule was an effort by the courts to preserve the meager assets of such institutions. Judge Musmanno further observed that conditions have now changed; that so-called charitable hospitals operate on the same basis as ordinary business establishments; that in 1963 "the fees received from patients in the still designated charitable hospitals in Pennsylvania constituted 90.92% of the total income of such hospitals," and that the plaintiff did, in fact, pay defendant $24.50 a day for services rendered her. On these facts, the court rejected defendant's claim of immunity based on financial considerations.

The court then turned to the remaining major contention of the defendant, specifically, that the rule of immunity as to charitable hospitals was so firmly established in the case law of Pennsylvania, including cases decided by the Pennsylvania Supreme Court, that, under the doctrine of *stare decisis,* the rule could not now be abandoned by the courts. In that regard Judge Musmanno, in a lengthy examination of cases, concluded that the immunity doctrine originated in an early English case that was soon overruled there, that the American courts seemed to adopt the rule of that case blindly, without examining the validity of the reasons ostensibly underlying it, and further noted that approximately half the states in this country have now rejected the doctrine of immunity. The court then continued:]

Failing to hold back both the overwhelming reasons of rudimentary justice for abolishing the doctrine, and the rising tide of out-of-state repudiation of the doctrine, the defendant hospital and the Hospital Association of Pennsylvania fall back for defense to the bastion of *stare decisis.* It is inevitable and proper that they should do so. Without *stare decisis,* there would be no stability in our system of jurisprudence.

Stare decisis channels the law. It erects lighthouses and flys the signals of safety. The ships of jurisprudence must follow that well-defined channel which, over the years, has been proved to be secure and trustworthy. But it would not comport with wisdom to insist that, should shoals rise in a heretofore safe course and rocks emerge to encumber the passage, the ship should nonetheless pursue the original course, merely because it presented no hazard in the past. The principle of *stare decisis* does not demand that we follow precedents which shipwreck justice. . . .

There is nothing in the records of the courts, the biographies of great jurists, or the writings of eminent legal authorities which offers the slightest encouragement to the notion that time petrifies into unchanging jurisprudence a palpable fallacy. [Emphasis added.] As years can give no sturdiness to a decayed tree, so the passing decades can add no convincing flavor to the withered apple of sophistry clinging to the limb of demonstrated wrong. There are, of course, principles and precepts sanctified by age, and no one would think of changing them, but their inviolability derives not from longevity but from their universal appeal to the reason, the conscience and the experience of mankind. No one, for instance, would think of challenging what was written in Magna Charta, the Habeas Corpus Act or the Bill of Rights of the Constitution of the United States. . . .

While age adds venerableness to moral principles and some physical objects, it occasionally becomes necessary, and it is not sacrilegious to do so, to scrape away the moss of the years to study closely the thing which is being accepted as authoritative, inviolable, and untouchable. The Supreme Court of Michigan said sagaciously in the case of *Williams v. City of Detroit,* 364 Mich. 231, that "it is the peculiar genius of the common law that no legal rule is mandated by the doctrine of *stare decisis* when that rule was conceived in error or when the times and circumstances have so changed as to render it an instrument of injustice."

The charitable immunity rule proves itself an instrument of injustice and nothing presented by the defendant shows it to be otherwise. In fact, the longer the argument for its preservation the more convincing is the proof that it long ago outlived its purpose if, indeed, it ever had a purpose consonant with sound law. "Ordinarily, when a court decides to modify or abandon a court-made rule of long standing, it starts out by saying that 'the reason for the rule no longer exists.' In this case, it is correct to say that the 'reason' originally given for the rule of immunity never did exist." *(Pierce v. Yakima Valley Hospital Ass'n, 260 P.2d 765.)*

A rule that has become insolvent has no place in the active market of current enterprise. *When a rule offends against reason, when it is at odds with every precept of natural justice, and when it cannot be defended on its own merits, but has to depend alone on a discredited genealogy, courts not only possess the inherent power to repudiate, but, indeed, it is required, by the very nature of judicial function, to abolish such a rule.* [Emphasis added.] . . .

We, therefore, overrule *Michael v. Hahnemann,* 404 Pa. 424, and all other decisions of identical effect, and hold that the hospital's liability must be governed by the same principles of law as apply to other employers. . . .

Reversed and remanded.

Precedent and Public Policy

We have seen that the formulation of common law requires a court to sift and examine prior cases in order to determine whether one rule of law has generally been adhered to in similar situations. If it has, the court in most instances can apply that rule without considering in detail whether it is good for the populace as a whole—that is, whether it brings about a result that is good public policy. This is so because most established rules of law are, in fact, based upon public policy considerations.

Occasionally, however, after a precedent has been discovered, a court will refuse to apply it in a particular case—or may even overrule it—for the reason that such application would, in its opinion, bring about essentially harmful results in future years. In such instances the rule is said to be "contrary to public policy." Insofar as the formulation of common-law rules in each state is concerned, the highest state court determines that state's public policy—defined as the "community common sense and common conscience" in an early case.[2]

In that case, a Mrs. Kinney was employed by a railroad as a car cleaner only after she agreed, by contract, not to hold the railroad liable for damages in case she was injured on the job by the railroad's negligence. An injury later occurred; and when she brought suit, the railroad relied on the "freedom of contract" principle as its defense—specifically, that plaintiff knew of the release clause at the time of con-

---

[2]*Pittsburgh, C., C. & St. L. Ry. Co. v. Kinney,* 115 N.E. 505 (1916).

tracting and was legally free to agree to such a release if she wished to do so. The Ohio Supreme Court, while reaffirming the freedom of contract principle generally, ruled against the railroad. It held that in this instance the release clause was contrary to public policy and therefore invalid as a defense.

In describing the harmful effects that would result if it gave effect to the clause, the court said:

> If a contract between employer and employee, whereby the employee assumes all risks no matter how negligent the employer may be, must be upheld by courts as a valid contract, the enormous increase in industrial casualties, the loss of life and limb that would suddenly and inevitably follow, would be almost inconceivable. We would have a veritable army of crippled unfortunates and maimed dependents, deprived of life's joys and blessings, filling our almshouses as paupers and charges upon the state's financial resources, entailing a burdensome system of taxation. Wholly apart from the higher humanitarian questions involved, the increased burden thus placed upon the state for charitable purposes would be, in and of itself sufficient to affect contracts of this character with a vital public interest. Courts should not hesitate to hold such contracts wholly null and void.

Questions and Problems

1. Mrs. Maddux was injured when the car she was riding in was struck by a car driven by Donaldson, and, almost immediately thereafter, by a second car driven by Bryie. When Mrs. Maddux sued the two negligent drivers, the facts of the case were such that it was impossible to determine which of her injuries were caused by the first collision, and which by the second collision. At the time of the suit, the Michigan common-law rule was that, in such a case, neither defendant could be held liable for any damages; accordingly, the trial court dismissed Mrs. Maddux's action. She then appealed to the Supreme Court of Michigan, claiming that the rule of non-recovery was too unfair to an injured plaintiff. Do you agree with this contention? If so, what do you think a better rule would be? (*Maddux v. Donaldson*, 108 N.W.2d 33, 1961.)

2. Tuttle was a barber in a small town in Minnesota, who alleged that Buck, a banker, had set up a rival barbershop in town for the sole purpose of putting Tuttle out of business. Because there were no prior cases in the U.S. on this subject, the trial court had to decide whether such conduct on the part of Buck constituted a wrong in the eyes of the law. (Among other things, Buck contended that his action was lawful because there was no common-law rule prohibiting conduct of this sort.) Assuming that there was no existing common-law rule, do you think that the court should therefore enter judgment in favor of Buck, or do you think the court could—and should—make new law by declaring Buck's conduct to be unlawful? Explain your reasoning. (*Tuttle v. Buck,* 119 N.W. 946, 1909.)

3. Mr. Henningsen bought a new Plymouth from his local New Jersey dealer, who had purchased it from the manufacturer, Chrysler Corporation. Ten days later Mrs. Henningsen was injured when the steering gear failed and the car ran into a brick wall. In Mrs. Henningsen's suit against Chrysler, she alleged that a manufacturer, by putting its products into the stream of commerce, impliedly warrants (guarantees) that they are "merchantable"

—i.e., reasonably fit for ordinary use—and further alleged that in this case the car was *not* merchantable because of the steering defect.

As a defense, Chrysler contended that the common-law rule in New Jersey (i.e., the rule of prior cases) was to the effect that a manufacturer was liable on a breach of warranty theory *only* to a person who purchased the car directly from the manufacturer. On the basis of that rule, Mrs. Henningsen would lose, since the car was purchased from a dealer rather than from Chrysler. A) Do you think the existing common-law rule should be changed to permit a subsequent buyer (such as Henningsen and his wife) to hold Chrysler liable? B) What would the reasons be for, and against, such a change? (*Henningsen v. Bloomfield Motors, Inc.,* 161 A.2d 69, 1960.)

4. Suppose, some years after the case of *MacPherson v. Buick Motor Co.* was decided, that a New York resident, Beatty, purchases an electric Whizbang calculator from his local dealer. Soon thereafter he suffers an eye injury when one of the keys flies off and shatters a lens in his glasses, in what is described as a "freak" accident. Beatty sues the Whizbang Manufacturing Company for damages in a New York court, basing his suit on the negligence theory. At the trial Beatty introduces evidence tending to show that the machine was negligently constructed, and he contends that his case falls squarely within the rule of the *MacPherson* case. If you were the judge hearing this case, would you agree? Why or why not?

5. In the case of *Flagiello v. Pennsylvania Hospital,* did the Supreme Court of Pennsylvania imply that the doctrine of *stare decisis* was, in general, a poor policy upon which to base rules of law, or was the court's decision a narrower one than that? Explain.

6. In a number of cases, the supreme court of State X had adopted the rule that a seller of land who overstated the *value of the land* to a prospective buyer was not guilty of fraud, even if he knew that the true market value of the land was much lower than the figure that he stated to the buyer. (In these cases, the reasoning of the court was that the value of any property is merely a matter of opinion, and that the buyer should realize this.) After this rule is adopted, a new case reaches the supreme court in which the buyer of land claims that the seller was guilty of fraud when he—the seller—intentionally misrepresented the *rental value* of the property. (E.g., Seller told Buyer, an out-of-state resident who had never seen the land, that "it can readily be rented for $100 a month," a statement that proved to be false.) If the supreme court felt that the seller in such a case should be made to pay damages on the theory that he *was* guilty of fraud, would the court have to overrule the prior decisions, or do you think the facts of the new case are sufficiently different so as to permit the court simply to apply a different rule to it? Explain your reasoning. (*Cahill v. Readon,* 273 P. 653, 1928.)

7. The courts of all states have adopted the rule that an employer is liable to third parties for injuries caused them that result from a negligent act committed by his employee, if the employee was doing the employer's work at the time of the accident. This liability is imposed even if the employer was careful about the selection of his employees, and even if the employer took reasonable care to supervise his employees so that such accidents would not occur. A) Why do you think this rule was ever adopted? and B) what argument, if any, can you make in support of the proposition that the common-law rule ought to be repudiated or modified? Explain.

In my own case the words of such an act as the [federal income tax law], for example, dance before my eyes in a meaningless procession; cross-reference to cross-reference, exception upon exception—couched in abstract terms that offer no handle to seize hold of—leave in my mind only a confused sense of some vitally important (but successfully concealed) purport which it is my duty to extract, but which is within my power, if at all, only after the most inordinate expenditure of time. I know that these monsters are the result of fabulous industry and ingenuity, plugging up this hole and casting out that net, against all possible evasion; yet at times I cannot help recalling a saying of William James about certain passages of Hegel: that they were no doubt written with a passion of rationality, but that one cannot help but wondering whether to the reader they have any significance save that the words are strung together with syntactical correctness.

Learned Hand, in "Thomas Walter Swan," *Yale Law Journal,* 1947*

Statutory Law 4

While a significant portion of our legal rules are common law in nature, most of our state and federal law results from the enactment of statutes by legislative bodies. All states, for example, have comprehensive statutes governing the subjects of corporation law, criminal law, and motor vehicle law. Similarly, at the federal level we find sweeping statutes in the areas of tax law, antitrust law, and securities regulation. And more recent federal statutes have been the 1964 Civil Rights Act, the National Environmental Policy Act of 1969, the Consumer Products Safety Act of 1972, and the Bankruptcy Reform Act of 1978.

In this chapter we will examine the processes by which *statutory* law is created and the significant respects in which its characteristics differ from those of common law.[1] Then we will turn our attention to the broad area of *statutory*

---

*Reprinted by permission of The Yale Law Journal Company and Fred B. Roth & Company from *The Yale Law Journal,* vol. 57, pp. 167–172.

[1] The term *statutory law,* when broadly used in contrast to *common law,* includes not only laws passed by state legislatures and by congress but, additionally, the state and federal constitutions, treaties, and municipal ordinances. In this chapter, however, the term is used in its more restricted sense.

interpretation, which was the source of Judge Hand's travail in the passage quoted on the preceding page. While most acts are not nearly as complex as the one to which he referred, all statutes do raise questions of interpretation as specific controversies arise under them.

Scope and Promulgation of Statutory Law

There are many reasons for the existence of statutory law, three of which deserve special mention. First, one of the primary functions of a legislature is to adopt measures having to do with the *structure and day-to-day operation* of the government. Thus many state statutes are of the "nuts and bolts" variety—relating to such matters as raising revenue, creating boards or commissions, and setting forth the powers of municipalities.

Second, because of their nature, certain activities can hardly be regulated by common-law principles and processes. In the area of criminal law, for example, it is absolutely essential for the general populace to know what acts are punishable by fine or imprisonment; and the only sure way to set forth the elements of specific crimes is by enacting *criminal statutes.* Similarly, the activities of corporations are so complex and so connected with the public interest that the only practical method of handling the special problems they present is by drafting detailed statutes, which, in total, comprise the broad *corporation laws* of the states.

The third function of a legislature is to *expressly change, or clarify, certain common-law rules* where it believes such modifications are desirable. Thus a state legislature might pass a statute making nonprofit corporations liable for the wrongs of their employees to the same extent as are profit-making corporations, thereby reversing the common-law rule of nonliability for such employers.

Legislative Limitations

As we shall see, Congress and the state legislatures have broad powers in enacting statutes. The powers are, however, subject to certain limitations: (1) *subject-matter* limitations, which are imposed by the federal Constitution; (2) *procedural requirements* in the various constitutions for the enactment processes; and (3) the constitutional requirement that statutes' provisions be *reasonably definite.* If a statute violates any of these requirements, it is usually void and of no effect. We will examine each of the limitations briefly.

Subject-matter Limitations: Under our system of dual sovereignty, fifty-one governments exist in this country—the federal government and the fifty state governments. This situation requires that the powers of the federal and state governments be delineated so as to prevent overlapping areas of authority. The lines of demarcation are set forth in the federal Constitution, where the powers of the federal government are spelled out in Section 8 of Article I. Of the numerous powers, the following are of particular importance:

The Congress shall have Power

To lay and collect Taxes, Duties, Imposts and Excises, to pay the Debts and provide for the common Defense and general Welfare of the United States; . . .

To borrow Money on the Credit of the United States;

To regulate Commerce with foreign Nations, and among the several States, and with the Indian Tribes;

To establish an uniform Rule of Naturalization, and uniform Laws on the subject of Bankruptcies throughout the United States;

To coin Money, regulate the Value thereof, and of foreign Coin, and fix the Standard of Weights and Measures; . . .

To establish Post Offices and post Roads;

To promote the Progress of Science and useful Arts, by securing for limited Times to Authors and Inventors the exclusive right to their respective Writings and Discoveries;

To constitute Tribunals inferior to the supreme Court; . . .

To declare War, grant Letters of Marque and Reprisal, and make Rules concerning Captures on Land and Water;

To raise and support Armies, but no Appropriation of Money to that Use shall be for a longer Term than two Years;

To provide and maintain a Navy;

To make Rules for the Government and Regulation of the land and naval forces;

To provide for calling forth the Militia to execute the Laws of the Union, suppress Insurrections and repel Invasions;

To provide for organizing, arming, and disciplining, the Militia, and . . .

To make all Laws which shall be necessary and proper for carrying into Execution the foregoing Powers, and all other Powers vested by this Constitution in the Government of the United States, or in any Department or Officer thereof.

Under section 8, the powers that appear therein have been expressly granted by the states to the federal government and are thus referred to as the "delegated" or "enumerated" powers. All other powers (called "reserved") rest in the state governments.

By and large, the lines of demarcation between the authority of the federal and state governments are quite clear. For example, an act of Congress that attempted to fix the general property tax rates of home owners in the various states would clearly be outside its jurisdiction and thus void. Conversely, state statutes prohibiting the importation of goods manufactured in other states, or imposing unreasonable taxes upon such goods, would be an invasion of the powers of the federal government under the interstate commerce clause and would likewise be void.

This is not to say, however, that disputes as to state/federal jurisdiction never arise. As one example, there is occasional difficulty in determining whether a particular business activity is essentially *inter*state, or *intra*state, in nature. More common is the question as to the constitutionality of state statutes which, though essentially regulating a local activity, at the same time do impose *some* burden on interstate commerce. This has been a continuing source of litigation, and the U.S. Supreme Court has taken the view that, in general, state regulation is permissible if it addresses a matter of legitimate "local concern," *and* if its effect on interstate commerce is "only incidental." For example, state regulations taken within the police power of the state, such as those limiting the length of double trailer units operated within its boundaries, may be permissible if the state can show that such regulations clearly contribute to highway safety.

State "economic legislation" has also been upheld in some circumstances, even if it burdens interstate commerce to some degree. This term refers to state statutes or regulations that attempt to balance the "local" rights of consumers or employees against those of manufacturers or employers. The case below presents a problem in this area.

Exxon Corp. v. Governor of Maryland

U.S. Supreme Court 437 U.S. 117 (1977)

During the 1973 nationwide oil shortage, evidence was produced indicating that out-of-state oil producers and refiners were favoring their company-operated gasoline stations in Maryland at the expense of independently operated stations. Responding to this evidence, the Maryland legislature passed a statute which, among other things, prohibited producers and refiners from operating retail gasoline stations in the state.

Exxon Corporation, a refiner who sold much of its gasoline to wholesalers and independent retailers in Maryland, also sold substantial quantities of gasoline through 36 retail stations that it owned in the state. Exxon, joined by Phillips, Shell, Gulf, and three smaller refiners, challenged the constitutionality of the statute. They contended that the statute violated both the due process and commerce clauses of the U.S. Constitution. The federal trial court agreed with these contentions, but the federal Court of Appeals reversed that judgment and ruled that the statute was valid. The oil companies appealed to the U.S. Supreme Court.

Stevens, Justice: . . . As brought out during the trial, the salient chracteristics of the Maryland retail gasoline market are as follows: Approximately 3,800 retail service stations sell over 20 different brands of gasoline. However, no petroleum products are produced in Maryland, and the number of stations actually operated by a refiner or an affiliate is relatively small, representing about 5% of the total number of Maryland retailers. . . .

[The court then held that statute did not violate the due process clause, saying that "(t)he evidence presented by the refiners may cause some doubt on the wisdom of the statute, but it is, by now, absolutely clear that the Due Process Clause does not empower the judiciary 'to sit as a superlegislature to weigh the wisdom of legislation.' . . . Appellants argue that (the statute) is irrational and that it will frustrate rather than further the State's desired goal of enhancing competition. But . . . this argument rests simply on an evaluation of the economic wisdom of the statute, and cannot override the State's authority to 'legislate against what are found to be injurious practices in their internal commercial and business affairs.' "[2] The court then turned to the contention that the statute violated the Commerce Clause of the Constitution].

Appellants argue that the divestiture provisions of the Maryland statute violate the Commerce Clause in three ways: (1) by discriminating against interstate commerce; (2) by unduly burdening interstate commerce; and (3) by imposing controls on a commercial activity of such an essentially interstate character that it is not amenable to state regulation.

Plainly, the Maryland statute does not discriminate against interstate goods, nor does it favor local producers and refiners. Since Maryland's entire gasoline supply flows in interstate commerce and since there are no local producers or refiners, such claims of disparate treatment between interstate and local commerce [are] meritless. Appellants, however, focus on the retail market, arguing that the effect of the statute is to protect in-state independent dealers from out-of-state competition. They contend that the divestiture provisions "create a protected enclave for Maryland independent dealers." As support for this proposition, they rely on the fact that the burden of the divestiture requirements falls solely on interstate companies. But this fact does not lead, either logically or as a practical matter, to a conclusion that the State is discriminating against interstate commerce at the retail level.

As the record shows, there are several major interstate marketers of petroleum that own and operate their own retail gasoline stations. These interstate dealers, who compete directly with the Maryland dealers, are not affected by the Act because they do not refine or produce gasoline. In fact, the Act creates no barriers whatsoever against interstate independent dealers; it does not prohibit the flow of interstate goods, place added costs upon them, or distinguish between in-state and out-of-state companies in the retail market. The absence of any of these factors distinguishes this case from those in which a State has been found to have discriminated against interstate commerce. [The court then turned to the oil companies' second argument.]

Appellants argue [that the statute] impermissibly *burdens* interstate commerce [by pointing to] evidence in the record which indicates that, because of the divestiture requirements, at least three refiners will stop selling in Maryland, and which evidence also supports their claim that the elimination of company-operated stations will deprive the consumer of certain special services [provided by company-operated stations]. Even if we assume the truth of both assertions, neither warrants a finding that the statute impermissibly burdens interstate commerce.

Some refiners may choose to withdraw entirely from the Maryland market, but there is no reason to assume that their share of the entire supply will not be promptly replaced by other interstate refiners. The source of the consumers' supply may switch from company-operated stations to independent dealers, but interstate commerce is not subjected to an impermissible burden simply because an otherwise valid regulation causes some business to shift from one interstate supplier to another.

[After ruling against the oil companies on their first two arguments, the court also rejected their contention that the sale of gasoline at retail was of such an interstate nature that it could not be regulated by a state. On this point the court said, "This Court has only rarely held that the Commerce Clause itself preempts an entire field from state regulation, and then only when a lack of national uniformity would impede the flow of interstate goods. The evil that appellants perceive in this litigation is not that the several states will enact differing regulations, but rather that they will all conclude that divestiture provisions are

---

[2]More will be said about the due process clause in the next chapter.

warranted. The problem thus is not one of national uniformity (and we cannot, therefore) conclude that the States are without power to regulate in this area." Finding the statute to be constitutional, the court affirmed the judgment of the court of appeals.]

Procedural Requirements: All state constitutions (and, to a lesser extent, the federal Constitution) contain provisions about the manner in which statutes shall be enacted. As a general rule, acts that do not conform to these requirements are void.

For example, virtually all state constitutions provide that revenue bills "shall originate in the House of Representatives," a requirement that also appears in the federal Constitution. Three other requirements normally appearing in state constitutions (1) restrict the enactment of "special" or "local" laws,[3] (2) require that the subject of every act be set forth in its title, and (3) prohibit a statute from embracing more than one subject. Additionally, all constitutions prescribe certain formalities in regard to the enactment processes themselves, such as specific limitations on the time and place of the introduction of bills, limitations on the amendment of bills, and the requirement that bills have three separate readings before final passage.

These kinds of provisions, while appearing to be unduly technical, actually serve meritorious purposes. For example, while legislatures normally strive to pass statutes of general application, it is necessary that some laws operate only upon certain classes of persons or in certain localities of a state. Such special or local laws are valid only if the basis of their classification is reasonable; two of the purposes of the constitutional provisions mentioned above are to insure such reasonableness and to guarantee that the classes of persons covered be given notice of the consideration of the bill prior to its passage. Similarly, the purpose of requiring that the subject of an act be expressed in its title is to insure that legislators voting on a bill are fully apprised as to its subject, thereby guarding against the enactment of "surprise" legislation. And the purpose of the requirement that a bill contain one subject is to prevent the passage of omnibus bills (those that bring together entirely unrelated, or incongruous, matters).

Requirement of Certainty: All statutes are subject to the general principle of constitutional law that they be "reasonably definite and certain." While the Constitution itself does not expressly contain such a provision, the courts have long taken the view that if the wording of a statute is such that persons of ordinary intelligence cannot understand its meaning, then the statute violates the due process clause of the Constitution and is thus invalid.[4] In such instances, it is said that the statute is "unconstitutionally vague."

---

[3] "A special or local law is one that, because of its restrictions, can operate on or affect only a portion of the citizens, or a fraction of the property embraced within a classification created thereby." 82 C.J.S., Statutes, § 14, Copyright © 1953 by West Publishing Co.

[4] *State v. Jay J. Garfield Bldg. Co.*, 3 P.2d 983 (1931).

As a practical matter, the majority of statutes that are challenged on the ground of vagueness or uncertainty are upheld by the courts. This is because most statutes are, in fact, drafted carefully and because the courts are extremely reluctant to declare a statute unconstitutional if they can avoid doing so. Thus, if the wording of a statute is subject to two possible but conflicting interpretations, one of which satisfies constitutional requirements and the other of which does not, the former interpretation will be accepted by the courts if they can reasonably do so.

Two examples will indicate the usual approaches taken by the courts. In the case of *McGowan v. State of Maryland,* 366 U.S. 420 (1960), it was held that a statute permitting Sunday sales of "merchandise essential to, or customarily sold at, or incidental to the operations of bathing beaches and amusement parks" was reasonably definite, and thus valid. There the court said that people of ordinary intelligence would be able to know what kinds of commodities were referred to by the act "as a matter of ordinary commercial knowledge, or by simply making an investigation at any bathing beach or amusement park" within the county. On the other hand, in the case of *Day v. Anderson,* 362 P.2d 137 (1961), a Wyoming statute that restricted the use of pleasure boats to streams having "an average flow for the month of July in excess of 1,000 cubic feet per second" was held to be invalid, the court saying that there was no reasonable way in which prospective boaters could determine which rivers and streams were excluded by such a provision.

Statutory Law and Common Law—A Contrast

Statutory law and common law differ in several significant respects. The most obvious of these are the *processes* by which each comes into being and the *form* of each after it becomes operative.

Processes and Form

Legislative acts become law only after passing through certain formal steps in both houses of the state legislatures (or of Congress) and, normally, by subsequent approval of the governor (or the president). The usual steps are (1) introduction of a bill in the house or senate by one or more members of that body; (2) referral of the bill to the appropriate legislative committee, where hearings are held; (3) approval of the bill by that committee and perhaps others; (4) approval of the bill by the house and senate after full debate; and (5) signing of the bill by the executive (or overriding an executive veto). At each of these stages the opponents of the bill are given considerable opportunity to raise objections, with the result that the bill may be voted down or may pass only after being substantially amended. *Common-law rules,* by contrast, are creatures of the judicial branch of government; they are adopted by the courts for settling controversies in those areas of law where the legislature has not spoken.

As a result of these differences, the products of the two processes—the rules themselves—are significantly different. A *statute* has an official text, usually drafted in specific terms, which becomes part of the state or federal code. *Common-law rules,* on the other hand, tend to be more general in nature and can be determined only by examining the fact-patterns and decisions of the prior cases in which they have been applied.

In addition to these obvious contrasts between the two types of law, there are others that are equally significant. We will note these briefly.

Social and Political Forces

The social and political forces within a state have a greater and more evident impact on statutory law than on common-law. Judges are somewhat more insulated from such pressures than are legislatures. Additionally, the steps required in the enactment of statutes enable representatives of vocal special-interest groups (who are frequently at odds with one another) to attract considerable publicity to their causes. And, of course, the raw political power that each is able to exert upon the legislators plays a significant, though not always controlling, part in the final disposition of a bill.

Legislative Options

While judges are required to settle controversies that come before them, legislatures generally have no duty to enact legislation. Thus legislatures have the option of refraining from the passage of laws where there is little public sentiment for them or where competing groups are so powerful that inaction is, politically, the better part of valor.

Legislative Scope

Subject only to the relatively few constitutional limitations placed upon it, the legislative power to act is very broad. Thus legislatures are not only free to enact statutes where case law is nonexistent, but they also can pass statutes that expressly overrule common-law principles. Examples of the latter are those statutes involving the legality of married women's contracts. Under English and early American common law, it was firmly established that married women lacked the capacity— the legal ability—to contract, and thus any agreements they entered into while married had no effect. Today, all states have enacted statutes that generally confer upon married women the same rights to contract as those enjoyed by other citizens.

As for jurisdictional scope, legislatures have the power to pass broad statutes encompassing all aspects of a given subject, whereas the courts can "make law" only in deciding the cases that come before them. Every state, for example, has comprehensive corporation acts, in which virtually all aspects of corporate activities, from incorporation procedures to dissolution procedures, are specified in detail. Similarly, every state has an all-encompassing criminal code, within which the criminal offenses in the state are defined.

We have seen that legislative bodies make law whenever they enact statutes. By doing so, they formally state what kinds of conduct they are requiring or prohibiting in specified situations and what results they expect from the passage of these laws on the rights and duties of affected parties.

But the true scope and meaning of a particular statute is never known with precision until it is formally construed by the courts in settling actual disputes arising under it. This searching for legislative intent, which usually necessitates a *statutory interpretation,* is thus another major source of our law.

Statutory Interpretation

Interpretation: A Necessary Evil?

Whenever a dispute arises where one or both of the parties is basing his or her case upon the wording of a particular statute, one might think that the court's job would be mechanical in nature; that is, once the facts were established, a careful reading of the statute would make it clear what result the legislature intended in such a situation. While this is often true, there are many instances in which it is not.

To bring the nature of the problem into sharper focus, consider the following situation. X flies a stolen airplane from one state to another and is convicted under a U.S. statute that makes the interstate movement of stolen motor vehicles a federal crime. In this statute, a motor vehicle is defined as "an automobile, automobile truck, automobile wagon, motorcycle, or any other self-propelled vehicle not designed for running on rails." Is an airplane a "motor vehicle" under this law? The problem is that the words of the statute are broad enough to embrace aircraft if they are given a literal interpretation; yet it is at least arguable that Congress did not really intend such a result. (The U.S. Supreme Court answered no to the question, with Justice Holmes saying that the term *vehicle* is "commonly understood as something that moves or runs on land, not something which flies in the air"—though he did admit that "etymologically the term might be considered broad enough to cover a conveyance propelled in the air."[5])

The "Plain Meaning" Rule

The primary source of legislative intent is, of course, the language that comprises the statute itself. In the relatively rare case where a court feels that the wording of an act is so clear as to dictate but one result, and that the result is not "patently absurd," the consideration of other factors is unnecessary. If, for example, a state statute provides that "every applicant for examination and registration as a pharmacist shall be a citizen of the United States," a state pharmacy board would have to refuse to process the application of an alien even though he or she may have *applied for* U.S. citizenship as of the date of the pharmaceutical examination.[6] In

---

[5]*McBoyle v. United States,* 283 U.S. 25 (1931).
[6]*State v. Dame,* Supreme Court of Wyoming, 249 p.2d 156 (1952).

cases of this sort (and occasionally in others where the language is somewhat less precise) the courts say that the statute possesses a *plain meaning* and that interpretation is thus unnecessary.

Aids to Interpretation

Most statutes, however, do not easily lend themselves to the "plain meaning" rule. This is true (1) because laws are usually drafted so as to contain an element of "deliberate imprecision," the legislature intending thereby to afford the courts some latitude in their application, and (2) because very few words (even in statutes that are highly restricted in scope) are susceptible to but one meaning. Thus in the majority of cases the courts recognize that some degree of *interpretation* is necessary and that a consideration of factors beyond the express language of a particular clause is advisable, if not mandatory, in determining the precise legislative intent.

At the outset, the court must give weight to prior judicial interpretations, if relevant. It will also look for guidance from (1) examination of the law's "textual context," which involves reading the statute as a whole rather than concentrating solely upon the language of the disputed clause; (2) examination of the statute's "circumstantial context"—that is, identification of the problem that prompted its enactment; and (3) reference to the law's "legislative history"—an examination of the reports of the legislative committees through which the bill passed prior to its final adoption.

Illustrating the *textual context* approach is a case in which the defendant was convicted of violating a section of a California statute which provided that "every person who loiters about any school or public place at or near which children attend or normally congregate is a public vagrant," subject to fine and imprisonment. On appeal, defendant contended that the statute was unconsitutionally vague in that its terms literally prohibited loitering for reasonable purposes as well as for unlawful ones. The Supreme Court of California rejected this contention because the preceding section of the statute provided that "every person who annoys or molests a child under the age of 18 is a vagrant," subject to fine and imprisonment. Viewed in that light, the court held that the section under which defendant was convicted meant only to prohibit loitering where the purpose was to molest or annoy a child, and that it was therefore constitutionally definite.[6]

In the first of the following cases, the court felt that the plain meaning rule was applicable. Do you agree? In the second case a broader approach is utilized, with the court giving particular attention to the factors comprising the statute's circumstantial context.

---

[6]*California v. Huddleson,* 40 Cal.Rptr. 581 (1964).

For over one hundred years prior to 1942, the City of Petersburg, Virginia, had maintained the Peoples Memorial Cemetery, which was located within the city limits. In 1942 the city purchased a tract of 1.01 acres of land adjacent to the cemetery with the intention of re-interring in it bodies which would have to be exhumed in order to permit the widening of a road that ran along another side of the cemetery.

The Temples, complainants, owned a home on St. Andrews Street in Petersburg, directly across the street from the newly acquired tract. Soon after they learned of the purchase, the Temples filed a bill in equity against the city asking that it be restrained from carrying out its plan to use the land for cemetery purposes.

Complainants relied on Section 56 of the Virginia Code, which provided in part as follows: "No cemetery shall be hereafter established within the corporate limits of any city or town; nor shall any cemetery be established within two hundred and fifty yards of any residence without the consent of the owner of the legal and equitable title of such residence . . . ."

The trial court ruled that Section 56 did not prohibit the enlargement of an existing cemetery, and refused to issue an injunction. The Temples appealed.

Temple v. City of Petersburg

Supreme Court of Appeals of Virginia, 29 S.E.2d 357 (1944)

Gregory, Justice: . . . We are called upon to ascertain the proper meaning of the statute, and to decide whether or not it has been violated by the city. Specifically the controversy concerns the meaning to be given to the word, "established," used therein. The appellants maintain that under the statute the enlargement of an exisiting cemetery, such as is sought here, in reality is the establishment of a cemetery, while the appellee contends that to enlarge an existing cemetery is not the establishment of a cemetery and, therefore, constitutes no violation of the statute. . . .

The principal and determinative issue to be determined in this case is whether or not the proposed enlargement of Peoples Memorial Cemetery, by the additional 1.01 acre tract, is prohibited by section 56 of the Code.

The appellants most strongly contend that the word, "established," as used in the statute, means "located," and that the evil intended to be inhibited is the location of a cemetery in a city or town upon ground not previously dedicated for cemetery purposes, or the location of a cemetery within 250 yards of a residence, whether by enlargement or otherwise. They contend that the purpose of the statute is to protect residences and lands from the ill effects growing out of close proximity to a cemetery. They further contend that it is unreasonable to say that residences and lands are to be protected against the "establishment" of cemeteries, but are not to be protected against the encroachment or enlargement of existing cemeteries; that the evil created by one is equally as real as that created by the other.

The position of the appellee is that the word "established" has such a clear and precise meaning that no question of statutory construction arises; that the statute provides that no cemetery shall be "hereafter established" in a city or town, and that this language does not mean that a cemetery already established shall not be hereafter enlarged. To hold otherwise [appellee contends], would be not to construe the statute, but in effect, to amend it.

It is elementary that the ultimate aim of rules of interpretation is to ascertain the intention of the legislature in the enactment of a statute, and that intention, when discovered, must prevail. *If, however, the intention of the legislature is perfectly clear from the language used, rules of construction are not to be applied. We are not allowed to construe that which has no need of construction.* [Emphasis added.]

If the language of a statute is plain and unambiguous, and its meaning perfectly clear and definite, effect must be given to it regardless of what courts think of its wisdom or policy. In such cases courts must find the meaning within the statute itself. . . .

In *Fairbanks, etc. Co. v. Cape Charles,* 131 S.E. 439, the court says: "Under the distribution of powers by the Constitution, it is the function of this court to interpret and not to enact laws. The latter power belongs to the Legislature alone."

The word "established" is defined in *Webster's New International Dictionary,* 2nd Ed., 1936, thus: "To originate and secure the permanent existence of; to found; to institute; to create and regulate;—said of a colony, a State or other institutions."

Just why the Legislature, in its wisdom, saw fit to prohibit the establishment of cemeteries in cities and towns, and did not see fit to prohibit enlargements or additions, is no concern of ours. Certain it is that language could not be plainer than that employed to express the legislative will. From it we can see with certainty that while a cemetery may not be established in a city or town, it may be added to or enlarged without running counter to the inhibition found in section 56. We are not permitted to read into the statute an inhibition which the Legislature, perhaps advisedly, omitted. Our duty is to construe the statute as written.

If construction of the statute *were* necessary and proper in this case, we would be forced to the same conclusion. Even if it be assumed that there is ambiguity in the language in section 56, the legislative history of its enactment and a consideration of Code sec. 53, a related statute, would remove all doubt as to what the legislature intended by its language in section 56.

Code sec. 53 affords a complete answer to the question of legislative intent in the use of the word "established" in section 56, for the former section makes a distinction between "establish" and "enlarge" in these words: "If it be desired at any time to establish a cemetery, for the use of a city, town, county, or magisterial district, or to enlarge any such already established, and the title to land needed cannot be otherwise acquired, land sufficient for the purpose may be condemned. . . ."

The foregoing language, taken from section 53, completely demonstrates that the Legislature did not intend the words "establish" and "enlarge" to be used interchangeably, but that the use of one excluded any idea that it embraced or meant the other. As used, they are mutually exclusive. To enlarge or add to a cemetery is not to establish one within the meaning of section 56.

The language of the statute being so plain and unambiguous, and the intention and meaning of the Legislature so clear, we hold that the City of Petersburg has not violated Code sec. 56, and the decree accordingly should be affirmed.

Affirmed.

Holy Trinity Church v. United States

United States Supreme Court, 143 U.S. 457 (1892)

In February of 1885 Congress passed a statute designed to prohibit the importation of foreigners and aliens under contracts to perform labor and service in the United States. The most important section of the act was as follows:

Be it enacted by the Senate and House of Representatives of the United States of America in Congress assembled, That from and after the passage of this act it shall be unlawful for any person, company, partnership, or corporation, in any manner whatsoever, to prepay the transportation, or in any way assist or encourage the importation or migration of any alien or aliens, any foreigner or foreigners, into the United States, its Territories, or the District of Columbia, under contract or agreement . . . made previous to the importation or migration of such alien or aliens, foreigner or foreigners, to perform labor or service of any kind in the United States, its Territories, or the District of Columbia.

In 1887 the Holy Trinity Church of New York City made a contract with one Warren, a pastor then living in England, under the terms of which he was employed to serve as its pastor. Pursuant to that contract, Warren immigrated to the United States and assumed his pastoral duties. Soon thereafter the United States instituted this action against the church to recover the fine provided by the federal statute.

In the Circuit Court of Appeals, the defendant church contended that Congress, by passing the act of 1885, did not intend to prohibit the kind of contract involved in the instant case. The court rejected that contention and found the church guilty. The church appealed to the United States Supreme Court.

Brewer, Justice: . . . It must be conceded that the act of the corporation is within the letter of this section, for the relation of rector to his church is one of service, and implies labor on the one side with compensation on the other. Not only are the general words labor and service both used, but also, as it were to guard against any narrow interpretation and emphasize a breadth of meaning, to them is added "of any kind;" and, further, as noticed by the Circuit Judge in his opinion, the fifth section, which makes specific exceptions, among them professional actors, artists, lecturers, singers and domestic servants, strengthens the idea that every other kind of labor and service was intended to be reached by the first section. While there is great force to this reasoning, we cannot think Congress intended to denounce with penalties a transaction like that in the present case. *It is a familiar rule that a thing may be within the letter of the statute and yet not within the statute, because not within its spirit, nor within the intention of its makers.* [Emphasis added.] This has often been asserted, and the reports are full of cases illustrating its application. This is not the substitution of the will of the judge for that of the legislator, for frequently words of general meaning are used in a statute, words broad enough to include an act in question, and yet a consideration of the whole legislation, or of the circumstances surrounding its enactment, or of the absurd results which follow from giving such broad meaning to the words, makes it unreasonable to believe that the legislator intended to include the particular act. . . .

[The Court then cited several cases illustrating the application of the above rule. In one of these, *United States v. Kirby,* 7 Wall. 482, the defendant was charged with violating a federal statute that made it a crime "to knowingly and wilfully obstruct the passage of the mail, or any driver or carrier of the same." The defendant, a Kentucky sheriff, admitted that he "obstructed" a mail carrier, one Farris, while the latter was on duty, but defended on the ground that the obstruction occurred solely as the result of his arresting Farris under a warrant that was issued by a Kentucky court after Farris had been indicted on a murder charge. The U.S. Supreme Court held that the arrest of Farris was not, under the circumstances, a violation of the statute. In its opinion the court said: "All laws should receive a sensible construction. General terms should be so limited in their application as not to lead to injustice, oppression or an absurd consequence. It will always, therefore, be presumed that the legislature intended exceptions to its language which would avoid results of this character. The reason of the law in such cases should prevail over its letter." . . . The court then turned its attention to the case at bar, and continued:]

Among other things which may be considered in determining the intent of the legislature is the title of the act. We do not mean that it may be used to add to or take from the body of the statute, but it may help to interpret its meaning. . . .

Now, the title of this act is, "An act to prohibit the importation and migration of foreigners and aliens under contract or agreement to perform labor in the United States, its Territories and the District of Columbia." Obviously the thought expressed in this reaches only to the work of the manual laborer, as distinguished from that of the professional man. No one reading such a title would suppose that Congress had in its mind any purpose of staying the coming into this country of ministers of the gospel, or, indeed, of any class whose toil is that of the brain. *The common understanding of the terms labor and laborers does not include preaching and preachers; and it is to be assumed that words and phrases are used in their ordinary meaning.* [Emphasis added.] So whatever of light is thrown upon the statute by the language of the title indicates an exclusion from its penal provisions of all contracts for the employment of ministers, rectors and pastors.

Again, another guide to the meaning of a statute is found in the evil which it is designed to remedy; and for this the court properly looks at contemporaneous events, the situation as it existed, and as it was pressed upon the attention of the legislative body. The situation which called for this statute was briefly but fully stated by Mr. Justice Brown when, as District Judge, he decided the case of *United States v. Craig,* 28 Fed. Rep. 795:

> The motives and history of the act are matters of common knowledge. It had become the practice for large capitalists in this country to contract with their agents abroad for the shipment of great numbers of an ignorant and servile class of foreign laborers, under contracts, by which the employer agreed, upon the one hand, to prepay their passage, while, upon the other hand, the laborers agreed to work after their arrival for a certain time at a low rate of wages. The effect of this was to break down the labor market, and to reduce other laborers engaged in like occupations to the level of the assisted immigrant. The evil finally became so flagrant that an appeal was made to Congress for relief by the passage of the act in question, the design of which was to raise the standard of foreign immigrants, and to discountenance the migration of those who had not sufficient means in their own hands, or those of their friends, to pay their passage.

It appears, also, from the petitions, and in the testimony presented before the committees of Congress, that it was this cheap unskilled labor which was making the trouble, and the influx of which Congress sought to prevent. It was never suggested that we had in this country a surplus of brain toilers, and, least of all, that the market for the services of Christian ministers was depressed by foreign competition. Those were matters to which the attention of Congress, or of the people, was not directed. *So far, then, as the evil which was sought to be remedied interprets the statute, it also guides to an exclusion of this contract from the penalties of the act.* [Emphasis added.] . . .

[The court then quoted from reports on the bill by the Senate Committee on Education and Labor, and the Committee of the House, which seemed to express their opinion that the terms *labor* and *service* meant only "manual labor" and "manual service." The court then concluded:]

We find, therefore, that the title of the act, the evil which was intended to be remedied, the circumstances surrounding the appeal to Congress, the reports of the committee of each house, all concur in affirming that the intent of Congress was simply to stay the influx of this cheap unskilled labor. . . .

Judgment reversed.

Before leaving the subject of statutory law, the Uniform Commercial Code, a **The Uniform** statute of particular significance, deserves special attention.[7] It is important (1) **Commercial Code** because it is a dramatic illustration of one way changes in law can occur in response to shortcomings that exist in prior law, (2) because the statute governs eight commercial law subjects, and (3) because it has been adopted by all the states except Louisiana, which has adopted articles 1, 3, 4, and 5 only. To see what the code is and why it came about, a brief look at the past is necessary.

Historical Background

By the latter part of the nineteenth century, there was considerable variety among the laws of the states applicable to business transactions within their borders. As interstate commerce increased, it became increasingly imperative that the bodies of law governing commercial transactions be made as uniform as possible.

To achieve this goal, the states in 1890 organized a continuing body called the Conference of Commissioners on Uniform State Laws. Commissioners, appointed by the state governors, were recognized experts in the various fields of commercial law—judges, law professors, and practicing attorneys, for the most part.

The hope was that if the conference drafted model acts from time to time that would ultimately govern all commercial transactions, and if these were adopted by the legislatures of all the states, the law applicable to business transactions would be uniform throughout the country. Two of the most important model acts, drafted about 1900, were the Uniform Sales Act (USA) and the Uniform Negotiable Instruments Law (NIL). Several other model acts of narrower scope, such as the Uniform Warehouse Receipts Act, were also subsequently drawn up.

The hope of total uniformity was never completely realized, for two reasons. First, a few states did not adopt the major acts, the USA and the NIL, and an even larger number failed to adopt the other model acts. Second, even though many states did enact a given uniform statute, the judicial interpretation of certain sections of the act sometimes differed from state to state. (Another problem that came to light subsequently was that many of the uniform acts, drafted and adopted in the early 1900s, were badly out of date by 1940. This was particularly true of the NIL, some provisions of which had little application to banking practices that evolved thirty or forty years after it was written.)

In 1941, in the light of these conditions, the National Conference of Commissioners on Uniform State Laws and the American Law Institute joined forces in an effort to draft a single "modern, comprehensive, commercial code, applicable throughout the country," covering eight areas of commercial law. For the next ten years, hundreds of legal experts in these selected areas worked on the project, which was completed in 1952.

---

[7]The complete text of the code is set forth in Appendix A. Additionally, full discussions of the major areas covered by the code—such as sales law and the law of commercial paper—appear elsewhere in this text.

The code was first adopted by Pennsylvania, in 1953. Thereafter, the New York and Massachusetts legislatures recommended that certain changes be made, and the drafters incorporated these modifications in the 1958 edition. A 1962 official edition, bringing about minor changes, was subsequently published; and it is this version that forty-nine of the states have since adopted. (An even more recent official text was published in 1972. Its changes were primarily in Article 9 [secured transactions]. The 1972 version appears in Appendix A to this text.)

Coverage

The code, commonly referred to as the UCC, consists of ten articles, or chapters:

Article 1	General Provisions
Article 2	Sales
Article 3	Commercial Paper
Article 4	Bank Deposits and Collections
Article 5	Letters of Credit
Article 6	Bulk Transfers
Article 7	Warehouse Receipts, Bills of Lading, and Other Documents of Title
Article 8	Investment Securities
Article 9	Secured Transactions; Sales of Accounts, Contract Rights, and Chattel Paper
Article 10	Effective Date and Repealer

Some Observations on the UCC

The eight substantive areas of law covered by the code are found in Articles 2 through 9. (Article 1 covers only introductory matters. Article 10 simply lists the section numbers of prior statutes of the adopting state, which heretofore covered those areas of law encompassed by the code and which are expressly repealed to eliminate statutory conflict.) From the business student's standpoint, the two most important chapters of the code are Articles 2 and 3.

Article 2 consists of 104 sections that govern virtually all aspects of the law of sales. This article supplants the sales law that was in effect prior to the adoption of the code, which in most states was the old Uniform Sales Act. (Because of the special relationship that exists between sales law and contract law, references to selected sections of this article are made in Part II of the text, and full coverage of the law of sales is in Part III.

Article 3, "Commercial Paper," supplants the earlier Uniform Negotiable Instruments Law, which had at one time been adopted in all the states. Its 80 sections govern such matters as the rights and obligations of the makers of notes and the drawers of checks and drafts, and the rights and duties of holders and indorsers of all types of negotiable instruments. (The subject of commercial paper is also covered in Part III.)

Articles 4 through 8 deal with more specialized situations, such as the duties that exist between depository and collecting banks and the resolution of problems resulting from the issuance and transfer of bills of lading and other documents of title. Article 9 is a lengthy chapter covering all kinds of secured transactions that were formerly governed by separate—and frequently dissimilar—state statutes on chattel mortgages, conditional sales, and other devices by which a creditor might seek to retain a security interest in goods that were physically in the possession of a debtor. (The subject of secured transactions is covered in Part VI.)

Questions and Problems

1. To protect and enhance the reputation of apples grown in Washington State, the Washington Department of Agriculture set up a strict mandatory inspection program, which required that all apples shipped out-of-state be tested and graded according to specified quality standards. All containers in which the apples were shipped were thus stamped with the applicable *state* grade.

In 1973 North Carolina passed a statute providing that all apple containers shipped into the state could bear *only* "the applicable *federal* grade or standard." (In all grades, the Washington State standards equalled or exceeded the federal standards.) The results of this statute were that 1) the 500,000 apples that were annually shipped into North Carolina from Washington would have to undergo a costly second inspection, and 2) high relabeling costs would have to be borne by Washington apple producers. Therefore, the Washington State Apple Commission challenged the law, contending that it imposed an unconstitutional burden on interstate commerce. A) What facts or conditions, in addition to those set forth, would you want to know in order to rule on the correctness of this challenge? B) Based solely on the facts stated, do you think the state law was unconstitutional? Explain. (*Hunt v. Washington Apple Advertising Commission,* 432 U.S. 333, 1977.)

2. In 1955 Colorado passed a statute that (among other things) made it unlawful for automobile manufacturers "to induce or coerce" Colorado new-car dealers into accepting delivery of unordered automobiles and trucks. General Motors, which annually shipped into Colorado more than $100 million worth of automobiles, challenged the statute in the federal courts, contending that it imposed an unreasonable and thus unconstitutional burden on interstate commerce. Colorado replied that the statute was merely a reasonable protection of its local dealers' businesses. Do you agree with the state's defense? Why or why not? (*General Motors Corporation v. Blevin,* 144 F.Supp. 381, 1956.)

3. Identify three significant types of limitations on the legislative powers of Congress and the state legislatures.

4. A student demonstrator and four labor pickets were convicted in the Hamilton County Municipal Court, Ohio, of violating a Cincinnati ordinance making it a criminal offense for three or more persons to assemble on a sidewalk "and there conduct themselves in a manner annoying to persons passing by." On appeal to the U.S. Supreme Court the five contended that the ordinance was unconstitutionally vague (i.e., that it was so vague that it violated

the due process clause). Do you agree with this contention? Discuss. (*Coates v. Cincinnati,* 402 U.S. 611, 1971.)

5. When the language of a statute does not fall clearly within the plain meaning rule, to what other factors or circumstances do the courts look in an effort to determine legislative intent?

6. After completing a flight in a hang glider, Sobeleski was arrested and charged with violation of a state statute that made it a crime to "pilot an aircraft" within the airspace of the state, unless certain documents were filed with specified airport officials prior to every flight. (Sobeleski had not filed any of the required documents.) What arguments could be made in support of the proposition that the quoted statute was *not* applicable to him? Explain.

7. For many years, in "dog-bite" cases, the common-law rule adopted by the Arizona courts was that the owner of a dog was absolutely liable to anyone who was bitten if the owner "knew or should have known of" the dog's dangerous propensities. (This was the rule of strict liability.) Thereafter, Arizona enacted a statute that varied from the common-law rule in two respects: a) dog owners were absolutely liable for dog bites even if they did *not* know of the dog's propensities; b) however, this liability extended only to "invitees or guests" of the dog owner, rather than to all persons who were bitten. In a subsequent case, an Arizona court of appeals had to decide whether the statute abrogated (replaced) the common-law rule, or whether the statute merely complemented the common-law rule—i.e., placed liability on dog owners, in certain situations, that was greater than that which the common law imposed generally. What factors do you think the court would consider in deciding this issue? Discuss. (*Jones v. Manhart,* 585 P.2d 1250, 1978.)

8. A creditor of a practicing physician, Dr. Prater, got a judgment against him. When the judgment was not paid, the creditor asked the court to order the sheriff to take possession of Dr. Prater's "two-seated automobile." After the seizure, Dr. Prater brought action to recover possession of the car, contending that it was exempt property under a Tennessee statute, passed before the invention of the automobile, which provided that "there shall be exempt from seizure . . . two horses; . . . one ox-cart; and . . . one horse wagon." Arguing that the purpose of the statute presumably was to leave in the debtor's hands those kinds of property necessary for him to earn a living, and noting that he used his car in his profession, Dr. Prater contended that the term *horse wagon* should be interpreted broadly enough to include automobiles of the type involved here. Do you agree with this contention? Why or why not? (*Prater v. Reichmann, Sheriff,* 187 N.W. 305, 1916.)

The interpretation of constitutional principles must not be taken too literally. We must remember that the machinery of government would not work if it were not allowed a little play in its joints.

Oliver Wendell Holmes, *Bain Peanut Co. v. Pinson*, 282 U.S. 499 (1931)

Constitutional Law 5

In the preceding chapter, two aspects of constitutional law were touched upon—specifically, that the U.S. Constitution prescribes the basic structure and authority of the federal government and that all state and federal laws must conform to applicable constitutional provisions. In this chapter we will examine these matters and their ramifications at greater length.

At the outset, however, it should be recognized that the subject of constitutional law is so far-reaching in scope that limits must be placed upon any discussion of it in an introductory text. We will examine briefly the general *nature and purposes* of the U.S. Constitution and then devote major attention to the broad area of *constitutional interpretation—the judicial process by which the Constitution is afforded "a little play in its joints."*

The Constitution— Leaving aside, for the moment, the rights of the individual that are protected by
Nature and   constitutional guarantees, the U.S. Constitution has two major purposes:
Purposes
1. It prescribes the organization and jurisdiction of the federal government.

2. It sets forth the authority of the legislative, judicial, and executive branches.

Organization and Jurisdiction

As we noted earlier, the matters within the jurisdiction of the federal government,
as distinguished from the states, are rather clearly spelled out under the Constitution. Congress, for example, has the undisputed power to enact legislation relative
to the recruitment and maintenance of the armed forces and to levy taxes necessary
to carry on the activities of the federal government.

This is not to say, however, that problems of federal-state jurisdiction never
arise; one such problem springs from the "commerce clause" of the Constitution.
Section 8 of Article I provides that Congress shall have power "to regulate commerce . . . among the several states." But since the Constitution does not further
define interstate commerce, the interpretation of the clause has been left to the
courts. Thus, when business firms claim they are not subject to a particular federal
statute (such as a minimum wage law) on the ground that their activities are
essentially intrastate in character, the courts have to examine the scope of each
firm's activities on a case-by-case basis. If it is established that a certain company
buys a substantial percentage of its products from sellers outside the state, or sells
a substantial percentage of its products to out-of-state buyers, it is clear that the
firm is in interstate commerce and thus subject to federal regulation.

A somewhat greater difficulty arises in regard to companies that buy few or no
goods from outside their own state and resell their goods exclusively, or almost
exclusively, to local customers. While such firms are not "engaged in" interstate
commerce, they may nonetheless be subject to federal regulation under the commerce clause—by virtue of Supreme Court interpretations—if their activities are
found to "substantially affect" interstate commerce. Under this broader view, a
motel, for example, might very well fall under the jurisdiction of the federal Civil
Rights Act even though only a fraction of its revenue is derived from interstate
travelers.[1]

Legislative, Executive, and Judicial Authority

The framers of the Constitution, drawing upon the ideas of Blackstone and Mon-
tesquieu, felt it imperative that the powers of the legislative, executive, and judicial
branches be essentially separate from one another. This separation of powers is
substantially brought about under the Constitution; and, by and large, the jurisdiction of each branch is clearly spelled out. It is obvious, for example, that Congress

---

[1] *Heart of Atlanta Motel, Inc. v. United States,* 379 U.S. 241 (1964).

—the legislative arm—cannot grant new trials at the request of disappointed litigants; such power rests solely with the judiciary. Conversely, the courts cannot engage in legislative functions, such as the determination of minimum wage rates. Nevertheless, some problem areas have arisen from time to time regarding the jurisdiction of the respective branches. We will briefly discuss three of these problems.

1. While the power of the Supreme Court to reverse decisions of the lower courts has never been questioned, its power to review the propriety of *legislative* and *executive actions* was, for a time, in doubt. The Constitution does not expressly grant such authority to the court, and it was not until the case of *Marbury v. Madison,* 5 U.S. 137, in 1803 that the court simply assumed that authority, in view of the fact that the Constitution provided no other method for the resolution of certain issues. Today, by virtue of that case, the authority of the court under its "right of judicial review" to inquire into the constitutionality of actions of the other two branches of government is well established.

2. Problems occasionally arise when one branch of government attempts to *delegate its authority* to an officer or agency of another branch. For example, Congress sometimes passes legislation creating a particular commission—a body normally within the executive arm of government—and indicating the general nature of the rules and regulations that it wishes the commission to promulgate. Such delegations by Congress are closely scrutinized by the courts; and if a statute does not set up reasonably definite standards governing the rules and regulations that are to be promulgated thereunder, the legislation will be declared an unconstitutional delegation of legislative power and thus void. However, as we will see in the next chapter, the tendency of the courts today is to uphold statutes that are challenged on this ground if it is reasonably possible to do so.

3. Another problem area involves the powers of the presidency, especially in regard to (A) the president's power to issue executive orders, and (B) the extent to which the doctrine of separation of powers immunizes presidential communications against orders by the judicial branch that they be produced.

In regard to the first question, it is well established that the power of the president to issue executive orders comes only from the U.S. Constitution and federal statutes. Thus such orders are lawful where they merely direct the manner in which an act of congress should be implemented. (By contrast, the attempted seizure of the nation's steel mills by President Harry Truman in 1952 by executive order was set aside by the U.S. Supreme Court, the court saying that neither constitutional nor statutory authority authorized such an action. The order was, therefore, a wrongful invasion by the executive branch of the legislative domain.)[2]

The U.S. Supreme Court, in its decision in the next case, sets forth the primary considerations bearing upon resolution of the second question—"How far does the

---

[2] *Youngstown Sheet and Tube Co. v. Sawyer,* 72 S.Ct. 863 (1952)

presidential claim of 'executive privilege' extend when a court is seeking the production of the chief executive's communcations?"

United States v. Nixon

U.S. Supreme Court, 418 U.S. 683 (1974)

In 1972 a number of persons were arrested while attempting to burglarize the head-quarters of the Democratic National Committee in the Watergate apartment complex in Washington, D.C. Thereafter it appeared that some of President Richard Nixon's staff members might themselves have violated federal criminal statutes by participating in what became known as the "Watergate coverup"—i.e., by attempting to obstruct the criminal proceedings against the burglars.

Prior to the trial of these staff members, Special Prosecutor Leon Jaworski asked the U.S. District Court for the District of Columbia to issue a subpoena to Mr. Nixon requiring him to produce specified tapes and documents of White House communications for use during the trial. That court overruled Mr. Nixon's claim that the doctrine of executive privilege immunized the office of the presidency against such orders, and it accordingly issued the subpoena. Mr. Nixon appealed that ruling to the U.S. Supreme Court.

Burger, Chief Justice: . . . Having determined that [the special prosecutor, in asking for the subpoena, satisfied certain requirements in the federal rules of criminal procedure], we turn to the claim that the subpoena should be quashed [voided] because it demands "confidential conversations between a President and his close advisors that it would be inconsistent with the public interest to produce." . . .

In the performance of assigned constitutional duties each branch of the Government must initially interpret the Constitution, and the interpretation of its powers by any branch is due great respect from the others. The President's counsel . . . reads the Constitution as providing an absolute privilege of confidentiality for all Presidential communications. Many decisions of this Court, however, have unequivocally reaffirmed the holding of *Marbury* v. *Madison* . . . that "it is emphatically the province and duty of the judicial department to say what the law is." . . .

Notwithstanding the deference each branch must accord the others, the "judicial Power of the United States" vested in the federal courts . . . can no more be shared with the Executive Branch than the Chief Executive, for example, can share with the Judiciary the veto power, or the Congress share with the Judiciary the power to override a Presidential veto. . . .

In support of his claim of absolute privilege, the President's counsel urges two grounds. . . . The first ground is the valid need for protection of communications between high Government officials and those who advise and assist them in the performance of their manifold duties; the importance of this confidentiality is too plain to require further discussion. Human experience teaches that those who expect public dissemination of their remarks may well temper candor with a concern for appearances and for their own interests to the detriment of the decisionmaking process. . . .

The second ground asserted by the President's counsel in support of the claim of absolute privilege rests on the doctrine of separation of powers. . . . However, neither the doctrine of separation of powers, nor the need for confidentiality of high-level communications, without more, can sustain an absolute, unqualified Presidential privilege of immunity from judicial process under all circumstances. . . . Absent a claim of need to protect military, diplomatic, or sensitive national security needs, we find it difficult to accept the argument that even the very important interest in confidentiality of Presidential communications is significantly diminished by production [of the material requested here.] . . .

Since we conclude that the legitimate needs of the judicial process may outweigh Presidential privilege, it is necessary to resolve those competing interests in a manner that preserves the essential functions of each branch. . . .

A President and those who assist him must be free to explore alternatives in the process of shaping policies and making decisions and to do so in a way many would be unwilling to express except privately. . . . [On the other hand,] the need to develop all relevant facts in [criminal cases] is both fundamental and comprehensive. The ends of criminal justice would be defeated if judgments were to be founded on a partial or speculative presentation of the facts. . . .

The allowance of the privilege to withhold evidence that is demonstrably relevant in a criminal trial would cut deeply into the guarantee of due process of law and gravely impair the function of the courts. . . .

We conclude that when the ground for asserting privilege as to subpoenaed materials sought for use in a criminal trial is based only on the generalized interest in confidentiality, it cannot prevail over the fundamental demands of due process of law in the fair administration of criminal justice. . . .

The order of the District Court is affirmed.

Constitutional Interpretation

Some provisions of the Constitution are so precise that they need little or no judicial interpretation. Such a clause is found in Section 2 of Article I, which provides in part that "no person shall be a representative who shall not have attained to the age of twenty-five years . . . ."

Many other provisions, on the other hand—particularly those that place limitations upon the powers of the state and federal governments—were deliberately drafted in general terms. The reason for this, of course, is that the drafters of any constitution cannot anticipate the exact problems that may arise fifty or a hundred years hence. Thus they must phrase government limitations and prohibitions in language which will afford the courts some leeway in applying them to specific controversies in later times and in foreseeable circumstances.

In the remainder of this chapter we will examine some of the problems inherent in the area of constitutional interpretation, with particular emphasis on the clauses that create and protect the basic rights of the individual by placing limits on government power. To indicate at the outset the kinds of problems we will discuss, consider the due process clause. The Fifth Amendment provides, in part, that no person shall "be deprived of life, liberty, or property without due process of law." But nowhere in the Constitution is *due process* defined. Thus the courts—called upon to review the propriety of a government action that results in the taking of life, liberty, or property—are given wide range in determining whether the action conformed to this constitutional mandate.

Similarly, other clauses guarantee that the citizens of each state shall be entitled to the "privileges and immunities" of citizens of the other states, and forbid the making of laws "respecting an establishment of religion" and those "abridging the freedom of speech." These clauses, too, must be interpreted on a case-by-case basis.

Some Preliminary Observations

We will see how the courts (and especially the U.S. Supreme Court) have interpreted some of the most important constitutional clauses in varying circumstances. First, however, mention should be made of several generalizations that underlie the whole area of constitutional interpretation.

Necessity for Challenge: The Constitution is not "self-executing." Thus, when the government passes (or takes action under) a statute that may exceed its constitutional powers, the persons who are aggrieved thereby must normally challenge the action in the courts. In other words, constitutional phrases are interpreted by the courts only when actual controversies require them to do so.

Power of Judicial Review: The Supreme Court has virtually unlimited power to decide which appeals it will hear. Where an appeal presents a basic constitutional question, review is normally granted. But most controversies present less significant questions; thus, of the approximately 5500 appeals that are filed with the Court each year, it usually agrees to hear only about 155. In the rejected cases the judgments of the lower courts are, in effect, upheld.

Judicial Restraints: While the Supreme Court theoretically possesses unlimited discretion in the area of constitutional interpretation, it is in fact subject to several restraints. Chief among these is the principle of *judicial self-restraint*—the philosophy that controversies must be settled, insofar as possible, in conformity with previously established principles. This does not mean that previous interpretations are never overturned; we shall see in subsequent cases that marked changes in interpretation occasionally do come about. It does mean that, barring compelling circumstantial changes, the rules of prior cases will normally be followed. Judicial self-restraint also imposes an implied duty on the justices to subordinate their personal economic and political beliefs to previously established interpretations (although, as we will see later, such factors can never be eliminated entirely from the interpretative processes).

Sources of Constitutional Guarantees. Insofar as the structure of the Constitution is concerned, the various provisions that guarantee the basic personal, property, and political rights of the individual do not all spring from the same source. Some of these provisions are found in the Constitution proper, some in the first ten Amendments (the so-called Bill of Rights), and some in later amendments—particularly the Fourteenth Amendment.

Scope of Constitutional Guarantees. The limitations upon governmental actions that are found in the First Amendment literally apply only to the federal government. That amendment, for example, commences with these words: "Congress shall make no law respecting an establishment of religion," followed—as we will see later—by an enumeration of additional rights that are protected against infringement. It would thus appear that *state* statutes or other actions limiting these rights would be permissible. However, the U.S. Supreme Court, by judicial interpretation, has taken the view that any such state actions are also invalid on the ground that such actions violate another constitutional provision, the "due process" clause of the Fourteenth Amendment (which we will examine later). The effect of this interpretation, then, is that neither congress nor the states can limit the freedoms set forth in the First Amendment.

We will now turn our attention to a number of problems of interpretation that some of the more important constitutional clauses have posed for the courts over the years, beginning with two clauses found in the Constitution proper. The remainder of the chapter will focus on selected provisions of the constitutional amendments.

Interpretation of Selected Provisions

Full Faith and Credit

Section 1 of Article IV of the Constitution provides in part that "Full faith and credit shall be given in each State to the public acts, records, and judicial proceedings of every other State." The import of this section is quite clear: the courts of one state must recognize judgments and other public actions of its sister states. Thus a business firm that obtains a valid judgment against a debtor in one state may enforce that judgment in the courts of any other state in which that debtor's property may be located. The full faith and credit clause is, however, subject to a number of limitations. For example, if the court that entered the judgment originally did not have jurisdiction of the defendant, the courts of other states will not recognize the judgment. And the courts in a state in which a foreign judgment is sought to be enforced will not enforce that judgment if it violates the public policy of that state.

Privileges and Immunities

Section 2 of Article IV of the Constitution provides, in part, that "The citizens of each State shall be entitled to all privileges and immunities of the several states." The basic import of this clause is that, in general, a state can not discriminate against citizens of another state solely because of their foreign citizenship. Thus a state cannot prohibit travel by nonresidents within its borders, nor can a state deny nonresident plaintiffs access to its court system.

The privileges and immunities clause is, however, subject to many judicially imposed limitations. For example, a state law may—within reasonable limits—subject nonresidents to certain limitations if the law involves protection of a matter of "legitimate local interest." Therefore a state statute may provide that in letting contracts for the construction of public buildings, preference may be given to raw materials or products produced within that state. Similarly, because state universities are essentially supported by taxation of residents, and also because of the interest that residents have in such schools, the charging of higher tuition for nonresident students does not violate the privileges and immunities clause.[3] And since corporations are not "citizens" within the meaning of this clause, nonresident corporations can be subject to higher tax rates than those applicable to domestic corporations (although such rates can not be confiscatory in nature).

In the following case, the U.S. Supreme Court was called upon to determine whether an Alaskan statute violated the privileges and immunities clause.

Hicklin v. Orbeck

U.S. Supreme Court,
437 U.S. 518 (1978)

Alaska passed a statute in 1972 (known as "Alaska Hire") for the avowed purpose of reducing unemployment within the state. The key provision of the statute required all employers engaged in specified lines of work to hire qualified Alaskan residents in preference to nonresidents. The types of employment covered by the act were, for the most part, activities relating to "oil and gas leases, and easements or right-of-way permits for oil or gas pipeline purposes." To implement the act, persons who had resided in the state for a minimum period of one year were furnished "resident cards" as proof of their preferred status.

Hicklin and others, plaintiffs, were nonresidents who had worked on the Trans-Alaska pipeline for short periods until late 1975, when the act was first enforced. In 1976, when plaintiffs were refused employment on the pipeline, they brought this action against Orbeck, the state official charged with enforcement of Alaska Hire, contending that the act violated the privileges and immunities clause. The Supreme Court of Alaska, by a vote of 3 to 2, held that the law was constitutional. Plaintiffs appealed.

Brennan, Justice: . . . The Privileges and Immunities Clause . . . establishes a norm of comity that is to prevail among the States with respect to their treatment of each other's residents. . . . Appellants' appeal to the protection of this Clause is strongly supported by this Court's decisions holding violative of the Clause state discrimination against nonresidents seeking to ply their trade, practice their occupation, or pursue a common calling within the State. For example, in [an early case this Court] . . . recognized that a resident of one State is constitutionally entitled to travel to another State for purposes of employment free from discriminatory restrictions in favor of state residents imposed by the other State.

Again, [in] *Toomer v. Witsell,* 334 U.S. 385 (1948), the leading exposition of the limitations the Clause places on a State's power to bias employment opportunities in favor of its own residents, [this Court] invalidated a South Carolina statute that required nonresidents to pay a fee 100 times greater than that paid by residents for a license to shrimp commercially in the three-mile maritime belt off the coast of that state. The Court reasoned that although the Privileges and Immunities Clause "does not preclude disparity of treat-

---

[3]*Johns v. Redeker,* 406 F2d 878 (1969). (The U.S. Supreme Court in effect affirmed this decision by denying certiorari.)

ment in the many situations where there are perfectly valid independent reasons for it, it does bar discrimination against citizens of other States where there is no substantial reason for the discrimination beyond the mere fact that they are citizens of other States." A "substantial reason for the discrimination" would not exist, the Court explained, "unless there is something to indicate that noncitizens constitute a peculiar source of the evil at which the statute is aimed." . . .

Even assuming that a State may validly attempt to alleviate its unemployment problem by requiring private employers within the State to discriminate against nonresidents—an assumption made at least dubious [by prior cases]—it is clear under the *Toomer* analysis that Alaska Hire's discrimination against nonresidents cannot withstand scrutiny under the Privileges and Immunities Clause. For although the Statute may not violate the Clause if the State shows [in the words of *Toomer*] "something to indicate that noncitizens constitute a peculiar source of evil," certainly no showing was made on this record that nonresidents were a peculiar source of the evil [that] Alaska Hire was enacted to remedy, namely, Alaska's uniquely high unemployment. What evidence the record does contain indicates that the major cause of Alaska's high unemployment was not the influx of nonresidents seeking employment, but rather the fact that a substantial number of Alaska's jobless residents— especially the unemployed Eskimo and Indian residents—were unable to secure employment either because of their lack of education and job training or because of their geographical remoteness from job opportunities. The employment of nonresidents threatened to deny jobs to Alaska residents only to the extent that jobs for which untrained residents were being prepared might be filled by nonresidents before the residents' training was completed.

Moreover, even if the State's showing is accepted as sufficient to indicate that nonresidents were "a peculiar source of evil," *Toomer* compels the conclusion that Alaska Hire nevertheless fails to pass constitutional muster, [because] the discrimination the Act works against nonresidents does not bear a substantial relationship to the particular "evil" they are said to present. Alaska Hire simply grants all Alaskans, regardless of their employment status, education, or training, a flat employment preference for all jobs covered by the Act. A highly skilled and educated resident who has never been unemployed is entitled to precisely the same preferential treatment as the unskilled, habitually unemployed Arctic Eskimo enrolled in a job-training program. If Alaska is to attempt to ease its unemployment problem by forcing employers within the State to discriminate against nonresidents—again, a policy which [itself] may present serious constitutional questions—the means by which it does so must be more closely tailored to aid the unemployed the Act is intended to benefit. Even if a statute granting an employment preference to unemployed residents or to residents enrolled in job-training programs might be permissible, Alaska Hire's across-the-board grant of a job preference to all Alaskan residents clearly is not. . . . [For these reasons,] Alaska Hire cannot withstand constitutional scrutiny.

Judgment reversed.

First Amendment; Establishment of Religion

The First Amendment provides: "Congress shall make no law respecting an *establishment of religion,* or prohibiting the free exercise thereof; of abridging the *freedom of speech,* or of the press; or the right of the people peaceably to assemble, and to petition the Government for a redress of grievances." (Emphasis added.)

The basic import of the "establishment clause" of the First Amendment is quite clear. The federal government is prohibited from establishing an official religion, and—as we have seen—the state governments, under interpretation of the due process clause, are subject to this same prohibition. Furthermore, through case decisions involving this clause, neither the federal nor state governments can enact legislation favoring one religious organization over another.

A much closer question is presented by statutes or regulations that merely permit the recitation of nondenominational prayers in schools on an entirely voluntary basis. Should the establishment clause also forbid this more innocuous form of state-sanctioned activity? It was not until 1962, in the case of *Engel v. Vitale,* 370 U.S. 421, that this precise question was presented. In that case the State Board of Regents of New York recommended that the following prayer be spoken aloud in the public schools at the beginning of each school day: "Almighty God, we acknowledge our dependence upon Thee, and we beg Thy blessings upon us, our parents, our teachers, and our Country." Thereafter this recommendation was implemented in a number of New York schools.

The action of the regents was challenged by a number of students' parents, who contended that it violated the establishment clause. The lower courts held against the parents, saying that the state action fell short of constituting the "establishment" of a religion. The U.S. Supreme Court, however, interpreted the establishment clause in a broader manner, and found the regents' action to be unconstitutional. The court said, in part, that "the constitutional prohibition against laws respecting an establishment of a religion must at least mean that in this country it is no part of the business of government to compose official prayers for any group of the American people to recite as a part of a religious program carried on by any government." The court based its conclusion to a great extent upon the "historical fact that governmentally established religions and religious persecutions go hand in hand," and inferred that the regents' action, if sanctioned, might be the foot-in-the-door that could lead to broader state intervention in the future.

First Amendment; Free Speech

Few peoples of the world enjoy more so-called political rights than citizens of the United States. Many of these rights spring directly from the first ten Amendments to the Constitution. Of these, none is given more sweeping protection by the courts than the right of free speech, which comes—as we have seen—from that part of the First Amendment providing that "Congress shall make no law . . . abridging the freedom of speech." As a result of this protection, citizens can, in general, criticize public officials and the laws of their government free of governmental interference.

The free speech guarantee has been interpreted in so many different situations that its precise effect is especially difficult to summarize briefly. Nonetheless, several general observations are possible.

First, this guarantee—while generally interpreted broadly by the courts—is still subject to certain limitations (as is true of all of our other constitutional guarantees). Justice Holmes illustrated this succinctly years ago in his observation that the freedom of speech clause does not sanction a false cry of "fire" in a crowded theater. Furthermore, free speech does not permit one to make false and defamatory statements about another. Thus, if A falsely tells B that C, an attorney, was disbarred at one time, C may recover damages from A in a slander action.[4] Similarly, state and federal statutes that make it a crime to disseminate obscene materials are constitutional (if their definitions of "obscenity" are in conformity with those of the U.S. Supreme Court). And it is well-established that "the constitutional guarantees do not permit unrestricted utterances or publication of remarks or literature which is seditious or hostilely subversive, (or) which advocate violent, forceful or terroristic changes (in government)."[5]

Second, the principle is often expressed in the cases that "the law abhors prior restraints." What this means is that, because of the extreme importance attached by the courts to the free speech guarantee, the courts will ordinarily hold prior restraints to be unconstitutional. Thus if a city council refuses to issue a permit for a rally or some other assembly of a particular group where unpopular speeches may be made, and if the group challenges the action in court, the clear tendency of the courts is to strike down the council's refusal on free speech grounds, rather than support the banning of the assembly. The inclination of the courts, then, is to *permit* the assembly, dealing with any unlawfulness that might grow out of it (such as injuries or destruction of property) to be redressed in subsequent civil actions brought against the wrongdoers themselves. The same approach generally is applicable where a local court issues an injunction against a similar gathering, and where the injunction is attacked in court. (Of course, as indicated earlier, the refusal to issue a permit, or the issuance of an injunction, may be *upheld* in the relatively rare case where a reviewing court is satisfied that the probability of force and violence—if the assemblage were to be held—is indeed very high.)

Third, symbolic (nonverbal) speech is given substantial protection by the courts today. For example, in one case reaching the U.S. Supreme Court, that court had to deal with a regulation adopted by a Des Moines school administrator prohibiting students from wearing black armbands in protest against the Vietnam War. The court ruled that the ban violated the free speech clause, where there was no showing that the wearing of the armbands had disrupted normal school activities.[6] Similarly, the free speech guarantee generally protects expressions espoused by peaceful picketing—although the number of pickets, and the places of picketing, are subject to reasonable regulation by the courts.

Lastly, "commercial speech" is being given increasing protection by the courts. In earlier years it was generally held that such speech (e.g., statements in advertisements) was not protected by the First Amendment, but today that position is eroding. Thus, in cases arising in 1975 and 1976, the U.S. Supreme Court struck

---

[4]The subject of slander, which is one type of tort, will be considered further in Chapter 7.

[5]16 *Am Jur 2d, Constitutional Law* §349 (Lawyers Co-operative Publishing Co., Rochester, New York; Bancroft-Whitney Company, San Francisco, California, 1964.)

[6]*Tinker v. Des Moines School District,* 393 U.S. 503 (1969).

down two restrictive Virginia statutes, saying that they violated the free speech guarantee. The statute in the first case made it a misdemeanor for anyone to publish an advertisement which encouraged or prompted the performance of abortions, and the second declared it to be "unprofessional conduct" for a pharmacist to advertise the prices of prescription drugs. And in *First National Bank v. Belotti,* 435 U.S. 765 (1978), the highest court ruled unconstitutional a Massachusetts statute that prohibited corporations from spending money to influence "the vote on any question submitted to the voters, other than one materially affecting any of the property, business, or assets of the corporation."

Due Process of Law

The Fifth Amendment, applicable to the federal government, provides in part that "No person shall . . . be deprived of life, liberty, or property without due process of law," and the Fourteenth Amendment contains a clause imposing the same limitation upon state action.

The primary purpose of the due process clauses, as they have been interpreted by the courts, is to prevent the federal and state governments from depriving individuals of certain basic rights in an unfair or arbitrary manner. While life, liberty, and property can be taken in certain circumstances, the main thrust of the due process clause—and the case law that has resulted under it—is that such deprivation should occur only by virtue of judicially acceptable proceedings. The underlying philosophy is aptly summed up in this statement:

> "Due process of law" implies at least a conformity with natural and inherent principles of justice, and forbids that one man's property, or right to property, shall be taken for the benefit of another, or for the benefit of the state, without compensation, and that no one shall be condemned in his person or property without an opportunity of being heard in his own defense.[7]

The guarantee springing from this clause extends to both criminal and civil proceedings. In the area of criminal law, a person who has been convicted of a crime may be successful in having the conviction set aside under the due process clause if the statute allegedly violated was so vague as to fail to prescribe "a reasonable standard of guilt." The case of *City of Columbus v. Thompson,* 25 Ohio St.2d 25 (1971), is one such example. There a Columbus "suspicious persons" ordinance was challenged. The ordinance defined a suspicious person as one "who wanders about the streets or other public ways or who is found abroad at late or unusual hours of the night without any visible or lawful business and who does not give satisfactory account of himself."

The Ohio Supreme Court, in setting aside the conviction of Thompson, held that the ordinance violated the due process clause in that it "leaves the public uncertain as to the conduct it prohibits" and "leaves judges and jurors free to

---

[7]*Holden v. Hardy,* 169 U.S. 366 (1898).

decide, without any legally fixed standards, what is prohibited and what is not in each particular case." Even where a conviction occurs under a statute whose language is reasonably precise, it may be set aside under the due process clause if the accused can show that the trial proceedings were so arbitrarily conducted as to deprive the person of a fair opportunity to present a defense.

Turning to the area of civil proceedings, we find that the due process clause is upheld as zealously as in criminal cases. For example, if a condemnation statute provides that the value of land taken from a private citizen shall be "conclusively determined" by an appointed board—thereby depriving the landowner of the right to contest the determination in the courts—it quite certainly violates the due process clause. Similarly, tax statutes may, in some circumstances, violate the due process clause. For example, while the courts generally construe the clause in favor of tax laws, statutes which impose taxes that are clearly shown to be confiscatory or discriminatory have been held to constitute the taking of property without due process of law.

In this general area, the courts require that there be both "procedural" due process and "substantive" due process. While the distinction is often a fuzzy one, procedural due process demands that the *proceedings* under which a statute or rule is carried out be fair, while substantive due process requires that the actual *provisions* of the statute or rule also be fair and reasonable. To illustrate the difference: the rules of a medical school specifying the kinds of misconduct that are grounds for dismissal may be clear and based on reason, yet a student who is dismissed under the rules may be successful in court in having the dismissal set aside if the student can show, for example, that the dismissal hearing was held without reasonable notice or in an arbitrary fashion, that he or she was not adequately permitted to refute the charges made, or that no appeal of the decision to higher school authorities was permitted. In any of these instances the requirement of *procedural* due process was probably not met.

A statute that contains a limitation of liability provision may not afford substantive due process if it can be shown that the limitations bear little relationship to the actual loss that may be incurred in actions to which it applies. In such an instance the limitation may be said to be inherently arbitrary, and thus unconstitutional from a *substantive* standpoint. The case below presents an issue of this sort in a modern setting—a case highly unique because of the vast "imponderables" that were involved.

When Congress passed the Atomic Energy Act of 1946, it contemplated that the development of nuclear power would be a government monopoly. A few years later, however, Congress concluded that the national interest would be best served if the government encouraged the private sector to become involved in the development of atomic energy for peaceful purposes under a program of federal regulation. The Atomic Energy Act of 1954 implemented this policy decision by providing for the licensing of private construction, ownership, and operation of commercial nuclear power reactors under supervision of the Atomic Energy Commission (AEC).	**Duke Power Company v. Carolina Environmental Study, Inc.** U.S. Supreme Court, 438 U.S. 59 (1978)

As private companies began to develop their nuclear plant facilities, they became aware that a major problem lay in the path of their industry—the risk of potentially vast liability in the event of a "nuclear accident of a sizeable magnitude." Private industry and the AEC were confident that such a disaster would not occur because of the comprehensive testing and study that had gone on, but the uniqueness of this form of energy production made it impossible totally to rule out the risk of a major nuclear accident.

Thus, in 1956 spokesmen for the private sector informed Congress that they would be forced to withdraw from the field if their liability were not limited by appropriate legislation. Congress responded in 1957 by passing the Price-Anderson Act, which limited the aggregate liability of licensees for a single "nuclear incident" to $500 million plus the amount of liability insurance that was then available on the private market, some $60 million.

The Price-Anderson Act was amended several times in subsequent years. In its final form the act provided, in essence, that liability in the event of a nuclear incident causing damages of $560 million or more would be spread as follows: $315 million would be paid from contributions by the licensees of the 63 private operating nuclear plants; $140 million would come from private insurance (the amount then available); and the remainder of $105 million would be borne by the federal government. The act thus clearly imposed a *statutory limit of $560 million* on the licensees' liability, but other language in the act provided that "in the event of a nuclear incident involving damages in excess of ($560 million), the Congress will thoroughly review the particular incident and will take whatever action is deemed necessary and appropriate to protect the public from the consequences of a disaster of such magnitude."

The Duke Power Company began construction of two nuclear power plants in 1973, one in North Carolina and one in South Carolina. This prompted the Carolina Environmental Study Group, joined by a labor union and 40 persons who lived close to the plants, to bring this action against the Nuclear Regulatory Commission and Duke Power. The purpose of the suit was to have the Price-Anderson Act declared invalid, the plaintiffs contending that the act violated the due process clause of the U.S. Constitution in several respects. The U.S. District Court agreed with the plaintiffs, ruling—among other things—that the limitation of liability was "not rationally related to the potential losses," and that the act "tended to encourage irresponsibility in matters of safety and enrivonmental protection." The defendants appealed to the U.S. Supreme Court.

Burger, Chief Justice: . . . As we read the Act and its legislative history, it is clear that Congress' purpose was to remove the economic impediments in order to stimulate the private development of electric energy by nuclear power while simultaneously providing [to] the public compensation in the event of a catastrophic nuclear incident. The liability limitation provision thus emerges as a classic example of an economic regulation—a legislative effort to structure and accommodate the burdens and benefits of economic life. "It is by now well established that (such) legislative acts . . . come to the Court with a presumption of constitutionality, and that the burden is on one complaining of a due process violation to establish that the legislature has acted in an arbitrary or irrational way." *Usery v. Turner Elkhorn Mining Co.,* 428 U.S. 1. That the accommodation struck may have profound and far-reaching consequences, contrary to appellees' suggestion, provides all the more reason for this Court to defer to the congressional judgment unless it is demonstrably arbitrary or irrational.

When examined in light of this standard of review, the Price-Anderson Act, in our view, passes constitutional muster. [The appellees do not challenge the need for a statutory limit on liability]; rather, their challenge is to the alleged arbitrariness of the *particular figure* of $560 million, which is the statutory ceiling on liability.

The District Court aptly summarized its position [that the amount of recovery was not rationally related to the potential losses, in these words]: "Abundant evidence in the record shows that although a major catastrophe in any particular place is not certain and may not be extremely likely, nevertheless, in the territory where these plants are located, damage to life and property for this and future generations could well be many, many times the limit which the law places on liability."

Assuming, *arguendo,* that the $560 million fund would not insure full recovery in all conceivable circumstances—and the hard truth is that no one can ever know—it does not by any means follow that the liability limitation is therefore irrational and violative of due process. The legislative history clearly indicates that the $560 million figure [was merely conceived of] as a "starting point" or working hypothesis. The reasonableness of the statute's assumed ceiling on liability was predicated on two corollary considerations—expert appraisals of the exceedingly small risk of a nuclear incident involving claims in excess of $560 million, and the recognition that in the event of such an incident, Congress would likely enact extraordinary relief provisions to provide additional relief, in accord with prior practice. . . .

[C]andor requires acknowledgment that whatever ceiling figure is selected will, of necessity, be arbitrary in the sense that any choice of a figure based on imponderables like those at issue here can always be so characterized. This is not, however, the kind of arbitrariness which flaws otherwise constitutional action. When appraised in terms of both the extremely remote possibility of an accident where liability would exceed the limitation, and Congress' now statutory commitment to "take whatever action is deemed necessary and appropriate to protect the public from the consequences of" any such disaster, we hold the congressional decision to fix a $560 million ceiling at this stage in the private development and production of electricity by nuclear power to be within permissible limits and not [violative] of due process.

The District Court's further conclusion that the Price-Anderson Act "tends to encourage irresponsibility on the part of builders and owners" of nuclear power plants simply cannot withstand careful scrutiny. [In a recent case] we outlined the multitude of detailed steps involved in the review of any application for a license to construct or to operate a nuclear power plant; nothing in the liability limitation provision undermines or alters in any respect the rigor and integrity of that process. Moreover, in the event of a nuclear accident the utility itself would suffer perhaps the largest damages. While obviously not to be compared with the loss of human life and injury to health, the risk of financial loss and possible bankruptcy to the utility is in itself no small incentive to avoid the kind of irresponsible and cavalier conduct implicitly attributed to licensees by the District Court. . . .

Accordingly, the decision of the District Court is reversed and the case is remanded for proceedings consistent with this opinion.

Equal Protection of the Laws

Section 1 of the Fourteenth Amendment, in its entirety, is as follows: All persons born or naturalized in the United States and subject to the jurisdiction thereof, are citizens of the United States and the State wherein they reside. No State shall make or enforce any law which shall abridge the privileges or immunities of citizens of the United States, nor shall any State deprive any person of life, liberty, or property, without due process of law; *nor deny to any person within its jurisdiction the equal protection of the laws.* (Emphasis added.) The general import of this clause is to forbid a legislature to enact laws imposing legal duties on certain classes of persons that are not imposed on others.

The equal protection clause, however, does not prohibit *all* class legislation. Occasionally problems are created by one class of persons (such as a particular type of retail establishment) which by reason of the nature of their business or the size of their operation may be subject to restrictions that are not necessary for others. Such class legislation, as viewed by the courts, does not offend the equal protection clause as long as the classification is based on reasonable and rational factors.

Literally, the equal protection clause applies only to the state governments. However, the Supreme Court has taken the view that *federal* statutes which arbitrarily treat one class of persons differently from other classes also violate the due process clause of the Fifth Amendment. The effect of this interpretation is to extend the equal protection clause to actions of the federal government as well as the state governments.

While the number of cases challenging legislation under the equal protection clause is virtually limitless, brief references to several of them are illustrative. In *Vigeant v. Postal Telegraph Cable Co.,* 157 N.E. 651 (1927), the highest court of Massachusetts struck down a statute making telegraph companies (but not similar companies) absolutely liable to any person injured by falling poles or wires. The court said, "A classification for the purpose of establishing liability with respect to persons injured by poles and wires without fault, which singles out telegraph companies, and excludes telephone companies, electric light, heat and power companies, does not stand on a reasonable basis."

In the now-celebrated case of *Brown v. Board of Education,* 347 U.S. 483 (1954), the U.S. Supreme Court was called upon to consider the constitutionality of state statutes that required the segregation of public school students on the basis of their color. Prior to this decision the court had applied the "separate but equal" doctrine to somewhat similar cases—i.e., the view that state regulations of this nature were not unconstitutional if the facilities afforded the minority members were equal to those afforded the majority race. The Supreme Court reversed this precedent in *Brown,* saying that the classification/segregation was inherently unreasonable—and thus in violation of the equal protection clause—no matter how adequate the minority facilities might be. (Today, almost 30 years after this decision, some school boards and federal courts across the nation are still struggling to devise desegregation plans in conformity with this and subsequent decisions of the Supreme Court in this area.) On the other hand, in *Foley v. Connelie,* 435 U.S.

291 (1978), the Supreme Court held that a New York statute requiring state police officers to be U.S. citizens *was* reasonable, and thus did not violate the equal protection clause.

Our "Activist" Courts

Critics of the Brown decision charged that the U.S. Supreme Court was, at best, trying to settle a problem that should have been resolved by Congress, or even worse, was extending federal authority over a matter that constitutionally was left in the hands of the states. And in the years since that decision the Court has decided a number of additional cases where, critics allege, the Court has become "too activist" in nature, or has become a "mini-legislature" bent on usurping congressional authority. In the case of *Baker v. Carr,*[8] for example, the Court ruled that state congressional districting plans which resulted in large numbers of voters being placed in one district, and markedly fewer voters in another district, violated the equal protection clause by granting too little representation to those voters in the more populous districts. In this decision the so-called "one man, one vote" principle was first implemented, in this setting, by the federal courts. And in the case of *Roe v. Wade,*[9] the Court in effect gave women the absolute right to an abortion during the first trimester of pregnancy, by striking down state statutes which permitted abortions only in cases of rape, incest, and medical necessity. Ruling that such statutes were a wrongful violation of the right of privacy—including the right of a pregnant woman to terminate her pregnancy for reasons of her choice—the court held them to violate the due process clause of the Fourteenth Amendment.

Questions and Problems

1. The Montana Fish and Game Commission adopted a regulation in 1976 that set the price of combination hunting licenses at $30 for residents and $225 for nonresidents. (A combination license permitted the taking of one elk, one deer, one black bear, and a specified number of game birds.) This regulation was challenged by nonresident hunters, who contended that it violated the privileges and immunities clause of the U.S. Constitution. The State of Montana contended, among other things, that the interest of Montana residents in the wildlife within its borders was a matter of state protection, and that this interest was substantial enough to justify the regulation. Do you think the U.S. Supreme Court agreed with this defense? Why or why not? (*Baldwin v. Fish and Game Commission of Montana,* 436 U.S. 371, 1978.)

2. The aviation commissioner for the City of Chicago adopted regulations which severely restricted the distribution of literature and solicitation of contributions at city airports. Among other things, the regulations (1) provided that persons who wished to do these things had to register with airport officials daily between 9 and 9:30 a.m.; (2) provided that

---

[8]369 U.S. 691 (1962)
[9]410 U.S. 113 (1973)

distribution and solicitation could be carried on only in specified public areas of the airports; and (3) prohibited the solicitation by more than one person from each group at a time. These regulations were challenged by a religious group on the ground that they violated the free speech guarantee of the constitution. Which, if any, of the above regulations do you feel did violate that clause? Explain. (*International Society for Krishna Consciousness, Inc. v. Rockford,* 585 F.2d 263, 1978.)

3. An Illinois criminal statute provided that violators would be subject to a fine and imprisonment for a specified period of time. It also provided that if a convicted person had no money to pay the fine, he was required to stay in prison for a longer time in order to "work off" the fine. Do you think that this statute might violate the equal protection clause? Explain. (*Williams v. Illinois,* 399 U.S. 235, 1970.)

4. A national bank in Ohio was charged with violating a federal criminal law that prohibited national banks from making loans to political candidates who were running for office in specified elections. At the trial, the bank contended that the federal law violated the equal protection clause of the constitution in that it applied to national banks and not to a number of other lending institutions. What additional factors, if any, would you want to examine in order to determine whether the bank's contention is correct? What result? (*U.S. v. First National Bank,* 329 F.Supp. 1251, 1971.)

5. An Arizona Motor Vehicle Safety Responsibility law provided for the suspension of a driver's license when a judgment for personal injuries was entered against the driver, and where the judgment was not satisfied (paid). The law also provided that even if the driver went into bankruptcy, the discharge in bankruptcy did not relieve the driver from the license suspension. A driver challenged this statute under the Supremacy Clause of the federal constitution, contending that the statute was contrary to certain provisions of the National Bankruptcy Act. (The Supremacy Clause provides, in effect, that state statutes that conflict with federal statutes are unconstitutional.) The State of Arizona argued that even if there were a conflict, it was justified for the reason that the purpose of the statute was "the protection of the public using the highways from financial hardship that may result from the use of automobiles by financially irresponsible persons," and that this purpose was clearly within the police power of the state. Does this argument save the statute? Why or why not? (*Perez v. Campbell,* 91 S.Ct. 1704, 1971.)

6. Today, the basic standards required by the due process clause of the Constitution are fairly clear, despite the fact that nowhere in the Consitiution is this clause defined. What is the explanation for this relative clarity?

7. A motorist was convicted of two traffic offenses in a mayor's court, and the convictions were affirmed by the state's supreme court. He appealed this judgment to the U.S. Supreme Court. He contended that he had been denied a trial before "a disinterested and impartial judicial officer as guaranteed by the Due Process clause," in view of the fact that a major part of the village's income was derived from the fines, costs, and fees imposed by the mayor's court. Do you believe that the appellant's contention is valid? Explain. (*Ward v. Village of Monroeville,* 34 L.Ed.2d 265, 1972.)

8. By what reasoning has the U.S. Supreme Court come to the conclusion that at least some of the provisions in the first ten Amendments to the Constitution apply to the state governments as well as to the federal government?

The rise of administrative bodies probably has been the most significant legal trend of the last century and perhaps more values today are affected by their decisions than by those of all the courts, review of administrative decisions apart. They also have begun to have important consequences on personal rights. . . . They have become a veritable fourth branch of the Government, which has deranged our three-branch legal theories as much as the concept of a fourth dimension unsettles our three-dimensional thinking.

Justice Robert H. Jackson, *Federal Trade Commission v. Ruberoid Co.,* 343 U.S. 470 (1952)

Lawmaking by Administrative Agencies

6

In the preceding chapters we have examined the major processes by which law is made—the formulation of common-law rules by the courts, the enactment of statutes by the legislative bodies, and the interpretation of statutes by the courts. But this examination does not present the total lawmaking picture. *Administrative agencies*—the hundreds of boards and commissions existing at all levels of government—also "make law" by their continual promulgation of rules and regulations.[1]

The number of administrative agencies has grown so rapidly in the last forty years that the practical impact of local, state, and federal agencies on the day-to-day activities of individuals and businesses is today probably at least as great as that of legislatures and courts. Every day, boards and commissions across the country engage in such traditional functions as assessing properties for tax purposes, granting licenses and business permits, and regulating rates charged in the transportation and public utility industries—actions that affect millions of Americans. And, more recently, newer agencies such as the Environmental Protection Agency (EPA),

[1]The specific activities of certain federal agencies, such as the Federal Trade Commission, will be examined in more detail in Part VIII.

Occupational Safety and Health Administration (OSHA), and the National Highway Traffic and Safety Administration (NHTSA) have spawned regulations having broad impact on the nation's businesses. The automobile industry has especially felt the brunt of many regulations (for better or for worse), with the result that the size and power—not to mention cost—of the cars we drive today are substantially mandated by federal regulation.

Rise of the Administrative Agency

At the risk of oversimplification, we can say that two major factors are responsible for the dramatic growth of the administrative agency in recent years. First (as we will see in greater detail in Part VIII), until about 1880 the basic attitude of the state and federal governments toward business firms was that of "hands-off"—a philosophy frequently characterized by the *laissez-faire* label. The theory was that trade and commerce could best thrive in an environment free of government regulation. By the end of the nineteenth century, however, various monopolistic practices had begun to surface; and, beginning in 1890 with the passage of the Sherman Act, the idea grew that a certain amount of government regulation of business was both necessary and desirable.

A second—and perhaps even more powerful—reason for the emergence of the modern administrative agency is that as our nation grew and became more industrialized, many complex problems sprang up that did not easily lend themselves to traditional types of regulation. Some were posed by technological advances such as the greatly increased generation and distribution of electrical power and the rapid growth of the airline industry. Others resulted from changes in social and economic conditions, particularly the rise of the giant manufacturers and the new methods by which they marketed their products on a national basis. The solution of these problems required expertise and enormous amounts of time for continuous regulation, which the courts and the legislatures simply did not possess. Faced with this situation, the legislative bodies sought new ways to regulate business (and to implement nonbusiness government programs, such as social security) that would be more workable.

The Agency— An Overview

In order to understand the basic workings of administrative agencies and the nature of the legal problems we will discuss later, it will be helpful to see how the typical agency is created and how it receives its powers. For this purpose, the Federal Trade Commission provides a good example.

By the turn of the century, it was apparent that some firms in interstate commerce were engaging in practices that, while not violating the Sherman Act, were nonetheless felt to be of an undesirable nature. While persons who were injured by these practices were sometimes able to obtain relief in the courts, the relief was sporadic and there was no single body that could maintain surveillance of these practices on a continuing basis.

Accordingly, in 1914 Congress passed the Federal Trade Commission Act, which created the Federal Trade Commission and authorized it (among other things) to determine what constituted "unfair methods of competition" in interstate commerce. Not only could the commission issue regulations defining and prohibiting such practices but, additionally, it could take action against companies that it believed to be violating such regulations. While the commission's regulations are not *statutes,* they are nonetheless *legal rules* in that they impose certain limits upon the activities of firms in interstate commerce. (The last case in this chapter affords us a brief look at some of the FTC's activities.)

The status of the administrative agency is unique among the traditional legislative-judicial-executive views of the branches of government; and, as Justice Jackson noted in the quotation at the beginning of the chapter, this has caused great difficulty for the courts over the years. The difficulty stems from the fact that most agencies are part of the *executive branch* of government, their members usually appointed by the president (or governor, in the case of state agencies); yet they engage in functions that are, to some extent, both *legislative* and *judicial* in nature. When they issue rules and regulations, they act like legislatures; and when they interpret and enforce those rules and regulations, they act very much like courts.

Status of the Agency

A major problem posed by this unique status involves the nature of the powers that a legislative body can lawfully delegate to an administrative agency. As we will soon see, most of the final rulings of boards and commissions can be appealed to the courts, and one of the grounds on which such appeals are made is that the statute under which the agency acted constituted an *unconstitutional delegation of legislative power.*

In deciding these cases, the test usually applied by the courts is whether the statute contains reasonable standards by which the agency is to be guided in performing its functions. If the statute lacks such standards, or if the standards are felt to be unconstitutionally vague, then the action of the agency will be set aside as an unlawful delegation of legislative power. On the other hand, if reasonable standards *are* set forth in the statute, and if the agency's action is within such standards, then the agency's ruling, regulation, or act is held to be valid.[2]

Two cases help illustrate the application of these rules. In *State v. Marana Plantations, Inc.,* 252 P.2d 87 (1953), a ruling of the Arizona Board of Health was challenged on the ground that the statute under which the board acted was an unlawful delegation of legislative authority. Section 5 of the statute provided that it was the duty of the board to "formulate general policies affecting the public health," and Section 6 gave the board the power "to regulate sanitation and sanitary

---

[2]In the latter case, a minor semantics problem is encountered with the *label* given to the authority or power that has been lawfully delegated. Some courts, clinging to the early view that legislative power can *never* be delegated, refer to such power as "administrative" rather than "legislative." More, however, refer to it simply as a "lawful delegation of legislative power."

policies in the interests of public health." The reviewing court held these sections of the act to be an unconstitutional delegation of the legislative power, inasmuch as the grants of power were so broad as to "permit the Board to wander with no guide nor criteria, with no channels through which its powers may flow. It may flood the field with such sanitary laws as its unrestrained discretion may dictate."

In the second case, which appears below, regulations issued by a federal agency were challenged on the same grounds as those in *Marana Plantations*. Here the federal law that created the Office of Price Administration early in World War II did contain some standards, and the question for the Supreme Court was whether they were sufficiently definite.

Yakus v. United States

U.S. Supreme Court,
321 U.S. 414 (1944)

In January 1942 Congress passed the Emergency Price Control Act, which provided for the establishment of the Office of Price Administration under the direction of a price administrator appointed by the president. The act also set up a comprehensive scheme for the promulgation by the administrator of regulations and orders fixing maximum prices of commodities and rents "as will effectuate the purpose of the Act and conform to the standards which it prescribes." The act was adopted as a temporary wartime measure and was extended in October 1942 by an amendatory act.

Acting under the statute, the administrator issued a price regulation in late 1942 which established specific maximum prices for the sale at wholesale of specified cuts of beef and veal. Subsequently, Yakus and others were tried in a U.S. district court and found guilty of selling beef at prices in excess of those prescribed in the regulation.[3]

Yakus appealed the conviction to the U.S. Supreme Court, where he challenged the constitutionality of the Emergency Price Control Act on four grounds. The first of these (the only one with which we are concerned) was based on the contention that the act "constituted an unconstitutional delegation to the Price Administrator of the legislative power of Congress to control prices."

Stone, Chief Justice: . . . Section 1 (a) declares that the Act is "in the interest of the national defense and security and necessary to the effective prosecution of the present war," and that its purposes are [in part]:

> to stabilize prices and to prevent speculative, unwarranted, and abnormal increases in prices and rents; to eliminate and prevent profiteering, hoarding, manipulation, speculation, and other disruptive practices resulting from abnormal market conditions or scarcities caused by or contributing to the national emergency; . . . [and] to protect persons with relatively fixed and limited incomes, consumers, wage earners, investors,

---

[3]Normally, when it appears that a firm's activities are not in conformity with an agency's order, a complaint is filed; and the agency itself, after an investigation and hearing, determines whether its order has been violated. The statute here involved, however, expressly provided that *criminal actions* be brought against suspected violators in the *federal courts*.

and persons dependent on life insurance, annuities, and pensions, from undue impairment of their standard of living. . . .

The standards which are to guide the Administrator's exercise of his authority to fix prices, so far as now relevant, are prescribed by § 2 (a) and by § 1 of the amendatory Act of October 2, 1942, and Executive Order 9250 promulgated under it. By § 2 (a) the Administrator is authorized, after consultation with representative members of the industry so far as practicable, to promulgate regulations fixing prices of commodities which "in his judgment will be generally fair and equitable and will effectuate the purposes of this Act" when, in his judgment, their prices "have risen or threaten to rise to an extent or in a manner inconsistent with the purposes of this Act."
The section also directs that:

> So far as practicable, in establishing any maximum price, the Administrator shall ascertain and give due consideration to the prices prevailing between October 1 and October 15, 1941 [with the power] to make adjustments for such relevant factors as . . . speculative fluctuations [and] general increases or decreases in costs of production [during the year 1941].

That Congress has constitutional authority to prescribe commodity prices as a war emergency measure, and that the Act was adopted by Congress in the exercise of that power, are not questioned here. . . .
Congress enacted the Emergency Price Control Act in pursuance of a defined policy and required that the prices fixed by the Administrator should further that policy and conform to standards prescribed by the Act. The boundaries of the field of the Administrator's permissible action are marked by the statute. It directs that the prices fixed shall effectuate the declared policy of the Act to stabilize commodity prices so as to prevent war-time inflation and its enumerated disruptive causes and effects. In addition the prices established must be fair and equitable, and in fixing them the Administrator is directed to give due consideration, so far as practicable, to prevailing prices during the designated base period, with prescribed administrative adjustments to compensate for enumerated disturbing factors affecting prices. In short, the purposes of the Act specified in § 1 denote the objective to be sought by the Administrator in fixing prices—the prevention of inflation and its enumerated consequences. The standards set out in § 2 define the boundaries within which prices having that purpose must be fixed. *It is enough to satisfy the statutory requirements that the Administrator finds that the prices fixed will tend to achieve that objective and will conform to those standards, and that the courts in an appropriate proceeding can see that substantial basis for those findings is not wanting.* [Emphasis added.]
The Act is thus an exercise by Congress of its legislative power. In it Congress has stated the legislative objective, has prescribed the method of achieving that objective—maximum price fixing—and has laid down standards to guide the administrative determination of both the occasions for the exercise of the price-fixing power, and the particular prices to be established. . . .
The standards prescribed by the present Act, with the aid of the "statement of the considerations" required to be made by the Administrator, are sufficiently definite and precise to enable Congress, the courts and the public to ascertain whether the Administrator, in fixing the designated prices, has conformed to those standards. [Emphasis added.]
Hence we are unable to find in them an unauthorized delegation of legislative power. . . .
The directions that the prices fixed shall be fair and equitable, that in addition they shall tend to promote the purposes of the Act, and that in promulgating them consideration shall

be given to prices prevailing in a stated base period, confer no greater reach for administrative determination [than has been found to be acceptable in prior cases]. . . .

Judgment affirmed.

Functions and Powers

Ministerial and Discretionary Powers

Before addressing ourselves to the legal questions that are presented when agencies' rules or orders are appealed to the courts, we will briefly look at the nature of agency activities. The activities of these government boards and commissions vary widely. The functions and powers of some agencies are only *ministerial*—concerned with routinely carrying out duties imposed by law. Boards that issue and renew drivers' licenses fall within this category, as do the many social security offices that give information or advice to persons filing for social security benefits.

But most agencies also possess broad *discretionary* powers—powers that require the exercise of judgment and discretion in carrying out their duties. Again there is variety in the specific powers of these agencies. Some agencies' discretionary power is largely *investigative* in nature. Two examples are the authority granted to the Internal Revenue Service to inquire into the legality of deductions on taxpayers' returns and the authority of some commissions to make investigations for the purpose of recommending needed statutes to legislatures. Other agencies are largely *rule making* in nature, with perhaps some investigative but little *adjudicatory* (enforcement) power.

But most "full-fledged" agencies, such as the Federal Trade Commission and the National Labor Relations Board, possess all three types of power—investigative, rule making, and adjudicative. Thus, typically, a board will conduct investigations to determine if conditions warrant the issuance of rules to require (or prohibit) certain kinds of conduct; then it will draw up the regulations and thereafter take action against individuals or firms showing evidence of violating them. In drawing up the rules the board acts quasi-legislatively, and in enforcing them it acts quasi-judicially.

The Investigative Power

Agencies frequently hold hearings before drafting regulations, and the investigative powers they possess in connection with such hearings are largely determined by the statutes by which they are created. Normally, agencies can order the production of accounts and records relative to the problem being studied and can subpoena witnesses and examine them under oath.

Rule-making Powers

The powers of rule-making agencies are also largely determined by statutes. Normally these powers are very broad, subject primarily to the condition that the resulting rules be kept within the general jurisdiction granted to the agency by the statute. If investigation indicates undesirable practices, an agency with rule-making power can show its disapproval simply by issuing a "policy statement" couched in general terms. It is more likely, however, to issue rules and regulations consisting of more precise definitions of the particular types of prohibited conduct. Examples include Federal Trade Commission regulations as to the kinds of television commercials that constitute unfair methods of competition and National Labor Relations Board regulations as to what specific kinds of employer conduct constitute unfair labor practices.

Adjudicatory Powers

One of the most important features of many modern administrative agencies is their *adjudicatory* (or "determinative") powers. Agencies having these powers can not only issue rules and regulations but also initiate action against persons and firms believed to be violating them. In such actions, the agency occupies the roles of both prosecutor and judge.

When an agency believes that a person has violated one of its rules, it holds a hearing to determine precisely what acts the defendant has (or has not) engaged in. The hearing, usually held by an "administrative law judge" appointed by the agency, is *quasi-judicial* in nature. Witnesses are called and examined under oath, and the basic rules of evidence are followed. The law judge then makes findings of fact, similar to those of a jury (or of a court sitting without a jury) and makes recommendations to the agency as to whether the defendant has violated the rule. While law judges' findings of fact are usually binding upon the agency, the recommendations are only advisory. Thus the full agency may accept, modify, or reject a law judge's interpretation of the regulation in making its final ruling.

Judicial Review

As noted earlier, most final actions and orders of administrative agencies can be appealed to the courts. In cases involving rulings of federal boards or commissions, appeals may be taken to the U.S. Court of Appeals having jurisdiction of the area in which appellant resides or does business; those involving state agencies are initiated at various levels of courts within the applicable state system.

Judicial review of agency actions is ordinarily permitted for either of two reasons: (1) that most of the statutes creating boards and commissions do, in fact, expressly provide for such review, and (2) that in the case of statutes which do not so provide, such a procedure is felt by the courts to be required by the due process clause of the state and federal constitutions.

Scope of Review

In the great majority of cases, the role of the reviewing court is almost precisely the same as that of an appellate court hearing appeals from a trial court. That is, it conducts a "limited review"—usually ruling only on questions of law rather than conducting a trial *de novo* (a new, full-fledged hearing). The court in this situation cannot set aside an agency action simply because it feels the action was unwise or imprudent, or because there may be a better solution to the particular problem than the one the agency adopted.

Questions of Law

As we have already seen, one major ground for appeal is based on the allegation that the power granted to the agency constitutes an unlawful delegation of legislative power. This presents a question of law properly within the reviewing court's jurisdiction, and the rule of thumb applicable to such a contention has been set forth earlier. Additionally, of course, an agency action can be challenged on the ground that it violates constitutional rights of the complaining party, such as those protected by the due process and equal protection clauses considered in Chapter 5. We shall now briefly turn to some of the other questions of law that are commonly raised on appeal.

Findings and Interpretations: In virtually all hearings, agencies are required to make certain *findings of fact,* based upon witnesses' testimony and other evidence presented. Typical questions of fact involve the value of a tract of land, whether a person claiming veterans' benefits is totally and permanently disabled, and the percentage of total industry sales that is attributable to the production of a single manufacturer within its industry.

Findings of fact by administrative agencies (as is true of jury verdicts in trial courts) are normally binding upon the reviewing courts. However, in the relatively rare case where there is "no substantial evidence" in the record to support a particular finding, a court has the power to set it aside as a matter of law.

After making findings of fact, an agency must apply the rules to the facts—a process usually requiring the agency to *interpret statutes* (or its own regulations) in order to determine whether the defendant's conduct violates them. Where a challenge is made to a particular administrative interpretation, the reviewing court has much greater authority to set it aside than is true in the case of a challenge to a finding of fact.

The reason for this is that the final interpretation of a legislative act or quasi-legislative regulation is always a *matter of law,* and the reviewing courts have the final say on matters involving legislative intent. Thus, for example, it is a question of law whether a manufacturer's pricing policies constitute a violation of Section 2 of the Clayton Act, and the reviewing court is free to adopt an interpretation contrary to that of the Federal Trade Commission if it feels that the case law interpreting that section requires it to do so.

Additional Questions: Other questions of law that can be raised in court are allegations that an agency's action constituted an abuse of discretion, fraud, or bad faith. The court cannot set aside an agency's action simply because it exercised bad judgment. But if the court finds that the agency's ruling or order is patently arbitrary or contrary to all reason, then it does have grounds for setting aside the ruling as an abuse of discretion. Similarly, if there is evidence that an order is the result of bribery, malice, prejudice, or some other intentional wrongdoing involving one or more of the agency's members, then it can be set aside on the grounds of fraud or bad faith or both.

The next case kills two birds with two stones, so to speak. First, it gives a look at specific kinds of advertising statements that may be challenged by the FTC, and, second, it presents additional questions of law that may at least be raised by one seeking to have an agency order set aside.

Jay Norris, Inc., had been in the mail order business for twenty-five years prior to 1978. It publicized its products by mail order catalogues, and by advertisements in national newspapers and magazines such as the New York Times and TV Guide.

In this action, the Federal Trade Commission charged that Norris had—through these and other publications—made false and misleading advertising claims about the "efficacy, performance and safety" of six widely varying products, as follows: (1) a propane "flame gun" that would "dissolve the heaviest snow drifts, whip right through the thickest ice"; (2) roach powder that was "completely safe to use" and "never loses its killing power—even after years"; (3) an "electronic miracle that makes your home wiring a huge TV or FM radio antenna for super reception"; (4) a "5-year" flashlight that carries an "absolute 5-year guarantee"; (5) a "minted Lincoln-Kennedy Commemorative" penny accompanied by a free "Plaque of Coincidences"; and (6) "carefully maintained" cars in "regularly maintained fleet use; thoroughly serviced."

After hearings, the administrative law judge found the claims to be false and misleading. In regard to the first three products, there was testimony from experts and consumers that the products did not perform as advertised. As to the other products, it was found that the actual flashlight guarantee of the manufacturer was for five years *or* ten hours, whichever came first; that the penny was not "minted," was not commemorative, had no numismatic or historical significance, and that the plaque was not free. In regard to the cars, it was found that they were former New York City taxicabs, and the "many owners had nothing but trouble with them."

The FTC accepted these findings and issued a cease and desist order which prohibited Norris "from representing the safety or performance of any product unless such claims are fully and completely substantiated by a reasonable basis which shall consist of competent and objective material available in written form." Norris petitioned the Court of Appeals to set aside the commission's order, contending that it was invalid on six grounds. Three of Norris's charges were that the order was (a) too broad; (b) unduly burdensome as well as vague and indefinite; and (c) a violation of the free speech guarantee of the First Amendment.

Oakes, Judge: Petitioner ... launches a multipronged attack against one rather poorly phrased paragraph of a lengthy Federal Trade Commission cease and desist order. ... We are not persuaded by any of the arguments [of petitioner,] but we do rephrase the order in the interest of clarity. ...

Jay Norris, Inc. v. F.T.C.

U.S. Court of Appeals, Second Circuit, 598 F.2d 1244 (1979)

Petitioner argues that the order is too broad because it covers all of the myriad of its products, when only six were shown to have been deceptively misrepresented. Petitioner also contends that the order is too vague and imprecise.

The broadness attack [is erroneous for two reasons.] First, the order covers only safety and performance representations, the specific characteristics that petitioner is wont to exaggerate. Second, as to the order's coverage of items other than those to which deception has been specifically found, it is well settled that this agency, like others, may fashion its relief "as a prophylactic and preventive measure." . . . In this case "all product" coverage is particularly appropriate because the six particular products specifically mentioned in the complaint are random samplings of Norris's inventory, which is constantly changing and which petitioner could manipulate to avoid the substantiation requirement if the order were directed only against specific products. As the Supreme Court said in *FTC v. Colgate-Palmolive Co.,* 380 U.S. 374 (1965), "It is reasonable for the commission to prevent similarly illegal practices in future advertisements." So, too, in tailoring a remedial order to fit future proclivities, the Commission may take into account petitioner's past history of noncompliance. . . .

Petitioner's argument that the order is vague and imprecise [is also in error.] Although the Supreme Court has held [in earlier cases] that "an order's prohibitions should be clear and precise in order that they may be understood by those against whom they are directed," the Court reiterated in the same breath that "it does not seem unfair to require that one who deliberatley goes perilously close to an area of proscribed conduct shall take the risk that he may cross the line." [Furthermore,] petitioner's vagueness fears can be assuaged because [if it is] sincerely unable to determine whether a proposed course of action would violate the order, it can [ask] the Commission to give it definite advice as to whether the proposed action would constitute compliance with the order. . . .

[Finally, the court rejected the argument that the Commission's order violated the free speech guarantee. In this regard, citing prior cases, the court said in part:] The use of the requirement of substantiation as regulation is clearly permissible. Commercial transactions are still subject to governmental regulation, and false or misleading commercial advertising does not have the same protection that similar noncommercial speech may have. [And] even since the briefs in this case were filed, the Supreme Court, on the basis that "restrictions on false, deceptive, and misleading commercial speech are permissible," upheld a Texas statute prohibiting the practice of optometry under an assumed name, trade name, or corporate name. *Friedman v. Rogers,* 99 S.Ct. 887 (1979).

[The court then rewrote the paragraph of the FTC order quoted in the facts of the case for purposes of clarification only, and affirmed the order as modified.]

Questions and Problems

1. Louisiana passed a statute to regulate commercial marine diving. Among other things, the statute created a Licensing Board, which thereafter promulgated rules and regulations relative to the qualifications of apprentice, journeyman, and master marine divers. One regulation provided that a person could be licensed as a master marine diver only if he had "continuously worked for a period of five years under supervision of a master marine diver." Under this regulation, the board refused to license a diver (as a master marine diver) who had had several years' diving experience in the U.S. Navy, and who had also had about eight years' commercial diving experience in Louisiana (but not under supervision of a master marine diver). The diver challenged the board's action, contending that the statute was an unconstitutional delegation of legislative authority in view of the fact that it permitted the board to set licensing qualifications without containing any statutory limitations on it, or any standards to which the board should look in setting its qualifications. Do you agree with this contention? Why or why not? (*Banjavich v. Louisiana Licensing Board of Marine Divers,* 111 So.2d 505, 1959.)

2. A South Carolina statute created a Board of Corrections to manage its penal institutions. It also provided for employment of a Director of the prison system, and further provided that it was unlawful "for any person to furnish any South Carolina prisoner with any matter declared by the Director to be contraband"—i.e., items that inmates could not possess. A person convicted of giving an inmate prohibited property contended that this statute was constitutionally invalid in that it contained no standards which would guide the Director in making up the list of contraband articles. (In other words, it was contended that the statute was unconstitutional because it gave arbitrary authority to the Director in this regard.) Do you think this is a valid objection? Explain. (*Cole v. Manning,* 125 S.E.2d 62, 1962.)

3. In the *Yakus* case, the U.S. Supreme Court ruled that the standards imposed upon the Office of Price Administration by the Energy Price Control Act of 1942 were reasonably definite and that the act therefore did not constitute an unlawful delegation of legislative power by Congress. What were the standards to which the court specifically referred?

4. The Federal Trade Commission Act authorizes the Federal Trade Commission to determine what kinds of business practices constitute "unfair methods of competition, and deceptive or unfair practices," and to prohibit such practices. Traditionally, when such a practice has been found to exist, the FTC has simply ordered the offending company to stop the practice. In 1975, however, when the FTC ruled that Listerine ads had—for many years—falsely stated that Listerine was "effective in preventing and curing colds and sore throats," the FTC ordered the manufacturer to stop such advertising, and, in addition, it ordered the manufacturer to insert in *future* advertising the statement that Listerine would *not* prevent or cure colds and sore throats. The manufacturer then asked the federal courts to rule that the FTC did not have the power, under the Federal Trade Commission Act, to issue such an order (known as "corrective advertising"). Do you think the manufacturer's argument is a good one? Why or why not? (*Warner-Lambert v. FTC* 562 F.2d 749, 1977.)

5. A New Jersey statute provided that every taxicab owner who wished to operate in a city within the state had to obtain consent of the "governing body" of the municipality. The statute also provided that the governing body could "make and enforce" ordinances to "license and regulate" all vehicles used as taxis. Under this law a New Jersey city passed an ordinance that set a flat rate taxicab fare of $1.15 for all trips made within the city, regardless of the miles involved. A taxicab owner who wanted to charge $1.50 for some trips attacked this ordinance on the ground that the statute did *not,* expressly or impliedly, give to cities the power to set taxi fares. (I.e., the gist of the attack was that legislatures could not delegate *rate-making* powers to municipalities.) What result? Discuss. (*Yellow Cab Corp. v. Clifton City Council,* 308 A.2d 60, 1973.)

6. One section of an Oklahoma law provided that no person shall "knowingly sell" alcoholic beverages to a minor. Certain penalties were provided for, in the event of violations. Another section of the law authorized the Oklahoma Beverage Control Board to promulgate rules and regulations to carry out the act. The board then adopted a rule that, in essence, provided that any liquor license could be revoked if the licensee sold liquor to a minor, even if he did *not* know the buyer was a minor. When the license of a liquor retailer, Wray, was revoked by the board as a result of his sale of liquor to a person who he did not know was a minor, he contended in the Oklahoma courts that the rule of the board was invalid because it conflicted with the quoted statute. Do you agree with this argument? Discuss. (*Wray v. Oklahoma Alcoholic Beverage Control Board,* 442 P.2d 309, 1968.)

7. A Pueblo, Colorado, police officer violated the Pueblo City Code by removing his personnel file from the city personnel office without permission of the city Civil Service Commission. The commission viewed the officer's conduct as a form of theft, and therefore discharged him. He appealed this ruling to a Colorado court, contending that the action of the commission was capricious and arbitrary—i.e., unreasonably harsh in view of the offense. If you were on the court, would you agree? Explain. (*Bennett v. Price,* 446 P.2d 419, 1968.)

8. The West Virginia Human Rights Act created a Human Rights Commission. The statute provided that "the commission shall encourage and endeavor to bring about mutual understanding and respect among all racial, religious and ethnic groups within the state and shall strive to eliminate all discrimination in employment and places of public accommodation by virtue of race, creed or religious belief." A later statute further listed certain specific discriminatory practices that were unlawful, including the refusal to rent property to minority group members. Thereafter the Human Rights Commission found a Mrs. Pauley guilty of such a violation. In addition to ordering her to stop the practice, the commission fined her $600. (Neither statute mentioned fines, nor the right of the commission to levy them.) When Mrs. Pauley appealed the ruling, the trial court agreed that the commission had neither the express nor the implied authority to fine violators. The commission appealed to the West Virginia Court of Appeals. What result? Explain. (*State Human Rights Commission v. Pauley,* 212 S.E.2d 77, 1968.)

[The reasonable man] is one who invariably looks where he is going, and is careful to examine the immediate foreground before he executes a leap or bound; who neither star-gazes nor is lost in meditation when approaching trap doors or the margin of a dock; . . . who never mounts a moving omnibus, and does not alight from any car while the train is in motion; . . . and who informs himself of the history and habits of a dog before administering a caress.
A. P. Herbert, *Uncommon Law: Fardell v. Potts**

Torts   7

Our primary concern in Part I of this text has been to familiarize the student with the aspects of our legal system that are common to, and that cut across, all branches of law. Thus we have examined the nature and sources of law generally and the processes by which rules of law are formulated, paying little or no attention to such specific subjects as contracts, sales, or agency. (The only deviation from this approach occurred in Chapter 5, where the subject of constitutional law was given special treatment because of the inherently supreme position it occupies.) Before moving on to Part II, however, we will discuss one other branch of law that merits special consideration—torts.

---

*Reprinted by permission of Lady Herbert.

A Preface

Two areas of law, criminal law and contract law, developed at an early time in England. While both were intended to eliminate, insofar as possible, various kinds of wrongful conduct, each was concerned with markedly different wrongs. The major purposes of criminal law, as noted earlier, were to define *wrongs against the state*—types of conduct so inherently undesirable that they were flatly prohibited—and to permit the state to punish those who committed such acts by the imposition of fines or imprisonment. The major purposes of contract law, on the other hand, were (1) to spell out the nature of the rights and duties springing from *private agreements between individuals,* and (2) in the event that one party failed to live up to these duties, to compensate the innocent party for the loss resulting from the other's breach of contract.

While criminal law and contract law were in their initial stages of development, it became apparent that neither one afforded protection to the large numbers of persons who suffered losses resulting from other kinds of conduct equally unjustifiable from a social standpoint—acts of carelessness, deception, and the like. Faced with this situation, the courts at an early time began to recognize and define other "legal wrongs" besides crimes and breaches of contract—and began to permit persons who were injured thereby to bring civil actions to recover damages against those who committed them. Acts that came to be recognized as wrongs under these rules (which were formulated by judges over the years on a case-by-case basis) are known as *torts* (the French word for "wrongs").

An Overview of Torts

At one time the English courts embraced the principle of "strict liability." Any person whose conduct caused injury to another was held liable in damages, even if the person was careful and had no intention of injuring anyone. Because of its onerous effects, this view was essentially abandoned around 1800, in favor of the "fault" approach, wherein an action was considered a tort only when it was felt to be wrongful or blameworthy in some respect.

In formulating the rules for determining whether fault existed, the courts originally equated fault with moral turpitude. In other words, conduct was considered legally wrongful when it violated the generally held moral standards of the community. Under this approach, the courts imposed liability upon persons who knowingly used property of others without the owners' consent, upon sellers who intentionally misrepresented their wares, and upon those who maligned the reputations of innocent persons by circulating false, defamatory statements about them.

The moral-fault approach brought about generally acceptable results—to such a degree, in fact, that it still serves as the primary basis for imposing tort liability. It did not, however, provide compensation for persons who suffered losses resulting from acts which were morally blameless but which nevertheless were so inimical to a stable society (or which so invaded the established interests of others) that the simplest concepts of reason and fairness demanded their redress by law. Take, for example, a case of innocent trespass, where X, a new home owner, cuts down an oak tree which the prior owner had assured him was on his property. In fact, the tree was on the land of a neighbor, Y. While X had no wrongful or immoral intent in this case, it would be grossly unfair if Y were denied a cause of action against him to recover the amount of his loss. To eliminate such injustices, the courts began to spell out additional common-law duties—beyond those arising out of the moral-fault approach—the breach of which would also constitute torts.

As our society has become increasingly industrialized and complex, with many relationships existing between individuals that were perhaps unthought of fifty years ago, the legal duties owed by one member of society to others have become considerably more numerous and varied. As a result, tort law encompasses such a wide range of human conduct that the breaches of some duties have little in common with others. For example, some actions are considered tortious (wrongful) only when the actor intended to cause an injury, while in other actions—especially those involving negligence—the actor's intentions are immaterial. Similarly, in some tort actions the plaintiff is required to show physical injury to person or property as a result of the defendant's misconduct, while in other actions such a showing is not required. The latter includes other kinds of legal injury, such as damage to reputation or suffering of mental anguish.

Scope and Complexity of Tort Law

Because of these diversities, *tort* can be defined in only the most general terms—as, for example, "any wrong excluding crimes and breaches of contract" or "any civil wrong committed upon the person or property of another, independent of contract." While such definitions are of little aid in illustrating the specific kinds of conduct ordinarily considered tortious, they do identify the one thread common to all torts: *the breach of a legal duty owed by the defendant to the plaintiff* (and, of course, a showing by the plaintiff of resulting injury). If no such duty is found to exist, or if the defendant's conduct has met the duty imposed by law, the essential element of a tort is lacking.[1]

With these general observations in mind, we will now examine a number of the more common tort actions.

The Most Common Torts

Negligence

The principles of negligence law are designed to protect persons from *unintentional* harm resulting from the careless conduct of others. Thus every person who engages in any kind of endeavor owes others the duty to use reasonable care while

---

[1] As indicated by these definitions, torts and crimes are essentially two different kinds of wrongs—the first being a wrong against the individual and the second a wrong against the state. However, as we will see, in many situations a single wrongful act can constitute both a tort and a crime.

carrying on his or her activities. If there is a failure to use such care, and injury to an innocent person results, the actor has committed the tort of *negligence.*

As we have seen earlier, the question of whether the defendant was or was not using the care of the "reasonable man" (that hypothetical fellow referred to in the quotation at the beginning of this chapter) is usually for the jury to decide. In *Schultz v. Cheney School District* in Chapter 1, for example, the jury found that the bus driver was exercising due care—i.e., acting nonnegligently—at the time of the accident. On the other hand, in *MacPherson v. Buick Motor Co.* in Chapter 3, the jury found that Buick's failure to inspect the wheels that it purchased from a supplier did constitute negligence on its part. (The tort liability of a manufacturer will be discussed further at the close of this chapter.)

Defenses: Probably the most common defense to a negligence action is that of *contributory negligence,* where the defendant is saying that even if he is guilty of negligence, the plaintiff should nevertheless be denied judgment for the reason that he, too, was guilty of an act of carelessness that contributed to his injury.

In the event that the jury finds defendant's allegation of contributory negligence to be true, the legal effect varies considerably from state to state. Until recently, the courts of most states followed the early common-law rule, under which a finding of contributory negligence was a *complete bar* to the plaintiff's action—even if that person's negligence was of a lesser degree than the defendant's. For example, assume that a personal injury suit has arisen out of an automobile collision that resulted essentially from the defendant running a red light. Under the early common-law rule, the defendant will be completely freed of liability if the plaintiff is found to have been driving left of center at the time of the accident, or even if the plaintiff had momentarily (and without excuse) looked away from the road and thus failed to see the defendant's car.

The harsh results brought about by the common-law rule in some circumstances —particularly where the plaintiff's negligence is found to be "slight" and the defendant's "gross"—have long been of major concern to lawmakers. Accordingly, within the last few years a majority of states have adopted *comparative negligence* rules either by statute or by judicial decision. While these rules vary substantially, they have one common concept: that in most situations a finding of contributory negligence does not totally bar the plaintiff's claim.

A common form of comparative negligence law is the "50 percent statute," which provides that a plaintiff can recover proportionate damages if his or her negligence is not greater than the defendant's. For example, if the jury finds that a plaintiff's total damages were $10,000 and that his negligence amounted to 40 percent, with 60 percent being attributable to the defendant, plaintiff's recovery would be reduced by 40 percent and he would receive a judgment for $6,000. On the other hand, if plaintiff's negligence were found to be greater, to any degree, than that of defendant's, he would recover nothing.

Proximate Cause: In every tort action the plaintiff must prove that the defendant breached a duty owing to him or her and that a legally recognized injury was suffered as a result. Additionally, however, there must be a showing of *direct causal connection* between the defendant's misconduct and the injury that the plaintiff sustained. We will discuss this requirement (generally referred to as *proximate cause*) now because the problem it involves arises most commonly in negligence actions.

Underlying the proximate cause requirement is recognition of the fact that a particular wrong may set off a chain of events so completely unforeseeable, and resulting in an ultimate injury so remotely related to the wrong itself, that common sense suggests the defendant should not be held liable for it. Take this extreme case. Two cars collide, and one of the drivers, D, is at fault. P, the driver of a third car, realizing that the way ahead is impassable, makes a "U" turn and drives away in the opposite direction. After traveling only one block, P's car is struck by a falling tree. P subsequently brings a negligence action against D to recover damages. In this suit the proximate cause of injury was the falling tree, not the negligent act of D. While it is true the injury to P would not have occurred without the collision, it was such an unforeseeable and unusual consequence of D's wrong that D has no liability for it.

The following case presents a somewhat different illustration of the proximate cause requirement: the troublesome situation in which an act of negligence by one party is followed by a second wrongful act by another.

George v. Breisig
Supreme Court of Kansas, 477 P.2d 983 (1970)

Breisig, the defendant, operated an automobile repair shop in Wichita. In early November of 1967 Roberts took his Oldsmobile into Breisig's garage for repairs. On November 13 Roberts asked if the car was ready, and Breisig said he hoped the repairs would be completed by the end of the day. If they were, Breisig said, he would park the car in the parking lot of his shop so Roberts could pick it up that evening.

About 7 p.m. Breisig finished the work and parked the car in the lot, leaving the keys in the ignition. Soon thereafter two teenage boys stole the car and drove it around town. They picked up two friends during the evening and left the car on a Wichita street overnight. The next day one of the friends, Williams, returned to the car and, while driving negligently, struck George, the plaintiff, who suffered serious injuries.

George brought this action against Breisig, claiming that leaving the keys in the unattended automobile constituted an act of negligence, particularly in view of the fact that the general neighborhood was "deteriorating" and that car thefts in the area were high. Breisig denied that his conduct constituted negligence; he further contended that even if it did, this negligence was *not the proximate cause* of plaintiff's injuries.

The trial court, agreeing with this contention, ruled that Williams's act of driving the stolen car negligently was an independent, intervening act for which Breisig had no liability. Accordingly, the court granted Breisig's motion for a directed verdict and plaintiff appealed.

Schroeder, Justice: ... The appellant concedes the instant case is one of first impression in Kansas, ... but [nevertheless] relies upon general rules in tort law heretofore discussed by this court with considerable detail in *Steele v. Rapp,* 183 Kan. 371. ...

The rule with which we are here concerned is stated in [that case] as follows:

> The rule that the causal connection between the actor's negligence and an injury is broken by the intervention of a new, independent and efficient intervening cause, so that the actor is without liability, is subject to the qualification that if the intervening cause was foreseen or might reasonably have been foreseen by the first actor, his negligence may be considered the proximate cause, notwithstanding the intervening cause. ...

Turning to the courts from other jurisdictions which have passed upon the question here presented, the majority of the courts hold there is no liability as a matter of law. Various reasons have been stated by the courts as supporting this conclusion. ...

It is well established that before one can be held responsible for his negligent act the actor's negligence must be the proximate cause of the injury sustained. [Emphasis added.] This leads to the fundamental law in negligence cases which was so aptly stated in words of Justice Cardozo speaking for the court in the landmark case of *Palsgraf v. Long Island R.R. Co.* (1928), 162 N.E. 99, where it was said:

"Proof of negligence in the air, so to speak, will not do. ... The risk reasonably to be perceived defines the duty to be obeyed, and risk imports relation; it is risk to another or to others within the range of apprehension. ..."

Negligence is not actionable unless it involves the invasion of a legally protected interest, the violation of a right. In every instance before an act is said to be negligent, there must exist a duty to the individual complaining, and the observance of which would have averted or avoided the injury. ...

Breisig may have owed a duty to Roberts, who owned the automobile in question, not to leave his automobile on the premises unattended, unlocked, with the keys in the ignition. *But Breisig's conduct was not a wrong and did not result in a breach of duty owing to the appellant merely because it may have been a breach of duty owing to Roberts.* [Emphasis added.]

This principle was made abundantly clear in *Shafer v. Monte Mansfield Motors* (1962), 372 P.2d 333. There the defendant left the ignition key in an automobile which was located in the rear of an unfenced lot along an alleyway containing several automobiles. A thief drove the car away and negligently collided with another automobile occupied by the plaintiff. The trial court granted judgment [for defendant, ruling as a matter of law that defendant's negligence, if any, was *not* the proximate cause of plaintiff's injury]. In affirming the trial court, it was said on appeal:

> The element with which we are here concerned is the scope of the duty owed by defendant. ... Before liability may be imposed for an act, the prevision of a reasonable person must be able to recognize danger of harm to the plaintiff or one in plaintiff's situation. *The risk which must be anticipated to convert an act into a wrong is a risk of harm not to anyone but to plaintiff or to another or others within the range of apprehension.* [Emphasis added.] ...

In view of the great weight of authority in other jurisdictions holding that as a matter of law the duty of one who leaves his keys in an unattended vehicle does not extend to a plaintiff injured in an accident with the converter of the car, and in the absence of further evidence that in this case the duty should be so extended, we hold that the trial court did not err in granting its judgment notwithstanding the verdict. . . .

Under the foregoing authorities, which we find to be persuasive, the act of Breisig in leaving Roberts' automobile on his property unattended, unlocked, and with the keys in the ignition, did not constitute a violation of any duty owed by Breisig to the appellant as a matter of law. *The fact the appellant was injured as a result of the negligent driving by a thief or his successor was not a reasonably foreseeable consequence of Breisig's conduct. Breisig's duty simply did not extend to the appellant.* [Emphasis added.] . . .

Assuming it was negligent for Breisig to leave the keys in Roberts' car on his property unlocked and unattended, the issue is not whether it was foreseeable that Roberts' vehicle would be stolen as the appellant urges in his brief; rather, the inquiry is whether the independent intervening act of negligence committed by Williams, the successor in possession to the thieves, in driving the stolen vehicle [a day after the theft] was reasonably foreseeable. Under the weight of authority such an independent intervening act of negligence is not foreseeable as a matter of law, thereby rendering Breisig's act of negligence to be a *remote cause* and the intervening act of negligence of Williams to be the direct and proximate cause of the injury sustained by the appellant. [Emphasis added.] . . .

Judgment affirmed.

Assault and Battery

One of the inherent rights of every member of society is that of personal security—the right to be free of physical attacks upon one's person. Accordingly, there is a duty upon every person to refrain from making such attacks upon others. If a person breaches this particular duty, he or she has committed the tort commonly known as *assault and battery.*

The essence of this tort is the *intentional,* unlawful physical touching of one person by another. Thus, if X strikes Y without provocation, or pushes him to the ground, or hits him with a thrown rock, X is guilty of an assault and battery, or, as it is sometimes called, a simple assault. (We are here using the term *assault* in the broad sense commonly ascribed to it today, which includes batteries. In a strictly technical sense, however, the terms *assault* and *battery* can be separated. In this sense, assault is the making of *a threat* to inflict immediate bodily injury, while battery refers to the actual physical contact that usually—but not always—follows the assault. Thus, if A unjustifiably fires a shot at B which misses him, A is guilty of an assault only.)[2]

Defenses: In some situations the application of physical force to another person is legally permitted. In such limited situations, the actor has a legally recognized "defense" to an action brought against him or her.

---

[2]An act that constitutes an assault and battery can also be a crime. If, for example, A wounds B by unlawfully shooting him, A's act is almost certainly a felony under the state's criminal law. Thus A has liability both in a criminal case brought by the state and in a civil (tort) case brought by B.

The most common defenses to assault and battery actions are those of "consent" and "privilege." Obviously, a person who engages in a prize-fight *consents* to the normal physical buffeting that is expected in the ring; the same is true of anyone who engages in the sports of football and basketball. The defense of *privilege* exists in the fact that under certain circumstances the use of physical force is socially justified—as in self-defense or in the removal of an intruder from one's home. In these situations, however, the degree of force must be no more than is reasonably necessary under the circumstances; a landowner, for example, has no right to shoot someone who is simply trespassing upon his or her property.

The case below highlights the narrow questions of fact that must often be decided in determining whether all of the ingredients of a particular tort—in this case, assault—are present.

Western Union Telegraph Co. v. Hill

Court of Appeals of Alabama, 150 So. 709 (1933)

Plaintiff, Hill, owned a business in Huntsville, Alabama. He had a contract with Western Union under which it was to regulate and keep in repair an electric clock in plaintiff's office. When the clock needed attention, plaintiff was to notify Western Union's office manager in Huntsville, Sapp, who in turn would contact a repairman to do the work.

One day Mrs. Hill told Sapp over the phone that the clock needed repair. When the repairman failed to show up, she took the clock to the Western Union office herself. There she found Sapp in charge, sitting behind a four-foot counter that separated him and the telegraph operators from the public.

Sapp arose as Mrs. Hill entered, and from his side of the counter asked what he could do for her. (He testified at the trial that he had just finished "two or three drinks," and that he was feeling "good and amiable.") Mrs. Hill produced the clock and asked when he was going to fix it. Sapp looked at her for a minute or two and said: "If you will come back here and let me love and pet you, I will fix your clock." He then reached forward in an effort to grasp Mrs. Hill's arm, but she jumped back out of the way, and no physical contact occurred.

In this action by Hill, alleging an assault upon his wife, there was conflicting evidence as to whether Sapp would have been physically able to touch Mrs. Hill—because of the width of the counter separating them—even if she had not moved back. The trial court left this question to the jury, and it returned a verdict in Hill's favor against Sapp and Western Union. (I.e., the jury found that a physical touching was possible, substantiating her claim of reasonable apprehension, and that an assault had thus occurred.) Judgment was for plaintiff, and Western Union appealed.

Samford, Judge: . . . The first question that addresses itself to us is, Was there such an assault as will justify an action for damages? . . .

In this state an assault and battery is: "Any touching by one person of the person of another in rudeness or in anger."

While every battery [ordinarily] includes an assault, an assault does not necesarily require a battery to complete it. What it does take to constitute an assault is an unlawful attempt to commit a battery, incomplete by reason of some intervening cause; or, to state it differently, to constitute an actionable assault there must be an intentional, unlawful, offer to touch the person of another in a rude or angry manner under such circumstances as to create in the mind of the party alleging the assault a well-founded fear of an imminent battery, coupled with the apparent present ability to effectuate the attempt, if not prevented. . . .

[The court then summarized the conflicting evidence as follows:] The counter [according to defendants' testimony] was four feet and two inches high, and so wide that Sapp, standing on the floor, leaning against the counter and stretching his arm and hand to full length [could barely touch] the outer edge of the counter. The photographs in evidence show that the counter was as high as Sapp's armpits. [Additionally,] the physical surroundings as evidenced by the photographs [tend to show that] Sapp could not have touched plaintiff's wife across that counter even if he had reached his hand in her direction, unless she was leaning against the counter. . . . However, there was testimony tending to prove that, notwithstanding the width of the counter and the height of Sapp, Sapp could have reached from six to eighteen inches beyond the counter in an effort to place his hand on Mrs. Hill. This evidence [when considered with her testimony as to her feeling of fear] presents a question for the jury. This was the view taken by the trial judge, and in the several rulings bearing on this question there is no error. . . .

[The trial court's definition of assault, and the verdict in favor of plaintiff, were thus upheld. However, the judgment was reversed and the case remanded for further proceedings because the trial court's instruction on another aspect of the case was held to be erroneous.]

Slander and Libel

One of the most important rights possessed by the individual is the "right to a good reputation." Accordingly, the law has imposed the general duty on all persons to refrain from making false and defamatory statements about others. A breach of this duty constitutes the tort of *slander* if the statement is made orally and *libel* if it is made in writing. Thus, if X falsely tells Y that Z was once convicted of the crime of embezzlement, X's statement is clearly slanderous—even if X honestly believes the statement to be true.

A plaintiff in a slander or libel action must prove not only that the statement complained of was false and defamatory—subjecting the person to ridicule or causing a loss of respect—but that it was communicated to a third party. Thus, if R falsely accuses S to his face of having committed a crime, and the statement is not overheard by others, no communication (or "publication") has occurred. On the other hand, if R makes the same accusation in a letter to S which is surreptitiously read by one of S's employees, the requirement of communication is satisfied.

Defenses: As noted above, a slander action will be dismissed if the statement complained of is in fact truthful, or, if false, is not really injurious to the plaintiff's reputation. Additionally, the defense of *privilege* is available in limited situations.

This defense is based on the recognition that, in certain circumstances, the usual protection afforded an individual's right to a good reputation must give way to even more compelling matters of public policy. It is felt, for example, that it is so important for legislative bodies to have available all possible information in considering the merits of a particular bill or proposed action that statements made by their members in legislative debates are *absolutely privileged.* Thus legislators have complete immunity from liability for false statements made in debate that clearly defame private citizens, even if they make them maliciously (knowing them to be untrue). This is also generally true for statements made by judges, witnesses, and jurors during court trials (although a witness testifying falsely under oath might subsequently be charged with the crime of perjury).

In some other circumstances the defense of privilege is recognized only where the person making the statement honestly believed it to be true, in which cases it is said that a "qualified privilege" exists. This defense is applicable to situations in which a private citizen makes a statement in regard to a matter in which he has a legitimate interest or duty. Thus if X writes a letter of reference to the Y corporation regarding the qualifications of Z for a certain position, in response to a request from the corporation, X is not liable to Z for any false statements that may be contained therein unless Z can prove that they were made maliciously—that is, with knowledge of falsity on the part of X.

False Imprisonment

If one person unjustifiably interferes with another's right to move about—the "right to come and go"—that person has committed the tort of false imprisonment. Thus, if X locks Y in his office, or prevents Y from leaving his office by the use of force or "by verbal compulsion and the display of available force," X has committed this tort. The same is true if X simply prevents Y, by the same means, from going onto property which Y is legally entitled to enter. The essence of the tort of false imprisonment, then, is the wrongful detaining of one person by another.

Defenses: Obviously, no tort has been committed if the detention is proven to be lawful, as, for example, where a policeman detains a person when he has reasonable grounds to believe that person has committed a crime. And even where such grounds do not exist, a defendant who is a private citizen may escape liability if it is determined that the plaintiff's detention was the result only of the defendant's words—i.e., that the defendant did not use or threaten to use force if the command was not obeyed.

Over the years, many cases have arisen in this area of law where a merchant has either detained a suspected shoplifter himself, or has caused a policeman to make such a detention. If the suspect were later proven innocent, in a criminal action, he or she often brought a false imprisonment or false arrest action against the merchant. Because the merchant/defendant was usually held liable in such cases under common-law principles, merchants generally were fearful of detaining suspects even when they were virtually positive that thefts had occurred. To help remedy this situation, most states have passed "antishoplifting" statutes of one

the torts we have considered. In its more limited and usual sense
is considered to be the wrongful invasion of the property righ
tort of "trespass to realty" is committed when one wrongfully
upon real property (land or buildings) owned by another; "tres
—or *conversion,* as it is usually called—occurs when a person
the personal property of another (such as an automobile) or u
with the owner's right to possess and enjoy such property b
consent.

Defenses: Since the gist of any trespass action is a *wrongfu*
another's property rights, any showing by the defendant tha
lawful is a complete defense. Since most states, for example,
expressly permit innkeepers to retain the personal property of g
paid for their lodging, the retention of such property by motels
circumstances is clearly not tortious. Another general defense
is a showing by the defendant that the plaintiff neither owned
the possession of the property which the defendant was accuse
or using.

Infliction of Emotional Distress

A person whose conduct inflicts severe mental or emotional di
is guilty of a tort if his or her actions were carried on intentio
outrageously. Thus, in *Turman v. Central Billing, Inc.,* 568 P.
collection agency was held liable to Mrs. Turman, who was blin
her in trying to collect a small debt assigned to it for collection
that she and the creditor had come to a satisfactory settlemen
which resulted in plaintiff's hospitalization for anxiety and seve
out by repeated phone calls—sometimes twice a day—in whic
"shouted" at her, used profanity, told her several times that
lose his job and house if she didn't pay, and called her "scum"

Fraud

The essence of the tort of *fraud* is the intentional misleadin
another, which results in a loss to the deceived party. Beca
fraudulent conduct occur where the sole purpose of the wrong
innocent party to enter into a contract which that person o
make, full consideration of this subject is undertaken in Cha

Some torts are so peculiarly related to the business world
business torts. We will list several of these, and then turn to a
liability of an employer for the torts committed by his or he

---

kind or another. The case below shows how these statutes are intended to work,
and how some problems of interpretation may arise under such statutes.

Jacques v. Sears, Roebuck & Company
Court of Appeals of New York, 285 N.E.2d 871 (1972)

In May of 1966 the plaintiff, Jacques, a self-employed carpenter, entered a Sears store in Syracuse to purchase business supplies. He picked up nineteen reflectorized letters and numbers worth ten cents apiece and put them in his pants pocket. He then selected a mailbox and had two extra keys made. He paid for the mailbox and keys, but left the store without paying for the letters and numbers. At the time he had over $600 in cash and a $400 check in his wallet.

A Sears' security officer, Varisco, had observed Jacques putting the items in his pocket and leaving the store without paying for them. As Jacques approached his car in the store parking lot, Varisco stopped him and told him that he was under arrest. Varisco took Jacques back to a security office, where he filled out a questionnaire in which he admitted having taken the letters without paying for them. He said he wished then to pay for the letters; that he was "sorry about the whole thing"; and that he "would never do anything like this again."

Sears' security officers called the Syracuse police, who arrived soon after the detention began. With the security officers accompanying them, the police took Jacques to police headquarters, booked him, and later released him on bail. Two days later he appeared in police court and stated that he was guilty of petit larceny. The court, however, refused to accept the plea and advised him to get a lawyer. The charge of petit larceny was subsequently dismissed on recommendation of the District Attorney because of "lack of proof of intent."

Jacques then brought this action for damages against Sears, alleging false imprisonment and false arrest. Sears contended that its detention of Jacques was "reasonable," and thus lawful under New York's "antishoplifting statute" (the text of which appears in the decision below). The trial court disagreed with Sears' interpretation of the statute, and entered a judgment of $1600 in favor of Jacques, the amount of the jury's verdict.

Sears appealed to an intermediate court, which reversed the judgment and dismissed the action. Jacques appealed to New York's highest court, contending (1) that the statute afforded a defense against a reasonable detention, but not against any arrest; or, in the alternative, (2) that the statute afforded a defense only against arrests resulting in convictions.

Breitel, Judge. . . . Section 218 of the General Business Law . . . provides merchants a defense in various types of actions, including actions for false arrest: "Defense of lawful detention. In any action for false arrest, false imprisonment, (or) unlawful detention . . . brought by any person by reason of having been detained on or in the immediate vicinity of the premises of a retail mercantile establishment for the purpose of investigation or questioning as to the ownership of any merchandise, it shall be a defense to such action that the person was detained in a reasonable manner and for not more than a reasonable time to permit such investigation or questioning by a peace officer or by the owner of the retail mercantile establishment, his authorized employee or agent, and that such peace officer, owner, employee or agent had reasonable grounds to believe that the person so detained was committing or attempting to commit larceny on such premises of such merchandise. . . ."

[This] section has been interpreted [unde
detention" a defense in an action against
plaintiff's asserted distinction between "arr
number of other legal authorities to suppc
'detention' have traditionally been used in
second contention, in the following paragr

The legislative history [of this statute] ind
arrest suits even where the criminal actions a
randum [in N.Y.Legis. Annual, 1960] stated
it will reduce . . . costs by helping to overcor
now attempt to interfere with or apprehe
caused by the vulnerability of merchants t
of the criminal case against a shop-lifter."

The general rule is that a private arrest
committed the crime for which the arrest
exception for merchants detaining or arres

Anti-shoplifting statues in other states v
interpreted to provide merchants with imr
there were reasonable grounds for the arre
a number of cases were cited.]

In this case, there was overwhelming
detention, from the initial arrest to the arriv
being stopped or arrested in the parking lot
out of the store in his pocket without pay
own handwriting when he filled out the w
time did he offer any exculpatory explanatic
a judge of the police court.

It makes no difference that, subjectivel
to commit a crime. Thus, it is assumed, a;
pocket to facilitate carrying other bulky ite
fingers on one hand, and that leaving the s
ently. . . . The point is that even he thoug
facts established as much. Certainly [unde
required to probe further the nature of tl

Similarly, defendants are not liable fo
custody. . . . Under the circumstances Se;
police. [Section 218 impliedly permits] th
reasonable circumstances and the executic
his initial arraignment. Of course, the limi
must be "on or in the immediate vicinity
the police. . . .

The order of dismissal is affirmed.

Trespass and Conversion

In its broadest sense, *trespass* is a gene
that injures another's person, propert

Business Torts

One of the most common of business-related torts, based on the amount of litigation in recent years, is that of "interference with contractual rights." This would occur, for example, where a manufacturer (M) has a long-term contract with a supplier, and a competitor of the manufacturer (C) brings pressure to bear on the supplier to stop its delivery of materials to M. C has committed a tort in this case if it is successful (and, probably, even if its efforts fail). A second business tort occurs in the more rare situation where one person engages in a competitive venture, not for the legitimate purpose of making a profit, but rather for the sole purpose of injuring the established business of another.

Another business tort results from acts by which one person violates the patent, copyright, or trademark rights which have been lawfully obtained by another. A fourth business tort, commonly called "disparagement" or "disparagement of quality," results from the circulation of an untrue statement that disparages the merchandise being offered by a competitor. The false statement must be in regard to a fact; thus a statement of opinion (for example, that a competitor's product is "ugly" or "looks awfully cheap") is not tortious. And, of course, there is no disparagement where a seller truthfully compares the physical specifications of a competitor's product with those of his or her own product.

Employers' Liability

Ordinarily, the application of the principles of tort law results in the imposition of liability upon the wrongdoer alone. There is one major exception, however, which springs from the principles comprising our master-servant law and our law of agency.

Under these principles, an employer is uniformly held liable for the torts of employees if the employees are acting "within the scope of their employment" at the time of the injury. Thus, if T, a truckdriver employed by the D Furniture Company, negligently injures P while delivering a piece of furniture to a customer's home, P has a cause of action against both T and the D Company.

Ordinarily, in such a case, P brings just one action against both defendants; if he is successful in proving the facts as alleged, he obtains a "joint and several" judgment against T and the D Company. This means that if he is awarded a judgment of $4,000, he can enforce the judgment against the assets of either party, or of both, until that sum is recovered. (The "scope of employment" problem is covered further in Chapters 29 and 30.)

Products Liability

Over the years, the courts have been plagued with the question of the extent to which a manufacturer ought to have liability to an ultimate consumer who is injured by the manufacturer's product—and the allied question of the legal theories

upon which such liability should be based. The various rules under which manufacturers' liability is determined comprise the developing area of law known as *products liability*. Some of these rules are based on negligence law; some on warranty
law; and some on the theory of "strict liability." While the courts of the various
states by no means agree as to the precise circumstances in which a manufacturer
might have liability under any of these rules, the generalizations appearing below
are accepted in most jurisdictions.

Negligence

The general view today is that there need be no privity of contract (contract
relationship) between a plaintiff and a defendant where an action brought against
a manufacturer is based on the charge of negligence. This view received its most
substantial impetus in this country, as we saw in Chapter 3, from the rule of the
MacPherson case. (The only limitation upon this rule is that the product in
question must be one that is likely to cause injury if negligently made.)

Insofar as manufacturers' liability is concerned, negligence—if any—is usually
predicated on negligent manufacture or negligent design. Thus if materials are used
that are not strong enough to resist stresses of normal use, or if defects in products
result from the inadequate training of production line employees, a case of negligent manufacture has been made out. Similarly, if a product is designed in such
a way that it creates a danger in ordinary use that is not anticipated by the
consumer, the manufacturer may be subject to liability. And, under the rule
adopted by most states, not only is there a duty to use reasonable care to design
a product so that an accident is unlikely, but, additionally, there is a duty to design
it so that injuries will be minimized if an accident does occur. To illustrate: X is
the driver of a car that explodes after being struck in the rear by a car being
negligently driven by Y. X may recover from Y for his initial injuries, and may
possibly recover from his car's manufacturer for those additional injuries resulting
from the explosion if, for example, the gas tank were located immediately ahead
of the rear bumper, or unreasonably close to a sharp frame member that was likely
to puncture it. (On the other hand, there is no requirement that a manufacturer
build cars that are accident-worthy in all situations; if this were the law, as some
courts have said, manufacturers could produce nothing but tanks.)

While the abandonment of the privity requirement has opened up a new avenue
of recovery to injured plaintiffs, the negligence theory still has its shortcomings.
In the first place, the plaintiff is frequently unable to make a showing of negligent
conduct on the part of the manufacturer at all. And second, the negligence theory
affords no relief to a buyer who purchases a product on the strength of statements
made by the manufacturer that later turn out to be false. In the latter case, however,
the plaintiff does have another string to his bow—the possibility of recovering on
the ground of a "breach of warranty."

Warranty Liability

Under the law of sales, it has long been established that if a seller makes a *warranty* about a product to the buyer which later proves to be false, the buyer can recover damages upon proving that the warranty was breached. In such a suit the buyer need *not* show negligence on the part of the seller. (In other words, a seller is liable if his warranty proves to be untrue even if he is not guilty of negligence in the manufacture or sale of the product in any way.) Warranties are of two kinds—*express* and *implied.*

Express Warranties: An *express warranty* is a statement of fact about the goods being sold (or a promise about performance capabilities) which results from specific statements made by the seller, orally or in writing. Thus, if S tells B that a used car has not been driven over 35,000 miles, an express warranty has been made. The same is true if S promises B that the exterior paint he is offering for sale will not chip, crack, or peel within three years after its application. In both these cases, if B purchases the goods in question and later proves that the statements were false, he can maintain a breach of warranty action against the seller—even if the seller honestly believed that his statement was true.

Implied Warranties: *Implied warranties* are those imposed by law, resulting *automatically* from the making of a sale in certain circumstances. The most important of these warranties in the area of sales law is the "implied warranty of merchantability." This warranty springs from Section 2-314 of the Uniform Commercial Code and provides that any *merchant* who sells a product is guaranteeing to the purchaser that the product is merchantable—fit for the ordinary purposes for which such a product is used. Thus, if B buys from the S Company a power lawn mower that simply won't work, or that runs only sporadically, obviously this warranty has been breached and B is entitled to recover the purchase price in a suit brought on this ground. Similarly, if B is injured by foreign matter in a soft drink purchased from the S Grocery, the drink is obviously not fit for its usual purpose—human consumption—and the grocer is liable for B's damages resulting from breach of the implied warranty. (A full discussion of the subject of warranties appears in Chapter 20.)

Strict Liability

In recent years it generally has been felt that the development of the negligence and warranty theories has not afforded ultimate consumers as much protection as they ought, in fairness, to have. In many negligence actions, for example, the plaintiff is not able to prove specific acts of negligence on the part of the manufacturer, and some warranty actions are dismissed simply because the plaintiff failed to give the defendent notice of the breach within a specified period of time.

In recognition of such deficiencies, the courts have increasingly imposed liability upon manufacturers on the *strict liability* theory—a concept similar to the ancient theory of the same name that was mentioned at the beginning of this chapter. The revival of this theory, beginning with several cases in the early 1960s, has received such widespread approval that today it is one of the most common grounds for the imposition of liability upon manufacturers (and, in some jurisdictions, upon all "remote" sellers of goods causing injury).

Under this principle, a purchaser of a product who is injured by its use has a cause of action against the manufacturer simply by showing (1) that the product was defective, (2) that the defect was the proximate cause of injury, and (3) that the defect caused the product to be unreasonably dangerous. (Proof of negligence, therefore, is *not* required.)

One of the landmark cases continues to be that of *Greenman v. Yuba Power Products, Inc.,* 59 Cal.2d 57 (1963). There the plaintiff purchased at retail a "Shopsmith combination power saw and drill" manufactured by the defendant company; he received serious head injuries when a piece of wood flew out of the machine while he was using it. While the Supreme Court of California conceded that plaintiff's action might fail if based on warranty alone, for the reason that he did not give notice of the breach of warranty as required by California law, the court held the manufacturer "strictly liable in tort." The court spelled out the theory in these words:

> *A manufacturer is strictly liable in tort when an article he places on the market, knowing that it is to be used without inspection for defects, proves to have a defect that causes injury to a human being.* [Emphasis added.] Recognized first in the case of unwholesome food products, such liability has now been extended to a variety of other products that create as great or greater hazards if defective.[3]

Here the court cited fourteen cases where similar results were reached, involving such defective products as automobiles, bottles, vaccines, and automobile tires.

In applying the strict liability principle, the courts are, in effect, extending the *implied warranty of merchantability* to the ultimate consumer in cases involving virtually all kinds of goods, which they had previously refused to do except in cases involving articles of food and drink. Nevertheless, actions based on strict liability are considered to be actions in tort rather than warranty—though the court in the *Yuba* case did refer to the unwholesome food product analogy. Whatever the

---

[3]Section 402A of the *Restatement of Torts 2d* adopts the strict liability view as follows:

(1) One who sells any product in a defective condition unreasonably dangerous to the user or consumer or to his property is subject to liability for physical harm thereby caused to the ultimate user or consumer, or to his property, if (a) the seller is engaged in the business of selling such a product, and (b) it is expected to and does reach the user or consumer without substantial change in the condition in which it is sold.

(2) The rule stated in Subsection (1) applies although (a) the seller has exercised all possible care in the preparation and sale of his product, and (b) the user or consumer has not bought the product from or entered into any contractual relation with the seller. [Copyright, 1965. Reprinted with permission of The American Law Institute.]

theory, the widespread acceptance of the strict liability principle has helped result in the imposition of liability upon manufacturers to an extent unanticipated even fifteen years ago. It has been estimated by some, for example, that product liability (i.e., juries' verdicts plus the total of liability insurance premiums) cost American businesses—and ultimately the consumer—nearly $100 billion in 1980.

One should not, however, jump to the conclusion that the strict liability theory is an answer to all plaintiffs' prayers. In the first place, some courts have limited its application only to cases in which personal injuries (as distinguished from property damage) have occurred. Secondly, in any action—including one in which personal injuries resulted—there is always the possibility that the manufacturer will escape liability by introducing evidence tending to prove that the defect occurred after the product left the plant, or by showing that the product was being misused at the time of the injury. And, because of the success that plaintiffs have enjoyed both in the number and amounts of recoveries in recent years, approximately half the states by statute have placed limits on the consumer's right to sue, and/or the amount that can be won, in product liability cases.

In the next case the defendant company contended that the strict liability theory was inapplicable to the controversy as a matter of law, for two reasons. See if you agree with both the trial and appellate courts in their rejection of this contention.

Wyatt v. Winnebago Industries, Inc.

Court of Appeals of Tennessee, 566 S.W.2d 276 (1978)

Danny Wyatt was injured while attempting to start the motor in a Winnebago Motor Home owned by a friend, Virgil Martin. He then brought this action for damages, based on strict liability in tort, against the manufacturer of the vehicle, Winnebago, and the manufacturer of the chassis, Chrysler Corporation.

The salient facts, as alleged in the complaint, were that plaintiff had Martin sit in the driver's seat with the ignition off and the gear selector in "park," while he (plaintiff) checked the wiring between the battery and the starter motor. When there appeared to be no loose connection, plaintiff got under the vehicle and told Martin he was going to use jumper cables to connect the battery directly with the starter. Plaintiff further alleged that although the gear selector was in park, the vehicle lurched forward and ran over him the moment he attached the cables to the starter, causing severe injuries. (Additional facts taken from plaintiff's deposition appear in the decision of the appellate court, below.)

The defendants, in their answer, denied liability on four grounds and asked for summary judgment—i.e., defendants asked the trial court to rule that they were not liable on the basis of the pleadings alone. The gist of the defenses was that defendants were not liable under the strict liability theory—even if plaintiff's statement of facts was correct—because (1) the motor home was not shown to be "unreasonably dangerous," and (2) even if it were unreasonably dangerous, plaintiff was aware of the defect prior to the accident. The trial court refused defendants' motion for summary judgment, and they appealed the correctness of this ruling.

Drowota, Judge: ... Defendants have raised several grounds, each of which, they contend, entitles them to summary judgment in this case. Each ground is alleged to negate an element of, or constitute a defense to, plaintiff's cause of action in strict liability. [The court here quoted § 402 A of the Restatement (Second) of Torts, and continued]:

We come first to defendants' contention that they should have been granted summary judgment because the alleged defect in the motor home did not render it "unreasonably dangerous." In order to recover, a plaintiff must show that the product was "in a defective condition unreasonably dangerous to the user." (Citations.) Prosser says the following with regard to this requirement:

> The prevailing interpretation of "defective" is that the product does not meet the reasonable expectations of the ordinary consumer as to its safety. It has been said that this amounts to saying that if the seller knew of the condition, he would be negligent in marketing the product. W. Prosser, Law of Torts § 99, 4th Edition.

In the instant case, we cannot say as a matter of law that a Winnebago Motor Home whose gear selector shows the vehicle to be in a gear other than that in which it actually is does not come within this definition of an unreasonably dangerous product.

[The appellate court thus held that the trial court was correct in ruling that the question of unreasonable danger in this case must be decided by a jury. The court then turned to defendants' second defense, the rule that a plaintiff can not recover under the strict liability theory if he "contemplated"—i.e., was aware of—the defect before using the product. The court addressed this issue as follows:] Defendant Winnebago relies heavily on the following excerpt from plaintiff's deposition:

> Now Virgil before I start this thing you get up in it, and you put this thing in park, the handbrake on, and make damned sure it doesn't run over me, because I'm going to start it; if that starter is not burned out I'm going to start this damned thing.

We do not read this as establishing that plaintiff contemplated the defect in the gear selector. On the contrary, his instruction to put the vehicle in "park" is some indication that plaintiff assumed the selector to be working properly. . . . The record before us supports the conclusion that plaintiff knew that his method of starting the vehicle would start it even if it was in gear, and that *had* he contemplated the defective gear selector he also would necessarily have contemplated the possibility of the accident which in fact occurred. (Emphasis added.) It does not, however, support the conclusion that he contemplated the defective selector. At most, a controverted question of fact is presented on that question. Again, . . . it is a point on which reasonable minds could clearly differ, at least on the record before us. . . . It follows that the trial court was correct in denying the motions for summary judgment. In affirming his decision, [however,] we emphasize that this opinion is intended not as a judgment of the strength or weakness of the merits of plaintiff's case, but [merely a ruling on the correctness of the trial court's disposition of the motions for summary judgment].

Affirmed.

Questions and Problems

1. A member of the Philadelphia Eagles football team was injured, and when the team refused to pay him for the remaining two years of his contract he asked for examination by a private physician to determine the exact extent of his injuries. The doctor found he was suffering from "stress polycythemia," a nonfatal disease. Later the Eagles' team physician

falsely and knowingly told reporters that the player had "polycythemia vera," which is fatal. When the player read newspaper accounts based on this false report he "broke down emotionally," could not cope with daily activities, and experienced marital difficulties. The player, after additional tests proved he had no fatal disease, sued both the team physician and the Eagles for damages for "intentional infliction of mental and emotional distress." The basic defense of both defendants was that the team physician's statement was, at most, reckless, and therefore not made intentionally to inflict distress. Discuss the validity of this defense. (*Chuy v. Philadelphia Eagles Football Club,* 595 F.2d 1265, 1979.)

2. As a train was pulling out of a station, a passenger ran after it in an effort to climb aboard. Two employees of the railroad boosted the passenger aboard, and in the process a parcel he was carrying fell to the ground. Unbeknownst to the trainmen, the parcel contained fireworks, which exploded when struck by the wheels of the car. The force of the explosion caused a scale at the end of the platform, many feet away, to topple over, injuring a Mrs. Palsgraf. In an action brought by Mrs. Palsgraf against the railroad, the railroad contended that even if its employees were found to be guilty of negligence in the particular situation, such negligence was not the "proximate cause" of her injuries. *Palsgraf v. The Long Island Railroad Company,* 162 N.E. 99 (1928). Do you think the railroad's contention is correct? Explain.

3. A woman slipped on a piece of wax paper that was on the floor of a Denver Woolworth store, and was injured by the fall. Testimony showed that a few pieces of such paper were on the floor in the area most of the time, and came from a pizza counter in the store where there were no seating facilities; customers thus had to eat standing at nearby tables. The manager of the store claimed there was no negligence, testifying that he had an employee "constantly" sweeping in the area. In the women's negligence action against Woolworth, do you think the company has established the fact that it was exercising "due care," and thus not negligent? Discuss. (*Jasko v. F. W. Woolworth Co.,* 494 P.2d 839, 1972.)

4. A patron in a gambling casino in the Aladdin Hotel had several drinks and, after losing his money, called the dealer a "hateful and degrading" name. The dealer reacted by punching the gambler in the nose. When the patron sued the Aladdin Hotel for damages resulting from the assault, the hotel contended that its employee, the dealer, was not acting within the scope of his employment at the time of the incident, and that it was therefore not liable for the injury. (I.e., the hotel claimed that this was essentially a personal dispute, and not one closely connected to the carrying on of its business.) Do you agree with this? Why or why not? (*Prell Hotel Corporation v. Antonacci,* 469 P.2d 399, 1970.)

5. The International Harvester Company sold a tractor on credit to Rich, a farmer, who gave the company a chattel mortgage on the tractor as security for the indebtedness. Rich got behind in his payments, and the company sent an employee, Dugan, to Rich's farm to "obtain some additional security" for the debt. When Rich refused to give additional security, Dugan said that he had no choice but to repossess the tractor. As Dugan attempted to drive it away, a scuffle ensued and Dugan knocked Rich down. Rich then sued Dugan and the company for damages resulting from this assault and battery. The company denied liability, claiming that even if Dugan's conduct were clearly unwarranted, it would not be liable for the reason that Dugan was acting outside the scope of his employment at the time the battery occurred. *Rich v. Dugan,* 280 N.W. 225 (1938). Under these circumstances, do you believe that the company's defense is valid? Explain.

6. Mrs. Manzoni purchased a bottle of Coca-Cola and became ill because of some spore mold that was in the drink. She sued the bottling company for damages on the "implied

warranty" theory—i.e., on the theory that the bottling company, by selling its products, thereby impliedly warranted that they were fit for human consumption, and that the product she purchased was obviously not fit for human consumption. The company contended it was not liable to Mrs. Manzoni for the reason that none of her evidence showed any negligence on its part in the preparation and bottling of the drink. Is this a good defense to an implied warranty action? Why or why not? (*Manzoni v. Coca-Cola Bottling Co.,* 190 N.W.2d 918, 1961.)

7. In what respects does the "strict liability" theory sometimes make it easier for a plaintiff to recover a judgment against a remote manufacturer than would be the case under the tort or warranty theories? Explain.

8. Kilmer bought a new Porsche from a Cedar Rapids dealer. Four days later the steering mechanism failed while she was negotiating an "S" curve. In the resulting accident a passenger, Holmquist, was severely injured. When he sued the dealer on the strict liability theory, the dealer pointed out the fact that there was no evidence at the trial showing any specific defect in the steering mechanism, even though the car was examined by experts after the accident, and the dealer thus contended that the strict liability theory was inapplicable. Holmquist, on the other hand, argued that the proof of the steering failure was itself proof of a defect. What result? Discuss. (*Holmquist v. Volkswagen of America, Inc.,* 261 N.W.2d 516, 1977.)

A Transitional Note

An Environmental-
Traditional Bridge

In Part I we took a sweeping look at the aspects of our legal system that are common to all branches of law: the sources of our legal rules, the primary lawmaking processes, and the manner in which rules of law are generally implemented by the courts. This *environmental* approach is clearly valuable in that it familiarizes us with the general workings of our legal system.

However, the various branches of law that directly control all the legal aspects of business transactions—such as contracts, sales, and corporation dealings—are comprised entirely of substantive rules. These are the currently-existing rules or principles that define and recognize the specific rights and duties flowing from the many diverse business (and nonbusiness) relationships and transactions existing in modern society.

It is imperative, then, that we devote the rest of this text to these basic rules and principles—a modest change of approach which is often characterized as *traditional* (rule-oriented) in nature.

Contract law, which will be considered in Part II, possesses several characteristics that make it the natural starting point for an examination of the other commercial law subjects. First is its all-pervasiveness, as a practical matter, in the average person's everyday activities. When a person buys a newspaper, leaves a car at a parking lot, or even purchases a ticket to an athletic event, a contract of some sort has been entered into. When someone borrows money, or asks a painter to paint his house, or insures his car, a contract has again most certainly been made—a more complex one than in the prior events. And the retailer (whether an individual running a corner store or a multimillion dollar corporation) has to make countless contracts of an infinite variety. The retailer must buy or lease office equipment, make agreements with employees, secure heat and light, and buy from suppliers most of the goods that stock the shelves. The formation of a partnership requires some kind of contract between the partners, and the formation of a corporation requires making two contracts (using the term broadly), one between the incorporators and the state and the other among the incorporators themselves.

Contract Law—Special Characteristics

Second, and equally important from the academic standpoint, is that the basic principles of contract law are the underpinning of the more specialized business-related subjects, such as sales and commercial paper. For example, the entire law of sales is applicable only to situations in which *sales contracts* have first been entered into; it is only where such contracts between sellers and buyers are found to exist that the more specialized rules of sales law—having to do with the buyers' and sellers' further obligations—are applicable.

The subject of contracts possesses yet a third virtue. Since it is essentially common law in nature, the controversies that are presented usually require the courts to examine earlier decisions handed down in cases involving similar fact-patterns. Thus the doctrine of *stare decisis* is illuminated; and an allied question—whether today's conditions have so changed as to justify a repudiation of the earlier decisions—affords an opportunity to analyze more fully the process of judicial reasoning.

By and large, the subjects of contracts and sales can be treated separately—for two reasons:

Contract Law and Sales Law—A Special Relationship

1. Sales law is applicable only to those contracts calling for the sale of tangible articles of personal property—goods such as automobiles, machine tools, grain, and items of clothing. Contract law, on the other hand, is applicable to virtually all other kinds of agreements—including leases, employment contracts, and real estate sales contracts.

2. As we have seen, our contract law is comprised of common-law rules, while sales is a statutory subject.

At this point, one might conclude that the subject matter covered by the two branches of law is so dissimilar that a study of the law of contracts would require no reference to the law of sales. In fact, such references are occasionally made, and experience has convinced us that potential confusion can be eliminated by realizing the need for this at the very outset.

First, of all the contracts that are entered into, a substantial number *are* sales contracts. And even more importantly, while the basic principles of sales law found in Article 2 of the Uniform Commercial Code are essentially consistent with those of contract law, several rules of sales law differ from well-established principles of contract law. These differences will be noted where we feel they are significant.

Part II

Principles of
Contract Law

Nature and Classification of Contracts

8

We noted earlier that the great majority of people live within the law, routinely respecting the rights of others and meeting the numerous obligations imposed by the law without being threatened by legal action. Happily, the same is true about duties that result from making contracts; most persons fulfill their contractual obligations voluntarily. Thus in the area of contracts, as in the other branches of the law, the legal disputes that do arise—particularly those that find their way into the courts—are the exception rather than the rule.

Despite the foregoing, a substantial number of cases involving contract law *do* have to be settled by the courts every year, and these cases most clearly bring into focus the principles of contract law. It is one thing to get a general idea about a principle that is stated in the abstract; it is quite another to see the practical results of its application to a concrete situation. It is at the latter stage that a principle or theory takes on real life; thus our examination of the principles of contract law will be interspersed with (and, we hope, enlivened by) a substantial number of selected cases.

Classification of Contracts

In the following chapters we will look at the "heart" of contract law—the various elements that the courts require to be present in order for a contract to exist. Then we will turn to such matters as the interpretation of contracts, the rights of third parties, and the many challenging questions that come under the general heading of performance.

Before proceeding to these basic matters, however, we should realize that the law recognizes many different kinds of contracts, each bearing a generally accepted label. Thus a court may refer to a contract as being "voidable" in one case, "executory" in another, and "bilateral" in a third. For this reason alone an early exposure to the most common types of contracts is useful. But even more important is the fact that a comparison of types of contracts that appear at first glance to be dissimilar in nature frequently brings to light certain commonly shared elements.

Nature of a Contract

A contract is a special sort of agreement—one that the law will enforce in some manner in the event of a breach. As will be seen in the following chapter, some agreements are not enforceable because their terms are too indefinite, or they are entered into in jest, or they involve obligations that are essentially social in nature. (Examples of the latter are making a "date" or a luncheon appointment.) Even seriously-intended, definite business agreements, however, are generally not enforceable unless three additional elements are present—what the courts refer to as consideration, capacity, and legality. (Generally, the law does not require contracts to be in writing. Exceptions will be noted in Chapter 14.)

A comprehensive definition of *contract* cannot be attempted until these four elements have been examined in some detail. But for the limited purpose of this chapter—to convey a general idea of what is being classified—we can simply say that *a contract is an agreement that a court will enforce.*[1]

Bilateral and Unilateral Contracts

Most contracts consist of the exchange of mutual promises, the actual performance of which is to occur at some later time. When a manufacturer enters into a contract in May with a supplier, calling for the supplier to deliver 10,000 steel wheels during September, each party has promised the other to perform one or more acts at a subsequent time. Such contracts, consisting of "a promise for a promise," are *bilateral* in nature.

The same terminology applies to offers (proposals) that precede the making of a contract. If the terms of an offer indicate that all the offeror wants at the present

---

[1]A more technical definition is the following: "A contract is a promise or set of promises for the breach of which the law gives a remedy, or the performance of which the law in some way recognizes as a duty." *Restatement, Contracts 2d,* § 1. Copyright, 1973. Reprinted with permission of the American Law Institute.

time is a return promise—rather than the immediate performance of an act—from the offeree, then the proposal can be called a *bilateral offer*.[2] Thus, if a professional football club sends a contract to one of its players in June, offering him $32,000 for the coming season, it is clear that all the club presently wants is the player's promise to render his services at a later time. Such an offer is bilateral; and if the player accepts it by signing and returning the contract, a bilateral contract has been formed.

Some offers, called *unilateral offers,* are phrased in such a way that they can be accepted only by the performance of a particular act. An example of such an offer would be the promise by a TV station to pay $5,000 to the first person who brings to its executive offices any piece of a fallen satellite, such as "Skylab." This offer can only be accepted by the actual physical production of a portion of the designated satellite at which time a *unilateral contract* is formed; a promise by an offeree that he or she will bring in the item later does not result in the formation of a contract.

True unilateral offers occur rather rarely. And, in cases where there is doubt as to the type of offer made, the courts generally construe them to be bilateral in nature—a view that is usually in keeping with the reasonable expectation of the offeree. One type of unilateral offer, however, *is* made frequently in the real world—the promise by a seller of property to pay a real estate agent a commission when the agent finds a buyer for it. The following case involves such a promise, which comes into being when the seller signs a "listing contract." In the court's decision, attention is focused upon the exact nature of the "act" that such an offer legally requires.

Judd Realty, Inc. v. Tedesco

Supreme Court of Rhode Island, 400 A.2d 952 (1979)

Frank Tedesco, defendant, wanted to sell a lot that he owned in Johnston, Rhode Island. On November 18, 1973, he listed the property with Judd Realty, plaintiff, giving it the exclusive right to sell the property for a period of six months—i.e., until the following May 18th. The stated price was $25,000. The "listing contract" signed by Tedesco contained this standard provision: "Should a purchaser be found during the life of this agreement by me, or by you, . . . I will pay you a commission of 8% of the price received."

About a week before the listing contract expired, plaintiff's president told defendant that she had a buyer for his property. A day or two later she had the prospective purchaser sign the customary "purchase and sale agreement," which was an offer by him to buy the property for $25,000. On May 15, two days before the listing contract expired, plaintiff's president took this offer and a $1,000 check drawn by the prospective purchaser to Tedesco. He told her then that he had decided not to sell. When he subsequently continued in his refusal to accept the offer to purchase, plaintiff brought this action to recover its commission.

The plaintiff claimed that it had produced a "purchaser" within the meaning of that term in the listing contract, even though no sale actually took place. Defen-

---

[2]The *offeror* is the person making the proposal; the *offeree* is the one to whom it is made.

dant, in support of the opposite view, contended that the term purchaser was an ambiguous one, in which case the court should follow the rule that the contract be construed against the drafter, the plaintiff. The trial court accepted defendant's contention, and thus ruled that the term "purchaser" meant "someone who actually purchases the property." On this basis it ruled there was no purchaser, and dismissed the complaint. Plaintiff appealed.

The higher court disagreed with the lower court's interpretation, saying that "It is well settled in Rhode Island that a broker has sufficiently performed, and is entitled to compensation under, a brokerage contract when the broker has produced a prospective purchaser who is ready, willing, and able to purchase at the price and terms of the seller." It thus reversed the judgment of the lower court and entered judgment for plaintiff. In that part of its decision appearing below the higher court emphasized that the contract ultimately formed between plaintiff and defendant was *unilateral* in nature.

Weisberger, Justice: . . . Williston distinguishes unilateral and bilateral contracts as follows: "An offer for a unilateral contract generally requires an *act* on the part of the offeree to make a binding contract. This act is consideration for the promise contained in the offer, and [the performance of the act] without more will create a contract. . . . On the other hand, an offer for a bilateral contract requires a *promise* from the offeree in order that there may be a binding contract." (Emphasis added.) 1 Williston, *Contracts* § 65, Third Edition.

Corbin also contrasts unilateral contracts with bilateral contracts in respect to brokerage agreements:

> "The most commonly recurring case is one in which the owner employs a broker to find a purchaser able and willing to buy, on terms stated in advance by the owner, and in which the owner promises to pay a specified commission for the service. This is an offer by the owner, the [acceptance of which occurs] by the actual rendition of the requested service [by the broker]. Here the only contemplated contract between the owner and the broker is a unilateral contract—a promise to pay a commission for services rendered [i.e. the production of a buyer].
>
> Cases are very numerous in which the owner, after the broker has fully performed the requested service, fails to make conveyance [of the property] to the purchaser, and refuses to pay the commission. Such a refusal is not the revocation of an offer; it is the breach of the fully consummated unilateral contract to pay for services rendered. If the requested service is merely the production of a purchaser able and willing to buy on definitely stated terms, the broker has a right to his commission *even though the owner at once refuses to accept the purchaser's offer.*" (Emphasis added.) 1 Corbin, *Contracts* § 50, (1963). . . .

We conclude that the trial justice erred as a matter of law in construing the word "purchaser" in the brokerage agreement to mean "someone who actually purchases the property." . . .

Judgment reversed.

Comment: While the *broker* had a cause of action against Tedesco, the *prospective purchaser* in this case does not. As a general rule, a person who lists property for sale has a perfect legal right—insofar as prospective purchasers are concerned—to reject all purchase offers (as long as the rejection is not based on the purchaser's race, color, religion, or national origin).

Express, Implied, and Quasi-Contracts

The essence of a contract is that an agreement (understanding) has been arrived at. If the intentions of the parties are stated fully and in explicit terms, either orally or in writing, they constitute an *express contract.* The typical real estate lease and construction contract are examples of contracts normally falling within this category.

Express contracts are frequently in writing and of considerable length, but this is not necessarily so. If B orally offers to sell his used car to W for $400 cash, and W answers, "I accept," an express contract has been formed. The communications between B and W, while extremely brief, are themselves sufficient to indicate the obligations of each.

An *implied contract* is one in which the promises (intentions) of the parties have to be inferred in large part from their conduct and from the circumstances in which it took place. It is reasonable to infer, for example, that a person who is getting his hair cut in a barbershop actually desires the service and is willing to pay for it. If the patron does not pay voluntarily, a court will have no hesitation in saying that by his conduct he had made an implied promise to pay a reasonable price, and will hold him liable on this obligation.

The "words-conduct" test is a good starting point in distinguishing between the two kinds of agreement, but it is an oversimplification. This is so because some agreements are reached through the use of both words and conduct, and because often the meaning of a particular word or phrase is itself subject to more than one interpretation.

A *quasi-contract* is said to exist in those exceptional circumstances where a court feels compelled to impose an obligation upon one person even though the person had no intention of making a contract. The classic illustration is that of a doctor who renders first aid to an unconscious man and later sends a bill for his services. It is perfectly obvious that the patient neither expressly nor impliedly promised to pay for the services when they were rendered; yet to permit him to escape liability entirely on the grounds that a contract was not formed would be to let him get something for nothing—a result the law generally abhors. To solve this dilemma, the courts pretend that a contract was formed and impose a quasi-contractual obligation on the person receiving the service.[4]

A quasi-contractual obligation is imposed only in circumstances where the failure to impose such an obligation would result in one party receiving an "unjust enrichment"—a benefit which, on the grounds of fairness alone, he or she ought to pay for. Suppose, for example, that A plants and cultivates crops on land

---

[4]The technical name for implied contracts is *contracts implied in fact,* and for quasi-contracts *contracts implied in law.* We are using the less formal labels to avoid confusion.

belonging to B, without B's knowledge. In such a case, B, upon learning the facts, is entitled to recover from A the reasonable value of the benefit (the profit which A made as a result of the use of the land), for otherwise A would be unjustly enriched.

Two limitations on the quasi-contractual principle should be noted.

1. It cannot be invoked by one who has conferred a benefit unnecessarily or as a result of negligence or other misconduct. Thus, suppose that the X Company contracts to blacktop Y's driveway at 540 Fox Lane for $900, and the company's employees instead mistakenly blacktop the driveway of Y's neighbor, Z, at 546 Fox Lane, in Z's absence. In such a situation Z has no liability to the X Company, since his retention of the blacktop, while a benefit to him, is not an unjust benefit or an unjust retention under the circumstances.

2. Quasi-contracts are contracts in fiction only, since they are not based upon a genuine agreement between the parties. Thus they are not "true" contracts; and except for the limited mention given them in this chapter, they will not be considered in the rest of the chapters on contracts.

The first of the following cases is typical of those in which the courts must consider the conduct of the parties, and the setting in which it occurred, in order to determine whether an express or implied contract—or no contract—was formed. The second presents a situation where the imposition of quasi-contractual liability might be proper.

Rockwell & Bond, Inc., v. Flying Dutchman

Court of Appeals of Michigan, 253 N.W.2d 368 (1977)

In 1972 John VanAlstyne, president of the Flying Dutchman Restaurant Corporation, defendant, decided to remodel the interior of its restaurant building. He asked Swanson Associates, an architectural firm, to draw up plans for the job, dealing at all times with Hofland, an agent of Swanson. Preliminary drawings were prepared and the project was "put out for estimates."

Rockwell & Bond, plaintiff, submitted an estimate of $55,000 to $60,000 based on these drawings, and was chosen as contractor for the job. Because the drawings were tentative in nature, the estimate excluded certain items. For example, it did not include mechanical and electrical costs (although VanAlstyne thought that it did). In any event, no written contract was ever drawn up between plaintiff and defendant covering the project.

Plaintiff began work in late April, using additional drawings that were prepared on a "day-to-day and week-to-week" basis to reflect the working decisions as they were made. VanAlstyne was present almost every day, and took an active role in the project. Hofland, representing the architect, was at the job site about three times a week. Numerous changes, revisions, and decisions were made as the work progressed.

When the work was almost completed, plaintiff billed defendant for $100,156 for labor and material. Defendant paid $54,337, but refused to pay more. Plaintiff then brought this action to recover damages for breach of contract. While the record of the trial proceedings was "complicated and confusing," the gist of defendant's defense was that an *express contract* had been formed, under which its obligation was a maximum of $60,000. Plaintiff denied this, contending instead that an *implied contract* for the larger sum had come into existence.

The trial court ruled that no express contract existed, apparently on the ground that the drawings and estimate were too vague to constitute such a contract. It further ruled that an implied contract in the amount of $100,156 *did* exist, and it awarded plaintiff damages of $45,819—the balance of the contract price. Defendant appealed. [The Supreme Court of Michigan, in that part of its decision appearing below, explains why both of the rulings of the trial court were correct.]

Gillis, Judge: . . . John Rockwell, president of plaintiff corporation, testified that it was his understanding that payments would be made on a "time and materials" basis [as distinguished from defendant's contention that a "fixed sum" contract was made]. He also stated that his company would never have given a firm estimate on drawings as incomplete as the ones initially submitted to him. . . . The types of materials and fixtures to be installed were determined on a daily basis as new drawings were prepared. . . . Defendant's own expert stated that any estimate based on the preliminary drawings would actually be a "guesstimate" because the materials used would greatly determine the cost. . . . The trial judge [thus correctly found that there was] no express agreement between the parties as to the price terms of the construction contract . . . [The court then turned to the implied contract question.]

A contract implied in fact has been defined as one that "arises under circumstances which, according to the ordinary course of dealing and common understanding of men, show a mutual intention to contract. A contract is implied in fact where the intention as to it is not manifested by direct or explicit words between the parties, but is to be gathered by implication or proper deduction from the conduct of the parties, language used, or things done by them, or other pertinent circumstances attending the transaction. The existence of an implied contract, of necessity turning on inferences drawn from given circumstances, usually involves a question of fact, unless no essential facts are in dispute." *Erickson v. Goodell Oil Co., Inc.,* 180 N.W.2d 798 (1970). . . .

[The trial judge] analyzed the conduct of the parties, including . . . VanAlstyne's constant presence at the job site and the need to make day-to-day determinations of desired materials due to the absence of necessary specifications in the initial drawings submitted to plaintiff, [and concluded that an implied contract had been formed, obligating defendant to pay] on a "time and materials" basis. We find no mistake in his conclusion, and ample support in the evidence. . . .

[While the judgment of the trial court was thus affirmed, in essence, the case was remanded to it for the purpose of making further "factual determinations" as to the exact extent of the work that yet remained to be done.]

Deskovick et al. v. Porzio

Superior Court of New Jersey, 187 A.2d 610 (1963)

Plaintiffs in this action are brothers, Michael and Peter Deskovick, Jr. Their father, Peter Deskovick, Sr., was hospitalized in 1958 until his death in 1959. During this period Michael paid the hospital and medical bills as they came in, under the impression that the father was financially unable to do so. (This impression was based on statements made by the senior Deskovick in which he indicated an apparently genuine fear that he would not be able to pay the expenses of the hospitalization.)

After the father's death it was discovered that, in fact, his estate was adequate to cover all of the payments made by Michael. The plaintiffs thereupon brought this action against the executor of their father's estate, Porzio, to recover the amounts paid out.

In the trial court, plaintiffs proceeded on the theory that an *implied contract* existed between them and their father in the foregoing fact-pattern. (No mention of quasi-contractual liability was made.) While the evidence was somewhat conflicting as to whether Michael intended to be repaid out of his father's estate at the time he made the payments, the trial judge ruled as a matter of law that no such intention was present, and directed a verdict for the defendant. On appeal, plaintiffs contended for the first time that the estate should be liable on the theory of *quasi-contract*. (As a general rule, the parties cannot raise new issues on appeal. It does not appear why this was permitted in this case.)

Conford, Justice: . . . If the question whether plaintiffs intended to be repaid at the time they advanced the monies in question were the sole material issue, we would conclude the trial court erred in taking the case out of the jury's hands [because of the conflicting evidence]. However, . . . their intention to be repaid was immaterial in the factual situation presented, for the following reasons.

It is elementary that the assertion of a contract implied in fact calls for the establishment of a consensual understanding as to compensation or reimbursement inferable from the circumstances under which one furnishes services or property and another accepts such advances. Here an essential for such a mutual understanding was absent *in that the decedent, on behalf of whom these advances were being made, was totally ignorant of the fact.* Whatever plaintiffs' subjective intent to be repaid, it could not supply the missing knowledge on the part of the beneficiary of the advances, required to sustain the inferential intent on his part to repay which would round out the postulated contract implied in fact. [Emphasis added.]

It is elementary that one who pays the debt of another as a volunteer, having no obligation or liability to pay nor any interest menaced by the continued existence of the debt, cannot recover therefor from the beneficiary. Nor can such a volunteer claim the benefit of the law of subrogation. If plaintiffs were mere volunteers, therefore, they would not, within these principles, be entitled to be subrogated to the creditor position of the hospitals and physicians whose bills they paid.

Notwithstanding the foregoing principles, however, we perceive in the evidence adduced at the trial, particularly in the version of the facts reflected in the deposition of Michael, adduced by defendant, a *quasi-contractual* basis of recovery which in our judgment ought to be submitted to a jury at a retrial of the case in the interests of substantial justice.

It is said that a "quasi-contractual obligation is one that is created by the law for reasons of justice, without any expression of assent . . . ." 1 *Corbin on Contracts* (1950), § 19, p. 38; 1 *Williston, Contracts* (1957), § 3A, p. 13. This concept rests "on the equitable principle that a person shall not be allowed to enrich himself unjustly at the expense of another, and on the principle that whatsoever it is certain that a man ought to do, that the law supposes him to have promised to do." The *Restatement of Restitution* (1937) undertakes to formulate a number of rules growing out of recognized principles of quasi-contract. Id., at p. 5 et seq. Section 26 (p. 116), entitled "Mistake in Making Gifts," reads: "(1) A person is entitled to restitution from another to whom gratuitously and induced thereto by a mistake of fact he has given money if the mistake (a) was caused by fraud or material misrepresenta-tion, ..." An innocent misrepresentation by the donee is within the rule. Id., comment, at p. 117. A "mistaken belief in the existence of facts which would create a moral obligation upon the donor to make a gift would ordinarily be a basic error" justifying restitution. Id., at p. 118. . . .

We think the foregoing authorities would apply in favor of sons, who, during their father's mortal illness, believing him without means of meeting medical and hospital bills as a result of what he had previously told them, and wishing to spare him the discomfort of concern over such expenses at such a time, themselves assumed and paid the obligations. The leaving by the father of an estate far more than sufficient to have met the expenditures would, in such circumstances, and absent others affecting the basic equitable situation presented, properly invoke the concept of a *quasi-contractual obligation* of reimbursement of the sons by the estate. Such circumstances would take the payors out of the category of voluntary intermeddlers as to whom the policy of the law is to deny restitution or reimburse-ment. [Emphasis added.] . . .

Judgment reversed and remanded.

Valid, Voidable, and Void Contracts

A *valid* contract is one in which all of the required elements are present. As a result, it is enforceable against both parties.

In some circumstances, one of the parties to a contract has the legal right to withdraw from it at a later time without liability. Such contracts are referred to as *voidable*. Contracts in which fraud is present fall within this category, because the law permits the one who has been defrauded to set aside the contract. Minors' contracts are another common example of voidable contracts.

Courts occasionally designate a third type of contract as being *void*. Such contracts are those which, so far as the law is concerned, never existed at all. Contracts are usually void for either of two reasons: (1) one of the parties is wholly incompetent at the time of contracting (such as a person who has been legally declared insane) or (2) the purpose of the contract is totally illegal (such as an agreement calling for the commission of a crime). The designation *void contract* is admittedly self-contradictory—an improper combination of terms. Nevertheless, this label is used by the courts to distinguish such contracts from those which are merely voidable; and in that sense it is a useful term.

Another type of contract is referred to as being "unenforceable." This means the contract was valid at the time it was made but was subsequently rendered unenforceable because of the application of some special rule of law. For example, if a debtor goes through bankruptcy proceedings, the person's nonexempt assets are distributed among creditors and the debtor ultimately receives a discharge in bankruptcy. Under bankruptcy law, this discharge prevents a creditor who was not paid in full from bringing legal action to recover the balance of the debt. The contract that created the indebtedness was rendered unenforceable by virtue of the discharge.

Executory and Executed Contracts

Once a contract is formed, it is *executory* until both parties have fully performed their obligations. When performance has taken place, the contract is said to have been *executed*. If one party has fully performed his or her part of the bargain but the other party has not, the contract is executed as to the former and executory as to the latter.

Formal and Informal Contracts

Some specialized types of contracts are referred to as being *formal*. The most common type is comprised of sealed contracts—ones that the parties have formalized either by making a physical impression on the paper on which the agreement was written or, in some instances, simply by having the word *seal* or the letters *L.S.* appear at the end of the document.[5]

The great majority of ordinary business contracts are not sealed and are therefore *informal* (or simple). Thus any unsealed contract can be referred to as "simple," even though it may be several pages long and contain complex provisions.

A Note about Remedies

In this chapter and the following ones, we are primarily concerned with the general principles that guide the courts in determining (1) whether a contract has been formed, and (2) if so, whether one of the parties has failed to live up to his or her part of the bargain. If the answers to both questions are affirmative, the next question is: What specific remedy will be afforded the party in whose favor judgment is given?

The subject of remedies was touched upon in Part I, where we traced the historical development of the branches of law and equity. There the emphasis was on remedies in general. Here we will focus briefly on the legal and equitable remedies most commonly sought in contract litigation.

Damages

In virtually all breach of contract actions, the injured party is entitled to the legal remedy of *damages*—sometimes called *money damages*. The law tries to put the successful plaintiff in the financial position that he or she would have occupied had there been no breach by the defendant. The usual (and frequently the only) way this can be done is by ordering the defendant to pay the plaintiff a sum of money.

The plaintiff generally is entitled to recover *compensatory damages*—a sum of money equal to the actual financial loss suffered as a direct result of the breach of contract. Thus, if a seller of corn reneges on his contract and the buyer has to pay an additional $1,500 to procure the same quantity of corn elsewhere, the buyer is

---

[5]The letters stand for *Locus Sigilli,* meaning "the place for the seal."

entitled to recover at least this difference from the seller. In any event, the plaintiff is required to prove the damages with "reasonable certainty," the precise amount usually being determined by the jury.

Damages that are *speculative* (not within the contemplation of the parties when the contract was made) are not recoverable. In a leading English case on this point, a mill was shut down by a broken crankshaft. The owner of the mill delivered the shaft to defendant, a drayman, and paid him to transport it to another city, where it could be used as a model for a new shaft by the manufacturer. The defendant neglected to deliver the shaft for several days, as a consequence of which there was a substantial delay before plaintiff received the new shaft. The milling company brought an action against the carrier to recover, among other things, the profits that it lost as a result of the shutdown of the mill. The higher court ruled that such profits were not recoverable, since a broken piece of machinery would not necessarily cause a mill to be shut down and since the defendant was not told that such was the case when he received the broken part.

The court said:

> If the special circumstances [the possible closing down of the mill] under which the contract was made were communicated by the plaintiffs to the defendants, and thus known to both parties, the damages resulting from the breach of a contract, which they would reasonably contemplate, would be the amount of injury which would ordinarily follow from a breach of contract under these special circumstances so known and communicated. But, on the other hand, if these special circumstances were wholly unknown to the party breaking the contract, he at the most could only be supposed to have had in his contemplation the amount of injury which would arise generally, and in the great multitude of cases not affected by any special circumstances, from such a breach of contract.[6]

In the event a breach of contract results in no financial loss to the innocent party, that person is awarded *nominal damages*—a judgment of a trifling sum, such as a few cents or one dollar. While this may be of little consequence to the plaintiff, it establishes that the defendant's conduct was wrongful, and it permits the court to order the defendant to pay court costs.

Sometimes the parties will specify in the contract the amount of damages one party can recover in the event of a breach by the other. Such damages, called *liquidated damages,* are ordinarily given effect as long as the sum agreed upon appears to have been a reasonable attempt by the parties to estimate in advance what the actual loss would be in the event of a breach. On the other hand, if the court feels that the sum was clearly excessive under the circumstances, then it is termed a "penalty" and may be ignored. In such a case the plaintiff is entitled to receive actual damages only.

---

[6]*Hadley v. Baxendale,* Court of Exchequer (1854).

Specific Performance

In exceptional circumstances a plaintiff may be entitled to a *decree of specific performance*—an order requiring the defendant to perform his or her contractual obligations. When equity began to emerge some centuries ago, one basic idea was that a plaintiff seeking an equitable remedy had to prove that his remedy at law—usually damages—was inadequate. If the plaintiff was asking for specific performance, this requirement could ordinarily be met only if the person could show that the subject matter of the contract was unique. These basic requirements still exist today.

As a practical matter, the great majority of contracts do not involve unique subject matter, and specific performance is not generally granted. For example: Suppose that X has agreed to sell a hundred shares of General Motors stock to Y at a price of $80 per share, but X later refuses to transfer the shares. Because the stock is freely obtainable elsewhere, the remedy of damages is considered adequate, and a request by Y for the specific performance of the contract will thus be denied. On the other hand, if a contract calls for the sale of stock in a close corporation (one in which stock is held by a small number of people—usually family members), a decree of specific performance probably will be granted.

Contracts calling for the sale of real property comprise the one major type of contract in which specific performance *is* customarily granted. Thus, if S contracts to sell his farm to B for $150,000 and later refuses to convey the property, a court will order him to do so if B requests such action. The theory is that each parcel of land is, of and by itself, necessarily unique—even though similar land may be available nearby.

In general, the law of sales parallels the principles set forth above—that is, a buyer of goods who is seeking a decree of specific performance against a reluctant seller must show that the goods are unique. In most sales contracts, such as those calling for the sale of a car or articles of furniture, this showing cannot be made and the buyer is entitled to recover damages only. Some exceptional contracts do meet the test of uniqueness—for example, the sale of family heirlooms, of a race horse with an exceptional reputation, or of a work of art by a famous artist. In these instances the award of damages clearly would not be adequate, and the purchaser would be entitled to receive the particular thing itself.[7]

Injunction

Another equitable remedy that may be granted in exceptional circumstances is the *injunction*—a court order that forbids the defendant to do certain specified acts. The seller of a business, for example, may promise the buyer that he will not engage in a competing business in the surrounding area for a specified period of time. As

---

[7]In the interest of accuracy, it should be noted that Sec. 2-716 of the Uniform Commercial Code authorizes the decree of specific performance in some circumstances even when the goods are not unique. Further consideration of this section appears in the sales chapters of Part III.

will be seen in Chapter 12, such promises are frequently enforceable; thus, if the seller violates the promise, the buyer is entitled to injunctive relief—an order restraining the seller from competing in violation of the terms of the agreement. Similarly, employment contracts frequently contain express promises on the part of employees that they will not work for a competing employer during the existence of the contract and, perhaps, for a year or two thereafter. Such promises can ordinarily be enforced against the employee, if necessary, by granting an injunction to the employer.

An injunction against an employee may also be granted where the employee contracts to work for a certain period of time, and later quits before that time is up. If this is not done with the employer's permission, it may ask a court for an injunction restraining the employee from taking other employment for the balance of the contract period. For example, in 1979, when the New England Patriots' coach, Chuck Fairbanks, was contacted by the University of Colorado in an effort to get him to jump his Patriots' contract with four years remaining on it, the Patriots were successful in getting a court order that prohibited the university from further efforts to get Fairbanks to sign a contract with it.[8] (In a sequel to this suit, the professional team released Fairbanks when the Flatirons club, a Colorado boosters' group, reportedly paid the Patriots $200,000, and Fairbanks waived his rights to a substantial sum of deferred compensation that he was otherwise entitled to receive from the Patriots.)

Rescission

Once a contract is made, the parties may later mutually agree to rescind (cancel) it. We will use the term *rescission,* however, to refer to a ruling by a court—again acting as a court of equity—formally declaring that a contract is terminated. For example, if one party learns that he was induced to enter into a contract because of the other party's fraud, he can bring suit requesting the remedy of rescission rather than await action by the other party to enforce the contract against him.

Questions and Problems

1. A corporation employed a contractor to build a barn. Later the contractor quit the job, leaving the subcontractor unpaid. A corporation officer then told the subcontractor to finish the job, and promised that the corporation would pay him for his time and materials. Later the subcontractor finished the job, but the corporation refused to pay the amount that the subcontractor demanded. (It was however, willing to pay a lesser sum.) In the ensuing lawsuit the corporation contended that no contract had ever been entered into here; the subcontractor, on the other hand, argued that the corporation had made a unilateral offer which he, the subcontractor, had accepted by the act of completing the barn. Do you agree with the corporation that no contract of any kind was entered into here? Why or why not? (*Redd v. Woodford County Swine Breeders, Inc.,* 370 N.E.2d 152, 1977.)

---

[8]*New England Patriots Football Club* v. *University of Colorado,* 592 F.2d 1196, (1979).

2. The law of Ohio required boards of education to furnish transportation to all children who lived more than four miles from the nearest high school. When one board refused to furnish such transportation to one of its eligible students, the student's father drove him to and from school for the school year. When the father then sued the board to recover his driving expenses, the board contended that no contract of any kind ever existed between it and him, and that it thus had no liability. Do you think an implied contract existed here, under which the board should be liable? If not, could the father recover on the quasi-contract theory? Why or why not? (*Sommers v. Board of Education,* 148 N.E. 682, 1925.)

3. In the *Deskovick* case, it seems clear that no *implied contract* (as distinguished from a quasi-contract) ever was formed between the Deskovick sons and their father. Which of the specific elements necessary to the formation of an implied contract were lacking in this case?

4. Pendergast entered into a contract with the Oakwood Park Homes Corporation under the terms of which he agreed to buy a new home in a housing development that it was building. Later, Pendergast employed Callano to plant a substantial amount of shrubbery at the home. Callano planted the shrubbery, but soon thereafter Pendergast died and Oakwood Park Homes canceled its contract with him. Callano, having received nothing from Pendergast or his estate, brought action against Oakwood Park Homes to recover the value of the shrubbery on the quasi-contract theory, claiming that Oakwood Park Homes would be unjustly enriched if it were not held liable to him in this situation. *Callano v. Oakwood Park Homes Corp.,* 219 A.2d 332 (1966). Is Oakwood Park Homes liable on this theory? Explain.

5. A schoolteacher owned some land on Lake Michigan. The land was eroding, and the teacher talked to a contractor about having a retaining wall built, but she never told him to go ahead with the job. Nevertheless, the contractor later built the wall without her knowledge. She refused to pay him for the job, whereupon he sued her—on the quasi-contract theory—to recover the reasonable value of the wall. Do you think she should be liable on this theory? What arguments can be made for, and against, recovery by the contractor on this theory? (*Dunnebacke Co. v. Pittman and Gilligan,* 257 N.W. 30, 1934.)

6. Mrs. B contracts in writing to buy S's home for $85,000. S later refuses to go through with the deal, whereupon Mrs. B brings an action asking for specific performance of the contract. At the trial, S's lawyer admits that S might be liable for damages for breach of contract, but he contends that a decree of specific performance—which would require S actually to deed the home to Mrs. B—is unjustified in view of the fact that there is nothing physically unique about S's home or its location. Is such a contention correct? Explain.

7. Madison Square Garden (MSG) made a contract with a professional boxer, Primo Carnera, under which he agreed to fight the winner of a Schmeling-Stribling contest which was to take place at a future date. Carnera also promised not to fight Max Baer or Jack Sharkey before the Schmeling-Stribling contest took place. When Carnera violated this last clause by signing a contract to fight Sharkey *before* the Schmeling-Stribling fight occurred, MSG asked for an injunction prohibiting Carnera from going through with the Sharkey fight. Carnera's lawyers contended MSG was entitled to damages for breach of contract, but was not entitled to an injunction. Do you agree that an injunction was not a proper remedy in this case? Why or why not? (*Madison Square Garden, Inc., v. Carnera,* 52 F.2d 47, 1931.)

The Agreement   9

The first and foremost element of any contract is an agreement—a reasonably definite understanding between two or more persons. It is for this reason that the liability or obligation resulting from the making of a contract (as distinguished from that imposed by the law of torts or the criminal law) is sometimes described as being "consensual." **Introduction**

The usual view taken by the law today is that if two or more persons, expressly or by implication, have reached a reasonably clear agreement as to what each party is to do, then that agreement shall be enforceable by the courts—assuming, of course, that the elements of consideration, capacity, and legality are also present.[1] On the other hand, if it is established in a particular case that an agreement has *not* been formed, neither party has contractual liability to the other. In such a situation, the court can dispose of the case without concerning itself about other contractual questions that may have been raised.

---

[1]Surprisingly, this has not always been the case. Several centuries ago, the English courts would not enforce agreements (even though the intentions of the parties were quite clear) unless the most rigid formalities had been adhered to—which included not only reducing the agreement to writing but affixing the parties' "seals" to the document.

Because the word *agreement* encompasses a broad spectrum of situations where some kind of understanding has been reached (ranging from the extremely concise to the hopelessly vague), the courts are faced with the problem of deciding just what kinds of agreements are sufficiently definite to warrant judicial relief if they are breached. The universal approach to this problem is to break the agreement down into two parts—the offer and the acceptance. The inquiries then become whether either party made an *offer* to the other and whether the offer was followed by an *acceptance*. Before turning our attention to the legal interpretations of these terms, we will offer a brief discussion of the parties' intentions as they relate to the offer and acceptance.

Intention of the Parties

In cases where the parties disagree as to whether their communications constituted an offer and an acceptance, the court will frequently emphasize the principle that the *intention of the parties* is controlling. If the court finds that their intentions were the same (that there was a "meeting of minds," as it is sometimes phrased), then there is a contract.

The idea that the courts must determine the intention of the parties in order to determine whether a contract exists brings about satisfactory results in most cases. However, one limitation or caution must be noted: in the exceptional situation where one party contends that his "actual" (or secret) intent was *different from* his "apparent" (or manifested) intent, it is the apparent intention that controls.[2] For example, if X writes a letter to Y containing a proposal which meets the legal requirements of an offer, and if Y promptly accepts the offer in a return letter, there is a contract—even if X later claims to have had some mental reservations about the proposal, or says that he really did not intend his letter to be an offer. Thus when it is said that there must be a *meeting of minds* to have a contract, we should understand this to mean that there must only be a legal, or apparent, meeting of minds.

There are two compelling reasons for this view:

1. It is virtually impossible for a court to determine what a person's actual intent was at a specific moment.

2. It would obviously be unfair to allow someone to indicate a particular intention to another person and then to come into court and claim that he or she did not mean what was apparently meant.

Requirements of the Offer

Inherent in the many definitions of the word *offer* is the idea that it is a proposal made by one person, called the offeror, to another, the offeree, indicating what the

---

[2] A person's manifested or apparent intent is frequently referred to by the courts as "objective" intent, while actual or secret intent is called "subjective" intent.

offeror will give in return for a specified promise or act on the part of the offeree. That is, the offeror must manifest a willingness to enter into a contractual relationship with the other party. Sometimes the manifestation is referred to as a "conditional statement" of what the offeror will do for the offeree. Used in this manner, the term *statement* is broad enough to include both *words* and *conduct* by which the offeror indicates a willingness to contract. Thus, if a person in a drugstore shows a magazine to the cashier and deposits 50 cents on the counter, it is quite clear that the person has made an *offer to purchase* the item without speaking a word. Similarly, when a company delivers an unordered article of merchandise under circumstances which indicate to the recipient that a charge will be made for the article if it is accepted, the company's act constitutes an *offer to sell* the product at the stated price. Of course, the recipient of such unsolicited merchandise does not incur a duty to pay for it unless he or she actually uses it or otherwise indicates acceptance of the sender's offer.[3]

The courts have never tried to specify the exact language or the particular kinds of conduct that must exist in order for one person to make an offer to another. Any attempt to do so would be utterly unrealistic. What the court has done, instead, is formulate certain general requirements that must be met in order for a particular communication (or act) to achieve the legal status of an offer. They are (1) a manifestation of an intent to contract, (2) a reasonably definite indication of what the offeror and the offeree are to do, and (3) a communication of the proposal to the intended offeree.

The Intent to Contract

Some language is so tentative or exploratory in nature that it should be apparent that an immediate contract is not contemplated. Such communications do not constitute offers; they are designated "preliminary negotiations" or "dickering." For example, the statement "I'd like to get $4,000 for this car" would normally fall into this category, as would a letter indicating "I will not sell my home for less than $56,000." If the addressee in either of these instances were to reply, "I accept your offer," a contract would not result since no offer would have been made. Along similar lines, it is usually held that requests for information—called inquiries —do not manifest a genuine intent to contract, and consequently such questions do not constitute offers in most circumstances. Thus, if A writes B, "Would you rent your summer home for the month of June for $300?" and B replies, "Yes, I accept your offer," there is no contract. (The most that can be said in this situation is that B has now made an offer to A, and it will ripen into a contract only if A subsequently accepts it.)

---

[3]If the unsolicited goods are sent *by mail,* ordinarily no duty to pay arises even if the recipient uses the goods. Sec. 3009 of Title 39 of the U.S. Code, the Postal Reorganization Act of 1970, provides in part that, except for "merchandise mailed by a charitable organization soliciting contributions," the mailing of any unsolicited merchandise "may be treated as a gift by the recipient, who shall have the right to retain, use, discard, or dispose of it in any manner he sees fit without any obligation whatsoever to the sender."

The decision in the well-known case below helps show how the courts try to draw the line between preliminary negotiations and offers in several common situations.

Richards v. Flowers et al.

District Court of Appeal, California, 14 Cal. Reptr. 228 (1961)

Mrs. Richards, plaintiff, wrote defendant Flowers on January 15, 1959, as follows: "We would be interested in buying your lot on Gravatt Drive in Oakland, California, if we can deal with you directly and not run through a realtor. If you are interested, please advise us by return mail the cash price you would expect to receive."

On January 19, 1959, Flowers replied: "Thank you for your inquiry regarding my lot on Gravatt Drive. As long as your offer would be in cash I see no reason why we could not deal directly on this matter. . . . Considering what I paid for the lot, and the taxes which I have paid I expect to receive $4,500 for this property. Please let me know what you decide."

On January 25, 1959, Mrs. Richards sent the following telegram to Flowers: "Have agreed to buy your lot on your terms will handle transactions through local title company who will contact you would greatly appreciate your sending us a copy of the contour map you referred to in your letter as we are desirous of building at once. . . ."

On February 5, 1959, Flowers entered into an agreement to sell the property to a third party, Mr. and Mrs. Sutton. Mrs. Richards, after learning of the Sutton transaction, called upon defendant to deliver his deed to her, claiming the above correspondence constituted a contract between him and her. Flowers refused to do so, denying that his letter of January 19 constituted an offer to sell, whereupon Mr. and Mrs. Richards commenced action, asking for specific performance of the alleged contract. (The Suttons intervened in this action to protect their interest by supporting Flowers's contention that a contract was not formed between him and plaintiffs.)

The trial court ruled that defendant's letter of January 19 did constitute an offer to sell, but it further ruled that plaintiff's telegram of January 25 was not a valid acceptance under a particular section of the California Code known as the "statute of frauds" (the provisions of which are not necessary to our consideration of this case). Accordingly the court entered judgment for defendant. The Richards appealed.

Shoemaker, Justice: . . . Under the factual situation in the instant case, the interpretation of the series of communications between the parties is a matter of law and an appellate court is not bound by the trial court's determination. Respondent Flowers argues that the letter of January 19th merely invited an offer from appellants for the purchase of the property and that under no reasonable interpretation can this letter be construed as an offer. We agree with the respondent. Careful consideration of the letter does not convince us that the language therein used can reasonably be interpreted as a definite offer to sell the property to appellants. As pointed out in *Restatement of the Law, Contracts,* section 25, comment a.: "It is often difficult to draw an exact line between offers and negotiations preliminary thereto. It is common for one who wishes to make a bargain to try to induce the other party to the intended transaction to make the definite offer, he himself suggesting with more or less definiteness the nature of the contract he is willing to enter into. . . ." Under this approach, our letter seems rather clearly to fall within the category of mere preliminary negotiations. Particularly is this true in view of the fact that the letter was written directly in response to appellants' letter inquiring if they could deal directly with respondent and requesting him to suggest a sum at which he might be willing to sell. From the record, we do not accept the argument that respondent Flowers made a binding offer to sell the property merely because he chose to answer certain inquiries by the appellants. Further, the letter appears to us inconsistent with any intent on his part to make an offer to sell. In response to appellants' question, respondent stated that he would be willing to deal directly with them rather than through a realtor as long as their "offer would be in cash." We take this language to indicate that respondent anticipated a *future offer* from appellants but was making no offer himself. [Emphasis added.]

Appellants refer to the phrase that he would "expect to receive" $4,500 and contend this constitutes an offer to sell to them at this price. However, respondent was only expressing an indication of the lowest price which he was presently willing to consider. Particularly is this true inasmuch as respondent wrote only in response to an inquiry in which this wording was used. We conclude that respondent by his communication confined himself to answering the inquiries raised by appellants, but did not extend himself further and did not make an express offer to sell the property. We have before us a case involving a mere quotation of price and not an offer to sell at that price. The cause, therefore, comes within the rule announced in such authorities as *Nebraska Seed Co. v. Harsh,* 1915, 152 N.W. 310, wherein the seller had written the buyer, enclosing a sample of millet seed and saying, "I want $2.25 per cwt. for this seed f.o.b. Lowell." The buyer telegraphed his acceptance. The court, in reversing a judgment for plaintiff buyer, stated: "In our opinion the letter of defendant cannot be fairly construed into an offer to sell to the plaintiff. After describing the seed, the writer says, 'I want $2.25 per cwt. for this seed f.o.b. Lowell.' He does not say, 'I offer to sell to you.' The language used is general, . . . and is not an offer by which he may be bound, if accepted, by any or all of the persons addressed"; and *Owen v. Tunison,* 1932, 158 A. 926, wherein the buyer had written the seller inquiring whether he would be willing to sell certain store property for $6,000. The seller replied: "Because of improvements which have been added and an expenditure of several thousand dollars it would not be possible for me to sell it unless I was to receive $16,000.00 cash. . . ." The court, in holding that the seller's reply did not constitute an offer, stated: "Defendant's letter . . . may have been written with the intent to open negotiations that might lead to a sale. It was not a proposal to sell." It would thus seem clear that respondent's quotation of the price which he would "expect to receive" cannot be viewed as an offer capable of acceptance. . . .

Since there was never an offer, hence never a contract between respondent Flowers and appellants, the judgment must be affirmed, and it becomes unnecessary to determine whether appellant's purported acceptance complied with the statute of frauds or whether appellants failed to qualify for specific performance in any other regard.

Judgment affirmed.

Preliminary Negotiations: The descriptions of goods in *mail-order catalogues* are almost universally held by the courts to be preliminary negotiations rather than offers, even though the goods are described in detail and a specific price is set for each article. The same view is usually taken of *price quotations* that companies send out to their customers. Therefore, when one orders goods from a catalogue or in response to a quotation, the order does not constitute an acceptance. The placing of the order is instead an *offer to purchase* made by the buyer, which the firm may accept or reject as it pleases.

Advertisements are also generally considered by the courts to be preliminary negotiations rather than offers to sell; this view persists even where specific prices are stated in the advertisement or the term *offer* appears therein. Thus, when a person goes to an advertiser's place of business and requests that an article be sold at the advertised price, a contract has not been formed. Under the general rule, such a request is simply an *offer to purchase,* which the advertiser can either accept or reject.[4] To prevent abuses, however, legislatures have sometimes enacted special statutes or ordinances which, in certain circumstances, impose criminal liability upon the advertiser who rejects such an offer. Under typical "false and misleading advertising" statutes, for example, an advertiser is guilty of a misdemeanor and subject to a fine if it is proven that he or she did not intend to sell at the advertised price at the time the advertisement was placed.

The placing of goods on sale at an *ordinary auction* does not constitute an offer to sell, and for this reason there is no obligation on the owner to sell the goods to the person who has made the highest bid—or to sell them at all. The bids of the prospective buyers are actually the offers; thus a particular bid does not ripen into a contract until it is accepted by the auctioneer, who is representing the owner. (A different situation is presented at auctions that have been announced as being "without reserve." In such instances the goods must be sold to the highest bidder.)

Up to this point, we have seen that the courts lay great stress on the actual language of a particular communication in determining whether it exhibited an intent to contract. Another factor the courts often have to consider is the background—the surrounding circumstances—in which the communication was made. Examination of the background sometimes makes it quite clear that an intent to contract was not present, even though the language taken by itself meets the requirements of an offer (as, for example, a statement made in jest or in anger).[5]

---

[4]In the interest of accuracy, it should be noted that there are occasional decisions in which advertisements *have* been held to constitute offers. Most (but not all) of these exceptional cases involve advertisements containing unique statements from which the courts have inferred a genuine intent to contract on the part of the advertiser. (*Lefkowitz v. Great Minneapolis Surplus Store, Inc.,* 86 N.W.2d 689, 1957, is one such case.) Additionally, advertisements promising *rewards for information* leading to the apprehension of persons who have committed crimes are almost universally held to constitute offers; these decisions apparently are based on grounds of broad public policy.

[5]A classic illustration is the case in which a $15 harness was stolen. The owner became angry, swore, and during the tirade made the statement that he would "give $100 to any man who will find out who the thief is." One of the persons who was present later gave the requested information and brought suit to recover the money, on the grounds that a contract had been formed. The higher court did not allow recovery, ruling that the quoted statement was not an offer under the circumstances. It was, instead, merely an "extravagant exclamation of an excited man." *Higgins v. Lessig,* 49 Ill. App. 459 (1893).

Of course, it is always possible that a statement will actually be made in jest (or in anger) under circumstances where this fact is *not* apparent to the offeree. Such a statement constitutes a valid offer and—if accepted—will impose contractual liability on the person making it.

Reasonable Definiteness

The requirement that the offer be *reasonably definite* is largely a practical one. The terms of an agreement have to be definite enough that a court can determine whether both parties lived up to their promises, in the event that a question of breach of contract arises. If the offer is too indefinite, the court is unable to do this.

In one case, a company told an injured employee that it would take care of him and offer him light work when his doctor certified that he was capable of doing such a job. The company later refused to rehire him, and he sued to recover damages, alleging that this was a breach of contract. In ruling against the employee, the court said that since no specific position was mentioned, and there was no discussion of rates of pay or hours of employment, it had no way of determining the amount of the employee's loss. The statement of the company, in other words, was held to be too indefinite to constitute an offer.[6] Similarly, if X writes Y, "I will sell you my car for $1,000, credit terms to be arranged," and Y replies, "I accept," there is no contract. X's statement does not constitute an offer, since there is no way of knowing what credit terms would be acceptable to her or whether any credit terms will ever be agreed on.

Despite the foregoing, the requirement of "reasonable definiteness" is relative rather than absolute. Therefore, it is not necessary that every obligation be set forth in a contract, so long as there is agreement on major points. Missing terms are sometimes supplied by the courts to "save" a contract; for example, the court might rule that there was *implied agreement* as to such matters. Thus, if a contract has been entered into by S and B, under the terms of which S agrees to do a particular job for B for $25, neither party can successfully contend that the agreement was too vague simply because no time of performance was specified. In this situation, it is implied that S will have a reasonable time in which to perform.

It is the policy of the courts to avoid setting aside a contract on the ground of indefiniteness if they are reasonably able to do so. The decision in the following case, while perhaps extending this policy close to its outer limits, is a good illustration of how the courts in some instances look to outside factors for help in resolving problems in this area of the law.

---

[6]*Laseter v. Pet Dairy Products Company,* 246 F.2d 747 (1957).

Rivers v. Beadle

District Court of
Appeal, California, 7
Cal. Rptr. 170 (1960)

Plaintiff, Vera Rivers, a California real estate broker, was contacted by the defendants, Mr. and Mrs. Beadle, who wished to buy three lots in San Rafael. Defendants intended to build houses on the lots and resell them at a profit.

Plaintiff agreed to represent the Beadles in making the purchase, without a commission, provided she was given an exclusive agency to sell the houses that were to be built. The following agreement was entered into:

March 3, 1955

In consideration of Vera Rivers Realty handling my purchase of 3 lots located at Center Avenue, corner K Street, San Rafael, without brokerage, as evidenced by attached copy of deposit receipt, I hereby agree as follows:

1. To build on each of said 3 lots a speculative home, which is to be placed on the market immediately for sale on completion of same.

2. To give to Vera Rivers Realty the exclusive right to sell each of such houses and pay a 3% commission of selling price, this exclusive right to sell to be effective immediately and to continue in effect for a period of one year from date of completion of each of such houses.

/s/ Philander B. Beadle
/s/ Eva May Beadle
/s/ Vera Rivers

Subsequently, defendants refused to build homes on the lots, and plaintiff brought action to recover damages for breach of contract. The trial court rejected defendants' contention that the agreement was too indefinite to enforce, ruling that "the term 'speculative home' means a home built with expectation of selling it for profit; . . . and that in relation to the area of said lots and the type of homes in said area, the homes, if constructed by the defendants, would have been homes that would sell for approximately $20,000." The court thereupon allowed damages based upon an allowance of 3 percent of $20,000 for each house, totalling for the three $1,800. Defendants appealed.

Bray, Justice: . . . "Vagueness of expression, indefiniteness, and uncertainty as to any of the essential terms of an agreement may prevent the creation of an enforceable contract. . . . Vagueness, indefiniteness, and uncertainty are matters of degree, with no absolute standard for comparison. It must be remembered that all modes of human expression are defective and inadequate. . . . In considering expressions of agreement, the court must not hold the parties to some impossible, or ideal, or unusual standard. It must take language as it is and people as they are. All agreements have some degree of indefiniteness and some degree of uncertainty. . . . [P]eople must be held to the promises they make. The court must not be overly fearful of error; it must not be pedantic or meticulous in interpretation of expressions. . . . If the parties have concluded a transaction in which it appears that they intend to make a contract, the court should not frustrate their intention, if it is possible to reach a fair and just result, even though this requires a choice among conflicting meanings and the filling of some gaps that the parties have left. . . . The application of such a rule as this is believed to come nearer to attaining the purpose of the contracting parties than any other, to give more business satisfaction and to make [a] contract a workable instrument." *Corbin on Contracts*, Vol. 1, § 95, pp. 288–292.

[In regard to a California statute, which required all contracts calling for the sale of land to be in writing, the court continued:] To be sufficient, the required writing must be one "which states with *reasonable certainty*, (a) each party to the contract, and (b) the land . . .

to which the contract relates, and (c) the terms and conditions of all the promises constituting the contract and by whom and to whom the promises are made." *Restatement, Contracts,* sec. 207. [Emphasis added.]

With these rules in mind, let us examine the contract. (a) It clearly sets forth each party to the contract. The parties are the defendants on the one hand, and Vera Rivers on the other.

(b) The subject matter is that in consideration of the waiving of a commission by Vera Rivers for her handling defendants' purchase of the described three lots, defendants agree to build on each lot "a speculative home" to be placed on the market for sale immediately on completion. That "speculative home" had a definite meaning to the parties will hereafter appear.

(c) The agreement also clearly shows "the terms and conditions of all the promises constituting the contract and by whom and to whom the promises are made." These are, first, that defendants agree to build the homes (although the time is not stated, such an agreement imports an understanding that it must be built within a reasonable time); secondly, that defendants will place the homes for sale on the market immediately upon completion, and that Vera Rivers has the exclusive right until the expiration of one year after the houses are completed to sell them, and defendants agree that on such sale Vera Rivers will receive a commission of 3 percent of the sale price. While the selling price is not fixed in the agreement (it could not be until the homes were built and their cost obtained), implied in the agreement, and well understood by the parties, is that the defendants would fix the selling price to return a profit to them. Vera Rivers was not concerned with the selling price. She was given the right to sell, if possible, the houses for whatever price defendants might place the houses on the market. There was nothing indefinite in this term of the contract.

"Speculative home" as here used is not indefinite or vague. It had a definite meaning to the parties. The evidence showed that this is a term well known in real estate circles and to defendants, as meaning simply a home built with expectation of selling it at cost plus a profit *and of the type and price of homes being then generally built and sold in the area.* [Emphasis added.] Applicable here is *Bettancourt v. Gilroy Theatre Co., Inc.,* 261 P.2d 351, where this court held that an agreement " 'to erect a *First class Theatre*' " was sufficiently definite and certain to create and impose a contractual obligation. . . .

It is true that some explanation has to be made of what the parties meant by a "speculative home," just as in *Bettancourt,* supra, explanation was required as to what the parties had in mind by " '. . . *First class Theatre.*' " In considering this question applicable here is the following from *Avalon Products, Inc. v. Lentini,* 219 P.2d 485: "The law leans against the destruction of contracts because of uncertainty and favors an interpretation which will carry into effect the reasonable intention of the parties if it can be ascertained. The description of the subject matter of an agreement may be indefinite but if it is capable of being identified and rendered definite and certain by evidence *aliunde* [from elsewhere], the contract is enforceable." A "speculative home" appears from the evidence to be sufficiently definite and certain to enable the defendants to know what they had undertaken to do.

The facts of our case differ greatly from those in *Ferrara v. Silver,* supra, 292 P.2d 251, where the contract provided that a " 'banquet room building' " was to be built, and we held that that expression was so vague that the contract could not be enforced. There the parties, at the time of entering into the agreement, did not have in mind any particular type, size or price of building. As the court there said, the parties did not have "in mind as a norm or standard" any building, such as the parties in *Bettancourt,* supra, did. *In our case the parties did have in mind a norm or standard. It was the type, materials and range of price of speculative homes in the general area.* [Emphasis added.] In determining the sufficiency of [a] contract, the purpose of the contract must be borne in mind. Its basic purpose was to enable the real estate broker to obtain a commission on the sale of the houses, to make up for the waiver of a commission then due for the purchase by defendants of the lots. While the description might be considered too vague were this a contract of purchase of a house or houses, it is not too vague for the purpose intended. The type, materials and price (within the norm or standard above mentioned) was left to the discretion of defendants, but they were to build the houses and the broker was to be permitted to sell them on commission. . . .

The evidence in our case shows that the term "speculative home" was one well known in the real estate business and known to the defendants. It should be pointed out that while the writing here was prepared by Vera Rivers, one of the defendants is and for a number of years has been a practicing lawyer. It is unreasonable to assume that he would enter into a contract which appeared indefinite to him, or whose terms he did not understand. He testified that when he signed it, the agreement was perfectly clear to him. . . .

Judgment affirmed.

Communication

An offer has no effect until it has reached the offeree. This requirement of *communication* is based on the obvious proposition that an offeree cannot agree to a proposal before knowing about it. To illustrate: A city council, via a public advertisement, offers to pay $200 to the person or persons who apprehend an escaped criminal. If X captures the fugitive on his farm, only to learn of the offer later, his act does not constitute an acceptance of the offer and he is not entitled to the reward under the principles of contract law. The relatively few cases that involve this kind of fact-pattern generally follow this view.[7]

The principle takes on broader scope—and is more difficult to apply—in situations where there has been clear-cut communication of some terms of the agreement but questionable communication of others. The so-called fine print cases illustrate the problem. For example, statements printed on the back of parking lot tickets frequently provide that "the company shall not be liable for loss of, or injury to, the automobile, regardless of cause," or words of similar import. The usual view is that such provisions have not been legally communicated to the owner of the car and that the owner is not bound by them unless they were actually brought to his or her attention when the contract was made.

We should not conclude from the foregoing that an *actual* communication of terms is required in all cases. If a court feels that the offeror has made a reasonable effort, under the circumstances, to call the terms of the offer to the offeree's attention, then a legal communication has occurred. A subsequent acceptance of the offer would be binding on the offeree in such a case, even though he or she might not have been aware of all its terms. The following case brings the nature of the problem into sharper focus.

[7]There are exceptions, however, where recovery has been allowed on noncontract grounds (for example, public policy, inherent fairness, and the like).

Smith, plaintiff, owned the Richmond Electric Garage. In the early part of 1918 he entered into a contract with Mrs. Green, defendant, under the terms of which he agreed to store her automobile for $37 a month and to deliver the car to her residence and take it back to the garage once each day, upon her request. It was also agreed, in the event the car was damaged while being driven by Smith's employees between the garage and Mrs. Green's home, that she would not hold Smith liable for damages done to her car.

In January 1920 Smith had printed what he called a "folder," which bore on the outside cover this inscription: "Service Rates of the Richmond Electric Garage. . . . Effective on and after January 1, 1920." The inside pages of the folder contained a schedule of charges for various services and the following clause: "Note: The owner agrees to accept our employees as his or her agent and *to absolve this garage from any liability whatsoever* arising while his or her car is in the hands of said employee at the request of the owner." [Emphasis added.]

Early in January Smith mailed out his monthly bills to all patrons and enclosed a folder with each bill. During that same month, Smith placed additional folders in all of his patrons' cars, including Mrs. Green's. Thereafter, Mrs. Green continued to have her car garaged as before.

On June 5, 1920, one of the garage's employees, while driving Mrs. Green's car back to the garage, negligently ran into a car driven by a Mr. Moore. Moore subsequently sued Smith and obtained a judgment against him in the amount of $2,735.

Smith paid that judgment and then brought action against Mrs. Green to recover that sum, basing his claim on the language of the "note" appearing inside the folder.

Defendant, Mrs. Green, did not appear at the trial because of her advanced age and infirmities. Her daughter, with whom Mrs. Green lived, testified that Mrs. Green had received several of the folders but that she "paid no attention to them." There was no evidence that Mrs. Green actually read the note at all.

The trial court rendered judgment for plaintiff, and defendant appealed. (Before the case was heard on appeal, Mrs. Green died and her executors prosecuted the appeal.)

Chinn, Justice: . . . As has been noted, plaintiff seeks to recover in this action upon an alleged contract by which, it is claimed in his declaration, defendant agreed to accept plaintiff's garage employees as her servants, and to indemnify and save him harmless from any and all liability whatsoever arising from the acts of any of said employees while moving her car to and from said garage. In the absence of agreement, the defendant is in no sense liable to the plaintiff for the injuries inflicted upon Mr. Moore under the circumstances disclosed by the record. . . . The real question is, therefore, Was there a valid and subsisting contract between the plaintiff and Mrs. Green, at the time Mr. Moore received his injuries, by which the defendant bound herself to indemnify the plaintiff against the consequences of all such acts of negligence on the part of his employees?

It is elementary that mutuality of assent—the meeting of the minds of the parties—is an essential element of all contracts, and, in order that this mutuality may exist, it is necessary that there be a proposal or offer on the part of one party and an acceptance on the part of the other. Both the offer and acceptance may be by word, act, or conduct which evince the intention of the parties to contract, and that their minds have met may be shown by direct evidence of facts from which an agreement may be implied.

Green's Executors v. Smith

Special Court of Appeals of Virginia, 131 S.E. 846 (1926)

It is manifest, however, that before one can be held to have accepted the offer of another, whether such offer is made by word or act, there must have been some form of communication of the offer; otherwise there could be no assent, and in consequence no contract. In the instant case the plaintiff relies upon the "note" printed in the folder as constituting the terms of the proposed contract, on the fact that said folder was mailed to Mrs. Green on several occasions with her monthly bills and placed in her car, as a communication of said terms, and on her conduct in continuing to keep her car in his garage as an implied acceptance of the terms specified in said note.

The question, therefore, of whether Mrs. Green agreed to, and is bound by, the terms of the "note" in the main depends upon whether the means employed by the plaintiff to communicate such terms were sufficient, under the circumstances, to constitute her act [of continuing the storage of her car with defendant] an implied acceptance of the said terms. [Emphasis added.] The rule as to when the delivery of a paper containing the terms of a proposed contract amounts to an acceptance, is thus stated in *13 Corpus Juris,* at page 277:

> A contract may be formed by accepting a paper containing terms. If an offer is made by delivering to another a paper containing the terms of a proposed contract, and the paper is accepted, the acceptor is bound by its terms; and this is true whether he reads the paper or not. When an offer contains various terms, some of which do not appear on the face of the offer, the question whether the acceptor is bound by the terms depends on the circumstances. He is not bound as a rule by any terms which *are not communicated* to him. But he is bound by all the legal terms which are communicated. This question arises when a person accepts a railroad or steamboat ticket, bill of lading, warehouse receipt, or other document containing conditions. He is bound by all the conditions whether he reads them or not, *if he knows that the document contains conditions. But he is not bound by conditions of which he is ignorant, even though the ticket or document contains writing, unless he knows that the writing contains terms, or unless he ought to know that it contains terms, by reason of previous dealings, or by reason of the form, size, or character of the document.* (Italics supplied.) . . .

There was nothing on the face of the folder, nor in its form or character, to indicate that it contained the terms of the contract which plaintiff has attempted to establish in this case, or any other contract imposing obligations of such a nature upon the defendant. The paper only purported to contain a schedule of rates for services at plaintiff's garage, and defendant had no reason, on account of her previous dealings with the plaintiff or otherwise, to know that plaintiff proposed, by mailing the folder to her along with his monthly bill, and placing a copy of it in her car, to commit her to a new contract of such unusual terms.

Considering the circumstances under which she received the folder, she was justified in assuming it to be only what it purported to be, and, as she already knew the rates prevailing at plaintiff's garage, was justified in paying no attention to it, as she did. There is no evidence that Mrs. Green ever read the "note" or knew it was printed in the folder until she received [a letter from the plaintiff after the accident], or that it was brought to her notice in any way prior to that time. If plaintiff proposed to form a special contract of this kind, he should have, at the least, called Mrs. Green's attention to the terms contained in the folder, as he undertook to do, upon the advice of counsel, after the accident . . . .

We are of the opinion that the plaintiff has failed to establish the contract alleged in his declaration in the manner that the law requires, and is not entitled to recover. . . .

Judgment reversed.

Because of the rule that an offer can be accepted at any time before it is legally terminated, it becomes necessary to see what events will cause the offer to die. The rules in this area of the law are rather mechanical in their operation, and we need touch upon them but briefly.

Termination by Act of the Parties

Most offers are terminated by the conduct of the parties themselves by (1) revocation, (2) rejection, or (3) lapse of time.

Revocation: A *revocation* is a withdrawal of the offer by the offeror. Like the offer itself, it is effective only when it has been communicated to the offeree. The mere mailing of a revocation, in other words, ordinarily does not terminate the offer.[8]

The ordinary offer can be revoked at any time—assuming, of course, that it is communicated to the offeree before an acceptance has occurred. This is generally true even if the offeror had promised to keep the offer open a certain length of time. Thus, if X makes an offer to Y, stating that the offer will remain open thirty days, X can revoke it the very next day if he wishes. While this may seem unfair to Y, the reason for this view lies in the fact that Y has not given "consideration" (something of value) in return for X's promise to keep the offer open.

There are two notable exceptions to the above. The first is the use of an *option* (or *option contract,* as it is frequently called). In an option, the offeree—either at the request of the offeror or acting on his or her own initiative—does give the offeror some consideration, usually a sum of money, in return for offeror's promise to keep the offer open. Once the money is accepted by the offeror, the offer cannot be revoked during the specified period of time.

The second exception arises under the law of sales. Sec. 2-205 of the Uniform Commercial Code provides that if an offer to buy or sell goods contains a promise that it will be held open for a stated period of time, it cannot be revoked by the offeror during that time even if the offeree has not given consideration for the promise. Two conditions must be met, however: (1) the offeror must be a merchant in that kind of goods, and (2) the offer must be in writing and be signed by the offeror. Additionally, the stated period of time cannot exceed three months.[9]

Rejection: A rejection occurs when the offeree notifies the offeror that he or she does not intend to accept. Like the offer and the revocation, it takes effect only when it has been communicated (in this case, to the offeror). Thus, if an offeree mails a letter of rejection but changes his mind and telephones an acceptance before the letter arrives, there is a contract.

One form of rejection is the *counter-offer*—a proposal made by the offeree to

---

[8]However, one state—California—provides by statute that a revocation is effective when "dispatched" (i.e., *when mailed,* in this case.)

[9]Offers conforming to these conditions, called *firm offers,* are discussed in more detail in Chapter 18.

the offeror that differs in any material respect from the terms of the original offer. Thus, if the price stated in an offer is $500, and the offeree replies, "I'll pay $400," the original offer is ended forever. To illustrate further: A seller offered to sell "2,000 to 5,000 tons" of iron rails at a price of $54 per ton. The offeree replied, "Enter my order for 1,200 tons." The seller refused the order, whereupon the offeree replied that he would take 2,000 tons. The seller refused to deliver, and in ensuing litigation the court ruled that the offeree's order for 1,200 tons constituted a counter-offer, which terminated the original offer. The offeree's second order for 2,000 tons did not, therefore, result in the formation of a contract.[10]

Subject to exceptions noted later in this chapter, if the offeree changes—or adds to—the terms of the offer, he or she has made a counter-offer. This is true even if the response says that he or she is accepting the offer. In the preceding case, for example, if the offeree's initial reply had been, "Accept your offer; ship 2,000 tons to our California plant," this would still constitute a counter-offer if the original offer contemplated delivery at some other point.

Lapse of Time: If revocation and rejection were the only recognized means of terminating offers, many offers would remain open forever. To prevent such an unworkable result, a third method of termination is recognized—termination by the *passage of a reasonable length of time.*[11] What is "reasonable" depends on the circumstances of each case; thus it is virtually impossible to formulate general rules in this area of law.

What we will do instead is list the circumstances or factors that the courts consider in reaching an answer in a given case.

1. A circumstance of particular importance is the language used in the offer. Obviously, if an offeror states, "I must hear from you very soon," the time within which the offeree must accept is somewhat shorter than if such language were not used.

2. Another important circumstance is the means of communication used by the offeror. Sending the offer by telegram normally imports an urgency that the use of the mails does not.[12]

3. Yet another factor of special importance is prevailing market conditions. If the price of a commodity is fluctuating rapidly, for example, a reasonable time might elapse within hours from the time the offer is received.

4. A final factor to be taken into consideration is the method by which the parties have done business in the past.

An offer in some circumstances may thus lapse soon after it has been made,

---

[10]*Minneapolis & St. Louis Ry. v. Columbus Rolling Mill,* 119 U.S. 149 (1886).

[11]A different rule applies to offers in which the offeree is given a *specific* time, such as five days, in which to accept. In such offers, the lapse of the stated period terminates the offer.

[12]Some courts, for example, adopt the general rule that an offer made via telegram lapses at the close of business hours on the day it is received. (This rule is not applicable, obviously, to offers that by their language expressly or impliedly grant a longer period of time.)

while in other circumstances it may remain open weeks or even months. While there are surprisingly few cases in this area of law, *Ward v. Board of Education,* 173 N.E. 634 (1930) is one of them. In that case Ina Ward received an offer of employment for the following school year on June 18, and she mailed her acceptance on July 5. In subsequent litigation, the higher court stated the applicable rule as follows: "It is a primary rule that a party contracting by mail, as she did, when no time limit is made for the acceptance of the contract, shall have a reasonable time, acting with due diligence, within which to accept." Applying that rule, where Ms. Ward had no explanation for her delay other than the fact that she was hoping to hear from another school board, the court held that the offer had lapsed prior to July 5 and there was, therefore, no contract.

Termination by Operation of Law

The rule that a revocation must be communicated to the offeree in order for it to take effect is based on the grounds of both fairness and logic. In ordinary circumstances, it seems reasonable that the offeree ought to be legally able to accept any offer until he or she has been put on notice that the offer has been terminated.

Certain exceptional events, however, will terminate an offer automatically—without notice to the offeree. These events fall into three categories: (1) death or adjudication of insanity of either party, (2) destruction of the subject matter of the contract, and (3) intervening illegality. The termination of an offer by any of these events is said to occur *by operation of law.*

To illustrate: On September 10, B offers a specific TV set to W for $525. On September 13, B dies. If W mails a letter of acceptance on September 14, there is no contract even if W is unaware of B's death. In the preceding example the result would be the same if, instead of B's death on September 13, the TV set were destroyed that day through no fault of B. As another example, X offers to loan $1,000 to Y for one year with interest at the rate of 12 percent. Before the offer is accepted, a state statute takes effect which limits the rate of interest to 8 percent. The offer is terminated automatically.

The various events that automatically terminate unaccepted offers generally do not terminate existing contracts (except those calling for the rendering of personal services, which we will discuss in Chapter 16). Thus, in the first example, if B's offer of September 10 had been accepted by W *before* B's death on September 13, B's estate would remain bound by the obligation to deliver the TV set.[13]

By the same token, the various terminations by operation of law do not generally apply to options (or option contracts). Thus, if B had promised on September 10 to keep his offer open for ten days, and if W had given B a sum of money in return for this promise, B's death on September 13 would *not* terminate the offer.

---

[13]Whether the destruction of the TV on September 13 (instead of B's death) would free B's estate from the duty to deliver another set or would free W from the obligation to pay for the set is controlled by the law of sales, especially sections 2-509 and 2-613 of the Uniform Commercial Code. These sections are discussed in the sales chapters in Part III.

Preliminary Considerations of the Acceptance

An offer ripens into a contract if, and only if, it is accepted by the offeree. Remember that a bilateral offer is accepted by the offeree making the return *promise* that the offeror has requested, while a unilateral offer is accepted only by the actual performance of the requested *act*.[14]

In most situations the offeree's response to the offer is so clearly an acceptance or rejection of it that no misunderstanding between the parties arises. But in a few situations legal difficulties do crop up—as, for example, where the offeree "accepts" the offer but then adds new terms to it or where the offeree's response is vague or indecisive. Another difficulty is the determination of the precise moment at which the acceptance becomes effective—specifically, whether the acceptance has to be actually communicated to the offeror before it becomes legally effective.

In the following discussion, emphasis is given to the acceptance of bilateral offers—those in which the offeror merely wants a return promise on the part of the offeree. Special problems raised by the acceptance of unilateral offers will be considered later in the chapter.

Requirements of the Acceptance

An acceptance is an expression on the part of the offeree by which the person indicates a consent to be bound by the terms of the offer. While the offeree usually states expressly that he or she is "accepting" the offer, it is not necessary that this particular term be used. Any language showing that the offeree is assenting to the proposal is sufficient.

Regardless of the particular words used by the offeree in his or her response to the offer, the response must meet certain requirements in order to constitute an acceptance. Generally, an acceptance must be (1) unconditional, (2) unequivocal, and (3) legally communicated to the offeror or to the offeror's agent.

New Conditions

We have already seen that when an attempted acceptance changes the terms of the offer, it becomes a *counter-offer* and a rejection rather than an acceptance. The same is true when the attempted acceptance adds new terms or conditions to those of the offer.

Many times the changed or new terms are readily apparent—for example, where goods are offered at a price of $20 and the offeree replies that he will pay $15, or

---

[14]Most offers are of either the one type or the other. However, there is one common type of offer that, under the law of sales, can be treated by the offeree as either bilateral or unilateral, at his or her option. Sec. 2-206 of the Uniform Commercial Code provides in part: "(1) Unless otherwise unambiguously indicated by the language or circumstances, . . . an order or other offer to buy goods for prompt or current shipment shall be construed as inviting acceptance either by a *prompt promise to ship or by the prompt or current shipment*" of the ordered goods. (Emphasis added.) Further discussion of this and other aspects of Sec. 2-206 is found in the sales chapters of Part III.

where the offeree replies, "I accept—deliver to Cody, Wyoming," when the offeror did not contemplate delivering the goods at all.

At other times the offeree's reply has to be scrutinized more carefully in order to determine its precise effect. To illustrate: Seller wrote Buyer, "I have about 80,000 feet of oak left yet, for which I will take $16 per M delivered on cars at Bridgewater 'log run.' I will take $8 per M for the mill culls I have at Bridgewater, as that is what it cost me, cut and deliver the same."

Buyer replied, in part, ". . . We will take your 4/4 oak at $16, mill culls out, delivered on cars at Bridgewater. We will handle all your mill culls, but not at the price you are asking. . . . We should be glad to handle yours at $4.50. . . . We will take the 80,000 feet and will depend on this. . . ."

Seller later refused to deliver either the lumber or the culls, contending that Buyer's reply did not constitute an acceptance. In ensuing litigation, the Supreme Court of North Carolina agreed with this contention.[15] In regard to the offer of the oak, the court held that Buyer's "acceptance" failed because of his addition of the "4/4" dimension requirement— particularly where the evidence indicated that 4/4 oak was an entirely different article than that which Seller had on hand. (In regard to the mill culls, the court had no difficulty in holding that Buyer's response constituted a counter-offer because of the price discrepancy.)

The following case presents an intriguing situation in which both parties originally assumed, quite understandably, that an agreement had clearly been reached —until the sharp-eyed bus driver began to compare the language of the school board's "acceptance" with the language of his offer. At that point, the fun began.

Lucier v. Town of Norfolk

Supreme Court of Errors of Connecticut, 122 A. 711 (1923)

Lucier, plaintiff, operated a school bus for the defendant town for the school years of 1915, 1916, 1918, and 1919. In the summer of 1920 plaintiff and defendant began negotiating a contract for the coming year.

After several communications between the parties, plaintiff was asked by the Norfolk Town School Committee to submit a bid covering the transportation of students for the 1920–1921 school year. On August 12, plaintiff submitted his bid, offering to provide transportation at "$175 per week each school week" for that year.

On August 17 the board passed the following resolution: "Voted to award the contract for transporting children to and from Gilbert school and to and from various points in town to Mr. E. A. Lucier for the sum of $35 per day." The next day, a member of the committee, one Stevens, told plaintiff that the board "had voted to award him the contract" and requested plaintiff to have his buses ready.

On the first day of school, September 7, plaintiff transported the students as agreed. On the evening of September 7 the board presented plaintiff with a formal contract for him to sign, the contract embodying the wording of the August 17 resolution. Plaintiff refused to sign the contract, on the ground that it was not in

---

[15]*Morrison v. Parks,* 80 S.E. 85 (1913).

accordance with his bid for compensation at the rate of $175 per week, but at the rate of $35 per day instead. Thereupon defendant refused to employ plaintiff and awarded the transportation contract to a third party.

Plaintiff brought action to recover damages for breach of contract, alleging that a contract was formed on his terms and was breached by defendant. (Specifically, plaintiff's argument was that his bid was accepted on August 18 when Stevens told him that the board "had voted to award him the contract.") Defendant contended that a contract was formed on *its* terms and that plaintiff was guilty of the breach. The trial court ruled that *no contract was formed in this situation* (but did award plaintiff $35 dollars, the reasonable value of his services performed on September 7). Plaintiff appealed.

Keeler, Justice: . . . Summarily stated, the contentions of the plaintiff are: that the negotiations between him and the school board [resulted] in a contract express or implied, and the minds of the negotiating parties met; that Stevens, by reason of his position, had authority to make a contract binding the town; and that [plaintiff's bid, followed by Stevens's actions] resulted in a contract being formed. . . .

[Other] than as to the price to be fixed for the service, there is no dispute between the parties as to the terms submitted in the notice to bidders, and the plaintiff bid with reference to them, his offer conforming to these terms, the price for the service being the only open item in the transaction. The dispute turns upon the question of a rate per week as contrasted with a rate per day. The committee received from the plaintiff a bid of $175 per week; this undoubtedly meant to it the same as $35 per day, a result arrived at by a simple act of division of the larger number by five, the number of school days in the ordinary school week. It would seem that the committee were justified in reaching this conclusion, in that the plaintiff's pay in the contract for the year just past had been at a sum per day, and the notice for bids had called for a bid by the day. . . . When, therefore, the committee received a bid by the week they very naturally in their vote awarding the contract to the plaintiff substituted what they deemed an equivalent sum by the day, to accord with the requirement of the notice. This also was evidently the understanding of Stevens, when he afterward informed the plaintiff that the contract had been awarded to the latter. Subsequent events showed that this construction of his bid was not intended by the plaintiff, and that he intended to insist on the distinction between pay by the day and pay by the week, in that the latter afforded him compensation for work which would not in fact be required, when in any week a school day came upon a holiday.

In the pleadings, each side claimed the equivalence in fact and in effect of the expressions in the bid with those in the vote, each resolving the question of intent favorably to the contention by each, and each consequently claimed a contract which had been broken by the other party. *Both are wrong. It clearly appears from the facts found that the trial judge correctly found that there was no meeting of minds, and hence no contract. The plaintiff had the burden of establishing his construction of the claimed contract and has failed.* [Emphasis added.]

But the plaintiff further insists that he was in effect informed by Stevens that his bid had been accepted by the committee, that the latter was bound by Stevens' statement, and that he [the plaintiff] acted in accordance with the information conveyed to him. Further, that Stevens was the agent of the committee, and had authority to bind it, and that the committee was so bound when Stevens told him that the contract had been awarded to him, which information was in his mind equivalent to a statement that his bid had been accepted in the form tendered. . . . So he says that whatever the committee really intended in the matter, it was bound by Stevens' statement that the contract had been awarded to him on the terms of his bid, even though the vote stated the price of the service at a sum differing therefrom. [The court rejected this contention of plaintiff, ruling that Stevens was simply informing plaintiff of the board's action so that he could get his equipment in readiness, and that Stevens did not intend—nor did he have the authority—to bind the board to anything other than the specific resolution as passed.]

Judgment affirmed.

A Note of Caution: In some situations the offeree's response does constitute an acceptance even though it contains one or more terms that were not set forth in the offer itself. This is true where a reasonable person, standing in the place of the offeree, would justifiably believe that the "new" terms were within the contemplation of, and were agreeable to, the offeror despite the failure to include them in the offer. Following are two illustrations.

1. For several years, X has been buying goods from the Y Company, and it has always granted him ninety days credit. If the Y Company offers a certain item to X for a price of "$500," and he replies by mail, "I accept on condition that I will have ninety days in which to pay," X's response very likely constitutes an acceptance. Under the circumstances—the manner in which they had been doing business in the past—X could assume that it was *implied* that the Y Company was granting him the usual credit.[16]

2. F offers to sell certain land to D for $55,000 cash. D replies by telegram, "I accept, assuming you will convey good title." This is an acceptance, even though F did not mention the quality of his title, because it is *implied* (under existing law) that a seller of land guarantees good or marketable title unless he or she indicates a contrary intention.

The purpose of the foregoing is simply to warn the student that it is possible for a term or condition to be literally new without necessarily being new in the legal sense. Thus, while the responses of the offerees in the preceding examples appear at first glance to constitute counter-offers, in the eyes of the law they add nothing new and therefore allow the replies to be valid acceptances.

Furthermore, under *sales law* (rather than contract law) an acceptance may be effective even though its terms clearly change, or add to, the terms of the offer. One major reason for this is the manner in which some kinds of sales contracts are entered into. For example, commercial buyers often use their own printed forms in ordering goods from manufacturers or wholesalers, and the latter companies frequently use *their* forms in notifying buyers of their acceptance. As one would expect, the terms and conditions of the two forms are rarely identical, and quite often the parties do not even attempt to iron out specific differences.

While the great majority of such sales contracts are satisfactorily performed

---

[16]The same result might obtain, even if there had been no past dealings between the two parties, if X could establish that the granting of credit was a widely accepted custom in the particular industry.

despite these variations, experience prior to the adoption of the Uniform Commercial Code showed that in a number of cases where one of the parties to a sales "contract" refused to perform, that party was able to escape liability on the ground that no contract had been legally formed because of the variance between the terms of the offer and the acceptance.

To reduce the number of such cases, particularly where the variance involved only minor terms, the drafters of the UCC adopted Sec. 2-207, which reads in part:

> 1. A definite and seasonable expression of acceptance or a written confirmation which is sent within a reasonable time operates as an acceptance even though it states terms *additional to or different from* those offered or agreed upon, unless acceptance is expressly made conditional on assent to the additional or different terms.

> 2. The additional terms are to be construed as proposals for addition to the contract. *Between merchants* such terms become part of the contract unless:

> > (a) the offer expressly limits acceptance to the terms of the offer;
> > (b) they *materially alter* it; or
> > (c) notification of objection to them . . . is given within a reasonable time after notice of them is received. . . . [Emphasis added.]

The provisions of this section are by no means self-explanatory. In order to understand the various situations to which they apply and the results of their application, one must study the official text of the UCC, the "comments" of the drafters, and the cases that have been decided since the section's adoption. While these cases often present difficult fact-patterns and, unfortunately, considerable conflict among the courts' interpretations of Sec. 2-207, it may nevertheless be helpful to see how this section would apply to the situation presented here.

Buyer Company orders 1,000 widgets from Seller Company for $2,000. Seller Company replies, "Accept your order 1,000 widgets at $2,000"; but on the back of Seller Company's form is a provision stating, "Any complaint regarding quality of goods must be made by buyer within six months of discovering defect." Later, Buyer Company wishes to get out of the deal and brings action, asking the court to rule that Seller Company's response is a counter-offer rather than an acceptance. In this case, Buyer Company will lose. Under Subsection 1 of Sec. 2-207, Seller Company's reply to the offer is clearly an acceptance (rather than a counter-offer), which results in the formation of a contract on the Buyer Company's terms. And, in this particular case, Seller Company's additional term *also becomes a part of the contract.* This is so because both parties are merchants, in which case (under subsection 2) the additional term becomes a part of the agreement *unless* 2(a), (b), or (c) is applicable. In this instance (a) and (c) clearly do not apply since the offer did not limit the acceptance to its terms, nor did the Seller Company object to the new term when it was notified of it. Thus the only question is whether the additional term "materially altered" the offer. Because most courts, in cases presenting new terms of the type involved in this example, have taken the view that such a term does *not* materially alter the offer, the result—as indicated above—is that the new term also becomes a part of the contract.

Unequivocal Assent

An acceptance is an expression on the part of the offeree indicating consent to be bound by the terms of the offer. As a general rule, this expression must be reasonably definite and unequivocal and must be manifested by some overt word or act.

Between the extremes of outright acceptance and flat rejection, there are many responses where the intent of the offeree is not at all clear. At best, such replies cause initial delay and uncertainty between the parties; at worst, litigation may ensue, with interpretation left to the courts. To illustrate: T offers to buy certain goods from H, and the latter replies by wire, "Order received; will give it my prompt attention." Subsequently, T refuses to buy the goods, claiming that H's response was not an acceptance. Since H's reply did not manifest a clear-cut intention to contract, it is likely to be ruled too equivocal to constitute an acceptance.[17] On the other hand, each case has to be decided on its own merits, including the circumstances surrounding the communications. Thus a different result might obtain in the foregoing example if the evidence indicated that H and T had in the past considered such language to be binding.

Silence: As a general rule, there is no duty on the offeree to reply to an offer. Silence on the part of the offeree, therefore, *does not usually constitute an acceptance.* This is true even when the offer states, "If you do not reply within ten days, I shall conclude that you have accepted," or contains language of similar import. The reasons underlying this view are fairly obvious: (1) the view is consistent with the basic idea that any willingness to contract must be manifested in some fashion, and (2) it substantially prevents an offeree from being forced into a contract against his or her will.

In exceptional circumstances, however, the courts may find that the general rule is unfair to the offeror—that under the facts of the particular case, the offeree owed the offeror a *duty to reject* if he or she did not wish to be bound. In such cases, silence on the part of the offeree does constitute an acceptance.

While it is difficult to generalize about these exceptional situations, two types of cases present little controversy.

1. If an *offeree* initially indicates that silence on his or her part can be taken as acceptance, there is no reason why that person should not be bound by the

---

[17]In a case of a similar nature, a school board advertised for bids for the construction of a school building. After fourteen bids were received, the board wired one contractor: "You are low bidder. Come on morning train." The board and the contractor were subsequently unable to agree to a formal contract, and litigation ensued. The Iowa Supreme Court ruled that the board's telegram did not of itself constitute an acceptance of the contractor's bid, saying that it indicated no more than a willingness on the part of the board to enter into contractual negotiations. *Cedar Rapids Lumber Co. v. Fisher,* 105 N.W. 595 (1906).

statement. For example: "If you do not hear from me by March 1, you can conclude that we have a contract."

2. If a series of *past dealings* exists between the parties, it can be assumed by the offeror that a failure to reject is the equivalent of an acceptance. For example: A retail jewelry store has, over the years, received periodic shipments of both ordered and unordered jewelry from a large supplier; during this time, the retailer-buyer has always paid for any unordered goods not returned within two weeks. A failure by the retailer to reject a particular shipment, or to give notice of such rejection, within two weeks would very likely operate as an acceptance under the circumstances.

In both the preceding kinds of cases, the courts are likely to say that the offeror "had reason to understand" that silence on the part of the offeree was to be taken as a manifestation of assent, and that the offeree should have been well aware of this fact.

There is another, smaller group of cases in which it has been held that the offeror is justified in believing silence to be a manifestation of assent. These are situations in which a retail buyer gives a salesperson an order (offer) for certain goods, which the salesperson forwards to his or her company. If a reasonable period of time elapses without the company taking action, some courts hold that the buyer can justifiably view such silence as an acceptance of the offer and can hold the company liable for damages if it refuses to deliver the goods. Such courts reason that a company which sends salespeople out to solicit offers owes a duty to buyers to reject their offers within a reasonable time if it does not intend to accept them. (The same rule has sometimes been applied to mail order houses when they have failed to reject buyers' orders within a reasonable time.)

When Acceptance Takes Effect

As we have seen, most communications—offers, revocations, and rejections—are not effective until they actually reach the party to whom they are addressed. A somewhat different rule, however, is applicable to acceptances.

Generally, an acceptance is effective when it is communicated to the offeror or to the offeror's agent. The application of this rule causes little trouble where no "agent" is involved; thus, where X receives an offer by mail from Y and immediately accepts by telephone, an actual communication has occurred and a contract is formed at that moment. Similarly, there is little trouble in the rare case where the offeror *expressly* designates an agent—some third party to whom the acceptance is to be given—and the offeree transmits acceptance to the designated person. But some situations are more complex, particularly where the offer does not indicate how the offeree is to respond. Here the courts have had to fashion special rules.

The Reasonable Medium Approach: If the parties are negotiating a contract through the mail or by telegram, there is necessarily a lapse of time between the moment the offeree starts a message of acceptance on its way to the offeror and the moment when it actually reaches that person. While most acceptances reach the offeror promptly and no questions arise, sometimes it is necessary to determine the precise moment at which the acceptance becomes effective. This is particularly true (1) where the acceptance is delayed en route or never reaches the offeror at all, and (2) where the offeror attempts to revoke the offer before receiving the acceptance.

Where the offer does not indicate how the offeree is to reply, the early rule was that the acceptance took effect upon dispatch only if the offeree used the same means of communication as that used by the offeror in extending the offer. (E.g., the acceptance of a mailed offer took effect the moment the offeree deposited the acceptance in the mail.) But if the offeree used any other means of communication, there was no contract until the acceptance actually reached the offeror.

The modern rule is that acceptance takes effect upon dispatch as long as the medium chosen by the offeree is "reasonable, under the circumstances." Under this rule, then, it is possible for a contract to exist the moment the acceptance is dispatched even if the means used by the offeree is different from that used by the offeror.

How do the courts determine whether the medium chosen by the offeree was a reasonable one? In general, a medium is reasonable if (1) it was the same one used by the offeror; or (2) it was one that was customarily used in similar transactions; or (3) if it had been customarily used in prior dealings between the parties. To illustrate: Y receives an offer in the mail from X, and at 5 p.m. that same day Y mails her acceptance. Because Y used the same means of communication that X used, *there is a contract at 5 p.m.*, even if the acceptance is delayed in the mail or does not reach X at all. Along similar lines, suppose that C, a businessman in Cheyenne, makes an offer on a Monday morning by phone to D in Denver. D mails a letter of acceptance that afternoon. The next morning, while his letter of acceptance is still in the mail, D receives a telegram of revocation. If D could prove that in the past he had routinely accepted such offers from C by mail, a contract was formed when D's acceptance was deposited in the mail. The later revocation thus had no effect.

Two further cases, presenting additional facts:

Case 1.   June 1—Y receives mailed offer from X.
         June 2—X mails letter of revocation.
         June 3—Y mails acceptance at 5 p.m.
         June 4—Y receives the revocation.
         June 5—X receives Y's acceptance.

Result A contract was formed at 5 p.m. on June 3, since use of mail by Y was clearly reasonable. (Since a *revocation* is usually not effective until it is received, the letter that X mailed on June 2 had no effect until June 4, when Y received it. And by that time a contract had already been formed.)[18]

---

[18]As noted earlier, in California (and perhaps a few other states) a revocation is effective when mailed—here, on June 2. In such states there would be no contract.

Case 2.   June 1—Y receives mailed offer from X.

June 2—Y mails letter of rejection.

June 3—Y changes his mind and at 10 a.m. calls X on the telephone and accepts the offer, telling X to disregard his letter of rejection.

June 4—X receives letter of rejection.

Result A contract was formed at 10 a.m. on June 3, when Y gave X actual notice of acceptance. (Since a *rejection* is usually not effective until it is received, Y's letter of rejection had no effect on June 2. The offer was thus open on June 3, when Y accepted it.)

A necessary corollary of the reasonable medium rule is that an acceptance by means of an *unreasonable medium* does not take effect upon dispatch. Nonetheless, such an acceptance still becomes effective when it actually reaches the offeror (assuming the offer has not been terminated in the meantime).

Some Words of Caution: Several observations about the reasonable medium rule are necessary.

1. As has been indicated, the rule does not apply to offers requesting acceptance through a specified medium. In such a case, an acceptance through a medium other than the one requested is *not* effective upon dispatch. Such an acceptance would, however, again normally be effective when actually received.

2. An offeror can always make it a condition of the offer that the acceptance must be actually received by him or her in order for it to take effect. In such instances, of course, the reasonable medium rule is inapplicable.

Even if the offeree clearly uses a reasonable means of acceptance, he may still be faced with a problem in proving the actual time of dispatch. In the case below this problem was resolved in the offeree's favor—although the decision was based upon evidence that was incomplete, to say the least.

Cushing v. Thomson

Supreme Court of New Hampshire, 386 A.2d 805 (1978)

An antinuclear protest group, the Clamshell Alliance, sent an application in March of 1978 to the New Hampshire Adjutant General's office, seeking permission to rent the national guard armory in Portsmouth the night of April 29. The alliance hoped to use the armory facilities for a dance it had scheduled on that date.

On March 31 the adjutant general mailed a "contract offer" to the alliance, agreeing to rent the armory upon specified terms. The offer required that a signed acceptance be returned to the adjutant general's office.

Cushing, a member of the alliance, received the offer at the alliance's office on Monday, April 3. That same day he signed it on behalf of the organization, put the acceptance in an envelope, and placed the letter in the office's "outbox."

At 6:30 in the evening of the next day, Tuesday, April 4, Cushing received a phone call from the adjutant general stating that he was withdrawing the offer on orders of Governor Meldrim Thomson. Cushing replied that he had already accepted the offer, but the adjutant general repeated the statement that the offer had been withdrawn. (The alliance's acceptance, postmarked April 5, reached the adjutant general's office on April 6.)

When the adjutant general continued in his refusal to give the alliance permission to use the armory, Cushing and other members of the organization brought suit against Governor Thomson and the adjutant general, seeking specific performance of the contract that had allegedly been formed. Defendants contended that there was no contract, claiming that they had revoked the offer prior to plaintiffs' "acceptance." Although there was no direct evidence indicating the precise moment at which the outgoing mail was placed in the hands of the U.S. Postal Service, the trial court found that this had presumably occurred prior to the time of the attempted revocation on Tuesday evening. It thus ruled that a contract had been formed, and granted plaintiffs a decree of specific performance. Defendants appealed.

Per Curiam:[19] ... The [primary] issue presented is whether the trial court erred in determining that a binding contract existed. Neither party challenges the applicable law. [The court quoted the rule from a prior New Hampshire decision as follows:] "To establish a contract of this character, there must be an offer and an acceptance thereof in accordance with its terms. Where the parties to such a contract are at a distance from one another and the offer is sent by mail, the reply accepting the offer may be sent through the same medium, and the contract will be complete when the acceptance is mailed ... and beyond the acceptor's control." Withdrawal of the offer is ineffectual once the offer has been accepted by posting in the mail.

The defendants argue, however, that there is no evidence to sustain a finding that plaintiff Cushing had accepted the adjutant general's offer before it was withdrawn. Such a finding is necessarily implied in the court's ruling that there was a binding contract. The implied finding must stand if there is any evidence to support it.

Plaintiffs introduced the sworn affidavit of Mr. Cushing in which he stated that on April 3 he executed the contract and placed it in the outbox for mailing. Moreover, plaintiff's counsel represented to the court that it was customary office practice for outgoing letters to be picked up from the outbox daily and put in the U.S. mail. No [other evidence bearing on this point] was submitted in this informal hearing, and ... the court's order appears to be [based] in part ... [on representations made by attorneys for both sides,] a procedure which was not objected to by the parties.

Thus the representation that it was customary office procedure for the letters to be sent out the same day that they are placed in the office outbox, supported the implied finding *that the completed contract was mailed before the attempted revocation [occurred]*. (Emphasis added.) Because there is evidence to support it, ... the trial court's finding that there was a binding contract ... must stand.

Decree affirmed.

Unilateral offers pose two unique problems insofar as offer and acceptance principles are concerned: (1) whether it is necessary for the offeree, having performed the requested act, to notify the offeror of that fact, and (2) whether the offeror

Acceptance of Unilateral Offers

---

[19]"Per curiam" is a phrase used to refer to an opinion of the whole court, as distinguished from an opinion written by any one judge.

has the right to revoke the offer after the offeree has commenced to perform but before the performance is completed.

The general rule on the first problem is that a unilateral offer is accepted the moment the offeree performs the requested act; giving notice that the act has taken place is usually not required. This rule does not apply, obviously, to offers that expressly request notification. In such offers, a contract is not formed until the requisite notice is given.

Another type of case requiring notice involves those exceptional situations where the act is of such a nature that the offeror "has no adequate means of ascertaining with reasonable promptness and certainty" that the act has taken place.[20] The typical cases in this category are *contracts of guaranty*—those in which one person guarantees a loan made to another. For example: A, in Columbus, asks B, in Miami, to loan $1,000 to C, a Miami resident, A promising to pay the debt if C fails to do so. In this situation, most courts take the view that while a contract is formed between A and B the moment that B makes the loan, A's resulting obligation is discharged (terminated) if B fails to notify him within a reasonable time that the loan has been made.

The traditional view on the second question has been that the acceptance of a unilateral offer occurs only when the act has been completed. Thus, in situations where the requested act requires a substantial period of time for completion, the offeror can revoke the offer at any time before full performance has taken place, even if the offeree has started to do the job. In such a case a contract is never formed. (However, under the quasi-contract theory, the offeree is ordinarily entitled to recover the reasonable value of his or her performance prior to the revocation. In the event that this partial performance is of no value to the offeror, the offeree will, of course, recover nothing.)

In recent years a growing number of courts have felt that the traditional view is unfair to the offeree in many circumstances, and they have abandoned it in favor of several other approaches. The most widely accepted of the newer views is that where the act is one that of necessity will take a period of time to complete, the *right of revocation is suspended* once the offeree starts to perform and remains suspended until the offeree has had a reasonable time to complete the act. This view is consistent with the traditional view to the extent that no contract is formed until the act has been completed, but it affords an interim protection to the offeree that the traditional view does not. Thus we have yet another illustration of the courts' freedom, within the framework of the common law, to modify those earlier principles whose application has brought about results of questionable merit.

Questions and Problems

1. A construction company wished to submit a bid on the construction of a school. It showed a subcontractor the masonry requirements for the job, and asked the subcontractor

---

[20]*Restatement, Contracts 2d,* § 56. Copyright 1973. Reprinted with permission of The American Law Institute.

to determine the lowest cost that it would do the work for. The subcontractor quoted a price, and the construction company replied, "Your bid is accepted. Come pick up the plans." Later, when the two companies tried to work out a written contract involving such matters as the manner of payment by the construction company, time for completion of the work, and bonding requirements, the construction company found that such an agreement could not be worked out, and it hired a different company to the masonry work. The subcontractor then sued the construction company for damages, claiming that its quotation of a price for the job, followed by the construction company's statement that "your bid is accepted," constituted an offer and an acceptance even though no written agreement was ever entered into. Do you agree? Why or why not? (*Savoca Masonry Co. v. Homes & Son Construction Co., Inc.,* 542 P.2d 817, 1975.)

2. The board of directors of the American Bank Stationery Co. passed a resolution authorizing the sale of its stock "to such persons as may be selected by the President" at $50 a share. Later the president told all of the salesmen at a meeting that the stock was available to them. One of the salesmen, McGinn, told the president he would like to buy 100 shares at $50 each. Shortly thereafter, the president told him that this was too large a number, but he could have a smaller amount if he wished. (McGinn never asked for a smaller amount.) When the president ultimately refused to sell McGinn any stock at all, he sued the company for damages for breach of contract, contending that the company's resolution was an offer, and that his request for 100 shares was an acceptance. Is McGinn correct? Explain. (*McGinn v. American Bank Stationery Co.,* 195 A.2d 615, 1963.)

3. Blakeslee, who wished to buy some land owned by the Nelsons, wrote a letter to them asking if they would accept "$49,000 net" for the property. The Nelsons replied that they would "not sell for less than $56,000," whereupon Blakeslee wired back, "Accept your offer of $56,000 net." *Blakeslee v. Nelson,* 207 N.Y.S. 676 (1925). Does a contract now exist between the parties? Explain.

4. Petersen was employed as building construction manager for the Pilgrim Village Company under a contract which provided that he was to be paid a stated salary per year, and, in addition, was to receive "a share of the profits" of the corporation while he remained in its employment. After several years on the job, during which time he received the stated salary, he asked for 10 percent of the profits made during that time, which he estimated to be $200,000. When the company refused that request, Petersen brought an action against it to recover "some share of the profits." At the trial, the company asked the court to rule that its promise as to the payment of profits was so vague and indefinite as to be unenforceable. *Petersen v. Pilgrim Village,* 42 N.W.2d 273 (1950). How should the court rule? Explain.

5. In the *Green* case, why, specifically, did the higher court rule that Mrs. Green was not bound by the note contained in the folder, even though she continued to permit the garage to store her car after she received the folder?

6. On June 1 X wrote a letter to Y offering to sell him a designated parcel of land in Salt Lake City for $75,000. The letter gave Y 10 days in which to accept, and was received by Y on June 2. On June 9 Y heard over radio station KSL in Salt Lake that the city had reportedly purchased the land, but that two councilmen would neither confirm nor deny the report. Y, feeling he had no time to investigate this information, mailed a letter of acceptance that same day. Is there a contract between X and Y? What is the specific issue in this case?

7. The Gator Company, a Florida firm, offered to buy 100 tons of scrap metal from the

Sooner Company, located in Norman, Oklahoma, at a specified price. The Sooner Company accepted this offer using one of its own forms, which contained this new term: "It is agreed that any disputes arising out of the performance of this contract will be governed by Oklahoma law." Later the Gator Company wanted to get out of the deal, and contended that the Sooner Company's "acceptance" was legally a counter-offer, and that thus a contract was never formed. Under sales law, Sec. 2-207 of the UCC, is the Gator Company correct? Why or why not?

8. Tayloe applied to an insurance company for a fire insurance policy on his home. The company forwarded Tayloe's application to Minor, its agent in Tayloe's area, with a letter telling Minor that he could go ahead and negotiate a policy with Tayloe. Minor then wrote Tayloe, saying that if he desired to effect the insurance coverage for which he had applied, "send me your check for $57 and the business is concluded." Tayloe received this offer on December 20 and deposited his check in the mail on December 21. On December 22, while Tayloe's check was in the mail, his residence burned down. *Tayloe v. The Merchants Fire Insurance Company,* U.S.S.Ct., 9 Howard 390 (1850). Was an insurance contract between Tayloe and the company in effect at the time of the fire? Explain.

Consideration   10

An elusive thing called *consideration* is the second element ordinarily required in a contract. Generally, if an agreement lacks consideration, neither party can enforce it, even if it is in writing.[1] As a practical matter, consideration is present in most agreements; but since this is not always the case, we need a basic understanding of the *doctrine of consideration* in order to determine when an agreement is legally binding.

We have dealt with this doctrine briefly in the preceding chapter. There we saw that an offeror who promises to keep an offer open a given number of days normally is allowed to revoke it before the specified time has elapsed. The promise is not binding because the offeror has received no consideration—something of value—

Introduction to the Doctrine

---

[1]From a technical standpoint, such agreements are not contracts. Nevertheless, courts and lawyers often refer to them as *unenforceable contracts*—indicating simply that neither party is bound by such agreements. (This use of the term should not be confused with our earlier, stricter definition—a contract that was valid when made but that subsequently was rendered unenforceable by a change of law.)

from the offeree.[2] A similar situation is presented when one person promises a gift to another. Suppose, for example, that on December 1 an employer promises an employee that he will pay him a Christmas bonus of $100 on December 20, and the employee replies, "I accept." Assuming that the employment contract does not mention bonus payments, the employer in this situation ordinarily cannot be held liable on his promise, because the employee's acceptance did not obligate him or her to do anything in return for the bonus.

These examples illustrate one of the basic ideas underlying the present-day requirement of consideration—that one party to an agreement should not be bound by it if the other party is not similarly bound. In neither of the preceding examples did the promisor receive anything of value from the promisee; as a result, neither promise was enforceable.[3]

Stating it positively, the concept of consideration requires that both parties to a contract shall have given and have received something as the "price" of their respective promises. For example: X promises to install a home air-conditioning unit for Y, and Y promises to pay X $1,100 for the job. Here the price X has received (in return for his obligation to install the unit) is the right to a payment of $1,100 from Y when the job is done; similarly, the price Y has received (for her promise to pay the $1,100) is her right to have the unit installed.

Present-day concepts of consideration have resulted from a mixture of logic and historical accident. Thus we will first look briefly at the historical developments in this area of the law. Following this, the rest of the chapter will be divided into two parts—the first presenting the basic concepts and the second exploring some of the exceptional situations in which the courts have either modified these concepts or abandoned them altogether.

A Historical Note

Ever since the forerunners of our modern courts began to take shape centuries ago, they had to wrestle with the question of what agreements ought to be enforced. The problem existed in the countries that operated under the civil system of law (the system of jurisprudence administered in the Roman empire and based strictly on codified law) as well as in the English-speaking nations that employed the common-law system.

Three basic periods stand out in the development of English and American law. The earliest English view, several centuries ago, was that contracts had to be "sealed" in order to be enforced. A *sealed contract* had to have a bit of wax affixed to it, on which the initials or other distinctive mark of each of the parties was

---

[2] This should be distinguished, of course, from the situation where an *option contract* has been formed—that is, where the offeree has given the offeror something of value, usually a sum of money, in return for the promise to keep the offer open.

[3] This creates one of the relatively few areas in which established legal views part company with moral views. On moral grounds, most people believe (laudably) that they are obligated to live up to their promises regardless of whether they receive something in return, and most people act accordingly.

imprinted. Contracts that lacked this formality were not legally recognized no matter how valid they were otherwise.

As trade and commerce began to grow in seventeenth century England, it became increasingly apparent that the strict requirement of a seal often led to undesirable results. Thus a second era emerged; the courts began to enforce unsealed promises (as well as sealed ones) as long as they were supported by what came to be called consideration.

This was the state of the English law at the time it was adopted by the United States. A third stage of development has now been reached in this country. Approximately forty states today take the view that virtually all promises must be supported by consideration in order to be enforceable, even if they are made under seal.[4]

The Basic Concept of Consideration

The courts agree substantially about the kinds of promises or acts constituting consideration in most situations. This is true because they have formulated, over the years, a number of definitions that have met with general approval. While these definitions (or tests) vary somewhat in detail, they ordinarily lead to the same conclusions when applied to agreements where the question of consideration has been raised. To determine the technical and usual meaning of the term, we will examine these tests and see how they are applied to specific situations.

The Detriment Test

Whenever a promisee seeks to hold a promisor liable on his or her promise, and the latter claims nonliability on the ground that the promise was not supported by consideration, the courts usually inquire whether the promisee incurred a *detriment* under the contract. If so, they decide that consideration is present and the promise is enforceable.

People incur legal detriments when they do (or promise to do) something that they are not otherwise legally obligated to do, or when they refrain from doing (or promise to refrain from doing) something that they have a legal right to do. A few illustrations will simplify this idea.

Example 1 (unilateral contract). X, a publisher, promises Y: "If you will loan $5,000 to my nephew for one year, I will run all your advertisements during that time at half the regular rate." Y makes the loan, but X refuses to provide advertising space at the reduced rate. If Y sues X to recover damages for breach of contract— that is, Y seeks to enforce X's promise—X is liable. Y's act of making the loan to the nephew constituted not only an acceptance of X's offer but a detriment to Y—the parting with something of value where he was not otherwise legally obligat-

---

[4]Of these states, about half have reached this result by enacting statutes that expressly abolish the private seal. The other half have reached a similar result through judicial decisions. The eight or ten states that have not adopted the general rule continue to enforce all sealed promises, even when consideration is lacking.

ed to do so. Thus X's promise, supported by consideration, is enforceable against him.

Example 2 (unilateral contract). A promises to pay C, his law partner, $750 if C will give up his part-time job in a dance band for the next nine months. C lives up to the terms of the offer, but A refuses to pay. If C brings suit to recover the $750, A is liable. Here again we have a unilateral contract, a promise in exchange for a negative act (or a forebearance)—the act of not playing in the band. C's refraining constituted both an acceptance of the offer and a legal detriment to him; thus, as in the prior case, we can see that A's promise was supported by consideration.

Example 3 (bilateral contract). M and B enter into a contract in April under the terms of which M agrees to build a swimming pool for B in June, B promising to pay $2,500 in return. M later refuses to perform, and B sues him to recover damages for breach of contract. M is liable; that is, his promise is enforceable. The return promise made by B (to pay M $2,500) was a detriment to B; thus M's promise was supported by consideration.

The detriment concept does not provide an answer to every question in which the enforceability of a promise is raised. Conditions sometimes exist, for example, where the courts feel justified in enforcing a promise on the grounds of *promissory estoppel* when consideration is clearly lacking, and there are even rarer situations in which a promise may be enforced where consideration is lacking and the doctrine of promissory estoppel is inapplicable.[5] The detriment concept also has received criticism from several authorities; and even the many courts that embrace it occasionally disagree on matters of interpretation and application. Nevertheless, the concept presents as simple a test as any yet devised, and the basic theory underlying it is generally accepted by courts and lawyers.

Identification of the Parties: The detriment test requires identification of the promisor and the promisee. In a unilateral contract this is easy to do, because there is only one promisor. In a bilateral contract, however, there are two promisors and two promisees (that is, each party is both promisor and promisee). In such a case, identification of the promisee—for the purposes of applying the test—must await the initiation of a lawsuit (or at least an examination of the two parties' situations in the event that a consideration question will be raised).

This can be illustrated by Example 3 above. Because of the manner in which that case arose, the question presented was whether M's promise was enforceable. Thus, for the purpose of applying the test, B was the promisee. Suppose, however, that B (rather than M) had reneged on the contract, by informing M in May that he did not want the work done. If litigation then ensued, M would bring the action, attempting to enforce B's promise. B would thus be the promisor and M the promisee. In such a suit, B would be liable, because his promise to pay was supported by M's promise to build. By his promise, M had incurred a legally

---

[5]The idea of promissory estoppel, and some of the other situations referred to here, will be examined in the second part of this chapter (special situations).

recognized detriment. (This manner of identifying the promisor and promisee should also make it clear that those terms are by no means synonymous with *offeror* and *offeree*. For example, when an offeree accepts an offer, he or she may make a return promise to the offeror. In regard to that promise, the offeree is the promisor.)

The Bargained-for Requirement: In order for a promisee's act (or promise) to constitute legal consideration, it must be the one asked for (expressly or impliedly) by the promisor. Consideration thus is "bargained for"—agreed to by both parties. Stating it another way, a promisee cannot unilaterally determine what promise or act constitutes consideration. Thus, if X promises to make a gift of $10 to Y on the following day, whereupon Y immediately purchases a shirt on the strength of the promise, Y's act of purchasing the shirt does not constitute the giving of consideration or the incurring of a detriment, and X's promise remains unenforceable. In such a case, the purchase constitutes nothing but mere reliance on the part of the promisee.

Detriment-Benefit Test

As we turn to specific cases, we will see that many authorities use the *detriment-benefit test* to determine the presence or absence of consideration. This test closely parallels the detriment test (though at first glance it seems substantially different) in that consideration is said to exist if either *the promisee has incurred a detriment* or *the promisor has received a benefit*. The parallel exists because in virtually every instance where the courts have found that the promisor received a benefit, they also have found that the promisee incurred a detriment. Thus the same results are usually reached under both tests.

The following cases present typical situations in which the basic concepts are applied.

Hamer v. Sidway
Court of Appeals of
New York, 27 N.E. 256
(1891)

William E. Story, Sr., promised to pay his nephew, William E. Story, II, $5,000 if he would refrain from drinking, using tobacco, swearing, and playing cards or billiards for money until he became twenty-one years of age. The nephew refrained from all the specified activities as he was requested to do, and on his twenty-first birthday he wrote his uncle a letter asking him for the money.

The uncle, in reply, assured the nephew, "You shall have the $5,000 as I promised you." The uncle went on, however, to explain that he had worked very hard to accumulate that sum of money and would pay it "when you are capable of taking care of it, and the sooner that time comes the better it will suit me."

Two years later the uncle died, without having made payment. The administrator of the uncle's estate, Sidway, refused to pay the $5,000, and suit was brought to recover that sum. (The plaintiff is Hamer, rather than the nephew, for the reason that at some time before litigation was begun the nephew had assigned—that is, sold—his rights against the estate to Hamer. Thus Hamer's right to recover is entirely dependent upon whether the nephew had a valid contractual claim against his uncle.)

The trial court ruled that the uncle's promise to pay the $5,000 was not supported by consideration on the part of the nephew (the promisee) and entered judgment for the defendant. The plaintiff appealed.

Parker, Justice: ... The defendant contends that the contract was without consideration to support it, and therefore invalid. He asserts that the promisee, by refraining from the use of liquor and tobacco, was not harmed, but benefited; that that which he did was best for him to do, ... and insists that it follows that, *unless the promisor was benefited,* the contract was without consideration—a contention which, if well founded, would [inject into the law, in many cases, an element so difficult to measure that needless uncertainty would result]. [Emphasis added.] Such a rule could not be tolerated, and is without foundation in the law. ...

Pollock, in his work on *Contracts*, page 166, says: " 'Consideration' means not so much that one party is profiting as that the other abandons some legal right ... as an inducement for the promise of the first." Now, applying this rule to the facts before us, the promisee used tobacco, occasionally drank liquor, and he had a legal right to do so. That right he abandoned for a period of years upon the strength of the promise of the [uncle] that for such forbearance he would give him $5,000. We need not speculate on the effort which may have been required to give up the use of those stimulants. *It is sufficient that he restricted his lawful freedom of action within certain prescribed limits upon the faith of his uncle's agreement,* and now, having fully performed the conditions imposed, *it is of no moment whether such performance actually proved a benefit to the promisor, and the court will not inquire into it;* ... [Emphasis added.] Few cases have been found which may be said to be precisely in point, but such as have been, support the position we have taken. ...

Judgment reversed.

Lampley v. Celebrity Homes, Inc.

Colorado Court of Appeals, Division II
594 P.2d 605 (1979)

Linda Lampley, plaintiff, began work at Celebrity Homes in Denver in May of 1975. On July 29 of that year Celebrity announced the initiation of a profit-sharing plan. Under that plan all employees were to receive bonuses if a certain "profit goal" were reached for the 1975 fiscal year—i.e., April 1, 1975 to March 31, 1976.

Plaintiff's employment was terminated in January of 1976. At the end of March, 1976, the company announced that the profit goal had been reached, and it made its first distribution of profits in May, 1976. When plaintiff was excluded from this distribution, she brought this suit for the share allegedly due her.

In the trial court Celebrity argued that its promise to pay the bonus was a mere "gratuity" on its part, on the ground that there was no consideration on the employee's part to support its promise. The trial court rejected this contention and entered judgment for plaintiff. Celebrity appealed.

Kelly, Judge: ... In further support of its claim that the plan is not a binding contract, Celebrity contends that there was no consideration [given by plaintiff.] Benefit to the promisor or detriment to the promisee, however slight, can constitute consideration. The plan states as its objective:

> "Our goal is . . . to produce added employee benefits gained through a higher quality of operation. Through teamwork in our day to day operation, we can achieve not only higher levels of profits, but also better performance for our customers, a better quality in design of products, fair treatment of customers, subcontractors, and suppliers."

This language indicates that the plan was established as an inducement to Celebrity's employees to remain in its employ and to perform more efficient and faithful service. Such result would be of obvious benefit to Celebrity, and thus consideration was present. . . . [The court also impliedly found a detriment, as follows]:

Lampley, who was employed for an indefinite term, was not obligated to remain until 1976, and it can be inferred from the evidence in the record that she was induced to do so, in part at least, by the profit sharing offer made to her by Celebrity. Thus, this case can be distinguished from [those] which hold that there can be no recovery where the company gets no more service as a result of such a promise than it would if no such promise had been made. The memorandum of the profit sharing plan was an offer to add additional terms to the original employment contract, and Lampley's continued employment with Celebrity [until January 1976] was an acceptance of the offer and the consideration for the contract.

Judgment affirmed.

Performance of Preexisting Obligations

A promisee has not incurred a detriment if that person merely performs, or promises to perform, an act that he or she was under a preexisting legal obligation to perform. One can be under a *preexisting obligation* through a general law of the state or federal government or because a prior contract has not yet been carried out.

Obligations Imposed by Law: Following is a simple illustration of an obligation imposed by law. X's store has been burglarized, and X promises a local policeman $75 if he uncovers, and turns over to the authorities, evidence establishing the identity of the culprit. If the policeman furnishes the requested information, he is not entitled to the reward. Under city ordinances and department regulations he already has a duty to do this; therefore it does not constitute a detriment to him.

Contractual Obligations: Greater difficulty is presented in situations where the preexisting obligation exists (or may exist) as the result of a prior contract between the parties. While such situations involve varying fact-patterns, the starting point can be illustrated as follows. D contracts to drill a seventy-foot well for G for $200. After he commences work, D complains that he is going to lose money on the job and may not finish it unless he gets more money. G then says, "All right. Finish up and I'll pay you $100 extra," and D completes the job. G now refuses to pay the additional $100, and D brings suit to hold G to his promise. In this situation most courts would rule that D's act of completing the well was simply the performance of his original obligation—that he incurred no detriment thereby, and cannot enforce G's promise to pay the additional money. Thus, as a general rule, modification of an existing contract requires consideration in order to be enforceable.[6] (Consideration would clearly have been present, of course, had the modification agreement required something extra of D—such as drilling the well to a depth of eighty feet.)

An entirely different situation is presented if the parties expressly or impliedly rescind (cancel) their prior contract. This will occur in the previous situation if, after D has aired his complaints, G says, "Let's cancel our contract right now and make a new one for $300." D agrees, and finishes the job. Here virtually all courts will permit D to recover the full $300, since an express cancellation has occurred. Because of such cancellation, D was entirely freed of his duty to complete a well. When, moments later, he assumed the same obligation by accepting G's promise to pay him $300, he incurred a detriment sufficient to support G's promise to pay the higher sum. The cancellation of the first contract *removed* D's preexisting obligation.

The following case is typical of those involving modification agreements. It shows how the courts inquire into the promisee's obligations under the original contract and determine whether these were enlarged by the second contract. (It also shows that even attorneys can get trapped by the principles of consideration.)

Quarture v. Allegheny County et al.

Superior Court of Pennsylvania, 14 A.2d 575 (1940)

Quarture, plaintiff, owned land in Pennsylvania. A portion of it was taken when the defendant county relocated and widened a state highway. Plaintiff needed legal help to recover damages from the county, and he employed a lawyer, Sniderman, to represent him in this effort.

A written contract was entered into, under the terms of which Sniderman was to "institute, conduct, superintend or prosecute to final determination, if necessary, a suit or suits, action or claim against the County of Allegheny on account of taking, injuring, and affecting (my, our) property in the relocation, widening, and opening of the State Highway known as Route No. 545." The contract further provided that Sniderman was to receive, as a fee for his services, "10 percent of all that might be recovered."

Sniderman represented plaintiff before the Board of Viewers of Allegheny County,

---

[6]Not all courts would reach the same result. A few would permit recovery by D on the ground that G's mere promise to pay more money constituted an *implied cancellation* of the first contract. (Most courts, however, require some additional evidence before ruling that an intent to cancel the first contract was present.) And a few states have adopted statutes providing that any *written* modification contract is enforceable, even if consideration is lacking. Had G's promise to pay the additional $100 been made in writing, courts in such states would have held him liable on it. Finally, while the *law of sales* is not applicable to this particular case, we should note that Section 2-209 of the UCC provides in part: "An agreement modifying a contract [calling for a sale of goods] needs no consideration to be binding." For example: S contracts to sell a hundred widgets to B for $400. If B later voluntarily agrees to pay $425 for them, B is bound by the higher figure, even though S's obligations under the contract are not changed. Thus the law of sales rejects the contractual principle stated above.

and the board awarded plaintiff $1,650 damages. Plaintiff was dissatisfied with this amount and wished to appeal that award.

Subsequently, a new agreement was entered into between plaintiff and Sniderman. This agreement provided that Sniderman would appeal the case to the court of common pleas and that Quarture would pay him a fee of 33 percent of whatever recovery might be obtained on appeal.

Plaintiff, represented by Sniderman, then brought this action in the court of common pleas, appealing the award of the Board of Viewers, and the court awarded him a judgment of $2,961. At this point Sniderman filed a petition with the court, asking it to distribute to him 33 percent of the judgment—$987.

Quarture objected, contending that his promise to pay the larger percentage was not supported by consideration and that Sniderman was thus bound by his original contract (a fee of 10 percent). The court rejected this contention and awarded Sniderman $987. Plaintiff appealed.

Stadtfeld, Justice: . . . Our first duty is to construe the original [contract]. What is meant by the terms "final determination?" . . . In the case of *Ex parte Russell,* 20 L.Ed. 632, it was said: "The final determination of a suit is the end of litigation therein. This cannot be said to have arrived as long as an appeal is pending."

The proceedings before the Board of Viewers cannot be considered as a "final determination," as their award is subject to appeal by either the owner of the property or by the municipality. If it were intended to provide for additional compensation in case of appeal from the award of viewers, it would have been a simple matter to have so provided in the contract. We cannot rewrite the contract; we must construe it as the parties have written it. . . .

The general principal is stated in *13 C.J. 351,* as follows: "A promise to do what the promisor is already bound to do cannot be a consideration, for if a person gets nothing in return for his promise but that to which he is already legally entitled, the consideration is unreal." Likewise, at p.353: "The promise of a person to carry out a subsisting contract with the promisee or the performance of such contractual duty is clearly no consideration, as he is doing no more than he was already obliged to do, and hence has sustained no detriment, nor has the other party to the contract obtained any benefit. Thus a promise to pay additional compensation for the performance by the promisee of a contract which the promisee is already under obligation to the promisor to perform is without consideration."

There are many cases in which this rule of law is laid down or adhered to, but one that clearly sets out the reason for the rule is *Lingenfelder v. Wainwright Brewing Co.,* 15 S.W. 844. In that case, plaintiff, an architect engaged in erecting a brewery for defendant, refused to proceed with his contract upon discovering that a business rival had secured one of the sub-contracts. The company, being in great haste for the building, agreed to pay plaintiff additional compensation as an inducement to resume work. It was held that the new promise was void for want of consideration, the court saying:

It is urged upon us by plaintiff that this was a new contract. New in what? Plaintiff was bound by his contract to design and supervise this building. Under the new promise he was not to do any more or anything different. What benefit was to accrue to defendant? He was to receive the same service from plaintiff under the new [contract] that plaintiff was bound to render under the original contract. What loss, trouble, or inconvenience could result to plaintiff that he had not already assumed?

No amount of metaphysical reasoning can change the plain fact that plaintiff took advantage of defendant's necessities, and extorted the promise of 5 percent on the refrigerator plant as the condition of his complying with his contract already entered into. . . . What we hold is that, when a party merely does what he has already obligated himself to do, he cannot demand an additional compensation therefor, and although by taking advantage of the necessities of his adversary he obtains a promise for more, the law will regard it as nudum pactum, and will not lend its process to aid in the wrong. . . .

While we do not question the value of the services rendered by Mr. Sniderman, we are nevertheless constrained by reason of our interpretation of the [first] agreement, to limit the right of recovery to the amount stipulated therein [in view of the fact that the carrying on of the appeal was nothing more than what the first agreement required of him]. It is unfortunate that [that] agreement did not stipulate additional compensation in case of an appeal.

Judgment reversed.

Unforeseen Difficulties: Before leaving the basic preexisting obligation principle, mention of the *unforeseen difficulties rule* is in order. This rule is illustrated most easily by reference to a leading case in which a builder, Schuck, contracted to dig a cellar under a portion of an existing house, to a depth of seven feet, for $1,500. (The contract was made after the parties examined an excavation across the street, where the soil appeared to be normal.) After commencing work, Schuck discovered that the ground below the three-foot level was "swamp-like, black muddy stuff," and that this condition would require the use of piling, which the parties did not contemplate under the contract. Thereupon the home owner, Linz, told Schuck to do whatever was necessary to dig a seven-foot cellar, adding that he would "pay him whatever additional cost" was involved. Schuck completed the job. In ensuing litigation, Linz denied that there was consideration on Schuck's part to support his promise to pay more than the $1,500. The court rejected this contention and permitted Schuck to recover his additional costs.[7]

In reaching this conclusion, the court stated that, in its opinion, the preexisting obligation rule should not be applied to a situation of this sort. To support its reasoning the court relied upon these statements from a prior decision:

It is entirely competent [legally possible] for the parties to a contract to modify or waive their rights under it and ingraft new terms upon it, and in such a case the promise of one party is the consideration for that of the other; but, where the promise to the one is simply a repetition of a subsisting legal promise, there can be no consideration for the promise of the other party, and there is no warrant for inferring that the parties have

---

[7]*Linz v. Schuck,* 67 Atl. 286 (1907). The facts of this case must be distinguished from those presented by the earlier well-drilling example. In that example, the well driller threatened to quit simply because he was losing money, not because of some unknown condition of the soil that required unanticipated efforts.

voluntarily rescinded or modified their contract. But where the party refusing to complete his contract does so by reason of some *unforeseen and substantial difficulties in the performance of the contract, which were not known or anticipated by the parties when the contract was entered into, and which cast upon him an additional burden not contemplated by the parties, and the opposite party promises him extra pay or benefits if he will complete his contract, and he so promises, the promise to pay is supported by a valid consideration.* [Emphasis added.] (*Bryant v. Lord,* 19 Minn. 396).

Situations where the rule is applied are admittedly exceptional. Courts of some jurisdictions do not recognize it at all. And among courts that do, its application is usually limited to construction contracts where the facts *closely parallel* those of the *Linz* case. These courts generally agree that such factors as increased costs, unexpected labor difficulties, or loss of expected sources of materials *do not fall within the rule;* thus promises to pay additional sums in recognition of these matters are usually unenforceable.[8]

Adequacy of Consideration

Whenever the enforceability of a promise is at issue, a finding that the promisee incurred a legally recognized detriment results in the promisor being bound by the contract. This is usually true even if the actual values of the promise and the detriment are unequal—as is reflected in the oft-repeated statement that "the law is not concerned with the *adequacy* of consideration." To illustrate: X contracts to sell an acreage in Montana to Y for $6,000. Y later discovers that the actual value of the land is under $3,000. Y is liable on his promise to pay $6,000, even though what he received was worth much less. Under the usual test, X incurred a detriment when he promised to convey the land—the surrender of his right to retain the property. The presence of this detriment constituted a consideration sufficient to support Y's promise to pay; and Y's claim of inadequacy is therefore of no relevance. The legal sufficiency of an act or promise, rather than its adequacy, is controlling.[9]

Mutuality of Obligation

In a *bilateral contract,* each party's promise is supported by the promise of the other. If, in a particular agreement, consideration is lacking on the part of one of

---

[8]However, modification of *sales contracts,* with both parties consenting, are enforceable even if they are not supported by consideration. This results from Sec. 2-209 of the UCC.

[9]Adequacy of consideration is, however, inquired into by the courts in exceptional circumstances. They will, for example, refuse to issue a decree of specific performance against a promisor in a contract felt to be "unconscionable"—that is, where the value of the consideration given by the plaintiff-promisee is so grossly inadequate that enforcement of the contract would "shock the conscience and common sense of reasonable people." Additionally, the courts will refuse to enforce promises where the inadequacy of consideration suggests that the promisor has been the victim of fraud (a subject covered in some detail in Chapter 13).

the parties, neither party is bound by it. For example: A and B enter into a written agreement under the terms of which A promises to employ B as his foreman for one year at a salary of $12,000 and B promises to work in that capacity for the specified time. The last paragraph of the agreement provides that "A reserves the right to cancel this contract at any time." Because A has thus not absolutely bound himself to employ B for the year, A has incurred no detriment (no unconditional obligation) by such a promise, with the result that B's promise to work for the year is not binding upon him. He can quit work at any time without liability to A. In such a case the requirement of *mutuality of obligation* has not been met, since A is said to have a "free way out" of the contract.

In the next case the right of cancellation was a restricted one. See if you agree with the distinction which the higher court makes between this kind of a clause, on the one hand, and one where the right to cancel is absolute, on the other.

Laclede Gas Company v. Amoco Oil Company
U.S. Court of Appeals, Eighth Circuit, 522 F.2d 33 (1975)

In 1970 a number of mobile home parks were being built by developers in Jefferson County, Missouri. At this time there were no natural gas mains serving these areas, so that persons living in them needed propane gas until the mains would be built.

In order to meet this demand, the Laclede Gas Company (Laclede) entered into a written contract with the American Oil Company (Amoco), under the terms of which Amoco would supply Laclede with propane for its customers living in the parks for a minimum period of one year. The contract contained a clause giving Laclede the right to cancel the agreement after one year upon 30 days written notice to Amoco, but it did not give Amoco any corresponding right to cancel the contract.

For several months Amoco made the required deliveries of propane to Laclede, but thereafter Amoco sent a letter to Laclede saying that it was "terminating" the contract. When Laclede brought this action to recover damages for breach of contract, Amoco contended that it was not bound by the contract because it lacked mutuality. (I.e., Amoco claimed that its promise to supply the propane was not supported by consideration on the part of Laclede because of the cancellation clause). The trial court agreed with this contention, and Laclede appealed.

Ross, Judge: The [trial] court felt that Laclede's right to "arbitrarily cancel the agreement" . . . rendered the contract void "for lack of mutuality." We disagree with this conclusion. . . .

A bilateral contract is not rendered invalid and unenforceable merely because one party has the right to cancellation while the other does not. There is no necessity that for each stipulation in a contract binding the one party there must be a corresponding stipulation binding the other.

The important question in the instant case is whether Laclede's right of cancellation rendered all its other promises in the agreement illusory, so that there was a complete [absence] of consideration. This would be the result had Laclede retained the right of immediate cancellation at any time for any reason.

However, in *1 Williston, Law of Contracts* § 104, Professor Williston notes:

Since the courts do not favor arbitrary cancellation clauses, the tendency is to interpret even a slight restriction on the exercise of the right of cancellation as constituting such detriment as will satisfy the requirement of sufficient consideration; for example, where the reservation of right to cancel is for cause, . . . or after a definite period of notice, or upon the occurrence of some extrinsic event. . . .

Professor Corbin agrees, and states simply that when one party has the power to cancel by notice given for some stated period of time, "the contract should never be held to be rendered invalid thereby for lack of mutuality or for lack of consideration." The law of Missouri appears to be in conformity with this general contract rule that a cancellation clause will invalidate a contract only if its exercise is *unrestricted.*

Here Laclede's right to terminate was neither arbitrary nor unrestricted. It was limited by the agreement in at least three ways. First, Laclede could not cancel until one year had passed after the first delivery of propane by Amoco. Second, any cancellation could be effective only on the anniversary date of the first delivery under the agreement. Third, Laclede had to give Amoco 30 days written notice of termination. These restrictions on Laclede's power to cancel clearly bring this case within the rule [and consideration on Laclede's part thus did exist]. . . .

Judgment reversed.

Illusory Contracts: Agreements that lack mutuality, such as employment contracts containing the *unrestricted* right of cancellation, are sometimes referred to as *illusory contracts.* Other such agreements are sales contracts under the terms of which the buyer has a "free way out"; that is, because of the language of the agreement, the buyer does not unconditionally promise to buy a specified amount of the goods from the seller. For example: S and B enter into a contract under the terms of which B promises to buy from S all the coal he "might wish" over the next six months, with S promising to sell such quantity at a specified price per ton. Because of the language used, intentionally or accidentally, B has not bound himself to buy *any* quantity of coal at all; thus he has incurred no detriment. This being true, neither promisor is liable to the other. The result is that if B later desires some coal, he is free to buy it from whomever he wishes. Conversely, if B orders coal from S, S ordinarily has no duty to supply it.

Requirements Contracts: The preceding concept soon began to cast doubt on the validity of all sales contracts in which buyers did not absolutely commit themselves to purchase some specified minimum quantity of goods. Many contracts, for example, were phrased in such a manner that the quantity of goods the buyer was committed to purchase depended on his or her subsequent needs (whatever they might prove to be) rather than on an obligation to take a fixed number of units at the outset. For example: An ice company contracts to sell to an ice cream manufacturer "all the ice you will need in your business for the next two years" at a specified price per ton.

The courts recognized the practicality of such contracts and wanted to enforce them if they could; but the theoretical difficulty was that these contracts did not, by their terms, absolutely bind the buyer to take even a single unit of the product or commodity in question.[12] The courts therefore sought a theory by which many of these contracts could be upheld without demolishing the concept of mutuality.

They accomplished this, in large measure, by adopting the following view. If the parties, by the language of the contract, indicate that the quantity of goods is to be dependent upon the *requirements of the buyer's business,* then the contract is not void for want of mutuality and both parties are bound by it. (The determination of the exact quantity of goods is simply postponed, of necessity, until expiration of the period in question.)[13] Under this theory, while the buyer might not require any of the item or commodity in question, consideration on the part of the buyer exists as follows. In the event that the buyer subsequently requires the product, he or she is obligated to buy it solely from the seller. (That is, the buyer gives up the right to buy it from others.) Thus contracts such as the one in the ice cream case are generally binding on both parties.[14]

Output Contracts: Output contracts are essentially similar to and governed by the same principles as requirements contracts. A seller contracts to sell his or her entire output of a particular article, or of a particular plant, for a specified period of time to the buyer at a designated unit price. The implied promise of the seller (in the event he or she does produce the articles) not to sell them to anyone other than the buyer constitutes a detriment to the seller. And the promise of the buyer to purchase the output, in the event there is any, constitutes a corresponding detriment to the buyer. As a result, such contracts are usually enforceable.[15]

---

[12]Unlike the ice cream illustration, for example, it was often highly questionable whether the buyer would require any of the product at all, particularly where the period of time was a short one. (And even in the ice cream case it was possible that the buyer would go out of business the next day.)

[13]In other words, such contracts are to be distinguished from illusory contracts, in which the quantity is solely dependent upon the buyer's whim or will.

[14]This discussion simply sketches out the basic distinction between illusory and requirements contracts. There are many cases, however, where the courts have difficulty determining whether the contract falls into one category or the other. This is due largely to the fact that the language is frequently vague— terms much less rigid than *require* or *need* are commonly used. As one illustration, the courts by no means agree as to the effect of contracts in which the buyer promises to purchase all goods that he or she "wants" over a specified period. Many feel that this creates a requirements contract; others do not. Thus questions of interpretation arise. And in determining the effect of such terms, an examination of the surrounding circumstances—which differ from case to case—is always relevant. For these reasons, particularly, the results of some cases unquestionably conflict with others (and the student of the law just has to make the best of it).

[15]Sec. 2-306 of the UCC implicitly adopts the general principles stated above in regard to requirements and output contracts. It also tries to limit certain abuses that have occasionally cropped up. For example, a seller under an output contract might take advantage of the buyer by increasing his or her productive capacity far beyond anything the buyer could have anticipated on entering the contract. (A similar hardship can exist in a requirements contract when the buyer's requirements skyrocket far above what was reasonably contemplated by the seller or when the buyer shuts down operations solely for the purpose of escaping liability on the contract) Sec. 2-306(1) tries to prevent such abuses by providing:

> A term which measures the quantity by the output of the seller or the requirements of the buyer means such actual output or requirements as may occur in good faith, except that no quantity unreasonably disproportionate to any stated estimate or in the absence of a stated estimate to any normal or otherwise comparable prior output or requirements may be tendered or demanded.

Settlement of Debts

After a debt becomes due, sometimes the creditor and debtor enter into a *settlement agreement*. This occurs when the creditor, either on his or her own initiative or that of the debtor, promises to release the debtor of all further liability if the debtor pays a specified sum of money. If, after the specified sum is paid, the creditor seeks to recover the balance of the debt on the ground that the agreement lacked consideration on the part of the debtor, the success of the suit usually depends on whether the original debt was "unliquidated" or "liquidated."

Unliquidated Debts: An *unliquidated debt* is one where a genuine dispute exists between the debtor and creditor as to the amount of the indebtedness. Compromise agreements as to such debts, if executed, are usually binding. For example: X claims that Y owes her $150 for work done under a contract, and Y contends that the job was to cost only $100. X then says, "I will settle for $120," and Y pays her that sum in cash. If X later sues to recover the balance, she will be unsuccessful, because she has made an implied promise to release Y upon payment of the $120. Y's payment of that sum constitutes a detriment to him, the promisee, because he thereby gave up the right to have a court rule on his contention that the debt was only $100. Since X's promise to release is thus supported by consideration, Y has a good defense to X's suit.

Payment by check. The above rule is also applicable to payments by check if the debtor indicates that the tendered payment is meant to be in full satisfaction of the indebtedness (rather than a partial payment). For example: Suppose that in the prior situation, before the parties had reached any agreement on the $120 figure, Y simply mailed X a check for $120, bearing the inscription "payment in full." If X cashes the check, she is—because of the inscription—impliedly promising to free Y of any balance. This promise is binding on X because Y, the promisee, by making the payment again gave up his right to contend in court that the debt was only $100.[16]

Liquidated Debts: In *liquidated debts,* those in which there is *no dispute* as to the amount of the indebtedness, compromise agreements are less frequently binding. For example: A is owed $150 by B. The two parties agree about the amount of the debt and about its due date of June 1. On June 2, A agrees to accept $120 as payment in full, and B pays that sum in cash. A thereafter brings suit to recover the balance of $30, and B contends that A is bound by the implied promise he made on June 2 to release him.

The majority view here is that A's promise to release is *not* binding, and he can

---

[16]If X, when cashing the check, had indorsed it "without prejudice and under protest," a few recent cases indicate that she may now be able to recover the balance. *Lange-Finn Construction Co. v. Albany Steel and Iron Supply Co., Inc.,* 103 N.Y.S.2d 1012 is one of these.

therefore recover the balance of $30. The reasoning is that the payment of $120 by B did not constitute a detriment to him, since it was less than what he admittedly owed. This rule is followed by most courts, even where the promise to release is in writing or where the creditor gives a written receipt for the money. (A number of courts, however, hold that A cannot recover the balance, on the theory that A, by making the composition agreement, thereby *waived* his right to collect any balance. And a few states have adopted statutes provide that all written settlement agreements are binding, even where the debt is unliquidated.)

Payment by check. Prior to the adoption of the UCC, the majority view—permitting recovery—was also applied by most courts to situations where the debtor made a compromise payment by check rather than by cash. Suppose, for example, that in the above case, where the debt was clearly $150, B sent A a check for $120 containing the words *payment in full,* and A simply cashed it. (i.e., A did not qualify his indorsement in any way.) The majority view was that the payment of the $120 by B did not constitute the giving of consideration, and thus A was not bound by the implied promise to release which he made when he cashed the check. Accordingly, A was permitted to recover the balance of $30.

For a short time following enactment of the UCC, there was some uncertainty as to whether Sec. 3-408 overruled the majority view. However, in the relatively few cases decided since enactment of the UCC, the courts have generally held that this section is not applicable to the specific situation being discussed here. They have, therefore, *generally continued to permit the creditor in a liquidated debt case to recover the unpaid balance, just as in the case where the debtor made the partial payment in cash.*

Composition Agreements: A different situation is presented when a debtor makes an agreement with two or more creditors, under the terms of which he or she agrees to pay each creditor who joins in the agreement a stated percentage of that person's claim, with the creditors agreeing in return to accept that percentage as full satisfaction of their claims. Such agreements, called *compositions* (or *creditors' composition agreements*), are ordinarily held to be binding on the participating creditors even though each of them receives a sum less than what was originally owed.

To illustrate: X owes Y $1,000 and Z $600. The three parties agree that X will pay each creditor 60 percent of the amount owed and that Y and Z will accept the 60 percent as payment in full. X then pays Y the $600 and Z the $360. If either Y or Z brings suit to recover an additional sum on the theory that his promise to release was not supported by X's payment of the lesser sum, the usual view is that the composition is binding; therefore, the creditor's suit will be dismissed. To reach this result, the courts of many states find consideration to be present in that the promise of each creditor to accept the smaller sum supports the promise of the other creditors to do likewise. Other courts reach the same result by simply ruling that such agreements are binding on the ground of public policy, without trying to find consideration.

Reliance and Moral Obligation

We have already seen that when a gift is promised to someone, the fact that the promisee spends money or incurs a debt on the strength of the promise does not constitute consideration, since the act was not bargained for. That is, *mere reliance* (the mere performance of an act by the promisee that the promisor did not request or anticipate) usually is not consideration.

Furthermore, as a general rule, the *moral obligation* that results from making a promise is not sufficient to cause it to be enforceable. Neither are the motives or feelings of the promisor. Thus an uncle's promise to pay $500 to his niece "in consideration of the love and affection that I have for you" is not binding. Nor is a promise made "in consideration of your many acts of kindness over the years." These acts (commonly referred to as acts of past consideration), having been performed earlier and, presumably, without expectation of payment, have not been bargained for. Thus they do not make a promise enforceable.

Special Situations

Up to this point, we have emphasized the usual situations where the courts require consideration to be present in order for promises to be enforced. (Occasional references to minority views were made only for purposes of completeness.) In the remainder of this chapter, we will focus on four exceptional situations where promises can be enforced by the same courts when consideration clearly is not present. The four are promissory estoppel, promises to charitable institutions, promises made after the statute of limitations has run, and promises made after a discharge in bankruptcy.

Promissory Estoppel

While it is well established that a promise to make a gift is generally unenforceable by the promisee even where the person has performed some act in reliance upon the promise, unusual circumstances exist where the application of this view brings about results that are grossly unfair to the promisee. In such circumstances, the courts occasionally will invoke the doctrine of *promissory estoppel* to enforce the promise.

The basic idea underlying this doctrine is that if the promisor makes a promise under circumstances in which he or she should realize that the promisee is almost certainly going to react to the promise in a particular way, and if the promisee does so react, thereby causing a substantial change in his or her position, the promisor is bound by the promise even though consideration is lacking. To illustrate: Tenant T leases a building from Landlord L from January 1, 1967, to December 31, 1968. In early December 1968, T indicates that he is thinking of remodeling the premises and wants a renewal of the lease for another two years. L replies, "We'll get to work on a new lease soon. I don't know about two years, but you can count on one year for sure." T then spends $500 over the next few weeks in having the first-floor rooms painted, but the parties never execute a new lease. If L seeks to evict T in March 1969 on the ground that no renewal contract had been formed, he will probably be unsuccessful—that is, he will be held to his promise regarding the year 1969. In this case, where L should have realized the likelihood of T's conduct in consequence of his promise, L is said to be "stopped by his promise"; he cannot contend that the lack of consideration on T's part caused his promise to be unenforceable.

To illustrate further: "A has been employed by B for forty years. B promises to pay A a pension of $200 per month when A retires. A retires and forbears to work elsewhere for several years while B pays the pension. B's promise is binding."[18]

The following case presents yet another situation where a resort to the estoppel doctrine seemed appropriate to the court.

Hoffman v. Red Owl Stores, Inc.

Supreme Court of Wisconsin, 133 N.W.2d 267 (1965)

In 1960 Hoffman, plaintiff, hoped to establish a Red Owl franchised grocery store in Wautoma, Wisconsin. During that year he and the divisional manager of Red Owl, Lukowitz, had numerous conversations in which general plans for Hoffman's becoming a franchisee were discussed. Early in 1961 Lukowitz advised Hoffman to buy a small grocery in order to gain experience in the grocery business before operating a Red Owl franchise in a larger community.

Acting on this suggestion, Hoffman bought a small grocery in Wautoma. Three months later Red Owl representatives found that the store was operating at a profit, at which time Hoffman told Lukowitz that he could raise $18,000 to invest in a franchise. Lukowitz then advised Hoffman to sell the store, assuring him that the company would find a larger store for him to operate elsewhere, that he would "be operating a Red Owl store in a new location by fall."

Relying on this promise, Hoffman sold the grocery and soon thereafter bought a lot in Chilton, Wisconsin (a site which the company had selected for a new store), making a $1,000 down payment on the lot. Hoffman then rented a home for his family in Chilton and, after being assured by Lukowitz that "everything was all set," made a second $1,000 payment on the lot.

In September 1961 Lukowitz told Hoffman that the only "hitch" in the plan was that he (Hoffman) would have to sell a bakery building he owned in Wautoma and that the proceeds of that sale would have to make up a part of the $18,000 he was to invest, thereby reducing the amount he would have to borrow. Hoffman sold the building for $10,000, incurring a loss thereon of $2,000.

About this time, Red Owl prepared a "Proposed Financing for an Agency Store" plan that required Hoffman to invest $24,100 rather than the original $18,000. After Hoffman came up with $24,100, by virtue of several new loans, Red Owl told him that another $2,000 would be necessary.

---

[18]*Restatement, Contracts* 2d., Section 90. Copyright 1973. Reprinted with permission of The American Law Institute. (The text of Section 90 itself appears in the decision in the next case.)

Hoffman refused to go along with this demand, negotiations were terminated, and the new store was never built. When Hoffman and his wife brought suit to recover damages for breach of contract, Red Owl defended on the ground that its promises were not supported by consideration on Hoffman's part (in view of the facts that no formal financing plan was ever agreed to by Hoffman and no franchise agreement obligations were undertaken by him). Hoffman contended that liability should nonetheless be imposed on the basis of promissory estoppel; the trial court agreed, entering judgment in his favor. Red Owl appealed.

Currie, Chief Justice: . . . Sec. 90 of Restatement, 1 Contracts, provides: "A promise which the promisor should reasonably expect to induce action or forbearance of a definite and substantial character on the part of the promisee and which does induce such action or forbearance is binding if injustice can be avoided only by enforcement of the promise."

[The Chief Justice then observed that the Wisconsin Supreme Court had never recognized the above rule, but continued:] Many courts of other jurisdictions have seen fit over the years to adopt the principle of promissory estoppel [embodied in Section 90], and the tendency in that direction continues. . . . The development of the law of promissory estoppel "is an attempt by the courts to keep the remedies abreast of increased moral consciousness of honesty and fair representations in all business dealings." *People's National Bank of Little Rock v. Linebarger Construction Co.,* 240 S.W.2d 12 (1951). . . .

Because we deem the doctrine of promissory estoppel, as stated in Section 90 of Restatement, 1 Contracts, [to be] one which supplies a needed tool which courts may employ in a proper case to prevent injustice, *we endorse and adopt it.* [Emphasis added.]

The record here discloses a number of promises and assurances given to Hoffman by Lukowitz in behalf of Red Owl, [and] upon which plaintiffs relied and acted upon to their detriment.

Foremost were the promises that for the sum of $18,000 Red Owl would establish Hoffman in a store, [and] in November, 1961, [the assurance] to Hoffman that if the $24,100 figure were increased by $2,000, the deal would go through. [In return,] Hoffman was induced to sell his grocery store fixtures and inventory in June, 1961, on the promise that he would be in his new store by fall. In November, plaintiffs sold their bakery building on the urging of defendants and on the assurance that this was the last step necessary to have the deal with Red Owl go through [and on which sale, incidentally, plaintiffs suffered the $2,000 loss earlier referred to].

We determine that there was ample evidence to sustain [the jury's finding that Hoffman relied on the promises of Red Owl], and that his reliance was in the exercise of ordinary care. . . .

[In regard to a contention by Red Owl that its promises were too vague and indefinite to be enforceable in this action, in view of the fact that the size, cost, and design of the proposed store building were never agreed upon, the court disagreed, saying:] We deem it would be a mistake to regard an action grounded on promissory estoppel as the [precise] equivalent of a breach of contract action. The third requirement [of promissory estoppel,] that the remedy can only be invoked where necessary to avoid injustice, is one that involves a policy decision by the court. Such a policy necessarily embraces an element of discretion.

We conclude that injustice would result here if plaintiffs were not granted some relief because of the failure of defendants to keep their promises which induced plaintiffs to act to their detriment. . . .

Judgment affirmed.

Promises to Charitable Institutions

The law generally looks with favor upon charitable institutions, such as churches, hospitals, and colleges. One result of this policy is that many courts try to enforce promises to pay money to such institutions (1) by bending the rules to find that consideration exists, (2) by extending the doctrine of promissory estoppel, or (3) if neither of these views can be justified, simply on the ground of public policy.

In regard to the first situation, the language contained in many pledge agreements provides that the promise to pay is made "in consideration of the promises of others" to make similar gifts. If a person signs such a pledge, most courts will hold him or her liable if the promisee (the institution) can show that at least one other person signed a pledge containing the same language during the same campaign. The theory is that the promise of each promisor is supported by the promise of the other.

The imposition of liability by extending the doctrine of promissory estoppel beyond its normal bounds can be illustrated by the following: In March, X signs a "subscription agreement" promising to pay $1,000 to the Presbyterian Church on June 30. In May, the church purchases new robes for its choir, an expenditure based on the promise of the $1,000. Many courts will hold that X is liable on the ground of promissory estoppel (whereas, if the promisee had been someone other than a charitable organization they would likely absolve X of liability on the ground that the purchase of the robes was an act of "mere reliance").

If the facts of a given case are such that neither of the above theories is applicable, many courts (though by no means all) will still enforce the promise on the ground of public policy.

Promises Made Subsequent to the Running of a Statute of Limitations

All states have statutes limiting the time a creditor has in which to bring suit against the debtor after the debt becomes due.[19] If the specified period of time elapses without the initiation of legal proceedings by the creditor, the statute is said to have "run." While the running of a statute does not extinguish the debt, it does cause the contract to be unenforceable—that is, it prevents the creditor from successfully maintaining an action in court to collect the debt.

New Promise to Pay: To what extent is the situation altered if the debtor, after the statute has run, makes a new promise to pay the debt? One might conclude that such a promise is unenforceable, since there is clearly no consideration given by the creditor in return. This, however, is not the case. *In all states, either by statute or by judicial decision, such a promise, if in writing, is enforceable despite*

---

[19]These periods of time vary widely among the states, and there is no typical statute. As a general illustration, however, some states give the creditor three years on an oral contract and six years on a written one.

the absence of consideration.[20] In such a case, the debt is said to have been "revived," and the creditor now has a new statutory period in which to bring suit. (If the new promise was to pay only a portion of the original indebtedness, such as $200 of a $450 debt, the promise is binding only to the extent of that portion—in this case $200.)

Part Payment or Acknowledgment: The debt is also revived if a part payment is made by the debtor after the statute has run. If, for example, a five-year statute had run on a $1,000 debt, and the debtor thereafter mailed a check for $50 to the creditor, the creditor now has an additional five years in which to commence legal action for the balance. A mere acknowledgment by the debtor that the debt exists will also revive the obligation to pay.

Imposition of liability in the above instances is based on the theory that the debtor has, by making the part payment or acknowledgment, *impliedly promised* to pay the remaining indebtedness. The debtor can escape the operation of this rule by advising the creditor, when making the payment or acknowledgment, that he or she *is not* making any promise as to payment of the balance.

Questions and Problems

1. Dr. Browning made a contract with Dr. Johnson, under which he was to sell his practice and equipment to Johnson for a specified price. Before the time for performance, Browning changed his mind and asked Johnson to relieve him of his obligation to sell. Thereafter a new contract was made, under the terms of which Browning promised to pay Johnson $40,000 in return for Johnson's cancellation of the first contract. Later Browning refused to pay the $40,000, contending that this promise of his was not supported by consideration on Johnson's part. Is Browning correct? If not, where is the consideration on Johnson's part? (*Browning v. Johnson,* 422 P.2d 319, 1967.)

2. Grombach was employed as a public relations representative for the Oerlikon Company. The written contract provided that Oerlikon had the right to cancel the contract by giving him written notice by May 1, 1953. If no such notice were given, the contract was to remain in effect for a specified number of additional years. On April 27, 1953, Oerlikon asked that its right of cancellation be extended to June 30 of that year, and Grombach agreed to this. On June 24 Oerlikon exercised its option and cancelled the contract. Thereafter Grombach sued for damages for breach of contract, contending that his promise to extend the right of cancellation until June 30 was not supported by consideration on the part of Oerlikon. Do you agree with this contention? Why or why not? (*Grombach v. Oerlikon Tool and Arms Corp. of America,* 276 F.2d 155, 1960.)

3. Vinson agreed to do a certain construction job for Leggett, the owner, for $3,950. After work was commenced, Vinson found out that he was going to lose money on the job.

---

[20] This rule on the enforceability of promises to pay debts barred by the running of the *statute of limitations* was, at one time, generally applied to promises to repay debts that were made by debtors after they had gone through *bankruptcy proceedings.* However, under the federal Bankruptcy Reform Act of 1978, effective October 1, 1979, this is no longer true. Thus, today such a promise to repay a debt is not binding unless supported by consideration.

Leggett examined Vinson's bills for materials to date and said, "Go ahead and complete the work like we said and I will pay you an additional $1,000." Vinson then completed the job. *Leggett v. Vinson,* 124 So. 427 (1929). Is Leggett bound by his promise? Explain.

4. Scales owned and operated a retail gas station on property which he leased for five years from Lang. When Scales got behind on his rent payments, the president of the Hy-Test Corporation, whose products Scales sold, wrote a letter to Lang saying, "Don't worry about the rent; we will pay it if Scales does not." Is this promise binding on the Hy-Test company? Explain.

5. A Pontiac dealer sold a new car to Knoebel under a contract that obligated him to make specified monthly payments. When Knoebel fell behind in his payments, the dealer repossessed the car, which he had a right to do. On July 26 the dealer told Knoebel that if he would pay off the amount then due ($498.99) by August 10, he—the dealer—would return the car to him at that time. On August 7 Knoebel went to the dealer with the money, but the dealer had sold the car to a third party. When Knoebel sued the dealer for damages for breach of contract (i.e., for failure to hold the car for him), the dealer argued that his promise to hold the car was not supported by consideration on Knoebel's part. Is this argument correct? Why or why not? (*Knoebel v. Chief Pontiac, Inc.,* 294 P.2d 625, 1956.)

6. A New York girl and an Italian count were engaged to be married. A short time before the wedding date the girl's father promised, in effect, that if the marriage took place he would pay them $2,500 a year as long as his daughter lived. The marriage took place and payments were made for ten years. When the father discontinued the payments, suit was brought against him for damages for breach of contract. He defended on the ground that the couple already had a preexisting obligation to get married when he made the promise (as a result of their engagement contract) and that their act of marriage did not, therefore, constitute consideration on their part. Is his argument valid? Discuss. (*DiCicco v. Schweizer,* 117 N.E. 807, 1917.)

7. Walquist was struck by a car driven by Christensen. The parties were in dispute as to whether or not the accident was Christensen's fault; they were also in disagreement as to the extent of Walquist's injuries. In this setting, they made an agreement: Christensen paid Walquist $500, and Walquist in turn released him from all liability. Later, when it turned out that Walquist's doctor bills alone came to $700, he sued Christensen to recover an additional sum. Christensen used the settlement agreement as a defense, but Walquist contended that Christensen's payment of $500 was not a sufficient consideration to support his promise to release, in view of the facts that his damages were, in actuality, considerably greater than $500. Is Walquist right? Why or why not?

8. Mrs. Harmon was a long-time employee of the FoxLane Company. Her son's illness had caused her to consider retiring, but she was not sure she was financially able to do so. The president of the company told her, "Marie, I have tried to work something out for you. While I hope you can stay with us for two more years, I want you to know that upon your retirement—whenever it occurs—the company will pay you your present salary as long as you live." Two months later she retired, and the company made several monthly payments. When it then stopped the payments, she sued it for damages. The company contended that its promise was not supported by consideration on her part (i.e., the company did *not* say "Retire now and we will pay.") Was there consideration on Mrs. Harmon's part? If not, is there any principle under which she might recover? Explain.

Contractual Capacity   11

Contractual capacity is the third element of a contract. In the cases encountered thus far, the contracting parties have been fully "competent." This means that in the eyes of the law, they have the capacity (the legal ability) to contract. When both contracting parties are competent, the contract is termed "valid" and both are bound by it—assuming, of course, that the other elements of a contract are present.

Some persons, however, have *no capacity to contract*. Typical examples are those who have been declared insane by a court, convicted felons while imprisoned, and children so young that their minds have not yet matured sufficiently to understand the meaning and obligation of an agreement. Any "contract" entered into by an individual in one of these categories is absolutely void—it does not exist in the eyes of the law. Neither the incompetent person nor the other contracting party incurs any obligation whatsoever from such an agreement (except in the rare instances when the agreement is subsequently approved by a court).

Between these extremes are several classes of persons who possess a *partial* (or limited) *capacity to contract*. Such persons' contracts are "voidable"; they can ordinarily be disaffirmed (or set aside) by the incompetent party if he or she desires to do so. In many circumstances an avoidance (a setting aside) entirely frees the incompetent party of contractual obligations, while in others it results in only a partial escape of liability. (Voidable contracts are binding on both parties until disaffirmed. In this respect they differ markedly from void contracts, which are inoperable from their inception.)

Minors, some types of insane persons, and intoxicated persons are the most common examples of those whose capacity to contract is limited and whose contracts are thus generally held to be voidable.[1]

Minors

Centuries ago, the English courts became aware of the fact that many of the contracts entered into by young persons evidenced a shocking lack of judgment; such persons assumed obligations and made purchases that they probably would not have done had they possessed greater maturity and experience. The courts, desirous of "protecting the young from the consequences of their own folly," began to wrestle with the question of how this protection could best be brought about.

They initially approached the problem by devising what came to be known as the *harm-benefit test*. Under this view, the courts permitted persons who had entered into contracts while under the age of twenty-one to disaffirm them if they were shown to be harmful to these individuals. This approach was followed for a time in the U.S. Its application, however, produced such conflict and uncertainty in the law that a new solution became necessary.

The Common-Law Rule

The U.S. courts finally adopted the sweeping rule that, virtually without exception, *all minors' contracts are voidable at their option.* The right thus given to minors to escape their contractual obligations is no longer dependent upon a showing that the contract is harmful or unwise or that they have been taken advantage of in some way. To effect a disaffirmance of any contract, all the minor has to do is indicate to the other party his or her intention not to be bound by it. The disaffirmance can be express or implied, and the right to disaffirm continues until the minor reaches the age of majority, plus a "reasonable time thereafter." (The right is entirely one-sided; since it is based solely on the fact of incompetence, the other party to the contract has no corresponding right to disaffirm.)

Definition of Minority

At common law the age of majority is twenty one, and as late as 1970 this definition was followed by over half the states. Since that time, however, forty states by statute

---

[1]The terms *minor* and *infant* are synonymous from a legal standpoint; both refer to persons who have not attained the age of majority. The former term is more common today, and we will use it exclusively.

have reduced the age of majority to eighteen for most purposes, including that of making valid contracts.[2] Therefore, the discussion and illustrations in this chapter will assume that one is a minor only until reaching the age of eighteen. (Of course, because of statutory variations, a person attempting to disaffirm a specific contract on the ground of minority should examine the applicable state statute.)

We will now examine the results of the general rule permitting minors to disaffirm contracts at their option in three basic situations: (1) ordinary contracts,[3] (2) contracts for the purchase of "necessaries," and (3) contracts in which the minor has misrepresented his or her age.

Minors' Liability on Ordinary Contracts

Executory Contracts: Few problems arise where the minor's repudiation occurs before either party has started to perform the obligations under the contract (that is, where the contract is still *executory*). Since the other party is caused little hardship in such a case, all states take the view that the disaffirmance entirely frees the minor of liability. For example, suppose that M, a minor, contracts on July 1 to buy a home stereo system from X for $1,200, the contract providing that the system will be delivered and the purchase price paid on July 15. If M notifies X on July 10 that he will not go through with the deal, the contract is at an end and X has no recourse against M. Similarly, if M contracts to paint Y's house for $400 and later refuses to do the job, the refusal absolves M of liability. If either X or Y were to bring suit against M to recover damages for breach of contract, the suit would be dismissed.

Executed Contracts: Surprising as it may seem, the same rule is also generally applied to executed contracts—those that have been fully performed before the repudiation takes place. Thus, in virtually all states, a minor can purchase a car for cash, drive it until he becomes an adult, and still disaffirm the contract (assuming, as is usually the case, that the car is not a necessity of life).

While virtually all courts agree as to the minor's *right to disaffirm* a contract in a situation such as the above, they do not agree about the *extent of the relief* that should be given to the minor in some circumstances. This can be illustrated by amplifying the facts about the car purchase. Suppose that the purchase price of the car was $2,800 and that the minor brings suit to recover that amount. At the trial, the seller offers evidence establishing that the value of the car at the time the minor offered to return it was $1,500. In such a case the seller can make at least two contentions: (1) that the minor should be charged with the benefit he

---

[2]These statutes almost uniformly confer upon eighteen-year-olds the rights to sue and be sued in their own names, to make wills, to marry without parental consent, and to choose their own domiciles; but generally they do not sanction the right to buy alcoholic beverages until the age of twenty-one is reached.

[3]We are speaking here of all contracts except those under which the minor is purchasing "necessities of life," such as articles of food and clothing.

received—that is, the reasonable value of the use of the car prior to disaffirmance, or (2) if this contention is rejected, that the minor should at least be charged with the depreciation of the car while it was in his hands.

The majority view. The courts of most states reject both contentions, permitting the minor to recover the full price of $2,800. Assuming that the automobile does not constitute a necessity, the majority rule is that the minor's only obligation is to return the consideration if he is able to do so. Under this view, the return of the car—even though it has greatly depreciated in value by reason of use or accident—entitles the minor to recover his *entire payment.* Furthermore, if the minor is unable to return the consideration, as would be the case if the car were stolen from him, he is still permitted to recover the $2,800 from the unfortunate seller. And regardless of whether the consideration has depreciated in value or cannot be returned, the minor is not charged with the benefit he has received from the possession and use of the consideration.[4]

This freedom from liability also would exist if the minor had purchased the car on credit rather than for cash. In this case, if the minor disaffirmed the contract before paying off the balance, and if the seller then brought action to recover that balance, the minor would again be freed of all liability (subject, again, only to the obligation to return the car if he is able to do so).

Some other views. The courts of a growing number of states, feeling that the majority view imposes unreasonable hardship on the other party to the contract, *do* impose liability on the minor under one of two theories. Some states hold the minor liable for the *reasonable value of the benefit* received prior to the disaffirmance, while others reach a similar result by holding the person liable for the depreciation that has occurred to the goods while in his or her possession. Going back to the original illustration, where the minor had paid cash for the car, the courts of these states would permit him to recover the purchase price *minus* the value of the benefit (or depreciation), whatever the jury finds this to be.

The following case illustrates the great protection the majority view gives to the minor, even where the loss in value is the result of negligence on his or her part.

Hogue et al. v. Wilkinson

Court of Civil Appeals of Texas, 291 S.W.2d 750 (1956)

In November 1953 Gordon Wilkinson, an eighteen-year-old, purchased a pair of chinchillas from Hogue and McCoy, the defendants, for $1,150. In December 1953 he purchased a second pair for $700. (At all times involved in this action the age of majority under Texas law was twenty-one.)

The chinchillas were delivered to Wilkinson soon after the contracts were made, and by December 1954 he had paid the total consideration of $1,850. By that time

---

[4]We are assuming, in this discussion, that the minor did not misrepresent his age—that is, did not indicate to the other party that he was eighteen when in fact he was not. Many sales contracts, particularly those of automobile dealers, contain a statement that "the buyer certifies he or she is eighteen years of age or older"; the position of minors signing such contracts will be discussed later in this chapter.

the number of chinchillas had increased to eight, the original pair having produced four offspring.

In March 1955 Wilkinson, still a minor, went to defendants' place of business and disaffirmed both contracts. At that time he offered to return the six chinchillas that were then living and demanded the return of the $1,850. (Between December 1954 and March 1955 one of the $700 pair and one of the young had died.)

Defendants would not accept the chinchillas and refused to return the money. Wilkinson then brought suit in April of 1955 asking for the return of the $1,850. (By that time, only two chinchillas were living.)

At the trial, the defendants contended that the inability of the plaintiff to return all eight of the chinchillas barred this action, particularly in view of the evidence that the deaths of the chinchillas resulted from the plaintiff's negligence. The court, acting without a jury, rejected this contention and entered a summary judgment for the plaintiff. Defendants appealed.

Fanning, Justice: . . . Appellants' contentions that the minor plaintiff was equitably estopped to disaffirm, that the deaths of the chinchillas that died were proximately caused by the negligence of the plaintiff, and that plaintiff failed to prevent the destruction of the chinchillas that died by reason of overheating, do not raise legal defenses under this record and under the authorities hereinafter outlined. . . .

There were no allegations by defendants that plaintiff committed any fraudulent or intentional acts by reason of which he would be estopped to disaffirm. Defendants contend in essence that the minor plaintiff was negligent and that his negligence proximately caused the death of the chinchillas, and that he could not restore the entire consideration, to-wit, all of the chinchillas he received.

In *Prudential Building & Loan Ass'n v. Shaw*, 26 S.W.2d 168, it was held that a minor shareholder could disaffirm a voidable contract for the purchase of shares and recover the full value paid in for such shares. On page 171 the court stated: "Of course, he must restore the consideration received by him in its then condition, *if he still has it.* Also if the consideration received by the infant or minor has depreciated on account of wear and tear *or is entirely lost,* nevertheless he is still entitled to recover the full amount of consideration paid by him. (Emphasis ours.) . . ."

In *Rutherford v. Hughes,* 228 S.W.2d 909, it is stated: "It is well established by the decisions that a minor is not estopped by his acts which mislead another to the latter's injury unless the acts were intentional and fraudulent, and also unless the party with whom he deals relied upon such acts and conduct."

[The court then ruled that the conduct of the plaintiff in caring for the animals, while perhaps constituting negligence on his part, was neither intentional nor fraudulent. Accordingly, the judgment of the trial court, permitting disaffirmance and full recovery of the $1,850, was affirmed.]

Rationale: There is no question but that the majority rule, as applied to given situations, frequently results in a severe financial loss to the party who has dealt with the minor. It is also evident that some young people, aware of the state law, enter into contracts with the intention of getting something for nothing. Nevertheless, most courts feel that the importance of protecting minors, by permitting disaffirmance in virtually all cases, outweighs the occasional hardship that such protection causes other parties. Thus we have once again a situation where the rights of some individuals, under certain circumstances, must give way to the rights of others because of public policy considerations.

A competent person can, of course, ordinarily escape such hardships by refusing to deal with minors.[5] All persons are presumed to know the law, so that (in theory at least) one who deals with a minor is on notice that it is at his or her peril. The courts frequently repeat that "it is the purpose of the common-law rule to discourage persons from contracting with minors," and the above rules no doubt tend to bring about this result.

A second solution for someone who wishes to make a sale is to refuse to deal with the minor and to contract instead with one of the minor's parents. In such a case the possibility of a disaffirmance is eliminated, since both parties to the contract are competent. A third solution, in situations where the competent party does not know whether the person with whom he or she is dealing is a minor, is to have that person make a statement, preferably in writing, that he or she is over the age of eighteen. (The protection afforded to the competent party by such a representation will be considered later in the chapter.)

Ratification: Once a minor reaches the age of majority, he or she has the ability to ratify any contracts made earlier. A *ratification* occurs when the minor indicates to the other party, expressly or impliedly, the intent to be bound by the agreement. Thus, if a minor, after reaching the age of eighteen, promises that he or she will go through with the contract, an express ratification has taken place and the right of disaffirmance is lost forever. Similarly, if a minor has received an article, such as a typewriter, under a contract and continues to use it for more than a "reasonable time" after reaching the age of eighteen, an implied ratification has occurred. Another situation in which a ratification can take place involves purchases made under installment contracts. Suppose, for example, that a minor has purchased a motorcycle, agreeing to pay the seller $25 a month until the purchase price has been paid in full. If he continues to make payments for any length of time after reaching the age of eighteen, it is probable that such payments will be held to constitute a ratification of the contract. It is obvious from the foregoing that any young person, upon becoming an adult, should review all contracts and, if he or she wishes to set any of them aside, should refrain from any conduct that would indicate to the other party an intention to be bound by them.

---

[5]Some persons, such as common carriers, have a legal duty to deal with everyone who requests (and is able to pay for) their services. Disaffirmance against such persons is generally not permitted once the contract has been executed. Thus, a seventeen-year-old who purchases and uses an airline ticket is not permitted to recover his or her fare.

Minors' Liability on Contracts to Purchase "Necessaries"

When a minor purchases goods that the law considers necessary to life or health, he or she incurs a greater liability than that imposed (by the majority rule) under contracts calling for the purchase of goods that are not necessities. The rule applicable to contracts calling for the purchase of "necessaries" is that the minor is liable to the other party for the *reasonable value of the goods actually used.* To illustrate: M, seventeen, buys a topcoat from C, contracting to pay the price of $150 one year later. At the end of that time, when the coat is completely worn out, C brings suit to recover the purchase price. If the court rules that the coat is a necessary, then it must determine what its reasonable value was at the time of the purchase, and M is liable to C in that amount. (In contrast, if the coat is held *not* to constitute a necessary, M is usually freed of all liability—as has been seen earlier.) This imposition of liability occurs only where the goods or services have been used by the minor; contracts calling for the purchase of necessaries can still be set aside as long as they are executory. Thus, if M contracts to purchase a coat from C, which is to be delivered one week later, he can set aside the contract without liability if he notifies C of his disaffirmance before the week is out—and, indeed, even later as long as he does not use the coat.

What Constitutes a Necessary? In answering the question of what constitutes a necessary, it is possible to draw a clear line in most cases. Minimum amounts of food, clothing, and medical services are clearly necessary. So, too, is the rental of a house or apartment by a minor who is married. Many items, on the other hand, are clearly luxuries—such as TV sets, sporting goods, and dancing lessons, under most circumstances.[6]

Cars are generally held not to be necessaries, but there is disagreement in regard to cars (and other items) used by the minor in his or her work. Most courts continue to follow the older rule in this area, holding that such items do not constitute necessaries. Recent decisions, however, have increasingly taken the view that *property used by the minor for self-support does constitute a necessity.*

It should also be noted that an item is a necessity only if it is actually needed at the time of purchase. Thus if a minor purchases an item that appears to be a necessity, such as an article of clothing, the minor still has no liability to the seller if he or she can prove that a parent or guardian was "willing and able" to furnish clothing of the type purchased under that particular contract.

The case below presents a problem typical of those arising in the "necessity" area.

---

[6]In determining whether a doubtful item is a necessary, the courts take into account the "station in life" occupied by the particular minor. Thus a fourth sport coat might be ruled a necessary for a minor who is a member of high society, while it would not be so ruled in regard to others.

Gastonia Personnel Corporation v. Rogers

Supreme Court of North Carolina, 172 S.E.2d 19 (1970)

Rogers was a minor who was studying civil engineering in a North Carolina college. When his wife became pregnant he had to quit school and go to work. In order to get suitable employment, Rogers signed a contract with an employment agency, Gastonia Personnel Corporation, the plaintiff. Under the terms of this agreement Rogers agreed to pay plaintiff a fee of $295 if it produced a "lead" that resulted in a job for him.

Soon thereafter one of plaintiff's personnel counselors put Rogers in touch with a Charlotte firm which hired him as a draftsman. Rogers subsequently disaffirmed the contract with plaintiff on the ground of minority, and refused to pay its fee. Plaintiff then brought suit to recover the $295 or, in the alternative, the reasonable value of its services. Plaintiff's primary contention was that its services constituted a necessity, under the circumstances of the case. The trial court ruled as a matter of law that the services were not a necessity, and dismissed the action. Plaintiff appealed.

Bobbitt, Chief Justice: . . . "By the fifteenth century it seems to have been well settled that an infant's bargain was [voidable] at his election, and also [well settled] that he was liable for necessaries." 2 *Williston, Contracts* § 223 (1959). . . . In accordance with this ancient rule of the common law, this court has held an infant's contract, unless for "necessaries" or unless authorized by statute, is voidable by the infant, at his election, and may be disaffirmed during infancy or upon attaining the age of [majority.] . . .

In general, our prior decisions are to the effect that the "necessaries" of an infant, and his wife and child, include only such necessities of life as food, clothing, shelter, medical attention, and so forth. In our view, the concept of "necessaries" should be enlarged to include such articles of property and such services as are reasonably necessary to enable the infant to earn the money required to provide the necessities of life for himself and those who are legally dependent upon him. . . .

The evidence [shows] that defendant, when he contracted with plaintiff, . . . was married, a high school graduate, within "a quarter or 22 hours" of obtaining his degree in applied science, and capable of holding a [draftsman's] job at a starting annual salary of $4,784. To hold, as a matter of law, that such a person cannot obligate himself to pay for services rendered him in obtaining employment suitable to his ability, education, and specialized training, enabling him to provide the necessities of life for himself, his wife and his expected child, would place him and others similarly situated under a serious economic handicap.

In the effort to protect "older minors" from improvident or unfair contracts, the law should not deny to them the opportunities and right to obligate themselves for articles of property or services which are reasonably necessary to enable them to provide for the proper support of themselves and their dependents. The minor should be held liable for the reasonable value of articles of property or services received pursuant to such contract. Applying the foregoing legal principles, which modify the ancient rule of the common law, we hold that the evidence offered by plaintiff was sufficient for submission to the jury for its determination of issues substantially as indicated below.

To establish liability, plaintiff must satisfy the jury . . . that defendant's contract was an appropriate and reasonable means for defendant to obtain suitable employment. If this issue is answered in plaintiff's favor, plaintiff must then establish the reasonable value of the services received by defendant pursuant to the contract. Thus, plaintiff's recovery, if any, cannot exceed the reasonable value of its services. . . .

Judgment reversed, and cause remanded.

Minors' Liability on Contracts Involving Misrepresentation of Age

We have assumed so far that the minor has not led the other party to believe he or she is an adult. If such misrepresentation does occur, the minor is guilty of a kind of fraud, and the courts of most jurisdictions will deny the protection that otherwise would be given that person.

Some states have provided by statute that a minor who has misrepresented his or her age is liable on the contract exactly as if he or she were an adult. Most states, however, have left the matter up to the courts, and a spate of rules has resulted. Without attempting to consider all of them, we can make one or two generalizations.

First, where the minor repudiates the contract while it is entirely executory, most courts permit the disaffirmance just as if there had been no misrepresentation. Although this does not penalize the minor for wrongdoing, it also does not cause particular hardship to the other party in most instances.

Second, where a contract calling for the purchase of a nonnecessary has been fully or partially executed before the attempted disaffirmance, many courts allow the disaffirmance only if it will not cause a loss to the other party.[8] Under this approach, each case is analyzed separately to determine the effect of the disaffirmance. Two illustrations follow.

Example 1. M, a minor, purchases a car from C, a competent party, for $2,500 cash, after telling C that she is eighteen. A year later, just before becoming eighteen, M wishes to disaffirm; at this time the market value of the car is $1,400. Despite the misrepresentation, disaffirmance will be permitted. C, however, will be allowed to withhold from the $2,500 the amount of the depreciation, $1,100, which—added to the $1,400 car—will restore him to his original position. M's recovery is thus only $1,400.

Example 2. M purchases a car from C under a contract providing, "Buyer certifies that he or she is eighteen years of age or older." The purchase price is $2,500, with $100 paid at the time of purchase and the balance of $2,400 payable in twenty-four monthly installments. Six months later, when the car is stolen, M notifies C that she wants to be relieved of the balance of the contract. Disaffirmance will probably not be allowed since this would cause a loss to C; thus a suit by C to recover the unpaid balance will be successful.[9]

Contracts That Cannot Be Disaffirmed

Not all contracts can be disaffirmed on the ground of minority. For example, disaffirmance of marriage contracts and contracts of enlistment in the armed forces

---

[8]In cases of "necessary" contracts, the usual rule normally continues in effect—the minor is liable for the reasonable value of the articles actually used.

[9]This example is based on *Haydocy Pontiac, Inc., v. Lee,* 19 Ohio App.2d 217 (1969). The minor in this case was held to be "estopped" from disaffirming, in view of her misrepresentation; and she continued to be liable for the "fair value of the property."

is not permitted, on the ground of public policy. For certain other contracts, such as those approved by a court or those made with banks or insurance companies, the same result is generally brought about by statute. For example, a North Carolina statute authorizes banks "in respect to deposit accounts and the rental of safe deposit boxes" to deal with minors as if they are adults. And another North Carolina statute authorizes minors of fifteen and over to make life insurance contracts to the same extent as if they were adults.

Torts and Crimes

The rules permitting minors to disaffirm most contracts do not apply to acts that are tortious or criminal in nature. Generally, minors are fully liable for any torts or crimes they commit (except, or course, minors of "tender years," such as two- or three-year-olds). Thus, if a minor drives a car negligently, anyone injured thereby can recover damages from him or her. Such liability cannot be disaffirmed. Similarly, if a minor operates a motor vehicle while intoxicated, the usual criminal penalties can be imposed (although in the criminal area, the penalties may be tempered under juvenile court procedures).

Insane Persons

Contract law recognizes two general classes of insane persons. The first class includes those who have been adjudicated insane—formally declared insane by a court after hearings and examination by psychiatrists. Any "contract" entered into by such persons after the adjudication is absolutely void (no liability can result from any such agreement, even if the insane person fails to disaffirm it).

The second class includes persons who, though never having been adjudicated insane, attempt to escape liability under a particular contract on the ground that they were *actually insane* at the time the contract was made. This raises a question of fact: whether the individual seeking to disaffirm was so mentally deranged at the time of contracting that he or she was incapable of understanding the nature and consequences of the agreement. If this condition is found to have existed, the contract is voidable and disaffirmance will be allowed.

The entertaining case below presents the typical kinds of evidence that a jury (or court) must evaluate in deciding whether the one seeking avoidance was actually insane ("insane in fact").

Hanks v. McNeil Coal Corporation

Supreme Court of Colorado, 168 P.2d 256 (1946)

Lee Hanks, a prosperous farmer and businessman in Nebraska, purchased a farm in Weld County, Colorado, and moved there with his family in 1918. A portion of the farm consisted of coal lands, and for a time Hanks operated a retail coal business in Boulder.

In 1937, Hanks sold a quarter section of the coal lands to the defendant corporation. In 1940 he was adjudicated insane, and a son, J. L. Hanks, was appointed conservator of his estate. Soon after his appointment, the son brought action to set aside the 1937 sale of the coal lands on the grounds that the senior Hanks was, in fact, insane at that time.

To support this contention, evidence was introduced that in 1922 Hanks became afflicted with diabetes, and that after that time he had become irritable, easily upset, highly critical of his son's work, and increasingly interested in "the emotional type of religion." He began to speculate in oil and other doubtful ventures with money needed for payment of debts and taxes. About 1934 he sent his son what he denominated a secret formula for the manufacture of medicine to cure fistula in horses, which was compounded principally of ground china, brick dust, burnt shoe leather, and amber-colored glass. If the infection was in the horse's right shoulder, the mixture was to be poured in the animal's left ear, and if in the left shoulder then in the right ear. In 1937 Hanks started to advertise this medicine through the press under the name of Crown King remedy. Thereafter he increasingly devoted his efforts and money to the compounding and attempted sale of this concoction, his business judgment became poor, and he finally deteriorated mentally to the point that on May 25, 1940, he was adjudicated insane.

The defendant corporation, on the other hand, introduced evidence indicating that Hanks was not insane in 1937. A Denver banker testified to making a substantial loan to Hanks in 1936 and again in 1939 to finance the purchase of feeder cattle, after personally interviewing and negotiating with Hanks himself. He said that on both occasions Hanks appeared to have very clearly in mind how he wanted to handle his cattle feeding, what kind of feed he wanted, and how much he had on hand. The president of a Boulder real estate and loan company, who had known Hanks fifteen years, testified to making him a loan in 1938 and meeting him a number of times thereafter. He said that Hanks appeared to be rational. Four attorneys who had various dealings with Hanks testified as to his apparent grasp of business affairs and rational conduct during and subsequent to the time of the sale involved here.

The trial court held that Hanks was sane at the time of the sale and dismissed the action. Plaintiff appealed.

Stone, Justice: There is always in civil, as well as in criminal, actions a presumption of sanity. Insanity and incompetence are words of vague and varying import. Often the definition of the psychiatrist is at variance with that of the law.

The legal test of Hanks' insanity is whether "he was incapable of understanding and appreciating the extent and effect of business transactions in which he engaged." *Ellis v. Colorado National Bank,* 10 P.2d 336. The legal rule does not recognize degrees of insanity. It does not presume to make a distinction between much and little intellect. One may have insane delusions regarding some matters and be insane on some subjects, yet capable of transacting business concerning matters wherein such subjects are not concerned, and such insanity does not make one incompetent to contract unless the subject matter of the contract is so connected with an insane delusion as to render the afflicted party incapable of understanding the nature and effect of the agreement or of acting rationally in the transaction.

Contractual capacity and testamentary capacity are the same. Clearly manifested symptoms of *senile dementia* before a will was made, continuing until the extreme degree of dementia was reached a few months later, is held not conclusive of incapacity to make a will, nor are *senile dementia* and improvident expenditures [proof] of lack of capacity to contract.

Patently Hanks was suffering from insane delusion in 1937 with reference to the efficacy of the horse medicine, but there is no evidence of delusions or hallucinations in connection with this transaction or with his transaction of much of his other business at that time; there is no basis for holding voidable his sale here involved on the ground of his insanity, and the trial court correctly so held. . . .

Judgment affirmed.

Contractual Liability

Generally, a person who is insane in fact when making a contract is in the same position as a minor. That is, as to ordinary contracts disaffirmance is allowed without liability, while as to necessities he or she remains liable for the reasonable value of the goods actually used (or services actually received).

In one limited situation, however, the insane person's rights are less than those of a minor. While a minor is allowed to disaffirm an ordinary contract without liability even if he or she is not able to return the consideration received, the insane person in such a case is *not* permitted to disaffirm if (1) the other party made the contract in good faith, not knowing of the insanity, and (2) the contract was a fair one—i.e., no advantage was taken of the insane person. Thus, if an insane person purchased a television set on credit, and it was stolen while in his possession, he or she remains liable for the purchase price if these two conditions are shown to exist.

Intoxicated Persons

People occasionally seek to escape liability under a contract on the ground that they were intoxicated when it was made. Success in doing so depends primarily on the degree of intoxication found to exist at that time. Disaffirmance is allowed only if a person can establish that he or she was so intoxicated as not to understand the nature of the purported agreement. Thus a question of fact is presented, for a lesser degree of intoxication is not grounds for disaffirmance.

If the required degree of intoxication is found to have existed, the intoxicated person's right to disaffirm, upon regaining sobriety, also substantially parallels that of a minor—again, however, with one basic exception. While we have seen that minors may, as a general rule, disaffirm contracts even though unable to return the consideration that they received, intoxicated persons are required by most courts to return the full consideration as a condition of disaffirmance in all cases (unless they are able to show fraud on the part of the other contracting party).

Questions and Problems

1. McAllister, while a minor, purchased a car under circumstances in which it was clearly not a necessity, and gave the seller his promissory note in payment. The note obligated McAllister to make specified monthly payments beginning with the time of purchase. Just

before reaching the age of majority, at which time McAllister had made no payments on the note, he lost possession of the car under circumstances which the trial court found to be "unknown." (It was clear, however, that the car was neither retained by McAllister, nor returned to the seller.) Three years after McAllister reached the age of majority, at which time he had still made no payments, the seller sued him on the note, and McAllister then informed the seller that he was disaffirming the purchase and the note. The seller argued that McAllister's attempted disaffirmance was invalid since he waited so long to exercise this right. Is the seller correct? Explain. (*Warwick Municipal Employees Credit Union v. McAllister,* 293 A.2d 516, 1972).

2. Robertson made an agreement with his son, a minor, that he would lend him enough money to finance his college education, and the son promised to begin repaying the loan after graduation. After the son graduated from college, at which time he was an adult, he wrote his father that he would repay the loan at $100 per month, and he made these payments for three years. Later he refused to pay the balance still due, contending that he was not liable on his original agreement since he was a minor when he entered into it. Under the circumstances, do you think the son's right to disaffirm still exists? Why or why not? (*Robertson v. Robertson,* 229 So.2d 642, 1969.)

3. Hughes, a minor, purchased a television set from Houghton and paid cash for it. Six months later, while Hughes was still a minor, the set was badly damaged by a fire in his apartment. Hughes now wants to return the set and recover the full purchase price. Under the majority rule, can he do so? Explain.

4. Ballinger and his wife, while minors, purchased a mobile home. In payment, they gave the seller of the home a promissory note which they signed as co-makers. Before reaching the age of majority they disaffirmed the contract and the note. The seller then brought suit against them to recover the reasonable value of the home, on the ground that it constituted a necessity of life. At the trial, the Ballingers introduced evidence showing that Ballinger's parents were more than willing to furnish them with living accommodations in their own home at the time they made the purchase, and thereafter. What bearing, if any, would this evidence have on the question whether the home constituted a necessity? Explain your reasoning. (*Ballinger v. Craig,* 121 N.E.2d 66, 1953.)

5. Daubert, a minor, was involved in an automobile accident in which he and the other driver, Mosley, were both injured. At the time of the accident Daubert was an army veteran, married and the father of a newborn child, and was gainfully employed. After the accident, and while still a minor, Daubert signed and gave to Mosley a release of all claims he might have against Mosley as a result of the accident. When Daubert later sought to disaffirm this release and recover the amount of his doctor bills from Mosley, Mosley contended that the release affected Daubert's necessities of life, and therefore could not be disaffirmed. Do you agree? Explain. (*Daubert v. Mosley,* 487 P.2d 353, 1971.)

6. Chauncey, aged 17, sold his 1949 Anteater automobile for $500 to Chang, an adult. Two weeks later Chauncey and Chang were both highly surprised to learn that the Anteater was a collector's item and easily worth $6,000. If Chauncey now seeks to disaffirm the sale, will the fact that Chang had no idea of the car's true value mean that Chauncey will not be successful in retaking it? Why or why not?

7. Robert Moore opened joint savings accounts in two banks, with the accounts listing a nephew and niece as co-depositors. These accounts, if valid, would result in the money in them passing to the nephew and niece as gifts upon Moore's death. After Moore died, other relatives brought a court action to set aside these joint accounts on the ground that Moore was incompetent to contract at the time that he established them. To support this contention, these relatives produced evidence that over a period of several weeks prior to the opening of the accounts Moore had often been found wandering on city streets late at night, not knowing where he was; that on one occasion he tried to extinguish the cooking units on his electric stove by pouring water on them; that a neighbor stopped transacting business with him "because he acted so queerly," and that he was once stopped on a street by a police officer because of "insufficient clothing." Do you think this evidence is sufficient to support the relatives' claim that Moore was incompetent when he made the transactions with the banks? Can you think of other evidence that might contradict this claim? Discuss. (*In re Moore's Estate*, 188 N.E.2d 221, 1962.)

8. St. Pierre, aged 17, sold a snowmobile to Derek, who resold it to Owens. St. Pierre, still a minor, now wishes to disaffirm the sale contract and recover the vehicle from Owens. Do you think St. Pierre should be allowed to do so, regardless of whether or not Owens knew the original owner was a minor? Discuss.

Illegality 12

The fourth element of a contract is *legality of purpose*—the attainment of an objective that is not prohibited by state or federal law. In this chapter we will examine some of the most common kinds of contracts that are ordinarily illegal under state law.[1] Within a given state, a contract is illegal because it is either (1) contrary to statute or (2) contrary to the public policy of that state, as defined by its courts.

All states have criminal statutes; these not only prohibit certain acts but provide for the imposition of fines or imprisonment on persons who violate them. Any contract calling for the commission of a crime is clearly illegal. Many other statutes simply prohibit the performance of specified acts without imposing criminal penalties for violations. Contracts that call for the performance of these acts are also illegal. (An example of the latter is lending money under an agreement that obligates the borrower to pay interest at a rate in excess of that permitted by statute.)

---

[1]Certain federal statutes that have a bearing on the legality of contracts in interstate commerce will be covered in Part VIII.

Still other contracts are illegal simply because they call for the performance of an act that the courts feel has an adverse effect on the general public. (Examples of contracts contrary to public policy are those under which a person promises never to get married or never to engage in a certain profession.)

As a general rule, contracts that are illegal on either statutory or public policy grounds are not enforceable in court. Certain exceptions to this rule will be discussed later in the chapter.

Contracts Contrary to Statute

Wagering Agreements

All states have statutes relating to gambling contracts. Under the general language of most of these statutes, making bets and operating games of chance are prohibited. Any obligations arising from these activities are "void" (nonexistent) in the eyes of the law and thus completely unenforceable.

In most instances wagering agreements are easily recognized. Simple bets on the outcome of athletic events and lotteries such as bingo (when played for money) are the most common of them.[2] In recent years a growing number of state statutes have been liberalized to permit these activities within narrow limits. For example, so-called friendly bets—those defined as not producing substantial sources of income—are frequently exempted, as are some lotteries operated by religious institutions. Additionally, a few states have sanctioned state-operated lotteries by special statutes.

Of course, many contracts whose performance is dependent upon an element of chance are clearly not wagers. This is particularly true of *risk-shifting* (as distinguished from *risk-creating*) contracts. If a person insures his home against loss by fire, for example, the contract is perfectly legal even though it is not known at the time the policy is issued whether the insurer will have liability under it. The contract is legal despite this uncertainty because the owner had an "insurable interest" in the home prior to taking out the policy—that is, he would have incurred a financial loss if a fire had occurred.[3] Thus an insurance policy is simply a contract by which an existing risk is shifted to an insurance company for a consideration paid by the owner.

Some other contracts present more difficult problems in determining legality. A case in point is a "futures contract" in the commodity markets, under which a seller contracts to sell, at a specified price, a quantity of goods, such as corn or wheat, that he presently does not own, with delivery to be made at a designated

---

[2]Definition of the term *lottery* is frequently left to the courts; a typical one is "any scheme for the distribution of property by chance, among persons who have paid or agreed to pay a valuable consideration for the chance, whether called a lottery, a raffle, a gift enterprise [or] some other name." *Wishing Well Club v. City of Akron*, 112 N.E.2d 41 (1951).

[3]A common statutory definition of this term is as follows: "Every interest in property, or any relation thereto, or liability in respect thereof, of such a nature that a contemplated peril might directly damnify the insured, is an insurable interest." Civil Code, California, S. 2546.

time in the future. While this may constitute a wager under certain circumstances, such contracts are generally held to be lawful on one of two grounds.

1. Many futures contracts are merely hedging transactions, which the seller engages in simply as a means of protecting a legitimate business profit. These are clearly not wagers.

2. Other futures contracts are not considered to be wagering agreements as long as the parties, at the time of contracting, intend that an actual delivery of the commodity (or of a contract under which delivery can be obtained) will be made at the specified time. This intention is ordinarily presumed to be the case in the absence of evidence to the contrary.

Thus the only illegal futures contracts are those where evidence clearly proves that an actual delivery was never intended, with the parties merely "agreeing to settle on differences"—that is, betting on the direction the market price will move in the future.

Licensing Statutes

All states have statutes requiring that persons who engage in certain professions, trades, or businesses be licensed. Lawyers, physicians, real estate brokers, contractors, electricians, and vendors of milk and liquor are but a few examples of persons commonly subject to a wide variety of such statutes. In many instances, particularly those involving the professions, passing a comprehensive examination (along with proof of good moral character) is a condition of obtaining a license. In others, only proof of good moral character may be required.

To find out whether an unlicensed person can recover for services rendered under a contract, one must check the particular statute involved. Some licensing statutes expressly provide that recovery by unlicensed persons shall not be allowed (no matter how competent their work).[4] Others, however, are silent on the matter, in which case their underlying purposes must be determined. Most courts take the view in such instances that if the statute is *regulatory*—its purpose being the protection of the general public against unqualified persons—then the contract is illegal and recovery is denied. On the other hand, if the statute is felt to be merely *revenue-raising,* recovery is allowed.

The reasoning behind this distinction, of course, is that allowing recovery of a fee or commission by an unlicensed person in the first category would adversely affect public health and safety, while the enforcement of contracts in the second category does not have this result. Thus an unlicensed milk vendor who has sold and delivered a quantity of milk will ordinarily not be permitted to recover the purchase price from the buyer. Similarly, an unlicensed physician, real estate agent, or attorney will be denied his or her fee. On the other hand, a corporation that has merely failed to obtain a license to do business in a particular city is still permitted

---

[4]A provision that contracts made in violation of the statute shall be void usually, though not always, has this effect.

to enforce its contracts, because city licensing ordinances are normally enacted for revenue-raising purposes.

The possibility that a regulatory statute might be passed for the protection of some persons, but not others, is presented in the case below.

Bremmeyer v. Peter Kiewit Sons Company

Supreme Court of Washington, 585 P.2d 1174 (1978)

The State of Washington awarded Peter Kiewit a prime contract to construct several miles of Interstate 90. The highway right-of-way was overgrown, and needed to have the trees and debris cleared before construction could begin. For this purpose, Peter Kiewit subcontracted the necessary clearing operation to Bremmeyer. Under the subcontract, Bremmeyer agreed to pay Peter Kiewit $35,000 for the right to fall, yard, buck, load and haul to a mill all the merchantable timber within the right-of-way. (Bremmeyer was to keep the proceeds of the sale as his compensation.)

Bremmeyer paid the $35,000 and began clearing the right-of-way, but before he had finished the job the state terminated Peter Kiewit's prime contract. Peter Kiewit, in turn, cancelled Bremmeyer's subcontract. Peter Kiewit received $1,729,050 from the state for "cancellation costs," but offered to pay Bremmeyer only $38 for cancellation of the contract. Bremmeyer refused the $38 and brought this action to recover the value of the merchantable timber that was still uncut at the time of termination.

In defense, Peter Kiewit's primary argument was that a state statute, RCW 18.27, required contractors to be registered with the state, and that Bremmeyer's failure to register barred his recovery. The trial court, citing a 1973 Washington State case, agreed with this contention and summarily dismissed the action. Bremmeyer appealed.

Stafford, Justice. . . . We first considered whether the legislature intended RCW 18.27 to bar actions by unregistered subcontractors against prime contractors in *Jeanneret v. Rees,* 511 P.2d 60 (1973). A majority of the court agreed the legislature intended to preclude such actions. [The court then went on to say, however, that it now felt that its decision in that case was based on too literal a reading of the statute, and thus was not necessarily controlling. The court continued.]

Continued reliance upon the literal expression of RCW 18.27 is particularly inappropriate in light of the legislature's amendment to the statute after our divided opinion in *Jeanneret.* . . . A new section now provides:

It is the purpose of this chapter to afford protection *to the public* from unreliable, fraudulent, financially irresponsible, or incompetent contractors. (Emphasis supplied by the court).

In view of this newly declared statutory purpose and the minimal protections afforded the public by the statute, we are convinced the legislature did not intend to protect prime contractors from actions initiated by unregistered subcontractors. The statutory purpose clearly provides protection *to the public,* i.e., the customers of building contractors. In light of the amendment, and considering the judicial history of RCW 18.27 we do not believe the legislature also intended to protect contractors *from each other.* . . .

Our conclusion that the legislature did not intend to bar actions by unregistered subcontractors against prime contractors is also supported by the practicalities of the contracting trade. Members of the trade are in a more nearly equal bargaining position with respect to *each other*. Not only is information concerning financial responsibility and competence readily attainable within the trade, but each contractor is knowledgeable concerning the financial protections needed for any particular job involved. . . .

Judgment reversed, and cause remanded for trial.

Sunday Contracts

At common law, contracts made on Sunday were perfectly legal. Today, however, most states have statutes prohibiting the transaction of certain kinds of business on that day. Under such statutes, as a result of judicial interpretation, contracts that are entered into on a Sunday may be illegal—even though performance is to occur another day. (However, active *enforcement* of the Sunday statutes varies widely, even among communities in the same state.)

It is difficult to summarize the kinds of contracts that are likely to be illegal on this ground, primarily because the statutes vary widely in scope. A few states, for example, have statutes that forbid carrying on "all secular labor and business on the Sabbath." Under such statutes, virtually all contracts made on a Sunday are illegal (and thus unenforceable as long as they remain executory).

At the other extreme, the statutes of some states merely prohibit the sale of certain kinds of goods on Sunday. Under these narrow statutes, all contracts made on Sunday (except those calling for the sale of the specified kinds of goods) are perfectly lawful.

Most states have adopted statutes between these extremes. Typical laws prohibit "common labor and the opening of a building for the transaction of business" on Sunday, "except in cases of work of necessity or charity."

While the legal status of a particular Sunday contract can be determined only by resort to the applicable statute and case law, several generalizations can be made about the status of such contracts under the "middle ground" statute referred to above.

1. The main thrust of such a statute is to prohibit Sunday sales of goods rather than to invalidate Sunday contracts generally. Thus such agreements as employment contracts and leases made on Sunday are probably lawful and enforceable.

2. Where a sale of goods in violation of the statute does occur, the transaction—if totally executed—will normally not be rescinded by a court despite its illegality. Thus, if B purchases a television set on Sunday from the S Company, with B making full payment and receiving possession on that day, neither he nor the S Company can subsequently rescind the agreement. On the other hand, if B contracts to buy the set on Sunday, with payment of the purchase price to be made later, B's executory promise to pay the price later is probably unenforceable on the ground of illegality. Some courts might even hold that B not only is free of the obligation to pay for the set but also can retain possession of it.

3. Particularly in regard to contracts other than those calling for the sale of goods, the tendency of the courts is to uphold Sunday contracts if it is reasonably possible to do so. Frequently they do this by ruling that the contract did not constitute the "transaction of business" within the intent of the statute or that it was "reasonably necessary" under the circumstances.

4. Many of the middle-ground statutes expressly provide that certain kinds of Sunday business activities are lawful. Section 3773.24 of the Ohio Revised Code, for example, provides in part that "this statute shall not apply to (A) traveling or the providing of services or commodities incidental thereto," (B) recreation, sports or amusement activities, and (C) state, county, or independent fairs.

Usury

Partly as a result of religious views going back to early biblical statements, and partly because of the practical hardships resulting from high interest rates charged desperate borrowers, all states have statutes establishing the maximum rate of interest that can be charged on ordinary loans. Charging interest in excess of the permitted rate constitutes *usury.*

The interest ceilings that are imposed by the usury statutes vary from state to state. Traditionally the basic statutes have varied from 6 percent to 12 percent per annum. However, as a result of inflationary pressures in recent years, the basic statutes now generally range from 10 percent to 16 percent per annum.

More importantly, many kinds of loans are not governed by the basic state statutes. For example, most states put no limit on the rate of interest that can be charged on loans made to corporations. And, under federal regulations, national banks are permitted to charge interest rates that are usually in excess of those permitted by the state usury laws.

Additionally, all states in recent years—again, partly because of inflationary pressures—have adopted special statutes permitting higher rates of interest on other specified kinds of loans. For example, most state laws today provide that interest rates charged by issuers of bank credit cards (such as Visa and Master Card), and by department stores on their revolving credit accounts, can be at an annual percentage rate of 18 percent. Similarly, home purchase and construction loans, car loans, and loans by credit unions may generally carry 18 percent interest rates.)[5]

The basic statutes also vary widely insofar as the effect of usury is concerned. Many states permit the usurious lender to recover the principal and interest at the lawful rate, but not the excess interest. In such states the lender suffers no penalty.

---

[5]It should also be noted that all states but one have adopted special statutes that expressly permit small loan companies, such as "personal loan companies," to charge rates of interest that are considerably higher than those of the general interest statutes. For example, a loan company that qualifies under such statutes may be allowed to charge interest at the rate of 3 percent *per month* on the first $150 of a loan, 2 percent per month on the amount from $151 to $300, and 1 percent on the balance. These statutes usually provide that if interest is charged in excess of the specified rates, the loan is void. In such a case, neither principal nor interest can be recovered.

In others, the lender is permitted to recover the principal only, forfeiting all interest. And in three or four states, the lender forfeits both interest and principal.

It is thus clear that no determination can be made as to the legality or effect of a given loan without inspecting the statutes of the state in which the transaction took place.

Resale Price Maintenance Contracts

In earlier years, sellers of goods often inserted in their sales contracts provisions forbidding the buyer to resell the goods below a specified price. For example, a manufacturer might sell 1000 widgets to a retailer for $900 under a contract obligating the retailer to charge a minimum price of $1.50 each upon resale.

All such clauses—"resale price maintenance" provisions—in contracts that involve the sale of goods in interstate commerce are clearly illegal today. Such transactions come under the federal antitrust laws, and the U.S. Supreme Court has ruled that this kind of a provision in a contract unreasonably restrains trade—and is thus a violation of Section 1 of the Sherman Act. Therefore, in the above example—assuming that interstate commerce is involved—the retailer is free to set the widgets at any price he wishes. Furthermore, the manufacturer in this situation might be subject to civil and/or criminal penalties under the Sherman Act.[6]

Contracts in Restraint of Trade

Contracts Contrary to Public Policy

Many contracts that unreasonably restrain trade or competition in interstate commerce are in violation of one or more federal statutes, such as the Sherman and Clayton acts.[7] Long before the enactment of these statutes, however, many other contracts in restraint of trade were illegal under the common law of the various states, and this continues to be the case today. Thus a contract that is not subject to Sherman or Clayton may still result in such restraint of trade that courts will set it aside under common-law principles. These principles are briefly summarized here.

Contracts under which one person agrees not to engage in a particular profession or trade, or not to operate a certain kind of business, comprise one group of contracts that are in restraint of trade. However, the promises—called *covenants not to compete*—made in such contracts are not necessarily illegal.

Generally, covenants not to compete are lawful if two conditions are met. First, the covenant must be of an "ancillary" nature, and, second, the restriction (the covenant) must be reasonable under the circumstances.

---

[6]Between 1937 and the end of 1975, resale price maintenance contracts in interstate commerce were generally lawful, because the Miller-Tydings Act essentially exempted such contracts from the operation of the Sherman Act. Effective March 13, 1976, however, Congress repealed the Miller-Tydings Act when it became clear that a major result of this exemption was an unacceptable stifling of price competition among retailers.

[7]These acts, and other federal statutes of a similar nature, are examined in Part VIII.

An ancillary covenant is one that is a subsidiary or auxiliary part of a larger agreement. Probably the most common example of an ancillary covenant is found in a contract to sell a business that contains a promise by the seller not to engage in the same type of business within a prescribed area for a certain length of time after the sale. Another common example is the covenant of an employee not to compete with the business of his employer for a specified period of time after the employment is terminated. (Nonancillary promises, on the other hand, stand alone; they do not protect any legally recognized interest. These covenants, such as a promise by a father to pay $10,000 for the son's promise not to engage in medical practice—are generally considered an unreasonable restraint of trade in all circumstances, and thus illegal and unenforceable on that ground.)

The requirement that an ancillary restraint be "reasonable" means that it must afford no greater protection to the party in whose favor it operates than is necessary under the particular circumstances. For example, a promise by the seller of a retail grocery in Kalispell, Montana, that he will not engage in the retail grocery business "within the City of Kalispell for the period of one year after the sale" is probably reasonable and thus lawful. If the seller violates his promise, the purchaser of the business is entitled to an injunction against him. (On the other hand, if the seller had promised not to engage in such a business "anywhere within the State of Montana for ten years," the restraint would be considered excessive, and thus illegal.)

Where ancillary restraints are found to be unreasonably broad, what relief, if any, is the covenantor entitled to? At the risk of overgeneralization, we can say that the courts of most states follow the traditional view, striking down the covenant entirely. If, for example, the grocery seller who promised not to compete anywhere in Montana for ten years wanted to reenter the grocery business, he could do so anywhere in the state, including Kalispell, at any time. The courts of a number of states, however, will "reform" the covenant, determining for themselves what a reasonable limitation would be and then applying it to the case. In the grocery case, involving the state-wide prohibition, for example, such courts might restrain the seller from doing business in Kalispell, but not elsewhere in the state, for a period of a year or two.

. The following case involves application of the foregoing principles.

Gann v. Morris

Court of Appeals of
Arizona, Ariz.App., 596
P.2d 43, (1979)

Alfred and Connie Gann bought a silk screening business in Tucson in 1974 from Gerry Morris. As part of the deal, Morris promised that he would not operate a competing business for the next ten years. (The exact provisions of this covenant not to compete appear in the decision below.) Thereafter, Morris violated this promise, and the Ganns sued to recover damages for breach of contract.

The trial court rejected Morris' contention that the promise not to compete was contrary to public policy, and thus illegal. Accordingly, the court entered judgment for the Ganns, and Morris appealed.

Richmond, Chief Judge: . . . The [sale] agreement provided in part:

> Seller agrees not to enter into silk screening or lettering shop business within Tucson and a 100-mile radius of Tucson, a period of ten (10) years from the date of this Agreement and will not compete in any manner whatsoever with buyers, and seller further agrees that he will refer all business contacts to buyers . . .

Seller urges that the contract, including the covenant not to compete, is unenforceable as a restraint of trade which violates public policy.

Covenants not to compete, although amounting to partial restraints of trade, will be enforced where they are ancillary to contracts for employment or sale of a business and are reasonably limited as to time and territory. What is reasonable depends on the whole subject matter of the contract, the kind and character of the business, its location, the purpose to be accomplished by the restriction, and all the circumstances which show the intention of the parties.

Courts distinguish between covenants incidental to employment contracts and those incidental to sales of businesses because the policy considerations necessarily differ. In the case of employment contracts, an employee is restricted from using his personal skills and experience, which may seriously impair his ability to earn a living. In light of the potential hardship and uneven bargaining position of the parties, courts scrutinize employer-employee agreements closely. [On the other hand,] courts have shown greater reluctance to interfere where the contract involves the sale of a business. In either case, whether the contract is reasonable is generally held to be a matter of law for the court to decide.

Where limited as to time and space, the covenant is ordinarily valid unless it is to refrain from all business whatsoever. Here, the seller agreed not to enter into the silk screening or lettering shop business within Tucson and a 100-mile radius of Tucson for 10 years. Although the covenant goes on to say that seller will not compete in any manner whatsoever, that language is clearly limited by the subject matter of the entire contract to the kind and character of the business sold.

The rationale for enforcing covenants not to compete is particularly valid in the case of a small business, operated by an individual who had developed a clientele and a reputation in a specialized business area. The sale of such a business necessarily includes the sale of good will, and the purchaser has the right to assure himself or herself as best they can of the transfer of the good will.

At the time of the sale in this case, one of the customers of the business had offices in Benson, Phoenix and San Manuel, an area extending beyond the 100-mile restriction in the agreement. Restrictions for 10 years or more have been upheld [in similar cases] where it was determined that the covenant was reasonable under all the circumstances.

From the foregoing, we conclude the scope of the covenant in this case [affords no more protection] than is necessary to protect the interest of the buyers of a small silk screening business, and [is thus a reasonable one]. The seller offered no evidence to the contrary. Under the circumstances, the buyers are entitled to enforcement of the covenant as written. . . .

Judgment affirmed.

Contracts with Exculpatory Clauses

In Part I we saw that the law of torts imposes certain duties on all persons, one of which is to carry out one's activities in a reasonably careful manner. If a person violates this duty by performing an act carelessly, he or she is guilty of the tort of negligence and is answerable in damages to anyone who was injured thereby.

Many people attempt to avoid this potential liability by the use of contracts containing *exculpatory clauses*—clauses providing that one party agrees to free the other of all liability in the event that he or she suffers a physical or monetary injury in a particular situation, even if the loss is caused by the negligence of the other party to the contract. In most circumstances these clauses are considered contrary to public policy and thus illegal; in other circumstances they may be lawful and enforceable.

Because the courts do not favor such clauses, they have recognized a number of grounds on which to base a finding that they are *contrary to public policy*. Exculpatory clauses in contracts that actually or potentially affect large segments of the populace usually fall in this category, as do contracts in which the party being released possesses a marked superiority of bargaining power over the other party.[8] Accordingly, such clauses in leases (under the terms of which the tenant agrees to free the landlord from all liability in case of loss) and in employment contracts usually are set aside by the courts on one or both of these grounds.

The decision in an 1886 landmark case is particularly instructive on the public policy aspects of employment contracts.[9] A brakeman was employed by a railroad under a contract containing a provision that

> . . . he hereby agrees with said railway, in consideration of such employment, that he will take upon himself all risks incident to his position on the road, and will in no case hold the company liable for any injury or damage he may sustain, in his person or otherwise, by accidents or collisions on the trains or road, or which may result from defective machinery, or carelessness or misconduct of himself or any other employee and servant of the company.

The brakeman subsequently was killed in an accident caused by a defective switch, and his estate brought an action against the railroad to recover damages.

Evidence at the trial indicated that the switch's defective condition was the result of negligence on the part of the railroad. The railroad contended that, even so, the quoted provision released it of liability. The trial court held that the provision was illegal on the ground that it was contrary to public policy, and entered judgment for the estate. The appellate court agreed, spelling out the public policy considerations in these words:

> It is an elementary principle in the law of contracts that the form of agreement and the convention of parties override the law. But the maxim is not

---

[8]If neither of these factors is present, exculpatory clauses frequently are held to be lawful, assuming they are given sufficient prominence in the contract. (The case of *Owen v. Vic Tanny's Enterprises, Inc.* 199 N.E.2d 280 [1964] is a case in point, and one containing a particularly instructive decision in this area of the law.)

[9]*Little Rock & Fort Smith Ry. Co. v. Eubanks,* 3 S.W. 808 (1886).

of universal application. Parties are permitted, by contract, to make a law for themselves only in cases where their agreements do not violate the express provisions of any law, nor injuriously affect the interest of the public. . . . The law requires the master to furnish his servant with a reasonably safe place to work in, and with sound and suitable tools and appliances to do his work. *If he can supply an unsafe machine, or defective instruments, and then excuse himself against the consequences of his own negligence by the terms of his contract with his servant, he is enabled to evade a most salutary rule.* [Emphasis added.]

[The defendant argues that this provision] is not against public policy, because it does not affect all society, but only the interest of the employed. But surely the state has an interest in the lives and limbs of all its citizens. Laborers for hire constitute a numerous and meritorious class in every community. And it is for the welfare of society that their employers shall not be permitted, under the guise of enforcing contract rights, to abdicate their duties to them. The consequence would be that every railroad company, and every owner of a factory, mill, or mine, would make it a condition precedent to the employment of labor, that the laborer should release all right of action for injuries sustained in the course of the service, whether by the employer's negligence or otherwise. The natural tendency of this would be to relax the employer's carefulness in those matters of which he has the ordering and control, such as the supplying of machinery and materials, and thus increase the perils of occupations which are hazardous even when well managed. And the final outcome would be to fill the country with disabled men and paupers, whose support would become a charge upon the counties or upon public charity.

Bailment Contracts: *Bailment contracts* are similar to leases and employment contracts in that they too are so widely used as to substantially affect the public interest. Accordingly, the status of exculpatory clauses in such contracts is essentially the same as those in leases and employment contracts—that is, highly suspect in the eyes of the law.

A *bailment* occurs when the owner of an article of personal property temporarily relinquishes the possession and control of it to another. The person who has parted with the possession is the *bailor,* and the one receiving it is the *bailee.* Typical bailments result from checking a coat at a nightclub and leaving a car at a garage for repairs.

Under general bailment law, a bailee is liable for any damages to, or loss of, the property that is the result of his or her negligence—the failure to use reasonable care under the circumstances. Bailees frequently attempt to escape this liability by the use of an exculpatory clause in the bailment contract. Companies operating parking lots, for example, customarily print on the back of identification tickets something like the following: "The company will endeavor to protect the property of its patrons, but it is agreed that it will not be liable for loss or damage to cars, accessories, or contents, from whatever cause arising."[10]

As suggested earlier, such a clause is contrary to public policy—at least to the extent that it purports to free the bailee from liability for loss caused by his or her negligence. The reasoning, of course, is analogous to that applied in the illustration involving the employment contract—specifically, that if such a clause were given effect, all bailees would utilize it, with a consequent lessening of care on their part. As a result, such provisions do not prevent a bailor whose property is damaged while in the bailee's hands from bringing suit. If it is established that the loss was occasioned by negligence on the part of the bailee, the bailor can recover damages.[11]

Other Illegal Contracts

Many other contracts are generally held to be contrary to public policy. Of these, one broad class deserves comment—contracts that "injure the public service." Promises to pay legislators money in return for their votes and similar promises to judges in return for favorable rulings are clearly injurious to the public and therefore illegal. On the other hand, *lobbying contracts,* under which a person is employed by a third party to influence a legislator's vote or an administrator's decision in the awarding of a contract, are not necessarily illegal. The legality of such contracts largely depends on the propriety of the means used by the lobbyist. If, for example, an engineer simply agrees, for a fee, to present to a lawmaker or administrator factual information tending to show the superiority of one product or material over another, the means are proper and the agreement is not contrary to public policy. A contract, however, that contemplates influencing a government official essentially by reliance on the lobbyist's long personal friendship with that person would be illegal.

In regard to *contingent fee contracts,* under which payment of the fee is conditional upon passage of a particular bill or awarding of a contract, many courts flatly deny the lobbyist recovery of his or her fee under any circumstances—on the ground that the tendency of such contracts to induce improper activities is, by itself, sufficient to cause them to be contrary to public policy. Other courts, in such cases, permit the lobbyist to recover if he or she can prove proper conduct—that is, conduct free of deception, undue pressure, and the like.

---

[10]While leaving a car at a parking lot creates a bailor-bailee relationship under ordinary circumstances, this is not always true. Many courts, for example, rule that such a relationship is not created if the patron is permitted to keep the car keys, on the theory that the lot operator in such a case is not given control of the car.

[11]Clauses that place a *limit* on the bailee's liability, in the event of a loss, are viewed more favorably by the courts. Such provisions, if reasonable, are usually not considered to be illegal. Additionally, some bailees are expressly permitted by statute to limit their liability by contract. Under federal law, for example, common carriers in interstate commerce are permitted to do so within limits approved by the Interstate Commerce Commission; thus the limitations commonly found in bills of lading and other transportation contracts are generally enforceable.

As a general rule, illegal contracts are unenforceable. This means that neither party **Effect of Illegal** to such a contract will be assisted by the courts in any way, regardless of the **Contracts** consequences to the parties involved. Thus, if S brings suit to recover the purchase price of a quantity of liquor that he has sold and delivered to B in violation of law, his action will be dismissed. Conversely, if B had paid the purchase price when the contract was made and S subsequently failed to deliver the liquor, any action brought by B to recover the price will also be unavailing.

Courts feel that such a hands-off policy is, in most cases, the best way to discourage the making of illegal contracts. There are exceptional situations, however, in which the courts feel that the results obtained under such a policy are so offensive as to warrant some measure of judicial relief. We will examine three of these situations.

Rights of Protected Parties

Some statutes have as their clear purpose the protection of a certain class of persons. Any contract made in violation of such a statute is enforceable by persons within that class, despite its illegality. For example: a Nebraska insurance company, not licensed to sell insurance in Colorado, issues a fire insurance policy on K's home in Denver. The home is destroyed by fire, and the company refuses to pay on the ground that the contract was illegal. The company is liable on its policy. It would be ludicrous if K, a person for whose benefit the licensing statutes were enacted, were to be denied recovery on the ground of illegality.

Parties Not Equally at Fault

In most illegal contracts the parties are considered to be equally at fault—that is, each should have known the contract was unlawful. If, however, one party to an illegal contract can show that he or she is innocent of wrongdoing, did not have knowledge of the illegality, and the fault was essentially that of the other party, the innocent party may be entitled to judicial assistance. In such a case, it is said that the parties were "not in *pari delicto*"—not at equal fault.

This exception applies particularly to situations where the party seeking judicial aid was ignorant of essential facts when the contract was made, through no fault of his or her own. For example: X forges a warehouse receipt, which makes it appear that he is the owner of certain goods stored at a warehouse. X takes the receipt to a trucking company and employs it to pick up the goods at the warehouse and to deliver them to his place of business. The trucking company does so, not knowing that X is not the owner of the goods. The company is entitled to receive its transportation charge from X, even though it was a participant in an illegal transaction.

Severable Contracts

Sometimes a single contract turns out on analysis to be two separate agreements. This can be illustrated by a contract under which a retiring restaurant owner agrees to sell to a former competitor his "ten pinball machines for $450 and one electric broiler for $75." In such a contract, the fact that one of the agreements may be illegal does not prevent the other from being enforced. Thus, if the sale of the pinball machines is prohibited by law, the seller is still under an obligation, enforceable in court, to deliver the broiler. However, most contracts that contain several promises on the part of both parties are not severable. The promises of the two parties usually are so interdependent that the court must rule that they resulted in the creation of a single, indivisible contract. In such cases, if any part of the contract is illegal, the entire agreement is unenforceable. The next case presents a typical fact-pattern involving this area of the law.

**Fong et al.
v. Miller**

District Court of
Appeal, California, 233
P.2d 606 (1951)

Ruby Miller, defendant, owned a cafe known as Gate Inn, located in Jackson, California, consisting of a bar and a restaurant. She wished to be relieved from the management of the restaurant; and on January 1, 1946, she entered into a contract with Horace and Fulton Fong, the plaintiffs, to achieve this end.

The contract, which was in essence a lease of the restaurant, basically provided that the Fongs would operate and manage the restaurant, in return for which they would receive all the proceeds from the restaurant plus one-fourth "of the net revenue derived from the operation of the bar and amusement machines" therein. (The record did not indicate whether the operation of the bar was to be taken over by the Fongs; apparently it continued to be operated by Miller.)

The contract also provided that any additional equipment or construction added to the restaurant would be paid for by the Fongs, which additions would remain their property except where the removal of them would damage the building in which they were located; that all licenses for the conduct of Miller's business would be taken out and maintained in her name, but that the Fongs would pay to her as rental for the restaurant premises a sum equal to one-half the total of all license fees required for the operation of all businesses operated upon the premises; and that the Fongs would pay all expenses of operating the restaurant.

The Fongs improved the restaurant by spending over $4,000 on additional equipment and over $1,000 in constructing living quarters to be used by their help. They then began the operation of the restaurant as agreed upon. Differences arose between the parties, and about two months after the Fongs moved in, Miller locked them out. Treating this eviction as a breach of contract, the Fongs brought action to recover the amounts expended in connection with the restaurant and $15,000 additional as compensation for loss of prospective profits. (At the trial the Fongs waived their claim to these profits.) The parties stipulated that the "amusement machines" referred to in the contract, which were being operated by Miller, were in fact slot machines, punchboards, a roulette table, and a blackjack table and that the term used in the contract was so understood. The trial court, deeming the contract to be tainted with illegality, denied relief to plaintiffs on that ground. From the judgment entered (granting them nothing), plaintiffs appealed.

Van Dyke, Justice: . . . We think the trial court was correct in its analysis of the contract and in its conclusions that no relief could be granted appellants, notwithstanding the respondent's alleged wrongful acts. As a general rule, to which there are exceptions, a party to an illegal contract can neither recover damages for breach nor by rescinding recover the performance that he has rendered or its value.

Under certain conditions, notwithstanding that one is a party to an illegal bargain, relief may be accorded if such party be not in *pari delicto,* but we are unable to conceive how appellants here could claim that they occupied that innocent position. Under the contract they were to operate the restaurant and to receive as their compensation therefor not only the profits from the restaurant, but [also] . . . a share of the profits from the bar and from the gambling devices. What they did in operating the restaurant may have been honest enough, but when they agreed that they were to be given for their services 25 percent of the profits derived from gambling they tainted their contract with illegality. This made it to their interest that the gambling should flourish in order that their profits therefrom might be enhanced. To say that such a consideration could be valid and that a contract requiring its payments would not be unlawful would be to say that a laborer might, because his labor was honest, lawfully agree that he should be paid from the profits of a crime which the parties contemplated his employer would engage in. The trial court correctly held that the appellants were in *pari delicto* and that the contract was unlawful and that the court should leave the parties where it found them.

Appellants argue that this contract possessed a dual nature and that one part of it, which they call a lease, could be completely separated from the unlawful agreement to receive a share in the profits of crime. But we think that the contract cannot receive such construction. Notwithstanding the agreement was to last for five years, and assuming that the appellants might lawfully receive the proceeds from the operation of the restaurant, it is yet quite clear from the terms of the contract itself that such profits were not the sole consideration moving to the appellants under the agreement. In addition to the profits from the restaurant, they were to receive a share in the profits of contemplated illegal action. That provision rendered the contract void. The contract made it clear that the consideration moving to respondent was the operation by appellants of the restaurant in connection with her liquor-selling and gambling business. "If any part . . . of several considerations for a single object is unlawful, the entire contract is void." Civ. Code. § 1608.

Appellants urge that by waiving their claim for future profits and confining their demands to the cost of their added equipment and reconstruction they freed their contract of the taint of illegality. But these things did not change the nature of the contract nor relieve the appellants from the rule invoked against them by the trial court. Appellants bitterly complain that the court's action leaves the respondent unjustly enriched. The complaint is a familiar one and is generally made by those who, deeming themselves wronged by their companions in illegal ventures, find themselves denied any right to enforce their unlawful agreements. Their pleas have always been unavailing. "This rule is not generally applied to secure justice between parties who have made an illegal contract, but from regard for a higher interest—that of the public, whose welfare demands that certain transactions be discouraged." *Takeuchi v. Schmuck,* 276 P. 345.

Judgment affirmed.

1. Wilson was a licensed Hawaii architect who rendered extensive professional services for the owner of a ranch. When he sought his $33,900 fee, the owner refused to pay because Wilson had failed to pay a $15 state "annual registration fee." Does this failure to pay render Wilson's contract illegal, as the ranch owner contends? Explain. (*Wilson v. Kealakekua Ranch, Ltd.*, 551 P.2d 525, 1976.)

2. Bonasera brought an action against Roffe to recover a real estate commission due him for finding a buyer for Roffe's property. Bonasera was not a licensed broker, and Roffe's defense was an Arizona statute providing that only licensed brokers could recover real estate commissions in that state. Bonasera contended that the statute was not applicable to him since he was not in the real estate business, his activity in this instance being but a "single, isolated transaction." *Bonasera v. Roffe*, 442 P.2d 165 (1968). Is the statute applicable to Bonasera? Explain.

3. A brewery rented a building "for use as a saloon" for a period of eight years. Five years later the state enacted a statute making the sale of liquor illegal. The brewing company claimed that passage of the statute freed it of its obligations under the lease for the three remaining years. Is this argument correct? Why or why not? (*Heart v. East Tennessee Brewing Co.*, 113 S.W. 364, 1908.)

4. What are resale price maintenance contracts, and why are they illegal today when used in interstate commerce?

5. Lally sold a barbershop located in Rockville, Connecticut, "together with all good will," to Mattis. The bill of sale contained a clause providing that Lally would not engage in the barbering business in any capacity for a period of five years "anywhere in the City of Rockville, or within a radius of one mile" of the shop's location on Market Street in Rockville. (The one-mile alternative was included because the shop was located only a quarter of a mile from the Rockville city limits.) After the sale, Lally operated a restaurant; but when this became unprofitable a year or two later, he opened a one-chair barbershop in his own home, three hundred yards from the shop Mattis had purchased. When Mattis's business fell off thereafter, he brought an action asking the court to enforce the restrictive clause in the contract. Lally contended that the clause in question constituted an unreasonable restraint of trade and was therefore unlawful. *Mattis v. Lally*, 82 A.2d 155 (1951). Is Lally's contention correct? Explain.

6. Soble, a lawyer, represented a client in a condemnation suit—ie., a suit in which the client's land was being taken by the state. Soble employed an expert real estate appraiser, Laos, to testify in the suit as to the value of the property. The contract between Soble and Laos provided that Laos was to receive a fee of $1500 if the court found the value of the property to be $200,000 or less, and $2500 if the valuation were set at any amount above $200,000. In subsequent litigation, the question arose as to whether this contingent fee contract was contrary to public policy and thus illegal. On what basis could it be argued that the contract *was* illegal? Discuss. (*Laos v. Soble*, 503 P.2d 978, 1972.)

7. When Mrs. Bova left her car at a parking lot operated by Constantine, she was given an identification ticket upon which was printed matter, which she did not read, as follows: "This station will endeavor to protect the property of its patrons but it is agreed that it will not be liable for loss or damage of cars, accessories or contents from whatever cause arising." When Mrs. Bova returned, the car was not in the lot. It had been stolen, and, when found, was in need of repairs totaling $154. In an action brought against Constantine to recover this amount, he contended that the clause on the identification ticket freed him of all

liability. *Agricultural Insurance Co. v. Constantine,* 58 N.E.2d 658 (1944). Was the clause lawful, and thus a good defense to the suit? Explain.

8. Describe three situations in which contracts may be enforceable even though they are illegal in some respect.

13 Reality of Consent

One who has a speaking acquaintanceship with the basic elements of a contract will logically assume that all contracts possessing such elements are clearly enforceable. While this assumption is usually true, there are some situations where it is not.

A contract that appears to be valid in all respects may yet prove unenforceable if it turns out that the apparent consent of one or both parties is in fact not genuine or if the contract is oral when the law requires it to be written. Contracts falling within the first category will be examined in this chapter and those of the second category in the following chapter.

Contracts that are tainted by *fraud, innocent misrepresentation, mistake, duress,* or *undue influence* can ordinarily be voided by the innocent parties. In such instance the courts are likely to allow rescission on the ground that there was no "reality of consent." That is, although it appears from the terms of the contract alone that the consent of both parties was genuine (real), in fact it was not.

We have seen earlier that one of the things the law tries to do is encourage conduct that is fair and good and discourage conduct that is deceitful or injurious either to a specific person or to society in general. Some types of conduct are felt

234

to be so detrimental to a stable society that they are flatly prohibited, and punishment for wrongdoers is prescribed. Hence our bodies of criminal law have been built up.

In other areas of the law, rules have come about that attempt to insure at least some degree of care and fairness when private citizens have dealings or other relationships with one another. We have seen, for example, that tortious conduct causes the wrongdoer to answer in damages to the injured party.

This continuing filament of thought, to the effect that a person should not be allowed to profit by conduct that is patently offensive, is woven into the law of contracts. It is most apparent in that part of law having to do with fraud and duress and, to a lesser extent, mistake and undue influence.

Fraud

Leaving aside, for the moment, any attempt to define the term, the essence of *fraud* is deception—the intentional misleading of one person by another. Perhaps the most common type of fraud occurs when one person simply lies to another about a material fact, as a result of which a contract is made. Thus, if S, the owner of a current model car, tells B that he purchased it new six months ago, S knowing that it was in fact "second hand" when he acquired it, S is guilty of fraud if B, believing this statement to be true, subsequently purchases the car. In this case, B—after learning the true facts—ordinarily can either rescind the contract and recover the purchase price or keep the car and recover damages from S.

One person can mislead another in so many ways that the courts have been reluctant to fashion a hard and fast definition of fraud; any precise definition almost certainly could be circumvented by persons intent on getting around it.[1] Instead, the courts generally recognize that the various forms of deception they wish to forestall usually contain common elements. When a court is called upon to decide in a given case whether the conduct of one of the parties was fraudulent, its usual approach is to see if the required elements are present. If so, fraud has been established and the victim will be afforded relief.

A party who claims to be the victim of fraud must show that the alleged defrauder made a misrepresentation of fact, and that the misrepresentation was made with the intent to deceive. The victim must also show that he or she relied on the misrepresentation and was thereby injured.

Misrepresentation of Fact

The term *misrepresentation* (or misstatement) is broadly interpreted to include any word or conduct that causes the innocent person to reach an erroneous conclusion

---

[1]Some helpful definitions do exist, of course. One provides that fraud is a "a false representation of a material fact made with knowledge of its falsity or culpable ignorance of its truth, with intention that it be acted upon by the party deceived and inducing him to contract to his injury." 17 C.J.S., Contracts, § 153, Copyright 1963 by West Publishing Co.

of fact. Thus a seller of apples who selects the best ones in a basket and puts them on top of others of inferior quality has, in the eyes of the law, made a "statement" to a prospective buyer that all the apples are of the same quality as those which are visible.

In order for a misstatement to be fraudulent, it must be about a "fact"—an actual event, circumstance, or occurrence. Statements about the age of a horse, the number of acres in a tract of land, and the net profit made by a business during a given year are all statements of fact—that is, statements about a fact. If the innocent person can prove that the particular statement made to him or her was false, the first element of fraud has been established.

Predictions: Statements as to what will happen in the future are clearly not statements of fact and therefore are not fraudulent even if they turn out to be in error. Thus, if a seller of stock tells a buyer that the stock is "bound to double in value within six months," the buyer is not entitled to relief in the event the increase in value does not come about. The same is true when the seller of a motel states that "it will certainly net $14,000 in the coming year." The reason for the view that such statements do not constitute fraud, of course, is that no one can predict what will happen in the future, and a reasonable person would not put faith in such statements.[2]

Opinion: Statements of opinion, like predictions, are also distinguished from statements of fact. Contracts cannot be set aside on the ground of fraud simply because one of the parties, prior to making the contract, expressed an opinion that later turned out to be incorrect.

Most statements of opinion, in which the declarant is merely expressing personal feelings or judgments on a matter about which reasonable persons might have contrary views, are usually easy to recognize. For example, statements that "this is an excellent neighborhood in which to raise children" or that "this painting will harmonize beautifully with the colors of your living room" involve conclusions with which others might disagree; thus they cannot be the basis of an action of fraud brought by one who relied upon them.

Other statements, however, are not so easily placed in the "opinion" or "fact" categories. A statement by the seller of a boat that it is "perfectly safe" or a statement by a home owner that "the foundation is sound" are closer to being

---

[2]One important type of statement about a present or future event or condition *does* impose a legal obligation on the one making it if it proves to be false: statements that are "warranties"—guarantees as to existing fact or assurances about future performance of a product by the seller. For example: A manufacturer of house paint states on the cans that "this paint, when applied according to the manufacturer's instructions above, will not crack, fade, or peel within two years of its application." If the statement proves to be false, a buyer who has purchased the paint in reliance on the statement can recover damages. The recovery in such a case would be on *breach of warranty* rather than on fraud, except in the rare situation where the buyer can prove that the seller knew the representation to be false when he or she made it. (Most, but not all, warranties are governed by the *law of sales.* Specific questions about the definition and application of express and implied warranties in regard to the sale of goods require reference to Secs. 2-312, 313, 314, 315 and 316 of the UCC.)

statements of fact than the previous representations about the neighborhood and the painting. But there are varying degrees of safety and soundness, so these statements too can be held in given situations to constitute only expressions of opinion—particularly if the declarant and the innocent party were on a relatively equal basis insofar as their experience and general knowledge of the subject matter were concerned. (On the other hand, if the declarant is considerably more knowledgeable than the other party, such statements are likely to be viewed as statements of *fact,* and thus fraudulent if false. For example, in the case of *Groening v. Opsata,* 34 N.W.2d 560, 1948, it was held that a false statement by the seller of a summer home located on an eroding cliff on the shore of Lake Michigan that "it isn't too close [to the lake]" and that "there is nothing to fear, everything is all right" constituted fraud, in view of the fact that the seller was a builder of homes in the area.)

Value: Statements about an article's *value* have also caused difficulties. Nevertheless, the courts today adhere to the traditional view (in most circumstances) that the value of an article or piece of property is a matter of opinion rather than fact. Two practical reasons are the basis for this view: (1) an awareness that many types of property are prized by some people but are considered of little value by others, and (2) a recognition of the fact that sellers generally overvalue the things they are attempting to sell and prospective buyers must accordingly place little or no reliance upon such statements.[3] Consequently, if a seller states that "this apartment building is easily worth $80,000," a buyer will not be permitted to rescind the contract on the ground of fraud, even though he relied on the statement and can prove later that the actual market value of the building at the time of sale was nowhere near the stated figure and that the seller knew this all the time.

Again, the general rule is not followed when the declarant's experience and knowledge of the particular subject matter is *markedly superior* to that of the other party—especially if it is so great that the declarant is considered an "expert" in the eyes of the law. In order to prevent such a person from taking grossly unfair advantage of those who are clearly less knowledgeable, and intentional misrepresentations *are* held to be fraudulent.

The next case presents an allegation of fraud in a modern setting.

The Chicago Medical School, defendant, issued a bulletin for the 1974–75 school year which stated that applicants would be selected "on the basis of academic achievement, Medical College Admission Test results, personal appraisals by a preprofessional advisory committee or individual instructors, and the personal interview, if requested by the Committee on Admissions." Steinberg received a bulletin, applied for admission, and paid the required $15 application fee.

After his application was rejected, Steinberg learned that the defendant, in fact,

Steinberg v. Chicago Medical School
Supreme Court of Illinois, 371 N.E.2d 634 (1977)

---

[3]Statements of gross overvaluation, like others that are grossly extravagant in nature ("this sport coat will wear like iron"), constitute mere "dealers' puffing."

used "nonacademic criteria" in admitting applicants, primarily the ability of the applicant or his family to pledge or make payments of large sums of money to the school. Steinberg then brought this action on behalf of all rejected applicants, claiming that defendant was guilty of fraud.

A number of issues were raised in the trial court. Two of these were (1) whether a contract was ever formed between the parties, and (2) if so, whether defendant's representations in its bulletin constituted fraud. The trial court ruled against plaintiff on all issues and dismissed the action. An intermediate court of appeals affirmed some rulings of the trial court but reversed others. Plaintiff appealed to the Supreme Court of Illinois. (Only those parts of the highest court's decision applicable to the two selected issues are set forth below).

Dooley, Justice: . . . An offer (and) an acceptance . . . are basic ingredients of a contract. Steinberg alleges that he and (others) received a brochure describing the criteria that defendant would employ in evaluating applications. He urges that such constituted an invitation for an offer to apply, that the filing of the applications constituted an offer to have their credentials appraised under the terms described by defendant, and that defendant's voluntary reception of the application and fee constituted an acceptance, the final act necessary for the creation of a binding contract.

This situation is similar to that wherein a merchant advertises goods for sale at a fixed price. While the advertisement itself is (usually) not an offer to contract, it constitutes an invitation to deal on the terms described in the advertisement. . . . When the merchant takes the money [there is] an acceptance of the offer to purchase. [The court then agreed with Steinberg's contention that the defendant's receipt of his application and fee constituted an acceptance of his application offer, and that a contract was thus formed. The court next turned to the question of fraud.]

Count III alleges that, with intent to deceive and defraud plaintiffs, defendant stated in its catalogs it would use certain criteria to evaluate applications; that these representations were false in that applicants were selected primarily for monetary considerations; that plaintiffs relied on said representations and were each thereby induced to submit their applications and pay $15, [and that plaintiffs were damaged as a result.]

These allegations support a cause of action for fraud. Misrepresentation of an existing material fact coupled with scienter (knowledge), deception, and injury are more than adequate. . . . Plaintiff's allegations of fraud meet the test of common-law fraud.

Not to be ignored is defendant's *modus operandi* as described in *DeMarco v. University of Health Sciences*, 352 N.E.2d 356 (1976):

"An analysis of those exhibits shows that in 1970, at least 64 out of 83 entering students had pledges made in their behalves totalling $1,927,900. The pledges varied in amounts from $1400 to $100,000 and averaged $30,123. In 1971, at least 55 out of 83 students had pledges made in their behalves totalling $1,893,000. The pledges varied in amounts from $3000 to $100,000 and averaged $34,418. In 1972, at least 73 out of an entering class of 92 had contributions made in their behalves totalling $3,111,000. The pledges varied in amounts from $20,000 to $100,000 and averaged $42,603. In 1973, at least 78 out of 91 students had contributions made in their behalves totalling $3,749,000. The pledges varied in amounts from $10,000 to $100,000 and averaged $48,064. In addition, there were amounts pledged and partial payments made for students who did not enter or dropped out shortly after entering."

It is immaterial here that the misrepresentation consisted of a statement in the medical school catalog, referring to future conduct, that "student's potential for the study and practice of medicine will be evaluated on the basis of academic achievement, Medical College Admission Test results, personal appraisals by a pre-professional advisory committee or individual instructors, and the personal interview, if requested by the Committee on Admissions." We concede the general rule denies recovery for fraud based on a false representation of intention or future conduct, but there is a recognized exception where the false promise or representation of future conduct is alleged to be the scheme employed to accomplish the fraud. Such is the situation here. . . .

[The higher court, disagreeing with the trial court, thus ruled that Steinberg's allegations, if true, did state a cause of action. It therefore remanded the case to the trial court for determination of the factual issues presented.]

Law: Under the early common-law rule of this country, *statements of law* made by lay persons were clearly held not to constitute "statements of fact" and thus could not be the basis for actions of fraud. If the seller of a vacant lot that carries a C-1 zoning classification assures the buyer that "this classification permits the erection of duplex rental units," a statement that the owner knows is not true, the buyer who purchases the property in reliance on the statement ordinarily cannot maintain an action for damages. The rule was based on two grounds: (1) the generally reasonable feeling that a statement made by a nonlawyer about a point of law should not be relied upon by the one to whom it is made, and (2) the somewhat more questionable maxim that "everyone is presumed to know the law."

While this is still the rule applied to most cases, it is subject to an increasing number of exceptions. One major exception is comprised of statements of law made by persons who—because of their professional or occupational status—can reasonably be expected to know the law relating to their specialty, even though they are not attorneys. Thus intentional misrepresentations of law by persons such as real estate brokers and bank cashiers as to legal matters within their particular specialties are frequently held to be fraudulent.

Silence: Because the essence of fraud is an affirmative misleading of one person by another, mere silence does not constitute fraud (that is, a misstatement of fact) in most situations. Thus, if the seller of a used car knew that it had been involved in an accident in the past, his failure to tell a prospective buyer of this fact would not, in and of itself, constitute fraud.[4] Similarly, a tenant who is attempting to sublet an apartment with the owner's consent would not be guilty of fraud by failing to tell a prospective renter that he or she had had numerous run-ins with the owner and had generally found that person difficult to deal with.

There are, however, exceptional situations in which the withholding of informa-

---

[4]The buyer can be somewhat protected, of course, in cases of this sort by asking if the car had ever been in an accident. If the seller answers falsely, he or she is clearly guilty of making a misstatement of fact.

tion by one party is so manifestly unfair that the silence may constitute fraud. In these situations a legal "duty to speak" exists. Of course, since the courts decide cases involving a wide variety of fact-patterns, they often do not agree completely on the precise circumstances in which silence constitutes fraud. However, for certain situations of special importance, they usually do hold that a legal duty to speak exists.

The first of these instances is the sale of property that contains a *latent, or hidden, defect*—one that a simple or casual inspection by a prospective purchaser ordinarily would not disclose. Common examples are a cracked motor block in an automobile and a termite infestation in a house. A property owner who has knowledge of such conditions is guilty of fraud if he or she does not apprise the prospective purchaser of them—assuming, of course, that the seller actually enters into a contract with an innocent buyer.

While the "latent defect" rule, abstractly stated, is highly commendable, the practical protection it affords is less than one might hope for. Frequently it is difficult for the buyer to prove that the defect actually existed at the time of purchase—particularly if a long period of time has elapsed before discovery of it. And even if this hurdle is cleared, the buyer has to establish that the seller knew, or should have known, of the defect when the sale occurred. The seller's contention that he or she was honestly unaware of the defective condition is frequently accepted by a jury.[5]

A second instance of the duty to speak occurs where one of the parties occupies a position of *trust and confidence* relative to the other. (This differs from the ordinary situation, where the parties are dealing "at arms' length.") For example, when a partnership is considering a land purchase, a partner who is part owner of the land under consideration has a duty to divulge his or her interest to the co-partner before the purchase is made. Similarly, a corporation officer who is purchasing stock from a shareholder has a duty to disclose any special facts of which he has knowledge, by virtue of his position, that would affect the value of the stock.

A third situation involves contracts of *uberrima fides*—those in which the "utmost good faith" is required because the relationship of the parties is such that one must rely upon information given by the other. Life insurance contracts are the most typical example, where the person applying for a policy has a duty, in answering the questions, to fully divulge all material information regarding his or her past and present physical condition.

A fourth and more limited instance occurs when one party during preliminary negotiations makes a representation of fact to the other that is then true, but the facts change before a contract is entered into. In such a case, the one who made the representation has a duty to notify the other of the changed condition before contracting.

---

[5]Normally the rule on hidden defects does not work in reverse. Thus, if the buyer possesses information about the property that causes its value to be higher than the seller believes it to be, the buyer does not have a duty to divulge this information to the seller (unless the buyer is an expert in the field by reason of training or experience).

Outside of these situations, most courts take the view that neither party has a duty to volunteer information to the other, even though it might bear materially on the other's decision of whether to contract. Thus the seller of a trash collection business probably has no duty to tell a prospective purchaser of indications that the city is going to institute a collection service of its own—especially if this information is as available to the buyer as it is to the seller.[6]

Some courts, however, impose a duty to speak in situations other than the four mentioned. For example, a few states have adopted the rule that where the seller of land knows of facts materially affecting its value or desirability, and additionally knows such facts are unknown to and not within reasonable reach of the purchaser, he or she must disclose such facts. This rule, applied by the California court in the following case, is somewhat broader than the "latent defect" rule in that it imposes liability in some situations where the latter rule does not. (In regard to the specific fact-pattern presented by the case below, however, the two rules overlap—that is, that most courts, while rejecting the broader "value or desirability" rule of the California court, would reach the same result by applying the latent defect rule.)

Drapeau, Justice: ... Plaintiffs purchased from defendant Fred A. Steele and his wife a resort in the San Bernardino mountains, consisting of a store, gasoline and service equipment, and several cabins. These improvements were located on United States government land in the San Bernardino National Forest, and along the state highway. For many years the resort had been known as "Bear Creek Lodge."

Kallgren v. Steele

District Court of Appeal, 2nd District, California, 279 P.2d 1027 (1955)

The improvements had been built upon the government land, and maintained there under a special use permit from the federal forest service, with an annual rental of $150. The permit provided that it could be terminated at any time for any reason by the forest service.

The purchase price of the Lodge was $12,000, with $6,000 [paid] in cash, and the remainder [to be paid] in monthly installments of $100 or more.

At the time of the negotiations for the sale, the parties went to the office of the forest service and explained what they were doing. The forest service made no objection to the transfer of the permit to plaintiffs. Apparently the permit was continued in Mr. Steele's name until plaintiffs paid him the last installment on the purchase price.

Then the forest service notified plaintiffs that the permit would be revoked at the end of five years. The reasons given for this drastic action were that the store and cabins were too close to the state highway, that they were in very poor condition, and that they impaired scenic values.

This was the first time that plaintiffs learned that any part of Bear Creek Lodge was *within or too close to the state right of way.* Defendant, Mr. Steele, knew about it all the time, but said nothing about it to plaintiffs. And due to the location of the buildings on the side of a precipitous mountain canyon it is impossible to move them farther away from the state highway.

Thus the forest service put an end to all of plaintiffs' rights in and to Bear Creek Lodge,

---

[6]*Jappe v. Mandt,* 278 P.2d 940 (1955).

except salvage value of the buildings if the cost of removing them should possibly be less than what they can be sold for. . . .

Plaintiffs brought this action for damages from defendants for fraud in concealing the fact that the improvements were in part within the highway right of way. Findings in the Superior Court were for plaintiffs, with damages fixed at $6,369.00. Defendants appeal from the judgment.

Reading the record, it appears quite likely that none of the parties gave much consideration to what the forest service might or might not do about the permit, or that the improvements would ever have to be moved on account of the state right of way. Bear Creek Lodge had been there for thirty years, and the parties just went ahead, without realizing that the tenancy was subject to the whim of some government officer clothed with a little brief authority.

This case presents an interesting example of the exercise of bureaucratic powers. If the improvements were too close to the highway, if their condition was poor, and if they impaired scenic values, it would seem but fair that the forest service should have advised plaintiffs of the impending revocation of the permit. The forest service knew of the sale, and that plaintiffs were proposing to invest $12,000 in Bear Creek Lodge.

However, the function of evaluating testimony and determining the rights of litigants based upon such testimony is not committed to courts of review in California. It is without conflict in the record that Mr. Steele did not mention the fact that any part of the improvements were within the state right of way, although he knew about it; and it is without conflict that the buyers didn't know about it when they bought the property, and didn't find out about it until just before they made the last installment payment. . . .

Defendant contends that the rule of *caveat emptor* [let the buyer beware] is applicable in this case, *and that there was no duty on his part to divulge any information to the plaintiffs. This contention is untenable in the law of fraud.* [Emphasis added.]

Fraud may consist in the misrepresentation or concealment of material facts, and may be inferred from the circumstances and condition of the parties contracting.

Deceit [fraud] is the suppression of a fact, by one who is bound to disclose it, or who gives information of other facts which are likely to mislead for want of communication of that fact.

As was said in *Kuhn v. Gottfried,* 229 P.2d 137: "Concealment may constitute actionable fraud where the seller knows of facts which materially affect the desirability of the property, which he knows are unknown to the buyer." . . .

Judgment affirmed.

Intent to Deceive

The second element of fraud is *knowledge of falsity* (or, as it is sometimes called, "scienter.") Thus the innocent party must ordinarily prove that the person making the statement knew, or should have known, that it was false at the time it was made. However, the knowledge of falsity requirement is also met if a person makes a statement "with a reckless disregard for the truth," even if the declarant did not actually know it was false. Thus, if the seller of a used car has no idea as to its mileage but nevertheless states that "it has not been driven more than 30,000 miles," his statement constitutes fraud if it is later proven that the true mileage materially exceeded that figure.

Reliance

The victim of a misrepresentation must show that he or she reasonably relied on the misstatement at the time of contracting. Sometimes this is not difficult to establish. The innocent party does not have to prove that the fact in regard to which the misrepresentation was made was the primary factor in inducing him or her to make the contract. It is sufficient that the misrepresentation involved a matter tending to influence the decision.

Reliance does not exist, of course, if the one accused of fraud can prove that the other party actually knew the true facts before making the contract. Also, a charge of fraud will fail if the victim's reliance was not reasonable under the circumstances. While the old rule of *caveat emptor* ("let the buyer beware") is of much less significance than formerly, a buyer still cannot blindly accept everything he or she is told. For example, if the buyer is given an opportunity to view the property, he or she is presumed to know about any "patent" (obvious) defects. Assume that the seller of a used television set tells the buyer it "produces an excellent picture on all channels." If the buyer viewed the set in operation prior to the sale and complained of reception on one channel, that person can hardly contend after the sale that he reasonably relied on the seller's representation.

Injury

A party seeking to recover *damages* based on fraud must ordinarily show that he or she suffered financial loss as a result of the misrepresentation. In the usual case involving the sale of property, the loss is the difference between the actual value of the property the buyer received and the value it would have had if the representation had been true. Many times, however, the defrauded party simply asks that the contract be *rescinded* (canceled), in which case the buyer returns the property and the seller returns the price. When rescission is asked, a showing of financial injury by the innocent party is usually not required.

Innocent Misrepresentation

If all the elements of fraud are present in a particular case, except that the person making the misstatement honestly (and reasonably) believed the statement to be true, that person is guilty of *innocent misrepresentation* rather than fraud. Under the rule of most states, the victim can rescind the contract on that ground, but is usually not given the alternative remedy of damages.

Mistake

Cases are continually arising where one of the parties to a contract attempts to have it set aside by the court on the ground that he or she was mistaken in some respect at the time the contract was made. Often the mistake involves opinion or judgment rather than fact, in which case no relief will be granted. For example, a person contracts to buy land for $30,000 thinking this is its true value. If he subsequently discovers that its actual value is much less, he has shown bad judgment and will not be permitted to rescind the contract. Similarly, if a person purchases stock in the belief that it will greatly increase in value in a short time, he obviously cannot have the contract set aside in the event that it does not perform as he had hoped. If rescission were permitted on grounds such as these, the basic value of all contracts would be destroyed.

However, in certain limited situations a plea of mistake will afford grounds for rescission of a contract, if the mistake was one of *fact*. The general rule is that if both parties were mistaken as to a material fact at the time of contracting, either party can rescind the agreement. On the other hand, if only one of the parties was mistaken, rescission will not be granted unless that person can show that the other party knew, or should have known, of the mistake at the time the contract was made. When both parties are mistaken, the mistake is said to be *mutual* or *bilateral;* when only one is mistaken, it is *unilateral.*

Bilateral Mistake

The following examples illustrate the general principle that a contract can be set aside if there is a mutual mistake as to the *existence,* the *identity,* or the *character* of the subject matter of the contract.

1. B purchases S's summer home on April 10. Subsequently, B learns that, unknown to either party, the home was destroyed by fire on April 1. Since both parties entered into the contract under the mistaken assumption that the subject matter of the contract actually existed at that time, B can have the contract set aside.

2. P owns two properties outside Woodsfield, Ohio. G, after viewing both acreages, makes P a written offer to purchase one for $18,000. P accepts the offer. It later develops that G had one property in mind while P, after reading the description contained in G's offer, honestly and reasonably believed that G was referring to the other property. Either party can rescind the agreement, because there was a mutual mistake about the identity of the contract's subject matter.

3. C purchases a gemstone from D for $25. At the time of contracting, both parties believe the stone is a topaz. In fact, it turns out to be an uncut diamond worth $700. Since both parties were mistaken about the true character of the contract's subject matter, D can have the contract rescinded, thereby recovering the stone.

The principle is not applicable to situations where both parties realize that they are *in doubt* as to a particular matter, but enter into a contract nonetheless. Thus, in Example 3 above, if neither C nor D had any idea what the stone was when they made the contract, neither party could subsequently rescind it when the stone turned out to be a diamond.

With these general rules of law in mind let us examine the problem presented by the following case.

Boskett was a part-time dealer in coins in New Jersey. He owned a 1916 dime which bore the letter "D," indicating that it had been minted in Denver. Because of the rarity of such coins, their market value was greatly in excess of their monetary worth.

Beachcomber Coins, plaintiff, was interested in buying the coin, and one of its owners examined the coin to determine its genuineness. After an examination of 45 minutes he was satisfied that the coin was, in fact, minted in Denver, and he purchased it on behalf of plaintiff for $500. Later plaintiff was advised by the American Numismatic Society that the "D" was a counterfeit. When Boskett, the seller, refused to take back the coin and refund the purchase price, plaintiff brought this action asking rescission of the contract.

The trial judge, sitting without a jury, found that there was a mutual mistake of fact (i.e., a mistake as to the coin's genuineness) that would ordinarily justify rescission of the contract. However, he further found that under customary coin dealing procedures a buyer of a coin who was permitted to examine it before purchase "assumed the risk" that it might be counterfeit. He therefore dismissed the action and plaintiff appealed.

Beachcomber Coins, Inc., v. Boskett

Superior Court of New Jersey, Appellate Division, 400 A.2d 78 (1979)

Conford, Judge: . . . The evidence and trial judge's findings establish this as a classic case [in which rescission should be allowed on the basis of] mutual mistake of fact. As a general rule, "where parties on entering into a transaction that affects their contractual relations are both under a mistake regarding a fact assumed by them as the basis on which they entered into the transaction, it is voidable by either party if enforcement of it would be materially more onerous to him than it would have been had the fact been as the parties believed it to be." *Restatement, Contracts,* § 502 (1932). . . .

Moreover, [the *Restatement* provides that] "negligent failure of a party to know or discover the facts as to which both parties are under a mistake does not preclude rescission or reformation on account thereof." The law of New Jersey is in accord. . . .

Defendant's contention that plaintiff assumed the risk that the coin might be of greater or lesser value is not supported by the evidence. It is [true that] a party to a contract can assume the risk of being mistaken as to the value of the thing sold. The *Restatement* states the rule this way:

> Where the parties know that there is doubt in regard to a certain matter and contract on that assumption, the contract is not rendered voidable because one is disappointed in the hope that the facts accord with his wishes. The risk of the existence of the doubtful fact is then assumed as one of the elements of the bargain.

However, for this rule to apply, the parties must be conscious that the pertinent fact may not be true and make their agreement at the risk of that possibility. [That rule is not applicable] in this case, because both parties were certain that the coin was genuine. . . .

[The court then turned to the trial judge's finding that it was customary in the coin dealing business for buyers of coins to assume the risk of genuineness. After examining the testimony on this point at the trial, the court concluded that it was too weak to support the finding of "custom and usage" under New Jersey law. The court thus reversed the judgment, and ordered rescission of the contract.]

Unilateral Mistake

Where only one party to a contract is mistaken about a material fact, rescission is ordinarily not allowed unless the mistake was (or should have been) apparent to the other party. Two examples follow.

1. A purchases a painting from B for $300; A believes it was painted by a well-known artist. A does not, however, disclose this belief to B. In fact, the painting is the work of an amateur and consequently worth no more than $50. Since only A was mistaken as to the identity of the artist, the mistake is unilateral and the contract cannot be rescinded. On the other hand, A would have been permitted to rescind if B had been aware of A's mistake and had not corrected it.

2. X furnishes three contractors with specifications of a building project and asks them to submit construction bids. C submits a bid for $48,000, and D submits one for $46,500. E's bid, because of an error in addition, is $27,000 rather than the intended $47,000. If X accepts E's bid, E can have the contract set aside if the jury finds (as is likely to be the case) that X either actually knew of the mistake when he accepted the bid, or that he should have been aware of the mistake because of the wide discrepancy in bids.

Cautions

The "bilateral-unilateral mistake" rule of thumb, while widely followed, by no means settles all cases that arise in the general area of mistake. In the first place, there is some disagreement as to what constitutes a bilateral mistake. A few courts, for example, take the view that such a mistake exists only where the parties have arrived at their erroneous conclusions independently of one another, rather than one party simply relying on information supplied by the other.

Second, the courts will sometimes settle cases purely on "equitable principles" —i.e., on the basis of overall fairness in particular situations—thereby placing little or no reliance on the bilateral-unilateral factor. For example: X and Y make a contract on June 12, at which time X is mistaken as to a material fact. If X should notify Y of the mistake on June 14, at which time Y has neither commenced performance of the contract nor otherwise relied upon its existence, rescission is often allowed even if Y was totally ignorant of the mistake when the contract was made. And, third, a few states have statutes relating to contracts entered into under mistake of fact that sometimes permit rescission where common-law principles would not.

Additional Types of Mistake

Occasionally a mistake involves the provisions of the contract itself rather than the contract's subject matter. For example, an offeree might accept an offer that he or she has misread, only to learn later that the offer was in fact substantially different than what it seemed. This is a unilateral mistake, and the offeree is bound by the resulting contract (unless the acceptance itself discloses the mistake to the offeror).

Mutual mistakes as to the value of an article being sold generally are held to constitute mistakes of opinion rather than fact, and rescission is not permitted in such cases. Thus, if B buys a painting from S for $10,000, both parties correctly believing that the artist was Andrew Wyeth, B obviously cannot have the contract set aside simply because he later learns that the painting's true value is only $5,000.

There is somewhat greater uncertainty insofar as mistakes of law are concerned. The courts at one time refused to permit rescission of contracts where a mistake of law existed, either bilateral or unilateral, on the theory that such a mistake was not a mistake of fact. (This idea was consistent with the view that a *misstatement of law* does not constitute a misstatement of fact, under the law of fraud.) Today, however, most courts treat *mistakes of law and fact* the same—that is, they will set aside contracts which both parties entered into under a mistake of law as well as those in which the mistake of one party was apparent to the other.

Duress

Occasionally a person will seek to escape liability under a contract on the ground that he or she was forced to enter into it. Often the courts find that the "force" is insignificant in the eyes of the law, and the complaining party is held to the contract. For example, if a person enters into a contract simply because he knows that failure to do so will incur the wrath of some third person, such as his employer or his wife, relief will not be granted. If, on the other hand, the degree of compulsion is so great as to totally rob him of free will, duress exists, and he can have the contract rescinded.

One definition of *duress* is:

> (1) any wrongful act of one person that compels a manifestation of apparent assent by another to a transaction without his volition, or (2) any wrongful threat of one person by words or other conduct that induces another to enter into a transaction under the influence of such fear as precludes him from exercising free will and judgment, if the threat was intended or should reasonably have been expected to operate as an inducement.[7]

A necessary element of duress is fear—a genuine and reasonable fear on the part of the victim that he or she will be subjected to an injurious, unlawful act by not acceding to the other party's demands. Thus, if a person signs a contract at gunpoint or after being physically beaten, duress exists, and the victim can escape liability on that ground. Duress also exists when a person makes a contract as a consequence of another person's threat of harm (say, of kidnapping his child) if the contract is refused.

---

[7]*Restatement, Contracts,* § 492. Copyright 1932. Reprinted with the permission of The American Law Institute.

Generally, the innocent party must show that the act actually committed or threatened was an illegal one. For instance, a contract entered into between a striking union and an employer cannot be set aside by the latter on the ground of duress if the strike was a lawful one—as, for example, if the strike occurred after an existing "no-strike" contract between union and employer had expired.

The threat of a criminal suit is generally held to constitute duress. For example: X proposes a contract to Y and tells him that if he refuses to sign the agreement, he (X) will turn over evidence to the prosecuting attorney's office tending to prove that Y had embezzled money from his employer six weeks earlier. To prevent this, Y signs the contract. Y can have the contract rescinded on the ground of duress, because a threat to use the criminal machinery of the state for such a purpose is clearly wrongful—regardless of whether or not Y had actually committed the crime in question. Threat of a civil suit, on the other hand, usually does not constitute duress.

While a contract cannot be set aside simply because there is a disparity of bargaining power between the parties, the courts are beginning to accept the idea that *economic duress* (or business compulsion) can be grounds for the rescission of a contract in exceptional situations. The decision in the next case sets forth three requirements that ordinarily must be met in order for a plaintiff to be successful in a suit asking rescission.

Totem Marine T. & B. v. Alyeska Pipeline

Supreme Court of Alaska, Alaska, 584 P.2d 15 (1978)

Totem Marine Tug and Barge, Inc., entered into a contract with Alyeska Pipeline Services under which Totem was to transport large quantities of pipeline construction materials from Houston, Texas, to Alaska. After Totem began its performance, many problems arose. One major difficulty was the fact that the tonnages to be shipped were six times greater than Alyeska had indicated. Additionally, long delays occurred in getting Totem's vessels through the Panama Canal, which resulted from Alyeska's failure to furnish promised documents to Totem by specified dates. After these and other problems, Alyeska cancelled the contract without cause.

At the time of the wrongful termination, Alyeska owed Totem about $300,000. Officers of Alyeska at first promised that it would pay Totem invoices promptly, but later they told Totem that it would have its money "in six to eight months." (Totem alleged that the delay in payment occurred after Alyeska learned through negotiations with Totem lawyers that Totem's creditors were pressing it for their payments, and that without immediate cash it would go into bankruptcy—allegations that Alyeska did not deny.)

After further negotiations, a settlement agreement was made in 1975, under which Alyeska paid Totem $97,000 in return for surrender of all claims against it. In early 1976 Totem brought this action to rescind the settlement agreement on the ground of economic duress, and to recover the balance allegedly due under the original contract. The trial court ruled as a matter of law that the circumstances under which the settlement occurred did not constitute duress, and dismissed the complaint. Totem appealed.

Burke, Justice: ... This court has not yet decided a case involving a claim of economic duress, or what is also called business compulsion. ... [In recent cases] this concept has been broadened to include myriad forms of economic coercion which force a person to involuntarily enter into a particular transaction. ...

There are various statements of what constitutes economic duress, but as noted by one commentator, "The history of generalization in the field offers no great encouragement for those who seek to summarize results in any single formula." Dawson, *Economic Duress,* 45 Mich.L.Rev. (1947). ... [However, many states adopt the view that] duress exists where: (1) one party involuntarily accepted the terms of another, (2) circumstances permitted no other alternative, and (3) such circumstances were the result of coercive acts of the other party. ...

One essential element of economic duress is that the plaintiff show that the other party, by wrongful acts or threats, intentionally caused him to enter into a particular transaction. ... This requirement may be satisfied where the alleged wrongdoer's conduct is criminal or tortious, but an act or threat may also be wrongful if it is wrongful in the moral sense. ...

Economic duress does not exist, however, merely because a person has been the victim of a wrongful act; in addition, the victim must have no choice but to agree to the other person's terms or face serious financial hardship. Thus, in order to avoid a contract, a party must also show that he had no reasonable alternative to agreeing to the other party's terms, or as it is often stated, that he had no adequate remedy if the threat were carried out. ...

Turning to the instant case, we believe that Totem's allegations, if proved, would support a finding that it executed a release of its contract claims against Alyeska under economic duress. Totem has alleged that Alyeska deliberately withheld payment of an acknowledged debt, knowing that Totem had no choice but to accept an inadequate sum in settlement of that debt; that Totem was faced with impending bankruptcy; that Totem was unable to meet its pressing debts other than by accepting the immediate cash payment offered by Alyeska; and that through necessity, Totem thus involuntarily accepted an inadequate settlement offer from Alyeska and executed a release of all claims under the contract. If the release was in fact executed under these circumstances, we think that ... this would constitute the type of wrongful conduct and lack of alternatives that would render the release voidable by Totem on the ground of economic duress. ...

Reversed, and case remanded.

Undue Influence

There are some circumstances in which a person can escape contractual liability by proving that his or her consent was brought about by the *undue influence* of the other party to the contract. While many kinds of influence are perfectly lawful, influence is "undue" (excessive) where one party so dominates the will of the other that the latter's volition actually is destroyed. A common example occurs where one person, as the result of advanced age and physical deterioration, begins to rely more and more upon a younger, more experienced acquaintance or relative for advice until the point is reached where his or her willpower and judgment are almost totally controlled by the dominant party. If the older, weaker person can show (1) that he was induced to enter into a particular contract by virtue of the dominant party's power and influence, rather than as the result of exercising his own volition or will, and (2) that the dominant party used this power to take advantage of him, undue influence is established and he is freed of liability on this ground.

A Statutory Postscript

Many contracts are made in which one party, usually the buyer of household goods, is persuaded to contract by the high-pressure selling tactics of the other party. In such cases the victim is usually unable to prove that the seller was guilty of fraud, and, as a general rule, the courts take the view that high-pressure salesmanship does not constitute duress. Thus, under common-law principles, the buyer is usually bound on the contract.

However, in a limited attempt to afford relief in some of these situations, over half the states have passed "home solicitation" statutes, and a good many cities in other states have adopted similar ordinances. While these statutes vary to some extent, particularly in regard to the exceptions that they contain, they essentially provide that contracts entered into as a result of home solicitations initiated by sellers—typically door-to-door salespersons—can be rescinded by the buyer simply giving notice by mail to the other party within three business days (the cooling off period) after making the contract. Most of these statutes apply to all home solicitation contracts involving the sale of consumer goods or services in which the price is $25 or more—though some statutes apply only to contracts that would result in a lien attaching to a home owner's property, such as in home improvement sales. In any event, the right to rescind is automatic; that is, the buyer need not allege or prove fraud or duress. (In relatively recent years, the Federal Trade Commission has adopted a three-day cooling off rule similar to the state statutes. This rule is of particular importance to buyers who have entered home solicitation contracts in those states where special statutes have not been adopted—assuming, of course, that interstate commerce is involved.)

Questions and Problems

1. Midwest Supply, a company in the business of preparing income tax returns, advertised "guaranteed accurate tax preparation." Waters, after reading the ad, contacted Midwest and was induced to apply for refunds that he was not legally entitled to. After Waters received the improper refunds, the Internal Revenue Service recovered the payments from him in addition to substantial penalties. Waters then sued Midwest to recover damages on the basis of fraud, alleging that (1) the statement in its ad was false; (2) the employees of Midwest had little or no training in accounting or income tax preparation; and (3) Midwest told its employees not to correct newswriters who described the employees as "specialists and tax experts." On these facts, is Midwest guilty of fraud? Discuss. (*Midwest Supply, Inc., v. Waters*, 510 P.2d 876, 1973.)

2. Whale applied for the position of rabbi with the Jewish Center of Sussex County, New Jersey. The application listed information regarding his education, ordination as a rabbi, and job experience from 1956 to 1977, all of which was true. The Jewish Center employed Whale, but soon thereafter brought action to rescind the contract on the ground of fraud,

alleging that Whale failed to disclose the fact that he had earlier been convicted of the crime of using the mails to defraud. Whale defended on the ground that in his resume accompanying the application he indicated further information and references would be furnished on request, but that the center did not avail itself of this opportunity. Is Whale's defense good? Why or why not? (*Jewish Center of Sussex County v. Whale*, 397 A.2d 712, 1978.)

3. Mrs. Goodson, a 54-year-old widow, signed a contract to sell her Wyoming ranch to Smith. Later, after finding out that the contract also included gas and oil rights (contrary to an oral agreement between the two that was entered into earlier), Mrs. Goodson sought to set aside the contract on the grounds of fraud and duress. To support her case, she alleged that the contract was made in an office where men of great stature and political influence were present (including a former governor of the state); that the men were boisterous and frequently interrupted her discussion with Smith; that she was tired and in a hurry to get back to her ranch, and that under these circumstances she had been unable to express her true intentions. (a) Do you think these facts show fraud? Discuss. (b) If there are additional facts you would need to know to rule on the question of fraud or duress, what would these facts be? (*Goodson v. Smith*, 243 P.2d 163, 1952.)

4. The seller of a building in Lusk, Wyoming, told an out-of-state buyer who had not seen the property that "it could readily be rented for $100 per month." The buyer, after making the contract, learned that the building had no rental value and that the seller knew this when he made his statement. When the buyer brought a fraud action against him, the seller contended that his statement was merely an expression of value, and thus a statement of opinion rather than one of fact. Rule on this defense, with reasons to support your ruling. (*Cahill v. Readon*, 273 P. 653, 1928.)

5. Clifford "tapped" a gas line of the Great Falls Gas Company with a device that permitted him to use gas that did not register on his gas meter. When the manager of the company discovered this, he told Clifford, "I have got the goods on you now. You are stealing gas. I will send you over the road to the penitentiary. You have burned it all winter and I want $200." Afraid that he would be sent to prison, Clifford paid the $200. Clifford later brought an action to recover a substantial portion of the $200 on the ground that his payment was induced by duress on the part of the gas company. *Clifford v. Great Falls Gas Co.*, 216 P. 1114 (1923). If Clifford can show that the value of the gas he used was actually far less than the $200 which the manager demanded, will Clifford be successful in his suit? Explain.

6. Black purchased two violins from White for $8,000, the bill of sale describing them as "one Joseph Guarnerius violin and one Stradivarius violin dated 1717." Unknown to either party, neither violin was made by Guarnerius or Stradivarius. Upon discovery of this fact, can Black set aside the purchase and recover payment? Explain.

7. The owner of a South Dakota ranch drove a prospective buyer around the property. He pointed out the boundaries of the ranch as clearly as possible, but because of the rough terrain it was not possible for the buyer to reach one or two parts of the property. Some time after the buyer purchased the land he wanted to set aside the contract on the ground of mistake, because he thought several strategically-located acres were part of the ranch which, in fact, were not. The seller defended on the ground that at no time during the negotiations did the buyer indicate that he was expecting to get the acres in question, and that he (the seller) thus was not aware of the buyer's mistake of fact. Is this a good defense? Explain. (*Beatty v. DePue*, 103 N.W.2d 187, 1960.)

8. What circumstances were responsible for the fact that many states have passed "home solicitation" statutes?

14   Contracts in Writing

Many people have the idea that contracts are never enforceable unless they are in writing. Insofar as the law is concerned, however, most oral contracts are just as enforceable as written contracts *if their terms can be established in court.*[1] In this chapter we will examine the relatively few kinds of contracts that *are* required by law to be in writing; then we will consider general problems relating to written contracts.

---

[1]Many actions based on oral contracts that are otherwise valid are dismissed by the courts because their terms cannot be sufficiently established. For this reason, all contracts of any importance ought to be in writing, even when not required by law. The practical weakness of oral contracts is probably what gives rise to the popular misconception that oral contracts are never enforceable, a feeling expressed in a statement attributed to Sam Goldwyn, the movie magnate, that "oral contracts aren't worth the paper they're written on."

In England, prior to the latter part of the seventeenth century, all oral contracts were enforceable as long as their existence and terms could be established. Under this approach, it became apparent that many unscrupulous plaintiffs were obtaining judgments against innocent defendants by the use of *perjured testimony*—false testimony given under oath. To illustrate: P claimed that D had breached a particular oral contract, a contract that D denied making. If P could induce his witnesses (usually by the payment of money) to falsely testify that they heard D agree to the alleged contract, and if D could neither refute such testimony by witnesses of his own nor otherwise prove that P's witnesses were lying, a judgment would ordinarily be granted in favor of P.[2] To eliminate this and other kinds of fraud, Parliament in 1677 passed "An Act for the Prevention of Frauds and Perjuries"—or, as it is commonly called, the "Statute of Frauds."

Section 4 of the statute provided, essentially, that five specified kinds of contracts had to be in writing in order to be enforceable,[3] and Section 17 required a sixth type of contract to be in writing (with certain exceptions). In this country, virtually all the states have reenacted the provisions of Sections 4 and 17 with but slight variations. Thus, when the question arises of whether a given contract has to be in writing today under the Statute of Frauds, reference is being made to the *state statute* operating in the jurisdiction within which the contract was made.

The Statute of Frauds

Contracts That Must Be in Writing

The typical statute today, closely following the language of Section 4 of the English act, requires the following kinds of contracts or promises to be in writing (or be evidenced by a written memorandum):

1. A contract calling for the sale of land or an interest therein.

2. A contract not to be performed within one year.

3. A promise by one person to pay the debt of another.

4. A promise made in consideration of marriage.

5. A promise by the administrator or executor of an estate to pay a debt of the estate out of his or her own funds.

Each of the above requirements raises questions of judicial interpretation: What is meant by *land*, by an *interest in land*, and so on. Only by examining these interpretations can one tell whether a particular contract falls within the statute or outside it. To illustrate: S, the owner of ten acres of land, orally contracts in July to sell the corn then growing on the land to B for $300. After the crop matures,

---

[2]D's situation was particularly difficult because, at the time we are speaking of, the parties to a civil suit were not permitted to testify in their own behalf; thus the testimony of their witnesses was all-important.

[3]The actual wording of the statute that brought about this result is: "*No action shall be brought* [upon the following contracts] unless the agreement upon which such action shall be brought, or some memorandum or note thereof, shall be in writing and signed by the party sought to be charged therewith or some other person thereunto by him lawfully authorized." (Emphasis added.)

S refuses to abide by the agreement, and B sues him to recover damages for breach of contract. S admits making the contract but pleads the "Statute of Frauds" as a defense; that is, S contends that the contract was required by the statute to be in writing. If the court rules that the growing crop constitutes land or an interest therein, the contract falls within the statute and S's defense will be sustained. On the other hand, if the court rules that the crop does *not* constitute land or an interest therein, the contract falls outside the statute and S is liable for damages even though the contract was not in writing. We will now examine the kinds of contracts that are held to fall within the five categories, with particular emphasis on the first three.[4]

Contracts Calling for the Sale of Land

As a practical matter, the most important contracts required by the statute to be in writing are those calling for the sale of land—that is, real estate. With an exception to be noted later, unwritten agreements of this kind are absolutely unenforceable. Thus, if X orally agrees to sell a farm to Y for a specified price, neither X nor Y can recover damages from the other if one of them refuses to go through with the bargain. This is true even in the unlikely event that both parties admit in court that they made the contract.

In most cases it is easy to determine whether a contract does or does not involve the sale of land. Land, or *real property,* essentially consists of the earth's surface, vegetation, buildings, and other structures permanently attached to the soil. Growing crops, being physically attached to the ground, are generally considered to be real property. Thus, if S, by a written agreement, contracts to sell his farm to B for $50,000, B is entitled to receive any crops then growing on it, as well as the land itself (unless the contract provides otherwise). On the other hand, if S contracts merely to sell the crop to B (a situation alluded to earlier), the crop is considered *personal property* and the contract does not have to be in writing under the statute. (It is possible, however, that such contracts would still be required to be in writing because of a special section of the Uniform Commercial Code, which will be discussed later in the chapter.)

Interests in land include real estate mortgages and easements. A *real estate mortgage* is a conveyance of an interest in land by a debtor to a creditor as security for the debt. An *easement* is the right of one person to use or enjoy the land of another in a limited manner. Easements can be created in two general ways— expressly or by implication. If created in an express manner, the granting of the right must be evidenced by a writing—either specific language in a deed or a written contract in place of a deed. An easement created by implication, on the other hand, need not be evidenced by a writing. (One example of such an easement

---

[4]The parties to very many oral business contracts do, in fact, perform their obligations in full, even though, because of the statute, they are not obligated to do so. The statute is important, then, in those relatively few situations where one of the parties decides to "stand on his or her legal rights" by refusing to perform under an oral—but otherwise valid—contract.

is an "implied easement of necessity." This is created when a landowner sells part of his or her property to another, the land being situated in such a way that the buyer has no access to it except by going across the seller's remaining land.) While real estate *leases* also convey interests in land and thus normally fall within the Statute of Frauds, most states have enacted special statutes providing that oral leases of a year's duration or less are valid.

Effect of Part Performance: As a general rule, the fact that one of the parties to an oral contract falling within the statute has *partially performed* his or her part of the bargain does not, in and of itself, cause the contract to be enforceable.[5] In the case of oral contracts involving the sale of land, however, most states adopt the view that such contracts are enforceable by the buyer if he or she has done three things: (1) paid part of the purchase price, (2) taken possession of the property, and (3) added substantial improvements to it. The reasoning here is that it would be manifestly unfair to the buyer if the seller were permitted to repudiate the contract under such circumstances. In fact, some states enforce the contract even if the buyer has not substantially improved the property.

Contracts Not to Be Performed within One Year

The section of the statute requiring that *agreements not to be performed within one year of the making thereof* be in writing is based on the fact that disputes over the terms of long-term oral contracts are particularly likely to occur; witnesses die, the parties' memories become hazy, and so on. Despite the logic underlying this provision, it has posed numerous problems in practice.

In deciding whether a particular agreement falls within this section, the usual approach taken by the courts is to determine whether it was *possible,* under the terms of the contract in question, for the contract to have been fully performed within one year from the time it was made. If so, the contract is outside the statute and need not be in writing. (The fact that performance *actually* may have taken more than one year is immaterial.) For example: A, on June 1, 1970, orally agrees to work for B in a certain capacity at a salary of $700 per month "as long as you [B] shall live." In June 1972 B discharges A without cause, whereupon A brings suit to recover damages for breach of contract. Since two years have elapsed since the making of the contract, B contends that the contract was within the statute and that A's action must therefore be dismissed. B's contention is incorrect. Since it was possible that B might have died within the first year—in which case the contract would have been fully performed—the contract is outside the statute and A is entitled to damages.

An entirely different situation would be presented if, in the above example, A had contracted on June 1, 1970, to work for B "for the next two years." In this case, the contract would have fallen within the statute. Thus, if B had discharged

---

[5]Of course, if both parties have fully performed the contract, the statute is no longer relevant, and neither party can rescind it on the ground that it was originally required to be in writing.

A without cause in February 1972, A could not recover damages. This contract falls within the statute because the agreement could not have been fully performed under any circumstances prior to May 31, 1972. True, it was again *possible* that B could have died within twelve months of June 1, 1970; but under the particular terms of the contract this event would not have caused the contract to be "fully performed" upon B's death. (The further question of whether B's estate would be freed of liability had B died during the first twelve months will be discussed in Chapter 16.)

The courts have occasionally engrafted exceptions to the requirements that "over one year" contracts must be in writing (just as they have done with most of the other statute of frauds requirements) where they feel that this is necessary to bring about just results. The case below is one that falls into this category.

Harmon v. Tanner Motor Tours of Nevada, Ltd.

Supreme Court of Nevada, 377 P.2d 622 (1963)

This litigation came about as a result of a dispute over which one of two competing common carriers had the exclusive limousine ground transportation franchise for servicing the Las Vegas, Nevada, airport for a period of ten years. The carriers were Tanner Motor Lines, Ltd., plaintiff, and Las Vegas-Tonopah-Reno Stage Lines, Inc. (LTR), one of the defendants.

Five legal issues were involved, one of which had to do with the enforceability of an oral contract entered into between Tanner and the Board of Clark County Commissioners (Board), which was the governing authority of the Las Vegas airport. (Only that part of the fact-pattern and decision of the case relating to this issue is considered below.)

In late 1959 Tanner submitted a written bid for the limousine service, and that bid was orally accepted by the board members. Despite this acceptance, the board entered into a written contract in 1960 with the second carrier, LTR, giving it the exclusive transportation rights.

Tanner then brought this action against Harmon, a representative of the board, and LTR, defendants, asking for specific performance of its 1959 contract. The defendants contended, among other things, that that oral contract was unenforceable under the statute of frauds, because its performance was to take more than one year. The trial court ruled against the defendants on all points, and entered a decree of specific performance. [I.e., the court ruled that Tanner's contract was valid; that he thus did possess the exclusive transportation rights, and it accordingly ordered the board to recognize these rights.] Defendants appealed.

Thompson, Justice: . . . [The Nevada statute of frauds] provides that every agreement which, by its terms, is not to be performed within one year from the making thereof, shall be void, unless such agreement, or some note or memorandum thereof, expressing the consideration, be in writing and subscribed by the party charged therewith. The Tanner proposal which the board accepted was to provide limousine airport transportation service over a ten year period. It could not be performed within one year and is, therefore, squarely within the mentioned statute [The court, however, continued:]

Following acceptance of the Tanner bid, the board [orally] assured Tanner that a formal written agreement would be prepared for signature. In reliance, Tanner continued to provide limousine service to the airport, paid $3,600 as the minimum guarantee for the ensuing year, and purchased two new 1960 limousines at the cost of about $9,000.

We acknowledge the general rule that, in the absence of fraud, a promise to reduce an agreement to writing is not, standing alone, a basis for invoking an estoppel against raising the statute of frauds in defense [i.e., such a promise alone does not make the oral agreement enforceable]. It is likewise true, as a general rule, that part performance of an agreement within the "one year provision" of the statute of frauds [does not alone make the oral agreement enforceable]. However, where both occur, i.e., a promise to reduce an agreement to writing *and* part performance, an estoppel is properly invoked [by the one seeking specific performance], and the main agreement [is enforceable]. We conclude, therefore, that the board cannot rely upon [the statute of frauds] as a defense to this action. . . . The lower court [did not err] in directing the board to execute a formal contract with Tanner and thereafter specifically perform the same. . . .

Affirmed.

Promises to Pay Debts of Another

The statute expressly provides that no action shall be brought "to charge the defendant upon any special promise to answer for the debt, default or miscarriage of another" unless the promise or some memorandum thereof is in writing. Such promises are most commonly found in "contracts of guaranty," two examples of which follow.

Example 1. R says to D, "Furnish all the lumber to P that he needs to build his garage, and I will pay for it if he does not." D furnishes the lumber, but P is unable to pay; thereupon D sues R on his promise. R's promise falls within the statute; and since it was not in writing, he escapes liability. This is a typical contract by which one person guarantees the debt of another.

Example 2. G owes H $600. J orally promises H that if she will not bring suit against G for one month, he (J) will pay the debt if G has not done so by that time. H refrains from bringing suit, and at the end of the month G still has not paid. If H now sues J on his promise, J will escape liability.

Some Notes of Caution: In practice, many difficulties have arisen in the interpretation and application of this provision of the statute. However, these observations can be made:

1. Only secondary, or collateral, promises are subject to the statute. In Example 1, if R had told D, "Furnish all the lumber that P needs and charge it to me," R's promise would have been enforceable even though it was made orally. The reason is that here R made a *primary* promise to pay—that is, the debt was his own, rather than P's, from the start. Thus R's promise was not "a promise to pay the debt of another."

2. Along similar lines, a promise is primary rather than secondary if the debtor is released from liability by the creditor. Redoing Example 2, we again have G owing

H $600. This time J orally tells H, "If you will free G, I'll pay the debt myself." H then expressly releases G. J is now liable on his promise, because when the release occurred, the debt became his alone; hence his promise to pay was primary rather than secondary.

3. Even if an oral promise is secondary and thus apparently within the statute, most courts recognize an exception to the rule of nonliability—when the promisor's main purpose in making the promise is to secure a benefit to himself (and where the benefit is thereafter actually received.) To illustrate: X orally tells Y, "Furnish Z with all the fuel oil that he will need for heating his home this winter and I will pay you for it if Z does not." Y furnishes the oil, but Z never pays for it. If Y can show that Z was a valuable employee of X, and that X made the promise in order to prevent Z from leaving his employment for a job in Florida, Y can hold X liable on his promise. In such a case, under the "main purpose" exception, Y is liable despite the statute.

Other Promises

Two categories of contracts—*promises made in consideration of marriage* and *executors' contracts*—are relatively insignificant today. However, they do fall within the statute. Thus, if A promises to pay B $5,000 when and if B marries C, A is liable only if his promise is in writing. The same is true in regard to prenuptial agreements, in which parties about to be married to each other expressly spell out their interests in the other's properties. Finally, if the administrator or executor of an estate promises personally to pay a debt of the deceased, the creditor can hold the promisor liable only if the promise is in writing.

<table>
<tr><td>

Contracts Calling for Sale of Goods

</td><td>

Section 17 of the English Statute of Frauds provided, in essence, that contracts calling for the sale of goods at a price of ten pounds or more were unenforceable unless either (1) the buyer paid part of the purchase price, (2) the seller delivered and the buyer accepted part of the goods, or (3) the contract was in writing. A similar provision has found its way into Article 2 of the Uniform Commercial Code; thus today there is another class of contracts (in addition to the five set forth in the basic Statute of Frauds) that generally must be in writing. Sec. 2-201 of the UCC provides in part:

</td></tr>
</table>

> 1. Except as otherwise provided in this section a contract for the sale of goods for the price of $500 or more is not enforceable ... *unless there is some writing sufficient to indicate that a contract for sale has been made between the parties* and signed by the party against whom enforcement is sought or by his agent or broker. ...

To illustrate this basic provision: B orally offers to buy a used car from the S Company for $1,700, and an officer of that company orally agrees to this proposal.

As long as nothing is put in writing, both B and the S Company are free to repudiate the agreement without liability to the other party.

Subsection 3 of Sec. 2-201, however, contains several exceptions to the writing requirement, only two of which will be noted here.[6] That subsection provides, in part, that "A contract which does not satisfy the requirements of subsection (1) but which is valid in other respects *is enforceable* . . . with respect to goods for which payment has been made and received (by the seller) or which have been received and accepted (by the buyer)." (Emphasis added.) Thus, going back to the example above, the contract would have been binding upon the S Company if B had paid the purchase price when the agreement was made, or within a reasonable time thereafter. Similarly, the contract would have been binding upon B if the S Company had delivered the car to B, and B accepted it, when the contract was made or within a reasonable time thereafter.

Other Statutes Requiring a Writing

In addition to the statute of frauds and Sec. 2-201(1) of the UCC, all states have additional statutes—usually narrow in scope—that require still other kinds of contracts to be in writing. For example, most states require real estate listing contracts to be in writing. Additionally, Sec. 8-319 of the UCC requires, in general, that contracts calling for the sale of securities (i.e., stocks and bonds) must be in writing, and Sec. 9-203 of the UCC imposes the same general requirement upon agreements that create security interests in favor of lenders of money or unpaid sellers of goods.

When Is the Writing Sufficient?

As a practical matter, any contract falling within the statute of frauds ought to be fully set forth in writing and signed by both parties. The statute, however, does not require the agreement itself to be in writing; it is sufficient if some *memorandum or note* thereof is in writing. And, as noted earlier, it need only be signed "by the party sought to be charged." To illustrate: S orally agrees to work as a secretary for D for three years, at a specified monthly salary. A week after the agreement is made, D mails S a signed confirming letter setting forth the terms agreed to earlier. In this situation, S can enforce the contract against D, but he cannot enforce it against her. In other words, she could recover damages from him if he discharged her without cause before the three years were up, but he could not recover damages from her if she quit the job before the specified time had elapsed.

Because of the requirement that only a memorandum or note of the contract need be in writing, rather than the contract itself, it is perfectly possible that an oral contract can be validated by the production in court of a confirming telegram, sales slip, check, invoice, or some other instrument in writing. In any event, when

---

[6]Further discussion of this section is found in the sales chapters.

the party who is seeking to enforce a contract does produce some written evidence of it (whether the contract itself or simply a note or memorandum thereof), there is always a question of whether the writing is "sufficient to satisfy the statute"— that is, complete enough to permit a court to interpret and enforce it. Generally, the courts require at least the following: (1) the names of both parties, (2) the subject matter of the contract, (3) the consideration to be paid, and (4) any other terms that the court feels are essential under the circumstances.

The Parol Evidence Rule

Whenever a contract (or memorandum thereof) is in writing, the writing ought to contain *all* the material terms of the agreement. One reason for this is to eliminate the possibility that the writing will be found "insufficient" under the statute and thus unenforceable. But an equally powerful reason is the *parol evidence rule.* This rule provides, in general, that when a contract has been reduced to writing, neither party can introduce evidence in court that an oral (parol) agreement, reached at the same time the written contract was made, actually contained terms *in addition to or in conflict with* those appearing in the written contract. Stating it more succinctly, the terms of a written agreement cannot be altered or added to by the use of parol evidence.

Some Exceptions to the Rule

The courts feel that application of the parol evidence rule sometimes brings about clearly undesirable results; therefore they have recognized certain exceptions. Following are the most important situations in which a party is permitted to introduce oral evidence:

1. The written contract itself appears to be incomplete.

2. The written contract is ambiguous, and the oral evidence tends to clear up the ambiguity.

3. The oral evidence tends to prove fraud on the part of the other party.

4. The evidence tends to prove that the parties made an oral agreement that modified the written contract *after* the written contract had been entered into (assuming that the agreement was supported by consideration).

Questions and Problems

1. A doctor owned a summer home in New York. He orally promised the Strandbergs that if they would live with him on weekends at the cottage, and keep it in good repair, the property would be theirs when he died. The Strandbergs performed their part of the bargain, a period of several years, but the doctor died without leaving a will. When the Strandbergs sued the executor of his estate to force him to deed them the property, the executor refused to do so on the ground that the doctor's promise involved a sale of land, and was therefore

unenforceable since it was not in writing. Do the Strandbergs have any basis for recovering, in this case? Explain. (*Strandberg v. Lawrence*, 216 N.Y.S.2d 973, 1961.)

2. Warner wished to build a lumber mill, which would require construction of a railroad switch and spur line from the Texas and Pacific Railroad's main line in Texas. In 1874, he entered into an oral contract with the railroad, under the terms of which he was to supply the ties and grade the ground for the switch, with the railroad promising to construct and maintain the switch and spur line "for Warner's benefit as long as Warner needed it." Warner built the mill, and the railroad built the spur line and switch and maintained service for several years. In 1887, however, the railroad tore up the switch and ties, leaving Warner without transportation facilities. When Warner sued to recover damages for breach of contract, the railroad contended that the oral agreement "was a contract not to be performed within one year" and within the statute of frauds, and therefore was not enforceable against it. *Warner v. Texas and Pacific Ry.*, 164 U.S. 418 (1896). Is the railroad's contention correct? Explain.

3. An automobile collision occurred between cars driven by Griffin and Martin. Immediately thereafter, Harris, a friend of Martin, arrived at the scene and orally promised Griffin that he would pay for the damage caused to Griffin's car if Griffin would not bring suit against Martin. Griffin refrained from bringing legal action against Martin and several months later brought suit against Harris to hold him liable on his agreement. Harris claimed that his promise was "a promise to pay the debt of another" and was thus unenforceable under the statute of frauds. *Harris v. Griffin*, 83 So.2d 765 (1955). Is Harris liable on his oral promise? Why or why not?

4. Wilson orally agreed to sell a thoroughbred horse, "Goal Line Stand," to Presti for $60,000. When Presti sent a check in payment, Wilson told him that he was going to hold the check for a month for tax purposes, rather than cash it immediately. (Possession of the horse was retained by Wilson.) Thereafter, while the check remained uncashed, a dispute arose between the parties. In subsequent litigation Wilson contended that the contract was unenforceable since it was only made orally; Presti, on the other hand, claimed that his giving of the check constituted payment, and that this made the oral contract enforceable. Is Presti's claim correct? Discuss. (*Presti v. Wilson*, 348 F.Supp. 543, 1972.)

5. The owner of a dairy company orally contracted to sell certain land to the Hancock Construction Company, but later refused to go through with the deal. When the construction company brought an action for specific performance (i.e., an action seeking the property), the dairy company defended on the ground that the contract was not in writing. The construction company pointed out, however, that after the contract was made it had engineering studies made of the property, and also had made application for a loan of over $292,000 in order to finance the purchase. The construction company then contended that these acts on its part constituted "part performance" of the contract, and thus made the oral contract enforceable. Is this contention correct? Why or why not? (*Hancock Construction Co. v. Kempton & Snedigar Dairy*, 510 P.2d 752, 1973.)

6. Lang orally contracted to purchase $600 worth of calendars from a printer, who was to put the inscription "Lang's Cody Inn" on them. After the printer had completed the work, but before the calendars were delivered, Lang told him he would not go through with the deal. When the printer brought suit for the contract price, Lang defended on the ground that this was a contract calling for the sale of goods of over $500, and that the contract was thus unenforceable under Article 2 of the UCC since it was not in writing. Is this a good defense? Explain.

7. S and B make an oral agreement over lunch, under which S agreed to sell, and B agreed to buy, S's farm for $200,000. That afternoon S went back to his office and typed up a letter addressed to B which set forth the terms of their agreement. Soon after B received the letter, he advised S that he would not go through with the deal. Will S be able to get damages for breach of contract from B? Why or why not?

8. What is the *parol evidence* rule, and what are three important exceptions to it?

Rights of Third Parties   15

As a general rule, the rights created by the formation of a contract can be enforced only by the original parties to the agreement. A contract is essentially a private agreement affecting only the contracting parties themselves; both legal and practical difficulties would arise if a stranger to the contract (a *third party*) were permitted to enforce it. Suppose, for example, that X employed B to paint her house and that B subsequently refused to do the job. If Y, one of X's neighbors, were to bring suit against B to recover damages for breach of contract, it would be ludicrous if he were permitted to get a judgment. Since Y was not a party to the contract, he clearly had "no standing to sue," and his suit would be dismissed.

However, in certain exceptional circumstances a third party is permitted to enforce a contract made by others, particularly (1) where it appears, expressly or by necessary implication, that the parties to the contract intended that that person receive the benefit of the contract, or (2) where one of the parties, after making the contract, assigned (transferred) his or her rights to a third party. In the former situation the third party is called a *third-party beneficiary,* and in the latter he or she is designated an *assignee* of the contract.

Third-party Beneficiaries

The law recognizes three kinds of beneficiaries—creditor, donee, and incidental. Generally, creditor and donee beneficiaries can enforce contracts made by others, while incidental beneficiaries cannot.

Creditor Beneficiaries

When a contract is made between two parties for the express benefit of a third person, the latter is said to be a *creditor beneficiary* if he or she had earlier furnished consideration to one of the contracting parties. To illustrate: A owes X $500. A later sells a piano to B, on the understanding that B, in return, is to pay off A's indebtedness to X. Here X is a creditor beneficiary of the contract between A and B, inasmuch as she originally gave consideration to A, which created the debt in her (X's) favor. Once A has delivered the piano, X is entitled to recover the $500 from B—by suit, if necessary.

Assumption of Mortgage: One typical situation involving a creditor beneficiary arises when mortgaged real estate is sold, with the purchaser agreeing to pay off the existing mortgage. For example: S owns a home subject to a $15,000 mortgage held by the Y Bank. S finds a buyer for the home, Z, who is willing to *assume the mortgage.* Thereupon S and Z enter into a contract, under the terms of which S agrees to convey the property to Z, and Z promises to pay S's existing indebtedness to the bank. The Y Bank now has become a creditor beneficiary of the contract between S and Z, since it originally gave consideration to S by making the loan, and it can hold Z liable on his promise to pay the indebtedness. (The assumption of the mortgage by Z does not by itself free S of his liability. Thus the bank can look to either party for payment in case Z defaults—unless it has expressly released S from his obligation.)

Donee Beneficiaries

Where a contract is made for the benefit of a third person who has not given consideration to either contracting party, that person is designated a *donee beneficiary* of the contract. To illustrate: P, an attorney, agrees to perform certain legal services for Q, with the understanding that Q will pay the $200 legal fee to R, P's son-in-law. Here P has made a gift of $200 to R, and R—the donee beneficiary of the contract—can enforce it against Q if Q refuses to pay him voluntarily.

Life Insurance Contracts: The most common type of contract involving donee beneficiaries is that of the ordinary life insurance policy. If A insures his life with the B Insurance Company, and the policy expressly designates C as the beneficiary of the proceeds of that policy, C—the donee beneficiary—can enforce the contract against the company. The fact that C has not furnished consideration to the company is immaterial; it is sufficient that A, the insured, has done so by making his premium payments.

Incidental Beneficiaries

Occasionally, where a contract does not designate a beneficiary in express terms, a third party will seek to enforce it on the ground that that person's interest in its performance was sufficiently substantial to constitute him or her a donee beneficiary by implication. In such a situation the court has to decide whether the contracting parties probably intended to confer a benefit upon the person occupying plaintiff's position. Unless the plaintiff can make a strong showing that he or she had a direct interest in the performance of the contract and that this fact was known to the contracting parties, the plaintiff's contention will probably fail. Without such a showing, the plaintiff is said to be merely an *incidental beneficiary* of the contract, and recovery is denied. Two illustrations may be helpful.

1. A city makes a contract with the X Company, under the terms of which the company promises to supply heat to a public building. It fails to do so during a three-day period, and a visitor there contracts pneumonia as a result. The visitor probably cannot recover damages from the X Company.

2. T leases an apartment from L, with the contract providing that L will keep T's premises in good repair. L breaches this promise, as a consequence of which one of T's guests is injured. While there is diversity of opinion, a majority of courts take the view that the purpose of the clause is to protect T only; thus the guest is ruled to be an incidental beneficiary and cannot recover damages from L.

Assignment of Rights

Assignments

All contracts create certain rights and duties. With exceptions to be noted later, the *rights* a person has acquired under a contract can be transferred, or *assigned,* by that person to a third party.[1] Suppose, for example, that A agrees to add a family room to B's home for $13,500 and that A performs the required work. A thereafter assigns his right to collect the $13,500 to C, in which case A is the *assignor* and C the *assignee.* C can now recover the $13,500 from B, just as A could have done had there been no assignment. It helps to diagram the situation as follows:

---

[1]While a person's *duties* under a contract can also be transferred to a third party in some circumstances, such a transfer is a *delegation* rather than an *assignment.* The delegation of duties will be discussed later in the chapter.

Status of the Assignee

Whenever an assignment takes place, the assignee acquires no greater rights than those possessed by the assignor. Putting it another way, the obligor can assert the same defenses (if any) against the assignee that he or she had against the assignor.

This can be easily illustrated by referring to the diagram above. If B refuses to pay C and C brings suit against him on the contract, B can escape liability if he can prove that A breached his contract in some material way—by failing to complete the job, for example, or by using materials inferior to those required by the contract. In such a case C's only redress is the right to recover from A any consideration he had given to A in payment for the assignment.[2]

What Rights Can Be Assigned?

Occasionally, when an assignee requests the obligor to perform his or her part of the bargain, the obligor refuses to do so on the ground that the assigned right was of such a nature that it could not be legally transferred without his or her consent. Usually, this contention is not accepted by the courts; most contractual rights can be assigned without the obligor's consent. This is especially true where the assigned right was that of *collecting a debt.* The reasoning is that it is ordinarily no more difficult for a debtor (obligor) to pay the assignee than to pay the assignor (the original creditor); hence the obligor has no cause to complain.

Some rights, however, *cannot* be assigned without the obligor's consent. Following are the most common of these situations:

1. The terms of the contract expressly prohibit assignment by one or both parties.

2. The contract is "personal" in nature; specifically, the right in question involves a substantial *personal relationship* between the original parties to the contract. If X, for example, agrees to be Y's secretary for one year, any assignment by Y of the right to X's services would be invalid unless she consented to it. In fact, many (perhaps most) employment contracts fall within this category.

3. The assignment would materially alter the duties of the obligor. For example: S, of Columbus, Ohio, agrees to sell certain goods to B, also of Columbus, with the contract providing that "S will deliver the goods to the buyer's place of business." If B assigned this contract to the X Company of Cheyenne, Wyoming, S's obligation would be drastically increased and he would not be bound by the assignment unless he consented to it.

Additionally, the assignment of some rights is prohibited by statute. For example, a federal law (31 U.S.C.A. § 203) generally prohibits the assignment of claims

---

[2]The rule that the assignee of a simple contract acquires no greater rights than those possessed by the assignor does not apply when a particular kind of contract—a *negotiable instrument*—is utilized by the parties. Under the law of commercial paper (which will be discussed in Part III) the purchaser of that special kind of instrument may qualify as a *holder in due course* of such instrument, in which case he or she can enforce the instrument against the obligor in certain situations where the seller of the instrument could not do so.

against the federal government, and some state statutes prohibit the assignment of future wages by wage earners. When the assignment of rights is prohibited by statute, such rights cannot be assigned even with the obligor's consent.

The following case poses a question of assignability in a modern business setting.

McDonald's, defendant, is the corporation that grants all McDonald fast food restaurant franchises. In 1959 defendant granted a franchise to a Mr. Copeland, giving him the right to own and operate McDonald's first store in the Omaha-Council Bluffs area. A few days later, in conformity with the negotiations leading up to the granting of the franchise, McDonald's sent a letter to Copeland giving him a "Right of First Refusal;" i.e., the right to be given first chance at owning any new stores that might be subsequently established in the area. In the next few years Copeland exercised this right and opened five additional stores in Omaha. In 1964 Copeland *sold and assigned all of his franchises* to Schupach, plaintiff, with McDonald's consent.

When McDonald's granted a franchise in the Omaha-Council Bluffs area in 1974 to a third party without first offering it to Schupach, he brought this action for damages resulting from establishment of the new franchise, claiming that the assignment of the franchises to him also included the right of first refusal.

A number of issues were raised in this litigation. Defendant contended, among other things, that the right it gave to Copeland was personal in nature, and thus was not transferable without its consent. Plaintiff alleged, on the other hand, that the right was not personal in nature, or, in the alternative, that its transfer was, in fact, agreed to by defendant.

On these issues the trial court ruled that the right was personal in nature. It also ruled, however, after analyzing voluminous correspondence between the parties, that defendant *had* consented to the transfer. It entered judgment for plaintiff, and defendant appealed. (Only that part of the higher court's opinion relating to these two issues appears below).

Schupach v. McDonald's System, Inc.
Supreme Court of Nebraska, 264 N.W.2d 827 (1978)

White, Justice: . . . McDonald's was founded in 1954 by Mr. Ray Kroc. Kroc licensed and later purchased the name McDonald's [and all other rights relating thereto] from two brothers named McDonald, who were operating a hamburger restaurant in San Bernardino, California. In 1955 Kroc embarked on a plan to create a nationwide standardized system of fast-food restaurants. . . .

At the trial, Kroc testified about the image he sought to create with McDonald's. . . . He wanted to create "an image people would have confidence in. An image of cleanliness. An image where the parents would be glad to have the children come and/or have them work there."

Kroc testified that careful selection of franchises was to be the key to success for McDonald's and the establishment of this image. . . . People were selected "who had a great deal of pride, and had an aptitude for serving the public, and had dedication."

Fred Turner, the current president of McDonald's, testified [in a similar vein]. . . . He stated that by 1957 it became apparent that McDonald's could only achieve its goal by careful selection of persons who would adhere to the company's high standards. He stated that an individual's managerial skills and abilities were a matter of prime importance in the selection process. . . .

Summarizing, the evidence is overwhelming, [and establishes the conclusion that] the Right of First Refusal was intended to be personal in nature, and was separately a grant independent of the terms of the franchise contract itself. [It also establishes the fact that] the grant depended upon the personal confidence that McDonald's placed in the grantee, and that to permit the assignability by the grantee without permission of McDonald's would serve to destroy the basic policy of control of the quality and confidence in performance in the event any new franchises were to be granted in the locality. . . .

[The court then reviewed the same correspondence which was examined by the trial court, and ruled that McDonald's had *not* given its permission to the transfer of the right. The judgment for plaintiff was therefore reversed.]

Form of the Assignment

As a general rule, no particular formalities need be observed in order for an assignment to be legally effective. Any words or conduct that indicate an intention on the part of the assignor to transfer his or her contractual rights are normally sufficient. Some assignments, however, are required by statute to be in writing. Thus the assignment of a contract that falls within the statute of frauds must be evidenced by a writing; similarly, under the statutes of most states, the assignment of one's rights to collect wages from an employer must also be in writing.

Absence of Consideration

Once a valid assignment has occurred, the assignee is entitled to enforce the contract against the obligor even if the assignee did not give consideration for the assignment to the assignor. The absence of consideration on the part of the assignee does have one significant effect, however; the assignor in such a case has the right to *rescind the assignment* at any time before the contract has been performed by the obligor, without liability to the assignee. (It is assumed here that the assignment was not meant to be a *gift*. If it were, rescission of the assignment would not, of course, be permitted.)

Notice of Assignment

A valid assignment takes effect the moment it is made, regardless of whether the obligor is aware that the assignment has occurred. However, the assignee should give *immediate notice* to the obligor whenever an assignment is made, in order to protect the rights received under it.

A primary reason for giving notice is that an obligor who does not have notice of an assignment is free to go ahead and render performance to the assignor, thereby discharging his or her contractual duties. Suppose, for example, that X is owed $500 by Y and that X assigns the right to collect the debt to Z. If Y, not knowing of the assignment, pays the debt to X (assignor), Z has lost her right to collect the indebtedness from Y. Any other result would be patently unfair to Y. Z's only redress in such a case is to recover payment from X, who clearly has no right to retain the money.

Notice of assignment can also be important in a case where successive assignments occur, as illustrated in the diagram below. R owes money to S. S assigns his right to collect the debt to A on June 10, then assigns the same right to B on June 15, B not knowing of the prior assignment.

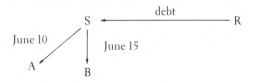

Suppose that the first assignee, A, does not give notice of assignment to R until June 25, while the second assignee, B, gives notice on June 20. In such a situation, a number of courts—though not a majority—would rule that B is entitled to payment of the debt, rather than A; in other words, the assignee who first gives notice prevails. (In states adopting this minority view, A's only redress is to recover the consideration, if any, that he gave to S in exchange for the assignment.) The majority view is that A, the first assignee, collects, even if he did not give notice first.

Delegation of Duties

Our discussion so far has been limited to the assignment of contractual *rights*. Under many assignments, however, the assignor can also transfer, or attempt to transfer, his or her contractual *duties* to a third party. Suppose, for example, that the X Company contracts to build a garage for Y for $2,500. Before commencing to perform its part of the bargain, the X Company assigns the *entire contract* to the Z Company, the latter promising to build the garage in place of the X Company. In this case, the X Company has both assigned its contingent right to collect the $2,500 and delegated its duty to build the garage. In the event that Y refuses to accept performance by the Z Company, the question is raised as to what kinds of duties can be delegated by the original promisor without the promisee's consent.

The courts' usual approach in making such a decision is to determine whether the work that was contracted for by the promisee substantially depended upon the personal skill, training, or character of the promisor. If so, delegation is not permitted. Thus the contractual duties assumed by a physician, attorney, or office manager clearly cannot be delegated without the consent of the promisee. Contracts of this nature are personal services contracts.

On the other hand, the delegation of duties *is* allowed without the consent of the promisee if the duties are essentially "routine"—that is, if the performance is standardized or nonpersonal in nature and can be performed as well by one person or firm as by another. For example, if the C Company contracts to sell 12,000 gallons of a standard type of crude oil to N, with deliveries to be made in designated installments over a one-year period, the C Company can delegate this duty or any portion of it to any other company that is as capable of performing the duty as the C Company itself. If such a delegation took place, N could not successfully claim that he was thereby freed of his duty to accept and pay for the oil. (The C Company would, however, remain liable to N for damages in the event that the company to whom the duty was delegated failed to live up to the contract; a party cannot terminate contractual obligations simply by delegating them to another.) Similarly, under many construction contracts the prime contractor can delegate all or a portion of the duties to subcontractors, since most of the duties created by such contracts are routine enough in nature that they can be performed as well by one construction firm as another. This is particularly true of large construction contracts, where the magnitude of the job itself is enough to put the promisee on notice that the prime contractor cannot do the entire job without assistance of other firms.

Questions and Problems

1. An agency of the State of Washington operated a ferry system providing service between the mainland and offshore islands. The ferry employees were unionized, and they worked under a contract between the union and the state. Just before a Labor Day weekend the union called a strike, which was a breach of its contract. As a result, tourist travel to the islands was substantially cut, and resort owners located on the islands sued the union to recover damages for breach of contract. Should the fact that the resort owners were not parties to the contract defeat their action? Why or why not? (*Burke and Thomas v. International Organization of Masters,* 585 P.2d 152, 1978.)

2. An insurance company issued a policy of automobile liability insurance to Enos. While Enos was driving the car he had an accident that injured a passenger, Julia Wagner. A doctor, Jones, treated her injuries. After being unable to recover his fee from Enos, Dr. Jones sued the insurance company to hold it liable. The company defended on the ground that he could not maintain the suit since he was not a party to the insurance contract. Is this a valid argument? Discuss. (*Franklin Casualty Insurance Co. v. Jones,* 362 P.2d 964, 1961.)

3. A labor union entered into a collective bargaining agreement with the Powder Power Tool Corporation, under which the company agreed to pay specified wages to various classes of its employees. When Springer, an employee and union member, was not paid the full wages to which he was entitled under the agreement, he brought action to recover the additional payments as specified. The company defended on the ground that Springer was not a party to the contract and thus could not maintain the action. *Springer v. Powder Power Tool Co.,* 348 P.2d 1112 (1960). Is the company correct? Explain.

4. The Brookfield Municipal Utility District (the District) made a contract with a land developer under the terms of which it agreed to furnish water and sewer service to a specific tract of land. A year later, after condominiums were built on the land, service was terminat-

ed. The condominium owners then sued the District for damages for breach of contract. The owners conceded they were not parties to the contract, but contended that they were beneficiaries of it, and thus entitled to sue. Is this a good argument? Why or why not? (*Greenway Park v. Brookfield Municipal Utility District*, 575 S.W.2d 90, 1978.)

5. Abramov, when leaving the employment of a partnership, signed a contract promising not to compete with the partnership for five years. Soon thereafter the partnership incorporated. Abramov later started a business in competition with the corporation, whereupon it brought action for an injunction ordering him to live up to the terms of the contract not to compete. The issue was whether the contract could be assigned by the partnership to the corporation without Abramov's consent. Decide, with reasons. (*Abramov v. Royal Dallas, Inc.*, 536 S.W.2d 388, 1976.)

6. Cullins worked for an insurance agency under an employment contract that prevented him from competing with that agency for a period of three years after leaving its employment. Later, another company, Smith, Bell & Hauck, Inc., purchased the insurance agency. When Cullins quit the agency and formed a new insurance firm, Smith, Bell and Hauck brought an action for an injunction ordering Cullins to live up to his contract not to compete. When Cullins defended on the ground that Smith, Bell and Hauck were not parties to the contract, they contended that an implied assignment of the contract from the insurance agency had taken place and, as assignees, they were entitled to enforce that contract. Is this a good argument? Discuss. (*Smith, Bell and Hauck, Inc., v. Cullins*, 183 A.2d 528, 1962.)

7. Folquet was employed as a school bus driver by the Woodburn Public School District for a contract period of five years at a salary of $125 per school month. The contract required Folquet to furnish and maintain a bus at his own expense, to conduct himself in a proper and moral manner, and to be responsible for the conduct of the pupils while in the bus. Forquet died before the five years elapsed, and his son, an adult, was appointed administrator of his estate. When the son offered to drive the bus for the remainder of the contract, the district refused to let him do so. The son then brought suit to recover damages for breach of contract. The school district contended that the contract was of a personal nature and thus could not be delegated or assigned to any other driver without its consent. *Folquet v. Woodburn Public Schools*, 29 P.2d 554 (1934). Is the school district's defense valid? Explain.

8. A company assigned its accounts receivable to an insurance company (Assignee #1) and later assigned the same accounts to a bank (Assignee #2.) The bank gave notice of the assignment to the account debtors before the insurance company did. In subsequent litigation the issue was which of the two assignees was entitled to collect the account receivables.

    a) If the majority ("American") rule were applied, who would win?
    b) If the minority ("English") rule were applied, who would win? (*Boulevard National Bank of Miami v. Air Metals Industries, Inc.*, 176 So.2d 94, 1965.)

16 | Discharge of Contracts

Sooner or later all contractual obligations come to an end. When this occurs in a particular case, the contract is said to be *discharged*. What is meant by this is that the *duties* of the contracting parties have been discharged.

There are many ways in which a discharge, or termination, can come about. Most of these result from the conduct of the parties themselves, while others involve events completely outside the control of either party. The *Restatement of the Law of Contracts* (Sec. 385) recognizes twenty-five separate and distinct ways in which a person's contractual obligations can be discharged. The most important are the following: (1) performance, (2) breach by the other party, (3) failure of a condition precedent, (4) occurrence of an express condition subsequent, (5) legal impossibility (implied conditions subsequent), (6) agreement of the parties, and (7) operation of law.[1]

---

[1]*Restatement of the Law of Contracts* (St. Paul, Minn.: American Law Institute, 1932).

Before examining the most common types of discharge, we will briefly discuss the nature of *conditions*. The law relating to conditions is so intertwined with the subject of discharge that it is virtually impossible to deal with one without understanding the other. First, all contracts are subject to certain implied conditions, and many contain express conditions as well. Second, whenever a condition is *breached* (not fulfilled) or *met* (fulfilled), the legal rights of the parties are invariably affected —and the duties of at least one of the parties are usually discharged in the process.

A Word about Conditions

The law recognizes three kinds of conditions—*conditions precedent, conditions subsequent,* and *conditions concurrent.* Each condition can be further classified as either *express* or *implied.*

Conditions Precedent

In many contracts the parties simply exchange mutual promises, neither promise being expressly conditioned or qualified in any way. Once such a contract is formed, each party is said to have assumed "a duty of immediate performance"—even though the performance of one or both parties is not to take place until some specified time in the future.

In some situations, however, the performance of the contemplated contract may be beneficial to one or both of the parties if, and only if, a certain event occurs (or does not occur) in the future. If a contract that is drawn up indicates, expressly or by implication, that the promises made therein are not to be operative until the specified event takes place, that event constitutes a *condition precedent.*

For example: X makes this offer to Y, "If the city rezones your property at 707 River Street from C-3 to C-1 within thirty days, I will pay you $18,000 cash for it." Y accepts the offer. While a contract has now been formed, it is clear that the specified event must occur before either party incurs a duty of immediate performance. Because the condition here resulted from the language of the contract itself, the rezoning constitutes an *express condition precedent.* Should the rezoning not occur within the stated time—in which case the condition is said to have failed—the obligations of both parties are discharged.

Occasionally, where a contract contains no *express* conditions, one of the parties will seek to be relieved from his or her obligations on the ground that the contract contains an *implied* condition precedent that was not met; the argument is that such a condition can be inferred from the circumstances surrounding the making of the contract. While the courts usually reject such contentions because of the danger that can result if they "remake" contracts, the contentions may be accepted in limited situations. For example: If E, an electrical contractor, agrees to install the wiring in a building being constructed by a prime contractor, it is necessarily implied that the construction of the building must proceed to the point where it is ready for wiring before E has an immediate duty of performance. Thus the construction of the building to that point is an implied condition precedent insofar as E's obligation is concerned.

Conditions Subsequent

Occasionally both parties to a contract are willing to incur a duty of immediate performance—with the qualification that if a certain event occurs before the time of performance arrives, their respective duties are to be discharged. In such cases the designated event is a *condition subsequent*.[2]

For example: S owns a grocery store located near a private school, Y College. In April S contracts to sell the store to B for $32,000, the contract providing that the first payment of $8,000 is to be due the following July 1, with payments thereafter to be made in the amount of $200 per month. The contract contains this further provision: "In the event that Y College is permanently closed at the end of the present school year, this contract shall be null and void." Here B has incurred an immediate duty of performance, but it will be terminated if the specified condition occurs. Hence the condition in this case constitutes a condition subsequent.

Most conditions subsequent (as is true of conditions generally) are express rather than implied. They can ordinarily be recognized by language providing that the contract is to be void, inoperative, or canceled if a certain event occurs in the future. (The relatively few situations in which *implied* conditions subsequent exist will be discussed later in the chapter.)

Conditions Concurrent

If a contract expressly provides (or if one can reasonably infer from its terms) that the performances of the parties are to occur at the same time, the conditions are said to be *concurrent* (or mutual). A common example is a land sale contract which provides that the seller is to deliver the deed on payment of the purchase price. The duty of each party is thus conditioned on performance by the other. The seller has no duty to deliver the deed until the buyer pays (or tenders) the purchase price, and the buyer has no duty to pay until the seller delivers (or tenders) the deed.[3]

We shall now turn our attention to the most common ways of discharging contractual obligations.

Discharge by Performance

Most contracts are discharged by performance—by each party completely fulfilling his or her promises. In such cases, obviously, no legal problems exist. Nevertheless, the subject of performance merits special attention for several reasons.

In the first place, many cases arise in which the actual performance of a promisor is, to some extent, defective. Sometimes the performance falls far short of what was

---

[2]Thus the essential difference in legal effect between the two basic kinds of conditions is that the occurrence of a condition precedent *imposes* a duty of immediate performance, while the occurrence of a condition subsequent *removes* such a duty.

[3]A tender is an *offer* to perform one's obligation.

promised; other times it deviates from the terms of the contract in only minor respects. As one might expect, the legal consequences of a major breach of contract are more severe and far-reaching than those resulting from a minor breach.

Secondly, in some cases the courts must determine whether the defective performance constituted a breach of a condition or a mere breach of a promise. A breach of a condition, no matter how slight, usually frees the nondefaulting party, while a breach of a promise generally does not unless it is a material one.

Promises: Degree of Performance Required

Many agreements consist simply of the exchange of mutual promises, with neither party's obligations expressly conditioned in any way. In most of these contracts, however, it is usually apparent from their nature that one of the parties is to perform his or her part of the bargain before the other is obligated to do so. For example: If X contracts to landscape Y's new home for $1,500, it can reasonably be inferred that the work is to be done by X before he can demand payment of Y. Thus, in general, when a promisor seeks to recover the contract price, that person must show that he or she has *fully performed* the promise in some cases or *substantially performed* it in others—depending on the nature of the obligation involved. If it is determined that this performance has fallen short of the applicable minimum standard, the promisor's obligation has not been discharged and recovery is denied.[4]

Total Performance: Some promises are of such a nature that they can be discharged only by complete performance. If a promisor's performance falls short of that called for under such a contract, even though the breach is minor, his or her obligation is not discharged. Suppose, for example, that B contracts in May to buy a car from S for $2,000—the contract providing that the price is to be paid in full by B on June 1, at which time S is to assign the car title to her. If, on June 1, B tenders S a check for $1,950, S has no obligation to transfer the title. A contract under which a seller of land is obligated to convey "merchantable title" falls into the same category; delivery of a deed conveying any interest or title less than that specified will not discharge the seller's obligation.

Substantial Performance: Many obligations are of such a nature that it is unlikely (indeed, not even to be expected, given the frailties of mankind), that a 100 percent performance will actually occur. The typical example involves a construction contract under which a builder agrees to build a home according to detailed plans and specifications. It is quite possible that the finished building will deviate from the specifications in one or more respects no matter how conscientious and able the

---

[4]In this regard, it is sometimes said that the actual performance of one's promises constitutes an *implied* condition precedent that must be met by that person.

builder is. In contracts of this sort, if the promisee-homemaker seeks to escape liability on the ground of nonperformance of the promisor-builder, it is ordinarily held that the promisor has sufficiently fulfilled the obligation if his or her performance, though imperfect, conformed to the terms of the contract in all major respects. This rule is known as the *doctrine of substantial performance.*

In order for the doctrine to be applicable, two requirements must ordinarily be met:

1. Performance must be "substantial"—that is, the omissions and deviations must be so slight in nature that they do not materially affect the usefulness of the building for the purposes for which it was intended.

2. The omissions or deviations must not have been occasioned by bad faith on the part of the builder. (This is ordinarily interpreted to mean that the omissions or deviations must not have been made knowingly by the builder).

Going back to the illustration involving the construction of a house, let us examine three cases where the builder is bringing suit against the owner to recover the last payment of $5,000 called for under the contract and where the owner is refusing to pay on the ground of inadequate performance.

Case 1. The owner proves that the following defects exist: (1) the plaster in all rooms is considerably softer than expected, because the builder used one bag of adamant for each hod of mortar instead of the two bags called for by the contract, and (2) water seepage in the basement is so great as to make the game room virtually unusable, as a result of the builder's failure to put a required sealant on the exterior of the basement walls. Here the defects are so material, and so affect the enjoyment and value of the home, that the builder has *not substantially performed* his obligations. Thus recovery will be denied, even if the breaches on the part of the builder are shown to be accidental rather than intentional.

Case 2. The owner proves that the following defects exist: (1) the detached garage was given but one coat of paint rather than the two required; (2) the water pipes in the walls were made by the Cohoes Company rather than the Reading Company as was specified (though otherwise the two types of pipe are virtually identical), and (3) the wallboard installed in the attic is ⅛ inch sheeting instead of the ¼ inch that was called for. Here the defects are so slight in nature, even when taken in total, that the builder has substantially performed the contract and can thus probably recover under the doctrine.

Case 3. Same facts as Case 2, but, in addition, the owner can show that one or more of the deviations were *intentional;* for example, he produces evidence tending to prove that the builder ordered the installation of the substitute pipe and wallboard knowing that they were not in conformity with the contract. Here the deviations are willful (rather than the result of simple negligence); therefore the builder is guilty of bad faith and the doctrine is not applicable.

Obviously, the requirement that performance be "substantial" is a somewhat elastic one, and neccessitates a comparison of the promisor's actual performance with that which the terms of the contract really required of him. In the following case the trial and appellate courts took different views on the question.

Butkovich & Sons v. State Bank of St.Charles

Appellate Court of Illinois, Second District, 379 N.E.2d 837 (1978)

This was essentially an action by a contractor, Butkovich, against a home owner, Grane, in which the contractor was seeking the balance due on a construction contract. The primary issue was whether the contractor had substantially performed the contract. (The State Bank of St. Charles was named a co-defendant only because it held a mortgage on Grane's home, and its interest would be affected if the contractor won a judgment which Grane was unable to pay.)

Butkovich contracted to do certain construction work on a home owned by Grane in Oak Brook, Illinois, for $19,290. The work involved enlargement of the existing basement; construction of a new room over that basement, and the laying of a new garage floor and patio. After the work was completed Grane refused to pay the balance due, $9,290, alleging that there were a number of defects in the work. The major allegations were that plaintiff (a) failed to install water stops; (b) failed to install reinforcing wire in one concrete floor; and (c) built the main floor of the addition at a level approximately nine inches lower than the plans called for.

The trial judge, viewing plaintiff's performance in its totality, ruled that he had substantially performed the contract despite the defects, and entered judgment for plaintiff. Defendants appealed.

Woodward, Justice: . . . The ordinary rule applied in cases involving building contracts is that a builder is not required to perform perfectly, but rather, he is held only to a duty of substantial performance in a workmanlike manner. The purchaser who receives substantial performance of the building contract must pay the contract price less a credit for any deficiencies existing in what he received [when measured against] what strict performance would have given him.

On the other hand, a contractor whose work amounts to less than substantial performance has no right to the contract price; in that situation the builder [has the right] to recover only reasonable compensation for value received by the purchaser over and above the injury suffered by the builder's breach. . . . Whether substantial performance has been given will depend on the relevant facts of each case. We shall therefore proceed to examine those facts in connection with this case.

A water stop [can be] caulking or a solid material poured up against a wall of fresh concrete . . . or a piece of vinyl material . . . that is placed in between the cement floor and the foundation wall. While admitting that the water stops were not installed, plaintiff argues that the contract makes no reference to water stops, that water stops are mentioned only in the specifications for the house, [and that] there was no testimony that the absence of water stops contributed to the water in defendant's premises. However, the Supplemental Conditions [in the contract] provide in part: "The contract shall consist of the specifications, the drawings, the proposal form and the Owner-Contractor Agreement." Finally, there was testimony that prior to entering the contract, the parties held lengthy discussions on the potential water problem. . . .

Plaintiff argues that the reinforcing mesh, like the water stops, was not mentioned in the contract, and that defendant offered no testimony that any damage was suffered as a result of such omission. However, Butkovich testified that page three of the specifications calls for reinforcing wire; it was placed in the garage floor, but he did not know about the basement floor; as a rule "we do not put it in the basement floor." . . .

Donald Smith, a licensed surveyor, testified that he found the defendant's residence [i.e., the addition] to be 8⅞ inches below the level required in the plans, and only three inches higher than the adjoining residence. . . .

Thus, considering the omissions from the contract, coupled with the evidence of the poor quality [of the cement work,] this court is of the opinion that the finding by the trial court that plaintiff substantially performed its contract with defendant is against the manifest weight of the evidence. Therefore, the decision . . . is reversed and the cause remanded for a new trial.

Reversed and remanded.

Substantial Performance; Amount of Recovery: If the rule of substantial performance is applicable to a particular case, the promisor/plaintiff is entitled to recover the *contract price minus damages.* (I.e., promisor may recover the amount that the promisee agreed to pay under the contract, minus damages—if any—which the promisee sustained as a result of the deviations.) Since the damages are typically inconsequential, the promisor usually recovers a high percentage of the contract price. By contrast, where the doctrine is not applicable, the recovery may be little or nothing. The general rules for such situations can be summarized as follows:

1. Where the performance falls short of being substantial and the breach is intentional, the promisor receives nothing. The rationale, of course, is that an intentional wrongdoer should not be rewarded—particularly where the promisee has not received the performance he or she was entitled to. (The rule of nonrecovery also has an affirmative aspect—it strongly "persuades" the promisor to actually finish the job, since he or she will receive nothing otherwise.)

2. In the somewhat rarer case where the performance is not substantial but the breach is unintentional, recovery is allowed on the basis of *quasi-contract.* For example, if the promisor is permanently injured when only halfway through the job, he or she is entitled to receive the reasonable value of the benefit received by the promisee as a result of the partial performance.

3. If the performance is clearly substantial but the breach is willful, there are conflicting views. Some courts deny any recovery, regardless of other circumstances, embracing the principle that aid should never be given the intentional wrongdoer. Most courts, while endorsing this principle in the abstract, in fact allow a quasi-contractual recovery where failure to do so would result in the promisee being unjustly enriched—particularly where the performance is of such a nature that it cannot be returned by the promisee.

Special Problems Relating to Performance

Personal Satisfaction Contracts: Under the ordinary contract, a person who has undertaken the performance of a job impliedly warrants only that he or she will perform in a "workmanlike manner"—i.e., that performance will be free of material defect and of a quality ordinarily accepted in that line of work. If performance meets this standard, he or she is entitled to recover the contract price even if the person for whom the work was done is not satisfied with it.

Some contracts, however, provide that "satisfaction is guaranteed," or contain other language of similar nature. In such cases, it is usually held that such satisfaction is a *condition precedent* that must be met in order for the promisor to recover under the contract; workmanlike performance alone will not suffice. In determining whether the condition has been met, the courts distinguish between two kinds of contracts: (1) those in which matters of personal taste, esthetics, or comfort are dominant considerations, and (2) those that entail work of mere "mechanical utility."

For contracts in the first category, the condition is fulfilled only if the *promisee is actually satisfied* with the performance that was rendered—no matter how peculiar or unreasonable that person's tastes may be. For example: X, an artist, contracts to paint a portrait of Y for $500 "that will meet with Y's complete satisfaction." When the portrait is completed, Y refuses to pay on the ground that he simply does not like it. If X brings suit to recover the $500, a question of fact is presented: Is Y's claim of dissatisfaction genuine? If the jury so finds, the condition has not been met and X is denied recovery. (Of course, if the jury finds that Y's claim of dissatisfaction is false—that is, he is actually satisfied and is simply using this claim as a ground to escape an otherwise valid contract—then the condition has been met and recovery is allowed.)

For contracts in the second category, where the performance involves work of mere mechanical fitness (or mechanical utility), an objective test is used. For example: M agrees to overhaul the diesel engine in T's tractor-trailer for $200, guaranteeing that T will be "fully satisfied" with the job. In this case, the condition precedent is met if the jury finds that *a reasonable person would have been satisfied* with M's job, even though T himself is dissatisfied.

Performance by an Agreed Time: If a contract does not provide a time by which performance is to be completed, the general rule is that each party has a reasonable time within which to perform his or her obligations. Whether the performance of a promisor in a given case took place within such a time is ordinarily a question for the jury. In practice this rule poses few problems and seems to produce acceptable results.

A more troublesome situation is presented by contracts that do contain a stated time of performance. For example: A printer agrees to print up 15,000 letterheads for a customer, with the contract specifying "delivery by April 10." If delivery is not made until April 14, and the customer refuses to accept the goods because of the late performance, the question for the jury is whether the stated time of performance legally constituted a condition precedent. If it did, the condition has obviously not been met and the customer has no obligation to accept the shipment.

The general rule is that such a provision, of and by itself, *does not create a condition precedent.* Usually, it is sufficient if the performance occurs within a reasonable time after the date specified. Thus, in the preceding illustration, the customer is very likely obligated to accept the letterheads where delivery was only four days late.

In some situations, however, the parties clearly intend that performance *must actually take place* by the specified time in order for the promisor to recover from the other party. In such situations, performance by the agreed upon time *does* constitute a condition precedent. The intention can be manifested in two ways (1) by the express wording of the agreement itself and (2) by implication (reasonable inference from the nature and subject matter of the contract alone).[5] Two examples may be helpful.

Case 1. P agrees to print up and deliver 15,000 letterheads to Q by April 10, the contract further providing that *time is of the essence.* By this clause, the parties have made the stated time of performance an express condition precedent. Thus, if P fails to deliver the letterheads until April 11, Q can refuse to accept the belated performance. P's failure to meet the condition frees Q of her obligations under the contract. Additionally, Q can recover damages from P in a breach of contract suit. (An alternative open to Q is to accept the late performance and "reserve her rights" against P—in which case she is entitled to an allowance against the purchase price to the extent that she has suffered damages as a result of the late performance.)

Case 2. A chamber of commerce purchases fireworks for a Fourth of July celebration it is sponsoring, with the contract providing that "delivery is to be made prior to July 4th." The fireworks arrive too late on July 4th to be used. From the nature of the *subject matter alone* it can be inferred that the stated time is a condition precedent, and the late delivery obviously did not meet that condition. In such a case it is said that time was made a condition "by operation of law" (that is, without regard to other factors).

As one might guess, courts seldom can rule, from the subject matter of the contract alone, that time was of the essence. A person making such a claim must ordinarily show (1) that delivery by the specified time was, in fact, material to him or her, and (2) that the other party knew, or should have known, this was the case.

There is, however, one kind of contract where the courts *are* likely to rule that performance by the specified time was a condition by operation of law. In the case of *commercial contracts* (those in which the seller and buyer are both merchants) the specified delivery date is frequently held to consitute a condition precedent "as a matter of law." This view is particularly likely to be applied where the buyer is purchasing goods for the purpose of resale. Thus, if a manufacturer contracted to sell one hundred television sets to a retailer with "delivery to be made by August 1," a delivery even one day late can be rejected by the buyer.[6]

---

[5]The latter possibility is eliminated in some jurisdictions. A number of states provide by statute that time is never of the essence unless the contract *expressly* indicates that it is.

[6]A note of caution. This view, while common, is not universally applied. Some courts, even in commercial contracts, will permit the seller to raise the question of whether delivery by the specified time was in fact material to the buyer in a given case. If it is found not to have been, delivery by the time specified does not constitute a condition precedent, and delivery within a reasonable time thereafter must be accepted.

Actual Breach

It would be contrary to common sense if a person who had materially breached a contract were nevertheless able to hold the other party liable on it, and the law does not tolerate such a result. As the preceding section indicates, the failure of a promisor to render performance that meets the minimum required by law (full performance in some cases and substantial performance in others) ordinarily results in the other party's obligations being discharged. In such cases the promisor's breach operates as "an excuse for nonperformance" insofar as the other's obligation is concerned.

This principle has found its way into the law of sales. Thus, if Seller S on May 1 contracts to deliver a thousand gallons of crude oil to Buyer B on August 15, and on that date S delivers only two hundred gallons with no indication that the balance will be delivered shortly thereafter, B can cancel the entire contract, returning the oil already delivered (see Secs. 2-610 and 2-711 of the UCC).

Anticipatory Breach

If one contracting party indicates to the other, before the time of performance arrives, that he or she is not going to perform his or her part of the bargain, an *anticipatory breach* has occurred; in most cases this has the same effect as an actual breach. For example: In March, X contracts to put in a sewer line for a city, with the contract providing that the work will be commenced by June 1. On April 10, X tells the city that he will not do the job. The city can immediately hire a new contractor to do the work and can institute a suit for damages against X as soon as the damages can be ascertained, without waiting until June to do so. (Such action is not mandatory; the city may ignore the repudiation in the hope that X will have a change of heart and actually commence the work on schedule.)

The doctrine of anticipatory breach does not apply to promises to pay money debts, such as those found in promissory notes and bonds. To illustrate: S borrows $500 from T on February 1, giving T a promissory note in that amount due September 1. If S tells T on August 6 that he will not pay the debt, T must nevertheless wait until September 2 before bringing suit to recover the $500.

We have already seen that the nonoccurrence (failure) of a condition precedent usually results in both parties to a contract being freed of their contingent obligations. In such cases it can be said that the contract is discharged.

Most conditions precedent are express rather than implied, usually created by clauses containing the words *if, in the event,* or *when.* Thus the following language creates an express condition precedent: "If X is able to obtain a building permit from the city within sixty days, it is agreed that Y will construct a swimming pool for her, according to the attached specifications, for $9,000."

In some situations the nonoccurrence of a condition precedent results in only one of the parties being freed of obligations. This is true when the other party has assumed the obligation of meeting the condition. Thus, where a promisor guarantees that the promisee will be satisfied with the performance to be rendered, only the promisee's obligations are discharged if satisfaction is not achieved; the promisor remains liable for damages for breach of contract.

Discharge by Occurrence of An Express Condition Subsequent

Where the wording of a contract makes it clear that the parties have agreed to terminate their obligations on the occurrence of a specified event, an *express condition subsequent* has been created. If the event occurs before performance takes place, the courts will respect this intention and rule that the obligations of both parties are thereby discharged.

While so far we have emphasized the differences between conditions precedent and conditions subsequent, either type of condition can be utilized to bring about the same result in a particular case. Suppose, for example, that N wants to buy R's land only if it is rezoned by the city. One way she can accomplish this, assuming that R is willing, is to agree to purchase the land for a designated price "if the land is rezoned from classification C-1 to C-3 within thirty days." Here a condition precedent is utilized. But she could instead agree to purchase the land with this proviso: "If the said land is not rezoned from C-1 to C-3 within thirty days, this contract shall be null and void." Here, through the use of a negative condition subsequent (the nonoccurrence of a specified event), N has achieved the same protection that was afforded her under the first contract.

Discharge by Legal Impossibility

Between the time of contracting and the time of performance, some event may occur that will make the performance of the contract—for one party, at least—considerably more difficult or costly than originally expected. When this happens, a promisor can contend that the occurrence legally discharged his or her obligations under the contract—that is, it created a *legal impossibility.*[7] For example: A, an accountant for a large corporation who "moonlights" in his spare time, contracts in May to perform certain auditing services for B during the first three weeks of August, A's regularly scheduled vacation. In June A is transferred to a city five hundred miles distant; as a result, he does not perform the promised services. If B were to seek damages for breach of contract, the issue presented would be whether A's transfer discharged his obligations under the contract.

In such a case, the courts resort to a two-step process. The first question to be decided is whether one of the parties had "assumed the risk" in some manner. For example, in the case above, a court might conclude—from a reading of the entire

---

[7]A related subject, the doctrine of commercial impracticability, will be discussed subsequently.

contract, or from testimony regarding the negotiations leading up to the contract—that B had agreed that A need not perform if he were transferred. If so, B had assumed the risk, and A need not perform.

If no assumption of risk is apparent (as is often the case), the court must proceed to the second question: whether it can rule, on the basis of the circumstances under which the contract was made, that the contract necessarily contained an *implied condition subsequent.* In other words, in the case above, A would be excused from performing the contract only if he could convince the court that he and B agreed by implication that the contract would be voided if he were transferred before the date of performance.

In most cases of this sort, the promisor's contention that an *implied condition subsequent* existed is rejected by the courts. The usual view is that such possibilities should have been guarded against by an express condition in the contract. Thus, in the example above, A will probably be held liable for breach of contract. Similarly, when a corporation promises to manufacture engines by a certain date under a contract containing no express conditions, the fact that it is unable to do so because of a strike at one of its plants is no legal excuse for its nonperformance of the contract. And when a contractor agrees to construct a building by a certain date, with a monetary penalty imposed for late completion, the law normally does not excuse late performance simply because unexpectedly bad weather delayed the work. Nor will a court normally free a builder from his obligations, in the absence of an express condition, merely because unexpectedly high labor or materials costs will cause him to suffer a loss if he is held to the contract.

"True" Impossibility

Up until recent years, implied conditions subsequent (i.e., conditions resulting in legal impossibility) have been recognized by the courts in only three situations: (1) in contracts calling for personal services, (2) where the subject matter of the contract is destroyed without the fault of either party, or (3) where the performance of the contract becomes illegal after the contract is formed.[8] We will examine each of these briefly.

Personal Services: In contracts calling for the rendering of *personal services,* such as the ordinary employment contract, the death or incapacity of the promisor (employee) terminates the agreement. The same is true of contracts that contemplate a *personal relationship* between the promisor and the other party. In such

---

[8]The view is rather commonly held among lay persons, and sometimes even finds its way into court decisions, that *any* "act of God" will discharge a promisor from his or her obligations. This generalization should be limited, however, to destruction-of-the-subject-matter cases, because it is by no means true in others. We have already noted, for example, that difficulties resulting from bad weather conditions are usually held not to constitute grounds for avoiding one's contractual obligations. (Because of such holdings, the typical construction contract usually contains a good many *express* conditions subsequent, excusing delays resulting from bad weather, strikes, and so on.)

cases the courts will accept the argument that the performer's promise was subject to the implied condition that his or her death prior to the time of performance (or illness at the time of performance) rendered the contract null and void.[9]

Destruction of the Subject Matter: The principle is well established that destruction of the subject matter of a contract, before the time for performance, terminates the contract. Where such a situation occurs, the courts will accept the argument that the destruction constituted an implied condition subsequent and will rule, as in the personal service contracts, that a legal impossibility has occurred. For example: If C contracted in January to move D's house in March, the contract would be discharged if the house were destroyed by flood in February. (In this regard, it can be said that the destruction of the subject matter of a contract by an "act of God" creates a legal impossibility.)

It is occasionally difficult to determine what is meant by the subject matter of a contract; the term often includes not only the precise subject matter involved but any other "thing" or property that performance of the contract necessarily depends on. For example: The X Company in January agrees to manufacture and deliver five hundred widgets to the Y Company in March. In February the X Company's only plant is destroyed by fire, with the result that the widgets cannot be manufactured. In this case the courts will ordinarily rule that the existence of the plant is so necessary to the fulfillment of the contract that its destruction excuses the X Company from its obligations. (Such a ruling would not be made, however, if the X Company operated several plants and if there was no indication in the contract, expressly or impliedly, that the parties intended for the widgets to come from the particular plant that was destroyed.)[10]

Subsequent Illegality: If, after a contract is made, its performance becomes illegal because of a change in the law, a legal impossibility is created. Thus if B in September contracts to sell fifty pinball machines to G in December, the contract would be discharged if a state statute prohibiting such a transaction took effect in November.

We will now examine two cases dealing with the subject of legal impossibility. (However, as noted earlier, this subject should also be considered together with a related view, the doctrine of "commercial impracticability," which is discussed immediately following these cases.)

---

[9]Note, however, that many obligations are not personal in nature. For example: If B contracts to sell his land to W for $30,000, and B thereafter dies, the agreement is not terminated. The reason is that B's estate, acting through the executor, is just as capable of delivering a deed to W as was B, had he lived. Nor would the contract be terminated if W rather than B had died. W's estate is just as capable of paying the $30,000 as W would have been, had he lived.

[10]Special problems arise in the "destruction" cases involving *sales of goods.* Specific provisions in Article 2 of the UCC (especially Sec. 2-509) govern situations of this sort.

The Allen Company, of Charleston, South Carolina, contracted to sell eight hundred bags of "Texas New Crop U.S. 1" blackeye peas to Pearce-Young-Angel at $16 per hundred pounds, for delivery on or before June 30, 1947. The contract was made in a long-distance telephone conversation between Mr. Allen and a Mr. Young, vice president of P-Y-A, on June 16, 1947, and was immediately confirmed by telegram.

A week later Allen arrived in Dilley, Texas, to purchase the peas he had contracted to sell. There he learned that torrential rains in the three days preceding his arrival had ruined the pea crop in the Dilley area. He immediately wrote to P-Y-A, explaining the circumstances and asking whether P-Y-A would prefer to have its order held for later delivery or have it cancelled.

P-Y-A replied that it did not wish to cancel the order and that "we expect delivery as confirmed." This letter was written by one Hamblin, who had assumed Young's position after the contract was made.

The Allen Company failed to deliver the peas, and P-Y-A, plaintiff, brought this action to recover damages for breach of contract. The Allen Company, defendant, contended that the peas—the subject matter of the contract—had been destroyed by an act of God, and that by reason of the subject matter's destruction it was relieved from its obligation to make delivery.

The trial court, hearing the case without a jury, made these findings of fact: (1) that the contract contemplated delivery of peas from any section of the State of Texas rather than peas grown only in a particular locality of the state, (2) that delivery of peas of the quality contracted for from the State of Texas was not prevented by an act of God, and (3) that peas of the quality contracted for were available for shipment within the terms of the contract. On these findings, judgment was entered for plaintiff, and defendant appealed.

Pearce-Young-Angel Co. v. Charles R. Allen, Inc.
Supreme Court of South Carolina, 50 S.E.2d 698 (1948)

Baker, Chief Justice: . . . Appellant recognizes that in pleading the act of God as a defense, the burden of proof is on the pleader of such defense; and further, that if there is any testimony in the record from which a reasonable inference can be drawn sustaining the findings of the trial judge, applying the applicable law, then the judgment will have to be affirmed.

The destruction of the subject-matter of a contract by an act of God vitiates the contract, since where the existence of a specific thing is necessary for the performance of a contract, the accidental destruction or nonexistence of that thing excuses the promisor. *Williston on Contracts,* Vol. VI, sec. 1946, p. 5,451.

". . . It is a well settled rule of law, that if a party by his contract charges himself with an obligation possible to be performed, he must make it good, unless its performance is rendered impossible by the act of God, the law, or the other party. . . ." *Dermott, Executor, v. Jones,* 69 U.S. 1. As stated in appellant's printed brief, surprisingly enough in a state which for so long a time has been predominantly agricultural, there are no South Carolina cases on the precise issue here involved. . . .

The rules of law applicable here are stated in the Annotation in *12 A.L.R.* at page 1,288, as follows:

Whether or not a contract for the sale of produce to be delivered at a certain future date contemplates that it shall be grown on a particular tract of land, so that a failure of the crop on that land will excuse non-delivery is often a close question of construction of the particular contract. The rule appears to be that if the parties contemplate a sale of the crop, or of a certain part of the crop, of a particular tract of land, and by reason of a drought or other fortuitous event, without fault of the promisor, the crop of that land fails or is destroyed, non-performance is to that extent excused; the contract, in the absence of an express provision controlling the matter being considered as subject to an implied condition in this regard; but that, if the contract does not specify or contemplate the crop of any particular tract of land, non-performance will not be excused merely because it happens that, on account of a drought or other fortuitous event, without his fault, the promisor is unable to perform the contract, the cases following in this respect the general rule that the mere inability of the obligor to perform will not ordinarily excuse non-performance. . . .

It appears to us that the finding by the Circuit Judge "that the contract did not contemplate delivery of peas from any particular locality . . . in the State of Texas" is wholly unsupported by the evidence. The appellant has conclusively shown by uncontradicted testimony that Mr. Young, the vice president and buyer of the respondent, and the one who handled all of the negotiations looking to the purchase of these peas, *knew that the appellant expected to obtain these peas from the section or locality of Dilley, Texas.* Not only did Mr. Young know this, but he knew that the subject-matter of the contract was to come from a *specific crop* then about to be harvested in the particular locality of Dilley, Texas. [Emphasis added.] And there is no contradiction of this fact, circumstantial or direct.

[These holdings were based on evidence in the trial court that Allen, in his conversation of June 16, stated to Young that the peas were "to be shipped from the locality of Dilley, Texas," and that when Young asked Allen, "How do you know that they are going to be No. 1?," Allen replied that the Dilley locality had been unusually dry until then, and that for this reason the peas from the area that would have otherwise been sold as fresh peas for canning were drying and would be sold as dry blackeyes.]

The appellant has shown by uncontradicted testimony that U.S. No. 1 blackeye peas were not procurable in the latter part of June, 1947, in the Dilley section of Texas because of the fact that the June blackeye pea crop of that section of Texas was destroyed by unexpected and torrential rains. . . . [On these facts, the court held that the crop failure *did* constitute a legal impossibility.]

Judgment reversed.

Comment: A possible criticism of the inclusion of this case is the fact that such a contract today would be governed by Article 2 of the UCC, since it involves the sale of goods. As will be noted in the discussion of the doctrine of "commercial impracticability," however, the applicable section of the UCC would bring about the same result as that reached by the court here. This is made particularly clear by a comment following Sec. 2-615 of the code, in which the drafters state that a seller of goods is excused under that section "*where a particular source of supply is shown by the circumstances to have been contemplated or assumed by the parties at the time of contracting.*" (Emphasis added.)

The La Gasse Company, plaintiff, made a contract with the City of Fort Lauderdale, under which it was to repair and renovate one of the city's swimming pools for a specified price. One night, when the job was almost completed, vandals damaged the pool so badly that most of the work had to be redone.

When the city refused to pay more than the contract price, plaintiff brought this action to recover compensation for the additional work. The trial court held that it was plaintiff's responsibility to redo the work, and entered judgment for defendant. Plaintiff appealed.

La Gasse Pool Construction Co. v. City of Fort Lauderdale

District Court of Appeal, Fourth District, 288 So.2d 273 (1974)

Downey, Judge: ... The question presented for decision is: Where the work done by a contractor, pursuant to a contract for the repair of an existing structure, is damaged during the course of the repair work, but the existing structure is not destroyed, upon whom does the loss fall where neither contractor nor the owner is at fault?

The general rule is that under an indivisible contract to build an entire structure, loss or damage thereto during construction falls upon the contractor, the theory being that the contractor obligated himself to build an entire structure, and absent a delivery thereof he has not performed his contract. If his work is damaged or destroyed during construction he is still able to perform by rebuilding the damaged or destroyed part; in other words, doing the work over again.

In the case of contracts to repair, renovate, or perform work on existing structures, the general rule is that total destruction of the structure ... without fault of either the contractor or owner, excuses performance by the contractor and entitles him to recover the value of the work done. The rationale of this rule is that the contract has an implied condition that the structure will remain in existence so the contractor can render performance. Destruction of the structure makes performance impossible, and thereby excuses the contractor's nonperformance.

But where the building or structure to be repaired is *not destroyed*, [and] the contractor's work is damaged so that it must be redone, performance is still possible, and it is the contractor's responsibility to redo the work so as to complete the undertaking. (Emphasis added.) In other words, absent ... some other reason for lawful nonperformance, the contractor must perform his contract. Any loss or damage to his work during the process of repairs which can be rectified is his responsibility. The reason for allowing recovery without full performance in the case of total destruction (i.e., impossibility of performance) is absent where the structure remains and simply requires duplicating the work. ... Accordingly, the judgment for [defendant] is affirmed.

Under the traditional views just discussed, most contracts did not present situations in which legal impossibility was recognized. Thus most contracting parties were not freed from their obligations even in cases where their performance was clearly made more difficult by events that occurred after the contracts were entered into. Today, however, courts are more likely to free contracting parties than was the case earlier, because of increasing recognition of the "doctrine of commercial impracticability."

Discharge by Commercial Impracticability

In the 1950's, when Article 2 of the UCC (Sales) was being written, its drafters felt that sellers of goods should be excused from their obligations in more situations than was the case under the impossibility doctrine. To achieve this, they adopted the doctrine of commercial impracticability, (or, as it is sometimes called, the doctrine of commercial frustration.")

Sec. 2-615 of the UCC reads, in part, as follows: "Delay in delivery or nondelivery in whole or in part by a seller . . . is not a breach of his duty under a contract for sale if performance as agreed has been made impracticable by the occurrence of a contingency the non-occurrence of which was a basic assumption upon which the contract was made." While a full discussion of the meaning of commercial impracticability cannot be undertaken here, it *can* be observed that certain events (in addition to those creating or causing a true impossibility) will cause the performance of a sales contract to be commercially impracticable—thereby freeing the seller of his or her obligations—even though they do not fall within the definition of impossibility under contract law. Examples of such events can be found in Comment 4 following Sec. 2-615 which provides that while increased cost alone does not excuse performance, such cost *does* excuse performance if "the rise is due to some unforseen contingency which *alters the essential nature of the performance.*" Further, "*a severe shortage of raw materials or of supplies* due to a contingency such as war, embargo, local crop failure, unforeseen shutdown of major sources of supply or the like, which either causes a *marked increase in cost* or altogether prevents the seller from securing supplies necessary to his performance, is within the contemplation of this section." (Emphasis added.)

After adoption of the UCC, the courts generally recognized commercial impracticability as an excuse for nonperformance in sales contracts only, continuing to require a showing of strict impossibility where other types of contracts were involved. Today, however, there is a growing tendency among the courts to apply the commercial impracticability yardstick to all kinds of contracts.

The Supreme Court of Alaska, in the case below, first speaks of impossibility in the true sense. But, perhaps because of some uncertainty on this score, it reflected the tendency noted above by buttressing its decision with references to the doctrine of commercial impracticability, even though the contract in question was not a sales contract.

Northern Corporation v. Chugach Electric Association

Supreme Court of Alaska, Alaska, 518 P.2d 76 (1974)

In August of 1966 the Northern Corporation, a contractor, entered into a contract with Chugach Electric Association. The contract called for Northern to install protective riprap on a dam owned by Chugach on Cooper Lake, Alaska, for $63,655. The job essentially involved the quarrying and transporting of large quantities of rock, and installing the rock on the upstream face of the dam.

The parties originally contemplated that the rock was to be drilled and shot at a designated quarry. However, when this rock was found to be unsuitable, the parties amended the contract in September so that Northern could use alternative quarry sites, and the contract price for the job was increased by $42,000. Northern then selected a site that was at the opposite end of the lake, intending to transport the rock across the lake on the ice during the winter of 1966–67. The contract apparently did not specify a means of transportation, but at the time of the contract amendment Chugach sent Northern a letter authorizing transportation across the lake. Work commenced in the new quarry in October, and all of the required rock was drilled and shot by the end of that month.

During the following winter Northern commenced hauling operations, but had to stop them because two of its vehicles went through the ice; a loader sank, and a tractor was recovered. Northern then told Chugach that ice was too unsafe for the job, but Chugach and its engineering firm insisted that the job be performed. Nevertheless, in March of 1967 Northern ceased operations, apparently with Chugach's approval.

After a long period of negotiations, Chugach advised Northern in January of 1968 that it would hold Northern liable for damages for breach of contract unless all rock was hauled by April 1. In late January, when ice conditions appeared to be much more favorable than the previous year, Northern started its hauling operation again. However, in February two half-loaded trucks broke through the ice, resulting in the deaths of the drivers and loss of the trucks. Northern then advised Chugach that it considered the contract "terminated for impossibilty of performance."

Northern then brought this action against Chugach, asking for (1) a ruling that the contract was impossible of performance, and (2) damages equal to the costs which it incurred in attempting to perform the contract. Chugach counterclaimed, contending that performance was not impossible, and that it was thus entitled to damages incurred between the date of completion specified in the amended contract, and the date of its termination by Northern. The trial court discharged both parties on the ground of impossibility, and denied both parties' claims for damages. Both parties appealed.

In the Supreme Court of Alaska, four issues were raised. Only two of these, appearing below, are considered here.

Boochever, Justice: . . . The issues on this appeal may be summarized as follows: . . .

1. Was the contract, as modified, impossible of performance?
2. If the modified contract was impossible of performance, is Northern entitled to reasonable costs in endeavoring to perform it? . . .

The focal question is whether the amended contract was impossible of performance. The September directive specified that the rock was to be transported "across Cooper Lake to the dam site when such lake is frozen to a sufficient depth to permit heavy vehicle traffic thereon," and the formal amendment specified that the hauling to the dam site would be done during the winter of 1966–67. . . . [Despite the foregoing] Chugach contends . . . that Northern was nevertheless bound to perform [under the contract itself,] and that it could have used means other than hauling by truck across the ice to transport the rock. The answer to Chugach's contention is that, as the trial court found, the parties contemplated that the rock would be hauled by truck once the ice froze to a sufficient depth to support the weight of the vehicles. The specification of this particular method of performance presupposed the existence of ice frozen to the requisite depth. Since this expectation of the parties was never fulfilled, . . . Northern's duty to perform was discharged by reason of impossibility.

There is an additional reason for our holding that Northern's duty to perform was discharged by impossibility. It is true that in order for a defendant to prevail under the original common law doctrine of impossibility, he had to show [not only that he could not perform, but also] that no one else could have performed the contract. However, this harsh rule has gradually been eroded, and the Restatement of Contracts has departed from the early rule by recognizing the principle of "commercial impracticability." Under this doctrine, a party is discharged from his contract obligations, even if it is technically possible to perform them, if the costs of performance would be so disproportionate to that reasonably contemplated by the parties as to make the contract totally impractical in a commercial sense. . . .

Removed from the strictures of the common law, "impossibility" in its modern context has become a coat of many colors, including among its hues the point argued here—namely, impossibility predicated upon commercial "impracticability." This concept—which finds expression both in case law and in other authorities—is predicated upon the assumption that in legal contemplation something is impracticable when it can only be done at an excessive and unreasonable cost. [The court here cited a California case in which the doctrine of commercial impracticability was applied, where the cost of the only alternative means of performance was ten times that of the means originally contemplated by the parties.] . . .

There is ample evidence to support [the trial court's findings that "the ice haul method of transporting riprap . . . was within the contemplation of the parties and was part of the basis of the agreement which ultimately resulted in the contract amendment,]" and that that method was not commercially feasible within the financial parameters of the contract. . . .

[The court then turned to the question of damages, and ruled that plaintiff *should* have been allowed damages to cover its costs incurred in attempting to perform the contract. It then set forth the rules that should be applied in determining this measure of damages.]

Judgment affirmed in part, reversed in part, and remanded.

Comment: 1. The court states that commercial impracticability is one form of impossibility. While this view blurs the line of demarcation that most courts have drawn between the two doctrines in the past, it is probably one that will have increasing acceptance in the future.

2. In a subsequent rehearing, the Alaska Supreme Court modified its decision in this case. The modification, however, had only to do with a restating of the rules applicable to the determination of damages; the holding as to impossibility and commercial impracticability was thus unchanged.

Discharge by Frustration of Purpose

Occasionally, after a contract is entered into, some event or condition will occur that clearly does not fall within the impossibility or commercial impracticability doctrines; yet one of the parties will argue that it so *frustrated the purposes of the contract* that its occurrence ought to free him nonetheless. (In other words, such a party is contending that the happening of the event caused the contract to be worthless to him or her.) To illustrate: D, a car dealer embarking on an ambitious expansion program, makes a contract with C, a contractor, under the terms of which he is to pay C $250,000 for the construction of new showroom facilities. Shortly thereafter, because of an unanticipated national defense emergency, the federal government orders a 90 percent reduction in the production of new automobiles. D contends that this action constitutes grounds for cancelling its construction contract, since he will obviously have few new cars to sell.

Here the courts are on the horns of a dilemma. On the one hand, they understand that the virtual stoppage of new car production substantially eliminates the purpose for which the contract was made—and may even drive D into bankruptcy if he is held to its terms. On the other hand, the adoption of a general rule to the effect that contracts are discharged whenever the *purposes* of one of the parties cannot be attained as a result of anticipated future occurrences would cast great uncertainty on the enforceability of almost all contracts.

While it is dangerous to generalize about the kinds of cases in which the doctrine of frustration may be accepted as grounds for avoiding contractual liability, it can safely be said that the courts—while giving the doctrine due consideration in their decisions—actually find it to be *inapplicable* in the great majority of cases. Thus, in the example above, D's contention that he was freed on the ground of frustration of purpose will probably (though not certainly) be rejected.

Once a contract has been formed, it is always possible for the parties to make a new agreement that will discharge or modify the obligations of one or both parties under the original contract. The new agreement can take any of several forms, the most common of which are rescission, novation, and accord and satisfaction.

Discharge by Parties' Agreement

Rescission

A contract can always be canceled by mutual agreement. When this agremeent occurs, the contract is *rescinded,* and the obligations of both parties are thereby discharged. An oral rescission agreement is generally valid and binding, even where the original contract was in writing—with one major exception. A rescission agreement must be in writing if it involves a retransfer of real property. (Additionally, under Sec. 2-209[2] of the UCC, modification or rescission of a written *sales contract* must be evidenced by a writing if the original contract so provides.)

Novation

A *novation* occurs when the party entitled to receive performance under a contract agrees to release the party who "owes" the performance and to permit a third party to take that person's place. It is simply a three-sided agreement that results in the substitution of one party for another. For example: X and Y have a contract. Later, they and Z agree that Z will perform X's obligations, with Y expressly releasing X from the original contract. X's obligations are now discharged.

Accord and Satisfaction

After a contract has been formed, the parties may agree that one of them will accept, and the other will render, a performance different from what was originally called for. Such an agreement is an *accord*. Thus, if B owes W $1,800, and they subsequently agree that B will air-condition W's home in satisfaction of the debt, an accord exists. The reaching of an accord does not, of and by itself, terminate the existing obligation. To effect a discharge, a *satisfaction* must take place—the actual performance of the substituted obligation. Thus B's indebtedness is discharged by "accord and satisfaction" only when he completes the air-conditioning job.

Discharge by Operation of Law

In addition to the types of discharge already discussed, other events or conditions can bring about a *discharge by operation of law*. The most common of these are bankruptcy proceedings, the running of a statute of limitations, and the fraudulent alteration of a contract.

Bankruptcy Proceedings[11]

As we mentioned earlier, bankruptcy actions today are governed by the federal Bankruptcy Reform Act of 1978. If an individual has been adjudged bankrupt after proper bankruptcy proceedings have taken place, he or she receives a *discharge in bankruptcy* from a court which covers most—but not all—of his or her debts. While the discharge technically does not extinguish the debts that are subject to it, it does so as a practical matter by prohibiting creditors from thereafter bringing court action against the debtor to recover any unpaid balance.

Running of Statutes of Limitations

All states have statutes providing that after a certain amount of time has elapsed, a contract claim is barred. The time limits vary widely from one jurisdiction to another. In some states, for example, claimants are given three years in which to bring suit on oral contracts and five years on written ones; in others, the times vary from two to eight years on oral contracts and from three to fifteen years on written ones.

In any event, if a contract claimant lets the applicable time elapse without initiating legal proceedings, the statute of limitations has run and subsequent court action by that person is barred. The period of time begins the day after the cause of action accrues. Thus, if X promises to pay Y $500 on June 10, 1976, in a state having a three-year statute, the statute begins to run on June 11, with the result that Y has until June 10, 1979, to institute suit. (As in the case of a discharge in

---

[11]The subject of bankruptcy is treated in Chapter 44.

bankruptcy, the running of the statute does not extinguish the debt or claim itself; it simply prevents the claimant from subsequently bringing a legal action to recover the indebtedness.)

Alteration

The law generally strives to discourage dishonest conduct. Consistent with this policy is the rule that the fraudulent, material alteration of a written contract by one of the parties discharges the other party as a matter of law. Suppose, for example, that A makes a written contract with B under the terms of which he is to sell 1,000 gallons of paint to B at a specified price per gallon. If B subsequently changes the quantity to 1,200 gallons without A's knowledge, A is excused from delivering any paint at all, if that is his desire. (A also has the right to enforce the contract according to its original terms or as altered—that is, he can tender either 1,000 or 1,200 gallons to B and hold him liable for the quantity chosen.)

Questions and Problems

1. Roper contracted in writing to buy a Wyoming ranch from Lewis for a specified price. At the same time that this contract was made Roper and Lewis also orally agreed, in rather general terms, that Lewis would also sell his 400 head of cattle and some ranch machinery to Roper. Later, when the cattle and machinery deal fell through, Roper brought court action asking for rescission of the ranch contract. Roper's contention was that performance of the cattle and machinery agreement was a *condition precedent* to his obligations under the ranch-purchase contract. Lewis disagreed, pointing out that (a) the written ranch contract did not mention the oral agreement, and (b) that, in fact, the parties never did come to specific terms as to the cattle and machinery prices. Would these factors cause the court to rule that performance of the cattle and machinery contract was *not* a condition precedent? Discuss. (*Lewis v. Roper,* 579 P.2d 434, 1978.)

2. Mr. and Mrs. Funk contracted to buy the Cox home in North Carolina. The contract provided that the contract was subject to the sale of the purchasers' present residence (i.e., the Funk's residence.) When Cox later brought an action demanding that the Funks go through with the contract and pay the purchase price, the Funks stated that they had not yet been able to sell their residence. The Funks thus contended that the actual sale of their old residence was a *condition precedent* to their obligation to buy the Cox home, and since the condition had not occurred, they did not yet have the duty to pay for the Cox home. Is this a good argument? Why or why not? (*Cox v. Funk,* 255 S.E.2d 600, 1979.)

3. Cayias owned a pool hall business, which he operated in a leased building. Wishing to sell the business, he listed it with the Associated Investment Company, a broker, under a contract providing that if the company found a buyer at a price agreeable to him, he would pay the company a commission of 10 percent of the purchase price. The company found a buyer willing to pay $3,000, and Cayias and the buyer entered into a contract calling for the sale of the business at that price. The contract provided, however, that if the buyer was not able to obtain a new lease on the building at a monthly rental of $150, "then and in that event the agreement shall become null and void." The purchaser thereafter was apparently not able to get a lease from the owner of the building at this figure, so the sale of the

business fell through. The company now sued Cayias, the seller, to recover its commission of $300. Cayias defended on the ground that (1) the quoted clause in the purchase agreement constituted a condition subsequent, and (2) since the condition (the inability of the buyer to get a lease) occurred with the result that the buyer was released, he (Cayias) was released from his obligation to pay a commission on the "sale." *Associated Investment Co. v. Cayias,* 185 P. 778 (1920). Rule on the correctness of Cayias's contention.

4. A contractor who built a country home for Kent for $77,000 sought to recover the unpaid balance of $3,400. Kent refused to make the final payment because the building contract required that all pipe in the home be of "Reading manufacture," and the pipe actually installed was made by a different manufacturer, the Cohoes Company. The contractor proved that the Cohoes pipe met all the specifications of the Reading pipe and that he was not aware of the Reading requirement in the contract when he installed the other pipe. *Jacobs and Young, Inc., v. Kent,* 129 N.E. 889 (1921). On these facts, does the doctrine of substantial performance apply to the plaintiff, the contractor? Explain.

5. The MTK Potato Company (the M Co.) contracted to buy a quantity of potatoes from the Tallackson Potato Company (the T Co.) Both companies were members of a potato "co-op." The contract provided a "payment schedule" under which the M Co. was to make its payments. Later the M Co. refused to go through with the deal, whereupon the T Co. sued it for damages for breach of contract. At the trial the M Co. tried to prove: (a) that when the contract was made it was understood by the T Co., the seller, that the M Co. expected to get the money to pay for the potatoes from the co-op, and (b) that, in fact, the co-op had never made any payments of money to it, the M Co. While the M Co. admitted that its receipt of the money from the co-op was not a condition of the contract, it did argue that the failure of the co-op to pay it (M Co.) the necessary sums of money constituted an "impossibility and/or a commercial impracticability" that thus freed it from its contractual obligations. Is this a good argument? Explain. (*Tallackson Potato Co. v. MTK Potato Co.,* 278 N.W.2d 417, 1979.)

6. A professional football player made a contract with Alabama Football, Inc. (Alabama) which at that time was a member of the World Football League. Under the contract Alabama agreed to pay the player a salary covering the years 1977, 1978 and 1979. Soon after the contract was made, the World Football League folded—ie., "ceased to exist." In subsequent litigation, Alabama contended that the failure of the league constituted a *legal impossibility* that freed it (Alabama) of its obligations to the player. Should the court accept this argument? Discuss. (*Alabama Football, Inc. v. Wright,* 452 F.Supp. 182, 1977.)

7.The Republic Creosoting Company contracted to sell and deliver to the City of Minneapolis a quantity of paving blocks, with deliveries to be made in the first six months of 1920. The contract did not contain any clause excusing a late delivery in the event of a strike, a boxcar shortage, or similar events beyond the company's control. Because of a nationwide boxcar shortage, the company was unable to deliver the blocks at the agreed upon time. The city considered this a breach of contract and purchased the blocks from another supplier at a higher price. The city then brought suit against the company to recover damages for breach of contract, and the company defended on the ground that the nationwide boxcar shortage constituted a legal impossibility. *Minneapolis v. Republic Creosoting Co.,* 201 N.W. 414 (1924). Rule on the validity of this defense (1) on the ground of impossibility, and (2) on the ground of commercial impracticability.

8. One railroad (the lessor) leased part of its depot facilities in Milwaukee to another railroad (the lessee) under a long-term contract. Thereafter, with several years on the contract remaining, Amtrak was formed by an act of Congress that resulted, among other things, in the lessee's passenger service in the Milwaukee area being very substantially reduced. As a result, the lessee has very little use for the depot facilities. When the lessor sued the lessee to recover $2 million rental fees for subsequent years, the lessee contended that the formation of Amtrak (and the sharp curtailment of its services) freed it from its remaining obligations under the *frustration of purpose* doctrine. The lessor contested this argument, and offered evidence to show (a) that when the contract was made the lessee was aware that Amtrak might come into existence; (b) that both parties realized that their need for the depot might be substantially cut, and (c) that the lessee, by joining Amtrak—which it was not required by law to do—was itself partly responsible for its cutback of services. Should this evidence convince the court to rule that the frustration of purpose doctrine is *not* applicable? (I.e., should this evidence cause the court to rule that the lessee is still bound by the contract?) Why or why not? (*Chicago, M.,St.P.&P.R. Co.* v. *Chicago & N.W.*, 203 N.W.2d 189, 1978.)

Part III

Commercial Transactions

Sales/Introduction to the Law of Sales 17

A college student purchases a stereo. A home owner buys several cans of house paint. A manufacturer of tires purchases raw rubber, sulphur, and other materials and ultimately sells tires to automobile owners. A mining company sells coal to an electric utility company. All of the above have at least two things in common. First, they are quite ordinary transactions, occurring countless numbers of times. Second, they involve sales of goods. Thus we can hardly question the relevance of studying the law of sales.

As is true of any area of the law, the principles governing sales of goods do not exist in a vacuum. Different areas of law frequently interact, and isolation is not often practicable. However, limitations must be placed on the scope of any discussion of legal principles. Otherwise, the discussion will be unstructured, unwieldy, and probably unusable. The chapters on the law of sales (Chapters 17 through 21) will be confined largely to those principles relating to the sales transaction itself, although closely related matters will occasionally be treated. For example, in this first chapter we will briefly mention *documents of title*. In most instances, however, related subjects are left for discussion elsewhere in the text.

Historical Note

Before discussing the law of sales as it is today, a brief historical digression is in order. All commercial law reflects to some extent the customs and traditions of business people. The influence of such customs on the law of sales is readily apparent from an examination of its origin. Most commercial trade in early England was conducted at "fairs," where merchants came together to buy and sell their goods. These merchants established their own courts at the fairs to settle disputes and enforce obligations among themselves. The *fair courts,* as they were called, developed a rather extensive body of rules, based in large part on commercial customs and practices existing at that time. This body of "unofficial" law was referred to as the "law merchant."

The fair courts were not officially recognized by the king's courts until early in the seventeenth century. By the end of that century, the king's courts had absorbed the fair courts, and the law merchant melted into and became part of the common law. For many years thereafter, the law of sales and other areas of law which had originated with the law merchant were entirely judge-made.

The first attempt in the United States to codify the law of sales occurred with the drafting of the Uniform Sales Act in 1906, which was eventually enacted by the legislatures of thirty-six states. By the 1940s, lawmakers recognized that the Uniform Sales Act and other uniform laws were in need of substantial revision to reflect more modern commercial practices. The Uniform Commercial Code (UCC) was promulgated to serve that purpose. It superseded the Uniform Sales Act and the other uniform laws and was eventually enacted in every state except Louisiana,[1] plus the District of Columbia and the Virgin Islands.

Scope of Article 2 of the UCC

Article 2 of the UCC deals with the sale of goods. It forms the basis for most of the following discussion of the law of sales.

Sales

A *sale* is defined in Sec. 2-106 of the UCC as "the passing of title from the seller to the buyer for a price." Thus Article 2 does not apply to leases or to other types of "bailments," because only temporary possession of the goods (rather than title) is transferred.[2] It does not apply to gifts, because no price is paid. (See the section on documents of title later in this chapter for a brief discussion of bailments, and Chapter 42 for a complete treatment of the subject. Gifts are dealt with in Chapter 40.)

---

[1]Louisiana has enacted *some parts* of the UCC, but it has not enacted Article 2, which governs sales of goods.

[2]Actually, Sec. 2-102 states that it applies to "transactions in goods." Therefore, one could argue that Article 2 is not limited to sales but includes all transactions in goods. However, the great majority of authorities agree that Article 2 applies only to "sales." Even so, in a few cases the courts have applied the sections of Article 2 that deal with warranties (which will be discussed in Chapter 20) to *leases* of goods.

Goods

In the majority of cases we will have no problem ascertaining whether the subject matter should be classified as a *good*. Occasionally, however, the term may present problems. Essentially, two requirements must be met before a particular item of property is classified as a good:

1. It must be *tangible*. In other words, it must have a physical existence. Thus intangible property such as a patent, copyright, trademark, investment security, or contract right would not come within the scope of Article 2.

2. It must be *movable*. This requirement obviously excludes real estate, which is tangible but not movable. (Of course, almost anything, even real estate, shovel by shovel, is capable of being moved if enough effort is expended. But the word is intended reasonably rather than literally.)

Using these two requirements we can easily envision the wide variety of products that are classified as goods, from airplanes to toothpaste.

Should things that are attached to real estate be considered goods? Because of the movability requirement this question would involve considerable conceptual difficulty were it not for Sec. 2-107 of the UCC, which sets forth the following basic rules:

1. A contract for the sale of *minerals or a structure* (such as a building or its materials) is a contract for the sale of goods if they are to be severed from the land by the *seller*. If, however, they are to be severed from the land by the *buyer*, the transaction is a sale of real estate and is governed by the principles of real estate law rather than by the UCC. Two examples may be of some help. First, suppose that S and B agree that S will sell to B a quantity of gravel to be taken from beneath the surface of land owned by S. If their agreement states that S will dig and remove the gravel, the transaction is a sale of goods. If, on the other hand, B is to dig and remove the gravel, the transaction is a sale of real estate. Second, suppose that S and B agree that S will sell to B a storage building (or perhaps the lumber from the building) located on land owned by S. If their agreement indicates that B will remove the building from the land, the transaction is a sale of real estate. If removal is to be by S, it is a sale of goods.

2. A contract for the sale of *growing crops or timber* is a contract for the sale of goods, regardless of who is to sever them from the land.

3. A contract for the sale of *anything else attached to real estate* is a sale of goods if it can be severed *without material harm* to the real estate. This rule is, perhaps, not as important as the two rules just discussed, simply because most of the problems regarding things attached to real estate have involved minerals, structures, timber, or growing crops. Situations might exist, however, where this third rule would be pertinent. For example: X and Y agree that X will sell to Y a window air conditioner that is now attached to X's home. (We are assuming it is attached, for otherwise the question would never arise—it would obviously be a sale of goods.) The air conditioner is bolted to a metal shelf supported by braces that are secured to the side of the house by bolts. It is fairly evident that the air conditioner can be removed without material harm to the real estate. Suppose, however, that the subject of the sale is a floor furnace. In this case a gaping hole in the floor would result. This might be a material harm, causing the sale to be treated as a sale of real estate rather than goods.

The rules regarding sales of goods attached to real estate presuppose that the items are being sold apart from the land. However, if two parties agree that one will sell a tract of land to the other, including a building or some timber located on the land, the sale is treated as a sale of real estate.

The UCC also gives special attention to three other potential problems of classification. It provides that (1) unborn animals are goods; (2) money treated as a commodity, such as a rare coin, is a good (though money used as a medium of exchange is not); and (3) things that are specially manufactured for the buyer are goods. Although item 3 seems clear-cut, the framers of Article 2 felt that such a sale might be seen as predominantly a sale of services rather than goods and therefore stated it definitely.

Sales of services (such as employment contracts) are obviously not within the scope of Article 2. However, as we saw in item 3 above, goods and services sometimes are so entwined that classification is no easy task. For example, when a hospital supplies blood to a patient, is the hospital selling a good or supplying a service? The blood itself meets the UCC requirements for a good, but the courts have to determine if the *predominant feature* of the transaction as a whole (including the transfusion) is that of selling a good or supplying a service.[3] Some courts have held that it is a sale of goods within Article 2; other courts have held it is not. A number of states have passed specific statutes which provide that a blood transfusion is not a sale of goods. The same problem arises where a beautician applies hair dye to a customer in a beauty parlor; and again the court decisions are in conflict. Although the UCC makes no statement regarding blood transfusions or hair treatments, it does specifically provide in Sec. 2-314(1) that food sold in a restaurant is a sale of goods (at least for the purpose of the implied warranty of merchantability).

The two cases that follow involve the difficult problem of determining whether the law of sales is applicable to "mixed" transactions.

De Filippo v. Ford Motor Co.

U.S. Court of Appeals, Third Circuit 516 F.2d 1313 (1975)

De Filippo and Fleishman, plaintiffs, became Ford dealers at Chestnut Motors, Inc., in West Philadelphia in 1969. Less than nine months later part of the facility, which had been leased from the previous dealer, was destroyed by fire. Plaintiffs and Ford discussed the possibility of plaintiffs acquiring another dealership in the city. On December 18, 1969, plaintiffs signed a contract under which they were to

---

[3]The issue in these cases has usually been whether a recipient of contaminated blood is protected by the *implied warranty of merchantability* (which will be discussed in Chapter 20). In those jurisdictions where the transaction is considered a service rather than a sale of goods, the injured party can recover damages only by proving that the hospital acted negligently.

purchase the assets, not including real estate, of Presidential Motors. They were to lease the real estate from Ford.

Certain provisions of the contract were more attractive than those for other dealers in the Philadelphia area. As a result, the other dealers protested to Ford. Ford, reconsidering the agreement with plaintiffs, refused to comply with some of its provisions. Plaintiffs brought suit in a federal district court, charging a violation of federal antitrust laws (to be discussed in Part VIII) and breach of contract. The district court held for plaintiffs on the antitrust issue and for defendant (Ford) on the breach of contract issue. (The latter holding was because the contract involved a sale of goods for a price of $500 or more and was signed only by plaintiffs, not by Ford. This rule will be discussed in the next chapter.) Plaintiffs received a judgment for over $2.5 million on the antitrust issue, and defendant appealed. The court of appeals reversed the antitrust decision of the lower court and upheld the breach of contract decision, thereby deciding completely against plaintiffs. The part of the opinion dealing with the breach of contract issue is reproduced below.

Aldisert, Chief Justice: . . . Whether the December 18th instrument was subject to the UCC Statute of Frauds for the sale of goods, as the trial court concluded, depends on whether the subject matter of the sale falls within the contemplation of "goods" as that term is defined in UCC § 2-105. Accordingly, our analysis begins with an examination of the documents involved in the December 18th transaction.

Accompanying the letter signed by plaintiffs were several exhibits, the principal one of which was entitled, "Assets to Be Sold and Computation Price". The document listed: parts and accessories, miscellaneous inventories, work in process, equipment, leasehold improvements, service vehicles, new vehicles, demonstrators, used vehicles, daily rental vehicles, leased vehicles, notes receivables, vehicle receivables, parts and service receivables, contracts covering services, and used car warranties. The exhibit also established a formula for deferring rent on the premises owned by Ford's subsidiary, Leaseco, specifically set forth a method for computing the cost of inventories, and provided: "The purchase price to be paid by the Buyer for the assets to be sold shall be the aggregate sum determined in accordance with the computations and the inventories to be made as specified herein, less $65,000."

. . . Although no [prior] Pennsylvania cases [deal with] the transfer of the assets of an automobile dealership, the Pennsylvania courts had held that the prior Sales Act governed the sale of a whole business. In addition, other jurisdictions have held that motor vehicles are "goods".

For their part, plaintiffs claim an analogue in *Field v. Golden Triangle Broadcasting, Inc.*, 305 A2d 689 (1973). There, the Pennsylvania Supreme Court was concerned with an agreement for the sale of two radio stations, including FCC licenses and various physical assets. The seller sought to invoke those provisions of the UCC which allow a seller to demand adequate assurance of performance and, in the absence thereof, to suspend his performance. The court stated: "We do not believe that Article 2 of the UCC applies to the instant contract. Rather than being an agreement for the sale of 'goods', this is a contract for the sale of the businesses of two radio stations, including their tangible and intangible assets, as a going concern."

We believe that *Field* offers plaintiffs little comfort . . . . The factual complex in *Field* is distinct from that in the instant case. There, only $30,000 of the total purchase price of $650,000—or 4.6 per cent—represented physical assets, including nonmovables such as towers and fences. This is to be contrasted with the proposed sale of Presidential Motors in which, we agree with Ford's assessment, the value of movables to be sold was well in excess of three times the value of assets not properly classified as "goods".

For the Statute of Frauds relating to the sale of goods to become applicable, we do not believe every asset subject to the sale must qualify under the "movable" test of UCC § 2-105. *Rather than a view of mechanical technicality or of mathematical nicety, a view of the reasonable totality of the circumstances should control the characterization of the contract for sale. If, viewed as a whole, it can be concluded that the essential bulk of the assets to be transferred qualify as "goods", then it is appropriate to consider the transaction a "contract for the sale of goods".* [Emphasis added.] To insist that all assets qualify as "goods" would substantially thwart the intentions of the drafters of the Uniform Commercial Code; it would sanction the absurd. The agreement of sale and purchase could cover physical, movable assets, thus qualifying as "goods", as well as other assets—such as receivables from their particular lines—not so qualifying. But to segregate "goods" assets from "nongoods" assets, and to insist that the Statute of Frauds apply only to a portion of the contract, would be to make the contract divisible and impossible of performance within the intention of the parties.

We believe it preferable to utilize a rule of reasonable characterization of the transaction as a whole. Applying this rule to the facts before us and carefully examining the list of assets to be sold, we note that title to no real estate was to pass in the transaction, nor was any value assigned for good will or the value of the business as a going concern. Accordingly, we have no hesitation in agreeing with the district court's applying UCC § 2-201 and its finding that the alleged contract was unenforceable for want of the signature of Ford Motor Company....

The judgment of the district court will be reversed with a direction to enter judgment in favor of appellant Ford Motor Company.

Bonebrake v. Cox
U.S. Court of Appeals,
Eighth Circuit, 499
F.2d 951 (1974)

Donald and Claude Cox owned a bowling alley called "Tamarack Bowl" in Missouri Valley, Iowa. It was gutted by fire in February 1968. They decided to rebuild and, on April 17, 1968, entered into a written contract with Simek, who agreed to sell and install the necessary equipment. When delivery and installation were incomplete and less than half the purchase price paid, Simek died. The Coxes obtained equipment elsewhere and hired others to finish the installation. Frances Bonebrake, administratrix of Simek's estate, sued the Coxes in federal district court to recover the balance of the contract price. The Coxes countersued for their damages. The trial court held for Bonebrake, the plaintiff, on the claim for the unpaid contract price and denied defendants' counterclaim. Judgment was in the sum of $28,000.

At issue in the case was whether certain provisions of the UCC should apply with respect to performance and damages. The trial court had held the UCC to be inapplicable, because a sale of goods was not involved. Defendants appealed.

Smith, Justice: ... We now consider whether the contract of April 17, 1968 comes under the Code.... The fire suffered by defendants' bowling alley on February 5, 1968 had destroyed its equipment. This contract with Simek was to replace those goods. The "following used equipment" was purchased: lane beds, ball returns, chairs, bubble ball cleaning machine, lockers, house balls, storage racks, shoes, and foundation materials. The equipment was to be delivered and installed by Simek. He warranted that the lanes would be "free from defects in workmanship and materials," and that they would "meet all ABC specifications." The purchase price was stated to be "for the total price of $20,000.00," two thousand dollars payable upon the execution of the contract, another payment "when work begins laying sub-floor, or foundation material; and the balance upon completion of this installation."

The language thus employed is that peculiar to goods, not services. It speaks of "equipment," and of lanes free from "defects in workmanship and materials." The rendition of services does not comport with such terminology.

The [trial court], however, ruled that the above-described contract "is not the type of contract which falls within the statutory scheme of the UCC. It involved substantial amounts of labor, as well as goods, with a lump sum price. The Code was meant to cover contracts for the commercial sale of goods, not nondivisible mixed contracts of this type."

In such holding there is error. Article 2 of the Code, here involved, applies to "transactions in goods." The definition of "goods" is found in § 2-105(1):

> "Goods" means all things (including specially manufactured goods) which are movable at the time of identification to the contract for sale other than the money in which the price is to be paid, investment securities (Article 8) and things in action. "Goods" also includes the unborn young of animals and growing crops and other identified things attached to realty as described in the section on goods to be severed from realty.

As Nordstrom [an authority on the law of sales] points out, this section is divided into two parts, the first affirmative, defining the scope and reach of Article 2, the second negative, excluding certain transactions. To come within the affirmative section, the articles (the "things") must be movable, and the movability must occur at the time of identification to the contract. The applicability of the Code to the April contract is clear from and within its four corners. The "things" sold are all items of tangible property, normally in the flow of commerce, portable at the time of the contract. They are not the less "goods" within the definition of the act because service may play a role in their ultimate use. The Code contains no such exception. "Services," continues Nordstrom, "always play an important role in the use of goods, whether it is the service of transforming the raw materials into some usable product or the service of distributing the usable product to a point where it can easily be obtained by the consumer. The definition should not be used to deny Code application simply because an added service is required to inject or apply the product." In short, the fact that the contract "involved substantial amounts of labor" does not remove it from inclusion under the Code on the ground, as the [trial court] found, that "The Code was [not] meant to cover . . . nondivisible mixed contracts of this type."

. . . *The test for inclusion or exclusion is not whether they are mixed, but, granting that they are mixed, whether their predominant factor, their thrust, their purpose, reasonably stated, is the rendition of service, with goods incidentally involved (e.g., contract with artist for painting) or is a transaction of sale, with labor incidentally involved (e.g., installation of a water heater in a bathroom).* [Emphasis added.] The contract before us, construed in accordance with the applicable standards of the Code, is not excluded therefrom because it is "mixed," and, moreover, is clearly for the replacement of equipment destroyed by fire, i.e. "goods" as defined by the Code.

[Reversed and remanded.]

Merchants

For the most part, Article 2 does not require the parties to be merchants. That is, if the transaction is a sale of goods, it is governed by most provisions of Article 2 regardless of whether either the seller or the buyer is a merchant. However, a few provisions of Article 2 do require either or both parties to be merchants. For this reason, we will now examine the UCC definition of a *merchant*.

Most people who see the word *merchant* probably think of someone engaged in the retail grocery business, the retail clothing business, or similar endeavors. While such people (or corporations) are indeed merchants, the UCC definition includes many others as well.

Sec. 2-104 of the UCC details three different ways in which a person or organization can be considered a merchant.

1. One who "deals in goods of the kind" is a merchant; thus, not only retailers but also wholesalers and probably even manufacturers are merchants. A party is considered a merchant, however, only for the types of goods dealt with regularly in his or her business. That is, a merchant in one type of goods is not a merchant for all purposes. Thus a retail shoe seller is a merchant with respect to transactions involving the purchase or sale of shoes. But if that person buys a new car or sells a secondhand lawn mower, he or she is not a merchant in those transactions.

2. Even if a person does not regularly "deal" in a particular type of goods, he is nevertheless a merchant if he "by his occupation holds himself out as having knowledge or skill peculiar to the practices or goods involved in the transaction." While most persons who fall within this provision are also merchants under the first provision by dealing in the particular goods, there are a few who do not really deal in goods but who are merchants within this second category. For example, if we assume that the word *deal* means "to buy and sell goods," a building contractor does not actually deal in goods. He buys building materials but does not resell them; instead he uses them in the performance of a service—constructing a building. However, he does, by his occupation, hold himself out as having "knowledge or skill peculiar to the practices or goods" involved in certain transactions and thereby is a merchant by definition. Of course, his status is irrelevant in any agreement to construct a building, because that agreement is essentially for services and not within the scope of Article 2. But his status as a merchant can be important with respect to a dispute arising from the sale contract between him and his materials supplier.

3. If a party is not a merchant under either of the first two categories, he or she may nevertheless be treated as one by *employing a merchant* to act in his or her behalf in a particular transaction. The UCC states that one is a merchant if one employs "an agent or broker or other intermediary who by his occupation holds himself out" as having knowledge or skill peculiar to the goods or practices involved in the transaction. Suppose, for example, that Smith, who does not regularly deal in grain, hires a professional grain broker to procure a large quantity of feed for Smith's cattle. In this situation Smith is considered a merchant.

The common thread running through all the above categories of merchants is the possession of or access to a degree of commercial expertise not found in a member of the general public. While the UCC usually treats merchants no differently from others, occasionally it applies different standards to them.

In the case that follows, the Supreme Court of Alabama deals with an issue that has posed a problem for several courts in recent years. Is a farmer who sells his crops a merchant?

The plaintiff, Loeb and Company, Inc., marketed raw cotton. The defendant, Charles Schreiner, was a farmer who had grown cotton and other crops since 1963.

In April 1973 plaintiff and defendant entered into an oral contract for the sale of 150 bales of cotton. Shortly thereafter the price of cotton more than doubled, and defendant refused to sell his cotton to plaintiff.

Since this contract was for the sale of goods for a price of $500 or more, it was required to be in writing and signed by defendant. (The rule will be discussed in the next chapter.) However, according to Sec. 2-201(2) of the UCC, if both seller and buyer are merchants, a later written confirmation of their oral agreement will satisfy this requirement, even if only the sender signs it—so long as the recipient does not make written objection to the terms of the confirmation within ten days after receiving it. In this case plaintiff had sent a confirmation to defendant, and defendant had made no objection. There was no doubt that plaintiff was a merchant. Thus, if defendant was also a merchant, the confirmation could be used to satisfy the statute of frauds even though defendant signed nothing. If he was not a merchant, however, the confirmation would not be a sufficient writing and the contract would be unenforceable.

The trial court ruled that defendant was not a merchant and that the contract was unenforceable. Plaintiff appealed.

Loeb & Company, Inc. v. Schreiner
Supreme Court of Alabama, 320 So.2d 199 (1975)

Almon, Justice: . . . Only a few courts have considered the question of whether a farmer is a "merchant." In *Cook Grains v. Fallis,* 395 SW2d 555 (1965), the Arkansas Supreme Court held that a soybean farmer was not a merchant when he was merely trying to sell the commodities he had raised. The court stated that there was not

> . . . a scintilla of evidence in the record, or proferred as evidence, that appellee is a dealer in goods of the kind or by his occupation holds himself out as having knowledge or a skill peculiar to the practices or goods involved in the transaction, and no such knowledge or skill can be attributed to him.

In *Oloffson v. Coomer,* 296 NE2d 871 (1973), the Third Division of the Appellate Court of Illinois stated in dictum that a farmer in the business of growing grain was not a "merchant" with respect to the merchandising of grain. However, in *Campbell v. Yokel,* 313 NE2d 628 (1974), the Fifth District of the Appellate Court of Illinois dealt with a case that involved an action against some soybean farmers on an alleged breach of an oral contract for the sale of soybeans. The court held that the soybean farmers, who had grown and sold soybeans for several years were "merchants" when selling crops and were therefore barred by § 2-201(2) from asserting the statute of frauds as a defense.

One court has suggested that whether or not a farmer is a "merchant" within the meaning of § 2-104 should turn upon whether or not he has engaged in a particular type of sale in the past. In *Fear Ranches, Inc. v. Berry*, 470 F2d 905 (10th Cir. 1972), a breach of warranty case, the court held that where the defendant cattle farmers made a sale to a nonmeatpacker for resale when they had previously sold all of their cattle to meatpackers, they were not "merchants" with respect to the sale to the nonmeatpacker. The court felt that the sale of cattle for resale was a sale of a different type of goods and made up a different type of business than the sale of cattle to meatpackers.

We hold that in the instant case the appellee was not a "merchant" within the meaning of § 2-104. We do not think the framers of the Uniform Commercial Code contemplated that a farmer should be included among those considered to be "merchants."

In order for a farmer to be included within the § 2-104 definition of "merchants," he must do one of the following:

1. deal in goods of the kind;
2. *by his occupation* hold himself out as having knowledge or skill peculiar to the practices or goods involved in the transaction; or
3. employ an agent or broker or other intermediary who by his occupation holds himself out as having such knowledge or skill.

Since the farmer in the instant case did not qualify as a merchant under 3 above, he would have to qualify under 1 or 2. It is not sufficient under 2 that one hold himself out as having knowledge or skill peculiar to the practices or goods involved, he must *by his occupation* so hold himself out. Accordingly, a person cannot be considered a "merchant" simply because he is a braggart or has a high opinion of his knowledge in a particular area. We conclude that a farmer does not solely *by his occupation* hold himself out as being a professional cotton merchant.

The remaining thing which a farmer might do to be considered a merchant is to become a dealer in goods. Although there was evidence which indicated that the appellee here had a good deal of knowledge, this is not the test. There is not one shred of evidence that appellee ever sold anyone's cotton but his own. He was nothing more than an astute farmer selling his own product. We do not think this was sufficient to make him a dealer in goods.

The official comment to § 2-104 states in part as follows:

> This Article assumes that transactions between *professionals* in a given field require special and clear rules which may not apply to a *casual or inexperienced seller or buyer*. It thus adopts a policy of expressly stating rules applicable "between merchants" and "as against a merchant", wherever [such rules] are needed instead of making them depend upon the circumstances of each case as in the statutes cited above. This section lays the foundation of this policy by defining those who are to be regarded as professionals or "merchants" and by stating when a transaction is deemed to be "between merchants." [Emphasis added by the court.]

Although a farmer might sell his cotton every year, we do not think that this should take him out of the category of a "casual seller" and place him in the category with "professionals."

If indeed the statute of frauds has, as claimed, permitted an injustice, it is a matter which addresses itself to the legislature.

The judgment is due to be and is hereby affirmed.

Comment: As Justice Almon pointed out, some courts have held that a farmer who sells his own crops is not a merchant. However, some other courts have reached an opposite conclusion. Two fairly recent examples are *Sierens v. Clausen,* 328 N.E.2d 559 (1975), and *Ohio Grain Co. v. Swisshelm,* 318 N.E.2d 428 (1973), in which the Illinois Supreme Court and the Ohio Court of Appeals, respectively, held that a farmer who regularly sells his crops is a merchant in such transactions.

When a sale of goods takes place, the seller may personally deliver the goods or the buyer may personally pick them up at the seller's place of business. It is more common, however, for the goods to be shipped to the buyer by way of a "carrier," such as a trucking, railway, or air cargo company. It is also quite common for a seller to store goods at a warehouse before selling them and for the buyer to pick them up there. In either case, whether the goods are shipped by a carrier or stored in a warehouse, the seller is turning over temporary possession of them to a third party. Such a transaction is called a *bailment.* The owner of the goods is sometimes called a *bailor,* and the party taking temporary possession is sometimes called a *bailee.* The above transactions are certainly not the only instances in which bailments occur, but they are two of the most frequent.

Documents of Title

When an owner of goods parts with possession in such a manner, he or she is given a receipt for them. If the goods are being shipped and the bailee is a carrier, this receipt is called a *bill of lading.*[4] Besides being a receipt for goods, it contains instructions to the carrier regarding destination and the like, as well as the terms of the shipping agreement. If the goods are being stored and the bailee is a warehouseman, the receipt is called a *warehouse receipt.* It too contains the terms of the storage agreement. Both bills of lading and warehouse receipts are sometimes referred to as *documents of title,* because they provide evidence of title to goods.

Documents of title are of two basic types: negotiable and nonnegotiable.[5] They are *negotiable* if, by their terms, the goods are to be delivered to "bearer" or to the "order" of a named person. Otherwise they are *nonnegotiable.* Following are examples of both types:

1. "Deliver to bearer" (the person who presents the document to the bailee). This is a negotiable document.

2. "Deliver to the order of Roscoe Sweeney" (to Roscoe Sweeney or to anyone else to whom he has transferred the document by endorsing it). This is a negotiable document.

3. "Deliver to Roscoe Sweeney." This is a nonnegotiable document.

A negotiable document is actually more than a mere receipt for the goods and a contract for their carriage or storage. The person who is in legal possession of a

---

[4]Technically, the bill of lading is called an *airbill* when air transportation is used.

[5]A negotiable bill of lading is sometimes called an "order bill" and a nonnegotiable one a "straight bill."

negotiable document is entitled to the goods described therein (that is, legal possession of the document is tantamount to ownership of the goods). Thus whoever is in legal possession and presents to the bailee a document stating that delivery is to be made to "bearer" is entitled to the goods. If the document states that delivery is to be to the "order of Roscoe Sweeney," whoever is in legal possession of the document and presents it to the bailee is entitled to the goods, if Roscoe Sweeney has properly endorsed it.

Legal possession of a nonnegotiable document, on the other hand, is not tantamount to ownership of the goods. Regardless of who presents the document to the bailee, that party will be governed by the instructions of the bailor. The bailee is under a duty to insure that he or she is delivering the goods to the party who is supposed to receive them under the bailor's instructions. (The difference between a negotiable and a nonnegotiable document is somewhat akin to the difference between a five-dollar bill and a copy of a contract.)

Questions and Problems

1. What is the law merchant? What part did it play in the development of our modern law of sales?

2. Why does Article 2 of the UCC not apply to bailments and gifts?

3. Helvey filed suit against Wabash County REMC for breach of a contract to supply electricity to Helvey's furniture factory. *Helvey v. Wabash County REMC,* 278 N.E.2d 608 (1972). During the course of the lawsuit the issue arose as to whether Article 2 of the UCC applied to the dispute. Discuss whether the contract between Helvey and Wabash is covered by Article 2.

4. Ernst and Williams agreed to trade an airplane owned by Ernst for an undeveloped residential lot owned by Williams. A dispute arose as to the time, place, and manner of delivering the airplane. Is this dispute governed by the provisions of Article 2? Explain.

5. Hauter agreed to sell 1,500 shares of General Manufacturing Co. common stock to Rogers for $15,000. Later, several terms of the contract became the subject of disagreement between Hauter and Rogers. Hauter filed suit. Does Article 2 govern the transaction? Explain.

6. Playboy Clubs International, Inc., operates a number of hotels and nightclubs. Playboy bought fabrics from Loomskill, Inc., which it was going to have made into costumes for its employees by a third party. A dispute arose between Playboy and Loomskill regarding the sale. *Playboy Clubs International, Inc. v. Loomskill,* 13 U.C.C. Rep. Serv. 765 (1974). Relevant to this dispute is a section in Article 2 which applies only if Playboy is considered a merchant. Does this section apply? Discuss.

7. *Loeb & Company, Inc. v. Schreiner* held that a farmer who sells his crops is not a merchant in those transactions. Argue the contrary position. Support your argument with references to the UCC and to statements made in the *Loeb* case itself.

8. Are there any circumstances in which a university might be considered a merchant? Discuss.

9. What part can documents of title play in a sale of goods? Explain.

10. How can one tell whether a document of title is negotiable or nonnegotiable? What is the basic difference between the rights of a person in legal possession of a negotiable document of title and the rights of a person in legal possession of a nonnegotiable document of title?

18 Sales/Formation and Interpretation of the Sales Contract

If a customer enters a retail store and purchases an item for cash, a sale of goods occurs. There is a contract, and that contract is performed the moment it is made. Many sales transactions are not so simple, however; often they consist of several stages extending over a period of time. (This is particularly true where the sale involves goods of substantial value.) The first stage in such transactions, the negotiation and formation of a contract, will be the focal point of this chapter.

In discussing contracts for the sale of goods we will draw heavily on our prior study of contract law in general, since the UCC has left much of the common law of contracts undisturbed. Often the UCC is either silent on a particular principle of contract law or merely restates an established rule. In such cases the common law or applicable statutes other than the UCC continue to govern.

However, a number of provisions of Article 2 of the UCC have markedly altered the common law of contracts as it applies to sales of goods. Our discussion will be directed at the important changes wrought by the UCC in the rules that apply to formation and interpretation of sales contracts, a few of which were mentioned in Part II of this book.

Irrevocable Offers

As a general rule, an offer to make a contract can be revoked by the offeror at any time before it is accepted, with one major exception. In the case of an *option* the offeror promises to keep the offer open in return for consideration given by the offeree. The general rule and exception apply with equal force to sales transactions. However, the UCC has added a second exception to the general rule by creating another type of irrevocable offer, referred to in Sec. 2-205 as a *firm offer*.

The following requirements must exist for an offer to be irrevocable under this section:

1. Obviously, it must be an offer to buy or sell goods.

2. It must be made *by* a merchant—though not necessarily *to* a merchant. That is, only the offeror need be a merchant.

3. It must be written and signed by the offeror.

4. It must give assurance that it will be held open.[1]

If all these requirements are met, the offer is irrevocable even if the offeree gives no consideration for the assurance that it will remain open.

The period of time during which the offeror cannot revoke the offer is the time stated in the offer so long as it does not exceed three months. If the offer contains an assurance that it will be held open but mentions no time period, it will be irrevocable for a reasonable time, again not exceeding three months. (The three-month limitation applies only where the offeree is relying on Sec. 2-205 to make the offer irrevocable. If he or she gives *consideration* for the offeror's assurance that the offer will remain open, an *option* exists, and the three-month limitation does not apply.)

Definiteness of the Agreement

Among the most significant modifications of the common law achieved by the UCC is a general relaxation of the degree of definiteness required in the agreement. Several provisions indicate that the drafters of the UCC wanted to make the formation of binding contracts somewhat easier than under common law. They recognized that business people frequently intend to enter into enforceable agreements in situations where it is impracticable to make those agreements as definite as required by common law.

A prime example of this approach is found in Sec. 2-204(3). This section broadly states that a sales contract is enforceable even if one or more terms are left open, so long as (1) the court feels that the parties *intended to make a binding contract,* and (2) the agreement and the surrounding circumstances give the court a *reasonably certain basis for granting an appropriate remedy* (such as money damages).

---

[1]But if the assurance is contained in a form supplied by the offeree, then the assurance itself must be separately signed by the offeror.

Of course, there is a line beyond which the court will not go. For instance, the larger the number of undecided terms, the less likely it is that a court will find that the parties intended to be legally bound. In fact, a seller and buyer who wish to make an agreement with one or more terms left for future determination would do well to state specifically whether they intend to be bound in the meantime.

Open Price Provisions: Other provisions of Article 2 deal more specifically with the problem of indefiniteness. Suppose, for example, that a seller wishes to be assured of a market for goods he or she is producing. Or perhaps a buyer is desirous of guaranteeing himself or herself an adequate supply of certain needed products. In either case price may be of only secondary importance. Thus buyer and seller might draw up a contract for the sale and purchase of goods at a future date, with the price to be agreed on later. The open price term may be especially desirable in a market where the going price is subject to fluctuation.

At common law many courts refused to enforce such an agreement because of its indefiniteness. Under Sec. 2-305 of the UCC, however, agreements of this nature are now enforceable if the court feels that the parties intended to be bound. Of course, if the evidence indicates that the agreement was merely tentative and the parties intended to be legally bound only if and when the price was ultimately set, there is no contract until that condition is met. The UCC cannot supply missing contractual intent.

Sometimes the court is called upon to enforce a contract in which the price, for one reason or another, was never actually set. If the parties had intended to be bound by the open price agreement, the court is faced with the task of providing a price term. Sec. 2-305 establishes a number of principles to guide the court in such a situation:

1. If the parties had expressly left the price for later agreement and then failed to agree, the price set by the court should be a "reasonable price at the time for delivery."

2. If the agreement had said nothing at all about price, and the price was never settled on, the method of determining it should depend on the circumstances. If the price had failed to be set through no fault of either party, the court should fix a "reasonable price at the time for delivery," as in item 1. But if the failure to set a price was caused by the fault of either party, the party not at fault can either treat the contract as cancelled or fix a "reasonable price." This price is binding and the court will uphold it, so long as it is found to be actually reasonable.

3. If the agreement had provided that the price was to be subsequently fixed according to a definite standard set or recorded by a third party, the rules for determining the unresolved price are exactly as they were in item 2. For example, the parties might have agreed that the contract price was to be the market price reported in a certain trade journal on a given date, but no such price was reported in the journal on that date. Or they might have agreed that an impartial third person was to set the price at a future date, but the third party later failed to do so. In either case, the price will be a "reasonable price at the time for delivery."

This reasonable price will be set by the court if neither party was at fault; if one party caused the agreed method to fail, the other party may set a reasonable price.

4. If the parties had agreed that one of them was to set the price at a later time, the deciding party is obligated to set the price in good faith. Although *good faith* is defined differently for merchants and nonmerchants, the most compelling evidence of good or bad faith generally is whether the price fixed was a reasonable market price at that time.[2] If the party responsible for setting the price fails to do so or if he or she fixes a price in bad faith, the other party can either treat the contract as cancelled or set a reasonable price.

Open Time Provisions: The absence of a time provision also does not cause a sales contract to be unenforceable. Sec. 2-309 states that, where a contract calls for some type of action (such as shipment or delivery) but does not specify the time for such action, the court shall infer a "reasonable time." Of course, a reasonable time in a given case depends on all the circumstances known to the parties. For instance, suppose that the parties did not set a specific time for delivery but that the seller knew the reason for the buyer's purchase and the use to which the buyer intended to put the goods. A reasonable time for delivery would certainly be soon enough for the buyer to put the goods to their intended use.

Open Delivery Provisions: A sales contract may also be enforceable even if certain delivery terms are to be decided at a later time. We have already discussed the absence of a delivery time. Another delivery term that might be absent is a provision for the place of delivery. Where the parties have not included this provision in their contract, Sec. 2-308 sets forth the following rules to serve as "gap-fillers."

1. The goods should be delivered to the buyer at the *seller's place of business.*

2. If the seller has no place of business, they should be delivered to the buyer at the *seller's residence.*

3. Where the contract refers to specifically identified goods, and both parties knew when making the contract that the goods were located at *some other place,* that place is where delivery should be made.

The UCC also attempts to account for other omitted details relating to delivery. For example, if the agreement contemplates shipping the goods but does not mention *shipping arrangements,* the *seller* has the right under Sec. 2-311 to specify these arrangements. His or her actions are subject only to the limitation that they be in good faith and within limits set by commercial reasonableness. Another example is the situation where goods are ordered but the parties make no agreement regarding the *assortment* (such as an order for two hundred dozen men's suits

---

[2]*Good faith* is generally defined in Sec. 1-201(19) of the UCC as "honesty in fact." In the case of a merchant, it is defined in Sec. 2-103(1)(b) as "honesty in fact *and* the observance of reasonable commercial standards of fair dealing in the trade." (Emphasis added.) Generally, the merchant definition will prevail, since open price terms are rare among nonmerchants.

that does not specify sizes or colors). Sec. 2-311 gives the *buyer* the right to select the assortment where the parties have not agreed otherwise. Again, the specification of the assortment must be made in good faith and in a commercially reasonable manner.

If the parties have not specified whether the goods are to be delivered all at once or in several lots, Sec. 2-307 obligates the seller to deliver them all at one time. However, the UCC does allow for an exception to this duty. If both parties, when making the contract, know that the circumstances are such that delivery in a single lot is not reasonably practicable, then the seller can deliver in several lots. For instance, the quantity involved may be so large that both realize a single delivery is not feasible. The seller must, of course, deliver in as few lots as commercially reasonable.

The Acceptance

Method of Acceptance: The UCC has not changed the common law rule that an offeror can specify the method by which acceptance is to be made. However, where the offeror has said nothing about the required method of acceptance, the UCC differs from common law. In Sec. 2-206(1)(a) it states that "an offer to make a contract shall be construed as inviting acceptance in any manner and by any medium *reasonable in the circumstances.*" (Emphasis added.) Although the UCC does not indicate the intended effect of this section, it might influence court decisions regarding the time that an acceptance takes effect. Under common law, if the offeror does not expressly authorize a particular medium of communication, the courts usually hold that an acceptance is effective when sent only if the offeree uses the *same medium* that the offeror has used. If some other medium is employed, the acceptance is effective only when actually received by the offeror (see Chapter 9). Sec. 2-206(1)(a) of the UCC indicates instead that for sales contracts an acceptance is effective immediately upon being sent if the means of communication used by the offeree are "reasonable in the circumstances."

Another important change from common law in the method of acceptance is found in Sec. 2-206(1)(b). Before the UCC was adopted, if a buyer offered to buy goods, using terms such as *for prompt shipment, for current shipment,* or *ship at once,* the offer was usually construed as being an offer for a *unilateral contract* (see Chapter 9). Actual shipment was therefore the only way in which it could be accepted. Under the UCC, however, an offer containing these or similar words is construed as inviting acceptance either by prompt shipment or by a prompt *promise to ship.* An offeree's return promise thus forms a contract under such circumstances, but prompt shipment must follow or the contract will be breached.[3] Thus Sec. 2-206(1)(b) blurs the distinction between bilateral and unilateral contracts. In so doing, it recognizes that the words used in a buyer's order often

---

[3]The buyer can still require acceptance of the offer only by the act of shipment itself, but he or she now must explicitly state this in the offer.

depend simply on which employee places the order or which book of printed forms has most recently been purchased from the office supply store.

This section also provides that, where a seller accepts an offer by actually shipping the goods, the act of shipment constitutes an acceptance even if the goods are not exactly what the buyer ordered. In such a case, the seller actually binds himself or herself to a contract and breaches it at the same time, thereby entitling the buyer to various remedies (which will be discussed in Chapter 21), including rejection of the goods. The shipment of "nonconforming" goods is not an acceptance, however, if the seller expressly indicates that he or she is not accepting the buyer's order but merely attempting to accommodate the buyer.

A further change with respect to unilateral contracts has been made in Sec. 2-206(2). According to the common law rule, an offeree who accepts by performing the required act does not necessarily have to notify the offeror of the acceptance. Such notice is required only in situations where the offeror would not otherwise be likely to learn that acceptance had taken place. Under the UCC, however, the offeree's performance of the act constitutes an acceptance only if the offeror is notified of it within a reasonable time.

Additional or Different Terms in Acceptance: At common law, an agreement results only if the offeree's acceptance strictly conforms to the terms of the offer. An acceptance containing terms not in the offer is treated as a counter-offer (and usually a rejection). Thus a contract is not formed unless the original offeror accepts the counter-offer.

The above rule generally makes good sense and works relatively well. However, when transactions involving the sale of goods were still under common law, the growing use of standard printed forms sometimes caused problems. Frequently business people have their forms drafted by an attorney and printed for convenient use. Thus order forms used by buyers contain buyer-oriented terms, while forms used by sellers to acknowledge or accept orders contain seller-oriented terms. Under common law, when the parties engaged in "form-swapping" in their dealings with one another (as they often did), the frequent result was that no contract existed.

To illustrate: Suppose that Buyer B ordered a quantity of goods at a certain price from Seller S. B's order form said nothing about warranties on the goods. S sent a form acknowledging the order and indicating that the goods would be shipped; but S's form contained a clause excluding warranties on the goods. At this point, there was no contract under the common law rule. S had made a counter-offer, and a contract would have resulted only if B had accepted that counter-offer. Most times this situation produced no problems, because conforming goods are usually shipped and paid for. But what if one party decided to back out of the agreement before the goods were shipped? The parties would have found, probably to their surprise, that no contract had ever been made. Or suppose that the goods were shipped and B accepted them, only to find later that they were defective in some way. Under common law, the courts probably would have held that B accepted S's counter-offer by accepting the goods and therefore was not covered by any warranty against defects.

The UCC attempts to solve such problems in Sec. 2-207. The section is certainly not limited to sales transactions in which printed forms are used; but it is in these situations that it is most useful, since most problems arise in the context of "form-swapping" (the "battle of the forms"). Sec. 2-207 sets forth the following rules:

1. If the offeree's response indicates a definite intent to accept the offer, it will be an acceptance even if it contains terms additional to or different from those found in the offer. This is where Sec. 2-207 makes a truly significant change in the common law. In the example above, S and B would have a contract, assuming that S's response clearly indicated an intent to accept B's order.

2. Sec. 2-207 does make one exception to this rule. If the offeree's attempted acceptance is expressly conditional on the offeror's consent to the additional or different terms, there is no acceptance and no contract. Thus, if S's response had not merely added the term excluding warranties but had also made his acceptance expressly conditional on B's consent to the exclusion, there would have been no contract.

3. If a contract exists at this point, is the warranty exclusion clause part of it? The immediate answer is that if B notices the clause and agrees to it, then it is included. But what about the usual case where B does not even notice the clause, or if he does notice it, he simply ignores it? In this situation, the UCC provides that additional terms are to be treated as "proposals for addition to the contract"; therefore, the warranty exclusion clause in S's form is simply a proposal. Under Sec. 2-207, it becomes part of the contract *only if both parties are merchants.* Thus, in determining whether there is a contract, it is not necessary that the parties be merchants. But their status as merchants *is* important in determining whether an additional term, such as the warranty exclusion, will become part of the contract. The drafters of the UCC evidently felt that additional terms should be included in the contract without express agreement only where the transaction is between two professionals.

4. Even if both parties are merchants, the additional term or terms will not become part of the contract if either of the following situations occurs:

a. If the additional term *materially alters* the contract, it will not be included. This, of course, is a question of fact to be decided in each individual case, and it often depends on what is customary in a particular industry or between particular parties. Thus, even though the UCC allows a contract to be formed despite the existence of new terms in the acceptance, the offeree is not allowed to slip anything important by the offeror. In the instant case, a term excluding warranties is almost certainly material unless such sales are customarily made without them.

b. Even if the additional term is only minor, it will not be included *if the offeror objects to it within a reasonable time.* Furthermore, if the term in question is not merely *additional* but also *different,* it will not be part of the contract. That is, where the term does not involve a new matter but is in direct conflict with the express terms of the offer, it will be assumed that the offeror objects to the change unless he or she indicates otherwise.

c. Again, even if the additional term is only minor, it will not be included if the offer had originally stated expressly that acceptance could be made only according to the terms contained in the offer.

5. Suppose that S and B reach their agreement orally, say over the telephone, and then one of the parties sends a letter or other written communication confirming the agreement. What if the confirmation contains terms additional to or different from those orally agreed on? In this situation we do not need to ask whether there is an acceptance and a contract. We know that the parties reached an oral agreement; thus the only question is whether the additional terms will be included in the contract.[4] This issue is decided in the same manner as where the additional terms are included in an acceptance.

6. Finally, Sec. 2-207 contains a provision that makes a binding contract possible even where one has not been formed by the parties' communications. The provision states that "conduct by both parties which recognizes the existence of a contract is sufficient to establish a contract for sale even though the writings of the parties do not otherwise establish a contract." Suppose that, in the earlier example, S's response is expressly conditioned on B's consent to the exclusion of warranties. There is not a contract at this point. Suppose further that neither party pays much attention to the terms contained in their forms and acts as though a contract exists, without saying anything more about terms. If S ships the goods and B takes delivery of them, there is probably a contract. But what are its terms? Under Sec. 2-207, the terms "consist of those terms on which the writings of the parties agree, together with any supplementary terms" found elsewhere in the UCC. Therefore, S's exclusion of warranties is not part of the contract because it was not agreed upon. In its place are the implied warranties that are set forth in other sections of the UCC (see Chapter 20 for details).

The following case illustrates a fairly common application of Sec. 2-207.

Just Born, Inc. v. Stein, Hall & Co.
Court of Common Pleas of Pennsylvania, 59 Pa. D. & C.2d 407 (1971)

During 1967, plaintiff, a candy manufacturer, made several purchases of gelatin from defendant. Plaintiff filed suit alleging that the gelatin was not fit for its intended use. Defendant contended that, according to their agreement, the dispute should be settled by submitting it to arbitration.

Williams, Justice: . . . The issue of whether the present dispute is subject to arbitration may be characterized as the "battle of conflicting forms" used by buyer and seller and arose in the following manner:

---

[4]We assume that any Statute of Frauds problems involved in the oral contract can be overcome, which they quite likely can. That is, the confirmation will often be considered a sufficient writing by the courts.

On six occasions between May and September 1967, plaintiff telephoned orders for various quantities of gelatin from defendant and followed these oral communications with written purchase orders specifying the terms of the agreement such as price, quantity and description of goods. Thereafter defendant sent a "Sales Acknowledgment Agreement" and shipped the gelatin to plaintiff's plant. On the first and sixth shipments, the "Sales Acknowledgment Agreement" arrived one day after the shipment of gelatin reached plaintiff; on the second, third and fourth shipments, the "Sales Acknowledgment Agreement" came before the gelatin arrived at plaintiff's plant; and on the fifth shipment, the "Sales Acknowledgment Agreement" came on the same day as the gelatin.

Plaintiff's purchase order forms were silent as to the mode of settling disputes. Defendant's "Sales Acknowledgment Agreements," on their front side, contained the following paragraph under the heading "Arbitration Clause": "Any controversy or claim arising out of or relating to this agreement, or the breach thereof, shall be settled by arbitration in New York, N.Y., pursuant to the rules, then obtaining, of the American Arbitration Association and the laws of New York. . . ."

Defendant contends that under the terms of the Uniform Commercial Code, § 2-207, the "Sales Acknowledgment Agreements" were definite and seasonable acceptances of plaintiff's purchase orders and that the arbitration clause contained therein was an additional term which should be construed as having become part of the contracts. Plaintiff cites § 2-207 for the opposite proposition, namely that the arbitration clause was an additional term which materially altered the offer to purchase the gelatin and thus did not become part of the contracts between plaintiff and defendant.

Section 2-207 provides:

(1) A definite and seasonable expression of acceptance or a written confirmation which is sent within a reasonable time operates as an acceptance even though it states terms additional to or different from those offered or agreed upon, unless acceptance is expressly made conditional on assent to the additional or different terms.

(2) The additional terms are to be construed as proposals for addition to the contract. Between merchants such terms become part of the contract unless:

(a) the offer expressly limits acceptance to the terms of the offer;

(b) they materially alter it; or

(c) notification of objection to them has already been given or is given within a reasonable time after notice of them is received.

(3) Conduct by both parties which recognizes the existence of a contract is sufficient to establish a contract for sale although the writings of the parties do not otherwise establish a contract. In such case the terms of the particular contract consist of those terms of the parties on which the writings agree, together with any supplementary terms incorporated under any other provision of this Act.

Applying § 2-207 to the facts of the case at bar, it is clear that a contract was formed by the exchange of forms between plaintiff and defendant, and that the arbitration clause contained in defendant's "Sales Acknowledgment Agreement" forms was an additional term. The Uniform Commercial Code, comment 2 to § 2-207 provides:

Under this Article a proposed deal which in commercial understanding has in fact been closed is recognized as a contract. Therefore, any additional matter contained in the confirmation or in the acceptance falls within subsection (2) and must be regarded as a proposal for an added term unless the acceptance is made conditional on the acceptance of the additional or different terms.

Defendant's "Sales Acknowledgment Agreements" did not contain language expressly conditioning its acceptance. Further, the actions of the parties in shipping and accepting delivery of the gelatin manifested a commercial understanding that their deal was closed. Both parties, in essence, agree to this proposition but disagree on the application of § 2-207(2) to the arbitration clause.

The pleadings indicate that both plaintiff and defendant are merchants; therefore, the arbitration clause would become a part of the contracts unless it runs afoul of the three caveats of § 2-207(2). Subsections 2-207(2)(a) and 2-207(2)(c) do not hinder the inclusion of the arbitration clause. Nowhere on plaintiff's purchase order forms did the offers to purchase the gelatin expressly limit acceptance to the terms of the offer. In addition, plaintiff admits that it made no objection to the additional clause as prescribed by subsection 2-207(2)(c).

The parties differ, however, as to whether the arbitration clause is a "material alteration" of the contract within the terms of subsection 2-207(2)(b). Defendant argues that the arbitration clause does not materially alter the contracts but merely sets forth the forum in which any disputes are to be decided without changing the substantive rights of either party with respect to the contracts. . . .

In *Application of Doughboy Industries,* 233 N.Y.S.2d 488 (1962), the New York court ruled that an arbitration clause contained in the seller's form but not in the buyer's form was a "material alteration" and under § 2-207 did not become a part of the contract between the parties. In determining that the arbitration clause was a "material alteration," the New York court based its conclusion on the well-settled principle that in New York an agreement to arbitrate had to be clear and direct and could not depend upon implication, inveiglement or subtlety. Elaborating on this principle, the court held: "It follows then that the existence of an agreement to arbitrate should not depend solely upon the conflicting fine print of commercial forms which cross one another but never meet. . . ."

The Pennsylvania policy with regard to arbitration agreements is similar to the New York law relied upon by *Doughboy.* In *Scholler Bros., Inc.* v. *Hagen Corp.,* 158 Pa. Superior Ct. 170, 173 (1945), it was held that:

> [A]s an arbitration agreement bars recourse to the courts where arbitrators are named in advance at common law, . . . and even if not named in advance, the assent to relinquish a trial by jury is not to be found by mere implication. . . .
>
> No technical or formal words are necessary to constitute a reference of a controversy to arbitration, but it must clearly appear that the intention of the parties was to submit their differences to a tribunal and to be bound by the decision reached by that body on deliberation.

Defendant wisely does not contend that there was actual assent or a meeting of the minds to include the arbitration clause in the present case, but urges that it be included by implication under § 2-207 of the code.

In our opinion, *Doughboy* is a proper interpretation of § 2-207 and is consistent with the principle of *Scholler* that an agreement to arbitrate is not to be found by implication. It should be noted that *Doughboy* has been uniformly followed in New York.

We conclude, therefore, that the arbitration clause contained in defendant's "Sales Acknowledgment Agreement" forms was an additional term which materially altered the offer and, as such, did not become a part of the contract between defendant and plaintiff. . . .

[This was a trial court decision. The result was that the dispute did not have to be submitted to arbitration, and the trial proceeded in this court.]

Consideration

A significant change has been made by the UCC in the law relating to modification of existing contracts. Under common law, a modification must be supported by new consideration. Sec. 2-209(1) of the UCC, however, states that "an agreement modifying a contract [for the sale of goods] needs no consideration to be binding." To illustrate: S and B have agreed that S will sell a certain quantity of goods to B at a certain price. S later finds that he is not going to be able to deliver by the agreed upon date. He contacts B, who agrees to an extension of the time for delivery. B subsequently has a change of heart and demands the goods on the original date. Under the UCC, B is bound by the agreed upon modification even though S gave no additional consideration for the extension of time.

Were it not for Sec. 2-209(1), most courts would hold that B is not bound by the modification. Indeed, the common law approach actually served a useful purpose in some cases. For instance, suppose that in the days before the UCC, B had depended on his contract with S to supply certain essential requirements in B's business. B had made other contractual commitments to his customers and to suppliers of other necessary materials. If S had decided to renege on his contract with B, B's business might have suffered greatly. Of course, B could have maintained a suit for breach of contract against S, but this right would have given him very little comfort. He wanted the goods, not a lawsuit. Thus S would have possessed a certain degree of power over B. If S had gotten B over a barrel, so to speak, and then threatened to hold up delivery unless B agreed to pay a higher price, S would have abused his bargaining power. Even if B had agreed, however, S could not have enforced the higher price under the common law rule because, under the preexisting duty rule, he had given no new consideration for B's promise to pay more.[5] It is easy to observe the merits of the rule requiring consideration in such a case. It protects against exploitation.

But because the common law rule swept too broadly and resulted in many modifications being held unenforceable even though no abuse of power or unfairness was present, Sec. 2-209(1) was enacted. While this section of the UCC does not require consideration, Section 1-203 does impose on the parties a general duty of good faith. Thus a coerced modification is unenforceable because it is made in bad faith. Further protection is given in Sec. 2-302, which provides that "unconscionable" agreements are not enforceable—and a coerced modification is in all likelihood unconscionable. (The concept of unconscionability will be dealt with more fully later in this chapter.)

Two situations exist where a modification without consideration must be *written* in order to be enforceable:

---

[5]This rule (discussed in Chapter 10) states that a promisee gives no consideration for a promise by merely doing or promising to do something he or she is legally obligated to do.

1. Under Sec. 2-209(2), the modification must be in writing if the original agreement had provided that it could be modified only by a writing.[6]

2. Under Sec. 2-209(3), the modification must be in writing if the whole contract, *as modified,* is required to be in writing under the Statute of Frauds.[7]

Statute of Frauds

Sec. 2-201(1) of the UCC states that a contract for the sale of goods for a price of $500 or more must be in writing to be enforceable. As is true of other Statute of Frauds provisions for nongoods transactions, this requirement can be satisfied either by having the contract itself in writing or by having a subsequent written memorandum of an oral agreement. In either situation, *the writing must be signed by the party against whom enforcement is sought.*

The UCC "Confirmation": When a sale of goods is involved, the UCC provides a third method for satisfying the requirement of a writing that is unavailable for transactions not governed by Article 2.[8] Suppose that two parties have orally agreed on a sale of goods. One of the parties then sends a signed letter or other written communication to the other party, saying: "This is to confirm that on June 20 we entered into an agreement for the sale of 175 men's suits on the following terms [the terms being stated in the letter]." If this is the only writing the parties make, can it be used to satisfy the requirements of the Statute of Frauds? In a lawsuit, it can almost certainly be used by the recipient against the sender, because the sender has signed it. But if the sender files suit, can the writing be used against the recipient? In transactions not governed by the UCC, the answer is no, because the recipient (defendant) did not sign it; for sales of goods, however (as in the above example), the answer sometimes is yes.

Under Sec. 2-201(2), a confirmation such as the above can be used by the sender against a nonsigning recipient if the following requirements are met:

1. The writing must be "sufficient against the sender." In other words, the *sender* must have *signed* the confirmation, and its contents must meet the relatively lenient sufficiency requirements discussed below.

2. Both parties must be *merchants.*

---

[6]But if a merchant and a nonmerchant are dealing with each other, using the *merchant's form,* the requirement in the original agreement that later modification be written must itself be separately signed by the nonmerchant.

[7]Another UCC provision, Sec. 1-107, alters the common law approach to consideration with regard to settlements of claims. However, we will not discuss this section (1) because it overlaps with Sec. 2-209 in many cases, and (2) because there is considerable confusion and very little authority regarding its effect.

[8]The UCC also provides for a similar alternative in transactions involving the sale of investment securities (see Sec. 8-319).

3. Recipient must have had reason to know of the contents of the confirmation *but had not objected to it in writing within ten days after receiving it.*

Sufficiency of the Writing: Regardless of which type of writing is involved in a given case—written contract, later memorandum, or confirmation under Sec. 2-201(2)—the UCC has greatly relaxed the requirements of the *sufficiency of the writing.* For transactions under other provisions of the Statute of Frauds (such as sales of land and contracts not performable within one year) the writing must contain *all* the essential terms of the agreement. For sales of goods, however, the UCC provides that the necessary writing merely has to be "sufficient to indicate that a contract for sale has been made between the parties." The only term that must be included in the writing is the *quantity.* Other terms that are orally agreed upon can be proved in court by oral testimony.[9] Terms that are not agreed upon at all can be supplied by Article 2 itself (as we saw earlier in this chapter).

In the case that follows, the court was concerned with whether a particular memorandum was sufficient to satisfy the requirement of a writing under Sec. 2-201.

Fortune Furniture Co. v. Mid-South Plastic Co.

Supreme Court of Mississippi, 310 So.2d 725 (1975)

Mid-South, the plaintiff, sued Fortune, the defendant, for the purchase price of plastic goods sold to Fortune by Mid-South. Fortune admitted owing Mid-South the amount sued for, $32,962.63, but filed a counter-claim for $39,028.79 (the amount and what it is based on are explained in the case) and demanded judgment against Mid-South for the $6,066.16 difference. The jury found for Fortune on its counter-claim, but the trial court sustained a motion by Mid-South for judgment notwithstanding the verdict (that is, the court overruled the jury's verdict—see Chapter 2 for a detailed explanation). Judgment was rendered for Mid-South in the amount demanded, and Fortune appealed.

Gillespie, Justice: . . . Fortune was engaged in manufacturing furniture in Okolona, Mississippi. On or before July 8, 1968, Phil Stillpass, who lived in New York, and W. E. Walker, who lived in Okolona, called at the office of Fortune and talked to Sidney Whitlock, President of Fortune, about plastics. Stillpass was in the business of selling plastics, and Fortune needed plastics in the manufacture of furniture. A tentative oral agreement was reached whereby a company by the name of Mid-South would sell plastics to Fortune. Whitlock told Walker and Stillpass to send him a letter containing the terms of the contract. On July 8, 1968, the following letter was mailed to Whitlock and received in due course:

---

[9]The oral testimony referred to here is intended to supplement an incomplete writing. If the writing does contain a particular term, oral testimony about anything supposedly agreed upon prior to execution of the writing is not admissible in court for the purpose of contradicting the clear terms of the writing. The UCC's "parol evidence rule," which is almost identical to the common-law rule (see Chapter 14 for details), appears in Sec. 2-202.

Mr. Sidney Whitlock, President
Fortune Furniture Manufacturers, Inc.
Okolona, Mississippi 38860.

Dear Sid:

This is to confirm the agreement entered into this date between myself and Phil
Stillpass on behalf of Mid-South Plastic Co. Inc. and you on behalf of Fortune Furniture Manufacturing Co. Inc.

    We agree to maintain expanded and 21 oz. plastic in the warehouse of Mid-South
Furniture Suppliers, Inc. in sufficient amounts to supply all of the plastic for your
plant's use, and if for any reason we do not have the necessary plastic you will be at
liberty to purchase the plastic from any other source and we will pay the difference
in price paid the other source and our current price.

    We also agree to pay Fortune a 2% rebate on the gross sale price of our plastic
as an advertisement aid to your Company which rebate to be paid at your request.

    We assure you that all fabrics you need will be in our warehouse at all times and
we appreciate your agreeing to buy all of your plastics from us.

Very truly yours,
W. E. Walker, President

Mid-South was organized with a corporate charter dated July 22, 1968. Stillpass was elected
chairman and secretary-treasurer and W. E. Walker was elected president. No one on behalf
of Mid-South, other than Walker and Stillpass, contacted Fortune concerning the sale of
plastics. Fortune began buying all its plastics from Mid-South. It was only when Mid-South
was unable to supply all of Fortune's needs that Fortune bought from other suppliers. The
difference between the amount paid to other suppliers for plastic when Mid-South was
unable to meet Fortune's requirements and Mid-South's price, plus the two percent rebate
provided in the letter, totaled $39,028.79, the amount of Fortune's counterclaim. . . .

    If the testimony on behalf of Fortune made a jury issue, the motion for judgment
notwithstanding the verdict should have been overruled. . . .

    [In determining whether Fortune should prevail on its counter-claim, the court had to
decide whether the above letter was a sufficient written memorandum. If so, Mid-South was
bound by the obligations stated therein.]

    In *Derden v. Morris*, 247 So2d 838 (Miss. 1971), this court held that there are three
requirements as to the memorandum necessary to [satisfy] the statute of frauds provisions
of the Uniform Commercial Code: (1) The memorandum must evidence a contract for the
sale of goods; (2) it must be signed by the party against whom enforcement is sought, and
(3) it must specify a quantity.

    Walker's letter provides for the sale of goods (expanded and 21 oz. plastic) and states
a quantity ("all of the plastic for your plant's use"). The Uniform Commercial Code
recognizes output or requirement contracts in section 2-306(1) as follows:

A term which measures the quantity by the output of the seller or the requirements
of the buyer means such actual output or requirements as may occur in good faith,
except that no quantity unreasonably disproportionate to any stated estimate or in
the absence of a stated estimate to any normal or otherwise comparable prior output
or requirements may be tendered or demanded.

The letter is signed by Walker, who was elected president of Mid-South upon its organization, and as already found, this contract was adopted by Mid-South. We hold that the letter satisfies the statute of frauds and was binding upon Mid-South.

All factual issues were resolved against Mid-South by the jury, whose verdict was justified by the evidence. We hold the trial court erred in sustaining the motion for a judgment notwithstanding the verdict and judgment is entered here reversing that judgment, reinstating the jury verdict, and judgment entered here in favor of Fortune for $6,066.16, with interest at the rate of six percent (6%) from May 4, 1973.

Reversed . . . .

Exceptions: Sec. 2-201(3) defines three situations in which a contract, if proved, will be enforceable despite the total absence of a writing, even when it involves a sale of goods for a price of $500 or more. The first exception can be used only by a seller; the other two can be used by either a seller or a buyer.

1. If the oral contract is for goods to be specially manufactured for the particular buyer, it may be enforceable if two requirements are met:

a. The goods must be of a type not suitable for sale to others in the ordinary course of the seller's business. For example: Suppose that C is an importer of small, foreign-made pickup trucks, and D is a manufacturer of "campers" that are mounted on pickups. C orally orders from D a number of campers made to fit the pickups imported by C (that is, they will fit no other pickups on the market). If C repudiates the bargain after the campers are made, D will be hard-pressed to sell them elsewhere. He might eventually be able to do so, but considerable effort would probably be required. Thus the goods cannot be sold in the ordinary course of his business.

b. The seller must either have substantially started the manufacture of the goods or have made commitments for procuring them. In each situation the required action must have been taken before the seller learned of the buyer's repudiation of the agreement.

2. If the defendant "admits in his pleading, testimony or otherwise in court that a contract for sale was made," it will be enforceable even though oral. (The common law court decisions on this point are conflicting, most courts holding that such an admission does not remove the requirement of a writing. Thus the UCC exception represents a significant innovation.) Observe that not just any admission will suffice; the admission by the defendant must become part of official court records.

3. An oral agreement will be enforced to the extent that payment has been made and accepted or that the goods have been received and accepted. Suppose, for example, that X and Y have made an oral contract for Y to sell X twenty-five television sets at a price of $300 each. Before any of the sets are delivered, X makes a prepayment of $1,800, which Y accepts. Y then refuses to honor the contract. Even if Y were not bound by the contract, X could of course get her money back under the unjust enrichment theory (see Chapter 8). But under the UCC her part payment will make the contract partially enforceable, and she will be able to maintain a suit for breach of a contract obligation to deliver six of the twenty-five television sets. Similarly, if X has made no payment but Y has made a partial shipment which X has accepted, the oral contract is again partially enforceable. That is, if Y delivers and X accepts six television sets, and X then repudiates the agreement, Y can maintain a suit for breach of a contract obligation to pay $1,800.[10]

In each of these three exceptions, the drafters of the UCC have recognized that in certain situations the purpose of the Statute of Frauds can be fulfilled without a written document. The requirement of a writing is primarily to forestall the possibility of a party successfully maintaining a fabricated breach of contract suit by the use of perjured testimony. In situations covered by the three exceptions, the likelihood that plaintiff's claim will be a complete fabrication is remote.

Other Statutes: Various other statutes besides the Statute of Frauds require a written contract where a sale of goods is involved. The most common are state and federal statutes intended to protect consumers against unscrupulous business practices. They usually apply to retail sales to consumers where credit is granted and require not only a writing but also a detailed disclosure of terms.

Interpretation of the Sales Contract

The language used by parties to a contract is not always clear and precise. And even where it seems to be straightforward initially, doubt can later arise as to the meaning of a particular word or phrase. Therefore, the need frequently arises for court interpretation of an agreement.

The basic rules used by the courts for interpreting sales contracts are the same as those employed in interpreting other contracts. Since the purpose of interpretation is to determine the *intent* of the parties, the courts decide on the basis of the parties' outward manifestations (their words and conduct) along with the surrounding circumstances. Their essential question is: What would a reasonable person mean in these circumstances by this word, this phrase, or this act?

Course of Performance, Course of Dealing, and Usage of Trade

For the purpose of interpretation, the UCC emphasizes the importance of course of performance, course of dealing, and usage of trade. While these tools were used

---

[10]Prior to enactment of the UCC, part performance of this type made the *entire contract* enforceable. Also, the statutory language in this exception does not address the situation in which the buyer has made a partial prepayment that cannot be allocated to a certain number of individual units of goods. For example, what if buyer makes and seller accepts a $1,000 downpayment on a single $6,000 automobile? In the few cases involving this question since enactment of the UCC, most courts have applied the common law rule and have held the entire contract to be enforceable despite the absence of a sufficient written document.

by courts prior to adoption of the UCC, they have been defined more succinctly by the drafters of this statute.

In Sec. 2-208(1), *course of performance* is defined in the following manner: "Where the contract for sale involves repeated occasions for performance by either party with knowledge of the nature of the performance and opportunity for objection to it by the other, any course of performance accepted or acquiesced in without objection shall be relevant to determine the meaning of the agreement." This aid to interpretation is based simply on how the parties themselves apparently understood the agreement while they were in the process of performing it.

Sec. 1-205 defines *course of dealing* as "a sequence of previous conduct between the parties to a transaction which is fairly to be regarded as establishing a common basis of understanding for interpreting their expressions and other conduct." In other words, if the parties in their past dealings have always attributed a particular meaning to certain words or actions, this fact may be used by the court to help ascertain what the parties mean in the present case.

The same section defines *usage of trade* as "any practice or method of dealing having such regularity of observance in a place, vocation or trade as to justify an expectation that it will be observed with respect to the transaction in question." Thus, if the parties haven't indicated otherwise by their words or conduct, they are treated as having implicitly consented to follow well-established customs of the locale or of the industry in which they are both involved.

These three aids are used by the court only to interpret or perhaps supplement an unclear or incomplete agreement. They are not used to contradict any clear expressions of the parties.

Unconscionable Agreements

Sec. 2-302 introduces to the law of sales the concept of the *unconscionable contract*. Under this section, a court can refuse to enforce any contract or any particular clause in a contract that it finds unconscionable (grossly unfair). It can also limit the application of any unconscionable clause so as to avoid an unconscionable result.

At common law, a number of doctrines are available under which a court can refuse to enforce a grossly unfair agreement, including fraud, duress, and undue influence (see Chapter 13). However, such theories have not always provided complete protection for victims of "overreaching." In many courts the requirements for proving fraud, duress, or undue influence are stringent. Furthermore, simple abuse of bargaining power, no matter how shocking, often does not "fit" within one of these theories.

While the doctrine of unconscionability had been recognized by the courts prior to the UCC, its use was quite rare. The UCC does not actually define *unconscionability,* but Sec. 2-302 is aimed at those contracts which are so unfair and so oppressively one-sided as to "shock the conscience" of the court—and the doctrine itself is still evolving. It appears from many of the recently decided cases that the principal beneficiaries of Sec. 2-302 will be consumers, particularly those who are economically disadvantaged. (Cases do exist in which unconscionability has been found in a contract between two merchants, but they are rare.)

Many of the unconscionable contract cases have focused on specific clauses. For example, in several decisions the courts have refused to enforce clauses in consumer sales contracts that grant exclusive jurisdiction to a court distant from the consumer's home. In a few cases the courts have even refused to enforce consumer sales contracts where the price was excessive. These cases usually involved a high-pressure salesperson, a poor and often illiterate consumer, a price several times the market value of the good, and various underhanded practices by the seller.

A number of courts have found contracts to be unconscionable even in the absence of a specific, unduly oppressive clause. The overall circumstances in these cases have generally included unequal bargaining power coupled with obviously unscrupulous dealings by one party. The following case provides an illustration.

Brooklyn Union Gas Co. v. Jimeniz
Civil Court of New York, 371 N.Y.S.2d 289 (1975)

Rafael Jimeniz, defendant, purchased a gas conversion burner from Brooklyn Union Gas Co., plaintiff. Defendant apparently owned or managed some type of tenement, and the gas burner was to be used in it. Plaintiff did not negotiate with defendant personally but induced defendant's tenants to pressure him into making the purchase. The written agreement was presented to the defendant in English only by an employee of plaintiff, David Mann. Defendant spoke and wrote Spanish fluently but had very limited comprehension of English. When he requested an explanation of the contract, he was told to just "sign it." He admitted signing it but testified that it never was explained to him. Mann, plaintiff's employee, had had defendant sign the contract at the tenement and not at plaintiff's main office, where a Spanish interpreter would have been available.

One month after signing the contract, defendant attempted to make a payment at plaintiff's office, but he was told that he need not pay for another year. The contract he had signed did, in fact, provide for payments to be deferred for twelve months. After the year had passed, defendant began making payments. During the second year the unit ceased functioning. Defendant complained to plaintiff, and one of plaintiff's repairmen found that a transformer had burned out. The repairman placed an order for the part with plaintiff's office. No further action was taken to supply the part, however, evidently because defendant had not made any payments during the first year. After a time, the unit having never been repaired, defendant ceased making payments. Plaintiff filed suit, and the trial court rendered the following decision.

Shilling, Justice: . . . The purported agreement presented to the court, on its face, seems to be a contract. Absent the testimony adduced at the trial, the normal conclusion would be that a contract had, in fact, been entered into by the parties. *However, the purported contract introduced by plaintiff showed three signatures, whereas the defendant's copy only shows his own signature.* [Emphasis added.] Under UCC § 2-302 "If the court as a matter of law finds the contract or any clause of the contract to have been unconscionable at the time it was made the court may refuse to enforce the contract."

That is the situation here—this court finds, as a matter of law, that the contract introduced by plaintiff is unconscionable and, thereby, under the UCC, unenforceable in this forum. The Court of Appeals has made it plain in *Wilson Trading Corp. v. David Ferguson, Ltd.,* 23 NY2d 398 (1968), that whether a contract or any clause of the contract is unconscionable is a matter for the court to decide against the background of the contract's commercial setting, purpose and effect. This court has the power and the discretion to determine whether a contract is unconscionable. . . .

An unconscionable sales contract contains procedural elements involving the contract formation process, including the use of high-pressure sales tactics, failure to describe terms of the contract, misrepresentation and fraud on the part of the seller, a refusal to bargain on certain critical terms, clauses hidden in fine print, and unequal bargaining power aggravated by the fact that the consumer, in many cases, can't speak English. . . . The term Caveat Emptor has been eroded by the UCC; no longer can a seller hide behind it when acting in an unconscionable manner. . . . In making an agreement, the contracting parties create obligations as between themselves—the law of contracts generally contemplate[s] that the parties will meet each other on a footing of social and approximate economic equality. The basic test of unconscionability of a contract is whether under the circumstances existing at the time of the creation of the contract the parties were in equality to each other on all levels. The court can look into the contract to make its determination and ascertain how the contract was made and if the contract was one-sided.

The defendant, in this case, was not looking for any arrangement but was induced to enter into this agreement by the plaintiff. The plaintiff, through its agent, made no attempt to explain to the defendant directly or indirectly what was involved. High pressure sales tactics were used and a Spanish speaking interpreter was not provided by the plaintiff before the contract was signed. Apparent throughout the trial of this matter was that the defendant had a reasonable though limited comprehension of day to day English language usage. On technical or legal issues, however, he demonstrated an uncertainty with various terms and difficulty in expressing himself often found in people in this city for whom English remains a second language . . . . [A]n interpreter was used throughout this trial.

The doctrine of unconscionability is used by the courts to protect those who are unable to protect themselves and to prevent injustice, both in consumer and nonconsumer areas. Unequal bargaining powers and the absence of meaningful choice on the part of one of the parties, together with contract terms which unreasonably favor the other party, may spell out unconscionability. In this case, the defendant had a limited knowledge of the English language and no knowledge of the technical or legal tools of English. The plaintiff never provided an interpreter to explain the contract. The bargaining positions, therefore, were unequal. The defendant was and is, under these facts, unable to protect himself. Since he cannot protect himself, the court must protect him and thus this court declares the contract unconscionable and a nullity.

[Judgment for defendant.]

Questions and Problems

1. On December 1, after some bargaining, R, a retail lumber dealer, offered to sell a quantity of lumber to B for $450. B, a computer programmer whose hobby was carpentry, intended to use the lumber to build a storage shed behind his home. After making the offer, R said: "Yeah, I think $450 is a pretty good price. As a matter of fact, it is so good that I can't hold it open very long. Tell you what—I'll hold the offer open until a week from today. That'll be December 8." On December 6, B had not yet accepted the offer. R had an opportunity to sell the lumber at a better price, and he did so. On the way home from his lumberyard in the afternoon, R stopped by B's house to inform him of this development. B was not at home, so R left a note telling B that the offer was no longer open. When B came home shortly thereafter, he found the note. The next morning, December 7, B stopped by R's lumberyard on his way to work. The lumberyard was not yet open, so B left a note:

R:

I had until the 8th to accept and I'm going to do just that. I'll take that lumber for $200 cash and the remaining $250 I'll pay off in 5 weekly installments.

B

When R got to the lumberyard a while later, he found the note and read it. That afternoon, B came to pick up the lumber, but R refused to sell it to him.

a. Discuss whether B's attempted acceptance was made while R's offer was still open. In your discussion, focus on both the common law and any applicable provisions of the UCC.

b. Assume now that the attempted acceptance was made while the offer was still open. Discuss whether this acceptance was actually valid, focusing again on both the common law and any applicable UCC provisions.

c. Assuming that the acceptance was valid, discuss whether the resulting contract would contain the credit terms stated by B, again considering both common law and the UCC.

2. Axelson, a merchant, offered to sell goods at $10 per unit to Roberts and promised to hold the offer open for six months. Roberts did not want to accept the offer immediately because he was not certain that he would need the goods. The market price was rising, however, so Roberts did want a commitment from Axelson to a fixed price. Roberts gave no consideration for Axelson's promise to keep the offer open; however, the circumstances were such that it was reasonable for Axelson to expect Roberts to rely on the promise. Roberts did so in a reasonable and substantial way by undertaking the project for which he needed the goods and making commitments to third parties based on the price offered by Axelson. Four months after the offer was made, Axelson notified Roberts that the rising market price forced him to revoke his offer of $10 per unit. Was Axelson entitled to revoke his offer? Discuss.

3. A and B agreed that A would sell his boat to B for $27,750. The contract provided that title was not to pass "until the entire purchase price and any extra or additional charges have been paid in full." *Silver v. The Sloop Silver Cloud,* 259 F.Supp. 187 (1966). Is this agreement sufficiently definite to be enforced? Discuss.

4. Define *battle of the forms,* and discuss its significance.

5. Dorton ordered substantial quantities of carpets from Collins & Aikman Corp. Collins & Aikman responded by sending a sales acknowledgment form. The language of the form purported to accept Dorton's offer to buy, but it also stated: "Acceptance of your order is subject to all of the terms and conditions on the face and reverse sides hereof." The acknowledgment listed several terms that were not in Dorton's offer, including the provision that disputes arising out of the contract must be submitted to arbitration. *Dorton v. Collins*

& Aikman Corp., 453 F.2d 1161 (1972). Was Collins & Aikman's acknowledgment an acceptance of Dorton's offer? Discuss.

6. Assume the acknowledgment in question 5 is a valid acceptance. Is the arbitration clause part of the contract? Explain.

7. Sec. 2-209 of the UCC eliminates the "preexisting duty" rule for modification of contracts for the sale of goods. This common-law rule is intended to provide protection against certain types of commercial exploitation. What is the nature of the exploitation at which it is aimed? Does the UCC offer any other form of protection to take its place? Explain.

8. Would a check bearing the notation, "This is a deposit on [a particular item of goods]" be a sufficient written memorandum under UCC Sec. 2-201? Discuss.

9. Would the check in question 8 be a sufficient written memorandum if the notation indicated it was a deposit "on a tentative purchase of" certain goods? Discuss.

10. Star Credit Corp. sold a freezer to Jones, a welfare recipient. The retail value of the freezer was $300, but the sale price in this transaction was $900 ($1,439 including credit charges). At the time of the sale, Star knew Jones's financial condition. *Jones v. Star Credit Corp.*, 298 N.Y.S.2d 264 (1969). On what grounds can the validity of this contract be challenged? Discuss whether the challenge will be successful.

Sales/Title, Risk of Loss, and Insurable Interest

The ultimate objective of a sale of goods is to transfer from one party to another the rights and responsibilities that accompany ownership. After negotiation and formation of the sale contract, some amount of time will usually pass before this objective is realized. Time may be needed to produce, procure, or manufacture the goods or simply to take them from inventory and ship them. And the buyer may not wish to receive the goods until some future date even if the seller is capable of immediate delivery.

Many events can occur during the lapse of time preceding the transfer of ownership. The goods may be destroyed by fire, flood, or other act of God. They may be lost or damaged in transit. The seller or buyer, or both, may attempt to obtain a casualty insurance policy on the goods. A government entity may levy a tax on them. During this time, the question often arises as to which of the contracting parties possesses various rights and is subject to various responsibilities regarding the goods.

Title to Goods

Prior to enactment of the UCC, all issues of rights and responsibilities were decided by answering a single question: Who had "title" to the goods at the relevant point in time? This procedure often produced fair and logical results, but sometimes it gave rise to poor ones. Different situations can involve different policy considerations and should not therefore be governed by a single standard. Moreover, the courts were never able to develop an objective method of determining the location of title. For these reasons the UCC has abandoned the concept that title determines all questions of rights and responsibilities and has adopted the approach of identifying specific problems and establishing rules for their solution that do not depend on who had title to the goods at a given time. Title is thus unimportant in resolving most legal issues arising under the UCC.

However, in some situations title is still a relevant consideration. A few UCC provisions, for example, do make specific mention of title to the goods. Furthermore, application of various laws other than the UCC can depend on the location of title. (For instance, the issue of title can determine the party upon whom certain tax liabilities rest.) These situations make it desirable for us to discuss specific UCC rules for locating title and a few special problems relating to title. Later in the chapter we will consider the UCC's treatment of two important and related legal problems—who bears the risk in case of casualty to the goods and who has sufficient interest in the goods to obtain insurance coverage.

Passage of Title

Under Sec. 2-105 of the UCC, goods must be *existing* before any interest in them can pass. Thus "future goods" (such as crops to be grown) can be the subject of a sale contract, but no title to them can pass to the buyer until they actually come into existence.

Other rules relating to passage of title are delineated in Sec. 2-401:

1. Goods must be not only existing but also *identified* before title can pass to the buyer. Generally speaking, identification occurs when specific goods are designated as being the subject of the sale contract. Thus, if a seller has an inventory of lumber and agrees to sell a certain described quantity, no title can pass to the buyer until the specific lumber to be sold is marked, segregated, or otherwise identified. This does not mean that title always passes when the goods are identified; identification is simply a condition that must be met before title can pass.

2. Subject to the requirement of identification, title can pass to the buyer in any manner and on any conditions expressly agreed on by the parties.

3. If the parties do not expressly agree as to passage of title, when and where this occurs depends on how the goods are to be delivered. If they are to be shipped to the buyer, title passes to the buyer when the seller "completes his performance with reference to the physical delivery of the goods." In this regard, two situations are possible:

    a. The parties might make a *shipment contract.* Under this type of agreement, the seller is authorized or required to ship the goods to the buyer but is not obligated to see that they actually reach that person. The seller's only obligation is to deliver the goods to a carrier, such as a trucking company; title passes when the goods are shipped.

b. On the other hand, the parties might make a *destination contract.* In this case the seller is obligated to see that the goods are actually delivered to the buyer. Title passes to the buyer only when that obligation is performed by tendering the goods at their destination. This is true whether the seller ships the goods by independent carrier or personally delivers them to the buyer.[1]

4. Sometimes the parties will agree that delivery to the buyer is to be accomplished *without physically moving the goods.* For example, the contract may require the buyer to pick up the goods at the seller's place of business or at a warehouse owned by a third party. In this situation, title passes at either of two different times, depending on whether a document of title is used.

a. If the seller is required to deliver a document of title (such as a warehouse receipt) to the buyer, title passes *when the document is delivered.* Thus the buyer can have title to the goods even if he or she leaves them in the possession of the warehouseman for a time.

b. If the seller is not required to furnish a document of title, passage of title occurs *when the sale contract is made*—if the goods are identified. If the goods are not identified at that time, title passes when identification does occur. (An example of the application of this rule is the situation where the buyer is to pick up the goods at the seller's premises.)

Special Problems Regarding Title

Sales by Persons with Imperfect Title: A situation occasionally exists where a party with no title or with imperfect title sells goods to another. To illustrate: Suppose that S sells goods to B. O then appears on the scene and claims to be the true owner or to have some interest in the goods.[2] If O is correct, S will ultimately be responsible for any loss he has caused O or B. Often, however, the real dispute is between O and B over who has the greater right to the goods.

In attempting to resolve the conflict between O and B, UCC Sec. 2-403 focuses on the type of title held by S, distinguishing between a void and a voidable title. If S has a *void* title (which is actually no title at all), he cannot transfer any interest in the goods to B. The most common example of this situation is where S is a thief. If S has stolen goods from O and then sold them to B, O can reclaim the goods from B. In such a case, it does not matter whether B has acted honestly.

The result may be different if S has a *voidable* title at the time he sells to B.

---

[1]Most sales contracts are of the *shipment* variety. Types of terms commonly used by sellers and buyers to indicate whether they are making a shipment or destination contract are discussed in Chapter 21.

[2]If O is a creditor of S and claims that the goods are the agreed-upon security for the debt, his right to the goods is governed by Article 9 of the UCC, dealing with secured transactions, which is the subject of Chapter 43. At this point we are not dealing with that situation.

Here S actually has title, but O has the power to void S's title for some reason. Common examples are:

1. S purchases the goods from O through fraud.

2. S purchases the goods from O in a "cash on delivery" transaction and pays with a check that bounces.

3. S is insolvent when he purchases the goods on credit from O. In this case, O's power to void S's title and reclaim the goods generally exists for only ten days after S receives the goods. However, under Sec. 2-702(2), if S has misrepresented his solvency to O in writing within three months before delivery, O's power to void S's title and reclaim the goods is not subject to the ten-day limitation.

4. S purchases the goods from O when O is a minor.

If O asserts his rights while S still has the goods, no particular problems arise. Suppose, however, that S has already sold them to B. Can O reclaim the goods from B? The answer is yes, unless B is classified as a *bona fide purchaser* (BFP). Sec. 2-403(1) states that "a person with voidable title has power to transfer *good* title" to a BFP. (Emphasis added.) This represents an important exception to the general rule that a person can transfer no better title than he or she has.

A BFP is defined as a "good faith purchaser for value." Thus two requirements must be met before B can be considered a BFP:

1. B must have acted in "good faith." This means essentially that B must not have known of the facts that caused S's title to be voidable.

2. B must have given "value" for the goods, that is, "any consideration sufficient to support a simple contract." B has given value, for instance, if he receives the goods in satisfaction of a preexisting claim against S. (Of course, an unreasonably small consideration might be evidence of bad faith on the part of the buyer.)[3]

The following case illustrates that under Sec. 2-403, a buyer cannot simply ignore suspicious circumstances and then claim to have acted in good faith.

Lane v. Honeycutt

Court of Appeals of North Carolina, 188 S.E.2d 604 (1972)

Lane, the plaintiff, was engaged in the business of selling boats, motors, and trailers. On February 21, 1970, he sold a new 20-foot boat, a 120-horsepower motor, and a boat trailer to a person who represented himself as John W. Willis. The purchaser took immediate possession of the goods in exchange for a check in the amount of $6,285. The check bounced. The boat, motor, and trailer somehow came into the possession of a John Garrett, who sold the items to the defendant, Honeycutt. Plaintiff filed suit against Honeycutt to recover the property. Defendant claimed that, even though the original purchaser had acquired only a voidable title because his check was dishonored, he (defendant) had acquired good title as a "good faith purchaser for value" under Sec. 2-403. The trial court ruled in favor of

---

[3]The requirement of value is easier to satisfy for a BFP than for a holder in due course of a negotiable instrument (see Chapter 25 for details).

plaintiff on the ground that defendant was not a good faith purchaser. Defendant appealed.

Vaughn, Justice: . . . We now review some of the evidence as it relates to how defendant came into possession of the property in order to determine whether there was evidence to support the court's finding that defendant was not a purchaser in good faith.

In the summer of 1970, defendant, a resident of Asheboro, North Carolina, rented a beach house from John R. Garrett in Garden City, South Carolina. Defendant had known Garrett for several years. Defendant's version of his transaction with Garrett with reference to the boat was, in part, as follows:

> Mr. Garrett first approached me about buying his house on the beach that I was staying in, and he told me he wanted $50,000.00 for it, and I told him I couldn't afford anything like that. He said, "Well, let me sell you a boat out there." And I said, "Well, I couldn't afford that, either."
>
> . . . As to whether or not, in other words, this boat looked like it was fairly expensive, well, I thought it would be a little more than it was. He told me the price and I was very pleasantly surprised. . . .
>
> . . . [H]e's a pretty sly businessman. I've bought stuff from him before, and he would make you think you were getting a steal. . . .
>
> I did not know John Willis and did not know him by one of his aliases. I never met him under the alias of John Patterson or any other alias, and I have never met him since that date. I don't know from whom Mr. Garrett got the boat, he didn't tell me the man's name. . . .
>
> . . . I first knew that the boat was stolen when the F.B.I. came to see me. . . . He (Agent Madden) told me who the true owner of the boat was at that time and he told me it was a stolen boat and Mr. Patterson was wanted by the F.B.I. . . . His real name is John William Willis. The F.B.I. told me that one of his aliases was John Patterson. . . .

Garrett told defendant he would let defendant have the boat for $2,500. Defendant then paid Garrett a deposit of $100. Garrett had nothing to indicate that he was the owner of the boat, motor or trailer. Garrett told defendant he was selling the boat for someone else. "This guy comes down, you know, and does some fishing."

Two weeks later defendant returned to Garden City, South Carolina, with $2,400, the balance due (on a boat, motor and trailer which had been sold new less than six months earlier for $6,285.00). On this occasion, [according to defendant],

> Mr. Garrett had told me—well, he always called him, "this guy" see, so I really didn't know of any name or anything, but he told me, "this guy does a lot of fishing around here, but I can't seem to get ahold of him." He said, "I've called him, but I can't get ahold of him, so since you have the money and you're here after the boat" . . . ; "[s]ince you have the money and I can't seem to find him," he said, "I don't believe he would object, so I'll just go ahead and sign this title for you so you can go on and get everything made out to you." He then signed the purported owner's name on the documents and he signed the title over to me then.

The so-called "document" and "title," introduced as defendant's exhibit No. 8, was nothing more than the "certificate of number" required by [state law] and issued by the North Carolina Wildlife Resources Commission. This "certificate of number" is not a "certificate of title" to be compared with that required for vehicles intended to be operated on the highways of this State. Upon the change of ownership of a motor boat, [the law] authorizes the issuance of a new "certificate of number" to the transferee upon proper application. The application for transfer of the number, among other things, requires the seller's *signature. . . .*

Defendant observed Garrett counterfeit the signature of the purported owner, John P. Patterson, on the exhibit. Following the falsified signature on defendant's exhibit No. 8, the "date sold" is set out as "June 12, 1970" and the buyer's "signature" is set out as "George (illegible) Williams." There was no testimony as to who affixed the "signature" of the purported buyer, George Williams, and there is no further reference to him in the record.

Defendant's exhibit No. 9 is a temporary registration certificate from the North Carolina Department of Motor Vehicles. The temporary certificate was dated 19 February 1970 (two days prior to the sale by plaintiff to "Willis" alias "Patterson"). It describes the vehicle as "trailer, homemade, 1970" and was issued to "John Palmer Patterson." The vehicle registration license number which appears on the temporary certificate is 7567KH. Defendant received this certificate from Garrett. The trailer defendant received from Garrett was a 1970 Cox trailer. It bore the same registration plate number, 7567KH. Defendant did not receive a certificate of title to the Cox trailer that he obtained from Garrett which plaintiff now seeks to recover. Plaintiff retained possession of the manufacturer's certificate of origin for the Cox trailer and, apparently no certificate of title has been issued for that vehicle.

We hold that the evidence was sufficient to support the court's finding that defendant was not a good faith purchaser. [In other words, defendant had not acted in good faith because he chose to ignore the extremely suspicious circumstances.] . . .

Affirmed.

Entrustment to a Merchant: One additional situation exists in which a seller can transfer a better title to a buyer than the seller actually has. Under Sec. 2-403(2), if an owner entrusts possession of goods to a merchant who deals in goods of that kind, the merchant has the power to transfer good title to a "buyer in the ordinary course of business." Suppose that Owner O leaves her typewriter to be repaired by M, who is in the business of both repairing and selling typewriters. M then sells O's typewriter to a customer, D. If D purchases the typewriter in an ordinary way from M, and if D has no knowledge that the typewriter actually belongs to O, D has good title. O's only remedy is to sue M for damages; she cannot reclaim the typewriter from D.[4] The "entrustment" necessary to bring this rule into effect can also occur if a buyer allows a merchant-seller to remain in possession of the goods after the sale. An obvious purpose of the rule is to facilitate the free flow of trade by relieving ordinary customers from the necessity of inquiring into the status of the merchant's title.[5]

---

[4]D's purchase would not be in the "ordinary course of business," however, if he received the typewriter as security for or in satisfaction of a preexisting debt owed to him by M. D also would not be buying in the ordinary course of business if the typewriter was part of a bulk purchase of all or a substantial part of M's inventory.

[5]But even though D can acquire greater title in this situation than M had, D's title can be no better than O's.

Protection of Seller's Creditors: If a seller for some reason retains possession of the goods after they have been sold, his or her creditors can be misled. Believing the seller's assets to be greater than they really are, a new creditor may grant credit or an existing creditor may fail to take timely protective measures. If the seller's retention of goods is an attempt to defraud his or her creditors, they can treat the sale as being void and the goods as being subject to their claims. Even "unsecured" creditors (those not having a lien on the specific goods) possess this power.[6]

The seller's retention of goods after the sale does not always constitute a fraud on creditors. Indeed, Sec. 2-402(2) states that *it is not fraud* for a seller to retain possession in good faith for a "commercially reasonable time." In other words, the retention must be for a legitimate purpose (such as making adjustments or repairs), and the seller must not keep the goods longer than is reasonably necessary to accomplish this purpose. If the criteria of good faith and a commercially reasonable time are met, the seller's unsecured creditors cannot void the sale.

Retention of possession is not the only way a seller can defraud his or her creditors. Sometimes the sale itself is fraudulent and can be voided by the creditors regardless of who has possession. For instance, a sale made for less than "fair consideration" (thereby depleting the seller's assets) is a fraud on the seller's creditors in either of the following two situations: (1) where the seller is *insolvent* (liabilities exceed assets) at the time of the sale or is made insolvent by the sale; or (2) where the evidence proves that the seller actually intended to hinder, delay, or defraud the creditors. These rules are intended to protect creditors from an attempt by the seller to conceal his or her assets through a sham transaction (usually with a friend or relative).

Bulk Transfers: Suppose that a merchant owing money to creditors sells his or her inventory to a third party. If the merchant uses the proceeds to pay the debts as they fall due, no problems arise. But what if the person pockets the money and disappears, leaving the creditors unpaid? Can these creditors lay any claim to goods that are now in the buyer's hands? If the buyer has paid a fair consideration, the sale is not fraudulent under the rules just discussed.

The merchant's creditors in such a situation are protected by the basic rules of Article 6 of the UCC:

1. A *bulk transfer* subject to the protective provisions of Article 6 is any transfer (sale) in bulk of a major part of the inventory of an enterprise whose principal business is the sale of merchandise from inventory.

2. Before the bulk transfer takes place, the seller must furnish a list of his or her creditors to the buyer. Then the seller and buyer must prepare a list of the property to be sold. Finally, the buyer must notify the seller's creditors of the bulk sale at least *ten days* before taking possession of or paying for the goods (whichever occurs first). This notice enables creditors to take steps to protect themselves; for example, they can impound the proceeds of the sale if they deem it necessary.

---

[6]The rights of "secured" creditors will be discussed in Chapter 43.

3. If the buyer fails to comply with this advance notice requirement, the sale is ineffective against the seller's existing creditors. (Those who become creditors after the notice is given are not entitled to any notice.) That is, in seeking to obtain satisfaction of their claims, the seller's creditors can treat the goods as still belonging to the seller. For example, a creditor might obtain judgment against the seller and then levy execution on the goods (have them seized) even though they are in the buyer's hands. The creditor must do so, however, within *six months* after the buyer takes possession.

4. Even if a bulk transfer is ineffective because proper notice has not been given, the buyer can transfer good title to a BFP.

Risk of Loss

A warehouse fire damages thousands of dollars worth of goods. A truck, train, ship, or airplane is involved in an accident that destroys a substantial quantity of goods. In these kinds of situations the question may arise as to who must bear the financial burden of the loss.

The question is especially provocative when the goods are the subject of a sale contract at the time of damage or destruction. The risk that the goods will suffer some casualty initially rests on the seller, but ultimately it passes to the buyer. The crucial issue is whether the risk had passed from the seller to the buyer at the time of the loss. If it had not yet passed, the financial loss is borne by the seller. (Whether the seller in such a case also remains responsible to fulfill the contract with the buyer is a separate issue, to be discussed in Chapter 21.) If it had already passed, the buyer must bear the loss. The buyer is obligated to pay for the goods if payment had not yet been made, and he or she is not entitled to a refund of any payment already made.

The existence of insurance coverage does not lessen the importance of this question; it simply means that the real issue is whose insurance company must bear the loss. Of course, insurance coverage may be inadequate or totally lacking in a given case. If the goods are damaged, lost, or destroyed while in possession of a bailee such as a carrier or warehouseman, the bailee will often be liable (see Chapter 42 for details). The risk of loss question in such a case is still important, however, because it determines who bears the burden of pursuing the bailee for a remedy.

As we mentioned earlier in this chapter, risk of loss does not automatically pass with title. In resolving the problem of who bears the risk, the UCC differentiates between two situations: (1) where the contract has not been breached when the loss occurs, and (2) where there has been a breach at the time of the loss.

Risk of Loss Where the Contract Is Not Breached

The rules for placing the risk of loss in the ordinary situation are found in Sec. 2-509, as follows:

1. As was the case with passage of title, the parties can make any agreement regarding risk of loss.

2. Where there is no agreement as to who bears the risk, the issue is based on *how the goods are to be delivered.* Where the sale contract requires or authorizes the seller to ship the goods by carrier, the timing of the passage of risk depends on the seller's obligation.

a. If the parties have made a *shipment contract,* in which the seller's obligation is completed upon shipment of the goods, risk of loss passes to the buyer when the goods are duly delivered to the carrier by the seller. This occurs when the seller puts the goods in possession of the appropriate carrier, makes reasonable arrangements for their transportation, obtains and promptly delivers any documents necessary for the buyer to take possession, and promptly notifies the buyer of the shipment.

b. If the parties have made a *destination contract,* in which the seller is obligated to see that the goods are actually delivered to the buyer, the risk of loss passes only upon fulfillment of that obligation by the seller tendering the goods at their destination.

Generally, when the goods are *delivered by carrier,* the rules governing risk of loss essentially correspond to those governing passage of title—though differences in wording between the two sections occasionally give rise to a situation where title and risk of loss do not pass at exactly the same time.

3. Sometimes the goods at the time of sale are being held by a *bailee* and are to be delivered *without being moved.* For example, they might be stored in a warehouse, the buyer intending to pick them up there or perhaps to leave them in storage until they are resold to someone else. In such a case, the placing of the risk of loss hinges primarily on whether the bailee has issued a document of title (warehouse receipt) and, if so, what type of document it is.

a. If a *negotiable* document of title has been issued for the goods, the risk of loss passes to the buyer when he or she receives the document. Since the holder of a negotiable document generally has an automatic right to receive the goods, it is logical to place the risk of loss on that person.

b. If a *nonnegotiable* document of title has been issued, the problem is different. A buyer with this kind of document is not as well protected as one who has a negotiable document. This person can, for example, lose his or her right to the goods to some third party, such as a creditor of the seller or a purchaser from the bailee. And the buyer does not actually have a right to the goods until he or she *notifies the bailee of the purchase.* (Indeed, the buyer does not have to accept a nonnegotiable document as performance by the seller; but if the buyer does not object, the seller can satisfy his or her performance requirements with such a document.) Logically, then, the buyer's receipt of a nonnegotiable document does not immediately shift the risk of loss to that person. In fact, the risk does not pass to the buyer until he or she has had a *reasonable amount of time* to present the document to the bailee and demand the goods; and, of course, the risk does not shift if the bailee refuses to honor the document.

c. When the bailee holds goods for which *no document of title* has been issued and the seller wishes to sell the goods without moving them, he or she can do so in either of two ways. *First,* the seller can give the buyer a writing that directs the bailee to deliver the goods to the buyer. Risk of loss in this instance is determined in the same way as if a nonnegotiable document of title had been issued. *Second,* the seller can obtain from the bailee an acknowledgment that the buyer is entitled to the goods. In this case, risk of loss passes to the buyer when the bailee acknowledges the buyer's right to possession.

4. Some situations are not covered by any of the foregoing rules. Two common examples are transactions in which the buyer picks up the goods at the seller's premises or in which the seller personally delivers the goods to the buyer (rather than shipping by independent carrier). In such cases, the time at which the risk of loss shifts to the buyer depends on whether the seller is a *merchant.*

If the seller is a merchant, his or her responsibility is somewhat greater than that borne by the nonmerchant; thus the risk of loss does not pass from seller to buyer until the buyer *actually receives the goods.* If the seller is *not* a merchant, the risk of loss passes to the buyer when the seller "tenders" delivery. (The concept of *tender* will be discussed in greater detail in Chapter 21, but it essentially means that the seller has placed at the buyer's disposal goods conforming to the contract requirements and has notified the buyer so as to enable that person to take possession.) Suppose, for example, that B purchases a new car from S, a dealer. S is supposed to install an AM-FM radio and speaker system before B takes possession of the car. S does the work and parks the car on his lot, then telephones B and informs her that the car is ready. Before B picks up the car, it is severely damaged by a hailstorm. S must bear the loss. Since he is a merchant, the risk does not shift to B until the latter actually takes possession. If S had been an individual selling his personal car, the loss would have been placed on B, because S had tendered delivery prior to the storm.

The case below illustrates a fairly common situation in which the issue of risk of loss becomes important.

Lumber Sales, Inc. v. Brown

Court of Appeals of Tennessee, 469 S.W.2d 888 (1971)

Under the terms of their destination contract, Lumber Sales, Inc., the plaintiff, was to deliver five carloads of lumber to Brown, the defendant. Brown admitted receiving four carloads but denied receiving the fifth, for which he refused to pay. The fifth carload was apparently stolen before defendant took possession of it. Plaintiff sued to recover the purchase price from defendant. The trial court held for plaintiff on the basis of its finding that the lumber had been delivered and the risk of loss had passed to defendant. Defendant appealed.

Puryear, Justice: . . . The railroad siding at which the lumber was to be delivered, according to agreement of the parties, is located about one half mile from the defendant's place of business and is known as a "team track" which designation means that it is available for use by several parties, which in this case, included the defendant. Track location 609-A on this siding is a point where a loading platform is located.

The uncontroverted evidence shows that during the early morning hours of November 27, 1968, the Louisville and Nashville Railroad Company, to which we will hereinafter refer as the carrier, placed a boxcar loaded with lumber consigned to the defendant on this siding at track location 609-A.

This boxcar was designated as NW54938 and it was inspected by an employee of the carrier between 8:00 A.M. and 8:30 A.M. on November 27, 1968, at which time it was found loaded with cargo and so designated upon the carrier's records.

At 11:07 A.M. on November 27, 1968, the carrier notified one of defendant's employees that the carload of lumber had been delivered at track location 609-A.

At approximately 4:00 P.M. on that same day an employee of the carrier again inspected this boxcar at track location 609-A, found one of the seals on it to be broken and resealed it at that time. The evidence does not show whether the car was still loaded with cargo at that time or not.

The following day, November 28th, was Thanksgiving Day and the record does not disclose that the carrier inspected the boxcar on that date. But on November 29, 1968, between 8:00 A.M. and 8:30 A.M. an employee of the carrier inspected the car and found it empty.

From evidence in the record before us it is impossible to reach any logical conclusion as to what happened to the carload of lumber without indulging in speculation and conjecture, but the defendant earnestly insists that he did not unload it and there is no evidence to the contrary.

The particular Code Section applicable here is Sub-section (1) of 2-509, as follows:

Risk of loss in the absence of breach.—(1) Where the contract requires or authorizes the seller to ship the goods by carrier . . . (b) if it does require him to deliver them at a particular destination and the goods are there duly tendered while in the possession of the carrier, the risk of loss passes to the buyer when the goods are there duly so tendered as to enable the buyer to take delivery.

The trial Court held that the risk of loss in this case did, in fact, pass to the defendant buyer.

Now let us further examine the evidence for the purpose of determining whether or not it preponderates against this conclusion of the trial Court.

There is competent evidence in the record which shows that on November 27, 1968, at 11:07 A.M. the carrier notified the defendant's employee, Mr. Caldwell, at defendant's business office, that the carload of lumber had been delivered at track location 609-A. Mr. Caldwell did not testify, so this evidence is uncontroverted.

There is no evidence in the record to the effect that the defendant declined to accept delivery at that time or asked for a postponement of such delivery until a later time.

The defendant testified that it would normally require about four or five hours for him and his employees to unload a carload of lumber and that on November 27, 1968, he and his employees were so busily engaged in other necessary work that he could not unload the lumber on that day and since the following day was Thanksgiving, he could not unload it until November 29th, at which time, of course, the carrier found the car to be empty. . . .

One Kenneth E. Crye, freight agent of the carrier, Louisville and Nashville Railroad Company, testified that on Thanksgiving Day, November 28th, he saw what he believed to be a railroad car being unloaded at track location 609-A, but he could not identify the car or the persons whom he believed to be unloading it. He qualified this testimony by saying that he was not positive that the car was being unloaded, but there was some lumber and some kind of activity on the platform, none of which appeared to be unusual.

From evidence in the record, a trier of fact could logically form one of two inferences:

(1) That the lumber was either stolen or unloaded by mistake by someone other than the defendant at some time between 8:30 A.M. and 11:07 A.M. on November 27th; or (2) that it was stolen or unloaded at some time after 11:07 A.M. November 27th . . . .

If the first inference should be formed then the issue should be found in favor of defendant, but if the second inference should be formed, then the issue should be found in favor of plaintiff if it could also be found that the loss occurred after defendant had sufficient time to protect himself against loss after notice of delivery.

We think the second inference is the more logical of the two, especially in view of the difference between the two intervals of time and also in view of Mr. Crye's testimony to the effect that on Thanksgiving Day, November 28th, he observed some activity at track location 609-A, which he believed to be unloading of a railroad car at that location.

Of course, we recognize and adhere to the rule that the burden of proof is upon plaintiff to prove delivery of the lumber and we are not required to indulge either of the above mentioned inferences because the trial Court . . . concluded that the plaintiff had successfully carried the burden of proof . . . and the evidence does not preponderate against that Court's conclusion.

Counsel for defendant argues that the lumber in question was not duly *"so tendered as to enable the buyer to take delivery"* as required by 2-509.

However, this argument seems to be based upon the premise that it was not convenient for the defendant to unload the lumber on November 27th, the day on which it was delivered at track location 609-A and defendant was duly notified of such delivery.

This was an ordinary business day and the time of 11:07 A.M. was a reasonable business hour. If it was not convenient with the defendant to unload the lumber within a few hours after being duly notified of delivery, then he should have protected himself against risk of loss by directing someone to guard the cargo against loss by theft and other hazards.

To hold that the seller or the carrier should, under the circumstances existing in a case of this kind, continue to protect the goods until such time as the buyer may find it convenient to unload them would impose an undue burden upon the seller or the carrier and unnecessarily obstruct the channels of commerce.

The language of Sub-section (1) (b) of 2-509 does not impose such a burden upon the seller, in the absence of some material breach of the contract for delivery, and we think a reasonable construction of such language only requires the seller to place the goods at the buyer's disposal so that he has access to them and may remove them from the carrier's conveyance without lawful obstruction, with the proviso, however, that due notice of such delivery be given to the buyer. . . .

[Affirmed.]

Effect of Breach on Risk of Loss

When one of the parties has breached the contract, that party sometimes is required to shoulder a risk that he or she otherwise would not have to bear. This risk is, of course, in addition to any damages that the party may have to pay. Sec. 2-510 sets forth three basic rules to cover such situations:

1. When a seller tenders or delivers goods that do not conform to the requirements of the contract, the buyer usually has a right to *reject* the goods. In such a case, the risk of loss does not pass to the buyer until the seller "cures" the defect or the buyer accepts the goods despite their nonconformity.[7] Suppose that S and B have made a shipment contract for the sale of some office furniture. The risk of loss in this situation ordinarily passes to the buyer when the goods are duly delivered to the carrier. However, in this case some of the furniture is improperly upholstered. On receiving and inspecting the furniture, B rejects the shipment. The risk remains with S until he reupholsters the defective pieces of furniture or substitutes good pieces for the bad ones. However, if B had accepted the shipment despite its defects, the risk would have passed to him on acceptance. (If, without fault of S or B, the nonconforming shipment had been damaged or destroyed before "cure" or acceptance, the loss would have fallen on S.)

2. In some situations, a buyer who has accepted goods can *revoke the acceptance.* Suppose, for example, that B does not discover the defect until after he has accepted the shipment. (The circumstances in which B has a right to revoke his acceptance will be discussed in Chapter 21. Here, assume that B does have this right.) If B revokes his acceptance, the risk of loss is treated as having remained with S from the beginning. However, the risk borne by S is *only to the extent that B's insurance coverage is deficient.* Suppose, for example, that the value of the goods is $10,000 but that B has insurance coverage of only $5,000. If the goods are destroyed through no fault of either party (for example, by flood or fire), S will bear a loss of $5,000 and B's insurance company will bear the remaining $5,000 loss. If B had had no insurance, S would have borne the entire loss. If B's insurance had covered the entire loss, S would have borne none of it.

3. Situations 1 and 2 involved a breach by the *seller.* What effect does a breach by the *buyer* have on the risk of loss? Stated simply, a breach of the contract by the buyer immediately shifts the risk of loss to him or her. Of course, the risk shifts only if, before B's breach, specific goods had already been identified as the subject of the contract. For example, S might ship conforming goods and B might wrongfully reject them on their arrival. Or, after specific goods had been identified, but before shipment, B might notify S that he will not comply with the contract. In either case, the risk of loss immediately shifts to B even if it would not have passed until later had B not breached the contract. B must bear the risk, however, *only for a reasonable time thereafter* and *only to the extent that S's insurance coverage is deficient.*

In the case that follows, the issue is what effect a buyer's breach of the sales contract has on risk of loss.

---

[7]The circumstances under which the buyer can reject goods are discussed in Chapter 21. In speaking of cure, we are assuming that the seller has a right to do so, which may or may not be the case. If he does not have the right, he cannot cure the defect and then force the buyer to take the goods. (See Chapter 21 for more details.)

Multiplastics, Inc. v. Arch Industries, Inc.

Supreme Court of Connecticut, 348 A.2d 618 (1974)

The plaintiff, Multiplastics, Inc., brought this action to recover damages from the defendant, Arch Industries, Inc., for the breach of a contract to purchase 40,000 pounds of plastic pellets.

Plaintiff, a manufacturer of plastic resin pellets, agreed with defendant on June 30, 1971, to manufacture and deliver 40,000 pounds of brown polystyrene plastic pellets for nineteen cents a pound. The pellets were specially made for defendant, who agreed to accept delivery at the rate of 1,000 pounds per day after completion of production. Defendant's confirming order contained the notation, "Make and hold for release. Confirmation." Plaintiff produced the order of pellets within two weeks and requested release orders from defendant. Defendant refused to issue the release orders, citing labor difficulties and its vacation schedule. On August 18, 1971, plaintiff sent defendant the following letter:

> Against P.O. 0946, we produced 40,000 lbs. of brown high impact styrene, and you have issued no releases. You indicated to us that you would be using 1,000 lbs. of each per day. We have warehoused these products for more than forty days, as we agreed to do. However, we cannot warehouse these products indefinitely, and request that you send us shipping instructions. We have done everything we agreed to do.

After August 18, 1971, plaintiff made numerous telephone calls to defendant to seek payment and delivery instructions. In response, beginning August 20, 1971, defendant agreed to issue release orders but in fact never did.

On September 22, 1971, plaintiff's plant, containing the pellets manufactured for defendant, was destroyed by fire. Plaintiff's fire insurance did not cover the loss of the pellets, and plaintiff brought action against defendant to recover the contract price.

The trial court concluded that (1) plaintiff had made a valid tender of delivery by its letter of August 18, 1971, and by its subsequent requests for delivery instructions; (2) defendant had repudiated and breached the contract by refusing to accept delivery on August 20, 1971; (3) the period from August 20, 1971, to September 22, 1971, was not a commercially unreasonable time for plaintiff to treat the risk of loss as resting on defendant under UCC Sec. 2-510(3); and (4) plaintiff was entitled to recover the contract price plus interest. Defendant appealed.

Bogdanski, Justice: . . . [Sec.] 2-510, entitled "Effect of breach on risk of loss," reads, in pertinent part, as follows: "(3) Where the buyer as to conforming goods already identified to the contract for sale repudiates or is otherwise in breach before risk of their loss has passed to him, the seller may to the extent of any deficiency in his effective insurance coverage treat the risk of loss as resting on the buyer for a commercially reasonable time." The defendant contends that § 2-510 is not applicable because its failure to issue delivery instructions did not constitute either a repudiation or a breach of the agreement. The defendant also argues that even if § 2-510 were applicable, the period from August 20, 1971, to September 22, 1971, was not a commercially reasonable period of time within which to treat the risk of loss as resting on the buyer. . . .

The trial court's conclusion that the defendant was in breach is supported by its finding that the defendant agreed to accept delivery of the pellets at the rate of 1,000 pounds per day after completion of production. The defendant argues that since the confirming order instructed the [plaintiff] to "make and hold for release," the contract did not specify an exact delivery date. This argument fails, however, because nothing in the finding suggests that the notation in the confirming order was part of the agreement between the parties. Since, as the trial court found, the plaintiff made a proper tender of delivery, beginning with its letter of August 18, 1971, the plaintiff was entitled to acceptance of the goods and to payment according to the contract. . . .

The remaining question is whether, under § 2-510(3), the period of time from August 20, 1971, the date of the breach, to September 22, 1971, the date of the fire, was a "commercially reasonable" period within which to treat the risk of loss as resting on the buyer. The trial court concluded that it was "not, on the facts in this case, a commercially unreasonable time," which we take to mean that it was a commercially reasonable period. The time limitation in § 2-510(3) is designed to enable the seller to obtain the additional requisite insurance coverage. . . . [Under the particular facts of this case,] August 20 to September 22 was a commercially reasonable period within which to place the risk of loss on the defendant. As already stated, the trial court found that the defendant repeatedly agreed to transmit delivery instructions and that the pellets were specially made to fill the defendant's order. Under those circumstances, it was reasonable for the plaintiff to believe that the goods would soon be taken off its hands and so to forego procuring the needed insurance.

We consider it advisable to discuss one additional matter. The trial court concluded that "title" passed to the defendant, and the defendant attacks the conclusion on this appeal. The issue is immaterial to this case. [Sec.] 2-401 states: "Each provision of this article with regard to the rights, obligations and remedies of the seller, the buyer, purchasers or other third parties applies irrespective of title to the goods except where the provision refers to such title." As one student of the Uniform Commercial Code has written:

> The single most important innovation of Article 2 is its restatement of . . . [the parties'] responsibilities in terms of operative facts rather than legal conclusions; where pre-Code law looked to "title" for the definition of rights and remedies, the Code looks to demonstrable realities such as custody, control and professional expertise. This shift in approach is central to the whole philosophy of Article 2. It means that disputes, as they arise, can focus, as does all of the modern law of contracts, upon actual provable circumstances, rather than upon a metaphysical concept of elastic and endlessly fluid dimensions. Peters, "Remedies for Breach of Contracts Relating to the Sale of Goods Under the Uniform Commercial Code: A Roadmap for Article Two," 73 Yale L.J. 199, 201. . . .

[Affirmed.]

Insurable Interest

Parties often obtain insurance coverage to protect themselves against the possibility that property in which they have an interest might be lost, damaged, or destroyed. An insurance policy is valid only if the party purchasing the protection has an "insurable interest." Whether a party has this in a given situation is primarily a matter of insurance law rather than sales law. Article 2 of the UCC does, however, contain certain rules regarding insurable interest in goods.

Seller's insurable interest. So long as the seller has title to the goods, he or she obviously has an insurable interest. But even if title passes to the buyer, the seller continues to have an insurable interest—and can insure the goods—so long as he or she has a "security interest" (a lien or mortgage to secure payment) in the goods.

Buyer's insurable interest. The buyer obtains an insurable interest and can insure the goods as soon as they have been identified as the subject of the sale contract.

Under these rules, seller and buyer can both have an insurable interest in the same goods at the same time. Of course, even if a party has an insurable interest and obtains insurance coverage, that person has no right to recover from the insurance company unless he or she actually sustains a loss.

In the following case, the defendant, an insurance company, sought to be relieved of responsibility for the plaintiff's damaged airplane on the ground that plaintiff no longer had an insurable interest in the craft.

Bowman v. American Home Assurance Co.

Supreme Court of Nebraska, 213 N.W.2d 446 (1973)

James Bowman, the plaintiff, and his partner Keith Moeller purchased a twin-engine Cessna airplane in 1969. Bowman obtained insurance on the plane from American Home Assurance Co., defendant. The insurance policy covered the period from December 23, 1969, through December 23, 1970. On December 12, 1970, Bowman contracted to sell the airplane to a James Hemmer, but the plane was destroyed before the transaction was completed. Bowman sued the insurance company to collect under the policy. The company claimed that Bowman did not have an insurable interest, and thus no effective insurance coverage, at the time of the accident. The trial court ruled in favor of plaintiff, and defendant appealed.

White, Chief Justice: . . . In December of 1970, Bowman and James Hemmer entered into negotiations for the sale of the plane to Hemmer. On December 12, 1970, Bowman and Hemmer agreed upon a price of $18,500 for the purchase of the aircraft and Hemmer paid $15,000 down. . . . Hemmer requested a bill of sale signed by both partners to protect himself, and to comply with the Federal Aviation Administration requirements for the transfer of an aircraft. Bowman testified that it was agreed that he was to remain the owner of the aircraft until "we were able to fill out the necessary paperwork." Hemmer, the buyer, testified numerous times that he was to be the owner when he received the bill of sale. This was to allow the buyer to comply with the Federal Aviation Administration requirements and make arrangements for insurance prior to the time he was to become the owner. Bowman also testified that he told Hemmer that he would leave his insurance in effect until it expired on December 23, 1970, only 11 days later. Bowman retained possession of the plane.

On December 15, 3 days later, Bowman contacted Hemmer and asked Hemmer if he wanted to go with him on a business trip to Kansas. The purpose of the flight was for Bowman to transact some business in Kansas. Upon their return to Fremont, Hemmer asked Bowman for permission to use the plane on the following Friday and Saturday. Bowman and Hemmer specifically examined Bowman's insurance policy to ascertain whether it would provide coverage while Hemmer flew the plane. Bowman then gave Hemmer permission and Hemmer took the plane to Columbus. On December 16, Hemmer flew the plane from

Columbus to Fremont to obtain the bill of sale, but it had not been signed so he returned to Columbus without it.

On December 18, Hemmer flew the plane to Mitchell, South Dakota, pursuant to the permission granted by Bowman. In attempting to take off from Mitchell, the tip of a wing caught in a snow bank causing extensive damage to the aircraft.

Hemmer testified that the Federal Aviation Administration regulations require that a registration certificate be in an aircraft before title to the plane can be transferred to a new owner, and that once the bill of sale is received, it is attached to a new registration application and sent to the Federal Aviation Administration. A pink copy of the new registration is placed in the aircraft to serve as a temporary registration. This paperwork had not been completed at the time of the loss because the bill of sale had not yet been received. The registration certificate in the aircraft at the time of the accident showed James Bowman as the owner.

The signature of Bowman's partner was obtained and the bill of sale was mailed to Hemmer on December 18, the day of the accident. Hemmer received the bill of sale on December 20. The bill of sale was in blank form and had not been filled out at the time Hemmer received it. It was understood that Hemmer was to fill out the necessary information on the bill of sale. Bowman filed an accident report after the accident and indicated he was the owner.

The controversy between the parties centers around two provisions of the Uniform Commercial Code. Section 2-501, UCC, provides in part: "(2) The seller retains an insurable interest in goods so long as title to or any security interest in the goods remains in him." . . .

Section 2-401, UCC, details the concept of passage of title: "(2) *Unless otherwise explicitly agreed* title passes to the buyer at the time and place at which the seller completes his performance with reference to the physical delivery of the goods, despite any reservation of a security interest and even though a document of title is to be delivered at a different time or place." . . . (Emphasis supplied.)

As section 2-501, UCC, provides, the seller has an insurable interest until title passes to the buyer. Under section 2-401, UCC, title passes to the buyer (1) at the time and place where the seller completes his performance with reference to the physical delivery of the goods or (2) at any other time explicitly agreed to by the parties. As dictated by the Uniform Commercial Code, the trial court submitted two factual questions to the jury. First, whether the seller had completed physical delivery of goods. Second, whether there was an explicit agreement between the buyer and the seller as to the time when title was to pass. A jury finding in favor of the insured upon either of these factual issues supports the verdict. Where reasonable minds might draw different inferences or conclusions from the evidence, it is within the province of the jury to decide the issues of fact and the jury verdict will not be set aside unless it is clearly wrong.

There was substantial evidence from which the jury could have inferred that the seller had not completed physical delivery of the goods. The evidence shows that the buyer was only given limited use of the plane to make the trip to South Dakota. The buyer even asked the seller for permission to use the plane for this one trip. The seller had only granted a limited possession of the plane to the buyer, even though the buyer had possession of the plane for 3 days prior to the accident.

The jury could have also inferred from the evidence that the buyer and seller had an explicit agreement that title was to pass upon the completion of the "necessary paperwork." The code itself provides no definition of the term "explicit" as used in section 2-401, U.C.C.

In *Harney v. Spellman*, 251 N.E.2d 265 (1969), the court defined "explicit" in reference to section 2-401, UCC, as follows: "The term 'explicit' means that which is so clearly stated or distinctly set forth that there is no doubt as to its meaning." . . .

Bowman testified that it was agreed that he was to remain the owner of the aircraft until "we were able to fill out the necessary paperwork." The only other testimony by Bowman on this subject was the testimony of Bowman on cross-examination that he thought a sale had occurred on December 12, 1970. On redirect, however, Bowman testified that he meant an agreement to sell the plane was entered into on December 12, 1970. The buyer testified numerous times that there was an agreement that he was to be the owner when he received the bill of sale. This was to allow the buyer to complete the Federal Aviation Administration requirements and make arrangements for insurance prior to the time he was to become the owner. From all this testimony the jury could infer that there was an explicit agreement. The credibility of the witnesses and weight to be given to their testimony are for the triers of fact. On the record as a whole, we cannot conclude that there was not sufficient evidence to support a jury finding that there was an explicit agreement as to the passage of title of the aircraft.

The evidence showed that the bill of sale sent to the buyer from the sellers on the day of the accident was not signed by both sellers until the day of the accident. The bill of sale was not received by the buyer until several days after the accident, and even at this time it remained in blank form. The parties knew that the buyer would fill in and complete the bill of sale after he received it. Thus, it is clear from the evidence that "completion of the necessary paperwork" involved more than the mere signing of the bill of sale by both sellers. It at least included receipt of the blank bill of sale by the buyer, but it could also have included the action of the buyer in filling out the necessary Federal Aviation Administration papers and completing the bill of sale. None of the above steps had been completed at the time of the accident, and therefore the time of the completion of the necessary paperwork had not occurred at the time of the accident.

In summary, the jury could reasonably have found from substantial evidence that either (1) the seller had not completed physical delivery of the goods under section 2-401, UCC, or (2) there was an explicit agreement for title to pass upon completion of the necessary paperwork which had not occurred at the time of the accident. Under either of these findings title had not passed to the buyer under section 2-401, UCC, and therefore under section 2-501, UCC, the sellers retained an insurable interest. For these reasons we affirm the judgment of the District Court.

Affirmed.

"Sale or Return" and "Sale on Approval"

Occasionally a seller and buyer agree that the buyer is to have a right to return the goods to the seller even though the goods conform to the sale contract. Such transactions possess certain unique characteristics warranting a separate discussion.

A sale of this type is either a "sale or return" or a "sale on approval." Which of the two forms the transaction takes can be expressly agreed upon by the parties. If the agreement provides for a return of conforming goods but does not designate which form is intended, the UCC provides specific rules for classifying the arrangement. Sec. 2-326 states: "Unless otherwise agreed, if delivered goods may be returned by the buyer even though they conform to the contract, the transaction is (a) a 'sale on approval' if the goods are delivered primarily for *use,* and (b) a 'sale or return' if the goods are delivered primarily for *resale."* (Emphasis added.) This is a common sense test. The purpose of a *sale on approval* is to allow the buyer who will be using the goods an opportunity to try them out before committing himself or herself to pay for them. The purpose of a *sale or return* is to allow the buyer of goods who intends to resell them to others an opportunity to return the unsold items.

In either type of transaction the sale contract can specify the period of time within which the buyer must make a decision. If no time is specified, the choice must be made within a *reasonable time.* Failure to decide within this time constitutes acceptance of the goods, and the buyer must pay for them.

In a sale on approval transaction, the buyer can express approval in several ways. For example, as we have already indicated, failure to express disapproval within the required time constitutes approval. Approval can also be given by any statements or actions signifying it. Of course, the buyer can make a *trial use* of the goods without implying approval—though the question sometimes arises as to whether a particular use is really just a trial. While this question must be answered on the basis of the facts of each case, the key is whether the use being made of the goods is consistent with the purpose of a trial.

The legal consequences of a sale or return and a sale on approval differ in several significant respects, among them:

1. In a sale or return, a valid sale exists until the buyer returns the goods. Thus title and risk of loss pass to the buyer as in any other sale and remain with that person until the goods are actually returned to the seller in substantially their original condition. But in a sale on approval, no sale exists until the buyer accepts the goods by giving approval. Up to that time, the arrangement is a bailment and the buyer merely a bailee, with the title and risk of loss remaining with the seller until the buyer gives approval.[8]

2. In a sale or return the buyer bears the expense of returning the goods. In a sale on approval the seller bears this expense; but if the buyer is a merchant, he or she must follow all reasonable instructions of the seller in making the return.

3. The rights of creditors also differ with the nature of the transaction. In a sale or return, the buyer is the "owner" of the goods in his or her possession. Therefore, the goods are subject to claims of the buyer's creditors rather than the seller's. When the goods are returned, they are subject to the claims of the seller's creditors. The contrary is true in the case of a sale on approval. Prior to approval the goods are subject to the claims of the seller's creditors and, with one exception to be discussed below, not to those of the buyer's creditors. Again, the situation reverses when approval occurs.

---

[8]Of course, if the goods are damaged, lost, or destroyed due to the buyer's negligence or intentional wrong, he or she is responsible regardless of where the risk of loss rests.

4. We said earlier that the parties can agree as they wish on whether a particular arrangement involving the return of conforming goods is a sale or return or a sale on approval. One important *exception* to this rule places significant constraints on that freedom. If the buyer maintains a place of business where he or she deals in goods of the kind involved, and if that place of business is conducted under any name other than that of the seller, then the goods in the buyer's possession are subject to the claims of his or her creditors.[9] This is true even though the parties have *agreed* that the arrangement is to be a consignment or a sale on approval and even though the seller is still the owner of the goods. In order to protect creditors of the buyer, who might be misled by the buyer's possession of the goods, the agreement of the seller and buyer can simply be *ignored.* It will still be effective, however, in regard to the rights and obligations existing between the seller and buyer.

In this situation, certain measures are available to the seller to protect his or her ownership rights in the goods. In other words, even though the goods are reachable by the buyer's creditors, a cautious seller can take steps to see that his or her interest prevails. Sec. 2-326(3) spells out alternatives for the seller, the best of which is compliance with the provisions of Article 9 (secured transactions) with respect to obtaining a "security interest" in the goods and filing public notice of that interest with the appropriate state official (See Chapter 43 for a detailed discussion of security interests.)

Questions and Problems

1. Briefly explain why the concept of *title* is not as important in the law of sales under the UCC as it was prior to enactment of the code.

2. In 1945, Lieber, then in the United States Army, was among the first soldiers to occupy Munich, Germany. There, he and some companions entered Adolph Hitler's apartment and removed various items of his personal belongings. Lieber brought his share, including Hitler's uniform jacket and cap and some of his decorations and personal jewelry, home to the U.S. after the war. In 1968 the collection was stolen by Lieber's chauffeur, who sold it to a New York dealer in historical Americana. The dealer sold it to the defendant, who purchased it in good faith. Through collectors' circles Lieber soon discovered the whereabouts of his stolen property. Lieber's demand for return of the property was refused, and he filed suit against defendant, seeking the return. *Lieber v. Mohawk Arms, Inc.,* 64 Misc.2d 206 (1970). Did Lieber or defendant prevail? Explain.

3. What is the distinction between void and voidable title under the UCC? Discuss.

4. A entrusted goods to B, who was a merchant in the business of selling such goods. B was not authorized to sell A's goods, but he did in fact sell them in his regular manner to C, who thought they belonged to B. C paid for the goods by paying a debt that B owed to X. A filed suit to reclaim the goods from C. Was A successful? Explain.

5. Briefly describe the purpose of the law concerning bulk transfers.

---

[9]The exception does not apply if the buyer is an affiliate of the seller doing business under the seller's name. In this case the buyer's creditors should be aware of the seller's interest.

6. Williams owned a motorboat, which he stored in a hobby shop. He agreed to sell the boat to Sanders. After making the agreement, Williams and Sanders went to the hobby shop, where Williams told the person in charge that Sanders would pick up the boat. Arrangements for the pickup were made between Sanders and the person in charge of the shop. When Sanders later returned to pick up the boat, it was gone. Sanders refused to pay for the boat, and Williams sued Sanders for the purchase price. Did he win his suit? Explain.

7. Lair Co. sold a TV antenna on credit to Crump. The contract provided that Crump could not remove the antenna from his premises while the price remained unpaid. The antenna was delivered and installed by Lair Co. Later it was destroyed by fire, and Crump refused to continue paying for it. When Lair Co. sued for the price, Crump claimed that risk of loss had not yet passed at the time of the fire. His reasoning was that, since the antenna was not shipped by carrier and not held by a bailee, risk would pass from Lair Co. (a merchant) to him only when he actually *received* the antenna. He argued that because of the restrictions placed upon his control of the antenna, Lair Co. technically had retained possession and he had not really received it. *Lair Distrib. Co. v. Crump,* 261 So.2d 904 (1972). Who prevailed? Explain.

8. X Company contracted to sell goods to Z Company. Both agreed that Z would pick up the goods at X's premises. The contract called for delivery "FOB purchaser's truck." X notified Z that the goods were ready for Z to pick up. Before Z called for them, however, they were destroyed. X Company sued for the purchase price. Did X win? Explain.

9. Shook bought electric cable from Graybar Electric Co. Shook was a contractor doing road work, and his place of operation continually changed. Graybar delivered the wrong cable to Shook, who promptly notified Graybar of the error and of the location where Graybar could pick up the cable. Graybar made no effort to take back the cable it had delivered, and after three months it was stolen. Graybar sued Shook to recover the purchase price for the cable. *Graybar Elec. Co. v. Shook,* 195 S.E.2d 514 (1973). Did Graybar prevail? Discuss.

10. Scarola purchased goods from Pearsall, not knowing that Pearsall had stolen the goods. Scarola obtained an insurance policy on the goods, which were later destroyed by fire. When Scarola sought to recover their value from the insurance company, the company asserted that Scarola had no insurable interest in the goods. Scarola sued. *Scarola v. Insurance Co. of North America,* 292 N.E.2d 776 (1972). Did he prevail against the insurance company? Discuss.

20   Sales/Warranties

A *warranty* is an assurance or guarantee that goods will conform to certain standards. If the standards are not met, the buyer can recover damages from the seller. Warranties can be either express or implied. An *express warranty* comes into existence because of the words or actions of the seller. An *implied warranty* is imposed upon the seller by law unless he or she takes the proper steps to disclaim it.

Warranties relate to either the soundness of the seller's title to the goods or the quality of the goods. Warranties of quality are by far the most important and the most frequently litigated of the two. Indeed, lawsuits by buyers alleging breach of a warranty of quality are probably more common than any other type of dispute in the law of sales. After a short initial section on title warranties, most of the rest of the chapter will be devoted to a discussion of express and implied warranties of quality.

Although English warranty cases date back as far as the fourteenth century, buyers in the early days did not have an easy time. Various legal obstacles made it difficult for a buyer to prevail; *caveat emptor* (let the buyer beware), a phrase often associated with early sales law, describes fairly well the state of the law until

354

relatively recent times. *Caveat emptor* certainly was the American tradition of the nineteenth century and even a bit beyond. The pendulum began to swing the other way, however, in the twentieth century. Without a doubt, *caveat emptor* is no longer an appropriate descriptive phrase for the law of sales. In fact, many sellers now feel that the pendulum has swung too far in the direction of sellers' liability. (Two of the most commonly voiced complaints in the business world today are "excessive" government regulation and "unrealistic" standards of responsibility for sellers' products.)

In the remainder of this chapter we will examine the law governing sellers' warranties.

Warranty of Title

In most sales of goods a warranty as to the validity of the seller's title automatically exists. Specifically, Sec. 2-312 of the UCC imposes two basic types of title warranties.

The first is a warranty that *the title conveyed shall be good and its transfer rightful.* This warranty is obviously breached if the seller has stolen the goods from some third party and has no title at all. But other breaches are not so obvious. Suppose, for instance, that after buying goods from S, B is approached by T, who claims that he is the rightful owner. Upon investigating, B finds that there is some basis for T's claim, although considerable doubt exists as to whether T or S was the true owner. This doubt can likely be resolved only by a lawsuit. Will B have to become involved in a lawsuit to determine if he bought a good title from S? Or has S breached his warranty of title by conveying a "questionable" title, thereby enabling B to return the goods to S and get his money back (leaving S and T to resolve their own problems)? The answer is that B purchased goods—not a lawsuit. If T's claim is reasonably well-founded (not completely frivolous), B has the option of returning the goods to S and getting his money back or defending against T's claim. If B takes the latter route and wins the lawsuit brought by T, B can recover his legal expenses from S. If B loses the lawsuit, he can recover from S not only his legal expenses but also the value of the goods lost to T.

The second type of title warranty is that *the goods shall be delivered free from any security interest or other lien or encumbrance of which the buyer at the time of contracting has no knowledge.* This warranty will be breached, for example, if S sells mortgaged goods to B without telling B of the mortgage (security interest or lien).

In an ordinary sale the seller is relieved from the obligations of the warranty of title only by indicating through specific language that he or she is making no assurances that the title is good. In certain situations, however, the circumstances themselves notify the buyer that the seller is making no such assurances; and there is no warranty of title in such cases. An example is a public sale by the sheriff of goods that have been seized to satisfy a debt.

Although not a warranty of title in the strict sense, an additional obligation is imposed upon some sellers by Sec. 2-312. Unless otherwise agreed, a seller who is a merchant in the type of goods involved is deemed to warrant *that the goods sold do not infringe upon the patent, copyright, or trademark of a third party.* Thus the seller is responsible to the buyer for any loss incurred by the buyer due to such a claim by a third party. But the buyer is responsible to the seller if the seller has manufactured the goods according to the *buyer's specifications* and is then subjected to a claim of infringement by a third party.

Express Warranties of Quality

As stated earlier, express warranties are those which exist because of the words or actions of the seller. To create an express warranty, the seller does not have to use the words *warranty* or *guarantee,* and the buyer does not have to show that the seller intended to make a warranty.

Under Sec. 2-313 of the UCC, express warranties can be created in three different ways: (1) by an affirmation of fact or a promise by the seller that relates to the goods, (2) by the seller's description of the goods, or (3) by provision of a sample or model.

Affirmation of Fact or Promise

An affirmation of fact or a promise relating to the goods may create an express warranty by the seller that the goods will conform to the affirmation or promise. For example, the seller might claim, "This boat is equipped with a two-year-old, 100 horsepower engine that was overhauled last month." The statement contains several affirmations of fact—that the boat is equipped with an engine, that the engine is two years old, that it has 100 horsepower, and that it was overhauled last month. Note that a seller's expression of *opinion or commendation* ("this is a first-class boat") does not constitute an express warranty. Nor does a statement that merely relates to the *value* of the goods ("this boat is worth $25,000 at retail").

Of course, some statements are on the borderline between fact and opinion. ("The steering mechanism on this boat has been thoroughly engineered" is a difficult statement to classify.) In such cases, the courts tend to find that the statement is an affirmation of fact when the buyer has only a limited knowledge of the type of goods involved. The greater the buyer's knowledge in relation to the seller's, the more likely it is that vague statements will be treated by the court as mere expressions of opinion. (This tendency of courts is natural, since vague, general statements are more likely to mislead the unknowledgeable than the knowledgeable.)

While an affirmation of fact relates to a past or present matter, a promise relates to the future. A promise that might give rise to an express warranty is, "I assure you that the engine on this boat will not stall, the way many boats do, when you run it in choppy water." Of course, since either an affirmation of fact or a promise may create an express warranty, there is no need to be overly concerned about the sometimes "fuzzy" distinction between an affirmation and a promise.

Description of Goods

A descriptive word or phrase used in a sale of goods may create an express warranty that the goods will conform to the description. For example, a sale of "pitted" prunes or "seedless" grapes is a warranty that the fruit will have no seeds. Use of recognized trade terms may also constitute a description. For example, the term "Scotchgard," used in connection with furniture upholstery, is descriptive of fabric that has been treated so as to make it water and stain resistant. Goods described by such a trade term are warranted to possess those characteristics generally associated with the term in the trade or business involved.

Sample or Model

Where a sample or model is provided to the buyer, and the evidence indicates that the parties treated it as establishing a *standard of quality* for the sale, there exists a warranty that the goods will conform to the sample or model.

A *sample* is taken from the mass to be sold, whereas a *model* represents the goods to be sold but is not taken from them. For example, one bushel of wheat drawn from a thousand bushels to be sold is a sample. Some goods do not lend themselves to being sampled. If, for example, the subject matter of the sale is an item that has not yet been manufactured or a large item that is difficult to move, a model might be used. While the UCC makes no distinction between a sample and a model, a sample is more likely to create an express warranty than a model. Since a sample is actually taken from the quantity to be sold, it is usually easier for the buyer to prove that a sample was intended to establish a standard of quality for the sale.

Basis of the Bargain

Under Sec. 2-313, an express warranty is created only if the affirmation or promise, description, or model or sample is "part of the basis of the bargain." The UCC contains no definition of that phrase. (One authority on the law of sales states that the phrase is not only undefined but undefinable.[1]) However, the phrase essentially refers to the fact that a statement, promise, description, sample, or the like gives rise to an express warranty only if the court feels that it was intended by the parties to be part of their contract.

Suppose that after the sale has been made, the buyer requests an assurance or promise from the seller that the goods meet certain standards. If it is given, does it become "part of the basis of the bargain"? Prior to enactment of the UCC, the answer probably would have been no; today it is probably yes. Under Sec. 2-209 (1), the seller's promise is a modification of the sale contract and becomes part of the contract even without additional consideration from the buyer.

---

[1]Robert J. Nordstrom, *Handbook of the Law of Sales* (St. Paul, Minn.: West Publishing, 1970), Sec. 66.

A related problem sometimes surfaces in a sales transaction. While negotiating a sale, a seller might make statements which the parties fail to include when they formalize their agreement in writing. Buyers who attempt to base a claim for breach of warranty on such statements are often thwarted by the *parol evidence rule* of UCC Sec. 2-202. Under this rule, if the court finds that the writing was intended as the final expression of the parties' agreement, the oral (parol) statements will not be admissible as evidence if they contradict the terms of the written document.

The following case illustrates how a company's advertising may expand the scope of an express warranty.

Community Television Services, Inc. v. Dresser Industries, Inc.

U.S. Court of Appeals, 8th Circuit, 586 F.2d 637 (1978)

In 1965, two television stations in South Dakota created a separate corporation, Community Television Services, Inc. (Community), for the purpose of constructing and operating a 2,000 foot tower that would broadcast signals for both stations. Community contracted with Dresser Industries, Inc. (Dresser), who designed, manufactured, and erected the tower for a price of $385,000. The tower was completed in 1969 and Community used it until 1975. During this time, Community regularly inspected and properly maintained the tower. On January 10 and 11, 1975, a severe winter blizzard occurred in the area where the tower was located. During the early morning hours of January 11, as the storm reached its height with wind speeds of up to 80 miles per hour near the top of the tower, the structure collapsed.

Dresser denied responsibility and Community sued in federal district court for breach of an express warranty. The verdict and judgment in the trial court were in favor of Community, the plaintiff, for damages of $1,274,631.60, and Dresser, the defendant, appealed.

Lay, Circuit Judge: . . . Expert witnesses called by both sides differed in their opinions as to the cause of the collapse. Community's experts testified that they had eliminated metallurgical or mechanical failure or abnormal wind loading as the cause of collapse. They theorized that the cause was high winds setting up a phenomenon known as mechanical resonance. They concluded that because of the resonance, the tower members "were inadequate to support the load that they sustained." On the other hand, Dresser's experts testified that a combination of ice, snow and wind subjected the tower to a total force greater than the ultimate capacity of its structural elements. They theorized that a substantial accumulation of ice on the upper fourth of the tower enlarged the tower members to a greater load than their designed wind loading capacity. Community attempted to refute Dresser's ice theory by calling several witnesses who testified that they did not see any such ice on or near the area where the tower collapsed. In turn, Dresser countered Community's theory through expert testimony that relatively constant winds were necessary for resonance to begin, and the winds were gusty and varied in speed and direction at the time of collapse. Furthermore, Dresser argued that the warranty did not guarantee against mechanical resonance, and experts testified that its prevention was beyond the current state of the art.

The specifications incorporated in the sale contract included a specified "Design Wind Load," which set forth the tower's capacity to withstand wind velocity as measured in pounds of pressure per square foot against the flat surfaces of its members. The specification reads: "The tower shall be designed to resist a uniform wind load per drawing T-5172, sheet S-1, 60 psf on flats." The trial court instructed the jury that this specification constituted an express warranty that the structure would withstand wind exerting pressure of 60 pounds per square foot on the flat surfaces of the tower. Dresser's advertising materials and the testimony of experts at trial revealed that the wind velocity necessary to create 60 pounds of pressure on the flat surfaces of the tower would be approximately 120 miles per hour. The evidence showed that the wind loading specifications referred, at least in engineering parlance, to "a force caused by the wind that is introduced parallel to the ground . . . [which] would be tending to blow the structure over."

Dresser argues that the trial court erred in failing to direct a verdict on the express warranty claim or grant it judgment notwithstanding the verdict, because expert testimony that the tower met the design specification was uncontradicted. Community's own experts stated unequivocally that in their opinion the tower conformed in a mathematical or analytical sense to the 60 pounds per square foot wind loading specification. If the warranty may be restricted to the technical specification set forth in the written contract, we would find Dresser's argument convincing. However, we agree with Community that the warranty was amplified, in advertising materials Dresser gave to Community prior to purchase of the tower, to promise more than mere compliance with technical measurements. In an advertising catalog, Dresser made the following supplementary affirmation:

> Wind force creates the most critical loads to which a tower is normally subjected. When ice forms on tower members thereby increasing the surface area resisting the passage of wind, the load is increased.
>
> Properly designed towers will safely withstand the maximum wind velocities and ice loads to which they are likely to be subjected. Dresser-Ideco can make wind and ice load recommendations to you for your area based on U.S. Weather Bureau data.
>
> In the winter, loaded with ice and hammered repeatedly with gale force winds, these towers absorb some of the roughest punishment that towers take anywhere in the country . . . yet continue to give dependable, uninterrupted service.

Although we agree with Dresser that a seller cannot be held to be the insurer of its product, Dresser nevertheless provided the catalog to Community to induce purchase of its product, and in the absence of clear affirmative proof to the contrary, the above affirmation must be considered part of the "basis of the bargain." Standing alone, the statements provide a warranty that Dresser's tower would be properly designed so as to safely withstand the maximum wind velocities and ice loads to which it would likely be subjected. Dresser did not indicate that this broad affirmation was superseded or cancelled by the technical specification in the contract. When the affirmation is read in tandem with the contract, as part of the "fabric" of the agreement of the parties, it enlarges the warranty created by the technical wind loading specification, giving evidence of its full intent and scope.

We find that the statements in the advertising catalog, which supplement the wind loading specification, could reasonably have been found by the jury to be an affirmation of fact or a promise concerning the actual durability or performance of the tower during the wind and ice storms to which it was likely to be subjected.

Although Dresser's defense was that the tower collapsed by reason of excessive loading due to ice on the tower members, no disclaimer or limitation of the warranty that a properly designed tower would safely withstand the maximum wind and ice loads to which it was likely to be subjected appeared in the advertising materials or the contract. Under the *integrated* warranty given, a purchaser could reasonably assume that the tower, if properly designed for its location, would withstand maximum wind speeds to which it was likely to be subjected, even if ice accumulated on the tower members. While the blizzard was a severe one, the evidence does not support the conclusion that the wind alone, or the combination of wind and ice which Dresser claimed caused the collapse, was not within the range of storm conditions to be reasonably contemplated for the tower's location. Breach of a warranty created by statements describing the specific capacity of goods is proved when the product is shown by direct or circumstantial evidence to have failed to perform reasonably and safely the function for which it was intended by the manufacturer. In view of the affirmation made in the catalog, there was sufficient evidence for the jury to reasonably find that the tower was not as durable as it was warranted to be.

[Affirmed.]

Implied Warranties of Quality

In Sec. 2-314 and Sec. 2-315 the UCC creates two types of implied warranties: the implied warranty of merchantability and the implied warranty of fitness for a particular purpose.

Merchantability

If the seller is a *merchant with respect to the type of goods being sold,* the law injects into the sale contract a warranty that the goods are "merchantable." When Jones, a carpenter, sells his 1968 Volkswagen to a neighbor, no implied warranty of merchantability exists because Jones is not a merchant in automobiles.

Merchantable means essentially that the goods must be *fit for the ordinary purposes for which such goods are used.* The warranty of merchantability requires, for example, that shoes have their heels attached well enough that they will not break off under normal use. The warranty does not require, however, that ordinary walking shoes be fit for mountain climbing. To be merchantable, goods must also do their ordinary job *safely.* A refrigerator that keeps food cold but that shorts out and causes a fire is not merchantable. But this warranty does not make the seller an insurer against loss, and the goods are not guaranteed to be accident-proof. A refrigerator is not unmerchantable simply because its door is capable of shutting on fingers. Similarly, the implied warranty of merchantability does not guarantee that goods will be of the highest quality available. They are required to be of only *average or medium grade,* around the middle range of quality. The merchantability warranty also requires the goods to be adequately packaged and labeled.

A number of cases decided prior to enactment of the UCC held that food purchased at a restaurant, hotel, or the like carried no such warranty because the subject matter of the sale was more a service than a good. The UCC, however, explicitly states that the implied warranty of merchantability extends to food sold at service establishments such as restaurants and hotels, whether the food is consumed on or off the premises. Applied to food in general, the implied warranty of merchantability can be equated with *wholesomeness.* A pork chop tainted with botulism, for instance, is not merchantable.

Many court cases have involved objects in food that caused harm to the consumer, ranging from a mouse in a bottled soft drink to a screw in a slice of bread. In such cases the courts traditionally have distinguished between "foreign" and "natural" objects. They usually find that if the object is foreign (such as the mouse or screw mentioned above), the warranty of merchantability has been breached. If, on the other hand, the object is natural (such as a bone in a piece of fish), no breach of this warranty has occurred. A *few* courts have rejected this distinction and have instead based their decisions on the "reasonable expectations of the consumer." The controlling factor in this approach is whether a consumer would reasonably expect such an object to be in the food. Thus one might reasonably expect to find a chicken bone in a piece of fried chicken but perhaps not in a chicken sandwich. Similarly, one probably would not expect to find a seed in an olive that has a hole in the end, indicating that it had been pitted.

The following two cases present specific illustrations of the kind of buyer protection provided by the implied warranty of merchantability. The first involves a printer who, thinking he had purchased a printing press, had actually bought a headache. The second shows how a buyer's detailed specifications may limit the scope of this warranty.

Sherman Burrus is a job printer doing business in East Peoria, Illinois, under the name of Metropolitan Printers. His business, in which he had been engaged since 1961, primarily involved the printing of letterheads, envelopes, brochures, and cards. In 1970 Burrus purchased a printing press from Itek Corp. for about $7,000. From the time the press was delivered to Burrus's place of business difficulties were encountered almost continuously. Although Itek's representatives had worked for several days in an effort to install the press and get it operating properly, it never did function satisfactorily.

Burrus's specific complaints were that the press did not feed properly, had paper jam-ups, failed to register properly (which is a process where one symbol is printed on top of another identical symbol without any visible overlap on the printed surface), streaked or smeared the printed surface, was not timed properly, produced crooked printing, and was slow in printing. Burrus and his employees spent many hours in an unsuccessful effort to correct the deficiencies of the press and to get it to work properly. One witness, a former employee of Burrus, testified that out of an eight-hour working day the press performed satisfactorily not more than two hours. About sixty days after buying the press, Burrus asked Itek to replace it. Mr. Nessel, a salesman for Itek, recommended to his company that the press be replaced, but Itek refused. Burrus, plaintiff, then sued Itek, defendant, for breach of the implied warranty of merchantability. The trial court held for plaintiff, and defendant appealed.

Burrus v. Itek Corp.
Appellate Court of Illinois, 360 N.E.2d 1168 (1977)

Scott, Justice: ... [W]e direct our attention to §2-314 of the Uniform Commercial Code, which provides: "(1) Unless excluded or modified (Section 2-316), a warranty that the goods shall be merchantable is implied in a contract for their sale if the seller is a merchant with respect to goods of that kind. . . ." . . .

. . . We need not analyze the evidence and set forth a recital of the same in order to determine that the defendant corporation is a merchant. It is obvious that the defendant is a merchant since its business is to sell printing presses.

Finding no evidence of any exclusions or modifications we can only conclude that a warranty of merchantability was implied in respect to the printing press purchased by the plaintiff.

Having found that an implied warranty of merchantability existed we are next confronted with the question as to whether or not the plaintiff proved that the same was breached.

We are of the opinion that the plaintiff did make proof of a breach of implied warranty. Again referring to our Commercial Code and in particular to section 2-314(2)(c) we find the following pertinent language:

(2) Goods to be merchantable must be at least such as . . .
(c) are fit for the ordinary purposes for which such goods are used; . . .

The plaintiff purchased from the defendant a press for the purpose of doing custom or job printing. He testified that his business required high quality printing, yet there is an abundance of evidence that the machine which he purchased contained a number of specific defects. All of the witnesses but one testified that the printing press did not feed paper properly. The feeder mechanism caused paper jams in the press and this resulted in large accumulations of wasted or nonusable paper.

The record contains evidence consisting of testimony and exhibits that support plaintiff's contention that the press purchased by the plaintiff did not register properly. On jobs requiring the use of two colors the machine left blank or white space between the colors which destroyed the contiguous effect that such a press was supposed to provide. There is in the record further evidence of streaking, smearing, slow printing, crooked printing, timing problems and loose and defective parts.

All of the defects in the press purchased by the plaintiff are not present in other presses of the same type whether they be machines sold by other companies or the defendant company.

As we have previously stated, the defendant's defense was based primarily on improper maintenance of the press by the plaintiff and improper operation. The fact that the defects complained of were apparent immediately after delivery is strong evidence against a finding that the problems were caused by improper maintenance. In the instant case there is also testimony from an expert witness that the press was at all times adequately maintained.

We fail to find in the record any evidence of the operation of the press by incompetent individuals. [Several people operated the press, but the primary operators were Burrus and a Mr. Wiese, who was also an instructor in the printing department at Illinois Central College.] The defendant acknowledges that Mr. Wiese could be considered an expert operator, yet the record reflects that Mr. Wiese encountered the same frustrating problems as were encountered by other operators.

It is true that the plaintiff made some modifications to the press, *i.e.,* an extra water roller, a piece of wood and some tape. [However, there was testimony by the defendant's own witness, Sowa, who was a senior service representative for Itek, that the plaintiff's slight modifications would not have appreciably affected the operation of the press.]

The defendant, while citing no authority, nevertheless argues strongly that specific defects such as were in the press and which caused the poor operation of the machine must be proven by expert testimony. With this contention we disagree for no mention of specific defects is found in the test of a breach of implied warranty of merchantability in our Commercial Code.

... [I]t is our opinion that the plaintiff more than amply proved a breach of implied warranty by the defendant in regard to the printing press.

The trial court in the instant case awarded damages to the plaintiff in the sum of $10,435. This sum included damages for the breach of the implied warranty of merchantability as to the press and also consequential damages for losses sustained by the plaintiff as the result of the press's defective operation. . . .

Judgment affirmed.

Anderson Halverson Corp., owner of the Stardust Hotel in Las Vegas, Nevada, ordered carpeting to be manufactured by Mohasco and installed in the hotel lobby and casino showroom of the Stardust. After installation the buyer refused to pay, claiming that the carpet "shaded" excessively, giving it a mottled effect and the appearance of being water stained. Mohasco, plaintiff, sued Anderson Halverson, defendant, to recover the price of $18,242.50. The trial court held in favor of defendant, and plaintiff appealed.

Mohasco Industries, Inc. v. Anderson Halverson Corp.
Supreme Court of Nevada, 520 P.2d 234 (1974)

Thompson, Justice: . . . One Fritz Eden, an interior decorator selected and hired by Stardust, designed a pattern for the carpet to be used in the hotel lobby and casino showroom. A sample run of the chosen pattern was taken to the hotel by Eden, and was approved. Eden then specified the material and grade of carpet which the Stardust also approved. The Stardust then issued a detailed purchase order designating the type and length of yarn, weight per square yard, type of weave, color and pattern. No affirmation of fact or promise was made by any representative of . . . the seller to . . . the buyer. The carpet which was manufactured, delivered and installed was consistent with the sample and precisely conformed to the detailed purchase order. There were no manufacturing defects in the carpet.

Upon installation, however, the carpet did shade and, apparently, to a much greater extent than the Stardust or its representative had anticipated. It is clear from the testimony that "shading" is an inherent characteristic of all pile carpeting. When the tufts of the carpet are bent in different angles, the light reflection causes portions of the carpet to appear in different shades of the same color. The only explanation in the record for the "excessive shading" was that Fritz Eden, the decorator for Stardust, decided not to specify the more expensive "twist yarn." That type yarn causes the tufts to stick straight up (or at least tends to do so) thus aiding in the elimination of excessive shading.

The trial court found that the sale of the carpet was a sale by sample which was made a part of the basis of the bargain and created an express warranty that the carpet delivered for installation would conform to the sample. Moreover, [the trial court found] that the express warranty was breached by the seller, thus precluding its claim for relief. . . .

That finding is clearly erroneous. The installed carpet conformed precisely to the description of the goods contained in the purchase order. Moreover, it conformed precisely to the sample which the buyer approved. Whether the sale be deemed a sale by description or by sample, in either event the express warranty of conformity was met. The seller delivered the very carpet which the buyer selected and ordered.

Although there is substantial evidence to support the trial court's finding that the installed carpet shaded excessively, that consequence may not be equated with a breach of an express warranty since the seller delivered and installed the very item which the buyer selected and ordered. Had the buyer, through its interior decorator, selected the more expensive carpet with "twist yarn," perhaps this controversy would not have arisen. The buyer, not the seller, must bear the consequence of that mistake.

As already noted, the judgment below rests upon an erroneous finding that the seller breached an express warranty that the whole of the carpet would conform to the sample which the buyer had approved. The buyer suggests, however, that the judgment should be sustained in any event since it is otherwise clear that the seller breached the implied warrant[y] of merchantability .... We turn to consider this contention.

Unless excluded, or modified, a warranty of merchantability is implied in a contract if the seller is a merchant with respect to the goods in question. We have not, heretofore, had occasion to consider the impact, if any, of the implied warranty of merchantability upon a case where the goods are sold by sample or description and the buyer's specifications are so complete that it is reasonable to conclude that he had relied upon himself and not the seller with regard to the merchantability of the goods. . . .

It is apparent that in a case where the sample or description of the goods may, for some reason, result in an undesirable product, the seller is placed in a dilemma. In Hawkland, A Transactional Guide to the Uniform Commercial Code, sec. 1.190206, at 65, the following example is given. Suppose a buyer provides his seller with minute specifications of the material, design and method of construction to be utilized in preparation of an order of shoes, and the seller delivers to the buyer shoes which exactly conform to the specifications. If the blueprints are in fact designs of defective shoes, the buyer should not be able to complain that the shoes are defective. For such an order might put the seller in the dilemma of being forced to breach either the express warranty of description or the implied warranty of merchantability.

The matter at hand is similar to the example just given. Although the carpet was not defective, it did shade excessively and was, in the view of the buyer, an undesirable product. Yet, it was the product which the buyer specified and ordered. The manufacturer-seller was not at liberty to add "twist yarn" and charge a higher price. The buyer relied upon its decorator, Fritz Eden, and the seller performed as directed. . . . [W]e hold that the implied warranty of merchantability is limited by an express warranty of conformity to a precise description supplied by the buyer, and if the latter warranty is not breached, neither is the former. [Emphasis added.] . . .

The judgment for [the buyer] is reversed, and since there is no dispute concerning the amount of the plaintiff's claim, the cause is remanded to the district court to enter judgment for the plaintiff against the said defendant for $18,242.50, together with appropriate interest and costs.

Fitness for a Particular Purpose

In Sec. 2-315, the UCC provides: "Where the seller at the time of contracting has reason to know any particular purpose for which the goods are required and that the buyer is relying on the seller's skill or judgment to furnish suitable goods, there is . . . an implied warranty that the goods shall be fit for such purpose." Suppose that a buyer purchases an item and then finds that it does not perform some particular function which he or she thought it would. Assume that no express warranties were made that would encompass the failure. Assume also that the particular function the item would not perform is not an "ordinary purpose" of such goods. In other words, assume that there has been no breach of the implied warranty of *merchantability*. The only remaining possibility that the seller might be liable to the buyer for breach of warranty is in the implied warranty of *fitness for a particular purpose*.

A close examination of the facts is required to ascertain whether such a warranty has been created here, because its creation depends on a number of quite narrow circumstances:

1. Sec. 2-315 states that the warranty exists only if the seller "has reason to know" of the particular purpose for which the goods are needed by the buyer. This requirement is obviously met if the seller *actually knew* of the intended purpose. But actual knowledge does not have to be proved. The requirement is also met if the circumstances are such that the seller, as a reasonable person, *should have known* that the buyer was purchasing the goods for a particular purpose.

2. The seller must also have had reason to know that the buyer was *relying on the seller's skill or judgment* to select or furnish suitable goods. That is, the buyer must have placed this type of reliance on the seller, and the seller must have known or should have known that the buyer was relying on him or her.

3. The facts leading to the conclusion that the seller either knew or should have known of the buyer's particular purpose and reliance must have existed at the time of contracting. The warranty does not exist if the seller learns the relevant facts after the sale contract is made.

4. The seller does not have to be a merchant for this warranty to exist, although in the usual case he or she will be one.

An illustration of the warranty of fitness for a particular purpose is found in *Catania v. Brown,* 231 A.2d 668 (1967). The buyer in this case owned a house with stucco walls. Because of the chalky and powdery nature of the walls, they were somewhat difficult to paint. The buyer went to the seller, specifically informing him of the problem and requesting his assistance. The seller recommended a certain brand of paint, which the buyer purchased. Despite the fact that the buyer carefully followed the seller's instructions in applying the paint, it blistered and peeled within a short time. Even though the paint was probably merchantable and would have been fit for its ordinary purposes, the Connecticut court held that an implied warranty of fitness for the particular purpose had been created and breached.

At issue in the following case is the existence of this kind of warranty. The court, in finding that no such warranty was present, based its decision on the failure of the buyer to fully inform the seller of all facts relevant to the purchase.

Johnson v. Lappo Lumber Co.

Court of Appeals of Michigan, 181 N.W.2d 316 (1970)

Johnson, plaintiff, raised hogs in an environmentally controlled barn. The building was a long structure consisting of several rooms, each of which contained pens where hogs of different ages and stages of growth were kept. It was located over a lagoon and had a floor made of slats with openings into the lagoon. The hogs were fed from troughs containing finely powdered feed. The building was completely enclosed except for openings near the ceiling.

Large ventilating fans were needed to maintain the proper temperature and to provide fresh air. Johnson contacted Lappo Lumber Co., which had furnished the building materials for the barn. Lappo referred him to the Fitzpatrick Electric Co., a wholesaler of electrical appliances. Fitzpatrick in turn called J. A. Goode. Co., a wholesaler of fans. Goode sent Bernard Jenkins, an expert on fans, to consult with the parties. Jenkins advised the purchase of certain fans with "open" motors that were not completely sealed off from the outside air. Johnson bought the fans as advised by Jenkins.

Johnson installed the fans immediately over the ends of the feed trough. Placing the fans in this position caused them to pick up the powdery feed and draw it into the fan motors. Because the motors had openings in them, they became clogged and could not operate properly. The failure of the fans caused a large number of hogs to die from lack of sufficient oxygen and many others to became so weakened that they were unmarketable. Johnson filed suit for breach of an implied warranty of fitness against Lappo, Fitzpatrick, Goode, and the manufacturer of the fans. The trial court held for defendants, and Johnson appealed.

Holbrook, Justice: . . . [T]he fans sold were not, in fact, reasonably fit for the particular purpose for which they were required. This being so, did Mr. Johnson make known to the defendants or any of them the particular purpose for which they were required, and did he, in fact, rely upon the seller's skill and judgment? This is the heart of the issue in the case. Allowing for some variations and inconsistencies in the testimony of the witnesses, the evidence clearly shows that the plaintiff did make known, and did rely, but only in part. Employees of both Lappo and Fitzpatrick bypassed the question altogether, and Bernard B. Jenkins, the manufacturer's representative employed by Goode, was called in. He was called in specifically to advise on the suitability of the fans which plaintiff proposed to buy for the purpose of ventilating the barn. Jenkins had considerable practical experience in the use of fans in agricultural and other buildings. . . . [W]hile Johnson had a right to rely upon Jenkins' conclusions, he had a corresponding duty, however, to supply the correct information to Jenkins when it was requested of him, and when that information was essential to the validity of the advice he sought. In this he failed. It was Mr. Johnson's testimony that Jenkins specifically inquired about the presence of unusual dust or moisture in the barn. The question was directly for the purpose of determining whether an open, closed, or "explosion" proof fan would be required. Mr. Johnson specifically informed Mr. Jenkins that the barn would be "Not necessarily any dustier than any other house, or home, or room or anything." He also told Jenkins that there would be no moisture problem. While there is some evidence to support plaintiff's claim that Jenkins had a plan of the barn, and that the location of the lagoon was indicated thereon, still the evidence preponderates that Johnson neither disclosed to Jenkins that the fans would be installed only inches away from the feeder nor that the barn would be directly over water and separated only by slats, and that finely ground feed would be employed. Mr. Johnson did disclose that the fans must each move 10,000 cubic feet of air per minute, but there is no proof whatsoever that the fans furnished were in any wise deficient in this requirement. It is entirely clear from the [evidence] that Mr. Johnson did not rely upon Mr. Jenkins' judgment as to the presence of dust and moisture in the barn, but rather upon his own judgment, and that in this respect Jenkins relied upon Johnson.

The testimony of the veterinarian, and indeed of Mr. Johnson, was that at the time, this particular method of raising hogs was new and rather unique, about which not a great deal was known. Consequently, the only information which Jenkins could have had upon which to base his judgment was that which he obtained from the plaintiff and Johnson had to be aware of this. It is manifestly clear from all of the testimony that had Mr. Johnson supplied the complete and correct information which Mr. Jenkins requested, the latter would without question have recommended closed-type fans with sealed motors and the unfortunate loss would never have occurred.

While anyone hearing or reading the testimony in this case is bound to feel great sympathy for the plight of Mr. Johnson, still his loss cannot be charged to any actionable misconduct, neglect or breach of warranty on the part of the defendants. . . .

Affirmed.

Conflicting and Overlapping Warranties

Two or more warranties sometimes exist in a single sales transaction. For example, an express warranty that a machine will perform in a certain way might be created by the use of a sample or model, and an additional express warranty relating to the machine's life span might be created by the statements of the seller. An implied warranty of merchantability or of fitness for a particular purpose, or both, might exist in addition to any express warranty.

When more than one warranty is created in a given transaction, the buyer does not have to choose between them. Ordinarily he or she can take advantage of *any and all* warranties accompanying the sale. Sec. 2-317 indicates that, where two or more warranties exist, courts should interpret them as being consistent with each other whenever such an interpretation is reasonable. In these situations the warranties are *cumulative;* that is, the buyer can use all of them. In the unusual case where two warranties are in conflict and cannot both be given effect, the court must attempt to determine the intent of the parties as to which warranty should prevail. The court is guided by several rules in determining this intention:

1. Exact or technical specifications take precedence over inconsistent samples or models or general language of description.

2. A sample drawn from the goods to be sold takes precedence over inconsistent general language of description.

3. An express warranty, regardless of how it was created, takes precedence over the implied warranty of merchantability if the two are inconsistent. (An express warranty does not take precedence over the implied warranty of fitness for a particular purpose, although it is difficult to envision a situation in which the two would be inconsistent.

These rules are not absolute and can be disregarded by the court if they will produce an unreasonable result.

Exclusion and Limitation of Warranties

Express Warranties

A seller who wishes to avoid liability on any type of express warranty obviously should not do anything that creates one. But as a practical matter this course of action may be rather difficult to carry out. The seller will have to avoid using samples or models that establish a standard of quality, avoid making statements or promises about the goods, and avoid giving any description of the goods. Any seller who is so concerned with escaping liability for product defects will probably not make many sales.

As an alternative the seller can include in the contract a "disclaimer," which attempts to disavow the existence of warranties or limit the circumstances in which warranty liability will exist.[2] If the warranty itself has actually become part of the contract, however, an attempt to disclaim liability will usually not be effective. Sec. 2-316(1) states that a disclaimer will be disregarded if it is inconsistent with the words or conduct that created the express warranty. Suppose that an express warranty has been created by some statement of the seller, by the use of a sample, or by the seller's description of the goods. The seller's disclaimer in the contract—"these goods are sold without warranties," or other words to that effect—is almost always inconsistent with the words or conduct that created the warranty. In sum, it is extremely difficult for a seller to disclaim an express warranty, assuming that it has been created and has become part of the contract.

Suppose, however, that the buyer claims an express warranty was created by an affirmation of fact, a promise, or a description made by the seller while the parties were negotiating the contract. But when the parties put the terms of their agreement in writing, this was not included. If the written document contains a disclaimer of warranties, the disclaimer will probably be effective in shielding the seller from liability should the goods fail to conform to his or her earlier statements. The reason is that, under the *parol evidence rule,* evidence of the prior oral affirmation, promise, or description will probably not be admissible in court, since it would contradict the clear terms of the written document.

Implied Warranties

As we mentioned earlier, the existence of an implied warranty depends on a given set of conditions or circumstances rather than on the words or conduct of the seller. However, even if the circumstances are such that an implied warranty would

---

[2]This is to be contrasted with a "limitation of remedies," a clause in the contract which merely attempts to limit the *remedies* available to one party if the other party breaches their agreement. If such a limitation clause focuses on the buyer's remedies for breach of warranty, it resembles a disclaimer. It is different, however, because a disclaimer relates to the *existence* of a warranty, not merely to the remedies available for breach of warranty. The rules regarding the validity of remedy limitations are somewhat less technical than those regarding disclaimers, and will be discussed in connection with the subject of remedies in Chapter 21.

ordinarily exist, a seller can disclaim liability for breach of the warranty by following these procedures (which sometimes differ between warranties of merchantability and of fitness for a particular purpose):

1. In the case of the *warranty of merchantability,* the language used by the seller to disclaim liability does not have to be in writing. If it is, however, it must be conspicuous (written in such a way that any reasonable person against whom it operates should notice it). For example, a disclaimer printed in larger type or in a different color than the remainder of the document will probably be considered conspicuous; and any term stated in a telegram is always considered conspicuous. In the case of the *warranty of fitness for a particular purpose,* the disclaimer must be in writing and must be conspicuous.

2. The disclaimer for the merchantability warranty must be more specific than that for the fitness warranty. It must expressly use either the word *merchantability* or other very explicit words, like *as is* or *with all faults.* The disclaimer for the fitness warranty can be merely a general statement, such as, "There are no warranties extending beyond the description on the face hereof."

Even if the seller does not make an express disclaimer, the existence of certain circumstances may sometimes exclude implied warranties. The most important circumstance concerns the buyer's *examination of the goods.* In this regard, a distinction must be made between defects that are *reasonably apparent* (that is, which a reasonable examination would reveal) and those that are *hidden* (which a reasonable examination probably would not disclose).

1. If, before making the contract, the buyer examined the goods (or a sample or model of them) as fully as he or she desired, or if the buyer refused to examine them at all, no implied warranty exists for *reasonably apparent* defects. Clearly, then, if the buyer had no opportunity to examine the goods before contracting, the seller is liable even for reasonably apparent defects. Indeed, even if the opportunity existed and the buyer chose not to take advantage of it, the seller is still responsible for reasonably apparent defects unless he or she had *demanded* that the buyer examine the goods and the buyer had expressly refused.

2. Even if the buyer did examine the goods, or expressly refused to examine them, the seller is still responsible for *hidden* defects unless it can be proved that the buyer actually knew about such defects before contracting. It should be noted that, when deciding whether a particular defect was reasonably apparent or hidden, a court will take into account the buyer's knowledge and skill. Such a factor obviously has a bearing on what an examination should have revealed to this buyer.

Implied warranties are sometimes excluded or modified by *trade usage* (industry-wide custom) or by a custom that has been established between the particular parties. However, an industry-wide custom will have no effect on the buyer if he or she is not a member of the particular industry and is unaware of the custom.

The type of consumer for which a product is intended can have an effect on the seller's attempts to escape warranty liability through a disclaimer or other limitation—as illustrated in the case below. This case also shows that courts do not look kindly on a seller's assertion that a disclaimer should be "implied" in a given transaction.

Hauter v. Zogarts

Supreme Court of California, 534 P.2d 377 (1975)

Defendants manufacture and sell the "Golfing Gizmo," a training device designed to help unskilled golfers improve their game. Defendants' catalogue states that the Gizmo is a "completely equipped backyard driving range." In 1966, Louise Hauter purchased a Gizmo from the catalogue and gave it to Fred Hauter, her thirteen-year-old son, as a Christmas present. While practicing with the Gizmo, Fred was knocked unconscious by the Gizmo's golf ball.

The Gizmo is a simple device consisting of two metal pegs, two cords—one elastic, one cotton—and a regulation golf ball. After the pegs are driven into the ground approximately twenty-five inches apart, the elastic cord is looped over them. The cotton cord, measuring twenty-one feet in length, is tied to the middle of the elastic cord. The ball is attached to the end of the cotton cord. When the cords are extended, the Gizmo resembles a large letter "T," with the ball resting at the base.

The user stands by the ball in order to hit practice shots. The instructions state that when hit correctly, the ball will fly out and spring back near the point of impact; if the ball returns to the left, it indicates a right-hander's slice; a ball returning to the right indicates a right-hander's hook. If the ball is "topped," it does not return and must be retrieved by the player. The labels on the shipping carton and on the cover of the instruction booklet urge players to "drive the ball with full power" and further state: "COMPLETELY SAFE BALL WILL NOT HIT PLAYER."

Fred Hauter testified at the trial that prior to his injury, he had practiced golf ten to twenty times at driving ranges and had played several rounds of golf. His father had instructed him in the correct use of the Gizmo. Fred had read the printed instructions accompanying the product and had used the Gizmo about a dozen times. Before the accident on July 14, 1967, he had set up the Gizmo in his front yard according to the printed instructions. The area was free of objects that might have caused the ball to ricochet, and no other persons were nearby. Fred then took his normal swing with a seven-iron. The last thing he remembers was extreme pain and dizziness. After a period of unconsciousness, he staggered into the house and told his mother that he had been hit on the head by the ball. He suffered brain damage and, in one doctor's opinion, is currently an epileptic.

The Hauters filed suit against the manufacturer and the seller, claiming among other allegations a breach of express and implied warranties. George Peters, a safety engineer and an expert on the analysis, reconstruction, and causes of accidents, testified for plaintiffs. In Peters's opinion, Fred Hauter had hit underneath the ball and had caught the cord with his golf club, thereby drawing the cord upwards and toward him on his follow-through. The ball had looped over the club, producing a "bolo" effect, and had struck Fred on the left temple. Peters concluded that the Gizmo was a "major hazard."

Ray Catan, a professional golfer, also testified for plaintiffs. He added that even if the club had hit the lower part of the ball, the same result probably would have occurred. He had personally tested the Gizmo, intentionally hitting low shots, and had found that his club became entangled in the cord, bringing the ball back toward him as he completed his swing. Catan described Fred Hauter as a beginner and stated that since a beginning golfer's swing usually is very erratic, the person rarely hits the ball solidly.

The jury returned a verdict for defendants, but the trial judge rendered a judgment notwithstanding the verdict (see Chapter 2) in favor of plaintiff. Defendants appealed.

Tobriner, Justice: . . . [After holding that defendants did breach their express warranty that the Golfing Gizmo was "completely safe" and would "not hit player," as well as their implied warranty of merchantability, the court continued by discussing defendants' allegations that their warranty liability had been "impliedly" limited.]

The Gizmo is designed and marketed for a particular class of golfers—"duffers"—who desire to improve their technique. Such players rarely hit the ball solidly. When they do, testified the golf pro, "it would be sort of a mistake, really." The safety expert classed the Gizmo as a major safety hazard. Furthermore, defendants *admit* that when a person using the Gizmo hits beneath the ball as Fred Hauter apparently did, he stands a substantial chance of seriously injuring himself. . . .

Defendants nevertheless seek to avoid liability by limiting the scope of their warranties. They claim that the box containing the Gizmo and the instructions pertaining to its use clarified that the product was "completely safe" only when its user hit the ball properly. They point to no language expressing such a limitation but instead claim that a drawing in the instructions depicting a golfer "correctly" using their product *implies* the limitation. . . .

[D]efendants' argument is wholly without merit. Furthermore, they fail to meet the stern requirements of [UCC § 2-316] which governs disclaimer and modification of warranties. Although § 2-316 has drawn criticism for its vagueness, its purpose is clear. No warranty, express or implied, can be modified or disclaimed unless a seller *clearly* limits his liability. This section is designed principally to deal with those frequent clauses in sales contracts which seek to exclude "all warranties, express or implied." It seeks to protect a buyer from unexpected and unbargained language of disclaimer by denying effect to such language when inconsistent with language of express warranty and permitting the exclusion of implied warranties only by conspicuous language or other circumstances which protect the buyer from surprise.

Because a disclaimer or modification is inconsistent with an express warranty, words of disclaimer or modification give way to words of warranty unless some clear agreement between the parties dictates the contrary relationship. . . .

Moreover, any disclaimer or modification must be strictly construed against the seller. Although the parties are free to write their own contract, the consumer must be placed on fair notice of any disclaimer or modification of a warranty and must freely agree to the seller's terms. A unilateral nonwarranty cannot be tacked onto a contract containing a warranty.

In the instant case, defendants do not point to any language or conduct on their part negating their warranties. They refer only to a drawing on the box and to the notion that golf is a dangerous game; based on that meager foundation, they attempt to limit their explicit promise of safety. Such a showing does not pass muster under the code, which requires clear language from anyone seeking to avoid warranty liability. We conclude, therefore, that the trial court properly granted plaintiffs judgment notwithstanding the verdict . . . .

[Affirmed.]

Privity of Contract   In the law of sales, *privity of contract* refers to the notion that the rights and liabilities created by a warranty extend only to those who were actually parties to the sale contract (see Chapter 7). Today, goods, especially consumer goods sold at retail, often travel through several steps before reaching the ultimate user. For instance, they might originate with a manufacturer and then pass through the hands of a wholesaler and retailer before coming to rest with the consumer. At one time, the privity of contract requirement was so strictly observed that only the *retailer* was responsible to the consumer for defects in goods. Today, however, it has been greatly relaxed and is in the process of disappearing. Generally speaking, *all parties* in the chain of distribution are responsible for the failure of goods to live up to the standards of any warranties that have been created.

Another problem with a strict privity of contract requirement is that defects in goods sometimes affect persons *other than the actual purchaser.* For example, the ultimate purchaser may lend the goods to someone, and that person may be injured because of the defect. Or an innocent bystander may suffer injury. Under strict application of the requirement, the protection provided by a warranty used to extend only to the actual purchaser. But Sec. 2-318 of the UCC has extended the protection to members of the buyer's family or household and to guests in the buyer's home, in situations where such individuals might reasonably be expected to use, consume, or be affected by the goods. However, this extension applies only when defective goods have caused a *physical injury to the individual.* Recently, the drafters of the UCC have proposed alternative versions of Sec. 2-318 to further relax the privity requirement, primarily by extending protection to *anyone* who could reasonably have been expected to use, consume, or be affected by the goods and who has been injured because of a defect. But only a few states have enacted these versions of Sec. 2-318.

From the above discussion we can see that most of the problems caused by the privity requirement have arisen in retail consumer transactions.

Products Liability in General   Any discussion of a seller's liability for defective products is woefully incomplete if limited to express and implied warranties. Warranties are only a small part of a broad area of the law frequently referred to as *products liability* (briefly discussed in Chapter 7).

During the last few decades the law of products liability has been one of the most rapidly changing areas in the entire history of the English common law system; and it is still changing. In fact, the law is in such a state of flux that it varies significantly from state to state. But it is clear that what once was a seller-oriented area of law is today buyer-oriented.

Breach of warranty is only one of several legal theories that a buyer can use against a seller of defective goods.[3] An example is the tort of *fraud,* which is

---

[3]The phrase *legal theory* here means a legally recognized basis of liability.

committed when a seller intentionally misrepresents the quality of goods. However, the two most important and frequently asserted theories (other than breach of warranty) are *negligence* and *strict liability,* both of which are part of the law of torts.

Negligence

To recover from a seller under the theory of negligence, the buyer must prove that the defect causing the injury was the result of some particular instance of negligence (carelessness) on the part of the seller. This theory offers the buyer several advantages over the warranty theory:

1. The buyer does not have to prove that a warranty existed.

2. Privity of contract is completely abolished as a requirement for recovery.

3. Under the warranty theory, the buyer must show that he or she notified the seller within a reasonable time after discovering the defect; no such requirement exists under the negligence theory.

4. A disclaimer by the seller in the sale contract usually does not enable that person to avoid liability for negligence.

The negligence theory also involves certain disadvantages for the buyer:

1. As indicated above, the buyer must initially prove some particular instance of negligence by the seller, and this can be difficult to do (although in some cases the burden is shifted so that the seller must *disprove* negligence).

2. The defense of contributory negligence (the claim that the injured party was also guilty of negligence, explained in Chapter 7) is available to a seller sued for negligence rather than for breach of warranty.

3. Perhaps most importantly, a buyer ordinarily can sue the seller for negligence only where the defective goods have caused *physical injury* to the buyer's person or property. If the injury is economic, breach of warranty is usually the only available theory.

Strict Liability

Of the various legal theories available to a buyer of defective goods, the doctrine of *strict liability* is the most recent. This theory, which has been recognized and applied in at least two-thirds of the states, possesses most of the advantages of both the warranty and negligence theories:

1. The buyer does not have to prove that a warranty existed or that the defect was caused by the seller's negligence. He or she must prove only that the goods were dangerously defective when they left the seller's hands and that this defect caused the buyer's injury.

2. As with the negligence theory, the seller's responsibility under the strict liability theory is usually not affected by a contractual disclaimer; nor is it affected by the

buyer's failure to give notice to the seller within a reasonable time after discovery of the defect.

3. Contributory negligence on the part of the buyer cannot be used as a defense by the seller. Thus a buyer's failure to inspect the goods or to discover the defect will not prevent his or her recovery of damages. Even misuse of the goods usually will not prevent recovery if the misuse is of a type which the seller could have reasonably foreseen. Practically the only defense to a strict liability claim is *assumption of risk*. If the buyer knows of the defect and the resulting danger but uses the goods anyway, the seller is not liable.

4. As with the negligence theory, privity of contract is not a requirement for recovery under the strict liability theory.

A few states allow the theory to be used only by the actual user or consumer of the goods. Most states, however, have extended the theory so it applies to anyone suffering a reasonably foreseeable injury because of the defect (such as the driver of a car struck from behind by another vehicle whose brakes were defectively manufactured).

The primary disadvantages of the strict liability doctrine are:

1. Like negligence, it generally has not been applied to purely economic injuries but only to physical injuries to person or property.

2. Unlike negligence, it ordinarily can be used only against a seller who is in the business of selling goods (a merchant).

Federal Consumer Legislation

Over the years Congress has enacted a number of federal regulatory laws dealing with the safety and quality of goods. For the most part these laws have focused solely on protecting ultimate consumers from physical harm, and until recently, they were enacted piecemeal and were rather narrow in scope. Examples include the Food, Drug and Cosmetic Act (1938), the Flammable Fabrics Act (1953), the Refrigerator Safety Act (1956), the Hazardous Substances Act (1960), and the Poison Prevention Packaging Act (1970).

Consumer Product Safety Act

In 1972 Congress enacted the Consumer Product Safety Act—the first law to deal with the safety of consumer products in general—and created a federal agency, the Consumer Product Safety Commission, to administer it.[4] This agency possesses broad powers and performs many functions, ranging from safety research and

---

[4]Some consumer products are not covered by the Act because they come under other federal laws. The most important of these are food, drugs, and cosmetics, which are regulated by a federal agency, the Food and Drug Administration, under the Food, Drug and Cosmetic Act. Automobiles are also excluded because of coverage by other legislation.

testing to preparing safety rules and standards. It has the power to ban products and to require special labeling in certain circumstances. It can levy civil penalties on those who violate the act and criminal penalties on those who violate it willfully.

Magnuson-Moss Warranty Act

In 1975 Congress passed the Magnuson-Moss Warranty Act. Like the other federal legislation discussed above, this statute is consumer-oriented. It applies only to purchases by ultimate consumers for personal, family, or household purposes, not to transactions in a commercial or industrial setting. The Warranty Act, which is usually enforced by the Federal Trade Commission (FTC), does not regulate the safety or quality of consumer goods. Instead it prevents deceptive warranty practices, makes consumer warranties easier to understand, and provides an effective means of enforcing warranty obligations. (While the federal Warranty Act is limited to consumer transactions, the UCC warranty rules are not. Thus in nonconsumer transactions the UCC rules continue in effect. But in consumer goods transactions the federal law has in some respects modified these rules.)

However, the Warranty Act does not *require* anyone to give a warranty on consumer goods. The Act applies only if the seller *voluntarily chooses* to make an express written warranty. The seller who does provide a written warranty must label it as either a "full" or a "limited" one. Under a *full warranty* the warrantor must assume certain minimum duties and obligations for products costing ten dollars or more.[5] For instance, he or she must agree to *repair or replace* any malfunctioning or defective product within a "reasonable" time and without charge. If the warrantor makes a reasonable number of attempts to remedy the defect and fails to do so, the consumer can choose to receive either a *cash refund* or *replacement* of the product without charge. *No time limitation* can be placed on a full warranty, and consequential damages (such as for personal injury or property damage) can be disclaimed only if the limitation is *conspicuous*. A written warranty that does not meet the minimum requirements must be designated conspicuously as a *limited warranty*. However, if a time limit (such as twenty-four months) is all that prevents the warranty from being a full one, it can be designated as a "full twenty-four month warranty."

The written warranty to which the act applies is much more narrowly defined than is an express warranty under the UCC. Specifically it is (1) any written promise or affirmation of fact made by a supplier to a purchaser relating to the quality or performance of the product and affirming or promising that the product is defect-free or will meet a specified level of performance over a period of time, or (2) a written undertaking to "refund, repair, replace or take other action" with respect to the product if it fails to meet written specifications. Obviously, many express warranties, such as those created by description or sample, will continue

---

[5]Only the person who actually makes the written warranty—no one else in the chain of distribution—is responsible under the Warranty Act.

to be governed only by the UCC even though a consumer transaction is involved.

Since the Warranty Act deals only with written warranties, it has no effect on the implied warranties of merchantability and fitness for a particular purpose defined by the UCC. However, the Act does depart from the UCC by *prohibiting a disclaimer of an implied warranty* (1) if an express written warranty is given, or (2) if within ninety days after the sale, a service contract is made with the consumer.[6] But a supplier providing an express written warranty with a time limitation can limit the duration of an implied warranty to the duration of the express warranty. A supplier who gives neither a written warranty nor a service contract can disclaim an implied warranty under the conditions imposed by the UCC.

The Warranty Act can be enforced by the FTC, by the Attorney General, or by a private party who has been damaged by a violation. The Act states, however, that in any agreement the supplier can provide for informal procedures by which a dispute between that person and the consumer can be settled. If the procedures follow guidelines established by the FTC, the consumer cannot resort to court action until those procedures have been exhausted.

Questions and Problems

1. Arthur sold goods to Edward. The bill of sale stated that seller transferred all of his "right, title, and interest," that "no other title to his knowledge existed," and that the "bill of sale was the original evidence of title." After the sale, a third party asserted an interest in the goods, and Edward sued Arthur for breach of the warranty of title. Arthur contended that the contract's language constituted a disclaimer of the warranty of title. Is Arthur correct? Discuss.

2. A salesclerk in a drugstore told a customer that she would get "fine results" from a hair dye she was purchasing. Does this language by itself create an express warranty of quality? Discuss.

3. Walcott & Steele, Inc., sold seed to Carpenter. State law required the package label to give the percentage of germination. The label on the seed bought by Carpenter carried the required statement, but the seed did not perform at the listed percentage. Carpenter sued for breach of an express warranty, which he claimed was created by the statement regarding percentage of germination. *Walcott & Steele, Inc. v. Carpenter,* 436 S.W.2d 820 (1969). Did Carpenter prevail? Discuss.

4. Central Gas Co. supplied natural gas to a variety of residential and commercial customers. Because of a defect in the meter owned by Central and located on Michener's property, gas escaped and caused an explosion. Damage resulted to Michener's property, and he sued Central for breach of the implied warranty of merchantability. Did Michener win his suit? Explain.

5. What is the foreign-natural distinction used in applying the implied warranty of merchantability to food? Have any courts taken a different approach? Explain.

---

[6]Under a *service contract* the seller agrees to service and repair a product for a set period of time in return for a fee.

6. Kassab, a cattle breeder, purchased feed which had been manufactured by Central Soya. The feed was intended for breeding cattle, but Central had accidentally included an ingredient that should be used only for beef cattle. After eating the feed, Kassab's cattle grew and prospered. Kassab was upset, however, when he discovered that the mistakenly-included ingredient had caused his entire herd of prize breeding cattle to be sterile. He sued Central for breach of the implied warranty of merchantability. Central claimed that there was no such breach because the feed had made the cattle gain weight exactly as it was supposed to do. *Kassab v. Central Soya,* 246 A.2d 848 (1968). Is Central's contention correct? Explain.

7. Meadows, a baseball player, needed sunglasses to wear while playing. He bought a pair of sunglasses manufactured by Optico, Inc., which had been advertised as being suitable for baseball players. When Meadows wore them in a game, he lost a fly ball in the sun and was then hit in the glasses by the ball. The glasses shattered, causing him to lose one eye. Suppose Optico can prove that the glasses were fit for the ordinary purposes for which such glasses are used. Might Meadows prevail in a lawsuit against Optico on the basis of any other type of warranty? Explain.

8. An item purchased by plaintiff from defendant was defective and thus not merchantable. However, the invoice used in the sale contained a clause specifically disclaiming liability for breach of the implied warranty of merchantability. The disclaimer clause itself was printed in the smallest lettering on the invoice, but it was preceded by the word *note* in letters larger than the remainder of the invoice. Will plaintiff prevail in his suit against defendant for breach of the implied warranty of merchantability? Discuss.

9. The strict liability theory gives the buyer most of the advantages of both the warranty and negligence theories. Discuss why this is true. Why would a buyer ever want to sue a seller on any theory other than strict liability?

10. Briefly summarize the major provisions of the Magnuson-Moss Warranty Act.

21 Sales/Performance and Remedies

In this final chapter on the law of sales we will discuss two subject areas: (1) performance of the sale contract (the obligations of both seller and buyer that are necessary to fulfill their agreement), and (2) remedies (the various avenues available to a seller or buyer if the other fails to live up to the contract obligations).

Performance of the Sale Contract

Generally speaking, the seller's obligation is to deliver conforming goods, and the buyer's obligation is to accept and pay for them. In Chapter 20, we dealt with the standards that goods must meet in order to be "conforming." While supplying goods that conform to the contract and to any applicable implied warranties is a very basic part of the seller's obligation, *total performance* involves a number of other aspects as well. In addition, several problem areas in the buyer's basic obligations of acceptance and payment require a closer look. The most important thing to remember is that the performance obligations of seller and buyer are ultimately controlled by the agreement of the parties themselves. The primary purposes of the UCC provisions in this area are to help in interpreting the agreement and to establish rules where the parties have not agreed on some point.

Seller's Obligations

Tender of Delivery: How does a seller deliver the goods? Must he or she actually put them into the buyer's hands? Has the seller performed the obligation if the buyer has changed his or her mind and refuses to take the goods? The answer to these questions is that the seller fully performs the delivery obligation by "tendering" delivery. According to Sec. 2-503(1), to make a tender of delivery the seller must "put and hold conforming goods at the buyer's disposition and give the buyer any notification reasonably necessary to enable him to take delivery." That is, the seller must keep the goods available for the period of time reasonably necessary to enable the buyer to take possession.

Tender must be made at a *reasonable hour.* Suppose, for example, that prices have risen since the making of the contract. The seller cannot perform by tendering delivery at three o'clock in the morning (unless the agreement so provided) in the hope that the buyer will reject the tender.

If the agreement makes no mention of the *place of delivery,* it should be at the seller's place of business or, if the seller has none, at his or her residence. However, if at the time the contract is made the goods are identified and both parties know that they are located at some other location, that place is the place of delivery.

Usually the parties will have agreed on the place of delivery, and most agreements fall within either of two categories:

1. The buyer agrees to pick up the goods at a particular place without the seller having any responsibility for moving them.

2. The seller undertakes responsibility for transporting the goods to the buyer.

The first category may involve an agreement that the buyer will call for the goods at the seller's premises. Or the goods may be in the possession of a bailee (such as a warehouseman), with the buyer being responsible for picking them up. Where the goods are held by a bailee, tender of delivery by the seller is a matter of paperwork. He or she must either deliver to the buyer a *negotiable document of title* (a warehouse receipt) or obtain the *bailee's acknowledgment* that the buyer is entitled to possession (see Chapter 17 for a discussion on documents of title). Delivery by the seller of a nonnegotiable document of title is a proper tender of delivery only if the buyer does not object. Similarly, a mere written direction to the bailee to hand the goods over to the buyer (with no acknowledgment by the bailee of the buyer's rights) is a sufficient tender only if the buyer does not object.

The second category of agreement, in which the seller ships the goods, is further divided into two types of contracts: shipment (the more common method) and destination (see Chapter 19). In a *shipment contract* the seller performs his or her obligation by tendering delivery at the point of shipment. Sec. 2-504 provides that, unless otherwise agreed:

1. The seller must put the goods in the possession of a carrier (such as a trucking or railway company), and the choice of carrier must be reasonable under the circumstances. Further, the seller's contract with the carrier for transporting the

goods must also be reasonable under the circumstances. (For example, a contract with the carrier that understates the value of the goods for insurance purposes is not considered reasonable.)

2. The seller must obtain and promptly deliver in proper form any document (such as a bill of lading) necessary for the buyer to take possession of the goods.

3. The seller must promptly notify the buyer of shipment.

If the seller fails to meet the above requirements, the buyer can reject delivery only if a material loss or delay resulted—unless the parties have agreed differently. For instance, they might agree that failure to give prompt notification is a ground for rejection regardless of the consequences of the failure.

The seller's obligation in a *destination contract* is not fulfilled until delivery is tendered at the destination. Since the seller's required performance extends to the buyer's doorstep, so to speak, special provisions regarding selection of a carrier are not needed for the buyer's protection. The general tender requirements already set forth are sufficient. At the point of destination, the seller must put and hold the goods at the buyer's disposition at a reasonable hour, for a reasonable period of time, and with proper notice. And, of course, the seller must furnish any required documents.

Commercial Shipping Terms: Sale contracts frequently contain terms that have well-established meanings in the commercial world but that are somewhat mysterious to the newcomer. For example, the contract may include phrases such as *FOB Detroit* or *FAS vessel, New York*. These indicate the parties' agreement on particular terms of shipment and are treated as shipping terms even when they appear only in connection with the price ("2.00/lb. FOB seller's plant"). Some of the more common terms are defined below.

FOB ("free on board"). If the named location following the FOB designation is the point of shipment, the agreement is a *shipment contract*. If the vehicle of transportation at the point of shipment is also referred to, the seller must not only put the goods into the possession of a carrier but also bear the expense of loading them on board. An example is "FOB Car 235Y, Mo. Pac. R.R. Depot, Dallas." If the named location following the FOB designation is the destination, the agreement is a *destination contract*.

FAS ("free alongside" vessel). FAS, frequently found in sale contracts where the goods are to be transported by seagoing vessel, indicates that a *shipment contract* has been made. The seller performs by delivering the goods alongside (on the dock next to) the vessel on which they are to be loaded but does not bear the expense of loading.

Ex-ship ("from the carrying vessel"). The phrase *ex-ship,* also a maritime term, is actually the reverse of FAS. It denotes a *destination contract* and indicates that the seller's obligation extends to unloading the goods at the port of destination.

CIF ("cost, insurance, and freight") and C & F ("cost and freight"). CIF and C & F are also found almost exclusively in maritime agreements. CIF indicates that the price paid by the buyer includes the cost of the goods, insurance while they are in transit, and all freight charges. C & F means that the price includes the cost of the goods and freight charges but not insurance. Although the terms indicate that the agreement is a *shipment contract,* their inclusion means that the seller assumes obligations in addition to those of an ordinary shipment contract. The C & F term obligates the seller to see that the goods are loaded and to pay the freight charges. The CIF term further obligates the seller to obtain appropriate insurance coverage.

The Perfect Tender Rule: At common law there developed a doctrine known as the *perfect tender rule.* Under this rule, the seller's tender of delivery was required to conform in every detail to the terms of the agreement. In other words, the doctrine of substantial performance (discussed in Chapter 16) did not apply to contracts for the sale of goods. An extreme illustration of the perfect tender rule is found in *Filley v. Pope,* 115 U.S. 213 (1885). The seller agreed to sell pig iron to the buyer, the contract calling for shipment to New Orleans from Glasgow, Scotland. When the time for shipment arrived, no ships were available at Glasgow. The seller's factory in Scotland was halfway between the ports of Glasgow and Leith; and since vessels were available at Leith, he sent the iron to Leith for shipment. The buyer rejected the goods when they arrived. The Supreme Court held that the buyer was entitled to do so, because a contract calling for shipment from Glasgow is not fulfilled by a shipment from Leith even though no delay results.

UCC Sec. 2-601 essentially restates the perfect tender rule by providing that "if the goods or the tender of delivery fail in *any respect* to conform to the contract," the buyer is not obligated to accept them. (Emphasis added.)

Exceptions to the Perfect Tender Rule: The perfect tender rule is not as absolute as it might at first seem. The parties themselves can, of course, limit the rule by agreement. For example, they might agree that a delivery of defective goods cannot be rejected if the seller repairs or replaces the defective parts.[1]

Even though Sec. 2-601 makes the perfect tender rule seem rigid, several other provisions of the UCC significantly relax this strictness. The most important of these modifications are discussed below.

Cure. At common law the seller had only one chance to make a perfect tender. Somewhat more latitude is given the seller by Sec. 2-508 of the UCC. This section applies to the situation where the seller makes a tender of delivery that is deficient in some way but where the *time for performance has not yet expired.* In such a case, if the seller promptly notifies the buyer of an intention to "cure," he or she can then make a conforming delivery *before* expiration of the time for performance.

---

[1]However, insofar as such a clause limits the application of an implied warranty, it must meet all the requirements of the UCC regarding disclaimers of warranty. In a consumer transaction it also must comply with the Magnuson-Moss Warranty Act.

In certain unusual circumstances, Sec. 2-508 allows cure even after the agreed upon time for performance has expired. This can occur where the seller makes a tender of delivery that does not conform to the contract because he or she had *reasonable grounds to believe that the nonconforming tender would be acceptable.* For example, suppose that S is a distributor of petroleum products who supplies B's factory with machine lubricants. S and B have dealt with one another over a period of time, with each contract calling for delivery of Z brand oil. On several occasions in the past, when Z brand was unavailable, S sustituted Y brand, which is equivalent to Z brand. On these occasions B did not object to the substitution. When the substitution occurred under the most recent contract, however, B rejected the oil, much to the surprise of S.[2] Since S had a reasonable basis for believing that the nonconforming delivery would be acceptable, he can make another tender of delivery if he promptly notifies B of his intention to do so. He must make the new tender within a reasonable time, but the time can extend beyond the contractual time for performance.

Installment contracts. An installment contract is defined in Sec. 2-612 as one requiring or authorizing the delivery of goods in separate lots to be separately accepted. A buyer can reject a particular installment only if the nonconformity *substantially impairs the value of that installment.* Furthermore, a nonconformity in a particular installment is a breach of the sale contract only if it substantially impairs the value of the *whole contract.* But if the buyer accepts the nonconforming installment without notifying the seller of cancellation, the contract is reinstated. This section of the UCC actually applies the doctrine of substantial performance to sale of goods contracts where delivery is in two or more separate lots.

Improper shipping arrangements. Remember that in a shipment contract the seller must (1) act appropriately in selecting and making a transportation contract with the carrier, (2) provide any documents necessary for the buyer to take possession of the goods, and (3) promptly notify the buyer of the shipment. However, failure by the seller to fulfill these obligations entitles the buyer to reject the delivery only if *material loss or delay* has resulted.

Substitute means of delivery. In some cases the parties specifically agree on the type of facilities to be used in loading, shipping, or unloading the goods. If, through no fault of either party, these agreed upon facilities become unavailable or impracticable, but a commercially reasonable substitute is available, the seller and buyer are required by Sec. 2-614 to use the substitute. (If the UCC had existed at the time of *Filley v. Pope,* the outcome of that case would have been different.)

Effect of Unforeseen Occurrences: The common law rules applying to contracts in general also apply to sale of goods contracts unless they have been altered by the UCC. Thus, if the specific subject matter of the sale contract has been destroyed through no fault of either party, or if performance has become illegal

---

[2]This situation involves a number of separate transactions rather than a single contract calling for delivery in several installments.

because of a change in the law, both parties are excused from their contractual obligations.

Suppose that Seller S and Buyer B have contracted for the sale of one hundred head of cattle. If the cattle are damaged or destroyed after risk of loss has passed to B (as would be the case in a shipment contract if the carrier is involved in an accident while transporting the cattle), then obviously S has already performed and B will have to pay for the goods. On the other hand, if a flash flood on S's land destroys the cattle before risk of loss has passed to B, then the financial loss will have to be borne by S, and B will not have to pay for the cattle.

A further question remains, however: Is S excused from performing his part of the bargain? If the contract was for the sale of one hundred head of cattle but not necessarily the specific cattle that were destroyed, the answer is no. Not only has S suffered the loss but he also must still perform the contract by delivering one hundred head of cattle. But if the contract was for the sale of the specific cattle that were subsequently destroyed, S is excused from his obligation and is under no further duty to perform. This common law rule is restated in UCC Sec. 2-613. In addition to the basic rule covering cases of *total* destruction, Sec. 2-613 also covers cases where the loss is only *partial.* In such a situation B has a choice. He can treat the contract as canceled, thereby excusing both parties from their obligations. Or he can accept the goods in their damaged condition with an allowance deducted from the contract price.

Commercial impracticability. The UCC also contains a provision, Sec. 2-615, to deal with certain types of unforeseen occurrences that do not result in damage to the specifically identified subject matter of the contract. If, because of un-foreseen circumstances, delivery of the goods becomes "commercially impractica-ble," the parties are excused from their obligations. Of course, a mere increase in costs or change in the market price is not sufficient to relieve the seller of his or her responsibility; the existence of such risks is one of the main reasons for making binding contracts. But where the difficulty is of an *extraordinary* nature, such as the destruction of a source of supply that had been agreed upon or contemplated by both parties, the seller is excused. In such a case, however, the seller must have taken *all reasonable steps* to assure himself or herself that the source would not fail. The seller also is excused from delivering if a severe shortage of raw materials due to such events as war, embargo, or local crop failure causes a drastic increase in cost or completely prevents the seller from securing necessary supplies. A seller seeking to be excused because of commercial impracticability must *promptly notify* the buyer of the problem.

Sometimes the commercial impracticablity affects only *part* of the seller's capac-ity to perform. For instance, the unforeseen occurrence might result in a material delay or in a diminution of the quantity of available goods. Where the available quantity is diminished, Sec. 2-615 requires the seller to *allocate deliveries* among customers, including all customers then under contract and, if he or she chooses, regular customers not currently under contract. The seller must give *prompt notification* of either a delay or an allocation and, in the case of an allocation, must make an estimate of the quota available.

Buyer's choices. When the buyer is notified of a significant delay or an allocation justified by commercial impracticability, he or she has a choice of canceling the contract or keeping it in effect. To cancel, the buyer can either notify the seller or merely remain silent. However, if the seller's inability relates only to a particular delivery in an installment contract, the buyer can cancel the contract only if the value of the *whole contract* is substantially impaired. If the buyer has a right to cancel but wishes to keep the contract alive, he or she must give written notice to the seller indicating agreement to the delay or allocation. This notice by the buyer actually amounts to a modification of the contract and must be made within a reasonable time, not exceeding thirty days.

Although the doctrine of commercial impracticability is always important, it takes on added significance during times of economic uncertainty. The following case involves an attempt to escape from a contract which had been made less profitable by the energy crisis.

Eastern Airlines, Inc. v. Gulf Oil Co.

U.S. District Court, So. Dist. of Florida, 415 F. Supp. 429 (1975)

For a number of years Gulf Oil Co. had been a major supplier of the jet fuel used by Eastern Airlines to operate its fleet. The most recent contract between the two was made in 1972, and obligated Gulf to supply Eastern's fuel requirements at certain specified cities.

Since jet fuel is refined from crude oil, the cost of producing the fuel is directly affected by the price of crude. Although the price of crude oil produced in the U.S. was regulated by the federal government, this price had been increasing and was expected by Gulf and Eastern to continue rising. In addition, the percentage of oil imported into this country from foreign sources had been growing. The price of imported oil could not be regulated by the U.S. government and, therefore, was more subject to market fluctuations. Because of these factors, Gulf and Eastern included in their 1972 contract a clause which permitted Gulf to charge higher prices on future deliveries of jet fuel to Eastern as the price of crude oil increased. However, this "escalator" clause in their contract permitted a rise in the jet fuel price only insofar as the government-regulated price of U.S.-produced oil increased.

After Gulf and Eastern made their agreement, the federal government partially decontrolled the price of domestically produced oil. In other words, the government removed the ceiling on the price of a portion of the oil produced in this country, thus permitting this price to rise to the world market level. Shortly thereafter, the foreign oil cartel, OPEC (Organization of Petroleum Exporting Countries), increased the price of its oil about 400 percent. This, of course, also caused the unregulated portion of U.S.-produced oil to rise dramatically. In producing jet fuel, Gulf was using some regulated domestic oil (on which there was a government-imposed price ceiling), some unregulated domestic oil, and some foreign oil. The escalator clause in the Gulf-Eastern contract only permitted jet fuel price increases in accordance with increases in the government-regulated price of domestic oil. Gulf ultimately found this clause to be quite inadequate to cover its increased costs of production.

In March, 1974, Gulf demanded that Eastern pay more for jet fuel than the escalator clause permitted, or Gulf would shut off Eastern's supply of fuel. Eastern refused to pay more and sued Gulf for breach of contract. Gulf defended on the ground that performance of the contract had become "commercially impracticable" and that it should therefore be excused from the contract as provided in UCC Sec. 2-615. The federal district court ruled as follows.

King, District Judge: . . . Official Comments 4 and 8 to UCC §2-615 [prepared by the drafters of the Code] provide:

> 4. Increased cost alone does not excuse performance unless the rise in cost is due to some unforeseen contingency which alters the essential nature of the performance. Neither is a rise or a collapse in the market itself a justification, for that is exactly the type of business risk which business contracts made at fixed prices are intended to cover. But a severe shortage of raw materials, or of supplies due to a contingency such as war, embargo, local crop failure, unforeseen shutdown of major sources of supply or the like, which either causes a marked increase in cost or altogether prevents the seller from securing supplies necessary to his performance, is within the contemplation of this section. . . .

> 8. The provisions of this section are made subject to assumption of greater liability by agreement and such agreement is to be found not only in the expressed terms of the contract but in the circumstances surrounding the contracting, in trade usage and the like. Thus the exemptions of this section do not apply when the contingency in question is sufficiently foreshadowed at the time of contracting to be included among the business risks which are fairly to be regarded as part of the dickered terms, either consciously or as a matter of reasonable, commercial interpretation from the circumstances. . . .

In short, for UCC §2-615 to apply there must be a failure of a presupposed condition, which was an underlying assumption of the contract, which failure was unforeseeable, and the risk of which was not specifically allocated to the complaining party. The burden of proving each element of claimed commercial impracticability is on the party claiming excuse.

The modern UCC §2-615 doctrine of commercial impracticability has its roots in the common law doctrine[s] of frustration of [purpose and] impossibility and finds its most recognized illustrations in the so-called "Suez Cases," arising out of the various closings of the Suez Canal and the consequent increases in shipping costs around the Cape of Good Hope. Those cases offered little encouragement to those who would wield the sword of commercial impracticability. As a leading British case arising out of the 1957 Suez closure declared, the unforeseen cost increase that would excuse performance "must be more than merely onerous or expensive. It must be positively unjust to hold the parties bound." *Ocean Tramp Tankers v. V/O Sovfracht (The Eugenia)*, 2 QB 226, 239 (1964). . . .

[R]ecent American cases similarly strictly construe the doctrine of commercial impracticability. For example, one case found no UCC defense, even though costs had doubled over the contract price. . . . Recently, the Seventh Circuit has stated: "The fact that performance has become economically burdensome or unattractive is not sufficient for performance to be excused. We will not allow a party to a contract to escape a bad bargain merely because it is burdensome. [T]he buyer has a right to rely on the party to the contract to supply him with goods regardless of what happens to the market price. That is the purpose for which such contracts are made," *Neal-Cooper Grain Co. v. Texas Gulf Sulfur Co.*, 508 F.2d 283 (7th Cir. 1974). . . .

With regard to Gulf's contention that the contract has become "commercially impracticable" within the meaning of UCC §2-615, because of the increase in market price of foreign crude oil and certain domestic crude oils, the court finds that the defense has not been proved. On this record the court cannot determine how much it costs Gulf to produce a gallon of jet fuel for sale to Eastern, whether Gulf loses money or makes a profit on its sale of jet fuel to Eastern, either now or at the inception of the contract, or at any time in between. Gulf's witnesses testified that they could not make such a computation. The party undertaking the burden of establishing "commercial impracticability" by reason of allegedly increased raw material costs undertakes the obligation of showing the extent to which he has suffered, or will suffer, losses in performing his contract. The record here does not substantiate Gulf's contention on this fundamental issue.

Gulf presented evidence tending to show that its "costs" of crude oil have increased dramatically over the past two years. However, the "costs" to which Gulf adverts are unlike any "costs" that might arguably afford ground for any of the relief sought here. Gulf's claimed "costs" of an average barrel of crude oil at Gulf's refineries (estimated by Gulf's witness Davis at about $10.00 currently, and about $9.50 during 1974) include intracompany profits, as the oil moved from Gulf's overseas and domestic production departments to its refining department. The magnitude of that profit was not revealed. . . .

[T]hese are not the kinds of "costs" against which to measure hardship, real or imagined, under the Uniform Commercial Code. Under no theory of law can it be held that Gulf is guaranteed preservation of its intracompany profits, moving from the left hand to the right hand, as one Gulf witness so aptly put it. The burden is upon Gulf to show what its real costs are, not its "costs" inflated by its internal profits at various levels of the manufacturing process and located in various foreign countries.

No criticism is implied of Gulf's rational desire to maximize its profits and take every advantage available to it under the laws. However, these factors cannot be ignored in approaching Gulf's contention that it has been unduly burdened by crude oil price increases. No such hardship has been established. On the contrary, the record clearly establishes that 1973, the year in which the energy crisis began, was Gulf's best year ever, in which it recorded some $800 million in net profits after taxes. Gulf's 1974 year was more than 25% better than 1973's record: $1,065,000,000 profits were booked by Gulf in 1974 after paying all taxes.

For the foregoing reasons, Gulf's claim of hardship giving rise to "commercial impracticability" fails.

But even if Gulf had established great hardship under UCC §2-615, which it has not, Gulf would not prevail because the events associated with the so-called energy crisis were reasonably foreseeable at the time the contract was executed. If a contingency is foreseeable, it and its consequences are taken outside the scope of UCC §2-615, because the party disadvantaged by the contingency [could] have protected himself in his contract. . . .

The record is replete with evidence as to the volatility of the Middle East situation, the arbitrary power of host governments to control the foreign oil market, and repeated interruptions and interference with the normal commercial trade in crude oil. Even without the extensive evidence present in the record, the court would be justified in taking judicial notice of the fact that oil has been used as a political weapon with increasing success by the oil-producing nations for many years, and Gulf was well aware of and assumed the risk that the OPEC nations would do exactly what they have done.

With respect to Gulf's argument that [partial decontrol of domestic oil prices by the U.S. government] was not "foreseeable," the record shows that domestic crude oil prices were controlled at all material times, that Gulf foresaw that they might be decontrolled, and that Gulf was constantly urging to the Federal Government that they should be decontrolled.

Government price regulations were confused, constantly changing, and uncertain during the period of the negotiation and execution of the contract. During that time frame, high ranking Gulf executives, including some of its trial witnesses, were in constant repeated contact with officials and agencies of the Federal Government regarding petroleum policies and were well able to protect themselves from any contingencies. . . .

Knowing all the factors, Gulf drafted the contract and tied the escalation clause to the [government-regulated price]. The court is of the view that it is bound thereby.

[Judgment for plaintiff Eastern; decree of specific performance issued against Gulf.]

Buyer's Obligations

When the seller has made a sufficient tender of delivery, the burden then falls on the buyer to perform his or her part of the contract.

Providing Facilities: Unless otherwise agreed, the buyer must furnish facilities that are reasonably suited for receipt of the goods.

Right of Inspection: Inspection of the goods by the buyer is a matter depending entirely upon the terms of the agreement. But if the parties have not limited inspection by their agreement, the buyer has a right to inspect the goods before accepting or paying for them—at any reasonable place and time and in any reasonable manner. When the goods are shipped to the buyer, inspection can occur after their arrival. Expenses of inspection must be borne by the buyer but can be recovered from the seller if the goods do not conform and are rejected.

Sometimes the parties' agreement obligates the buyer to make payment before inspecting the goods. For example, when a contract calls for COD ("collect on delivery"), there is no right of inspection before payment unless other terms of the contract expressly grant such a right. Contracts can also require "payment against documents," which means that, unless otherwise agreed, payment is due on receipt of the required documents of title regardless of when the goods themselves actually arrive. CIF and C & F contracts, for example, require payment on receipt of documents unless the parties have agreed to the contrary. Where a contract calls for payment before inspection, payment must be made unless the goods are so obviously nonconforming that inspection is not needed.

When payment is required before inspection, it does not constitute a final acceptance of the goods. Rejection of the goods can still occur if the buyer inspects after the required payment and finds that they are nonconforming.

Acceptance: When conforming goods have been properly tendered, the buyer's basic duty is to accept them, which means simply that the buyer takes the goods as his or her own. This acceptance can occur in three different ways:

1. The buyer can expressly indicate acceptance by words. For example, there is an acceptance if the buyer, after having had a reasonable opportunity to inspect,

signifies to the seller either that the goods are conforming or that he or she will take them despite their nonconformity.

2. Acceptance also occurs if the buyer has had a reasonable opportunity to inspect the goods and has failed to reject them within a reasonable period of time.

3. The buyer accepts the goods by performing any act inconsistent with the seller's ownership. For example, using, consuming, or reselling the goods usually constitutes an acceptance. However, reasonable use or consumption for the sole purpose of testing is not an acceptance.

Partial Acceptance: If part of the goods are conforming and part are nonconforming, the buyer can make a partial acceptance; he or she cannot, however, accept less than a commercial unit. A *commercial unit* is defined in Sec. 2-105 as a unit of goods recognized in commercial practice as being a "single whole" for purposes of sale, the division of which materially impairs its value. It can be a single article (such as a machine), a set of articles (such as a suite of furniture or an assortment of suits in different sizes), a quantity (such as a bale, gross, or carload), or any other unit treated in use or in the relevant market as a single whole.

Payment: Seller and buyer can agree upon credit arrangements or agree that payment is due when the buyer receives a document of title, regardless of when the goods arrive. But if the parties do not expressly agree on a time for payment, it is due when the buyer receives the goods.

While the price is ordinarily payable in money, the parties can agree that some other medium of exchange (such as other commodities) will be used. In addition, the buyer can use any method of making payment that is generally acceptable in the commercial world (such as a check). But the seller can demand payment in *legal tender* (currency) if he or she desires. A seller who makes such a demand must allow the buyer a reasonable amount of time to obtain legal tender. If the buyer pays by check and the check is accepted by the seller, the buyer has performed the obligation of payment unless the check is dishonored (bounced) by the bank.

Some buyers pay with a *letter of credit* (used primarily in foreign commerce). The buyer obtains the letter of credit from his or her own bank, and the bank guarantees to the seller that payment will be made when the proper documents are tendered.

Remedies for Breach of the Sale Contract

Thus far we have focused our discussion on the performance of the sale contract by both parties. But suppose the contract is instead breached by one of the parties. What avenues are open to the other party?

Anticipatory Repudiation

A breach of contract can occur at any stage in the transaction after the contract is made, even before the time for performance falls due. If, before time for performance, one party clearly communicates to the other the intention not to perform, that party has breached the contract by an *anticipatory repudiation.* The party receiving the repudiation can then suspend his or her own performance, treat the contract as having been breached, and pursue the appropriate remedies. Or the person can wait a reasonable length of time for performance in the hope that the repudiating party will change his or her mind.

Sometimes there is not a clear-cut repudiation but the circumstances are such that one party has reasonable doubts about whether the other is going to perform. In such a case the party who has a reasonable basis for feeling insecure can demand in writing that the other party give *assurance of performance.* Adequate assurance of performance must then be given within a reasonable time (not exceeding thirty days) after receipt of the demand. Failure to give this assurance in response to a justified demand constitutes an anticipatory repudiation.

In the case below there was clearly an anticipatory repudiation by the seller. The key question, however, was whether the buyer continued to await the seller's performance for longer than a commercially reasonable time.

Oloffson, plaintiff, was a grain dealer; Coomer, defendant, was a farmer. In April 1970 Coomer agreed to sell forty thousand bushels of corn to Oloffson at $1.1225 per bushel, delivery to be in October and December. On June 3, Coomer informed Oloffson that he was not going to plant corn because the season had been too wet. He told Oloffson to arrange elsewhere to obtain the corn if Oloffson had already obligated himself to deliver to any third party. The market price for a bushel of corn on June 3 was $1.16. Oloffson asked Coomer in September about delivery of the corn, and Coomer repeated that he would not be able to deliver. Oloffson persisted, however, and mailed Coomer confirmations of their April agreement, which Coomer ignored. Oloffson's attorney then requested that Coomer perform, and Coomer also ignored this request. When no corn was delivered on the scheduled delivery dates, Oloffson covered his obligation to his own buyer by purchasing twenty thousand bushels at $1.35 per bushel and twenty thousand bushels at $1.49 per bushel.

Oloffson sued Coomer and recovered damages in the trial court of $1,500, the difference between the contract price ($1.1225) and the market price on June 3 ($1.16) multiplied by forty thousand bushels. Oloffson appealed, claiming that his damages should have been computed as the difference between the contract price and the market price on the dates the corn should have been delivered.

Alloy, Justice: . . . It is clear that on June 3, 1970, Coomer repudiated the contract "with respect to performance not yet due." . . . As a consequence, on June 3, 1970, Oloffson, as the "aggrieved party," could then:

(a) for a commercially reasonable time await performance by the repudiating party; or
(b) resort to any remedy for breach, even though he has notified the repudiating party that he would await the latter's performance and has urged retraction; . . .

Oloffson v. Coomer

Appellate Court of Illinois, 296 N.E.2d 871 (1973)

If Oloffson chose to proceed under subparagraph (a) referred to, he could have awaited Coomer's performance for a "commercially reasonable time." As we indicate in the course of this opinion, that "commercially reasonable time" expired on June 3, 1970. The Uniform Commercial Code made a change in existing Illinois law in this respect, in that, prior to the adoption of the Code, a buyer in a position as Oloffson was privileged to await a seller's performance until the date that, according to the agreement, such performance was scheduled. To the extent that a "commercially reasonable time" is less than such date of performance, the Code now conditions the buyer's right to await performance. . . .

Since Coomer's statement to Oloffson on June 3, 1970, was unequivocal and since "cover" easily and immediately was available to Oloffson in the well-organized and easily accessible market for purchases of grain to be delivered in the future, it would be unreasonable for Oloffson on June 3, 1970, to have awaited Coomer's performance rather than to have proceeded under Section 2-610(b) and, thereunder, to elect then to treat the repudiation as a breach. Therefore, if Oloffson were relying on his right to . . . cover under Section 2-711(1)(a), June 3, 1970, might for the foregoing reason alone have been the day on which he acquired cover. . . .

[Thus, since the court felt it unreasonable for Oloffson to continue to await performance after the repudiation on June 3, his damages were computed by using the market price on that date rather than later.]

Affirmed.

Buyer's Remedies

Where Seller Fails to Deliver: When the seller breaches the contract by failing to deliver the goods according to the contract, the following remedies are available to the buyer:

1. The buyer can cancel the contract, which relieves him or her of any contractual obligations.

2. The buyer can recover any prepayments made to the seller.

3. The buyer can *cover* (buy the goods elsewhere in a commercially reasonable manner) and receive damages. The damages include (a) the amount by which the cover price exceeds the contract price; (b) any incidental expenses—out-of-pocket costs such as additional transportation and handling expenses; and (c) any consequential losses, such as the buyer's lost profits, that should have been foreseen by the seller as resulting from the breach. Deducted from the buyer's damages, however, are any expenses saved because of the seller's breach. If the buyer does not wish to cover, he or she can receive the amount by which the market price exceeds the contract price, plus any incidental and consequential damages, minus any expenses saved. The market price is determined as of the time when the buyer learned of the breach and as of the place where delivery should have been tendered.

4. In most cases the buyer will be unable to recover the goods themselves from the seller and will have to be content with money damages. In certain circumstances, however, the buyer can obtain a court decree entitling him or her to possession of the particular goods contracted for. If the goods are *unique* (such as

an heirloom), the buyer can recover them by obtaining a decree of *specific perfor-mance* (an order commanding the seller to live up to the agreement). Even if the goods are not unique, the buyer can recover them (a) where they have been specifically identified and (b) where the buyer has made reasonable but unsuccess-ful efforts to cover or where the circumstances reasonably indicate that such efforts would be fruitless (such as where the goods are in very short supply). The technical name for the buyer's recovery of goods in this type of situation is *replevin.*

Where Seller Delivers Nonconforming Goods: If the seller delivers goods that are defective or in some other way do not conform to the contract, the buyer must notify the seller within a reasonable time after discovering the nonconformity in order to be able to pursue available remedies. The buyer's remedies in this situation are:

1. The buyer can cancel the contract.

2. The buyer can recover any prepayments made to the seller.

3. The buyer can *reject* the delivery. Under the perfect tender rule, the buyer can usually reject if the tender or the goods fail in any respect to conform to the contract. Where the defects are of a type that can be discovered by reasonable inspection, sometimes the buyer can reject only by specifying them in the notice to the seller. This duty to specify defects exists (a) where they can be cured if the seller learns of them promptly or (b) where the specification is requested by one merchant from another merchant.

4. If the buyer has already accepted delivery, however, he or she cannot thereafter reject it. Of course, acceptance is more than just receiving the goods; it means taking them as one's own. However, in a few circumstances the buyer can *revoke his or her acceptance:*

    a. An acceptance can be revoked only if the nonconformity *substantially impairs the value* to the buyer of the delivery or commercial unit in question. For example, a cracked engine block substantially impairs the value of a car, while a malfunctioning clock in the dashboard does not.

    b. Where the buyer *knew* of the nonconformity when accepting, he or she can revoke the acceptance only if it was made on the reasonable assumption that the nonconformity would be cured, but it has not been. On the other hand, where the buyer *did not know* of the nonconformity when accepting, he or she can revoke if the acceptance had been made because of the difficulty of discovering the nonconformity at an earlier time or because of the seller's assurances that there were no defects.

    c. Revocation of acceptance must occur within a reasonable time after the buyer discovers the basis for it and before any substantial change occurs in the condi-tion of the goods (other than by their own defects).

5. The effect of a rejection or a revocation of acceptance is the same: the goods are not the buyer's and he or she does not have to pay for them. After a justified

rejection or revocation the seller usually makes arrangements to take back the goods. The buyer must return the goods on request if the seller refunds any payments made on the price and reimburses the buyer for reasonable expenses incurred in inspecting, receiving, transporting, and caring for them. While in possession of the goods the buyer has certain rights and duties with respect to them:

a. The first duty is to follow all reasonable instructions given by the seller regarding the goods. A seller's instructions are unreasonable if he or she does not guarantee payment of expenses after the buyer has demanded it.

b. If the seller does not pick up the goods or give instructions as to their handling within a reasonable time, the buyer has three alternatives—storing the goods for the seller's account, reshipping them to the seller, or reselling them for the seller's account. (In unusual situations the buyer is actually under a *duty to try to resell* the goods for the seller when reasonable instructions are not given. This duty arises if the buyer is a merchant, the seller has no agent or place of business in the buyer's locality, and the goods are perishable or otherwise threaten to rapidly decline in value.) The buyer has a right to recover reasonable expenses in handling the goods in these situations, just as when following the seller's instructions. One note of caution: a buyer who resells goods without being entitled to do so has legally accepted them.

6. The buyer can cover if he or she wishes, and damages will be computed in the same manner as when the seller breaches by failing to deliver.

7. Finally, the buyer can *accept and keep the goods* despite their nonconformity and still recover all damages caused by the nonconformity. This is frequently the situation in *breach of warranty* cases where the product has already been used or consumed when the defect is discovered. The buyer's damages in such cases are the difference between the actual value of the goods and the value they would have had if they had conformed to the warranty, plus incidental and consequential damages. Consequential damages in a breach of warranty case include bodily injury and property damage caused by the breach and often constitute the largest portion of the buyer's damages. If the goods are not yet paid for, the purchase price is offset against the damages.

A plaintiff is allowed to recover from the defendant only those damages which are the reasonably direct and foreseeable consequence of the breach of contract. This issue is not always easy to resolve, as illustrated by the following case.

Baden v. Curtiss Breeding Service

U.S. District Court, Montana, 380 F.Supp. 243 (1974)

Baden, a rancher, purchased bull semen from Curtiss Breeding Service for the purpose of artificial insemination. The semen was defective and no calves were born. Baden, plaintiff, sued Curtiss, defendant, for breach of warranty, contending that his consequential damages should include not only the value of the 1972 calf crop which was not born but also the 1974 calf crop that might have been expected

from the calves born in 1972. The opinion of the trial court on this point appears below.

Smith, Justice: . . . Under the code the rule with respect to consequential damage is: "All that is necessary, in order to charge the defendant with the particular loss, is that it is one that ordinarily follows the breach of such a contract in the usual course of events, or that reasonable men in the position of the parties would have foreseen as a probable result of breach." In the case of semen sold for artificial insemination, the seller knows that if the semen is defective the inseminated cow may not become pregnant and the capital investment devoted to that cow in that year may be totally unproductive. Certainly the loss of a calf or calves is one that ordinarily follows the use of defective semen and one which the parties would reasonably foresee. I have difficulty, however, in extending this foreseeability to the loss of the second calf crop, that is, the calves which would have been produced in 1974 by the 1972 calf crop had there been one.

When a rancher discovers that his cows are barren he may be expected to keep his capital, that is, the ranch, equipment and livestock, busy in what seems to him to be the most productive way. The fact that a calf crop is lost does not mean that the ranch operation stops. Replacements for the cow herd are bought and are bred and the operation continues. The capital is kept busy, and it appears to me that reasonable men in the position of the parties here would not foresee the loss of a second calf crop as a proximate result of the defective semen, nor do I think they would foresee that a plaintiff would so conduct his operation that a second calf crop actually raised necessarily would be of less value than the one which the plaintiff had hoped to raise. . . .

Many variables affect the commercial production of beef animals. Always present are the factors of the fertility of the heifer, the fertility of the bull, the efficacy of the breeding, the risks of calving, disease, and accident. These risks make the projection of the result of the breeding in any one season somewhat uncertain. But if projections are extended beyond the first calving and into the calving of the calves (a period of over two and one-half years from the first breeding), the effects of the variables are greatly magnified and the projection becomes more uncertain.

Any rule of damages which permits the recovery for losses beyond the first calf crop makes the selling defendant accept in some degree another variable, and that is the risk of the buying plaintiff's management.

Allowing recovery for consequential damages up to the first calf crop does permit plaintiffs to produce evidence to show the effect of the variables in the first year and does make defendant accept what may be inequities in the appraisal of those variables. It may seem arbitrary to hold that the uncertainties up to the first calf crop may be tolerated but that no matter what the proof is the uncertainties beyond that point will not be. At some point, however, the degree of uncertainty permitted becomes a question of law. The fact is that as to the first calf crop we deal with cows that were born and did live long enough to become fertile. In the case of the second calf crop we must project a supposititious calf into a period of supposititious fertility followed by a supposititiously successful breeding which is in turn followed by a supposititiously successful calving, and hence motherhood. In my opinion the need for these suppositions is sufficient to warrant a distinction between the loss of the first calf crop and the loss of the second and to permit the line to be drawn where I have drawn it.

[Judgment for plaintiff for damages caused by loss of 1972 calf crop only.]

Seller's Remedies

Where Buyer Breaches before Receiving the Goods: Following are the remedies for the seller where the buyer has repudiated or otherwise breached the contract before receiving the goods:

1. The seller can cancel the contract.

2. If the goods are in the seller's possession or control but have not yet been identified, he or she can take the steps necessary to identify them (separate them from inventory, tag or label them, and so on). If they are in an unfinished condition, the seller can complete their manufacture if it is reasonable to do so for the purpose of minimizing the loss—or cease manufacture and resell for scrap or salvage value.

3. The seller obviously is entitled to *withhold delivery* and in some cases even *stop delivery* where the goods have already been shipped but have not yet been received by the buyer. Because of the burden to the carrier, the seller can stop delivery in transit only if a carload, truckload, planeload, or larger shipment is involved. Also, if the carrier has issued a *negotiable bill of lading* (see Chapter 17), the seller can stop delivery only by surrendering the document to the carrier. Thus stoppage in transit cannot occur if the seller has already sent a negotiable bill of lading to the buyer.

4. The seller can *resell* the goods in a commercially reasonable manner at either a private or public (auction) sale. If the resale is *private,* the buyer must be given prior notice of it; if it is *public,* the buyer must be given prior notice unless the goods are perishable or otherwise threaten to rapidly decline in value. A purchaser who buys in good faith at a resale takes the goods free of any rights of the original buyer even if the seller has not conducted the resale in a commercially reasonable manner. When the seller has resold the goods in a proper manner, the damages to which he or she is entitled include the amount by which the contract price exceeds the resale price plus incidental damages such as additional transportation and handling expenses.[3] Any expenses saved because of the buyer's breach are deducted from the seller's damages. If the seller *does not resell,* the damages are computed in either of two ways, depending on which is more advantageous to the seller: (a) the amount by which the contract price exceeds the market price at the time and place for tender (rather than the actual resale price), plus incidental damages, minus expenses saved; or (b) the profit that the seller would have made had the contract been performed, plus incidental damages, minus expenses saved.

5. Under some circumstances the seller can sue to recover the *purchase price* from the buyer, even though the buyer did not receive the goods. This can occur, for example, where (a) the seller shipped conforming goods that were lost or destroyed after risk of loss had passed to the buyer, (b) the seller made reasonable but unsuccessful efforts to resell at a reasonable price, or (c) the circumstances indicate that efforts to resell would be unsuccessful. Any incidental damages caused by the

---

[3]The seller is not accountable to the buyer for any profit made on the resale.

buyer's breach are added to the purchase price. If the seller receives a court judgment against the buyer for the purchase price, and then, because of changed conditions, is able to resell the goods before the buyer pays the judgment, the proceeds of the sale must be credited to the buyer. Payment of the judgment entitles the buyer to any of the goods not resold.

Where the Buyer Breaches after Receiving the Goods: The seller's remedies where the buyer's breach occurs after he or she receives the goods are:

1. If the buyer accepts the goods and does not pay for them, the seller can recover the purchase price plus any incidental damages resulting from the breach.

2. If the buyer wrongfully rejects or revokes acceptance and does not pay, the seller's remedies depend on *whether he or she retakes possession* of the goods. If possession is retaken, the remedies are basically the same as if the buyer had breached *before* receiving the goods. In addition to canceling the contract, the seller can resell the goods, keep them and recover damages, or recover the purchase price plus incidental damages if resale is impossible. If the seller does *not* retake possession, the remedies are the same as if the buyer had accepted the goods. In other words, the seller can recover the purchase price plus incidental damages.

Insolvency

Suppose that the buyer has prepaid all or part of the purchase price and the seller becomes insolvent before shipping the goods. Under Sec. 2-502 of the UCC, in some circumstances the buyer can compel the seller to turn over the goods to him or her.

Similarly, if the buyer becomes insolvent during the course of a sales transaction, under Sec. 2-702 the seller can refuse to deliver except for cash. If the goods have already been shipped and are still in transit, the seller can usually stop delivery unless he or she has already forwarded a negotiable document of title to the buyer. The seller is even given the right in some situations to reclaim the goods after they have been received by the buyer.

There are times, however, when the UCC, which is state law, will not prevail. A seller or buyer who becomes insolvent will often go into bankruptcy, a proceeding governed by federal law. Since the federal bankruptcy law prevails over state laws, the remedies granted in the UCC may have little practical significance in cases of insolvency.

Prior Agreement as to Remedies

The parties to a sale contract can provide in their agreement for remedies to be available in the event of breach. Under Sec. 2-718, they can agree on liquidated damages (the measure of damages to be payable in case of breach). Their provision must be reasonable, taking into account the anticipated or actual harm caused by the breach, the difficulties of proof of loss, and the inconvenience of otherwise obtaining an adequate remedy. If the contract sets an unreasonably large amount of liquidated damages, the amount will simply be ignored by the court.

More generally, Sec. 2-719 states that "the agreement may provide for remedies in addition to or in substitution for" those provided in the UCC. For example, the parties might agree that buyer's only remedy for breach of warranty will be to bring the goods back to the seller for repairs. Sec. 2-719 also provides that if the clause limiting remedies "fails of its essential purpose," it will be ignored by a court and the remedies normally available under the UCC will apply. A remedy limitation "fails of its essential purpose" if circumstances cause the limitation to substantially deprive one party of the value of his or her bargain. Thus, in the example above, if the seller does not repair the defective item within a reasonable period of time, the limitation clause will be ineffective and the buyer can resort to whatever remedies the UCC gives him in the circumstances. Furthermore, a limitation of remedies will be ignored by a court if it is so unfair and represents such a gross abuse of bargaining power that it is deemed *unconscionable*. Sec. 2-719 provides that, in a sale of *consumer goods,* a clause which limits the availability of damages for *bodily injury* is *presumed* to be unconscionable. Even though a remedy limitation clause is different from a warranty disclaimer (as explained in Chapter 20), such a clause in a consumer transaction must comply with the Magnuson-Moss Warranty Act when applicable.

The following case involves a sale contract containing a limitation on the buyer's remedies. In addition, the case contains a thorough discussion of "revocation of acceptance," which is the UCC remedy this particular buyer was trying to obtain in spite of the limitation clause in his contract.

Conte v. Dwan Lincoln-Mercury, Inc.

Supreme Court of Connecticut, 374 A.2d 144 (1976)

On March 25, 1970, Conte purchased a 1970 Lincoln Continental from Dwan, who was an authorized Lincoln Continental dealer under a franchise agreement with the manufacturer, Ford Motor Co. The following day, after being notified that the car was ready, Conte went to pick it up but refused to do so because it was dirty and a door was out of alignment. The next day Conte did take possession of the car, a warranty booklet, and other printed material inside the vehicle. The written sale agreement made by Conte and Dwan included a provision that there were no warranties applicable to the automobile, except the most recent printed Ford Motor Co. warranties, "and they shall be expressly in lieu of any other express or implied warranty, condition or guarantee on the new vehicle, chassis or any part thereof, including any implied warranty of merchantability or fitness ..." The basic Ford warranty provided that with respect to each 1970 passenger automobile the dealer would repair or replace any part, except tires, that was found to be defective in factory materials or workmanship in normal use within twelve months from the date of original retail delivery.

The day after Conte took delivery of the automobile he noticed that the motor and transmission were leaking oil and that the cigarette lighter and windshield wiper did not work. The next morning the car was brought in to Dwan, the windshield wiper was fixed and the plaintiff was told that he should make a list of his problems and

Dwan would take care of them. Within a week, the electric windows did not operate and paint blistered on the vehicle. Between the time that Conte took delivery in March, 1970, until May 3, 1971, Dwan had attempted to repair the car eight times as shown by Dwan's records. Between October 25, 1970, and May, 1971, it became undriveable five times on the road and was towed to Dwan for repairs. At one time when the car was driven, Conte received an electrical shock. Subsequently, an alternator was replaced and a fan belt repaired. Soon after he purchased the automobile and until May, 1971, Conte corresponded directly with Ford about his problems. On October 27, 1970, Conte met with a representative of Ford and was assured, in the presence of Dwan's service manager, that his automobile would be repaired to his satisfaction. The last repair order for the automobile was May 3, 1971, when, two weeks after an alternator was replaced, the automobile had to be towed and a fan belt repaired. Upon being informed that the car had been repaired, Conte told Dwan to keep it because it was dangerous and he wanted his money back or another automobile. After that, Conte never picked up his car. In May 1971, after the automobile had been in the garage six to eight weeks in one year of ownership, after being told each time that it was in good working order, after Ford sent its representative to ascertain the problem and have the car put in good working condition, and after it had been towed to the garage five times, Conte refused, in May, 1971, to accept any further assurance from Dwan and Ford that the automobile was in good and safe order and refused to take delivery of the vehicle after the last purported repairs.

Conte, plaintiff, then filed suit against Dwan, defendant. The trial court held in favor of plaintiff and defendant appealed.

Barber, Justice: . . . The Uniform Commercial Code—Sales is the law of this state. . . . It . . . provides a specific remedy permitting a buyer under proper conditions to force the seller to retake nonconforming goods even if the buyer has already accepted them. Under the code, a buyer's revocation of acceptance is a distinct course of action not to be confused with rescission by mutual consent; nor is it an alternative remedy for breach of warranty. When a buyer justifiably revokes acceptance, he may cancel and recover so much of the purchase price as has been paid. On the other hand, the basic measure of damages for breach of warranty is the difference between the value of the goods accepted and the value that they would have had if they had been as warranted.

Section 2-608 . . . sets up the following conditions for the buyer who seeks to justify revocation of acceptance: (1) a nonconformity which substantially impairs the value to the buyer; (2) acceptance (a) with discovery of the defect, if the acceptance is on the reasonable assumption that the nonconformity will be cured, or (b) without discovery of the defect, when the acceptance is reasonably induced by the difficulty of the discovery or the seller's assurances; (3) revocation within a reasonable time after a nonconformity was discovered or should have been discovered: and (4) revocation before a substantive change occurs in the condition of the goods not caused by their own defects. The buyer has the burden of establishing any breach with respect to the goods accepted. . . .

Whether goods are substantially impaired by nonconformity and whether revocation of acceptance is given within a reasonable time are questions of fact subject to the jury's determination. The reason why a "substantial impairment of value" must exist before a buyer may justifiably revoke his acceptance is to preclude revocation for trivial defects or defects which may easily be corrected. Each case must be examined on its own merits to determine what is a "substantial impairment of value" to the particular buyer. *Tiger Motor Co. v. McMurtry,* 224 So.2d 638. The facts of *Tiger,* similar to those stated here, disclose a situation where, after the plaintiff had bought and accepted an automobile, it consumed an excessive amount of oil, provided low gas mileage, and continued to jump or misfire, even after the installation of new equipment such as a new fuel pump, a new carburetor, new piston rings, and a "short block." The court held that the evidence supported the conclusion of the trier of fact that there had been a substantial impairment of value to the buyer and that the buyer was justified in revoking his acceptance a year after the sale. Similarly, the jury in the present case could reasonably have concluded from the evidence before it that the nonconformity of the automobile purchased by the plaintiff substantially impaired its value to the plaintiff and that he was entitled to a return of the purchase price from Dwan.

Not only must there be a substantial impairment of value to the buyer, but the revocation must take place "within a reasonable time after the buyer discovers or should have discovered" the defect. What is a reasonable time for taking any action [under the Code] depends upon the nature, purpose and circumstances of such action. Although the plaintiff did not revoke his acceptance until fourteen months after the sale, it is significant that he was in almost constant touch with the dealer concerning the condition of the vehicle, relying on the dealer's continued assurances that the automobile would be repaired satisfactorily. When it became apparent to the buyer that repeated attempts at adjustment had failed, he unequivocally notified Dwan that he was revoking his acceptance. Under the circumstances of this case, involving an almost continuous series of negotiations and repairs, the delay in the notice did not prejudice the dealer and the delay was not unreasonable. Under the Uniform Commercial Code, the dealer did have the right to attempt to cure any defects in the automobile, but this opportunity does not last for an indefinite period of time. One policy of the Code is to encourage the parties to work out their differences and so to minimize losses resulting from defective performance. Continued use of the automobile was inevitable while there was an attempt to cure the defects as they became apparent and such use did not defeat the revocation in this case. The jury could have reasonably concluded that the revocation was timely and justifiable. The plaintiff was, therefore, entitled to recover the amount of the purchase price which he had already paid. This basic remedy for justifiable revocation was not effectively limited by the warranty provision [in the contract] that the buyer was only entitled to the repair and replacement of defective parts. The Code provides that it shall be liberally construed, and recognizes that it is the very essence of a sales contract that at least minimum adequate remedies be available. In this case, the limited remedy of the warranty had failed of its essential purpose because even after numerous attempts to repair, the automobile still did not operate as a new automobile should, free from defects. [Thus, since the limitation of remedy in the sale contract had "failed of its essential purpose," this contractual provision was ignored by the court, and the remedies provided in the UCC were available to the buyer.]

[Affirmed.]

Questions and Problems

1. Explain the significance of the notation *FOB* as a shipping term.

2. Smith purchased a new car. Almost immediately after taking delivery he discovered that the car had a defective transmission, and he promptly took the car back to the dealer. When he told the dealer that he wanted to return the car and cancel the sale, the dealer offered

to replace the transmission. Smith refused the dealer's offer of "cure," left the car with the dealer, and made no further payments. The dealer fixed the car, resold it, and sued Smith for damages. *Zabriskie Chevrolet, Inc. v. Smith,* 240 A.2d 195 (1968). Did the dealer prevail? Discuss.

3. After a series of negotiations between Gulf and Sylvan, they made a contract providing for delivery in three separate lots, to be separately accepted and evidenced by three separate purchase orders sent on the same date. No problems arose in the first two deliveries, but the buyer noticed a minor defect in the third delivery and rejected it, citing the perfect tender rule as his authority. Moreover, he claimed that the seller had breached the entire contract. *Gulf Chemical & Metallurgical Corp. v. Sylvan Chemical Corp.,* 12 U.C.C. Rep. Serv. 117 (1973). Is he correct? Explain.

4. What part does foreseeability play in commercial impracticability, according to UCC Sec. 2-615?

5. A dairy farm contracted with a public school district to supply the latter with half-pints of milk. Between the time of contracting and the time for performance, the price of raw milk rose 23 percent. Other increases in the market price had occurred in the past. The dairy filed suit for a declaratory judgment, asking the court to relieve it from its obligation to deliver the milk under Sec. 2-615. *Maple Farms, Inc. v. City School Dist. of the City of Elmira,* 352 N.Y.S.2d 784 (1974). What was the result? Discuss.

6. Eckerd purchased a new mobile home from Zippy Mobile Home Sales. After the purchase but before moving into the home, Eckerd discovered a slight leak in one of the plumbing fixtures. He moved into the mobile home and then repaired the leak. Shortly thereafter, Eckerd became dissatisfied with the home because it was not large enough for his family. He went to Zippy and indicated that he was rejecting the mobile home because of defective plumbing. Zippy's manager said that he could not reject because he had already accepted. Who is correct? Explain.

7. What is a commercial unit? Explain its importance.

8. Under their sale contract Seller S was required to deliver goods to Buyer B on October 25. On April 30, S called B and demanded more money for the goods. B refused, and S said, "Well, if that's the way you want it." On May 30, B filed suit against S for breach of contract. S contended that B was not entitled to file suit until after the date for performance, October 25. Is S correct? Explain.

9. Plymouth Chemical Co. used propane gas as an essential raw material in producing certain chemicals. It had a long-term supply contract for such gas with Commonwealth Gas Co. A shortage of propane gas occurred, and most suppliers were no longer committing themselves to long-term contracts. Commonwealth breached the contract, and Plymouth sued for specific performance. Commonwealth claimed that Plymouth should be allowed to sue for damages but not for specific performance. Is Commonwealth correct? Explain.

10. After Buyer's breach of contract, Seller resold the goods at a private sale but did not give prior notice of the sale. The resale netted Seller $1,000 less than he would have received under the contract with Buyer. Seller sued Buyer for the $1,000. Buyer claimed that Seller could not recover the $1,000 deficiency because he had not notified Buyer of the sale. Is Buyer correct? Explain.

22 Commercial Paper/Types, Parties, and Basic Concepts

The term *commercial paper* refers to written promises or obligations to pay sums of money that arise from the use of such instruments as drafts, promissory notes, checks, and trade acceptances. (The most common instruments are checks and promissory notes.) Although a possibility exists that during our lifetime we will live in an almost checkless society, the present use of commercial paper in our credit-oriented economy is of enormous significance. In fact, if all business obligations represented by commercial paper were due and payable at this very moment, there would not be nearly enough U.S. currency available to pay these debts in full.

Commercial paper has been used for many centuries, probably as early as 1500 B.C., according to archeologists, who tell us that crude promissory notes existed in very early civilizations. By the thirteenth century merchants in the middle east were making significant use of both promissory notes and bills of exchange, and by the beginning of the seventeenth century, both kinds of instruments were commonly used in England.

Because the early English courts refused to recognize commercial paper at that time, the merchants created their own methods of enforcing rights arising from this kind of paper. The rules they developed were enforced by traders at their "fair" or "borough" courts, and together they made up what is known as the *law merchant* (see Chapter 17 for details).

During the eighteenth and nineteenth centuries these principles came to be substantially recognized by English and American courts and thus became part of the common law of both countries. In 1896 the American Bar Association drafted the Uniform Negotiable Instruments Law (NIL) for state consideration, and by the early 1920s this act was adopted by all the states. This caused our negotiable instruments law to be "codified."

Development of the Law

The Uniform Commercial Code

Today the old NIL has been superseded in all states by Article 3 of the Uniform Commercial Code, entitled "Commercial Paper." (Louisiana has not adopted the UCC in its entirety, but it has enacted Articles 1, 3, 4, and 5.) While the adoption of the UCC has resulted in a substantial updating of the earlier rules to conform to modern-day practices, the most important provisions of Article 3 are not much different from those of the original NIL. In any event, legal questions growing out of the use of negotiable instruments today are governed almost entirely by Article 3 of the UCC—although references to Article 4 are also necessary if problems arise that deal with the relationship existing between the drawer of a check and the bank upon which it is written.

Purposes of Commercial Paper

During the early part of the Middle Ages, merchants and traders had to carry gold and silver to pay for the goods they purchased at the various international fairs. Obviously these precious metals were continually subject to loss or theft through the perils of travel.

To eliminate dangers of this sort, merchants began to deposit their gold and silver with bankers. When they needed funds to pay for goods they had purchased, they "drew" on them by giving the seller a written order addressed to the bank, telling it to deliver part of the gold or silver to the seller. These orders, called bills of exchange, *were thus substitutes for money.* Today, checks and the drafts and promissory notes that are payable on demand serve this same basic purpose.

The second major purpose of commercial paper is to serve as a *credit device;*

this came about as a logical extension of the initial use of commercial paper. Soon after bills of exchange became established as substitutes for money, merchants who wished to purchase goods on credit discovered that sellers were sometimes willing to accept bills of exchange that were not payable until a stated time in the future—such as "ninety days after date." If the seller was satisfied as to the commercial reputation of the bill's drawer (the purchaser), he would take such an instrument (called a *time bill* or *draft*) and wait until the maturity date to collect it. In this way the seller/payee extended credit to the buyer/drawer.

Soon thereafter ways were devised by which payees could sell these instruments to third parties, usually banks, and receive immediate cash in return. Since the banks would then have to wait for the maturity dates before receiving payment, the payees would have to sell them the paper at a discount—that is, at perhaps five or ten percent less than the face amount. This meant, in effect, that the purchasing banks were charging the sellers interest in advance as compensation for their role in the transaction.

Today, because of the widespread use of time notes and drafts, the credit aspect of commercial paper is as important to the business community as its "substitute for money" aspect.

| Types of Commercial Paper | There are numerous ways to classify the basic types of commercial paper. Of these, the classification specified by Article 3 of the UCC probably merits top billing. |

The UCC Classification

Sec. 3-104 specifies four types of instruments—drafts, checks, certificates of deposit, and notes.

Drafts: A *draft,* or bill of exchange, is an instrument whereby the party creating it (called the *drawer*) orders another party (the *drawee*) to pay money to a third party (the *payee*). For example: X owes Y $100, and Y owes Z the same amount. Y signs a written order directing X to pay the $100 to Z and gives it to Z. Z presents the instrument to X, who then pays him. Here Y is the drawer, X the drawee, and Z the payee.

In order for a draft to work, one of two general conditions must exist. Either the drawee must owe the drawer a debt (in which case the drawer is simply telling the drawee to pay the debt or a portion of it to a third party) or some kind of agreement or relationship must exist between the parties under which the drawee has consented to the drawing of the draft upon him or her. If neither of these conditions existed, obviously the drawee would not obey the order to pay the amount of the draft to the payee or to any subsequent holder of the instrument.

One type of draft is the *trade acceptance,* which is ordinarily used in connection with a sale of goods. We can illustrate this by referring to the specimen trade acceptance reproduced here. The Frymire Corporation has sold goods to the Paul

Jones Company. Because the Paul Jones Company wishes to utilize a negotiable instrument rather than paying cash for the goods immediately, the Frymire Corporation (drawer) draws a trade acceptance on the Paul Jones Company (drawee) for the purchase price of the goods. The instrument orders the Paul Jones Company to pay the stated sum to the order of the Frymire Corporation at a stated time in the future—in this case, on the following July 25th. (The Frymire Corporation is thus both the drawer and the payee of the instrument.) It is then presented to an officer of the Paul Jones Company, who *accepts it* by signing that company's name on it in the space provided for this purpose. The acceptance, which constitutes a promise by the Paul Jones Company (the drawee-acceptor) to pay the instrument when it becomes due, is then returned to the Frymire Corporation. It can now negotiate the instrument to a third party, such as the Frymire Corporation's bank, and receive cash immediately. Use of instrument in this manner—by sellers of goods—explains why it is called a *trade* acceptance. (Other kinds of drafts are also frequently accepted by their drawees; these will be discussed in Chapter 27.) Another frequently used draft is the *bank draft,* which is utilized when one bank draws on its funds in another bank.

Trade Acceptance   A *trade acceptance* is a draft or bill of exchange drawn by the seller of goods on the purchaser of those goods and accepted (signed) by the purchaser. The purpose of the transaction is to enable the seller to raise money on the paper before the purchaser's obligation matures under the sales contract.

Checks: A *check* is a particular type of draft. Under Sec. 3-104(2), it is by definition a "draft drawn on a bank [and] payable on demand." It is distinguished from other drafts primarily in that it must be drawn on a bank and must be payable on demand. As one might guess, checks are by far the most commonly used form of

```
                              Hinsdale, Illinois
$ 500.00                                           July 18,            19 80

    Ninty days after above date-------------------------------- PAY TO THE ORDER OF

    Nelle Cotten

    Five hundred and no/100------------------------------------------ DOLLARS
                              WITH EXCHANGE

                      VALUE RECEIVED AND CHARGE TO ACCOUNT OF

TO    Bank of Hinsdale                          )
                                                }           Bernice Gordon
NO.        1          Hinsdale, Illinois        )

STOCK FORM 590-S  BANKFORMS, INC
```

Draft A *draft* is an instrument by which the party creating it (the drawer) orders another party (the drawee) to pay money to a third party (the payee).

drafts. It is estimated, for example, that approximately 37 billion checks will be written during the year 1981 in the United States alone.

One particular form of check is the *cashier's check,* which is drawn by a bank on itself, payable on demand to a payee. Because this check is drawn by the bank ordering itself to pay, the bank must honor the check upon proper presentment. For this reason, in transactions involving the sale of property—where the owner/seller requires some form of guaranteed payment to accompany all offers to purchase—bidders commonly submit cashier's checks along with their bids.

Notes: A *note* is a promise by one party (called a *maker*) to pay a sum of money to another party (the *payee*). Notes differ from drafts in two primary respects. They always contain promises to pay money (as distinguished from orders), and they have two parties—maker and payee—rather than three.

Because notes are used in a variety of transactions, they come in many different forms. For example, a note used in a real estate transaction secured by a mortgage on the property being purchased is a *real estate mortgage note.* A note containing a promise to make payments in specified installments, such as payments for a new car, is an *installment note.* And a note secured by personal property is a *collateral note.* While all of these are *promissory notes* in a general sense, that term when used alone usually refers to the simplest kind of notes, those merely containing promises by one person to pay money to another.

Check   A *check* is the most common type of draft; it is an order (draft or bill of exchange) drawn on a bank and payable on demand.

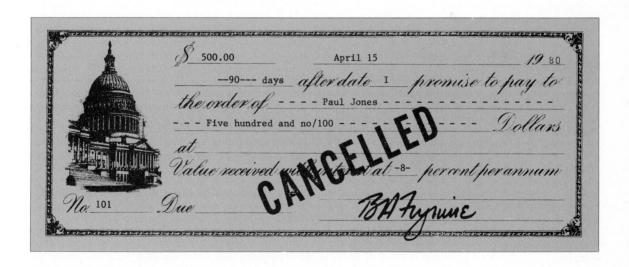

Promissory Note   A *promissory note* is an instrument by which the maker promises to pay a sum of money to another party (the payee).

Certificates of Deposit: A *certificate of deposit* is an acknowledgment by a bank of receipt of money with a return "promise" on the bank's part to repay it at a fixed future date or, in some instances, on demand.

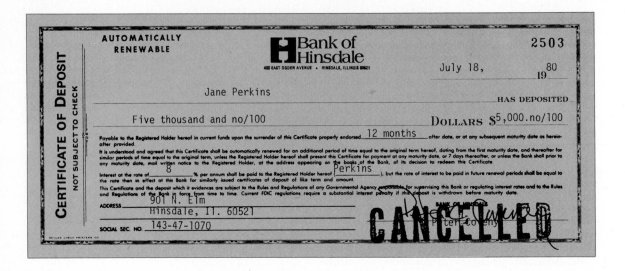

Certificate of Deposit A *certificate of deposit* is an instrument by which a bank acknowledges receipt of money and promises to return it at a later date or on demand. Certificates of deposit may be negotiable or non-negotiable, depending upon their terms.

Promises to Pay and Orders to Pay

A second method of classifying commercial paper uses only two categories. All instruments involving the payment of money, regardless of their specialized names within the business community, contain one of two elements—*promises* to pay money or *orders* to pay money. Instruments containing promises to pay can be broadly classified as *notes* and those containing orders to pay as *drafts*. As already indicated, the certificate of deposit is a special type of note and the check a special type of draft.

Demand and Time Instruments

A third method of classifying commercial paper is based solely on the time at which the instrument is payable. Instruments that are payable whenever the holder chooses to present them to the maker (in the case of a note) or to the drawee (in the case of a draft) are called *demand* (or *sight*) *instruments*. Those payable at a specific future date are *time instruments*. Notes, drafts, and certificates of deposit can be either demand or time instruments, while checks—by definition—must be payable on demand.

Negotiable and Nonnegotiable Instruments

Using the term *commercial paper* in its broadest sense, all such paper is either negotiable or nonnegotiable—a classification that depends entirely on whether the paper contains all the elements that are formally required by Sec. 3-104 of the UCC. Thus, which category the instrument falls into depends entirely on its form and content.

In many instances the negotiable/nonnegotiable classification of commercial paper transcends all others in importance, for two primary reasons:

1. The rules of Article 3 of the UCC apply (with rare exception) only to instruments that meet the tests of negotiability. By contrast, nonnegotiable instruments are governed by the ordinary principles of contract law. In other words, the rights and liabilities of makers, drawers, and indorsers of negotiable instruments are controlled by one body of law, while those of parties to nonnegotiable instruments are governed by another.

2. It is possible under the rules of Article 3 for a holder of a negotiable instrument to enjoy a special status, that of a *holder in due course* (HDC). Such a holder takes the instrument free of many defenses that exist between its original parties. (*Defenses* are matters pleaded by defendants as a reason in law or fact why the plaintiff should not recover what he or she seeks.) The holder of a nonnegotiable instrument (such as a simple contract), on the other hand, can never qualify as an HDC. Such a holder takes it subject to these defenses.

While an examination of the precise rights of the HDC must await the subject of defenses in Chapter 26, the basic distinction between the status of such a holder and that of a mere assignee will be brought to light here.

Assignee versus Holder in Due Course

Under contract law, the assignee of a simple contract acquires no better rights under the contract than those possessed by the assignor. For example: X contracts to buy a bulldozer from Y for $25,000 under an installment contract. After delivery, Y assigns the contract (the right to collect the price) to a third party, Z. If the machine proves defective, X can successfully assert this fact as a defense against Z, just as he could have asserted it against Y had there been no assignment. This means that the assignee, Z, is not entitled to a judgment against X. The same would be true if X had simply given Y a nonnegotiable note or draft in payment for the bulldozer; Z's rights would be no better than those possessed by Y.

On the other hand, if X had given Y a *negotiable* note, draft, or check in payment for the machine, and if Y had then transferred the instrument to Z under circumstances that qualified Z as a holder in due course, then Z would be entitled to recover the full amount of the instrument from X, despite the fact that Y had breached his contract with X by delivering a defective machine.

The above is a simple illustration of one of the basic commercial paper concepts —*that it is possible for a third party/HDC to acquire greater rights under an instrument than those possessed by the payee/transferor.* This does not mean, however, that the HDC is always legally entitled to payment from the primary party. Sometimes the primary party has available a "real" or "universal" defense, which he or she can successfully assert against any holder, even the HDC. And the holder-in-due-course doctrine itself has been sharply limited in recent years. (These limitations will be explained more fully in Chapter 26.)

Parties to Commercial Paper

We have already seen that notes have two original parties—the maker and the payee—while drafts and checks have three—the drawer, the drawee, and the payee. But after an instrument is issued, additional parties can also become involved. (The liability incurred by each of these parties is spelled out in Chapter 27.)

The Acceptor

Frequently, after a draft is issued, it is presented by the payee (or a subsequent holder) to the drawee (the person to whom the order is addressed) for that person's "acceptance." Under the UCC some types of drafts require a presentment, while for others the presentment is at the option of the holder. In any event, the drawee who "accepts" the draft is called the *acceptor* (or drawee/acceptor), and he or she becomes a primary party to the instrument. (As we have seen, an acceptance occurs when the drawee signs his or her name somewhere on the face of the instrument.) In this capacity, the acceptor's liability is roughly akin to that of the maker of a note.

Indorsers

Often the payee of a note or draft transfers it to a third party soon after acquiring it, instead of presenting it to the primary party for payment. When such a transfer occurs, the payee/transferor almost always "indorses" the instrument by signing his or her name on the back of it before delivering it to the third party; by so doing, the payee becomes an *indorser.* For example, if P, the payee, receives a check from D, P can indorse it to a third party, Z, in payment of a debt that P owes to Z (or for any other reason).

Indorsees

The *indorsee,* of course, is the person who receives an indorsed instrument; in the example above, the indorsee is Z. Z can indorse the instrument to another party, in which case Z also becomes an indorser.

The Bearer

From both a legal and a practical standpoint, the term *bearer* is of limited (though well-defined) significance. A *bearer* is any person who has physical possession of an instrument that legally qualifies as a *bearer instrument.* For example, if a note is expressly made "payable to bearer" or is simply payable to "cash," whoever possesses it is the bearer.

Another type of bearer instrument comes into existence when an instrument is originally payable to the order of a named person, and the named person indorses it by signing his or her name on the back. An indorsement such as this, called a *blank indorsement,* converts the paper into a bearer instrument; therefore, the subsequent taker of the instrument also is a bearer.

Holders

The term *holder* is broader in scope and of greater legal significance than the term *bearer.* Sec. 1-201(20) of the UCC defines a *holder* as a person who possesses a negotiable instrument which is either payable to bearer or payable to the specific person as payee or indorsee. Thus the term includes not only persons possessing bearer instruments but also payees and indorsees possessing order instruments. To illustrate: X pays a utility bill by drawing a check "payable to the order of Columbia Gas of Ohio" and mailing it to that company. While Columbia Gas cannot be called a bearer (since the check is not payable to bearer), as payee it clearly qualifies as a holder.

Holder in Due Course: Under Sec. 3-302, a *holder in due course* is a holder who has given value for the instrument, has acquired it before it was overdue, and has taken it in good faith. And, as indicated earlier, it is the HDC who is afforded most-favored status under the code.[1]

Ordinary Holder: A person who qualifies as a holder but does not meet all the HDC requirements is called an *ordinary holder.* Unlike the HDC, an ordinary holder cannot enforce the instrument against the primary party if the latter has a personal defense, such as fraud on the part of the payee. In other words, the ordinary holder takes the instrument subject to all defenses, much like the assignee of a nonnegotiable instrument. However, also like the assignee, the ordinary holder can enforce the instrument against the primary party if the latter has no defense available.

---

[1]The precise rights of the holder in due course, ordinary holder, and holder through a holder in due course will be examined in Chapter 25.

Holder through a Holder in Due Course: If a holder fails to qualify as an HDC, he or she can still enjoy the special rights of a holder in due course by showing that any prior holder qualified as an HDC. Such a person is called a *holder through a holder in due course.*

Questions and Problems

1. X contracts to paint Y's house for $1200 in June. On June 20, when X is half-way through with the job, Y is called to Europe on a business trip. Before leaving, Y makes out a promissory note for $1200 that is payable July 15, and hands it to X. The next day X sells the note to a local bank for $1100 (i.e., he "discounts" the note). In late July, when the bank demands payment from Y, Y refuses to pay the instrument because X never finished the job. If the note in question turns out to be nonnegotiable in form, what effect—if any—does this have upon Y's liability to the bank? Explain.

2. What were the major factors that were responsible for the creation of commercial paper in the Middle Ages?

3. Often the holder of a promissory note that is not due until some future date will "discount" it at a bank. What are the advantages to the holder, and to the bank, in doing this?

4. Tom is owed $1000 by Dick, but he (Tom) in turn owes Harry $400. When Harry presses Tom for payment, Tom gives Harry this letter addressed to Dick: "Out of the $1000 you owe me, please pay $400 of it to Harry as soon as he requests it." Does this letter look like a *draft,* or more like a *note?* What is the primary reason for your answer?

5. The Scarlet Corporation orders 10 snowmobiles from the Gray Company at a total cost of $12,000. If a *trade acceptance* were to be used here (instead of a cash payment by the Scarlet Corporation), who would be (a) the drawer, (b) the drawee, and (c) the acceptor?

6. X sells a used car to Y and takes a promissory note from Y in payment. When the note comes due Y is financially unable to pay it. X then brings suit on the note, and Y's only defense is that the note is *nonnegotiable* in form. (That is, there was nothing wrong with the car that he received.) If Y can clearly prove that the note *is* nonnegotiable, is his defense good? (I.e., will the court dismiss the action?) Why or why not?

7. You see this statement in a text: "As a general rule, bearer instruments are governed by contract law, and order instruments by Article 2 of the UCC." Is this statement essentially true? Why or why not?

8. B is the maker of a negotiable promissory note, and he issues it to C. C later negotiates it to D. In such a situation, D may qualify as a *holder in due course,* or he may be only an *ordinary holder.* If D were forced to bring suit against B in an effort to obtain payment of the note, under what circumstances might D's success depend entirely upon whether he was the one type of holder, or the other? Explain.

Commercial Paper/ Negotiability

23

In many situations, whether an instrument is negotiable or nonnegotiable is of little importance. Suppose, for example, that P is willing to sell goods to M on credit, taking a promissory ninety-day note signed by M as evidence of the indebtedness. Suppose further that M's financial reputation is good, and that P is perfectly willing to hold the note himself until it matures. In these circumstances P might well be satisfied with a nonnegotiable note, for his chances of being paid on the due date, and his legal rights against M if payment is not made voluntarily, are about as good as those he would possess if the note were negotiable.

In many other circumstances, however, the negotiability or nonnegotiability of an instrument is of vital importance, for a number of reasons. First, as we briefly suggested in the preceding chapter, when legal problems arise as to the enforceability of the instrument, the rights and obligations of the parties are resolved under Article 3 of the UCC if the instrument is negotiable and under ordinary contract law if it is not. And since the holder-in-due-course concept is recognized only under Article 3, any person seeking to enforce the instrument under this concept must (among other things) show at the outset that the instrument meets the tests of negotiability.

In addition, as a practical matter, commercial paper cannot serve its "substitute for money" and "extension of credit" roles unless it is freely transferable (that is, unless prospective purchasers of the paper, especially financial institutions, are willing to accept it routinely). And acceptability comes about only if the paper has "strong" characteristics. That is, the promises or orders contained therein must be unconditional in nature, and the other provisions of the paper must leave no doubt as to such matters as the date of maturity and the amount of money which the holder is entitled to receive at that date.

Because of these legal and practical considerations the law has formulated over the years certain express requirements that commercial paper must meet in order to be negotiable. As a result of these requirements, the negotiability or nonnegotiability of an instrument is entirely dependent upon its *form and content*.

Requirements of Negotiability

Today the requirements of negotiability are expressly set forth in Sec. 3-104. Subsection 1 reads as follows:

> Any writing to be a negotiable instrument within this Article must (a) be signed by the maker or drawer; and (b) contain an unconditional promise or order to pay a sum certain in money and [must contain] no other promise, order, obligation, or power given by the maker or drawer except as authorized by this Article; and (c) be payable on demand or at a definite time; and (d) be payable to order or to bearer.

Each of these requirements, together with later sections that help interpret Sec. 3-104, will now be examined.

The Writing and Signing Requirements

The Writing: Just as there is no such thing as "oral money," an oral promise or order to pay money obviously cannot serve as a substitute for it. Under contract law it is true that an oral promise to pay money can be enforced as long as its existence can be established in court. However, in the commercial world, where large numbers of promises and orders must be transferred daily, the need for such obligations to be evidenced in tangible written form becomes obvious. Under Sec. 1-201(46), this "writing" can be handwritten, printed, or typewritten, or it can consist of "any other intentional [method of] reduction to tangible form."

Normally, of course, the substance on which the writing appears is paper, but the UCC does not require this. Thus we occasionally read in the newspaper about the holder of a "check" written on a watermelon or some similar object who was able to obtain payment at the drawee bank upon physical presentment of the object. These cases, of course, are rarities; they do, however, bring a welcome degree of humor and ingenuity to the subject of commercial paper (though the bank officials involved might not entirely share this view).

The Signing: As we have seen, a negotiable instrument must be signed by the maker in the case of a note or by the drawer in the case of a draft. Ordinarily there is little trouble with this requirement, since such a party almost invariably affixes his or her signature (in longhand) to the instrument at the outset.

In some instances, however, questions do arise. Sec. 1-201(39) is designed to alleviate these by stating that the term *signed* means "any symbol executed or adopted by a party with [the] present intention to authenticate a writing." Thus a signing can occur through the use of one's initials, a rubber stamp, or some other type of "signature," such as the mark X, so long as it is made with the intention of giving assent to the writing's terms. (Problems that relate to forgeries and the unauthorized signing of principals' names by their agents will be examined in Chapter 27.)

The Promise or Order Must Be Unconditional

In order for an instrument to be treated as a substitute for money or as a credit extension device, the holder wants assurance that no conditions will be imposed on the instrument's payment. Whether such conditions exist in a given case, thus causing the instrument to be nonnegotiable, depends on the totality of the terms and provisions that make up the instrument.

As one might imagine, an almost infinite variety of clauses or notations find their way into some instruments and raise legitimate questions as to whether they condition the basic promise or order to pay. We will consider here the most common of these.

Express Conditions: A small percentage of notes and drafts contain clauses that *expressly condition* the primary promise or order to pay. Obviously these clauses destroy negotiability of the instrument at the outset. A note signed by M, maker, which is payable "upon the marriage of my daughter" or "on the date of the next Rose Bowl game," falls into this category, for it is expressly made payable upon an event that may never occur. Even if the event is very likely to occur (or does, in fact, occur subsequently), it does not save the negotiability of the instrument.

Permitted Provisions: A more common situation is one where the basic obligation is itself unconditional but where the instrument contains language or clauses which will *possibly* condition the primary obligation—depending, of course, on how the clauses are legally interpreted.

Sec. 3-105 resolves many of these problems of interpretation. (See page 936 of the Appendix.) By referring to subsection 1, we see eight express types of clauses or notations that may appear on an instrument without conditioning its payment. Thus, clauses falling within this subsection do not destroy negotiability.

Subsection 1 permits the maker or drawer to note on the face of the instrument its purpose ("January rent"), or the consideration received in exchange for the instrument ("Payment for 100 bushels wheat.") It also permits the maker or drawer to indicate that the instrument has arisen out of a separate agreement, if such is the case, or is secured by a mortgage on specified property. Thus the UCC recognizes that these kinds of references should have no adverse legal or practical effect on the instrument's negotiability.

Subsections f and g contain two "fund" provisions. F permits inclusion on the face of an instrument a clause which merely "indicates a particular account to be debited or any other fund from which *reimbursement* is to be made." Two examples: (1) D draws a check on which he writes the words, "Charge to petty cash," and (2) the X Corporation, a manufacturer holding several construction contracts with the U.S. Navy, writes on an obligation, "Charge to Navy Contract SX-102." In both instances it is clear that the instruments pledge the general credit of the parties issuing them, and that the extra notations merely refer to funds (or assets) out of which the parties will reimburse themselves after they have paid the instruments. The instruments, therefore, remain negotiable.

Subsection g refers to certain instruments that are *payable out of* specified funds, as distinguished from instruments merely containing references to funds from which reimbursement is to be made. While most instruments that are payable out of specified funds are nonnegotiable (see below), g provides one major exception: where the instrument is issued by a government, governmental unit or agency.[1] Thus a state-issued bond, payable out of the revenue of that state's turnpike commission, is a negotiable instrument. Subsection g expressly provides that such a promise to pay is not conditional, even though the fund in fact may not be large enough to permit payment of the full face value of the bond when it matures. Government obligations are given this special treatment because government funds almost always are adequate to honor the obligations, while this is less likely to be the case where the maker is an ordinary corporation or individual.

Unpermitted Provisions: Subsection 2 of § 3-105, in contrast to subsection 1, refers to two kinds of clauses or provisions that *do* destroy the negotiability of any note or draft. The first of these involves language which indicates that the promises or orders which they contain are *subject to* some other agreement, such as a mortgage or rental agreement. Specifically, subsection 2a reads as follows: "A promise or order is not unconditional if the instrument states that it is subject to or governed by any other agreement." Prior to the adoption of the UCC, some courts took the view that the negotiability of an instrument that was subject to some other agreement depended upon the actual terms of that agreement. This meant that a prospective purchaser would have to search out that other agreement in order to know what the status of the instrument was—a most impractical requirement in the commercial world. Subsection 2a makes such instruments *nonnegotiable as a matter of law*—i.e., regardless of what the terms of the other agreement actually are. This subsection thus underscores the general idea that the negotiability or nonnegotiability of an instrument must be determinable from the face of the instrument alone.

---

[1] A second exception: instruments payable out of the "entire assets of a partnership, unincorporated association, trust or estate by or on behalf of which the instrument is issued."

The second kind of clause that destroys negotiability under subsection 2b is that which makes the instrument *payable out of a specified fund* (with the two narrow exceptions noted in our discussion of § 3-105(1)(g) above.) Because the payment of such instruments is subject to the possibility that there may be no such fund in existence at maturity, the promise or order is obviously conditional in nature, and 2b expressly so provides. Thus if X in June promises to pay $5000 to the order of Y on the following December 1st "out of the proceeds of the sale of my Ford Motor stock," the instrument is nonnegotiable when issued to Y, and remains nonnegotiable even if the stock is sold before December 1 for more than $5000.

The "fund" rules of § 3-105 can be summarized as follows:

1. An instrument that refers to a fund out of which reimbursement is to be made is negotiable.

2. An instrument that is payable out of a fund is nonnegotiable, except for instruments payable out of governmental funds and those payable out of the entire assets of a partnership, unincorporated association, trust or estate.

We have seen that an instrument, otherwise negotiable, is rendered nonnegotiable if its terms are subject to another agreement. The case below raises the reverse question: Can an instrument that is nonnegotiable on its face (i.e., on the basis of its express provisions) be made *negotiable* by reference to some other agreement?

The State of Oklahoma has a statute that prohibits any seller of consumer goods from taking a negotiable instrument—other than a check—in conjunction with a consumer credit sale. If a seller violates the statute, the purchaser can recover three times the amount of the credit charge from the seller.[2]

Walls v. Morris Chevrolet, Inc.

Court of Appeals of Oklahoma—Division 1, 515 P.2d 1405 (1973)

Walls, plaintiff, brought action against Morris Chevrolet, defendant, claiming that it took a negotiable instrument from him in connection with his purchase of a car, in violation of the above-mentioned statute. Defendant contended that the papers signed by Walls did not include a negotiable instrument, and it therefore filed a demurrer to Walls's petition. (The papers consisted of two instruments written on the same sheet of paper: a promissory note and a security agreement.)

The trial court agreed with defendant company that the note in question was not negotiable. Accordingly, the court sustained the demurrer and dismissed Walls's petition. Walls appealed.

Bailey, Justice: . . . First, both parties assume that the note, considered by itself, is not negotiable. So do we. The sum payable from the face of the note does not appear to be a sum certain because of the privilege stated in the note [which provides for a] refund of any

---

[2]The purpose of this statute presumably is to give protection to purchasers of consumer goods by preserving their defenses against third parties in the event that the seller breaches his contract. For example: if a car dealer made a warranty to a buyer that later proved to be false, with the buyer giving the seller a *nonnegotiable* note in payment, the buyer could thus assert the defense of "breach of warranty" against any subsequent holder of the instrument.

unearned finance charge . . . upon prepayment of the balance. . . . In this instance the amount of the discount is not stated in the note and cannot be computed from its face. . . .

To overcome the absence of a sum certain on its face, the plaintiff argues (1) that the amount of the finance charge *appears in the accompanying security agreement;* (2) that the security agreement and the note *should be considered one instrument* because [they are written] on the same sheet of paper; and (3) that, so construed, *the missing term is supplied and both the note and security agreement are [therefore] negotiable.* [Emphasis added.]

For the proposition that the note and security agreement must be considered one instrument for purposes of determining negotiability, plaintiff relies upon the apparently pre-Code case of *Commerce Acceptance of Oklahoma City v. Henderson,* 446 P.2d 297 (Okl. 1968). In that case the Oklahoma Supreme Court held that the terms in a conditional sales contract *destroyed the negotiability of a note attached to it,* saying: "The Conditional Sales Contract and 'NOTE' must be considered one instrument, since admittedly [they were not separated] until after [they were assigned] to plaintiff." We think this quoted language continues to have vitality under the Code.

However, . . . the Commerce Acceptance Case makes it clear that a note may be made *non-negotiable* by the added terms of an attached agreement, *not* that it may be made *negotiable* by those terms when it lacks an element of negotiability on its face. *We have been cited to no case, nor have we found one, in which a note on its face non-negotiable has been found to be negotiable by reference to an attached security agreement.* [Emphasis added.]

It is our opinion that a note cannot depend upon another agreement for elements of negotiability whether that agreement is attached to the note or separate from it, except in those rare instances where such an incorporation is sanctioned by the Uniform Commercial Code expressly or by necessary implication. . . .

Sec. 3-105 in subdivision (2) provides that a note is not negotiable if the instrument "(a) states that it is subject to or governed by any other agreement." . . . Sec. 3-119(2) provides: "A separate agreement does not affect the negotiability of an instrument." Bender's U.C.C. Service . . . states in part:

> Section 3-119(2) makes it clear that the conditional or unconditional character of an instrument is to be determined from the terms of the instrument itself. . . . An instrument is non-negotiable if it contains "any language which, fairly construed, requires the holder to look to the other agreement for the terms of payment." . . .

We think that these Code provisions are controlling in this instance where the attached note and security agreement could be detached and treated as separate instruments.

We are particularly concerned about the incongruous result which might be reached in this case if we held that the security agreement here imparted the necessary element of negotiability to the promissory note so that it became negotiable. Though on the same sheet of paper, the security agreement and the note are so situated on the paper that they could be detached from each other and each would appear to be an agreement complete in itself. There is nothing in the terms of either agreement to make it illegal or even inappropriate for a holder to so separate them. In that event any subsequent holder of the note could not determine its negotiability from the note itself but this would depend upon a now separate instrument, the security agreement. Presumably such a note, though negotiable when attached (if we should so hold) would be non-negotiable when separated . . . . This is a bad result, to be avoided if possible. . . .

Judgment affirmed.

Definite Promise or Order to Pay: Occasionally an instrument refers to the existence of a debt, but its language raises the question of whether the instrument really constitutes a promise or order that the debt be paid. For example, one person may hand to another a written IOU. A statement of this kind, or any other statement that merely acknowledges the existence of a debt, does not constitute a promise to pay, and the instrument thus fails to meet the requirements of negotiability.

Amount to Be Paid Must Be a Sum Certain in Money

If an instrument is to be a substitute for money and have an equivalent degree of acceptability, the necessity that the amount be a *sum certain* is obvious. This requirement of certainty is met if the holder can determine from the terms of the instrument itself the amount he or she is entitled to receive at maturity.

The UCC recognizes that some instruments contain provisions that at least raise the question of whether they violate this requirement, and Sec. 3-106 is meant to "save" the negotiability of many of these instruments by providing that

> The sum payable is a sum certain even though it is to be paid (a) with stated interest or by stated installments; or (b) with stated different rates of interest before and after default or a specified date; or (c) with a stated discount or addition if paid before or after the date fixed for payment; or (d) with exchange or less exchange, whether at a fixed rate or at the current rate; or (e) with costs of collections or an attorney's fee or both upon default.

Subsections a, b, c, and e are self-explanatory. Subsection d refers to instruments that are payable in foreign currency. The holder of this kind of instrument may want payment in his or her own country's currency, which requires application of the exchange rate in effect between the two countries. Such instruments, whether payable at fixed exchange rates or at "current rates," are deemed by subsection d to meet the "sum certain" requirement.

Payment to Be Made Only in Money: With exceptions to be discussed later in this chapter, instruments must be payable only in *money*. Thus, in general, any contract that requires the obligor to perform an act other than, or in addition to, the payment of money is nonnegotiable.[3] Three examples of such contracts are: (1) M, in return for a loan, promises to deliver "sixty bushels of U.S. #1 blackeye peas ninety days after date"; (2) M signs a note that obligates him to pay at maturity $1,000 *and* to deliver to the holder at that time sixty bushels of U.S. #1 blackeye

---

[3]However, contracts that require the *delivery of goods* at a future date often do possess the quality of negotiability. Thus, while many bills of lading and warehouse receipts fail to qualify as negotiable instruments under Article 3 of the UCC, because they do not contain promises to pay money, they do qualify as negotiable documents of title under Article 7 of the code.

peas; and (3) M signs a note that obligates him to pay $1,000 *or* to deliver the peas at maturity.

Money is defined in Sec. 1-201(24) as a "medium of exchange authorized or adopted by a domestic or foreign government as a part of its currency." It thus follows that any instrument payable in the currency of a recognized government is payable in money regardless of where the instrument is to be paid. In that regard, Sec. 3-107(2) provides that an instrument payable in this country whose amount is stated in a foreign currency (such as 2,000 German marks) can be satisfied by the payment of an equivalent number of American dollars at the due date, unless the instrument *expressly* requires payment in marks. In either event the instrument is negotiable. In no case, however, can the instrument be payable in something other than money. To illustrate:

1. An instrument drafted in Mexico City and payable in Austin, Texas, expressly calls for payment in one hundred Mexican dollars. The instrument is payable in money. (See Sec. 3-107[1] for details.)

2. An instrument payable in U.S. government bonds is not negotiable, since government bonds are not a medium of exchange recognized by the U.S. government.

Payable on Demand or at a Definite Time

Under Sec. 3-108, to be negotiable an instrument must be either payable on demand or at a definite time. This requirement recognizes that the holder of an instrument wants to know with certainty when he or she will be entitled to payment. Any appreciable uncertainty as to time of payment makes the instrument commercially unacceptable and defeats the concept that a negotiable instrument is a substitute for money.

Instruments payable *on demand* include (1) those which are expressly so payable, (2) those whose terms make the instrument payable "at sight" or "on presentation" by the holder, or (3) those in which no time for payment is stated, as, for example, the following: "I promise to pay to the order of P one hundred dollars. (signed) M."

Instruments that are not payable on demand, called *time instruments,* must be payable at a definite time in order to be negotiable. When issuing this kind of note or draft, the maker or drawer usually wants assurance that there will be no obligation to pay until the specified time period has elapsed. Thus the terms clearly indicate a definite future time for payment, such as "payable one year from date" or "payable July 1, 1981."

While no problems of negotiability are presented by these kinds of instruments, problems do arise when the note or draft contains additional terms that apparently conflict with the definite time requirement. Sec. 3-109 clears up most of these problem situations, as follows:

(1) An instrument is payable at a definite time if by its terms it is payable
    (a) on or before a stated date or at a fixed period after a stated date; or

(b) at a fixed period after sight; or (c) at a definite time subject to any acceleration; or (d) at a definite time subject to extension at the option of the holder, or to extension to a further definite time at the option of the maker or acceptor or automatically upon or after a specified act or event.

(2) An instrument which by its terms is otherwise payable only upon an act or event uncertain as to time of occurrence is not payable at a definite time even though the act or event has occurred.

We will now briefly examine subsections a and b of § 3-109(1), together with a case that involves an interpretation of these provisions. Following the case we will return to the "acceleration" and "extension" provisions of subsections c and d.

Subsections 1a and 1b: Subsections a and b are virtually self-explanatory. An instrument payable on or before a specified date gives the maker, drawer, or acceptor the option of paying before the stated maturity date if he or she wishes. Subsection 1a simply points out that such uncertainty does not violate the definite time requirement. Subsection 1b refers to a common provision in drafts that they are payable a specified time (frequently sixty or ninety days) "after sight." That is, the time period does not begin to run until "sight" (the moment the draft is accepted by the drawee) occurs. Although the time at which the acceptance will occur is unknown when the instrument is first issued, this subsection provides that the instrument nonetheless meets the definite time requirement.

In the following case we have the primary question of: "When is the instrument due?" rather than "Is the instrument negotiable?" The case is nonetheless useful because in answering the primary question the higher court clearly implied that the note did qualify as a negotiable instrument under the code.

Ferri v. Sylvia

Supreme Court of Rhode Island, 214 A.2d 470 (1965)

Mr. and Mrs. Sylvia, the defendants, signed a promissory note payable to Maria Ferri, plaintiff. Under the terms of the note, dated May 25, 1963, the Sylvias promised to pay plaintiff $3,000 "within ten (10) years after date." At some unspecified time thereafter, but long before the ten years had elapsed, plaintiff brought action to recover on the note. The Sylvias defended on the ground that the instrument had not yet matured.

The trial court ruled that the maturity date was "uncertain" and therefore admitted oral testimony by both parties "as to their intentions and prior agreements." On the basis of that testimony the court ruled that plaintiff had the right to demand payment at any time after May 25, 1963. Judgment was thus entered for plaintiff, and defendants appealed.

Joslin, Justice: . . . The question is whether the note is payable at a fixed . . . time. If the phrase "within ten (10) years after date" lacks explicitness or is ambiguous, then clearly parol [oral] evidence was admissible for the purpose of ascertaining the intention of the parties. . . . While the trial justice in admitting and accepting the extrinsic evidence apparently relied on [this principle], it is not applicable because the payment provisions of the note are not uncertain nor are they incomplete.

[Under] the law merchant it was generally settled that a promissory note or a bill of exchange payable "on or before" a specified date fixed with certainty the time of payment. The same rule has been fixed by statute first under the Negotiable Instruments Law, ... and now pursuant to the Uniform Commercial Code. The Code in Sec. 6A-3-109 (1) reads as follows: "An instrument is payable at a definite time if by its terms it is payable (a) on or before a stated date . . . ."

The courts in the cases we cite were primarily concerned with whether a provision for payment "on or before" a specified date impaired the negotiability of an instrument. Collaterally, of course, they necessarily considered whether such an instrument was payable at a [definite] time, for unless it was, an essential prerequisite to negotiability was lacking.

They said that the legal rights of the holder of an "on or before" instrument were clearly fixed and entitled him to payment upon an event that was certain to come, even though the maker might be privileged to pay sooner if he so elected. They held, therefore, that the due date of such an instrument was fixed with certainty and that its negotiability was unaffected *by the privilege given the maker* to accelerate payment. [Emphasis added.] ... Judge Cooley in *Mattison v. Marks* [cited earlier], observing that notes of this kind were common in commercial transactions, said:

> It seems certain to us that this note is payable at a time certain. It is payable certainly, and at all events, on a day particularly named; and at that time, *and not before,* payment might be enforced against the maker. . . . True, the maker may pay sooner if he shall choose, but this option, if exercised, would be a payment in advance of the legal liability, and nothing more. [Emphasis added.]

On principle no valid distinction can be drawn between an instrument payable "on or before" a fixed date and one which calls for payment "within" a stipulated period. This was the holding of *Leader v. Plante,* 95 Me. 339, where the court said: " 'Within' a certain period, 'on or before' a day named and 'at or before' a certain day, are equivalent terms and the rules of construction apply to each alike." ...

For the foregoing reasons it is clear that the parties unequivocally agreed that the plaintiff could not demand payment of the note until the expiration of the ten-year period. It is likewise clear that any prior . . . oral agreements of the parties relevant to its due date were so merged and integrated with the writing as to prevent its being explained or supplemented by parol evidence. . . .

Judgment reversed.

Acceleration Clauses: Instruments due at a fixed future date sometimes have clauses providing that the date of maturity shall be *moved ahead* if a specified event occurs prior to the stated due date. An instrument issued this year with a maturity date two years hence might contain, for example, either of these acceleration clauses: (1) "This instrument shall become immediately due and payable upon the maker's (or acceptor's) bankruptcy"; or (2) for a note payable in monthly installments: "If any installment is not paid when due, the entire instrument is due and payable."

Under Sec. 3-109(1)(c) all instruments with acceleration clauses meet the definite time test, even if the events upon which the acceleration is based are to some extent within the holder's control. To illustrate: "Should the holder deem himself insecure at any time prior to the maturity date, he can demand payment at such time and the entire instrument shall thereupon immediately become due and payable." However, the right of the holder to accelerate an instrument containing a clause such as this is subject to the good faith requirement contained in Sec. 1-208—that the clause "shall be construed to mean that he shall have the power [to accelerate] only if he in good faith believes that the prospect of payment or performance is impaired."

Extension Clauses: Extension clauses are the reverse of acceleration clauses; that is, they appear in notes or drafts having a fixed future maturity date and provide that, under certain circumstances, the date shall be *extended further*. Before enactment of the UCC this kind of clause posed a number of questions for the courts about their effect on negotiability. Virtually all these questions have been eliminated by UCC Sec. 3-109(1)(d), which provides that an instrument is negotiable if by its terms it is payable "at a definite time subject to extension at the option of the holder, or to extension to a further definite time at the option of the maker or acceptor or automatically upon or after a specified event."

Thus extension clauses that give the *obligor* (maker or acceptor) the right to extend the time of payment meet the definite time test only if they contain a new fixed maturity date. (The same is true for clauses that extend the time of payment automatically on the occurrence of a specified event.) On the other hand, clauses giving the *holder* the right to extend the time of payment need not contain a new fixed maturity date.

This distinction is logical. If the *obligor* had the right to extend payment without limit, neither that person nor any potential purchaser could determine with certainty when the holder had the absolute right to be paid. But when the *holder* has the option, he or she is free to demand payment at the maturity date or at any time thereafter. (Actually, the holder of any instrument is free to postpone the time of payment even if no extension clause appears.)

We can illustrate the primary effects of subsection d as follows:

1. "It is expressly agreed that the holder of this note at the date of maturity can extend the time of payment until the following Thanksgiving or even later if she wishes." *Result:* Negotiability is not destroyed, even though it is not known how long the extension will be, since the option is solely that of the holder.

2. "The maker has the unconditional right to postpone the time of payment of this note beyond its November 1, 1978, maturity date, but for no longer than a reasonable time after such date." *Result:* The definite time requirement is not met and the negotiability of the instrument is thus destroyed, since the right to extend is the maker's and since no further definite time is contained in the extension clause.

Payable upon Happening of Specified Event: As was indicated earlier, an instrument that is payable upon the happening of an event that may never occur (such as "upon the marriage of my daughter") is nonnegotiable for the reason that the promise or order to pay is clearly *conditional* in nature. The instrument remains nonnegotiable even if the event subsequently does occur (although it would, of course, become *payable* at that time.)

Sec. 3-109(2) goes one step farther by providing that "an instrument which by its terms is . . . payable only upon an act or event uncertain as to time of occurrence is not payable at a definite time even though the act or event has occurred." To illustrate: A draft is payable "upon the death of X." Even though X's death is an event that is certain to happen, the draft is nonnegotiable when issued, and remains nonnegotiable even after X's death. (Again, however, as in the prior example, the draft would become payable at that time.)

Payable to Order or to Bearer

It is fundamental to the concept of negotiability that the instrument contain language clearly indicating that the maker or drawer intends it to be fully capable of being transferred to some person or persons other than the one to whom it was originally issued. This is why Sec. 3-104(1)(d) states that the instrument must "be payable to order or to bearer." *Order* and *bearer* are frequently referred to as the "words of negotiability" (although any other words indicating a similar intention will also meet this requirement of the code).[4]

Order Instruments: Sec. 3-110 defines *order instrument* and helps interpret Sec. 3-104(1)(d). Essentially Sec. 3-110(1) provides that "an instrument is payable to order when by its terms it is payable to the order or assigns of any person therein specified with reasonable certainty, or to him or his order."[5] Additionally, the instrument can be payable "to the order of (a) the maker or drawer; or (b) the drawee; or (c) a payee who is not maker, drawer, or drawee; or (d) two or more payees together or in the alternative; or (e) an estate, trust or funds . . .; or (f) an office or an officer by his title as such . . .; or (g) a partnership or unincorporated association . . . "

The requirements of the order instrument are met by such language as "pay to the order of Jennifer Howell" and "pay to Melanie Howell or order." However, an instrument "payable to Charles Menkel" is not an order instrument and therefore is nonnegotiable.

---

[4]We are here concerned with the order/bearer requirement only as it affects *negotiability* of an instrument, but the requirement also affects the manner in which instruments are to be *transferred.* As we will see in the next chapter, a bearer instrument can be "negotiated" to a third party without being indorsed by the transferor, while an indorsement is essential for order instruments.

[5]*Assigns* simply means all third parties to whom the instrument might subsequently be transferred.

Bearer Instruments: A note or draft that fails to qualify as an order instrument is nonetheless negotiable if it is payable to the *bearer*. Sec. 3-111 provides that "an instrument is payable to bearer when by its terms it is payable to (a) bearer or the order of bearer; or (b) a specified person or bearer; or (c) 'cash' or the order of 'cash,' or any other indication which does not purport to designate a specific payee."

Under this section the following all qualify as bearer instruments: "payable to bearer," "payable to the order of bearer," and "payable to X or bearer." However, an instrument that is payable only to a specified person ("payable to X") is not payable to bearer and hence is nonnegotiable.[6]

The following case presents the general question of whether postal money orders meet the tests of negotiability. In making its decision the court had to determine, among other things, if such instruments meet the "payable to order" requirement. As is often the case in real life, a second but related clause appearing in the instruments also entered the picture.

Joseph MacDonald stole sixty-three domestic money order blanks and an "all purpose dating stamp" from two post offices. Thereafter he completed the money orders so that they were payable to a fictitious person, wrote in a fictitious initial of a supposed employee of one of the post offices, and impressed the mark of the stolen validating dating stamp on the instruments.

On the back of each money order appeared the following:

PAYEE MUST ENDORSE BELOW ON LINE MARKED 'PAYEE.'

OWNERSHIP OF THIS ORDER MAY BE TRANSFERRED TO ANOTHER PERSON OR FIRM IF THE PAYEE WILL WRITE THE NAME OF SUCH PERSON OR FIRM ON THE LINE MARKED 'PAY TO' BEFORE WRITING HIS OWN NAME ON THE SECOND LINE. MORE THAN ONE ENDORSEMENT IS PROHIBITED BY LAW. BANK STAMPS ARE NOT REGARDED AS ENDORSEMENTS.

PAY TO _____

THIS ORDER BECOMES INVALID AFTER 20 YEARS. THEREAFTER NO CLAIM FOR PAYMENT WILL BE CONSIDERED

A number of the money orders were indorsed to the First National Bank, defendant, and were honored by it. The bank presented the orders to the U.S. and was paid the full amount of $100 for each of the money orders by the U.S. The U.S., after learning the facts, brought action against the defendant bank to recover the amount of money it had paid out to that bank.

United States v. The First National Bank of Boston
U.S. District Court, District of Massachusetts, 263 F. Supp. 298 (1967)

---

[6]In Chapter 22 we said that in general Article 3 of the UCC does not apply to nonnegotiable instruments. The exception to this rule is the kind of instrument mentioned here. According to Sec. 3-805, Article 3 "applies to any instrument whose terms do not preclude transfer and which is otherwise negotiable within this Article but which is not payable to order or to bearer, except that there can be no holder in due course of such an instrument."

Wyzanski, Chief Justice: This case . . . presents . . . the question whether when a stolen postal domestic money order . . . is bought by a good faith indorsee [the defendant bank], and that indorsee has received payment from the United States, the United States may recover back its payment from the indorsee. . . .

[The] broadest contention [of defendant bank] is that today the postal domestic money order, unlike its pre-1951 prototype, is a negotiable instrument within the meaning of the Uniform Commercial Code and that it is therefore proper to apply to it Sec. 3-418 of the Code which provides that "payment . . . of any instrument is final in favor of a holder in due course, or a person who has in good faith changed his position in reliance on the payment . . . ."

There is difficulty in sustaining this broad contention. [It is true that the money order meets the requirement that it be "payable to order or bearer," in view of the fact that the] order states that "ownership . . . may be transferred to another person or firm" [by indorsement]. However, the money order adds . . . that "More than one indorsement is prohibited by law."

Such a restriction is contrary to § 3-301 of the Uniform Commercial Code, which provides that "the holder of an instrument whether or not he is the owner *may transfer and negotiate it,"* and is out of harmony with § 3-206(1), which provides that "No restrictive indorsement prevents further transfer or negotiation of the instrument." *Thus it cannot be said that in all respects a postal domestic money order is like the ordinary negotiable instrument covered by modern codes and statutes.* [Emphasis added.]

[While the court thus rejected the defendant bank's contention that the money orders were negotiable (because of the clause restricting their circulation), in the remaining part of its decision the court nonetheless *ruled in favor of the bank,* citing three "policy considerations" that it felt should prevent the United States from recovering from an innocent bank in these particular circumstances.]

Miscellaneous Order/Bearer Problems: An "apparent" order instrument may exist where the payee's name is omitted ("payable to the order of _____"). Such a note or draft is an incomplete instrument, failing to qualify as either an order or a bearer paper. It is not payable to order, for it does not meet the requirement of Sec. 3-110(1) that it be payable to a "person specified with reasonable certainty." Neither does it qualify as a bearer instrument under Sec. 3-111(c)—although if it is subsequently completed by the addition of a payee's name, at that time it will ordinarily meet the order definition.

In rare instances—usually through inadvertence of the maker or drawer—a hybrid order may occur ("pay to the order of Melanie Howell or bearer"). Under Sec. 3-110(3) such an instrument is an order instrument "unless the bearer words are handwritten or typewritten." The assumption is that if the words *or bearer* are simply part of the printed form, presumably the maker or drawer intended that the name of the payee written in the blank space should control. But if the words *or bearer* are added by the maker or drawer, then presumably they should control and the instrument is thus a *bearer* note or draft.

The negotiability of most instruments is settled by reference to the basic sections we have examined. Occasionally, however, instruments present special problems—sometimes because they contain terms not covered by the preceding sections, sometimes because terms are omitted that normally are present, and sometimes because they contain provisions that are in apparent conflict. Secs. 3-112 through 3-118 are designed to resolve most peripheral problems of this sort. We will discuss below the more important of these rules.

Terms and Omissions Not Affecting Negotiability

Selected Sec. 3-112 Rules

Omissions: Sec. 3-112 provides in part that the negotiability of an instrument is not affected by "the omission of a statement of any consideration, or of the place where the instrument is drawn or payable." This provision thus rejects the possible view that such omissions cause an instrument to be incomplete and therefore nonnegotiable. (Along similar lines, Sec. 3-114 states that the negotiability of an instrument is not destroyed simply because the date of issue does not appear—unless, of course, the date of maturity is tied to the date of issue, as when an undated note is "payable sixty days after date.")

Additional Powers and Promises: We have seen that under Sec. 3-104(1)(b) any instrument containing a promise or order *in addition to* the "promise or order to pay a sum certain in money" causes the instrument to be nonnegotiable "except as authorized by this Article." Several of these additional promises are expressly authorized by Subsections b and c of Sec. 3-112.

Subsection b states that the negotiability of an instrument is not affected by a statement that collateral has been given as security for the obligation. Nor is it affected by a promise on the part of the maker, drawer, or acceptor to *maintain,* to *protect,* or to *give additional collateral* in specified circumstances. To illustrate: The maker of a time note has given the payee a warehouse receipt for six hundred bags of beans in the X Warehouse as security. The note further provides that "if a decline in the market value of this collateral should cause the holder of this instrument to deem himself insecure, the maker shall deliver additional collateral upon demand." This note is negotiable.

The reason why Sec. 3-112 provides that the stipulations noted above do not destroy negotiability lies in the fact that the stipulations actually *enhance* the value of the basic obligation, rather than limiting or conditioning it. Thus the instruments are more freely acceptable in commerce and even better able to fulfill their role as substitutes for money or as credit instruments than would be the case were the clauses absent.

1. Sain Builders gave a $4,000 promissory note to Samuel Feinberg, with whom it had an existing contract. Feinberg later negotiated the note to a Mr. D'Andrea. The note contained

Questions and Problems

a clear-cut promise to pay, and was negotiable in all other respects, but in the lower left hand corner Sain Builders had written in the words "as per contract." Does this inscription destroy negotiability of the instrument? Why or why not? (*D'Andrea v. Feinberg,* 256 N.Y.S.2d 504, 1965).

2. City X is authorized to borrow money to finance certain improvements within the city; residents benefiting from such improvements are to pay special assessment taxes. City X signs a note with a local bank for $250,000, payable in three yearly installments at a rate of nine percent interest. The note states that "payment is conditional upon payment of special assessment taxes based on improvements made with money received from this loan." If you are the local bank president and are asked by your loan officer whether the note is negotiable, what would your answer be? Explain.

3. A law firm performed legal services for a client. Later the client wrote this letter: "I agree to pay to your firm as attorney's fees for representing me in obtaining property settlement agreement and tax advice, the sum of $2,760, payable at the rate of $230 per month for twelve (12) months beginning January 1, 1970. (Signed) Barbara Hall Lodge." Is this written promise a negotiable instrument? Why or why not? (*Hall v. Westmoreland et al.,* 182 S.E.2d 539, 1971).

4. Following is a promissory note, written entirely in longhand: "I, the undersigned, hereby promise to pay to the order of Kevin Smith or bearer on January 2, 1983, one hundred dollars. Should I become bankrupt at any time, the entire sum shall be immediately due and payable upon demand of the holder. (Signed) Mark Gibson."

(a) Is this instrument payable to order, or to bearer? Explain.
(b) Does the acceleration clause destroy negotiability of the instrument? Explain.

5. Holly Hills Acres, Ltd., executed a promissory note and a mortgage securing it and delivered both instruments to the payee, Rogers and Blythe. Part of the note read as follows: "This note with interest is secured by a mortgage on real estate . . . made by the maker hereof in favor of the said payee, and shall be construed and enforced according to the laws of the State of Florida. The terms of said mortgage are by this reference made a part hereof." Does this writing affect the negotiability of the note? Why or why not? (*Holly Hill Acres, Ltd., v. Charter Bank of Gainesville,* 17 UCC Rep. 144, 1975).

6. In the case of *Walls v. Morris Chevrolet,* on page 415, the maker of the note argued that the note met the "sum certain" requirement in view of the fact that the attached security agreement did indicate the precise amount of the finance charge involved. Give two reasons why the appellate court rejected this contention.

7. M is the maker of a note "payable on or before June 1, 1983."

(a) Does this clause give the *maker* the right to pay the instrument before the due date, or does it give the *holder* the right to demand payment before the due date? What is the basis for your answer?
(b) Does the clause destroy the negotiability of the note? Explain.

8. Grinch is the maker of a note payable on May 1, 1984. The note contains a clause giving him the right to extend the time of payment "no more than six months" by giving notice of extension to the holder. Does this clause destroy the negotiability of the instrument? Why or why not?

Commercial Paper/   24
Transfer and Negotiation

In Chapter 23 we dealt with only one basic topic—the requirements for negotiability. We noted, however, that commercial paper is designed primarily for the purpose of circulating freely in the business world. In this chapter we will look at the various ways such paper can be transferred from one holder to another and at the basic UCC rules that apply to such transfers.

A negotiable instrument has no legal significance of and by itself. In other words, its legal life does not begin until it is issued by the maker or drawer to the first holder.[1] After it has been issued to that person, it can be further transferred by him or her in one of two ways—by *negotiation* or by *assignment*.[2] While we shall

Assignment and Negotiation

---

[1]*Issue* is defined in Sec. 3-102(1)(a) as "the first delivery of an instrument to a holder."

[2]By contrast, the transfer of a nonnegotiable instrument *always* constitutes an assignment, no matter how the transfer is effected. This is because the negotiation provisions of Article 3 apply only to *negotiable instruments* (as is true of all other provisions of that article).

be concerned in this chapter primarily with the legal requirements of a negotiation and the significant rights and duties that flow from it, we will first distinguish between the two kinds of transfers.

If a payee or other holder of an instrument transfers it to a third party in such a manner that the transfer qualifies as a negotiation under the UCC, the transferee is by definition a holder of the instrument. This makes it possible for the transferee to qualify as a holder in due course (HDC) if he or she meets the other HDC requirements of Article 3. As an HDC the person can acquire *greater rights* under the instrument than those possessed by the transferor.

Assignment

If the transfer fails to qualify as a negotiation, it is merely an *assignment,* and the transferee is an *assignee* rather than a holder. As such, his or her status is governed by the common law contract rules discussed in Chapter 15, under which the transferee's rights cannot be greater than those of the transferor. Obviously, then, the purchaser of a negotiable instrument will almost always want to be sure that the transfer qualifies as a negotiation rather than an assignment.

Negotiation

The definition of *negotiation* and the requirements that must be met in order for the transfer of a particular instrument to qualify as a negotiation are found in Sec. 3-202(1): "Negotiation is the transfer of an instrument in such form that the transferee becomes a holder. If the instrument is payable to order it is negotiated by delivery with any necessary indorsement; if payable to bearer, it is negotiated by delivery [alone]."[3]

The requirements that must be met, then, in order for a particular transfer to qualify as a negotiation depend entirely upon the form of the instrument at the time of transfer. Before we examine the various kinds of indorsements that can be used, we will illustrate the basic delivery/indorsement requirements.

Case 1. M issues two notes to X, one "payable to bearer" and the other "payable to cash." Because both notes are obviously bearer instruments, X can further negotiate either or both of them to a subsequent purchaser, Y, simply by handing them or mailing them to Y without an indorsement of any kind. (In practice, the purchaser of a bearer instrument normally requests the transferor to indorse it, but the indorsement is not required by the UCC.)

Case 2. Same facts as for Case 1, except that the two notes are stolen from X's home by a thief, T. Because *delivery* means a voluntary delivery by the transferor, T's acquisition of the notes in this manner does not constitute a delivery; hence,

---

[3]The issuance of an instrument to the payee technically constitutes a negotiation in view of the fact that the payee (as we saw in Chapter 22) is one of the persons who qualifies as a holder under Sec. 1-201(20). However, in actual practice *negotiation* refers only to transfers that occur after an instrument has been issued.

no negotiation has occurred. However, a further delivery of either note by T to a third party does constitute a negotiation. This points up one of the dangers arising from the use of a bearer instrument. While a thief (or a finder) does not acquire title to the instrument by virtue of the theft (or finding), he or she can *transfer title* to a subsequent innocent purchaser. In such a case, the original owner, X, has lost all rights to the instrument itself.

Case 3. D draws a check that is "payable to the order of P" and mails it to P. P writes her name on the back of the check (an indorsement) and transfers it to her grocer, G, in payment for groceries. The transfer from P to G constitutes a negotiation of this order instrument, since indorsement and delivery have both occurred. However, if P had delivered the instrument without indorsement, it would not suffice. (G's rights in such a case will be discussed near the end of this chapter.)

Case 4. B draws a check that is "payable to the order of C" and mails it to C. T, a thief, steals the note, signs C's name on the back, and delivers it to R, a retailer, in payment for liquor. The transfer from T to R is not a negotiation (nor is it even an assignment) because a forged "indorsement" is no indorsement. Nor would a further transfer by R constitute a negotiation; no one can qualify as a holder under a forged indorsement on an order instrument.

Essentially there are four kinds of indorsements: blank, special, qualified, and restrictive.

Blank, Special, Qualified, and Restrictive Indorsements

Blank Indorsements

Under Sec. 3-204(1) a *blank indorsement* is one that specifies no particular indorsee; ordinarily it consists only of the name of the payee. Thus, if a check is payable "to the order of Mary Glenn," she can indorse it in blank by simply writing or stamping her name on the back of the indorsement.[4]

A blank indorsement converts an order instrument into a bearer instrument. Thus, if Mary Glenn delivers the check to Harold Baker after indorsing it, Baker can further negotiate the check by delivery only. A blank indorsement makes the instrument virtually as transferable as cash, and for that reason the instrument should ordinarily be indorsed only at the time it is actually delivered to the transferee.

A person who receives an instrument bearing a blank indorsement can protect himself or herself against the possibility of loss of title through subsequent negotia-

---

[4]Indorsements are ordinarily written on the instrument itself. However, under Sec. 3-202(2), if there are so many indorsements on the back of an instrument that there is no room for more, subsequent indorsements can be written "on a paper so firmly affixed thereto as to become a part thereof." Such a paper, called an *allonge,* must be firmly pasted or stapled to the instrument; attachment by paper clip alone will not suffice.

tion by a thief. Sec. 3-204(3) provides that a "holder may convert a blank indorsement into a special indorsement by writing over the signature of the indorser in blank any contract consistent with the character of the indorsement." Thus, where the instrument was indorsed "Mary Glenn" and delivered to Harold Baker, Baker can write above the Glenn signature such words as "pay to the order of Harold Baker." The instrument is now "indorsed specially" and cannot be negotiated further without Baker's indorsement. (Special indorsements will be discussed later in the chapter.)

Effect of Indorsement: A blank indorsement has three effects:

1. It transfers title to the instrument to the indorsee on delivery.

2. It extends certain warranties to the indorsee and all subsequent holders.

3. It imposes a legal obligation on the indorser to pay the amount of the instrument to the person holding it at maturity if the maker, acceptor, or drawee does not pay (and if certain other conditions are met). This obligation is sometimes called "conditional" or "secondary" liability of the blank indorser.[5]

The following case involves the negotiation of a note by a hospital—through the use of a blank indorsement—to a bank, and a subsequent retransfer of the instrument by the bank back to the hospital. (Following this case, our examination of the other types of indorsements will be resumed.)

Westerly Hospital v. Higgins

Supreme Court of Rhode Island, 256 A.2d 506 (1969)

Higgins, in consideration for services rendered by the plaintiff hospital in connection with the birth of a child to his wife, executed a promissory note payable to the order of the hospital. The note, cosigned by Mrs. Higgins, was payable in eighteen monthly installments.

An authorized officer of the hospital indorsed the note by *blank indorsement* and negotiated it to the Industrial National Bank (hereafter referred to as Industrial), with the hospital receiving cash in return. The indorsement contained a clause under which the hospital guaranteed payment of principal and interest in the event that the maker, Higgins, should default on the obligation.

Higgins made only the three initial payments to Industrial. As a result of this default the hospital paid Industrial the balance due, as it was obligated to do by the guarantee clause. Industrial then redelivered the note to the hospital, which subsequently brought action against Higgins to recover the balance.

At the trial Higgins contended that the redelivery of the note by Industrial to the hospital did not constitute a negotiation, that the hospital was therefore not a holder of the instrument, and that it consequently could not bring this suit. These contentions were based on evidence indicating that (1) at the time Industrial

---

[5]The warranty and conditional liabilities mentioned here arise from Secs. 3-417(1) and 3-414(1) respectively. Their nature and extent are covered in Chapter 27.

redelivered the note one of its employees indorsed the instrument on Industrial's behalf, and (2) such indorsement was invalid because the employee *possessed no authority* to make the indorsement.

The trial court, for reasons appearing in the decision below, rejected Higgins's contentions and entered judgment for the plaintiff hospital. Higgins appealed.

Roberts, Chief Justice: . . . The defendant contends that the trial justice's ruling granting . . . judgment to plaintiff was error because a genuine issue existed as to whether Westerly Hospital *or Industrial* was in fact the proper party to bring the instant action on the note. We cannot agree with this contention. . . .

The face of the instrument reveals that Westerly Hospital was the payee of the note made by defendant and his wife as co-makers. It further discloses that an indorsement of guarantee was executed in blank [by the] plaintiff hospital. The note was then delivered to Industrial [which then became a holder of the instrument]. . . . Thereafter, when defendant defaulted, Industrial redelivered the note to plaintiff in return for the payment of the remaining amount of defendant's obligation that had been guaranteed by plaintiff hospital, [and it is the validity of this second transfer that is at issue here].

The defendant argues that this delivery of the note [by Industrial] back to plaintiff was not sufficient to constitute a negotiation [for the reason that the representative of Industrial who indorsed the instrument on Industrial's behalf did not possess the authority to do so]. Thus, according to defendant, . . . Westerly Hospital was precluded from becoming a holder of the instrument, . . . and Industrial was the proper party to bring the action on this note [rather than the hospital].

However, [Sec. 3-204] of the Uniform Commercial Code states, in pertinent part, that "An instrument payable to order and indorsed in blank becomes payable to bearer and may be negotiated by delivery alone until specially indorsed." Here Westerly Hospital as payee of the note caused its indorsement to appear thereon without specifying to whom or to whose order the instrument was payable. Instead, a blank indorsement, one specifying no particular indorsee, was made. The legal effect of such an indorsement and delivery was to authorize Industrial as the transferee and holder of the note *to further negotiate the note without indorsement but by mere delivery alone. It is clear that any attempt on its part to achieve negotiation by indorsing the note to plaintiff would have been mere surplusage.* [Emphasis added.]

In our opinion, then, the redelivery of the note in question by Industrial to Westerly Hospital accomplished a negotiation of the instrument, and the fact that a purported special indorsement to Westerly Hospital was not legally executed is of no consequence and does not affect plaintiff's status as the holder of the note. It is our conclusion that in these circumstances [the ruling of the trial court was correct].

Judgment affirmed.

Special Indorsements

Under Sec. 3-204(1), "a special indorsement specifies the person to whom or to whose order it makes the instrument payable." To illustrate: A check is payable to the order of P, and he indorses it, "Pay to the order of X, (signed) P." An instrument indorsed in this manner remains an order instrument, and X's indorsement will be necessary for a further negotiation to occur. An indorsement need not, however, include words of negotiability; thus an indorsement "Pay to X, (signed) P" has the same legal effect as "Pay to the order of X, (signed) P."

A special indorsement on a bearer instrument converts it into an order instrument. To illustrate: A note is "payable to bearer." The first holder, H, indorses it, "Pay to the order of X, (signed) H" and then delivers it to X. X's indorsement is now necessary for a further negotiation of the instrument. However, if X indorses it in *blank,* it is now reconverted to a bearer instrument.

The primary effect of a special indorsement, then, is that it requires the indorsement of the special indorsee before it can be negotiated further.

Qualified Indorsements

Blank and special indorsements are "unqualified" indorsements for the reason that indorsers who use them incur what is called conditional liability on the instruments negotiated in this manner. Specifically, such indorsers are promising to pay the instruments themselves if the holder is unable to obtain payment from the maker, acceptor, or drawee at maturity. A blank or special indorser, then, is actually guaranteeing payment of the instrument in addition to transferring title to it.

A *qualified indorsement,* by contrast, is one whose wording indicates that the indorser is not guaranteeing payment of the instrument. The usual qualified indorsement is "*without recourse,* (signed) X," and the precise effect is illustrated as follows: P receives a check in the mail, drawn on an out-of-town bank and payable to his order. He indorses it "without recourse, (signed) P" and negotiates it to H. H deposits the check in his account at a local bank, but a week later the bank returns it to him because the drawer did not have sufficient funds in his account. Because P indorsed the instrument qualifiedly, H cannot recover the amount of the dishonored check from him.

Except for eliminating the conditional liability of the indorser, a qualified indorsement has the same general effect as an unqualified (blank or special) indorsement. "Without recourse" indorsements thus transfer title to the indorsee, permitting further negotiation of the instrument. They also impose a warranty liability on the indorser that is quite similar to the liability of the blank and special indorsers (see Chapter 27 for details).

Restrictive Indorsements

It is difficult to make broad generalizations about restrictive indorsements, because the UCC recognizes four distinctly separate kinds. Nonetheless, two observations do apply to all of them:

1. Under Sec. 3-206(1) restrictive indorsements are similar to the other indorsements discussed in this chapter in that they do not (despite their name) restrict the further negotiation of any instrument so indorsed.

2. They differ from the other indorsements by restricting the rights of the indorsee in order to give certain protection to the indorser.

According to Sec. 3-205:

An indorsement is restrictive which either (a) is conditional; or (b) purports to prohibit further transfer of the instrument; or (c) includes the words "for collection," "for deposit," "pay any bank," or like terms signifying a purpose of deposit or collection; or (d) otherwise states that it is for the benefit or use of the indorser or of another person.

Conditional Indorsements: As the name indicates, *a conditional indorsement* is an order to pay the instrument only if a specified event occurs. As such, the indorsement imposes a condition on the indorsee's right to collect the proceeds of the instrument. This kind of indorsement is not common, but it is useful in certain situations, particularly when combined with a special indorsement. To illustrate: "Pay to the order of Karen R. Jones upon her delivery to me of one hundred shares of AT&T stock as per our agreement of last November. (Signed) Paul Miller."

Such an indorsement has three basic effects:

1. It does not prohibit further negotiation of the instrument, regardless of whether the condition has or has not occurred.

2. Until the stated condition does occur, however, neither the restrictive indorsee nor any subsequent holder has the right to enforce the instrument.

3. In the event that a holder does receive payment from the maker (or drawee) when the condition has not yet occurred, both the maker (or drawee) and the holder remain liable to the restrictive indorser for the amount of the instrument.

Special bank rules. Because of the large volume of commercial paper handled in the bank collection process, certain banks in that process are permitted to disregard any restrictive indorsements (including, of course, conditional indorsements). This result flows from Sec. 3-206(2), which provides that "an intermediary bank, or a payor bank which is not the depositary bank, is neither given notice nor otherwise affected by a restrictive indorsement of any person excepting the bank's immediate transferor or the person presenting for payment." To illustrate: D, in Worthington, Ohio, draws a check on his Worthington bank and mails it to P, payee, in Bozeman, Montana. P indorses it conditionally and cashes it at his Bozeman bank. The check, now in the bank collection process, is forwarded to a Billings bank, thence to a Chicago bank, and ultimately to the drawee bank in Worthington. Under Sec. 3-206, the Worthington bank may honor the instrument even if the condition specified in the indorsement has not occurred. Neither that bank nor the Billings or Chicago banks could be held liable to the restrictive indorser in such a situation.[6]

Indorsements Purporting to Prohibit Further Negotiation: Sec. 3-205(b) refers to indorsements that intend to prohibit further negotiation—for example, "Pay to

---

[6]Here the Bozeman bank is the "depositary bank," the Billings and Chicago banks "intermediary banks," and the Worthington bank the "payor" (and drawee) bank.

the order of X only, (signed) P." Under pre-UCC law such an indorsement terminated negotiability of the instrument, and no subsequent purchaser could qualify as a holder. While this kind of indorsement is used rarely today, the drafters of the UCC reversed the common-law view. Sec. 3-206(1) provides expressly that "no restrictive indorsement prevents further transfer or negotiation of the instrument." Thus a "pay to X only" or "pay to the order of X only" indorsent has the same legal effect as a special indorsement, and an instrument indorsed in this manner can be further negotiated by X upon proper indorsement and delivery by him or her.

"For Collection" and "For Deposit" Indorsements: Indorsements for collection and for deposit are by far the most commonly used types of restrictive indorsements. Instruments indorsed in either way are almost always put directly into the bank collection process. Under Sec. 3-206(3), in such situations any depositary bank receiving the instrument is responsible for acting consistently with the terms of the indorsement, which ordinarily means that it must credit the restrictive indorser's account.

The protection afforded to the restrictive indorser is best illustrated by a situation where the transferee/depositary bank fails to live up to the duty imposed by Sec. 3-206: D draws and delivers a check payable to P. P indorses the check, "For deposit, (signed) P" and gives the check to his accountant, A, to deposit in P's bank. P's bank gives A cash for the check (or credits A's account), and the cash is not in fact turned over to P (or the funds in A's account are not subsequently made available to P). P can now maintain an *action of conversion* against the bank, and the bank will be liable because it clearly has acted inconsistently with the terms of the restrictive indorsement.

Special bank rules. As indicated in the discussion of conditional indorsements, drawee and intermediary banks holding restrictively indorsed paper do not have the responsibility that is imposed on depositary banks. Thus, under Sec. 3-206(2), drawee and intermediary banks in possession of instruments indorsed "for collection" or "for deposit" are neither given notice of nor affected by such indorsements. In other words, these banks cannot be held liable to the restrictive indorser if the restrictive indorsee/depositary bank fails to act consistently with the terms of the indorsements.

A similar type of restrictive indorsement is the *pay any bank or banker indorsement.* This is expressly deemed a restrictive indorsement under Sec. 3-206(3), and the rules applicable to it are the same as those for the other types of restrictive indorsements discussed in this section.

Trust Indorsements: The fourth type of restrictive indorsement is one which by its terms shows an intent to benefit the indorser or some third party; it is frequently referred to as a *trust or agency indorsement.* For example: "Pay to A as agent of P, (signed) P," and "Pay to A in trust for B, (signed) P." In these situations, two results flow from the indorsements. (1) When the restrictive indorsee, A, receives payment of the instrument, he holds the proceeds in trust for the named beneficiary. (2) Any subsequent purchaser of the instrument takes it free of the restriction, and thus qualifies as an HDC unless he or she has actual knowledge that A's negotiation of the instrument is a breach of A's fiduciary duty.

The case below serves notice on bank officers of the unfortunate circumstances that may befall a bank when an employee (or, perhaps, *ex*-employee) takes an instrument without noticing that it has been restrictively indorsed.

American Fidelity Fire Insurance Company, plaintiff, was a surety of the Quantum Development Corporation. (A *surety* is a person or firm who has made himself or itself responsible for the debts or other obligations of another.)

Quantum Development went into bankruptcy in March of 1973. Soon thereafter American Fidelity, responding to its obligations as surety, delivered a certified check in the amount of $84,858 to the clerk of the bankruptcy court, who delivered the check to Charles Joy, the receiver of the bankrupt firm. The check was made payable to "Charles R. Joy, Receiver," and the bankruptcy judge ordered Joy to put the bulk of the money into certificates of deposit in Quantum Development's name, and the balance into a checking account for Quantum Development.

Joy took the check to the manager of a branch of the Bank of Nova Scotia (BNS), a Mr. Chandler, and purchased $75,000 worth of certificates of deposit with the check. (The balance of approximately $9,000 was placed in a checking account in Joy's name.) Although Joy indorsed the check "For Deposit in Quantum Acct. Quantum Bankruptcy, Charles R. Joy," the bank made out the CDs in the name of Joy *personally*.

Six months later, when the CDs matured, Joy cashed them at the bank and vanished with the money. Thereafter American Fidelity brought this action against BNS to recover the value of the CDs. (The decision below is that of the trial court.)

In Re Quantum Development Corp.; American Fidelity Fire Ins. Co. v. Joy; Lang v. Bank of Nova Scotia

U.S. District Court, Virgin Islands, D. St. Croix, 397 F.Supp. 329 (1975)

Young, Justice: . . . As heretofore noted, the check which Joy presented to Mr. Chandler was payable to "Charles R. Joy, Receiver," and bore on the back the indorsement "For Deposit in Quantum Acc. Quantum Bankruptcy, Charles R. Joy." A perusal of § 3-205 of the Uniform Commercial Code, intended to provide a functional definition of the term "restrictive indorsement," leaves little doubt that the foregoing fits within the prescription:

> "An indorsement is restrictive which either . . . (c) includes the words 'for collection,' 'for deposit,' 'pay any bank,' or like terms signifying a purpose of deposit or collection; or (d) otherwise states that it is for the benefit or use of the indorser or of another person."

The indorsement clearly indicates that it was for the benefit or use of the Quantum bankruptcy estate.

The recognized purpose of a restrictive indorsement *is to restrict the use to which the indorsee may put the proceeds of the instrument when a party pays them to the indorsee.* [Emphasis added.] [Although] no section of the UCC specifically requires an indorsee-bank to examine the restriction and to ensure that its payment is not inconsistent therewith, . . .

such duty and resulting liability for the failure to carry out such duty can be fairly inferred from a number of Code sections.

Section 3-206(2), for example, permits an intermediary bank, or a payor bank *which is not the depositary bank,* to disregard any restrictive indorsement except that of the bank's immediate transferor. . . . [But] it is clear under the facts of the instant case [that] BNS stands in the position of the depositary bank rather than an intermediary bank. Thus, at least by negative implication, . . . the Code provides a remedy in conversion against a *depositary bank* which fails to pay or apply the proceeds in accordance with the terms of a restrictive indorsement. [Emphasis added.] . . .

By his own admission, Mr. Chandler never examined the indorsement on the check, which indorsement was made in his presence. Instead, he merely instructed his secretary to make out the CDs in accordance with Mr. Joy's wishes. Certainly, such actions on the part of BNS's branch manager do not comport with reasonable commercial standards. The very least Chandler could have done was to ensure that the inscription on the CDs corresponded to that on the original check. Although he noticed that the check was made out to Joy in his representative capacity, Chandler made no effort to ascertain for whom Joy was a receiver. . . .

Ignoring the restrictive indorsement inscribed on the back of a check in the substantial amount of over $84,000, the bank proceeded to issue to Mr. Joy in his personal and individual capacity the CDs in the amount of $25,000 each. Although the bank officials in no way participated in the extreme breach of trust of which Mr. Joy was guilty, their placing the CDs in Joy's individual name provided the opportunity and encouragement which Joy may have needed to perpetrate his scheme. . . .

Judgment for the plaintiff to be paid by the defendant BNS for the sum of $77,664.54 plus interest.

Miscellaneous Negotiation Problems

A discussion of several peripheral problems not covered by the general rules will conclude the subject of negotiation.

Multiple Payees: Under Sec. 3-116(a), instruments are sometimes payable to two or more alternative persons ("pay to the order of A or B"). Negotiation of such an instrument requires only the indorsement of either of the payees. On the other hand, under Sec. 3-116(b), if the instrument is payable to the parties jointly ("pay to A and B"), then both indorsements are required for a further negotiation of the instrument.

Correction of Names: Sec. 3-203 is self-explanatory; it provides that "where an instrument is made payable to a person under a misspelled name or [a name] other than his own, he may indorse in that name or his own or both; but signature in both names may be required by a person paying or giving value for the instrument."

Transfer of Unindorsed Order Paper: If an order instrument is transferred without the indorsement of the payee, the transferee is not a holder of the instrument and therefore cannot negotiate it. He or she does, however, have the right (by legal action, if necessary) to require the transferor to indorse the instrument. Upon receiving the indorsement the transferee qualifies as a holder.

There is one exception to the rule that the transferee of an unindorsed order paper cannot negotiate the instrument further. Sec. 4-205 permits a depositary bank that received such a check either to supply its customer's indorsement or simply to note on the instrument that it has credited the check to its customer/depositor's account. In either case the bank is a holder and can negotiate the instrument further.

The following case shows how well this exception worked out for the defendant, a depositary bank.

Cole v. First National Bank of Gillette
Supreme Court of Wyoming, 433 P.2d 837 (1967)

Clarence and Wilma Cole, plaintiffs, purchased a home from Wyoming Homes of Gillette, Wyoming. As a down payment on the contract Mrs. Cole gave a Wyoming Homes salesman a $4,000 check.

The check was drawn by Buffalo Auto Supply (a company owned by the Coles) on that company's account in the First National Bank of Buffalo, Wyoming, and it was payable to the order of Wyoming Homes. The salesman took the check to the First National Bank of Gillette and, without indorsing it, deposited it in the Wyoming Homes account with that bank.

The Gillette bank stamped the check "First National Bank, Gillette, Wyoming, For Deposit Only" and put it into the bank collection process. The check reached the drawee bank in Buffalo, and the $4,000 was duly charged to the Buffalo Auto Supply account. Thereafter the Coles claimed that Wyoming Homes (1) had failed to give consideration and (2) was guilty of fraud in the sale of the home.

The Coles brought action against the First National Bank of Gillette on the theory that it was merely a transferee of the check and had only the rights of the transferor, Wyoming Homes, in view of the fact Wyoming Homes did not indorse the check on depositing it in the Gillette bank. As a result, the Coles contended that the Gillette bank was not a holder in due course, or even a holder of the check as defined by the UCC, and that the bank thus took the check subject to the defenses of failure of consideration and fraud.

The trial court rejected plaintiffs' contentions and entered summary judgment for the defendant. The Coles appealed, claiming that the Supreme Court of Wyoming should, as a matter of law, reverse that judgment.

Harnsberger, Chief Justice: . . . Appellants' first argument is that under [a number of cited sections of the UCC] the appellee owned merely an equitable title to the check which was subject to all defenses available to its maker.

In the view we take, only § 34-4-205 is of major importance, with the possible exception of § 34-4-201, W. S. 1957 (1965 Cum. Supp.). Section 34-4-205 clearly authorized the Gillette bank, as the depositary bank taking the check for collection, *to place a statement on the check to the effect that the item was credited to the account of a customer, which statement is said to be as effective as the customer's endorsement.* [Emphasis added.] This was done. The section is as follows:

(1) A depositary bank which has taken an item for collection may supply any indorsement of the customer which is necessary to title unless the item contains the words "payee's endorsement required" or the like. In the absence of such a requirement a statement placed on the item by the depositary bank to the effect that the item was deposited by a customer or credited to his account is effective as the customer's indorsement.

(2) An intermediary bank, or payor bank which is not a depositary, is neither given notice nor otherwise affected by a restrictive indorsement of any person except the bank's immediate transferor.

Any question as to whether Wyoming Homes was such a "customer" within the meaning of § 34-4-205 is answered by § 34-4-104(e), W. S. 1957 (1965 Cum. Supp.), reading, "'Customer' means any person having an account with a bank or for whom a bank has agreed to collect items and includes a bank carrying an account with another bank."

It follows that the Gillette bank having credited the amount of the check to the account of its payee and a final settlement of the item having been made, the bank did not step into the shoes of the payee or become subject to any equities between the check's maker or its payee. *Thus matters of possible failure of consideration or of fraud relate solely to matters between the Coles and Wyoming Homes, to which transactions the appellee was not a party.* [Emphasis added.]

The judgment of the trial court is affirmed.

Rescission of Indorsements: Sometimes the indorsement and delivery of an instrument are made under circumstances in which the indorser, under ordinary contract law, has the right to rescind the transaction. The most common situations are those where: (1) the indorser is a minor, (2) the indorsement and subsequent delivery are brought about by fraud or duress on the part of the indorsee, and (3) the negotiation is part of an illegal transaction. Under Sec. 3-207:

1. Such negotiations are "effective" (that is, the indorsee qualifies as a holder and thus is capable of negotiating the instrument further).

2. However, until the instrument is negotiated to a party who qualifies as an HDC, the indorser can rescind the indorsement. To illustrate:

a. P, a minor, indorses a note to H, the holder. As long as the note remains in H's hands, P can rescind the indorsement and recover the instrument.

b. P, a minor, indorses a note to H, the holder. After H negotiates the instrument to X (holder 2), P seeks to disaffirm the indorsement and recover the note from X. If X qualifies as an HDC of the instrument (under rules to be examined in the next chapter), P cannot set aside the negotiation.

Questions and Problems

1. The X Corporation issues a check "payable to the order of Gladys Nall." Gladys indorses the instrument in blank (e.g., "Gladys Nall") and negotiates it to the Y Company. Before the Y Company has time to indorse the check it is stolen by Z and transferred to H, who has no knowledge of the theft. The X Corporation then learns of the theft and stops payment on the check. In a subsequent suit brought by H against the X Corporation to recover the amount of the instrument, the X Corporation contends that H is not a holder of the instrument since the Y Company had not indorsed it. Is this contention correct? Why or why not?

2. D draws a draft payable to the order of P. P indorses it to A as follows: "Pay to A without recourse, (signed) P." A indorses the instrument to B as follows: "Pay to B upon her delivery of her 1980 Citation, (signed) A." B indorses the instrument, "Pay to the order of C, (signed) B," and gives it to C.

   a. Classify each of the above indorsements.
   b. Since P indorsed the instrument "Pay to A . . ." instead of "Pay to the order of A . . . ," does this mean that A's subsequent transfer of it to B is not a negotiation? Explain.
   c. Which of the transferees (i.e., A, B, and C)—if any—qualify as holders?

3. The D Company purchases its oil from a jobber, the P Company. In payment for its December purchases of oil the D Company sent a check to the P Company for $975, the check being payable "to the order of the P Company." An authorized employee of the P Company indorsed the check, by rubber stamp, "Pay to the order of Gulf Oil, the P Company." X, a janitor of the P Company stole the check and forged this indorsement on it: "Gulf Oil, by John Andrews, assistant treasurer." If this instrument should later be cashed by a bank under circumstances in which it had no reason to suspect the forged indorsement, would the bank be a holder of it? Why or why not?

4. Your car is damaged in an accident caused by X. X's insurance company asks you to get three repair estimates. From the three, the company chooses the ABC Auto Repair Company and drafts a check payable to both you and ABC Auto Repair. You then decide that you want the R Company to repair your car. What difficulties, if any, do you have if you wish to use the insurance company's check as payment to R Company for the repair of damage to your car?

5. You receive a check that is payable to your order. You indorse the check in blank, intending to deposit it in your account later in the day. What risks have you created by indorsing the check this way?

6. A check is drawn payable to *cash* and is thus a bearer instrument "on its face." Is there any legal way, under the UCC, to convert this instrument to an order instrument? Explain.

7. A check is drawn payable to the order of Chauncey Ricks, who is a minor. Chauncey indorses the check to X, and X in turn indorses it to Y. Y later learns that Chauncey is a minor, and also that he has disaffirmed the contract in payment for which he had negotiated the check to X. Does the fact that Chauncey disaffirmed his contract with X prevent Y from qualifying as a holder of the instrument? Why or why not?

8. The Soong Company of San Francisco draws a $1500 check on its local bank payable to the order of the West Company of Baltimore, and mails it to the West Company. An officer of the West Company, which is in the process of liquidation, indorses the check under court order: "Pay to John Chandler, trustee of the X Company, (signed) the West Company." Chandler cashes the check at a Baltimore bank, which gives him cash for it. The bank then sends it to the San Francisco bank via a Chicago bank. If Chandler fails to turn the $1500 over to the West Company, and if a new trustee is appointed, does the new trustee have any right to hold either the Baltimore bank or the Chicago bank liable for the amount of the instrument? Explain.

25 Commercial Paper/ Holders in Due Course

Under ordinary contract law the assignment of a contractual (nonnegotiable) right passes to the assignee the same rights possessed by the assignor—no more and no less. The assignee thus takes the right or claim subject to all defenses that might exist between the original parties to the contract, regardless of whether the assignee knows of them at the time of acquiring the right. As a result, contractual claims are not transferred in large numbers in the business community, for most prospective assignees will purchase a claim only after satisfying themselves that the original obligor on the contract does not have a defense against it. This is usually a time-consuming process and often an impossible one.

The purchasers of negotiable instruments, by contrast, acquire them free of many defenses that exist between the original parties to the instrument. In fact, a major purpose of Article 3 of the UCC is to facilitate the negotiation of commercial paper by (1) spelling out the requirements that must be met by the purchaser of a negotiable instrument in order for that person to acquire the most favored status of a holder in due course (HDC) and (2) identifying the specific kinds of defenses that are cut off when a purchaser of the instrument attains this status.

Before proceeding further, we should understand the typical situation where an HDC acquires greater rights than those possessed by his or her transferor. To illustrate: M, a building contractor, has contracted to purchase certain plumbing fixtures from the P Company, a plumbing supply firm, for $2,250. M makes a negotiable promissory note for that amount, due sixty days later, and gives it to P Company. After receiving the note, P Company negotiates it immediately to the B Bank, receiving cash in return (probably somewhat less than $2,250). When the note comes due, M refuses to pay it because many of the fixtures delivered by the P Company are defective. In this situation the B Bank—if it qualifies as an HDC—*is entitled to a judgment against M for the full $2,250, even though its transferor, the P Company, probably would have recovered nothing from M* had it held the instrument itself until maturity.

The bank is entitled to a judgment in full because M's defense—breach of contract on the part of the payee—is one of the defenses that are cut off by negotiation of the instrument to an HDC. (These "personal" defenses will be discussed along with "real" defenses in the next chapter.)

Two further observations about HDCs and other holders should be made here.

Assignees and Holders: There is nothing inherently "wrong" with the assignment of a simple contractual right or the transfer of any other nonnegotiable instrument, because in both of these situations the assignee/transferee is entitled to payment from the obligor if the obligor has no defense to the instrument. Thus in the above illustration, if M had signed and given to the P Company a simple (nonnegotiable) note, and if the company had sold it to the bank, the bank (assignee) would have been entitled to payment at maturity *if* the plumbing fixtures delivered by the P Company were not defective in any way. In such a situation M would have no defense against the P Company and hence no assertable defense against the bank. (In this respect, it is sometimes said that "nonnegotiability alone is not a defense." This means that a maker or drawer cannot escape liability simply by showing that the instrument held by the plaintiff is nonnegotiable. Instead, the nonnegotiability of an instrument permits its maker or drawer to assert a defense against the holder *if one exists.*)

Limitations on the Holder in Due Course: Despite the favorable position that the HDC usually occupies, even holders in due course do not *always* prevail against the obligor. In the first place, if the obligor has a "real" defense—such as forgery—he may assert this defense against *all* holders. Second, and perhaps more important-ly, *several recently-enacted consumer protection statutes and/or orders of regulatory agencies have cut down the right of holders in due course by permitting obligors to assert personal defenses against them in certain situations.* (These limitations on the holder in due course doctrine will be discussed in the following chapter.)

Holder in Due Course Requirements

Sec. 3-302 of the UCC is the definitive HDC section, containing the three basic requirements for HDC status. According to Sec. 3-302(1): "A holder in due course is a holder who takes the instrument (a) for value; and (b) in good faith; and (c) without notice that it is overdue or has been dishonored or of any defense against or claim to it on the part of any person." The major purpose of these requirements is to define the kind of person who deserves, as a matter of policy, to take the instrument free of certain defenses (such as breach of contract by the payee). Some purchasers of instruments are denied this favored treatment, for example, because they either knew or should have known of an existing defense at the time of purchase.

Before examining each of the requirements, we should remember that a person seeking HDC status must first qualify as a *holder,* defined by Sec. 1-201(20) as "a person who is in possession of . . . an instrument . . . drawn, issued or indorsed to him or to his order or to bearer or in blank." Thus a transferee who acquires an instrument other than by issue or negotiation fails to qualify as an HDC at the outset, regardless of the other circumstances under which the acquisition took place.

Value

The term *value* is defined in Sec. 3-303, which states that a holder (usually a purchaser) has given value (a) to the extent that the agreed-upon consideration has been performed (by him or her) or to the extent that he or she acquires a security interest in or a lien on the instrument other than by legal process, or (b) when he or she takes the instrument in payment of, or as security for, an antecedent claim against any person, whether or not the claim is due, or (c) when he or she gives a negotiable instrument in payment for it. The reasoning underlying the value requirement is that if a person receives a note or a check without having given value for it, he or she obviously will suffer no out-of-pocket loss by being unable to recover from the primary party in the event that the latter has a personal defense available.

The following examples will most easily illustrate the basic import of Sec. 3-303.

1. P, the payee of an out-of-town check, cashes it at his own bank. The bank, by giving P cash, has obviously given value.

2. P, a retailer, is the payee of a $900 note issued by M. P makes a contract with a third party, H, under which H is to deliver 30 cameras to P in exchange for the note. Before the delivery date P runs into financial difficulties and H, fearing that the note might be attached by P's creditors, demands that it be negotiated to him immediately. P delivers the note to H, and H later delivers the cameras. H is a holder for value, since he performed the agreed-upon consideration (i.e., delivered the cameras). H is thus entitled to enforce the instrument against the maker, M, at maturity even if M has a personal defense against P.

3. Same facts as 2, above, except that after H received the note he had delivered

only 20 cameras, at which time H learned that M had a defense against P. Here H would be accorded HDC status only to the extent of $600 (i.e., the extent to which the "agreed-upon consideration has been performed").

4. Same facts as 2, above, except that after H received the note he failed to deliver any of the cameras before learning of M's defense against P. Here H has not given value for the instrument (i.e., H's original *promise* to deliver the cameras does not constitute value. (This illustration points up the fact that the term *value* in Article 3 of the UCC is not synonymous with *consideration* under contract law.)

Depositary Banks and Value: A problem sometimes arises when a check is placed in the bank collection process and then is not honored by the drawee bank. For example: P, a New York resident, receives a check payable to her order, the check being drawn by D on a Georgia bank. P deposits the check to her account in her New York (depositary) bank, and the check is duly forwarded through two intermediate banks to the drawee bank in Georgia. If that bank dishonors (refuses to pay) the check because D has insufficient funds in his account, it will return the instrument through the same channels to the depositary bank in New York.

At this point one of two things will be done. Probably the depositary bank will charge (debit) P's account and return the check to her. The bank can do this because the bank-depositor contract almost always provides that the crediting of an account on any check deposited by the bank's customers is conditional upon the check being honored by the drawee bank. In this situation the question does not arise as to whether the depositary bank is an HDC, or even a holder, for it is out of the picture once it returns the check to P.

The question of whether the depositary bank has given value for the check can arise, however, in the rarer situation where the depositary bank does not or cannot charge its depositor's account. In that situation the bank itself may have to bring action against the drawer; and if the drawer has a personal defense against the payee, the bank will have to show that it qualifies as an HDC in order to overcome the defense.

The initial rule in such a situation is clear: the mere crediting of an account by a bank does not constitute the giving of value. So if P has not withdrawn funds after depositing the check at the depositary bank, that bank is clearly not an HDC and therefore is not entitled to judgment against D (assuming again that D has a personal defense against P).

A different result is reached, however, if P, after depositing the check, withdrew funds from her account to such an extent that the particular credited item was reached (using the first-money-in, first-money-out theory) before the bank learned of D's defense.[1] To illustrate: Suppose that the check in question is in the amount of $75 and that when P initially deposited it, she already had $300 in her checking account. In this case the depositary bank will have given value if, after deposit of

---

[1] *First-in, first-out* is the theory that when money deposited in a bank is followed by subsequent deposits, any withdrawals (by the depositor writing checks) thereafter are presumed to come from the funds that were deposited first.

the $75 check, it honored checks drawn by P on her account, totalling $375, before it learned of D's defense. (On the other hand, if the withdrawals total only $335, the bank is a holder for value only to the extent of $35.)

"Good Faith"

The requirement that one must take the instrument in good faith in order to qualify as an HDC is contained in Sec. 3-302(b). *Good faith* itself is defined (not too helpfully) in Sec. 1-201(19) as "honesty in fact in the conduct or transaction."

The wide-ranging circumstances in which a maker, acceptor, or drawer of an instrument can at least argue that the plaintiff/holder did not take the instrument in good faith make it difficult to accurately explain this term.[2] In some situations, for example, a purchaser might take an instrument under circumstances that are somewhat suspicious but of such a minor nature that he or she honestly does not believe the instrument is defective. Under these circumstances the purchaser might well satisfy the good faith requirement. At the other extreme, the circumstances under which a person acquires an instrument might be so unusual that it is quite clear he or she is not acting honestly in the transaction and hence is guilty of bad faith. An example of the latter is: The buyer of a $1,500 instrument purchases it from the payee for $200 in cash, a grossly inadequate consideration.

The case below is typical of those arising in the "good faith" area.

Norman v. World Wide Distributors, Inc., and Peoples National Fund, Inc.

Superior Court of Pennsylvania, 195 A.2d 115 (1963)

A salesman of World Wide Distributors called on the Normans on January 22, 1961, and outlined a "program of direct advertising" that his company was carrying on. He told the Normans that if they would purchase a breakfront (a type of cabinet) for a specified price, and if they would thereafter write letters to their friends asking them to request World Wide salesmen to contact them and explain the same plan to them, World Wide would pay the Normans $5 for each letter they wrote. Additionally, World Wide promised to pay the Normans $20 for each sale made to any of their friends in this way. The salesman also told the Normans that they would make enough money out of the plan not only to pay the purchase price in full but also to put their daughter through college.

Without reading it, the Normans signed a "purchase agreement"; they also signed in blank an attached judgment note. They were told by the salesman that the note would be made out to be payable in thirty monthly installments for a total of $1,079.40 (the price of the breakfront plus interest). After leaving the Norman home, the salesman filled in the amount to read $1,079.40 and made it payable to

---

[2]Partly as a result of this difficulty, the courts frequently attack the question from the other side, by determining if the purchaser took the instrument in *bad faith*—a standard that is somewhat easier to apply. Either way, however, the test is subjective, asking, "Did the purchaser take the instrument honestly?" rather than "Did the purchaser act with the care of the reasonable, prudent person?" (This test is sometimes referred to as the "pure heart, empty head" concept.)

"H. Waldran Trading As State Wide Products." (State Wide was the name of a prior firm which Waldran and others had operated under the same kind of plan.) The note was made payable at the office of Peoples National Fund, the principal defendant in this action, and the due date was filled in as January 25, 1961—three days after the Normans had signed it. Peoples National purchased the note on either January 22 or 23, and the following February 7—by virtue of the confession of judgment clause in the note—they obtained judgment against the Normans on the note without the necessity of a hearing or a trial.

The Normans brought action against Peoples to have the judgment set aside. They claimed fraud on the part of World Wide in the wrongful completion of the note; and they also testified that when they demanded payment from World Wide of $300 for sixty letters they had written, they received only $80 and a variety of excuses as to why the balance was not paid them. Additionally, the Normans produced evidence indicating that the owners of World Wide had had a long history of failing to make good on their referral plan obligations and that the company had never intended to live up to the promises it made.

The Normans further contended that the principal defendant in this action, Peoples, was not a holder in due course of the note *because it took the instrument in bad faith.* The trial court agreed with the Normans and declared the judgment against them null and void. Peoples appealed.

Woodside, Justice: . . . The referral plan was a fraudulent scheme based on an operation similar to the recurrent chain letter racket. It is one of many sales rackets being carried on throughout the nation which are giving public officials serious concern. The plaintiffs introduced evidence to show that at the end of 20 months of operation, it would require *17 trillion* salesmen to carry on a referral program like World Wide described to the plaintiffs.

Peoples contends that even though World Wide may have been guilty of fraud, it can collect on the note because it was a holder in due course.

[The court then quoted the UCC holder in due course requirements along with Sec. 1-201(19) of the code, defining *good faith* as "honesty in fact in the conduct or transaction concerned." The court expressly noted that Peoples would have to meet the good faith requirement in order to be an HDC, and continued:]

He who seeks protection as a holder in due course must have dealt fairly and honestly in acquiring the instrument as to the rights of prior parties, and where circumstances are such as to justify the conclusion that the failure to make inquiry arose from a suspicion that inquiry would disclose a vice or defect in the title, the person is not a holder in due course.

When the defense of fraud appears to be meritorious as to the payee, the burden of showing it was a holder in due course is on the one claiming to be such.

The appellant here had knowledge of circumstances which should have caused it to inquire concerning the payee's method of obtaining the note. Peoples knew enough about the referral plan to require it to inquire further concerning it. The fact that the appellant's vice president called the makers of the note and denied any connection with the referral plan indicates his own suspicion concerning it. The frequency with which the principals changed the name under which they were operating—three times in approximately one year—should have added to this suspicion. Furthermore, the appellant paid $831 for a $1,079.40 note payable three days after date. See *Gimbel Brothers, Inc. v. Hymowitz*, 51 A.2d 389 (1947). Under all the circumstances, *Peoples was bound to inquire further into the operation of the seller of these notes, and having made no inquiry, it is held as though it had knowledge of all that inquiry would have revealed.* [Emphasis added.]

The appellant argues that the plaintiffs are estopped from raising against it any defenses which they might have raised against World Wide, because they did not complain to the appellant when its vice president called them. The appellant's hands are not clean enough to raise this point. Estoppels are used in law as a means to prevent fraud, and never to become its instruments.

Decree affirmed.

Overdue or Dishonored Instruments and Defenses or Claims against Them

Sec. 3-302(1)(c) provides that, to be an HDC, a holder must take the instrument "without notice that it is overdue or has been dishonored or of any defense against or claim to it on the part of any person."[3] Notice received *after* the instrument has been acquired does not, of course, prevent a holder from attaining HDC status.

The basic thrust of this section is that a holder should not receive the protection afforded an HDC if he or she acquires an instrument knowing, or having reason to know, that something is wrong with it. The most extreme (and somewhat unlikely) case is where, say, H purchases a note from P, the payee, knowing at the time of purchase that P has breached his contract with M, the maker of the note. In such a situation there is no reason whatever why H should take the note free of the defense. Another obvious situation is that of an instrument bearing a fixed maturity date, where H purchases the instrument at some time *after* the date. Here the fact that the instrument was not paid at maturity is a clear indication to a prospective purchaser that there is probably a reason why payment was not made.

Sec. 3-304 is an aid to the interpretation of the "notice that an instrument is overdue" and "notice of defense against or claim to" language found in Sec. 3-302. Subsection 1 of Sec. 3-304 sets forth the most common circumstances in which notice exists as a matter of law, with the result that a purchaser does *not* qualify as an HDC. Subsection 2, by contrast, specifies certain information that a purchaser may possess and still qualify as an HDC.

Because of its length, Sec. 3-304 cannot be set forth or discussed here in full; instead, we will mention only a few of its salient provisions. (The section can be read in its entirety in Appendix A.)

Notice That Paper Is Overdue or Has Been Dishonored: As we saw in Chapter 22, all negotiable instruments are either time or demand instruments. Those bearing a fixed future date of maturity, such as "payable July 1, 1980," are time

---

[3]Sec. 1-201(25) provides in part that "a person has 'notice' of a fact when (a) he has actual knowledge of it, or (b) when he has received a notice or notification of it, or (c) when from all the facts and circumstances known to him at the time in question he has *reason to know* that it exists." (Emphasis added.)

instruments; those stating that they are payable on demand or having no stated maturity date are demand instruments.

A person who purchases a *time instrument* even one day after its stated maturity date takes it with notice that it is overdue. Thus, if a note payable on September 1 is acquired by H on September 2, H does not qualify as an HDC. Sec. 3-304(3) provides in part that "the purchaser has notice that an instrument is overdue if he has reason to know (a) that any part of the principal amount is overdue or that there is an uncured default in payment of another instrument of the same series." And the purchaser has such notice here because the instrument carried its maturity date on its face.

The question as to when *demand instruments* are overdue has caused difficulties, since such instruments obviously do not contain a stated maturity date. The rule in Sec. 3-304(3)(c) is that a purchaser takes a demand instrument with notice that it is overdue if the person knows (or has reason to know) that he or she is purchasing it "after demand has been made" or if the person acquires it more than "a reasonable length of time after its issue." To illustrate: M is the maker of a demand note. A holder (either the payee or a subsequent holder) demands payment from M. Payment is refused, whereupon the holder negotiates the note to a third party, X. If X knows (or should know under the circumstances) of M's refusal to pay, which is a "dishonor" of the instrument, X is not an HDC.

A person who purchases an instrument more than a "reasonable time after its issue" fails to qualify as an HDC even if the instrument has not been dishonored. Sec. 3-304(3)(c) contains the only provision that specifically defines a reasonable time, and it applies only to checks. A reasonable time in regard to checks drawn and payable in the U.S. "is presumed to be 30 days." To illustrate: D draws a check on June 1 payable to the order of P. Thereafter one or more negotiations take place, the last one, with H, occurring on July 15. In this case H has almost certainly not taken the check within a reasonable time after its issue. (But note that the thirty-day limit is not absolute; rather, thirty days is "presumed" to be the deadline. This means that in exceptional circumstances a person might acquire a check beyond that time and still qualify as an HDC.)

As to demand instruments other than checks—demand notes and sight drafts— the UCC does not define *reasonable time,* thereby leaving the decision to the courts. In determining reasonable time, the courts take into account business and community customs and the particular facts of each case (for example, interest-bearing notes circulate longer than noninterest-bearing notes, and reasonable times generally are longer in rural areas than in cities). Under case law before adoption of the UCC, many courts presumed as a rule of thumb that demand notes were overdue sixty days after issue (in the absence of unusual circumstances), and demand drafts became overdue in a somewhat shorter time.

An analysis of more recent cases indicates that this rule-of-thumb is less often applied today. Some recent decisions have held that demand notes in particular circumstances are overdue within a much shorter period of time, and others have held that they are not overdue even when purchased a year or more after their date of issue. About all we can say now is that each case is decided on the basis of its own particular fact-pattern, with widely varying results.

Notice of Claim or Defense: Sec. 3-304(1) reads in part as follows:

> The purchaser has notice of a claim or defense if (a) the instrument is so incomplete, bears such visible evidence of forgery or alteration, or is otherwise so irregular as to call into question its validity, terms or ownership or to create an ambiguity as to the party to pay; or (b) the purchaser has notice that the obligation of any party is voidable in whole or in part, or that all parties have been discharged.

Subsection a addresses itself to situations where some unusual aspect about the face of the instrument itself should indicate to a reasonable person that a defense very likely exists. Under this section, the fact that an instrument is incomplete to *some* extent or bears *some* evidence of a possible forgery or alteration does not necessarily prevent the holder from qualifying as an HDC. Rather, the disqualification occurs only where the irregularity is one that is so material as to call into question the instrument's validity, terms, or ownership.

On the subject of incompleteness, it is well established that any third party who acquires an instrument so incomplete that one of the requirements of negotiability is missing is not an HDC. Thus, if H takes a check from P, payee, the amount of which is entirely blank, H does not qualify as an HDC since the instrument was not negotiable at the time she acquired it. Similarly, if H takes an instrument "payable twenty _____ after date," she is not an HDC.[4]

On the other hand, an instrument that is incomplete in only a minor respect is not considered so irregular as to prevent a purchaser from attaining HDC status. For example: A note is complete in all respects except that it contains this clause: "Payable at _____ (the location)." Here the purchaser qualifies as an HDC because the place where an instrument is payable is not a required element of negotiability; thus the fact that this particular blank is not filled in does not of itself cause a reasonable person to question the instrument's validity. The same is true of a check that does not bear its date of issue; this alone is not a disqualifying irregularity.

This approach also applies to altered terms in an instrument. Unexplained alterations that are both material and apparent (such as a line drawn through the original payee's name, with a second name substituting for it) will disqualify a taker from HDC status. But alterations so skillfully done that they are not readily apparent will not keep the instrument taker from qualifying as a HDC. Similarly, an instrument bearing some evidence of erasure and subsequent correction of a necessary element will not necessarily put a purchaser on notice of a defense; for example, the purchaser might have inquired about the erasure and received an

---

[4]If, in either of these cases, H completes the instrument and negotiates it to X, another holder, X probably will qualify as an HDC if he meets the other requirements. X's rights in these circumstances will be discussed in the next chapter.

adequate explanation of it. Thus every case arising under this section has to be settled on the basis of its own facts.

The gist of Sec. 3-304(1)(b) is that a person who purchases an instrument knowing of a defense, or having reason to know of it, takes the instrument with "notice" of such fact and is thereby disqualified as an HDC. Thus if it is proven that the purchaser acquired a note knowing that the payee had breached his contract with the maker, or had reliable information that the payee may have breached the contract, the purchaser is not an HDC, and consequently takes the instrument subject to the maker's defense.

In the next case it may be argued that the plaintiffs did not actually know that a defense (breach of contract) existed before they purchased the instrument. But let us see what other information the plaintiffs did possess at that time, and how the court viewed the legal effect of that information.

Salter v. Vanotti
Colorado Court of Civil
Appeals, Div. III 599
P.2d 962 (1979)

Mr. and Mrs. Vanotti, defendants, signed an agreement to purchase a lot in an Arizona development from Cochise College Park, Inc. (Cochise), the developer of the area. As part of the transaction the Vanottis signed a negotiable promissory note (payable to Cochise) in the amount of $4,392, payable in monthly installments. Cochise thereafter negotiated the note to the Salters, plaintiffs.

The Vanottis made three monthly payments on the note, after which time they visited the property and found that it was not as Cochise had represented it to be.

In this action by the Salters to recover the unpaid balance of the note, the Vanottis alleged that they had several defenses against Cochise, and they further alleged that the Salters were not holders in due course of the note. On this basis the Vanottis claimed that they could assert their defenses against the Salters.

The trial court agreed that the Vanottis' defenses against Cochise were valid, and also agreed that the Salters were not holders in due course (for reasons appearing in the decision below). Accordingly, it dismissed the action. Plaintiffs appealed.

Silverstein, Chief Judge: ... The trial court found that defendants had three defenses: (1) that defendants had attempted to exercise their rights under the money back guarantee, as provided in the Property Report, and that the attempt was not honored by Cochise; (2) that defendants did not receive a copy of the Property Report prior to, or at the time they entered into the agreement as required by [federal law], and (3) that the contract had been breached [by Cochise] by failure to deliver a deed after three payments had been made. ...

The primary issue on appeal is whether plaintiffs are holders in due course of the note. Under the Uniform Commercial Code a holder in due course must, [among other requirements] take the instrument ... without notice ... of any defense against or claim to it on the part of any person. § 3-302. "The purchaser of an instrument has notice of a claim or defense if (b) the purchaser has notice that the obligation of any party is voidable in whole or in part ..." § 3-304. And, "a person has 'notice' of a fact when (c) from all the facts and circumstances known to him at the time in question he has reason to know that it exists." § 1-201(25).

The significant "facts and circumstances" are these: Prior to purchasing the defendants' note, plaintiffs had bought seven similar notes from Cochise, and bought three more

simultaneously with the purchase of defendants' note; at the time the note was delivered to plaintiffs, they also received the additional documents which set forth defendants' rights under the contract, and one of plaintiffs [admitted] "I had all the supporting documents."
. . .

Here plaintiffs knew, from the documents delivered with the note, that defendants had a right to rescind the contract within six months from the date of the contract, that apparently defendants had not received a copy of the Property Report, and that defendants were entitled to a deed after making three monthly payments on the note. Plaintiffs further knew that they were not in a position to deliver such a deed, since only a photocopy was forwarded to them, [and yet] took no steps to investigate these facts. . . . The protection afforded a holder in due course cannot be used to shield one who simply refuses to investigate when the facts known to him suggest an irregularity concerning the commercial paper he purchases. This is especially so where, as here, the note was not purchased for value, but was discounted forty percent. . . .

[And, in regard to plaintiffs' claim that they took the instrument in good faith], under the UCC if a holder takes an instrument with notice "that the obligation of any party is voidable in whole or in part," § 3-304, that notice is sufficient to prevent the holder from qualifying as a holder in due course, regardless of good or bad faith. And, since plaintiffs had such notice they were not holders in due course, and thus, held the note subject to any valid defenses.

Judgment affirmed.

Related Holder in Due Course Problems

Holder through a Holder in Due Course

Any taker of an instrument who does not meet all the requirements for a holder in due course is usually called an *ordinary holder* (or sometimes a *mere holder*). This person takes the instrument subject to all outstanding defenses—that is, like an assignee, the ordinary holder acquires only the rights of prior parties, no greater ones.

However, if an ordinary holder takes an instrument from someone who is an HDC, or takes an instrument where *any* prior party qualified as an HDC, he is now a "holder with all the rights of an HDC."[5] Thus if H purchases a note that is clearly overdue, or receives it as a gift, he can still enforce the instrument against the maker, even though the maker has a defense, if he (H) can show that any prior holder met the requirements of an HDC.

One exception to the above does exist, however. If a purchaser of an instrument negotiates it to a subsequent holder and ultimately repurchases it (from either that holder or a later holder), his or her status is determined at the time of first acquiring it. To illustrate: H purchases an instrument, failing to qualify as an HDC for some reason. Later she negotiates the instrument to a holder who does qualify as an

---

[5]This results from Sec. 3-201(1), which provides that "the transfer of an instrument vests in the transferee such rights as the transferor has therein." This section, based on assignment law, is referred to as the *shelter provision* of the code.

HDC. If H reacquires the instrument subsequently, she is not accorded "holder with the rights of an HDC" status. In other words, H cannot improve her position by reacquiring from an HDC.

The Payee as a Holder in Due Course

Before adoption of the UCC, some courts took the view that the payee of an instrument could not qualify as an HDC even if he or she gave value for the instrument, purchased it before it was overdue, and took it without notice of any defense or claim. Other courts disagreed. The UCC has resolved this conflict by flatly providing in Sec. 3-302(2) that "a payee may be a holder in due course," assuming, of course, that the person has met the three basic HDC requirements.

To merely say, however, that a payee can be an HDC is not particularly helpful. If a payee has actually given value and taken the instrument before it is overdue, in the majority of instances the maker or drawer *does not have a defense,* with the result that the payee is entitled to payment regardless of whether he or she qualifies as an HDC.

The real question, then, is: Can a payee qualify as an HDC when the maker or drawer does in fact have a defense of some kind available? In most "real life" situations, the answer is no, because the defense usually arises from some misconduct of the payee himself. To illustrate: P contracts to paint D's home. At the end of P's first day of work D gives him a check for $1,300, the full amount of the job, because D will be out of town for the next month. If P, the payee, never finishes the job he will not be an HDC because he obviously knows of the defense ("breach of contract") that D possesses, since it arose out of his (P's) misconduct.

In a few highly exceptional situations, however, a defense may exist which is not the fault of the payee, and of which he has no notice when he receives the instrument. One example: D, drawer, signs a check payable to the order of P, payee, but leaves the amount of the check blank, since the total value of P's services is not yet determined. D gives the check to his agent, A, with instructions to fill in the amount—but for no more than $500. P submits a bill for $700. A fills in the amount of $700 and issues the check to P. In this situation D has the defense of "unauthorized completion," since his agent did not follow his instructions. However, as we will see in more detail in the next chapter, this defense cannot be asserted against an HDC, who is entitled to the amount of the check as finally completed. In this situation, despite the existence of a defense, P qualifies as an HDC (since he gave value and took the instrument before it was overdue and without notice of the unauthorized completion). He is thus entitled to recover the full $700.

Questions and Problems

1. Drexler was an officer of Eldon's Super Fresh Stores (Eldon's) in Farribault, Minnesota, and also its attorney. For several years Drexler had maintained a personal trading account with the Merrill Lynch brokerage company.

Eldon's drew a $4,150 check payable to the order of ML and gave it to Drexler (for reasons not appearing in the record of the case). Drexler took the check to ML and purchased 100 shares of stock in a corporation with it. The stock was issued in Drexler's name, but he permitted ML to retain possession of it as he had done with similar purchases in the past.

Later a dispute arose between Eldon's and Drexler as to the ownership of the stock in ML's possession. Eldon's claimed that ML could not be a holder in due course of the check, contending that the check—being drawn by Eldon's instead of by Drexler—should have indicated to ML that it should not have given value to Drexler personally. Do you agree that ML was *not* a holder in due course? Discuss. (*Eldon's Super Fresh Stores, Inc. v. Merrill Lynch, Pierce, Fenner & Smith, Inc.,* 207 N.W.2d 282, 1973).

2. Willman was the maker of several notes payable to the order of a designated payee, and he issued them to the payee. Later the payee wanted to borrow money from a Mr. Wood, and in order to get the loan the payee had to pledge the notes (that is, deliver them) to Wood as security for the loan. (The amount of the loan was substantially less than the total amount of the notes.)

In subsequent litigation by Wood against Willman, the maker of the notes, the question arose whether Wood was a holder in due course to the full extent of the notes, or only to the extent of the amount of the loan which he (Wood) had made to the payee. How would you rule on this issue? What is your reason? (*Wood v. Willman,* 423 P.2d 82, 1967).

3. On July 1, M signs a note, as maker, in the amount of $1,000, payable ninety days after date. He issues it to P, payee, in payment for the purchase of P's motorcycle. One month later P, needing cash to pay a debt, negotiates the note to H, who pays P $600 cash and agrees orally to pay an additional $400 within thirty days. Before the thirty days are up, H learns that M has rescinded the motorcycle purchase, claiming that the motorcycle has serious engine problems and that P knew this at the time of the sale.

a. In this situation does H qualify as a holder in due course under the UCC? Explain.
b. Assuming, for the sake of argument, that H is a holder in due course, to what extent (if any) can M assert as a defense his claim that the motorcycle was defective at the time of the sale? Explain.

4. In the above case, would your answers be different if H had purchased the note on October 20 (with the other facts of the case unchanged)? Explain.

5. P receives a check payable to her order, drawn on an out-of-town bank. She deposits the check in her account at the X Bank, which forwards it to the drawee bank. The drawee bank soon returns the check to the X Bank, marked "insufficient funds." The X Bank now attempts to charge P's account and to require P to take back the instrument, rather than bringing an action against the drawer itself. As a general rule can the X Bank do this? Explain.

6. A demand note, dated June 1, is issued to P on that date. On June 15, P demands payment from M, the maker, and payment is refused. On June 20, P negotiates the instrument to S. Later, S sues M on the note, and M proves that S knew, or had reason to know, of the dishonor at the time he acquired the instrument. S contends he still qualifies as an HDC since he clearly acquired the instrument within a reasonable time of its issue. Is S correct? Explain.

7. M is the maker of a promissory note. P, the payee, negotiates the note to H before maturity. H gives value for the instrument and takes it in good faith and without notice of any claim or defense. Before the note matures, H gives it to his daughter, D.

a. Is D an HDC? Explain.

b. If M has a personal defense against P, will this prevent D from obtaining judgment against him? Explain.

8. Cey makes out a promissory note payable to the order of the Griffey Corporation, and issues it to the corporation in payment for work to be done by it later. The Griffey Corporation negotiates the note for value to Concepcion, who qualifies as a holder in due course. Thereafter Concepcion becomes indebted to the Griffey Corporation, and in payment of this dept he negotiates the instrument back to the Griffey Corporation. When the note matures Cey (maker) refuses to pay the Griffey Corporation for the reason that the Griffey Corporation never did the work that it contracted to do for him (Cey) in the first place.

a. Was the Griffey Corporation an HDC when it first received the note? Explain.

b. Does the Griffey Corporation have all the rights of an HDC in view of the fact that it acquired the note from someone (Concepcion) who *was* an HDC? Why or why not?

26

Commercial Paper/
Defenses

In Chapter 25 we briefly discussed the two general classes of defenses, referring to them by the commonly used terms *personal* and *real.* While the UCC calls them, respectively, *limited* and *universal,* we will continue to use the older and more common terms.

Personal defenses, under the UCC, can be asserted only against ordinary holders; generally they cannot be asserted against an HDC or against a holder with all the rights of an HDC. In fact, it is the cutting off of these defenses that gives the HDC his or her status as a favored holder.

Real defenses can be asserted against all holders, including HDCs and holders with all the rights of an HDC.[1] A defendant/maker who has available a real defense is under no liability to the plaintiff even if the latter is an HDC. This is why we said earlier that HDCs are not always entitled to judgments in actions brought against makers, acceptors, or drawers of negotiable instruments.

---

[1] Throughout this chapter, when we refer to the rights of an HDC, we will assume that whatever is said applies equally to holders with all the rights of an HDC.

454

Sec. 3-306 of the UCC lists all the personal defenses (those that are ordinarily   **Personal Defenses**
assertable only against ordinary holders). The major part of that section follows:

> Unless he has the rights of a holder in due course, any person takes the in-
> strument subject to (a) all valid claims to it on the part of any person; and
> (b) all defenses of any party which would be available in an action on a sim-
> ple contract; and (c) the defenses of want or failure of consideration, non-
> performance of any condition precedent, non-delivery, or delivery for a
> special purpose; and (d) the defense that he or a person through whom he
> holds the instrument acquired it by theft, or that payment or satisfaction to
> such holder would be inconsistent with the terms of a restrictive indorse-
> ment.

We will now examine the most common kinds of personal defenses under this
section.

Breach of Contract

Breach of contract is the most common defense falling within the provision of Sec.
3-306(b). Many instruments are issued to payees in payment for goods (or services)
that the payees are obligated to deliver (or perform) under contracts with the
makers or drawers of the instruments. If the contract is breached by the payee, the
maker of the note can refuse to pay it, and the drawer of a check can stop payment
on it, claiming that the failure of the payee to perform the contract relieves him
or her of liability.

The case of *Salter v. Vanotti,* in the prior chapter, is a perfect illustration of
these rules. In that case it may be recalled that the seller of land (Cochise) breached
its contract with the buyers (the Vanottis) in at least two respects: (a) by failing
to permit them to cancel the purchase, as the contract provided, if they were not
satisfied with the land; and (b) by failing to deliver a deed to them after they had
made three monthly payments. Those breaches afforded the Vanottis their personal defenses.

Breach of warranty—a form of breach of contract—occurs when goods are
delivered by a merchant seller under a sales contract, in payment for which the
seller receives a negotiable instrument from the buyer. Under sales law such a seller
impliedly warrants that the goods are at least merchantable. If they turn out to be
so defective that they are unmerchantable (will not perform in the expected manner), this constitutes a breach of warranty and gives the buyer (the maker or drawer
of the instrument) a defense that he or she can assert against any holder who is
not an HDC.

Lack or Failure of Consideration

Failure of consideration is essentially a breach of contract. *Lack (or want) of
consideration* (as we saw in Chapter 10) exists in a commercial paper context where

a maker or drawer of an instrument issues it to the payee in any case where the payee does not give "consideration" under ordinary contract law principles. In such situations "want of consideration" can be asserted by the maker or drawer against an ordinary holder. To illustrate: D, a distant relative of P, drafts a check and makes a gift of it to P so that P can attend college. P negotiates the check to H. P does not go to college, and D, in disgust, stops payment on the check. If H sues D on the instrument, D can successfully assert the defense of "want of consideration"— but only if H fails to qualify as an HDC.

The defense that exists in the next case clearly falls within the breach of warranty/failure of consideration category.

United Securities Corp. v. Bruton

District of Columbia Court of Appeals, 213 A.2d 892 (1965)

Cora Bruton, defendant, purchased two wigs from The Wig Shoppe, giving in payment her promissory note for $322.98. Two weeks later she returned one of the wigs, complaining of defects in its workmanship. After paying approximately half of the note, she refused to make further payments. Action was brought by United Securities Corporation, to whom The Wig Shoppe had sold the note two days after its execution, for the balance of the note.

The trial court found that United Securities was not a holder in due course and gave judgment for defendant. On appeal, United Securities relied upon Title 28, Section 409, of the District of Columbia Code, 1961 edition, which provides that "every holder is deemed *prima facie* to be a holder in due course," and claimed it was denied the benefits of that presumption by the trial court.

Hood, Chief Justice: . . . Appellant [United Securities] overlooks the fact that [the section referred to above] has been superseded [by] the Uniform Commercial Code. Section 28:-3-307(3) provides: "After it is shown that a defense exists, a person claiming the rights of a holder in due course has the burden of establishing that he or some person under whom he claims is in all respects a holder in due course."

Although the entire transaction occurred prior to the effective date of the Uniform Commercial Code, the trial occurred after the effective date, and the burden of proof, a procedural matter, was controlled by the law existing at date of trial. . . .

In the case before us a defense of defective workmanship in the article sold was shown. Appellant made no attempt to meet the merits of that defense, but sought to avoid the defense by its claim of being a holder in due course. Under present law the burden was on appellant to prove that it was "in all respects a holder in due course." The only evidence offered by appellant to establish its status as a holder in due course was that it "purchased" the note on the date shown on the endorsement. It offered no evidence of the price paid and no explanation why the note was payable at its office, or why the note was purchased so promptly after its execution, or what was the relationship between it and the payee. Under these circumstances the court could, as it did, find that appellant had failed to sustain its burden of proving it was a holder in due course.

Judgment affirmed.

Other Personal Defenses

Fraud in the Inducement: Two kinds of fraud are recognized in the area of commercial paper; one creates a personal defense and the other a real defense. *Fraud in the inducement* falls into the personal category. It arises where a person who signs a negotiable instrument (knowing it to be such) has been induced to sign by some intentional misrepresentation of the other party. For example: B agrees to purchase S's year-old car for $3,500 after being assured by S that the car is a demonstrator that S had purchased just six months earlier from a new car dealer. At the time of purchase B gives S $1,500 in cash and a promissory note for the balance of $2,000. Soon thereafter B learns that S had actually purchased the car from a private owner, a farmer, who in fact had driven it extensively before selling it to S. S's intentional misrepresentation constitutes fraud in the inducement, and B can assert this defense against S and against any subsequent holder who does not qualify as an HDC.

Illegality: Like the general defense of fraud, some types of *illegality* constitute personal defenses and others constitute real defenses. This is so because although certain transactions are illegal (prohibited) under state statutes or ordinances, the applicable statutes do not always provide that the prohibited transactions are void. If a statute voids the transaction, the defense is real; if it does not, the defense is merely personal. To illustrate: A retailer sells goods to D on a Sunday in violation of a state statute prohibiting the sale of goods by merchants on that day. However, the statute does not provide that such sales, or the contracts or papers connected with them, are void. The next day the retailer negotiates the check to H, who subsequently learns that the buyer/drawer has stopped payment on it. The buyer can assert the defense of illegality against H only if H is an ordinary holder. (Illegality as a real defense will be discussed later in the chapter.)

Nondelivery of an Instrument: Sometimes an instrument finds its way into the hands of a subsequent holder through loss or theft. In such a case the maker or drawer of the instrument has available the defense of *nondelivery*. To illustrate: M is the maker of a bearer instrument that is stolen from her home by X and negotiated to H. If H is merely an ordinary holder, he takes the instrument subject to the defense of nondelivery and therefore cannot enforce it against M.

Unauthorized Completion: Although it is ordinarily a bad practice, the maker or drawer of an instrument sometimes signs it while it is incomplete in some respect (for example, leaving blank the amount or the payee's name). He or she usually gives it to a third party (often an employee but sometimes the payee) with instructions as to how the blank should be filled in (such as, "fill in the amount for no more than $400"). The instrument is then completed *contrary to instructions* and later is acquired by a subsequent holder. If the latter fails to qualify as an HDC, the maker or drawer usually can assert the defense of *unauthorized completion* and avoid liability. However, under Sec. 3-407(3), if the subsequent holder does qualify as an HDC (by taking the instrument without knowledge of the wrongful completion and by meeting the other HDC requirements), he or she can enforce the instrument as completed. Thus, where the maximum authorized amount is $400, if the third party completes the instrument to read $1,000, a subsequent HDC can recover the full $1,000 from the maker or drawer. Therein lies the danger in signing an incomplete instrument.

Prior Payment: When a note or draft is paid by the maker or acceptor, it is routinely surrendered to that person, regardless of whether it is paid at or before maturity. Either way the instrument normally stops circulating. However, the maker/acceptor may neglect to ask for the return of the instrument, or, after its return, it may be stolen. If payment of the instrument occurred before maturity, and if the instrument bears no notation of payment, it is possible that it will get into the hands of an innocent third party. When that holder demands payment at maturity, the maker or acceptor has available the defense of *payment* or *payment before maturity* and is therefore not liable if the holder fails to qualify as an HDC. (Obviously, however, if the holder is an HDC, the maker or acceptor must pay a second time.)

Incapacity (Except Minority): As we saw in Chapter 11, the law recognizes various types and degrees of incapacity. However, unless a maker's or drawer's incapacity is so extreme that under local law the contract or instrument is completely nullified, the defense of *incapacity* is only personal—except in the case of a minor (which will be discussed later in the chapter).

Duress: Similarly, there are varying degrees of duress under the law, most of which are merely personal in nature. Thus, if a person signs an instrument under a vague threat or through fear of economic retaliation, the defense is only personal in nature. (Duress as a real defense will also be discussed later in the chapter.)

Real Defenses

Real or "universal" defenses can be successfully asserted against all holders, including holders in due course. We will now describe the more common types of real defenses, including the "offshoots" of some of the personal defenses already discussed.

Forgery

A fundamental legal principle of commercial paper, appearing in Sec. 3-401(1), is that a person cannot be held liable on an instrument unless his or her name appears on it. In the case of *forgery* the person's name does appear, probably as maker or drawer, but it is signed by another person who has no authority to do so. (An unauthorized signature or indorsement is defined in Sec. 1-201(43) as "one made without actual, implied, or apparent authority and includes a forgery.")

The "pure" forgery case occurs where a person who has no authority from (and usually no relationship with) the purported drawer or maker simply commits a criminal act by signing the latter's name to an instrument. For example: A thief steals a book of personalized checks belonging to D. The thief drafts a check and signs D's name as drawer. In this case D has no liability to any holder of the instrument. Sec. 3-404(1) provides that "any unauthorized signature is *wholly inoperative* as that of the person whose name is signed unless he ratifies it or is precluded from denying it." (Emphasis added.) *Ratification* consists of any conduct on the part of the person whose name has been signed without authority which indicates to third parties that he or she will assume liability on the instrument despite the unauthorized signing. It occurs rarely; and when it does, it is usually in a situation where a principal-agent relationship exists between the purported drawer and the forger.[2]

A situation related to forgery exists when an agent exceeds his or her authority by signing the principal's name on an instrument as drawer or maker. If the principal can show that the agent had no express, implied, or apparent authority to sign, and if the principal does not subsequently ratify the signature, he or she can assert the defense of *unauthorized signing* against any holder, even an HDC. (See Chapter 30 for a treatment of the rules which the courts use in determining whether express, implied or apparent authority exists.)

Fraud in the Execution

Unlike fraud in the inducement, in the case of *fraud in the execution* a person is caused to sign a negotiable instrument under circumstances in which he or she honestly and reasonably believes it to be something other than a negotiable instrument, as, for example, a lease or receipt of some kind.

This commonly occurs when an experienced, high-pressure salesman talks a home owner who has little education (or perhaps who is even illiterate) into signing a promissory note by telling him or her that it is only a request for an estimate or an application of some kind. The salesman's company then negotiates the instrument to a holder. Here the home owner/maker has a real defense, good against any holder, if the following conditions are met. The maker must show not only that he or she honestly believed the signing was for something other than a negotiable instrument but also that he or she was not guilty of negligence under the circumstances in failing to realize that the document was a negotiable instrument. The phrase *under the circumstances* takes into account such factors as the signer's age, experience, and schooling. Thus the maker who is very inexperienced in the business world, or aged, or with failing eyesight may have a real defense, while such a defense would not exist if he or she was a business person who hurriedly signed the note after a cursory look (or perhaps without reading it at all) because of a rush to attend a meeting.

---

[2]Under Sec. 3-404(1), the primary situation in which a drawer of an instrument may be precluded from asserting the defense of forgery is where he or she is guilty of negligence that contributed to the forgery. This topic will be discussed in Chapter 28.

Material Alteration

Sec. 3-407, entitled "Alteration," covers two essentially different situations—alteration of a completed instrument and completion of a blank instrument contrary to instructions. (The latter topic was discussed earlier, under the heading "Personal Defenses.")

Alteration of a Completed Instrument: Sometimes, after a completed instrument is issued by the maker, one or more of the terms are changed without his or her knowledge by a holder, and the instrument is thereafter negotiated to a subsequent holder. The issue is thus raised whether the last holder can recover on the instrument—and, if so, to what extent. The answer to these questions depends on two factors: (1) whether the alteration was material, and (2) whether the holder qualifies as an HDC.

Sec. 3-407 essentially defines a material alteration as one that changes the contract of the parties in any respect. A change in the amount of the instrument even by the addition of one cent, or an advance of the date of payment even by one day, is thus material. On the other hand, a correction of the spelling of the payee's name or the addition of the address of the maker would not be material. (If the alteration is not material, all holders are entitled to enforce the instrument as it was originally drawn.)

If the alteration *is* material, the holder's rights depend on whether he or she is an HDC. It is possible to be an HDC when the alteration is so skillfully done that it is not readily apparent to the subsequent purchaser.

Under Sec. 3-407(3), an HDC can enforce the instrument according to its "original tenor"—that is, as originally drawn. To illustrate: M is the maker of a note payable to the order of P in the amount of $1,000. P alters the amount to read $3,000 and negotiates the instrument to H, an HDC. At maturity, H is entitled to recover $1,000. (Since H cannot recover the balance of $2,000 from M, it is said that the defense of material alteration is a defense "to the extent of the alteration.") If, on the other hand, H is not an HDC, he recovers nothing. This is so because a material alteration that is also fraudulent—as is usually the case—is a complete defense against an ordinary holder

Other Real Defenses

Illegality: As we indicated in the section on personal defenses, some kinds of transactions are not only prohibited by statute but expressly made *void* or *void ab initio* (from the beginning). The defense of *illegality* in these situations is a real defense, assertable against both ordinary holders and HDCs. In a number of states, for example, checks and notes given in payment of gambling debts fall into this category.

The next case illustrates the fact that while crime does not pay, it frequently provides the innocent drawer of a check with a most welcome real defense.

Middle Georgia Livestock Sales (MGLS) bought some cattle at an auction and gave the seller its check in payment. Soon thereafter MGLS discovered that the seller had stolen the cattle, and that it therefore had not acquired title to them. MGLS accordingly stopped payment on the check—i.e., it ordered the drawee bank not to honor it when it was presented for payment.

Without knowledge of these facts another bank, the Commercial Bank and Trust Company, cashed the check for the seller/thief, and routinely presented it for collection to the drawee bank. That bank, because of the stop payment order, refused to pay it and returned the check to Commercial. Commercial then brought this action against MGLS, the drawer, who claimed that it possessed a real defense.

The trial court granted judgment for the plaintiff, and MGLS appealed.

Commercial Bank & Trust Co. v. Middle Georgia Livestock Sales

Georgia Court of Appeals, 182 S.E.2d 533 (1971)

Been, Justice: . . . The sole question in this case *is whether a holder in due course for value of a check given by an innocent [drawer] for the purchase of cattle which turned out to be stolen may recover the value of such check from the [drawer].* [Emphasis added.] This in turn involves a construction of the controlling section of the Uniform Commercial Code, § 3-305(2)(b) providing that a holder in due course takes the instrument free from defenses of any party thereto with whom it has not dealt except "such other incapacity, or duress, or illegality of the transaction as renders the obligation of the party a nullity."

Under the Commercial Code "a holder in due course is subject to the defense of illegality when under the applicable local law such illegality makes the obligation of the defending party a nullity or void, but he is not subject to the defense when the illegality makes the obligation merely voidable." Anderson's Commercial Code, vol. 1, § 3-305:14, p. 607.

This means that the illegality is considered as of statutory origin and its "existence and effect is left to the law of each state. If under the local law the effect is to render the obligation of the instrument entirely null and void, the defense may be asserted against a holder in due course. If the effect is merely to render the obligation voidable at the election of the obligor, the defense is cut off." . . .

In *Pac. Nat. Bk. v. Hernreich* (398 S.W.2d 221) the court held that the instruments must be not merely unenforceable but void *ab initio* under applicable state law to present a defense against a holder in due course. The case then turns on the question of whether the sale of stolen [cattle], presuming the seller possessed guilty knowledge of the fact but the buyer did not, represents an "illegal consideration" so as to render it absolutely void. "A contract to do an immoral or illegal thing is void." Code § 20-501. A sale of stolen goods, although to a bona fide purchaser for value, cannot transfer any lawful interest in the property and does not divest the title of the true owner.

Knowingly disposing of stolen property is, like the actual asportation, a type of theft and a statutory offense. Being prohibited by statute, it is an illegal transaction with the meaning of Code Ann. 109A-3-305(2)(b) supra, which under the Uniform Commercial Code leaves the determination of what transactions are illegal to be decided under the statute law of the forum. This accords with decisions of our courts. In *Smith v. Wood,* 36 S.E. 649, it was held: "A note given for something . . . which the law absolutely prohibits and makes penal is based upon an illegal consideration, and is consequently void in the hands of any holder thereof. The thing for which the note is given is outlawed, and the note standing upon such a foundation is outlawed also." [In accord is] *Johnston Bros. & Co. v. McConnell,* 65 Ga.189, dealing with a sale of fertilizer prohibited by statute, and holding that contracts for the sale of articles prohibited by statute are not only void as between the parties themselves but gather no vitality by being put in circulation. "To hold otherwise would be to have them transferred as soon as executed, enabling parties claiming to be innocent, and perhaps really so, to collect money upon a consideration the foundation of which would have its existence in the positive violation of a criminal law."

It follows that the note is unenforceable even in the hands of a holder in due course, and the trial court erred in granting summary judgment for the plaintiff. [Emphasis added.]

Judgment reversed.

Incapacity of a Minor or Insane Person: When the maker or drawer of an instrument is a minor, he or she can escape liability on the ground of *incapacity*. Whether this defense is real or personal depends upon applicable state law (and as we saw in Chapter 11, state laws differ in their treatment of minors' rights). Still, the defense of *minority* is in most states a real defense. Under this view, if it is asserted by the maker or drawer of an instrument—even against an HDC—the holder recovers nothing. Similarly, if a person signs a note or draft after having been adjudicated insane by a court, his or her defense is also real, the instrument being void *ab initio.*

Extreme Duress: Most kinds of duress constitute only personal defenses. *Extreme duress,* however, is another matter; it exists where the force or threat of force is so overwhelming that the victim is entirely deprived of his or her will. A real defense exists, for example, if a person signs an instrument at gunpoint.

Discharge in Bankruptcy: In some situations the general defense of *discharge* is available to one of the parties to an instrument; yet the instrument can still circulate, and an HDC can still take it free of the defense. One kind of discharge, however, is always a real defense: the *discharge in bankruptcy.* The person who has been discharged under bankruptcy proceedings has no further liability on any outstanding instrument, even if it is held by an HDC.

Lack of Title: When a party to an instrument is being sued, he or she may be able to prove that the plaintiff is not even a holder. This defense obviously rules out any recovery by the plaintiff. Thus, if an instrument is payable to the order of P, and P's indorsement in blank is forged, no subsequent purchaser qualifies as a holder; nor can such a purchaser recover anything from the instrument's maker or drawer. Where lack of title is established, the plaintiff simply has no standing to sue; that is, the person is not the owner of the instrument he or she is attempting to enforce.

Limitations on Holder in Due Course Doctrine

The basic holder in due course concept, which permits an HDC to take an instrument free of all personal defenses, is a necessity if commercial paper is to circulate freely. In certain situations, however, the HDC doctrine has brought about results that have been the subject of increasing scrutiny and dissatisfaction. A typical example is the situation where a person purchases a consumer good, such as a TV set, from a retailer and gives the retailer an installment note in payment for it. The retailer then negotiates the instrument to a third party (usually a lending institution), who probably qualifies as an HDC. In such a case, if the TV does not work properly (or even if it is never delivered), the *buyer remains fully liable to the HDC.* The person's only recourse is to harass the retailer until he or she delivers a workable set or to recover damages for breach of contract—certainly an unsatisfactory solution for the buyer. In recent years two general kinds of limitations on the HDC doctrine have come into existence in an effort to give the purchaser of consumer goods some relief.

State Statutes

Some state legislatures have enacted statutes that give the consumer a measure of protection. Because of their diversity, these statutes can only be summarized briefly.

A few states have adopted the Uniform Consumer Credit Code (not to be confused with the UCC), which prohibits a seller of consumer goods from taking a negotiable instrument—other than a check—as evidence of the buyer's obligation. (*Walls v. Morris Chevrolet, Inc.,* in Chapter 22, is a case in point.) Some other states have enacted legislation that flatly abolishes the HDC doctrine in many situations. And a number of states have legislation requiring instruments that evidence consumer indebtedness to bear the words "commercial paper," and providing that such instruments are nonnegotiable.

The Federal Trade Commission Rule

The statutes mentioned above have brought about consumer protection that varies from state to state, and in some states they give less protection than was originally expected. For that reason, in 1975 the Federal Trade Commission (FTC) promulgated a "Rule to Preserve Buyers' Claims and Defenses in Consumer Installment Sales." This rule, usually referred to as the FTC Holder in Due Course rule, took effect in May of 1976.

In general, the FTC rule applies to two situations: (1) where a buyer of consumer goods executes a sales contract that includes giving a promissory note to the seller, and (2) where a seller of consumer goods arranges for a direct loan by a third party—usually a bank or other commercial lending institution—to the customer in order for the sale to be made.

In regard to the first situation, the rule provides in part:

> In connection with any sale or lease of goods or services to consumers, in or affecting [interstate] commerce . . . it is an unfair or deceptive trade practice . . . for a seller, directly or indirectly to (a) *Take or receive a consumer cred-*

it contract which fails to contain the following provisions in at least ten point, bold face type [emphasis added]:

NOTICE

ANY HOLDER OF THIS CONSUMER CREDIT CONTRACT IS SUBJECT TO ALL CLAIMS AND DEFENSES WHICH THE DEBTOR COULD ASSERT AGAINST THE SELLER OF GOODS OR SERVICES OBTAINED PURSUANT HERETO OR WITH THE PROCEEDS HEREOF. RECOVERY HEREUNDER BY THE DEBTOR SHALL NOT EXCEED AMOUNTS PAID BY THE DEBTOR HEREUNDER.[3]

In regard to the direct loan by a third party situation, the rule provides in part:

In connection with any sale or lease of goods or services to consumers, in or affecting [interstate] commerce . . . it is an unfair or deceptive trade practice . . . for a seller, directly or indirectly to (b) accept, as full or partial payment for such sale or lease, the proceeds of any purchase money loan . . . unless any consumer credit contract made in connection with such purchase money loan contains the following provision in at least ten point, bold face type [emphasis added]:

NOTICE

ANY HOLDER OF THIS CONSUMER CREDIT CONTRACT IS SUBJECT TO ALL CLAIMS AND DEFENSES WHICH THE DEBTOR COULD ASSERT AGAINST THE SELLER OF GOODS AND SERVICES OBTAINED WITH THE PROCEEDS HEREOF. RECOVERY HEREUNDER BY THE DEBTOR SHALL NOT EXCEED AMOUNTS PAID BY THE DEBTOR HEREUNDER.

While the FTC Rule permitting assertion of defense has widespread applicability, it does not, by any means, bring about the death of the HDC doctrine. For example, the rule does not apply to contracts of commercial buyers (as distinguished from consumer buyers), and commercial contracts account for a great deal of commercial paper activity. Additionally, the rule applies only to consumer purchases on credit; thus purchases in which checks are given in full payment are not subject to it. Finally, the rule permits the assertion of only those personal defenses which the purchaser could assert against the seller of the goods (such as fraud or breach of contract).

Questions and Problems

1. A corporation borrowed $25,000 from a bank, with the corporation giving its promissory note to the bank as evidence of the debt. As a part of the deal, the bank demanded that four individuals—including one Rochman—indorse the instrument as accommodation indorsers, who would thereby guarantee payment by the corporation. Rochman told the bank that he would indorse the note only if a Raymond D'Onofrio would also indorse it, and the bank agreed to this condition. Rochman then indorsed the note, but the bank never did get

---

[3]The failure by a seller who is a "dealer" to include the required notice in each consumer credit contract subjects that person to a possible fine of up to $10,000 and to possible liability in a civil suit brought by the customer to recover damages incurred as a result of such failure.

D'Onofrio's indorsement. When the maker of the note (the corporation) later defaulted, the bank sued Rochman as indorser. Assuming that the bank is not an HDC, can Rochman successfully assert his defense against the bank? (I.e., the defense that his liability was conditioned upon D'Onofrio's indorsement?) Explain. (*Long Island Trust Company v. International Institute for Packaging Education, Ltd.,* 344 N.E.2d 377, 1976.)

2. A salesman for a corporation demonstrated a water softening device to the Hutchinsons. Before leaving, the salesman asked them to sign a form so that he could show it to his employer as proof that he had made the demonstration. The Hutchinsons signed, and later learned that they had actually signed a promissory note. The note was subsequently negotiated to a bank, which qualified as an HDC. When the bank sued the Hutchinsons after the note came due, they claimed that they had a real defense in view of the fact that they honestly did not think they were signing a promissory note. The bank sought to overcome that defense by producing evidence that showed the Hutchinsons were intelligent people, and could easily have discovered the true nature of the instrument if they had just read it. If this evidence is true, what effect—if any—does it have upon the Hutchinsons' defense? Explain. (*Reading Trust Co. v. Hutchinson,* Court of Common Pleas of Pennsylvania, 1964.)

3. D owned a small ranch that needed a new fence around its borders. He bought the materials and hired P to put up the fence. After the fence was completed, D wrote P a check for $1,000. Two days later a rainstorm caused part of the fence to fall, indicating that the work had not been done properly. D stopped payment on the check. However, between the time D had given P the check and the time he had stopped payment on it, P had negotiated the check to H, a holder in due course. If H sues D on the check, is he entitled to the $1,000? Explain.

4. D, drawer, signs a check in blank for her son, since she is going to be out of town for two weeks; she authorizes him to fill in an amount "not over $200." D's son loses the check before he has had a chance to complete it. F, finder, fills in his own name as payee and $400 as the amount. F then negotiates the instrument to H, who pays him $350 for it. D's son notifies D that he has lost the check, and D immediately stops payment. H now wishes to enforce the check against D.

    a. What is the name of D's defense?
    b. If H does not qualify as a holder in due course, is he entitled to recover $200, $400, or nothing from D? Explain.

5. Under what circumstances is the defense of illegality a personal defense?

6. D, who is seventeen years old, purchases a suit from the P Company and pays for it by issuing that company a check for $100 (of which he is the drawer). The P Company later negotiates the check to the H Company. Before the H Company can cash the check, D stops payment on it. The H Company now seeks to hold D liable on the check, and D defends on the ground of minority. If the H Company can clearly qualify as a holder in due course, is it entitled to recover? Explain.

7. M issues a promissory note to P for $500. P alters the amount of the note to $5,000 and negotiates it to H. At the date of maturity H demands payment of $5,000 from M, and M refuses to pay H anything. If H is a holder in due course, is he entitled to receive $500, $5,000, or nothing from M? Explain.

8. What "evil" is the FTC Rule meant to eliminate, and to what two basic situations does it apply?

27

Commercial Paper/Liability of the Parties

All parties to commercial paper fall into one of two categories, as was noted in Chapter 22. Makers of notes and acceptors of drafts are *primary* parties, and all others are *secondary* parties.

As a general rule, a primary party is absolutely liable on the instrument, while a secondary party is only conditionally liable on it. Before we examine the ramifications of this rule—and its exceptions—in this chapter, however, we have to recall how a person becomes a "party" in the first place.

Sec. 3-401(1) of the UCC provides that "no person is liable on an instrument unless his signature appears thereon." Sec. 3-403 provides that a signature may be made "by an agent or other representative," but Sec. 3-404 goes on to say that "any unauthorized signature is wholly inoperative as that of the person whose name is signed unless he ratifies it or is precluded from denying it."

Agency Problems

Usually, the maker, acceptor, drawer, or indorser does in fact personally sign the instrument, and in such instances there is no trouble with the above sections. However, in cases where the instrument is signed by an agent or other representative, two related problems arise. The first involves the liability of the principal (the person whom the agent is representing, and whose name is signed to the instrument), and the second involves the personal liability of the agent or representative himself. (These problems—or potential problems—take on an added significance when one realizes that all commercial paper issued by corporations necessarily involves corporate names being signed by their agents, since all corporate activity can be carried on only through actions of agents and employees.)

In approaching the most common principal/agent liability problems, let us assume initially that the signature on the instrument is in proper form—i.e., it identifies the principal and indicates that the signing is being done by an agent (for example, "P, principal, by A, agent" or "X Company by T, treasurer). Here the *principal alone is liable,* assuming that the agent possessed the authority to sign the instrument [Sec. 3-403(1)].[1] (If the agent did *not* have that authority, the agent alone is liable on the instrument [Sec. 3-440(1)].)

Three additional situations are governed by Sec. 3-403(2). The first of these is where the agent signs his or her own name to the instrument, intending to bind the principal, but the instrument "neither names the person represented nor shows that the representative signed in a representative capacity." For example: Adkins, who is Polaski's agent, signs a note "Adkins." Because Polaski's name does not appear on the note, he has no liability on it. The liability is thus Adkins' alone.

The two remaining situations are (a) where the instrument does name the principal, but does not show that the agent signed in a representative capacity, and (b) where the instrument does not name the principal, but does show that the agent signed in a representative capacity. (An example of a would be where Polaski's name appears as principal, but Adkins—after signing his own name—fails to add the word "agent," "vice-president," or some other title indicating an agency status. An example of b would be where Polaski's name does not appear at all, and the only signature is "Adkins, agent.")

Sec. 3-403(2)(b) applies to both of these situations. It provides that "except as otherwise established between the immediate parties, the representative (agent) is personally obligated on the instrument." Thus if the agent is being sued by a third-party holder—i.e., someone to whom the instrument has been negotiated—the agent is fully liable. (On the other hand, as a result of the exception, if the agent is being sued by the *payee,* the agent is permitted to introduce evidence—if there is such evidence—showing that the agent was only signing in a representative capacity, and that the payee knew this to be the case. In such a circumstance the agent is not liable.)

In the case below the holder of a number of corporate checks brought action

---

[1]For a discussion of the different kinds of authority an agent might possess, see Chapters 29 and 30.

against the corporation's president in an effort to hold him personally liable on them. Note the factors to which the higher court looked *in addition to* the form of the signature in concluding that the instrument *did* indicate that the president was signing only in a representative capacity.

Pollin v. Mindy Mfg. Co. and Apfelbaum

Superior Court of Pennsylvania, 236 A.2d 542 (1967)

In September 1966 the Mindy Mfg. Co. issued to its employees payroll checks that were drawn on the Continental Bank and Trust Co. of Norristown, Pennsylvania. Thirty-six employees indorsed their checks to Pollin, who operated a check cashing business. Payment on these checks was refused by the drawee bank (Continental) because Mindy did not have sufficient funds in its account. These checks were returned to Pollin, who then brought suit against Mindy and Robert Apfelbaum, Mindy's president.

Each check was "boldly imprinted" at the top: "Mindy Mfg. Co."; each clearly stated that it was a payroll check; and "Mindy Mfg. Co." was also imprinted in the lower right-hand corner of each check, with two blank lines appearing below it. Apfelbaum had simply signed his name on one of the blank lines, *without indicating his position or his capacity in any way*. It was on this basis that the trial court ruled Apfelbaum to be personally liable.

The trial court entered judgments against both the Mindy company and Apfelbaum. Apfelbaum appealed this judgment, claiming that he signed only in a *representative capacity* and thus could not be held personally liable on the checks.

Montgomery, Justice: . . . Judgment against [Apfelbaum] was entered by the lower court on the authority of Section 3-403 of the Uniform Commercial Code . . . which provides, "An authorized representative who signs his name to an instrument . . . (b) except as otherwise established between the immediate parties, is personally obligated if the instrument names the person represented but *does not show that the representative signed in a representative capacity* . . .," and our decisions thereunder. [Emphasis added.]

The issue before us, therefore, is whether a third party to the original transaction, the endorsee in the present case, may recover against one who affixes his name to a check in the place where a [drawer] usually signs without indicating he is signing in a representative capacity, without giving consideration to other parts of the instrument or extrinsic evidence. This appears to be a novel question under the Uniform Commercial Code.

If this were an action brought by the payee, parol [oral] evidence would be permitted to establish the capacity of the person affixing his signature under Section 3-403 previously recited and our decisions in *Bell v. Dornan* and *Pittsburgh National Bank v. Kemilworth Restaurant.*

However, since this is an action brought by a third party our initial inquiry must be for the purpose of determining whether *the instrument* indicates the capacity of appellant as signer. Admittedly, the instrument fails to show the office held by appellant. However, we do not think this is a complete answer to our problem, since the Code imposes liability on the individual only ". . . if the instrument . . . does not show that the representative signed in a representative capacity . . .". *This implies that the instrument must be considered in its entirety.* [Emphasis added.]

Although Section 3-401(2) of the Code provides that "A signature is made by use of any name, including any trade or assumed name, upon an instrument, or by any word or mark used in lieu of a written signature," which would be broad enough to include the printed name of a corporation, we do not believe that a check showing two lines under the imprinted corporate name indicating the [place for the] signature of one or more corporate officers would be accepted by any reasonably prudent person as a fully executed check of the corporation. It is common to expect that a corporate name placed upon a negotiable instrument in order to bind the corporation as [drawer], especially when printed on the instrument, will be accompanied by the signatures of officers authorized by the by-laws to sign the instrument. While we do not rule out the possibility of a printed name being established as an acceptable signature, we hold that such a situation is uncommon, and in the present case the two lines under the printed name dictate against a valid corporate signature [in the absence of a signature by an officer].

Next we must give consideration to the distinction between a check and a note. A check is an order of a depositor on a bank in the nature of a draft drawn on the bank and payable on demand. It is revokable until paid or accepted for payment. A note is an irrevocable promise to pay on the part of the maker. The [drawer] of a check impliedly engages not only that it will be paid, but that he will have sufficient funds in the bank to meet it. In the present instance the checks clearly showed that they were payable from a special account set up by the corporate defendant for the purpose of paying its employees. This information disclosed by the instrument of itself *would refute any contention* that the appellant intended to make the instrument *his own order* on the named bank to pay money to the payee. [Emphasis added.] The money was payable from the account of the corporation, over which appellant as an individual had no control.

Considering the instrument as a whole we conclude that it sufficiently discloses that appellant signed it in a representative capacity. . . .

Judgment reversed and entered for appellant-defendant.

Liability of Primary Parties

For the remainder of this chapter we will make two assumptions: (1) that the party whose liability is being examined signed the instrument, personally, and (2) that such party does not have an assertable defense against the holder. On this basis we will first examine the liability of *primary parties* (makers of notes and acceptors of drafts).

Liability of the Maker

Contractual Liability: The maker of a note is *primarily* (absolutely) *liable* on it. That is, the party has the duty to pay the instrument at its maturity date even if the holder does not demand payment at that time. Sec. 3-413(1) provides that "the maker or acceptor engages [promises] that he will pay the instrument according to its tenor at the time of his engagement or as completed pursuant to Section 3-115 on incomplete instruments."

Furthermore, the maker—unlike the indorser—*is not discharged in any way by the fact that the instrument is presented for payment late;* thus, even if a note is presented for payment many months or even years after its due date, the maker remains fully liable on it (until the Statute of Limitations has run).

There is, however, one exception to this rule. Under Sec. 3-502(1)(b), where the note is payable at a specified bank, and where presentment is not made at maturity, and where the bank becomes insolvent after the maturity date but before present-ment for payment actually occurs—with the result that the maker is "deprived of funds" during the delay—the maker "may discharge his liability by written assign-ment to the holder of his rights against . . . the payor bank in respect [to] such funds." To illustrate: A note is made payable at the X Bank on March 1, at which time the maker has sufficient funds on deposit to meet the note. Presentment is not made on March 1 even though the UCC requires it.[2] On March 10 the bank fails. Presentment is finally made by the holder on March 11, at which time, of course, he does not obtain payment, because the bank has closed. In this case the maker can assign his rights against the funds in the bank (to the extent of the amount of the note) to the holder and thereby be discharged of further liability. Thus, if the bank does not pay out a hundred cents on the dollar, the loss falls on the holder, because of the late presentment.

Liability on Admissions: By signing a promissory note, the maker *admits* (guaran-tees) certain facts. Sec. 3-413(3) provides in part that the maker "admits against all subsequent parties . . . the existence of the payee and his then capacity [capacity at the time of signing the note] to indorse." Thus, if no such payee exists and a purchaser suffers a loss thereby, or if the payee is a minor who negotiated the instrument and subsequently recovered it from the transferee/holder by rescinding his or her indorsement, such holder can recover from the maker any damages incurred as a result of the nonexistence of the payee or as a result of the rescission.

Liability of the Acceptor

As we saw in Chapter 22, time drafts are frequently presented to the drawee prior to maturity for his or her *acceptance.* Under the UCC, in some instances present-ment for acceptance is mandatory while in others it is optional. In any event, when the drawee accepts the instrument he or she becomes liable on it for the first time.[3]

Once an acceptance occurs, the liability of the drawee/acceptor is virtually identical to that of the maker of a note. Under Sec. 3-413(3), by accepting, he or she admits the existence of the payee and that person's then capacity to indorse. More importantly, under Sec. 3-413(1) the drawee/acceptor promises to pay the instrument at its maturity date. Again the obligation to pay is not cut off or diminished by a late presentment for payment.[4] The only exception to this rule of

---

[2]Presentment here is due on March 1 because, under a rule to be examined later, an instrument that is payable at a fixed future date must ordinarily be presented for payment *on that date.*

[3]While acceptance does not take place in the case of checks, they can be "certified," an act that is similar to acceptance (see Chapter 28 for details).

[4]The primary rules prescribing the various times at which presentments for acceptance and/or payment should be made are discussed later in the chapter.

continuing liability arises in the same circumstances as those connected with the liability of the maker of a note—where the draft is payable at a bank and where that bank becomes insolvent between the time presentment should have been made under the code and the time it actually was made. Again, the drawer can discharge his or her liability to the holder by giving that person an assignment of funds, just as the maker of a note can do in similar circumstances.

Two further observations regarding acceptances are needed:

1. Until a draft is accepted, the drawee has no liability on the instrument to the payee or to any other holder. As we will see later in this chapter, the drawee usually owes the *drawer* a legal duty to accept the instrument, but failure to accept is not a breach of duty owed to any *holder* of the draft. Thus, if a holder presents the draft for acceptance and the drawee refuses to accept, the holder cannot bring action against the drawee (though he or she can bring action against the drawer, who is a secondary party).

2. As a general rule, a refusal by the drawee to accept a draft that is properly presented constitutes a "dishonor" of the instrument, which triggers the liability of secondary parties on the instrument—the drawer and all indorsers except those indorsing "without recourse" (that is, without guaranteeing payment). The precise elements and ramifications of a dishonor will be examined later in this chapter.

General Liability of Secondary Parties; Promissory Liability

Secondary parties are *drawers* of drafts and checks and *indorsers* of all instruments. The liability of these parties is significantly less than that of primary parties.

Primary parties *absolutely promise* to pay the instruments they have signed. Secondary parties promise to pay *only if certain conditions are met:* (1) due presentment, (2) dishonor, and (3) notice of dishonor. Essentially, the secondary party (except for the "without recourse" indorser) is saying, "I will pay this instrument to anyone holding it *if* it is presented to the primary party (or the drawee), and *if* he or she dishonors it (usually by failing to pay), and *if* I am given notice of the dishonor." These conditions, unless waived, must be met in order for the secondary party to be held on his or her *promissory liability.*[5] The conditions need not be met, however, if a person is seeking to hold the secondary party on his or her *warranty liability* (which will be examined later in this chapter).

Liability of Drawers

All drawers, like makers and acceptors, admit the existence of the payee and his or her then capacity to indorse. Of more importance, however, is the drawer's promissory liability.

---

[5]Some drafts provide that the drawer waives presentment, dishonor, and notice of dishonor. In this discussion, however, we will assume that no such waiver exists. (Also, under Sec. 3-511, delay in presentment and notice of dishonor are excused in certain circumstances.)

As we have indicated, the contractual liability of the drawer of a draft or check is conditional in nature; that is, by drawing the instrument the person agrees to become liable on it only under specified conditions. Sec. 3-413(2) provides in part that "the drawer engages that upon dishonor of the draft and any necessary notice of dishonor . . . he will pay the amount of the draft to the holder or to any indorser who takes it up." Because dishonor necessarily involves, as a first step, presentment of the draft to the acceptor (or the drawee if there is no acceptor), three conditions must be met: (1) presentment for acceptance and/or payment, (2) dishonor (refusal to accept or pay, as the case may be), and (3) notice of dishonor to the drawer.

Presentment of Drafts

While checks and promissory notes require only presentment for payment in order to hold the drawer and indorsers liable, drafts often involve two presentments—*presentment for acceptance* and, later, *presentment for payment.* Under Sec. 3-501(1)(a), presentment for acceptance is *required* in three situations. This section provides that, unless excused, the presentment is necessary to charge the drawer and indorsers (1) "where the draft so provides," (2) where it "is payable elsewhere than at the residence or place of business of the drawee," or (3) where its "date of payment depends upon such presentment."[6] The section also provides that "the holder may *at his option* present for acceptance *any other draft payable at a stated date*" (which excludes drafts payable on demand). (Emphasis added.)

The following situation illustrates these two presentments (the presentment for acceptance in this case falling into the "optional" category). D draws a draft on X, payable to the order of P. The draft is dated and issued on May 1 and is payable the following September 1. After P receives the draft, he wants some assurance that the instrument will actually be paid at maturity; he gets this assurance by presenting the draft to X, the drawee, at some time before the date of maturity (say on May 20) for acceptance. X accepts the instrument by signing it on its face, thereby becoming liable as an acceptor, and returns the draft to P. P can then either retain the instrument until its maturity date or negotiate it further.

Regardless of whether P negotiates it further, the person who is the holder of the draft at maturity will present it at that time to X (the drawee/acceptor) for payment. X will most likely pay as promised, and the question of secondary party liability will not arise. Occasionally, however, an acceptance or payment of a draft is refused by the drawee or acceptor, which brings us to the subject of dishonor.

Dishonor of Drafts

For most drafts, a dishonor can occur in either of two ways—by a *refusal to accept* or by a *refusal to pay at maturity.* Thus, in the above case, if X had refused

---

[6]An example of the kind of instrument referred to is one "payable ninety days after sight." *Sight* means acceptance, so the ninety days does not begin to run until acceptance is made.

acceptance on May 20, a dishonor would have taken place at that time, and the drawer (and indorsers, if any) would have been held on their secondary liability. A dishonor would also have occurred if X had accepted the draft on May 20 but had refused payment when the draft was presented on September 1. (Note that refusal of the drawee to accept an instrument constitutes a dishonor not only in those cases where presentment for acceptance is mandatory but also, with time drafts, where presentment is optional.)

Time of Presentment

Sec. 3-503 brings together the rules that set the time limits within which presentments for acceptance and/or payment must be made. While it is standard procedure to introduce those rules at this point (i.e., as they effect the liability of the drawer), we have chosen to summarize them in the following section, Liability of Indorsers, instead. The reason for this delay is twofold. First, in the great majority of cases, drawers of drafts are *not* freed of liability by a late presentment for acceptance or payment; nor are drawers of checks freed by a late presentment for payment.[7] Second, by contrast, indorsers *are* entirely freed of their conditional liability by a late presentment. The rules specifying the times when presentments and notices of dishonor must be made thus generally have far more relevance to the liability of indorsers than to any other parties.

Liability of Indorsers

Unqualified indorsers have two kinds of liability—*conditional liability* and *warranty liability*. Qualified ("without recourse") indorsers, on the other hand, incur warranty liability only. These two general kinds of liability will be discussed in order.

Conditional Liability

All unqualified indorsers promise that they will pay the instrument themselves if (1) the instrument is properly presented for acceptance and/or payment, (2) the instrument is dishonored, and (3) a proper notice of dishonor is given them. Thus, in general, the *conditional or secondary liability* of the indorser is much like that of the drawer of an instrument—with one important difference. If either a required

---

[7]For example, about the only situation in which the drawer is discharged to any extent by a late presentment for acceptance is where (1) the presentment was required, (2) it was not made "on or before" the due date of the instrument, and (3) the drawee became insolvent after the maturity date but before the presentment actually occurred. In this situation the drawer can discharge his or her liability by giving an assignment of funds to the holder, just as the maker and acceptor of an instrument payable at a bank can do in similar situations. But in real life the drawee rarely becomes insolvent during the delay, and the drawer's liability is undiminished. Similarly, the drawer of a check is not freed of liability by a late presentment for payment to the drawee bank except where the bank has become insolvent during the delay—also a rare event.

presentment for acceptance or a presentment for payment is made late, the indorser is entirely freed of contractual liability to the holder of the instrument.[8] The same is true where a proper presentment for acceptance and/or payment is made, but the holder gives the indorser a late notice or no notice at all of the dishonor.

How Presentments Are Made: Under Sec. 3-504(1), presentment is a demand for acceptance or payment made upon the maker, acceptor, drawee, or other payor by or on behalf of the holder. It can be made by mail (in which case the time of presentment is the time at which it is received); through a clearing house; at the place specified in the instrument; or, if no place is specified, at the place of business or at the residence of the maker. (In the latter case, if neither the maker "nor anyone authorized to act for him is accessible" at such place, then presentment is excused.) The importance of these rules is that if an attempted presentment is made in any manner other than these authorized ways, a refusal of the maker, acceptor, or drawee at that time does not constitute a dishonor.

Time of Presentment: As we have indicated, a required presentment must be made not only in a proper manner but also at a *proper time* if indorsers are to be held on their conditional liability. What is a proper time depends upon the type of presentment (presentment for acceptance or presentment for payment), and the time at which the instrument is payable.

Sec. 3-503(1) sets forth the rules for determining the times at which *all* presentments must be made. In the interest of brevity, we will concern ourselves only with those parts of this section that apply to presentments for payment. (This section appears in full on page 945 of the Appendix.)

Subsections c and e of Sec. 3-503(1) provide us with the two basic rules. In essence, they are as follows: (1) If an instrument is payable at a specified time (e.g., "November 20, 1982"), presentment must be made *on that date* if secondary parties are to be held liable. (2) As to all other instruments—demand notes, demand drafts, and checks—presentment must be made *within a reasonable time after the secondary party signed the instrument.*

Sec. 3-503(2) goes on to provide that "a reasonable time for presentment is determined by the nature of the instrument, any usage of banking or trade, and the facts of the particular case." For the time of presentment of *checks,* however, the section is more specific. In regard to uncertified checks drawn and payable within the U.S., Sec. 3-503(2) provides that "with respect to the liability of the drawer" of such checks, a reasonable time is presumed to be "30 days after [its] date or issue, whichever is later." And "with respect to the liability of an indorser" a reasonable time is presumed to be "seven days after his indorsement."

---

[8]We are assuming throughout this section that the requirements of dishonor and notice of dishonor are not waived. In some situations, however, the purchaser of an instrument will not take it unless the transferor's indorsement provides that "presentment, dishonor, and notice of dishonor are hereby waived" (by the indorser). In such cases the discussion is inapplicable.

We will now examine several of the more common fact-patterns to which these rules apply.[9]

1. *Promissory note, payable at a fixed future date.* On March 3, M signs a note as maker and issues it to P, payee. The note is payable the following September 5th. P indorses the instrument in blank later in March and negotiates it to H. H presents the note to M for payment on September 10, and it is dishonored (i.e., M simply does not pay it). Here H cannot hold the indorser, P, liable. Under Sec. 3-503(1)(c), where an instrument "shows the date on which it is payable, presentment is due on that date"; thus any presentment after September 5 is late, and all indorsers are freed of their conditional liability.

2. *Promissory note, payable on demand.* On February 2, M signs a note as maker and issues it to P, payee. The note is payable "on demand." On March 2, P indorses the instrument via a blank indorsement and negotiates it to H. On May 20, H presents the note to M for payment, and it is dishonored. H now brings action against P on her indorsement. Since the note is a demand note and thus governed by Sec. 3-503(1)(e), H—in order to hold P—must show that his presentment on May 20 was within a reasonable time after P indorsed the instrument. (As indicated earlier, a reasonable time as to demand notes and drafts "is determined by the nature of the instrument, any usage of banking or trade, and the facts of the particular case." Under this clause, for example, it is generally held that an interest-bearing demand note can be presented somewhat later than one bearing no interest.)

3. *Regular (uncertified) check.* D draws a check on his account in the B Bank payable to the order of P on April 6, and he issues it to P on that date. P, by a blank indorsement, negotiates the check to X on April 15, and X, by blank indorsement, negotiates it to H on April 20. On April 26, H presents the check to the drawee, the B Bank, and payment is refused for some reason; H then gives immediate notice of the dishonor to both indorsers, P and X. Under the "seven day" rule of Sec. 3-503(2) that applies to indorsers of ordinary checks, the last indorser (X) is liable to H, but the prior indorser, P, is not. Since P indorsed on April 15, he could be held on his conditional liability only if the check were presented to the drawee bank, or at least put into the bank collection process, within seven days—by April 22. In this case presentment on April 26 was thus late as to P but effective as to X, since the presentment was within seven days of X's becoming an indorser. And if action were brought by H against D (drawer) as well, obviously the presentment *as to him* would be timely, since it would conform to the "within thirty days of issue" rule applicable to drawers.

Notice of Dishonor and Protest: When a dishonor occurs, either by a refusal to accept or by nonpayment, any indorser is freed of conditional liability unless he or she is given a *notice of dishonor* within the time specified by Sec. 3-508. That

---

[9]The next court case in this chapter also is concerned with "time of presentment," although it appears in a later section.

section provides in part that "any necessary notice must be given by a bank before its midnight deadline, and by any other person before midnight of the third business day after dishonor."[10] The indorser receiving the notice then has the same prescribed time in which to give notice to his or her immediate indorser, if any.

Sec. 3-508 also provides that notice can be given "in any reasonable manner, and may be oral or written." However, it must at least identify the instrument and state that it has been dishonored.

Under Sec. 3-509, in some situations a *protest* (a formal, notarized notice of dishonor) can be made. Protest is required only where the dishonored instrument is drawn in or payable in a foreign country. As to other instruments, use of protest in lieu of ordinary notice of dishonor is optional.

The following case, an action brought by an indorser of an accelerated note to have a judgment set aside, presents a typical situation in which a court must determine whether the holder of an instrument presented it for payment within the time allowed by law. The further question of due notice of dishonor is also discussed.

Hane v. Exten
Maryland Court of Appeals, 259 A.2d 290 (1969)

A note was issued by Theta Electronic Laboratories payable to George and Marguerite Thomson. The instrument was a time installment note with an acceleration clause providing that if any installment payment was missed, the entire note became due on demand. The note also contained a confession of judgment clause, which permits the holder to obtain judgment against the maker and indorsers, in the event of default by the maker, without the necessity of first bringing suit against the parties.

The note was indorsed by three persons, one of whom was Exten, and thereafter it was negotiated to Hane. A payment was missed by Theta in late 1965. Eighteen months later Hane demanded payment of the entire instrument from Theta, and payment was refused. Hane then obtained a judgment by confession against Theta and indorsers.

Exten then brought action to have the judgment set aside, claiming that the presentment for payment and notice of dishonor were not in conformity with the UCC. The lower court decided in Exten's favor, and Hane appealed.

Singley, Justice: . . . This case raises the familiar question: Must Hane show that [there was a timely presentment of the note, and that the] Extens were given notice of presentment and dishonor before he can hold them on their endorsement?

The court below, in finding for the Extens, relied on the provisions of [Sec. 3-414(1) of the UCC] which provides:

Unless the indorsement otherwise specifies (as by such words as "without recourse"), every indorser engages that upon dishonor and any necessary notice of dishonor and

---

[10]The midnight deadline rule requires that if payment cannot be made because of insufficient funds or because a stop payment order has been issued, the drawee bank must give notice to its transferor no later than *midnight of the next business day.* If that transferor is also a bank, it must in turn give notice by midnight of the day following its receipt of the original notice.

protest he will pay the instrument according to its tenor at the time of his indorsement to the holder or to any subsequent indorser who takes it up, even though the indorser who takes it up was not obligated to do so.

Section 3-501(1)(b) provides that "Presentment for payment is necessary to charge any indorser" and § 3-501(2)(a) that "Notice of any dishonor is necessary to charge any indorser" [in each case subject, however, to the provisions of § 3-511, which recite the circumstances under which notice of dishonor may be waived or excused, none of which is here present]. Section 3-502(1)(a) makes it clear that unless presentment or notice of dishonor is waived or excused, *unreasonable delay* will discharge an indorser. [Emphasis added.]

There was testimony from which the trier of facts [the trial judge] *could find as he did that presentment and notice of dishonor were unduly delayed.* [Emphasis added.]

It is clear that Hane held the note from November, 1965, until some time in April, 1967, before he made demand for payment. UCC § 3-503(1)(d) provides that "Where an instrument is accelerated, presentment for payment is due within a reasonable time after the acceleration." "Reasonable time" is not defined in § 3-503, except that § 3-503(2) provides, "A reasonable time for presentment is determined by the nature of the instrument, any usage of banking or trade and the facts of the particular case," but § 1-204(2) characterizes it: "What is a reasonable time for taking any action depends on the nature, purposes, and circumstances of such action."

Reasonableness is primarily a question for the fact finder. *We see no reason to disturb the lower court's finding that Hane's delay of almost 18 months in presenting the note "was unreasonable from any viewpoint."* [Emphasis added.]

As regards notice of dishonor, § 3-508(2) requires that notice be given by persons other than banks "before midnight of the third business day after dishonor or receipt of notice of dishonor." Exten, called as an adverse witness by Hane, testified that his first notice that the note had not been paid was the entry of the confessed judgment on 7 June 1967. Hane's brother testified that demand had been made about 15 April 1967. He was uncertain as to when he had given Exten notice of dishonor, but finally conceded that it was "within a week." The lower court found that the ambiguity of this testimony, coupled with Exten's denial that he had received any notice before 7 June *fell short of meeting the three day notice requirement of the UCC.* [Emphasis added.] The date of giving notice of dishonor is a question of fact, solely for determination by the trier of facts. We cannot say that the court erred in its finding.

In absence of evidence that presentment and notice of dishonor were waived or excused, Hane's unreasonable delay discharged the Extens, § 3-502(1)(a) .... Hane makes much of the fact that he is a holder in due course. We doubt that he was, since there is some evidence that he took the note with notice that it was overdue, § 3-302(1)(c). ... Whether Hane was or was not a holder in due course has no relevance to the issue here presented. In either case timely presentment and notice of dishonor were required to hold the Extens. Whether Hane was or was not a holder in due course is of no significance unless there was a defense which could have been asserted against the payee.

Judgment [for Exten] affirmed.

When Presentment Is Excused or Delay Permitted: Sec. 3-511(1) provides: "Delay in presentment, protest or notice of dishonor is excused when the party is without notice that it is due or when the delay is caused by circumstances beyond his control and he exercises reasonable diligence after the cause of the delay ceases to operate." The phrase *without notice that it is due* has particular application to an instrument containing an acceleration clause. It is entirely possible that a holder will take an instrument *after* the time of payment has been accelerated but having no knowledge of the acceleration at the time of taking it. The phrase *circumstances beyond his control* excuses delay in presentment or in notice of dishonor when the delay is caused by such things as extreme weather conditions or the emergency closing of businesses in a certain area by act of the governor of the involved state.

Additionally, Sec. 3-511(2) provides that presentment or notice of dishonor is entirely excused if the party to be charged (1) has waived presentment or notice; (2) has personally dishonored or stopped payment on the instrument; or (3) "if by reasonable diligence the presentment . . . cannot be made, or the notice given."

General Liability of Secondary Parties; Warranty Liability

Warranty Liability

Every indorser makes certain warranties (or guarantees) about the instrument he or she is negotiating. These warranties create what is sometimes called the unconditional liability of secondary parties, meaning that the liability is *not* conditioned upon proper presentment, dishonor, and notice of dishonor.

Unqualified Indorsers: The warranties made by all unqualified indorsers are set forth below. (With an exception to be noted later, the same warranties are also made by qualified indorsers.)

Sec. 3-417(2) provides in part that a person who negotiates an instrument by indorsement and who receives consideration for it makes five warranties to the indorsee and subsequent holders.[11] Under this section the indorser essentially warrants that:

(a) he or she has good title to the instrument;

(b) all signatures are genuine or authorized;

(c) the instrument has not been materially altered;

(d) no defense of any party is good against him or her (the indorser); and

(e) he or she has no knowledge of any insolvency proceeding instituted against the maker, acceptor, or drawer of an unaccepted instrument.

We will briefly illustrate the first four of these warranties (the fifth being but rarely encountered).

A breach of *warranty of title* often involves a forged indorsement. For example: D draws and issues an instrument payable to the order of P. The instrument is stolen from P, and the thief forges P's indorsement on the back of it. He then sells the instrument to X, an innocent purchaser. X, by blank indorsement, negotiates the instrument to H. H presents the instrument for payment, but payment is refused because the maker, acceptor, or drawee has learned that P's indorsement

---

[11]The liability of a person who negotiates an instrument *by delivery only* (without indorsing it) will be discussed later in the chapter.

is a forgery. Because of the forged indorsement of P, H has not acquired title to the instrument and cannot hold the maker (or acceptor or drawee, in the case of a draft or check) liable on it. However, he can hold X liable on the warranty of title theory, because X did not have title either, because of the forged indorsement. X is liable on this warranty even if he had no reason to suspect the forgery and (as is true of all other warranties) even if the presentment for payment by H to the primary party was late.

The warranty that *all signatures are genuine or authorized* is almost self-explanatory. Suppose, for example, that P received a note of which M was the apparent maker. P later indorsed the note to H, and H recovered nothing from M because M was able to prove that her signature on the note was a forgery. (It may take a lawsuit against M to establish the fact of the forgery, or the evidence may be so convincing that H forgoes a lawsuit against M.) H can now hold P (the indorser) on his warranty that all signatures on the instrument at the time of the indorsement were genuine. Again, H need not show that P knew of the forgery when he indorsed; it is the fact of the forgery that is controlling.

We discussed the defense of *material alteration* in Chapter 26, where we saw that a maker or acceptor might escape liability on an instrument by showing that it was materially altered after he or she had made (or accepted) it. The ordinary holder who presents for payment in this situation will probably recover nothing from the maker or acceptor, and an HDC may make only a partial recovery (especially if the alteration involved a raising of the amount of the instrument). However, either holder can hold any indorser liable on the breach of warranty theory and thereby recover whatever loss he or she sustained—assuming, of course, that the alteration occurred before the indorsement.

The warranty that *no defense is good against the indorser* refers to the kinds of defenses that do not fall within the first three subsections of Sec. 3-417(2)—as, for example, the defense of illegality. To illustrate: After a Saturday night poker game A ends up owing B $175; A gives B a check for that amount in payment. The following Monday A learns from a lawyer friend that gambling debts are totally unenforceable in his state, so he stops payment on the check. In the meantime B has indorsed the check to C. In this situation, after being refused payment by the drawee bank, C can hold B (the indorser) liable for breach of the warranty that no defense existed against him.

Qualified Indorsers: The warranty liability of the person who indorses "without recourse" is exactly the same as that of the unqualified indorser—with one exception. While the unqualified indorser flatly guarantees that no defense of any party is good against him or her (refer back to Sec. 3-417(2)(d)), the qualified indorser warrants only that he or she "has no knowledge of such a defense" (Sec. 3-417(3)). Thus, if a check were given in payment of a totally illegal obligation and subsequently a party indorsed the instrument "without recourse," that indorser would not be liable upon dishonor unless it were established that he or she *knew of the defense* at the time of indorsement.

However, this warranty applies only to defenses falling within Subsection d.

Thus, if the qualified indorser were being sued for breach of the warranty that all signatures were genuine (Subsection b), the person would be liable if the drawer's or maker's signature were a forgery, even if he or she did not know of the forgery.

The next case shows particularly well how the application of Sec. 3-417(3) works out in real life.

Fair Finance Co. v. Fourco, Inc.

Court of Appeals of Ohio, 237 N.E.2d 406 (1968)

Fourco, defendant, sold goods to a buyer and had the buyer, in payment thereof, sign a promissory note payable to the order of Fourco. (For this reason, Fourco is usually referred to in the decision as the vendor-payee.)

Fourco indorsed the note "without recourse" and negotiated it to Fair Finance, plaintiff. When plaintiff sought payment from the maker (the buyer of the goods), it was discovered that the defendant (the payee and qualified indorser) had computed the interest at too high a rate in determining the face amount of the note. The maker was thus obligated to pay to plaintiff only the corrected amount due, and plaintiff then sought recovery of the balance from defendant/indorser.

The lower court found that defendant had no notice of the fact that the interest provided for in its note was usurious (in excess of that permitted by Ohio law). In view of this fact, the court ruled that defendant, having transferred the instrument by qualified indorsement, was not liable to plaintiff for the balance of the interest. Plaintiff appealed.

Hunsicker, Justice: ... Is this, then, a matter which is provided for in the Uniform Commercial Code?

Section 1303.53, Revised Code (U.C.C. 3-417), says in part:

(B) Any person who transfers an instrument and receives consideration warrants to his transferee and if the transfer is by indorsement to any subsequent holder who takes the instrument in good faith that: ... (4) no defense of any party is good against him; and

(C) By transferring "without recourse" the transferor limits the obligation stated in division (B)(4) ... to a warranty that he has no knowledge of such a defense. ...

Fair Finance Company admits that Fourco, Inc., had no [actual] knowledge of the defense of improper computation until after an attempt to obtain payment by court action against the maker was instituted. There is no claim of fraud in the sale and purchase of this promissory note. Counsel for the Fair Finance Company, in their statements to the trial court and to this court, [however,] said: "We do claim unintentional misrepresentation." [Fair Finance's claim] of misrepresentation arises from the fact that interest on the note was [accidentally] calculated by the vendor, Fourco, Inc., at the beginning of the interest period and taken in advance instead of at the end of the interest period.

Is the claim of "unintentional misrepresentation" such that it is exempt from the provisions of Section 1303.53(B)(4) and (C), Revised Code, set out above? We find no reported cases in Ohio, or elsewhere, interpreting this section of the Uniform Commercial Code. Counsel have cited several cases from other jurisdictions which bear on the question, [but these] were decided prior to the adoption of the Uniform Commercial Code. ...

The vendor in the instant case, Fourco, Inc., used its own printed note to obtain the written promise of the maker. The terms of that note concerning the computation of interest were its handiwork. The computation of interest was not made by the maker but by the vendor of the note who now wishes, because of its own error and improper computation of interest, to be relieved of liability because of the endorsement, "without recourse." Is this such a lack of knowledge of a defense as releases the vendor-indorser from liability? *We think it is not,* for we believe that where an indorsement of a promissory note "without recourse" is made by a vendor-payee, who computes the interest incorrectly in determining the face value of that note at the time of sale, and where the form of note and terms thereof are those of the vendor-payee, *such vendor-payee has knowledge of that wrongful computation, and the defense arising therefrom, within the terms of Section 1303.53(C), Revised Code.* [Emphasis added.]

It is the conclusion of this court that the judgment must be reversed, and, as there is no dispute as to the facts, final judgment shall be ordered entered herein for the appellant, Fair Finance Company, for the amount admitted by the parties hereto as being the improper computation of interest by Fourco, Inc.

Judgment is reversed.

Liability of Transferor without Indorsement

Selected Transferor/Indorser Problems

A person who negotiates a bearer instrument by mere delivery (without indorsing it) has no conditional liability on the instrument. Thus, if the primary party is unable to pay the instrument at maturity, the transferor is not liable to the holder.

However, a transferor by mere delivery does have the same warranty liability as an unqualified indorser, with one important exception. While the warranties of indorsers run to all subsequent holders of the instrument, the warranties of the person who transfers without indorsement run only to his or her *immediate transferee.* To illustrate: P receives a bearer note of which M is apparently the maker. P negotiates the note to X by delivery only, and X in turn negotiates it by delivery only to H. If M's signature turns out to be a forgery, H can hold X, his immediate transferor, liable on his warranty that all signatures are genuine, but he cannot hold P, the prior transferor. (Of course, if X has to pay damages to H arising out of the breach of his warranty, X can then hold P because P's warranty did run to him.)

Order of Indorsers' Liability

Where two or more indorsements appear on an instrument, it is presumed, under Sec. 3-414(2), that the indorsers are liable in the order in which their signatures appear. Suppose that a note is indorsed by X, and the names of Y and Z appear successively below her indorsement. If Z is held liable to the holder, H, following a dishonor, Z can proceed against Y and Y against X. X will then be limited to an attempt to recover the amount of the instrument from the maker.[12]

While the holder of a dishonored instrument usually seeks to hold the last

---

[12]It is only *presumed* that the indorsers are liable in the order in which their signatures appear; a contrary agreement may exist among the indorsers. Thus, in the example above, X will not be liable to Y if she can prove that such an agreement existed between her and Y at the time of her indorsement.

indorser liable, the holder is not limited to such a proceeding. For example, in the above case, if, upon dishonor, H *gives proper notice* to X, Y, and Z, he can then "skip" Y and Z if he wishes and bring suit directly against X, the first indorser.

Liability of Accommodation Indorsers

Sometimes a person will indorse an instrument merely for the purpose of lending his or her credit to the instrument. *Such a person is an accommodation indorser.* To illustrate: P is the holder of a check of which she is the payee, and she wishes to cash it at a bank where she is unknown. At the bank's suggestion P asks A, an acquaintance who is a local merchant and depositor at the bank, to indorse the check along with her. A does so, becoming an accommodation indorser; the bank then cashes the check, giving the amount of the instrument to P in cash. (In this case, P is known as the *accommodated party.*)

In general, an accommodation indorser has the same liability to subsequent holders as does any other indorser. Thus the accommodation indorser has both conditional and warranty liability to any subsequent holder (including a holder who knew that he or she was signing merely as an accommodation indorser). Once there is a dishonor of the instrument and proper notice is given to the accommodation indorser, that person is immediately liable to the holder. That is, the holder does not have to bring suit against the primary party in an effort to obtain payment before initiating action against the accommodation indorser.

Discharge of the Parties

Examination of the rules regarding the liability of secondary parties has already presented several situations in which these parties are discharged—such as failure to make a required presentment or failure to give a notice of dishonor. Now we will briefly describe the important additional ways in which parties to commercial paper can be discharged.

Discharge by Payment: The vast majority of negotiable instruments are discharged by payment. Under Secs. 3-601(1)(a) and 3-603, payment in good faith to the holder by a primary party or by the drawee of an unaccepted draft or check usually discharges all parties on the instrument. Payment by any other party, such as an indorser, only discharges the indorser and subsequent parties on the instrument. The party making payment can still seek recovery from prior parties on the instrument.

If a payment is less than the amount owed, the party making the payment is discharged only to the extent of the payment, as determined by the rules of debt settlement (see Chapter 10). Under Sec. 3-604, if a party tenders payment, but it is refused, the party is not discharged from liability. However, the holder cannot later recover interest from the time of the tender; nor can he or she recover legal costs or attorney's fees.

Alteration: Under Sec. 3-407, alteration of an instrument by a holder discharges any party whose obligation is affected by the alteration, except that a holder in due course can enforce the instrument according to its original terms.

Cancelation and Renunciation: Sec. 3-605(1)(a) reads as follows: "(1) The holder of an instrument may even without consideration discharge any party (a) in any manner apparent on the face of the instrument or the indorsement, as by intentionally cancelling the instrument or the party's signature by destruction or mutilation, or by striking out the party's signature." To illustrate: Marking an instrument "paid" constitutes a cancellation of the instrument itself, as does intentional destruction or mutilation of it. Similarly, striking out a party's indorsement cancels that party's liability (but not the liability of prior parties). Under Sec. 3-605(1)(b), *renunciation* occurs when a holder gives up his or her rights against a party to the instrument in a particular way—either by renouncing them in a signed writing given to such party or by surrendering the instrument to that party.

Discharge of a Prior Party: As a general rule, the intentional cancellation of an instrument discharges all parties to it. Additionally, the discharge of a particular party by cancellation or renunciation normally discharges all subsequent parties as well. These results flow from Sec. 3-606, which provides in part that "the holder discharges any party to the instrument" when he or she "releases or agrees not to sue any person whom [that] party has a right of recourse against." To illustrate: A note bears three indorsements: X, Y, and Z, in that order. If the holder, H, gives a valid release to the first indorser, X, both subsequent indorsers, Y and Z, are thereby discharged. It is possible, however, for H in such a situation to release X but to expressly "reserve his rights" against Y and Z. If this occurs, and if H later collects the amount of the instrument from either Y or Z, then that party still retains the right of recourse against X, the first indorser. Thus H's release of X, where he reserves his rights against subsequent indorsers, does not insulate X from liability to the subsequent indorsers.

Discharge by Reacquisition: If a person acquires an instrument that he or she had held at a prior time, all intervening indorsers are discharged as against the reacquiring party and as against subsequent holders who do not qualify as holders in due course. To illustrate: P indorses a note to A, and A indorses it to B. If P reacquires the note, indorsers A and B are freed of all liability to P. And if P thereafter recirculates the instrument, A and B will have liability to subsequent holders only if they are HDCs.

1. A promissory note was signed by three makers, as follows: "Leo Palmer; George Johnson, Secy; Hubert Alligood." All three men were officers of a corporation for whose benefit the note was issued, but the name of the corporation did not appear anywhere on the instrument. When the instrument was not paid at maturity, the payee-holder brought suit against

Questions and Problems

Johnson personally. As a defense, Johnson offered evidence showing that the plantiff knew, when he received the instrument, that Johnson was simply signing as a representative of the corporation. Should this evidence be allowed? Why or why not? (*Kramer v. Johnson,* 176 S.E.2d 108, 1970).

2. A promissory note was issued by the Gold Company, payable to the order of X, and bears the following signatures as makers: (1) "The Gold Company, by George Blue, President," and (2) "Derek Vance." The note was subsequently negotiated by X to the Last National Bank. When the note was not paid at maturity, the bank sought to hold Vance personally liable on it. At the trial, Vance offered evidence showing that the payee, X, knew that he (Vance) was secretary-treasurer of the Gold Company, and that he also knew that Vance was simply signing as a representative of the company. Should this evidence be admitted? Explain why or why not.

3. As part of a real estate transaction, a $20,000 check was issued by Francis Kirby, of which he was the drawer. When difficulties about the transaction arose later, the holder of the check telephoned the drawee bank to find out whether Kirby had sufficient funds in his account to cover the check. A bookkeeper of the bank replied that the funds were insufficient. In subsequent litigation, the question arose as to whether the holder's inquiry to the bank constituted a valid "presentment for payment" under the UCC. Do you think the telephone call was a valid presentment? Why or why not? *(Kirby v. Bergfield,* 182 N.W.2d 205, 1970).

4. Lucile Fisher was an accommodation indorser of a check that was drawn on a Missouri bank. The check was cashed by the payee at the Nevada State Bank (which was also Mrs. Fisher's bank). The check was put in the channels of collection by the Nevada State Bank, but was "lost in transit" for almost three months before it finally reached the drawee bank in Missouri. At this time the instrument was dishonored by the drawee bank because of insufficient funds in the drawer's account. The drawee bank promptly returned the check to the Nevada State Bank, which gave Mrs. Fisher notice of dishonor the next day. When the Nevada State Bank sought to hold Mrs. Fisher liable as indorser, she contended that she was freed of liability in view of the fact that 90 days had elapsed between the time she indorsed the check and the time that she was given notice of dishonor by the Nevada State Bank. Do you agree with this contention? Explain. (*Nevada State Bank v. Fisher,* 565 P.2d 332, 1977).

5. M was the maker of a $5,000 note issued in 1978, due "June 1, 1980." The note was payable at the XYZ Bank. The holder of the note presented it for payment on June 1, 1980, only to learn for the first time that the bank had failed three months earlier. In a suit by the holder against M, M proved that he lost 50 percent of his money that was in the bank when it failed—assuming that for some reason federal deposit insurance did not cover the loss—and he argues that he is thus liable to the holder only in the amount of $2,500. Is M correct? Why or why not?

6. A corporation issues a note payable to the order of X. The note is stolen from X, and the thief forges X's indorsement on the back. The thief transfers the note to Y, an innocent purchaser, who indorses it "without recourse, Y" and transfers it to Z. The corporation refuses to pay the note after learning of the forgery of X's name, whereupon Z sues Y, the qualified indorser, claiming breach of warranty of title. Y claims he is not liable because he had no knowledge of the forgery whatever. Is this a good defense? Why or why not?

7. D draws a check "payable to bearer" and issues it to X. X negotiates it to H the next day by delivery only (i.e., without indorsing it) and H immediately presents the check to the drawee bank for payment. If the check is dishonored because of insufficient funds and if H gives X prompt notice of the dishonor, is X liable to H? Explain.

8. A note held by H bears the successive indorsements of Alpha (payee), Bravo, and Charlie. The note is not paid at maturity, whereupon H talks his old friend Bravo into taking up the instrument (i.e., Bravo pays H the full amount of the note to H, who returns it to Bravo). What effect, if any, does this have on the liability of (1) the maker; (2) Alpha; and (3) Charlie?

28

Commercial Paper/Checks and the Bank-Depositor Relationship

While checks are simply one type of commercial paper, they do possess certain characteristics that set them apart from promissory notes and drafts. Although some of these special aspects have been discussed in prior chapters, others have not. In this chapter we will first summarize the special attributes of checks and then examine the legal relationship existing between the drawer of a check and the drawee bank (the bank on which the check is drawn).

Checks

Under Sec. 3-104 of the UCC, a check is by definition "a draft drawn on a bank payable on demand." (The *demand* requirement thus means that a "postdated check"—e.g., one issued to the payee on March 10 but dated April 5—is, technically speaking, a draft rather than a check.) In any event, the primary consequence of postdating is that the drawee bank should not honor the instrument until the specified date arrives.

Checks generally have a shorter life than other instruments and thus circulate more quickly than ordinary drafts and promissory notes. This is reflected in Sec.

3-503, which provides that (1) for the drawer of a check, it is presumed that a reasonable time after issue is no more than thirty days, and (2) in order to hold an indorser liable on an ordinary check, the reasonable time following the indorsement is presumed to be only seven days.

In regard to the thirty-day provision, the general rule for drawers of drafts—that a late presentment excuses them of liability only if they have suffered a loss as a result of the delay—will be illustrated as it specifically applies to checks. D draws and issues a check to P on March 1; after several negotiations the check is presented by H, the last holder, to the drawee bank on June 18. Payment is refused at that time (perhaps because D has insufficient funds in her account or because a creditor of D, through legal proceedings, has attached D's funds in the bank). In this case, though presentment has been made more than two months after the thirty-day deadline (March 31), D remains fully liable to H on the instrument *unless* the drawee bank failed after March 31 and before the late presentment on June 18. (In that limited situation D can discharge her liability by giving an assignment of funds to H in the amount of the instrument, in the same manner that the maker of a note payable at a bank can—see Chapter 27.)

The Check Is Not an Assignment of Funds

As a practical matter, checks are drawn (and accepted by the payee and subsequent holders) on the assumption that the drawer has funds in his or her account at the drawee bank sufficient to pay the instrument when it is presented. In the great majority of instances this is, in fact, the case. Federal Reserve Board figures indicate that of every thousand checks drawn, only six or seven are dishonored because of insufficient funds.

Despite the likelihood that a given check will actually be honored, under Sec. 3-409 the issuance of a check does not constitute an "assignment of funds" in the drawee bank. Until final payment is made by the drawee bank, the issuance and circulation of the instrument have no effect on the funds in the drawer's account; nor do they discharge the underlying debt in payment for which it was issued.

Thus, while a check may be accepted by the payee in payment of a debt owed by the drawer, and while the payee may even give the drawer a receipt marked "paid in full," the receipt is conditional upon the check actually being honored by the drawee bank when presented. The same thing is true for bank credits. Thus where a payee deposits a check in his or her account in a bank (the depositary bank) and receives credit for the deposit, and that bank forwards the check to an intermediary bank, which credits the depositary bank's account, then the entire process is reversed if the drawee bank dishonors the check. That is, the check is returned to the payee through the same channels, each bank charging its transferor bank with the amount of the instrument. Ultimately the check is returned to the depositary bank, which charges the account of its depositor, the payee, with the amount of the check and returns it to him or her. The payee can now sue the drawer on the check or on the underlying debt itself.

Certification of Checks

In our discussion of drafts we noted that checks (unlike many drafts) are not presented for acceptance. However, they are occasionally presented to the drawee bank for *certification;* and if certification is made, the bank's liability is the same as that of the acceptor of a draft.

One of the most common uses of certified checks is where a seller of goods, such as a used car dealer, is selling to a buyer with whom he or she has had no business dealings. In such a case the seller will probably want the buyer to have his or her personal check certified before taking it in payment. From a practical standpoint the primary result of certification is that the seller no longer has to worry that the check will be dishonored because of insufficient funds. Frequently, certified checks are required by law from purchasers of real estate at sheriff's sales, and occasionally they are required from persons who are paying fees owed to a state or agency thereof.

Mechanics and Effect: In the absence of a special agreement, a bank has no legal duty to certify a check drawn on it; its only duty is to pay the holder in conformity with the terms of the instrument. A bank that accedes to a request for certification does so by stamping the word *certified* on the face of the check, together with the name of the bank and the date, and including the handwritten signature or initials of the officer making the certification. At that time the bank charges the drawer's account with the amount of the check and transfers the funds to its certified check account.

Certification has three basic effects:

1. The certifying bank is now primarily liable on the instrument (it absolutely promises to pay the instrument when it is presented for payment).

2. The certification of a check at the request of a holder discharges the drawer and any indorsers who indorsed prior to certification. To illustrate: A check drawn by D is issued to P; P indorses it to H, and H obtains certification from the drawee bank. At this point D (the drawer) and P (the indorser) are released of all liability on the instrument. On the other hand, if the *drawer* requests the certification, he or she remains secondarily liable; that is, in the unlikely event that the certifying bank subsequently cannot or will not honor the check when it is presented for payment, the drawer is liable to the holder. (While it is unlikely that any indorsements will appear on the instrument when certification is requested by the drawer, if there are any, the same rule applies to the indorsers; like the drawer, they are not released of secondary liability by the certification.)

3. Once a check is certified, the drawer no longer has the right to stop payment on it. This is true no matter who obtained the certification. (UCC Sec. 4-403, Comment 5.)

Revocation of Certification: Under pre-UCC law a bank had the right to revoke a certification (sometimes called the right to "uncertify") if it could show that certification was obtained by fraud or made under a mistake of fact on its part—provided that the holder at the time of revocation had not substantially changed his or her position in reliance on the certification. This is still the general rule today, with one modification. Because Sec. 3-418 provides that "payment or acceptance of any instrument is final in favor of a holder in due course," it is probable that revocation cannot be made if the holder at the time of attempted revocation qualifies as an HDC, regardless of whether that person had changed his or her position subsequent to the certification.

A bank can be liable to a depositor or a depositor liable to a bank solely through Article 3 of the UCC (dealing with commercial paper)—as we saw in previous chapters. However, the bank-depositor relationship is a broad one; thus the general rights and duties of the two parties spring from several sources in addition to that article. These sources include the following:

The Bank-Depositor Relationship

1. A *creditor-debtor relationship* exists between the depositor and the drawee bank, and sometimes the bank's obligations are essentially those of debtors generally.

2. In some transactions a *principal-agent relationship* exists between the depositor and the bank, and in these situations the bank has the same obligations as those imposed on all agents—for example, the duty to use reasonable care and the duty not to profit at the principal's expense.

3. In limited situations involving controversies between the depositor and the bank, *Article 4 of the UCC* (dealing with bank deposits and collections) enters the picture.

For most of this chapter we will be concerned with setting forth the primary duties of a bank. However, in the last part of the chapter we will examine some specific situations that commonly cause bank-depositor controversies.

The Bank's Duties

The Duty to Honor Orders: The drawee bank is generally obligated to honor checks drawn by the depositor so long as he or she has sufficient funds in the account and so long as payment has not been stopped by the depositor/drawer.[1] The bank's failure to honor a check usually makes it liable to the depositor, under ordinary breach of contract principles, for damages resulting from the refusal to pay. As we will see in more detail later, the bank also is obligated to obey the stop payment orders of its drawers.

Stale checks. The duty to honor checks is not absolute, however. For example,

---

[1] A bank can, if it wishes, honor a drawer's check even if there are insufficient funds in the drawer's account. In such a case an *overdraft* is created, and the bank has the right to recover from the drawer the amount of the overdraft.

the bank obviously does not have to honor checks if there are insufficient funds in the drawer's account. The bank also does not have to honor *stale checks*. UCC Sec. 4-404 provides that "a bank is under no obligation to a customer having a checking account to pay a check, other than a certified check, which is presented more than six months after its date, but it may charge its customer's account for a payment made thereafter in good faith." This section suggests that a drawee bank presented with a check beyond the six-month time limit should secure a confirmation from the drawer before honoring it; failure to do so raises at least the possibility that the bank might not be able to show "good faith" in making the payment. (But see the *Granite Equipment Leasing Corp.* case later in the chapter for a fuller discussion of the good faith requirement.)

Duty to Pay after Death of Drawer: While the general rule under common law is that the death of a principal automatically terminates the authority of the agent to act in his or her behalf, the drafters of the UCC have taken a different position on checks. Sec. 4-405 provides in essence that the death of a customer (drawer) does not revoke the bank's authority to pay that customer's checks "until the bank knows of the fact of death . . . and has reasonable opportunity to act on it." Since the bank might not actually know of a customer's death for a long time after it has occurred (possibly weeks or even months), if it honors any of the customer's checks during this period, it is generally not liable to the drawer's estate for funds so paid out.

A second provision of Sec. 4-405 pertains to a different situation—where the bank does receive notice of the drawer's death soon after it has occurred. In this case the drawee bank still has the right to honor checks for a limited time. Sec. 405(2) provides: "Even with knowledge [of death] a bank may for ten days after the date of death pay or certify checks drawn on or prior to that date unless ordered to stop payment by a person claiming an interest in the account."

Duty to Pay on Only Genuine or Authorized Signatures: As we will see in more detail later, a drawee bank that honors a check bearing a forged drawer's signature cannot legally charge the purported drawer's account even if the bank did not know of the forgery when it honored the instrument. Thus, if D's signature is forged to a check drawn on the X Bank, and that bank subsequently honors the instrument by paying a holder and charging D's account, D, upon discovery of the forgery, can require the bank to recredit her account in the amount of the instrument.

Duty to Use Reasonable Care as Agent: A bank has the duty to use reasonable care in handling commercial paper when acting as an agent for a depositor. This relationship is usually created when a bank's customer deposits in his or her own account a check drawn by a third party (often on some other bank). In such a case, under Sec. 4-201(1), it is presumed that the bank receiving the check is taking it simply as agent for its depositor rather than purchasing it outright—and this presumption continues even if the bank permits the depositor to make immediate withdrawals against it. As a result of this relationship, the bank owes the depositor (among other things) the duty to use reasonable care in handling and forwarding the instrument through the bank collection process.

The following case invited a Pennsylvania appellate court to make forays into such varied but related matters as the law of bailments, the legality of "exculpatory clauses" in general, and the great public necessity for competent (nonnegligent) banking services.

On the evening of June 16, 1973, Max Shectman prepared a bank deposit of $5,669 in receipts from his business, Phillips Home Furnishings, Inc. He then picked up his wife at her place of employment and proceeded to an office of Continental Bank, where he had done his banking for thirty years. Upon arriving at the bank, he placed his deposit in the bank's night depository safe in the wall of the bank building and returned home. Five days later, having received no confirmation of his deposit, Shectman phoned the bank, only to learn that it had no record of the deposit and no explanation of what might have happened to it. (At the subsequent trial, the two employees who had opened the safe the morning after the deposit was made filed affidavits in which they stated that no bag belonging to Shectman was found.)

Phillips Home Furnishings, Inc., v. Continental Bank
Superior Court of Pennsylvania, 331 A.2d 845 (1974)

When Shectman made further inquiries of the bank, one of its officers showed him a copy of the "night depository agreement" he had signed a year earlier. That agreement stated in part:

> Bank grants to the undersigned the privilege of using the Night Depository gratuitously and solely as an accommodation to the undersigned; and the exercise of the privilege by the undersigned will be at the sole risk of the undersigned. Bank will employ such safeguards ... as it deems proper, [but] without any liability to the undersigned for their sufficiency.... Bank shall be under no liability with respect to anything placed in the Night Depository, except for the amount of cash and checks actually taken into its possession upon opening the Night Depository Safe.

The bank, relying upon this agreement, refused to credit Shectman's account. He then brought action to recover damages for the bank's failure to credit the account. The lower court found the night depository agreement to be legal and binding, and it entered judgment for the bank. Shectman appealed.

Jacobs, Justice: ... The first issue thus presented is whether a bank may contractually absolve itself from all liability in connection with the use of a night depository facility, so that its customers are required to use the facility at their own risk. Other courts which have examined this question have concluded that there is nothing inherently wrong with permitting a bank to make its Night Depository Service available under terms and conditions which place the risk of loss on the customer. The courts in these cases find no reason in law or social policy why a bank cannot make the facility available on those terms and conditions mutually agreed upon.

In Pennsylvania, however, the rule has developed ... that the bailor-bailee relationship is one in which the law will protect the former party from attempts by the latter to exculpate himself from the consequences of his own negligence. This rule is particularly applicable here because neither party disputes that the relationship was one of bailment. . . . In *Downs v. Sley System Garages,* 194 A. 772, we stated the "well-recognized rule . . . that a bailee cannot relieve himself of a liability for his own negligence." . . .

We, however, will not rest our decision upon so thin a reed, because we find a much stronger foundation in the bank-customer relationship and the public policy which encircles it and similar relationships.

[The court then conceded that exculpatory clauses were lawful in certain circumstances, and continued:] However, the law also recognized that lying behind these contracts is a residuum of public policy which is antagonistic to carte blanche exculpation from liability, . . . and thus developed the rule that these provisions would be strictly construed . . . against the party seeking their protection. . . . Where a disparity of bargaining power has grown out of economic necessity for certain goods or services or from a monopolistic position of a seller, courts have found exculpatory clauses inimical to the public interest. Where an agreement does not represent a free choice on the part of the plaintiff, where he is forced to accept the clause by the necessities of his situation, *courts have refused to enforce such agreements as contrary to public policy.* [Emphasis added.] . . .

In Pennsylvania, both the courts and the legislature have implicitly agreed that the public necessity for banking services belies the concept that the bank-customer relationship is one of equal parties evenly bargaining. [The court then noted that the position of banks was similar to that of common carriers and cited Pennsylvania cases in which it was held: "This court has consistently decided that it is against public policy to permit a common carrier to limit its liability for its own negligence." The court also noted that Sec. 4-103 of the UCC prevents a bank from disclaiming or limiting its liability for lack of good faith or failure to exercise ordinary care in connection with bank deposits and collections.]

We, therefore, . . . hold that a bank cannot contractually exculpate itself from the consequences of its own negligence or lack of good faith in the performance of any of its banking functions. We find the public need for professional and competent banking services too great, and the legitimate and justifiable reliance upon the integrity and safety of financial institutions too strong, to permit a bank to contract away its liability [in the manner attempted here].

[The court then reversed the judgment of the lower court and remanded the case with instructions that further evidence be considered bearing on the question of whether the bank was in fact guilty of negligence.]

The Depositor's Duties

The depositor has the general obligation to keep sufficient funds in his or her checking account to permit the bank to honor all checks drawn on the account. In this respect the drawer of a check has a greater potential liability than the drawer of a draft. The drawer of a draft is liable only in a civil action to the holder of a draft where it is not paid by the drawee at maturity. The drawer of a check, however, has not only civil liability but also criminal liability for writing a "bad" check (if it is proved that the drawer issued the check with the intent to defraud). Under the statutes of many states there is a presumption of intent to defraud if the drawer does not "make good" to the holder of the check within a specified number of days after the dishonor occurs. Finally, as we will see in more detail later in the chapter, a depositor owes his or her bank the general duty to report forgeries and alterations within a reasonable length of time after he or she knows, or should know, of them.

Stop Payment Orders

Selected Bank-Depositor Problems

As we have indicated, it is possible for the drawer of a check to countermand the order contained in it by issuing the drawee bank a "stop payment" order. The purpose of this, of course, is to prevent the payee or other holder from receiving immediate payment from the bank. Usually the stop payment order is given only after the drawer discovers some default on the part of the payee (such as fraud or the delivery of defective goods under a sales contract) or after the check has been lost.[2] The order is binding for only a limited time period. Sec. 4-403(2) provides that "an oral order is binding upon the bank only for fourteen calendar days unless confirmed in writing within that period. A written order is effective for only six months unless renewed in writing."

Assuming a valid stop payment order has been issued, two basic questions remain:

1. What is the effect of such an order on the drawer?

2. What is the bank's liability in the event that it fails to obey the order?

Effect of Stop Payment Order on Drawer: Assuming that a stop payment order is given in time to permit the bank to act on it, the immediate effect is that the holder of the check fails to obtain payment when he or she presents it to the drawee bank. This does not necessarily mean, however, that the drawer is freed of liability on the instrument.

If the payee, after being refused payment, brings suit against the drawer, he or she may be able to prove that the drawer had no legal grounds for stopping payment; that is, the court may determine that the drawer had no assertable defense against the payee. In such case the payee is entitled to recover the amount of the instrument in full. The drawer also might have liability in a situation where he or she does in fact have a personal defense against the payee but where the holder who was refused payment qualifies as an HDC. In a suit against the drawer such a holder would also be entitled to full payment of the instrument.

Even in these instances the stop payment order is of some benefit to the drawer, for it at least assures that person of the right to present, in a court proceeding, his or her reason for believing that the holder is not entitled to payment. And, of course, in many such proceedings the drawer can prove an assertable defense and escape all liability to the holder/plaintiff.

Bank's Liability for Disobeying Stop Payment Order: If the drawee bank honors

---

[2]We are speaking throughout this section of *uncertified checks.* Once a check has been certified, at the request of either the drawer or a holder, no stop payment order can thereafter be effective.

a check after a valid stop payment order has been issued against it, the bank is liable to the drawer for any loss he or she suffers by reason of the wrongful payment. However, if the drawer has to bring legal action against the bank in order to have the account recredited in the amount of the check, he or she has the burden of proving the amount of loss.

Often it is not difficult for the drawer to prove that he or she suffered a loss. Such is the case where the payee obtained payment and the drawer is able to establish clearly that he or she had either a personal or real defense that could have been asserted against the payee. In this situation, if the stop payment order had been obeyed by the bank, it is obvious that the payee would never have been able to enforce the instrument against the drawer. The result is that the bank must recredit the drawer's account in the amount of the check.[3]

In some situations, however, it can be shown that the drawer did not suffer a loss by reason of the bank's failure to honor the stop payment order. Such is the case where, in the suit by the drawer against the bank, the facts indicate that the drawer did not have a defense of any kind against the payee. In this situation no loss was incurred by the drawer, because even if the stop payment order had been obeyed by the bank, the payee would still have been entitled to payment on the check (by legal action against the drawer, if necessary). The payee therefore had the right to the proceeds of the check in any event, and the drawer's suit against the bank will thus fail. The same result will occur (in the suit by the drawer against the bank) if it is determined that although the drawer had a personal defense against the payee, the person who obtained payment was a holder in due course—someone to whom the payee had negotiated the instrument and who met all the HDC requirements.

The following case is particularly instructive in that it raises two important questions: (1) Is a bank generally free to honor a check after a stop payment order has expired, and (2) if so, does it have this right even when the check is presented several months after the expiration?

Granite Equipment Leasing Corp. v. Hempstead Bank

New York Supreme Court, Nassau County, 326 N.Y.S.2d 881 (1971)

Granite Equipment Leasing Corp. kept a checking account with Hempstead Bank. On October 10, 1968, Granite drew a check payable to Overseas Equipment Co., Inc. After Overseas advised that the check had not been received, Granite wrote the bank on October 15, 1968, to *stop payment* on it. On that same day Granite authorized the bank to wire the funds to the payee in the same amount as the stopped check, and the bank did so. Granite did not renew its stop payment order. On November 10, 1969, without notice or inquiry to Granite, the bank accepted

---

[3]Written stop payment orders sometimes contain clauses to the effect that the drawer agrees not to hold the drawee bank liable if it should honor the check "through inadvertence or oversight." Such disclaimers are generally invalid. Sec. 4-103(1) provides in part that "no agreement can disclaim a bank's responsibility for its own lack of good faith or failure to exercise ordinary care" in a particular transaction.

the check on which payment had been stopped the year before, paid the indicated funds to a collecting bank, and charged Granite's account.

Granite now seeks to recover from the defendant, Hempstead Bank, the amount of the check. The bank defends on the ground that, under UCC Sec. 4-403, the stop payment order had expired for want of renewal and that, acting in good faith, it was entitled under UCC Sec. 4-404 to pay the stale check.

Harnett, Justice (of the trial court): Under the Uniform Commercial Code, does a bank have a duty of inquiry before paying a stale check? Does it matter that the stale check had been previously stopped under a stop payment order which expired for lack of renewal? So this case goes.

[The court here stated the facts, and continued:]

There is no doubt the check is stale. There is no doubt the stop payment order was properly given at the outset, and that it was never renewed. Granite essentially maintains the bank had a duty to inquire into the circumstances of that stale check, and should not have paid in face of a known lapsed stop order without consulting its depositor.

The UCC, which became effective in New York on September 27, 1964, provides that:

(1) A customer may by order to his bank stop payment of any item payable for his account ... (2) ... A written [stop] order is effective for only six months unless renewed in writing. UCC Sec. 4-403.

The Official Comment to UCC Sec. 4-403 notes that:

the purpose of the [six-month limit] is, of course, to facilitate stopping payment by clearing the records of the drawee of accumulated unrevoked stop orders, as where the drawer has found a lost instrument or has settled his controversy with the payee, but has failed to notify the drawee. ...

... Granite cannot be permitted to predicate liability on the part of the bank on its failure to inquire about and find a stop payment order which had become terminated in default of renewal. *Feller v. Manufacturers Trust Co.*, 4 NY2d 951, held that a drawee bank was not liable to a drawer for payment of a check two months after expiration of a stop payment order which had not been renewed. See also, *William Savage, Inc. v. Manufacturers Trust Co.*, 20 Misc2d 114, holding a bank not liable for payment on an eleven month old check after expiration of a stop payment order.

Neither may Granite predicate a claim of liability upon the bank's payment of a stale check. The legal principles applicable to this circumstance are codified in UCC Sec. 4-404, which provides that:

a bank is under no obligation ... to pay a check, other than a certified check, which is presented more than six months after its date, but *it may charge its customer's account for a payment made thereafter in good faith.* [Emphasis supplied.]

[After overruling a cited case, the court continued:] There is no obligation under the statute on the bank to search its records to discover old lapsed stop payment orders. The bank does not have to pay a stale check, but it may pay one in "good faith." Significantly, UCC Sec. 1-201(19) defines "good faith" as "honesty in fact in the conduct or transaction concerned." In the absence of any facts which could justify a finding of dishonesty, bad faith, recklessness, or lack of ordinary care, in the fact of circumstances actually known, or which should have been known, the bank is not liable to Granite for its payment of the check drawn to Overseas.

One statute invalidates stop payment orders not renewed within six months. Another statute allows payment in good faith of stale checks. Granite cannot combine the two statutes to reach a synergistic result not contemplated by either separately.

Granite's complete remedy lies in its pending Florida action against Overseas to recover the extra payment.

Judgment in favor of defendant dismissing the complaint.

Payment on a Forged Indorsement

If a drawee bank honors a depositor's check that bears a *forged indorsement,* the bank must recredit the drawer's account upon his or her discovery and notification of the forgery. To illustrate: D draws a check on the X Bank payable to the order of P. The check is stolen from P by T, and T forges P's indorsement on the back of the instrument. Thereafter T negotiates the instrument to Y, and Y obtains payment from the X Bank, which has no knowledge of the forgery. The bank then charges D's account and returns the check to D at the end of the month along with D's other cancelled checks. If D later learns of the forged indorsement and notifies the bank within a reasonable time after this discovery, the bank must recredit D's account in the amount of the check; the bank in this case has obviously paid out the money to a person who was not the holder of the instrument. Usually the bank will recredit the account voluntarily; but if it does not, under Sec. 3-419(1) and (2) the drawer can bring an action of conversion against it to recover the amount of the check.

Bank's Rights against Surrendering Party: Since it is the bank rather than the drawer who initially suffers the loss in the case of a forged indorsement, the question arises whether the bank can recover payment from the person who surrendered the check to it for payment (Y in the above illustration). The general rule is that the bank can recover, even if the person who surrendered the instrument for payment did not know of the forgery. Sec. 4-207(1)(a) provides that a customer "who obtains payment or acceptance of an item . . . warrants to the payor bank . . . that (a) he has good title to the item." Obviously, a person who surrenders an instrument for payment with a forged indorsement does not have title, so he or she is liable to the drawee bank in the amount of the check on the breach of warranty theory. (After making good to the bank, the person who surrendered the instrument can, of course, proceed against the forger, if that individual can be found.)

Payment on a Forged Drawer's Signature

A substantially different situation is presented when the drawee bank honors a check on which the *drawer's signature* is a forgery. To illustrate: F, forger, draws a check on the Z Bank payable to the order of himself and forging the signature of G, one of the bank's depositors, as the drawer. F indorses the check to H, and H presents the check to the X Bank for payment. The X Bank, not knowing of the forgery, honors the instrument and charges G's account. At the end of the month the forged check is returned to G along with his other cancelled checks.

At this point, assuming that the forgery had occurred without any negligence on the part of G and that G has promptly notified the bank of the forgery, the bank must *recredit* G's account in the amount of the check. This is true because (1) a forged signature is wholly inoperative and (2) a drawee bank is presumed to know the signatures of its depositors. (The latter is based in part on the fact that when a depositor opens a checking account, he or she signs a signature card that is held by the bank and that can be used to determine whether checks subsequently presented to the bank in the depositor's name are genuine.)

Negligent Drawer: The rule that the drawee bank is liable to its depositor in the case of forgery does not apply if the bank can show that the drawer was guilty of negligence that substantially contributed to the forgery.

Two primary situations exist in which negligence on the part of the drawer may be found to exist:

1. If the drawer (usually a corporation in this instance) signs its checks by means of a mechanical check writer, it may be shown that the drawer failed to use reasonable care in preventing unauthorized persons from gaining access to the machine. For example, if the device is left in an area where it is readily accessible to a large number of employees and the forgery is made by one of these employees, the drawer cannot require the bank to recredit its account.

2. It has long been established that a customer owes to the drawee bank the duty of examining his or her cancelled checks within a reasonable time after they have been returned to discover if any of the signatures are forgeries. If the person fails to do so, he or she may well be barred from holding the bank liable. This is especially true where a series of forgeries occurs after the initial one that went undetected.

Sec. 4-406(1) contains the basic provision requiring the drawer to "exercise reasonable care and promptness" in examining checks and statements. Sec. 4-406(2) sets forth specific rules that apply to various "failure to examine" situations. Because these subsections are difficult to understand in the abstract, we will present a hypothetical case along with the appropriate rules:

On February 2, D, drawer, receives thirty cancelled checks from the drawee bank that have been charged against his account during the month of January. His signature has been forged on one check by E, an employee of D who has access to D's checkbook. On February 10, E forges another check and cashes it at the drawee bank. On March 2, this check is returned to D with others honored by the bank during February. During the month of March, E forges and cashes five more checks; these are charged to D's account and returned by the bank to him on April 2, along with his other checks cashed during March.

On April 5, *D for the first time examines all the checks returned to him in February, March, and April.* He discovers the seven forgeries and immediately notifies the bank of them; later he asks the bank to recredit his account for all the forged checks. The bank refuses to do so, contending that it has no liability in view of D's failure to discover the first forgeries promptly.

In this situation D can probably hold the bank liable for the first two checks but not for the following five. Sec. 4-406(2)(b) states in essence that when a forged check is returned to the depositor and that person does not discover it within *fourteen days from the time of return,* he or she is "precluded from asserting" any *subsequent* forgeries against the bank that are forged "by the same wrongdoer." Thus, since the first forged check was returned to D on February 2, he had until February 16 to give the bank notice in order to protect himself against subsequent forgeries. Since he did not meet this deadline, the liability for the forged checks that were honored after that date is shifted from the bank to D.[4]

Bank's Rights against Surrendering Party: As we have seen, if the drawer promptly examines his or her cancelled checks for forgeries and notifies the drawee bank of them, the bank rather than the drawer suffers the loss. The question then arises (as it did in the forged indorsement case) as to whether the bank can recover the amount of the check from the person who surrendered it for payment. The rule here (unlike that involving the forged indorsement) is that if the person did not know of the forged drawer's signature when receiving payment, the bank *cannot* hold him or her liable. Under Sec. 4-207(1)(b), a person who surrenders an instrument for payment guarantees to the drawee bank only that "he has *no knowledge* that the signature of the ... drawer is unauthorized." (Emphasis added.) Thus, unless the bank can prove such knowledge, its only recourse is an action against the forger (if that person can be identified and located).

Payment on an Altered Check

While it happens rather rarely, it is possible that the amount of a check will be raised and the instrument will be presented to the drawee bank and paid in its altered form. To illustrate: N draws a check for $75, and P (payee) or a subsequent holder alters the amount—both figures and words—to $175. If the bank charges N's account with the full $175, N can recover from the bank the amount of the alteration—$100. The general rule is that the drawee bank can charge the drawer's account only with the original amount of the check.

The exception to this rule is similar to that involving the forged drawer's signature. If the drawee bank can establish negligence on the part of the drawer that substantially contributed to the alteration, then the drawer is barred from recovering the difference. Two common kinds of negligence follow:

---

[4]As to the first two checks, since they had already been paid by the drawee bank before the February 16 deadline, it is probable that the bank cannot shift its loss to the drawer—though Sec. 4-406(2)(a) keeps this possibility open in exceptional circumstances.

1. One kind of negligence occurs where a drawer drafts an instrument so carelessly that it invites alteration. For example, the amount might be written in such a way that there is ample space to insert a digit before (or after) it. Or the place where the amount is to appear in words is left entirely blank.

2. Another kind of negligence occurs where the drawer does not inspect his or her cancelled checks within a reasonable time after they are returned and thus fails to give the bank the notice of alteration that it is entitled to receive. Under Sec. 4-406(1), (2), and (3), the drawer in this situation is barred from asserting the fact of alteration against the drawee bank—in the same circumstances and to the same extent as the drawer who negligently failed to detect forged signatures on his or her cancelled checks.

Bank's Rights against Surrendering Party: We have seen that where no negligence exists on the part of the drawer, the loss (the amount of the alteration) is borne by the drawee bank. However, as a general rule, the bank is entitled to recover that loss from the person who surrendered the instrument for payment. Sec. 4-207(1)(c) provides that, with limited exceptions, a customer who obtains payment of an item warrants to the payor bank "that the item has not been materially altered." Thus the person who surrenders the check is usually liable on the breach of warranty theory even if he or she did not know of the alteration at the time of obtaining payment.

Questions and Problems

1. On July 1, D draws a check payable to the order of P and issues it to P. P forgets about the check until August 10, at which time she presents it to the drawee bank for payment. Under what circumstances might D's liability be reduced as a result of the late presentment? What is D's only obligation in such circumstances?

2. What are the three basic effects of certifying a check?

3. You are manager of a branch bank, and one of your tellers comes to you with a check that an apparent holder wishes to have cashed. The check is drawn by one of your depositors, but it is seven months old. What are your bank's rights and duties in regard to this check?

4. On June 10, D (drawer) issues an oral stop payment order on a particular check to his drawee bank, just before leaving town for a short vacation. When he returns at noon on June 20, he goes to the bank and signs a written stop payment order. It turns out, however, that the bank had already honored the check at 10 a.m. that day. The bank now wishes to charge D's account with the amount of the check, in view of the fact that it had honored the check before the written order was issued. Can the bank charge D's account in these circumstances? Explain.

5. D issues a valid stop payment order, but the drawee bank, without excuse, fails to obey the order and charges D's account with the amount of the check. D sues the bank to force it to credit her account in the amount of the check. The bank can totally escape liability to D if it proves that she suffered no loss as a result of its failure to obey the stop payment order. What are the circumstances under which the bank can prove this?

6. D issues a check payable to the order of P. A few days later the drawee bank cashes the check at the request of H (who surrenders it to the bank). The instrument apparently bears the blank indorsement of P, the payee, at the time of surrender. The bank later learns, however, that P's indorsement is a forgery, so it credits D's account as required by law and now seeks to recover the amount of the check from H. H defends on the ground that he neither knew nor had reason to know that the indorsement was forged. Is H's defense valid? Explain.

7. D issues a check payable to the order of P. One week later the drawee bank cashes the check at the request of H, the surrenderer. At the time of the surrender the amount of the check was "$700," and that is the amount that the drawee bank gave to H when he cashed it. Later the bank learns that the original amount of the check was *$100,* and that P apparently was the party who made the alteration. The bank, having no reason to suspect the alteration, now seeks the $600 difference from H; H contends that he, too, was innocent of the alteration. Is this defense of H good? Why or why not?

8. The general rule is that a drawer's account cannot be charged with checks that are proven to be forgeries, unless the drawer has been guilty of negligence that contributed to the forgeries. Give examples of the two general types of misconduct on the part of the drawer that may constitute such negligence.

Part IV

Agency

Agency/Nature, Creation, Duties, and Termination
29

In a legal context the term *agency* ordinarily describes a relationship in which two parties—the principal and the agent—agree that one will act as a representative of the other. The *principal* is the person who wishes to accomplish something, and the *agent* is the one employed to act in the principal's behalf to achieve it.

Nature of the Agency Relationship

At one time or another, almost everyone has come into contact with the agency relationship. Anyone who has purchased merchandise at a retail store almost certainly has dealt with an agent—the salesclerk. Similarly, anyone who has ever held a job probably has served in some type of representative capacity for the employer.

The usefulness of the agency relationship in the business world is obvious. With few exceptions, no single individual is capable of performing every act required to run a business enterprise. Furthermore, many businesses are organized as corporations (see Chapter 35 for details), which by definition can act only by employing agents. As a result, most business transactions throughout the world are handled by agents.

The term *agency* is often used loosely to describe many different types of relationships in which one party acts in a representative capacity for another. *Principal* and *agent* are also sometimes used loosely to denote the parties to various types of arrangements. However, throughout our discussion these terms will be used narrowly to describe a particular type of relationship. The *principal-agent relationship,* as we will use it, means a relationship in which the parties have agreed that the agent is to represent the principal in negotiating and transacting business; that is, the agent is employed to make contracts or enter similar business transactions in behalf of the principal. The term will ordinarily be used in discussions of contractual liability.

Two other closely related relationships are those of *master-servant* and *employer–independent contractor.* In these arrangements the subordinate usually has been employed to perform *physical work* for his or her superior, and the matter in dispute usually concerns *tort liability.*[1] Of course, a person may be hired to represent the employer in commercial dealings and also to perform physical tasks. In such a case he or she is an agent with respect to the authority to transact business and either a servant or an independent contractor with respect to the performance of physical tasks. Although courts sometimes loosely use the term *agent* to describe someone who performs physical duties, we will continue using the term in its narrow sense and thereby avoid confusion.

Most of our discussion in these two chapters will involve the principal-agent relationship; the master-servant and employer–independent contractor relationships will, however, be dealt with in the latter part of the next chapter.

Formalities Required

Creation of the Agency Relationship

The agency relationship is *consensual*—that is, based on the agreement of the parties. Many times it is created by a legally enforceable employment contract between the principal and the agent. A legally binding contract is not essential, however. An agency relationship that gives the agent authority to represent the principal and bind him or her by the agent's actions can generally be established by any words or actions that indicate the parties' consent to the arrangement. Consideration is not required.

In fact, no formalities are required for the creation of an agency relationship in most circumstances. For example, it is not usually necessary to spell out the agent's authority in writing; oral authority is ordinarily sufficient. Exceptions do exist, however. The most common one occurs when an agent is granted authority to sell real estate. In a majority of states an agent can make a contract for the sale of real estate that will bind the principal only if the agent's authority is stated in writing.[2]

Even though formalities are usually not required for the creation of an agency,

---

[1]This statement is admittedly something of an oversimplification, because a few torts, such as fraud and slander, are not of a physical nature. Questions of liability for such torts may occur even if the subordinate's tasks are entirely nonphysical.

[2]In addition, in those few states (about ten) where the *seal* still retains some significance, an agent can execute a sealed document only if his or her authority was given in a sealed document. (See Chapter 8 for the discussion of seals.)

it is certainly wise to express the extent of an agent's authority and any other relevant matters in writing. This precaution often prevents misunderstandings between the principal and agent or between the agent and third parties with whom he or she is dealing. The formal written authorization given by a principal to an agent is frequently referred to as a *power of attorney.* When a formal power of attorney is used, the agent is sometimes referred to as an *attorney-in-fact.* This is simply another term for an agent, and should not be confused with attorney-at-law (a lawyer). Courts generally scrutinize powers of attorney very carefully and interpret their language strictly. The following case illustrates this approach.

On June 12, 1972 Joseph Weinberg purchased a condominium unit and had the title placed in his name and that of his intended bride, Rachela Weiser, as "joint tenants with rights of survivorship." (This means that they were co-owners and that when one died the other would receive the interest of the deceased.) About a month later, on July 16, Weinberg executed and delivered to his son, Arthur Winters, a general power of attorney as follows:

Bloom v. Weiser
District Court of Appeal of Florida, 348 S.2d 651 (1977)

> "KNOW ALL MEN BY THESE PRESENTS:
> "THAT I, JOSEPH WEINBERG, residing at 400 Diplomat Parkway, Hallandale, Florida, have made, constituted and appointed, and by these presents do make, constitute and appoint my son, ARTHUR A. WINTERS, my true and lawful attorney for me and in my place, name and stead giving and granting unto my said attorney full power and authority to do and perform all and every act and thing whatsoever requisite and necessary to be done in and about the premises as fully, to all intents and purposes, as I might or could do if personally present, with full power and substitution and revocation, hereby ratifying and confirming all that my said atorney or his lawful substitute shall lawfully do or cause to be done by virtue hereof." Acting as Weinberg's agent pursuant to this power of attorney, Winters on July 18 executed and delivered to Miriam Bloom, Weinberg's daughter, a deed purporting to transfer Weinberg's one-half interest in the condominium to her. Weinberg died shortly thereafter.

Miriam Bloom, plaintiff, then filed suit against Rachela Weiser, defendant, claiming (1) that the June 12 deed giving Weiser a one-half interest was void because it was obtained by undue influence and (2) alternatively, that Bloom had a one-half interest by virtue of the July 18 deed which terminated Weiser's right of survivorship. The trial court ruled for defendant on both of plaintiff's contentions, and plaintiff appealed.

Haverfield, Justice: . . . [After agreeing with the trial court that there was no evidence to support plaintiff's claim that defendant obtained her interest in the June 12 deed by undue influence, the court then turned to plaintiff's second contention.] . . . The established rule is that a power of attorney must be strictly construed and the instrument will be held to grant only those powers which are specified. We are of the view that for a power of attorney to authorize a conveyance of real estate, the authority of the agent to do so must be plainly stated. Reviewing the power of attorney granted Winters, we find the instrument contains no specific grant of power authorizing him to convey real estate. Therefore, the July 18 deed executed by Winters and purporting to convey Weinberg's one-half interest in the subject condominium unit to Miriam Bloom is void.

It is interesting to note that the instant power of attorney ... contains almost the identical wording of the power of attorney found to be insufficient to authorize the agent to convey or dispose of real estate in *Graham v. State,* 51 N.Y.S.2d 437 (1944) where the court at page 441 explained:

> A power of attorney to convey real estate is an instrument of title. Either expressly or by necessary implication it should state the authority of the agent without leaving it to be established by parol, inferred from coincidences or based on speculation. [This rule] is for the protection of the public. It is not merely a matter between principal and agent. The deed and the agent's authority are instruments of equal dignity. The language of the so-called power of attorney herein confers no authority on Robert H. Dunnet. It lacks an operative clause. It is not a general power of attorney; he is authorized to act only "in and about the premises." It is not a special power of attorney; no premises or things to be done appear on the face of the instrument. The document states nothing to which the grant of powers can be related. Drawn, as it would seem, on the usual blank form of special power of attorney, it omits after the words, "for me and in my name, place and stead," the usual statement of specific acts authorized.

The July deed being void, the trial court properly entered judgment [in favor of] Rachela Weiser.

[Affirmed. Thus, defendant Rachela Weiser owns the condominium.]

Capacity

If an agent, acting in behalf of a principal, makes a properly authorized contract with a third party, the contract is viewed legally as being one between the principal and the third party; that is, it is the *principal's* contract, not the agent's. For this reason the principal's capacity to make contracts may be important in determining the validity of the contract in question. The minority, insanity, or other incapacity of the principal has the same effect on contracts made through an agent as it does on contracts made personally.

On the other hand, the agent's capacity is usually immaterial. The reason is the same—the contract made by the agent for the principal is the principal's contract. A minor, for example, can serve as an agent; his or her lack of contractual capacity ordinarily has no effect on a contract made in behalf of the principal.[3]

Duties of Principal and Agent

The principal-agent relationship is a *fiduciary* relationship—one of trust. Each party owes the other a duty to act with the utmost good faith. Each should be

---

[3]Of course, the agent's lack of contractual capacity has an effect on his or her own contract of employment with the principal, if one exists. The agent's capacity can also be important if for any reason the third party attempts to hold the agent personally responsible on a contract made with that party.

entirely open with the other, not keeping any information from the other that has any bearing on their arrangement. Other duties are considered below, some of which are merely specific applications of the general fiduciary obligation.

Duties Owed by Principal to Agent

The primary duty owed by the principal to the agent is simply that of complying with the terms of their employment contract, if one exists. Failure of the principal to do so will render him or her liable to the agent for damages; if the breach is material, it will justify the agent in refusing to act for the principal any further. For example: P and A have agreed that A is to be paid a specified percentage of the sales she makes for P. If P refuses or fails to pay A, A can rightfully terminate their arrangement and hold P responsible for damages.

In addition, the principal is under a duty to reimburse the agent for any expenditures reasonably incurred by the agent in furthering the interests of the principal. For example, if P directs A to travel from Chicago to Los Angeles to transact business for P, but does not provide her with any funds for travel expenses, P will be under a duty when A returns to reimburse her for amounts she reasonably expended in making the trip, such as her round-trip air fare.

Duties Owed by Agent to Principal

Obedience: It is the duty of the agent to obey the clear instructions of the principal, so long as such instructions are legal. If the instructions are ambiguous, the agent cannot disregard them altogether, but he or she can fulfill the duty by acting in good faith and interpreting them in a manner that is reasonable under the circumstances.

Where the instructions are both legal and clear, the agent is justified in departing from them on only rare occasions. One such occasion is when an *emergency* occurs and following the principal's original instructions is not in that person's best interests. The agent should, of course, consult with the principal and obtain new instructions if possible. But if there is no opportunity to consult, the agent is justified in taking reasonable steps to protect the principal, even if it means deviating from prior instructions. Indeed, the agent may even be under a duty to depart from instructions if following them in the emergency can be considered so unreasonable as to be negligent. (The agent's authority to act in emergencies will be discussed more fully in the next chapter.)

Reasonable Care: Unless special provisions in the agreement say otherwise, an agent is normally expected to exercise the degree of care and skill that is reasonable under the circumstances. In other words, the agent has a duty not to be negligent. For example, suppose that B has funds which he wishes to lend to borrowers at current interest rates. He employs C to act in his behalf in locating the borrowers. C lends B's money to T without investigating T's credit rating and without obtaining from T any security for the loan. T turns out to be a notoriously bad credit risk and is actually insolvent at the time of the loan. If B is later unable to collect from T, C will probably be liable to B, because he failed to exercise reasonable care in making the loan.

Under some circumstances, an agent may be under a special duty to exercise more than an ordinary degree of care and skill. For example, if a person undertakes to serve in a capacity that necessarily involves the possession and exercise of a special skill, such as that of a lawyer or stockbroker, he or she is required to exercise the skill ordinarily possessed by competent persons pursuing that particular calling.

In any agency relationship, the principal and agent can by agreement change the agent's duty of care and skill, making it either stricter or more lenient.

Duty to Account: Unless principal and agent agree otherwise, it is the agent's duty to keep and make available to the principal an account of all the money or property received or paid out in behalf of the principal. In this regard, an agent should never mix his or her own money or property with that of the principal. The agent should, for example, set up a separate bank account for the principal's money. If the agent commingles (mixes) his or her own money or property with the principal's in such a way that it cannot be separated or identified, the principal can legally claim all of it.

Duty to Notify: Another important duty of the agent is to notify the principal of all relevant facts—just about any information having a bearing on the interests of the principal—as soon as reasonably possible after learning of them. For example, if A (the agent) discovers that one of P's (the principal's) creditors is about to foreclose a lien on P's property, A should promptly notify P. Or if A learns that one of P's important customers, who owes P a substantial amount of money, has just filed for bankruptcy, A should contact P as soon as possible.

Loyalty: Perhaps the most important duty owed by the agent to the principal is that of loyalty. Violation of this duty can occur in numerous ways. A few of the more significant actions constituting a breach of the duty are discussed below.

Quite obviously, the agent should not *compete* with the principal in the type of business he or she is conducting for the principal, unless the principal expressly gives consent. To illustrate: X, who owns a textile manufacturing business, employs Y to act as his sales agent. Y will be violating his duty of loyalty if, without X's consent, he acquires a personal interest in a textile manufacturing business that competes with X's.

The law presumes that a principal hires an agent to serve the principal's interests and not the personal interests of the agent. Thus the agent should avoid any existing or potential conflict of interest. For example, if B is hired to sell goods for R, he should not sell to himself. Or if he is hired to buy goods for R, he should not buy them from himself. It is difficult, if not impossible, for the agent to completely serve the principal's interests when his or her own personal interests become involved. Of course, such things can be done if the principal is fully informed and gives consent.

In a similar fashion, the agent should not further the interests of any third party in his or her dealings for the principal. The agent also should not work for two parties on opposite sides in a transaction unless both parties agree to it.

If the agent, in working for the principal, acquires knowledge of any *confidential information,* he or she should not disclose this information to outsiders without the principal's consent. To illustrate: G hires H, a lawyer, to represent G in defending a lawsuit filed against G by T. T alleges that his factory was damaged in a fire caused by certain chemicals, purchased by T from G, that were highly flammable and not labeled with an adequate warning. In order to properly defend G, H must learn the secret formulas and processes for producing the chemicals. After learning them, he should not disclose them to anyone without G's consent, either at that time or at any time in the future.

The following case illustrates the strictness of the duty of loyalty owed by an agent to the principal.

Thompson v. Hoagland

Superior Court of New Jersey, 242 A.2d 642 (1968)

Thompson, the plaintiff, was a real estate broker. On June 11, 1963, he entered into a written "exclusive right-to-sell" agreement with Mr. and Mrs. Hoagland, the defendants, for their seventy-six-acre tract of land in Franklin Township for a period of 365 days. (An "exclusive right-to-sell" agreement gives the broker or agent the right to receive a commission if he or she procures a buyer at the stated price during the specified time, regardless of whether the owner sells the property to that buyer. And if the property is sold, the broker is entitled to the commission even if the owner or some other broker procured the buyer.) The sale was authorized at a price of $65,000, with terms specified. The commission was to be 10 percent of the sale price.

Several weeks later the Hoaglands decided that they wanted to change the sale price to $80,000, but Thompson refused—which he had the right to do. A few months later Thompson obtained a buyer, Dr. Abrams, who was willing to pay the $65,000 price; but the Hoaglands refused to sell and refused to pay Thompson his commission.

Thompson brought suit to recover the commission. The trial court dismissed the suit because Thompson had allegedly failed to inform the Hoaglands that he had engaged in several partnership arrangements and joint investments in real estate with Dr. Abrams. Thompson appealed.

Conford, Justice: . . . Plaintiff argues that it is immaterial in any event whether he ever informed defendants of his association with Dr. Abrams since the proof is clear that that circumstance was not material to their refusal to sell—they having decided to sell to no one at the figure listed in the agreement. We do not agree. If the failure to apprise defendants of the relationship bore upon a circumstance which could have generated a fair suspicion as to whether plaintiff had exercised his very best efforts as defendants' agent to obtain the best price possible for the property, this constituted an absolute defense to any action for a commission, whether or not defendants were in fact prejudiced by the nondisclosure. For reasons to be indicated, we are satisfied that plaintiff's relationship to Dr. Abrams was of a character requiring full apprisal of defendants thereof and their consent, express or implied, to the submission of an offer by him, in consequence of the fiduciary status of plaintiff toward defendants inherent in the broker-principal relationship.

Only recently the Supreme Court restated the fundamental relationship between broker and principal as follows:

> The broker was and is looked upon as a fiduciary and is required to exercise fidelity, good faith and primary devotion to the interest of his principal. He cannot permit his interests to interfere with those of his principal. As the Court of Errors and Appeals said in *Young v. Hughes,* 32 N.J.Eq. 372, pp. 384–385, the rule which applies to trustees has been equally applied to the relation between the real estate broker and his principal. He must show perfect good faith and openness of dealing. *The rule was not intended to be remedial of actual wrong done alone, but also to be preventive of the possibility of it.* (Emphasis ours.) . . .

It is a corollary of the principle discussed above that failure of the broker to inform the principal that the purchaser he produces is an *alter ego* of the broker or a relative or partner renders the transaction voidable as between broker and principal at the option of the principal. The rule is prophylactic in purpose, and, by the better view, not qualified by the actual *bona fides* [good faith] of the broker in the matter or the absence of harm to the principal. In this context the principal is entitled to be informed of "any circumstance that might reasonably be expected to influence the complete loyalty of the agent to the interest of his principal."

We are satisfied that the close and continuing business relationship between plaintiff and Dr. Abrams, amounting in substance, although not with legal technicality, to a partnership in land speculation, was such as to foster a temptation on the part of plaintiff to favor the interests of his associate at the expense of undivided loyalty to defendants in submitting a purchase offer by the former. This brought the case within the spirit of the rule cited above making an undisclosed partner of the broker an impermissible source of an offer of purchase to be submitted to a principal-seller in purported satisfaction of the brokerage undertaking.

In view of the foregoing, if plaintiff failed to make the necessary disclosure it would be inconsequential that defendants refused to accept the offer because they did not desire to sell at the stipulated price to anyone at all. . . .

Judgment reversed; the case is remanded for a new trial.

Comment: Although the appellate court agreed that Thompson should have disclosed to the Hoaglands his relationship with Dr. Abrams, some of the evidence indicated that he had indeed made the disclosure. The appellate court therefore remanded the case for a new trial on the ground that the trial court should not have summarily dismissed the case. That is, since an issue of fact was present, the jury should have been allowed to decide whether the disclosure had been made and, if so, whether it was sufficient.

Termination of the Relationship

Like most private consensual arrangements, the agency relationship usually comes to an end at some point. Termination can occur because of something done by the parties themselves or by operation of law (something beyond their control). Our discussion will focus on the termination of the relationship between the principal and the agent, ignoring for the moment the effects of termination on third parties who might deal with the agent. (The circumstances under which third parties should be notified of the termination and the type of notice required will be dealt with in the next chapter.)

Termination by Act of the Parties

Fulfillment of Purpose: Many times an agent is employed to accomplish a particular object, such as the sale of a tract of land belonging to the principal. When this object is accomplished and nothing else remains to be done, the agency relationship obviously terminates.

Lapse of Time: If principal and agent have agreed originally that the arrangement will end at a certain time, the arrival of that time obviously terminates their relationship. If nothing has been said as to the duration of the agency, and if nothing occurs to terminate it, the relationship is deemed to last for a period of time that is reasonable under the circumstances. This generally is a question of whether, after passage of a particular period of time, it is reasonable for the agent to believe that the principal still intends for him or her to act as earlier directed. Of course, if the principal *knows* that the agent is continuing to make efforts to perform, and if the principal does nothing about the situation, the agency relationship may remain alive for a period of time longer than would otherwise be held reasonable.

Occurrence of Specified Event: In a similar fashion, if the principal and agent have originally agreed that the agency, or some particular aspect of it, will continue until a specified event occurs, the occurrence of the event obviously results in termination. For example: P authorizes A to attempt to sell P's farm, Blackacre, for him "only until B returns from New York." When B returns, A's authority to sell Blackacre as P's agent comes to an end. An analogous situation occurs when principal and agent have agreed that the agency, or some aspect of it, will remain in existence only during the continuance of a stated condition. If the condition ceases to exist, the agent's authority terminates. For instance: X directs Y, X's credit manager, to extend $10,000 in credit to T, so long as T's inventory of goods on hand and his accounts receivable amount to $50,000 and his accounts payable do not exceed $25,000. If T's combined inventory and accounts receivable drop below $50,000, the agency terminates insofar as it relates to Y's authority to grant credit to T.

Mutual Agreement: Regardless of what the principal and agent have agreed to originally, they can agree at any time to end their relationship. It makes no difference whether the relationship has been based on a binding employment contract or whether no enforceable employment contract exists; their mutual agreement terminates the agency in either case. It is a basic rule of contract law that the parties can rescind (cancel) the contract by mutual agreement.

Act of One Party: Since the agency relationship is consensual, it can usually be terminated by either the principal or the agent if that person no longer wants to be a party to the arrangement. In most circumstances termination occurs simply by one party indicating to the other that he or she no longer desires to continue the relationship. This is true even if the parties had originally agreed that the agency was to be irrevocable.

If no binding employment contract exists between the two of them, the party terminating the agency normally does not incur any liability to the other by this action. If an enforceable employment contract does exist, one party may be justified in terminating it if the other has violated any of the duties owed under it. Of course, if there are no facts justifying termination, the party taking such action may be responsible to the other for any damages caused by the breach of contract. But the agency relationship is ended nevertheless.

One major exception exists to the ability of either party to terminate the relationship. If the agency is not just a simple one but instead is an *agency coupled with an interest* (that is, the agent has an interest in the subject matter of the agency), the principal cannot terminate the agent's authority without the agent's consent.[4] (Note, however, that an agent is not considered to have an interest in the subject matter simply because he or she expects to make a commission or profit from the activities as agent.) To illustrate: P borrows $5,000 from A. To secure the loan, P grants A a *security interest* (sometimes called a *lien* or a *mortgage*) in P's inventory. As part of the agreement, P makes A his agent for the sale of the inventory in case P defaults on the loan. Since A has an interest in the subject matter of the agency (the inventory), the arrangement is an agency coupled with an interest, and P cannot terminate A's authority to sell without A's consent (unless, of course, P repays the loan, in which case A no longer has an interest in the subject matter).

The reason for the exception is that the agent is not really acting for the principal in this situation. By exercising this authority, the agent is acting in his or her own behalf to assert a personal interest.

Termination by Operation of Law

Death or Insanity: The death or insanity of the *agent* immediately terminates an ordinary agency but not an agency coupled with an interest. In the latter case the executor of the agent's estate (in the case of death) or the guardian (in the case of insanity) can exercise the power given to the agent.

The death or insanity of the *principal* also terminates an ordinary agency but

---

[4]Considerable confusion and conflict exist in the law with regard to an agency coupled with an interest (also referred to as an "agency for security," a "power coupled with an interest," and a "power given for security"). We have therefore tried to keep our discussion simple enough to avoid these pitfalls.

usually does not terminate an agency coupled with an interest. In most cases the termination of an ordinary agency by the principal's death or insanity occurs immediately, regardless of whether the agent knows what has happened.

Bankruptcy: The insolvency or bankruptcy of the *agent* does not always terminate the agency, but will do so in those circumstances where it impairs the agent's ability to act for the principal. To illustrate: B is authorized by I, an investment house, to act as its agent in advising I's local clients about investments. If B becomes bankrupt, he will no longer be authorized to act for I. The reason is simple; the agent in this situation should realize that the principal probably would not want him to act in its behalf any longer if it knew the facts.

Suppose, however, that the *principal* becomes insolvent or bankrupt, and the agent knows about it. In this case the agent might no longer have authority to act for the principal—but only under circumstances where the agent ought to realize that the principal would no longer want such transactions to be conducted in his or her behalf. For example: P has authorized A to buy an expensive fur coat on credit for P. If P becomes bankrupt, this will probably terminate the agency when A learns of it. A should reasonably infer that under the circumstances P will no longer want him to make such a purchase. However, if A is P's housekeeper and has been authorized to buy groceries for P's household, P's bankruptcy probably will not extinguish that authority. The inference that A should reasonably draw when learning the facts is that P will want her to continue buying necessities such as food until informed otherwise. It is simply a matter of reasonableness.

With regard to an agency coupled with an interest, the question of whether the bankruptcy of either principal or agent terminates the agent's authority involves a number of complexities under Article 9 of the UCC and under the federal bankruptcy statutes. A discussion of such complexity is beyond the scope of this chapter.

Change of Law: If a change in the law makes the agency or the performance of the authorized act *illegal,* the agent's authority is ordinarily extinguished when he or she learns of the change. To illustrate: S is a saleswoman for T, a toy manufacturer. If a federal agency determines that certain of T's toys are dangerous and bans them, S's authority to sell them to retailers probably will be terminated when she learns of the government ban. That is, upon learning the facts, S should reasonably assume that T will no longer want her to sell the banned items.

Even if the change in the law does not make the agency or the authorized act illegal, termination can still occur if the agent learns of the change and should reasonably expect that the principal will no longer want him or her to act in the manner previously authorized. For instance: A is authorized to purchase fabricated aluminum from a foreign supplier. The federal government imposes a new tariff on imported aluminum that results in substantially higher prices. It is likely that A's authority to buy foreign aluminum will be terminated when he learns of the change.

An agency coupled with an interest is also terminated by a change in the law resulting in illegality (although the problem does not arise very frequently). Where no illegality results from the change, there is no termination.

Loss or Destruction of Subject Matter: Obviously, the loss or destruction of the subject matter of either an ordinary agency or an agency coupled with an interest will terminate the agent's authority. If, for example, X employs Y to sell grain belonging to X that is being stored in a particular storage elevator, the destruction by fire of the elevator and the grain will ordinarily extinguish Y's authority.

Whether the agent's authority terminates automatically or only when he or she learns of the facts depends on the nature and terms of the original agreement between principal and agent. In the instant case, if, instead of a fire, X himself sells the grain to a buyer (which actually amounts to X revoking Y's authority), Y's authority may or may not be automatically terminated. If X has given Y *exclusive authority* to sell, that authority ends only if X notifies Y that he has sold the grain himself. On the other hand, if the authority is not exclusive and Y should realize that X may try to sell the grain himself, Y's authority will terminate when X sells the grain even if Y does not know of the sale.

If the subject matter of the agency (such as the grain) is not lost or destroyed but is merely damaged, Y's authority is terminated if the circumstances are such that Y ought to realize that X would not want the transaction to be carried out.

Miscellaneous Changes of Conditions: The various occurrences we have dealt with that terminate an agency by operation of law are by no means an exclusive list. For instance, in some circumstances the outbreak of war, a sudden change in the market value of the subject matter of the agency, or an unexpected loss of some required qualification by the principal or the agent (such as a license) may terminate the agency. Again, if all the circumstances known to the agent are such that he or she, as a reasonable person, ought to realize that the principal would no longer wish him or her to continue in the endeavor, the authority is ended. The agent simply must act in a reasonable fashion until there is an opportunity to consult with the principal.

Questions and Problems

1. Explain the difference between attorney-in-fact and attorney-at-law.

2. What formalities are required for the creation of the principal-agent relationship?

3. Fortner, a minor, employed Jones, an adult, as his agent for the purpose of selling his motorcycle for $400. Jones sold the motorcycle to Todd for $400. Fortner later changed his mind and tried to disaffirm the sale. Todd claimed that Fortner could not do so because Jones was an adult. Is Todd's contention correct? Explain.

4. Pointer hired Anderson as his agent for the purpose of buying a thousand shares of stock in Zeta Co. Unknown to Pointer, Anderson owned a thousand shares of Zeta stock. Anderson sold his stock to Pointer at the current market price of $20 per share. When Pointer

found this out, he demanded that Anderson take back the stock and refund the price. Is Anderson required to do so? Explain.

5. Carter promised to pay Hines a commission if he would sell a tract of land for Carter. Hines sold the land to Jackson, who had employed Hines to purchase land for him, also for a commission. When Carter learned of this dual arrangement, he refused to pay Hines the promised commission. Was Carter entitled to make such a refusal? Discuss.

6. Swenson instructed Thompson, his banker, to invest some money for him. Thompson purchased mining stock with the money. The stock proved to be virtually worthless. Swenson sued Thompson for his loss. Is Thompson liable? Discuss.

7. Clay was hired by Green to sell Green's boat for not less than $700, out of which Clay was to receive a 10 percent commission. Clay sold the boat for $800 and offered Green $630 in settlement ($700 less 10 percent). Green demanded an additional $90 as the amount due him. Was Green justified in claiming the additional money? Explain.

8. Harkins, a salesman for Watson, was paid a commission on sales made for Watson. Harkins took an order from Boswell for merchandise. Watson accepted the order and shipped the merchandise. In the meantime, Boswell changed his mind and repudiated the transaction, claiming he no longer needed the goods. When they arrived, he refused to accept or pay for them and shipped them back to Watson. Watson claimed that Harkins was not entitled to a commission because the sale had not been completed. Is Watson correct? Explain.

9. What is the meaning and significance of the phrase *agency coupled with an interest?*

10. When will an agent's bankruptcy terminate the agency relationship?

30

Agency/Liability of the Parties

We have already discussed the formation and termination of the agency relationship and the duties existing between the parties. Now we will focus our attention on the legal consequences of this relationship, primarily the *contractual liability* of those involved: principal, agent, and third parties. Near the end of the chapter we will deal with a superior's liability for the torts and crimes of his or her subordinates.

Liability of the Principal

The principal is, of course, liable to the agent if he or she breaches a valid employment contract with the agent or violates any other duty owing to the agent. However, the most important questions in this area relate to the principal's liability to the third parties with whom the agent has dealt. If A, acting in behalf of P, makes a contract with T, what is P's legal responsibility to T? If P does not perform as indicated in the contract, is P required by law to compensate T for T's losses resulting from P's breach?

The answers to these questions usually depend on the court's decision on another question: Was the agent acting within the scope of his or her authority in making this particular contract? We will now examine the approach taken by the courts in arriving at an answer.

Authority

Hiring someone to act as your agent does not mean that the person can represent you in any way he or she sees fit. An agent ordinarily can act for the principal in such a way as to make the principal legally responsible only when he or she is *authorized* by the principal to act that way. The agent's authority can be divided into two basic types: actual and apparent. *Actual authority* is, of course, the authority that the agent does, in fact, have. For convenience it can be further divided into *express authority* and *implied authority*. On the other hand, *apparent authority* is something of a contradiction in terms. It describes a concept which, because of unusual circumstances giving rise to an appearance of authority, occasionally holds the principal responsible for certain of the agent's actions that were not really authorized at all.

Express Authority: *Express authority* is the most obvious and the most common type of authority—that which is directly granted by the principal to the agent. To illustrate: P authorizes A to sell P's farm for at least $25,000. If A sells the farm to T for $30,000, P is bound by the transaction and must honor it. The obvious reason is that A's actions are within the scope of his express authority. Conversely, under most circumstances, P will not be required to honor the transaction if A sells the farm for $20,000.

Implied Authority: As is the case with most business transactions, the principal and agent rarely, if ever, contemplate and provide for every possible event that might occur during the existence of their relationship. The law seeks to allow for this fact through the concept of implied authority. *Implied authority* is primarily a matter of what is *customary*. In other words, where the principal has said nothing about a particular aspect of the agent's authority, whether the agent has such authority normally depends on what type of authority a person in a similar position customarily has. Of course, the principal has the final word as to what authority the agent possesses and can grant more or less authority than such an agent usually has. The concept of implied authority serves only to fill in gaps where the principal has not spoken specifically on the subject but where it is reasonable to assume that the principal would have granted such authority if he or she had thought about it.

Many examples of implied authority can be found. For instance, unless the principal has given indications to the contrary, a traveling salesperson ordinarily has authority to take orders but not to make a binding contract to sell the principal's goods. He or she often will be in possession of samples but there usually is no implied authority to sell them. If, however, the salesperson is one who possesses goods *for immediate sale* (such as a salesclerk in a retail store or a door-to-door sales agent who actually carries the principal's merchandise), he or she ordinarily has authority to sell them and collect payment. But this type of agent still does not have implied authority to grant credit or accept payment from the customer for prior credit purchases. Such authority usually exists only if expressly given by the principal, because it is simply not customary for a salesperson to do these things.

Another common application of the concept of implied authority enables an agent to perform those acts which are merely incidental to the main purpose of the agency. (Some legal writers have, in fact, used the term *incidental authority*.) Again, the key is what is customary. The rule regarding such authority is: *Unless the principal has indicated otherwise, his or her agent has implied authority to do those things which are reasonably and customarily necessary to enable that person to accomplish the overall purpose of the agency.*

To illustrate: O, the owner of a retail clothing store, hires M to act as manager of the store and gives M express authority to act in certain ways. For instance, M probably will be expressly authorized to purchase inventory and make sales. In addition, M will have implied authority to handle matters that are incidental to the main purpose of the agency. Thus, if the plumbing in the store begins to leak, M can hire a plumber, and O is bound to pay for the services. Similarly, unless instructed otherwise, M can hire an electrician to repair a short in the wiring or a janitorial service to clean the floors. He can also hire a salesclerk or other necessary assistants.

Of course, if the transaction is out of the ordinary or involves a substantial expenditure, the agent should first consult with the principal, because the agent's implied authority may not extend to such matters. Thus, if the electrician hired by M to repair a shorted wire informs him that the wiring in the building is badly worn and does not comply with city building code requirements, M should not act on his own to contract for the rewiring at a substantial cost. Instead he should consult with O before taking further action.

Interesting questions regarding an agent's authority are sometimes raised by the occurrence of an *emergency*. Although it is often said that the scope of an agent's implied authority is "expanded" in emergency situations, this is only sometimes true. If an emergency occurs and there is no opportunity to consult with the principal, the agent has implied authority to take steps that are reasonable and prudent under the circumstances—including actions that may be contrary to prior instructions by the principal.

To illustrate: A has been ordered by P to purchase badly-needed raw materials from country X and to ship them through country Y, which has the nearest port facility where the goods can be loaded on vessels. A makes the purchase but then learns from a usually reliable source that a revolution is imminent in country Y and will probably break out while the goods are en route. Fearing that transportation may be impaired or that the goods may be seized by the revolutionaries, A attempts to contact P but is unable to do so. Since he knows that P needs the goods quickly, A arranges for shipment to another port through country Z. Shipment over the other route will be slightly more expensive and time-consuming but also presumably safe, and P will still receive the goods in time to meet his needs.

In this case, A was impliedly authorized to act as he did—even if no revolution actually occurred. What is important is that two elements were present: (1) A, the agent, was *unable to consult with his principal;* and (2) he acted *reasonably,* in light of all the knowledge available to him, to protect the interests of his principal.

Apparent Authority: Thus far we have dealt with situations where the agent has actual authority, either express or implied. Now we will examine the peculiar concept of *apparent authority.* As we mentioned earlier, speaking of apparent authority as a specific type of authority is something of a contradiction, because the phrase describes a situation where the agent actually has no authority. If the agent acts outside the scope of his or her actual (express or implied) authority, the principal is normally not responsible on the unauthorized transaction. However, if the principal, *by his or her own conduct,* has led reasonable third parties to believe that the agent actually has such authority, the principal may be responsible. In discussing implied authority, we were concerned with what appeared reasonable to the *agent.* But for apparent authority, our concern is with the viewpoint of reasonable *third parties.* Obviously, some situations can fall within the scope of either implied or apparent authority. In such cases we usually speak in terms of implied authority; apparent authority is used as a basis for holding the principal responsible only where no express or implied authority is present.

The importance of apparent authority can be illustrated by two examples:

1. S, a salesman for R, has in his possession R's goods (not just samples). It is customary for an agent in S's position who is handling this type of goods to have authority to actually sell and collect payment for them. While making his rounds, S calls the home office. R tells him that he is afraid some of the items S has are defective and instructs him not to sell the goods in his possession but merely to take orders for a period of time. Contrary to instructions, S sells the goods. R is bound by the transactions and will be responsible to T, the buyer, if the goods actually are defective. It appears that R has acted in a reasonable fashion under the circumstances. However, by allowing S to have possession of the goods, he has led T to believe that S is authorized to sell—because it is *customary.* T has no way of knowing that S's actual authority has been expressly limited to something less than what is customary. The basis of R's liability is *not* S's implied authority, because S *knew* that he had no authority and was acting contrary to express instructions. Instead, the basis for R's liability is *apparent* authority—arising out of the fact that T has been misled by the *appearance of authority.*

2. When the agency is terminated, the agent's *actual authority* is also terminated. But this does not automatically dispose of the problem of *apparent authority.* It is sometimes necessary to notify third parties of the termination in order to keep the principal from being liable under the concept of apparent authority. As a general rule, where termination has occurred *as a matter of law* (see Chapter 29 for details), all authority ceases automatically and the principal is not responsible for the agent's further actions regardless of whether the third party has been

notified.[1] Most problems involving termination and apparent authority arise when the agency has been ended *by act of the parties* (such as the principal firing the agent). Where termination is by act of the parties, the principal may still be bound by the agent's actions (because of apparent authority) unless and until the third party is notified of the termination. The principal must notify third parties with whom the agent has dealt in the past by letter, telegram, telephone, or some other method of *direct communication* if their identities are reasonably easy to ascertain. Regarding all other third parties, the principal can protect himself simply by giving *public notice.* An advertisement in a local newspaper is the most common form of such notice, but other methods may be sufficient if they are reasonable under the circumstances.

Ratification

If an agent's action is not within the scope of his or her actual (express or implied) authority, and if the facts are such that no apparent authority is present, the principal generally is not liable to the third party for that action. Even in the absence of actual or apparent authority, however, the principal may become responsible if he or she *ratifies* (or *affirms*) the agent's unauthorized actions. An unauthorized act ratified by the principal is treated by the courts in the same manner as if it had been actually authorized from the beginning. The two forms of ratification—express and implied—are discussed below.

Express Ratification: If, upon learning of the agent's unauthorized dealings, the principal decides to honor the transaction, he or she can simply inform the agent, the third party, or someone else of that intention. In this situation an *express ratification* has obviously occurred.

Implied Ratification: Even if the principal has not expressly communicated the intent to ratify, the person can nevertheless be deemed to have done so if his or her words or conduct reasonably indicate that intent. *Inaction* and *silence* may even amount to ratification if, under the circumstances, a reasonable person would have voiced an objection to what the agent had done. The following five examples will help clarify the concept of *implied ratification.* For each example, no actual authority exists, and there are no facts present to indicate apparent authority.

    Example 1. A, who is a driver of a truck owned by P, enters into an unauthorized agreement with T, under which A is to haul T's goods on P's truck. Sometime later, while A is en route, T becomes concerned about the delay and calls P. Upon learning of the transaction, P does not repudiate it but instead assures T that "A is a good driver and the goods will be properly cared for." P has ratified the agreement.

---

[1]However, a few courts have held that where the agency is terminated by the principal's *death,* his or her estate can continue to be liable for the agent's actions, under the doctrine of apparent authority, until the third party learns of the death.

Example 2. Same facts as Example 1. This time, however, T does not call P. The goods arrive safely at their destination, and T sends a check for the shipping charges to P. This is when P first learns of the transaction. If P cashes or deposits the check and uses the money, he will be deemed to have ratified the agreement. Even if he simply retains the check for an appreciable period of time and says nothing, he will probably be held to have ratified.

Example 3. A makes an unauthorized contract to sell P's goods to T. Upon learning of the contract, P says nothing to A or T but assigns the right to receive payment for the goods to X. P has ratified the agreement.

Example 4. Same facts as Example 3. This time, however, P does not assign the right to receive payment. Instead he ships the goods to T. P has ratified the agreement.

Example 5. Same facts as Example 4, but the goods are shipped to T without P's knowledge. P then learns of the transaction, and when T does not make payment by the due date, P files suit against T to collect the purchase price. P has ratified the transaction. (P would not have ratified if he had filed suit to rescind the sale and get his goods back.)

Requirements for Ratification: Certain requirements must be present for ratification to occur. Following are the most important of them:

1. The courts generally hold that a principal can ratify only if the agent, in dealing with the third party, has indicated that he or she is acting *for a principal* and not in his or her own behalf.

2. At the time of ratification, the principal must have *known* or had *reason to know* of the essential facts about the transaction. What this means is that the principal must have had either actual knowledge of the relevant facts or sufficient knowledge so that it would have been easy to find out what the essential facts were. The requirement of knowledge is usually important when the third party tries to hold the principal liable by claiming that some words or actions of the principal had amounted to ratification.

3. Ratification must occur within a *reasonable time* after the principal learned of the transaction. What constitutes a reasonable time will, of course, depend on the facts of the particular case. However, a court will automatically rule that a reasonable time period has already expired, and thus that there can be no ratification, if there has been a fundamental change in the facts that had formed the basis of the transaction. An example would be damage to or destruction of the subject matter of the transaction. Similarly, the principal will not be permitted to ratify if the third party has already indicated a desire to withdraw from the transaction. The third party has the right to withdraw prior to ratification and, when he or she does so, any later attempt by the principal to ratify will be treated as being too late.

4. If the principal ratifies, he or she must ratify the *entire transaction* rather than ratifying that part which is to his or her advantage and repudiating that which is to his or her disadvantage. For example, a principal ratifying a contract for the sale of goods to a third party is obligated on any warranties that accompany the goods.

5. The transaction obviously must be *legal,* and the principal must have the *capacity* required to be a party to the transaction.

6. If any *formalities* (such as a writing) would have been required for an original authorization, the same formalities must be met in ratifying the transaction. Of course, if formalities are required, the ratification will have to be express—it cannot be implied. Since most authorizations do not require any special formalities, this usually poses no problem.

The following two cases both deal with the question of apparent authority. The second case also involves the issue of ratification.

Industrial Molded Plastic Products, Inc., v. J. Gross & Son, Inc.

Superior Court of Pennsylvania, 398 A.2d 695 (1979)

Industrial Molded Plastic Products (Industrial) is in the business of manufacturing custom injection molded plastics by specification for various manufacturers. Industrial also manufactures various "fill-in" items during slack periods, such as electronic parts, industrial components, mirror clips, and plastic clothing clips. J. Gross & Sons (Gross) is a wholesaler to the retail clothing industry, selling mostly sewing thread, but also other items such as zippers, snaps, and clips.

Sometime in the Fall of 1970, Mr. Stanley Waxman (Gross' President and sole stockholder) and his son Peter (a 22-year-old salesman for Gross) appeared at the offices of Industrial's President, Mr. Judson T. Ulansey. They suggested to him that they might be able to market Industrial's plastic clothing clips in the retail clothing industry, in which they had an established sales force. At this initial meeting, there was no discussion of Peter Waxman's authority or lack thereof in the company. After this meeting, Stanley authorized Peter to purchase a "trial" amount of clips (not further specified) to test the market, but neither this authorization nor its limitation was communicated to Ulansey. All subsequent negotiations were between Ulansey and Peter Waxman only. Deceiving both his father and Ulansey, Peter held himself out as Vice-president of Gross, and on December 10, 1970, signed an agreement obligating Gross to purchase from Industrial five million plastic clothing clips during the calendar year of 1971, at a price of $7.50 per thousand units, delivery at Industrial's plant in Blooming Glen, Pennsylvania. Before the execution of this agreement, Ulansey telephoned Stanley Waxman, who told Ulansey that Peter could act on behalf of Gross. There was no discussion of the specific terms of the agreement, such as the quantity purchased.

Industrial immediately began production of the five million clips during "fill-in" time. As they were manufactured, they were warehoused in Industrial's plant as specified in the contract. In February, 1971, Peter Waxman picked up and paid for 772,000 clips. Stanley Waxman, who had to sign Gross' check for payment, thought that this was the "trial amount" he had authorized Peter to buy. These were the only clips which Gross ever took into its possession. On numerous occasions during the year Ulansey urged Peter to pick up more of the clips, which were taking up more and more storage space at Industrial's plant as they were being manufactured. Peter told Ulansey that he was having difficulty selling the clips and that Gross had no warehousing capacity for the inventory that was being accumulated. At no time, however, did Peter repudiate the contract or request Industrial to halt production. By the end of 1971, production was completed and Industrial was warehousing 4,228,000 clips at its plant.

On January 19, 1972, Industrial sent Gross an invoice for the remaining clips of $31,506.45. However, Gross did not honor the invoice or pick up any more of the clips. Ulansey wrote to Stanley Waxman on February 7, 1972, requesting him to pick up the clips. Receiving no response, Ulansey wrote to Stanley Waxman again on February 23, 1972, threatening legal action if shipping instructions were not received by March 1, 1972. Finally, on March 30, 1972, Peter Waxman responded with a letter to Ulansey, which stated that Gross' failure to move the clips was due to a substantial decline in the clothing industry in 1971 and competition with new lower-cost methods of hanging and shipping clothes. The letter asked for Industrial's patience and predicted that it would take at least the rest of the year to market the clips successfully. At this point, Industrial sued. Stanley Waxman learned of the five million clip contract for the first time when informed by his lawyer of the impending law suit. At this time, Peter began an extended (four years) leave of absence from Gross.

The trial court ruled in favor of Industrial, the plaintiff, but awarded damages of only $2,400. Both parties appealed, plaintiff claiming that it should be entitled to the entire contract price of over $31,000, and defendant claiming that it should not be liable at all.

Hoffman, Judge: . . . Gross contends that it was not bound by the agreement to purchase the clips because Peter Waxman had no authority to sign the contract for Gross. However, Peter was an agent of Gross and did have express authority to purchase for Gross, as its president instructed him to purchase a "trial amount" of clips. A principal's limitation of his agent's authority in amount only, not communicated to the third party with whom the agent deals, does not so limit the principal's liability. Although the agent violates his instructions or exceeds the limits set to his authority, he will yet bind his principal to such third persons, if his acts are within the scope of the authority which the principal has caused or permitted him to possess. Such limitations will be binding [only] upon third persons *who know of them.*

An admitted agent is presumed to be acting within the scope of his authority where the act is legal and the third party has no notice of the agent's limitation. The third person must use reasonable diligence to ascertain the authority of the agent, but he is also entitled to rely upon the apparent authority of the agent when this is a reasonable interpretation of the manifestations of the principal.

Here, the limitation on Peter's authority was not communicated to Industrial. As Stanley Waxman brought Peter into the initial meeting soliciting business from Industrial, Ulansey could reasonably presume his authority to act for Gross in consummating the deal. Gross complains that Ulansey was not diligent in ascertaining Peter's authority, but in fact Ulansey telephoned Stanley Waxman precisely for the purpose of verifying Peter's authority. As Stanley said that Peter was authorized to act on behalf of Gross, the principal thus completed clothing the agent in apparent authority to bind the corporate entity on the agreement. If anybody was lacking in diligence, it was Stanley Waxman in not inquiring as to the amount of the contract Peter proposed to sign. Thus, we affirm the conclusion of the court below that Gross was bound by the agreement to purchase the clips.

[The court then held that the trial court had incorrectly computed damages, and that Industrial was entitled to the total contract price of $31,506.45 plus interest from the invoice date.]

Wing v. Lederer

Appellate Court of Illinois 222 N.E.2d 535 (1966)

Plaintiff Jacob A. Wing, a licensed tree surgeon, brought suit against the defendants, Philip C. Lederer and Peter Sonza-Novera, to recover the sum of $500 for services rendered.

In the early spring of 1964 Mrs. Lederer asked her yardman, Novera, whether a certain maple tree on the Lederer property needed care. He answered that it did, that he knew a man in the business, and that he would send him to her. Novera then contacted the plaintiff, had him come to the property, and showed him the tree, which had some dead branches near its top.

Plaintiff pointed out some other tree and shrubbery work that needed to be done. The testimony was in conflict as to whether Novera told plaintiff to do what was necessary or whether he told him to talk to the lady of the house.

During the summer plaintiff did a considerable amount of work but neither saw nor talked to Lederer, Mrs. Lederer, or Novera while working on the premises. Plaintiff did not contact the Lederers until he sent them a bill in November for $500. The bill was not paid, but Mrs. Lederer called plaintiff on several occasions to discuss it with him. Plaintiff never returned her calls. Nothing further was heard from plaintiff until he sent another bill in October 1965. That bill was not paid, and plaintiff brought suit.

The trial court held that Lederer, but not Novera, was liable to the plaintiff. Lederer appealed.

Davis, Justice: . . . Lederer had unquestionably constituted Novera his agent to recommend someone to take care of the maple tree. There is no issue as to the existence of an agency between Lederer and Novera, but only as to the latter's authority. The authority of the agent may come only from his principal. There is no dispute as to the actual authority conferred upon Novera. He was told to recommend someone to take care of the maple tree and to have that person talk to Mrs. Lederer. Both the principal and the agent understood this to be the extent of the agent's authority. It clearly did not include the hiring of a tree man for any purpose, and under no circumstances could it be parlayed to include the hiring of such man to do whatever he thought was necessary.

Nor can it be said that Lederer clothed Novera with apparent authority to hire plaintiff to do the work which was done. Apparent authority in an agent is such authority as the principal knowingly permits the agent to assume or which he holds his agent out as possessing—it is such authority as a reasonably prudent man, exercising diligence and discretion, in view of the principal's conduct, would naturally suppose the agent to possess. The plaintiff had no contact with Lederer either before or during the time in which the work was done, and Lederer neither did nor failed to do anything which would justify the plaintiff in assuming that Novera had authority to hire him.

One dealing with an assumed agent is duty bound to ascertain the extent of the agent's authority. Such circumstance alone should put the person dealing with such agent on guard in that anyone dealing with such agent must, at his own peril, ascertain not only the fact of the agency, but also the extent of the agent's authority.

Even assuming that the plaintiff's version of his conversation with Novera was correct, he conceded that Novera pointed out to him only the work to be done on the maple tree. It was the plaintiff who mentioned other work which should be done on the trees and shrubbery. Apparently, from the size of the bill, the other work was substantial and, in view of such circumstance, the plaintiff had a duty to confirm that a part time yardman had the authority to direct him to do whatever was necessary.

The plaintiff contends that, absent any original authority on the part of Novera, Lederer, by accepting the work which the plaintiff did, and by retaining the benefit thereof, ratified the acts of his agent in hiring the plaintiff. The rule is that where an agent has acted outside of the scope of his authority, a principal may ratify the act and render it obligatory upon himself; and that subsequent assent and ratification is equivalent to an original authorization and confirms that which originally was an unauthorized act. The ratification may either be express or inferred from the surrounding circumstances, but it must come from the acts or conduct of the principal. However, a principal may not be held to have ratified that which was done unless he acts with full knowledge of all the material facts.

Ratification rests on intention. The mere retention of the benefits of a transaction cannot be held to constitute ratification if the principal does not have the privilege of repudiating the unauthorized act. Absent such choice, the principal's conduct in accepting such benefits does not indicate that he assents to what has been done or intends to confirm it. In all of the cases cited by plaintiff, the ratification by a principal was made when he had full knowledge of the facts and a choice of either accepting or rejecting the benefits of the transaction.

Lederer had no choice! His trees had been pruned and sprayed long before he had knowledge of what had been done. He could not undo that which had then been done and his acceptance of the work was not by choice but by necessity. The fact that he did not stop the plaintiff from doing the work is no evidence of ratification, since it is undisputed that Lederer did not have knowledge of the services during the time they were being rendered. Lederer cannot be held to have ratified the hiring of plaintiff even if it is assumed that Novera hired him to do whatever was necessary.

If plaintiff predicates his right to recover upon a quasi contractual obligation on the part of Lederer, he must fail since he neither plead sufficient facts to warrant such recovery nor proved the reasonable value of the materials and services rendered.

For the reasons we have indicated, the judgment of the trial court is reversed and judgment is hereby entered in favor of the defendant, Lederer.

Importance of Agent's Knowledge

In deciding the question of a principal's liability to a third party, sometimes a key issue is whether the principal has received notice of a particular fact. For example, P is obligated under a contract to make payment to T. T assigns her right to receive this payment to X, an assignee. Assuming that T's right is assignable, P is bound to honor the assignment and pay X instead of T only if he has received notice of the assignment. But what if P's agent, A, receives this notice rather than P himself? If A promptly relays the information to P, there is usually no problem. What happens, though, if A fails to do so and P, not knowing of the assignment, pays T instead of X? Is P liable to X because P's agent had received notice?

Ordinarily, in any case where notice to the principal is important, *notice to the agent is treated as notice to the principal if the agent's receipt of the notice is within the scope of his or her actual or apparent authority.* In other words, in such cases the law will treat the principal as if he or she had received notice even if the agent did not transmit it. Obviously, however, this does not apply where the third party who notifies the agent knows that the agent is acting adversely to the interests of the principal (as where the third party and the agent are conspiring to defraud the principal).

Liability of the Agent

When the agent is acting for the principal, the agent ordinarily incurs no personal responsibility if he or she acts in a proper fashion. However, circumstances do exist where the agent can become liable.

Breach of Duty: If the agent violates any of the duties owed to the principal, he or she naturally is liable for the damages caused by the breach. Where the duty which has been violated is that of loyalty, the penalties may be even more severe. A disloyal agent is not only responsible to the principal for any resulting loss sustained by the latter but also usually forfeits his or her right to be compensated for services rendered. Furthermore, the agent must turn over to the principal any profits made from his or her disloyal activity.

Exceeding Authority: The agent who exceeds his or her actual authority is personally responsible unless the principal ratifies the unauthorized actions. Whether this responsibility is to the principal or to the third party depends on the circumstances. If the agent exceeds his or her actual authority, but the principal is liable to a third party on the ground of apparent authority, the agent's liability is to the *principal.* On the other hand, if the agent exceeds his or her actual authority and the facts are such that the principal is not liable to a third party under apparent authority, then the agent's liability is to the *third party.*

Assuming Liability: If the agent personally assumes liability for a particular transaction, then he or she obviously is responsible. For instance: A is attempting to purchase goods for P on credit. T, the seller, is wary of P's credit rating and refuses to grant credit unless A also becomes obligated. A signs the agreement as P's agent and in his own individual capacity. A is in effect a *co-principal* and therefore personally liable to T if P defaults.

Nondisclosure of Principal: If the agent, in dealing with a third party, fails to disclose that he or she is *acting for a principal or* fails to disclose the *principal's identity,* the agent is personally responsible to the third party. Additionally, the agent will sometimes be liable if he or she acts for a nonexistent principal or for one not having legal capacity. (These subjects will be dealt with specifically later in the chapter.)

Commission of a Tort: If the agent commits a *tort,* he or she is personally responsible to the injured party for the resulting harm. This is true regardless of whether the agent was working for the principal at the time. (Sometimes the principal also is responsible. This problem will be discussed later in the chapter.)

Relatively little need be said about the liability of the third party. Since that party is acting in his or her own behalf, he or she is personally responsible to the other party to the transaction. This ordinarily means that:

Liability of the Third Party

1. If the third party fails to live up to his or her part of the bargain, that person will be liable to the principal.

2. The third party owes no responsibility to the agent unless the agent has personally become a party to the transaction.

3. The third party is liable for his or her torts to any party injured as a result thereof.

In discussing the principal-agent relationship we have thus far assumed that the principal exists when the agent executes the transaction in question and that both the existence and the identity of the principal are disclosed to the third party. This is usually, but not always, the case. The special problems that arise in connection with *nonexistent, partially disclosed,* and *undisclosed principals* are discussed below.

Nonexistent, Partially Disclosed, and Undisclosed Principals

Nonexistent Principals

If an agent purports to act for a principal who does not exist at the time, the agent is usually liable to the third party. Of course, since there is no principal, the agent is not really an agent at all; he or she merely *claims* to be one.

While this situation does not occur frequently, it is by no means rare. A common instance of the nonexistent principal is that of a person attempting to act for an organization that is not legally recognized as a separate entity. (A *legal entity* is an organization—such as a corporation—that is recognized by the law as having the rights and duties of a person, although it is not flesh and blood. It can, for example, make contracts, sue, and be sued in its own name.) Thus a member of an unincorporated association, such as a church, club, fraternity, or the like, may attempt to contract in behalf of the association. Since the "principal" is not legally recognized as one, the members who make the agreement are personally responsible. It is for this reason that many churches and other such organizations form corporations.

The contracts of *corporate promoters* (those who play a part in the initial organization of a corporation) have posed similar problems. Quite often, these people make various types of agreements before the proposed corporation is formed. They may, for example, enter contracts for the purpose of raising capital, purchasing a building site, or procuring the services of an attorney, an accountant, or other professionals. The liabilities of the promoter, of the corporation once it is formed, and of the third party are discussed in Chapter 35.

A similar situation occurs when a principal has existed but is now dead or lacks contractual capacity when the agent contracts with the third party. As we mentioned in Chapter 29, such an occurrence often terminates the agency, and the principal (or that person's estate) is not bound. If the agency is not terminated, the principal's status affects his or her own liability in the same way as if the principal had personally dealt with the third party.

Whether the *agent* is personally liable depends on the circumstances. If the principal is *dead or has been declared insane by a court* at the time of the transaction, the agent invariably is held personally liable to the third party. On the other hand, if, at the time the transaction is made, the principal is either a *minor* or *insane* (but not officially declared insane by a court), the agent is personally responsible to the third party in only two situations:

1. The agent is liable if he or she has made representations to the effect that the principal has contractual capacity. This is true even if the agent is honestly mistaken.

2. The agent who has made no such representations is still liable to the third party if he or she *knew or had reason to know* of the principal's lack of capacity *and* the third party's ignorance of the facts.

Partially Disclosed Principals

As we indicated earlier, an agent usually is responsible to the third party if the agent discloses the fact that he or she is acting for a principal but does not *identify* that person. If the agent acts with authority, the principal is also responsible and may be held liable when the third party learns his or her identity.[2] Since the third party knows that the agent is acting for someone else, the third party is, in turn, liable to the principal. In sum, the liability of the principal and the third party is the same as in the case of a completely disclosed principal. The only difference is that in the case of a partially disclosed principal, the *agent is also liable,* unless the agent and the third party agree otherwise.

Undisclosed Principals

Individuals and business organizations sometimes prefer not to have their connection with a transaction be known. If an agent acts in behalf of a principal but does

---

[2]There is conflict among the courts on whether the third party must make a choice (or *election*) between the agent and the principal in such a case or whether he or she can hold both of them responsible.

not disclose to the third party the fact that he or she is representing another, it is said that the agent acts for an *undisclosed principal.* In other words, the third party, not knowing that a principal-agent relationship exists, thinks that the agent is dealing solely for himself.

In a case such as this, the agent is personally liable to the third party. If and when the principal makes himself known, that person is also liable to the third party if the agent acted within the scope of his authority. In such event, the third party must *elect* whether to hold the agent or the principal responsible.[3]

Thus far we have focused on the liability of the undisclosed principal and the agent. But what about the liability of the *third party?* Since the *agent* is a party to the contract, he or she can enforce the agreement against the third party. Once revealed, the *principal* ordinarily can also enforce the agreement. In three situations, however, the third party can refuse to perform for the undisclosed principal and can continue to treat the agent as the sole party to whom he or she is obligated:

1. If the third party has already performed for the agent before the principal is revealed, the third party is not required to render a second performance.

2. If, prior to the transaction, the third party has indicated that he or she will not deal with the one who is the undisclosed principal, the third party is not required to perform for that principal. Similarly, the third party is not responsible to the undisclosed principal if the former has indicated beforehand or in the agreement that he or she will not deal with *anyone* other than the agent.

3. In all other situations the undisclosed principal is treated in much the same way as an *assignee* from the agent (see Chapter 15 for a discussion of assignees). He or she can demand performance from the third party only if the contract is of a type that can be assigned. Thus, if the contract calls for personal service by the agent or if the agent's personal credit standing, judgment, or skill played an important part in the third party's decision to deal with that individual, the third party cannot be forced to accept the undisclosed principal as a substitute.

Tort Liability

Until now, our discussions of legal responsibility have focused almost exclusively on the parties' contractual liability. Now we will turn to their *tort liability.*

Rationale

Obviously, if either the superior, the subordinate, or the third party personally commits a tort, that person is liable to the one injured by the wrongful act. If the

---

[3]Different jurisdictions apply different rules as to what constitutes an *election.* Demanding payment from the agent or the principal or even filing suit against one of them usually *is not* considered the third party's "point of no return." Obtaining satisfaction of the claim obviously *is* an election. However, courts differ on whether *obtaining a court judgment* (which has not yet been collected) constitutes an election. Of course, if the third party obtains a judgment against the agent before knowing the principal's identity, there is no binding election and the third party can still pursue the principal.

subordinate commits a tort, the additional question often arises whether his or her *superior* is also liable to the injured third party. Indeed, this is often the most important question, because ordinarily the superior is insured or otherwise more financially capable of paying damages.

If the superior personally is at fault, that person obviously is liable because he or she has committed a tort. This can be seen in the following situations:

1. If the superior *directs* the subordinate to commit the tort (or even if the superior *intends* that the tort be committed), he or she is responsible.

2. If the superior carelessly allows the subordinate to operate potentially dangerous equipment (such as an automobile or truck), even though he or she knows or should know that the subordinate is unqualified or incapable of handling it safely, the superior is responsible for any resulting harm. The phrase *negligent entrustment* is often used to describe this situation.

3. Similarly, the superior is held liable if he or she is negligent in *failing to properly supervise a subordinate.*

Most often, however, the superior has not directed or intended the commission of a tort and has no reason to suppose that he or she is creating a dangerous situation. Therefore, the third party usually seeks to impose *vicarious liability* (liability imposed not because of one's own wrong but solely because of the wrong of one's subordinate) on the superior. The imposition of liability on the superior for a tort committed by a subordinate is based on the doctrine of *respondeat superior* ("let the master answer").

The theoretical justification for holding the superior responsible is that he or she can treat the loss—or the premiums for liability insurance—as a cost of doing business. The cost is thus reflected in the price of his or her product, and the loss is ultimately spread over a large segment of the population.

When the superior is required to pay damages to a third party because of the tort of a subordinate, the superior usually has a legal right to recoup the loss from that subordinate. As a practical matter, this is an illusory right in many cases, because the subordinate frequently is unable to pay.

Of course, the superior is not always responsible for the torts of subordinates. In this regard, two issues must ordinarily be dealt with:

1. Was the relationship that of master-servant or employer–independent contractor?

2. If a master-servant relationship existed, was the servant acting within the scope of his or her employment at the time of committing the alleged tort?

Master-Servant or Employer–Independent Contractor

Legal Significance of the Distinction: The imposition of vicarious liability often depends on the nature of the relationship involved. If it is found to be that of master and servant, the master is liable for a tort committed by his or her servant if it was committed in the scope of the servant's employment for the master.

On the other hand, if the relationship is found to be that of employer and independent contractor, the employer generally is not liable for a tort committed by the independent contractor. Those few instances in which the employer *is liable* for such a tort are:

1. If the task for which the independent contractor was hired is *inherently dangerous,* the employer will be responsible for harm to third parties caused by the dangerous character of the work. The employer's responsibility in such a case is based on the tort concept of *strict liability.* That is, the responsibility exists solely because of the nature of the activity, regardless of whether any negligence or other fault brought about the damage. Activities deemed to be inherently dangerous include blasting, using deadly chemicals, or working on buildings in populated areas where people must pass below the activity.

2. If the employer owes a *nondelegable duty,* he or she cannot escape ultimate responsibility for performing that duty by obtaining an independent contractor to perform it. Thus, if the independent contractor is negligent or commits some other tort in the performance of such a task, the employer is liable to the injured third party. Nondelegable duties are those duties owed to the public which courts feel to be of such importance that responsibility cannot be delegated. Examples are (1) a duty imposed by statute, such as the statutory duty of a railroad to keep highway crossings in a safe condition; (2) the duty of a city to keep its streets in a safe condition; (3) the duty of a landlord who has assumed responsibility for making repairs to the premises to see that those repairs are done safely; and (4) the duty of a business proprietor whose premises are open to the public to keep the premises in a reasonably safe condition.

Making the Distinction: The determination of whether a particular subordinate is a servant or an independent contractor depends essentially on the issue of *control.* If the superior has hired the subordinate merely to achieve a result and has left decisions regarding the method and manner of achieving that result up to the subordinate, the latter is an independent contractor. On the other hand, if the superior actually controls or has the right to control the method and manner of achieving the result, then the subordinate is a servant. Thus a construction contractor hired to erect a building is usually an independent contractor, while a secretary hired to type and take dictation is usually a servant.

However, the delineation is not always easy, and sometimes it produces problems of extreme conceptual difficulty. The most important question, of course, is whether the superior *controls or has the right to control the method and manner of doing the work.* Where the matter of control is not so obvious as to make the determination readily apparent, other factors can be taken into account. Some facts which would increase the likelihood of a subordinate being viewed as an independent contractor are: (1) The subordinate has his own independent business or profession; (2) The subordinate uses his own tools, equipment, or workplace to perform the task; (3) The subordinate is paid by the job, not by the hour, week, or month; (4) The subordinate has irregular hours; and (5) The subordinate is performing a task that is not part of the superior's regular business. None of these facts automatically makes a subordinate an independent contractor; each is simply a factor to be weighed along with all the other evidence.

In recent years, "franchising" has become a common method of doing business. In a franchise arrangement, the "franchisor" owns and promotes a trademark. Agreements are made with "franchisees," independent entrepreneurs who own and operate local outlets (such as fast-food restaurants). The franchising agreement will give the franchisee the right to use the franchisor's trademark and will place various restrictions on the way the local outlet is operated. The franchisee will be required to pay a royalty for his use of the trademark, which usually is a percentage of the franchisee's gross sales, and the franchisor usually promises to provide national advertising and various kinds of assistance. In the following case, the court considers the important question of whether a franchisee is an independent contractor or a servant of the franchisor.

Singleton v. International Dairy Queen, Inc.

Superior Court of Delaware, 332 A.2d 160 (1975)

Christine Singleton, nine years old, went to the local Dairy Queen store in Newark, Delaware. After purchasing ice cream, she started to leave. As she attempted to open the door, not by touching the glass but by pushing on a metal crossbar designed for the purpose, the bottom part of the door glass cracked and fell outward. Because of her forward motion, Christine fell through the door and onto the broken glass, suffering severe lacerations and other injuries.

In Christine's behalf, her father sued W. R. Hesseltine, the owner of the local Dairy Queen franchise, and International Dairy Queen, Inc., the franchisor. The franchisor ("Dairy Queen") filed a motion for summary judgment prior to trial, claiming that the documentary evidence established as a matter of law that Hesseltine was an independent contractor. In other words, Dairy Queen asserted that there was no issue of fact as to its liability and that it should be dismissed from the case, because even if plaintiff proved that the franchisee had been negligent in not maintaining a safe premises (which almost certainly would be the case), Dairy Queen could not be held liable for that tort. Following is the trial court's decision in ruling upon Dairy Queen's motion.

Longobardi, Judge . . . [The court first noted that Hesseltine had recently remodeled the store and that, in connection with the remodeling project, Hesseltine's personal architect had based his plans and specifications on plans furnished by Dairy Queen. The use of Dairy Queen's plans was required by the franchise agreement.] . . .

In addition to the requirement that any structure had to be built according to Dairy Queen's plans, the franchise agreement also contains the following pertinent conditions: (a) Dairy Queen imposes "rules and controls" for the "conduct of the Dairy Queen business"; (b) Dairy Queen has the right to inspect the premises; (c) The "mix" formulas are subject to Dairy Queen's regulation; (d) The franchise agreement cannot be assigned without prior approval; (e) Only the words "Dairy Queen" are to be displayed as the trade name of the store; (f) Dairy Queen reserves the right to inspect the premises for the purpose of quality control of the product "and the conditions of manufacture or sale thereof"; (g) Suppliers of "mix" have to be approved by Dairy Queen. All other products have to be purchased from Dairy Queen's approved suppliers; (h) Dairy Queen requires the store be kept in a "high state of repair"; (i) All employees have to wear uniforms approved by Dairy Queen; (j) All advertising cartons and containers used in the business must be marked to indicate they are being used under the authority of Dairy Queen; (k) Freezers must be purchased from "authorized" manufacturers; (l) Dairy Queen dictates portion control which can vary from time to time as they see fit; (m) All freezers used on the premises must have a name plate containing only the name "Dairy Queen"; (n) Dairy Queen reserves the right to dictate what additional items may be sold besides the dairy product from the freezer; (o) The franchisee must keep records and make monthly reports on the number of gallons of mix, from whom they were purchased and the date the mix was received; (p) Dairy Queen has the right to cancel the franchise agreement for many reasons, not the least of which is the franchisee's failure to meet the requirements proposed by Dairy Queen for the "physical properties"; (q) Dairy Queen renounces liability or responsibility for the "business operations" of the franchisee.

Private franchising, the multibillion dollar entrepreneurial goliath, thrives so long as it can maintain control of its service, product and trade name. The franchise agreement attests to the skill of corporate counsel in reserving as many rights as is possible to maintain control and to protect the product or service covered by the trademark. The necessity to maintain control for the purpose of protecting its product, service, know-how and name, however, may also result in a master-servant relationship wherein the franchisor becomes liable for the torts of the franchisee. [Other cases] have decided that when the control becomes excessive the borderline is breached and a master-servant relationship is created.

In the instant case, the control exercised by Dairy Queen appears to be excessive. When an entity can control the size, shape and appearance of its franchisor's establishment, impose the nationally known sign "Dairy Queen" as the only sign for the premises, require all containers to show the name of the parent company, dictate portion control, the size and shape of containers, the uniforms of the employees, subject the franchisor to the obligation to obey subsequent rules and regulations, reserve the right to inspect the premises . . . , name the suppliers and even dictate what else may be sold on the premises, there appears little else to establish agency. The very lifeblood of the agent is in the hands of the franchisor. What greater control can there be than portion control or the nebulously defined sanction of termination by the unilateral action of the franchisor? In addition, Hesseltine himself [said in his pretrial deposition that] Dairy Queen did control the day to day operations through their inspections. [The court then ruled that, in light of Hesseltine's testimony in his deposition as to Dairy Queen's control over him, which conflicted with the statement in the written franchise agreement that Dairy Queen had no such control, there was a fact issue as to the nature of their relationship.] . . .

The dispute is not resolved merely because the agreement says Dairy Queen is not responsible for the "business operations" of franchisee. The label by which parties to a relationship designate themselves is not controlling. In addition, the franchise agreement is so broadly drawn it requires additional discovery or testimony at trial to decide what the parties meant and understood by its terms. These are issues which are best resolved at trial during which the parties are given an opportunity for a full and rigorous examination of the facts.

In addition, there is a fact question as to Hesseltine's being an "apparent" servant of Dairy Queen . . . . [O]ne who represents . . . that another is his servant and causes a third person to justifiably and reasonably rely upon the care and skill of such apparent [servant] is subject to liability to the third person for harm caused by the lack of care or skill of the one appearing to be a servant as if he were such. [Thus, the court held that there were fact issues, to be decided at trial, as to both an "actual" and an "apparent" master-servant relationship.]

Defendant Dairy Queen's motion for summary judgment is denied.

Comment: Although we can only speculate, it is very likely that, after this decision, Dairy Queen either settled with the Singletons or was held liable along with Hesseltine after a trial.

Scope of Employment

If the subordinate is deemed to be a servant, the master is liable to third parties for those torts committed by the servant in the *scope of his or her employment* (sometimes called *course of employment*) for the master. There exists no simple definition of the scope of employment concept. Obviously, a servant is acting within the scope of employment while performing work that he or she has been *expressly directed to do by the master.* To illustrate: M has directed S to drive M's truck from New York to Albany via a certain route. While on that route, S drives negligently and injures T. M is liable to T.

In the absence of a specific directive given by the master, an act usually is in the scope of employment if it is *reasonably incidental to an activity that has been expressly directed.* Thus, in the above example, if S had stopped to buy gasoline and had negligently struck a parked car belonging to T, M would have been liable to T.

Deviations: The master sometimes can be held liable even though the servant has deviated from the authorized activity. The master's liability in such cases depends on the *degree* and *foreseeability* of the deviation. If the deviation is great, the master usually is not responsible. Suppose that S, in driving M's truck from New York to Albany, decides to go a hundred miles off his authorized route to visit an old friend. On the way there, S negligently collides with T. In this situation, M is not liable.

But what if S had been to see his friend and was returning to his authorized route when the collision occurred? Three different viewpoints have been taken by various courts. Where there has been more than a slight deviation from the scope of employment, as in this case, some courts have held that the reentry into the scope of employment occurs only when the servant has *actually returned to the authorized route or activity.* Others have held that there is reentry the moment that the servant, with an intent to serve the master's business, *begins to turn back toward the point of deviation.* However, a majority of courts have held that reentry occurs when the servant, with an intent to serve the master's business, *has turned back toward and come reasonably close to the point of deviation.*

If the deviation from the authorized route or activity is only slight, many courts have held that the servant is still within the scope of the employment if the type of deviation was *reasonably foreseeable* by the master. For example: While driving from New York to Albany, S stops at a roadside establishment to get something to eat or to buy a pack of cigarettes. While pulling off the road, he negligently strikes a parked car. In this situation M is liable. Although buying something to eat or smoke may not be necessary to drive a truck from New York to Albany (as is the purchase of gasoline) and although S was not really serving his master, the deviation was only slight and was of the type that any master should reasonably expect.

Many examples of the scope of employment issue—such as the next two cases—involve auto accidents (though certainly the issue is not limited to them). These two cases illustrate some typical problems in this area.

Bridger v. International Business Machines Corp.

U.S. Court of Appeals, 5th Circuit, 480 F.2d 566 (1973)

Bridger, plaintiff, brought this suit to recover damages for injuries to himself and for the death of his wife, caused when the car they occupied was struck from the rear by a car driven by Billy Farris Teasley, an employee of International Business Machines Corporation (IBM), defendant. Both sides moved for summary judgment; the trial court granted IBM's motion, holding that the facts established as a matter of law that Teasley was not acting within the scope of his employment with IBM at the time of the accident. Bridger appealed.

Thornberry, Justice: . . . Teasley was a "customer service engineer" or serviceman for IBM, performing repairs and service on IBM products (typewriters, dictation equipment, and the like) on the owners' premises. He was required to be at the day's first job by 8:30 a.m. and was permitted to cease work in time to return to IBM's Macon, Georgia, office by 5:15 p.m., although he was not required actually to return to Macon at the end of the day. For any work done outside these hours, Teasley was paid overtime. Although all customer service engineers were subject to call seven days a week, twenty-four hours a day, to perform emergency service work, Teasley had not received an emergency call for at least two years prior to the date of the accident, and the equipment he was trained to repair was not normally serviced after regular hours. Moreover, it is unclear from the record whether IBM could relay an emergency call to Teasley in the field; Teasley's supervisor testified only that "*now* we are actually using radios to contact them."

Teasley drove his own car when making service calls, and was paid $2.70 per day for maintenance, whether he drove his car or not. In addition, IBM paid him mileage for the distance between his home in Warner Robins, Georgia, to the first job of each day, the distance he drove between job sites during the day, and the distance from the last job site back to Warner Robins, regardless of whether he actually returned to Warner Robins after finishing his last job.

On the day of the accident in question, after spending about two hours at IBM's Macon office, Teasley performed service work at Robins Air Force Base in Warner Robins for almost two hours. Thereafter he drove to the Agriculture Stabilization and Conservation Service office in Perry, Georgia, and did repair work there for approximately four hours. It is undisputed that this was his last service call for the day and that he received no emergency calls that night. He left Perry at roughly 5:00 p.m. and took the easternmost of four alternate routes to Warner Robins, located roughly twelve miles northeast of Perry. At the town of Bonaire, Georgia, he drove east to the Flamingo Club, where he drank beer until ten o'clock that night. He then resumed his trip toward Warner Robins. Shortly after reaching the highway to Warner Robins, his car struck [Bridger's] car from the rear, severely injuring Mr. Bridger and killing his wife. Teasley claimed and received mileage for the trip from Perry to Warner Robins.

. . . Undeniably, Teasley was performing a purely personal mission while he was at the Flamingo Club for almost five hours drinking beer, and IBM cannot be liable for any tort he committed while engaged in that mission. Under Georgia law, however, the employer's liability for his employee's torts is suspended only during the employee's "deviation" from his duties; upon the employee's resumption of his work, the employer's liability re-attaches. Thus, the issue here is whether the trial court properly held that the evidence conclusively established that Teasley had not resumed the discharge of his duties at the time of the accident.

In *Southern Gas Corp. v. Cowan,* 81 S.W.2d 488, the Georgia Court of Appeals held that facts substantially similar to those of the case at bar authorized a jury finding that an employee-driver was acting within the scope of his employment at the time of an automobile accident. Bowman, a salesman and serviceman for Southern Gas, collided with the plaintiff while driving home in a company-owned car roughly two hours after his last call of the day. The company paid operating expenses for the car, which Bowman could keep at home for his personal use subject to emergency business calls. Relying primarily on the fact that Bowman kept the car for his personal use subject to emergency calls, the court of appeals held that this evidence warranted a jury finding that Bowman was acting within the scope of his employment while driving home in the company car:

> To the extent that he was subject to call at all hours and had the automobile there to use in case he was so called, the keeping of the automobile at his home was in furtherance of his employment duties. . . . Bowman's driving of the company's automobile from the place of his last call to his home where he would keep it subject to using it on company business in the event he was called out by the company was within the scope of his employment.

The court expressly reserved [did not decide] the question whether Bowman would have been acting within the course of his employment while performing personal errands after reaching his home.

The holding in *Cowan* is somewhat ambiguous. Bowman was arguably benefiting his employer *both* by keeping the car subject to use on emergency business *and* by storing his employer's car at his home overnight. Whether either of these possible benefits was enough to impose vicarious liability on an employer, or whether both of them were necessary, was unclear until the *Cowan* court decided *Price v. Star Service and Petroleum Corp.,* 166 S.E.2d 593. There, an employee of Star Service had been involved in a collision while driving home from a Sunday church service in a company car. The opinion contains no mention of whether the employee was on call at the time of the accident. It was argued that the employee was benefiting his employer simply by driving the company car home for storage; but the court squarely rejected that argument, holding that company ownership of the car, standing alone, is an insufficient basis of employer liability. That holding makes it evident that the fact that Bowman was on call was the deciding factor in imposing liability on the employer in *Cowan*. It follows that, if Teasley was subject to call after resuming his trip home to Warner Robins, he was, no less than was Bowman, acting within the scope of his employment.

The trial court distinguished *Cowan*, however, on the ground that Teasley was not subject to emergency call. Noting that Teasley had not received an emergency call in at least two years, and pointing to IBM's doubtful ability to contact Teasley in the event of an emergency, the trial court held that the requirement of availability in emergencies was "never enforced and . . . not expected to be enforced" and was "at best a theoretical requirement." In our view, the question whether Teasley was on call was properly a question for the jury in the instant case. Merely because no emergency calls had been *made* is no evidence that IBM would not "enforce" the requirement that servicemen answer such calls if they were made. Nor is it as clear to us as it was to the trial court that IBM had no way of contacting Teasley in the event an emergency call was made. As noted above, Teasley's supervisor testified on deposition that "*now* we are actually using radios to contact them." While it is reasonable to infer from this statement that at some point in the past IBM did not use radios to contact its servicemen, the statement says nothing about whether IBM had any means of contacting its servicemen before the installation of the radios. In brief, the question whether Teasley was in fact subject to emergency call—which, as we have seen above, is a critical factor in determining his employer's liability—was a disputed issue of fact that was inappropriate for the decision by the trial court on motions for summary judgment. Accordingly, the judgment below is reversed and remanded for further proceedings consistent with this opinion.

Comment: Merely "commuting" to and from work is generally held *not* to be in the scope of employment. The above case shows that an exception to this general rule is made when the servant uses a vehicle for work purposes and is "on call" during nonworking hours.

Rappaport v. International Playtex Corp.
Supreme Court, Appellate Division, New York, 352 N.Y.S.2d 241 (1974)

During October 1971 Davis was employed as a salaried outside salesman by Playtex in a sixteen-county area surrounding Syracuse, New York. He had been so employed for twenty-one years. His duties included selling the employer's products directly to retail stores and preparing reports and orders relating to such sales. He did not have an office but worked out of his home at Cazenovia, New York. He was required to own and operate a motor vehicle as a condition of employment (for which he received a flat monthly reimbursement), most of his work travel being by car. He had no set hours of employment but worked whenever it was necessary, including weekends; he was, in fact, urged by his district manager to work evenings and weekends.

On October 10, a Sunday, Davis worked part of the morning at his home. He left for his then separated wife's home at Cazenovia, arriving about 1:30 p.m. and departing two hours later with the unfinished paper work of the morning still in his car. His destination was the Canastota home of Madeline Reynolds, whom he later married. According to Davis, the purpose of the trip to the Reynolds home was "to do paper work and visit at my friend's house, and have dinner at my friend's house. . . . I do my weekly call reports for two days over there on Sunday, and I have that with me and also I have some other records and orders that I have to make out, [and] so on, key accounts and books to close." The evidence indicated that it was normal for Davis to do paper work wherever he happened to be.

While traveling to the Reynolds home, Davis was involved in a collision with Barnum. Barnum died from his injuries; and Rappaport, the executor of Barnum's estate, brought suit against Playtex, the defendant. The trial court denied defendant's motion to dismiss, and defendant appealed that action.

Cooke, Justice: ... Under the doctrine of *respondeat superior,* an employer will be liable for the negligence of an employee while the latter is acting in the scope of his employment and "[a]n employee acts in the scope of his employment when he is doing something in furtherance of the duties he owes to his employer and where the employer is, or could be, exercising some control, directly or indirectly, over the employee's activities." As a general rule, an employee driving to and from work is not acting in the scope of his employment, but an exception to this rule would exist, in the case of an employee who uses his car in furtherance of his work and while he is driving to a business appointment, since such a person is working and under his employer's control from the time he leaves the house in the morning until he returns at night.

Davis testified at the examination before trial that he was enroute to Canastota to visit Madeline Reynolds and to do more paper work, the further work to be done after dinner. With relation to a trip, involving both business of the employer and a private purpose of the employee, it was said in *Matter of Marks v. Gray,* 167 N.E. 181 at page 183:

> To establish liability, the inference must be permissible that the trip would have been made though the private errand had been canceled. ... The test in brief is this: If the work of the employee creates the necessity for travel, he is in the course of his employment, though he is serving at the same time some purpose of his own. *Clawsen v. Pierce-Arrow Motor Car Co.,* 131 N.E. 914. If, however, the work has had no part in creating the necessity for travel, if the journey would have gone forward though the business errand had been dropped, and would have been canceled upon failure of the private purpose, though the business errand was undone, the travel is then personal, and personal the risk.

... While the [evidence] indicate[s] that Davis intended to perform employment related paper work at his girl friend's house following dinner and that he customarily did such work there on Sundays, he also stated that he normally did his paper work wherever he happened to be. The only reasonable inference that can be drawn is that the business purpose alone would not have launched the subject journey, and that, had Davis not known Madeline Reynolds socially or had the dinner engagement been canceled, the trip to her home at Canastota would not have been undertaken. Accordingly, it cannot be said that the employer's business was even a "concurrent cause" of the fateful trip ... and, therefore, Davis was not in the scope of defendant's business at the time and *respondeat superior* does not apply.

[Reversed. Case dismissed.]

Intentional Torts: Thus far we have assumed the tort to be that of *negligence* (simple carelessness). Most cases in fact *are* concerned with the servant's negligence. However, a servant's *intentional tort,* such as assault and battery, libel, slander, fraud, trespass, or the like, can also subject the master to liability. The test is the same. The master is liable if the servant was acting within the scope of his or her employment at the time. It should be emphasized, though, that a master is *less likely* to be responsible if the servant's tort was intentional rather than merely negligent. The reason is that when a servant intentionally commits a wrongful act, he or she is more likely to be motivated by personal reasons rather than by a desire to serve the master. Those cases where the master *has* been held liable for his or her servant's intentional torts usually fall within one of three broad categories.[4]

Where the tort occurs in a job in which force is a natural incident. An example is a bouncer in a saloon, who is naturally expected to use force occasionally. But if *excessive* force is used, the master is liable.

Where the servant is actually attempting to promote the master's business but does it in a wrongful manner. For example, two competing tow truck drivers are attempting to beat each other to the scene of an accident to get the business for their respective masters. One intentionally runs the other off the road. The master of the one committing the tort is liable.

Where the tort results from friction naturally brought about by the master's business. For instance, the servant, who works for a building contractor, argues with an employee of a subcontractor about the method for laying a floor. They become angry, and the servant strikes the other party. The building contractor, as master, is probably liable.

Concluding Note on Tort Liability

Two problems of a miscellaneous nature regarding a master's tort liability remain to be discussed:

1. A minor is not necessarily the servant of his or her parents. Thus, in the absence of a special statute, the parent is not liable for the torts of a minor child unless the child was acting as a servant in the scope of employment for the parent. The parent can, of course, be held liable for his or her own wrongful act in negligently supervising the child. Also, several states have passed statutes making parents liable within set limits for intentional property damage caused by a minor child.

2. Although the subject of bailments is beyond the scope of this discussion, it should be mentioned that a bailee is not necessarily the servant of the bailor. A *bailment* occurs when the owner of an item of property (the bailor) turns over temporary custody (not ownership) of the item to the bailee for any reason. The bailor ordinarily is *not* liable to third parties for torts committed by the bailee while using the bailor's property. The bailor *is* liable, however, if he or she was negligent in entrusting the item to one whom he or she knew not to be qualified or capable of handling it safely. Otherwise, the bailor generally is liable only if the bailee was acting as the bailor's *servant* in the scope of employment at the time of the tort. Two exceptions exist with regard to *bailments of automobiles:*

   a. A few states follow the *family purpose doctrine.* Under that judge-made doctrine, a member of the family is treated as the servant of the head of the

---

[4]See Philip Mechem, *Outlines of Agency,* 4th ed. (Chicago: Callaghan & Co., 1952), § 395.

household when driving the family car, regardless of whether such a relationship actually existed.

b. A few states have passed *owner-consent statutes,* which hold the owner of an automobile liable to a third party injured by the negligence of anyone who is driving it with the consent of the owner. This liability exists regardless of any master-servant relationship and regardless of whether the owner was personally negligent.

Criminal Liability

As a general rule, a superior cannot be *criminally* prosecuted for a subordinate's wrongful act unless the superior expressly authorized it. Thus, if S, a subordinate, while acting within the scope of her employment, injures T, and T dies, S's superior can be held liable in a civil suit for damages but cannot be subjected to criminal liability. Any criminal responsibility rests on the shoulders of the subordinate. The rule exists because crimes ordinarily require intent, and the superior in this situation has no criminal intent.

Exceptions to the rule usually fall within one of two categories:

1. The statute making the particular act a crime may specifically provide for placing criminal responsibility on the superior. For example, the federal antitrust laws provide for criminal penalties to be levied against corporations, which can commit crimes only through their human agents.

2. A superior can sometimes be criminally prosecuted under statutes that do not require intent for a violation. A specific example is the offense of selling adulterated food under the federal Food, Drug and Cosmetic Act. Other examples can be found in some state laws regulating liquor sales and the accuracy of weights of goods sold on that basis.

Questions and Problems

1. Simpson gave Ricks written authority to sell Simpson's residential lot for $5,000. Ricks procured a buyer willing to pay that price, made a contract with the buyer in Simpson's behalf, and executed a deed conveying the land to the buyer. When Simpson learned of Ricks's actions, he disavowed the transaction, claiming that Ricks had exceeded her authority. Is Simpson correct?

2. A check was made payable to "Mrs. Robert Jenkins." Robert Jenkins endorsed his wife's name on the check and cashed it. The teller at the bank where he cashed the check watched Jenkins endorse his wife's name. Jenkins used the money to buy an outboard motor for his boat. Jenkins and his wife were having marital difficulties and separated shortly thereafter. When Mrs. Jenkins learned of her husband's actions in cashing the check, she sued the bank to recover the money that had been paid to her husband. Did she prevail?

3. Suppose that in Question 2 Mrs. Jenkins had been standing silently beside Mr. Jenkins at the time he endorsed her name in front of the teller. What would be the result if she later sued the bank? Discuss.

4. In 1959, Bert Bell, Commissioner of the National Football League (NFL), entered into an agreement with representatives of the NFL Players Association, which provided for certain pension benefits for players who had retired from the NFL prior to 1959. The bylaws of the NFL required any such agreement to be approved by the owners of at least ten of the twelve NFL teams. During negotiations leading to the agreement, Bell stated that he would resign if the agreement were not approved. The agreement was not approved and the pension benefits were not paid. Those players who would have received benefits under the agreement sued both the NFL and the players association, claiming that the NFL was bound by the agreement because Bell had acted with apparent authority. *Soar v. National Football League Players Ass'n,* 438 F. Supp. 337 (1975). Should the players have won their lawsuit? Discuss.

5. Roberts, a salesclerk in a jewelry store, wanted to take a short break. He asked Jones, the store janitor, to watch the store for a few minutes while he was gone. Jones, dressed in soiled work clothes, sold a silver tray priced at $300 to a customer for $250. Roberts returned shortly thereafter and learned what Jones had done. As soon as Roberts was able to contact the customer, he demanded the return of the tray or payment of the additional $50. Does the customer have to comply with the demand?

6. Suppose that in Question 5, Roberts had asked Richardson, the bookkeeper, to watch the store rather than the janitor. Would the result be any different in this case? Would it matter whether the buyer was a new customer or a regular customer who knew the store's employees? Discuss.

7. Rodriguez was a salesman at a retail carpet outlet owned by Carpet World, Inc. He usually was the only employee in the store, and the company's sales manager only made occasional visits to the store. Although he had no hiring authority, Rodriguez hired Amy Schoonover on a salary and commission basis. Amy worked for two months, earning salary and commissions of $714, but was never paid. Rodriguez disappeared, and Amy sued Carpet World for her unpaid compensation. *Schoonover v. Carpet World, Inc.,* 588 P.2d 729 (1978). Is Carpet World liable? Discuss.

8. Bruton lent a D-8 Caterpillar rent-free to David Eckvall, who wanted to clear some land owned by Eckvall. It was agreed that Eckvall would provide an operator and pay for fuel and routine maintenance. Nothing was said about major repairs. While Eckvall was using the Cat, it broke down. Without contacting Bruton, he took it to Automatic Welding & Supply (AWS), where extensive repairs were made at a cost of $2,340. When the repairs were almost completed, Bruton happened to come into the AWS shop on other business and saw his Cat. He spoke to an AWS mechanic and learned of the scope of the repairs, but nothing was said about cost. After the repairs were completed, the Cat was returned to Eckvall's property where he used it for some time thereafter. AWS billed Bruton for the repairs. Bruton denied liability, and AWS sued. *Bruton v. Automatic Welding & Supply,* 513 P.2d 1122 (1973). Is Bruton responsible for the $2,340? Discuss.

9. Chipman, an employee at Barrickman's service station, was towing a disabled car for Barrickman. Estell, Chipman's girlfriend, was a passenger in the tow truck. She was just along for the ride, without Barrickman's knowledge. The tow truck was involved in an accident and Estell, who was injured, sued Chipman and Barrickman. *Estell v. Barrickman,* 571 S.W.2d 650 (1978). The trial court dismissed the suit against Barrickman, because he had an official "no rider" rule, even though he didn't always enforce it. Estell appealed. How should the appellate court rule? Discuss.

10. Hartford Ice Cream Co. manufactured ice cream. Son operated a grocery store, selling, among other items, Hartford's ice cream. Hartford delivered the ice cream to Son by truck, and the driver was instructed to collect the price on delivery. On one occasion, Son claimed that the ice cream being delivered had not been properly refrigerated, and he refused to accept or pay for it. The driver tried to take the money from Son's cash register, but Son managed to lock the register before this could be done. The driver then started to carry away the entire cash register, and a struggle for its possession developed. Although Son prevented the driver from removing the cash register, Son was severely beaten by him. Son sued both the driver and Hartford Ice Cream Co. for the damages caused by the beating. *Son v. Hartford Ice Cream Co.*, 129 Atl. 778 (1925). Is Hartford liable for the actions of the driver? Discuss.

Part V

Business
Organizations

Forms of Business Organizations

31

A business can operate in any of several different organizational forms, the most **Introduction** common of which are the sole proprietorship, the partnership, the limited partnership, and the corporation. Certain other types of organization are of limited usefulness and are therefore not frequently employed. These include the joint stock company, the business trust, the joint venture, and the syndicate.

In this chapter we will outline the basic structure of each form and indicate the factors one should consider in selecting the appropriate form. Later chapters will explore in much greater detail the two predominant types of organizations in use today: the partnership and the corporation.

Sole Proprietorship

A person who does business for himself or herself is engaged in the operation of **Structure of the** a *sole proprietorship.* (In reality, anyone who does business without creating an **Various Forms** organization is a sole proprietor.) The sole proprietorship is obviously the most

545

elementary organizational form. The owner *is* the business. No legal formalities are necessary to create this form, and any business affairs not handled personally by the owner are handled through his or her agents. The sole proprietorship is usually associated with small, local enterprises, but there is no legal or theoretical limit to the scope or complexity of its operations.

Partnership

A *partnership* is an association of two or more persons who carry on a business. The partners are co-owners of the business, and as such they have joint control over its operation and the right to share in its profits. A partnership is created by agreement of the parties. Although the agreement need not be formal, it is usually desirable that a formal partnership agreement be executed. The Uniform Partnership Act (UPA), adopted in forty-seven states, sets out rules to govern the operation of a partnership in the absence of a formal agreement or if certain areas are not covered in the formal agreement. Thus the parties can vary many of the rules set forth in this statute. They cannot, however, vary the rules relating to their liability to a third party (a nonpartner, such as a creditor) unless the third party agrees.

The partnership is suitable for almost any type of business and is very widely used. It will be discussed in much greater detail in Chapters 32 to 34.

Limited Partnership

A *limited partnership* is a partnership comprised of at least one general partner and at least one limited partner. The general partner is treated by the law the same as a partner in an ordinary partnership. The limited partner, on the other hand, is only an investor. He or she merely contributes capital and does not exercise any powers of management. This form of organization was created for the purpose of allowing a person to invest in a partnership and share in its profits without becoming personally liable to partnership creditors. *Limited liability* is the key characteristic of the limited partnership.

Since an owner of a business can avoid full personal liability for business debts only if this is provided for by statute, it naturally follows that a limited partnership is purely a creature of statute. It can be created only where permitted by statute, and it must meet all required statutory formalities. For example, a "certificate of limited partnership" must be filed with a designated official in the state in which the organization is to do business. If the formalities are not all met, a limited partner usually is treated as a general partner, with resulting personal liability to partnership creditors. A limited partner is also treated as a general partner if he or she takes part in managing the business. The Uniform Limited Partnership Act (ULPA), adopted by forty-eight states, governs the organization and operation of such partnerships. Limited partnerships are allowed under other statutes in the states that have not enacted the ULPA.

Corporation

The corporation is perhaps the most important form of business organization, not only because it is so widely employed but also because most large businesses operate as corporations. Like the limited partnership, the corporation is entirely a creature of statute. It simply cannot exist unless provided for by an applicable statute and unless the requirements of that statute are met. Every state does, in fact, have statutes governing the formation and operation of corporations.

Essentially, a corporation consists of its *shareholders* (the owners of the business) and its *board of directors* (those people elected by the shareholders to manage the business). The directors commonly employ agents (such as *officers* and other subordinate employees) to oversee the daily operation of the business.

An outstanding characteristic of the corporation is that its shareholders are not personally liable for business obligations beyond the amount of their respective investments. The reason is that the corporation is recognized as a *legal entity* separate and apart from its owners. Corporations will be extensively dealt with in Chapters 35 to 38.

Other Organizational Forms

Joint Stock Company: A *joint stock company* is an unincorporated association that closely resembles a corporation but for most purposes is treated as a partnership. It can exist even where there is no governing statute. Management of the enterprise is usually delegated to one or a few persons. Ownership of the business is evidenced by shares of transferable stock, and each of the shareholders is as liable for business obligations as a partner in a partnership. However, the shareholders are not generally treated as agents of one another (as is true of partners). This form of organization is not widely used today.

Business Trust: The *business trust* (sometimes called the "Massachusetts trust," after the state of its origin) is another organization created by agreement. Legal ownership and management of business property rest with one or more "trustees," and the profits are distributed to "beneficiaries." The business trust originated as an attempt to obtain certain advantages of corporate status, such as limited liability, without incorporation. It was a fairly popular arrangement for a few years during the early 1900s, but it is seldom used today, for two primary reasons:

1. A number of states enacted statutes subjecting the business trust to many of the same burdens placed upon corporations, such as payment of certain corporate taxes.

2. In many states, the beneficiaries were treated as partners by being held personally liable to business creditors.

Joint Venture: A *joint venture* (sometimes called a "joint adventure" or a "joint enterprise") is essentially just a partnership created for a limited purpose or duration. It is treated virtually the same as a partnership.[1] Of course, the implied authority of one participant to obligate the enterprise to third parties under the rules of agency law is more limited than in most partnerships because of the restricted scope of the organization's operation. (An example is the association formed a number of years ago by Pennsalt Chemicals Corporation and Olin Mathieson Chemical Corporation. The two companies formed Penn-Olin Chemical Company, a joint venture, solely for the purpose of producing and selling sodium chlorate in the southeastern United States.)

Syndicate or Investment Group: The terms *syndicate* and *investment group* are often used to describe a group of investors in a particular enterprise (such as financing a professional football team or a real estate development). The precise nature of the organization depends entirely on the terms of the parties' agreement and the actual operation of the enterprise. The parties can be partners, members of some other type of association, or simply joint owners of a property interest with no legally recognized business relationship. One pitfall in such arrangements is that the investors may find themselves liable to third parties as partners without having realized the possibility of that occurrence.

Selecting the Appropriate Form

Choosing the appropriate form from among the suitable alternatives is a necessary and important step in the organization of a business enterprise. This choice should be made only after careful analysis of the needs and desires of the owner or owners of the business—and with the aid of legal counsel. Several of the available alternatives may be suitable; there usually will not be one form that *must* be used. Since the organizational form is only a vehicle, the owners should choose the one that enables them to reach their objectives in the easiest, most direct, and most inexpensive way.

Following are some of the factors that should be considered in choosing the most appropriate organizational form. The discussion is devoted primarily to the most frequently used forms: sole proprietorship, partnership, and corporation.

Liability of Owners

The significance of the owners' potential liability for business debts varies with the circumstances. In a given case, its importance depends not only on the degree of probability that substantial claims will arise against the business but also on the practical likelihood of owners having to meet these claims from personal assets not

---

[1]Technically speaking, there must be a *business purpose* rather than a *social purpose* for a joint venture to exist. In many cases, however, courts have used the terms *joint venture* or *joint enterprise* to describe a situation in which persons are engaged in some common pursuit even if the transaction is not for a business purpose. The most common example is a car pool, where passengers in an automobile share expenses of and control over a trip for a common purpose. The courts have applied the *joint venture* concept to impose joint liability for the negligent driving of one of the participants.

devoted to the business and on the proportion of their wealth that they intend to risk in the business. More specifically:

1. The potential liability (in proportion to capital) is much heavier in some businesses than in others.

2. Those who expect to risk their total accumulated wealth in an enterprise are less in need of limited liability than those who possess substantial assets not being committed to the business.

3. The practicability of obtaining agreements from business creditors to look only to business assets in satisfying their claims varies greatly from one situation to another.

4. The practicability of obtaining liability insurance covering tort claims varies significantly among different types of businesses.

As mentioned earlier, freedom from personal liability for business obligations ordinarily is enjoyed by shareholders of a corporation and by limited partners in a limited partnership. Owners are not usually shielded from liability by any other organizational forms.[2]

By itself, though, the *form* of the organization does not always determine the issue of owners' liability. It is sometimes more dependent on simple bargaining power, particularly in smaller businesses. For example, a corporation with relatively few shareholders and limited assets may be unable to obtain credit solely on the basis of its own credit standing. A creditor in such a case will frequently require as a condition of granting credit that the shareholders personally obligate themselves to satisfy the claim in the event of default by the corporation. On the other hand, a sole proprietorship, partnership, or other organization with ample business assets and financial strength might be able to obtain the agreement of a creditor to look only to business assets for satisfaction of its claim. (In the latter instance, of course, it is unlikely that the owners would ever be required to expend personal assets not committed to the business even if such an agreement were not made.)

Control

The power to make business decisions is of interest to almost anyone undertaking to organize a business. As a purely legal matter, the sole proprietor exercises the most control over the enterprise, for he or she *is* the business. The individual degree of control naturally decreases as other owners enter the picture. Thus a partner must share control with copartners. When an organizational form that employs centralized management (such as a corporation) is used, the owners surrender even more control. Business decisions in a corporation are delegated to the board of directors, who may or may not be shareholders. Of course, in the small corporation, where shares of stock are held by only a few persons and are not

---

[2]However, beneficiaries of a *business trust,* assuming that they refrain from exercising control over the business, are shielded from liability in a few jurisdictions.

publicly sold (called a *close corporation*), most or all of the shareholders might be on the board of directors. Thus the owners of a close corporation usually do not relinquish as much direct control as do the owners of a corporation with widely distributed shares. (Close corporations will be further explored in the chapters on corporations.)

Control, like limited liability, is not necessarily determined only by legal structure. Control of the enterprise often is shaped by other practical matters such as finances and personality. For example, even in a large enterprise, a shareholder who owns a substantial percentage of a corporation's stock frequently can exercise a great deal of indirect control even if he or she is not a member of the board. (Of course, such a person probably can win election to the board if he or she so desires.) At the other end of the continuum, the sole proprietor, who theoretically possesses total control over a business, often surrenders some of that control in borrowing substantial sums of money. Few lenders will allow their capital to be used in a business without retaining a certain amount of control over how it is used. Thus a creditor may impose various conditions in the loan agreement and will almost certainly acquire a lien on business assets that will limit or exhaust the credit of the enterprise.

Sometimes a partner, a shareholder, or other business associate exerts a degree of control much greater than his or her actual financial interest. This can occur because the person possesses either experience or a persuasive personality.

Continuity

Most business owners are concerned about the extent to which their business interests will be passed on to their heirs when they die. The entire interest of a sole proprietor passes to his or her heirs. However, if several heirs exist, disputes will probably occur about the continued operation of the business and the heirs will end up selling it and dividing the proceeds. A sole proprietor who wants the business to continue in the family after his or her death will have to plan very carefully (and even then continuity is often impossible).

As we will see later, the partnership is a fragile structure that dissolves on the death or withdrawal of a partner. However, a carefully planned and drafted agreement can strengthen the partnership as a continuing enterprise by providing, for example, that remaining partners have the right to purchase the interest of a retiring or deceased partner.

A corporation, because its shares of stock are transferable, possesses the continuity usually lacking in a partnership.[3] Neither a shareholder's sale of stock nor his or her death terminates the corporation. The purchaser or heir simply becomes the owner of the interest in the business represented by those shares. In most cases

---

[3]Usually the interests of limited partners in a limited partnership, as well as the owners' interests in joint stock companies and business trusts, also are freely transferable.

a corporation continues until the shareholders vote to dissolve it; theoretically, it can continue forever.

While continuity is usually desirable, under some circumstances it may be undesirable. For example, suppose that a small business is organized as a close corporation. All the shareholders know one another personally, and each plays a significant part in the everyday operation of the business. One shareholder transfers all his stock to a third party, and the other shareholders find themselves forced to share control with someone they don't know and never contemplated dealing with. For this reason, it is advisable to include certain restrictions on the transfer of shares in close corporations, particularly in family-owned corporations. (Restrictions on transferability will be discussed in Chapter 37.)

Capital Requirements

Expansion of the business and the resulting need for additional capital is perhaps the most common reason for changing the organizational form from a sole proprietorship or partnership to a corporation.

If an interest in a sole proprietorship is sold to raise capital, the owner is no longer a "sole" proprietor. Therefore, a sole proprietor wanting to remain one can raise capital only by borrowing. But borrowing as a method of satisfying capital requirements has limitations that are quickly reached. They include not only the exhaustion of one's credit but also the onerous burden of fixed interest charges.

A partnership presents more possibilities for raising capital:

1. The existing partners themselves are possible sources of additional funds.

2. New partners who will bring more capital into the enterprise can be admitted.

3. In most (but not all) cases, a partnership can secure more funds through borrowing, because the cumulative value of all the partners' assets usually exceeds that of a sole proprietor, thereby improving the business's credit standing.

Definite limitations exist, however, on the capital-raising ability of a partnership. Existing partners provide sources of new funds only insofar as they are willing and financially able to further invest in the business. Bringing in new partners results in a smaller share of profits for each partner. But, perhaps most importantly, the point may quickly be reached at which there are simply *too many partners* to operate efficiently. The larger the number of owners, the greater the need for centralized management. Ultimately, the same limitations on borrowing to satisfy capital requirements exist in a partnership as in a sole proprietorship, although the limits may not be reached so quickly.

In most cases, the corporation is the most suitable form of organization if large amounts of capital are required. As with any other organization, the amount of capital that can be raised by borrowing depends on the financial strength and credit standing of the business. Almost limitless possibilities for capital procurement exist, however, in the issuance of *capital stock* (see Chapter 35)—assuming, of course, that the business has been profitable and it appears that financial success will continue, thus making new issues of stock attractive to investors.

Cost and Convenience of Doing Business

Because of the tremendous increase in the degree of government regulation to which business is subjected, it would be naive to state that doing business in any organizational form is simple or convenient. We can observe, however, that the sole proprietorship involves fewer organizational costs and formalities than other available forms. Even though a partnership can be organized without formalities, it usually is not as simple or as convenient to operate as a sole proprietorship. In a partnership, the rights of other owners must always be considered, as well as their voices in the decision-making process. For all its advantages, the corporation involves more formalities and organizational costs than any other form. This is true not only because the required statutory formalities must be strictly adhered to but also because the corporation is subject to a wider variety of government regulation than the other forms. Greater fees to the government are usually required, and greater attorneys' fees are usually the rule because of the necessity of legal counsel to insure that all formalities are met.

The question of cost and convenience of doing business is not ordinarily the determining factor in the choice of an organizational form. If the objectives of the organizers are best achieved by incorporation, the inconveniences to be encountered will probably not change the decision. But the organizers will have to decide whether the advantages of the corporate form are worth the additional cost and inconvenience. However, in several states today some formalities of operating a *close corporation* have been substantially relaxed. This will be considered in further detail in Chapter 36.

Taxation

The subject of business taxation is one of such complexity that only a few of the most basic principles can be given in a text of this nature.

Any business, regardless of its form, is subject to certain types of taxation (for example, property taxes and sales taxes). However, corporations encounter certain types of taxation not dealt with by other organizations (such as franchise taxes).

By far the most important type of taxation to consider is the federal income tax. However, the form of organization offering the most income tax advantages differs from case to case. Under the Internal Revenue Code, federal income taxation of businesses depends on how the enterprise actually operates rather than on what it is called. For this purpose, all business organizations are classified as either sole proprietorships, partnerships, or corporations. Other types of associations are taxed as either partnerships or corporations, depending on their characteristics. Thus an organization will be taxed as a corporation if it has a *majority* of the following corporate characteristics:

Continuity of life. The death, bankruptcy, or resignation of a member does not dissolve or otherwise interrupt its continuity.

Centralization of management. Management is centralized in one or more persons who act in a representative capacity.

Limited liability. No member is liable beyond his or her investment for the firm's debts.

Free transferability of interests. A member can freely transfer his or her interest without obtaining the consent of other members.

Because of this approach, joint stock companies and business trusts are usually taxed as corporations. Sometimes limited partnerships and other associations are also taxed as corporations.

The income tax treatment of sole proprietorships and partnerships differs significantly from that of corporations. Since the sole proprietor *is* the business, the net income of the business is taxed as personal income. Similarly, the net income of a partnership is taxed as personal income to the partners, each being responsible for the tax on his or her share.

In ordinary circumstances, the income of a corporation is taxed in a substantially different manner. Initially, the net income of the corporation itself is subject to taxation. When any of this income is subsequently distributed to shareholders as dividends, the amount received by each shareholder is taxed as personal income. The result is actually a form of *double taxation.*

In past years, the "double taxation" of corporate income persuaded some businesses (usually small ones) not to incorporate. In 1958, however, Congress attempted to diminish the importance of the income tax as a factor in choosing a form of organization. The Internal Revenue Code was amended in that year to allow certain small business corporations (sometimes called "Subchapter S corporations") to be taxed in a manner similar to that of partnerships. (Subchapter S corporations will be discussed in more detail in Chapter 35.)

Questions and Problems

1. Must a partnership strictly follow all the provisions of the Uniform Partnership Act? Discuss.

2. Exalted Co. was organized as a limited partnership with A and B as general partners and C, D, and E as limited partners. The business became insolvent after a period of time. The business assets of Exalted and the personal assets of A and B were exhausted by the claims of Exalted's creditors. To satisfy the unpaid portion of their claims, the creditors then attempted to reach the personal assets of E. They produced evidence showing that while the business was in operation, E had spent an average of ten hours per week keeping its books. Were these creditors able to reach E's personal assets? Discuss. Would it have made any difference if E had been paid by Exalted for keeping the books?

3. In Question 2, would your answer be any different if E had provided consulting services to A and B with respect to operating the business? Would it have made any difference if E had been paid by Exalted for these services? Discuss.

4. Are there any similarities between a limited partnership and a corporation? Discuss.

5. X was a limited partner in Plateau Co., a limited partnership. After the business had been operating for several months, X discovered that the required certificate had not been filed with the designated state official. Is X personally liable to Plateau's business creditors because of this mistake? Is there anything X can do? Discuss.

6. What are the characteristics of a joint stock company?

7. A, B, C, D, and E organized a syndicate for the operation of an apartment building. From this statement alone do we know anything about the rights and liabilities of A, B, C, D, and E? Discuss.

8. Why is the personal liability of the owners of a business not always dependent solely on the form of their organization?

9. What part do capital requirements play in selecting a form of business organization?

10. What is meant by the phrase *double taxation?*

Partnerships/Nature, Formation, and Property

32

Historical Background

The Nature of the Partnership

The precise origin of the partnership form of business organization is unknown. It has been stated that "some form of partnership is probably as old as the first exhibition of the gregarious instinct of man."[1] We do know that the basic partnership concept of two or more persons combining their skills and property for mutual reward has existed in every organized society.

The English common law of partnership, from which the American law has developed, traces its derivations back to the Roman law and to the law merchant.[2] For several hundred years the rules of law regarding partnerships in England and America were developed almost solely by the courts. Shortly after the turn of the century, in 1914, work was completed on the Uniform Partnership Act (UPA). The UPA codified most of the common-law rules relating to partnerships and

---

[1]Walter Jaeger, "Partnership or Joint Adventure," *Notre Dame Lawyer* 37 (1961), p. 138.

[2]The law merchant, discussed earlier, was the body of rules created by English merchants that ultimately was absorbed into the English common law.

555

significantly altered a few of them. It has been adopted by forty-seven states, the exceptions being Louisiana, Georgia, and Mississippi.[3]

Defining a Partnership

Section 6 of the UPA defines a *partnership* as "an association of two or more persons to carry on as co-owners a business for profit." This definition can be broken into five constituent elements.

Association. The term *association* indicates that a partnership is a voluntary arrangement formed by agreement.

Person. Under the UPA the term *person* includes not only individuals but also corporations, other partnerships, and other types of associations. Problems traditionally have occurred over the question of whether a *corporation* can be a partner; and although the UPA attempts to solve them by including corporations within its definition of a person, it is not the controlling authority on the point. To determine whether a corporation has the power to enter a partnership, one must look to the corporation laws of each individual jurisdiction. Until recent years, the general rule was that a corporation could not be a partner. The Model Business Corporation Act has taken the contrary view, however, and the legislatures in about half the states have passed corporation laws based on that Act, thereby allowing corporations to be partners.[4] With regard to minors and insane persons, the same basic rules apply to partnership agreements as to other types of contracts. Thus a minor can treat the partnership agreement with the other partners as voidable. The minor usually can also repudiate personal liabilities to creditors beyond the amount of his or her investment in the business. But this investment *is* subject to the claims of partnership creditors, although it is the maximum liability that the minor ordinarily can incur.

Co-owners. The partners are defined as co-owners of the business, which distinguishes them from those who are merely agents, servants, or other subordinates. Each partner has a voice in the management of the enterprise and a right to share in the profits.

To carry on a business. The term *business* has been defined in Section 2 of the UPA as including "every trade, occupation, or profession."

For profit. An association cannot be a partnership unless the purpose of forming it is to make profits directly through its business activities. Associations for other purposes (including religious, patriotic, or public improvement purposes, or furtherance of the *separate* economic interests of members) are not partnerships, even if they engage in business transactions. Thus the local chapter of a fraternal lodge cannot be a partnership, and the rights and duties of partners cannot attach

---

[3]The UPA, which appears in its entirety in Appendix B, and other "uniform" laws were created by the American Law Institute and the National Conference of Commissioners on Uniform State Laws. Since these groups possessed no legislative power, the laws were proposed to each of the state legislatures.

[4]The Model Business Corporation Act, drafted by the American Bar Association, serves as a model for state legislatures that are revising their corporation laws.

to its members. For example, individual members are not personally liable for debts incurred for the lodge by its officers unless an agency relationship has been expressly created.

The Entity Theory versus the Aggregate Theory

For centuries there have been two theories of the nature of the partnership association. One theory is that the partnership is a separate *legal entity*—in other words, a "legal person." Traditionally the viewpoint of those in the commercial world, it was the approach taken by the Roman civil law. A legal person can own and dispose of property, make contracts, commit wrongs, sue, and be sued. In our legal system most adults are obviously considered legal persons. The English courts, however, found difficulty with the concept of a partnership as a legal person. They evidently felt that no one but the Crown could create a legal entity. Corporations, being creations of the Crown, were deemed to be separate legal entities. This remains true in America today; corporations are created by authority of the government, not simply by agreement, and are regarded as legal persons.

Partnerships, on the other hand, are formed simply by the express or implied agreement of the partners. And since the English courts would not allow private parties to create a legal person separate from their own identities, the traditional approach of the common law in both England and the United States was to treat the partnership as an aggregation of individuals. Under this theory, commonly called the *aggregate theory,* a partnership was not recognized as a separate legal entity. That is:

1. The partnership could not own property; the property of the business had to be owned individually by one partner or by two or more partners as co-owners.

2. The partnership could not sue or be sued in its own name, and a court could not render judgment separately against the partnership; such actions had to be in the name of one or more individual partners.

3. One partnership could not sue another where the two had a member in common, because a party cannot be both plaintiff and defendant in the same legal proceeding.

Although most American courts followed the aggregate theory, a few contrary decisions were rendered. In reality, the courts sometimes employed the different theories as rationalizations of results reached on other grounds. Professor Judson Crane, a leading authority on partnership law, has observed that "the entity may be recognized or disregarded according to the demands of justice in the particular situation."[5]

The UPA does not expressly adopt either the entity theory or the aggregate theory. In a sense it has retained the aggregate theory by defining a partnership as "an *association of two or more persons* to carry on a business for profit."

---

[5]Judson Crane, *Handbook on the Law of Partnership,* 2d ed. (St. Paul, Minn.: West Publishing Co., 1952), Sec. 3.

(Emphasis added.) On the other hand, it has used the entity approach for selected purposes. For example, the UPA recognizes the concept of *partnership property* and allows a partnership to own and convey property in the partnership name. Also, it places liability for acts of the partners in conducting partnership business primarily on the partnership itself and the partnership property and only secondarily on individual partners and their individual property. The UPA says nothing of procedural matters such as lawsuits in the partnership name, but most states have enacted other statutes allowing suit to be brought by or against the partnership in the partnership name. In many instances, the procedural rules in federal courts also allow suits in the partnership name.

Many legal problems, such as taxation, are not governed by the UPA. Depending on the particular problem presented, courts and certain other statutes sometimes treat the partnership as a separate legal entity. For instance, under the Internal Revenue Code of 1954, the entity rule more often than not does apply with respect to federal taxation.[6]

Formation of a Partnership

As previously mentioned, the partnership is formed by agreement, either express or implied. It is not a creature of statute, as is a corporation. Few, if any, statutory requirements must be met in order to *form* a partnership. While the UPA governs many aspects of the *operation* of a partnership, it is intended primarily to fill in the gaps of the partnership agreement. Many UPA rules are applicable only if the partners do not agree otherwise.

The agreement obviously must have a *legal object,* but a partnership can be formed even if one or more of the other elements of a valid contract is absent. A valid contract usually does exist as a practical matter, but it is not required. A partnership can be created without a written document, although any part of the agreement falling within the Statute of Frauds does require a writing for enforceability.

Despite the fact that a written partnership agreement is usually not required, it is highly desirable. Formation of a business is a substantial undertaking and should not be left to the oral declarations of the parties—for several reasons:

1. There are many inherent problems in *proving* the exact terms of an oral agreement.

2. Numerous problems (such as those relating to taxation) can be satisfactorily resolved only by a carefully drafted written instrument.

3. If the parties go through the process of drafting a formal document with the aid of an attorney, they are much more likely to foresee many problems they otherwise would not have thought about. For example, matters such as procedures

---

[6]Zolman Cavitch, *Business Organizations* (New York: Matthew Bender and Co., 1969), Vol. 1, Sec. 11.02.

for expulsion of a partner or for settlement of disputes between partners are easily overlooked because they seem so remote when the partnership is first formed.

The formal partnership agreement, often referred to as the *articles of partnership*, should clearly reflect the intent of the partners as to the rights and obligations they wish to assume in the business. What is contained in these articles will depend on the nature of the business and the desires of the partners, but ordinarily the written instrument should include such items as the following:

1. Name of the firm. The partnership is not required to have a firm name, but it is usually a good idea to have one. The name can be that of one or more of the partners, or it can be fictitious. (But it cannot be deceptively similar to that of another business for the purpose of attracting its customers.) If the name is fictitious, it usually must be registered. Most states have *fictitious name statutes* (sometimes called *assumed name statutes*) that require any firm, including a partnership, to register with a state official the fictitious name under which the firm is doing business. The purpose of such statutes is to enable creditors of the firm to learn the identities of those responsible.

2. Nature and location of the business.

3. Date of commencement and duration of the partnership.

4. Amount of contributions in money or property each partner is to make (in other words, the amount of their investments in the business).

5. Time within which the contribution of each partner is to be made.

6. Salaries and drawing accounts of each partner, if such are desired.

7. Division of work and duties of each partner, including rights in management.

8. Admission requirements for new partners.

9. Each partner's proportionate share of net profits while the business is continuing to operate and upon dissolution.

10. Any proposed restrictions on the power of individual members to bind the firm.

11. Clear delineation of partnership assets as distinguished from individual partners' assets.

12. Bookkeeping and accounting methods to be used and location of and access to books.

13. Requirements and procedures for notice to partners and partnership creditors in case of dissolution.

14. Which partner or partners will be in charge of winding up the business upon dissolution.

15. Procedures for settling disputes between partners, such as submitting them to arbitration.

The following case illustrates the value of a carefully planned and drafted partnership agreement. In this case a partnership of physicians was able to terminate an unsatisfactory relationship with one of their group who simply could not get along with the others. This would have been much more difficult had it not been for their well-planned partnership agreement.

Gelder Medical Group v. Webber

Court of Appeals of New York, 363 N.E.2d 573 (1977)

The Gelder Medical Group, a partnership engaged in practicing medicine and surgery in Sidney, New York, was first formed in 1956. Some 17 years later, defendant Dr. Webber, then 61 years old and a newcomer to Sidney, was admitted to the partnership following a one-year trial period in which he was employed by the group as a surgeon.

As had the other members of the group who had joined since its inception, Dr. Webber had agreed that he "will not for five years after any voluntary or involuntary termination of his association with said Gelder Medical Group, practice his profession within a radius of 30 miles of the Village of Sidney, as a physician or surgeon . . . without the consent, in writing, of said Gelder Medical Group." The partnership agreement also provided a procedure for the involuntary withdrawal of partners. It stated that "In the event that any member is requested to resign or withdraw from the group by a majority vote of the other members of the group, such notice shall be effective immediately and his share of the profits to the date of termination shall be computed and he shall be paid in full to the date of termination of his employment pursuant to his agreement with the association."

Dr. Webber's association turned out to be unsatisfactory to his partners. His conduct, both professional and personal, became abrasive and objectionable to his partners and their patients, a cause of "intolerable" embarrassment to the group. A psychiatrist who examined Dr. Webber a number of times on the referral of the partnership stated that Dr. Webber had "what would be termed an adjustment reaction of adult life with anxiety and depression." While the psychiatrist concluded that the adjustment reaction soon cleared, he summed up his description of Dr. Webber as a perfectionist who was a "rather idealistic, sincere, direct, frank individual who quite possibly could be perceived at times as being somewhat blunt."

Although the difficulties were from time to time discussed with Dr. Webber, the unhappy relationship persisted. In October, 1973, the discord culminated with the group's unanimous decision to terminate Dr. Webber's association with the partnership. After Dr. Webber refused to withdraw voluntarily, the group, in writing, formally notified him of the termination. It was effective immediately, and, on the basis of an accounting, Webber was paid $18,568.41 in full compliance with the partnership agreement.

In about two months, Dr. Webber, disregarding the restrictive covenant, resumed his surgical practice as a single practitioner in Sidney. The group, to protect its practice, promptly sued to enjoin Dr. Webber's violation of the restrictive covenant. Dr. Webber instituted his own lawsuit for damages resulting from his expulsion. The two lawsuits were consolidated. The trial court and the intermediate level appellate court both ruled in favor of the partnership, granting an injunction prohibiting Dr. Webber from violating the noncompetition clause and dismissing his claim for damages. Dr. Webber appealed.

Breitel, Chief Justice: The applicable law is straightforward. Covenants restricting a professional, and in particular a physician, from competing with a former employer or associate are common and generally acceptable. As with all restrictive covenants, if they are reasonable as to time and area, necessary to protect legitimate interests, not harmful to the public, and not unduly burdensome, they will be enforced.

Similarly common and acceptable are provisions in a partnership agreement to provide for the withdrawal or expulsion of a partner. While there is no common-law or statutory right to expel a member of a partnership, partners may provide, in their agreement, for the involuntary dismissal, with or without cause, of one of their number.

Turning to the Gelder Group agreement, no acceptable reason is offered for limiting the plainly stated provisions for expulsion, freely subscribed to by Dr. Webber when he joined the group, and none is perceived. When, as here, the agreement provides for dismissal of one of their number on the majority vote of the partners, the court may not frustrate the intention of the parties at least so long as the provisions for dismissal work no undue penalty or unjust forfeiture, overreaching, or other violation of public policy....

[The court then held that the covenant not to compete was reasonably limited as to time and area, and was not unduly burdensome.] ...

Hence, Dr. Webber's attempts to free himself from the covenant not to compete ... must be rejected. It is true, as the group stated in its letter of termination to Dr. Webber, that the termination was a tragedy which it regretted. But the expulsion clause was designed to function when the conflict between the group and one of its members was insoluble, and the necessity for its use must always be unfortunate....

Affirmed.

Determining the Existence of a Partnership

When the parties have clearly expressed their intentions in a written instrument, there is ordinarily no difficulty in determining whether a partnership exists. But when the parties have not been explicit in declaring their intentions, problems frequently arise. The most fundamental, of course, is whether a partnership has even been *created*. This issue arises with surprising frequency, because of its importance in regard to the rights and obligations of the "partners" and third parties as well. For example, a creditor may seek to hold several persons liable for the transactions of one of them on the ground that they are partners. Or one party might claim that he and another are partners and that the other party has violated a resulting fiduciary duty by having a conflicting business interest.

When the existence of a partnership is disputed by an interested party, such existence becomes a question of fact to be decided on the basis of all the circumstances. No single factor usually is controlling, and the court's ultimate decision commonly is based on several considerations, the most important of which are: (1) sharing of profits, (2) joint control of the business, and (3) joint ownership and control of capital or property.

Sharing of Profits: A distinction should be made between gross revenues and net profits. It has been consistently held by the courts, and reiterated in the UPA, that an agreement to share the *gross revenues* from a particular enterprise does not in itself indicate the existence of a partnership. Sharing of *net profits,* however, usually creates a very strong inference that the parties have formed a partnership. Indeed, where there has been no sharing of profits or agreement to share them, the court is very likely to find that no partnership exists.

In certain situations, profits are shared by persons who obviously never intended to become partners. Under such circumstances the fact that profits are shared or that the parties have agreed to share them will not by itself create a presumption that a partnership was intended. These situations are:

Where the profits are received by a creditor in payment of a debt. For example: O, the owner of a business in financial difficulty, owes debts to X, Y, and Z. In settlement of these debts, X, Y, and Z agree to accept a certain percentage of O's profits for a period of time. No inference of partnership is created by the sharing of profits, and no partnership exists between O, X, Y, and Z (unless, perhaps, X, Y, and Z take title to a portion of the business property and take part in managing the business).

Where the profits are received as wages by an employee. Suppose that X is the owner of a business and A, B, and C are her employees. As an incentive to the employees, X establishes a plan whereby they share in the profits of the business. There is no presumption of a partnership so long as the evidence as a whole indicates an *employment* relationship; that is, X withholds federal taxes from the employees' salaries, exercises control over them, and does not allow them any management powers or co-ownership of business property.

Where the profits are received as rent by a landlord. If the probable returns of a business being undertaken by a party are uncertain, that party may wish to avoid the burden of fixed charges as much as possible by leasing necessary equipment or real estate at a variable price. It is not uncommon, if the owner of the equipment or real estate is willing, for a rental agreement in such a case to provide that the rent will be based in whole or in part on the profitability of the business. Such an arrangement does not of itself make the owner a partner with the person carrying on the business. However, if the owner of the property also takes part in managing the business, this might be enough for a court to rule that a partnership has been formed.

Where the profits are received as an annuity by the spouse or representative of a deceased partner. If a successful partnership is dissolved by the death of a partner, it is often desirable to continue (rather than liquidate) the business because of the value of the goodwill it possesses as a going concern. Thus, it may be agreed, either in the original articles of partnership or by contract after a partner's death between the spouse, executor, or administrator and the surviving partners, that the dead partner's interest will not be liquidated. In consideration for allowing this interest to remain in the business, the spouse or representative might receive a share of the profits. Such facts do not by themselves make that person a partner. If, however, such a party exercises powers of control and management, a court might find that a partnership has been created.

Where the profits are received as interest on a loan. If a creditor who has lent money to a person or persons carrying on a business agrees to receive a share of profits in lieu of interest, the courts generally have held that the lender has not become a partner unless he or she also participates in management. In a number of cases the courts also have held that no partnership exists even where the lender has been given a degree of control in the business, so long as the control is of a limited nature for the sole purpose of protecting the loan.

Where the profits are received as consideration for the sale of property. When an item of property having an uncertain value is sold to someone who expects to use it in carrying on a business, it is sometimes agreed that the price payable to the seller will include a share of the profits made from use of the property. Two common examples are *goodwill* and *trademarks*. The seller usually retains no ownership of the property or control over its use;[7] nor is he or she usually expected to share any losses incurred by the buyer. In many instances this is simply the best way of computing the value of a particular property right. No partnership is created by such an arrangement.

Joint Control and Management: Although sharing of profits is a cardinal element of the partnership, another factor often felt to be important by the courts is whether the parties have *joint control* over the operation of the business. For instance, where sharing of profits by itself is not sufficient to indicate existence of a partnership, the addition of the factor of joint control might well cause a court to hold that a partnership has been created. *Exercise of management powers* is obviously very strong evidence of control. But the fact that management powers have been expressly delegated to one or more of the partners does not mean that those who do not manage are not true partners if the other facts indicate that they are. In a sense, agreeing to relinquish control is itself an exercise of the right of control.

Joint Ownership of Property: Another factor that frequently finds its way into court opinions is *joint ownership of assets*. Of the three basic tests for existence of a partnership, this is the least important, although it certainly is taken into account by the court, along with all the other evidence. The UPA takes the position that co-ownership of property does not, of itself, establish a partnership. An inference of partnership is also not necessarily created by the fact that the co-owners share any profits made by the use of the property. This seems at first to be inconsistent with our earlier discussion of the presumption of partnership that is usually engendered by profit sharing. But there is no real inconsistency. In the case of co-owners of property, the sharing of profits made from the property is a basic part of co-ownership. In most cases the owner of property wishes to receive whatever income it generates; thus it is reasonable to assume that co-owners will want to share the income from their jointly-owned property. A partnership should

---

[7]However, if there is no sale of the trademark but only a *license* (a permission to *use* the trademark), the licensor does retain ownership and, usually, a measure of control over how it is used. But the receipt of profits by the licensor as consideration for the license does not by itself make that person a partner in this case either.

not be presumed simply because they act in a way totally consistent with simple co-ownership.

On the other hand, if the property and its use are only part of a larger enterprise, and the parties share profits from the whole enterprise, an inference of partnership is justified. For instance, co-ownership of a commercial building and sharing of its rental income by A and B does not necessarily make them partners. If, however, they use part of the building as premises for the operation of a going business of some type, sharing not only the rental income from the remainder of the building but also the profits and management of the business, they are quite likely to be considered partners.

The two cases below illustrate the type of evidence considered by courts in determining whether a partnership has been formed where no formal agreement has been made. In the first case there was no express agreement at all. In the second there was an express oral agreement to be partners, but the nature of the business venture changed over a period of time, thus prompting a question whether the original partnership agreement extended to the transformed enterprise.

Grissum v. Reesman

Supreme Court of Missouri, 505 S.W.2d 81 (1974)

Nora E. Grissum, plaintiff, filed this suit against Dale Reesman, defendant, who was administrator of the estate of plaintiff's deceased brother, Elwood Grissum. Plaintiff was the sole beneficiary under her brother's will. She was to receive a considerable amount of property under the will and, as a result, state inheritance taxes and federal estate taxes in rather large sums would be due. She asked the court to declare that she and her brother had been partners in a farming operation and that the property in question belonged to the partnership. If the court ruled in her favor, the interest that she had owned in the partnership would not pass to her by her brother's will, because it was already hers. Such a holding would save her approximately $57,000 in taxes. The trial court did hold for plaintiff. The State of Missouri (which was also a defendant because of the matter of state taxes) appealed. The primary question on appeal was whether a partnership had existed.

Eager, Justice: . . . The theory of plaintiff's case was and is that a partnership was created orally between her brother and herself, back in the 1930s, to operate the farmland then owned or to be acquired, to accumulate property, and to share the benefits 50-50. . . . These two continued to farm the land together until Elwood's death in 1970. There was ample evidence that Nora did the cooking, housework and all related chores, kept the books for the operation, did most of the banking, wrote all checks and paid all the bills, fed the livestock, sorted cattle and hogs and, at times, did actual, hard farm labor. This continued through all the years. She was regularly consulted about the purchase of livestock and land; she frequently (or usually) accompanied her brother on trips for the purchase or sale of livestock, and such deals were made by agreement. The farm truck bore the legend: "Elwood & Nora Grissum Farms—Boonville Mo." Elwood had this placed on the truck. A sign was placed by Elwood over the harness shed bearing the [same] legend . . . . This was visible to anyone approaching the house from the highway. . . . Elwood Grissum told sundry people, over the years, both in the presence of Nora and out of her presence, that they were partners on a 50-50 basis. A nephew of Elwood . . . who worked with him a great deal over a period of many years, asked Elwood why they could not "go partners"; the reply was that Elwood could not do so because he already had a partner, his sister. This nephew was told at sundry times that the arrangement was a partnership; on more than one occasion he heard Nora ask Elwood when he was going to fix up the business so that she would be protected, and his answer was that they would go in and fix it up if they ever got time. In other conversations, Elwood stated on many occasions to other farmers, his doctor, and perhaps others that (in substance) he and his sister were partners in their farm enterprise "50-50," or "all the way through," or that they "owned the whole thing together," or were partners in everything. Some of these statements were made on various occasions to the same individuals. One was made so as to include the real estate. Nora, at times, made similar statements in her brother's presence. On one occasion Elwood told his nephew that he thought Nora should "come up" with her partnership half of the work (apparently meaning farm labor), and the nephew replied that she was doing more than her half. Elwood and Nora discussed and decided together on livestock deals and the general operation of the farm. The statements relating to the partnership extended back at least as far as the 1940s and they continued to within a very few weeks of Elwood's death. Nora and Elwood told their banker that everything they had was a "joint venture." All entries into the safety deposit box, except one in 1949, were made by Nora. On one occasion Elwood stated that he would have to consult Nora before buying some cattle because she was his partner; he later bought them.

A joint bank account was opened in the names of Elwood and Nora Grissum in June, 1967, with a deposit of $13,128.68, proceeds of the farm operations. Prior to that time the account had been kept in the name of Elwood Grissum. The joint account was continued until Elwood's death with all farm money deposited in it. When money was borrowed Elwood signed the notes alone. The farm insurance was applied for and issued in both names . . . from at least as early as 1957 and presumably before. It was stipulated that Elwood filed individual federal income tax returns . . . from "about" 1966 through 1969 . . . . We are not advised what was done before that. For the year 1970, four returns were filed: an individual return for Elwood to the time of his death, a partnership return, a fiduciary return, and an individual return for Nora. The point of all this is that Elwood did, for some years prior to his death, report farm income on individual returns. We shall discuss this later. . . . [L]and was acquired in the name of Elwood in 1937 (presumably from his father and mother), in 1942, 1946, 1947, 1948, 1949 and 1952. . . . It is obvious that most of these tracts were purchases made to increase the farming operation. The occupancy and operation of the farm or farms started in the depression in the 1930s, with one eighty-acre tract; at Elwood's death the [property value] had increased to approximately $286,000. During all this period Nora had lived and worked on the farm. It is certainly true that both Elwood and Nora derived all their living expenses from the operation of the farm, for no other source of income is indicated. It also seems obvious that neither drew down any profits, as such, but that all excess went into the expansion of the farm operation and (some) beginning in January, 1969, into joint certificates of deposit. . . .

[A] partnership agreement may be implied from conduct and circumstances; . . . evidence of a sharing of profits constitutes prima facie evidence of the existence of a partnership and in the absence of other evidence becomes conclusive; . . . the parties are not required to know all of the legal incidents of a partnership . . . ; a partnership consists of a factual relationship between two or more persons who conduct a business enterprise together. We note further that when the essentials of such an agreement have been established, expressly or by implication, it is not to be avoided because of uncertainty or indefiniteness as to minor details and, in the absence of express agreement, it will be presumed that profits are to be shared equally. . . .

The element of profits and a sharing of profits is essential. It is important to note here that although the operation was prosperous, neither party ever drew down any profits, but put all money over and above farm expenses and living expenses into additional equipment and land, until in 1967 and 1969 when they established the joint account and bought the joint certificates of deposit. The joint account recognized Nora's interest in the farm operating funds, and the joint certificates recognized her interest and ownership in the accumulated funds. It would appear, therefore, that Nora shared in any and all profits just as much as Elwood did, but that neither saw fit to make use of them individually. It is a fair inference that either had the *right* to take profits at any reasonable time. It is probable that minor losses may have occurred over the years; if so, they were taken care of out of the general funds.

We recognize that three things speak to some extent in opposition to a partnership, namely: (1) the individual income tax returns filed by Elwood; (2) the fact that title to the real estate stood in his name; and (3) that an individual bank account in Elwood's name was maintained until 1967, although Nora drew checks upon it regularly in Elwood's name by herself. It is generally recognized that partnership property may be held in an individual name. That element is of no great materiality. When we consider the background of these individuals, the fact that they cannot be held to have known the usual or legal requirements or incidents of a partnership, and the fact that it was probably a matter of convenience to transact those certain phases of the partnership business in an individual name, we find that these things are not sufficient to prevent a conclusion that a partnership in fact existed. Certainly Nora was not an employee, for she received no wages; she was not a wife, and it was not her duty as such to perform all such services and labor. We are *clearly convinced,* and hold, that a partnership existed with the ownership of the property and the profits to be shared on an equal basis. . . .

The judgment is affirmed.

Shawn v. England

Court of Appeals of
Oklahoma, 570 P.2d 628
(1977)

In the summer of 1973 Gary England was a weathercaster for television station KWTV Channel 9, Oklahoma City, and Bill Shawn—a stock broker with E. F. Hutton and Company—was a stock market reporter and commentator for the same station.

For some time England had made occasional reference to what he called a "thunder lizard" while telecasting the weather. Usually he did so during thunderstorms as an interest provoker, particularly during his early morning reports. The make-believe creature engaged Shawn's imagination and eventually it occurred to him that it might be profitable to design and promote the sale of a stuffed thunder lizard which the kids could hold during thunderstorms as a sleep-inducing comforter.

One day Shawn broached the idea to his friend England, who immediately thought he saw merit in it. After some discussion the parties decided they needed a commercial artist to help design the mythical animal. To Shawn's mind came a long-time friend and artist, Larry May, with whom he had attended grade, junior high and high school. Shawn contacted May, told him of the idea, and upon inquiry learned that the commercial artist was not only interested but willing to help "poor boy" the project by contributing the art work.

The three individuals staged their initial meeting at May's office and at that time discussed ways to achieve maximum publicity for the fictional lizard. They accepted

England's proposal that the three consider themselves equal partners in their venture and divide any profits realized three ways. During the next several months the threesome met nearly every week for a so-called "brainstorming session." At one early meeting they decided to have a drawing contest wherein they would ask the youngsters and adults alike to send in drawings of what they envisioned the thunder lizard to be with the promise of a prize to the winner. The contest met with a good response and May, as judge, picked a nine-year-old boy's drawing for the prize. A little later while continuing pursuit of still better promotional ideas the trio hit upon the idea of a weather fact cartoon book featuring thunder lizard drawings, which after further thought was transformed into a coloring book for the kiddies.

Gary England began gathering material for the coloring book and after accumulating considerable weather data the three men concluded that the publication of a regular weather booklet about the weather in Oklahoma would have even more profit potential than a coloring book in that it would have broader appeal. And so they turned their joint efforts to the development of a weather book.

By January of 1974 England had not only gathered considerable data for the booklet but had written the manuscript. Shawn was given the responsibility of having it typed and edited and he accomplished the assignment promptly. England made additional changes in the text and added pictures here and there in an effort to finalize it for publication.

In the meantime, England met with the management of KWTV and discussed the possibility of it underwriting and helping promote the booklet. England reported back that the station agreed to "bankroll" the project by buying enough copies to pay for the initial production of the work—estimated to be about 13,000 copies—and proceeds from sales exceeding this were to be the profit of the three-man partnership.

Then it happened. In April of 1974, at one of their regular Saturday morning meetings, Shawn was abruptly informed he was no longer needed and the partnership was ended. He tried to get the other two to reconsider, but they insisted on terminating his relationship with them. England and May said that there were too many people in the deal and that the partnership arrangement only applied to the "thunder lizard" idea.

Shawn, plaintiff, sued England and May, defendants, claiming that their original partnership agreement extended to the weather book. He sought to recover a one-third share of all profits to be made from the book. In the trial court a jury found that there was a partnership and that plaintiff should receive one-third of the profits, but the judge granted defendants' motion for judgment notwithstanding the verdict. Plaintiff appealed.

Brightmire, Presiding Judge: . . . In arguing that there was no partnership, defendants acknowledge that "all parties to this controversy concede that a partnership existed for the specific purpose of marketing a 'thunder lizard' doll" but this partnership, they insist, was terminated with the "abandonment of that plan." The crux of their argument is that profit sharing was restricted to the thunder lizard doll and perished with the toy and since there was no new agreement made with regard to later projects, namely, the thunder lizard color book or the weather book, Shawn failed to prove any factual foundation for recovery. It makes no difference legally, goes defendants' argument, that Shawn thought the initial partnership continued because the fact of the matter is that it could not have continued since it was never discussed after the first meeting. Defendants' conclusion is, therefore, that the only way plaintiff could have succeeded in this lawsuit was to have presented proof that the disputants specifically articulated an express agreement to participate as partners in the marketing of the weather book—an event which never occurred. . . .

In our opinion plaintiff was justified in thinking the partnership status established in the summer of 1973 continued until the day defendants terminated it. The fact that the particular creation at the partnership's inception was abandoned did not prevent it from serving as the metamorphic progenitor of the genre's ultimate yield—namely, the weather booklet. It was a weather related idea that brought the parties together; it was a weather related idea that became the focal point of their first discussions; and it was the same weather related theme which one finds threading through all nine months of weekly meetings.

If in advance of this lawsuit defendants considered the partnership ended with the abandoned lizard plaything they took care to conceal it. Not only did they fail to disclose their thoughts about this but conducted themselves in a manner that demonstrated the very opposite. They continued to welcome plaintiff to their meetings and accept the benefit of his knowledge, experience and thinking. They assigned him a task to perform with reference to the weather booklet as though he was still partner in the enterprise. And when at last it began to look like success of the venture was near at hand two members of the triumphant trinity decide to tell the third, "We don't need you anymore!" This act, we think, is comparable to that of a pilot at the end of a transoceanic flight who, as soon as he sees the runway and commences his final approach, ejects his navigator from the aircraft with the declaration, "I don't need you anymore!"

Moreover, there is another circumstance which we think undermines defendants' position and that is that each admitted he considered himself a partner with regard to the weather booklet ventured both before the ouster of Shawn and afterwards, notwithstanding the absence of further definitive discussion of their status after the initial partnership agreement was made. Certainly if between themselves defendants had reason to believe the original partnership status continued throughout the course of their meetings then why would not plaintiff be entitled to entertain the same belief? Neither defendant testified to any circumstance or fact that would have led the plaintiff to believe that the original arrangement did not obtain as to all results of the "brainstorming" sessions particularly with reference to figuring out weather related projects to promote for profit production purposes. No evidence does the record contain justifying defendants' conclusion that the thunder lizard doll project was an isolated endeavor disconnected from what went on afterwards. On the contrary, a fair evaluation of the evidence leads comfortably to the conclusion that the weather booklet was a natural end product of a creative ideological evolution that began with the thunder lizard.

Under the facts, it seems to us, and certainly it must have seemed to twelve jurors, as though defendants used the efforts and the mental ability of the plaintiff for as long as they thought they needed him and then, when they got their book about ready to publish and thought they had marketing arrangements made, arbitrarily decided to eliminate his interest in joint venture assets by terminating it. This they could not do. If a partner decides to dissolve a partnership and appropriate the business to himself, he must first fully compensate his copartner for his share of the gain to be realized from the fulfillment of a prospective business undertaking the consummation of which is imminent. . . .

[Reversed, and judgment rendered for plaintiff for one-third of the profits, in accordance with the jury's verdict.]

A partnership commonly requires various types of property for the operation of **Partnership** its business, including, for example, real estate, equipment, inventory, or intangi- **Property** bles such as cash or securities. The prevailing rule at common law was that a partnership, not being a separate legal entity, could not own real estate. Somewhat inconsistently, it was also generally held that a partnership *could* own other types of property. Under the UPA, a partnership is recognized as an entity insofar as property ownership is concerned and can own either real estate or other types of property. The UPA uses the phrase *tenants in partnership* to describe the status of individual partners with respect to the partnership property. (The rights that individual partners have regarding partnership property will be discussed in the next chapter.)

Although today a partnership can (and quite often does) own such property itself, it is not essential that it own *any property at all.* The partners themselves may wish to *individually* own the property needed for the operation of the business.

For a number of reasons it is sometimes important to determine whether an item of property belongs to the partnership or to an individual partner. Among them:

1. Creditors of the partnership must resort to partnership property for satisfaction of their claims before they can take property of individual partners.

2. The right of a partner to use partnership property is usually limited to purposes of furthering the partnership business.

3. The question of ownership can also be important with regard to taxation, distribution of assets upon dissolution of the partnership, and other matters.

Factors in Determining Ownership

The ownership of property is determined by *agreement* of the partners. Sound business practices dictate that the partners should explicitly agree on the matter and keep accurate records of their dealings with property. Unfortunately, partners often fail to clearly indicate their intentions as to whether ownership of particular items of property rests with the partnership or with one or more individual partners. In such cases, the courts consider all pertinent facts in an attempt to discover the partners' *intent.* Where it appears that the matter of property ownership never occurred to the partners, so that they actually had no definite intention, the court determines which of the possible alternatives—partnership or individual ownership —more closely accords with their general intentions and objectives for the business as a whole and which is fairer both to partners and to third parties.

In the absence of a clear agreement as to ownership, the strongest evidence of property ownership is the name in which the property is held, often referred to as the *legal title.* If an item of property is held in the name of the partnership, courts will hold it to be partnership property in almost every case. This principle most often plays a part where *real estate* is involved, because a deed has been executed in the name of some party and usually has been "recorded" (made part of official county records). Such formal evidence of ownership is frequently not available for property other than real estate, but if it is available, it will play the same important role. For example, this principle applies to motor vehicles, for which there is usually a state-issued certificate of title.

Problems regarding ownership seldom arise if title to the property in question is held in the partnership name. Those that do arise usually occur in either of two situations: (1) where the property is of a type for which there is no deed, certificate, or other formal evidence of ownership; or (2) where title is held in the name of one or more individual partners, but there is a claim that it is actually partnership property. In the first instance, evidence must be presented to establish just where ownership actually rests. In the second, evidence must be introduced to overcome the presumption of individual ownership and prove that the property actually belongs to the partnership. No single factor is controlling; the court's determination ordinarily is based on the cumulative weight of several factors. Discussion of some of the more important ones follows.

Purchase with Partnership Funds: The funds generated by the business operations of a partnership are partnership property. Additionally, the funds paid into the partnership by individual partners and used by the partnership as working capital are *presumed* to be partnership property. The courts will hold such funds to be individual property only if very strong evidence is produced to show that the payment was intended as a *loan* to the partnership by a partner, rather than a contribution to capital.

An item of property *purchased with partnership funds* is also presumed to be partnership property. The use of partnership funds in making a purchase often plays an important part in a court's decision that ownership resides in the partnership. Indeed, proof that partnership funds were used to buy the property is sufficient to establish the partnership as owner *even if this is the only evidence presented.* Moreover, the presumption created by use of partnership funds is very difficult to overcome. If property has been purchased with such funds, it will take a great deal of contrary evidence to establish that the property does not actually belong to the partnership—even if it is held in the name of an individual partner or other person.[8]

The Way the Property Is Used: Evidence indicating that the property has been used in the business of the partnership is considered by the courts, but by itself it is not sufficient to enable a court to hold that the property belongs to the partnership. For example, if the property is held in the name of an individual

---

[8]On the other hand, if the fact that the property is held in the name of an individual has *misled an innocent third party,* such as a creditor, a different result may be reached. To illustrate: A tract of land was purchased with funds belonging to the B Company, a partnership; but title is held in the name of X, one of the partners. When X applies to C for credit, C innocently relies upon the fact that title to the land appears to rest with X, and C grants credit to X and obtains a lien on the land. If X defaults, C can reach the land for satisfaction of his claim. Even though it is really partnership property, it will be treated as X's individual property insofar as C is concerned. Of course, X will be held responsible to the partnership for the loss of its property.

partner, the fact that it has been used for partnership purposes is not enough to make the partnership the owner. Courts realize that it is not uncommon for an individual partner to allow his or her property to be used in the partnership business without intending to surrender ownership of it.

Treatment in the Partnership Records: If the property is carried in the partnership books as an asset of the firm, this strongly tends to indicate that it is partnership property. The inference is even stronger if an unpaid balance on the property is carried in the records as a partnership liability.

Other Factors: Any number of other factors might influence a court's decision that an item is partnership property:

1. If property had been purchased with funds of an individual partner, the fact that partnership funds were later used to improve, repair, or maintain the property *tends* to show that it now belongs to the partnership. (But additional evidence usually is required, because most courts have been unwilling to infer that the property is owned by the partnership *solely* on the basis that partnership funds were later used to maintain it.)

2. The fact that *taxes* on the property have been paid by the partnership can be important.

3. The receipt by the partnership of *income* generated by the property is evidence that the partnership is the owner.

4. Any other conduct of those involved is considered if it tends to indicate their intent regarding property ownership.

In the case below the court was concerned with two questions: (1) whether a particular parcel of real estate was partnership property, and (2) if so, whether the contract to sell the property, signed by only one partner, was binding on the partnership.

Kay v. Gitomer
Court of Appeals of
Maryland, 251 A.2d 853
(1969)

Albert J. Kay and Benjamin F. Eckles, brothers-in-law, decided to go into the plumbing and contracting business as partners but never entered into a formal partnership agreement. Mr. and Mrs. Kay and Mr. and Mrs. Eckles pooled their resources and purchased real estate consisting of "lot 5," on which was located a small shed, and the rear fifty feet of "lots 1 to 4," on which was located a frame bungalow. Lots 1 to 4 adjoined lot 5. Title to the property was not taken in the name of the partnership, but rather was in the names of Kay and Eckles, individually, as co-owners. The partnership of "Kay and Eckles, Building Contractors," established its office in the bungalow on lots 1 to 4. It is not clear whether lot 5 was ever actually used in the partnership business, but Kay and Eckles did rent it out as a parking lot.

The partnership was financially unsuccessful during the first few years of its operation, and Eckles and Kay decided to sell lot 5 to raise cash. Kay by himself signed a contract to sell lot 5 to Gitomer. A dispute then arose as to the terms of the sale, and Kay and Eckles refused to sell. Gitomer, as plaintiff, sued for a decree of specific performance, which would require Kay and Eckles, defendants, to convey the lot 5 title to him. The trial court held for plaintiff, and defendants appealed. The first question to be decided by the appellate court was whether lot 5 was actually partnership property.

Singley, Justice: ... The resolution of the questions presented can be accomplished by equating the facts of this case to the pertinent provisions of the Uniform [Partnership] Act. . . . § 8(1) provides:

> All property originally brought into the partnership stock or subsequently acquired, by purchase or otherwise on account of the partnership is partnership property.

In *Williams v. Dovell,* 96 A.2d 484 (1953), we held that the Uniform [Partnership] Act does not prevent a partnership from acquiring real estate by having the partners take title as co-tenants [that is, co-owners], and in *Vlamis v. De Weese,* 140 A.2d 665 (1958), that where record title to real estate was in the name of the partners [individually] as [co-owners] "... The criterion of whether property not held in the partnership name is partnership property is the intention of the parties to devote it to partnership purposes, to be found from the facts and circumstances surrounding the transaction considered in connection with the conduct of the parties in relation to the property."

The testimony of Mr. Kay, taken at a pretrial deposition, was read into the record below without objection:

> Q. Now, Mr. Kay, what was the intention in your mind when you purchased Lot 5 in Block H in Easley's subdivision on Fenton Street in connection with the ownership of the real estate and the partnership that you had formed or were forming with your brother-in-law, B. F. Eckles?
> A. We figured it would be a fairly good place to work out of in the business that we sort of hoped to develop and let's say a likely spot for maybe the appreciation of the property rather than a depreciation in its value.
> Q. Well, was it your intention that the partnership of you and Mr. Eckles would have the beneficial ownership of this property?
> A. We had the use of it.
> Q. Was that your intention?
> A. Oh, yes.

It was stipulated that the capital account of the partnership consisted principally of land at a cost of $38,583.62 and improvements at a cost of $15,000, which were equally reflected on the accounts of the two partners. The United States income tax return filed by the partnership for the calendar year 1960, which was an exhibit in the case, disclosed that the *partnership had recognized as income $55.00 received as rent from lot 5, then used as a parking lot, and had taken as deductions* $750.00 in depreciation on the frame building on lots 1 to 4, *$704.66 in real estate taxes which included the taxes on lot 5,* and $690.00 in interest on the mortgage on lots 1 to 4. *It was stipulated that of taxes paid by the partnership in 1961, $524.99 related to lots 1 to 4 and lot 5.* [Emphasis added.]

This is the evidence on which the lower court relied in finding that when Kay and Eckles took title to lots 1 to 4 and lot 5 on 18 June 1959, they intended the real estate to be the property of the partnership which they had formed. There was no necessity for it to have been purchased with partnership funds. It constituted Kay's and Eckles' contribution to partnership capital, for, in the language of the Uniform [Partnership] Act, it was "originally brought into the partnership stock."

[The court thus held that the evidence in the record was sufficient to support the trial court's conclusion that lot 5 was partnership property and not owned by Kay and Eckles as individuals. The court then held that the contract signed only by Kay did bind the partnership in this case and that Gitomer was entitled to specific performance.]

Decree affirmed.

Questions and Problems

1. Discuss whether the UPA adopts the *entity* or *aggregate* theory of the nature of a partnership.

2. Wishing to invest their money, Johnson and Watkins combined funds in equal portions and purchased a substantial amount of corporate stock as well as corporate and government bonds. They owned these securities jointly, shared equally in all dividends and other investment income, and jointly made all decisions relating to the management of their investments. Are they partners? Discuss.

3. Nelson was employed by Cox as an accountant for Cox's large chicken-raising business. Nelson contributed no capital to the business and followed Cox's orders in performing his duties. Nelson's pay, however, was to be one-third of each month's profits from the business. Does a partnership exist between Nelson and Cox? Explain.

4. X, Y, and Z were partners in an automobile dealership. Their partnership agreement provided for continuation of the business in the event of the death of any partner. X died, and Y and Z agreed with X's widow that she would receive a lump sum payment of $50,000 and a 25 percent share of the business's profits as compensation for X's share in the partnership. It was agreed, however, that she would not be required to perform any duties for the business and would take no part in management. Is X's widow a partner of Y and Z? Explain.

5. Shaw was the owner of a shopping center. He rented a store in the center to Winn and agreed to accept, as rent, 20 percent of the net profits of the business. Did this agreement make him a partner? Explain.

6. Wyman and Harvey, college students, each contributed $500 for the purchase of a refreshment stand near the beach of a summer resort. They spent the summer operating the stand and, at the end of the summer, divided the approximately $5,000 profit they had made. They had not entered into a written agreement at any time, and nothing had ever been said about their being partners. Did a partnership between them exist during the summer? Discuss.

7. Corley and Foster were partners in a grain brokerage business, Southwest Grain Brokers. They invested $10,000 of the profits from the business in the stock of Zeron Corp. The Zeron stock certificates were issued jointly to Corley and Foster in their individual names. Corley died, and his widow, as the sole heir of his estate, claimed a one-half interest in the Zeron stock. Will her claim be upheld? Discuss.

8. What is an *assumed name statute?*

9. Discuss why anyone wishing to form a partnership should obtain legal advice and prepare a written partnership agreement.

10. Give three reasons for the importance of determining whether a particular item of property belongs to the partnership or to one or more partners as individuals.

Partnerships/Operating the Business

33

One of the most basic rights of a partner is that of participating in the management of the enterprise. Unless the partnership agreement provides otherwise, all partners have equal rights in the conduct and management of the partnership business. This is true regardless of the amount of their capital contributions or services to the business.

Many partnership agreements expressly provide that a particular partner will be the "managing partner," exercising control over the daily operations of the business. Such agreements also can be implied from the conduct of the partners. For example: Ajax Co. is a partnership composed of partners A, B, C, D, and E. Over a substantial period of time, C, D, and E have left the management of the business to A and B, who possess recognized ability and experience as managers. If C, D, and E suddenly complain about a management decision made by A and B, the court probably will find that there was an implied agreement to give management powers completely to A and B and that they were therefore justified in acting without first consulting C, D, and E.

Relations between Partners
Management Rights

Unless it has been expressly or impliedly agreed otherwise, differences among the partners regarding management are usually settled by a *majority vote*. A few matters, however, such as admission of a new partner or amendment of the articles of partnership, require the consent of *all* the partners unless they have previously agreed that a less-than-unanimous vote will suffice.

Individual Partners' Rights in Specific Partnership Property

Although a partner does not actually *own*, as an individual, any part of the partnership property (the partnership is the owner), he or she does have *rights* in specific partnership assets. However, the interests of the partnership as a business entity are of greater importance than the rights of any of the individual partners. Let us assume that a partnership owns a piece of equipment and that this ownership is undisputed. If one of the partners wishes to make use of the property or otherwise control it, he or she is subject to a number of limitations.

1. The first limitation is that of the *partnership agreement*. If the agreement between the partners stipulates the rights each is to have with respect to partnership property, then the individual who wants to use or control the property is bound by the agreement. For example, the agreement might provide that one of the other partners has the exclusive right to possess or deal with the property.

2. Where there has been no agreement regarding partnership property, certain limitations are imposed by law on individual partners. Under the UPA, each partner has an *equal right to possess partnership property for partnership purposes*. Without the consent of all the other partners, an individual is not entitled to exclusive possession or control of partnership assets. Furthermore, the equal right of possession enjoyed by each partner is limited to purposes that further the partnership business, unless the other partners consent to a use for some different purpose.

3. A partner's right to possess and control partnership property for partnership purposes *cannot be transferred by that person to a third party outside the partnership*. The reason is simple. In this situation the third party would be exercising a right that for all practical purposes would make him a new partner, and a new partner can be brought into the partnership only by agreement of all the partners. For similar reasons, this right cannot be reached by a partner's personal creditors. Additionally, it does not pass to the executor or administrator of a partner's estate when he or she dies; instead it passes to the surviving partner or partners.

A partner's rights with respect to specific partnership property should not be confused with his or her interest in the partnership. The *interest in the partnership* is each partner's share of the profits and surplus, and it is subject to different rules than the right to use partnership property. (This concept will be more fully developed later in the chapter.)

The case below illustrates how an individual partner's right to use partnership property is restricted.

Haft, Weiss, and Wine together owned, as co-tenants, a long-term leasehold on a tract of land on which was located a shopping center. (A *leasehold* is the property interest owned by a lessee, who has leased property from the lessor; and *co-tenants* are essentially co-owners of the leasehold.) Each party as an *individual* owned an undivided interest in the leasehold. After acquiring the leasehold, Hart, Weiss, and Wine formed a joint venture called Pike Associates, for the purpose of managing and operating the shopping center for a period of twenty-five years. In their written agreement they expressly agreed "to invest, as their respective shares of the capital of the Joint Venture herein created, all of their respective rights, titles and interests in and to the aforesaid leasehold interest in the Property."

Weiss was also involved in other business enterprises, and he borrowed money from Madison National Bank and Fidelity Associates, Inc., to be used in these other enterprises. To secure the loan from Madison, Weiss gave Madison a lien on his *interest in the joint venture.* To secure the loan from Fidelity, he gave Fidelity a deed of trust (a mortgage or lien) on his *interest in the leasehold itself.* When Weiss did not pay the debts, Fidelity sought to foreclose its mortgage on the leasehold. Madison sued Fidelity (the named defendant, Newrath, was the individual acting for Fidelity in attempting to foreclose the mortgage) to prevent Fidelity from foreclosing. Madison claimed that Fidelity's mortgage was invalid because it was a mortgage on partnership property for Weiss's individual debt. The trial court held that Pike Associates was not a partnership and that the leasehold was jointly owned by Haft, Weiss, and Wine *as individuals,* as it had been before Pike Associates was formed. Thus Weiss *could* mortgage his interest in the leasehold. Madison National Bank appealed.

Finan, Justice: . . . [The court first pointed out that in almost all situations there is no legal distinction between a joint venture, as Pike Associates had been labeled, and a partnership.]

The Uniform Partnership Act, which has been in effect in Maryland since 1916, defines a partnership as "an association of two or more persons to carry on as co-owners a business for a profit." Of similar import is . . . the classic definition of Chancellor Kent, who defined a partnership "as a contract of two or more competent persons to place their money, effects, labor and skill, or some or all of them, in lawful commerce or business and to divide the profit and bear the loss in certain proportions." We think Pike Associates, serving the purpose of several individuals, who had contributed personal assets to bring it into being, for the building, financing, leasing, managing and operating for mutual profit a major shopping center over a period of 25 years or more, comes within the ambit [bounds] of the Uniform Partnership Act. This being the case, the lower court's theory that Weiss' interest in the leasehold was that of a tenant in common and that he could [mortgage] it by way of a deed of trust as individually owned property does not hold water. Weiss' interest in the leasehold was contributed by him as his share of the capital contribution to Pike Associates, and, as such, it became partnership property.

Section 8 of the Uniform Partnership Act provides:

(1) All property originally contributed to or subsequently acquired by purchase or otherwise on account of the partnership is partnership property. . . .

Section 25 . . . provides that "a partner's right in specific partnership property is not subject to attachment or execution except upon a claim against the partnership . . . .

In view of what we have expressed, the deed of trust given by Weiss to Fidelity in July of 1967 to secure the $165,000 note is invalid, as he sought to [mortgage], as individually owned property, that which was partnership property. . . .

Decree reversed and case remanded . . . .

Comment: As we will see later, partners *can* assign or mortgage their *interests in the partnership,* even though they cannot assign or mortgage their rights in a specific item of partnership property to secure an individual debt. Thus Madison's mortgage was valid and Madison prevailed over Fidelity, whose mortgage was not valid.

Profits and Losses and Other Compensation

As previously mentioned, a partner's "interest in the partnership" is his or her share in the profits of the business as well as a share of what the excess would be at a given time if all the partnership's debts were paid and all the accounts were tallied up and settled. The proportion of partnership profits to be received by each partner is ordinarily determined by an express provision in the articles of partnership. This proportion can be determined on the basis of each partner's contribution of capital, property, or services or by any other method the partners wish to use. If the agreement makes no provision for distributing profits, they will be divided *equally*. The rule requiring equal division in the absence of contrary agreement applies without regard to the amount of capital, property, or service contributed by each partner.

The agreement may also provide for the sharing of losses, although it is often silent on the matter, since few people enter a business expecting to lose money. If the agreement says nothing about losses, they are shared *in the same proportion as profits*. Thus, if nothing is agreed as to either profits or losses, both are shared equally.

The articles of partnership may provide for salaries or other compensation to be paid an individual partner or partners for services rendered in behalf of the partnership. If, however, the agreement does not so provide, a partner is *not entitled to any compensation for such services*. The law presumes in such cases that the parties' intent was that a share of the profits be each partner's only compensation. The sole exception to this rule occurs after the partnership has been dissolved. A partner who is in charge of winding up the affairs of the dissolved partnership is entitled to reasonable compensation for these services.

Unless otherwise agreed, a partner is *not entitled to interest on his or her contribution of capital* to the partnership (the partner's investment). But if the partners originally agreed upon a date for repayment to individual partners of their capital contributions, a partner has a right to receive interest on his or her contribution from that date if it remains unpaid. As we saw in the previous chapter, a partner's payment of money to the partnership is presumed to be a capital contribution rather than a *loan*. However, if a payment is clearly a loan, then the partner is entitled to receive interest computed from the date of the loan.

If an individual partner, acting reasonably in the ordinary and proper conduct of partnership business, makes a payment or incurs personal liability to a third party, the partner is entitled to be *reimbursed* or *indemnified* by the partnership. For example, suppose that the partnership has contracted to sell goods to a buyer. The buyer breaches the contract and refuses to accept the goods. While attempting to find another buyer, it is necessary for the partner handling the transaction to store the goods or to ship them elsewhere. If that partner personally pays such expenses, he or she is entitled to be reimbursed by the partnership.

Basic Fiduciary Duties

Each partner maintains a *fiduciary* relationship with the partnership and with every other partner in matters pertaining to the partnership. This relationship is much the same as the one existing between principal and agent. (The analogy is particularly appropriate, because each partner is an agent of the partnership.) Since such a relationship requires the highest standards of loyalty, good faith, and integrity, a partner who acts in his or her own self-interest and to the detriment of the partnership is accountable to it for any profits made from the endeavor. The seriousness with which courts view this fiduciary relationship is very well described in the following statement by Judge Benjamin Cardozo (who later became a member of the U.S. Supreme Court):

> [Partners] owe to one another, while the enterprise continues, the duty of the finest loyalty. Many forms of conduct permissible in a workaday world for those acting at arm's length, are forbidden to those bound by fiduciary ties. A [partner] is held to something stricter than the morals of the marketplace. Not honesty alone, but the punctilio of an honor the most sensitive, is then the standard of behavior. As to this there has developed a tradition that is unbending and inveterate. Uncompromising rigidity has been the attitude of courts of equity when petitioned to undermine the rule of undivided loyalty by the "disintegrating erosion" of particular exceptions. . . . Only thus has the level of conduct for fiduciaries been kept at a level higher than that trodden by the crowd. It will not consciously be lowered by any judgment of this court.[1]

A partner may engage in his or her own enterprises outside the partnership, so long as the articles of partnership do not prohibit such activity and so long as the outside involvement does not cause the partner to neglect partnership affairs. But a partner cannot *compete* with the partnership. (For example, a partner in a grocery business obviously cannot legally run a competing store in the neighborhood.) Going one step farther, a partner cannot even *acquire* a business interest adverse to the

---

[1]*Meinhard v. Salmon,* 164 N.E. 545 (1928).

interests of the partnership. Thus it has been held that a partner cannot acquire a partnership asset without the consent of the other partners. To illustrate: A lease on real estate held by the partnership is about to expire. One of the partners, acting on his own and for his own benefit, cannot secretly secure from the owner a renewal of the lease for himself. In a similar vein, if a partner in a partnership whose business is purchasing and selling real estate purchases and resells in his or her own name (or in the name of a relative) a lot that he or she should have purchased for the partnership, the partner is accountable to the partnership for the profit.

The fiduciary relationship also demands that each partner be utterly scrupulous when transacting business on his or her own behalf with the partnership or with another partner in matters pertaining to the partnership. To illustrate: If the partners decide to sell an item of partnership property to one of the partners, the purchasing partner is under a duty to disclose all material facts relevant to the transaction. If this partner has any information relating to the present or prospective value of the property, he or she must reveal it to the other partners. The same holds true where one partner is selling his or her interest in the partnership to another partner. Such transactions are not of an "arms-length" nature, with each party looking out after its own interests. They are, to the contrary, transactions in which individual self-interest must take a back seat to the requirements of complete disclosure and rigid fairness.

A partner can also be held responsible to the partnership for losses resulting from negligence. The partner is not liable simply because of bad judgment but is liable if the business is harmed because of carelessness or neglect.

Partnership Books

All matters relating to record keeping should be dealt with in the articles of partnership. If the agreement is silent in this regard, the partnership books are required to be kept at the partnership's *principal place of business.* Every partner must at all times have access to the books and the opportunity to inspect or copy any of them.

If the partners have named one of them to be the managing partner or if they have given record-keeping duties to a particular partner, that partner must keep complete and accurate accounts and can be held liable for the failure to do so. He or she also has the burden of proving that the records are correct; and if an accurate account is not kept, any doubts that may arise when partnership affairs are being closed will usually be resolved against the responsible partner.

The type of records and the degree of detail required will depend on the express or implied agreement of the partners. For example, the strict rule on record keeping might not be applied if the other partners had free access to the books and did not complain that they were kept less than perfectly. Also, where the partnership agreement is silent on the matter, the nature of the business and other circumstances might cause a relaxation of the rule requiring complete and accurate books (for example, where the partners are virtually illiterate and the business they run is limited to remote logging camps in the mountains).

Right to an Account

Under certain circumstances a partner can institute a legal proceeding called an *account* or an *accounting*. In such a suit, all records of the partnership must be formally produced and all balances computed under court supervision. Since each partner ordinarily has free access to the books, this kind of lawsuit usually is filed only when the partnership has been dissolved.

There are circumstances, however, in which a partner may demand a formal account from his or her co-partners without seeking the dissolution of the partnership. Then, if the co-partners refuse or if the partner making the demand is dissatisfied with the accounting, he or she may institute legal action. Under Sec. 22 of the UPA, a partner has the right to a formal account as to partnership affairs under any of the following circumstances:

1. He or she has been *wrongfully excluded* by the other partners from the partnership business or from possession of partnership property.

2. The right to a formal account has been provided for in an *agreement* between the partners.

3. One of the other partners has derived a *personal benefit* from a transaction related to partnership business without his or her consent.

4. Other circumstances render it "just and reasonable" (for example, if he or she has been traveling for a long period of time on partnership business and the other partners are in possession of the company's records).

General Application of Agency Rules

Relations with
Third Parties

In partnership transactions with third parties, the law of agency governs the liabilities of the partnership, the partners, and the third party. Technically, *the partnership is the principal and each partner an agent* with respect to partnership affairs. Statements are also found in many cases to the effect that each partner is an agent for the other partners (who are principals), as well as for the partnership as an entity. Of course, this is often the practical result anyway, since the other partners can be held personally liable if partnership assets are insufficient to satisfy the partnership liability.

The partnership is liable to third parties for a partner's transactions that are contractual in nature if the partner had actual or apparent authority. (Actual authority can, of course, be express or implied.) Partnership liability can also exist if the partnership, acting through the other partners, ratifies an unauthorized transaction of a partner. (More will be said later about partnership liability for a partner's contracts.)

As in agency law generally, the partnership is liable to third parties harmed by the tort or other wrongful act of a partner only if the tort was committed while the partner was acting in the ordinary course (or scope) of the partnership business.

However, even if a partner's tort did not involve partnership business, any other partner participating in, directing, or authorizing the wrongful act is personally liable along with the one actually committing it.

The courts are somewhat more reluctant to impose *criminal liability* on a partnership or on the other partners for the act of one of them. Such liability is, of course, placed on any partner who participated in, directed, or expressly authorized the act of the other. However, the partnership as an entity (and other partners who did *not* participate in, direct, or expressly authorize the wrongful act) will be liable for the crime of a partner only if (1) it was committed in the ordinary course of the partnership business *and* (2) proof of criminal intent is *not* required for conviction. Examples include illegal liquor sales, mislabeling of goods, and unsafe transporting of explosives.

Examples of a Partner's Implied Authority

Most questions concerning partnership liability for acts of individual partners stem from commercial dealings and other transactions of a contractual nature. The partnership, as principal, is usually liable for a partner's transaction only if it is *authorized.* Such authority can be expressly granted in the partnership agreement or by the other partners at a later time.

Even where no express authority has been given, under the UPA a partner can bind the partnership in transactions that are for the purpose of "carrying on the partnership business in the usual way." This *implied authority* exists with regard to those types of transactions that are *customary* in conducting the kind of business in which the partnership is engaged. In the articles of partnership or by other agreement the partners can expressly limit the authority of a partner to act for the partnership. If such a limitation restricts a partner's implied authority by prohibiting transactions that would otherwise be normal and customary, third parties are bound by the limitation only if they know of it. For example, suppose that a partnership is in the business of buying and selling real estate. It is customary in such a business for a partner to have authority to sell for the partnership real estate that is held for resale. Suppose, however, that the articles of partnership provide that such sales can be made only by two or more partners acting together. A third party who does not know of this restriction and who buys from a single partner is not affected by the limitation, and the partnership is bound by the transaction under the doctrine of *apparent authority.*

The following transactions are of such a usual and customary nature that a partner *ordinarily* is impliedly authorized to undertake them. These are only examples; other instances of implied authority exist, but they depend more on particular circumstances. Furthermore, these transactions might not be impliedly authorized in certain situations, particularly where the nature of the business is such that they are not usual and customary. Ultimately, the type of business conducted by the partnership and all the surrounding circumstances determine the extent of a partner's implied authority.

Borrowing Money: In determining whether a partner has implied authority to borrow money in behalf of the partnership, most courts have traditionally distinguished between *trading* and *nontrading* partnerships. Implied borrowing authority has been held to exist in trading partnerships but not in nontrading ones. A partner in a nontrading partnership usually has been held to have authority to borrow money only if this authority has been expressly granted by a majority of the other partners.

Essentially, a *trading partnership* is one that engages in the business of buying and selling goods. All others, ranging from professional partnerships such as those of lawyers and physicians to partnerships for the purpose of carrying on a real estate, insurance, or loan business, are classified as *nontrading partnerships.* In view of the increasing complexity of the business world, the simple division into trading and nontrading categories is of doubtful usefulness. Today many types of partnerships require working capital, even though their business is not limited to merchandising.

The courts, perhaps sensing the inadequacies of the simple dichotomy between trading and nontrading partnerships, have expanded the trading category to include businesses such as those of tailors, plumbing and construction contractors, manufacturers, and dairy farmers. The courts will probably continue to use the terms *trading* and *nontrading,* but their importance will diminish. If a court holds a business to be a trading partnership, the authority of a partner to borrow money is automatically present unless the other partners expressly limit this authority and make such limitation known to third parties. In other types of partnerships, the courts will probably look at all the surrounding circumstances. If it is usual and customary for a partner in this particular partnership, or perhaps even in similar partnerships, to have borrowing authority, then such authority will probably be found to exist by many courts.

What has been said about implied authority to borrow money applies also to the execution of promissory notes and other types of instruments purporting to obligate the partnership to make a future payment of money. In fact, many of the cases decided on this point have involved such instruments.

Selling Partnership Property: A partner has implied authority to sell goods, real estate, or other property belonging to the partnership if sales of such items are within the ordinary course of the partnership's business. For example, suppose that a partnership engages in the wholesale grocery business and also owns real estate for investment purposes. In this case a partner has implied authority to sell groceries held for resale but usually does not have implied authority to sell the real estate. The latter authority will have to be expressly granted by a majority of the other partners. On the other hand, if the business of the partnership consists of buying and selling real estate, a partner *does have* implied authority to sell partnership real estate.

The addition of other facts might change the above example. For instance, if the other partners had in the past always allowed one partner to make all investment decisions on his own, that partner might have implied authority to sell the grocery partnership's real estate.

Even if the sale of a certain type of property, such as goods, is part of the ordinary business of the partnership, a partner generally does not have implied authority to sell most or all of the items held in inventory if this will result in a suspension of the business.

Hiring Employees: A partner ordinarily has implied authority to hire employees whose services are necessary for carrying on the business of the partnership, to make reasonable agreements for their compensation, and to discharge them.

Making Purchases: A partner usually has implied authority to purchase items that are reasonably necessary to the operation of the partnership's business.

Receiving and Enforcing Performance of Obligations: If the partnership is entitled to some type of performance, such as a payment of money or delivery of goods, a partner ordinarily has implied authority to accept performance of the obligation in behalf of the partnership. In addition, a partner has implied authority to take legal action for the partnership if the other party defaults on the obligation.

In the first case below, the court applies basic agency concepts contained in the UPA to plaintiff's claim against a partnership on a promissory note executed by a single partner. In the second case, a partner's improper motive transformed several authorized transactions into a breach of his fiduciary duties.

Burns v. Gonzalez
Court of Civil Appeals of Texas, 439 S.W.2d 128 (1969)

Gonzalez and Bosquez were partners in Inter-American Advertising Agency (hereafter called "the partnership"). The sole business of the partnership was the sale of broadcast time on XERF, a radio station located in Ciudad Acuna, Mexico. The radio station was owned and operated by a Mexican corporation, Compania Radiodifusora de Cahuila, S.A. (hereafter called "the corporation"). The corporation, in turn, was entirely owned by Gonzalez and Bosquez.

In 1957 a contract was made between the corporation and partnership, on the one hand, and Roloff and Burns, on the other. Under this contract Roloff and Burns were to pay $100,000 in return for two fifteen-minute segments of broadcast time daily over XERF for so long as the franchise of the radio station remained in force. Roloff and Burns paid the $100,000 during 1957 and 1958. In June 1962 Roloff assigned all of his rights under the contract to Burns, who apparently intended to sell the broadcast time to others.

Because of labor disputes and other problems, the radio station was shut down at various times. With some exceptions, the broadcast periods described in the 1957 contract were not made available to Burns or to the persons to whom he sold them. In November 1962 the radio station was in receivership, and it became unlikely that the broadcast periods in question would be available for at least two years. On November 28, 1962, Bosquez, purporting to act in his own behalf and in behalf of the partnership, executed a promissory note for $40,000 payable to Burns on November 28, 1964. This note was given to Burns to compensate him for the income he would have derived from selling the broadcast time during the two-year period ending November 28, 1964. Another purpose of the note was to settle any claim for breach of contract that Burns might have against the corporation.

The note was not paid when due, and Burns sued both the partnership and Bosquez and Gonzalez as individuals. The trial court rendered judgment for Burns against Bosquez, who made the note, but it held that neither the partnership nor Gonzalez was liable. Bosquez did not appeal the judgment against him, but Burns appealed the court's denial of recovery from the partnership and from Gonzalez.

Cadena, Justice: . . . Under Sec. 9(1), U.P.A. "Every partner is an agent of the partnership for the purpose of its business, and the act of every partner, including the execution in the partnership name of any instrument, *for apparently carrying on in the usual way the business of the partnership* of which he is a member binds the partnership, unless the partner so acting has in fact no authority to act for the partnership in the particular matter, and the person with whom he is dealing has knowledge of the fact that he has no such authority." (Emphasis added [by the court.]) In this case, in fact, Bosquez had no authority to bind the partnership by executing a negotiable instrument. [Evidently, Gonzalez and Bosquez had agreed that Bosquez could not take such action alone.] But, since this express limitation on the authority of Bosquez was unknown to Burns, then, under the language of Sec. 9(1), his act in executing the note would bind the partnership if such act can be classified as an act "for apparently carrying on in the usual way the business of the partnership."

As we interpret Sec. 9(1), the act of a partner binds the firm, absent an express limitation of authority known to the party dealing with such partner, if such act is for the purpose of "apparently carrying on" the business of the partnership in the way in which other firms engaged in the same business in the locality usually transact business, or in the way in which the particular partnership usually transacts its business. In this case, there is no evidence relating to the manner in which firms engaged in the sale of advertising time on radio stations usually transact business. Specifically, there is no evidence as to whether or not the borrowing of money, or the execution of negotiable instruments, was incidental to the transaction of business, "in the usual way," by other advertising agencies or by this partnership . . . . It becomes important, therefore, to determine the location of the burden of proof concerning the "usual way" of transacting business by advertising agencies. . . .

[The court then concluded that the burden of proof fell on the third party rather than on the nonparticipating partner. Thus Burns had the burden of proving that execution of the note by Bosquez was for the purpose of "apparently carrying on in the usual way the business of the partnership."]

The language relating to carrying on in the usual way the business of the partnership is no more than a statement of the rule concerning vicarious liability based on "apparent" authority. . . .

Our conclusion is supported by the fact that the liability of partners with respect to third persons is largely determined by reference to the principles of the law of agency. One who asserts that the particular act of an agent is within the scope of the agent's authority has the burden of proving the extent of such authority. . . . The principle for imposing liability on the nonacting party, be he partner or ordinary principal, is that he has "held out" the actor as being empowered to perform acts of the nature of the act in question. . . .

There are many statements to the effect that members of a "trading" partnership have implied authority to bind the partnership by issuing commercial paper, while members of a "nontrading" partnership have no such implied authority. But we do not base our holding on the ground that the partnership here was of the nontrading type. It is apparent that the attempted distinction between the two types of partnership is nothing more than a short-hand rendition of the notion that B is liable for the act of C if B has "held out" to other persons that C is empowered to perform acts of that particular nature. The nature of the distinction is revealed by the language of Chief Justice Stayton in *Randall v. Meredith,* 13 S.W. 576 (1890):

> If the partnership contemplates the periodical or continuous or frequent purchasing, not as incidental to an occupation, but for the purpose of selling again the thing purchased, either in its original or manufactured state, it is a trading partnership; otherwise, it is not.... There is no doubt that all partnerships which fall within this definition are trading partnerships, and it may be that it is broad enough to cover all that should be so classed. If these were not embraced within this definition, in which each partner is clothed with power to borrow money, they may be recognized by the character of the business pursued, which makes frequent resort to borrowing a necessity, not existing by reason of embarrassments, or on account of some fortui-tous event, but for the advantageous prosecution of even a prosperous business....
>
> An act may be necessary for the carrying on of the business of a partnership, but when done by one partner the firm cannot be bound by it, unless he has express or implied power to do the act. Whether he has the implied power depends on whether the act be necessary to carry on the business in the ordinary way. A part-ner's power is to do only what is usual, and not what is unusual because neces-sary....
>
> Whether the work was done in the usual course of business, or was necessary, was not the [proper] inquiry.... The work may have been done in the usual course of business, or necessary, but this would not confer on the partner power to borrow money to pay for it, unless the exercise of that power was usual in the ordinary con-duct of such a business.

It appears that the tests announced in *Randall* for determining whether a partnership is to be classed as trading or nontrading is exactly the same test for imposition of liability embodied in Sec. 9(1). This explains the fact that the U.P.A. makes no mention of the distinction between trading and non-trading firms....

The power of a partner to issue commercial paper arises not from the existence of the partnership, but from the nature of the partnership business and the manner in which such business is usually conducted. This is the plain meaning of Sec. 9(1).

The only thing we know of the nature of the partnership here is that it was restricted to the sale of broadcast time over XERF on a commission basis. There is nothing to show that the transaction of such business required "periodical or continuous or frequent purchas-ing" or made "frequent resort to borrowing a necessity, not existing by reason of embarrass-ments, or on account of some fortuitous event, but for the advantageous prosecution of even a prosperous business." The assets of the partnership consisted of a few desks, chairs, typewriters and office supplies.

We disagree with the contention put forward by Burns to the effect that Bosquez was the managing partner. At best, the record reflects that both Bosquez and Gonzalez were active in the management of the business. As a matter of fact, with the exception of the

... 1962 note ..., the record discloses that all instruments significantly affecting the relations between the partners and Burns were signed by both Bosquez and Gonzalez.

Since the evidence does not disclose that Bosquez, in executing the 1962 note, was performing an act "for apparently carrying on in the usual way the business of the partnership," there is no basis for holding that the note sued on was a partnership obligation. . . .

The judgment of the trial court is affirmed.

Early in 1966 Oswald and Leckey, certified public accountants, executed a partnership agreement to conduct an accounting practice. After forming the partnership each partner continued to bill the clients that he personally served. The relationship between Oswald and Leckey was not harmonious and the partnership was dissolved in June 1968. Oswald, plaintiff, filed suit for an accounting to determine each partner's share of a partnership bank account. In the lawsuit, Oswald claimed that Leckey, defendant, had improperly "written down" several accounts while they were partners. An account is "written down" when the amount actually billed is less than the amount due as shown on the books. The trial court ruled that defendant had not acted properly in writing down the accounts and that he was responsible to the partnership for the amount of the write-downs. Defendant appealed.

Oswald v. Leckey
Supreme Court of
Oregon, 572 P.2d 1316
(1977)

Bryson, Justice: . . . The first item in contention is defendant's "write-down" of several accounts he serviced. Defendant collected $4,610.85 less on these accounts than the books showed was due. The partnership agreement does not specify the responsibility of partners in collecting partnership debts. Thus, this issue must be decided by the general principles of partnership law.

Partners have authority to make compromises with partnership debtors, even after dissolution. This power to compromise claims is stated briefly as follows: "A partner may receive payment of obligations due to the partnership, may compromise with firm debtors, and release them. . . ." Crane & Bromberg, Law of Partnership 456, §80 (1968).

So defendant had the power to compromise claims, but in exercising this power he had to follow the fiduciary duty imposed on him as a partner, "to act with the utmost candor and good faith." Although defendant testified that his "write-downs" were consistent with his past practices and with good practice, he also testified:

Q. And in our opinion, knowing these clients, what would have happened if you had billed it out at the amounts that you had written off?
A. Well, these are clients that were under my responsibility and that came with me when I left the partnership. And I would have been out a substantial number of clients and future work, future income.

In other words, in adjusting downwards the amounts due for work in progress, defendant was partly motivated by a desire to retain certain clients. This falls far short of the duty of good faith imposed on partners. We conclude, as did the trial court, that defendant ought to pay the partnership the difference between the amount stated on the books and the amount actually collected by defendant on these accounts. . . .

Affirmed.

Examples of Authority Not Usually Implied

The following actions are those for which implied authority usually does not exist. Again, these are only examples, and other actions also might not be impliedly authorized, depending on the nature of the business and the surrounding circumstances. Furthermore, the activities below might be impliedly authorized if the circumstances are such that the activity is usual and customary in the particular business involved. Remember, too, that any of these acts may be *expressly* authorized by the other partners if they so desire.

Assumption of Debts: In most cases, a partner does *not* have implied authority to assume, in the name of the partnership, liability for the debt of another. Such authority *may* exist, however, if the nature of the business includes this type of transaction. For instance, it might be customary for a partnership that sells stocks, bonds, and other securities to guarantee the securities it sells. This is, in effect, an assumption of the obligation of the company that originally issued the securities, but a partner can nevertheless have implied authority to make such a guarantee where it is a normal part of the partnership's business.

Purchases of Corporate Stock: The courts have generally held that a partner does not have implied authority to purchase or agree to purchase, for the partnership, stock in a corporation. Of course, such authority may exist if this type of transaction is within the usual scope of the business (for example, if the partnership's business is the sale of corporate stocks).

Gratuitous Undertakings: Since partnerships are formed for the purpose of operating a profit-making enterprise, a partner usually does not have implied authority to involve the partnership in a charitable undertaking or to give away partnership property. Such authority ordinarily has to be expressly given by the other partners. Exceptions might exist where it is customary for a business to provide certain free services to customers in an effort to generate goodwill and enhance future business. Thus it might be customary for a brokerage firm to furnish free market information to prospective customers.

Actions Expressly Disallowed by the UPA

In Sec. 9, the UPA specifically designates several types of actions that are completely unauthorized. In other words, a partner cannot bind the partnership by these acts regardless of the nature of the business or what is customary. Furthermore, even a *majority* of the partners do not have the power to bind the partnership by these acts; there must be express agreement by *all* the partners.[2]

---

[2]One exception exists. The consent of a partner who has abandoned the business need not be obtained.

Confession of Judgment: Action by all partners is required to confess judgment. A *confession of judgment* is the agreement of a debtor that allows the creditor to obtain a court judgment for a specified sum against the debtor without the necessity of legal proceedings. Agreement of all the partners is required because of the unusual and severe nature of a confession of judgment.[3]

Arbitration: Unanimous consent is also required to submit a claim by or against the partnership to *arbitration*. Although arbitration is now a common and accepted method of settling commercial disputes, this has not always been the case. Courts were not particularly receptive to the idea of arbitration at an earlier time, an antagonism reflected in the UPA when it was drafted in 1914.

Acts Restricting Partnership Business: The UPA also requires unanimous agreement by the partners to perform certain types of acts that restrict the operation of the partnership business. For example, consent of all partners is required before the partnership property can be placed in trust for the partnership's creditors. Such a transaction is commonly referred to as an *assignment for the benefit of creditors,* and it represents one way an insolvent business can settle with its creditors without formal bankruptcy proceedings.

Agreement of all partners is also necessary to dispose of the goodwill of the partnership. The courts have construed this provision as requiring unanimous consent to a covenant not to compete. For example, the partnership might sell part of its business and agree not to compete with the buyer. Such an agreement would bind the partnership only if it was made by all the partners.

The UPA also states that consent of all partners is required to "do any other act which would make it impossible to carry on the ordinary business" of the partnership. An example is an agreement to cancel the lease of the premises where the partnership conducts its business.

Satisfaction of Creditors' Claims

One of the cardinal characteristics of the partnership form of business is that the individual partners are *personally liable* for the obligations of the partnership. But this liability is secondary. A creditor having a claim against a partnership must first look to *partnership property* for satisfaction of the claim. The creditor can reach the assets of individual partners only after partnership assets are exhausted. Moreover, the assets of an individual partner must first be used to satisfy claims of his or her personal creditors before partnership creditors can assert their claims.

Quite naturally, then, creditors of an individual partner must first look to the personal assets of that partner for satisfaction of their claims. In fact, such creditors *cannot* reach specific items of partnership property. If some debt remains after a

---

[3]In some states a confession of judgment is not permitted at all.

partner's personal assets have been exhausted, the creditor's only recourse with regard to the partnership is to obtain a "charging order" against the partner's *interest in the partnership* (that is, the partner's right to share in the profits and surplus of the partnership). A charging order issued by a court will order that partner's share of the profits to be paid to his or her creditor until the debt is fully discharged. If the debt has not been completely paid when the partnership is dissolved, the charging order will require payment to the creditor of that partner's share in the surplus, if any remains when all partnership affairs are settled.

Special Rules Regarding Liability to Third Parties

The Incoming Partner: When a new partner is admitted into an existing partnership, he or she naturally becomes responsible along with the other partners for all partnership obligations that arise *after* the admittance. The new partner is also responsible for partnership obligations that arose *before* he or she became a partner, but this liability does not extend beyond his or her interest in the partnership. Partnership creditors whose claims against the partnership arose prior to admission of the new partner cannot reach his or her individual assets for satisfaction of the claims.

Partner by Estoppel: Even if a person is not a member of a particular partnership, under certain circumstances there may be personal liability to third parties as if the individual were a partner. If someone has represented himself or herself as a partner to a third party, (or allowed such a representation to be made), that person is liable as a partner if the third party grants credit to the partnership because of the representation. This liability results because the individual is "estopped" (prohibited) from denying that he or she is a partner in a suit brought by the third party.

To illustrate: Regency Co., a partnership, wished to obtain credit. Fearful of being unable to do so, the partners in Regency Co., X and Y, appealed to Jones, a businessman whose name and financial capabilities were well known in the business community. Out of friendship, Jones agreed that X and Y could tell prospective creditors that he was a member of the partnership in order to obtain credit. Subsequently, X and Y represented to the First National Bank that Jones was a partner. Relying on the representation, the bank granted the loan to the partnership. Even though Jones is not actually a partner, he is liable to the bank as if he were one. However, he is not treated as a partner for any other purpose. No partnership relations have been created between Jones and X and Y, and he is not liable as a partner to third parties who have not relied on the representation.

Assignment of a Partner's Interest

As previously discussed, a partner's right to possess and control partnership property cannot be assigned to a third party. However, a partner's interest in the partnership *can* be assigned to a third party without the consent of the other partners.

The assignee of a partner's interest is merely entitled to receive the profits to which the assigning partner would otherwise be entitled. If the partnership is subsequently dissolved, the assignee is entitled to receive whatever share of the surplus the assigning partner would have been entitled to receive. But the assignee acquires *nothing else*. He or she does not become a partner unless all the partners consent to the admission. Therefore, the assignee acquires no management powers, does not become an agent of the partnership, and, while the partnership exists, is not entitled to inspect the partnership books or to receive a formal account of partnership transactions.

Before enactment of the UPA, the assignment by a partner to a third party of his or her interest in the partnership was generally deemed to automatically *dissolve* the partnership, unless the partnership agreement provided otherwise. Under the UPA, this is not the case. The UPA recognizes that a partner may wish to assign the interest with absolutely no intention of bringing an end to the partnership. For example, a partner may wish to assign this interest to an individual creditor as security for a loan. On the other hand, in some circumstances a partner's assignment can be considered evidence of an intent to dissolve the partnership. For example, if, after the assignment, the assigning partner neglects partnership affairs and acts as if there is no longer any business relationship with the other partners, a court will be justified in holding the partnership to be dissolved. But the mere act of assignment, with nothing more, does not bring about dissolution. (The subject of dissolution will be treated more fully in the next chapter.)

Questions and Problems

1. X, Y, and Z were partners in Snappy Delivery Service Co. The partnership owned three delivery trucks. X borrowed one of the trucks to haul some of his personal belongings and never returned it to the business. Y and Z demanded the return of the truck, but X refused. X said that he owned a third of the partnership; and since the partnership owned three trucks, one of them naturally belonged to him personally. Is X correct? Explain.

2. Anderson, Richards, and Williams formed a partnership for the purpose of producing rock music concerts. The three partners initially contributed $2,000, $4,000, and $3,000, respectively, to the partnership for use as working capital. The partnership agreement made no provision for the division of profits. At the end of the first year, the partnership had made a profit of $4,500. What is each partner's share of the profits? Explain.

3. Suppose that in Question 2 the partnership agreement had provided that profits were to be divided equally but had made no provision for the division of losses. If the partnership loses $3,000 the first year, what proportion of this loss must each partner bear? Explain.

4. Wilkes, Watkins, and Weston formed a partnership for the express purpose, as provided in the partnership agreement, of engaging in the retail shoe business. Even though the business was relatively successful, Wilkes and Watkins wanted to change the nature of their business from a shoe store to a men's clothing store. Weston objected. Can Wilkes and Watkins take such action over Weston's objection? Discuss.

5. In Question 4, suppose that Wilkes and Watkins had merely wanted to expand their business to include athletic shoes as well as dress and casual shoes. Could they do so over Weston's objection? Discuss.

6. What is the distinction between a trading and a nontrading partnership? What is the significance of this distinction?

7. A, B, C, and D owned a used car business as partners. D sold a car to Johnson, guaranteeing in writing that any defects in the car would be repaired free of charge during the ninety-day period following the sale. Johnson brought the car back a month later, claiming that the transmission was not operating properly. A, B, and C stated that the warranty was no good because D had not been given express authority to make warranties. Must the partnership honor the warranty made by D? Discuss.

8. Suppose that in Question 7 the partnership agreement had expressly provided that a partner does not have authority to make warranties in connection with the sale of cars. Would this fact make any difference? Would Johnson's knowledge of the provision be of any importance? Explain.

9. Jurgenson and Taylor were partners in an automobile repair business. Driver brought his car to Jurgenson and Taylor's garage to have the brakes repaired. Jurgenson repaired the brakes. Two days later Driver had a collision caused by failure of the brakes. The brake failure was due to Jurgenson's negligence in doing the repair work, so Driver sued the partnership. Is the partnership liable? Explain.

10. Suppose that in Question 9 Driver's suit against the partnership was successful. The assets of the partnership, however, were not sufficient to satisfy the judgment awarded to Driver by the court. Driver then sought to hold the individual partners personally liable for the unpaid portion of the judgment. Could he hold them personally responsible? Explain. Suppose that Jurgenson and Taylor had admitted Leonard as a new partner in the business. If Driver also tries to hold Leonard personally liable, what will be the importance of the time of Leonard's admission as a new partner? Discuss.

Partnerships/Termination 34

Complete termination of the partnership as a business organization is comprised of two elements: dissolution and winding up. *Dissolution* does not of itself bring the partnership business to a close; it is, rather, the "beginning of the end." Essentially, the word *dissolution* designates that point in time when the object of the partners changes from that of continuing the organization in its present form to discontinuing it.[1] The partnership is not terminated at that time, but its object has become termination.

The second element of termination, commonly referred to as *winding up*, involves the actual process of settling partnership affairs after dissolution. After both dissolution and winding up have occurred, the partnership as an organization will have terminated.

---

[1]Later in the chapter we will discuss the situation where certain of the partners wish to continue the *business*, even though the partnership as an organization is dissolved. It might be continued as a new partnership or in some other organizational form. In such a case, the termination of the partnership consists primarily of bookkeeping entries and purchase of the interests of noncontinuing partners.

Dissolution

Causes of Dissolution

The events that cause dissolution can be divided into four categories: (1) act of the parties not in violation of their agreement, (2) act of the parties in violation of their agreement, (3) operation of law, and (4) court decree.

Act of the Parties Not in Violation of Their Agreement: In many circumstances dissolution of a partnership can be brought about by the partners themselves without violating their partnership agreement (articles of partnership) and without the necessity of any formal legal proceedings. For example, the agreement may provide that the partnership will exist for only a specified period of time. Upon expiration of this period, the partnership obviously will dissolve in accordance with the original agreement, unless all the partners agree to amend the articles of partnership and extend the prescribed duration.[2] Similarly, the articles of partnership may provide that the arrangement is for some expressly indicated purpose or undertaking. If that purpose is accomplished or can no longer be pursued, dissolution occurs.

Where the partnership agreement makes no provision for a definite duration or undertaking, the partnership is commonly referred to as being *at will* (any partner can withdraw at any time without incurring liability to the other partners). Withdrawal by any of the partners results in dissolution.

The articles of partnership may provide for still other methods of dissolution. For example, even if a definite duration or undertaking is expressed in the agreement, it may nevertheless expressly provide for dissolution at the request of any partner who so desires. By the same token, the agreement may allow for exclusion of a partner by the other partners for specified reasons. The terms of the partnership agreement may even permit exclusion of a partner by the others whenever they feel it will be in the best interests of the business. Dissolution results in any of these situations, although the other partners can, and often will, immediately reorganize and continue the business.

Since a partnership is *created* by agreement, it can be *dissolved* by agreement. Regardless of the terms of the articles of partnership, dissolution can be accomplished at any time by agreement of *all* the partners. Such agreement must be unanimous, unless the articles of partnership have provided for dissolution by a less-than-unanimous vote.[3] Otherwise, the agreement would be violated by those partners who caused the dissolution.

---

[2]Continuance of the business by the partners after expiration of the agreed term constitutes an implied partnership agreement even in the absence of an express amendment of the articles of partnership. The partnership will then be one "at will," which means that the individual partners are legally free to withdraw at any time thereafter. So long as they actually continue, however, the partnership exists and the terms of the implied partnership agreement are those of the original agreement, insofar as they are applicable.

[3]However, if a partner has assigned his or her interest in the partnership to a third party, or if a partner's personal creditor has subjected the partner's interest in the partnership to a "charging order," the consent of that partner is not required for dissolution.

Act of the Parties in Violation of Their Agreement: Irrespective of the terms of the partnership agreement, any partner can at any time withdraw from the partnership and cause its dissolution. If this withdrawal violates the partnership agreement, however, the withdrawing partner is liable to his or her co-partners for any *damages* resulting from the wrongful dissolution. In such a case dissolution can occur without any formal court decree, but the nonwithdrawing partners may choose to seek one, particularly if there is disagreement about whether the dissolution was actually wrongful or about the amount of damages.

By Operation of Law: The partnership automatically dissolves if an event occurs that makes it illegal to carry on the business. The *business itself* may become illegal, as where a partnership for the purpose of selling liquor loses its liquor license. Or it may become illegal for *these particular partners* to carry on the business together, as where an individual partner in a medical practice has his or her license revoked.

Dissolution also occurs automatically on the *death* of a partner or on the *bankruptcy* of either a partner or the partnership itself. The articles of partnership may, of course, provide for continuation of the *business* in the event of death or bankruptcy of a partner. Dissolution still occurs, however; the agreement in such a case simply provides for reorganization and continuation instead of liquidation.

By Court Decree: Sec. 32 of the UPA specifically enumerates several situations in which dissolution of a partnership can be accomplished by seeking and obtaining a formal court decree. They can be divided into two broad categories: (1) situations in which a *partner* can obtain a decree of dissolution, and (2) situations in which a *third party* can obtain such a decree.

Decree obtained by a partner. When a partner has become *insane,* either that person or another partner can obtain a court decree dissolving the partnership. In such a case dissolution does not occur automatically (as it does in the case of death or bankruptcy). A formal court decree is required in the instance of insanity because a person's mental competency is inherently subject to doubt and dispute, whereas death and bankruptcy are more certain events. The decree can be sought (1) when a partner has already been declared insane by a court in a sanity hearing or (2) when such a formal adjudication has not yet occurred. In the latter case, the court asked to dissolve the partnership will itself determine whether the partner is insane. The court will not dissolve the partnership in either case, however, unless it appears probable that the insanity will continue for a substantial part of the partnership's duration.

Dissolution also can be obtained by court decree if a partner becomes in any other way *incapable of performing his or her part of the partnership agreement.* This provision is usually applied to disabilities other than insanity (such as prolonged illness, a paralytic stroke, or a serious accident) when it appears that the disability will continue for a substantial period of time and will materially obstruct or negatively affect the objectives of the partnership. The court decree in this case can be sought by either the partner suffering the disability or any other partner.

A partner can obtain a decree of dissolution when one of the other partners has been guilty of *serious misconduct*. Breach of the partnership agreement is, of course, one example of such misconduct. Even if the partnership agreement has not been breached, under the UPA a decree of dissolution can be obtained if another partner has been "guilty of such conduct as tends to affect prejudicially the carrying on of the business" or if the other partner "so conducts himself in matters relating to the partnership business that it is not reasonably practicable to carry on the business in partnership with him." Examples of such conduct are fraud in dealing with partnership property or funds, substantial overdraft of a drawing account by a partner who has been temporarily left in charge of the business, and serious neglect of partnership affairs.

Where misconduct has occurred, the guilty partner cannot obtain dissolution by court decree; this right belongs solely to one or more of the other partners. Furthermore, if the other partner or partners so desire, they can simply withdraw and cause dissolution. A court decree is not essential, and the guilty partner cannot sue them for damages even if their withdrawal is contrary to the partnership agreement. Although formal court action is not essential in cases of misconduct, it is often desirable where any doubt exists as to whether the misconduct is serious enough to warrant dissolution or where disagreement exists regarding damages or the value of partners' interests.

Finally, any partner can obtain a decree of dissolution when it becomes evident that the business is *unprofitable* and will probably not be profitable in the future.

Decree obtained by a third party. Two types of third parties are considered to have a sufficient interest in partnership affairs to obtain a decree of dissolution in certain circumstances: (1) an *assignee* of a partner's interest in the partnership and (2) a partner's *personal creditor* who has subjected that partner's interest to a charging order. Either of these third parties, however, can obtain a decree of dissolution in only two situations: (1) after expiration of the period of time or accomplishment of the purpose specified in the articles of partnership, in cases where the articles include such a provision, or (2) at any time, if the partnership is a partnership "at will" when the third party acquires his or her interest.

Effect of Dissolution on Partners' Authority

Despite the fact that dissolution does not sound the instantaneous death knell of the partnership, it is frequently important to ascertain the precise moment when it occurs. The reason is simple. When dissolution takes place, certain significant changes occur in the nature of the partners' relationships with each other and with outsiders. Of paramount significance is the effect dissolution has on the *authority of partners to bind the partnership*. In most cases, of course, a partner acting without authority must personally shoulder the burden of any liability resulting from such action.

Upon dissolution, the authority of individual partners to act in behalf of the partnership usually ceases, *except for acts necessary to complete unfinished transactions or those appropriate for winding up partnership affairs.* For example, suppose that a partnership, before dissolution, had made a contract to sell goods.

After dissolution, a partner would have authority to arrange for shipping those goods in accordance with the existing contract. However, he or she would not have authority to make new contracts without the consent of the other partners, unless these contracts were in furtherance of liquidating the business. Thus the partner probably would be authorized to make contracts for the sale of existing inventory. Similarly, he or she usually would be able to do such things as hire an accountant to take inventory and perform an audit, pay partnership debts and receive payment of obligations owing to the partnership, and make reasonable compromise agreements with debtors and creditors. Obviously a partner's authority to borrow money would be severely restricted after dissolution. Borrowing in order to pay existing obligations would probably be authorized in many situations, but borrowing for any other reason probably would not.

If, instead of liquidating the business, some of the partners intend to continue it as a new partnership or other type of organization, these limitations on authority may cause short-term difficulties. During the changeover period, certain transactions not within the scope of this limited authority may be necessary to keep the business going. In such a case, the consent of *all* partners must be obtained to authorize this kind of transaction.

In the absence of a contrary agreement among the partners, the type of authority still existing after dissolution can be exercised by *any* of the partners. If they choose, however, they can agree that such authority rests only with a certain partner. (The person delegated this type of responsibility is sometimes referred to as the *liquidating partner* or *winding up partner.*) Then, if third parties are so notified, they can hold the partnership liable only if they deal with the designated partner.

Regarding the effect of dissolution, three exceptional situations must be mentioned:

1. Under some circumstances it is important to determine whether the partner transacting business for the partnership after dissolution has *knowledge* of certain facts. If dissolution is caused either by the *act* of any partner (whether in violation of the partnership agreement or not), the *death* of any partner, or the *bankruptcy* of any partner, the partnership will be bound by any transaction made by a partner who *did not know* the facts that caused dissolution.[4] This liability exists even if the transaction was not merely a completion of unfinished business and was not otherwise appropriate for winding up partnership affairs. (Of course, the transaction must be of a type that would have been binding upon the partnership if dissolution had *not* occurred.)

2. In some situations the *absence of notice to third parties* may result in partnership liability for unauthorized transactions entered into after dissolution. If the transaction is of a type that would have bound the partnership if dissolution had

---

[4]Sec. 3 of the UPA makes a distinction between *knowledge* and *notice.* However, we feel that this distinction makes no difference in the majority of cases and that its technicality is of too refined a nature for our discussion.

not taken place, the firm will be liable for it *after* dissolution if the third party being dealt with has not been properly notified of the dissolution. If, before dissolution, the third party has extended credit to the partnership, a transaction with this person after dissolution will bind the partnership unless he or she is proven to have had knowledge of the dissolution. The best way to prevent such a possibility is to directly notify all the partnership's creditors that dissolution has occurred. Since their names and addresses will almost certainly be in the partnership records, no undue inconvenience will result. If the third party had not extended credit to the partnership in the past but did know of its existence prior to dissolution, *the partnership is not liable for transactions with that party* made after dissolution if he or she either knows of the dissolution or if the fact of dissolution has been advertised in a newspaper of general circulation in those places where the partnership has regularly done business.[5] These rules regarding notice to third parties are simply an application of the principle of *apparent authority.*

3. Under the UPA, the partnership is not bound in any circumstances where the postdissolution transaction is made by a partner who is personally *bankrupt.* In such a case it does not matter whether the third party knows of the partner's bankruptcy or of the resulting dissolution; the UPA's view is that one should know the status of the person with whom one is dealing.

Effect of Dissolution on Existing Liabilities

A cardinal rule of partnership law is that dissolution in and of itself does not alter the existing liabilities of the partnership or of individual partners. In some circumstances the event causing dissolution may also cause a discharge from certain liabilities, but it is not the dissolution itself that causes the discharge. Contracts in force at the time of the event that causes dissolution may or may not be discharged, depending upon the rules of contract law. For instance, the death of a partner might terminate an existing partnership contract if the contract had called for some type of personal service by the deceased partner. And bankruptcy of the partnership will not only result in dissolution but also will discharge partnership liabilities that are in excess of the combined assets of the partnership and all the partners. Whether existing liabilities in other situations will be discharged depends entirely on the circumstances.

Winding Up Partnership Affairs

As indicated earlier, *winding up* is the second and final step after dissolution in the termination of a partnership.

---

[5]Before enactment of the UPA, some courts had recognized other methods of publicizing the dissolution, but the UPA speaks only of advertisement by newspaper.

The Right to Wind Up

The question of which partners have the right to wind up partnership affairs can be determined by agreement of the partners.[6] In the absence of an agreement, all partners have an equal right to settle partnership affairs, with two notable exceptions. A partner who has *wrongfully caused dissolution* and a partner who is *personally bankrupt* do not have the right to exercise any control over the winding up process.

Distribution of Assets

When dissolution has occurred and the business is to be terminated, the winding up process entails such activities as liquidating partnership property (turning it into cash), collecting outstanding accounts, paying outstanding debts, and any other actions required to bring partnership affairs to a close.

After all partnership assets have been liquidated, they are distributed to those having claims against the partnership. The order in which they are distributed is of little importance if the partnership has been profitable and all claims can be paid in full. Where partnership assets are insufficient to completely satisfy all claims, however, the issue obviously becomes quite significant.

As previously noted, when partnership assets are insufficient to pay partnership debts, assets of individual partners can be used insofar as necessary. Before this can happen, however, any claims of that partner's individual creditors must be satisfied.

Claims against the partnership are paid in the following order:

1. First to be paid are claims of outside creditors of the partnership.

2. Next are claims of individual partners for repayment of loans they have made to the partnership. Interest is ordinarily payable unless it had been agreed that the loan would be interest-free.

3. Claims of individual partners for return of contributions they have made to the partnership's working capital are third in line. Interest is not payable on contributions to capital unless the partners had agreed otherwise.

4. If any partnership assets remain after satisfying the other claims these are distributed as profits to the partners in the proportion in which profits were to be shared.

To illustrate: Jones and Smith are partners in the retail clothing business. The partnership has not been profitable and is dissolved. The financial position of the partnership after all assets have been reduced to cash is summarized as follows (assuming no interest payable on partners' loans or capital contributions):

---

[6]If the partners disagree as to who shall wind up, a court may appoint a qualified disinterested third party as a *receiver* to handle the winding up process.

Assets		Liabilities and Partner's Equity		
Cash	$200,000	*Liabilities*		
	$200,000	Accounts payable	$225,000	
		Loans from partners		
		Jones...................	25,000	
		Smith.................	10,000	$260,000
		Partners' equity		
		Jones (contribution to		
		capital)	$50,000	
		Smith (contribution to		
		capital)	50,000	100,000
				$360,000

As we can see, the operations of the partnership have resulted in an overall loss of $160,000. Assuming that losses are to be divided equally, Jones and Smith will each have to personally bear an $80,000 loss. The following summary indicates the personal financial positions of Jones and Smith:

	Jones	Smith
Assets	$150,000	$200,000
Liabilities	−75,000	−250,000
	$75,000	($50,000)

Here we see that Smith is insolvent. Since his individual assets must first be used to pay his individual debts, he is financially unable to pay partnership obligations. As a result, Jones must use his personal assets to pay the remaining partnership debts to partnership creditors. This obligation amounts to $25,000, since partnership accounts payable were $225,000 and partnership assets were $200,000. The losses actually borne by each partner are summarized as follows:

	Jones	Smith
Loans to partnership (unpaid)	$ 25,000	$10,000
Contributions to partnership capital (unreturned)...........................	50,000	50,000
Use of individuals assets to pay partnership creditors	25,000	—
	$100,000	$60,000

Since each partner should have borne a loss of $80,000, Jones now has a claim against Smith for $20,000. Whether this claim will be collectible, as a practical matter, is a problem Jones must face.

Continuing the Business

The business of a partnership is not always terminated after dissolution, even though the partnership as an organization comes to an end. Where the operations of the partnership have been profitable and customer goodwill has been built up, the business will be more valuable as a going concern than it will if it is liquidated. Thus some of the partners may wish to continue the business—and they can do so unless continuation would be illegal for some reason. If they decide to continue, the winding up process will consist primarily of bookkeeping entries and the purchase by continuing partners of the interests of withdrawing partners. Customers may never know there has been any change, unless some change is made in the firm name. And creditors of the dissolved partnership will continue to be creditors of the reorganized partnership.[7]

If the articles of partnership provide for continuing the business after dissolution, these provisions dictate the procedures to be followed. For instance, the articles of partnership may state that withdrawal or death of a partner will not dissolve the partnership. This is not quite what happens, though. Regardless of the articles, withdrawal or death of a partner still causes dissolution. But instead of the business terminating, it is reorganized according to the provisions of the articles that govern the settling of affairs between the continuing partners and the withdrawing one (or the estate of the deceased partner).

When the articles of partnership make no provision for continuing the business, the procedure for doing so is guided by the UPA. In this regard, the UPA makes a distinction between two situations: (1) where dissolution has occurred *without* a wrongful act by any partner, and (2) where it *has been caused* by such a wrongful act.

The most common situations of no wrongful act are dissolution caused by death of a partner or by the withdrawal of a partner in a situation where he or she had the right to do so. In such a case, the continuing partners must immediately settle with the withdrawing partner or the estate of the deceased partner (the term *withdrawing partner* hereafter will also include the estate of a deceased partner) if the latter so desires. If settlement is made *immediately,* it consists only of a payment to the withdrawing partner of an amount equal to the value of that partner's interest in the partnership at the time of dissolution. This, of course, will be his or her share of any existing surplus of partnership asset value (including goodwill) over partnership liabilities. If settlement is *postponed,* the withdrawing partner receives not only the value of his or her interest in the partnership (comput-

---

[7]The situation may be different if the business is reorganized and continued in some form other than a partnership, such as a corporation. In such a case, all those who were partners in the dissolved partnership will be liable for debts incurred by the partnership before dissolution, unless the creditors release them. This is true for those persons continuing the business (who may now be officers, directors, and/or stockholders in the new corporation) and for those who have left it. The corporation itself is a separate legal entity not liable for these old debts unless it assumes them. This frequently occurs, however, because the new corporation ordinarily is controlled by at least some of the former partners, and it will often assume the old debts in return for a release by creditors of the former partners.

ed as of the moment of dissolution) but also an additional amount to compensate for the delay. The additional amount is computed in one of two ways, depending on the choice of the withdrawing partner—either as *interest* on the amount due since dissolution or as an amount equal to that partner's proportionate share of partnership *profits* earned since dissolution.

In the second situation, where dissolution has been caused by a partner's wrongful act, somewhat different rules are applied. The wrongfully withdrawing partner is still entitled to receive the value of his or her interest in the partnership, but the value of partnership *goodwill* is not included in computing this value. Further, the damages caused by the wrongful dissolution are deducted from the total amount. If settlement is not made immediately, the rules for compensating the withdrawing partner for the delay are the same as in the first situation.

Notice of dissolution to third parties is as important when the business is continued as when it is terminated. Those continuing the business must take it upon themselves to provide proper notification (as explained earlier). If they do not, they may be bound by certain later acts of a former partner who has left the business. Also, if those continuing the business reorganize it as a *corporation* rather than as another partnership, they will need to notify their business creditors of the change in status. If this is not done, and new obligations to these creditors are incurred (the creditors still thinking they are dealing with a partnership), the former partners might find themselves personally liable for the new obligations as if they were still partners. If proper notice is given, of course, they will be able to claim the limited liability that is enjoyed by those who are officers, directors, or stockholders in a corporation.

The following two cases illustrate the application of several important legal principles regarding the dissolution and winding up of partnerships.

Smith v. Kennebeck

Supreme Court of Missouri, 502 S.W.2d 290 (1973)

Thomas Smith and his brother, Charles, formed a partnership in 1963. On February 11, 1964, they dissolved this partnership and formed a new one with Kennebeck as an additional partner. The new partnership agreement provided that ownership ratios would be: Thomas Smith, 50 percent; Charles Smith, 25 percent; and Kennebeck, 25 percent. It was agreed that the value of assets transferred from the old partnership to the new one was $15,000. Kennebeck contributed $5,000, so that the new partnership began with assets of $20,000.

The new partnership operated for several months, until November 10, 1964, when Thomas Smith and Kennebeck notified Charles Smith that they were dissolving the partnership and forming a corporation to operate the business. Charles did not want the partnership dissolved. Thomas and Kennebeck offered Charles the same 25 percent interest in the proposed corporation that he had in the partnership and a salary of $100 per week (he had been paid $75 by the partnership). Charles did not accept their offer.

After this dissolution against Charles's wishes, Thomas and Kennebeck continued the business. They employed Bo-Tax Co., which had been doing bookkeeping work for the partnership, to compute the value of Charles's interest in the partnership as of the date of dissolution, November 10, 1964. Although the value of Charles's interest as agreed in the articles of partnership was $5,000, Bo-Tax computed the value as $2,646. The statement prepared by Bo-Tax showed the profit only to November 10, 1964, even though work was apparently in process on previously received orders and was completed after that date. (Records of work in process were not given to Bo-Tax by Thomas and Kennebeck.) There was also evidence of profit on completed orders as of November 10 which was not included.

When they were unable to settle their dispute, Charles filed suit against his brother Thomas and against Kennebeck, asking the court to formally dissolve the partnership, to require winding up, and to order a formal accounting and determination of the value of Charles's share. The testimony at the trial included the following statement by Thomas Smith:

Q. Did you make a full and complete inventory of everything on hand on the date of dissolution?

A. I found out since then that we missed a few things but I felt if Charley had an objection he should hire an accountant; I felt this was something he should have to do. He was going to do it anyway, no doubt.

The trial court held that there had been a dissolution and a valid winding up, and that Charles, the plaintiff, was entitled only to the amount computed by Bo-Tax. Charles appealed.

Hyde, Justice: . . . "Winding up" means the administration of the assets for the purpose of terminating the business and discharging the obligations of the partnership to its members. In this case instead of administration of the partnership assets, it appears the two remaining partners kept all the partnership assets and continued the business, only making plaintiff an offer for his share which appears to be based on an inadequate estimate of the value of his interest.

The Bo-Tax Co. computation does not appear to be a proper basis for determining plaintiff's interest. The Bo-Tax agent who made it was not a certified public accountant. It was reviewed by Ernst & Ernst, who did not examine the books of the partnership, and their report shows the Bo-Tax accountant had not seen a copy of the partnership agreement which stated the value of plaintiff's capital interest at $5,000. Moreover, it states profits only through November 10, 1964 and does not consider profits on uncompleted work on contracts on hand at that time or all profits on completed contracts. The [trial] court apparently considered the Bo-Tax statement to be a "winding up" account as it found plaintiff only "entitled to the value of his share as computed on November 10, 1964." We cannot hold that was a valid "winding up" of the partnership [or] that plaintiff was only entitled to the amount shown by it. It is insufficient not only because it did not take into consideration the work on then existing contracts but also because the individual defendants continued the business as partners until its incorporation and then had the corporation continue it without any other offers or effort to settle plaintiff's claim for his interest. Plaintiff brought this action, in less than a month after defendants' articles of incorporation were signed. Plaintiff asked, among other relief sought, that the court wind up the partnership by appointment of a receiver. It is said in Crane and Bromberg, Law of Partnership (1968) § 83A: "A partner may compel liquidation after dissolution 'unless otherwise agreed.' " This was included in the relief plaintiff sought. . . .

Since our view is that the evidence fails to show there ever was a valid winding up of the partnership but instead shows a continuation of the business without plaintiff's consent, plaintiff's rights were as stated in Crane and Bromberg Law of Partnership § 86:

> The situation changes if the business is not [terminated] but continued, whether with or without agreement. In either case [that is, with or without agreement], the noncontinuing partner (or his representative) has a *first election* between two basic alternatives, either of which can be enforced in an action for an accounting. He can force a liquidation, taking his part of the proceeds and thus sharing in profits and losses after dissolution. Alternatively, he can permit the business to continue (or accept the fact that it has continued) and claim as a creditor (though subordinate to outside creditors) the value of his interest at dissolution. This gives him a participation in all values at dissolution, including asset appreciation and good will, and means he is unaffected by later changes in those values. If he takes the latter route, he has a *second election* to recover in addition either interest (presumably at the local legal rate) or profits from date of dissolution.

In a recent Illinois case, *Polikoff v. Levy,* 270 N.E.2d 540, 547 (1971), involving dissolution of a joint venture which the court held was governed by substantially the same rules which govern a partnership, it was said: "In an accounting on dissolution of a partnership or co-venture, the same type of account is required as that of a trustee. The account should list all receipts and disbursements made and the original vouchers, bills and cancelled checks should be tendered or available for inspection to support the items listed. It should include a listing of original contributions and current assets and liabilities." No such accounting was made or offered in this case and the evidence shows the Bo-Tax figures were inadequate to be the kind of accounting required. . . .

Although defendants offered plaintiff an interest in the corporation equal to his interest in the partnership he had no obligation to accept it and his refusal did not affect his right to have the partnership properly wound up. It certainly appears that there was work in process and orders on hand as well as some completed orders which were not taken into consideration in determining the amount of plaintiff's interest by the Bo-Tax statement; and this was the only basis for the amount offered plaintiff for his interest and found by the [trial] court to be the amount due him. Therefore, we must hold there was no valid winding up of the partnership and that the true value of plaintiff's interest must be determined.

Reversed and remanded.

Cauble v. Handler

Court of Civil Appeals
of Texas, 503 S.W.2d
362 (1974)

Tom Handler, the defendant, and Thomas Cauble were partners in the retail furniture and appliance business, each owning a 50 percent interest. Thomas Cauble died and Anice Cauble, administratrix of his estate, brought this suit against Handler. In the suit the administratrix, as plaintiff, asked for an accounting of partnership assets.

After the trial court rendered judgment allowing recovery by plaintiff in a certain amount, she appealed, claiming primarily that the trial court had erroneously used book value in computing the deceased partner's share and in refusing to allow recovery of a share of the profits made by Handler since Cauble's death.

Brewster, Justice: . . . The [trial] court erred when he used the cost price or book value of the partnership assets in determining the value of the inventory. The following is from the opinion in the case of *Johnson v. Braden,* 286 S.W.2d 671: . . . "Market values of the company assets are wholly absent from the record, and Johnson, on cross-examination, demonstrated that the plaintiff's audit was based on book values. *It should have been based on market value.*" (Emphasis added [by the court.]) . . .

[B]ook values are simply arbitrary values and cannot be used. . . .

The defendant contends that plaintiff offered no evidence during the trial tending to establish the reasonable cash market value of the partnership assets at date of dissolution and that the burden of proof was on the plaintiff to establish such value. He contends that since the record contains no evidence as to the market value of the inventory that the court's action in using book or cost value could not be reversible error.

We agree that the burden of proof in this accounting case was on the plaintiff to show that Handler was indebted to the deceased's estate and to show the amount of such debt. Plaintiff thus had the burden to prove the market value of the partnership assets.

When the estate of a deceased partner sues the surviving partner for an accounting of partnership assets the burden of proof is upon the plaintiff to prove the amount for which the surviving partner should account to the deceased's estate. Once the amount that should be accounted for is established, it then becomes the duty of the surviving partner to account to or to pay to the estate of the deceased partner that sum. . . .

We do not agree, however, that there was no legitimate evidence offered during the trial that could be properly considered by the trial court on the issue of market value of the partnership inventory involved.

Prior to trial time the learned trial court had, pursuant to plaintiff's motion, appointed an auditor . . . to state the account between the parties and to make a report thereof to the court.

During the trial the plaintiff offered in evidence Exhibit B of the auditor's report which read as follows: "Inventory as of May the 18th, 1971, inventory at lower cost or market, $90,227.61." This constituted some legitimate evidence as to the market value of the inventory at the time in question.

Much of plaintiff's argument . . . is devoted to her contention that the trial court erred in failing and refusing to allow her a share of the profit made by Handler by continuing the partnership business between date of dissolution and date of judgment.

We sustain this contention.

The undisputed evidence shows that Handler continued to operate and to control the partnership business after the death of Cauble and down to the trial date, and that he used and sold the assets of the partnership during all that period. The record does not show that this was done with the consent of the administratrix of the deceased's estate.

Exhibit E of the court appointed auditor's report was offered into evidence and it showed that during the period from May 19, 1971, to May 21, 1972, Handler made a net profit of $40,163.42 out of operating the partnership business after dissolution. The fact that this net profit was made is undisputed. As demonstrated above this auditor's report was legitimate evidence of the amount of those profits. . . .

The trial court, in its judgment, refused to allow the plaintiff to recover one-half of the profits that were made by Handler after the dissolution of the partnership by his continued operation of the business. Instead the trial court awarded plaintiff a recovery of some interest in the amount of $3,764.89. . . .

[T]he representative of the estate of the deceased partner [had] the right to elect, if she so desired, to have the partners assets liquidated, the debts paid, and the share of [the deceased] partner in the surplus paid to [her] in cash.

The plaintiff in this case did not elect to have this done. . . .

[The court then quoted from "Law of Partnership" by Crane and Bromberg, as follows:]

> Alternatively, he can permit the business to continue (or accept the fact that it has continued) and claim as a creditor (though subordinate to outside creditors) the value of his interest at dissolution. This . . . means he is unaffected by later changes in those values. *If he takes the latter route, he has a second election to receive in addition* either interest . . . *or profits from date of dissolution.* This second election shields him from losses . . . .

> The second election may seem one-sided. It serves as "a species of compulsion . . . to those continuing the business . . . to hasten its orderly winding up." In part it is compensation to the outgoing partner for his liability on partnership obligations existing at dissolution; this liability continues until satisfaction, which would normally occur in the process of winding up. . . .

> The second election rests partly on the use of the outgoing partner's assets in the conduct of the business. . . . [H]is right to profits ends when the value of his interest is properly paid to him. (Emphasis added [by the court.])

Section 42 of . . . the Texas Uniform Partnership Act . . . gives the representative of the estate of a deceased partner a right to share in the profits, if he elects to do so, if the other partner continues to operate the business after dissolution.

The great weight of authority is to the effect that Sec. 42, . . . giving the option to take profits to the noncontinuing partner, is applicable regardless of whether the business is continued with or without the consent of the noncontinuing partner or the representative of his estate. . . .

It is manifestly clear that the plaintiff in this case elected, as she had a right to do under Sec. 42, to have the value of Cauble's partnership interest at the date of dissolution ascertained and to receive from the surviving partner, Handler, as an ordinary creditor, an amount equal to the value of Cauble's interest in the dissolved partnership at date of dissolution, plus the profits attributable to his right in the property of the dissolved partnership. . . .

Although the undisputed evidence showed that Handler made over $40,163.42 by operating the partnership business after dissolution, the Court refused to allow plaintiff to recover from Handler the Cauble estate's share of those profits, which plaintiff had a right to do. In lieu of profits, which plaintiff elected to recover, the Court awarded her six percent interest on what he found to be the cost or book value of the Cauble interest in the partnership at date of dissolution. This . . . amounted to $3,764.89, which sum was considerably less than [one-half of] the $40,163.42 in profits that Handler made out of his operation of the partnership business after dissolution.

This error was obviously prejudicial to plaintiff.

Reversed and remanded for a new trial.

Questions and Problems

1. Discuss the difference between the terms *dissolution* and *winding up.*

2. Henderson and Alden were partners in a partnership that owned and operated a chain of movie theaters. Alden died, and his widow, who was his sole heir, informed Henderson

that she would take her husband's place as a partner in the business. Henderson would not agree to this. Mrs. Alden stated that, as an alternative to becoming a partner, she would simply take half of the theaters in the chain, since her husband had owned a one-half interest in the partnership. Henderson refused to agree to this proposal and insisted on buying her interest even though the partnership agreement between Henderson and Alden had said nothing about the purchase of a deceased partner's interest. What is the effect of Alden's death on the partnership? Discuss.

3. In Question 2, what rights does Henderson have after Alden's death? Explain.

4. In Question 2, what rights does Alden's widow have regarding the partnership? Discuss.

5. What is the nature of a partner's authority to bind the partnership after dissolution? Give three examples of actions that might fall within the scope of this authority.

6. Does the fact that a partnership is dissolved necessarily mean that the business itself will cease to operate? Explain.

7. Parsons and Raymond were partners in the construction business. The business was not successful and the partnership was dissolved. After all the partnership's assets were liquidated, the partnership had a cash balance of $400,000 and accounts payable of $500,000. A $60,000 loan from Parsons to the partnership remained unpaid, and the unreturned capital contributions of Parsons and Raymond to the partnership were $75,000 and $50,000, respectively. Parsons had personal assets of $800,000 and liabilities of $400,000. Raymond had personal assets of $300,000 and liabilities of $200,000. Assuming that losses are to be divided equally, how much of each partner's assets should be used to pay partnership creditors? Explain.

8. In Question 7, how would your answer change if Raymond's liabilities were $250,000 instead of $200,000? Explain.

9. A partnership was created by Atkins, Benson, and Collier, who agreed to share profits equally. Nothing was agreed as to the sharing of losses. The partners decided to dissolve the partnership after a year of operation, at which time the partnership's books revealed the following: Atkins had loaned the partnership $10,000 and had made a capital contribution of $20,000; Benson had made a $10,000 capital contribution; Collier had made no capital contribution; the partnership had assets of $80,000 and owed outside creditors $55,000. Explain how distribution of assets should be made to the partnership's creditors and to the partners.

10. What is the proper basis for valuation of partnership assets after dissolution? Discuss.

35

Corporations/
Nature and Formation

**The Nature of
the Corporation**

Suppose for a moment that you have been given the authority to create a new organizational form for conducting a business enterprise. You probably would want to create an artificial being with a legally recognized identity of its own, so that it could make contracts, own property, sue and be sued, and do all the other things necessary for running a business. This artificial being, having existence only on paper but nevertheless recognized by law as a "person," could have perpetual existence. It would be completely unfettered by the limitations of a flesh-and-blood existence. There would be no worries about death and its effect upon the continuing vitality of the business. True, it would have to act through human agents, but these agents could be replaced with no effect on the artificial being.

You probably would want the ownership of this new organizational form to rest in the hands of investors who would have no management responsibilities. In this way, an investor's interest in the business could be sold to another investor with no effect on the operation of the enterprise. And management would be centralized, thus improving the efficiency of the business.

Investors could be attracted by making their ownership interests freely transferable and by shielding them from liability for business debts. The possibilities for raising capital would be practically endless. New shares in the ownership of the business could be issued as needed for capital requirements; and if the business had been successful, investors would buy them.

But despite the worthiness of your creation, it possesses one fatal flaw: it is not new. It has already been conceived of and put into practice. *It is called a corporation.*

Historical Background

The concept of granting legal recognition to a group of individuals was developed to a very limited degree in Babylonian law as early as the twenty-first century B.C. More formal acceptance of the idea is found in ancient Roman law, although its application to commercial ventures was yet to come. At this time, the organizations acknowledged by the sovereign were formed primarily for religious, educational, governmental, and other noncommercial purposes.

Under canon law (the law of the Roman Catholic church), the corporation was employed by the church as a convenient vehicle for property ownership. Indeed, canon law made an extremely important theoretical contribution in the thirteenth century, when Pope Innocent IV developed the concept of the corporation as an artificial person legally separate from the natural persons composing it.

Recognition of the corporation in English common law had evolved to a fairly sophisticated state by the fourteenth century. However, the corporation had not yet been substantially utilized for commercial purposes; its use as an instrument of commerce did not become commonplace in England until the sixteenth century. Shortly thereafter, in the seventeenth century, the "concession theory" appeared in English law, treating the corporation as a concession of the government and thus justifying increased regulation and taxation.

The famous overseas trading companies of the sixteenth and seventeenth centuries, such as Hudson's Bay Company and the British East India Company, were chartered by the English government for purposes of exploration, colonization, and foreign trading. These companies, which were given substantial governmental powers and many trading privileges, became the models for our present-day business corporations.

During the first few decades after the Revolutionary War, corporations in the United States were formed only by special acts of state legislatures. In the nineteenth century, however, states began to enact "general incorporation" laws, under which persons could form corporations by following specified procedures and without special legislative action. By the end of that century general incorporation was the established rule.

The federal government can also charter corporations—insofar as it is "necessary and proper" for carrying out other express federal powers. Examples of federally chartered corporations are the national banks, the Tennessee Valley Authority, and the American Red Cross. Additionally, many of the federal regulatory statutes, such as the securities, antitrust, and labor laws, weigh heavily upon the operations of corporations. However, despite increasing involvement by the federal government in the affairs of corporations, their organization and operation are still largely a matter of state law. Each state has its own corporation laws, and they are not entirely uniform. The Model Business Corporation Act (hereafter referred to as the Model Act), drafted by the American Bar Association in 1946 and substantially revised in 1969, has provided a basic guideline for the modern corporation laws of over half the states. In the remaining states, the basic principles of corporation law are sufficiently similar that they can be discussed with some degree of generalization.

The Corporation as a Legal Entity

Perhaps the most important characteristic of the corporation is its recognition as a legal entity—an artificial being or person. This has many ramifications, the most important of which are discussed below.

Normal Business Operations: The corporation can own property, make contracts, sue and be sued in court, and generally perform all normal functions that an individual can perform.

Liability for Debts: The individuals who own the corporation (the "stockholders" or "shareholders") and those who manage it (the "officers" and members of the "board of directors") generally are not personally liable for its debts. Conversely, the corporation is not liable for the personal debts of those who own and manage it. The legal identity of the corporation is thus distinct from the identities of its owners and managers. (Of course, these individuals can assume personal liability for corporate obligations if they so choose.)

Procedural and Jurisdictional Matters: Recognition of the corporation as a separate entity also can play an important role in certain procedural and jurisdictional maters. For instance, one basis for federal court jurisdiction is "diversity of citizenship," where the plaintiff and defendant in a lawsuit are citizens of different states. For this purpose, a corporation is deemed to be a citizen of both the state where it was incorporated and the state where it has its principal place of business (if a different state). This principle holds true without regard to the citizenship of those who own and manage the corporation.

Income Taxation: The income of the corporation is taxed under the federal income tax laws. And because the corporation and its shareholders have separate identities, the distribution of this income to shareholders as "dividends" is again taxed, this time as personal income to the individuals receiving it. In 1958, however, Congress lessened the burden of this "double taxation" with respect to *Subchapter S corporations.* If certain requirements are met, the corporation can choose to be taxed in the same manner as a partnership. In other words, *the corporation itself pays no income tax,* but each shareholder's portion is taxed as *personal income* to that person.[1] Several requirements must be met for qualification as a Subchapter S corporation, the most important of which are:

1. There must be fifteen or fewer shareholders (though there is no limit on the amount of assets).

2. All shareholders must be individuals or estates of individuals. Thus a partnership or another corporation cannot be a shareholder in a Subchapter S corporation.

3. There must be only one class of stock.[2]

4. All shareholders must file a written consent with the Internal Revenue Service.

Constitutional Rights: As a "person," the corporation enjoys many of the same rights and privileges under the Constitution that are granted to individuals. For example, it has the right to be secure from "unreasonable searches and seizures"; the right not to be deprived of life, liberty, or property without "due process of law"; the right not to be tried twice for the same offense ("double jeopardy"); and the right not to be denied "equal protection of the laws." On the other hand, the corporation does *not* enjoy the privilege against "self-incrimination."

The following case deals with the question of whether a corporation possesses freedom of expression under the first amendment to the Constitution.

The Massachusetts state legislature passed a statute prohibiting corporations from making expenditures "for the purpose of. . .influencing or affecting the vote on any question submitted to the voters, other than one materially affecting any of the property, business or assets of the corporation." The statute further specified that "no question submitted to the voters solely concerning the taxation of the income, property or transactions of individuals shall be deemed materially to affect the property, business or assets of the corporation." Maximum criminal penalties for violating the statute were a fine of $50,000 against the corporation and a fine of $10,000 and/or one year's imprisonment for any responsible officer, director, or agent of the corporation.	**First National Bank of Boston v. Bellotti** U.S. Supreme Court, 98 S.Ct. 1407 (1978)

This statute was passed to exclude corporations from the public debate concerning a voter referendum on a Massachusetts constitutional amendment to permit a state income tax. Although the proposed tax would be on the income of *individuals,* not corporations, The First National Bank of Boston and several other corporations wanted to publicly express their opposition to it. Bellotti, the Massachusetts Attorney General, notified these corporations that he would enforce the statute against them if they carried out their plans. The corporations filed suit in a Massachusetts state court against Bellotti, claiming that the statute was unconstitutional. The Massachusetts courts ruled against the corporations and they appealed from the

---

[1]Each shareholder pays federal income tax on his or her proportionate share of the income regardless of whether it is actually received.

[2]Classes of stock will be discussed in Chapter 37.

highest state court to the U.S. Supreme Court. In the Supreme Court's opinion which follows, the corporations are referred to as "appellants" and Bellotti as "appellee."

Powell, Justice: . . . In appellants' view, the enactment of a graduated personal income tax, as proposed to be authorized by constitutional amendment, would have a seriously adverse effect on the economy of the State. The importance of the referendum issue to people and government of Massachusetts is not disputed. Its merits, however, are the subject of sharp disagreement.

As the Court said in *Mills v. Alabama,* 384 U.S. 214, 218 (1966), "there is practically universal agreement that a major purpose of the First Amendment was to protect the free discussion of governmental affairs." If the speakers here were not corporations, no one would suggest that the State could silence their proposed speech. It is the type of speech indispensable to decisionmaking in a democracy, and this is no less true because the speech comes from a corporation rather than an individual. The inherent worth of the speech in terms of its capacity for informing the public does not depend upon the identity of its source, whether corporation, association, union, or individual.

The court below nevertheless held that corporate speech is protected by the First Amendment only when it pertains directly to the corporation's business interests. In deciding whether this novel and restrictive gloss on the First Amendment comports with the Constitution and the precedents of this Court, we need not survey the outer boundaries of the Amendment's protection of corporate speech, or address the abstract question whether corporations have the full measure of rights that individuals enjoy under the First Amendment. The question in this case, simply put, is whether the corporate identity of the speaker deprives this proposed speech of what otherwise would be its clear entitlement to protection. We turn now to that question. . . .

[The statute] permits a corporation to communicate to the public its views on certain referendum subjects—those materially affecting its business—but not others. It also singles out one kind of ballot question—individual taxation—as a subject about which corporations may never make their ideas public. The legislature has drawn the line between permissible and impermissible speech according to whether there is a sufficient nexus, as defined by the legislature, between the issue presented to the voters and the business interests of the speaker.

In the realm of protected speech, the legislature is constitutionally disqualified from dictating the subjects about which persons may speak and the speakers who may address a public issue. If a legislature may direct business corporations to "stick to business," it also may limit other corporations—religious, charitable, or civic—to their respective "business" when addressing the public. Such power in government to channel the expression of views is unacceptable under the First Amendment. Especially where, as here, the legislature's suppression of speech suggests an attempt to give one side of a debatable public question an advantage in expressing its views to the people, the First Amendment is plainly offended. Yet the State contends that its action is necessitated by governmental interests of the highest order. We next consider these asserted interests. . . .

. . . Appellee advances two principal justifications for the prohibition of corporate speech. The first is the State's interest in sustaining the active role of the individual citizen in the electoral process and thereby preventing diminution of the citizen's confidence in government. The second is the interest in protecting the rights of shareholders whose views differ from those expressed by management on behalf of the corporation. However weighty these interests may be in the context of partisan candidate elections, they either are not implicated in this case or are not served at all, or in other than a random manner, by the prohibition in [this statute.]

Preserving the integrity of the electoral process, preventing corruption, and sustaining the active, alert reponsibility of the individual citizen in a democracy for the wise conduct of government are interests of the highest importance. Preservation of the individual citizen's confidence in government is equally important.

Appellee advances a number of arguments in support of his view that these interests are endangered by corporate participation in discussion of a referendum issue. They hinge upon the assumption that such participation would exert an undue influence on the outcome of a referendum vote, and—in the end—destroy the confidence of the people in the democratic process and the integrity of government. According to appellee, corporations are wealthy and powerful and their views may drown out other points of view. If appellee's arguments were supported by record or legislative findings that corporate advocacy threatened imminently to undermine democratic processes, thereby denigrating rather than serving First Amendment interests, these arguments would merit our consideration. But there has been no showing that the relative voice of corporations has been overwhelming or even significant in influencing referenda in Massachusetts, or that there has been any threat to the confidence of the citizenry in government. . . .

To be sure, corporate advertising may influence the outcome of the vote; this would be its purpose. But the fact that advocacy may persuade the electorate is hardly a reason to suppress it: The Constitution protects expression which is eloquent no less than that which is unconvincing. . . . Moreover, the people in our democracy are entrusted with the responsibility for judging and evaluating the relative merits of conflicting arguments. They may consider, in making their judgment, the source and credibility of the advocate. But if there be any danger that the people cannot evaluate the information and arguments advanced by appellants, it is a danger contemplated by the Framers of the First Amendment. In sum, a restriction so destructive of the right of public discussion, without greater or more imminent danger to the public interest than existed in this case, is incompatible with the freedoms secured by the First Amendment.

Finally, the State argues that [the statute] protects corporate shareholders, an interest that is both legitimate and traditionally within the province of state law. The statute is said to serve this interest by preventing the use of corporate resources in furtherance of views with which some shareholders may disagree. This purpose is belied, however, by the provisions of the statute, which are both under- and over-inclusive.

The under-inclusiveness of the statute is self-evident. Corporate expenditures with respect to a referendum are prohibited, while corporate activity with respect to the passage or defeat of legislation is permitted, even though corporations may engage in lobbying more often than they take positions on ballot questions submitted to the voters. Nor does [the statute] prohibit a corporation from expressing its views, by the expenditure of corporate funds, on any public issue until it becomes the subject of a referendum, though the displeasure of disapproving shareholders is unlikely to be any less.

The fact that a particular kind of ballot question has been singled out for special treatment undermines the likelihood of a genuine state interest in protecting shareholders. It suggests instead that the legislature may have been concerned with silencing corporations on a particular subject.

Nor is the fact that [the statute] is limited to banks and business corporations without relevance. Excluded from its provisions and criminal sanctions are entities or organized groups in which numbers of persons may hold an interest or membership, and which often have resources comparable to those of large corporations. Minorities in such groups or entities may have interests with respect to institutional speech quite comparable to those of minority shareholders in a corporation. Thus the exclusion of Massachusetts business trusts, real estate investments trusts, labor unions, and other associations undermines the plausibility of the State's purported concern for the persons who happen to be shareholders in the banks and corporations covered by [the statute.]

The over-inclusiveness of the statute is demonstrated by the fact that [it] would prohibit a corporation from supporting or opposing a referendum proposal even if its shareholders unanimously authorized the contribution or expenditure. Ultimately shareholders may decide, through the procedures of corporate democracy, whether their corporation should engage in debate on public issues. Acting through their power to elect the board of directors or to insist upon protective provisions in the corporation's charter, shareholders normally are presumed competent to protect their own interests. In addition to intra-corporate remedies, minority shareholders generally have access to the judicial remedy of a derivative suit to challenge corporate disbursements alleged to have been made for improper corporate purposes or merely to further the personal interests of management.

Assuming, *arguendo,* that protection of shareholders is a "compelling" interest under the circumstances of this case, we find no substantially relevant correlation between the governmental interest asserted and the State's effort to prohibit appellants from speaking.

Because [the statute] prohibits protected speech in a manner unjustified by a compelling state interest, it must be invalidated.

Reversed.

Comment: The contribution of corporate funds to political parties and candidates for public office has also caused controversy over the extent of a corporation's constitutional rights. Many state statutes forbid such contributions in connection with state political elections. In addition, the Federal Elections Campaign Act prohibits corporate campaign contributions in connection with federal elections. Campaign contributions are, in fact, a form of expression protected by the Constitution. However, these statutes have been upheld as a permissible limitation on corporate speech. The courts have ruled that the risks of corrupting the political process by corporate campaign contributions are substantial enough to justify the limitation of corporate rights. The risk of corruption has been viewed as greater in the case of campaign contributions than in the case of corporate participation in public political debate.

Disregarding the Corporate Entity

The general rule that a corporation possesses an identity separate from its owners and managers is almost always applied. In some unusual circumstances, however, courts may ignore the separate status of the corporation and its owners. This disregard of the corporate identity, which is sometimes referred to as "piercing the corporate veil," occurs most often when the corporation is used as a vehicle for *perpetrating a fraud or other prohibited act.* The court will not allow the separateness of the corporate identity to be used merely as a tool to accomplish an illegitimate objective. Suppose, for example, that the sole or principal shareholder of the corporation sets fire to corporate property, and the corporation then sues to recover on its fire insurance policy. The court will disregard the separateness of the corporation and the shareholder and will not allow the corporation to recover from the insurance company.

Another situation in which a court will probably disregard the corporate entity occurs when the corporation has been formed with insufficient capital to meet reasonably expectable business obligations *and* the shareholders themselves have intermingled and confused their personal identities with the corporation's identity. This confusion might, for instance, take the form of intermingling corporate and personal funds or failing to maintain corporate records separate from personal records. In such a case, an unpaid corporate creditor who is harmed by the inadequacy of corporate assets may be able to reach the personal assets of stockholders to satisfy its claim.

Corporations are sometimes formed by a single individual or by several members of a family who own all the stock. This fact by itself will not cause a court to ignore the separateness of the corporation from its owners; one-person and family-owned corporations are entirely permissible. However, those situations in which courts disregard the separateness of the corporation are much more likely to occur when a one-person or family-owned enterprise is involved.

Subsidiary corporations. Often a corporation, as the "parent," forms or acquires another corporation as a "subsidiary" for some particular purpose. Even if the parent corporation owns most or all of the stock in the subsidiary, and even if the officers and directors of the two corporations are the same, the parent and its subsidiary are normally viewed by the law as *separate entities.* Care must be taken, however, to maintain this separateness, specifically:

1. All required formalities should be followed in separately incorporating and operating the subsidiary.

2. The subsidiary should be financed with sufficient capital to meet its reasonably foreseeable business needs.

3. All business transactions and business records of the two corporations should be kept separate.

4. Advertising and other public statements should not intermingle or confuse the separate identities of the two.

Failure to observe any of the above precautions may in some cases lead a court to disregard the separateness of the parent and subsidiary and to treat them as a single entity. This could result in the parent being held liable for the debts of the subsidiary or for wrongful acts of the subsidiary's managers and employees.

The following case illustrates the courts' stern attitude toward those who use the corporation as a mere tool to escape legitimate obligations.

Tigrett v. Pointer

Court of Civil Appeals
of Texas, 580 S.W.2d
375 (1979)

Ruby Tigrett suffered an on-the-job injury while working for Heritage Building Company. In April 1974 she sued the company to recover workmen's compensation benefits. At that time the company liabilities exceeded its assets. On May 1, 1974, substantially all of the corporation's assets were transferred to its president and sole stockholder, Gerald Pointer. This transfer was made in consideration of a reduction of the company's indebtedness to him. On the same day, he transferred the same assets to another one of "his" corporations, Heritage Corporation. No money ever changed hands—it was shown on the books of the transferee, Heritage Corporation, as a loan to it by Pointer in the same amount as the reduction of Pointer's loan to Heritage Building Company.

Tigrett's lawsuit against Heritage Building Company ultimately resulted in a judgment against the company for approximately $20,000. By that time, of course, the company had no assets from which to satisfy the judgment. Tigrett then filed suit against Pointer and Heritage Corporation, the transferee. The trial court held that Pointer and the transferee were not liable, and Tigrett appealed.

Guittard, Chief Justice: . . . Heritage Building Company was chartered in 1955 for the purpose of purchasing, subdividing and selling real estate, erecting and repairing buildings, and accumulating and lending money for these purposes. It was capitalized for $1,000 in cash, and 10,000 shares of stock were issued . . . .

It has been said that each case involving disregard of the corporate entity must rest on its own special facts. . . . Of course, domination of corporate affairs by the sole stockholder does not in itself justify imposition of personal liability. Personal liability may be imposed on the sole stockholder only in extraordinary circumstances. Various statements of the circumstances justifying personal liability are found in judicial opinions, but common to all is the concept that the corporate form may be disregarded when it is used to perpetrate a fraud or is relied on to justify wrong or injustice. . . .

Accordingly, even though corporate formalities have been observed and separate accounts of corporate property kept, one who has dealt with the corporation may challenge the corporate entity by showing that he has been the victim of some basically unfair device by which the corporate form of business organization has been used to achieve an inequitable result. . . .

Among the unfair devices which have been considered in piercing the corporate veil is inadequate capitalization. One authority states that if a corporation carries on a business with so little capital that it is likely to have insufficient assets to pay its debts, it would be inequitable to allow the stockholders to set up such a flimsy organization to escape personal liability. *W. Fletcher, Cyclopedia of the Law of Private Corporations,* §44.1 (1974). Another commentator has pointed out that the policy of the law supporting limited liability is to induce investors to risk their capital in the corporate enterprise, and that to extend limited liability without requiring adequate capital would give the privilege without receiving the benefit of the investment and would have the contrary effect of encouraging entrepreneurs to subject as little of their capital as possible to the risks of the business. Drye, *Inadequate Capitalization as a Basis for Shareholder Liability,* 45 So.Cal.L.Rev. 823, 845 (1972).

Inadequate capitalization by itself may not be a sufficient ground to pierce the corporate veil. Thus, a party who has contracted with a financially weak corporation and is disappointed in obtaining satisfaction of his claim cannot look to the dominant stockholder or parent corporation in the absence of *additional compelling facts.* [Emphasis added.] *Grossly* inadequate capitalization, however, as measured by the nature and magnitude of the corporate undertaking, is an important factor in determining whether personal liability should be imposed. [Emphasis added.] [Pointer argues] that in this case the minimum capitalization of $1,000 was more than adequate for the type of business carried on by Heritage Building Company, since construction projects on real property are generally financed by loans without personal liability, with the realty standing as collateral. This argument is conclusively rebutted by the company's financial statement of April 30, 1974, which shows loans from Pointer to the company aggregating $484,218, designated as "capital." Although Pointer might have been able to carry on the business without advancing the money other than the amount he paid for the stock, he chose not to do so. Instead, he advanced money to the corporation from time to time in the form of loans aggregating more than four hundred times the initial capitalization. These loans were in addition to borrowings secured by liens on real estate and other property held by the company. There is no evidence that the company had ever obtained a loan from a financial institution without full security. It is most unlikely that a commercial lender or any other person without a shareholder's interest would have made such unsecured loans to a company with so little capital. Neither does it appear that Pointer's loans were made at times of financial stress, but rather pursuant to a practice Pointer had followed for many years of advancing funds needed in the company's operations. Pointer testified that he had loaned money to his corporations for years, and one of his employees, who served as a director of all the corporations, testified that all of Pointer's corporations were indebted to him. Thus, the evidence conclusively shows that the initial capital stock was grossly inadequate as compared to the funds which Pointer actually invested in the enterprise.

Another ground for disregarding the corporate entity is a dominant stockholder's preference of himself as a creditor, in violation of his fiduciary duty to an insolvent corporation. [Pointer contends] that a debtor, even though insolvent, may prefer one of several creditors by conveying property in satisfaction of the debt, and insists that the evidence establishes that at the time of the transfer, Heritage Building Company was indebted to Pointer in an amount greater than the value of the assets transferred.

The rule that a debtor may prefer one of several creditors does not apply to an insolvent corporation when it can no longer continue to do business in the usual way. Its assets then become a trust fund for the benefit of all its creditors; consequently, its stockholders have no right, directly or indirectly through the managing officers, to pay or secure some of the creditors at the expense of others. . . .

[As stated earlier, the fundamental question is whether Pointer has used] a basically unfair device by which the fiction of separate corporate personality is likely to be or actually has been used to achieve an inequitable result. Such a device is clearly shown by the undisputed evidence in this case. Pointer organized Heritage Building Company with a minimum of capital stock and advanced the necessary working funds from time to time in the form of loans. When the corporation ran into financial difficulty, he used his dominant position as president, director, and sole stockholder to withdraw substantially all assets from the corporation without making any provision for payment of plaintiff and other creditors. This maneuver was a violation of his fiduciary duty as officer and director of an insolvent corporation to preserve the assets for the benefit of all the creditors. It was particularly inequitable and unfair in that he preferred himself as a creditor, although in view of the inadequate capitalization, his loan to the corporation must be treated as an advance of capital, or, at most, as a claim subordinate to those of other creditors. Although no one of these circumstances, standing alone, would justify piercing the corporate veil, when taken together, they demonstrate conclusively that while Pointer observed the form of the corporate enterprise, he ignored his substantive duties as a corporate officer and director and acted solely in his own interest. Consequently, we hold that the trial court erred in failing to hold him liable individually for the corporation's debts.

[Reversed. Note: Heritage Corporation, to which the assets had been transferred, was held liable along with Pointer because it was dominated by Pointer and was a part of the overall "device."]

Classifications of Corporations

Domestic, Foreign, and Alien Corporations: A corporation that has been incorporated in a particular state is referred to as a *domestic corporation* in that state. One that has been incorporated in some other state is a *foreign corporation,* and one that has been incorporated in another country is an *alien corporation.*

Private and Public Corporations: *Private corporations* are those formed by private parties. (Most corporations fall within this category.) They are usually organized for private business purposes but may be formed for public service purposes as well, such as the supplying of electricity.[3] *Public corporations* are those formed by the government, usually for political or governmental purposes. Incorporated cities and towns are common examples of public corporations. (Even though they are not really public corporations at all, private business corporations whose shares of stock are offered for sale to the public are frequently referred to as "public" or "publicly-held" corporations.)

Nonprofit Corporations: Most private corporations are formed for the purpose of generating profits from some type of business enterprise. Some, however, are formed without a profit-making purpose. *Nonprofit corporations* (sometimes called *not-for-profit* or *eleemosynary corporations*) are in the nature of private charities. Churches, private hospitals, and private universities are frequently organized as nonprofit corporations.

Professional Corporations: Until recently, state corporation laws generally did not allow persons to form corporations for the purpose of engaging in the practice of a profession (law, medicine, and so on). Since 1961, however, most states have enacted statutes allowing the creation of *professional corporations.* Probably the most important result of these statutes has been that practitioners of the professions can now enjoy certain federal tax advantages as "employees" of the corporation that they could not enjoy as sole proprietors or members of a partnership.

Stock and Nonstock Corporations: Although corporations ordinarily issue shares of stock which represent ownership interests in the company, a few do not.

---

[3]Private corporations organized for public service purposes are sometimes referred to as *quasi-public corporations.*

Creation of a so-called "nonstock" corporation usually is done only in the case of a social or charitable organization.

Close Corporations: The *close corporation* is a corporation whose shares of stock are held by either a single shareholder or a small, closely-knit group of shareholders.[4] The shareholders themselves are usually active in managing the business. Since shares of stock in a close corporation are not offered for sale to the public, the raising of capital is usually not the reason for its creation. Instead, the close corporation is most often formed to achieve limited liability or tax advantages for its owners while at the same time retaining the type of control characteristic of a sole proprietorship or partnership.

Promoters' Activities

Formation of the Corporation

For various reasons the word *promoter* sometimes elicits unfavorable reactions from people. The negative connotations of the word are generally unwarranted, though, because promoters usually serve a legitimate and socially useful function. In essence, a promoter is the *motivating force* behind the creation of the corporation. He or she recognizes the business opportunity, analyzes it to determine its economic feasibility, and brings together the necessary resources and personnel.

In planning for the proposed corporation, the promoter often finds it necessary to employ the services of attorneys, accountants, architects, or other professionals. He or she may also have to borrow money or contract for the purchase of real estate, equipment, patent rights, or other property. And in some circumstances the promoter may find it desirable prior to incorporation to contract with persons to serve as officers and employees upon formation of the corporation. Several legal questions can arise in connection with such transactions. For example: Is the promoter personally liable on these contracts? Is the corporation liable once it is formed? The approach taken by the courts is summarized as follows:

1. If the proposed corporation *is* later formed, it can adopt the contract and become a party to it, in which case the corporation itself will be bound. If the promoter makes the agreement in his or her own name, with no reference to the proposed corporation, but intends to assign the contract to the corporation when it is formed, then the promoter obviously continues to be liable after incorporation unless released by the third party. If the promoter has made the agreement in the name of, or with reference to, the proposed corporation, many courts nevertheless hold the promoter personally liable after incorporation unless the third party has indicated an intent to release him or her. The reasoning of these courts is that the promoter made the contract as an *agent for a nonexistent principal.* But some courts have, in the latter situation, held the promoter to be automatically discharged when the corporation is formed and adopts the agreement.

---

[4]It is also variously called a *closed, closely-held, one-person,* or *family corporation.*

2. If the proposed corporation is *not* formed, or if it is formed and does not adopt the agreement, then the promoter usually is personally liable, with certain exceptions:

a. The evidence may indicate to the court that both the promoter and the third party intended only an informal agreement and that neither of them intended to be legally bound if the corporation did not come into existence and become a party.
b. The agreement may expressly provide that the promoter will not be liable if the corporation is not formed or does not adopt the transaction.
c. The third party may later release the promoter from liability.

Many times two or more promoters are involved. Prior to the actual creation of the corporation these promoters are viewed by the law as being engaged in a *joint venture*. As a result, they maintain the same kind of fiduciary relationship that exists between partners. In their dealings with one another they must exercise the highest standards of honesty and openness.

Once the corporation is formed, the promoters also owe the same type of fiduciary responsibility to the corporation itself and to all interested parties. Complete disclosure must be made, for example, to the board of directors and to all investors (shareholders). Promoters are not allowed to make secret profits on the promotional scheme.

The two cases that appear below involve the activities of corporate promoters. The first deals with misuse of corporate assets by a promoter. The second involves a contract between the promoters themselves made prior to incorporation.

Krause v. Mason

Supreme Court of
Oregon, 537 P.2d 105
(1975)

Mr. and Mrs. Mason, defendants, had been engaged in the sale of carpets in Oregon for several years under the name of "Mason Custom Carpets." In March 1973 they approached Mr. and Mrs. Krause, plaintiffs, regarding a business venture for the distribution and sale of "area carpets" (carpets that are cut and bound, not wall-to-wall) in the northwest. Shortly thereafter, the parties formed an Oregon corporation, Golden Age Distributors, Inc., for this purpose. It was agreed that each of the four parties would receive five thousand shares of stock in Golden Age. Plaintiffs were to each pay $5,000 in cash for their shares, and defendants were to each contribute $5,000 worth of carpets for their shares.

Not long after the corporation was formed, one of the defendants, Donald Mason, informed plaintiffs that he was flying to Georgia that weekend to purchase carpets for Golden Age. For this purpose, plaintiffs gave him $7,900 of their personal funds, as part payment for their shares of stock in Golden Age. Mr. Mason used these funds to buy carpets not only for Golden Age but also for his and his wife's own business, Mason Custom Carpets. The carpets bought for the Masons' own business were resold at a profit. (Later, the Masons apparently gave to Golden Age carpets that were the equivalent of those which should have been purchased earlier for Golden Age but which had been purchased for Mason Custom Carpets instead.)

During the next month, plaintiffs asked Mr. Mason for an account of what had been done with the money they had supplied. Mason refused to tell them. Plaintiffs, acting in behalf of the corporation, sued the Masons for misappropriating corporate assets. The trial court ruled for defendants, and plaintiffs appealed to the Oregon Supreme Court.

Bryson, Justice: . . . Defendants' fiduciary duty was breached when defendants used plaintiffs' capital contributions to purchase carpets for their own Mason Custom Carpets and when carpets rightfully belonging to Golden Age were sold by defendants for their private gain.

Defendants were promoters of Golden Age and owed a fiduciary duty to Golden Age. In addition, Donald Mason knew that the $7,900 which he obtained from plaintiffs constituted a portion of plaintiffs' consideration for shares of Golden Age stock and was to be used for the purchase of Golden Age's inventory of carpets.

> It is the duty of the promoters to retain in their hands the property whi ch is to constitute corporate assets until the corporation is formed, . . . and then to turn over to it the assets so held. 1 Fletcher, Cyclopedia of Private Corporations § 192 at 731 –32 (rev. ed. 1963).

Generally, fiduciaries, such as defendants, are liable to account for any gain or profits which they may realize from their breach of a fiduciary duty.

The mere fact that defendants in this case may have subsequently replenished the corporation's supply of carpets with like physical assets does not entitle defendants to retain the profits which they made as a result of their original wrongful conduct. If the physical assets in this case were no longer physically recoverable, defendants would be liable for the entire proceeds of the various sales, including the value of the assets sold and any gain derived therefrom. To permit defendants to retain the profits in this case would reward them for their own wrongdoing. We conclude that the trial court erred in not requiring defendants to account for any profits they may have realized as a result of their breach of duty to the corporation. . . .

Reversed and remanded . . . .

Following the death of her husband, Helen Joplin acquired a retail liquor business, which she operated as a sole proprietorship. She later persuaded Sidney Henderson to join the business. It was agreed that a corporation would be formed, with Henderson purchasing 25 percent of the corporate stock and Joplin receiving 75 percent in return for the assets that she would transfer from the sole proprietorship to the corporation. It was further agreed that Joplin would be president and treasurer of the corporation and Henderson would be vice president, secretary, and general manager. Each was to receive a salary from the corporation of $700 per month.

The corporation was formed in 1967, and the business was prosperous until 1970, when competition became increasingly intense. In late 1970, having become discouraged as to the future prospects of the business, Henderson proposed to Joplin

Henderson v. Joplin
Supreme Court of Nebraska, 217 N.W.2d 920 (1974)

that she buy him out or he buy her out or that they sell to someone else. She refused the offer and fired Henderson. (This she was able to do, of course, because of her controlling interest in the corporation.)

Henderson, plaintiff, sued for breach of contract. The trial court ruled in his favor, and defendant Joplin appealed.

McCown, Justice: . . . The defendant contends that the cause of action for breach of the preincorporation contract belongs to the corporation and not to the plaintiff. She also asserts that agreements between directors or stockholders purporting to control the actions of directors after they are elected in handling the ordinary business of a corporation are void. The modern rule is contrary. 1 Fletcher Cyclopedia Corporations (1963 Rev.Ed.), section 191, page 714, states: "No public policy forbids contracts for promoting and managing a corporation according to law and for lawful purposes or for determining among themselves what the stock shall be and how it shall be divided, or for election of themselves as officers and employment by the corporation when formed."

A large majority of jurisdictions hold that such agreements are not invalid unless inspired by fraud or unless they will prejudice other stockholders. Nebraska has clearly adopted the majority rule where the control agreement was between two stockholders owning a majority of the stock of the corporation. In *E. K. Buck Retail Stores v. Harkert,* 157 Neb. 867, 62 N.W.2d 288, this court said:

> We conclude that stockholders' control agreements are not invalid per se. If they are based on a sufficient consideration between the contracting stockholders they are valid and binding if they do not contravene any express constitutional or statutory provision or contemplate any fraud, oppression, or wrong against creditors or other stockholders, or other illegal object. Where such a situation appears it is not illegal or against public policy for two or more stockholders owning the majority of the shares of stock to unite upon a course of corporate policy, or upon the officers, including directors, whom they will elect.

It is difficult, if not impossible, to put the law as to the liability on promoters' contracts into any definitive terms as to a particular class of contract. Such agreements are covered by the general principles of contract law, and ordinarily, are governed by the intention of the parties as expressed. We think it clear that the agreement here, while technically a preincorporation agreement between promoters, was intended to serve as a stockholders' agreement after incorporation. There is no evidence whatever that there was any fraud or prejudice against anyone, and the two contracting parties were to be and became the holders of all the stock.

This case has many factual similarities to the North Carolina case of *Wilson v. McClenny,* 136 S.E.2d 569. In upholding the validity of a preincorporation agreement between promoters dealing with the designation of officers and directors of a company to be formed, and the salaries to be paid, that court said:

> A competent person, gainfully employed in his chosen field, will not ordinarily give up a secure position to take another with a new enterprise without some assurance as to his future. No corporation could ever be created without a preliminary agreement between the parties proposing to form it as to the mode and manner of doing so. . . . The promoters of a corporation occupy a relation of trust and confidence towards the corporation which they are calling into existence as well as to each other,

and the law requires of them the same good faith it exacts from directors and other fiduciaries. . . . There is no evidence here that the contract between the plaintiff and defendant was not made in good faith or that, at the time it was made, it was not in the best interest of the corporation. Prima facie, it was a valid exercise of the promoters' right to contract.

That case also makes it clear that any agreement of this kind for the employment or continued employment of a corporate officer contains the implied condition that the agreement may be terminated at any time for cause. While there was some attempt to establish cause for the plaintiff's discharge, the jury verdict removes the issue from doubt, and the evidence supports the jury verdict that the plaintiff's employment as general manager . . . was terminated by the defendant without just cause and constituted a breach of the agreement. . . .

Affirmed . . . .

Incorporation

The word *incorporation* refers to the procedural mechanics of forming a corporation. Although the details of these procedures differ from state to state, substantial similarity exists with respect to their basic outline.

Articles of Incorporation: The first step in the formative process is preparation of *articles of incorporation,* a legal document that should be prepared by an attorney and that must be signed by the *incorporators.* A few states require the signature of only one incorporator, but most states follow the traditional requirement of three signatures. The incorporators are those individuals who *technically* apply to the state for incorporation. They must be adults, but they need not have any interest in the business enterprise itself. Often they are the persons actually forming the corporation, but they can be completely disinterested parties (such as secretaries in the office of the attorney who is preparing the articles).

The following is a summary of those matters which generally should be included in the articles of incorporation.

1. *The name of the corporation.* This name cannot be the same as, or deceptively similar to, that of any other corporation legally doing business within the state.

2. *The duration of the corporation.* In most states this can be perpetual. And in the few states that do place limitations on the number of years a corporation can exist, it is usually only a formality to renew the corporation's existence on expiration of the stated time period.

3. *The purpose or purposes for which the corporation is organized.* While most states allow the formation of a business corporation for any lawful purpose, a few still prohibit corporations from practicing medicine, law, or other professions. Also, many states do not allow banks, loan companies, insurance companies, public

utilities, or railroads to be formed under the general incorporation statutes. These types of businesses are often required to incorporate under other, specialized statutes.

4. *The financial structure of the corporation.* Detailed information must usually be included about the methods by which the corporation will raise capital needed for its operations.

5. *Provisions for regulating the internal affairs of the corporation.* Examples of such provisions are the location of shareholders' meetings, quorum and voting requirements at shareholders' and board of directors' meetings, removal of directors, and filling director vacancies.

6. *The address of the corporation's registered office and the name of its registered agent at this address.* The registered office is simply the corporation's official office in the state, and the registered agent is its official representative. The purpose of requiring a corporation to have a registered office and registered agent is to assure that there will be an easily identifiable place and person for the receipt by the corporation of summonses, subpoenas, and other legal documents.

7. *Information relating to the first board of directors of the corporation.* The board of directors is the group of individuals who manage the affairs of the corporation. The number of directors constituting the initial board must be indicated in the articles. Additionally, the articles usually must include the names and addresses of those individuals who will serve as directors until the first annual shareholders' meeting or until another board of directors is otherwise selected.

8. *The name and address of each incorporator.*

Certificate of Incorporation: The articles of incorporation must be filed with the designated state official (usually the secretary of state). If they are in conformance with all legal requirements and if all required fees are paid, the state official will issue a *certificate of incorporation* (sometimes called a *charter*). This certificate represents the permission given by the state to conduct business in the corporate form. The corporation comes into existence when the certificate of incorporation is issued. After issuance, the certificate and an attached copy of the articles of incorporation are returned to the incorporators or their representatives.

Initial Organization: Under the laws of most states, the incorporators must hold an "organizational meeting" after issuance of the charter. In states where the first board of directors is not named in the articles of incorporation, the incorporators elect the directors at this meeting. In all states, authorization will usually be given to the board of directors to issue shares of stock. Perhaps the most important purpose of the meeting, however, is to adopt bylaws.[5]

Bylaws are the rules or "private laws" that regulate and govern the actions and

---

[5]In some states, however, formulation of the initial bylaws is a function of the shareholders, and in others it is a function of the board of directors.

affairs of the corporation. Although they ordinarily are *not* filed with a state official, bylaws must not conflict in any way with the provisions of the articles of incorporation. The relationship between the articles and the bylaws is analogous to the relationship between the constitution and the statutes of a state. A corporation's bylaws sometimes amount to only a brief statement of rules for internal management of the corporation. Often, however, the bylaws are extremely detailed, sometimes even including a restatement of applicable statutes as well as provisions from the articles of incorporation. As an example of the type of details frequently included in the bylaws, many provisions relate to the specifics of conducting directors' and shareholders' meetings.

The board of directors also holds an organizational meeting, at which time it transacts whatever business is necessary to launch the operations of the enterprise. In some states the incorporators do *not* hold an organizational meeting, and in these states the board of directors adopts bylaws and performs the other tasks described earlier as functions of the incorporators. In the states in which incorporators *do* meet, the directors at their initial meeting usually approve all actions taken by the incorporators. In addition, the agenda of the first directors' meeting includes such matters as approval of the corporate seal, election of corporate officers, adoption of preincorporation agreements made by the promoters, selection of a bank for depositing corporate funds, and other pertinent items of business.

Effect of Improper Incorporation Procedures

If all requirements for incorporation have been followed to the letter, it is said that a *de jure corporation* exists. The existence of such a corporation cannot be challenged by either the state or any other party so long as the corporation acts lawfully in the conduct of its business.

Occasionally there occurs some deviation from the procedures required for incorporation. If the deviation is relatively insignificant (in other words, if there is "substantial compliance" with procedures) and if no harm to the public interest results, the corporation still has de jure status. (An example of such an inconsequential procedural defect is a mistake in the address of one of the incorporators in the articles of incorporation.)

On the other hand, the defect may be sufficiently important that there is not substantial compliance with mandatory incorporation procedures. In such a case, there will not be a de jure corporation. There might, however, be what is commonly referred to as a *de facto corporation.* If the corporation has de facto status, the *state* can challenge the validity of its existence, but no other party can do so. (If it has neither de jure nor de facto status, the validity of its existence can be challenged by the state or by any other interested party, such as a creditor seeking to hold a shareholder personally liable for a corporate debt.) The requirements for the existence of a de facto corporation are:

1. There must be a state statute under which the corporation could have been validly incorporated.

2. There must have been a genuine, good-faith attempt by the incorporators to follow statutory requirements.

3. There must have been some type of business transacted by the enterprise *as a corporation.*

Historically, issues relating to de facto corporations have not arisen very frequently, and the importance of the concept in actual practice appears to be further diminishing.

Even if a corporation has neither de jure nor de facto status, particular situations exist where a party can be estopped (prohibited) from denying the validity of its existence. If, for example, the individuals operating a business represent their enterprise as being a corporation, they can be estopped from denying the corporate status in a particular lawsuit. (This concept is often denoted by the phrase *corporation by estoppel.*)

Doing Business in Other States

A corporation that has been incorporated in one state may wish to do business in other states as well. Before doing so, the corporation must apply for and receive a *certificate of authority* in each state where it plans to do business. The process of obtaining the certificate is largely a formality, and the initial steps in applying for it often are taken at the organizational meeting of the board of directors. However, the corporation is also usually required to maintain a registered office and registered agent in each state where it does business.

The penalties levied by various states against foreign corporations that have not obtained a certificate of authority include fines, denial of the privilege of filing lawsuits in the courts of that state, and placement of personal liability for corporate obligations incurred in that state on the directors, officers, or agents involved.

Financing the Corporation

After incorporation, the corporation must obtain the funds necessary to launch and initially operate the business. When the business has been in operation for a substantial period of time, a wider range of financing alternatives are available, including retained earnings, short-term borrowing, and accounts receivable financing. At the beginning, however, fewer alternatives exist.

The principal method of initially financing a corporation is by the issuance of *securities,* which are sold to investors. The board of directors usually authorizes their issuance during its initial organizational meeting. The most common types are "equity securities" and "debt securities."

Equity securities take the form of "shares of capital stock" (often referred to today simply as "shares"). The investors who purchase them (the "shareholders" or "stockholders") are actually the owners of the corporation. That is, each share represents an interest in the ownership of the corporation. If the board of directors assigns a specific value to each share of capital stock, the stock is known as *par value stock;* if no value is fixed, it is called *no-par value stock.* The par value is a completely arbitrary figure and may be only nominal. It may or may not have any relation to the actual value of the stock as reflected by the financial condition of the corporation, and it may or may not have any relation to the amount actually received by the corporation from purchasers of the shares. (More will be said about the various types of shares in Chapter 37.)

Debt securities are usually called "bonds." The investors who purchase them are not purchasing any ownership interest in the corporation. They are instead lending money to the corporation, thereby creating a debtor-creditor relationship.

Registration of Securities

When a corporation issues securities to meet either its initial capital requirements or its later financial needs, it usually must comply with the securities laws of those states in which they are offered for sale.[6] The laws of some states simply prohibit fraud in the sale of securities. In many states, however, the issue of securities must be *registered* with the state agency empowered to administer the law. To register, the corporation must supply extremely detailed financial and other information about itself. These state agencies commonly have broad discretionary powers to pass judgment on the merits of a particular issue of securities—even to forbid such issuance—and penalties for failing to register with them can be quite severe.[7]

Many issues of securities, such as those sold in interstate commerce or through the mails, must also be registered under the Securities Act of 1933, a federal law. Here again, detailed financial and other information must be supplied. This information must be given both to the appropriate federal agency—the Securities and Exchange Commission (SEC)—and to the persons to whom the securities are offered for sale. The SEC does not pass judgment on the merits of a particular issue of securities but attempts only to assure full and complete disclosure of relevant information. The underlying rationale is that the light of publicity will serve to deter misconduct in the sale of securities. Under the Securities Act of 1933, failing to register or willfully making false statements in the registration is punishable by a fine of up to $5,000 and/or imprisonment of up to five years. Civil actions for damages can also be brought by injured private parties.

The purpose of both state and federal securities laws is protection of the investing public. Although compliance with these laws is costly and time-consuming, failure to comply can be even more costly. What is more, the protection afforded by these laws benefits not only the investors but also the corporations themselves by encouraging investment in corporate enterprises.

Both state and federal securities laws provide for certain types of *exemptions* from registration requirements. And because preparation of the required registra-

---

[6]These state laws are often referred to as *blue-sky laws,* because they are largely antifraud statutes intended to prevent the sale of worthless securities ("pieces of the blue sky").

[7]For example, the sale of unregistered securities in the state of Texas is a felony punishable by a fine of up to $5,000 and/or imprisonment for up to ten years.

tion statement involves a substantial expenditure of time and money, corporations are usually eager to take advantage of an exemption if possible. One of the most important exemptions is that provided for *private offerings*. Under the Securities Act of 1933, and under most state laws as well, registration is not required if the securities being issued are not publicly offered for sale. Securities are usually offered for sale to the public only by well-established companies. Newly-organized corporations ordinarily seek funds from a narrower range of investors. Thus, securities issued by well-established companies are more likely to fall within the scope of state and federal regulatory measures. Registration requirements do, however, apply with equal force to the securities of a new corporation unless it can legitimately qualify for an exemption.

The following U.S. Supreme Court decision is the leading one on the private offering exemption.

SEC v. Ralston Purina Co.

U.S. Supreme Court, 346 U.S. 119 (1953)

Ralston Purina Co. offered shares of "treasury stock" for sale to its "key employees." (*Treasury stock* refers to shares that the corporation had sold and then later repurchased.) It did not file a registration statement with the Securities and Exchange Commission. The SEC filed suit in federal district court, seeking an injunction to prevent the unregistered offerings. The district court dismissed the suit, holding that no public offering was involved and thus no registration was required. The court of appeals affirmed, and the SEC appealed to the Supreme Court.

Clark, Justice: . . . Section 4(1) of the Securities Act of 1933 exempts "transactions by an issuer not involving any public offering" from the registration requirements of § 5. We must decide whether Ralston Purina's offerings of treasury stock to its "key employees" are within this exemption. . . .

Ralston Purina manufactures and distributes various feed and cereal products. Its processing and distribution facilities are scattered throughout the United States and Canada, staffed by some 7,000 employees. At least since 1911 the company has had a policy of encouraging stock ownership among its employees; more particularly, since 1942 it has made authorized but unissued common shares available to some of them. Between 1947 and 1951, the period covered by the record in this case, Ralston Purina sold nearly $2,000,000 of stock to employees without registration and in so doing made use of the mails.

In each of these years, a corporate resolution authorized the sale of common stock "to employees . . . who shall, without any solicitation by the Company or its officers or employees, inquire of any of them as to how to purchase common stock of Ralston Purina Company." A memorandum sent to branch and store managers after the resolution was adopted, advised that "The only employees to whom this stock will be available will be those who take the initiative and are interested in buying stock at present market prices." Among those responding to these offers were employees with the duties of artist, bakeshop foreman, chow loading foreman, clerical assistant, copywriter, electrician, stock clerk, mill office clerk, order credit trainee, production trainee, stenographer, and veterinarian. The buyers lived in over fifty widely separated communities scattered from Garland, Texas, to Nashua, New Hampshire and Visalia, California. The lowest salary bracket of those purchasing was $2,700 in 1949, $2,435 in 1950 and $3,107 in 1951. The record shows that in 1947, 243 employees bought stock, 20 in 1948, 414 in 1949, 411 in 1950, and the 1951 offer, interrupted by this litigation, produced 165 applications to purchase. No records were kept of those to whom the offers were made; the estimated number in 1951 was 500.

The company bottoms its exemption claim on the classification of all offerees as "key employees" in its organization. Its position on trial was that "A key employee . . . is not confined to an organization chart. It would include an individual who is eligible for promotion, an individual who especially influences others or who advises others, a person whom the employees look to in some special way, an individual, of course, who carries some special responsibility, who is sympathetic to management and who is ambitious and who the management feels is likely to be promoted to a greater responsibility." That an offering to *all* of its employees would be public is conceded. [Emphasis added.]

The Securities Act nowhere defines the scope of § 4(1)'s private offering exemption. Nor is the legislative history of much help in staking out its boundaries. [The Court then pointed out, however, that the congressional committee considering the Securities Act before its final passage felt that the private offering was one of those transactions "where there is no practical need" for application of the Act or "where the public benefits are too remote."]

Decisions under comparable exemptions in the English Companies Acts and state "blue sky" laws, the statutory antecedents of federal securities legislation, have made one thing clear—to be public, an offer need not be open to the whole world. In *Securities and Exchange Comm. v. Sunbeam Gold Mines Co.,* 9 Cir., 1938, 95 F.2d 699, 701, this point was made in dealing with an offering to the stockholders of two corporations about to be merged. Judge Denman observed that:

> In its broadest meaning the term "public" distinguishes the populace at large from groups of individual members of the public segregated because of some common interest or characteristic. Yet such a distinction is inadequate for practical purposes; manifestly, an offering of securities to all redheaded men, to all residents of Chicago or San Francisco, to all existing stockholders of the General Motors Corporation or the American Telephone & Telegraph Company, is no less "public", in every realistic sense of the word, than an unrestricted offering to the world at large. Such an offering, though not open to everyone who may choose to apply, is none the less "public" in character, for the means used to select the particular individuals to whom the offering is to be made bear no sensible relation to the purposes for which the selection is made . . . . To determine the distinction between "public" and "private" in any particular context, it is essential to examine the circumstances under which the distinction is sought to be established and to consider the purposes sought to be achieved by such distinction.

The courts below purported to apply this test. The District Court held, in the language of the *Sunbeam* decision, that "The purpose of the selection bears a 'sensible relation' to the class chosen," finding that "The sole purpose of the 'selection' is to keep part stock ownership of the business within the operating personnel of the business and to spread ownership throughout all departments and activities of the business." The Court of Appeals treated the case as involving "an offering, without solicitation, of common stock to a selected group of key employees of the issuer, most of whom are already stockholders when the offering is made, with the sole purpose of enabling them to secure a proprietary interest in the company or to increase the interest already held by them."

Exemption from the registration requirements of the Securities Act is the question. The design of the statute is to protect investors by promoting full disclosure of information thought necessary to informed investment decisions. The natural way to interpret the private offering exemption is in light of the statutory purpose. Since exempt transactions are those as to which "there is no practical need for . . . [the law's] application," the applicability of § 4(1) should turn on whether the particular class of persons affected need the protection of the Act. An offering to those who are shown to be able to fend for themselves is a transaction "not involving any public offering."

The Commission would have us go one step further and hold that "an offering to a substantial number of the public" is not exempt under § 4(1). We are advised that "whatever the special circumstances, the Commission has consistently interpreted the exemption as being inapplicable when a large number of offerees is involved." But the statute would seem to apply to a "public offering" whether to few or many. It may well be that offerings to a substantial number of persons would rarely be exempt. Indeed nothing prevents the Commission, in enforcing the statute, from using some kind of numerical test in deciding when to investigate particular exemption claims. But there is no warrant for superimposing a quantity limit on private offerings as a matter of statutory interpretation.

The exemption, as we construe it, does not deprive corporate employees, as a class, of the safeguards of the Act. We agree that some employee offerings may come within § 4(1), e.g., one made to executive personnel who because of their position have access to the same kind of information that the Act would make available in the form of a registration statement. Absent such a showing of special circumstances, employees are just as much members of the investing "public" as any of their neighbors in the community. Although we do not rely on it, the rejection in 1934 of an amendment which would have specifically exempted employee stock offerings supports this conclusion. The [congressional committee considering the amendment] said that "the participants in employees' stock-investment plans may be in as great need of the protection afforded by availability of information concerning the issuer for which they work as are most other members of the public."

Keeping in mind the broadly remedial purposes of federal securities legislation, imposition of the burden of proof on an issuer who would plead the exemption seems to us fair and reasonable. Agreeing, the court below thought the burden met primarily because of the respondent's purpose in singling out its key employees for stock offerings. But once it is seen that the exemption question turns on the knowledge of the offerees, the issuer's motives, laudable though they may be, fade into irrelevance. The focus of inquiry should be on the need of the offerees for the protections afforded by registration. The employees here were not shown to have access to the kind of information which registration would disclose. The obvious opportunities for pressure and imposition make it advisable that they be entitled to compliance with § 5. [Thus the offering was "public" and registration was required.]

Reversed.

Questions and Problems

1. Progress Tailoring Co. advertised that it manufactured garments, although these garments actually were manufactured by its wholly-owned subsidiary. The Federal Trade Commission instituted proceedings in which it sought to stop such advertising on the ground that it was deceptive. *Progress Tailoring Co. v. FTC*, 153 F.2d 103 (1946). Did the FTC prevail? Discuss.

2. A federal statute prohibited railroads from giving rebates to those using the railroad for shipping goods. X Corp. shipped substantial quantities of goods by rail. The officers and

principal shareholders of X Corp. formed a separate corporation for the purpose of obtaining what were, in actuality, rebates. Did X Corp. violate the antirebate law by receiving rebates through the separate corporation? Explain.

3. Discuss why a nonprofit organization such as a church, fraternal club, or hospital might want to incorporate.

4. Boss, a promoter, signed a contract for architectural services as "agent for a Minnesota corporation to be formed which will be the obligor." The architectural drawings were prepared, but the proposed corporation was never formed, and the architects sued Boss for their fee. *Stanley J. How & Associates v. Boss,* 222 F. Supp. 936 (1963). Will the architects recover from Boss? Discuss.

5. Acting in his own behalf and not in behalf of any proposed corporation, Caparella purchased equipment subject to a debt, used it, then turned it over to a subsequently-created corporation, of which he became president. The creditor sent bills to the corporation, but the corporation never responded. The creditor then sued the corporation. Will the creditor prevail? Explain.

6. Under what types of circumstances might it be useful to use "dummy" incorporators (those having no real interest in the corporation to be formed)?

7. Baum Holding Co. was formed in Nebraska in 1922, when there was no state statute authorizing the formation of holding companies (corporations whose operations consist only of the ownership of interests in other corporations). In 1941 a holding companies statute was enacted, but the company made no attempt to comply with its provisions. Sometime thereafter, several shareholders who were dissatisfied with the way the company was being run filed suit challenging the validity of the corporation's existence. *Baum v. Baum Holding Co.,* 62 N.W.2d 864 (1954). Should they prevail? Discuss.

8. Plaintiff entered the "corporation's" building on business and fell into an unlit, unguarded elevator shaft. Although the organizers of the "corporation" had filed its articles before the accident, no arrangements had been made for the issuance of shares of stock, no meeting of shareholders had been held, officers had not been elected, and the corporation had not done any business as a corporation. The plaintiff sued the individual organizers for his injuries. Should he recover? Explain.

9. What is a major difference between the authority of the SEC and the authority of many state securities agencies?

10. In the *Ralston Purina* case, the court stated, "That an offering to *all* of its employees would be public is conceded." (Emphasis added.) Explain why this is so.

36 Corporations/Corporate Powers and Management

Corporate Powers As an "artificial person," a corporation possesses the power to do most of the things an individual can do in the operation of a business enterprise, such as own property, make contracts, borrow money, and hire employees. Corporate powers derive from several sources, traditionally classified as follows.

Statutory powers. State corporation laws ordinarily contain a list of activities in which corporations are permitted to engage—their statutory powers.

Express powers. Express powers are those set forth in the articles of incorporation. The articles frequently restate the powers granted by the statutes of their jurisdiction and then enumerate other powers specifically related to the corporation's business. Of course, the powers stated in the articles must not conflict with the statutory powers, but this rarely happens, because most of the statutes are drafted in a rather broad fashion.

Implied powers. With some exceptions, a corporation also has implied powers to do any other things reasonably necessary for carrying on its business. These powers simply serve to fill in gaps that exist in the statutory and express powers.

Problem Areas

Rather than discuss in detail all the various powers possessed by corporations, we will begin with the general notion that a corporation can do just about everything an individual can do in operating a business, and we will proceed to examine a few of the problem areas with respect to these powers.

Lending Corporate Funds: A corporation generally has implied power to make use of idle funds by lending them and charging interest. It also has the power to lend funds or extend credit (with or without interest) to customers or to other corporations in which it owns shares or with which it has contractual relations. But when no such relationship exists, the corporation does *not* have the implied power to cosign or guarantee the obligations of others merely as an *accommodation* to them (that is, with no value received in return)—though this power can be expressly provided for in the articles of incorporation. Additionally, the statutes of a significant number of states prohibit corporations from making loans to their directors or officers.

Charitable Contributions: In the early cases, the courts generally held that corporations did not have implied power to make contributions to charity. Their reasoning was that since the primary purpose of business corporations is to make profits, gifts could be made only if expressly authorized by the corporation's articles. This older view has undergone radical change, however, both by statute and by more recent court decisions. As a result, the general rule today is that corporations do possess implied power to make charitable contributions.

Joining a Partnership: Traditionally, a corporation did not have the power to become a member of a partnership. It was felt by the courts that allowing a corporation to become a partner would effectively delegate to the other partners a degree of control over corporate affairs that should be exercised only by duly elected directors. The courts not only refused to recognize the joining of a partnership as an implied power, but in many cases (though not all) they refused to recognize such power even if it was expressly granted in the articles of incorporation. Curiously (and illogically) the courts usually did permit a corporation to become a member of a joint venture, thereby sometimes allowing a clever manipulation of words to control the result. The modern trend, however, is to empower corporations to join partnerships. This trend is observable in numerous recent changes in state corporation statutes.

Torts and Crimes: A corporation obviously has power to act only through human agents and servants. Like any other employer, it is liable for the torts of its servants committed in the scope of their employment. In some situations, corporations also are responsible for the *criminal acts* of their subordinates.[1] Corporate criminal liability may exist, for example, in the following situations:

1. Where the illegal act is committed by an officer or other high-ranking managerial employee.

2. Where the illegal act is authorized or ratified by the board of directors or by vote of the stockholders.

3. Where the particular crime does not require proof of criminal intent, such as engaging in an activity without a required license.

4. Where the statute defining the criminal offense provides specifically for corporate responsibility or for responsibility by employers in general. For example, the federal antitrust laws provide expressly for the imposition of criminal penalties on corporations.

The "Ultra Vires" Doctrine

A corporation is organized for particular purposes. An important principle in the area of corporate powers is that *a corporation is empowered to act only insofar as is necessary to further the purposes for which it was organized.* All that has been said regarding corporate powers must be qualified by this principle. Thus even such ordinary powers as making contracts and owning property can be exercised only within the limits of a corporation's expressed purposes.

Any act by a corporation that is beyond the scope of its business as defined in the articles of incorporation is said to be *ultra vires.*[2] Many of the cases in which the *ultra vires* doctrine has been at issue have involved corporate contracts made for unauthorized purposes. The treatment accorded *ultra vires* contracts by the courts is summarized below.

1. In past years, some courts treated *ultra vires* contracts as *absolutely void,* with no rights or duties created on either side.

2. Most courts, however, did not apply an absolute rule of invalidity to *ultra vires* contracts unless they were illegal as well. Where the contracts were merely *ultra vires* but not otherwise illegal, these courts varied their treatment according to how far performance had progressed. For example, a fully-executed *ultra vires* contract, where both parties had completely performed, was treated as valid and left undisturbed. On the other hand, where the contract was entirely executory, neither party having performed, the *ultra vires* nature of the agreement could be raised by either party; and this defense would prevent enforcement of the contract. Where the contract was partially executed, it would be enforceable under some circumstances.

---

[1] A corporation obviously cannot be imprisoned, but it can be fined or dissolved. And, of course, those *individuals* who actually commit the crime are also subject to criminal penalties, including imprisonment when appropriate.

[2] *Ultra vires* acts should not be confused with illegal ones. All illegal corporate acts are inherently *ultra vires;* but not all *ultra vires* acts are illegal. In fact, most are not illegal but are merely beyond the scope of corporate powers.

(For example, where one party had received benefits under the contract, that party would be estopped from asserting the defense of *ultra vires*.)

3. Although some courts still take the approach discussed in item 2, a majority of states have passed statutes in recent years greatly diminishing the significance of the *ultra vires* doctrine. Most of these statutes follow the lead of the Model Act, which abolishes *ultra vires* as a contractual defense. In other words, in these states the *ultra vires* nature of the contract does not affect its validity as far as the parties themselves are concerned. However, other legal consequences continue to ensue from an *ultra vires* contract, including (a) a suit by shareholders for an injunction to prevent performance where it has not yet taken place, (b) a suit by the corporation itself or by shareholders acting in its behalf to recover damages from the directors and officers responsible for the action, and (c) a suit by the state either for an injunction or for dissolution of the corporation.

The diminishing importance of the *ultra vires* doctrine can be observed in other ways as well. For example, corporate attorneys have become increasingly adept at including within the statement of purpose in the articles of incorporation all remotely conceivable activities. This ordinarily is more convenient than amending the articles at a later time. In addition, several states have changed their corporation laws so as to permit incorporation for "any lawful purpose," with no requirement that the articles state specific purposes.

Corporate Management

When one speaks of corporate "management" one is usually referring to the board of directors, officers, and managerial employees who oversee the details of corporate operation. Although shareholders generally do not take part in the daily running of the corporation, they do, as owners, have ultimate control over its policies.

The structure of corporate control can be viewed as pyramidal in nature, the shareholders forming the broad base of the pyramid. The shareholders exercise their control, for the most part, by selecting the individuals who serve on the board of directors. The board, in turn, usually selects corporate officers and other managerial employees at the top of the pyramid.

Shareholders' Functions

As we have already indicated, shareholders as such do not usually have the power to dictate the details of daily corporate operation. Such power resides with the board of directors, which often delegates much of the responsibility to officers and other employees. In most situations, the remedy for shareholder dissatisfaction with the manner in which corporate affairs are being handled is to elect a new board of directors. The most important shareholder functions are (1) election and removal of directors, (2) amendment of articles and bylaws, and (3) approval of certain extraordinary corporate matters.

Election and Removal of Directors: Although the initial board of directors is either named in the articles of incorporation or selected by the incorporators, its term ordinarily extends only until the first meeting of shareholders. The selection of directors then becomes a shareholder function.

Except for death or resignation, a director usually serves until the expiration of his or her term of office, and frequently is reelected to one or more subsequent terms. However, shareholders have always had the inherent power to remove directors at any time *for cause* (fraud, misconduct, neglect of duties, and so on)—subject, of course, to court review. On the other hand, the traditional common-law rule was that a director could not be removed *without cause* during his or her term unless the shareholders had expressly reserved that right at the time of election. Today, however, this rule has been changed by statute in a majority of states so as to permit shareholders to remove directors at any time *with or without cause.* Removal of a director either for cause or without cause is accomplished by majority vote. However, if "cumulative voting" was used to elect the director, removing him or her may be somewhat more difficult. The concept of cumulative voting and its effects will be discussed shortly.

Amendment of Articles and Bylaws: Shareholders have the power to amend the articles of incorporation. Of course, since the corporation's articles must be filed with the secretary of state, any later amendments must also be filed.

In different states the bylaws are initially adopted by either the incorporators, the directors, or the shareholders. But regardless of which body possesses the power of original adoption, the shareholders are empowered to amend or even repeal them subsequently.

In many jurisdictions the directors have the power to amend or repeal the bylaws, but this power is really subordinate in nature. In other words, even when the directors are given such authority by statute, by the articles, or by the bylaws themselves, the ultimate power rests with the shareholders. Because they possess an inherent power with respect to bylaws, they can override the directors' actions even if such actions were authorized.

Approval of Extraordinary Corporate Matters: Although the authority to conduct most corporate affairs is held by the directors, certain matters are of such an unusual nature as to require shareholder approval. This approval is ordinarily given in the form of a "resolution" voted on at a shareholders' meeting. Extraordinary matters requiring shareholder approval include (1) sale or lease of corporate assets *not* in the regular course of the corporation's business, and (2) merger, consolidation, or dissolution of the corporation.[3]

Exercise of Shareholders' Functions

Shareholders as such are not agents of the corporation and therefore cannot bind the corporation by acting *individually;* their powers must be exercised *collectively.*

---

[3]Mergers, consolidatons, and dissolutions will be discussed in Chapter 38.

The most common vehicle for the exercise of shareholder functions is the *share-holders' meeting*. In recent years, however, most states have amended their corporation laws to allow shareholders to take action by *written consent*. This consent must ordinarily be signed by all shareholders entitled to vote on the matter.[4] But the shareholders' meeting still remains the most common forum for shareholder action.

Types of Meetings: Shareholders' meetings are either *annual* or *special*. Corporations are usually required by state law to hold annual meetings; the most important item of business at these meetings is usually the election of some or all of the directors. Between annual meetings, special meetings may be called to transact business that cannot or should not wait until the next annual meeting.

Time and Place of Meetings: The time of annual meetings and the place for annual and special meetings may be set forth in the articles, but they are more commonly found in the bylaws. Most annual meetings are held in the spring. Older statutes often required shareholders' meetings to be held in the state of incorporation, but this generally is no longer a requirement.

Notice of Meetings: State laws usually require written notice of any shareholders' meeting to be sent to each shareholder a reasonable time prior to the meeting, although shareholders can waive this requirement by signing a waiver before or after the meeting. In some instances a shareholder's *conduct* may constitute a waiver of notice. For example, where a shareholder receives no formal notice but knows of the meeting and attends without protesting the lack of notice, he or she waives the requirement of notice.

The notice generally must state the place, day, and hour of the meeting; and in the case of a special meeting, the notice must state the purpose or purposes for which the meeting is being called. The business transacted at a special meeting must be limited to the purposes set forth in the notice.

Quorum: Before action can validly be taken at a shareholders' meeting, a *quorum* must be present. Quorum requirements are expressed in terms of either a specific portion of outstanding shares or a specific portion of shares entitled to vote. These requirements are usually set forth in the articles or the bylaws within limits defined by state statute. As an example, the Model Act allows the articles of incorporation to set the quorum requirement so long as it is not less than one-third of all outstanding shares. The Model Act further provides that, if the articles are silent on the matter, a majority of outstanding shares constitutes a quorum.

Voting: Action at a shareholders' meeting is taken by voting. The number of votes a shareholder has is determined by the number of shares he or she owns. Assuming

---

[4]A few states allow shareholder action by a less-than-unanimous written consent.

that a quorum is present, the majority vote of the *shares represented at the meeting* (not the shares outstanding or entitled to vote) is usually sufficient for ordinary matters. More than a majority is sometimes required by state law or by the articles or bylaws for certain unusual matters such as mergers or consolidations. When a greater-than-majority vote is required, it is usually expressed in terms of all shares entitled to vote, not just those represented at the meeting.

State laws frequently require that a corporation keep a record of all its shareholders, listing their names and addresses as well as the number and type of shares held by each. Usually corporations are also required to prepare a *voting list* (a list of shareholders who can vote and the number of votes each is entitled to) prior to each shareholders' meeting. The record of shareholders and the voting list must be kept at a designated place (such as the principal corporate office) and must be available for inspection by shareholders.

Impartial individuals referred to as *tellers* (or sometimes as *judges* or *inspectors*) are usually present to supervise elections at shareholders' meetings. Although tellers are not generally required by law, many state statutes do require them if a shareholder so requests or if they are called for in the bylaws.

Methods for Concentrating Voting Power: Several methods exist by which a shareholder who owns a relatively small portion of the corporation's shares can increase his or her voting power.

Cumulative voting. Practically every state provides for cumulative voting by shareholders. A few states *require* it, but most merely *permit* it if the articles of incorporation provide for it. Cumulative voting applies only to the *election of directors,* and it is designed to increase the likelihood of minority representation on the board. ("Minority" refers to the owner(s) of a less-than-controlling number of shares, not to an ethnic minority.) The following example will illustrate the mechanics of cumulative voting: J is the owner of a hundred shares of stock in Gemini Corp. At the annual shareholders' meeting, three directors are to be elected. The slate of candidates includes A, B, C, D, E, and F. J wants to elect A, B, and C, or at least one of them. If "straight" voting is used, J can cast a hundred votes each for A, B, and C (that is, one vote per share for each directorship to be filled). But if cumulative voting is allowed, J can take the total three hundred votes that he is entitled to cast at the election and cast them *all* in favor of A or divide them in any manner he wishes.

We previously mentioned that a director may be removed from office by majority vote. This is true if the director is being removed *for cause,* even though he may have been elected by minority interests through cumulative voting. However, if a corporation uses cumulative voting and if the attempted removal is *without cause,* a director cannot be removed from office if the vote *against removal* would be sufficient to elect that director by cumulative voting.

Shareholder agreements. Agreements in which a group of shareholders decide prior to a meeting to cast their votes in certain ways are sometimes employed to concentrate voting power. These agreements are usually valid and enforceable.

Voting trusts. Another method of concentrating voting power is the voting trust. This is formed by an agreement in which the "record ownership" of shares is transferred to trustees whose sole function is to vote the shares. "Voting trust certificates" are given by the trustees to the original shareholders, entitling them to all rights of share ownership other than voting rights.

Proxies. Shareholders can vote their shares at a meeting either in person or by proxy. A *proxy* is simply a signed, written document authorizing a person present at the meeting to vote the shares of a shareholder. Proxies (which create an agency relationship) are useful both to alleviate problems of distance between a shareholder's residence and the site of a meeting and to concentrate voting power. For example, one person might solicit and accumulate proxies authorizing him or her to vote in behalf of a number of shareholders. Proxies are usually solicited by corporate managers prior to each shareholder's meeting. (More will be said later, particularly in Chapter 37, about the duties of one who solicits proxies.)

The two following cases involve challenges to the procedures followed in connection with shareholders' meetings. In the first case the challenge was raised *before* the meeting took place. In the second case the challenge was raised *after* the meeting, and the court scrutinized the action that had been taken at the meeting.

Two factions were fighting for control of Loew's. One faction was headed by Joseph Tomlinson (the "Tomlinson faction"), the other by the president of Loew's, Joseph Vogel (the "Vogel faction"). At the annual shareholders' meeting in February 1957 a compromise was reached by which each faction nominated six directors, who in turn nominated a thirteenth, neutral, director. But the battle had only begun. After several more months of controversy, on July 17 and 18, two of the six Vogel directors and the neutral director resigned.

Campbell v. Loew's, Inc.
Court of Chancery of Delaware, 134 A.2d 852 (1957)

On July 19 the Tomlinson faction asked that a directors' meeting be called for July 30 to consider the problem of filling director vacancies. On the eve of this meeting one of the Tomlinson directors resigned. This left five Tomlinson directors and four Vogel directors in office. A quorum was seven. Only the five Tomlinson directors attended the July 30 meeting. They purported to fill two of the director vacancies and to take other action. (In a separate case, this court had ruled that for want of a quorum the two directors were not validly elected and the subsequent action taken at that meeting was invalid.)

On July 29, the day before the directors' meeting, Vogel, as president, sent out a notice calling a shareholders' meeting for September 12 for the purposes of (1) filling director vacancies, (2) amending the bylaws to increase the number of directors from thirteen to nineteen and the quorum requirement from seven to ten, (3) electing six additional directors, and (4) removing Stanley Meyer and Joseph Tomlinson as directors and filling the resulting vacancies.

In August, Vogel sent out another notice for the September 12 shareholders' meeting, along with a "proxy statement" (essentially a request sent to shareholders asking that they grant proxies to the sender, authorizing him or her to cast their votes in a particular way). The notice and proxy statement were accompanied by a letter from Vogel soliciting shareholder support for the matters stated in the notice and particularly seeking to fill the vacancies and newly created directorships with "his" nominees.

Campbell, a shareholder, promptly filed this suit. He requested an injunction to either prevent the holding of the shareholders' meeting or to prevent the meeting from considering certain matters. The trial court ordered that the meeting be postponed until October 15 to allow time to decide the case. It ultimately rendered the following decision.

Seitz, Chancellor: [The court first ruled that Vogel did have the power to call the shareholders' meeting for the purposes of filling director vacancies and amending the bylaws. It then turned to the question of whether the meeting could be called for the purpose of removing Meyer and Tomlinson from the board.] . . .

Plaintiff next argues that the shareholders of a Delaware corporation have no power to remove directors from office even for cause and thus the call for that purpose is invalid. . . .

While there are some cases suggesting the contrary, I believe that the stockholders have the power to remove a director for cause. This power must be implied when we consider that otherwise a director who is guilty of the worst sort of violation of his duty could nevertheless remain on the board. It is hardly to be believed that a director who is disclosing the corporation's trade secrets to a competitor would be immune from removal by the stockholders. Other examples, such as embezzlement of corporate funds, etc., come readily to mind. . . .

Plaintiff next argues that the removal of Tomlinson and Meyer as directors would violate the right of minority shareholders to representation on the board and would be contrary to the policy of the Delaware law regarding cumulative voting. Plaintiff contends that where there is cumulative voting, as provided by the Loew's certificate, a director cannot be removed by the stockholders even for cause.

. . . [I]t is certainly evident that if not carefully supervised the existence of a power in the stockholders to remove a director even for cause could be abused and used to defeat cumulative voting.

Does this mean that there can be no removal of a director by the stockholders for cause in any case where cumulative voting exists? The conflicting considerations involved make the answer to this question far from easy. Some states have passed statutes dealing with this problem but Delaware has not. The possibility of stockholder removal action designed to circumvent the effect of cumulative voting is evident. This is particularly true where the removal vote is, as here, by mere majority vote. On the other hand, if we assume a case where a director's presence or action is clearly damaging the corporation and its stockholders in a substantial way, it is difficult to see why that director should be free to continue such damage merely because he was elected under a cumulative voting provision.

On balance, I conclude that the stockholders have the power to remove a director for cause even where there is a provision for cumulative voting. I think adequate protection is afforded . . . by the existence of a remedy to test the validity of any such action, if taken.

. . . [Thus,] the meeting was validly called by the president . . . .

I next consider plaintiff's contention that the charges against the two directors do not constitute "cause" as a matter of law. It would take too much space to narrate in detail the contents of the president's letter. I must therefore give my summary of its charges. First of all, it charges that the two directors (Tomlinson and Meyer) failed to cooperate with Vogel in his announced program for rebuilding the company; that their purpose has been to put themselves in control; that they made baseless accusations against him and other management personnel and attempted to divert him from his normal duties as president by bombarding him with correspondence containing unfounded charges and other similar acts; that they moved into the company's building, accompanied by lawyers and accountants, and immediately proceeded upon a planned scheme of harassment. They called for many records, some going back twenty years, and were rude to the personnel. Tomlinson sent daily letters to the directors making serious charges directly and by means of innuendos and misinterpretations.

Are the foregoing charges, if proved, legally sufficient to justify the ouster of the two directors by the stockholders? I am satisfied that a charge that the directors desired to take over control of the corporation is not a reason for their ouster. Standing alone, it is a perfectly legitimate objective which is a part of the very fabric of corporate existence. Nor is a charge of lack of cooperation a legally sufficient basis for removal for cause.

The next charge is that these directors, in effect, engaged in a calculated plan of harassment to the detriment of the corporation. Certainly a director may examine books, ask questions, etc., in the discharge of his duty, but a point can be reached when his actions exceed the call of duty and become deliberately obstructive. In such a situation, if his actions constitute a real burden on the corporation then the stockholders are entitled to relief. The charges in this area made by the Vogel letter are legally sufficient to justify the stockholders in voting to remove such directors. In so concluding I of course express no opinion as to the truth of the charges. . . .

[Thus, the court held that the meeting had been validly called and the shareholders could vote on the removal of Meyer and Tomlinson from the board.]

Comment: At the October 15 shareholders' meeting, the Vogel group prevailed by a large margin, but the Tomlinson faction was able to obtain some representation on the board through cumulative voting. However, at the urging of the Vogel group, shareholders eliminated cumulative voting the next year. (For a fascinating account of the struggle for control of Loew's, read the chapter "Proxy Battle" in *My Life in Court* by Louis Nizer, who served as attorney for the Vogel faction.)

In Re William Faehndrich, Inc.
Court of Appeals of New York, 161 N.Y.S.2d. 99 (1957)

In the words of the court, "this proceeding presents a regrettable conflict between an elderly father, William Faehndrich, and his 47-year-old son, Rudolph." In 1912 the father founded a business of manufacturing, importing, and marketing cheeses, which he conducted under his own name. In 1925 he incorporated the business with a capitalization of $5,000 represented by 50 shares of $100 par value stock. In 1929 the authorized capitalization was increased from $5,000 to $100,000 and the authorized number of shares from 50 to 1,000. No new shares were actually issued at that time.

Rudolph entered the business in 1926 at the age of 16. He assumed greater and greater responsibility as the years went by, and he apparently contributed substantially to the growth and success of the business. In 1941 he became president, his father then holding the offices of secretary and treasurer.

In 1953, possibly because of the father's advanced age (he was then 74) and his desire to afford protection to Rudolph, two stock certificates (the formal documents that evidence ownership of corporate shares) were prepared and issued. Certificate No. 1 was for 157 shares in the name of the father, and certificate No. 2 was for 161 shares in the name of the son. They were both signed by the father and son as officers. According to the son, these two certificates represented all the outstanding shares of stock. The father claimed, however, that 50 shares had been issued years before, 45 to him and 5 to his daughter. But no certificates representing these shares could be found.

As a result of growing differences between father and son (which appeared to have been aggravated by the latter's concern over the father's transfer of property to a younger brother), Rudolph, as president of the corporation, had a notice sent to his father, advising him of a special meeting of the stockholders. The notice, dated December 28, 1955, said:

> Please take notice that a meeting of the stockholders of William Faehndrich, Inc., will be held at the office of the corporation, 11 Harrison Street, New York 13, N.Y. on the 8th day of January, 1956, at 5:15 p.m. for the purpose of electing directors of the corporation for the ensuing year, or for such action or further business as may arise at said meeting.

The corporation's bylaws provided, apparently from the inception of the corporation, that the presence of the holders of *two-thirds* of the capital stock was required for any special meeting of stockholders.

The father failed to attend. The son asserted that his father had been in the office a short time before the meeting and that he had reminded him of the meeting; the father claimed he had been ill. Rudolph, of course, was present at the meeting. He voted his 161 shares of stock in favor of himself and his wife, and they were elected directors. They thereupon held a directors' meeting, at which they elected Rudolph president and treasurer and his wife vice president and secretary, thereby replacing the father as secretary-treasurer and terminating his employment. The father was thereafter notified of all the action thus taken.

The father filed suit, asking the court to declare (1) that the election was illegal and must be set aside; (2) that the offices of the newly-elected directors be declared vacated; and (3) that a new election for directors be ordered, inspectors of election be appointed, and a new certificate for 45 shares be issued in his name and one for 5 shares in the name of his daughter. The trial court held that the election was invalid because the notice of the meeting had been insufficient—that is, it did not "carry home" to the father that it was the son's "purpose" to remove him as a director, officer, and employee of the corporation and that, to effect that end, the son was going to rely upon "the asserted invalidity" of the provision in the bylaws for a quorum of two-thirds of the capital stock. This decision was affirmed by the intermediate-level appellate court, and the son appealed to the Court of Appeals (the highest court in New York).

Fuld, Justice: . . . Sympathy-provoking though the facts may appear, they afford no ground for relief . . . ; the petition should have been dismissed. . . .

The notice of the stockholders' meeting, admittedly received, fairly and adequately apprised the petitioner [the father] of the purpose of the meeting; in so many words, it recited that the meeting was called "for the purpose of electing directors". It is quite likely that the father did not fully realize the significance of such an election or the consequences to himself that would flow therefrom, but it may not be said that the notice of the meeting was insufficient or misleading in any way. If the purpose of the meeting be clearly stated, there generally is no duty to specify the course of conduct contemplated by the directors after their election, and no requirement to explain the consequences that will follow from the action they plan to take. There likewise was no necessity that there be notification that the by-law provision with respect to the two-thirds quorum requirement would be considered or treated as invalid. A stockholder is presumed to have knowledge of the by-laws of his corporation and of their legal effect.

Once we conclude that the notice of meeting was adequate and fair, the question arises as to whether a quorum was present at the January, 1956 meeting. A bylaw of the corporation, as already noted, required a quorum of two-thirds of the shares at special meetings of the stockholders and, concededly, that amount of stock was not represented. However, the bylaw provision, since it was not authorized by the certificate of incorporation as originally filed or by any amendatory certificate, is invalid, "because it contravenes an essential part of the State policy" as reflected in its statutes. Thus, the provision is in direct opposition to . . . section 55 of the Stock Corporation Law which fixes a quorum, for a meeting to elect directors, at a number "not exceeding a majority" of the shares . . . .

Accordingly, . . . whether a quorum was present at the meeting depends on whether Rudolph's 161 shares constituted a majority of the outstanding stock. The petitioner was unable to produce any corporate records whatsoever showing that he was a holder of more than the 157 shares standing in his name. And the corporation's tax returns disclosed its capital to be $31,800, which is entirely accounted for by the stock certificates for 157 shares and 161 shares at $100 a share. . . .

The corporate records here presented establish that Rudolph owns a majority of the corporation's outstanding stock and, accordingly, that a quorum was present at the stockholders' meeting in question. It necessarily follows, therefore, that the election of the directors at that meeting was indisputably valid and that the officers thereafter designated by those directors are properly and legally in office.

In sum, then, since the notice of meeting in the case before us adequately and fairly stated its purpose, and no suggestion of impropriety in conducting the meeting or the election is even advanced, no legal ground exists for vacating the election or setting it aside.

[Reversed.]

Board of Directors: Choice and Functions

Number: State statutes have traditionally required that there be at least *three* directors. In recent years, however, the laws in a majority of states have been changed so as to permit fewer directors in corporations that have fewer than three shareholders. Subject to these statutory limitations, the number of directors is usually set forth in either the articles or the bylaws.

Qualifications: In most states directors no longer have to meet minimum age requirements, although in a few states they do. Requirements that directors be residents of the state of incorporation, still found in a few states, are also becoming much less common. In the past, most states required that directors be shareholders. This requirement also is vanishing; statutes in a majority of states now provide that directors need not be shareholders unless they are so required by the articles or bylaws. In actual practice, most directors *are* shareholders; however, there is a growing trend toward obtaining the services of disinterested outsiders as "watchdogs" on the board of directors. Also, it is permissible for an individual to be both a director and a corporate officer, and this frequently occurs.

Election and Term: The initial board ordinarily serves until the first annual shareholders' meeting, when new directors are elected by majority vote of the shareholders.

The term of office for corporate directors is one year (that is, until the next annual shareholders' meeting) unless the board is "classified" (divided into classes, with only one class elected each year, the result being that the directors serve "staggered" terms). Today, most states permit a classified board. When this system is used, the most common practice is to have *three* classes, with one-third of the directors being elected each year for a three-year term. Classification prevents replacement of the entire board at the same time, thereby providing greater management continuity.

We mentioned earlier that removal of a director during his or her term is a shareholder function. The power to remove a director *for cause* can also be given, in the articles or bylaws, to the board of directors itself, although the shareholders have inherent power to review the action. But the board cannot be empowered to remove a director *without cause.*

When vacancies occur on the board (through death, resignation, or removal) or when an amendment to the articles or bylaws creates a new place on the board, filling of the opening generally is also a shareholder function. But several states now allow such openings to be filled by the board itself if it is so authorized by the articles or bylaws.

Management Functions: Even though the corporation generally is bound by the actions of the board, the directors are not agents of the corporation or of the shareholders who elect them. There are two reasons for this. First, their powers are conferred by the *state* rather than by the shareholders. And second, they do not have *individual* power to bind the corporation, as agents do; instead, they can only act *as a body.* Directors thus occupy a position unique in our legal system.

With the exception of certain extraordinary matters mentioned earlier, the board of directors is empowered to manage all the affairs of the corporation. It not only determines corporate policies but also supervises their execution. The management powers of the board of directors usually include the following:

1. Setting of basic corporation policy in such areas as product lines, services, prices, wages, and labor-management relations.

2. Decisions relating to financing the corporation, such as the issuance of shares or bonds.

3. Determination of whether (and how large) a dividend is to be paid to shareholders at a particular time.

4. Selection, supervision, and removal of corporate officers and other managerial employees.[5]

5. Decisions relating to compensation of managerial employees, pension plans, and similar matters.

Exercise of Board's Functions

As we previously mentioned, most states now allow *shareholders* to act by unanimous written consent in addition to annual and special meetings. A majority of states (but not as many as allow shareholder action by written consent) also now allow the *board of directors* to act by unanimous written consent. The traditional, and still most common, method for board action, however, is the board of directors' meeting.

Time and Place of Board Meetings: Board meetings are of two types—regular and special. The time and place of *regular meetings* is ordinarily established by the bylaws, by a standing resolution of the board, or simply by custom. Unless expressly required, notice of such meetings does not have to be given to directors. If the need arises, *special meetings* can be called between regular meetings. Prior notice is required in most cases, since special meetings by their very nature are not regularly scheduled.[6]

Quorum: Before action can validly be taken at a board of directors' meeting, a quorum must be present. Most state statutes are flexible on the matter of what constitutes a quorum. They usually provide that a quorum will be a majority of the authorized number of directors unless the articles or bylaws say otherwise. Some state statutes also place a maximum and a minimum on the quorum requirement.

Voting: As is true at shareholders' meetings, action at a board meeting is taken by voting. But a director's voting power is not determined by the size or nature of any financial interest he or she has in the corporation. Instead, each director has *only one vote.* Board action usually requires only a *majority vote,* although some states permit the articles or bylaws to require a greater-than-majority vote for certain actions. (The "majority" referred to here is a majority of the directors actually attending a meeting at which a quorum is present.) Unlike shareholders, directors cannot vote by proxy.[7] However, a small number of states have recently

---

[5]Several states now permit the shareholders to select corporate officers if so provided in the articles or bylaws.

[6]State laws usually provide, however, that a director waives any notice requirement if he or she actually attends the meeting, unless such attendance is for the express purpose of objecting that the meeting was not lawfully called.

[7]The lone exception is Louisiana, which does allow a director to vote by proxy in some circumstances.

changed their laws to permit a director to fully participate in a meeting by telephone. In such cases, a "conference call" must be used, so that the absent director and those present at the meeting can all speak and listen as a group.

The case below discusses the rationale behind the concept that directors must act *as a board* rather than as individuals. It also illustrates the requirement that directors be given proper notification of board meetings.

Stone v. American Lacquer Solvents Co.

Supreme Court of Pennsylvania, 345 A.2d 174 (1975)

Harold E. Stone became chairman of the board of directors of American Lacquer Solvents Co. (hereafter referred to as American) on December 7, 1967. On that date, American's board of directors adopted a resolution that upon Stone's death, his wife, Rachel, would be paid an $8,000 annual pension by American until her death or remarriage. The resolution was adopted in consideration for services to be rendered to American by Stone, and it further provided that it could not be revoked without his consent.

In March 1968 Stone and his wife encountered marital difficulties. Stone contacted Shaw, the president and general manager of American, and told him that he wanted the pension resolution cancelled. Shaw contacted the company's legal counsel and, acting in accordance with his advice as to the procedure to be followed, prepared a letter from Stone to the board of directors of American, saying, "It is my wish that the Resolution dated December 7, 1967 concerning a pension for my wife Rachel be rescinded." Stone signed and personally delivered the letter to Shaw on March 3.

On March 11, 1968, Shaw convened a special meeting of the board of directors of American. Five of the seven members of the board attended the meeting; and when Stone's letter was brought to their attention, they voted unanimously to rescind the resolution of December 7, 1967. Stone was not notified of the meeting and did not attend.

Stone died on November 1, 1968; and when American refused to pay his widow, Rachel, the pension provided for in the resolution, she sued for specific performance. The trial court ruled that the resolution had been validly rescinded by the board at the meeting of March 11, 1968, and hence the plaintiff had no claim. She appealed the decision.

Eagen, Justice: ... As a general rule the directors of a corporation may bind a corporation only when they act at a legal meeting of the board. If they purport to act at a meeting which is not a legal meeting, their action is not that of the corporation, and the corporation, absent ratification or acquiescence, is not bound.

As to special meetings of the board of directors of a corporation, the general rule in Pennsylvania is that such a meeting held without notice to some or any of the directors and in their absence is illegal, and action taken at such a meeting, although by a majority of the directors, is invalid absent ratification or estoppel. However, this notice requirement may be waived by a director either prior or subsequent to the special meeting, provided such waiver is in writing. Additionally, any action which may properly be taken at a meeting of a board of directors of a corporation may be effected and is binding without a meeting, if a consent in writing setting forth the action so taken is signed by each and every member of the board and filed with the secretary of the corporation.

A reading of the trial court's opinion filed in support of its decree upholding the legality of the Board's action of March 11, 1968, rescinding the Board's prior Resolution providing for the payment of the pension to the plaintiff was based on three grounds, any one of which, if correct, would warrant its ruling.

First, the court concluded that Stone's letter of March 3, 1968, constituted a consent to the Board's subsequent action rescinding the pension Resolution. The difficulty with this position is that the applicable statute requires that such a consent be executed *after* the meeting and that it specifically set forth the action taken, and that it be filed with the secretary of the corporation. Stone's letter does not meet these requirements.

Secondly, the court concluded [that] Stone's letter of March 3, 1968, constituted a waiver of receipt of notice of the meeting of March 11, 1968. The difficulty with this position is that the letter does not refer to the meeting or indicate in any way that notice thereof is waived. The letter amounts to no more than an expression of desire or consent to rescind the pension Resolution.

In connection with its conclusion that Stone's letter constituted a waiver of notice of the meeting, the court reasoned that no purpose would be served by Stone's presence at the meeting since the other Directors were merely acceding to Stone's wishes and request. This analysis overlooks the rationale for the salutary rule that all directors receive notice of special meetings. That rationale is that "each member of a corporate body has the right of consultation with the others, and has the right to be heard upon all questions considered, and it is presumed that if the absent members had been present they might have dissented, and their arguments might have convinced the majority of the unwisdom of their proposed action and thus have produced a different result." We agree with this rationale and, in view of the presumption embodied therein, we cannot concur in the trial court's premise that Stone and the other Directors were of one mind as regards the pension rescission. In relation to this, we specifically note that another member of the Board of Directors failed to attend the meeting of March 11, 1968, and there is nothing in the record to show if he received notice of the meeting, or ever consented to the action taken at the meeting.

Finally, the court concluded that the rescinding resolution of the Board was voidable only and that Stone's silence and failure to object thereto prior to his death amounted to a ratification. The difficulty with this position is that there is nothing in the record to show that Stone was ever made aware that the meeting of March 11, 1968, had been held or knew the rescinding resolution had been adopted by the Board. Under the circumstances, it cannot be said a ratification was effected. . . .

[R]eversed and . . . remanded for further proceedings. . . .

Pomeroy, Justice (concurring): The sparsely developed record before us fails to establish that decedent Stone had the requisite notice of the special board meeting of the board of directors here challenged, or that he received knowledge of the rescission of the pension arrangement for his wife which was approved at that meeting. Hence I am constrained to concur in the Court's conclusion that the meeting was not lawfully convened and that there is no evidence of a subsequent ratification by Stone of the action taken at that meeting. I further agree that Stone's letter requesting the rescission was not a consent to board action within the meaning of Section 1402(7) of the Business Corporation Law. Unlike the majority, however, I do not believe that the statute's application turns on the fact that the letter was signed prior to the special meeting. The purpose of Section 1402(7), as its language makes clear, is to permit a board of directors to act without the necessity of any meeting when all directors consent in writing to such action. Here, there has been no written consent signed by all the directors. It is this factor, not the timing of the execution of the writing, which takes the letter outside the scope of the statute. Accordingly, I concur in the result.

Delegation of Board Powers to Officers and Employees: We said earlier that all functions of the board of directors must be exercised by the board as a whole, usually by majority vote. This does not mean, however, that the board itself must carry out all the details of corporate management; it can, and quite often does, *delegate authority* to carry out its decisions. The most common instance of such delegation is the authority given by the board to corporate officers and other managerial employees. Not only is authority usually given to carry out board decisions, but managerial personnel also are generally given authority to make management decisions. The delegation of decision-making authority is usually a practical necessity, because daily business activities require too many decisions for each one to be made by the board. The powers delegated by the board, however, must not exceed two boundaries:

1. They must relate only to ordinary corporate affairs, not to matters of an unusual nature.

2. They must not be so broad as to give an officer or employee complete managerial discretion. In other words, the delegated authority must be either relatively limited in scope or accompanied by adequate guidelines.

Thus, even though certain management functions are often delegated to officers and other employees, the ultimate power to manage the corporation still rests with the board. And the authority delegated to managerial personnel is, of course, subject to board supervision.[8] The duties owed by the board of directors to the corporation and its shareholders will be discussed in the next chapter, but we would like to emphasize here that a delegation of authority by the board does not relieve it of the responsibility to fulfill these duties.

Other Delegations of Board Powers: Most state corporation laws permit the board of directors to select a certain number of its members (usually two or more) to serve as the "executive committee." The rules governing delegation of authority to an executive committee are somewhat similar to those governing delegation to managerial personnel:

1. An executive committee is usually authorized to make management decisions relating only to ordinary business affairs. Power to make decisions on unusual matters generally cannot be delegated to the committee. Examples of unusual

---

[8]This is a statement of the *law*. However, in actual practice, because of personalities or financial interests, the boards of some corporations serve primarily as a "rubber stamp" for decisions initiated by high-ranking managerial employees.

matters include: (a) amending corporate bylaws, (b) filling vacancies on the board, and (c) submitting to shareholders matters that require their approval.

2. The delegation of authority to an executive committee cannot be too broad in scope.

3. The committee can usually exercise its delegated powers only during the intervals between meetings of the whole board of directors.

Officers and Other Managerial Employees

Officers: The officers of the corporation are usually selected by the board of directors, although in a few states they can be chosen by the shareholders. Most commonly, the corporate officers are the president, one or more vice presidents, secretary, and treasurer. Some corporations also have other officers, such as chief executive officer, chairman of the board, general manager, comptroller (sometimes called "controller"), and general counsel.

Qualifications. In the past, many state laws required the president to also be a director. This requirement no longer exists in most states. In actual practice, however, the president almost always is a director as well. And when a corporation has a chairman of the board, he or she obviously must be a director. Other qualifications for the various officers can be included in the articles or bylaws if desired. In most states the same individual can hold more than one office. For example, it is not unusual for the offices of secretary and treasurer to be occupied by the same person. Limitations are frequently placed, however, on certain types of dual office holding. Most states, for instance, prohibit the same person from serving simultaneously as *president and secretary,* or as *president and vice president.*

Term of office. In a few states the term of office is limited by statute to a specific duration, such as one year. But in most states the only limitations are those expressed in the articles or bylaws. For the most part, officers hold their positions at the pleasure of the board and can be removed by the board *either with or without cause* and *regardless of any enforceable employment contract.* Of course, if the termination of an officer constitutes a breach of contract, the corporation can be held liable for damages to the discharged officer.

Other Managerial Employees: A corporation of almost any size requires the services of many employees to conduct its daily affairs. Some of these employees occupy supervisory positions and exercise certain managerial functions even though they are not officers. Selection of a few of the higher-ranking supervisory personnel is often done by the board of directors, but the task of hiring employees is generally delegated to the officers or even to other employees.

Applicability of the Law of Agency: Officers and other employees are agents of the corporation, and all the rules of agency law apply to the relationships created. Thus the corporation is bound by the actions of its officers and employees if they are acting within the scope of their authority—whether it is express, implied, or apparent. The express authority of *officers* comes only rarely from state laws or the articles of incorporation. It most frequently emanates from the corporate bylaws or from a resolution of the board of directors. The express authority of *other employees* most commonly comes from the officers or from higher-ranking employees. Implied and apparent authority are created in essentially the same way as in any other principal-agent relationship.

Management of Close Corporations

As indicated in the previous chapter, a close corporation is one whose shares of stock are held by either a single shareholder or a small, closely-knit group of shareholders. Since all these shareholders usually hold positions as directors and officers, the management of a close corporation in practice more closely resembles a sole proprietorship or partnership than a corporation. In fact, close corporations with more than one shareholder are frequently referred to as "incorporated partnerships."

However, the nature of a close corporation should not be misconstrued. In the eyes of the law, *it is still a corporation* and must meet the same legal requirements as other corporations. While this has sometimes caused certain practical problems for close corporations, the problems have usually been overcome by the exercise of organizational ingenuity. For example, the law traditionally required at least *three* directors. But what if only *two* individuals own shares of stock and are interested in the operation of the corporation? One method of resolving the problem has been to set the number of directors at three in the articles of incorporation but then to operate with a permanent vacancy on the board. Another method has been to persuade a disinterested party to serve as a director in name only, with authority delegated to an executive committee composed of the two interested directors. And if the delegation of powers is too broad, there is really no one to complain.

Given that the law recognizes the validity of close corporations, one might wonder why the parties are forced to resort to these clever devices. And, indeed, modern corporation laws are beginning to recognize this dilemma. As indicated earlier, for example, a majority of states now require only one or two directors where there are only one or two shareholders. Furthermore, in recent years a few states have enacted special laws to deal with the unique nature of close corporations. The most striking of these is a provision found in a handful of states permitting the shareholders of a close corporation (as defined in the particular statute) to manage the enterprise *without a board of directors*. The primary purpose of these recent statutory innovations is to allow more internal flexibility in the management of a close corporation, thereby enabling the enterprise to operate with approximately the same degree of freedom and owner control that is found in partnerships while retaining the advantages of doing business as a corporation (such as limited shareholder liability for business debts).

In the following case, the legal basis for plaintiffs' claim was a violation by defendants of their "fiduciary" duties as "controlling" shareholders. The various duties of those who manage and control a corporation will be dealt with more fully in Chapter 37. For present purposes, however, this case highlights some of the special problems involved in managing a *close corporation.*

Two brothers, Paul and Peter Hallahan, joined forces with Charles and Errol Thompson, also brothers, to launch a drinking and eating establishment in Hyannis, Massachusetts, known as the Quarter Deck Lounge. For two weeks before opening for business in June 1975, David Thompson, a cousin of the Thompson brothers and a carpenter by trade, helped the four joint venturers make renovations of the premises to be occupied by the Quarter Deck. After opening, the four decided to incorporate their business, intending that there be four equal shareholders. In late July 1975, they filed articles of incorporation which established Haltom Corp., of which Charles Thompson was the president, Errol Thompson the treasurer, and Paul Hallahan the "clerk." These three were also directors. Haltom issued one hundred shares of stock, 23¾ shares to each of the four, and five shares to David Thompson as partial payment for the carpentry work he had performed. It was understood that power was to remain equally divided among the four, and that David Thompson would not actively participate in the business. However, shortly thereafter David Thompson signed a proxy for his five shares in favor of Charles Thompson.

In November 1975, the Alcoholic Beverages Control Commission approved the transfer of the Quarter Deck's liquor license from the names of Paul Hallahan and Errol Thompson to the name of Haltom Corp. At this point, relations deteriorated between the Hallahans and the Thompsons. Charles and Errol Thompson called a stockholders' meeting at Paul Hallahan's home, without notice of the business to be transacted at the meeting. When the meeting convened, the Thompsons said that they had received complaints about the Hallahans' performance as bartenders. On those grounds, voting their shares and those of David Thompson, the Thompson brothers fired the Hallahans as employees of the corporation. The Hallahans had not received any complaints from customers or from the Thompsons prior to the meeting.

The Hallahan brothers, plaintiffs, filed suit against the corporation and the three Thompsons. The trial court ruled in favor of plaintiffs and ordered David Thompson to return his five shares of stock to the corporation in exchange for $500. ($100 per share was the price set in the articles of incorporation for repurchase by the corporation.) Defendants appealed.

Kass, Justice: ... The findings we have summarized describe a close corporation as defined in *Donahue v. Rodd Electrotype Co.,* 328 N.E.2d 505. Haltom has a small number of stockholders, no ready market for its corporate stock, and substantial majority stockholder participation in the management, direction, and operations of the corporation. Within such a corporation the principal stockholders owe to each other and minority stockholders the rigorous fiduciary duty of partners and participants in a joint venture. For persons in a partnership relation, as Judge Cardozo poetically phrased it, "not honesty alone, but the punctilio of an honor the most sensitive, is then the standard of behavior." *Meinhard v.*

Hallahan v. Haltom Corp.

Appeals Court of Massachusetts, 385 N.E.2d 1033 (1979)

Salmon, 164 N.E. 545, 546 (1928). The peremptory discharge of the Hallahans without warning, when compensation as employees was the principal benefit which they could hope to enjoy from the enterprise, is short of that standard. Depriving minority stockholders of corporate offices and employment is a particularly effective "freeze-out" device. An investor in a close corporation typically depends on his salary as the principal return on his investment, since the "earnings of a close corporation . . . are distributed in major part in salaries, bonuses, and retirement benefits." 1 F. H. O'Neal, Close Corporations §1.07 (2d ed. 1971). . . . [W]e must inquire whether the controlling group demonstrated a legitimate business purpose for its action. No such purpose appears in the unchallenged findings of the trial judge which, on the contrary, recite a peremptory seizure of control without prior warning. . . .

[Requiring David Thompson to return his five shares to the corporation] restored the balance of control among the Hallahans and the Thompsons which the trial judge found the parties had envisioned and which they had a fiduciary duty to each other to maintain. The action of the trial judge was consistent with the generic similarity of the duties of stockholders in a close corporation to each other and partners in a partnership . . . .

Judgment affirmed. [The court mentioned that, under Massachusetts law, the owners of fifty percent or more of a corporation's shares can obtain court-ordered dissolution. It can probably be assumed that either the Thompsons or the Hallahans subsequently obtained an order dissolving the corporation.]

Questions and Problems

1. Can a corporation be a partner? Explain.

2. Explain how the *ultra vires* doctrine has diminished in importance in recent years.

3. Charlestown Co. was dissolved, and its shareholders elected a committee to work with the board of directors in winding up the business. The laws of New Hampshire, where the case arose, provided that "the business of every such corporation shall be managed by the directors thereof, subject to the bylaws and votes of the corporation, and under their direction by such officers and agents as shall be duly appointed by the directors or by the corporation." The board ignored the committee. A shareholder filed suit challenging the board's failure to recognize the committee. *Charlestown Boot and Shoe Co. v. Dunsmore,* 60 N.H. 85 (1880). Did the board act properly? Discuss.

4. The directors of Omega Corp. proposed an amendment to the bylaws that would create a new class of shares with rights equal to an existing class. A special meeting was called to consider the amendment. The notice of the special meeting gave a brief statement about the amendment but did not mention the new class. The amendment was adopted at the meeting, but its validity was then challenged by a shareholder. Is the amendment valid? Discuss.

5. The bylaws of Thompson Co. set the quorum requirement for directors' meetings as a "majority of the directors." The number of directors provided for in the articles was eleven, but because of one death and one resignation, the board actually had only nine directors in office when it held a meeting in January 1976. Five directors attended. The action taken at the meeting was challenged by a shareholder on the ground that there had not been a quorum. Is the shareholder correct? Discuss.

6. Prince Co. owns a manufacturing plant, several trucks, and other items of equipment; it also owns two tracts of land of about five hundred acres each, which it holds as an investment. Prince Co. was in need of cash, so Girard, who is both president and treasurer, sought to obtain a loan for the company from City National Bank. As security for the loan, the bank wanted a mortgage on one of the tracts of land. Can Girard execute the mortgage without express authority from the board of directors? Discuss.

7. The president of Hessler, Inc., made a contract with an employee, Farrell, in which retirement benefits were promised to him. In the past, the president had been allowed to manage the company's affairs more or less independently of the board; he also owned approximately 80 percent of the corporation's stock. When Farrell retired, the corporation refused to pay the benefits, and Farrell sued. The corporation claimed that the agreement made with Farrell by the president was invalid because it had not been approved by the board of directors. *Hessler, Inc. v. Farrell*, 226 A.2d 708 (1967). Is the corporation correct? Discuss.

8. Acting for the company, the executive committee of Ace Corp.'s board of directors made a contract with Henson, who was to perform services for Ace. The corporation's bylaws provided that all contracts must be approved "by the board of directors," but elsewhere in the bylaws it was stated that "the executive committee shall conduct the corporation's business." Is the contract valid? Discuss.

9. Plymouth Co. made an agreement with United National Bank in which Plymouth was to receive a substantial loan. In consideration of the loan, it was agreed that Plymouth's shareholders would elect two directors designated by United, one of whom would be comptroller and have complete charge of all the corporation's finances. Is the agreement valid? Explain.

10. Should a corporation's board of directors be permitted to hire an employee under a contract guaranteeing lifetime employment? Discuss.

37

Corporations Rights and Liabilities of Shareholders and Managers

Successful operation of the corporate enterprise usually involves the concerted efforts of many people. Although success demands that their efforts be focused on essentially the same goals and objectives, their own *individual* interests inevitably come into play on some occasions. For this reason, we will now discuss the rights and liabilities of the parties to the corporate venture, with respect to one another, and with respect to the corporation as an entity.

Rights of Shareholders

Voting Rights

As indicated in the previous chapter, shareholders exercise their ultimate control by voting. Unless otherwise provided in the articles, a shareholder has one vote for each share. The right to vote does not have to be expressed in the articles of incorporation; it is inherent in the ownership of shares. Of course, the articles can expressly exclude or limit the right to vote—for example, by providing for the issuance of a certain number of special shares without voting rights.

Treasury stock (shares that have been issued and later repurchased by the corporation) carries no voting rights, since a corporation cannot logically act as a shareholder of itself. If these shares are subsequently resold, however, they once again carry voting rights.

Dividends

A person who purchases corporate shares is making an investment from which he or she obviously intends to receive a profit. Depending on the nature of the business and the type of shares purchased, the shareholder may expect such profit to arise either from increases in the market value of the shares, or from dividends, or perhaps from both.

Dividends are simply payments made by the corporation to its shareholders, representing income or profit on their investment. The payment is usually in the form of money, but it can consist of some type of property, such as the securities of another company that the corporation has been holding as an asset.

Sometimes the corporation pays a *stock dividend,* which is the issuance to shareholders of additional shares of the corporation's own stock. Such a distribution is *technically not a dividend,* because it does not represent a transfer of any property from the corporation to its shareholders. Instead, each shareholder simply becomes the owner of a larger number of shares. Although shareholders may not benefit immediately from a stock dividend, because the value of the preexisting shares is diluted, they usually do benefit in the long run due to the tendency of such shares to later increase in value.

The laws of the various states differ substantially with respect to the circumstances in which dividends can legally be paid. Generally, however, the following limitations are imposed:

1. Dividends cannot be paid if the corporation is insolvent or if the payment itself will cause the corporation to become insolvent. Depending on the particular state statute involved, *insolvency* is defined either as (a) the inability of the corporation to pay its debts as they become due, or (b) the possession of insufficient assets to meet all outstanding liabilities.

2. Dividends ordinarily can be paid only from a particular source. For example, some states allow dividends to be paid only from "current net earnings." This means that the source of funds for the payment must be the net profits of the corporation for the current year or the year just ended. Many states, however, permit dividends to be paid from any existing "surplus." In effect, this means that the payment must not be made out of the original capital investment in the corporation.

Shareholders do not have an absolute "right" to receive dividends. It is true that many corporations actually have long-established policies regarding payment of dividends. But whether a dividend is to be paid ("declared") in a given situation, and how large it is to be, are largely left to the discretion of the board of directors and usually cannot be challenged. A challenge to their decision ordinarily can be made only if (1) funds were not legally available for the dividend, or (2) the division among shareholders was not fair and uniform, or (3) the special rights of any particular class of stock were not observed.

Preferences

We have referred several times to different "classes" of corporate stock. The rights enjoyed by individual shareholders sometimes depend on the class of shares they own. In a given situation, a corporation might issue only one class of stock or it might issue several, depending upon the needs of the business.

Corporate stock is generally classified either as common or preferred. *Common stock,* the most basic and frequently issued type, enjoys no special privileges or preferences. *Preferred stock,* on the other hand, guarantees to its owner some type of special privilege or "preference" over the owners of common stock. The most frequently granted preferences relate to *dividends* and to *distribution of assets upon liquidation.*

Dividend Preferences: A preference as to dividends does not mean that the owners of the preferred shares are guaranteed the right to receive dividends. What it does mean is that, *if a dividend is declared,* owners of preferred stock have a priority over owners of common stock. For example: Zeta Corp. has issued one class of common stock and one class of preferred stock (the preferred stock being "$3 preferred"). In any given year, the owners of the common stock cannot be paid a dividend until the owners of the preferred stock have received a dividend of $3 per share. The preference can also be expressed as a percentage, such as "4 percent preferred." If this is the case, the owners of common stock cannot be paid a dividend until the preferred shareholders have received a dividend equal to 4 percent of the par value of their shares.

Shares that are preferred as to dividends may or may not be cumulative. When a dividend preference is *cumulative,* it means that if dividends are not paid in any year in the amount of the preference, they accumulate and must be paid in a future year before any dividend is paid to common shareholders. A majority of courts have held that preferred stock *is* cumulative unless there is an express statement in the articles of incorporation that it is not.

Furthermore, shares that are preferred as to dividends may or may not be participating. If preferred shares are *participating,* their holders are not only entitled to the original dividend, but, after the common shareholders receive a specified amount, they also share with the owners of common stock any additional dividends. Most of the time there is an express statement in the articles of incorporation that preferred stock is nonparticipating. But even without such a provision, a majority of courts have held preferred stock to be nonparticipating—in most states the only way for preferred stock to be participating is for the articles of incorporation to say that it is.

Liquidation Preferences: Owners of preferred stock sometimes are also given a preference as to the distribution of corporate assets in the event that the corporation is dissolved. It is customary to limit this preference to the par value of the preferred shares plus any unpaid dividends. And, of course, a liquidation preference gives preferred shareholders a priority only over common shareholders, not over creditors of the corporation.

Preemptive Rights

At Common Law: Suppose that Jupiter Corp. has a capitalization of $100,000, consisting of 1,000 shares of $100 par value common stock. X owns 100 shares of this stock. The corporation is in need of additional capital funds, so the shareholders authorize the issuance of another 1,000 shares. (This authorization is accomplished by a vote of the shareholders to amend the articles of incorporation.) If X is not given an opportunity to purchase shares of the new issue of stock, her proportionate interest in the corporation obviously will be reduced, and this will decrease her voting power and may result in her receiving a smaller amount of income from dividends.

For these reasons, the courts traditionally have recognized a concept known as the *preemptive right.* When a corporation issues new stock, the common-law preemptive right gives each shareholder an opportunity to purchase the number of new shares that will maintain his or her proportionate interest in the corporation. A shareholder possessing a preemptive right must be given notice and a reasonable amount of time to exercise the right by purchasing new shares. Anyone who fails to exercise this right within a reasonable time loses the right with respect to that particular issue of stock. A thirty-day period for exercising the right has been frequently used and is generally deemed reasonable.

Preemptive rights are of vital importance in a *close corporation,* where each shareholder possesses a substantial interest in the enterprise and usually takes an active role in management. But the significance of preemptive rights diminishes when the corporation's stock is *publicly sold and traded* (i.e., when the company is a so-called "publicly-held" corporation). In the latter case, the number of shareholders is often quite large and each shareholder usually owns a relatively small portion of the total outstanding shares.

Courts have not recognized preemptive rights in all circumstances. Following are two of the most important situations in which such rights have been held not to exist.

Treasury stock. If a corporation sells shares that it has been holding as treasury stock, it is obvious that this is not a "new issue" of shares and that there is no reduction in the proportionate interests of existing shareholders. Therefore, shareholders do not have preemptive rights with respect to sales of treasury stock.

Shares issued for consideration other than money. A corporation may sometimes have a good reason for accepting something other than cash as the consideration for shares that it issues. This occurs very frequently in connection with a *merger.* As we will see in Chapter 38, the merger of two corporations can be achieved by various means. In some cases the acquiring corporation may issue new shares of its stock, which will then be exchanged for the assets or the shares of the acquired corporation. In other situations not involving a merger, a corporation might issue shares to be used in the purchase of patent rights, real estate, equipment, or other property. Or shares may be issued and used as part of a compensation package to recruit a top executive. In these examples and in other instances of noncash share issuances, the corporation is ordinarily pursuing legitimate objectives that may be hindered, if not completely defeated, by the exercise of preemptive rights on the part of existing shareholders. For this reason, courts have generally held that preemptive rights do not apply to noncash issuances.

Statutory Treatment: In the earlier-mentioned example of Jupiter Corp., the recognition of X's preemptive right was an easy matter. But the financial structure of many modern corporations is much more complex than that of Jupiter. This is particularly true of publicly-held corporations, which often have several different classes of stock, each carrying different rights and preferences. This diversity of classes, coupled with the large number of shareholders, often makes it impractical to give complete recognition to preemptive rights. Furthermore, as previously mentioned, preemptive rights are often not of vital importance in publicly-held corporations. For these reasons, most state statutes today permit the articles of incorporation to determine the matter of preemptive rights. The articles can limit the circumstances in which these rights exist or can abolish them altogether. In actual practice, most publicly-held corporations have abolished preemptive rights in their articles.

Transferability of Shares

Shares of corporate stock are recognized by the law as items of property. As is true of other kinds of property, shares ordinarily can be sold or otherwise transferred as the owner wishes. Thus a shareholder has the right to transfer his or her shares to someone else unless a valid restriction has been placed on such transferability.

Restrictions: In some circumstances, it may be desirable for the corporation to restrict the shareholder's right to transfer his or her shares. Such restrictions are commonly employed by *close corporations,* because the shareholders themselves, who are few in number, actively manage the corporation and deal personally with one another on a daily basis. For example, assume that A, B, and C are the only shareholders of Prestige Corp. A and B will not want to wake up one morning and find that C has transferred his interest to D, a complete stranger with whom they will then have to share the management of the business.

Most restrictions on transferability take the form of *options to purchase,* which provide that a shareholder who wishes to sell his or her shares must first offer them to the corporation or to the other shareholders. Such restrictions are generally valid if a *reasonable time limit* is set for the exercise of the option. Provisions aimed at restricting transferability can be included in the articles or bylaws, but they are more often established by agreements among all the shareholders.

The existence of a transferability restriction should always be indicated explicitly on the *stock certificate*. The stock certificate is the formal document that provides evidence of the ownership of particular shares. It also provides evidence of the *agreement between the corporation and the shareholder* as to preferences, voting rights, and other terms. If the certificate does not include a notice of transfer restrictions, a purchaser of the shares is not bound by the restriction unless it can be proved that he or she knew of it.

Method of Transfer: There is nothing particularly unique about the way in which shares are transferred from one party to another. The terms of the sale or other type of transfer are negotiated, a contract is made, and the current shareholder endorses the stock certificate to the transferee. No other formal steps are required to effectuate the transfer. Practical considerations, however, dictate that the corporation should always be notified of the transaction, since the new shareholder will have no right to vote or receive dividends unless the corporation's records are changed to reflect his or her ownership.

Inspection Rights

Unless limited by statute, every shareholder possesses the basic right of *access to corporate records.* This includes not only the right to inspect and copy corporate records personally but also the right to employ accountants, attorneys, stenographers, or other assistants as may reasonably be required to get the necessary information.

The right of inspection is one that possesses a definite potential for abuse. It could be used, for example, merely for harassment during a struggle for control of the corporation. Or a competitor could purchase a few shares and use the right to obtain trade secrets or other confidential information. Furthermore, even if the purposes for the inspection are legitimate, the existence of a large number of shareholders might cause unrestricted inspection rights to be impractical.

For these reasons, limitations are often placed on the inspection right. An illustration of the types of limitations that are frequently imposed is found in Sec. 52 of the Model Act:

> Any person who shall have been a holder of record of shares . . . *at least six months* immediately preceding his demand *or* shall be the holder of record of . . . *at least five percent* of all the outstanding shares of the corporation, *upon written demand stating the purpose thereof,* shall have the right to examine, in person, or by agent or attorney, *at any reasonable time or times, for any proper purpose* its relevant books and records of accounts, minutes, and record of shareholders and to make extracts therefrom. [Emphasis added.]

It may well be imagined that the question of whether a shareholder's proposed inspection is for a "proper purpose" is fraught with many difficulties. In the following case, the court is faced with the problem of whether a shareholder's desire to inspect corporate records must actually have an *economic* motivation.

Pillsbury v. Honeywell, Inc.

Supreme Court of
Minnesota, 191 N.W.2d
406 (1971)

Honeywell, a Delaware corporation, operated a manufacturing facility in a city in Minnesota where Pillsbury lived. On July 3, 1969, Pillsbury learned that Honeywell produced munitions for use in the Vietnam War. He had long opposed the war and believed that America's involvement therein was wrong. He was shocked at the knowledge that Honeywell had a large government contract to produce antipersonnel fragmentation bombs. Upset by the knowledge that such bombs were produced in his own community by a company he had known and respected, Pillsbury was determined to stop Honeywell's munitions production.

On July 14, Pillsbury bought several shares of Honeywell stock. He later admitted that the sole purpose of the purchase was to give himself a voice in Honeywell's affairs so that he could persuade the company to cease munitions production.

Shortly thereafter, Pillsbury made a formal demand on two different occasions that Honeywell permit him access to its shareholder ledger and all corporate records dealing with weapons manufacture. Honeywell rejected these demands. Pillsbury sued to require Honeywell to produce the records, claiming that a shareholder who disagrees with management has an absolute right to inspect corporate records for the purpose of communicating with other shareholders and soliciting proxies from them. Honeywell, on the other hand, argued that a "proper purpose" for inspection must be one that involves an economic concern.

The trial court agreed with Honeywell and held that it did not have to allow inspection by Pillsbury. Pillsbury appealed.

Kelly, Justice: . . . [A] stockholder is entitled to inspection for a proper purpose germane to his business interests. While inspection will not be permitted for purposes of curiosity, speculation, or vexation, adverseness to management and a desire to gain control of the corporation for economic benefit does not indicate an improper purpose.

Several courts agree with [Pillsbury's] contention that a mere desire to communicate with other shareholders is, per se, a proper purpose. This would seem to confer an almost absolute right to inspection. We believe that a better rule would allow inspections only if the shareholder has a proper purpose for such communication. This rule was applied in *McMahon v. Dispatch Printing Co.*, 129 A. 425 (1925), where inspection was denied because the shareholder's objective was to discredit politically the president of the company, who was also the New Jersey secretary of state.

The act of inspecting a corporation's shareholder ledger and business records must be viewed in its proper perspective. In terms of the corporate norm, inspection is merely the act of the concerned owner checking on what is in part his property. In the context of the large firm, inspection can be more akin to a weapon in corporate warfare. The effectiveness of the weapon is considerable:

> Considering the huge size of many modern corporations and the necessarily complicated nature of their bookkeeping, it is plain that to permit their thousands of stockholders to roam at will through their records would render impossible not only any attempt to keep their records efficiently, but the proper carrying on of their businesses. *Cooke v. Outland,* 144 S.E.2d 835 (1965).

Because the power to inspect may be the power to destroy, it is important that only those with a bona fide interest in the corporation enjoy that power. . . .

[Pillsbury] had utterly no interest in the affairs of Honeywell before he learned of

Honeywell's production of fragmentation bombs. . . . But for his opposition to Honeywell's policy, [Pillsbury] probably would not have bought Honeywell stock, would not be interested in Honeywell's profits and would not desire to communicate with Honeywell's shareholders. His avowed purpose in buying Honeywell stock was to place himself in a position to try to impress his opinions favoring a reordering of priorities upon Honeywell management and its other shareholders. Such a motivation can hardly be deemed a proper purpose germane to his economic interest as a shareholder. . . .

We do not mean to imply that a shareholder with a bona fide investment interest could not bring this suit if motivated by concern with the long- or short-term economic effects on Honeywell resulting from the production of war munitions. Similarly, this suit might be appropriate when a shareholder has a bona fide concern about the adverse effects of abstention from profitable war contracts on his investment in Honeywell.

In the instant case, however, the trial court, in effect, has found from all the facts that [Pillsbury] was not interested in even the long-term well-being of Honeywell or the enhancement of the value of his shares. His sole purpose was to persuade the company to adopt his social and political concerns, irrespective of any economic benefit to himself or Honeywell. This purpose on the part of one buying into the corporation does not entitle [him] to inspect Honeywell's books and records. . . .

[Affirmed.]

Liabilities of Shareholders

As we saw earlier, one of the basic attributes of the corporate form of doing business is the limited liability of the owners. That is, shareholders are usually not personally liable for the debts of the corporation; they may lose their investment in the corporation if it is a failure, but usually their liability ends there. We also saw that in a few exceptional circumstances the separate identity of the corporation can be disregarded and liability imposed on the shareholders. We will now examine a few other situations in which the personal liability of shareholders can become an issue.

Liability on Stock Subscriptions

A *stock subscription* is an offer by a prospective investor (a "subscriber") to buy shares of stock in a corporation. The ordinary rules of contract law apply to such offers, and they can thus be revoked prior to acceptance by the corporation—with two important exceptions:

1. Stock subscriptions are frequently made by the promoters before formation of the corporation. It is not uncommon for several promoters to agree that their subscriptions cannot be revoked for some period of time. In such a case, the subscriptions are irrevocable for the agreed time.

2. The statutes of a majority of states provide that a subscription is irrevocable for a certain time period, unless the subscription itself expressly provides that it can be revoked. For example, the Model Act provides for a six-month period of irrevocability.

A stock subscription can be made either before or after incorporation. Where it is made prior to formation of the corporation, some states hold that acceptance of the offer occurs automatically when the corporation comes into existence. In other states, the subscription must be formally accepted by the board after incorporation. Where the subscription is made for shares in an existing corporation, there obviously must be a formal acceptance by the board. (Of course, the sale of shares by an existing corporation often does not involve stock subscriptions at all. Instead, the corporation itself is frequently the offeror.)

In any event, an accepted stock subscription is a contract, and the subscriber is liable for damages to the corporation if he or she breaches that contract by refusing to pay the agreed price.

Liability for Watered Stock

We mentioned in a previous chapter that corporate stock can be issued either as "par value" or "no-par value" shares. Par value shares cannot lawfully be issued unless the corporation receives consideration at least equal to the par value. In the case of no-par shares, the consideration must be at least equal to the "stated value" (a value placed upon the shares by the board or by the existing shareholders).

The consideration can be in the form of money, property, or services actually rendered (not just promised) to the corporation.[1] The board of directors generally determines the value of property or services received in return for shares, and this determination ordinarily will not be reviewed by a court so long as it appears to have been made in good faith.

Shares issued for less than the par or stated value are referred to as *watered stock.* A shareholder is personally liable for the deficiency (the "water"). This liability is usually to the corporation itself, but in some states an owner of watered stock is liable directly to the corporation's creditors when their claims cannot be satisfied out of corporate assets. Thus a shareholder can incur liability even if he or she has paid the agreed price for the shares, if that agreed price was less than the par or stated value. Of course, this rule applies only to the initial purchase of shares from the corporation upon their issuance, not to later purchases from the shareholder ("on the market") or to purchases of treasury shares.

Liability for Illegal Dividends

Shareholders usually are liable for the return of any dividend that was improperly paid, as indicated below:

1. If the dividend is paid while the corporation is *insolvent,* shareholders are *always* liable for its return.

---

[1] In some states, the preincorporation services rendered by promoters or others can be treated as consideration for shares.

2. In the case of any other illegal dividend, a shareholder usually is required to account for its return only if he or she *knew* of the illegality when receiving payment. Examples of such illegal dividends are those that cause the corporation to become insolvent (as opposed to those made when the corporation is already insolvent) and those paid from an unauthorized source.

The liability of a shareholder for the return of an illegal dividend ordinarily is to the corporation itself. If the corporation is insolvent, however, the shareholder's liability often is to the corporation's creditors instead. Of course, those directors responsible for paying the illegal dividend also incur liability. When directors are subjected to such liability, however, they generally are allowed to recoup their loss from those shareholders who *knew* the dividend was illegal when they received it.

In the following discussion the rights of directors will be dealt with separately from the rights of officers and other managerial employees. The reason for this is that some of the rights possessed by directors are unique to their position.

Rights of Corporate Managers

Directors

Recognition and Participation: A director who has been properly elected possesses several rights of a very basic nature—for instance, the right to be recognized as a director by his or her associates, the right to receive notice of board meetings, and the right to attend and participate in them. A duly-elected director who is excluded from recognition or participation by his or her associates can obtain a court order enforcing these rights.

Inspection: The right of directors to inspect all corporate records is somewhat similar to the inspection right possessed by shareholders. However, the reasons for allowing inspection by directors are even stronger than those for allowing shareholder inspection. Directors *must* have complete access to corporate records in order to fully discharge their decision-making responsibilities. It obviously would be unfair to hold them responsible for paying an illegal dividend, for example, if corporate financial records had not been completely at their disposal.

Because of this compelling need for access to corporate books, most states hold that a director's right of inspection is *absolute and unqualified* (that is, not subject to the various limitations that are often placed on a shareholder's inspection right). Of course, a director's abuse of this right can provide a basis for his or her removal from the board, as illustrated in *Campbell v. Loew's, Inc.* in the previous chapter. And a director is liable for any damage to the corporation resulting from abuse of the right (such as its use for an improper purpose). But in the majority of states where the director's inspection right is absolute, *neither the other directors, the officers, nor the shareholders can restrict his or her examination of corporate records.*[2]

Compensation: The traditional rule was that directors were not entitled to compensation for their services to the corporation. This rule was predicated on the assumption that directors were usually shareholders and would receive their compensation in the form of dividends. It also took into account the fact that some directors also served as corporate officers and received compensation for their services in those positions.

The basis for this rule is not applicable to many modern corporations, however. It is not uncommon today for individuals having little or no stock ownership to serve as directors. Furthermore, a great many directors serve only as directors and do not hold other positions with the corporation.

For these reasons, there is a growing trend in modern corporations toward compensation of directors as such. The traditional rule provides no real obstacle to this trend, because it simply holds that directors have no inherent *right* to be compensated. They can in fact be paid if there is a valid authorization for such payment in the articles or bylaws. Indeed, the statutes of some states today go even farther, providing, for example, that the board of directors can fix the compensation of its own members unless the articles or bylaws state otherwise. Directors are, of course, responsible for any abuse of this power.

Indemnification: The performance of their management responsibilities sometimes causes directors to become involved in legal proceedings. For example, the directors may be sued by a shareholder who claims that they acted negligently in managing the corporation. Or they may be charged by the government in a civil or criminal suit with a violation of the antitrust laws.

The costs of such lawsuits to the individual director, in terms of both expenses and potential liability for damages or fines, may be quite substantial. Under the common-law rule a director had no right to be indemnified (reimbursed) by the corporation for expenses or other losses. Today, however, the statutes of most states do permit indemnification of corporate directors in some circumstances. An excellent illustration of the modern statutory trend is found in Sec. 5 of the Model Act, which can be summarized as follows:

1. In general, the corporation is authorized (but not required) to indemnify a director regardless of whether he actually committed a wrongful act, "if he acted in good faith and in a manner he reasonably believed to be in . . . the best interests of the corporation." This rule applies to an ordinary civil lawsuit or to a legal proceeding brought by an administrative agency.

2. Special rules are applied, however, to a "shareholders' derivative suit"—a lawsuit brought by one or more shareholders *in behalf of the corporation* (rather than

---

[2]The courts in a *few* states, however, have held that a director's inspection right can be denied where his or her motive is obviously hostile or otherwise improper.

in their own behalf). In this type of case, indemnification usually is not permitted if the director is actually found guilty of negligence or misconduct in the performance of his or her duties.

3. If the director is criminally prosecuted, indemnification is authorized only if the director (a) "acted in good faith and in a manner he reasonably believed to be in . . . the best interests of the corporation," *and* (b) "had no reasonable cause to believe his conduct was unlawful."

Officers and Other Managerial Employees

Corporate officers and other individuals who have managerial responsibilities are simply *employees* of the corporation.[3] It naturally follows, therefore, that the rights they have with respect to compensation and other matters are determined by their employment contracts.

Since their positions involve them in corporate decision making, officers and other managerial employees are subject to many of the same risks of litigation as are directors. Thus the rules regarding indemnification are the same for directors, officers, and managerial employees. That is, everything we have said about indemnification of directors applies with equal force to all others occupying management positions.

Those who manage the corporate enterprise owe to the corporation and its shareholders a number of basic duties that can be classified under the headings of *obedience, diligence,* and *loyalty.* A corporate manager incurs personal liability for the failure to fulfill any of these duties. In addition to these fundamental duties, certain special liabilities are imposed by federal securities laws. Unlike the previous section on the *rights* of corporate managers, our discussion of *liabilities* makes no distinction between directors and other types of managers. The duties and liabilities of all who manage the corporation are essentially the same.

Liabilities of Corporate Managers

Obedience

Corporate managers have a duty to see that the corporation obeys the law and confines its operations to those activities that are within the limits of its corporate powers. If they knowingly or carelessly involve the corporation in either an illegal or *ultra vires* act, they are personally liable for any resulting damage to the corporation.[4]

---

[3]The word *employee* is used in a nontechnical sense. Managers and supervisors are not considered "employees" under some other specialized laws, such as those governing labor-management relations. But such laws are not our concern here.

[4]Of course, any manager who participates in the commission of an illegal act also may be personally subject to fines or other penalties imposed by the particular law.

Diligence

The duty of diligence is sometimes referred to as the duty of "due care." It is, in effect, a duty "not to be negligent."

Two standards have been employed for measuring a manager's diligence. In a few states, a director or other manager is required to exercise the kind of care in handling corporate affairs that an ordinarily prudent person would exercise under similar circumstances in the conduct of his or her own affairs. A majority of states, however, consider this test to be too strict. They follow the rule that a corporate manager must exercise only the kind of care that an ordinarily prudent person would exercise in a similar position and under similar circumstances.

Examples of the type of conduct that might violate the duty of diligence are (1) the repeated and unexcused failure of a director to attend board meetings, (2) the failure to properly examine corporate financial records before making an important decision, and (3) the failure to adequately supervise an inept subordinate.

In making business decisions, a director, officer, or other manager is entitled to rely on the advice of experts such as attorneys and accountants. On the other hand, a manager cannot "hide behind" the attorney or accountant and fail to exercise his or her own sound business judgment. In other words, reliance on expert advice protects the manager from responsibility only if it is reasonable and prudent to rely on that advice under the circumstances. It would not be reasonable, for example, to rely on an attorney's advice that price-fixing is perfectly legitimate.

Although held to a standard of reasonable care, a manager is generally not liable for "honest mistakes." For example, no breach of duty occurs where a manager, acting in good faith, involves the corporation in a transaction that initially appears to have a reasonable probability of success but that actually turns out to be unprofitable. The rule that protects a corporate manager from responsibility for honest errors of judgment is often referred to as the *business judgment rule*. Of course, whether a particular act is merely an honest mistake or whether it amounts to negligence is a question of fact that depends on all the surrounding circumstances. Often it is a matter of degree. Thus, if an act is so obviously foolish or absurd as to show an entire lack of judgment or good sense, the manager is not shielded by the business judgment rule.

Each of the following cases involve claims that corporate directors had been negligent in their management of the business.

Shlensky v. Wrigley
Appellate Court of
Illinois, 237 N.E.2d 776
(1968)

Shlensky, the plaintiff, is a minority shareholder in Chicago National League Ball Club, Inc. The corporation owns and operates the major league professional baseball team known as the Chicago Cubs. The individual defendants are directors of the Cubs. Defendant Philip K. Wrigley is also president of the corporation and owner of approximately 80 percent of the corporation's shares.

Shlensky filed suit in behalf of the corporation (a derivative suit), claiming that it had been damaged by the failure of the directors to have lights installed in Wrigley

Field, the Cubs' home park. No trial was held, however, because the trial court dismissed his complaint on the ground that it did not set forth a claim that the law would recognize even if his version of the facts were correct. Shlensky appealed.

Sullivan, Justice: . . . Plaintiff alleges that since night baseball was first played in 1935 nineteen of the twenty major league teams have scheduled night games. In 1966, out of a total of 1620 games in the major leagues, 932 were played at night. Plaintiff alleges that every member of the major leagues, other than the Cubs, scheduled substantially all of its home games in 1966 at night, exclusive of opening days, Saturdays, Sundays, holidays and days prohibited by league rules. Allegedly this has been done for the specific purpose of maximizing attendance and thereby maximizing revenue and income.

The Cubs, in the years 1961–65, sustained operating losses from its direct baseball operations. Plaintiff attributes those losses to inadequate attendance at Cubs' home games. He concludes that if the directors continue to refuse to install lights at Wrigley Field and schedule night baseball games, the Cubs will continue to sustain comparable losses and its financial condition will continue to deteriorate.

Plaintiff alleges that, except for the year 1963, attendance at Cubs' home games has been substantially below that at their road games, many of which were played at night.

Plaintiff compares attendance at Cubs' games with that of the Chicago White Sox, an American League club, whose weekday games were generally played at night. The weekend attendance figures for the two teams was similar; however, the White Sox week-night games drew many more patrons that did the Cubs' weekday games. . . .

Plaintiff further alleges that defendant Wrigley has refused to install lights, not because of interest in the welfare of the corporation but because of his personal opinions "that baseball is a 'daytime sport' and that the installation of lights and night baseball games will have a deteriorating effect upon the surrounding neighborhood." It is alleged that he has admitted that he is not interested in whether the Cubs would benefit financially from such action because of his concern for the neighborhood, and that he would be willing for the team to play night games if a new stadium were built in Chicago. . . .

Plaintiff . . . argues that the directors are acting for reasons unrelated to the financial interest and welfare of the Cubs. However, we are not satisfied that the motives assigned to Philip K. Wrigley, and through him to the other directors, are contrary to the best interests of the corporation and the stockholders. For example, it appears to us that the effect on the surrounding neighborhood might well be considered by a director who was considering the patrons who would or would not attend the games if the park were in a poor neighborhood. Furthermore, the long run interest of the corporation in its property value at Wrigley Field might demand all efforts to keep the neighborhood from deteriorating. By these thoughts we do not mean to say that we have decided that the decision of the directors was a correct one. That is beyond our jurisdiction and ability. We are merely saying that the decision is one [for the] directors [to make] . . . .

Finally, we do not agree with plaintiff's contention that failure to follow the example of the other major league clubs in scheduling night games constituted negligence. Plaintiff made no allegation that these teams' night schedules were profitable or that the purpose for which night baseball had been undertaken was fulfilled. Furthermore, it cannot be said that directors, even those of corporations that are losing money, must follow the lead of the other corporations in the field. Directors are elected for their business capabilities and judgment and the courts cannot require them to forego their judgment because of the decisions of directors of other companies. Courts may not decide these questions in the absence of a clear showing of dereliction of duty on the part of the specific directors and mere failure to "follow the crowd" is not such a dereliction.

For the foregoing reasons the order of dismissal entered by the trial court is affirmed.

Francis v. United Jersey Bank

Superior Court of New Jersey, 392 A.2d 1233 (1978)

Pritchard & Baird Intermediaries Corp. ("Pritchard & Baird") was engaged in the business of being a "reinsurance broker." (If an insurance company has a very large individual risk or a number of similar risks on which it has given coverage, it often protects itself from too heavy a loss by shifting the risk to another large insurer or group of insurers. It does this by "reinsuring," that is, by purchasing insurance on all or part of the underlying risk from one or more other insurers. A reinsurance broker brings the parties together in a reinsurance arrangement.) Charles Pritchard, Sr., the founder of the company, was for many years its principal shareholder and controlling force. In 1970 he took his sons, Charles, Jr. and William, into the business. Because of the father's advancing age, the two sons played an increasingly dominant role in the affairs of the corporation. After the father's death in 1973, the sons took complete control.

Pritchard & Baird had been a successful company under the control of Charles, Sr., even though he engaged in various questionable business practices. He commingled the funds of different clients, commingled the company's funds with his own personal funds, and kept incredibly poor records. However, his clients were always taken care of and his creditors were always paid. After his sons took over, they continued his sloppy business practices but did not continue taking care of clients and paying creditors. In essence, they "looted" the company of millions of dollars and by the end of 1975 had plunged it into bankruptcy.

Francis was appointed as trustee in bankruptcy for Pritchard & Baird. In this capacity he sought to recover for Pritchard & Baird's creditors several million dollars which had been wrongfully taken from the company. He brought suit against two defendants: (1) the father's estate, of which United Jersey Bank was administrator; and (2) the estate of Lillian Pritchard. Lillian Pritchard was the wife of Charles, Sr., who died after the bankruptcy proceedings began, and had served as a director of the corporation from its creation until its bankruptcy. Apparently because of the size of Lillian Pritchard's personal estate, the primary question in the case was whether she had acted negligently in her role as a director by not discovering and stopping the illegal actions of her sons. If so, her estate would be liable for that negligence. The trial court's opinion follows. (Note: There was no mention of the whereabouts of the two sons.)

Stanton, Judge: . . . Directors are responsible for the general management of the affairs of a corporation. They have particular responsibility with respect to distributions of assets to shareholders and with respect to loans to officers and directors. It is true that in this case the directors were never asked to take explicit and formal action with respect to any of the unlawful payments made to members of the Pritchard family. I am satisfied that, in terms of her actual knowledge, Mrs. Pritchard did not know what her sons were doing to the corporation and she did not know that it was unlawful. She did not intend to cheat anyone or to defraud creditors of the corporation. However, if Mrs. Pritchard had paid the slightest attention to her duties as a director, and if she had paid the slightest attention to the affairs of the corporation, she would have known what was happening.

Financial statements were prepared for Pritchard & Baird every year. They were simple statements, typically no longer than three or four pages. The annual financial statements accurately and clearly reflected the payments to members of the Pritchard family, and they clearly reflected the desperate financial condition of the corporation. For example, a brief glance at the statement for the fiscal year ending on January 31, 1970 would have revealed that Charles, Jr. had withdrawn from the corporation $230,932 to which he was not entitled, and William had improperly withdrawn $207,329. A brief glance at the statement for the year ending January 31, 1973 would have shown Charles, Jr. owing the corporation $1,899,288 and William owing it $1,752,318. The same statement showed a working capital deficit of $3,506,460. The statement for the fiscal year ending January 31, 1975, a simple four-page document, showed Charles, Jr. owing the corporation $4,373,928, William owing $5,417,388, and a working capital deficit of $10,176,419. All statements reflected the fact that the corporation had virtually no assets and that liabilities vastly exceeded assets. In short, anyone who took a brief glance at the annual statements at any time after January 31, 1970 and who had the slightest knowledge of the corporation's business activities would know that Charles, Jr. and William were, in simple and blunt terms, stealing money which should have been paid to the corporation's customers.

. . . [T]he inherent nature of a corporate director's job necessarily implies that he must have a basic idea of the corporation's activities. He should know what business the corporation is in, and he should have some broad idea of the scope and range of the corporation's affairs. In terms of our case, Mrs. Pritchard should have known that Pritchard & Baird was in the reinsurance business as a broker and that it annually handled millions of dollars belonging to, or owing to various clients. Charged with that knowledge, it seems to me that a director in Mrs. Pritchard's position had, at the bare minimum, an obligation to ask for and read the annual financial statements of the corporation. She would then have the obligation to react appropriately to what a reading of the statements revealed.

It has been urged in this case that Mrs. Pritchard should not be held responsible for what happened while she was a director of Pritchard & Baird because she was a simple housewife who served as a director as an accommodation to her husband and sons. Let me start by saying that I reject the sexism which is unintended but which is implicit in such an argument. There is no reason why the average housewife could not adequately discharge the functions of a director of a corporation such as Pritchard & Baird, despite a lack of business career experience, if she gave some reasonable attention to what she was supposed to be doing. The problem is not that Mrs. Pritchard was a simple housewife. The problem is that she was a person who took a job which necessarily entailed certain responsibilities and she then failed to make any effort whatever to discharge those responsibilities. The ultimate insult to the fundamental dignity and equality of women would be to treat a grown woman as though she were a child not responsible for her acts and omissions.

It has been argued that allowance should be made for the fact that during the last years in question Mrs. Pritchard was old, was grief-stricken at the loss of her husband, sometimes consumed too much alcohol and was psychologically overborne by her sons. I was not impressed by the testimony supporting that argument. There is no proof whatever that Mrs. Pritchard ever ceased to be fully competent. There is no proof that she ever made any effort as a director to question or stop the unlawful activities of Charles, Jr. and William. The actions of the sons were so blatantly wrongful that it is hard to see how they could have resisted any moderately firm objection to what they were doing. The fact is that Mrs. Pritchard never knew what they were doing because she never made the slightest effort to discharge any of her responsibilities as a director of Pritchard & Baird.

Defense counsel have argued that Mrs. Pritchard should not be held liable because she was a mere "figurehead director." . . . In legal contemplation there is no such thing as a "figurehead" director. This has been clearly recognized for many years so far as banking corporations are concerned. 3A *Fletcher, Cyclopedia of the Law of Private Corporations,* §1090, has this to say:

> It frequently happens that persons become directors of banking houses for the purpose of capitalizing the position in the community where the bank does business, without any intention of watching or participating in the conduct of its affairs. It is a dangerous practice for the director, since such figureheads and rubber stamps are universally held liable on the ground that they have not discharged their duty nor exercised the required amount of diligence exacted of them.

There is no reason why the rule stated by *Fletcher* should be limited to banks. Certainly, there is no reason why the rule should not be extended to a corporation such as Pritchard & Baird which routinely handled millions of dollars belonging to, or owing to, other persons. . . .

I hold that Mrs. Pritchard was negligent in performing her duties as a director of Pritchard & Baird. Had she performed her duties with due care, she would readily have discovered the wrongdoing of Charles, Jr. and William shortly after the close of the fiscal year ending on January 31, 1970, and she could easily have taken effective steps to stop the wrongdoing. Her negligence caused customers and creditors of Pritchard & Baird to suffer losses amounting to $10,355,736.91. There will be a judgment against her estate in that amount.

Loyalty

Directors, officers, and other corporate managers are deemed to be *fiduciaries* of the corporation they serve. Their relationship to the corporation and its shareholders is one of trust. They must act in good faith and with the highest regard for the corporation's interests as opposed to their personal interests. Several problems that commonly arise in the context of the duty of loyalty are discussed below.

Use of Corporate Funds: Obviously, a director or other party who occupies a fiduciary position with respect to the corporation must not use corporate funds for his or her own purposes.

Confidential Information: A director or other manager sometimes possesses confidential information that is valuable to the corporation, such as secret formulas, product designs, marketing strategies, or customer lists. The manager is not allowed to appropriate such information for his or her own use.

Contracts with the Corporation: A corporate manager who enters into a contract with the corporation should realize that it is not in an "arms-length" transaction.

That is, the manager must make a full disclosure of all material information he or she possesses regarding the transaction. Furthermore, if the contract is at all unfair to the corporation, it is *voidable* at the corporation's option.

For obvious reasons, courts have not looked kindly upon contracts in which a *director* has a personal interest. (The contract might be with the director personally or with another company in which he or she has a financial stake.) If a contract of this nature was authorized at a board meeting where the presence of the interested director was necessary for a quorum or where this director's vote was required for a majority, most states hold the contract to be voidable at the corporation's option *regardless of its fairness.*

Corporate Opportunity: The *corporate opportunity* rule prohibits corporate managers from personally taking advantage of business opportunities that, in all fairness, should belong to the corporation. An obvious violation of this rule occurs when a manager has been authorized to purchase land or other property for the corporation but instead purchases it for himself.

Application of the corporate opportunity rule is sometimes not so clear-cut, however. A much more difficult problem is presented, for instance, when a director or other manager is confronted with a business opportunity arising from an *outside source* rather than from direct corporate authorization. For example: C is a director of Ace Air Freight, a corporation engaged in the business of transporting freight by air. C learns that M, a third party, has a used airplane in excellent condition that he is offering for sale at a low price. Can C purchase the airplane for himself? If the plane is of a type suitable for the corporation's freight business, the answer probably is no. He is obligated to inform the corporation of the opportunity.

This example illustrates the so-called "line of business" test employed by most courts in resolving such problems. Under this approach, a corporate manager cannot take personal advantage of a business opportunity that is *closely associated with the corporation's line of business.* Furthermore, the rule includes opportunities not only in the area of current corporate business but also in areas where the corporation might naturally expand.

Of course, if the corporation is actually offered the opportunity and *rejects* it, an individual manager can then exploit it. Similarly, if the corporation is legally or financially *unable* to accept an opportunity, a manager can take personal advantage of it.

The following case illustrates the type of "double dealing" which the corporate opportunity doctrine is designed to prevent.

Bio-Lab, Inc. was formed in 1972 by Joseph Morad, Joseph Thomson, George Coupounas, and Dr. June Shaw for the purpose of establishing a plasmapheresis business. In this business, red blood cells are separated from the plasma of a paid blood donor and returned to the donor's circulatory system. The plasma is then sold to biological manufacturing companies. Initially, Bio-Lab opened an office in

Morad v. Coupounas
Supreme Court of Alabama, 361 So.2d 6 (1978)

Birmingham with Morad, who had approximately five and one-half years experience in the plasmapheresis business, as president. Coupounas, a resident of Massachusetts, was to handle the books.

By mid-1973, dissension had arisen among the directors and stockholders of Bio-Lab over Morad's compensation. In June 1973, Thomson purchased Dr. Shaw's stock so that the ownership of Bio-Lab was divided as follows: Morad, 42 percent; Thomson, 28 percent; Coupounas, 30 percent. Several months later Coupounas and Dr. Shaw were removed from the board of directors and replaced by Morad's wife, Pamela, and two other individuals.

In February 1974, Morad, his wife, and Thomson incorporated another plasmapheresis business, Med-Lab, Inc., that began operating in Tuscaloosa in September 1974. Since that time, Morad has served as president of both Bio-Lab and Med-Lab, working "full-time" for both corporations, according to the corporate tax returns. Both corporations were profitable.

In May 1976, Coupounas, eliminated from any interest in the Tuscaloosa venture, filed suit individually, and for the benefit of Bio-Lab, against Med-Lab, Morad, Morad's wife, and Thomson, alleging a breach of fiduciary duty to Bio-Lab in the formation of Med-Lab. The trial court rendered judgment for Coupounas and ordered the defendants to offer him 30 percent of the stock of Med-Lab. Defendants appealed.

Faulkner, Justice: ... In *Lagarde v. Anniston Lime & Stone Co.*, 28 So. 199 (1899), this Court first formulated its doctrine of corporate opportunity. There it was stated:

> ... [I]n general the legal restrictions which rest upon such officers in their acquisitions are generally limited to property wherein the corporation has an interest already existing, or in which it has an expectancy growing out of an existing right, or to cases where the officers' interference will in some degree balk the corporation in effecting the purposes of its creation.

The last restriction in *Lagarde*, that which prohibits "balking the corporate purpose," is really quite broad in its formulation. . . .

[W]hether or not an officer has misappropriated a corporate opportunity and thereby balked the corporate purpose does not depend on any single factor. On the contrary,

> "[n]umerous factors are to be weighed, including the manner in which the offer was communicated to the officer; the good faith of the officer; the use of corporate assets to acquire the opportunity; the financial ability of the corporation to acquire the opportunity; the degree of disclosure made to the corporation; the action taken by the corporation with reference thereto; and the need or interest of the corporation in the opportunity. These, as well as numerous other factors, are weighed in a given case. The presence or absence of any single factor is not determinative of the issue of corporate opportunity." *Paulman v. Kritzer*, 219 N.E.2d 541 (1966).

... Here the trial court specifically found that one of the corporate purposes of Bio-Lab was to expand into specific new areas, including Tuscaloosa. Ample evidence in the record supports this conclusion. Bio-Lab's certificate of incorporation declared that one of the purposes of the business was "to have one or more offices." While this open-ended, boilerplate language standing alone might not be sufficient to support the trial court's findings, testimony and exhibits produced at trial show that expansion to Tuscaloosa was anticipated for Bio-Lab's future.

As pointed out above, one of the factors to be considered by the trial court is the corporation's financial ability to undertake the new enterprise, although financial ability must be carefully considered and will not necessarily be determinative. . . .

Testimony on the issue of financial ability was given at trial by Herbert Raburn, a certified public accountant, familiar with the books of both Bio-Lab and Med-Lab. Counsel for Morad sought to have Raburn testify that Bio-Lab could not have obtained a loan to finance expansion to Tuscaloosa. In fact, no one had ever sought a loan for this purpose. Because no loan had been sought, the trial court refused to allow Raburn to testify on this point, and observed that any testimony on what a particular bank would do, would be, under the circumstances, highly speculative. We agree. Raburn admitted that he knew only "in general terms" what banks look for in making loans. Consequently, he was not qualified to testify whether or not Bio-Lab could have gotten a loan.

Furthermore, Raburn's testimony revealed that $44,000 had been required to establish Med-Lab. At the end of 1974 Bio-Lab had only $24,300 available for this purpose. But, Raburn also testified that in 1974 Bio-Lab had paid a "rather high" dividend of $20,000. His testimony indicated that the payment of dividends is often restricted when a corporation wishes to expand. Thus, if the dividend had not been paid, Bio-Lab clearly should have had the financial ability to expand to Tuscaloosa, with or without a loan. In light of this testimony the trial court's finding that defendants improperly formed Med-Lab to the detriment of Bio-Lab is clearly supportable and will not be disturbed by this Court on appeal.

We do not, however, feel that the trial court was justified in ordering defendants to offer 30 percent of Med-Lab's stock to Coupounas. The traditional remedy in cases of this sort is a constructive trust imposed for the benefit of the corporation. . . . One purpose for preserving the use of a constructive trust in this sort of situation is to avoid forcing individuals into business together under strained circumstances. Such a situation would only be counterproductive. The policy underlying the use of a constructive trust is well illustrated by this case. Coupounas and defendants were not getting along prior to the formation of Med-Lab. It is hardly likely that their relations have improved through the course of this lawsuit. While the courts should strive to place the parties in their proper financial positions, they should not force individuals into business arrangements they clearly do not want. Here, a constructive trust for the benefit of Bio-Lab was the appropriate remedy.

[Affirmed. Note: Although the court affirmed the decision in favor of Coupounas, it returned the case to the trial court with an order that the trial court impose a constructive trust on Med-Lab. What this means is that Med-Lab's profits would belong to Bio-Lab.]

Controlling Shareholders: In some situations, *controlling shareholders* are placed under fiduciary duties similar to those owed by directors, officers, and other managers. If a single shareholder, or a group of shareholders acting in concert, owns a sufficient number of shares to control the direction of corporate affairs, the possibility exists that they will try to exercise this control so as to further their own personal interests at the expense of the corporation and the other shareholders. Corporate control must not be abused, however, and the controlling shareholders are required to act in the best interests of the corporation as a whole and with complete fairness to minority shareholders.

An Oregon case, *Browning v. C. & C. Plywood Corp.*, 434 P.2d 339 (1967), provides an example of a breach of this duty. In that case, the controlling shareholders attempted to dilute a minority shareholder's interest by voting to issue new shares of stock at a time when they *knew* that the minority shareholder was unable to buy his proportionate part of the new issue. The court struck down the scheme.

Liabilities under Federal Securities Laws

The Securities Act of 1933 and the Securities Exchange Act of 1934 place a number of specific duties and liabilities upon corporate managers and others.[5] In many cases, an activity that violates one of these federal regulatory provisions also amounts to a breach of duty under the state common-law rules previously discussed. Even in such instances, however, these federal statutes are of extreme importance because they (1) define some types of duties with greater precision than existed at common law, (2) provide for penalties that may not have existed under state law, and (3) provide for enforcement by a federal agency, the Securities and Exchange Commission (SEC). Several of the more important federal statutory provisions relating to duties and liabilities are discussed below.

Registration Statements: As indicated in Chapter 35, the 1933 Act requires corporations to file a registration statement with the SEC when nonexempt issues of securities are offered for sale in interstate commerce or through the mails. Under Secs. 5 and 11, if a violation occurs, either by filing a misleading registration statement or by failing to file one at all, the corporate managers involved in the securities issuance can be held personally responsible. Others involved, such as accountants, attorneys, and underwriters, may also be liable.

Use of Inside Information: Sec. 10b of the 1934 Act essentially prohibits *fraud* in the sale or purchase of securities.[6] Pursuant to this section, the SEC has promulgated Rule 10b-5, which makes the 10b prohibition more specific.

One of the most important features of Rule 10b-5 is that it effectively prohibits the use of "material inside information" in the sale or purchase of securities. The purpose of this rule is to prevent an "insider" from using inside information to take advantage of the other party to the transaction. In most cases, insiders are directors, officers, or holders of large amounts of stock. It is not required, however, that any such position be held in order for a person to be liable under Rule 10b-5. Others employed by the corporation, as well as friends, relatives, or business associates of true insiders, can also incur liability. The key is whether the person has actually acquired material information about the corporation that is not available to the

---

[5]These acts are hereafter referred to as the "1933 Act" and the "1934 Act."

[6]This provision applies to fraud in the sale or purchase of securities *after* their initial issuance. Another provision, Sec. 17 of the 1933 Act, prohibits fraudulent practices with respect to the original issuance.

other party to the transaction. If so, he or she must either reveal the information or refrain from selling or buying the corporation's securities until the information becomes generally available to investors.

We have said that the duty of disclosure with respect to inside information applies only if the information is "material." By its nature, the word *material* is rather difficult to define with precision. A determination must be made on the basis of all the circumstances of the particular case. Broadly speaking, however, material information has been judicially defined as "information which, if generally known, would probably affect the market price of the corporation's securities." It has been defined by other courts as "information which would probably affect the decision of a reasonable investor as to whether to sell or buy the securities." An example of the type of information likely to be considered material is knowledge that the corporation is planning to merge with another company. Other examples of material information include knowledge that the corporation has just discovered a major mineral deposit or that it is about to be sued by the Department of Justice for an alleged violation of the antitrust laws.

Short-Swing Profits: Under Sec. 16b of the 1934 Act, *short-swing profits* are defined as any profits made on either the sale and subsequent purchase or purchase and subsequent sale of equity securities where both purchase and sale take place within a six-month period. This section does not actually prohibit short-swing profits; it does, however, prevent certain insiders from keeping any short-swing profits made on transactions in the shares of their own corporation. Such profits made by these insiders must be turned over to the corporation. The insiders who are required to turn over their short-swing profits to the corporation are (1) directors, (2) officers, and (3) owners of 10 percent or more of any type of shares issued by the corporation.[7]

Sec. 16b is essentially a preventive measure designed to discourage the misuse of inside information. *It applies, however, without regard to whether the particular insider actually possessed material inside information.* But it applies only to the types of insiders who are specifically listed. Short-swing profits made by others are not subject to the statute.

Proxy Solicitation: In the previous chapter we saw that corporate managers often solicit proxies from shareholders prior to a shareholders' meeting. In the "proxy statement" sent to shareholders, the managers request authority to cast votes in behalf of the shareholders for particular board candidates and for particular proposals the managers have made. The shareholders are, of course, under no obligation to grant this request; they can attend the meeting themselves or choose not to vote at all.

Sec. 14a of the 1934 Act prohibits making any false or misleading statements in the proxy material sent to shareholders. Furthermore, the proxy statement must

---

[7]Under Sec. 16a, these types of insiders are also required to make periodic reports to the SEC of *any* personal transaction in the shares of their corporation.

disclose all material facts relating to the matters to be voted on. *In other words, when corporate managers solicit proxies, they must reveal to the shareholders, in a clear and truthful manner, all facts that will probably affect the voting decision.* Violation of this section subjects the responsible managers to personal liability.

Questions and Problems

1. Hanrahan, a shareholder of Puget Sound Corp., demanded the right to inspect corporate records prior to a shareholders' meeting. His purpose was to obtain the names and addresses of other shareholders so that he could urge them to elect directors who would seek a merger of Puget Sound with another corporation. Puget Sound refused the demand, and Hanrahan sued to enforce his right of inspection. *Hanrahan v. Puget Sound Power & Light Co.,* 126 N.E.2d 499 (1955). Will Hanrahan win? Explain.

2. Pioneer Savings & Loan Co. issued an additional 100,000 shares of common stock. The circumstances were such that Pioneer's existing shareholders should have been accorded preemptive rights. Because of a mistake, however, several of these shareholders had not been given an opportunity to exercise those rights. Upon discovering the situation, Pioneer sought to cancel the entire issue of stock. *Barsan v. Pioneer Savings & Loan Co.,* 121 N.E.2d 76 (1954). Can it do so? Discuss.

3. Explain the difference in the relative importance of preemptive rights in a close corporation and in a publicly-held corporation.

4. An amendment to the articles of Constantin & Co. stated that "the holders of the preferred stock shall be entitled to receive, and the company shall be bound to pay thereon, but only out of the net profits of the company, a fixed yearly dividend of Fifty Cents (50¢) per share." The dividend was not paid in a particular year, and a preferred shareholder sued to compel its payment. Assuming that the company actually made a net profit that year, will the shareholder prevail? Discuss.

5. The articles of Apex Co. provided that, if preferred shareholders failed to receive a dividend in any given year, they "shall be entitled to the same voting power as the holders of the common stock." Except for this situation, the preferred shares of Apex carried no voting rights. One year the preferred shareholders did not receive a dividend. At the next shareholders' meeting, where the preferred shareholders were to exercise their newly-acquired voting power, an issue arose as to the extent of this power. The preferred shareholders contended that the meaning of the quoted provision was that they *as a class* should have the same voting power as that possessed by the common shareholders *as a class.* Under this interpretation, each share of the preferred would be worth eighty-nine votes, rather than the ordinary one vote per share to which the common shareholders would be entitled. Are the preferred shareholders correct? Discuss.

6. The directors of Southwest State Bank were warned by the bank examiner that the bank was in a precarious condition. After the warning, the directors made no audit of the bank's affairs for the next year, did not check the cashier's statement as to loans made, and thus did not discover that the cashier was frequently using forged notes in the names of third parties to cover his embezzlements. The bank's directors were sued for negligence by a shareholder. What is the result? Explain.

7. Reese, a director of Lafleer, Inc., was seventy-five years old and in failing health. He was suspicious of the activities of the company's vice president, but because of his poor health he no longer attended board meetings and did nothing about the matter. It was later discovered that the vice president had involved the company in a number of prohibited activities, including illegal campaign contributions. The company was damaged by these activities, and a shareholder sued not only the vice president but also Reese. Is Reese liable? Discuss.

8. Johnson, the president of Continental Co., badly mismanaged its affairs and caused the company to sustain heavy losses. The board of directors had allowed Johnson a free hand in running the company. A shareholder filed a derivative suit against Johnson and all the directors for negligence. One of the directors, Wembley, claimed that he should not be held responsible. His defense was that, because of the great distance between his home and Continental's headquarters (2,500 miles), he had not attended a board meeting in almost a year. Should Wembley's defense shield him from liability? Discuss.

9. Explain the rationale behind the corporate opportunity rule.

10. Carlton owned 1 percent of the shares of Zepco, Inc. He was not an officer or director. He sought to buy a piece of equipment worth $30,000 from Zepco for $25,000. Zepco's board of directors voted 9–2 to sell the equipment to him for $25,000. After the sale, another Zepco shareholder sued Carlton to force him either to return the equipment or to pay an additional $5,000. What was the result? Discuss.

38

Corporations/Merger, Consolidation, and Termination

In the preceding chapters we examined the nature and formation of the corporation, its basic operation, and the rights and liabilities of its individual participants. This final chapter will focus on more unusual aspects of corporate operation. Initially we will discuss changes in the fundamental structure of the corporation brought about by mergers and consolidations. Then we will deal with the various circumstances in which the corporate existence can be terminated.

Mergers and Consolidations

The terms *merger* and *consolidation* are often used interchangeably to describe any situation in which two or more independent businesses are combined under a single ownership. Technically, however, there is a difference in meaning between the two terms. A *merger* is the absorption of one existing corporation by another; the absorbing corporation continues to exist while the one being absorbed ceases to exist. A *consolidation,* on the other hand, is a union resulting in the creation of an entirely new corporation and the termination of the existing ones. Symbolically, a merger can be illustrated by the equation $A + B = A$, while a consolidation is represented by $A + B = C$.

Even though we distinguish between mergers and consolidations, the distinction has very little practical significance. Whether a particular combination is a merger or consolidation, the rights and liabilities of the corporations and their shareholders and creditors are the same. For this reason, the popular term *merger* will sometimes be used in the following discussion to describe both combinations.

Reasons for Merging

The reasons for merging two corporations vary greatly, depending on the particular circumstances. The most common reasons are discussed below.

General Advantages of Size: In many cases the motive for a merger is the acquisition of some or all of the benefits that result from an increase in size. An ability to buy and produce in larger amounts, for example, may bring about greater efficiency and lower overhead costs.

Because the combination possesses greater resources than its constituent companies had possessed separately, it may be able to obtain capital more easily and to engage in more extensive advertising and research. Furthermore, the larger organization sometimes finds it easier to attract the best managers, technical advisers, and other personnel.

These advantages of size are usually legitimate. Occasionally, however, the motives of corporate managers in pursuing mergers may be less valid. Sometimes growth is sought merely for its own sake, without any resulting increase in efficiency. For instance, a merger might produce a much more impressive set of financial statements for the acquiring company, not through any improvement in its performance but simply because of the "larger numbers" brought about by the acquisition. And, of course, the personal rewards of the corporate managers may increase accordingly.

Eliminating Competition: Some mergers are motivated by the desire to lessen the rigors of competition. The most obvious example, of course, is the acquisition of a direct competitor for the purpose of suppressing competition between the two.[1] Mergers brought about solely for this purpose are somewhat less common than in the past, however, due in large part to the active enforcement of antitrust laws.

Acquisition of Know-how: A large corporation might acquire a much smaller one in the same or a related line of business for the purpose of obtaining needed patents or other technological know-how owned by the latter. In addition, some of the individuals employed by the smaller company might possess needed capabilities.

---

[1]A merger between two competitors is referred to as a "horizontal" merger.

Guaranteed Supplies or Outlets: A company might seek to assure itself of an adequate supply of an essential item by acquiring a producer of that item. Conversely, a guaranteed outlet might be the motivating factor behind the acquisition of a company that purchases a product supplied by the acquiring firm.[2]

Diversification: One corporation sometimes wishes to acquire another in a totally unrelated line of business solely for the purpose of diversifying. Doing business in several diversified lines removes some of the economic risks that exist when a corporation commits all its resources to a single industry.[3]

Defensive Mergers: Occasionally a corporation actually seeks to be acquired by another. For example, suppose that X Corporation is attempting to acquire Y Corporation. However, the managers and shareholders of Y Corporation are opposed to the takeover because of differing business philosophies. Y Corporation thus arranges a merger with Z Corporation to avoid the takeover attempt by X.

Another merger that might be classified as "defensive" is illustrated as follows. Suppose that Jones, the founder of General Steel Corp. and its primary manager throughout its existence, now wishes to retire. Jones is afraid that "his" company will not be managed properly in his absence, so he arranges for General Steel to be acquired by a larger company whose management capabilities he trusts.[4]

Tax Savings: Although tax considerations are beyond the scope of this discussion, the lessening of federal income tax liability sometimes is an important reason for undertaking a particular merger.

Unused Capital: Sometimes a merger may simply be an investment outlet for unused capital. For example, a corporation may have accumulated profits that it does not choose to pay out as dividends. Acquisition of another corporation may be an attractive investment opportunity for these funds.

Procedures

The procedure for a merger or consolidation is governed by statute. Every state has a statute that authorizes the combination of two or more *domestic* corporations. In almost every state, the statutory procedures also allow the combination of a domestic and a *foreign* corporation. The procedures vary somewhat from state to state, but they can be outlined generally as follows:

---

[2]Mergers between firms in a supplier-customer relationship are referred to as "vertical" mergers.

[3]Mergers between companies in unrelated lines of business are called "conglomerate" mergers.

[4]Of course, Jones is probably a controlling shareholder in General Steel Corp. and thus has the power to carry out his wish.

1. The board of directors of each corporation must adopt a resolution approving the merger or consolidation. This resolution should set forth:

   a. The names of the combining corporations and the name of the corporation that will result from the combination.

   b. The terms and conditions of the proposed combination.

   c. The method and basis to be used in converting the securities of each corporation into securities of the resulting corporation.

   d. In the case of a merger, any changes caused thereby in the articles of incorporation of the surviving corporation. In the case of a consolidation, the resolutions of the respective boards should include the entire articles of incorporation for the resulting new corporation.

2. The plan must then be approved by the shareholders of each corporation, at either an annual or a special meeting. The vote required for approval varies among the states from a simple majority to four-fifths of the outstanding shares; a *two-thirds* vote is the most common requirement.

3. After shareholder approval, the plan for the combination must be submitted to the appropriate state official (usually the secretary of state) in a document referred to as the "articles of merger" or "articles of consolidation."

4. If all documents are in the proper form, the state official issues a "certificate of merger" (or consolidation) to the surviving or new corporation.

Merger with a Subsidiary

In a majority of states, the procedures have been greatly simplified for the merger of a subsidiary corporation into its parent. These streamlined procedures allow such a merger to be consummated *without shareholder approval*.

If the parent owns *all* the subsidiary's shares, the only requirements are that (1) the parent's board of directors adopt a resolution setting forth the plan for the merger, (2) articles of merger be filed, and (3) a certificate of merger be issued. If some of the subsidiary's shares are owned by others, there is an additional requirement that these minority shareholders be given prior notice of the merger. These simplified procedures can be used, however, only if the parent owns a *very large portion* of the subsidiary's shares (90 or 95 percent in most states).

Effects of Merger or Consolidation

The effects of a merger or consolidation can be summarized as follows:

1. The corporations who are parties to the merger become a single corporation.

2. All of the corporate parties to the merger, other than the surviving or new corporation, cease to exist.

3. The surviving or new corporation possesses all the rights, privileges, and powers of the combining corporations.

4. The surviving or new corporation acquires all the property of the combining corporations without the necessity of a deed or other formal transfer.

5. The surviving or new corporation is liable for all the debts and obligations of the combining corporations.

6. In the case of a merger, the articles of incorporation of the surviving corporation are deemed to be amended to the extent, if any, that changes in these articles are stated in the articles of merger. In the case of a consolidation, the articles of consolidation serve as the articles of incorporation for the new corporation.

The Appraisal Right

At common law a merger, consolidation, or other combination required the *unanimous* approval of the shareholders of each corporation. In an effort to lessen the severity of this restriction on corporate action, all the states at a fairly early time passed statutes providing for approval by less-than-unanimous vote.

One result of this change, however, was that any shareholders who disapproved of a merger might find themselves unwilling investors in a corporation different from the one whose shares they originally had purchased. Out of concern for fairness to these shareholders, provisions were included in the state laws giving them the right to sell their shares back to the corporation for cash. This right has generally become known as the *appraisal right.*

A dissenting shareholder must strictly follow the required procedures, or this appraisal right will be lost. The most important requirement is that the dissenting shareholder *object to the merger and demand payment within the designated time period.* For example, the Model Act provides that a dissenting shareholder must give the corporation written notice of objection to the proposed combination either prior to or at the meeting where the matter is voted upon. If the merger is approved at the meeting, the Model Act requires that the dissenting shareholder make written demand for payment from the corporation within the next ten days.

When the merger or consolidation takes place, the surviving or new corporation must make a written offer to each dissenting shareholder regarding the purchase of his or her shares. Under the Model Act, this offer must be made within ten days after the effective date of the combination and must be accompanied by the most recent balance sheet and income statement of the corporation whose stock is owned by the dissenting shareholder.

The overriding concern of the dissenting shareholder is, of course, the price to be paid for his or her shares. The requirement found in most state statutes is that the corporation pay the "fair value" of the shares, computed as of the date of the merger. If the dissenting shareholder feels that the offer does not reflect the fair value of the shares and refuses to accept it, the corporation can institute a court action to have the value determined. The shareholder can personally file such a suit only if the corporation fails to do so within a specified period of time (under the Model Act, sixty days after the merger). In the court proceeding, the judge sometimes appoints an official "appraiser" to hear evidence and recommend a fair value.

Other Types of Combinations

Thus far our discussion has been limited to "statutory" mergers and consolidations, in which all of the requisite formalities have been carried out. However, corporations can achieve the same practical results by less formal means, particularly through *asset acquisition* and *stock acquisition.* In legal circles these transactions are often called "practical mergers" or "de facto mergers" (as contrasted with "statutory" mergers and consolidations). In everyday usage they are more frequently referred to simply as "mergers."

Purchase of Assets: Suppose that X Co. wishes to acquire all or most of the assets of Y Co. It may purchase these assets with cash or with a combination of cash and promissory notes. Or it may make the purchase by issuing shares of its stock to Y in return for Y's assets.[5]

Although the practical effect of such an asset acquisition is to merge one company into the other, the *acquiring company* usually does *not* have to obtain shareholder approval. Ordinarily, the only situation in which the approval of the acquiring company's shareholders must be obtained is when the assets are to be bought with shares and there are not enough authorized but unissued shares to make the purchase. In such a case the shareholders will have to amend the articles of incorporation to authorize the issuance of additional shares.

The rules are substantially different, however, with respect to the *acquired company.* The sale of all or most of its assets puts its shareholders into a position very different from the one they previously occupied. Therefore, they must approve the sale. Indeed, in the past, the common-law rule required unanimous approval. This strict requirement was relaxed, however, along with the relaxation of the approval requirement for formal mergers and acquisitions. Today, the general rule is that the shareholders of the acquired company must approve the sale by the same vote required for a merger or consolidation. And the dissenting shareholders of the acquired company possess an appraisal right just as in a formal merger or consolidation.

After the sale, the corporation that has sold its assets may simply choose to dissolve. It may, however, decide to start its operations anew (either in the same or some other line of business). A third alternative is for the corporation to continue in existence as an "investment company" (or "holding company"). In the latter case, its sole (or at least primary) function will be to own and receive income from securities, such as those it may have received as the purchase price for its assets.

The following case illustrates that, on occasion, when a corporation buys the assets of another company, it may find that it has also bought a problem for itself. In this case, an individual with a claim against the selling company attempted to hold the buying company liable for that claim.

---

[5]A word of caution is in order when X issues shares of its stock to purchase Y's assets. It is entirely possible that this issuance may have to be registered under state and federal securities laws.

Ray v. Alad Corporation

Supreme Court of California, 560 P.2d 3 (1977)

In 1968 Alad Corporation, which manufactured ladders, sold its factory, equipment, inventory, trade name, and goodwill to Lighting Maintenance Corp. for $207,000. The principal stockholders of Alad, Mr. and Mrs. William Hambly, agreed not to compete with the purchaser in the ladder business for 42 months. Alad Corporation was dissolved and Lighting created a new corporation which was also named Alad Corporation. The new Alad used the acquired assets to continue the ladder manufacturing business, with only one week's interruption. The same factory workers were used, but Lighting's managers took over the running of the new Alad. Mr. Hambly, who had been general manager of the original Alad, provided consulting services to the new Alad for six months. The new company used the "Alad" name on all the ladders it produced, employed the salespeople and manufacturer's representatives who had sold ladders for the original Alad, and solicited the same list of customers.

In 1969 Herbert Ray was injured in a fall from one of the ladders manufactured prior to 1968 by the original Alad. Claiming that the ladder was defective, he sued the new Alad. The trial court granted summary judgment in favor of defendant Alad, and plaintiff appealed. (In the Supreme Court's opinion below, the original Alad is referred to as "Alad I" and the new Alad as "Alad II.")

Wright, Justice: . . . Our discussion of the law starts with the rule ordinarily applied to the determination of whether a corporation purchasing the principal assets of another corporation assumes the other's liabilities. As typically formulated the rule states that the purchaser does not assume the seller's liabilities unless (1) there is an express or implied agreement of assumption, (2) the transaction amounts to a consolidation or merger of the two corporations, (3) the purchasing corporation is a mere continuation of the seller, or (4) the transfer of assets to the purchaser is for the fraudulent purpose of escaping liability for the seller's debts.

If this rule were determinative of Alad II's liability to plaintiff it would require us to affirm the summary judgment. None of the rule's four stated grounds for imposing liability on the purchasing corporation is present here. There was no express or implied agreement to assume liability for injury from defective products previously manufactured by Alad I. Nor is there any indication or contention that the transaction was prompted by any fraudulent purpose of escaping liability for Alad I's debts.

With respect to the second stated ground for liability, the purchase of Alad I's assets did not amount to a consolidation or merger. This exception has been invoked where one corporation takes all of another's assets without providing any consideration that could be made available to meet claims of the other's creditors or where the consideration consists wholly of shares of the purchaser's stock which are promptly distributed to the seller's shareholders in conjunction with the seller's liquidation. In the present case the sole consideration given for Alad I's assets was cash in excess of $207,000. . . . There is no contention that this consideration was inadequate or that the cash given to Alad I was not included in the assets available to meet claims of Alad I's creditors at the time of dissolution. Hence the acquisition of Alad I's assets was not in the nature of a merger or consolidation.

Plaintiff contends that the rule's third stated ground for liability makes Alad II liable as a mere continuation of Alad I in view of Alad II's acquisition of all Alad I's operating assets, its use of those assets and of Alad I's former employees to manufacture the same line of products, and its holding itself out to customers and the public as a continuation of the same enterprise. However, California decisions holding that a corporation acquiring the assets of another corporation is the latter's mere continuation and therefore liable for its debts have imposed such liability only upon a showing of one or both of the following factual elements: (1) no adequate consideration was given for the predecessor corporation's assets and made available for meeting the claims of its unsecured creditors; (2) one or more persons were officers, directors, or stockholders of both corporations.

. . . We therefore conclude that the general rule governing succession to liabilities does not require Alad II to respond to plaintiff's claim. . . . [However,] we must decide whether the policies underlying strict tort liability for defective products call for a special exception to the rule that would otherwise insulate the present defendant from plaintiff's claim.

The purpose of the rule of strict tort liability is to insure that the costs of injuries resulting from defective products are borne by the manufacturers that put such products on the market rather than by the injured persons who are powerless to protect themselves. However, the rule does not rest on the analysis of the financial strength or bargaining power of the parties to the particular action. It rests, rather, on the proposition that the cost of any injury and the loss of time or health may be an overwhelming misfortune to the person injured, and a needless one, for the risk of injury can be insured by the manufacturer and distributed among the public as a cost of doing business. . . . Justification for imposing strict liability upon a successor to a manufacturer under the circumstances here presented rests upon (1) the virtual destruction of the plaintiff's remedies against the original manufacturer caused by the successor's acquisition of the business, (2) the successor's ability to assume the original manufacturer's risk-spreading rule, and (3) the fairness of requiring the successor to assume a responsibility for defective products that was a burden necessarily attached to the original manufacturer's good will being enjoyed by the successor in the continued operation of the business. . . .

. . . The injury giving rise to plaintiff's claim against Alad I did not occur until more than six months after the filing of the dissolution certificate declaring that Alad I's "known debts and liabilities have been actually paid" and its "known assets have been distributed to its shareholders." This distribution of assets was perfectly proper as there was no requirement that provision be made for claims such as plaintiff's that had not yet come into existence. Thus, even if plaintiff could obtain a judgment on his claim against the dissolved and assetless Alad I he would face formidable and probably insuperable obstacles in attempting to obtain satisfaction of the judgment from former stockholders or directors.

The record does not disclose whether Alad I had insurance against liability on plaintiff's claim. Although such coverage is not inconceivable, products liability insurance is usually limited to accidents or occurrences taking place while the policy is in effect. Thus the products liability insurance of a company that has gone out of business is not a likely source of compensation for injury from a product the company previously manufactured.

. . . While depriving plaintiff of redress against the ladder's manufacturer, Alad I, the transaction by which Alad II acquired Alad I's name and operating assets had the further effect of transferring to Alad II the resources that had previously been available to Alad I for meeting its responsibilities to persons injured by defects in ladders it had produced. These resources included not only the physical plant, the manufacturing equipment, and the inventories of raw material, work in process, and finished goods, but also the know-how available through the records of manufacturing designs, the continued employment of the factory personnel, and the consulting services of Alad I's general manager. With these facilities and sources of information, Alad II had virtually the same capacity as Alad I to estimate the risks of claims for injuries from defects in previously manufactured ladders for purposes of obtaining insurance coverage or planning self-insurance. Moreover, the acquisition of the Alad enterprise gave Alad II the opportunity formerly enjoyed by Alad I of passing on to purchasers of new "Alad" products the costs of meeting these risks. Immediately after the takeover it was Alad II, not Alad I, which was in a position to promote the paramount policy of the strict products liability rule by spreading throughout society the cost of compensating otherwise defenseless victims of manufacturing defects.

Finally, the imposition upon Alad II of liability for injuries from Alad I's defective products is fair and equitable in view of Alad II's acquisition of Alad I's trade name, good will, and customer lists, its continuing to produce the same line of ladders, and its holding itself out to potential customers as the same enterprise. This deliberate, but legitimate, exploitation of Alad I's established reputation as a going concern manufacturing a specific product line gave Alad II a substantial benefit which its predecessor could not have enjoyed without the burden of potential liability for injuries from previously manufactured units. . . . By taking over and continuing the established business of producing and distributing Alad ladders, Alad II became an integral part of the overall producing and marketing enterprise that should bear the cost of injuries resulting from defective products.

We therefore conclude that a party which acquires a manufacturing business and continues the output of its line of products under the circumstances here presented assumes strict tort liability for defects in units of the same product line previously manufactured and distributed by the entity from which the business was acquired.

The judgment is reversed.

Purchase of Stock: A frequently employed method for achieving a combination is the purchase by one corporation of the shares of another. This generally is accomplished by action of the acquiring company's board of directors, without any need for approval by its shareholders. The aim of the purchaser, of course, is to obtain a sufficient number of shares so that it *controls* the acquired company. If ownership of the acquired company's shares is widely dispersed, control can be achieved by the purchase of less than 50 percent of those shares.

Various reasons exist for choosing this method of combination. One situation in which the device is useful occurs when the managers of the target company oppose the transaction. In a stock purchase the acquiring company can bypass these managers and deal directly with the shareholders of the corporation it seeks to control.

The acquiring company can negotiate *individually* with the target company's shareholders. Problems sometimes arise, however, if the acquiring company extends its offer only to the *controlling* shareholders of the target corporation. If the price paid to these shareholders exceeds the market value of their shares, the excess may be viewed as a price paid for the power to control the corporation. According to the courts of some states this power is a *corporate asset,* and the price paid for it rightfully belongs to the corporation rather than to those who possess the power at the time. Under this view, a "sale of control" is a breach of the fiduciary duty owed to minority shareholders of the target corporation. The controlling shareholders thus have to account to the corporation for the amount received in excess of market value.

Many states, however, do not take this approach. In fact, a majority of them do not view a "sale of control" as a breach of duty by controlling shareholders unless (1) the controlling shares are sold to a purchaser whose purpose is to take advantage of the minority (known as a sale to a "corporate looter"), or (2) the sale of shares is accompanied by the sale of a corporate directorship or office.

In view of the problems that often accompany an offer made only to controlling shareholders, it is usually advisable to make the offer to *all* the shareholders of the target company. In fact, the controlling shareholders, for their own protection, may *insist* on it.

However, if the number of shareholders is large, individual offers to all of them may not be feasible. Thus, the acquiring corporation may wish to make a *tender offer*—a publicly advertised offer addressed to all shareholders of the target company. The offered price does not have to be in terms of cash, but it almost always is. In fact, the tender offer usually is made at a cash price somewhat higher than the current market value.

Of course, the acquiring corporation probably will not want to be obligated to purchase shares unless it is assured of gaining control. Therefore, the tender offer may provide that it will be valid only if accepted by the holders of a stated number of shares. On the other hand, the purchaser may not want to buy any more shares than are necessary to achieve control. Thus the tender offer may also expressly limit the number of shares to be purchased and may provide that if more than this number are made available, they will be purchased on a proportionate basis from all shareholders accepting the offer.

After a controlling stock interest has been obtained, the acquiring company may want to continue the separate existence of the acquired company, operating it as a subsidiary. Alternatively, the parent may wish to effectuate a formal statutory merger or perhaps to purchase the subsidiary's assets and terminate its existence.

As might be expected, an attempted "takeover" of one corporation by another through the use of a tender offer will occasionally result in a pitched battle for control. The parties to such a struggle must proceed with caution to avoid engaging in any illegal activities during the heat of battle. In the following case, legal problems under the federal securities laws resulted from a defensive tactic used in an attempt to defeat a tender offer.

Crane Co. v. Westinghouse Air Brake Co.

U.S. Court of Appeals, Second Circuit, 419 F.2d 787 (1969)

In an effort to acquire control of Westinghouse Air Brake Co. (hereafter "Air Brake"), Crane Co. made a tender offer to Air Brake's shareholders for a price of not more than $50 per share with an expiration date of April 19.

American Standard, Inc. (hereafter "Standard"), owned a substantial interest in Air Brake (just under 10 percent) and wanted to consummate a merger with that company. Obviously, Standard did not want Air Brake to be taken over by Crane.

Standard knew that the holders of Air Brake stock would probably delay until the last moment in order to make a decision based on the latest market information (that is, to compare the value of the $50 tender offer with the market price on the day the offer was to expire). Standard also knew that the surest way to defeat Crane's tender offer was to run the market price up to $50.

On April 19 Standard purchased, in a series of transactions ranging in size from 100 to 9,700 shares, a total of 170,200 Air Brake shares at an average price of $49.08 per share. These purchases were made in the open market. Standard did not want its interest in Air Brake to pass the 10 percent mark, so it then secretly resold 100,000 of these shares at $44.50 each.

Although the market price of Air Brake shares was $45.25 per share on the New York Stock Exchange at the beginning of the day on April 19, it quickly reached $50. Consequently, Crane's tender offer was unsuccessful, because few Air Brake shareholders accepted the offer.

Crane filed suit, asking the court to prohibit the planned merger of Standard and Air Brake because of alleged violations of the Securities Exchange Act of 1934. The trial court ruled for defendants, and Crane appealed.

Smith, Justice: . . . It is reasonable to conclude that many Air Brake stockholders who might otherwise have chosen to tender to Crane chose not to do so because their own holdings in Air Brake looked better as the price went up. . . .

Standard had "painted the tape" in Air Brake stock. . . .

Standard's extraordinary buying here, coupled with its large secret sales off the market, inevitably distorted the market picture and deceived public investors, particularly the Air Brake shareholders. The effect of these purchases was to create the appearance of an extraordinary demand for Air Brake stock and a dramatic rise in market price, as a result of which Air Brake shareholders were deterred from tendering to Crane. Concentrated open market bidding in a takeover battle may not in itself violate present laws and regulations, a question we do not decide here. Standard's action here, however, in concealing from the public—and in particular from the Air Brake stockholders—the true situation as to the market it was making in Air Brake stock resulted in violations of section 9(a)(2) . . . of the Act. . . .

We must determine the application of section 9(a)(2) . . . to the relatively new device of the tender offer, rarely used before 1965, and to the methods here used to combat it. . . .

Section 9(a)(2) makes it unlawful:

To effect, alone or with one or more other persons, a series of transactions in any security registered on a national securities exchange creating actual or apparent active trading in such security or raising or depressing the price of such security, for the purpose of inducing the purchase or sale of such security by others. . . .

Section 9(a)(2) was considered to be "the very heart of the act" and its purpose was to outlaw every device "used to persuade the public that activity in a security is the reflection of a genuine demand instead of a mirage." 3 Loss, Securities Regulation 1549-55 (2d ed. 1961).

Section 9(a)(2) . . . contain[s] requirements of both manipulative motive and willfulness. The section does not condemn extensive buying or buying which raises the price of a security in itself. Nor are the requirements of manipulative purpose and willfulness to be interpreted apart from the statute's design to prevent those with a financial interest in a security from manipulating the market therein. The requisite purpose and willfulness is normally inferred from the circumstances of the case. . . .

When a person who has a "substantial direct pecuniary interest in the success of a proposed offering takes active steps to effect a rise in the market" in the security, we think that a finding of manipulative purpose is prima facie established. Here we have even more than a motive to manipulate joined with the requisite series of transactions. In furtherance of its interest in defeating the Crane tender offer and consummating its own merger with Air Brake, Standard took affirmative steps to conceal from the public its own secret sales off the market at the same time it was dominating trading in Air Brake's shares at a price level calculated to deter Air Brake shareholders from tendering to Crane. . . .

An ordinary investor watching the tape could only conclude that there was a wide-based demand for Air Brake stock and that it would be unprofitable to tender his stock to Crane at that time. Not only did Standard fail to provide Air Brake shareholders with the information that it planned or was in fact purchasing large amounts of Air Brake stock at a price which made the Crane offer look unappealing on the crucial expiration date, but it further distorted their only ready source of market information—the stock tape—by secret private sales off the stock exchange. . . .

[Thus Standard violated section 9(a)(2), and its merger with Air Brake should be prohibited.

Reversed.]

Of course, the making of a tender offer does not necessarily mean that an intense contest for control will result. However, there is still the need for great caution even when the takeover attempt is a rather calm affair. For example, anyone making a tender offer must disclose all relevant, material facts to the shareholders of the target company. The failure to do so may violate state law, federal securities law, or sometimes both. The following case involves a shareholder's claim that state law was violated by a misleading disclosure.

Lynch v. Vickers Energy Corporation
Supreme Court of Delaware, 383 A.2d 278 (1978)

On September 30, 1974, Vickers Energy Corp. made an offer to purchase all outstanding common stock of TransOcean Oil, Inc. at $12 per share. At the time of the tender offer, Vickers already owned 53.5 percent of TransOcean's common stock. As a result of the offer, Vickers acquired 4,228,141 of the 5,888,999 shares held by others, thus increasing its interest in Trans Ocean to 87 percent.

Shortly thereafter, Libby Lynch, who had sold her 100 shares to Vickers in response to the offer, filed suit in her own behalf and in behalf of other TransOcean minority shareholders. In her suit against Vickers and its directors, plaintiff contended that defendants had not made a full and frank disclosure of the value of TransOcean's net assets and asked the court to award damages based on the difference between the tender offer price and the shares' fair value. The trial court granted summary judgment in favor of defendants, and plaintiff appealed.

Duffy, Justice: . . . Vickers, as the majority shareholder of TransOcean, owed a fiduciary duty to plaintiff which required "complete candor" in disclosing fully "all of the facts and circumstances surrounding the tender offer. . . .

In our view, the tender offer failed to disclose fully two critical facts: (1) that a "highly qualified" petroleum engineer, who was a member of TransOcean's management, had calculated the net asset value to be worth significantly more than the minimum amount disclosed in the offer; and (2) that Vickers' management had authorized open market purchases of TransOcean's stock during the period immediately preceding the $12 per share tender offer for bids up to $15 per share.

We turn first to the net asset value disclosures. The Tender Offer Circular contained the following statement concerning TransOcean's net asset value:

> Management of the Company [TransOcean] has informed the Offeror [Vickers] that, based on a calculation of discounted present value of the Company's reserves and values attributable by the Company's management to the Company's un-developed acreage and other assets, management of the Company estimates that at this date the Company's net asset value adjusted for such factors is *not less than* $200,000,000 (approximately $16.00 per share) and could be substantially greater. While the foregoing evaluation is based on the current judgment of the manage-ment of the Company, it should be recognized that because of the highly uncertain conditions affecting oil and gas values and because of the many assumptions it was necessary for the management of the Company to make in its evaluation, the evalu-ation is necessarily arbitrary and there can be no assurance that the values ultimately realized from such assets will be consistent with the estimate of the management of the Company.

. . . However, at the time of offer, defendants were in possession of another estimate, prepared by Forrest Harrell, a petroleum engineer and a vice-president of TransOcean, fixing the net asset value at $250.8 million, which computes to approximately $20 per share, and from which one could conclude that the value could be as high as $300 million. Both of these estimates were, of course, substantially higher than the minimum amount stated in the tender offer.

The Trial Court closely examined the Harrell report and concluded that nondisclosure thereof was not fatal; the Court reasoned that the " 'not less than $200,000,000 . . .' phrase used in the offering circular qualified by the phrase . . . 'and could be substantially greater . . .' furnished the TransOcean stockholders with adequate facts on which to make an educated choice . . . ."

This approach to the controversy was, in our view, mistaken in two respects: First, to reach such a conclusion it was necessary for the Court to weigh the merits of the Harrell report and, in the context of this case, that was error. The Court's function was not to go through Harrell's estimates of oil reserves and recoveries, for example, and make its own judgment about whether these should be "substantially discounted," nor should it have substituted its judgment for Harrell's about the rate which the Federal Power Commission would approve for a sale of natural gas. The stockholders and not the Court should have been permitted to make such qualitative judgments.

The Court's duty was to examine what information defendants had and to measure it against what they gave to the minority stockholders, in a context in which "complete candor" is required. In other words, the limited function of the Court was to determine whether defendants had disclosed all information in their possession germane to the transac-tion in issue. And by "germane" we mean, for present purposes, information such as a reasonable shareholder would consider important in deciding whether to sell or retain stock. The objective, of course, is to prevent insiders from using special knowledge which they may have to their own advantage and to the detriment of the stockholders.

Defendants concede that they owed plaintiff a fiduciary duty of complete frankness but assert that they discharged that duty by accurately disclosing that TransOcean's net asset value was "not less than $200,000,000 . . . and could be substantially greater." Technically speaking, the language may be accurate; but that kind of generality is hardly a substitute for hard facts when the law requires complete candor. And when, as here, management was in possession of two estimates from responsible sources—one using a "floor" approach defining value in terms of its lowest worth, and the other a more "optimistic" or ceiling approach defining value in terms of its highest worth—it is our opinion that complete candor required disclosure of both estimates. If management believed that one estimate was more accurate or realistic than another, it was free to endorse that estimate and to explain the reason for doing so; but full disclosure, in our view, was a prerequisite.

. . . We conclude, therefore, that it was a breach of the fiduciary duty of candor for defendants to fail to disclose the Harrell estimate to those persons to whom they owed the duty and whose stock Vickers was attempting to acquire.

The same rationale applies to defendants' failure to disclose that, prior to the tender offer of $12, Vickers had authorized open market purchases of TransOcean's shares at a price of $15 per share. The Trial Court discounted that allegation, reasoning that "the record is clear that the $15 limit set for such purchases of TransOcean stock was just that, namely a ceiling on board authorization of such purchases so that new resolutions would not have to be sought from time to time if required to meet the market price of TransOcean." The inference is that the authorization price was nothing more than a procedural convenience and not an accurate reflection of Vickers' opinion as to the true value of TransOcean's shares. Accordingly, the [Trial] Court ruled that nondisclosure thereof was not fatal.

But, again, the [Trial] Court incorrectly weighed the quality of the information before it ruled on the claim of nondisclosure. Whether the authorization price accurately stated Vickers' opinion as to true value of TransOcean's shares, or whether it was a tool of convenience established to facilitate the acquisition of TransOcean's shares in a fluctuating market, is not relevant in a context involving the fiduciary obligation of full disclosure. What is important is the fact that the authorization price was germane to the terms of the tender offer, and as such it should have been disclosed to the minority shareholders.

[W]e do not hold that the Harrell estimate was a more accurate estimate of TransOcean's net asset value, nor do we determine that $15 per share was a more reasonable price for the TransOcean stock. We hold only that the minority shareholders had the right to this information and to make their respective judgments about its significance before they were asked to sell their shares to Vickers.

[Reversed and remanded to lower court for computation of damages.]

Termination

As we saw earlier, a primary characteristic of the corporation is that it can have a perpetual existence. (While a few states do place time limits on the duration of the certificate of incorporation, this is of no real consequence because renewal is usually only a formality.) This is not to say, however, that a corporation *must* exist forever. A number of different circumstances can bring about an end to its existence.

In discussing the termination of a corporation, a distinction must be made between "liquidation" and "dissolution." *Liquidation* is the conversion of the corporation's assets to cash and the distribution of these funds to creditors and shareholders. *Dissolution* is the actual termination of the corporation's existence as an artificial person—its "legal death." A liquidation can occur without an actual dissolution, as where the corporation sells its assets to another company. The shareholders might then choose to dissolve the corporation, but it would not be required. On the other hand, dissolution sometimes takes place before liquidation. The remainder of our discussion will be devoted primarily to the various circumstances that bring about dissolution, with a final mention of the process of winding up corporate affairs after dissolution.

Voluntary Dissolution

A corporation can voluntarily terminate its own existence. Dissolution can be accomplished by the incorporators in some unusual circumstances, but the shareholders are ordinarily the only ones with such power. The board of directors does *not* have the power to dissolve the corporation.

By Incorporators: If the corporation has never gotten off the ground, it can be voluntarily dissolved by the incorporators. This can occur where the corporation has not done any business and no shares have been issued. In such a situation, the incorporators dissolve the corporation by filing "articles of dissolution" with the appropriate state official, who then issues a "certificate of dissolution."

By Shareholders: If the shareholders wish to discontinue the corporation's existence for any reason, they can do so. The most common reason for voluntary dissolution is that the enterprise has proved unprofitable.

The procedures for voluntary dissolution vary somewhat from state to state, but their general outline is basically the same. The process is usually initiated by resolution of the board of directors. A meeting of the shareholders is then called, at which time the matter is voted on. The vote required for approval varies among the states in the same manner as for mergers and consolidations, from a simple majority to four-fifths, with a *two-thirds* vote being the most common requirement. After shareholder approval, articles of dissolution are filed and the certificate of dissolution is issued.

Dissenting shareholders can challenge the dissolution in court. However, a court will issue an injunction prohibiting dissolution only if these shareholders are able to prove that the controlling shareholders dissolved the corporation in *bad faith*, with the intent of defrauding the minority.

Involuntary Dissolution

In some circumstances, a court action can be instituted for the purpose of dissolving the corporation. A legal proceeding of this nature can be brought by a shareholder or by the state. Dissolution ordered by a court in such a proceeding is often referred to as an "involuntary" dissolution.

By Shareholders: The laws of the various states generally provide that one or more shareholders can file a lawsuit requesting that the court dissolve the corporation. Those situations in which a shareholder can obtain dissolution by court order are:

Oppression of minority shareholders. In most states, oppression of minority shareholders by those in control is a ground for judicial dissolution. Oppressive conduct generally includes any act by which controlling shareholders seek to take unfair advantage of the minority. One example is the purchase of corporate assets by controlling shareholders, who then lease them back to the corporation for exorbitant rental fees.

Deadlock. Most states authorize dissolution by the court if it is proved that the corporation is unable to function because of a management deadlock. This is not a common occurrence and ordinarily could only happen in a closely-held corporation. In order for there to be an unbreakable management deadlock, of course, there would have to be equal ownership interests by two separate factions and a board of directors with an even number of members split into equal, opposing groups.

Mismanagement. Courts are generally reluctant to interfere with decisions made by corporate managers. However, a court may order dissolution of the corporation if it is being so grossly mismanaged that its assets are actually being wasted.

The following case illustrates the difficulty a shareholder may encounter in seeking to have the corporation involuntarily dissolved because of alleged mismanagement.

Goldmine Corp's. principal asset was a 900-acre tract of land fronting on the Mississippi River in Louisiana. Acquired in 1941 for $65,000, the property was appraised at $3,000 per acre in 1975, giving it a value at that time of $2,700,000. Since its acquisition the land had been used solely for growing sugar cane, a business which in recent years had not been very profitable. However, since 1966 various industrial interests had expressed a desire to buy the land, the latest proposed price being $3,600 per acre.

Without even investigating the merits of these offers, Goldmine's directors voted to reject them. The directors apparently were motivated by a feeling that the land would probably continue to increase in value, but they made no effort to obtain information that would enable them to intelligently weigh the proposals and determine the best interests of the shareholders.

Ten of Goldmine's shareholders, who collectively owned 40 percent of its stock, filed suit seeking to have the corporation dissolved by court order. They were opposed by four shareholders who collectively owned the remaining 60 percent. These four also served as the company's directors. Louisiana law provided several grounds for involuntary dissolution, the following two of which were asserted by plaintiffs as applying to Goldmine's situation: (1) "The objects of the corporation have wholly failed, or are entirely abandoned, or their accomplishment is impracticable;" or (2) "It is beneficial to the interests of the shareholders that the corporation should be liquidated and dissolved."

The trial court dismissed the suit, and plaintiffs appealed.

Gruenberg v. Goldmine Plantation, Inc.
Court of Appeal of Louisiana, 360 So.2d 884 (1978)

Stoulig, Judge: ... Meanwhile, back at the farm, the sugar cane crop was yielding dismal dividends which, over the past 10 years, averaged a net profit of less than one-half of 1 percent and the only reason the operation did not result in a loss for most of these years was that no charge for the use of the land was included in the operating expenses. ...

From the minority standpoint, approximately $1,080,000 of their collective funds are tied up in a farming operation that has no future and from which they realize sparse returns. Aware of the tax consequences of liquidating, they nonetheless reason that 50 percent plus of something they can use is better than 100 percent of a paper asset beyond their reach.

In the light of this situation, we consider whether plaintiffs have sustained the proof to support their demands for involuntary dissolution. ... First we hold the evidence does not support our concluding the objects of incorporation have "wholly failed" or "been abandoned" or that "their accomplishment is impracticable." Sugar cane has been grown continuously on this property since 1941 .... Although the future of sugar cane farming on plantations the size of Goldmine is at best speculative and the record leaves no doubt that the highest and best use of this land at present is for industrial purposes, we cannot conclude that the accomplishment of sugar farming is impracticable.

Low profits per se do not render the accomplishments of the objects of the corporation impracticable. ... To us "impracticability" connotes an element of obsolescence as well as a low return operation. Therefore relief is not available [on this ground].

We next consider whether the record supports the view that dissolution would be more beneficial to the shareholders. It can be urged validly in this case that the low returns of the past have been more than offset by the appreciation of the corporate assets. With the completion of the river bridge at Luling within the next few years, the land value, according to [an expert appraiser], should increase tremendously. Thus the proof required [for this ground] is lacking.

... We appreciate the frustrations of the minority who are locked into a financial situation in which they have a substantial interest but no control. They suggest the shareholders be equated to partners and be permitted to disengage from the corporation as they could were Goldmine operated as a partnership. Our substantive law provides for involuntary dissolution but offers no remedy for the minority shareholder with substantial holdings who is out of control and trapped in a closed corporation. We will not arrogate the legislative function to provide relief. ...

Affirmed.

By the State: Since a corporation derives its right to exist from the state where it is incorporated, it seems natural that the state should also be able to take away that right. This power can be exercised, however, only in certain circumstances, The grounds for dissolution by the state (which are remarkably similar in the various jurisdictions) are discussed below.

Failure to comply with administrative requirements. All states insist that corporations comply with various administrative requirements. With respect to some of these duties, noncompliance may be cause for dissolution at the instance of the state. The most common examples are (1) failure to file required annual reports with the secretary of state, (2) failure to pay franchise fees or other state taxes, and (3) failure to appoint or maintain a registered agent. Many states acknowledge the relative insignificance of such omissions by providing for easy reinstatement upon compliance and payment of any penalties owed.

Ultra vires acts. The performance of acts that are beyond the corporation's powers constitutes a reason for dissolution. This principle is of little practical importance today, however, because most articles of incorporation now grant such broad powers that *ultra vires* acts are rather infrequent.

Dormancy. If a corporation never commences business after it is formed, or if it becomes dormant by abandoning its operations, the state can seek its dissolution in court. But the absence of corporate activity does not automatically bring about dissolution; it simply gives the state a basis for obtaining court-ordered dissolution.

Antitrust violations. In many jurisdictions, a corporation's violation of the state (not federal) antitrust laws is a cause for dissolution.

Fraudulent formation. Several states provide for dissolution where the corporation obtained its certificate of incorporation by misrepresenting material facts.

The attorney general of the state usually acts as its representative when a court action seeking dissolution is filed. But where the basis for dissolution is merely the failure to comply with an administrative requirement, some states authorize the secretary of state or other official to cancel the certificate of incorporation without court action.

Winding Up

Where Dissolution Is Voluntary: When voluntary dissolution occurs, the corporation's directors become *trustees* who hold corporate assets for the benefit of creditors and shareholders. They usually are allowed to wind up corporate affairs without court supervision. The directors in this situation have four duties:

1. They must not undertake any new business. Their authority is limited to the fulfillment of existing corporate obligations.

2. They must make a reasonable attempt to collect debts owed to the corporation.

3. After liquidation of corporate assets, they must pay creditors insofar as these assets are sufficient to do so.

4. When the claims of corporate creditors have been satisfied, they must distribute any remaining funds to shareholders. This distribution is required to be in the proportion of shareholders' respective interests and in accordance with any special rights enjoyed by preferred shareholders.

The directors can be held personally responsible for the breach of any of these winding-up duties. However, if they are unwilling to serve as trustees in liquidating the corporation, a "receiver" will be appointed and supervised by a court for the purpose of winding up corporate affairs. The court can also take such action if a creditor or shareholder shows cause why the directors should not be allowed to perform this function.

Where Dissolution Is Involuntary: In any case where dissolution is involuntary, the liquidation of corporate assets and other winding-up activities are always performed by a court-appointed receiver.

Questions and Problems

1. X Co. manufactures casual and dress shoes of all types. It wishes to expand its product line by getting into the athletic shoe business. What factors should its board of directors consider in deciding whether to get into the new line by internal expansion or by acquiring an existing maker of athletic shoes?

2. Discuss the rationale behind the appraisal right.

3. Pierce Co. was merged into Rayex Co. One of Pierce's creditors was not paid before the merger took place. The creditor demanded payment from Rayex, but its directors refused, saying that Pierce no longer existed and Rayex had not agreed to take over Pierce's obligations. Is the position taken by Rayex correct? Explain.

4. Explain why the court in *Ray v. Alad Corp.* placed such emphasis on Alad II's use of Alad I's trade name, goodwill, and customer lists, and its continuation of the same product line.

5. Chemco, Inc., was merged into Atlas Industries according to a merger plan adopted by the controlling shareholders of both companies. Under the plan, Chemco's controlling shareholders received cash in return for their Chemco shares. Chemco's minority shareholders, on the other hand, were given Atlas shares in return for their Chemco shares. Although the amount of cash received by the controlling shareholders was reasonable and fair, several members of the minority filed suit, challenging the plan because of its different treatment of controlling and minority shareholders. Will their suit be successful? Discuss.

6. Tandem Corp. purchased all the assets of Kilmer Company for cash. After the sale, a creditor of Kilmer demanded payment from Tandem. The creditor asserted that by buying Kilmer's assets Tandem had automatically assumed Kilmer's obligations. Is the creditor correct? Discuss.

7. Portsmouth, Inc., had two classes of shares outstanding: common shares, and nonvoting preferred shares. At the annual meeting, Portsmouth's shareholders voted to merge the company into International Conglomerate, Inc. Only the common shareholders, whose shares carried voting rights, were allowed to vote. As had been the case at past meetings, the preferred shareholders, who did not have voting rights, were not allowed to vote. The preferred shareholders challenged the validity of the merger, claiming that this situation was "different" than earlier ones and that they should have been allowed to vote. Will their challenge be successful? Explain.

8. What are the advantages of the tender offer as a method for obtaining control over another corporation?

9. What type of corporation seems the most susceptible to a deadlock? Explain.

10. National Equipment Rental Co. was dissolved, its assets liquidated, and all its liabilities paid. Remaining for distribution to shareholders was $5,000,000. Two classes of shares were outstanding: 150,000 shares of $35 par value common and 100,000 shares of $35 par value 8 percent preferred. National's articles of incorporation were silent on the matter of a preference as to assets on liquidation. What division will be made of the $5,000,000?

Part VI

Property and Bailments

Real Property   39

All of the world's material wealth consists of *property* of one type or another. The acquisition of property has been and continues to be one of the primary goals of a major portion of the world's population. What is more, a substantial percentage of all the civil lawsuits ever commenced have arisen out of disputes over some sort of property. For these reasons, the rules of law governing the ownership of property are among the most fundamental in our legal system.

In a society without a system of laws, "ownership" of property would consist merely of physical possession plus the strength and wits to keep it. In an organized society, however, with rights and duties determined by law, the concept of ownership is considerably more sophisticated, in terms of both its complexity and the orderliness of its protection. In the modern sense, then, ownership is comprised of a group of rights (such as possession, use, enjoyment, and transfer) that are *protected and guaranteed by governmental authority.*

All property is divided into two basic categories: real property and personal property. Essentially, *real property* (often called "real estate" or "realty") is land and most things affixed to it. *Personal property,* on the other hand, consists of every item of tangible or intangible property not included within the definition of

699

real property. Real property is the subject matter of this chapter, and personal property is dealt with in the following chapter.

The Nature of Real Property

The most important element of real property is, of course, the land itself. Things affixed to the land take the form of either vegetation or fixtures.

Land

The definition of *land* includes not only the surface of the earth but also everything above and beneath it. Thus the ownership of a tract of land theoretically includes both the air space above it and the soil from its surface to the center of the earth.

Air Rights: A landowner's rights with respect to the air space above the surface are called *air rights.* In earlier times, questions concerning air rights arose infrequently and usually involved rather novel issues. For example, in a 1925 Montana case, *Herrin v. Sutherland,* 241 P. 328, it was held that shooting a bullet over the land of another constituted a trespass.

Recently, however, air rights have come to involve more practical considerations. In densely populated metropolitan areas, for instance, air space is often quite valuable from a commercial standpoint. Thus the owner of an office building might sell a portion of its air space to a party who wishes to build and operate a restaurant or group of apartments atop the building. And railroad companies with tracks running through downtown areas, where building space is at a premium, have begun to sell the space above their tracks for office building construction.

For obviously practical reasons, modern courts have held that a landowner's air rights are not violated by airplanes flying at reasonable heights. If, however, a flight is low enough to actually interfere with the owner's use of his land (such as when the plane is taking off or landing), there is a violation of these air rights.

Subsurface Rights: The most practical result of the rule extending a landowner's property rights to the center of the earth is that he or she owns the *minerals* beneath the surface. When the land is sold, the buyer acquires any existing minerals, such as coal, even if they are not expressly mentioned. These minerals in the ground can also be owned *separately.* Thus a landowner might sell only the minerals or sell the rest of the land and expressly retain the minerals.

In some states (such as Texas and Pennsylvania) oil and natural gas are treated like other minerals with respect to ownership. That is, they can be owned while they are still in the ground.[1] The courts in a few states (such as California) take a contrary view, holding that oil and gas are not owned by anyone until pumped

---

[1]Ownership of oil, gas, or other minerals while still in the ground is referred to as *ownership in place.*

out of the ground. Of course, regardless of the type of mineral or the particular jurisdiction, an owner who first *removes* the minerals and *then sells* them is making a sale of personal property, not real property.[2]

Vegetation

For the purpose of classification as real or personal property, vegetation has traditionally been divided into two categories: (1) that which grows naturally (such as trees or wild grasses and bushes), and (2) that which requires cultivation (such as corn, wheat, or other growing crops). Naturally-growing vegetation is treated as *real property,* and cultivated vegetation is treated as *personal property.* Valuation for the purpose of levying real property taxes is an example of a situation where the distinction can prove important.

In a sale transaction, however, any type of vegetation—natural or cultivated—passes to the buyer along with the land unless the seller expressly excludes it from the sale. Also, regardless of the type of vegetation and regardless of whether severance from the soil is to be accomplished by the seller or buyer, the general rule today is that if growing vegetation (such as timber or crops) is sold by itself, and not with the land, the transaction is a sale of *personal property.*[3]

Fixtures

A *fixture* is an item that was originally personal property but that has been attached to the land (or to another fixture) in a relatively permanent fashion. Fixtures are viewed by the law as *real property.* Thus title to them passes to the buyer of real property unless the seller expressly excludes them from the transaction. In other words, even if the documents employed in the transaction describe only the land and are silent with respect to fixtures, title to them nevertheless passes to the buyer. Items that are not fixtures, however, do not pass along with a sale of land unless they are expressly included in the terms of the transaction.

To illustrate: Jones contracts to sell his farm to Williams; the contract describes only the boundaries of the land. Located on the farm are a house and a barn. These buildings are fixtures and will pass to Williams as part of the real property, as will the fence around the land. Inside the house, Jones's clothing and furniture are not fixtures, but the built-in cabinets and plumbing are. The hay stored in the barn is not a fixture, but the built-in feeding troughs are.

As is true of minerals, when a landowner removes a fixture from the soil or from the building to which it was attached and then sells the item *by itself,* it is considered a sale of *personal property* rather than real property. In fact, if a landowner removes a fixture with the intention that removal will be permanent,

---

[2]In other words, the owner is selling *goods* (tangible personal property).
[3]See UCC Sec. 2-107.

the item reverts back to its original status as personal property regardless of whether it is sold.

Determining Whether an Item Is a Fixture: Although the decision on whether a particular article is a fixture is often obvious (as in the case of a house), many items are difficult to classify. In general, a court will hold that an item is a fixture if there was *an intent that it become a permanent part of the real property.* Of course, this intent must be determined from all the circumstances of the case. Following are three factors that are often considered in determining whether something is a fixture:

1. An item is usually classified as a fixture if it is attached to a building in such a manner that it cannot be removed without damage to the building. Examples include shingles on the roof, built-in cabinets or appliances, a floor furnace, or a floor covering that is cemented in place.

2. An item is usually considered a fixture if it was specially made or altered for installation in a particular building. Examples include specially-fitted window screens, drapes custom-made for an odd-sized window, and a neon sign created for particular business premises.

3. Sometimes local custom dictates whether an item is a fixture. For example, in some parts of the country it is customary for houses to be sold with refrigerators. Where this custom exists a landowner's intent when installing the refrigerator is probably that it be a permanent addition. Thus it is a fixture. (The same principle applies, of course, to any other "customary" item.)

Tenant's Fixtures: When an owner of real property leases it to another, the owner is usually referred to as a *landlord* (or lessor) and the other party as a *tenant* (or lessee). Most items affixed to the property by the tenant are not considered fixtures and can be removed when the lease expires.[4] Here again it is simply a matter of intent. In most cases, a tenant does not intend to make a permanent addition to the landlord's property when installing some type of item.

Many of the items that do not become fixtures if installed by a tenant *do* become fixtures if installed by the landlord. For instance, gasoline pumps in a leased service station are not fixtures if installed by a tenant but probably are fixtures if installed by the owner of the premises.[5] A similar example is bookshelves fastened to the wall of an apartment.

The following case illustrates the importance of *clearly* setting forth the parties' understanding regarding fixtures in a land sale transaction.

---

[4]If the removal causes any damage to the leased premises, however, the tenant must pay the landlord for such damage.

[5]An item installed by a tenant in connection with a business he or she is conducting on the leased premises is often called a *trade fixture.* But the word *fixture* in this case is misleading, since the item is not a true fixture and is not considered part of the real property.

Richard Cook and other, unnamed, individuals purchased sixty-two acres of farmland from Otto Beermann in April 1974. Negotiations leading up to the transaction were conducted between Cook and Ernie Albertson, who was Beermann's real estate broker. Albertson received all of his instructions from Rodney Smith, Beermann's attorney. When Cook inspected the property he observed an irrigation well complete with pump and motor. The pump was positioned in the well. The motor, which was supplied with fuel by an underground natural gas line running from the house, was bolted to a concrete pad directly adjacent to the well. The irrigation pipe and sprinkler system were unassembled and stacked behind the house, approximately 1,500 feet from the well. Cook informed Albertson that he would have no use for the pipe or sprinkler system.

The sale agreement, prepared by Albertson and signed by the purchaser, provided that the sale included "all fixtures and equipment permanently attached to said premises." The space provided for listing personal property included in the sale was left blank. Also in the agreement was a typewritten provision that had been added to the printed form which stated, "The irrigation equipment is not included in this sale." The agreement was accepted in behalf of Beermann by Smith, his attorney.

Before the purchasers took possession of the property, Beermann notified them that the pump and motor did not go with the real estate. The purchasers disagreed, claiming that the exclusion of "irrigation equipment" referred only to the pipe and sprinkler system, not to the pump and motor. Beermann then sold the pump and motor to a third party. Cook and the other purchasers, as plaintiffs, sued defendant Beermann for the value of the pump and motor. In the trial court, plaintiffs were awarded damages of $1,750. Both sides appealed, defendant claiming that plaintiffs should receive nothing, and plaintiffs contending that $1,750 was inadequate.

Spencer, Chief Justice: . . . The first question presented is whether the pump and motor were fixtures or items of personalty. . . . We said in *Frost v. Schinkel,* 238 N.W. 659, that where the owner puts in improvements, the law at once raises a presumption of intention to make them a part of the land. Rules for determining what is a fixture are construed strongly against the vendor and in favor of the purchaser.

It seems clear the pump and motor were fixtures. The motor was bolted to a concrete pad which measured approximately 8 to 10 feet in length and 4 feet in width. Natural gas to power the motor was supplied from an underground line. The pump was inside the well casing and secured by bolts.

Finding the pump and motor to be fixtures, it becomes necessary to determine whether they were excluded from the sale by the terms of the contract. The purchase agreement provides: "The irrigation equipment is not included in this sale." Both Cook and Albertson testified the term "irrigation equipment" referred to the irrigation pipe and sprinkler system and not to the pump and motor. Smith, defendant's attorney [in the real estate transaction, not in the present lawsuit], testified as to the following conversation with plaintiffs' attorney after the dispute arose: "Well, you told me you were having problems about a motor in a well and I told you, at that time, that I didn't know that there was a motor in the well, but had I known I would have assumed it went with the property."

Defendant contends the testimony of his attorney, as well as that of Cook and Albertson, should have been excluded as violative of the parol evidence rule. The attorney was his representative in this transaction and made alterations in the contract before approving it for defendant. Actually, the contract was made by the attorney.

Cook v. Beermann

Supreme Court of Nebraska, 271 N.W. 2d 459 (1978)

In *Ely Constr. Co. v. S & S Corp.,* 165 N.W.2d 562 (1969), we said: "In interpreting a written contract, the meaning of which is in doubt and dispute, evidence of prior or contemporaneous negotiations or understandings is admissible to discover the meaning which each party had reason to know would be given to the words by the other party." . . .

Defendant argues that even if the pump and motor could be considered "fixtures and equipment permanently attached to the premises," the irrigation pipe and sprinkler system which were stacked on the property definitely would not be included in this category. From this premise he argues that the provision "excepting irrigation equipment" from the sale must be read to apply to the pump and motor because it would be superfluous otherwise. *Actually, there is authority that the irrigation pipe and sprinkler system were also fixtures even though they were not physically attached to the real estate.* [Emphasis added.] We said in *Frost v. Schinkel,* 238 N.W. 659, 671 (1931): "It should be a safe rule to say that parts of property which are not physically attached to realty, but which are absolutely necessary to the operation of machinery and equipment which is physically attached, become themselves governed by the same rules as that which is annexed to the [land]."

The contract was ambiguous. The parol testimony was properly admitted to ascertain the meaning of the term "irrigation equipment." The testimony preponderates that there was no intention to exclude the pump and motor from the sale. The clause excluding "irrigation equipment" was inserted in response to Richard Cook's assertion that plaintiffs had no need for the irrigation pipe and sprinkler system.

[Judgment for plaintiffs affirmed. However, the trial court was ordered to increase plaintiffs' damages to $3,500.]

Interests in Real Property

Ownership of real property is not an "all or nothing" proposition. The total group of legal rights constituting complete ownership can be divided among several individuals. The particular set of rights owned in a given situation is referred to as an *interest* (or sometimes an *estate*) *in real property.* The following discussion will show that some real property interests entitle the owner to possession (these are called *possessory interests*), while others do not (these are called *nonpossessory interests*).

Possessory Interests

Fee Simple: When a person has complete ownership of real property, his or her interest is described as a *fee simple.*[6] In everyday usage, when someone is spoken of as the "owner" or as "having title," it generally means that the individual owns a fee simple interest. The characteristics of a fee simple interest are: (1) Ownership is of unlimited duration. (2) So long as the owner abides by the law and does not interfere with the rights of adjoining landowners, the owner is free to do whatever he or she chooses with the property.

If O, the owner of a fee simple interest in real property, conveys (transfers) the

---

[6]Various other phrases are also employed. It is sometimes said that the person is the "fee owner" or that he or she owns the land "in fee," "in fee simple," or "in fee simple absolute."

property to B, it is presumed that the entire fee simple is being conveyed. B will acquire a lesser interest only if the terms of the conveyance clearly so indicate. Thus a conveyance of the property "from O to B," with nothing said about the type of interest being conveyed, is deemed to transfer the entire fee simple interest to B.

Fee Simple Defeasible: Some interests in real property are classified as fee simple interests despite the fact that ownership is not absolute. Suppose, for example, that O conveys a fee simple interest to B, subject to the limitation that B's interest will cease upon the occurrence of a specified event. B's interest in this case is called a *fee simple defeasible.* It is a fee simple in every respect except that it is subject to the possibility of termination.

One of the most common limitations of this type relates to the *use* that is to be made of the land. For instance, the terms of the conveyance from O to B may state that B's ownership will continue only if the land is used for recreational purposes.

Suppose that the terms of the conveyance from O to B provide that the fee simple ownership will automatically revert back to O upon the occurrence of a designated event (such as the cessation of use for a particular purpose). While B's interest continues (conceivably forever), O is also the owner of an interest in the property, generally referred to as a "future interest." In this example, the particular type of future interest is called a "possibility of reverter." It is actually just an expectancy, and it may never ripen into a fee simple.

On the other hand, suppose that the terms of the conveyance from O to B provide that, on the occurrence of a designated event, fee simple ownership will shift from B to X. Here, while B's interest continues, X owns a future interest that may or may not ripen into fee simple ownership. A future interest owned by a third person, such as X, is usually referred to as an "executory interest."

Life Estate: A *life estate* is an interest in real property the duration of which is measured by the life of some designated person. For example, O, the fee simple owner, might convey the property to B "for B's lifetime." During his lifetime B would own a life estate. Similarly, if O's conveyance to B was "for the life of X," B would still own a life estate. (The latter is a much less common situation.)

If O, the fee simple owner, conveys any type of lesser interest (such as a life estate) to B, O obviously remains the owner of a future interest, which in this case is called a "reversion." When the lesser interest terminates, O again owns the fee simple interest.

Owning a life estate is not the equivalent of owning a fee simple for one's lifetime. It is true that the owner of the life estate (called the "life tenant") has the right to *normal use* of the property. For example, the life tenant can use it as a residence, farm it, conduct a business on it, allow another to use it in return for the payment of rent, or make any other reasonable use of it. However, the life tenant cannot do anything that will permanently damage the property and thus harm the owner of the future interest.

As an example of the limitations on a life tenant's use of the property, the right to cut timber on the land is generally quite restricted. The timber can be cut if it is required for fuel, fencing, or agricultural operations. But it cannot be cut for the purpose of *sale* unless (1) the life estate was conveyed to the life tenant specifically for that purpose, or (2) selling timber is the only profitable use that can be made of the land, or (3) the land was used for that purpose at the time the person became a life tenant, or (4) the owner of the future interest expressly permits the cutting.

Similarly, a life tenant can take oil and gas from existing wells and other minerals from existing mines. But this party cannot drill *new* wells or open *new* mines without authorization either in the document creating the life estate or at a later time from the owner of the future interest.

Although a life tenant is responsible to the owner of the future interest for any permanent damage he or she personally causes to the land, there is no such responsibility for damage caused by accidents, by third parties, or otherwise without the life tenant's fault.

A life tenant is also under a duty to pay taxes on the property. If this duty is neglected and the land is taken by the taxing authority, the life tenant is liable to the owner of the future interest.

Leasehold Estate: A "lease" of real property occurs when the owner grants to another the temporary right to possess the property in return for the payment of "rent."[7] In such a case, the owner is referred to as the *lessor* (or *landlord*) and the occupier as the *lessee* (or *tenant*). The interest acquired by the lessee is termed a *leasehold estate.*[8]

Although a leasehold is an interest in real property, it is treated for some purposes as personal property. For example, the lessee is not liable for real property taxes unless he or she has agreed to be responsible for them.

Under the parties' agreement, a leasehold can be created for *a stated period of time,* such as one year, ten years, ninety-nine years, or any other duration. Among the various names given to this type of leasehold, one of the more frequent is "tenancy for years." (This term is used even if the agreed duration is less than a year.) Such a leasehold automatically terminates on the expiration of the stated term.

If the parties do not agree on a definite duration for the lease but do agree that rent is to be paid at *specified intervals,* it is usually said that a "periodic tenancy" exists. (When the rent is to be paid monthly, the periodic tenancy is often called a "tenancy from month to month." A periodic tenancy with a rental period of one year is referred to as a "tenancy from year to year.") On the expiration of each rental period, this type of leasehold is *automatically renewed* for another rental period unless terminated by one of the parties. Termination of a periodic tenancy

---

[7]Although the granting of a *right to drill* for oil and gas is often called a *lease* in popular usage, it is not truly a lease because it does not convey a possessory interest in real property.

[8]The "owner" in this situation might be the owner of a fee simple, of a fee simple defeasible, of a life estate, or even of a leasehold.

is accomplished by giving notice prior to expiration of a rental period. Under the common-law rule, unless the parties agree otherwise, this notice must be given at least one full rental period (but no more than six months) beforehand in order to constitute termination. Today, however, many states have statutes that prescribe a specific length of time for such a notice, such as thirty days. This specified time governs unless the parties have agreed on a different time period.

Where the agreement of the parties provides that either of them can terminate the lease *at any time*, the leasehold interest is called a "tenancy at will."

The owner of the property can sell or otherwise transfer his or her interest to some third party, but the transferee takes the property subject to the lessee's interest. In other words, such a transfer does not terminate the leasehold.

The lessee can also transfer the leasehold to another, unless such a transfer is forbidden by the terms of the lease (and many leases do contain this prohibition). A lessee's transfer of the entire unexpired portion of the leasehold is an "assignment." But if the lessee transfers less than the entire remaining portion of the leasehold, the transfer is a "sublease." The distinction is important, because an *assignee* becomes directly liable for rent to the lessor, whereas a *sublessee* is liable only to the sublessor (the original lessee). Of course, in either case the original lessee remains ultimately responsible to the lessor for the payment of rent.

Nonpossessory Interests

Easement: Essentially, an *easement* is the right to make some limited use of another's real property without taking possession of it. Stated another way, it is the right to do a specific thing on another's land. Sometimes an easement is referred to informally as a "right-of-way."

Easements are either "appurtenant" or "in gross." An *easement appurtenant* is one created specifically for use in connection with another tract of land. For example: A and B own adjoining tracts. A grants B an easement to cross A's land to get to and from a highway. Here the easement on A's land is appurtenant, because it was created for use in connection with B's land. In this situation, A's land is called the "servient estate" and B's the "dominant estate."

An *easement in gross,* on the other hand, is one *not* used in connection with another tract of land. For example, a telephone company has an easement in gross when it acquires the right to run poles and wires across A's land.

Whenever a tract of land subject to either type of easement is sold, the purchaser must continue to recognize the easement if he or she knew or should have known of its existence at the time of purchase. Even without such knowledge, the purchaser's ownership is subject to the easement if the document creating it had previously been "recorded" (filed with the appropriate county official).

An easement appurtenant is said to "run with the land." This means that if the land being benefited by the easement (the dominant estate) is sold, the easement goes along with it. The owner of an easement appurtenant cannot sell or otherwise transfer it *by itself,* apart from the dominant estate. However, the owner of an easement in gross now is generally allowed to transfer it to another party.

Profit: A *profit*, technically called a "profit à prendre," is a nonpossessory interest in land consisting of the right to go upon the land and take something from it. Examples include the right to mine minerals, drill for oil, or take wild game or fish. Like easements, profits can be either appurtenant or in gross. The rules regarding transfer of the dominant and servient estates, as well as transfer of the profit by itself, are basically the same as for easements.

A *right to take* minerals, which is a profit, must be distinguished from an actual *sale* of the fee simple interest in the minerals in the ground. The form the transaction takes depends on the intent of the parties, as evidenced primarily by the language used. Of course, in those states where oil and gas are not deemed capable of being owned while in the ground, any transaction in which the buyer is to drill for oil and gas is a profit.

License: In essence, a *license* is simply the landowner's permission for someone else to come upon his or her land. It does not create an interest in real property, because the landowner can revoke it at any time. But even though the grantee of the license does not have a legally enforceable *right* to go upon the land, the license (prior to its revocation) does keep the grantee from being considered a trespasser. Two examples of situations where licenses exist are:

1. The purchaser of a ticket to a movie or other amusement or sporting event has a license to enter the premises.

2. Sometimes a license is created when there is an ineffective attempt to create an easement or profit. For example, since these are required to be in writing, an oral easement or profit is merely a license.

Lien: A person who borrows money usually has to grant the lender an interest in some item of property to secure payment of the debt. When the property to be used as security is real property, the landowner grants the lender an interest by executing a "mortgage." The interest created by the mortgage is called a *lien*.

If the landowner (the "mortgagor") defaults on the obligation, the lender (the "mortgagee") has a right to "foreclose" the lien. This means that the land can be seized and sold, the proceeds being used to pay off the debt.

Concurrent Ownership

Any interest in real property that can be owned by one individual can also be owned jointly by two or more individuals.

The most frequently encountered types of co-ownership are the *tenancy in common* and the *joint tenancy*. In a tenancy in common the co-owners are called "tenants in common" or "co-tenants." In a joint tenancy they are called "joint tenants." Unless a joint tenancy has been explicitly created, any co-ownership is presumed to be a tenancy in common.

The most important distinction between these two types of co-ownership has to do with disposition of a co-owner's interest when he or she dies. The interest of a tenant in common passes to that person's *heirs*. The joint tenancy, on the other hand, is characterized by a "right of survivorship," which means that the interest of a deceased joint tenant passes to the *other joint tenant(s)*.

In either a joint tenancy or a tenancy in common, none of the co-owners owns any segregated portion of the land. Instead, each owns an undivided fractional interest in the entire tract of land. Of course, the co-owners can agree to *partition* the land; but if they do so, their relationship as co-owners ends, and each becomes the owner of a specifically designated section of the property. If one or more of the co-owners want to partition the land but the parties are unable to reach unanimous consent on the matter, any of them can initiate a lawsuit to have the court order the property partitioned in a fair manner.

Sales of Real Property

Next to leases, sales are the most commonly occurring real estate transactions. Whether such sales involve a residential house and lot, a farm, or other real property, they are the most monetarily significant transactions many people ever experience.

Most real estate sales involve the transfer of a fee simple interest, but the same rules and procedures also apply to transfers of most other interests in real property.[9] Throughout the following discussion we will assume that the transaction is of the most common type—the sale of a fee simple interest.

Brokers

When a landowner wishes to sell property, the first step usually is to contact and employ a real estate broker (or "agent"). Although this is not required (the land-owner can, of course, sell the land without help), it is usually desirable unless the owner already has a buyer lined up.

The function of the broker is to find a buyer. This is usually the extent of the broker's authority; he or she ordinarily is not given authority to actually sell or even to make a contract to sell. In return for finding a buyer the broker is entitled to be compensated by receiving an agreed-upon "commission," which is usually a percentage of the selling price.

A formal employment contract setting out the terms of the arrangement should be made with the broker. Indeed, in many states a broker has no legally enforceable right to a commission unless the agreement to pay it is in writing.

The arrangement with the broker can be of several types:

1. It can be an *open listing*. This means that the broker is entitled to a commission only if he or she is the *first one* to procure a buyer who is "ready, willing, and able" to buy at the stated selling price. In this situation the owner is free to sell the land

---

[9]The exception is the transfer of a *leasehold interest*, which is accomplished by less complex means. All that is necessary to create a leasehold is the making of a contract; no deed is required.

personally or through another broker without incurring liability to the employed broker.

2. On the other hand, it can be an *exclusive agency.* In this case the owner gives assurance that no other broker will be hired during the term of the agreement. If the owner does employ another broker who procures a buyer, the sale is valid but the original broker is still entitled to the agreed commission. However, the owner is entitled to sell the land *personally,* without the aid of the employed broker or any other broker. If the owner makes the sale without assistance, the employed broker is not entitled to a commission.

3. The type of arrangement most advantageous to the broker is an *exclusive right to sell.* Under such an agreement, if the property is sold during the arrangement's duration *by anyone,* whether done with the aid of the employed broker or some other broker, or by the owner acting alone, the employed broker is entitled to the agreed commission.

The Contract

When a buyer is found, a contract for sale will ordinarily be made. This contract is usually evidenced by a detailed formal document signed by both seller and buyer, though this is not essential. To be enforceable, a contract for the sale of land does, of course, have to be *in writing* in almost all circumstances. But this requirement can be satisfied by informal instruments such as letters or telegrams. The writing, whether formal or not, must contain *all the essential terms* of the agreement and must be signed by the party against whom enforcement is sought.[10] If any of the essential terms are missing, the writing is considered insufficient; oral testimony will not be allowed to fill in the gaps, and the contract is unenforceable.

Specifically, the terms that must be included in the written contract for sale are (1) the *names* of the seller and buyer and an indication of their intent to be bound, (2) a *description* of the property sufficient to identify it, and (3) the *price.*

More will be said about the required description in the later discussion of deeds. (Incidentally, if the seller does ultimately convey title by giving a deed, it is immaterial whether there was an enforceable contract. The contract simply prevents one party from reneging prior to transfer of title.)

Title Examination and Insurance

One of the main reasons for initially making a sale contract rather than immediately transferring ownership is to give the buyer an opportunity to investigate the seller's title (often called a *title examination*). This essentially involves an examination of all officially recorded documents concerning the property. The examination is

---

[10]The signature can be that of the party's authorized agent. However, in most states, a contract for the sale of real estate signed by an agent is enforceable only if the agent's authorization is also in writing. (The same is true for the signing of a deed, which will be discussed later in this chapter.)

usually made by an attorney employed either by the purchaser or by the lending institution from which the purchase price is being borrowed.

The attorney may personally search the public records and on the basis of this investigation issue a "certificate of title" giving his or her opinion as to the validity of the seller's title. Or the attorney may examine an *abstract,* which is a compilation of the official records relating to a particular parcel of land. Privately owned "abstract companies" or "abstracters" produce such abstracts and keep them current.

The sale contract often requires the seller to provide evidence of a good title. The certificate of title is used as such evidence in some parts of the country, while in other areas the abstract and the attorney's opinion based thereon provide the required evidence. It is also becoming more frequent for the contract to require the seller to provide the buyer with "title insurance." This may be used as the sole evidence of title, or it may be required in addition to other evidence. Title insurance, which is purchased from a company engaged in the business of selling such insurance (often called a "title company"), simply provides that the issuing company will compensate the buyer for any loss if the title ultimately proves defective. Of course, the title company will issue such a policy only if its own attorneys feel, after making a title examination, that the title is good.

Survey

Unless a survey has been made very recently, the seller is often required under the contract to have a new survey made. A licensed surveyor will be employed to make sure that the described boundaries are correct and that no buildings or other encroachments lie on the boundary line.

Financing

Many times the purchaser will not have sufficient funds available to pay the agreed price. In such cases, after the contract is made but prior to the transfer of title, the buyer must obtain the necessary financing. Savings and loan associations are one of the most frequently used sources of such funds, especially for the purchase of residential property. In this situation, as we mentioned earlier, the purchaser (mortgagor) will execute a mortgage to the lender (mortgagee). And since the mortgage itself conveys an interest in real property (a lien), it has to be written and signed by the mortgagor.

The Closing

The actual transfer of ownership often takes place at the *closing* (or *settlement*)— the meeting attended by the seller and buyer as well as other interested parties such as their attorneys, the broker, and a representative of the mortgagee. At the meeting the seller signs and delivers to the buyer a *deed* that transfers the ownership; and the buyer pays the purchase price. (As a practical matter, however, the representative of the mortgagee may actually pay the seller.) It is also common for the mortgage to be executed at the closing and for other incidental financial matters to be settled (such as apportionment of property taxes and insurance that the seller may have prepaid).

Sometimes a closing occurs in a different manner, by the use of an "escrow agent." The *escrow agent* is a disinterested third party to whom the seller has delivered the deed and to whom the buyer has made payment.[11] This party's instructions generally are to close the deal by delivering the deed to the buyer and the payment to the seller on receipt of the required evidence of good title.

The Deed

Types of Deeds: As we stated earlier, title to real property is conveyed by means of a written deed. Several types of deeds exist, each involving particular legal consequences:

1. From the buyer's point of view, the *general warranty deed* is by far the most desirable kind to obtain, since it carries certain warranties or guarantees that the title is good. These warranties—called "covenants of title"—may be expressed in the deed, but even if not expressed they are *implied* if the document is actually a general warranty deed. Whether a particular deed is one of general warranty depends on the language used in it. The wording necessary to create such a deed varies from state to state. In Michigan, for example, the verb phrase *convey and warrant* makes it a general warranty deed. The warranties, which overlap somewhat, usually consist of the following:

a. *Covenant of seisin.* The seller (called a "grantor" in the deed) guarantees that he or she has good title to the land conveyed.

b. *Covenant against encumbrances.* The grantor guarantees that there are no encumbrances on the land except as stated in the deed. (An *encumbrance* includes any type of lien or easement held by a third party.) Even if the grantee (the buyer) knows of an existing encumbrance when receiving the deed, this warranty is breached unless the deed states that the title is "subject to" the particular encumbrance.

c. *Covenant for quiet enjoyment.* The grantor guarantees that the grantee (or those to whom the grantee later conveys the property) will not be evicted or disturbed by a person having a better title or a lien.

2. In the *special warranty deed,* there is a warranty only that the title has not been diminished in any way by a personal act of the grantor. For example, suppose the grantor had previously executed a mortgage on the land that the deed does not mention. If the grantee later has to pay off the mortgage or if it is foreclosed and the grantee loses the property, the grantor will be liable to the grantee for damages.

---

[11]It is fairly common for an institution such as a title insurance company to serve as escrow agent.

On the other hand, if the grantor has not personally encumbered the title but an outstanding title or interest in the land is later asserted by some third person, the grantor incurs no liability. This situation might arise, for instance, if the land is encumbered by a valid lien created by someone who owned the land prior to the grantor. The special warranty deed is a sufficient performance of the seller's obligations under the sale contract unless that contract specifically required a general warranty deed.

3. In a *quitclaim deed,* the grantor does not really purport to convey any title at all to the grantee. The deed says, in essence, "If I have any present interest in this land, I hereby convey it to you." This deed is not a sufficient performance of the grantor's obligations under the sale contract unless the contract so provides. Quitclaim deeds are often used as a form of *release.* For example: A owns the land, but X arguably has some type of interest in it, and A negotiates with X for a release of X's claim. One way of accomplishing the release is for A to obtain a quitclaim deed from X. Quitclaim deeds are also frequently employed by government entities (such as cities and counties) when they sell land.

4. The *deed of bargain and sale* purports to convey title but does not contain any warranties. Even though differing in form, this deed conveys the same type of title as a quitclaim deed. It also is not a sufficient performance of the grantor's obligations under the sale contract unless the contract so provides.

Requirements of a Valid Deed: Although the requirements of a valid deed vary slightly among the states, they are generally as follows:

1. The deed must name a *grantor and grantee.* The grantor must have legal capacity. If the grantor is married, it is generally desirable to have the grantor's spouse named as a grantor as well, for several reasons. In most states, if the property is occupied by husband and wife as their "homestead" (that is, their home), both must join in a conveyance of the property even if only one of them owns it. Furthermore, regardless of whether the property is their homestead, the laws of many states give one spouse certain types of rights with respect to the property of the other, and these rights are extinguished only if the grantor's spouse joins in the deed.[12]

2. Consideration is *not* a requirement for a valid deed. The owner can give away the property if he or she wishes. Of course, a *sale contract* must be supported by consideration, as must any other executory contract. A promise to make a gift of land or of anything else is generally not enforceable; but a completed gift by delivery of a deed is perfectly valid, assuming that there is no intent to defraud the grantor's creditors. Even though there is no requirement that a grantee give

---

[12]For the same reasons, the buyer should have taken the precaution of getting the seller's spouse to sign the sale contract.

consideration for a deed or that consideration be stated in the deed, it is customary for the deed to contain a *recital of consideration*—a statement of what consideration is being given by the grantee. It is also customary for the recital to state merely a nominal consideration (such as $10) rather than the price actually paid.

3. The deed must contain *words of conveyance*—words indicating a present intent to transfer ownership to the grantee, such as "I, Joe Smith, do hereby grant, sell, and convey . . ."

4. The deed must contain a *description of the land sufficient to identify it.* Although this description should be (and usually is) stated in the deed, it is permissible for the deed to refer to a sufficient description contained in another document. With respect to the sufficiency of the description, the following observations should be made:

a. There is a generally observable tendency for the courts to require a greater degree of certainty in a deed than in a sale contract. For example, in the case of residential property, a sale contract usually is enforceable if the description is merely a *street number* in a particular city and state. In many states, however, such a description is not sufficient for a deed to be a valid conveyance of title to the property.

b. Land can be adequately described in several different ways, but regardless of the method employed the property must be identified in such a way that there can be no mistake about precisely which parcel of land is being conveyed. One common method of description, especially in rural areas, is by "metes and bounds." *Metes* means measures of length; *bounds* refers to the boundaries of the property. A metes and bounds description essentially just delineates the exterior lines of the land being conveyed. It may make use of a "monument" (a natural or artificial landmark such as a river or street) to constitute a boundary or to mark a corner of the tract. A metes and bounds description begins at a well-identified point and runs a stated distance at a stated angle, tracing the boundary until it returns to the starting point.

c. Metes and bounds descriptions are not usually employed in urban areas, however. Most property within a city has been surveyed and divided into numbered lots on a "plat" (map) that is recorded (filed) with a designated county official. A city lot thus can be described by reference to the plat and the lot number.

d. In some areas of the country, where the land was originally owned and surveyed by the federal government, a sufficient description can be accomplished by a detailed reference to the official government survey.

5. The deed must be *signed by the grantor.* For the reasons already discussed, it is also usually desirable to obtain the signature of a married grantor's spouse.

6. There must be *delivery* of the deed to the grantee.

In the following case, we will see how problems can arise from "homemade" deeds. The case also illustrates that a court will, where it is possible to do so, attempt to make sense out of an imprecisely drafted deed.

Margaret and Carl DeBow owned a tract of land known as the Lakeland Allotment. There was a "plat" subdividing the land into lots, but no actual subdivision had ocurred. The property was mostly farmland, and the DeBows lived in the farmhouse and operated an antique shop in the barn behind the house. There also were several other sheds and garages on their property. In 1968 they built and moved into a new home west of the land in question. They then asked Marie Baker (Margaret's sister) and her husband George to leave their home in Cleveland, Ohio, move to the farmhouse on the Lakeland Allotment, and operate the antique shop. They agreed to do so, and Margaret prepared a deed conveying the property to the Bakers.

Before preparing the deed, Margaret had "walked off" (measured) the land to be transferred, and asked the Bakers if they thought it was sufficient footage to include the buildings located on the land. Margaret stated that if the land she measured off was not sufficient to include the buildings, "we can clear it up later." The deed prepared by Margaret began "at a point where the east line of the proposed Michigan Avenue intersects the south line of West Erie Street" and then followed the directional and distance description matching a lot on the Lakeland Allotment plat. Michigan Avenue was an unopened street and Margaret admitted that she did not know exactly where it began when she prepared the deed.

The Bakers moved into the farmhouse and reopened and operated the antique shop in 1971. During the same year Carl DeBow died. In 1973 Margaret married Mr. Zingelman, her present husband. It appears that this remarriage contributed in some way to the problems that later arose. Sometime in 1973 George Baker became upset with Margaret because she parked her truck in the garage which the Bakers claim is located on their property. There was a falling out between the families about this time. Margaret informed the Bakers that part of the barn, the garage, and sheds located on the land extended onto her adjacent land. By early 1975, Margaret's attorney informed the Bakers that the part of the barn which projected onto Margaret's property would be forcibly removed unless the Bakers chose to purchase for $10,000 the strip of property which would clear up the location problem of the buildings. The Bakers, plaintiffs, then sued to enjoin Margaret from parking her truck in the garage and from cutting off part of the barn.

At the trial, the testimony of two surveyors disclosed that all of one shed and garage and a portion of another shed and 13 feet of the barn extended onto Margaret's property. The lower court, however, enjoined Margaret from any further trespass and ordered her to convey to the Bakers the strip of land which would then place the buildings on the Baker property, in order to effectuate the original intent of the parties in their conveyance of 1971. Margaret, the defendant, appealed.

Cercone, Judge: . . . Defendant's argument stems from the legal principles and cases stating that when the language of a deed is clear and unambiguous, the intent of the parties must be gleaned solely from the instrument. Where a portion of a building is not included in the description of the deed and it is not clear from the deed that the parties meant for the entire building to pass, only that portion of the building passes that is covered in the description. In the case before us, defendant argues that the description in the deed was clear, . . . [and] that since there was no mention of any of the buildings in the deed, the judge should not have allowed parol evidence concerning the alleged inducement by Margaret for her sister to move to Pennsylvania.

Baker v. Zingelman
Superior Court of Pennsylvania, 393 A.2d 908 (1978)

Although this is a correct statement of the law, we must remember the lower court sat in equity. It is a general proposition of equity that when a person grants a thing, he intends to grant also that without which the thing cannot be enjoyed. We must assume the parties intended a reasonable result. The description in the deed before us was not prepared by a professional, but by defendant, who admitted she did not know exactly where Michigan Avenue began at the time of the deed preparation. There very easily could have been a mistake or ambiguity in the deed concerning the description, regardless of the omission of the word "building." Where such an ambiguity exists, the surrounding circumstances may be considered to determine the intent of the parties, and the subsequent acts of the parties are important to manifest their intentions. The actions of the parties subsequent to the deed were that the Bakers moved into the farmhouse and operated the antique shop in the barn. They obviously relied on the deed as having conveyed to them their interest in the property and in the buildings. It was only after the sisters' "falling out" that the boundary dispute arose. The proposed sale of the strip of land which would clear the building at a price of $10,000 seems extremely unreasonable in light of the fact that the deed of 1971 conveyed the majority of the land without any consideration passing.

Even if the language of the deed can be construed as being precise and clear on its face, the cases do make exceptions where encroachments are minor and where it would be illogical and unreasonable for the grantor to have conveyed only part of buildings. Here, plaintiffs were living in the house and operating the antique shop in the barn unhindered until the argument occurred. It is extremely unlikely that 13 feet of the barn, one garage, and part of two other sheds were deliberately excluded from the conveyance.

Taking all these facts into consideration, we must agree with the lower court that the defendant intended to convey sufficient footage to cover the house, barn, and related buildings to her sister and her husband at the time of the original deed in 1971.

[Judgment for plaintiffs, the Bakers, is affirmed.]

Acknowledgment: An *acknowledgment* is a formal declaration before a designated public official, such as a notary public, by a person who has signed a document, that he or she executed the document as a voluntary act. The public official places his or her signature and seal after the declaration and the declarant's signature. The resulting instrument, referred to as a *certificate of acknowledgment,* is attached to the document to which it relates.

In most states an acknowledgment is not required for a deed to be valid, but it is required as a prerequisite to "recording."

Recording: *Recording* is the act of filing the deed with a public official, referred to in different states as the "recorder of deeds," "register of deeds," or any of several other titles. The official copies the deed into the record books, indexes it, and returns the original to the person who filed it.

As between the grantor and grantee, an otherwise valid deed is perfectly good even if it is not recorded. The purpose of recording procedures, which exist in every state, is to give notice to the world at large that the transfer of title has taken place. Frequently referred to as "constructive notice," this means that third parties are treated as having notice regardless of whether they actually do.

State recording statutes generally provide that an unrecorded deed, though valid between grantor and grantee, is void with respect to any subsequent bona fide purchaser. (A *bona fide purchaser* [BFP] is a good faith purchaser for value.) For example, suppose that O sells a tract of land to B, and B does not record her deed. O then sells the same land to C by executing another deed. If C pays for the land rather than receiving it as a gift, he is giving *value*. If C does not know of the earlier conveyance to B when he purchases, he is acting in *good faith*. Thus C qualifies as a BFP and has good title. In this situation B has no title. But if B had recorded her deed prior to C's purchase, B would have title even if C later gave value and acted in good faith. The reasoning is that C could have discovered B's interest if he had checked the records.

Although there is some conflict on the point, the courts in a majority of states hold that C qualifies as a BFP even if he does not record his own deed. (Of course, if he does not do so, he runs the risk of having the same thing happen to him that happened to B. If there was a "C," there could later be a "D.")

Regarding the status of C as a BFP, another point must be made. If B, the first grantee from O, is actually *in possession of the land* when C acquires his interest, this possession serves as notice to C. Thus, even if B did not record and C did not have actual knowledge of B's interest, C nevertheless is not a BFP.

Recording statutes apply not only to the sale of a fee simple interest but also to the conveyance of any other type of interest in land. For example, if O executes a mortgage to B, giving her a lien on the property, B should record her mortgage. If she does not, she risks losing her interest to a subsequent BFP.

Furthermore, the word *purchaser* actually means a grantee of any type of interest in the land, even such interests as liens or easements. Suppose, for instance, that O sells to B, who does not record her deed. O later borrows money from C and executes a mortgage purporting to give C a lien on the land. By making the loan to O, C is giving value. If C receives the mortgage without knowledge of the earlier conveyance to B, he is acting in good faith and is treated as a BFP. Thus C's mortgage is valid, and B's ownership is subject to it. If B had been a mortgagee herself instead of an actual grantee of the title, the same rules would apply to the conflict between B and C, the two mortgagees.

Gift

Other Methods of Ownership Change

As indicated earlier, ownership of an interest in land can be acquired by gift. This is accomplished by delivery of a deed from grantor to grantee under circumstances showing an intent to make the gift.

Inheritance

Upon an owner's death, title to the person's real property can pass according to the terms of his or her validly executed "will." If the owner dies "intestate" (without a valid will), such ownership passes to those relatives designated as heirs under state law (called "statutes of descent and distribution" or "statutes of intestacy").

Eminent Domain

Eminent domain is the power of the government to take private property for a "public purpose" (such as a highway). This power can be exercised without the owner's consent, but he or she must be paid the "fair value" of the property. The process by which the government takes the property is referred to as "condemnation." Any type of interest in real property can be so taken ("condemned").

The federal government derives the power of eminent domain from the U.S. Constitution. Individual states draw the power from their own constitutions. Additionally, states have delegated the power of eminent domain by statute to local governments (such as counties and cities) and to railroads and public utilities.

Adverse Possession

Under some circumstances, a party can acquire ownership of land by taking possession of it and staying in possession for a certain number of years. The required time period is established by statute and varies from state to state, ranging from five years in California to thirty years in Louisiana.

Ownership acquired in this manner is frequently referred to as *title by adverse possession* or *title by limitation*.[13] Since it is not acquired by deed, there is nothing to record. Thus the recording statutes do not apply, and title by adverse possession, once acquired, cannot be lost to a subsequent BFP. Of course, even though such title is not *acquired* by deed, it can be *conveyed* by deed to someone else. Such a deed would be subject to all the rules applicable to deeds in general, including the recording statutes.

Not all types of possession will ripen into ownership. The possession must be "adverse," which means, in effect, that it must be actual, hostile, open and notorious, and continuous.[14]

Actual: The requirement that possession be *actual* simply means that the possessor must have exercised some type of *physical control* over the land that indicates a claim of ownership. The person need not actually live on the property, although this certainly constitutes actual possession. What is required is that the possessor act toward the land as an average owner probably would act, taking into account

---

[13]The latter phrase is explained by the fact that the prescribed time periods are, in essence, statutes of limitations setting forth the maximum length of time an owner has to sue someone who is wrongfully in possession of the owner's land.

[14]Some courts have also said that the possession must be "exclusive" and "under claim of right." These requirements will not be discussed because they overlap with the four listed here and really add nothing to what is required for adverse possession to exist.

the nature of the land. For example, if it is farmland, the farming of it constitutes actual possession. Erecting buildings or other improvements may also be sufficient.

Construction of a fence or building that extends over the true boundary line and onto the land of an adjoining property owner generally constitutes actual possession of that part of the land encompassed by the fence or located under the building. Thus, if the other requirements of adverse possession are met, the party erecting the fence or building will become the owner of the area in question after the prescribed period of time.

Hostile: The requirement that the possession be *hostile* does not mean that it must be accompanied by ill feelings. What it means is that possession must be *nonconsensual;* it is not adverse if it occurs with the consent of the true owner. Thus a lessee's possession of the lessor's property under a lease agreement is not hostile.

Similarly, if two parties are co-owners of a tract of land, each of them has a right to possession. Therefore, possession by one co-owner is not hostile as to the other unless the possessor notifies the other that he or she is claiming sole ownership.

Open and Notorious: The possession must be *open and notorious* rather than secretive. In other words, it must be a type of possession that will be easily noticeable by the true owner if a reasonable inspection is made.

Continuous: In order for adverse possession to ultimately ripen into ownership, it must be *reasonably continuous* for the required period of time. The possessor does not have to be in possession every single day of the period. For instance, he or she could leave temporarily with an intent to return, and the law would treat the possession as not having been interrupted.

In answering the question of whether possession has been continuous, a court will take into account the nature of the land and the type of use being made of it. Thus farming the land only during the growing season each year constitutes continuous possession.

Also, the uninterrupted possession by two or more successive possessors can sometimes be added together, or "tacked," to satisfy the statutory time requirement. For "tacking" to be permitted, there must have been "privity" between the successive possessors. This simply means that the possessions by different persons must not have been independent of each other; rather, there must have been a transaction between them which purported to transfer the property. To illustrate: In State X the required period for adverse possession is ten years. O is the true owner. B meets all the requirements for adverse possession except that he stays on the land only six years. B then purports to sell or otherwise transfer the land to C. If C stays in possession for four more years, continuing to meet all the requirements for obtaining title by adverse possession, C becomes the owner of the land.

The following case illustrates the applicability of the adverse possession doctrine to a common problem—a boundary dispute between "unneighborly" neighbors.

Kline v. Kramer

Court of Appeals of
Indiana, 386 N.E.2d 982
(1979)

The Klines and the Kramers were adjoining landowners who both claimed owner-ship of a strip of land one to four feet wide and 309 feet long. The disputed strip formed the northern boundary of the Kramer property and the southern boundary of the Kline property. Both claimed ownership through previous owners. The Klines, who acquired their property in 1972, based their claim to the strip on the legal description contained in their deed. The Kramers, who purchased their prop-erty in 1968, claimed the strip on the theory of adverse possession. The position of the Kramers was that the ten-year period of possession necessary to establish ad-verse possession had been satisfied by the previous owners of the Kramer property, Harry and Hazel Britt.

The Kramers, plaintiffs, filed suit against the Klines, defendants, seeking to estab-lish ownership of the boundary strip. The trial court granted the plaintiffs' motion for summary judgment, ruling that they had title by adverse possession, and the de-fendants appealed.

Staton, Judge: . . . Harry Britt testified at the hearing on Kramer's motion for summary judgment that when he purchased the present-day Kramer property in 1947, a fence existed along the northern boundary of the land. Britt maintained the fence during his period of ownership. Photographs of the fence-line were introduced into evidence at the hearing in which Britt identified old fence posts he had set in maintaining the existing fence and familiar trees which had grown in the fence-line during his tenure on the land. While Britt testified that he never contemplated that he was claiming land that belonged to his neighbor, the fence in fact described a line which ran roughly one to four feet north of and parallel to the legally-described northern boundary of his property.

   Britt testified that he felt that he owned the property up to the fence line and that he used it to plant crops and pasture cattle. It was his belief that he had bought "what was inside the fence." Similarly, Britt stated that when he sold the land to the Kramers in 1968 he intended to convey to them all the land enclosed by the fence.

   F. Richard Kramer testified that he believed that he had purchased the property up to the fence that ran along the northern edge of his acreage. In 1972, Kramer inadvertently allowed his tractor to roll through the fence, tearing out a middle portion of it. Kramer repaired the break in the fence by stretching new fencing between the remaining old fence and fence posts to the east and west of the break. This new portion of the fence was set in the exact location of the old fence, according to Kramer, who noted that the new section followed a trail which cattle had worn along the old section.

   Kramer concluded his testimony by stating that he had made improvements which encroached on the disputed stretch of land, that he had no knowledge of the true boundary line until Kline had conducted a survey of the land, and that he had paid taxes on his property according to the tax receipts sent to him by the County Treasurer.

   . . . The trial court's entry of summary judgment was predicated on its conclusion that the Kramers had acquired title to the property through adverse possession. The ten year possessory period necessary to acquire title on that basis is a statute of limitations which runs against the titleholder. If the titleholder fails to oust the intruder within the ten year period, title to the property vests in the intruder, assuming all other elements of adverse possession are satisfied.

   . . . The Klines contend that summary judgment was improper because the undisputed evidence reveals the absence of the elements necessary to acquire title by adverse possession. Specifically, the Klines maintain that the Kramers' predecessors-in-interest, the Britts, whose possessory period provides the foundation for the Kramers' claim, lacked the necessary adverseness, hostility, and intention to claim title to the strip. This argument is premised largely on the testimony of both Harry and Hazel Britt that they never intended to lay claim to any land that belonged to their neighbor to the north. Accordingly, the Klines argue, the Britts held the land by mistake and lacked the adverse intent or hostility which is requisite to establishing a claim of adverse possession.

We note that in the law of adverse possession, "adverse" is synonymous with "hostile." So long as an occupant of another's land does not disavow his or her right to possession of the property nor acknowledge that the possession is subservient to the title held by the true owner, the possession is adverse or hostile.

. . . While it is true that the Britts did not intend to claim the land of their neighbors, the record clearly reveals that they intended to claim all the land within the parameters of the fence which ran along the northern boundary of their property. They did not recognize that their ownership was subservient to their neighbor's title, nor did they acknowledge that they had no legal right to possession of the property. In all respects they acted as the sole owner of the property, maintaining the fence and using the land in a manner consistent with its normal purposes. This evidence clearly establishes that the Britts intended to claim title to the disputed strip of land. The only mistake involved in the Britts' possession was their belief that they were merely acting in a manner consistent with their ownership rights, a fact which does not negate the conclusion that their possession was adverse.

This uncontroverted evidence also establishes the Britts' "intent to claim title" to the contiguous strip of land, as the Klines have characterized the element of adverse possession. This element is more aptly defined as "a claim of ownership." The element is satisfied by entering upon and occupying the land with the intent to hold the land as one's own. The trial court was thus justified in finding that the Britts' possession was both hostile and under a claim of ownership. . . .

[Affirmed. The Kramers, plaintiffs, own the boundary strip because of adverse possession.]

Prescriptive Easements

An easement can be acquired in a manner quite similar to acquisition of title by adverse possession. Such an easement is called a *prescriptive easement* or *easement by prescription*.

Possession obviously is not an element in the acquisition of a prescriptive easement, since an easement is not a possessory interest. What is important, instead, is *use*. A prescriptive easement is created if, for example, X actually exercises an easement on O's land for the required time period, and the use X makes of the land is hostile, open and notorious, and continuous. The required period of time is usually the same as for acquisition of title by adverse possession.

1. Talley and Warren were adjoining landowners. Talley drilled a producing oil well on his land close to the boundary line between his and Warren's property. Warren sued Talley for trespass. Although the entire well was on Talley's property, Warren proved that the well

Questions and Problems

was drawing oil not only from beneath Talley's land but also from beneath Warren's. Will Warren prevail? Discuss.

2. In the above situation, suppose that Talley had drilled a "slant well," which began on his land but ended beneath Warren's land because it had been drilled at an angle. What will be the result if Warren sues for trespass in this case? Discuss.

3. Jenkins sold a ten-acre tract of land to Watkins. In the past, Jenkins had engaged in the business of raising rabbits, and at the time of the sale a number of rabbit hutches were still on the land. They were not attached to the soil but merely rested upon it. Each hutch had a wire-covered wooden frame and a tin roof; each measured approximately 4 ft. by 4 ft. by 4 ft. These hutches were never mentioned in the transaction. When Jenkins moved from the premises after the sale, he claimed that the rabbit hutches were still his and that he was entitled to take them. Watkins disagreed. Who is correct? Discuss.

4. Discuss whether wall-to-wall carpeting should be considered a fixture.

5. What are some probable reasons for the rule that the owner of a fee simple interest is presumed to be selling the entire interest unless the terms of the conveyance clearly indicate tranference of a lesser interest? Explain.

6. Kempin was the owner of a life estate in a sixty-acre parcel of land. A valuable stand of growing timber was situated on the property, and substantial deposits of lignite were located beneath it. Kempin began cutting the timber, both for firewood and for the purpose of sale. He also undertook to mine the lignite, some of which he intended to use for fuel and some of which he intended to sell. Moskovitz, who was to become the fee simple owner on Kempin's death, sued Kempin to enjoin him from all of the above activities. Who will prevail? Explain.

7. Explain the difference between easements, profits, and licenses.

8. In connection with the employment of a real estate broker, what is the difference between an open listing, an exclusive agency, and an exclusive right to sell?

9. Poindexter sold his farm to Samuelson, who did not record his deed. Several weeks later, before Samuelson had taken possession of the land, Poindexter sold the same property to Rosser, who made a large down payment and knew nothing of the earlier sale to Samuelson. Does Samuelson or Rosser have title to the land? Explain. Would it matter whether Rosser recorded his deed? Explain. Would it make any difference if Samuelson had already taken possession of the land when Rosser bought it? Explain.

10. Arnold and Ross were adjoining landowners. The opening of a cave was located on Arnold's land, but the cave ran beneath Ross's land. Ross did not know of the cave's existence. For a continuous period of twenty-five years, Arnold used the entire cave for various purposes, including storage. On a number of occasions, doing business as the Marengo Cave Co., he also guided visitors through the cave for a fee. Ross finally learned of the cave and of the use Arnold had been making of it. He demanded that Arnold cease his use of the part of the cave beneath Ross's land. Arnold refused, claiming that he had acquired title to the cave by adverse possession. The pertinent state statute provided for acquisition of such title after twenty years. Ross filed suit to establish ownership of the cave. *Marengo Cave Co. v. Ross,* 10 N.E.2d 917 (1937). Who owned the portion of the cave located beneath Ross's land? Discuss.

Personal Property   40

As a general proposition, ownership of personal property is a somewhat simpler matter than ownership of real property, primarily because the law does not formally recognize the numerous types of interests that it does for real property. Ordinarily a person either is the owner of an item of personal property or is not.[1]

One example of this simpler approach is found in the case of a *lease*. A lease of real property actually conveys an interest in the property to the lessee. This, however, is not true of a lease of personal property. In this situation the lease merely creates a *bailment;* the lessee has temporary possession but no ownership interest in the property itself.[2]

An important exception to the "all-or-nothing" concept of personal property ownership is the "security interest." For the purpose of guaranteeing payment, a debtor may grant to a creditor an interest in one or more items of personal

Ownership of Personal Property

---

[1]Of course, the legal question of *who* actually is the owner may not be so simple.
[2]Bailments will be discussed in Chapter 42.

property. The debtor retains title, but the creditor also owns an interest in the property until the debt is paid.[3]

Another exception is that personal property, like real property, can be jointly owned by two or more persons. Also like real property, the most common types of co-ownership of personal property are the "tenancy in common" and the "joint tenancy." Two important points about these types of ownership should be recalled from the previous chapter:

1. The most important distinction between them is the "right of survivorship," which exists in the joint tenancy but not in the tenancy in common.

2. Whenever property is co-owned, the arrangement is generally presumed to be a tenancy in common, and very explicit language is required to make it a joint tenancy.

The remainder of the chapter will deal with the methods by which ownership of personal property is acquired. However, we will not discuss the subject of *sales of goods* in this chapter. Although it obviously involves the transfer of title to personal property, the subject is of such importance and complexity that it has been separately discussed in Chapters 17 through 21.

Gifts of Personal Property

A gift occurs when an owner of property (called the *donor*) voluntarily transfers ownership of the property to another (the *donee*) without receiving any consideration in return. A promise or expression of an intent to make a gift in the future is not the same thing as an actual gift. By its very nature, such a promise is not made in return for consideration, as required by contract law. Accordingly, it usually confers no rights on the promisee and cannot be enforced.

In order to transfer ownership by gift, the donor must actually carry out the promise or expression of intent. If this is done, the absence of consideration is irrelevant. Thus two requirements exist for making a valid gift: (1) an *intent* to transfer ownership, and (2) *delivery of possession* to the donee.[4]

Intent: The language and conduct of the donor, considered in the light of all the surrounding circumstances, must indicate an intent to transfer *ownership,* not merely possession or the right to use the property.

Delivery: Many lawsuits involving gifts of personal property have centered on the question of whether there had been a delivery of possession to the donee. The most frequent problems in this area are summarized below:

1. *Retention of control.* If the donor attempts to retain a degree of control over the property, there usually is not a legally effective gift. As one court stated, there must be "a complete stripping of the donor of dominion or control over the thing

---

[3]Security interests are discussed in Chapter 43.

[4]There is also a requirement that the donee accept the gift, but acceptance is presumed unless the donee expressly rejects the gift. This issue obviously arises only on rare occasions.

given."[5] To illustrate: Suppose that X indicates he wants to give a diamond ring to Y. If X then places the ring in a safe-deposit box to which both X and Y have access, there is not a sufficient delivery. Another example is found in the case of *Lee v. Lee,* 5 F.2d 767 (1925): The widow of a grandson of General Robert E. Lee prepared a written document stating that she was giving to her two sons a trunk containing several items which had belonged to the general. She deposited the trunk with a storage company, with instructions to the company obligating it to deliver the trunk to either her or her sons. In holding that there had not been an adequate delivery, the court said, "[T]here was not that quality of completeness present in the transaction which distinguishes a mere intention to give from the completed act, and where this element is lacking the gift fails."

2. *Delivery to an agent.* If delivery of the property is made to the donor's *own agent,* with instructions to deliver to the donee, there is not a completed gift until the donee actually receives the item. The reason, again, is that the donor does not part with sufficient control until the donee takes possession. If the donor delivers possession to the *donee's agent,* however, a valid gift has been made.

3. *Property already in possession of the donee.* If the donee already possesses the property when the donor indicates an intent to presently make a gift, the gift is immediately effective. There is no need to make a formal delivery in this situation.

4. *Constructive delivery.* In most cases, delivery of actual physical possession is required. In two types of circumstances, however, a "constructive" (or "symbolic") delivery will suffice:

a. If it is *impractical or inconvenient* to deliver actual physical possession because the item is too large or because it is located at too great a distance from the parties, constructive delivery is allowed. In such cases it ordinarily takes the form of a delivery of something that gives the donee *control* over the property. For example, if the item being given is a car, delivery of the car's key to the donee is sufficient. Similarly, delivery to the donee of a key to a building, room, or container in which an item is located constitutes a valid delivery if physical delivery of the property itself is impractical or inconvenient.

b. Constructive delivery is permissible for a gift of *intangible* personal property, for the obvious reason that there is nothing physical to deliver. Some types of intangible property rights are evidenced by written documents that by either law or business custom are accepted as representing the intangible right itself. Examples are bonds, promissory notes, corporate stock certificates, insurance policies, and savings account books. For these types of property rights, delivery of the written instrument evidencing the right is treated as delivery of the right itself. If the property right is an ordinary contract right not represented by any commercially recognized document, most courts allow constructive delivery of it by delivery of a writing setting forth the *present intent* to assign the right to the donee.

---

[5]*Allen v. Hendrick,* 206 Pac. 733 (1922).

Of course, a gift will not be valid if the donor's action was induced by fraud, duress, mistake, or undue influence. In addition, the courts always examine very carefully any gift occurring between persons in a "fiduciary" relationship. Thus, if X owes a higher degree of trust to Y because of a fiduciary relationship, and X receives a gift from Y, the law places the burden upon X to prove that all was fair. The following case illustrates this important principle.

Gordon v. Bialystoker Center & Bikur Cholim, Inc.

Court of Appeals of New York, 385 N.E.2d 285 (1978)

Ida Gorodetsky, who was 85 years old at the time, suffered a stroke and was admitted to Brookland-Cumberland Hospital in August 1972. Her closest relatives, two brothers and a niece, had not seen her for several years, and she had lived alone since 1962. From the time of her stroke until her death four months later, Ida remained partially paralyzed, confused, and sometimes semicomatose.

At the suggestion of one of Ida's acquaintences, the Bialystoker nursing home sent one of its social workers to visit the elderly lady in the hospital in October 1972. After learning that Ida had funds of her own, the director of the nursing home sent the social worker back to visit Ida on November 3 for the purpose of having her sign a withdrawal slip. A request had already been made for her admittance to the home, and the purpose of the withdrawal slip was to obtain funds for her care at the home. Using the withdrawal slip, the home obtained a $15,000 check from Ida's account payable to the home "for the benefit of Ida Gorodetsky."

On November 13 Ida was moved to the infirmary of the nursing home. That same day, within an hour and a half of admission, she was visited by a group consisting of the home's executive director, its fund raiser, one of its social workers, and a notary public. She was presented with a collection of instruments on each of which she placed her mark. These instruments included an application for admission to the home, an admission agreement, a withdrawal slip for the $12,864.46 remaining in her bank account, an assignment of that amount to the home, and a letter making a donation to the home of any part of the $27,864.46 remaining after paying expenses for her lifetime care.

Ida died on December 5 while still a resident of the nursing home. Her brother, Sam Gordon, administrator of her estate, filed suit against the nursing home to recover these funds, less the amount necessary to pay her expenses. The trial court ruled for the defendant nursing home on the ground that a valid gift had been made. The intermediate level appellate court reversed, ruling in favor of plaintiff administrator, and defendant appealed to New York's highest court.

Jones, Justice: ... It is indisputable that on November 13, 1972, when the gift on which defendant predicates its claim to the funds in dispute was made, there existed between the donor and donee a fiduciary relationship arising from the nursing home's assumption of complete control, care and responsibility of and for its resident. As the executive director of that institution testified at some length, the residents of the nursing home are dependent on the home "to take care in effect of their very livelihood, their existence;" they "rely upon the people in the home to take care of them . . . ; they have no means of taking care of themselves;" and ask and receive help from the staff of the home. According to the witness, "every one of the residents' particular needs . . . is administered to them by the help, the nurses or the doctors" of the home and in many instances—as was the case with the decedent—"they have no other source of getting that kind of help and don't get any help other than from the institution." The acceptance of such responsibility with respect to the aged and infirm who, for substantial consideration availed themselves of the custodial care offered by the institution, resulted in the creation of a fiduciary relationship and the applicability of the law of constructive fraud. Under that doctrine, where a fiduciary relationship exists between parties, transactions between them are scrutinized with extreme vigilance, and clear evidence is required that the transaction was understood, and that there was no fraud, mistake, or undue influence. Where those relations exist there must be clear proof of the integrity and fairness of the transaction, or any instrument thus obtained will be set aside, or held as invalid between the parties. As was said long ago, in articulating the concept of constructive fraud: "It may be stated as universally true that fraud vitiates all contracts, but as a general thing it is not presumed but must be proved by the party seeking to relieve himself from an obligation on that ground. Whenever, however, the relations between the contracting parties appear to be of such a character as to render it certain that they do not deal on terms of equality but that either on the one side from superior knowledge of the matter derived from a fiduciary relation, or from an overmastering influence, or on the other from weakness, dependence, or trust justifiably reposed, unfair advantage in a transaction is rendered probable, there the burden is shifted, the transaction is presumed void, and it is incumbent upon the stronger party to show affirmatively that no deception was practiced, no undue influence was used, and that all was fair, open, voluntary and well understood. This doctrine is well settled." (*Cowee v. Cornell*, 75 N.Y. 91, 99-100). So here, the defendant, rather than plaintiff, bore the burden of proof on the issue whether Ida's gift of funds was freely, voluntarily and understandingly made. *Examination of the record demonstrates that that burden had not been met.* [Emphasis added.]

... The home was aware of the patient's mental and physical infirmities and weakness. Nothing to that point had remotely suggested that the patient might be disposed to make a gift to the home, or indeed that she even knew of its existence. The parties were brought together only in contemplation of the patient's transfer to the home; the transaction between them had no other meaning. That the patient was inescapably reposing confidence in the home from the moment of their first encounter was implicit in the circumstances.

We reject out of hand defendant's contention that, as a charitable organization, it should not be made subject to the same evidentiary burden that would be imposed on a profit-making institution. However worthy may be the objectives to which its funds are dedicated, no justification exists for relieving it of the obligation, when circumstances suggest a substantial risk of overreaching, of affirmatively demonstrating that assets it has acquired have come to it from a willing and informed donor, untainted by impermissible initiative on the part of the donee.

... [T]he testimony offered, in conjunction with the other evidence in the case, was insufficient as a matter of law to sustain the burden of proof resting on the nursing home.

[The judgement of the intermediate level appellate court is affirmed; defendant nursing home must return to Ida's estate all funds beyond what was necessary to pay her expenses.]

Special Treatment of Joint Bank Accounts

The requirement that the donor part with all control over the property is frequently an issue in cases involving a bank account jointly owned by the donor and the donee. For example, suppose that X deposits money belonging to him in a bank account that is in the name of X and Y. Both X and Y have the right to withdraw funds from the account. Obviously there is a completed gift from X to Y of all money actually taken from the account by Y. But because of the retention of control by X, money that is not withdrawn from the account by Y is not considered a gift.

Suppose, however, that the agreement between X and the bank provides that on the death of X or Y, the funds remaining in the account will go to the *survivor* (that is, a "joint tenancy" is created).[6] If X dies first, the question will arise whether a valid gift of the remaining funds has been made by X to Y. A few courts have held that in such a situation there is not a sufficient relinquishment of control by X to create a gift. However, they also have usually held that Y is nevertheless entitled to the money as a *third party beneficiary* of an enforceable contract between X and the bank. On the other hand, a majority of courts have simply relaxed the delivery requirement in this type of case and have held that there is a valid gift to Y despite the retention of some control by X.

Of course, as is true of any other gift, X must have *intended* to make a gift to Y. In the case of a joint tenancy bank account (one with a right of survivorship), there is a *presumption* of intent on the part of X to make a gift to Y, and this presumption can be rebutted only by evidence clearly showing that X did *not* intend to make a gift. For instance, the evidence might show that the joint account was established solely to give Y access to X's funds so as to enable Y to help X handle his financial affairs.

Gifts *Inter Vivos* and *Causa Mortis*

Gifts are classified as either *inter vivos* or *causa mortis*. A gift *inter vivos* is simply an ordinary gift between two living persons. A gift *causa mortis* is also between living persons, but it is made by the donor in contemplation of his or her death from some existing affliction or impending peril.

The requirements for making either type of gift are the same.[7] In the case of a gift *causa mortis,* however, two special rules apply:

1. The gift is automatically revoked if the *donee dies before the donor,* with the result that ownership reverts back to the donor.

2. The gift is automatically revoked if the *donor does not die from the current illness or peril.*

---

[6]The phrase *joint account* is often used in a nontechnical sense to describe any bank account in the name of two persons. Such accounts are either a joint tenancy with survivorship rights or a tenancy in common, depending on the terms of the agreement with the bank.

[7]The only way to make a valid gift conditional on the donor's death without an immediate transfer of possession is by executing a formal *will.* Personal property can be transferred to heirs by will or under statutes of descent and distribution in the same way as real property.

Acquiring Unowned Property

As a general rule, unowned personal property falls into either of two categories: (1) wild animals, fish, and birds; and (2) abandoned property. Ownership of either category is acquired by the first person who takes possession with an intent to become the owner. The technical name for such acquisition is *occupation*.

With respect to wild game, two points should be made:

1. If the one taking possession is a trespasser on the land where the game is found, that party does not acquire ownership.[8] In such a case, the owner of the land acquires title to the game.

2. All states have passed laws that regulate hunting and fishing. Additionally, the hunting of certain migratory birds is regulated by federal law. No title is acquired by the violator to any game taken in violation of such laws.

Property is deemed to be *abandoned* if it is found under circumstances indicating that the owner left it with the intent to relinquish ownership. In other words, the evidence must indicate that the property was left by someone who did not want it anymore. The nature of the property, its location, and the length of time it had apparently been there are all factors to be considered. As in the case of wild game, a trespasser does not acquire ownership of abandoned property found on the premises where the individual is trespassing.

Finding

A careful distinction should be made between property that has been abandoned and property that has been lost or mislaid. An item of personal property is characterized as *lost* if it is discovered under circumstances indicating that it was *not* placed there voluntarily by the owner (such as a purse, billfold, or ring found on a street or sidewalk or on the floor of a hotel or theater lobby). Property is characterized as *mislaid* (or *misplaced*) if it is discovered under circumstances indicating that it *was* placed there voluntarily by the owner and then forgotten (such as a suitcase under the seat of an airplane or bus or a purse on a table in a restaurant).

Most courts hold that the *finder of lost property* has the right to its possession, whereas the *owner of the premises where the property is discovered* has the right to possession of *mislaid* property. The reasoning behind this distinction is that, since mislaid property was voluntarily put in a particular place by the owner, that person is likely to remember where it was left and return for it. Therefore, giving the owner of the premises the right to possession of mislaid items increases the probability that their true owner will be able to reclaim them. But if the finder is a *trespasser,* then the owner of the premises always has the right of possession, even if the goods are lost.

It should be emphasized that the finder of lost property and the owner of the

---

[8]Essentially, a *trespasser* is one who goes upon another's premises without consent.

premises where mislaid property is discovered do not immediately acquire owner-ship of the property. What they acquire is merely a right to possession of the property as against *everyone but the true owner*. This right does not ripen into ownership unless the true owner fails to appear and reclaim the property within the period of time established by state statute.

In a number of states, statutes have been passed requiring the finder or the owner of the premises (as the case may be) to take certain steps, such as publishing a newspaper notice, in an attempt to locate the owner. In the absence of such a statute, however, there is simply the duty to make a *reasonable effort* to locate the owner and to exercise *reasonable care* in handling and preserving the property.[9] Although there is no right to a reward unless one was offered, there is a right to reimbursement from the owner for the reasonable expenses of caring for the property.

As previously mentioned, in the last few years several states have passed statutes concerning lost or mislaid property. The following case provides an excellent illustration of such a statute and how it was applied to a bank customer's unexpect-ed discovery.

Paset v. Old Orchard Bank & Trust Co.

Appellate Court of Illinois, 378 N.E.2d 1264 (1978)

On May 8, 1974, the plaintiff, Bernice Paset, a safety deposit box subscriber at the defendant Old Orchard Bank (the bank), found $6,325 in currency on the seat of a chair in an examination booth in the safety deposit vault. The chair was partially under a table. The plaintiff notified officers of the bank and turned the money over to them. She then was told by bank officials that the bank would try to locate the owner, and that she could have the money if the owner was not located within one year.

The bank wrote to everyone who had been in the safety deposit vault area either on the day of, or on the day preceding, the discovery, stating that some property had been found and inviting the customers to describe any property they might have lost. No one reported the loss of currency, and the money remained un-claimed a year after it had been found. However, when the plaintiff requested the money, the bank refused to deliver it to her, explaining that it was obligated to hold the currency for the owner.

The plaintiff filed suit asking the court to declare that the Illinois "estray" statute applied to her find and that she was now the owner of the money according to that statute. The trial court concluded that the money was "mislaid," not "lost," and that the statute did not apply. The court ruled that the bank should continue to hold the money indefinitely as trustee for the true owner, and plaintiff appealed.

Simon, Justice: . . . The bank's position is that the estray statute is not applicable because the money was not lost in the sense the word "lost" is used in that statute. The bank

---

[9]This assumes, of course, that the identity of the true owner is not known. If the person in possession knows who the owner is, there is a duty to return the property to the owner. Failure to do so constitutes the tort of *conversion* (and may be a criminal offense as well).

contends that, under the common law, the money was mislaid by its owner rather than lost, and that the estray statute does not apply to mislaid property. . . .

This appeal requires a determination of whether a finder of cash in an examining booth in a safety deposit vault may be a keeper under the Illinois estray statute and an analysis of the extent to which the common law concepts of lost and mislaid property apply to the statute.

The estray statute provides in pars. 27 and 28:

> If any person or persons find any lost goods, money, bank notes, or other [personal property] of any description whatever, such person or persons shall inform the owner thereof, if known. . . . If the owner is unknown and if such property found is of value of $15 or upwards, the finder or finders shall, within 5 days after such finding, appear before some circuit judge residing in the county, and make affidavit of the description thereof, the time and place when and where the same was found, that no alteration has been made in the appearance thereof since the finding of the same, that the owner thereof is unknown to him and that he has not secreted, withheld or disposed of any part thereof. The judge shall enter an order stating the value of the property found as near as he can ascertain. A certified copy of such order and the affidavit of the finder shall, within 10 days after the order has been entered, be transmitted to the county clerk to be recorded in his estray book, and filed in his office.
>
> . . . If the value thereof exceeds the sum of $15, the county clerk, within 20 days after receiving the certified copy of the judge's order shall cause an advertisement to be set up on the court house door, and in 3 other of the most public places in the county, and also a notice thereof to be published for 3 weeks successively in some public newspaper printed in this state and if the owner of such goods, money, bank notes, or other [personal property] does not appear and claim the same . . . within one year after the advertisement thereof as aforesaid, the ownership of such property shall vest in the finder.

The Illinois estray statute's principal purposes are to encourage and facilitate the return of property to the true owner, and then to reward a finder for his honesty if the property remains unclaimed. . . .

Traditionally, the common law has treated lost and mislaid property differently for the purposes of determining ownership of property someone has found. Mislaid property is that which is intentionally put in a certain place and later forgotten; at common law a finder acquires no rights to mislaid property. The element of intentional deposit present in the case of mislaid property is absent in the case of lost property, for property is deemed lost when it is unintentionally separated from the dominion of its owner. The general rule is that the finder is entitled to posssession of lost property against everyone except the true owner. . . .

As is usual in cases involving a determination of whether property is lost or mislaid, this court is not here assisted by direct evidence, for, obviously, the true owner is not available to state what his intent was. Also, because all the evidence here has been presented by affidavit or stipulation, this court is in as advantageous a position as the trial judge to determine whether the money was lost or mislaid. Our conclusion is that the estray statute should be applied, and ownership of the money vested in the plaintiff finder.

Thus, we do not accept the bank's initial argument that the money was mislaid rather than lost. It is complete speculation to infer, as the bank urges, that the money was deliberately placed by its owner on the chair located partially under a table in the examining booth, and then forgotten. If the money was intentionally placed on the chair by someone who forgot where he left it, the bank's notice to safety deposit box subscribers should have alerted the owner. The failure of an owner to appear to claim the money in the interval since its discovery is affirmative evidence that the property was not mislaid.

Because the evidence, though ambiguous, tends to indicate that the money probably was not mislaid, and because neither party contends that the money was abandoned, we conclude that the ambiguity should, as a matter of public policy, be resolved in favor of the presumption that the money was lost. This conclusion is in harmony with the above mentioned purposes of the estray statute, for it construes the statute liberally rather than technically, with the result that the statute is brought into play rather than rejected. Such an application of the statute better effectuates the legislature's goal of restoring property to a true owner; it provides incentive for a finder to report his discovery by rewarding him if the true owner does not appear within the statutorily-determined time limit. Accordingly, we reject the bank's first contention that the money was mislaid and the estray statute irrelevant, and conclude that the money was "lost," and so encompassed by the Illinois estray statute.

. . . Further, whether the property was discovered in a public or private place should not be permitted to preclude the application of the estray statute. The statute itself makes no distinction between "public" and "private" places of finding. . . .

Therefore, looking at both the common law and estray statute, we [conclude] that where property is found in a bank safety deposit vault area, the bank as owner of the premises should hold the property on a temporary basis as custodian until ownership is determined. This is a just result not inconsistent with the purposes of the estray statute, for the return of property to its true owner is best promoted by requiring the finder to leave the property temporarily with the owner of the premises where it was found. . . .

[T]he estray statute provides the proper method for resolving the eventual question of ownership of the property if the true owner does not claim it. * * * Therefore, we conclude that the estray statute vested ownership in the finder of the property in this case when the owner did not appear after the legislatively designated time of one year—at which point the bank's temporary custody and possession was terminated. . . .

Judgment reversed.

Accession

An *accession* is an addition to or a change in an item of personal property. Difficult legal questions sometimes arise where an accession is made by one person to property owned by another *without the owner's consent*.[10] This may occur in two different types of fact situations, discussed below.

Increase in Value by Labor: Sometimes the accession takes the form of an increase in the value of the property brought about entirely or almost entirely by the *labor* of another. In this instance, ownership passes to the party performing the labor only if (1) the *identity* of the property has been changed, or (2) the value of the property is *many times greater* than it was prior to the accession.

An example of a change in identity is shown in the situation where A takes B's grapes and makes them into wine. An example of a sufficiently great increase in

---

[10]Where the accession occurs *with* the owner's consent, there is no effect on the title to the property.

value is found in the case where A takes a piece of stone belonging to B and carves a statue from it.

There is a definite tendency on the part of courts to deal more harshly with someone who caused the accession while knowing that it was wrong. A greater magnitude of change is often required to pass title to such a party than to someone who caused the accession in the honestly mistaken belief that the action was rightful.

Increase in Value by Addition of Other Property: When one person permanently affixes something to another's property without the latter's consent, ownership of the resulting product goes to the owner of the "principal" item. To illustrate: If A takes B's car and puts a new engine in it, the car and the new engine are owned by B. On the other hand, if A takes B's engine and installs it in A's car, the car and the engine belong to A.

In either of these situations, where the increased value is due primarily to labor or where it is due to the addition of other property, the party who wrongfully caused the accession is responsible for any loss to the other party. Thus, if the circumstances are such that the improver gained title to the item as a result of the accession, that individual must compensate the original owner. If the improver acted in *good faith* (honestly), he or she is required to pay the original owner only for the value of the property in its original condition. But if the improver acted in *bad faith* (with knowledge that the act was wrongful), he or she is required to pay to the other party the value of the property in its improved state.

Where the accession itself does not cause title to pass to the improver, but the original owner simply chooses not to reclaim the property, the situation is treated the same as if the accession *had* caused title to pass. Where the accession does not cause title to pass to the improver, and the original owner *reclaims* the improved property, the improver is not entitled to any compensation at all, regardless of whether he or she acted in good faith.

Confusion

A *confusion of goods* occurs where there has been such an intermingling of the goods of different persons that the property of each can no longer be distinguished. It usually occurs in connection with fungible goods, such as grain, oil, or chemicals. It can, however, occur with respect to nonfungible goods, such as cattle or quantities of packaged merchandise.

If the goods of A and B have been confused (1) by agreement between A and B, (2) by an honest mistake or accident, or (3) by the act of some third party, a *tenancy in common* is created. Here, A and B each own an undivided interest in the mass according to the particular proportions they contributed to it.

Suppose, however, that A caused the confusion by *deliberately wrongful or negligent conduct*. In this case, if the goods of A and B are all exactly the same (such as the same grade of oil), A will get his portion back if he can prove how much that portion is. On the other hand, if the goods are *not* all identical (such as cattle), A will get nothing unless he can prove which specific items are his.

After there has been a confusion, the quantity of goods might be diminished by fire, theft, or other cause so that not enough is left to give each owner a complete share. If one owner caused the confusion by deliberately wrongful or negligent conduct, that person must bear the entire burden of the decrease. If the confusion came about by agreement, by accident or honest mistake, or by an act of a third party, the burden of the decrease is borne proportionately by both owners.

In the following case, the problem of confusion of goods is presented in a factual setting of extraordinary significance—the injection of natural gas into an underground reservoir.

Humble Oil & Refining Co. v. West

Supreme Court of Texas, 508 S.W.2d 812 (1974)

In 1938 the Wests, plaintiffs, conveyed to Humble, the defendant, a tract of land in a natural gas field located in southeast Texas. From the conveyance, however, the Wests reserved a one-sixth royalty interest. In other words, the Wests were entitled to one-sixth of the value of all natural gas extracted from the land.

Because of the nature of this particular subsurface reservoir, saltwater entered it as natural gas was removed. Thus, if all the natural gas were removed, the reservoir could not be used in the future for gas storage. To prevent the total destruction of the reservoir's storage capacity, Humble began injecting gas into the reservoir in 1969.

In 1970 the Wests filed suit against Humble, requesting an injunction to prohibit gas injection by Humble. Alternatively, they asked that the court declare them to be entitled to a one-sixth royalty on *all* gas—both native and "extraneous" (injected)—subsequently taken from the reservoir.

The trial court refused to grant an injunction but granted the Wests' alternative request. The Court of Civil Appeals reversed, holding that an injunction should have been granted. Humble appealed.

Steakley, Justice: [First, the court held that the Wests were not entitled to the injunction, because the granting of such an injunction would result in the destruction of the natural gas storage capacity that was vital to the southeast Texas area. Then the court dealt with the second issue.] . . .

. . . "[O]nce severed from the realty, gas and oil, like other minerals, become personal property. . . . [T]itle to natural gas once having been reduced to possession is not lost by the injection of such gas into a natural reservoir for storage purposes."

. . . Humble's ownership of the gas as personal property is not altered either upon injection of the gas into the reservoir or upon later production of the gas.

. . . However, by injecting this extraneous gas into the reservoir prior to production of all native gas, Humble has commingled extraneous gas, in which Humble has an exclusive property interest, and native gas, in which the Wests have a royalty interest. The question thus becomes one of determining whether Humble's intentional "confusion" of the two bodies of gas should result in the forfeiture of its exclusive rights to the extraneous gas. If such a forfeiture is proper, the Wests would be entitled to a royalty on all gas produced, consistent with the trial court judgment.

As a general rule, the confusion of goods theory attaches only when the commingled goods of different parties are so confused that the property of each cannot be distinguished. Where the mixture is homogeneous, the goods being similar in nature and value, and if the portion of each may be properly shown, each party may claim his aliquot [proportionate] share of the mass. Additionally, the burden is on the one commingling the goods to properly identify the aliquot share of each owner; thus, if goods are so confused as to render the mixture incapable of proper division according to the pre-existing rights of the parties, the loss must fall on the one who occasioned the mixture. Stated differently, since Humble is responsible for, and is possessed with peculiar knowledge of, the gas injection, it is under the burden of establishing the aliquot shares with reasonable certainty.

Humble sought to discharge this burden by offering expert opinion evidence in estimation of the volume of native gas as of January 1, 1969; its commitment in the trial court was to continue the payment of royalties to the Wests on the basis of this proof until production of the commingled gas equaled the volume of the gas in place at such time. As to this, the Wests contend that the obligation of Humble to account for their royalty interests may not rest upon expert opinion evidence and that, at the least, upon its election to utilize the reservoir for storage and hence to commingle native and extraneous gas, Humble came under the obligation of paying royalties on all gas thereafter produced from the reservoir.

The counter position of Humble is that the opinion testimony of the geology and engineering witnesses is reasonably certain; that their testimony was based upon more than acceptable well control for mapping the reservoir, and that there existed sufficient data upon which to compute reservoir pressure, reservoir temperature, gas formation volume factor, reservoir porosity and permeability and connate water saturation. Thus, Humble asserts that the Wests' aliquot share of the gas in the reservoir prior to injection of the extraneous gas is subject to a reasonable estimate and that the expert testimony sufficiently established the volume of the reserves.

In the context of their asserted right to equitable relief, the Wests emphasize, on the other hand, that Warnack, Humble's geologist witness, admitted that a certain "judgment or opinion decision" had to be made in calculating the reservoir size. They stress that the witness acknowledged that wide discrepancies may exist in determining the size of a reservoir and insist that his calculations were based upon limited and unacceptable information. Also, they note that Whitson, the petroleum engineer called to testify by Humble, made critical calculations of porosity and permeability by means of mathematical averages; further, that experts agree that the limits of a reservoir are difficult of exact determination.

As we have indicated, it is our view that the act of commingling native and extraneous gas did not impose upon Humble the obligation of paying royalties on all gas thereafter produced from the reservoir, if the evidence establishes with reasonable certainty the volume of gas reserves upon which the Wests would have been entitled to royalties, absent injection of extraneous gas. The burden of this showing devolves upon Humble after proof by the Wests of their royalty interests, together with proof of Humble's commingling of extraneous and native gas. The threshold question for determination is whether the requisite computation of reserves is capable of establishment with reasonable certainty; and, if so, the further question to be resolved is whether the burden defined above is discharged by Humble under the evidence. We have concluded that the [case] should be generally remanded to the trial court for determination of these issues at the trial level, as well as for consideration of any other issues the parties may raise in the light of our rulings.

. . . [R]eversed. . . .

Comment: When the case was heard again in the trial court, the oil company's expert witnesses testified, based upon their studies, as to the maximum amount of gas which could have been in the reservoir as of the date storage operations began. West, the plaintiff, introduced no evidence to contradict this estimate. It was held that the company did not have to pay royalties on gas extracted beyond this estimated maximum. *Exxon Corporation v. West,* 543 S.W.2d 667 (1976).

Question and Problems

1. How does a lease of personal property differ from a lease of real property with respect to the type of interest received by the lessee?

2. Closter was despondent and had decided to commit suicide. Before doing so, he inserted into an envelope a promissory note that he owned. On the note he wrote that he was giving it to Schutz. Closter then shot and killed himself. Schutz, who occupied another room in the same boardinghouse, heard the shot, rushed to his friend's room, and found his body there. Schutz saw the envelope lying on the desk where Closter had placed it. Thinking that it might be a suicide note, Schutz opened it and found the promissory note containing Closter's expression of donative intent. Schutz pocketed the envelope and note. The existence of the note later came to light, and Liebe, the administrator of Closter's estate, filed suit to collect on the note from Battman, who had originally executed it. Schutz claimed that *he* was the owner of the note and was entitled to collect on it from Battman. *Liebe v. Battman,* 54 Pac. 179 (1898). Who won? Discuss.

3. Walters suffered a heart attack. Fearful of impending death, he gave his diamond ring to his sister while he was still in the hospital. Walters' condition improved, and he was discharged from the hospital two months later. He asked his sister to return the ring, but she refused. Not wanting to cause a family quarrel, he said nothing more. Five years later he died from heart disease. Does the ring belong to his sister? Explain. Would it make any difference if he had never asked for the return of the ring? Discuss.

4. Why is delivery essential to the making of a valid gift? Discuss.

5. Hillebrant indicated to Brewer that he was making a gift to Brewer of a herd of cattle. Hillebrant then obtained Brewer's branding iron and branded the cattle with Brewer's registered brand. Before the cattle were delivered to Brewer, however, Hillebrant changed his mind. Brewer sued, claiming that a completed gift of the cattle had been made. *Hillebrant v. Brewer,* 6 Tex. 45 (1851). Was Brewer correct? Discuss.

6. Harkness was elderly and bedridden. So that his close friend Kuntz could pay his bills for him a joint account was established with money belonging to Harkness. The account was a joint tenancy with right of survivorship. It was used for its intended purpose until Harkness died two years later (that is, Kuntz never used the funds for any purpose other than to pay bills for Harkness). When Harkness died, Kuntz claimed the money remaining in the account, asserting that it was his as a gift. Harkness's heirs disagreed. What is the result? Explain.

7. Explain the distinction between lost, mislaid, and abandoned property, as well as the rationale behind the different rules applied when such property is found.

8. Five young boys were playing on a railroad track. Crawford, the youngest of the group, saw an old sock stuffed with something. He picked it up but did not investigate its contents. It was snatched from him by Cashman, an older boy, and soon a lively game of "keep away"

developed around the sock. The sock broke open during the game, and the boys discovered $800 inside. The money was turned over to Keron, the police chief. Keron then turned the money over to the court and filed suit, asking the court to decide who owned it. Crawford claimed all the money as the "finder," since he first picked it up. The other boys merely claimed an equal share. *Keron v. Cashman,* 33 Atl. 1055 (1896). What was the result? Discuss.

9. X and Y consented to the mixing of their wheat in a grain storage elevator owned by Z. What is the status of the ownership of the wheat? Explain. Would the answer be different if Z had caused the confusion accidently? Explain. Would the answer be different if X had intentionally caused the confusion with knowledge that he had no right to do so? Explain.

10. How might a party who caused an accession to another's property in good faith fare better than one who did so acting in bad faith? Explain.

41 Wills, Trusts, and Estates

When Pablo Picasso died in 1973, he left a tremendous fortune—millions of dollars in assets he had accumulated during his lifetime. To whom did he leave it? The answer to this question and a brief discussion of the artist's estate problems serve as an introduction to the coverage of wills, trusts, and estates. Picasso died *intestate;* that is, at the time of his death he had not prepared a document—a will—in which he could have provided specific and detailed instructions about what to do with his property. If properly planned, drafted, and executed, a will would largely have eliminated the bitter controversy that arose among those close to him over disposition of his wealth.

Picasso apparently felt that making a will was an act in contemplation of death and therefore an unpleasant subject to be avoided. He resisted all efforts by those who anticipated protracted legal proceedings to persuade him to make a will and thereby provide for an orderly disposition of his property. When any person of considerable means refuses to provide for the estate's distribution on death, controversy is as certain as death itself.

Few of us will amass large fortunes in our lifetimes. On the other hand, few of us will die penniless. Many who take the time and trouble to total up their assets are surprised at the actual value of what they had considered to be modest holdings.

738

Real estate, acquired early in life, may appreciate dramatically. Life insurance, both individual and group, may be owned in substantial amounts. Access to the stock market through mutual funds is commonplace; and one's personal property, slowly acquired over a period of years, may constitute a sizable asset. It is therefore useful to have some knowledge of wills, trusts, and other estate planning devices in order to make a more informed judgment about one's personal situation.

Wills

A will transforms a person's wishes about the disposition of his or her property into a valid, legal instrument. This section will cover formal, written wills in some detail and mention other types briefly. Following are some commonly-used terms with which the student may be unfamiliar. A man who makes a will is a *testator;* a woman is a *testatrix.* A person who dies is a *decedent.* A decedent leaving a valid will is said to die *testate;* a person leaving no will dies *intestate.* It is customary for a testator to designate a personal representative to carry out the provisions of the will. This person is known as an *executor* if male and an executrix if female. If there is no will, the court will appoint an *administrator* (or *administratrix*) to handle the decedent's estate. With regard to the testator's property, disposition of real estate is called a *devise,* money passing under a will is a *legacy,* and other property is disposed of by *bequest.* Another important term is *testamentary capacity.* In most states the testator must have attained a specific minimum age, usually eighteen.[1] In all states the testator must possess the mental capacity to dispose of the property intelligently. The minimum age requirement presents little difficulty; the mental capacity requirement is frequently litigated. In general, testators have the capacity to make wills if they have attained the statutory age, if they know what property they own, and if they resonably understand how and to whom they want to leave their property. The following case illustrates this principle:

Holladay v. Holladay
Court of Appeals of Kentucky, 172 S.W.2d 36 (1943)

This action was a will contest involving the will of Lewis Holladay. A college graduate, Holladay made his home on his mother's farm with her and a sister until his mother's death in 1929. He remained on the farm until he died in 1940 at age 66. He was survived by a brother, Joe, and three sisters. Joe was the sole beneficiary under Lewis's will. When he submitted the will for probate, the sisters opposed the proceeding on a number of grounds. The primary basis for the contest was the allegation by the sisters, the contestants, that Lewis did not possess sufficient mental capacity to execute a will.

Sims, Justice: Upon a verdict rendered in the Clark Circuit Court a judgment was entered adjudging that a paper executed by Lewis Holladay was his last will and testament. This appeal is prosecuted from that judgment.

---

[1] In Georgia, fourteen, and in Louisiana, sixteen.

. . . Lewis Holladay had a college education and made his home on his mother's farm with her and a maiden sister, Miss Denia, until his mother's death in 1929. His mother was quite old and her death greatly upset him. The testimony for contestants is that Lewis was far from normal mentally years before his mother died, but was much more unstable afterwards. It was testified he shot and killed his pet dog without reason in 1917 or 1918. During electrical storms he would take his seat under a tree, saying it was safer there than in the house. He was afflicted with stomach ulcers and could not sleep at nights and would roam over the premises and farm, and on occasion would stand like a statue in the county road even at midnight, requiring travelers to drive around him. At times he would go to the barn during the night and throw down hay for his stock when it was not in the barn but was out on pasture. He would bathe at night in a pond which was little more than a hog wallow, saying it gave him relief. It was testified that if the least thing went wrong, such as some meat falling down or the spilling of some lard from a bucket, he became so upset that it was necessary to put him to bed to quiet him. Pages could be consumed in reciting the testimony relative to his queer, weird and unnatural actions. There were many suicides and much insanity on both sides of his family, and it appears in the evidence that he threatened to destroy himself.

Opposing such testimony, twenty-six of his neighbors, friends, business acquaintances and associates testified he was perfectly sane and normal; that he was a good farmer and a successful business man. These twenty-six witnesses made up a cross section of the community and included people from all walks of life; doctors, bankers, veterinarians, livestock buyers, farmers and shop keepers, practically all of whom had business or social contacts with him. Upon the written request of his sisters, he and his brother, Joe, were named administrators of his mother's $23,000 estate, which testator wound up practically without assistance from Joe. In 1930, the year he wrote his will, Lewis contracted with his sisters that he would bid $137.50 per acre for his mother's farm of 146 acres if it were sold at public auction; and he carried out his contract and purchased the farm. He raised and sold registered sheep; was the moving spirit in some important and successful litigation in 1929 involving damages to farm lands in the community when a water dam broke. From 1929 to 1933 he served twice on the petit jury and twice on the grand jury; and in the interim between 1927 and 1940 he wrote more than 2,000 checks aggregating $29,000.

. . . The court did not err in refusing to give contestants' proffered instruction on the alleged insane delusions Lewis had against his sisters. His feelings toward them were unkind and even bitter, but they were based upon facts and not delusions. His sisters had objected to the fee allowed him as administrator of his mother's estate, although it was slightly less than the statutory limit of 5 percent. They had insinuated that when he and Joe, the morning after the death of their brother Felix, went through the deceased's personal effects they were looking for his will with the sinister motive of destroying it if they found one in favor of the sisters. Miss Denia had intimated that Lewis had sensual plans in bringing in a housekeeper after his mother's death. Then after Lewis had agreed to bid $137.50 per acre on his mother's farm, his three sisters attempted to raise the price. This combination of incidents had turned Lewis against his sisters, but it cannot be said his feelings were insane delusions, which are ideas or beliefs springing spontaneously from a diseased or perverted mind without reason or foundation in fact. A belief which is based upon reason and evidence, be it ever so slight, cannot be an insane delusion. . . .

. . . The judgment is affirmed.

The Formal Will

The term *formal* indicates that the will has been prepared and executed in compliance with the state's law of wills. That is, certain rigid formalities are prescribed and must be carefully observed. The right to make a will is not exactly granted by statute, but the procedures for drafting, executing, and witnessing the formal written document are governed by statute. Such statutory requirements, although basically similar, vary from state to state. Therefore the drafter must be thoroughly acquainted with the law of the state in which the testator's will is to be effective and must be sure to comply with its provisions. Noncompliance usually means that the will is declared invalid. If this happens, the decedent's property passes in accordance with the state's law of descent and distribution. (Such statutes and their application will be discussed later in another section.)

General Requirements: A will must be written; it must be signed by the testator or testatrix or by someone for him or her; and, in the majority of states, the signing must be witnessed by two competent persons.[2] Most states require an *attestation clause,* a paragraph beneath the testator's signature to the effect that the will was *published*—that is, declared by the testator to be the last will and testament, signed in the presence of the witnesses who, in the presence of each other, themselves signed as attesting witnesses. These are the formalities required by statute, and they must be strictly observed. The witnesses do not need to read or know the contents of the will. The testator or testatrix simply announces to them that the document is the will and that he or she is going to sign it. This process is called *publishing the will.*

Specific Provisions: The main function of a will is to provide for the disposal of property. However, it can appoint an executor and cancel all previous wills if it so states. It can also provide for an alternative disposition of property in the event the primary beneficiary predeceases the testator. If the testator or testatrix is married, the surviving spouse is usually appointed as the executor or executrix; if unmarried, a close relative or friend may be designated. It is essential for the will to state that it revokes any and all prior wills. The existence of two or more wills can create insurmountable problems. Sometimes none are admitted to probate (the court proceedings whereby a will is proved and the estate of the decedent is disposed of).

A will can also cover the disposition of property in the event that husband and wife die nearly simultaneously. If, after an accident, for example, the husband outlives the wife only by a matter of hours, he will take under her will either as the beneficiary or as the surviving spouse. Then, upon his death, the property will pass to his heirs or his side of the family. This may not be what the couple would have wanted. Their wills can prevent such an unwanted disposition by providing that if there is insufficient evidence to prove which spouse predeceased the other,

---

[2]A few states require three witnesses.

the clause making the spouse the beneficiary is cancelled. The property will then be disposed of as each one desired.

The will can also name a guardian for minor children. If both husband and wife die, the guardian they have appointed in their wills can be confirmed by the court if he or she is qualified and willing to serve in that capacity. This will obviate the necessity for a court-appointed guardian and a possible controversy between the two competing, though well-meaning, sides of the family.

Modification: While it is possible in some states to change one's will by erasure, by striking out portions, or by interlineation, such procedures are risky undertakings at best. The proper method is to modify by means of a *codicil.* This is an addition to the will and must be executed with the same formalities as the original document. Consequently, if extensive modification is necessary, the testator would be well-advised to consider making a new will.

Revocation: A will speaks (becomes effective) only at the death of the testator. In other words, a will cannot operate to transfer property until the testator dies. The testator can therefore revoke the will during the period between execution of the instrument and death. Revocation can be accomplished in several ways. Typical statutory language governing it is as follows:

> A will shall be revoked by the testator by tearing, canceling, obliterating, or destroying such will with the intention of revoking it, or by some person in such testator's presence, or by such testator's express written direction, or by some other written will or codicil, ...[3]

Whatever means the testator may select for revoking a will, there must be a clear intent to revoke. For example, if someone else destroys the will without the testator's approval, there is no revocation. Executing a new will with a clause expressly revoking all prior wills and codicils is a customary method of revoking a will. In any case, a revocation must comply with the appropriate statute.

Thompson v. Royall

Supreme Court of Appeals of Virginia, 175 S.E. 749 (1934)

Mrs. M. Lou Bowen Kroll executed a will on September 4, 1932. The will consisted of five typewritten pages and was signed by her and three witnesses, as required by statute. On September 19 she called her attorney, S. M. Coulling, to her home and asked him to destroy the will. He suggested, instead, that she retain it to be used as a memorandum in case she decided to make a new will in the future. Then, to satisfy Mrs. Kroll's intention that the will be cancelled, he wrote the following, in longhand, across the cover page of the will, which was stapled to the five pages of the will itself:

> This will null and void and to be only held by H. P. Brittain instead of being destroyed as a memorandum for another will if I desire to make same. This 19 Sept. 1932.

---

[3]Ohio Revised Code, Sec. 2107.33.

Mrs. Kroll signed her name immediately below this writing in Coulling's presence. (The H. P. Brittain referred to was named as executor in the will.) Mrs. Kroll died in October of 1932, having made no new will, leaving an estate of $200,000.

When the beneficiaries under the will offered it for probate, the heirs of Mrs. Kroll who were not beneficiaries challenged its validity, claiming that it had been validly revoked on September 19. In the trial court the jury found that the attempted revocation did not conform to Virginia's statute relative to the revocation of wills and that the will was consequently valid. The heirs appealed.

Hudgins, Justice ... For more than 100 years, the means by which a duly executed will may be revoked have been prescribed by statute. These requirements are found in section 5233 of the 1919 Code, the pertinent parts of which read thus: "No will or codicil, or any part thereof, shall be revoked, unless ... by a subsequent will or codicil, or by some writing declaring an intention to revoke the same, and executed in the manner in which a will is required to be executed, or by the testator, or some person in his presence and by his direction, cutting, tearing, burning, obliterating, canceling, or destroying the same, or the signature thereto, with the intent to revoke."

The notations, dated September 19, 1932, are not wholly in the handwriting of the testatrix, nor are her signatures thereto attached attested by subscribing witnesses; hence under the statute they are ineffectual as "some writing declaring an intention to revoke." The faces of the two instruments bear no physical evidence of any cutting, tearing, burning, obliterating, canceling, or destroying. The only contention made by appellants is that the notation written in the presence, and with the approval, of Mrs. Kroll, on the back of the manuscript cover in the one instance, and on the back of the sheet containing the codicil in the other, constitute "canceling" within the meaning of the statute.

... [O]ther authorities that might be cited, hold that revocation of a will by cancellation within the meaning of the statute contemplates marks or lines across the written parts of the instrument, or a physical defacement, or some mutilation of the writing itself with the intent to revoke. If written words are used for the purpose, they must be so placed as to physically affect the written portion of the will, not merely on blank parts of the paper on which the will is written. If the writing intended to be the act of canceling does not mutilate, or erase, or deface, or otherwise physically come in contact with, any part of written words of the will, it cannot be given any greater weight than a similar writing on a separate sheet of paper, which identifies the will referred to, just as definitely as does the writing on the back. If a will may be revoked by writing on the back, separable from the will, it may be done by a writing not on the will. This the statute forbids....

The attempted revocation is ineffectual, because testatrix intended to revoke her will by subsequent writings not executed as required by statute, and because it does not in any way physically obliterate, multilate, deface, or cancel any written parts of the will.

For the reasons stated, the judgment of the trial court is affirmed.

Affirmed.

Revocation can also be caused by operation of law. Marriage, divorce, or the birth of a child subsequent to making a will may affect its validity by revoking it completely or partially. State laws on wills are by no means uniform—the birth of a child may revoke a will completely in State A but only partially in State B.

Marriage and divorce affect wills differently from state to state. Consequently, a knowledge of applicable statutes is essential.

Holographic Wills

Nineteen jurisdictions allow testators to execute their own wills without formal attestation. The wills must be entirely in their own handwriting, including the signature. These holographic wills differ from formal wills in that no attestation clause or witnesses are required. However, most states allowing holographic wills require that the testator's handwriting and signature be proved by two witnesses familiar with them during probate of the will. Competent witnesses would include persons who had received correspondence from the testator. A holographic will is purely statutory—that is, it must be made in accordance with the appropriate state's law and is subject to prescribed conditions and limitations. The principal requirement is that it be entirely in the testator's own handwriting. In *Estate of Thorn,* a testator in a holographic will used a rubber stamp to insert "Cragthorn" in the phrase "my country place Cragthorn." The will was held to be invalid since it was not entirely in the testator's handwriting.[4] In some jurisdictions the holographic will must be dated in the testator's handwriting. The requirements of testamentary capacity and intent are the same as those for formal wills, but a holographic will is otherwise informal and may even take the form of a letter if it conveys testamentary intent (the mental determination or intention of the testator that the document constitute the person's will).

Nuncupative Wills

About half the states permit oral wills. In general, statutes impose strict limitations on the disposal of property through a nuncupative will. Most states require that it be made during the testator's "last sickness"; that it be written down within a short period; that it be proved by two witnesses who were present at its making; and that the value of the estate bequeathed not exceed a certain amount, usually quite small. Some states also require that the decedent have been a soldier in the field or a sailor at sea in actual contemplation or fear of death.[5]

Nuncupative wills are difficult to establish, and the restrictions placed on them are intended to discourage their use. There is always the possibility of mistake or fraud and, except on rare occasions, a testator can easily plan sufficiently ahead to use the more traditional and acceptable type of will.

---

[4]183 Cal. 512, 192 P. 19 (1920).

[5]Commonly known as soldiers' and sailors' wills.

State laws govern the disposition of a decedent's estate when the decedent has died without a will—intestate. Such laws are called statutes of descent and distribution. They provide for disposition of the decedent's property, both real and personal, in accordance with a prescribed statutory scheme. Real property descends; personal property is distributed. Consequently, the law of the state where the decedent's real estate is located will determine the heirs, by class, to whom it will descend. The decedent's personal property will be distributed in accordance with the law of the state in which he or she is domiciled. In addition to prescribing the persons who will inherit a decedent's property, statutes of descent and distribution also prescribe the order and proportions in which they will take. The effect of this is that intestate decedents permit the state to select their heirs by default.

Intestacy—Statutes of Descent and Distribution

The Surviving Spouse

Without exception, statutes of descent and distribution specify the portion of a decedent's estate that will be taken by his or her lawful, surviving spouse. Variation in this area is significant from state to state. Formerly, under common law, the surviving spouse was entitled only to a life estate (ownership for life) or *dower* (to the widow) or *curtesy* (to the widower) in the real property owned by the decedent. Personal property was divided among the surviving spouse and any children of the marriage. Today, the law of dower and curtesy has been either abolished or altered significantly by statute in all jurisdictions. Typically, if a husband or wife dies intestate, the statutes provide that the surviving spouse takes one-half or one-third of the estate if there are children or grandchildren. If there are no children or grandchildren, in most jurisdictions the surviving spouse takes the entire estate. However, the states vary considerably in their treatment of this matter. In one jurisdiction, for example, children of the decedent take the real estate, to the exclusion of a surviving spouse, with the spouse taking one-third of the personal property. If there are no children or descendants of children the spouse takes the entire estate. In another, if there are children or representatives of deceased children, the surviving wife takes a child's share but not less than one-fifth of the estate.

In general, if there are children the surviving spouse must share the estate with them. The number of children or grandchildren will determine the share which is to pass to the surviving spouse. If there are no children or grandchildren, or none have survived the decedent, the surviving spouse takes everything.

Descendants of the Decedent

There is no disparity in the statutes that govern the shares of an intestate's children or other lineal descendants (those in a direct line from the decedent—children and grandchildren). It is generally the case that, subject to the statutory share of a surviving spouse, children of the decedent share and share alike, with the children of a deceased child taking that child's share. This latter provision is known as a *per stirpes* distribution. Suppose, for example, the decedent dies leaving two children,

A and B, each of whom has two children. If both A and B survive the decedent, each will take half his estate. However, if A predeceases the decedent, the grandchildren of the decedent will take their parent's share, each of them taking one-fourth of the estate. The estate considered here is what remains after the surviving spouse, if any, has taken his or her share. If the descendants are all of one class, that is, children or grandchildren, they will take *per capita,* each getting an equal share. Thus, if the intestate had five children all of whom survive him, each will take one-fifth of what is left after the surviving spouse's share has been provided for.

The Surviving Ascendants

There is also general agreement that children of the decedent and subsequent generations of lineal descendants will take to the exclusion of other blood relatives such as parents or brothers and sisters. With regard to the ascendants of the intestate (parents and grandparents), there is much less uniformity in state law. In most states, where decedents leave no descendants, their parents will take the estate, with brothers and sisters (known as collaterals) taking if the parents are not living. In other jurisdictions, brothers and sisters share with the parents. Nephews and nieces may take the share of a predeceased parent if other brothers and sisters of the decedent are still living. If not, the nephews and nieces, as sole survivors, share and share alike in a *per capita* distribution. In any event, a distribution to ascendants and collaterals is made only if there are no surviving descendants or spouse.

Other than the surviving spouse, relatives by marriage have no claim on the decedent's estate. If the intestate has died leaving no heirs or next-of-kin whatsoever—no spouse, children, grandchildren, ascendants, or collaterals—the estate will pass to the state by a process known as *escheat.* This rarely happens, but it is provided for by law.

Administration of the Estate

Administration of decedents' estates is accomplished by a proceeding in probate if they die leaving a will. The word derives from the Latin *probatio,* proof. In the law of wills it means the proof or establishment of a document as the valid last will and testament of the deceased. In most states, the court having jurisdiction is called the probate court, and the principal question to be decided by judicial determination is the validity or invalidity of the will. Once the will has been admitted to probate—that is, determined to be valid—the probate court insures efficient distribution of the estate. Creditors and taxes are paid first. Then the remaining assets are distributed impartially to heirs, devisees, legatees, and others, in accordance with the testator's wishes.

Early in the chapter we mentioned the "personal representative" of the decedent (called the executor if appointed by will and the administrator if appointed by the court). The function of the personal representative is to administer the estate under the supervision of the court—to collect decedent's assets, to pay or settle any lawful claims against the estate, and to distribute the remainder to those who will take under the will. If there is no will, the state's law of descent and distribution will determine how the estate is to be distributed.

Probate and the administration of decedents' estates are strictly regulated by statute and can be complex procedures when the estate is substantial and the interest in property of the deceased is not clear. Many parties may be affected by the administration process, so attention to detail and compliance with the state's probate law or code are essential. A personal representative who has effectively handled the estate and wound up its affairs may petition the court and be discharged from any further responsibilities.

Avoiding Administration

Quite frequently, the formal administration of decedents' estates can be wholly or partially avoided. In fact, it is safe to say that less than half the deaths in this country result in administration proceedings. Obviously, if the decedent died with no assets or a very small estate, there is no need for an involved administration. Most jurisdictions permit the handling of decedents' affairs without official administration in such cases.

There are, however, still other situations in which probate or formal administration can be avoided, at least for a portion of the decedent's assets. For example, if some or all of the property was co-owned with others as a "joint tenancy" with a right of survivorship, it passes to the surviving owners and not to the estate.[6] Joint tenancy bank accounts or securities or a residence owned as a joint tenancy or as a tenancy by the entirety would all pass to the surviving owner. This method of owning property is sometimes referred to as the "poor man's will." It should be noted, however, that even though the decedent's interest in such property bypasses the estate, it can still be subject to an estate or inheritance tax.

If the decedent owned one or more life insurance policies, they will not be subject to administration if a beneficiary has been named. If one has not been named or if the one named has predeceased the decedent, the proceeds pass to the estate.

Continuing a Business by Will

A testator who is the sole proprietor of a successful business or a partner in an ongoing partnership can insure that the individual business is continued or that the interest and membership in the partnership pass to a chosen successor. This can be done by will if thorough advance planning has taken place. Sole proprietors seldom are meticulous about keeping business assets separate from personal assets. Upon death it might be difficult to differentiate between them. To pass on a

[6]See Chapters 39 and 40 for a discussion of concurrent ownership and the right of survivorship.

partnership interest, care must be exercised to insure compliance with the pre-existing formal partnership agreement. Therefore, certain problems are inherent in bequeathing a business interest. Nevertheless, it is something a person in business might wish to consider. Anticipation, planning, and competent advice are essential.

Trusts

The trust is a versatile legal concept that is typically used to conserve family wealth from generation to generation, to provide for the support and education of children, and to minimize the tax burden on substantial estates. Trust law recognizes two types of property ownership, legal and equitable. One person can hold legal title to property while another can have the equitable title.

To establish a trust, the party intending to create a trust, called a *settlor* or *trustor,* transfers legal ownership of property to a *trustee* for the benefit of a third party, the *beneficiary.* The trustee is the legal owner of the property, called the *res* or *corpus,* but it is owned in trust to be used and managed solely for the benefit of others, who own the equitable title. A trust established and effective during the life of the settlor is known as an *inter vivos* or "living" *trust.* If it is created by the settlor's will, to be effective on that person's death, it is a *testamentary trust.* Trusts are also classified as *express, implied, private,* or *charitable,* depending on the purpose they serve and how they are created.

The Express Private Trust

An express private trust is created when a settlor, with clear intent to do so, and observing certain formalities, sets up a fiduciary relationship involving a trustee, the beneficiaries, and management of the trust *res* for a lawful purpose. There is little uniformity in the statutes that govern trusts and their creation. It is a general requirement, however, that trusts be established by a writing or, if oral, subsequently proved by a writing. The writing need not be formal so long as it clearly identifies the trust property and the beneficiary and states the purpose for which the trust is created. The intent of the settlor to create a trust must be clear from the circumstances and the action taken. No particular language is required, but the settlor's instructions should be direct and unambiguous. If the purpose of the trust is to put children through college, this should be stated clearly. Language that "requests," or "hopes," or "desires" that the trustee do certain things is considered to be precatory in nature (a mere request and not an order or command) and may not be binding on the trustee. Further, words or phrases that fall short of appointing a trustee or imposing positive responsibilities should be avoided. Suppose that A names B as the beneficiary of her life insurance proceeds and, in a letter telling B that she has done so, expresses the "hope" that B will use the money to put A's daughter through college. Such language is purely precatory; it is doubtful that a trust was intended. The following case illustrates the problems created by the use of precatory language and conflicting provisions.

James Cantrell owned valuable real estate in Nashville. The third paragraph of his will after making minor bequests not relevant to this case, read in material part as follows:

> Third: I give, devise and bequeath all the rest, residue and remainder of my estate and property of whatsoever kind and nature, wherever situated, both real and personal, to which I am entitled, or which I may have the power to dispose of at my death, to my wife, Clara Augusta Cantrell to be her absolute estate forever; ...

The fourth paragraph provided that:

> It is my *request* (emphasis supplied), that upon her death my said wife, Clara Augusta Cantrell, shall give, devise and bequeath my interest (in the specified real estate) to each of my brothers, Harvey W. Cantrell, Lee Cantrell and Julian W. Cantrell, or their heirs. ...

Mrs. Cantrell survived her husband, and she provided in her will that the Nashville property would go to her nephew and his wife. After Mrs. Cantrell's death a dispute arose between the nephew and Mr. Cantrell's brothers over the precise extent of Mrs. Cantrell's interest in the property. The nephew contended that she received a fee simple (absolute) interest in the property under her husband's will. The brothers claimed that she took the property subject to a trust in their favor at her death. The trial court ruled in favor of the nephew, and the brothers appealed.

Green, Chief Justice: . . . Such being the will before us, we think the case falls under the authority of Smith v. Reynolds, 173 Tenn. 579, 121 S.W.2d 572, 574. In that case the court reviewed earlier decisions and re-affirmed the rule that a clear and certain devise of a fee, about which the testamentary intention was obvious, would not be cut down or lessened by subsequent words which are ambiguous or of doubtful meaning. Although the will said that the estate devised to his wife "is by my wish returned to my nearest blood kin" at her death, the court held that the wife took the fee, it having been clearly and without ambiguity given to her previously in the instrument. The court said that the testator did not use the word wish as a command. And further that a trust would not be declared on the basis of precatory words where the will showed an intention to leave property absolutely. . . .

In 1 Bogert on Trusts and Trustees, § 48, it is said:

"The words 'request,' 'desire,' and the like, do not naturally import a legal obligation. But the early view in England was that such words, when used in a will, were to be given an unnatural meaning, and were to be held to be courteous and softened means of creating duties enforceable by the courts. According to that opinion words of request prima facie created a trust. But since the beginning of the nineteenth century the English courts have changed their stand upon this question, and now hold that the natural significance of precatory words is not a trust, but that such an obligation may be shown by other portions of the instrument or by extrinsic circumstances. The American courts have adopted this natural construction of precatory expressions."

We find nothing in the record indicating an intention on the part of James G. Cantrell that his will should be construed otherwise than we have done. It is true that those parties recommended by him to the beneficence of his wife were his relatives, but there is nothing to indicate that they were in need. Moreover, he had remembered them by another substantial devise in his will.

Comford v. Cantrell

Supreme Court of Tennessee, 151 S.W.2d 1076 (1941)

For the reasons stated, and upon the authorities cited, the decree of the chancellor must be affirmed.

The Trust Property

The subject matter of a trust, the *res,* may be any property of value. Money, interests in real estate, securities, and insurance are commonly used. However, settlors must own the property at the time they create the trust. They cannot transfer in trust property they expect to acquire and own at a later date. When the property is tranferred to the trustee it becomes his or hers to manage for the benefit of the beneficiaries and in accordance with the terms of the trust. If the essential elements of a valid trust are missing or if the trust fails, the property will revert to the settlor, if living, or to that person's estate, if deceased.

The Trustee

A trustee is, of course, essential; a trust without one cannot be effective. However, the courts will not let an otherwise valid trust fail for want of a trustee. If the named trustee dies or declines to serve or is removed for cause, the court will appoint a replacement. The court will also appoint a trustee when the settlor fails to name one in the trust. No special qualifications are necessary. But since trustees take title to property and manage it, it follows that they must be capable of owning property. Minors and incompetents can, of course, own property. But they are also under a disability in regard to contractual capacity. Consequently, since their contracts are voidable, they cannot function as trustees. Settlors can appoint themselves trustees and, in fact, designate themselves as beneficiaries. The settlor cannot, however, be the sole trustee and the sole beneficiary of a single trust. This relationship would merge both legal and equitable titles to the trust property in the trustee, and he would hold it free of any trust.

If a corporation (an artificial person), is not prohibited by its charter from doing so, it can act as a trustee. Trust companies and banks, for example, frequently serve as trustees for both large and small trusts.

Beneficiaries

The express private trust is ordinarily created for the benefit of identified, or identifiable, beneficiaries. A father can establish a trust for the care and education of his minor children—and will name them in the trust instrument. However, a settlor can simply specify as the beneficiaries a class of persons, such as "my minor children" or "my brothers and sisters." In either case, the persons who are to benefit are readily identifiable. Trusts have also been held to be valid when established for domestic animals, household pets, and even inanimate objects. Such trusts present problems, since nonhuman and inanimate beneficiaries are incapable of holding title to property. Additionally, there will be no beneficiary with the capacity to enforce the provisions of the trust against the trustee. This is not to say that a charitable trust for animals in general or a trust for humane purposes will fail. (We will discuss the charitable trust in a following section.)

The beneficiary does not have to agree to accept the benefits of the trust. It will be presumed that beneficiaries accept the trust unless they make a specific rejection. Their interest in the trust can, in general, be reached by creditors, and they can sell or otherwise dispose of their interests. However, beneficiaries can transfer only the interests they hold—the equitable title. If a beneficiary holds more than a life estate, and the trust does not make other provisions, this interest can be disposed of in a will or can pass to the beneficiary's estate after death.

Managing the Trust

The administration of a trust is highly regulated by statute. Therefore, trustees must know the law of their jurisdictions. In general, they must make every effort to carry out the purpose of the trust. They must act with care and prudence and use their best judgment, and at all times they must exercise an extraordinary degree of loyalty to the beneficiary—the degree of loyalty required of those in a fiduciary position.

In carrying out the purposes of a trust, the trustees ordinarily have broad powers that are usually described in the trust instrument. In addition, they may have implied powers that are necessary to carry out their express duties. For example, trustees can have express authority to invest the trust property and pay the beneficiary the income from such investments. They can also have the implied power to incur reasonable expenses in administering the trust.

Insofar as it is possible trustees should exercise the care and skill of a "prudent person" in managing the trust. Ordinarily this will not require that they possess special skills or a high degree of expertise, or that they be financial wizards. A reasonable goal for a trustee is to exercise the diligence necessary to preserve the corpus and realize a reasonable return on income from "prudent" investments at the same time. State laws often specify the types of investments a trustee can make. In Georgia, for example, trust law authorizes investment in bonds or securities issued by the state and by the U.S. government and certain of its agencies and in certain banks or trust companies insured by the Federal Deposit Insurance Corporation. With certain exceptions, any other investment of trust funds must be under an order of the superior court or at the risk of the trustee. If the trust instrument gives the trustee wide discretion to invest in "other" securities, many jurisdictions allow this. However, the trustee can still be held accountable for a failure to exercise prudence and care. In other words, the law discourages bad investments.

The relationship between the trustee and the beneficiary is fiduciary in nature. Consequently, in managing trusts, trustees must act solely for the benefit of the beneficiaries. The fiduciary duty of loyalty requires that trustees always act in the best interests of the beneficiaries. For example, trustees cannot borrow any portion of the trust funds or sell their own property to the trust. Neither can they purchase trust property for themselves. Even though the trustee's personal dealings with the trust may prove to be advantageous to the beneficiary, the duty of loyalty is breached and the trustee can be charged with such breach. The rules in this matter may seem harsh, but they are designed to prevent a trustee from making a personal profit at the expense of the trust.

The Spendthrift Trust

Settlors may be concerned that beneficiaries may be incapable of managing their own affairs either because of inexperience and immaturity or simply because they are "spendthrifts." Settlors can therefore determine that beneficiaries will not sell, mortgage, or otherwise transfer their rights to receive principal and income and that the beneficiaries' creditors will not reach the income or principal while it is in the hands of the trustee. Such a provision no longer applies after the income or principal has been paid over to the beneficiary. Further, modern statutes limit the spendthrift trust. They either limit the income that is protected from creditors, or they permit creditors to reach amounts in excess of what the beneficiary is considered to need.

Trust Termination

Settlors can revoke a trust at any time if they have reserved that power. However, most trusts are terminated when the stated period has elapsed or when the trust purpose has been served. In a trust for the care of minor children, it logically ends when the beneficiaries have reached their majority. In a trust for the college education of the beneficiary, it will terminate when that goal has been reached. In any event, upon termination of a trust, any balance of funds remaining reverts to the settlor or is disposed of in accordance with the instructions contained in the trust.

Charitable Trusts

The purpose of a charitable trust is the general benefit of humanity. Its beneficiaries can be education, science, religion, hospitals, homes for the aged or handicapped, and a host of other charitable or public entities. Charitable trusts are much like private trusts. Furthermore, the courts of most jurisdictions will find another suitable purpose for a charitable trust when the settlor's stated purpose is impossible or difficult to achieve. The courts do so under the doctrine of *cy pres,* meaning so near or as near. The doctrine is used to prevent a charitable trust from failing for want of a beneficiary. To illustrate, suppose that a testator establishes a testamentary trust for the support and maintenance of orphans in a specified orphanage. If the specified orphanage ceased to exist before the testator's death, the court could use the *cy pres* doctrine, find that the trustor's intent was to benefit orphans generally, and apply the trust to some other orphanage in the area. The *cy pres* doctrine applies only where there is definite charitable intent, never to private trusts.

Implied Trusts

An implied trust, constructive or resulting, is created by law. While the distinction is not always clear, a *constructive trust* is usually imposed upon property by the courts to correct or rectify fraud or to prevent one party from being unjustly enriched at the expense of another. In reality, it is a fiction or remedy to which a court of equity will resort to prevent injustice. Suppose that A and B have agreed to purchase a tract of land jointly with the deed to list both of them as grantees. If, despite the agreement, A secretly buys the land alone, and the deed fails to list B as grantee, the court will impose a constructive trust on the property to the extent of the half interest B should have. This procedure assumes that B is ready and willing to pay half the purchase price. In another case, directors of corporations who take advantage of their positions to make secret profits from corporate opportunities will be constructive trustees for the corporations to the extent of the profits they make. Constructive trusts commonly arise out of the breach of a fiduciary relationship where no trust intent is present or required.

The *resulting trust* arises out of, or is created by, the conduct of the parties. It is imposed in order to carry out the apparent intentions of the parties at the time they entered into the transaction that gave rise to the trust. The most frequent use of the resulting trust occurs when one party purchases property but records the title in the name of another. For example, A wants to purchase a tract of real estate but does not want it subjected to the hazards of his business ventures. He therefore buys the land but has the deed made out in the name of a friend, B. There is no problem if B conveys the real estate to A on demand in accordance with their understanding of the nature of the transaction. However, if B refuses to convey the land, the courts can impose a resulting trust on B for A's benefit. Some difficulty can arise if, in the situation above, A has title taken in the name of his wife or a close relative, because it could be valid to presume that A intended the land as a gift. And if A had purchased in the name of another to defraud his creditors, it is likely that the courts would refuse to impose the resulting trust, being reluctant to afford relief to a wrongdoer.

Estate Planning

"*Estate Planning* is applying the law of property, trusts, wills, future interests, insurance, and taxation to the ordering of one's affairs, keeping in mind the possibility of retirement and the certainty of death."[7] We have discussed both wills and trusts, the most commonly used estate planning devices. In this final section we will briefly explore other aspects of the estate planning process, touching first on the philosophy that has previously guided or misguided many in the disposition of their property—a disposition that usually occurs after death, with dire results for the surviving heirs. The general public equates estate planning with death and

---

[7]R. J. Lynn, *An Introduction to Estate Planning* (St. Paul, Minn.: West Publishing 1975), p. 1.

finds that the subject is one about which it is very easy to do nothing. Rethinking the problem will be easier if one realizes that lifetime planning is more important than death planning. The aim is not merely to dispose of one's estate at death but to organize resources during life in order to provide for the present and future well-being of one's family.

The major consideration in preserving estate integrity today is the impact taxes may have when little thought has been given to methods for reducing estate shrinkage. In fact, it is quite likely for the decedent's survivors to find that, on settling the estate, the principal heir has been Uncle Sam. It is, of course, unlawful to evade taxes. However, there is nothing illegal about doing everything possible to avoid paying unnecessary taxes. Various planning devices can keep unwanted heirs, in the form of estate and inheritance taxes, and the expense of probate and administration to a minimum. However, estate planning is a complex process, best accomplished by experts in the field. Do-it-yourself or fill-in-the-blanks wills can be risky propositions; and trusts, while ordinarily useful devices, can be of no effect if ineptly created.

Giving Can Be Saving

One of the keys to cutting estate taxes is to give away some assets before death. Benefit is derived because the gifts shift income to children or perhaps retired parents who may be in lower tax brackets. For some time the rich have found it worthwhile to donate large portions of their estates. Yet middle-class families, many of whom have acquired substantial estates, often have the mistaken idea that only the rich must be concerned with estate taxes. Giving, as an estate planning device, may be hard to accept for the donor who has spent a lifetime slowly accumulating an estate. Nevertheless, it is something to consider, keeping in mind one's personal situation. Amateur philanthropy, however, can be dangerous. Property given outright to a poor manager can be wasted away. On the other hand, a gift with too many strings attached can be something less than useful to the donee.

Life Insurance

Life insurance, in its various forms, can serve many purposes in estate planning. Ownership can be so arranged that the proceeds will not become part of the insured's estate to be taxed. It is a good means of providing liquid funds so that forced sales of other property to pay estate charges or debts can be avoided. In general, life insurance is not subject to probate and administration expenses and is a good way to make *inter vivos* (lifetime) gifts to children, to grandchildren, or, if the donor is so inclined, to charity. Many kinds of policies are available—term, whole life, and endowment, for example—and there may be a place for one or more types in an estate plan. For the average wage earner life insurance is the major, perhaps the only means of providing security for the family. Indeed, it may be all that is necessary, other than a valid will. With regard to business ventures, the members of a partnership often enter into buy and sell agreements with a view to continuing the partnership after the death of a partner. The partnership agreement sometimes provides that the estates of deceased partners will sell their interests to surviving partners and that the partners will buy such interest. Insurance is frequently used by the partnership to fund the agreement.

Trusts

Trusts are an excellent estate device, capable of accomplishing much more than other tools used in the construction of an estate plan. The use of trusts is usually motivated by tax benefits. For example, if property is transferred outright to the estate owner's children, and they transfer it to their children, there will be estate taxes and other expenses at the death of the children—a double bite, so to speak. However, if the property is transferred to the owner's children in trust for their lives, with the remainder to the grandchildren, no tax will be levied on the death of the children. A generation will be skipped in the tax chain. And if the transfer is properly made, *inter vivos,* the estate tax may be substantially reduced for both generations.

There are several other reasons for using trusts. Those with "spendthrift" provisions will protect beneficiaries from their own mismanagement. A trust can be set up so that a beneficiary cannot dispose of property the settlor wants to keep in the family. Insurance proceeds can be handled effectively by a trust because of its flexibility. A variety of beneficiaries can be provided for, with payments being increased or diminished depending on the individual needs of each beneficiary. However, in using the trust and other devices, familiarity with tax laws—particularly the Tax Reform Act of 1976—is absolutely essential.

The Marital Deduction

For federal estate tax purposes the marital deduction should not be overlooked as a useful device in estate planning involving substantial assets. It reflects the social concept that property belonging to either husband or wife should be treated as belonging one-half to each and is derived from community property law. The marital deduction provisions of the tax code permit up to one-half the adjusted gross estate (or $250,000, whichever is larger) to pass to the surviving spouse without federal estate tax in the estate of the first spouse to die. Substantial tax savings can be realized since, due to the progressive estate tax rates, the two estates taxed separately yield a lower tax than the two estates taxed together. The income-splitting provisions of the 1948 marital deduction, as amended by the 1976 Tax Reform Act, permit this tax saving treatment if the surviving spouse so elects. However, the 1976 act is quite complex; competent counsel and advice should be sought early in the estate planning process.

Questions and Problems

1. Decedent, Matilda Manchester, prepared the following document, wholly in her own handwriting:

"I, Matilda Manchester, leave and bequeath all my estate and effects, after payment of legal, funeral and certain foreign shipment expenses (as directed) to the following legatees, viz."

Then followed a statement of devises and bequests to divers persons. It ended as follows:

"Whereunto I hereby set my hand this fourteenth day of January, 1914." Decedent did not sign the document, her name appearing only in the opening clause as shown above. The paper was folded and sealed in an envelope which was endorsed by the decedent: "My Will, Ida Matilda Manchester." *Estate of Manchester,* 163 P. 358 (Cal.1917). Should the document be admitted to probate as a valid holographic will?

2. A father purchased 100 shares of stock for each of his two children, using money he had withdrawn from their savings accounts. The shares of stock were issued to the mother and registered in her name. When the mother died, a question arose as to ownership of the stock. *Markert v. Bosley,* 207 N.E.2d 414 (1965). What are the childrens' rights in this matter?

3. A state's law required that all formal wills must be "subscribed at the end thereof by the testator" and that attesting witnesses must "sign the instrument as a witness, at the end of the will." The will in question consisted of three pages. The first page was a printed form entitled "Last Will and Testament." Typed on the form were two testamentary provisions and the appointment of executors. On the same form, in the spaces provided, appeared the signature of the testatrix and an attestation clause signed by three witnesses. There were two additional typewritten pages containing testamentary clauses, each of the two pages being signed at the bottom by only the testatrix. The attesting witnesses had not signed the additional pages, their signatures appearing only on the first, "form" page. *Estate of Howell,* 324 P.2d 578 (Cal.1958). Does the document qualify as a will?

4. A testator wanted to revoke his will by having his wife burn it. In his presence she burned an envelope which she fraudulently represented to him to contain his will. *Brazil v. Silva,* 185 P. 174 (1919).

    a. If she was the sole legatee under his will, is she likely to take his estate?
    b. If the testator had two children, are they, in effect, disinherited?

5. A widow died intestate. There had been four children; but one, who had two children, predeceased his mother. How will the estate be divided among the widow's descendants?

6. A trustee sold to herself, at an advantageous price, property belonging to the trust. She then resold the property and deposited a substantial profit in her personal bank account. Discuss the propriety of this transaction.

7. The will of Lauren M. Townsend, after a statement of several specific bequests, provided: " . . . that the remainder be made into a fund, the interest of which shall be used to help defray the expense of educating some girl or boy in music or art. I appoint Paul Gill to have charge of selecting the recipient of this last bequest. *"Estate of Huebner,* 15 P.2d 758 (Cal.1932). Is the quoted language sufficiently specific to create a charitable trust?

8. When the testatrix died, her will consisted of four pages—dated, signed by her, and properly attested by two witnesses. However, a fifth page was attached on which was typed: "CODICIL—Having forgotten my nephew James, I hereby give and bequeath to him the sum of $1,000." It was signed by the testatrix but had no attestation clause; nor had any witnesses signed it. What is the effect of this fifth page?

9. A testator provided in his will: "To my brother, John, I leave my house in Jackson County and the sum of $5,000. I do this trusting that he will provide a place for our older sister, Mary, for so long as she lives; and I request that he use this legacy to improve her lot in life." Upon the testator's death, Mary claimed that the house and money were conveyed to John in trust and must be used for her benefit. Do you agree? Explain.

10. A man died intestate, leaving a widow and the following property:

   a. His residence, which he held as a joint tenant with his surviving spouse.
   b. A thousand-acre farm of which he was the sole owner.
   c. A savings account of $5,000, which was jointly owned by him and his wife.
   d. Two automobiles—he was the sole owner of one and joint owner, with his wife, of the other.
   e. A life insurance policy in the amount of $10,000 on which his son was listed as the beneficiary and on which he had reserved the right to change the beneficiary.

Which of the above assets are subject to administration as a part of his estate? Explain.

42   Bailments

The term *bailment* initially evokes a feeling of puzzlement in most people. Once it is described, however, it is immediately recognized as a simple and commonplace occurrence in everyday life. Taking a dress to a dry cleaner, lending a car to a friend, and delivering goods to a railroad for shipment are all actions that result in the creation of bailments.

While several different kinds of bailments are recognized by the law, they all share certain basic elements. A *bailment* can be defined as the delivery of possession of personal property from one person to another under an agreement by which the latter is obligated to return the property to the former or to deliver it to a third party. The person transferring the possession is the *bailor*, and the one receiving it is the *bailee*.

In this chapter we will first examine those bailments to which the usual bailor/bailee rules apply—ordinary bailments—and then briefly look at those bailments which, because of their unique characteristics, are called "special" or "extraordinary" bailments.

The delivery of property by one person to another does not always constitute a bailment. For example, as a general rule, the delivery of property by an employer to his or her employee (such as furnishing a truck to an employee/driver) is not a bailment, since the employee is said to have mere "custody" rather than the exclusive right of possession. Thus, because the rights and duties of parties to bailments sometimes differ from those existing between parties to other similar transactions, the basic elements of a bailment must be recognized at the outset.

Ordinary Bailments

Elements of a Bailment

As our definition has indicated, a bailment necessarily involves (1) a delivery of possession (but not title), (2) of personal property, (3) under an agreement that the recipient will later return the property or dispose of it in some specified manner. Each of these requirements has been the subject of considerable judicial interpretation, which is summarized here.

The Delivery of Possession Requirement: As interpreted by the courts, *delivery of possession* generally requires not only a physical delivery (transfer) of possession but also a transfer that (1) gives the recipient a substantial measure of control over the property, and (2) is knowingly accepted by the recipient.

If either of these two conditions is lacking, the transaction is not a bailment. For example, when a patron hangs his or her coat on a coatrack at a restaurant, it is almost uniformly held that the restaurant owner is not a bailee of the coat. Since the patron is physically able to remove the coat at any time without notice to the restaurant management, the restaurant does not have exclusive possession and control of the property. If, however, the coat is checked with an attendant of the restaurant, a bailment has come into existence.

For the same reason, leaving a car at a parking lot is generally held to constitute a bailment only if the car owner is required to leave the car keys with the parking lot company. Where this is not required, the company does not have a sufficient amount of control over the car to be constituted a bailee of the property. Thus, in a situation where the car owner is permitted to lock the car and keep the keys, the parking lot company is generally viewed as a mere *lessor* of space and the car owner as a *lessee.*

In the great majority of bailments there is a physical delivery of the property to the bailee. However, in some situations a *constructive* (theoretical) *delivery* will suffice. This might occur, for example, where the owner of a car gives X his certificate of title to the car—not for the purpose of transferring title to X but rather to permit X subsequently to obtain possession of the car from a third party. Also, while in the great majority of bailments the bailor is the owner of the bailed property, this is not necessarily the case. All that is required is that the bailor have a "superior right of possession" vis-à-vis the bailee. Thus, if X loans his power lawn mower to Y for the summer and Y takes the mower to a repair shop in September before returning it to X, a bailor-bailee relationship exists between Y and the repair shop while it is being repaired.

As we have indicated, a physical delivery of property by one person to another does not create a bailment unless the recipient knowingly accepts the property. To illustrate: B has several Christmas presents in the trunk of his car when he leaves it at a parking lot under circumstances in which a bailment exists as to the car. In this situation, if B does not in some way indicate the presence of the gifts to the lot attendant, there is no bailment as to those items.

In exceptional circumstances bailments are sometimes found to exist even where one of the usual elements is lacking. A majority of courts today hold, for example, that the placing of property (such as stock certificates) in a bank safe-deposit box creates a bailor-bailee relationship between the owner of the property and the bank, even though the bank does not have exclusive possession of the property or actual knowledge of the contents of its customers' boxes. Along similar lines, it is generally held that the finder of property (such as a diamond ring) is a bailee of the property even though its owner obviously did not "deliver" the item to the finder. In such a case, because of the lack of the voluntary element, the finder is termed a *constructive* (theoretical) *bailee* of the property.

The Personal Property Requirement: As has been indicated in Chapter 39, all property is either "real" or "personal" in nature. By definition, bailments involve transfers of personal (movable) property only. In other words, while owners of land frequently transfer possession of it to others for limited periods of time, such transactions do not constitute bailments.

Most bailments involve items of tangible personal property, such as automobiles, tools, and jewelry. It is possible, however, for intangible personal property to be the subject of a bailment. This occurs, for example, when a stock certificate representing ownership of shares of stock in a corporation is delivered by a debtor to a creditor as security for the debt.

The Bailment Contract Requirement: A bailment necessarily involves an agreement between the parties that the property ultimately is to be returned by the bailee to the bailor or is to be delivered to a designated third party. The contract can be either express or implied, and, as a general rule, the law does not require it to be in writing. As a practical matter, however, it is generally advisable to have the bailment contract in writing if the value of the bailed property is at all substantial and particularly if a professional or commercial bailor or bailee is being dealt with. Most commercial bailors, such as automobile rental agencies, utilize written contracts routinely.[1]

As a general rule, one of the requirements of a bailment contract is that the

---

[1] A recent federal law, the Consumer Leasing Act, applies to many leases of personal property in or affecting interstate commerce. This statute, which became effective March 23, 1977, is an effort by Congress to require lessors to make a full disclosure of contract terms to their lessees and to adequately explain the lessees' rights under such contracts. In general, the law applies to all types of leased property if the lease period is of at least four months' duration and the value of the property does not exceed $25,000.

bailee return the *identical* goods to the bailor at the end of the bailment period. Thus, if a Buick dealer delivers a car to X under a contract providing that X will deliver to the dealer his used motor home within a month in return, the transaction is a sale rather than a bailment. The transaction is also held to be a sale if the contract gives X the option of returning the car or delivering the motor home at the end of the month.

The rule requiring delivery of the identical property is subject to two well-recognized exceptions:

1. If the subject matter of the transaction is *fungible goods,* such as grain or gasoline, with the contract obligating the recipient simply to deliver the same quantity of goods of the same description at a later time to the person making the original delivery, the transaction still constitutes a bailment. This rule is especially applicable to grain storage situations, with the result that grain elevators taking in grain for storage are bailees even though the grain they later return to their customers is different from that which they initially received.

2. The second exception is presented by the situation where the owner of property delivers it to a prospective purchaser under an agreement giving the latter a specified time in which to decide whether to purchase it at a stated price. This transaction, called a *bailment with the option to purchase,* is held by the courts to fall into the bailment category despite the fact that the recipient of the property has the right to give the bailor the agreed price in cash rather than the specific property that was originally bailed.

The two cases below present typical situations in which the courts are called upon to determine whether a bailment relationship has been created. They also serve as an introduction to the topic of the bailee's liability, which will receive further attention later in the chapter.

The Broadview Apartments Co. v. Baughman

Court of Special Appeals of Maryland, 350 A.2d 707 (1976)

Baughman, plaintiff, was a tenant of Broadview Apartments in Baltimore. Under a separate agreement he paid Broadview $15 a month so he could park his car in the Broadview Garage. The enclosed, two-level garage was located beneath the apartment building. It had separate entrances and exits for both the lobby level and the basement level. There was no attendant at the entrance and exit on the lobby level, but there was one on the basement level. Plaintiff was aware of only two security devices: there was a security guard on duty twenty-four hours a day, and each "renter" of the garage was provided with a key to the garage doors (although the doors were not closed at all times).

On the night of November 23, 1966, Baughman parked his car in his assigned spot on the lobby level, locked the car, and took his keys with him. He testified that he did not recall seeing the security guard that evening. When he returned the next day, his car was gone. He notified the police that it was missing, but the car was never recovered.

Baughman brought this action against Broadview to recover the value of the car, essentially alleging that (1) Broadview was a bailee of the car, (2) under the law of bailments he had made out a *prima facie* case of negligence (that is, proof of loss of the car was proof of negligence on the part of Broadview unless it could prove that it was not negligent), and (3) Broadview had not proven that it had exercised reasonable care under the circumstances.

The trial judge, hearing the case without a jury, agreed with plaintiff's contentions and entered judgment in his favor. Broadview appealed, again asserting that it was not a bailee of the car.

Melvin, Justice: .... A bailment is the relation created through the transfer of the possession of goods or chattels, by a person called the bailor to a person called the bailee, without a transfer of ownership, for the accomplishment of a certain purpose, whereupon the goods or chattels are to be dealt with according to the instructions of the bailor.... To constitute a bailment there must be an existing subject-matter, a contract with reference to it which involves possession of it by the bailee, delivery, actual or constructive, and acceptance, either actual or constructive. *Dobie on Bailment and Carriers* as quoted in *Refining Co. v. Harvester Co.,* 196 A. 131.

... Once the bailment relationship is proven, certain responsibilities flow from the relationship. The bailee in accepting possession of the bailed property assumes the duty of exercising reasonable care in protecting it....

[The court agreed that if a bailment existed in this case, the plaintiff had made out a *prima facie* case of negligence against the defendant company. The court then continued.]

From the above it is readily apparent that the answer to the threshold question of whether a bailment exists will have not only a procedural but oftentimes a substantive impact on the outcome of the case. If no bailment is shown, and the owner of the property is a mere licensee or lessee of the storage space, then in order to recover against the defendant garage the plaintiff would have to prove specific acts of negligence on the part of the defendant....

The courts have uniformly found a delivery of possession to the parking lot operators, and therefore a contract for bailment, where the keys are surrendered with the car or where the car is parked by an attendant.... Some other factors which have been considered to be important are: (1) whether there are attendants at the entrances and exits of the lots, (2) whether the car owner receives a claim check that must be surrendered before he can take his car, (3) whether the parking lot operator expressly assumes responsibility for the car. No single factor has been viewed as determinative of the issue....

In the instant case we think the evidence is *legally insufficient to establish that a bailor-bailee relationship existed.* [Emphasis added.] Plaintiff merely rented a parking space monthly; he parked his own car, locked the car and took the keys with him. There was no testimony that Broadview had a set of keys for the car or had any right or authority to move or exercise any control over the car. Plaintiff entered into the monthly lease arrangement with full knowledge of how the garage operated. He was not required to check his car in or out, and there was no evidence whatsoever that control of the car was ever turned over to the operators of the garage, or that they ever accepted delivery or control. Nor was there any evidence that Broadview expressly contracted or asserted that the car would be safe from theft while in the garage....

On the record before us, as we have indicated, there is insufficient evidence to warrant a finding of a bailor-bailee relationship between the parties. The trial court was wrong in finding there was such a relationship. There being no bailment, the burden was upon the plaintiff to produce sufficient evidence of specific acts of negligence on the part of Broadview or its employees ... from which the trier of fact could predicate a judgment in his favor.

The record is devoid of any such evidence. The mere fact that Broadview may have employed a security guard and that plaintiff's car was missing is not enough. . . .

Judgment reversed.

Judith Lissie and a fellow employee brought this action against their employer, the Southern New England Telephone Company, to recover the value of their coats, which were lost while left in a coatroom during their regular working hours.

The plaintiffs were employed in an office on the second floor of defendant's building in Hartford. Because employees were not permitted to leave their coats by their desks or in their work area, and because there were no facilities available for the coats on the second floor, employees were instructed to leave their coats in one of two areas on the first floor.

On November 29, 1972, plaintiffs left their coats in a designated area on the first floor. They were unable to see the coats in the coatroom from their working area on the second floor. On that day, after working until 8 p.m., plaintiffs discovered that their coats were missing from the room on the first floor where they had been left after plaintiffs had returned from lunch at 2 p.m.

Other facts established at the trial were essentially undisputed. The defendant company did not charge a fee for hanging the coats; nor did it have an attendant or custodian on duty at the coatroom to receive the coats. The plaintiffs knew that the area in which they hung their coats was unguarded. On the day in question members of the general public had access to the coatroom until 5 p.m. without being required to show identification. After 5 p.m. ingress to the building could be obtained only by ringing a bell and showing identification. The coatroom in question did not have security supervision from 2 p.m. to 5 p.m. on the day in question, although the company did have one security guard on duty during that time who was responsible for patrolling defendant's entire complex of four acres.

The trial court ruled that the defendant company was a bailee of the coats, that on the basis of the facts there was a presumption that the loss was the result of negligence on the part of the company, and that the company failed to rebut (refute) this presumption. The company appealed.

Sponzo, Judge: . . . Whether an arrangement between employer and employee for storing personal property during working hours, such as the one revealed by the facts in this case, gives rise to a bailment is an issue of first impression in this court. The essential element of bailment is the express or implied assumption of control over the property by the bailee. Whether or not a transaction creates a bailment is determined by the degree of custody or control given the [one having possession]. Applying that principle to the instant case it is apparent that the defendant required the plaintiffs to leave their coats in the first floor coatrooms and prohibited them from bringing their coats into their working area on the second floor. The defendant had knowledge that during working hours the plaintiffs' coats, together with the coats of other employees, would be left in those areas specifically designated by it. By requiring its employees to comply with that procedure *the defendant implicitly assumed exclusive, albeit temporary, custody and control* over their personal property

Lissie v. Southern New England Telephone Co.

Superior Court of Connecticut, 359 A.2d 187 (1976)

during working hours. [Emphasis added.] The trial court correctly concluded that . . . a bailment [was created]. . . .

We are in agreement with the trial court that the bailment . . . was one for mutual benefit. The standard of care required in a mutual-benefit bailment is due care. When a bailor establishes that his property has not been returned, . . . a presumption arises that the loss of the bailed property was due to the bailee's negligence, [regardless] of the standard of care [that is applicable]. . . .

Whether the bailee . . . has rebutted the presumption of negligence is a question for the trier of the facts. Although there was testimony by the plaintiffs that their coats were stolen and testimony on behalf of the defendant regarding security measures taken for the protection of its premises, we cannot say that the trial court erred in finding that defendant failed to rebut the presumption of negligence. No evidence was presented as to the conduct that materially contributed to the loss, and the evidence of security measures instituted by defendant does not establish conclusively that it fulfilled the duty of using reasonable care to prevent plaintiffs' loss. The trial court correctly concluded that the defendant failed to rebut the presumption of negligence on its part as bailee. . . .

Judgment affirmed.

Types of Bailments

We have already seen that bailments can be classified as either ordinary or special. *Ordinary bailments,* the type with which we are here involved, can in turn be subdivided because of the great variety of uses to which they are put.

A traditional classification is based on the degree of usefulness or profit that each party to the transaction receives. On that basis bailments are classified as being (1) bailments for the *sole benefit of the bailee,* (2) *mutual-benefit* bailments, and (3) bailments for the *sole benefit of the bailor.*

As will be seen later in the chapter, this classification is useful in determining the degree of care the bailee is legally obligated to exercise over the goods while they are in his or her possession. It also is helpful to some extent in determining the bailors' and bailees' rights in particular transactions.

Bailments for Sole Benefit of Bailee or Bailor: Bailments for the sole benefit of the bailee are self-explanatory. Examples of such transactions are the loan of a car to a friend or a power mower to a neighbor.

Bailments for the sole benefit of the bailor are also easy to recognize. Such a bailment occurs whenever the owner of property, for his or her own convenience, delivers it to another person under circumstances where it is clear that the latter is not going to charge the owner anything for the safekeeping of the article. For example, a secretary leaves her car in her employer's garage while she is on vacation in Hawaii.

Mutual Benefit Bailments: Because persons do not ordinarily enter into bailments unless they receive some sort of gain from the transaction, mutual benefit bailments are by far the most common kind. Transactions falling into this category can be further broken down into a number of narrower classes, depending on the specific rights and duties created by the bailment contract. In many mutual benefit bailments, for example, the bailee is a *compensated bailee;* that is, he or she receives a fee for storing the bailor's property. This is not necessarily true, however. The case of *Lissie v. Southern New England Telephone Company* earlier in this chapter is a typical example of a mutual benefit bailment where the benefit received by the bailee (the telephone company) did not arise out of the payment of a fee to it by the bailors (the company's employees). Instead, its benefit resulted from the greater ease with which its employees could do their jobs in an area uncluttered with their personal belongings.

Mutual benefit bailments also often involve the payment of a fee by the *bailee to the bailor;* this is true, for example where one leases a car or tools from a company in the rental business. Again, however, this is not necessarily the case. Thus, if a hotel maintains a checkroom for its dining room patrons without charge, the leaving of a coat by a patron with the checkroom attendant would still be a bailment for the benefit of both parties.

Mutual benefit bailments also vary in regard to the bailee's right to use the property. Thus, in the case of a tool rental, the bailee is obviously permitted to use the rented property, for that is the very purpose for which he or she has entered into the contract. In the case of a parking lot, on the other hand, the bailee/parking lot operator clearly has no such right. Additionally, in many mutual benefit bailments the bailee is under a contractual duty to perform some service on the property (such as altering a dress), while in other situations no service is contemplated.

Rights of the Bailee

Rights and Duties of the Parties

Right to Possession: If the bailment agreement gives the bailee the right to possession for a specified period of time and if the bailor is receiving consideration in return, the bailee ordinarily has the right to retain possession for the entire time. And if the bailor wrongfully retakes possession before the agreed time has expired, the bailee is entitled to damages from him or her for breach of the contract.

The bailee also has another general right involving possession of the property— the right to recover the goods (or damages) from any third party who wrongly interferes with his or her possessory interest. Thus, if the goods are stolen by a third party, the bailee can personally initiate legal action to recover them. Similarly, if the property is damaged by a third party, the bailee has the right to recover damages from that person.

Right to Use the Property: Whether the bailee has the right to use the bailed property depends on the express terms of the contract or, if there are no such terms, on the general purposes of the bailment. If the contract is one for *storage,* for example, the bailee usually has no right to use the property while it is in his or her possession. On the other hand, if the bailee is *renting* the property (such as tools), he or she obviously has the right to use it in a normal manner.

Right of Compensation: Except for bailments in which the bailee is renting property for personal use, he or she normally has the right to some form of compensation for the safekeeping of the property. If the person is a commercial or professional bailee (one who is in the business of storing property) the compensation is usually spelled out in the contract. Where this is not the case, the bailee is entitled to the reasonable value of his or her services. If the purpose of the bailment is to have the bailee render a specified service (such as tuning up a car's motor), the amount of the compensation for the labor expended again depends on the express or implied terms of the contract.

Duties of the Bailee

Under general bailment law all bailees have two basic duties—that of taking reasonable care of the property and that of returning it upon termination of the bailment.

Duty to Exercise Care: In most circumstances a bailee has the duty to use *reasonable care under the circumstances* to protect the property. If it is damaged or destroyed because of the bailee's failure to use such care, he or she is guilty of the tort of negligence and therefore liable for the loss. On the other hand, if the loss occurs through no fault or negligence of the bailee, he or she has no liability to the bailor. The question of whether the bailee was exercising the requisite degree of care at the time of the loss is ordinarily one of fact rather than one of law.

The circumstances to be taken into account by the court include the *degree of benefit* the bailee was receiving from the bailment. The rule of thumb is that a bailee under a mutual benefit bailment is required to exercise the same care that a reasonable person would use for his or her own property in a similar situation. In a bailment for the sole benefit of the bailor the standard of care required of the bailee is somewhat less than this, and in a bailment for the sole benefit of the bailee it is somewhat greater.

To illustrate: X borrows a $40 pocket calculator from Y, a business associate, to use at home that evening. On his way home from work X makes a short business call in a residential neighborhood, leaving the calculator in his unlocked car. During the fifteen-minute stop the calculator is damaged by children on their way home from school. In this situation X may well be liable to Y even though the "reasonable person" probably would not have been considered negligent for leaving a calculator *of his own* unattended for such a short period of time. In other words, because the bailment was solely for X's benefit, the court may well find that he did not exercise appropriate care insofar as Y was concerned.

Other factors to be considered in determining whether the bailee used due care in a particular situation include the value of the bailed property, the degree of the property's susceptibility to injury or theft, and the amount of experience the bailee has had in dealing with similar property in the past.

Due Care and the Presumption of Negligence: In some cases, where the bailor is seeking damages from the bailee in a negligence action, he or she is able to prove *specific acts of negligence* on the part of the bailee (for example, a compensated bailee leaving valuable property unattended). In many cases, however, the bailor does not know the specific cause of the damage; thus he or she is unable to prove that a specific act of negligence on the part of the bailee caused or contributed to the loss. In such situations, as has already been indicated to some extent in the case of *Lissie v. Southern New England Telephone Co.,* the courts have uniformly adopted the rule that the proof of damage or loss to the property in and of itself raises a "presumption of negligence" on the part of the bailee. (Courts in such cases often say that the bailor has made out a *prima facie* case of negligence.) Where the presumption of negligence rule is applicable, this means that in the eyes of the law the bailee is guilty of negligence unless the bailee can clearly prove he or she was *not* at fault. If this is done, it is said that the bailee has "rebutted" (overcome) the presumption and thus is not liable to the bailor.

The following case indicates how the presumption of negligence rule often aids the bailor—as it is intended to do—where he or she is unable to prove specific acts of negligence on the part of the bailee.

For a fee of $40 a month the defendants, Byrd and Barksdale, agreed to feed and keep Buchanan's horse on their five-acre tract in Irving, Texas. The tract contained a caretaker's house, a barn with ten stalls whose gates opened into a fenced "run-a-round," and small fenced pastures used only for exercise (due to lack of sufficient grass for grazing). Defendants boarded seven horses there, four of which were their own. The horses and facilities were cared for by Byrd's brother-in-law, who lived on the premises.

On the night of March 4, 1972, the horses were in one of the pastures rather than in their stalls. About midnight all of them got out of the pasture, apparently through an open gate. They left the premises, and Buchanan's horse and one owned by the defendants were killed by a train a mile away. Buchanan then brought this action for damages.

At the trial without a jury, defendant Byrd testified that the pasture gate and fences were secure when he left the premises after dark on March 4; that his brother-in-law customarily checked the barn, gates, and fences, but that he had been away from home for the evening and had returned about midnight; that he did not know whether his brother-in-law had checked them that night; but that his brother-in-law found the pasture gate open the next morning after neighbors notified him that the horses were out. (The brother-in-law did not testify.)

Byrd also testified that the gate and fences were in good condition when he examined them on March 5, that he did not know whether the horses opened the gate or whether it was left open on the night of March 4, and that he had no idea how the horses got out.

The trial court ruled that a mutual benefit bailment had been entered into, that

Buchanan v. Byrd
Supreme Court of
Texas, 519 S.W.2d 841
(1975)

proof of the loss of the horse raised a presumption that the defendant bailees were guilty of negligence, and that the defendants' testimony did not overcome this presumption. Judgment for plaintiff, Buchanan, was entered for $1,930, and defendants appealed to the court of civil appeals. That court reversed the judgment, and Buchanan appealed to the Supreme Court of Texas.

Daniel, Justice: ... In a bailment for mutual benefit, a rebuttable presumption of negligence and a *prima facie* case of liability is established by a bailor against the bailee upon proof that the bailed chattel was not returned. ...

"Where goods have been committed to a bailee, and have either been lost or been returned in a damaged condition, ... the fact of negligence may be presumed, placing on the bailee at least the duty of producing evidence of some other cause of loss or injury." *Wigmore on Evidence,* 3rd Ed., Sec. 2508. [As was stated in] *Trammell v. Whitlock,* 242 S.W.2d 157, "The rule is said to be based on the just and common sense view that the party in possession or control of an article is more likely to know and more properly charged with explaining the damage to it or disappearance of it than the bailor who entrusted it to his care. ... "

Defendants contend, and the court of civil appeals agreed, that they had explained and rebutted the presumption of their negligence by evidence that the pasture gate and fences were in good repair; that no damage to the premises was found or repaired after the horses' escape; that a caretaker lived on the premises; and that neither plaintiff nor his daughter [principal user of the horse] had ever made any complaint about the condition of the premises. We disagree.

Proof of the good condition of the pasture and gate and fences does not explain the open gate or the permitting of seven horses to run loose at night in a small barren pasture from which there had been previous escapes, one of which was through an open gate. Proof that the brother-in-law caretaker lived on the premises was no rebuttal of presumed negligence when the evidence showed that the caretaker was away until about midnight; that it was not known whether he checked the gate that night; and that he found the gate open when the horses were reported to be out the next morning. Defendants' only evidence directed at the crucial question of the open gate was defendant Byrd's testimony that *he did not know whether the horses opened the gate or whether it was left open.* [Emphasis added.] ...

The salutary purposes of the presumption would be nullified if it can be met by mere proof that a bailee did not know how the loss occurred. [Emphasis added.] That being the effect of defendant bailees' explanation in this case, we hold that it did not meet or rebut the presumption of negligence which was established. ...

Accordingly, the judgment of the court of civil appeals is reversed and the judgment of the trial court [for plaintiff] is affirmed. ... [The case was, however, remanded to the trial court to consider whether the damages allowed plaintiff were excessive, as claimed by defendants.]

Duty to Use Care—Special Considerations: Following are two additional matters related to the general obligation of the bailee to use reasonable care.

First, bailees often attempt to free themselves of this duty by express provisions in the bailment contract. Many parking lot tickets, for example, provide, "It is expressly agreed that the owner of the automobile assumes all risk for damage to, or loss of, the automobile regardless of cause," or contain other provisions indicating that the bailor will not hold the bailee liable even if he or she is guilty of negligence. Such provisions, called *exculpatory clauses,* are generally held not to be binding upon the bailor for one or both of two reasons:

1. As indicated in the contracts portion of this text (Part II) it is often held that such provisions are *not legally communicated* to the bailor unless there is proof that he or she actually read them.

2. Even if the provisions are legally communicated, they are usually held by the courts to be *illegal* (contrary to public policy) and thus unenforceable. This view is especially applicable where the bailee is a compensated bailee and where the provision appears in a bailment contract prepared by the bailee and presented to the bailor on a "take it or leave it" basis.

Second, a bailee in certain exceptional circumstances may be legally liable to the bailor for damage to the property even if there was no negligence at all on the bailee's part. This is true particularly where the bailee has exceeded the terms of the bailment contract—that is, where the bailee at the time of the damage or loss was clearly using the property in some unauthorized manner. To illustrate: Vance, a resident of Sacramento, California, borrows a pickup truck from his neighbor, Perez, to move some furniture from Stockton to Sacramento. After Vance reaches Stockton and loads the furniture, he decides to go on to Modesto, about twenty-five miles farther, to visit his brother. If the truck is damaged in an accident while Vance is in Modesto, he is fully liable to Perez for the damage done even if the accident was not his fault in any respect.

Bailee's Duty to Return the Property: While the duty to use reasonable care to avoid loss is based on principles of *tort law,* the second general duty of the bailee—to return the property to the bailor (or to a specified third party)—is essentially *contractual in nature.* Because of this duty, if the bailee upon termination of the bailment is unable to return the property (for example, if it had been stolen), he or she ordinarily is liable for damages on the breach of contract theory. This contractual duty is not absolute, however, with the result that the obligation to return is excused if the goods are shown to have been lost or stolen without fault on the part of the bailee.

Rights of the Bailor

Essentially, the rights of the bailor arise out of the duties owed that person by the bailee in a given situation. Thus the recent discussion of the bailee's duties gives a fair indication of the bailor's rights in particular kinds of bailments.

To summarize, the general rights of the bailor are: (1) to have the property returned at the end of the bailment period, (2) to have the bailee use reasonable care in protecting the property while it is in his or her possession, and (3) to have the bailee use the property (if use is contemplated) only in conformity with the express or implied terms of the bailment agreement. Additionally, the bailment contract may also entitle the bailor to a specified compensation (as in the car rental cases) and, where the performance of work on the property by the bailee is contemplated, the right to have such services performed in a workmanlike (nondefective) manner.

Duties of the Bailor

Liability for Defects in Bailed Property: Leaving aside any specific duties imposed by the bailment contract (which have been touched on in the discussion of bailee's rights) one of the basic obligations owed by the bailor is the duty *to refrain from knowingly delivering to the bailee property that contains a hidden defect* likely to cause injury to the bailee, without giving notice of the defect to the bailee. In this regard a distinction is made between the bailor's obligation in a mutual benefit bailment and in a bailment for the sole benefit of the bailee. In a mutual benefit bailment the bailor owes the duty to notify the bailee of any defects in the property that he *actually knows of* or *should know of.* In a bailment for the sole benefit of the bailee, on the other hand, the bailor is liable for injury to the bailee or the bailee's property only when it is shown that the bailor *actually knew* of the defect and did not notify the bailee of it. The greater obligation of the bailor in a mutual benefit bailment thus arises in a situation where the careless bailor actually did not know of the defect at the time of the bailment, but where he or she would have known of it had the property been reasonably inspected prior to the bailment.

In the general situation discussed above, the failure of the bailor to use the requisite degree of care subjects him or her to liability on the *negligence theory.* A somewhat different obligation is incurred by a bailor in a bailment for hire (where the bailee rents the property for personal use). Here, in addition to possible liability based on negligence principles, the bailor can also incur *warranty liability.* In such bailments there is ordinarily an implied warranty made by the bailor that the property is fit for its intended use. The distinction between the two possible grounds for liability is this: If a bailee can proceed only on the negligence theory, he or she must prove not only that the goods were defective but that the bailor knew or should have known this fact. Unless both criteria are met, the bailee cannot recover from the bailor. On the other hand, if the implied warranty theory applies, the bailee need only prove that the property was not fit for the intended purposes of the bailment, regardless of whether the bailor knew or should have known of the condition causing the unfitness.

The imposition of liability by the courts on bailors in "for hire" bailments was given impetus by enactment of the Uniform Commercial Code in the 1960s. As we saw in Chapter 20, under Article 2 of the code (sales), sellers of goods today have reasonably clear implied warranty liability to buyers in given situations—especially if they are merchant sellers. While this liability is literally applicable only to sellers of goods (rather than to bailors), the courts have increasingly held that commercial bailors in bailments for hire are also subject to this kind of warranty liability. The following case is one of the first in which the reasoning that underlies this view was spelled out in persuasive fashion.

Hertz leased nine trucks to Contract Packers of Jersey City "on a long term basis." Under the contract the trucks were kept at Contract Packers' premises, but Hertz was obligated to service, repair, and maintain them. The arrangement was that once a year or every 18,000 miles, whichever came first, Hertz was to provide "preventive maintenance," which consisted of a comprehensive checking out of the mechanical condition of each truck. Additionally, the trucks were "gassed up" at the Hertz garage at the end of each day, at which time drivers reported any troubles they had had with the trucks during the day. Hertz either repaired these trucks overnight or substituted others until the repairs could be completed.

The plaintiff, Cintrone, an employee of Contract Packers, was injured while riding in one of the trucks driven by another employee of Contract Packers when the brakes of the truck failed and the vehicle ran into a railroad bridge.

Cintrone brought this action against the defendant/bailor, Hertz Leasing, alleging that his injuries resulted (a) from negligent inspection on the part of the defendant, and/or (b) from breach of defendant's implied warranty that the vehicle was fit and safe for its intended use. The trial court dismissed plaintiff's warranty claim, and the jury found no negligence on the part of Hertz. Plaintiff appealed from this adverse judgment.

Cintrone v. Hertz Truck Leasing and Rental Service, Inc.
Supreme Court of New Jersey, 212 A.2d 769 (1965)

Francis, Justice: . . . Plaintiff [contends] that the contractual relationship between Hertz and his employer gave rise to an implied continuing promissory warranty by Hertz that the truck in question was fit for the purposes for which plaintiff's employer rented it, i.e., operation and transportation of goods on the public highways. He urges further that . . . the failure of the brakes and the consequent accident created a factual issue for jury determination as to whether there was a breach of the implied warranty. Therefore he claims the court below erred in refusing to submit that issue for jury consideration.

. . . [I]f the relationship in the present case between Contract Packers and Hertz were manufacturer or dealer and purchaser, an implied warranty of fitness for operation on the public highway would have come into existence at the time of the sale. Moreover, under those cases, breach of the warranty which caused personal injury to an employee [of the bailee] would be actionable by the employee. It must be recognized, however, that the occasions have been relatively few when the courts have been asked to imply warranties in personal injury cases as an incident of transactions other than sales of [goods]. . . .

There is no good reason for restricting such warranties to sales. Warranties of fitness are regarded by law as an incident of a transaction because *one party to the relationship is in a better position than the other to know and control the condition of the property transferred* and to distribute the losses which may occur because of a dangerous condition the chattel possesses. [Emphasis added.] These factors make it likely that the party acquiring possession of the article will assume it is in a safe condition and therefore refrain from taking precautionary measures himself. . . .

In this connection it may be observed that the comment to the warranty section of the Uniform Commercial Code speaks out against confining warranties to sales transactions. The comment says: "Although this section is limited in its scope and direct purpose to warranties made by the seller to the buyer as part of a contract of sale, the warranty sections of this Article are not designed in any way to disturb those lines of case law which have recognized that warranties need not be confined either to sales contracts or to the direct parties to such a contract. They may arise in other appropriate circumstances, such as in the case of bailments for hire. . . ." See Comment [Sec. 2-313 of the UCC]. . . .

We may take judicial notice of the growth of the business of renting motor vehicles, trucks and pleasure cars.

The nature of the U-drive-it enterprise is such that a heavy burden of responsibility for the safety of lessees and for members of the public must be imposed upon it. The courts have long accepted the fact that defective trucks and cars are dangerous instrumentalities on the highways. . . . Therefore the offering to the public trucks and pleasure vehicles for hire necessarily carries with it a representation that they are fit for operation. This representation is of major significance because both new and used cars and trucks are rented. In fact, as we were advised at oral argument the rental rates are the same whether a new or used vehicle is supplied. In other words, the lessor in effect says to the customer that the representation of fitness for use is the same whether the vehicle supplied is new or old. . . .

In the case before us, it is . . . obvious that when a company like Contract Packers rents trucks for limited or extended periods for use in its occupation of transportation of goods, it [like other bailees] relies on the *express or implied representation of the [bailor] that they are fit for such use.* [Emphasis added.] . . .

When the implied warranty or representation of fitness arises, for how long should it be considered viable? Since the exposure of the user and the public to harm is great if the rented vehicle fails during ordinary use on a highway, the answer must be that it continues for the agreed rental period. The public interests involved are justly served only by treating an obligation of that nature as an incident of the business enterprise. The operator of the rental business must be regarded as possessing expertise with respect to the service life and fitness of his vehicles for use. That expertise ought to put him in a better position than the bailee to detect or to anticipate flaws or defects or fatigue in his vehicles. Moreover, as between bailor for hire and bailee, the liability for flaws or defects not discoverable by ordinary care in inspecting or testing ought to rest with the bailor just as it rests with a manufacturer who buys components containing latent defects from another maker, and installs them in the completed product, or just as it rests with a retailer to the point of sale to the consumer. . . .

The warranty or representation of fitness is not dependent upon existence of Hertz' additional undertaking to service and maintain the trucks while they were leased. That undertaking serves particularly to instill reliance in Contract Packers upon mechanical operability of the trucks through the rental period. But the warranty or representation that the vehicles will not fail for that period *sprang into existence on the making of the agreement to rent the trucks,* and was an incident thereof, *irrespective* of the service and maintenance undertaking. [Emphasis added.] . . .

Accordingly, we are of the opinion that the leasing agreement gave rise to a continuing implied *promissory warranty* that the leased trucks would be fit for plaintiff's employer's use for the duration of the lease, . . . and that the evidence *created a factual issue for determination by the jury* as to whether defendant Hertz had been guilty of a breach of that warranty which produced the collision and plaintiff's injury. . . .

Judgment for the defendant is reversed, and the case is remanded for a new trial to be had in accordance with the views outlined.

Bailor's Limitations on Liability

Exculpatory clauses often appear in contracts prepared by commercial bailors, purporting to free them from damages resulting from their negligence or breach of the implied warranty of fitness. These clauses, like similar provisions in bailees' contracts considered earlier, are generally held to be contrary to public policy. Thus in most situations they do *not* insulate the bailor from liability when negligence or breach of warranty is proven, even if they were called to the bailee's attention at the time the contract was formed.

Termination of Bailments

Bailments are most commonly terminated by: (1) mutual agreement, at any time; (2) elapse of the stated bailment period; (3) unilateral termination by either party, where bailment is not for a definite time; (4) accomplishment of the purpose for which the property was bailed; and (5) any act of the bailee that is entirely inconsistent with the terms of the bailment agreement.

Special Bailments

Some bailees are called *special* or *extraordinary* bailees. They fall into this category either because the law imposes a greater liability upon them than is true of ordinary bailees or because they furnish services that are more unique or specialized than those of ordinary bailees. The two most common kinds of special bailees are *common carriers* and *warehousemen;* closely allied to them are *innkeepers* (or *hotelkeepers*).

Common Carriers

In general, carriers are persons or companies who undertake the transportation of goods for a consideration. *Common carriers* are those which are willing to furnish transportation facilities to the general public, while *contract carriers* have the right to select the companies or persons to whom they will furnish their services.

The delivery of goods to a common carrier clearly creates a bailment relationship —the shipper being the bailor and the carrier the bailee. But common carriers have duties beyond those of most other bailees:

1. Unlike most bailees they have a contractual obligation to transport the bailed property.

2. They possess what is called *strict* or *extraordinary liability*.

Liability of the Common Carrier: Under common-law rules—that is, in the absence of a limitation of liability in the bailment contract—a common carrier is absolutely liable for all loss or damage to the goods unless it is able to prove that the damage was caused by one of the following: (1) an act of God, (2) an act of a public enemy, (3) an act of public authorities, (4) an act of the shipper, or (5) the inherent nature of the goods.

The strict liability of the common carrier can be contrasted with the usual liability of the ordinary bailee by a simple illustration. Suppose that the X Co.

delivers a quantity of electronic equipment to the Burlington Northern Railroad in Minneapolis for shipment to its Seattle, Washington, distribution center. While the train is stopped in Mandan, North Dakota, the crewmen on board are overcome by armed robbers and the equipment is stolen. The railroad is liable for the loss, despite the fact that it was not negligent, solely because the cause of the loss did not fall within any of the five listed exceptions to the rule of absolute liability. An ordinary bailee in such a situation would not be liable to the bailor.

Under federal statutes and Interstate Commerce Commission regulations, common carriers in interstate commerce are permitted to limit their liability for loss or damage by provisions in their shipment contracts (bills of lading). In order for the standard limitations that appear in such contracts to be valid, the carriers must (among other things) offer shippers the option of higher limits of liability. Shippers who choose this greater protection pay a somewhat higher freight charge than would normally be the case.

Warehousemen

Warehousemen are persons in the business of storing others' property for compensation. *Public warehousemen* are those obligated to serve the general public without discrimination.

Warehousemen are distinguished from ordinary bailees in two major respects, first because of their issuance of warehouse receipts and second because their activities are subject to more governmental regulation than is true of ordinary bailees. (Their liability for loss or damage to the property, however, is in general the same as that of ordinary bailees rather than that of common carriers.)

When goods are delivered by their owner to a warehouse, the owner/bailor receives a document (the warehouse receipt) which is an acknowledgment by the warehouseman that he has received the described property. This receipt also contains the conditions of the bailment contract.

Warehouse receipts are either negotiable or nonnegotiable, depending upon their express terms. (See Chapter 17 for more information about such documents of title.) A receipt is negotiable if it provides that the bailee/warehouseman will deliver the goods to the bearer of the receipt or to "the order of" any person named in the receipt. This kind of receipt facilitates the sale of the property by the original owner/bailor. Thus, if X delivers goods to a warehouse, he can then sell them to Y by indorsing and delivering the warehouse receipt to Y; and Y can be confident of obtaining the property when he presents the negotiable receipt to the warehouseman.

Under ordinary bailment law, warehousemen have only the liability of ordinary bailees. That is, they are generally liable for loss or damage to the property only if the loss is shown to be a result of their negligence. However, all states today have special statutes containing extensive regulations that must also be adhered to by warehousemen, such as those prescribing minimum building standards and requiring the maintenance of fire prevention systems. Furthermore, warehousemen who operate in interstate commerce are subject to additional federal regulations.

Innkeepers

The taking of articles of personal property to a hotel or motel room by a guest does not create a bailment relationship between the guest and the hotel. This is true even when the guest locks the door to the room and temporarily departs, for two reasons:

1. The innkeeper (the hotel or motel owner and their agents) normally does not have knowledge of the specific articles that are deposited in the room.

2. Even if this knowledge does exist, the innkeeper's "possession" is not exclusive; the guest is free to remove the property at will without notice to the innkeeper.

Despite this lack of a bailment relationship, under common-law principles the innkeeper had the same liability regarding the safety of guests' property as that imposed on common carriers. That is, he was automatically liable for damage or loss of the property unless it occurred as a result of one of the five limited causes listed earlier.

Today, in all states, this extraordinary liability has been greatly cut down or eliminated entirely by statute. While state statutes vary in detail, their basic provisions can be summarized to some extent.

The typical statute requires innkeepers to maintain facilities for the safekeeping of guests' "valuables"—such items as money, jewelry, and negotiable instruments. If a guest deposits an item of this sort with the innkeeper or the innkeeper's agent, a bailment exists and the innkeeper usually has extraordinary liability as to such property. That is, he or she is automatically liable for loss or damage unless it is due to one of the five limited causes. (Many statutes, however, do place dollar limitations on innkeepers' liability in such situations.)

As to any property that is *not* deposited for safekeeping but is left in the guest's room, the statutes vary. Many provide that the innkeeper's common-law liability is reduced to that of an ordinary bailee. That is, proof of loss or damage to the property raises a presumption that it was caused by negligence on the part of the innkeeper or that person's agents, with the innkeeper having the opportunity to rebut the presumption by evidence establishing that the cause of loss was not his or her fault. Other statutes do not remove innkeepers' common-law liability for loss of such property but do severely limit the amount of recovery—such as $25 or $50—to which the guest is entitled in such instances.

Questions and Problems

1. Hanson agreed to loan $1,000 to Kristofferson only after Kristofferson agreed to *pledge* a diamond ring valued at $3,000 with Hanson. (A pledge is a transfer of possession—but not title—of personal property from a debtor to a creditor as security for the debt. When the debt is paid, the property is returned to the debtor.) Soon after the loan was made, the ring was stolen while in Hanson's possession. In subsequent litigation between the parties, Hanson contended that he was *not* a bailee in this situation for the reason that his obligation to return the ring was not absolute—i.e., he would not have to return it if Hanson defaulted on his loan. Is Hanson's contention correct? Why or why not?

2. Miss X left her expensive leather handbag in a medical clinic waiting room when she was called into her doctor's office for her appointment. When she returned to the waiting room forty-five minutes later, the handbag was gone. She later brought suit against the clinic to recover its value. At the trial the clinic receptionist and X's doctor testified that they did not see the handbag at any time during the day of her appointment.

a. Assuming the receptionist and the doctor were telling the truth, would this testimony necessarily rule out a bailor-bailee relationship? Explain.

b. If the receptionist had testified that she had noticed Miss X placing the handbag in a corner of a couch before entering the doctor's office, would this fact clearly establish a bailment? Discuss.

3. Scarlet, a Ford dealer, delivered a new Mustang automobile to his neighbor, Gray, for ten days; the understanding between the two men was that at the end of that period Gray would have the option of (a) giving his 1913 Ford to Scarlet in payment for the Mustang, or (b) paying Scarlet $4,600 in cash for the Mustang.

a. During the ten-day period while Gray is in possession of the Mustang, is he a bailee of the car? Discuss.

b. Would your answer be any different if the agreement had simply given Gray, at the end of the ten-day period, the option of either returning the Mustang or paying $4,600 cash for it? Explain.

4. In the *Southern New England Telephone Company* case the court ruled, among other things, that the bailment entered into between the company and its employees (in regard to the employees' coats) was a mutual benefit bailment. In view of the fact that the company was not charging a fee for the service, do you think the court was correct? Explain.

5. Give examples of two kinds of bailments in which the bailee clearly does not have the right to use the bailed property.

6. X leaves his car at the Y Company's parking lot and returns an hour later to find it has been badly damaged while in the Y Company's possession. In this situation, X's right to recover damages from the parking lot company might be seriously jeopardized if—legally speaking—the relationship between X and the Y Company was merely one of lessee and lessor rather than bailor and bailee. Explain why this is so.

7. In regard to the *Byrd* case, what was the specific reason for the court's ruling that the evidence of Byrd (the defendant/bailee) did not rebut the presumption of negligence on his part?

8. David Crystal, Inc., delivered goods to a trucking company for transportation. While in the trucking company's possession, the goods were lost when the truck carrying them was hijacked in New York City. In an action by David Crystal against the trucking firm, a common carrier, it defended on the ground that truck hijackers are "public enemies," and that it is thus not liable for the loss. Do you agree with this argument? Why or why not? (*David Crystal, Inc., v. Ehrlich-Newmark Truck Co.,* 314 N.Y.S.2d 559, 1970.)

Part VII

Secured
Transactions
and Bankruptcy

Secured Transactions 43

A very large part of the business that is carried on in this country is done "on credit." While there are many types of transactions in which credit is extended by one person or firm to another, probably the two most common of these arise from sales of goods (in which the buyer promises to pay the purchase price in install-ments) and loans of money. In these transactions a *debtor-creditor* relationship results, with the buyer (or borrower) being the debtor, and the seller (or lender) being the creditor.

Sometimes a seller or lender is willing to extend credit without receiving any security from the creditor. Unsecured debts frequently arise at the retail sale level, where, for example, a department store will sell goods to a buyer who is permitted to charge them to his account by the use of a credit card. Unsecured credit may also be extended by wholesalers and manufacturers, and by lenders, especially where the debtor has established a good credit rating with the creditor as a result of past dealings.

In all unsecured credit cases, once the creditor delivers the goods or makes the loan to the debtor he has lost all his rights to the goods or money. This means that if the debtor subsequently defaults, the creditor cannot immediately claim or attach any specific goods or money in the debtor's possession. Instead, he is initially limited to bringing an action to recover the amount of the indebtedness. After getting a judgment in such a suit the creditor has the right to have any unencumbered property then in the debtor's possession sold under court order to satisfy his debt.[1] However, it may be that he will have to share these limited proceeds with other judgment creditors (or, worse still, it may be that the debtor may not own any property at all by the time the judgment is obtained). Thus an unsecured creditor runs a distinct risk that he may ultimately recover little or nothing from the debtor.

Secured Credit Transactions: To minimize the risks mentioned above, many sellers and lenders routinely require the debtor to enter into a *security agreement* at the time credit is extended—i.e., an agreement by which the debtor conveys to the creditor a legally-recognized interest in specific personal property owned by the debtor. Once such an interest is created, the creditor has the right to have the specific property sold if the debtor defaults on his payments, and to receive as much of the proceeds of the sale as is necessary to pay off the debt. (If the proceeds are not sufficient to pay the total indebtedness, the creditor then has an *unsecured* claim as to the unpaid balance).

The dual purpose of a secured transaction, then, is to give to the creditor (1) a *specific interest* in the debtor's property, and (2) a *priority claim* in that property as against other creditors who may seek to have the property sold in satisfactions of their claims. This priority, usually obtained by giving "notice" to all other creditors and third parties who may subsequently become creditors, is called "perfection." (The subject of perfection will be discussed in more detail later in the chapter.)

To illustrate a typical secured transaction situation; R, a retailer, needs to purchase some inventory from W, a wholesaler; but R does not want to pay cash for the goods. R and W therefore sign a security agreement under which W will transfer title to the inventory to R, with R paying 10 percent down and the balance in monthly payments and with W retaining a security interest in the inventory in the event of R's default. At this point a debtor-creditor relationship has been created; W, the secured party, has the inventory collateral of R as security for the debt. W now files a financing statement to give notice to all others of his security interest in the collateral. If R defaults, W can repossess the remaining inventory to satisfy the debt. Furthermore, assuming that W's filing has given him priority, the collateral will go first to pay off R's debt with W, and whatever remains will go to other creditors.

Pre-UCC Secured Transactions Law

Before adoption of the UCC, the law on secured transactions was concerned primarily with the person who had "title" to the property and the "form" of the

---

[1]Unencumbered property is that which the debtor owns outright—that is, free of any security interest, mortgage, or other lien of a third party.

transaction. A separate body of law and a separate terminology existed for each form used. To determine the rights of the creditor, the debtor, and third parties, one had to know what type of security device had been used. (The most common of such devices were the conditional sales contract, the chattel mortgage, the trust receipt, and the pledge; other devices were the factor lien and the assignment of account.) To add to the complexity, notices given to third parties about the outstanding security interest varied insofar as their priorities were concerned. The laws also varied as to when a creditor had to resell repossessed property and when he or she could keep it in satisfaction of the debt.

Because of the complexity and conflict that existed in pre-UCC secured transaction law, the basic goals which the drafters of the UCC sought to accomplish were clear—simplicity and uniformity.

Under Article 9 of the UCC the various forms of the security transaction were abandoned, and a simple terminology was created. The same terms now appear in security agreements, financing statements, and any other such documents. Following are the terms needed for an understanding of the basic concepts of secured transactions law.

Article 9 Terminology

Secured party. Under Sec. 9-105(1)(m), a secured party is a lender, seller, or other person in whose favor a security interest exists—including a person to whom accounts or chattel paper have been sold. This person was formerly referred to as a chattel mortgagee, conditional seller, entruster, factor, or assignee of accounts.

Debtor. Under Sec. 9-105(1)(d), a debtor is a person who owes payment or other performance of the obligation that is secured, regardless of whether he or she owns or has rights in the collateral, and includes the seller of accounts or chattel paper. Formerly this person was referred to as a chattel mortgagor, conditional buyer, trustee, borrower, or assignor of accounts.

Security interest. Under Sec. 1-201(37), a security interest is an interest in personal property or fixtures that secures payment or performance of an obligation—that is, the interest granted the secured party. Formerly this term was referred to as the "lien" in a chattel mortgage, the "title" in a conditional sales contract, the "security interest" in a trust receipt, and the "sale" or "transfer" in an assignment of accounts.

Security agreement. Under Sec. 9-105(1)(l), a security agreement is a security arrangement between the debtor and the secured party—the agreement that creates the security interest. Formerly this agreement was referred to as a chattel mortgage, conditional sales contract, trust receipt, factoring agreement, or assignment contract.

Collateral. Under Sec. 9-105(1)(c), collateral is the property subject to a security interest, and includes accounts and chattel paper that have been sold.

Perfection. The taking, by a secured creditor, of those steps which are required under the UCC in order for his or her security interest to be valid as against other creditors.

Financing statement. Under Secs. 9-401 and 9-402, the financing statement is the instrument filed to give public notice of the security interest in the collateral.

Following is an illustration of the basic concepts using this terminology. The secured party and debtor usually enter into a security agreement by which the secured party receives a security interest in one or more pieces of the debtor's collateral, to be available in the event of the debtor's default. To gain priority over others who may also want a security interest in this same collateral, the secured party files a financing statement as notice of his or her claim. The secured interest is now perfected. (While the usual security device is expressly labelled "security agreement" to conform to this terminology, older forms creating security interests (the chattel mortgage or conditional sale) are still used occasionally. In such cases these devices, too, are treated today as ordinary security agreements.)

Scope of Article 9

Article 9 covers security agreements that are created in *personal* property. Therefore, security interests in *real* property, such as those created by the mortgage of a farm or a home, are not governed by this article.[2]

Many times the personal property has a tangible existence, which we call "goods." But security interests are also commonly created in certain kinds of personal property that have no physical existence, which are called "intangibles"— e.g., accounts receivable and common stock.

Goods

Under Article 9 there are four kinds of goods, as follows:

Consumer goods. Under Sec. 9-109(1), goods are consumer goods if they are used or bought for use primarily for personal, family, or household purposes.

Equipment. Under Sec. 9-109(2), goods are equipment if they are used or bought for use primarily in business (including farming or a profession).

Farm products. Under Sec. 9-109(3), goods are farm products if they are crops or livestock or supplies used or produced in farming operations, or products of crops or livestock in their unmanufactured state (such as eggs, milk, or sap used in the production of maple syrup), and if they are in the possession of a debtor engaged in raising, fattening, grazing, or other farm operations.

Inventory. Under Sec. 9-109(4), goods are inventory if they are held by a person for sale or lease, or if they are to be furnished (or are already furnished) under service contracts, or if they are raw materials, work in process, or materials used or consumed in a business.

---

[2]In the interest of accuracy it should be noted that *some* security interests in personal property fall outside the scope of Article 9. For example, under special statutes an auto mechanic usually obtains a lien on the car while it is in his possession, and under Article 2 of the UCC an unpaid seller of goods may have an interest of the goods while they are en route to the buyer. Such interests are governed by the special statutes that create them.

In addition to the above, Article 9 also covers security interests in *fixtures* (which, as we saw in Chapter 39, are articles of personal property that subsequently are attached to real estate in such a manner that they become a part of that real estate). To illustrate: a security interest in an electric motor in a store's inventory continues to exist if the motor is subsequently installed in a manufacturer's plant.[3]

Intangible Personal Property

Section 9-102 specifically covers a large number of interests in personal property in addition to those in goods. These types of property are "documents, instruments, general intangibles, chattel paper or accounts." (Additionally, as we will see subsequently, this section also applies to any *sale* of accounts or chattel paper.)

Documents of title. Under Sec. 1-201(15), documents of title include bills of lading, dock warrants, dock receipts, warehouse receipts or orders for delivery of goods, and any other documents which in the regular course of business or financing are treated as adequate evidence that the person in possession is entitled to receive, hold, and dispose of them and the goods they cover. (Documents may be negotiable. If so, under Sec. 9-309, the maximum perfection afforded the secured party can be achieved only by that person taking possession of the documents; it cannot be achieved by filing.)

Instruments. Under Sec. 9-105(1)(i), *instrument* means a negotiable instrument (defined in Sec. 3-104) or a security (defined in Sec. 8-102) or any other writing evidencing a right to the payment of money.

General intangibles. Under Sec. 9-106, general intangibles are any personal property (including "things in action"—the right to collect money or property) other than goods, accounts, chattel paper, documents, instruments, and money. Examples are goodwill, literary rights, trademarks, patents, copyrights, and the like.

Chattel paper. Under Sec. 9-105(1)(b), chattel paper is a writing or writings evidencing both a monetary obligation and a security interest in or lease of specific goods.

Accounts. Under Sec. 9-106, an account is any right to payment for goods sold or leased or for services rendered which is not evidenced by an instrument or chattel paper, regardless of whether it has been earned by performance.

The provision referred to above covering the "sale" of accounts or chattel paper covers this type of situation: R, a retailer, sells goods to P, a purchaser, on credit. That is, P either promises to pay the price later (i.e., buys "on account") or gives R a promissory note (a type of "chattel paper"). At the time of the sale R may or may not require P to enter into a security agreement giving him (R) a security interest in the goods. In either case, R may thereafter want to transfer the account or the note to a third-party lender (L) to secure credit which he (R) is seeking from

---

[3]This is not true, however, in the case of ordinary building supplies, such as lumber that is used in building a house. In this case the lumber is not a fixture, and any security interest is lost when it becomes a part of the building.

L. In such a case, if R enters the required security agreement and transfers the account or note to L, L now has a security interest in *these documents*.

Creating a Security Interest

Under Sec. 9-203, in order for the business person to be sure of having an enforceable security interest that attaches to the collateral, three events must occur:

1. There must be a *security agreement* entered into which describes the collateral. This agreement must be in writing (and signed by the debtor), with one exception: where tangible collateral—e.g., jewelry, cattle, or furniture—is put in the possession of the secured party. Such delivery of possession is called a *pledge*.

2. The secured party must give *value*. In most cases, value is any consideration that supports a simple contract—e.g., the delivery of goods or the transfer of money to the debtor. Under Sec. 1-201(44), value also includes any security for preexisting obligations, and any binding commitment to extend credit in the future.

3. The debtor must have *rights* (any current or future legal interest) in the collateral.

The following case illustrates the importance of these three criteria insofar as the creation of a security interest is concerned.

M. Rutkin Electric Supply Co. Inc. v. Burdette Electric, Inc.

Superior Court of New Jersey (Chancery Division), 237 A.2d 500 (1967)

Defendant Burdette Electric, Inc., was adjudicated an insolvent corporation on June 26, 1964, and a receiver was appointed.

Among the accounts receivable held by Burdette was one owed by B. J. Builders, Inc. This account receivable was allegedly assigned by Burdette to Milton Rabin, the assignment being made because of certain advances of money Rabin had made to Burdette prior to the bankruptcy proceedings. *In this action Rabin now claims an enforceable security interest in the account receivable.*

A *financing statement* signed by Burdette and Rabin was filed with the secretary of state on March 6, 1964. At the trial, Rabin was instructed to produce a *security agreement* in support of this transaction. He failed to do so, and the lower court necessarily concluded that no written security agreement was ever executed by Burdette. Accordingly, it dismissed Rabin's action.

To determine whether the assignment was effective, the appellate court had to deal with the issue of whether there was creation of a security interest that could be assigned.

Mintz, Justice: . . . The debtor, Burdette Electric, had rights in the collateral, and Rabin, the alleged secured party, advanced value. But, as noted earlier, Rabin has failed to produce a written security agreement to document his acquisition of a security interest in the B. J. Builders account receivable. Thus Rabin's claim fails unless he can prove the existence of some form of enforceable "agreement" which provides that his security interest in the account receivable be created. . . .

New Jersey Study Comment, Note 2, to UCC § 9-204 indicates that in order to ascertain whether an "agreement" to attach a security interest has legal sufficiency, . . . Chapter 9's statute of frauds must also be considered. The Study Comment reads:

> The requirement that there must be an agreement must be read *not only* in connection with § 1-201(3), but also in connection with § 9-203 which requires that the security agreement be written (see, Comments, § 9-203) unless the collateral is in the possession of the secured party. So much of § 9-204(1) as requires an "agreement" expressing an intent that a security interest be created makes no change in New Jersey law. . . .

Accordingly, in order for an "agreement" to arise, signifying the creation of an enforceable security interest, *either the collateral must be in the possession of the secured party or the debtor must have signed a security agreement which contains a description of the collateral.* [Emphasis added.] An account receivable is an intangible and as such cannot be "possessed" within the meaning of the Code.

Hence, "possession" is unavailable to Rabin as a means of signifying an agreement with the insolvent that the security interest attach. A security interest in an account receivable must be evidenced by a security agreement signed by the debtor and containing a description of the collateral. . . . In the instant situation, since Rabin can proffer no writing signed by the debtor giving, even sketchily, the terms of the security agreement, it is unenforceable. The financing statement signed by the parties and duly filed with the Secretary of State is no substitute for a security agreement. It alone did not create a security interest. It was but notice that one was claimed. . . .

Hence, the alleged assignee Rabin has no enforceable security interest in the account receivable in question and the same is vested in the receiver. Rabin's claim that he holds a security interest through an assignment is unsubstantial and only colorable [having the mere appearance of reality] at best. Accordingly, it is the subject of summary disposition in this proceeding [as the trial court concluded].

Perfection of the Security Interest

Under Sec. 9-201, the security agreement binds the debtor and secured party the moment that it is made, without the taking of any additional steps. In general, however, the agreement does not protect the creditor against the rights of third parties until the agreement is *perfected.* Because the creditor's usual purpose in using a security agreement in the first place is to protect him or her against such parties—such as the debtor's other secured creditors, general creditors and purchasers of the collateral—the rules in regard to perfection take on particular importance.

The secured party perfects his or her interest in one of three ways, depending on the type of collateral that is involved. In many situations the secured party has a choice of means of perfection, while in others there is only one method that can be used. The three methods of perfection follow:

1. As a general rule, perfection requires the creditor to file a *financing statement* at a specified filing location. This is by far the most commonly used method, and will be further discussed below.

2. Occasionally, an interest can be perfected by *mere attachment*—that is, automatically—when the security interest is created. In general, this occurs only when a buyer of consumer goods purchases them on credit, in which case the seller has a "purchase-money security interest." Sec. 9-302(1)(d) provides that the unpaid seller here needs not file a financing statement or take possession of the goods to be protected. (However, two basic exceptions to the consumer goods rule are security interests in fixtures and in motor vehicles.)

3. A security interest may also be perfected by transfering possession of the collateral from the debtor to the secured party. (A good example of this is a pledge.)

Where a financing statement is utilized in the perfection, as is usually the case, the requirements of Sec. 9-402 must be met. That section initially provides that "A financing statement is sufficient if it gives the names of the debtor and the secured party, is signed by the debtor, gives an address of the secured party from which information concerning the security interest may be obtained, gives a mailing address of the debtor and contains a statement indicating the types, or describing the items, of collateral." (However, the section goes on to provide that additional information is needed for some types of collateral, so that a reading of the full section is necessary to determine the sufficiency of a financing statement in a given situation.)

Sec. 9-402 also provides that a separate document or a copy of the security agreement properly filed is itself sufficient as a financing statement if it meets certain requirements:

1. The document or agreement must be signed by the debtor.

2. It must contain the names and addresses of both the debtor and the secured party.

3. It must contain a description of the type or types of collateral. Under Sec. 9-402(1), when the collateral of the security interest is crops, timber to be cut, minerals, accounts under Sec. 9-103(5), or goods that are to become fixtures, additional requirements must be met.

Filing

As we have seen, the UCC stresses filing as the usual means of perfection—although the secured party may accomplish the same result by taking possession of the collateral, if it is of such a nature to easily permit this, and if the debtor agrees. However, if the collateral is classified as instruments or money, the secured party *must* take possession of it (and assuming, of course, a written security agreement).

In all cases where filing is utilized, the place for doing so depends on the classification of the collateral. (Thus, in a particular case, reference must be made to the types of classification set forth earlier, and a careful reading of Sec. 9-401.) The primary rules regarding the place of filing will now be summarized.

Where to File: Most states have two filing locations—a central one (usually with the secretary of state) and a local one (usually with the county clerk). The rule of thumb is that financing statements dealing with consumer goods or the business of farming should be filed locally; all the rest should be filed centrally. For local filing, the financing statement should be filed in the county of the debtor's residence. If the debtor is not a resident, proper filing is usually in the county where the goods are kept.

Determining that the debtor is a farmer, merchant, or consumer is not enough to classify the collateral. The determination depends on how the collateral is used by the debtor. For example, a refrigerator is a *consumer good* if it is sold to a householder, *inventory* if it is in the hands of a merchant selling appliances, *equipment* if it is used by a doctor for storing drugs in his or her office, and *farm equipment* if it is used to store eggs for resale.

Occasionally a good is used for more than one purpose. A bulldozer, for example, could be used by the owner in his farming operation and in his road-building business. Under these circumstances, the classification and filing are based on the primary use being made of the property. And under Sec. 9-401, once properly filed, a change in the use of the collateral does not impair the security interest of the secured party.

Additional filings are usually required when the collateral consists of crops, timber to be cut, minerals (including oil and gas), or fixtures. Frequently this filing must be locally in another filing system, such as the place where real estate records are filed. However, state statutes vary on this point.

How Good Is Perfection?

As has been mentioned, the primary purpose of a proper perfection is to give the secured party a superior claim in the collateral as against third parties. In this section we will discuss the effect of an unperfected security interest, and—especially—the extent and the limitations of a perfected interest.

The Unperfected Security Interest

Generally speaking, under Sec. 9-301, an *unperfected security interest* is of little value when challenged by third parties. For example: A lends B $500 and takes as security interest a prize bull belonging to B. A does not perfect the security interest by filing or by taking possession of the bull. Later, X Bank lends B $500, also taking a security interest on the bull. X Bank files its financing statement. Under Sec. 9-312(5), if B defaults, X Bank's perfected security interest will prevail over A's unperfected interest even though A's security interest was created first.

Under Secs. 9-301(3) and 9-307(3), there are other third parties (in addition to the one described above) who prevail over the unperfected secured party, among them:

1. A "lien creditor" (one who has acquired a lien on the property by attachment, levy, or the like, or who is able to attach the property of the debtor for creditors, or who is able to take the property as a trustee in bankruptcy) prevails even if he or she has knowledge of the security interest.

2. A buyer of goods, instruments, documents, and chattel paper from a person who does not deal in these types of collateral (referred to as a purchase "not in the ordinary course of business") prevails if the buyer gives value and takes delivery without knowledge of the security interest.

3. A buyer of farm products who buys from a person dealing in these products prevails, providing the buyer gives value and takes delivery without knowledge of the security interest.

4. A transferee of accounts or general intangibles prevails if he or she gives value and takes delivery without knowledge of the security interest.

Perfection and the Floating Lien Concept

Except in one instance, the UCC accepts and perpetuates the "floating lien" concept. It does this in Sec. 9-204 by permitting the security agreement (and, where appropriate, the perfected financing statement) to provide that all obligations covered by the security agreement are also secured by after-acquired collateral, future advances, proceeds, and goods with which the collateral has been commingled. This can have an important effect on the priority of the secured party's security interest in the collateral, since after-acquired property and future advances date from the time of the original perfection under Sec. 9-312(7).

A simple illustration will demonstrate the floating lien concept: A, the secured party, extends credit to X, the debtor, under a security agreement that covers "all the equipment in X's plant" and that contains an after-acquired property clause along with a clause applying this equipment as security for future advances. The security agreement is made on April 2, and A files a financing statement centrally on that date. X's profits have been good, and on June 1, X purchases a new piece of equipment for $50,000—in cash. On June 15, X decides to replenish his raw material inventory; he gets a loan from B, another secured party, for $25,000, putting up his new piece of equipment as security for it. On the same date, B files a financing statement centrally. On June 30, X needs some additional funds to meet the payroll and approaches A for a $25,000 loan. A knows of the new piece of equipment but does not know of B's security interest. A lends X the $25,000. On August 1, X's business is hit by a recession and X is in default to both A and B. Which secured party, A or B, has priority security interest in the new piece of machinery? The answer is A, for two reasons:

1. The after-acquired property clause included the new piece of equipment as security for the original loan on April 2; thus it can be acquired by A for satisfaction of that debt.

2. Although B's security interest in the new piece of equipment was perfected prior to A's future advance on June 30, the security agreement and perfection on April 2 included future advances, and the June 30 advance *dates back to the April 2 perfection,* thus giving A priority.

The secured party's right to proceeds is extremely important when the debtor sells the collateral to a third party under circumstances in which the secured party loses his or her interest in the collateral. In such a case, any payments made by the third party to the debtor—which are called *proceeds*—can be claimed by the secured party in satisfaction of the debt. Under Secs. 9-203 and 9-306, this right of the secured party is automatic unless the parties agree otherwise, and it is usually continuous until the debt is paid.

In certain business operations, goods under a perfected security interest are commingled with other goods and become part of the product or mass. What then happens to the security interest? Sec. 9-315(1) provides that the security interest *continues* in the product or mass if the goods lose their identity in processing or manufacturing or if the financing statement covering the original goods also covers the product into which the goods have been manufactured or processed. And under Sec. 9-315(2), in the same situation, if more than one security interest attaches to the product or mass, they all rank equally according to the cost ratio of their contribution to the total.

The rules relating to after-acquired property, future advances, commingled or processed goods, and proceeds make it possible for the lien to "float" also on a *shifting stock* of goods. And under Sec. 9-205, the lien can start with raw materials and pass to work in process, to finished inventory, to accounts receivable or chattel paper, and to any cash proceeds under one perfected security interest.

Perfected Collateral Moved to Another Jurisdiction

The UCC also stresses the floating lien concept in dealing with perfection of a security interest in collateral that is later moved across county or state lines. The basic section in this regard is Sec. 9-103, which is complicated by its length and by the fact that under some of its provisions state law is controlling. In general, however, the following statements are true:

1. Under Sec. 9-103(1)(b), whether a security interest is perfected when brought into a new jurisdiction depends on the law of the jurisdiction where the collateral was located when the last event occurred on which the assertion of the security interest is based.

2. Under Sec. 9-103(1)(c), in dealing with perfection of a purchase-money security interest, if the parties to the transaction at the time the security interest is created understand that the collateral will be kept in *another jurisdiction,* then the law in that jurisdiction governs the perfection for thirty days after the debtor receives possession—if the collateral is moved to that jurisdiction within the thirty-day period. Of course, if the collateral is not moved within that period, the secured party may lose the priority of perfection. Thus it is advisable for that party to file in both the jurisdiction where the security interest was created and the one to which it will eventually be moved.

3. Generally, under Secs. 9-103(1)(d) and 9-103(3)(e), collateral perfected in one jurisdiction and then moved into another remains perfected for the period of original perfection or for four months in the new jurisdiction, whichever expires first. The security interest continues to be perfected in the new jurisdiction after this time only if before expiration of the four-month period the secured party properly files in the new jurisdiction. (Only the secured party's signature is required for the new filing.) This is particularly important in dealing with collateral filed locally and then moved to a different county or state, such as farm equipment or mobile goods other than motor vehicles (which are governed by certificate of title laws).

To illustrate: B Bank has extended credit to a road-building construction firm, taking a security interest in the equipment of the firm. The bank files a financing statement in State X. The firm receives a big construction contract in State Y and moves its equipment there. B Bank's perfection is good in State Y for up to four months. After this time the bank will lose its priority to any other secured party who, in extending credit, takes a security interest in the same collateral and files properly during this period—unless B Bank files properly in State Y sometime during the four-month period. Knowledge of where the collateral is kept is thus important to a secured party.

How Long Is Perfection Effective?

Under Sec. 9-403(2), a filed financing statement is effective for five years from the date of filing. After this period, according to Sec. 9-403(3), the security interest generally becomes unperfected unless the secured party files a *continuation statement* within six months prior to the expiration date. This continuation, good for five more years, can again be continued, using the same procedure. Thus the secured party can continue the perfected interest indefinitely.

Limitations on Perfection as Protection In some instances, the perfection of a security interest does *not* protect a secured party as against certain third parties. The most important of these situations are illustrated below.

Buyers in the Ordinary Course of Business: Under Sec. 9-307, the UCC protects, as a class, buyers of goods, on the assumption that the average consumer who buys goods from a merchant should not be required to find out if there is an outstanding security interest on the merchant's inventory. Thus the code provides that a person who buys "in the ordinary course of business" from a merchant seller takes the goods free of any security interest to which they might be subject. *This is true even if the consumer knows of the existence of the interest at the time of purchase.* (The rule does not apply, however, to those who buy farm products from a person engaged in farming operations, for such goods are not considered inventory.)

To illustrate: M, a merchant in the appliance business, seeks a loan from B Bank, putting up his inventory of refrigerators, stoves, freezers, and other appliances as security for the loan. B Bank perfects its security interest by filing a financing statement centrally with the secretary of state. A week later, C, a consumer, purchases a freezer from M for cash. Since C has purchased in the ordinary course of the seller's business, *he takes the property free of B Bank's security interest.*

Buyers Not in the Ordinary Course of Business: A second class of buyer who receives protection in some circumstances as against a secured party is the buyer who does not buy in the ordinary course of business (sometimes referred to as the "next-door neighbor buyer"). Sec. 9-302(1)(4) provides that, in regard to a purchase-money security interest in consumer goods, perfected interest is automatically effective; that is, the creditor does not have to file or take possession of the collateral. However, under Sec. 9-307, the perfection is not good against a buyer who does not buy in the ordinary course of business if the following conditions are met:

1. The buyer must buy without knowledge of the security interest.

2. He or she must give value (as previously defined).

3. The purchase must be for the buyer's own personal, family, or household purposes.

4. The purchase must take place before the secured party files a financing statement.

To illustrate: M, a merchant in the appliance business, sells a freezer out of his inventory to C, a consumer, under a conditional sales contract, because C cannot pay the full purchase price. Since this is a purchase-money security interest in consumer goods, M makes no filing. C takes the freezer home but decides he does not like it and sells it to his friend, F, who purchases the freezer for his own use without knowledge of M's security interest. If C defaults, M will lose his security interest in the freezer and become a general creditor of C, since F has met the UCC requirements and therefore has an automatic perfected interest in the freezer.

Buyers of Chattel Paper: Another class of persons who receive some protection as against a secured party despite perfection of the party's security interest are purchasers of *chattel paper.* This protection is afforded by Sec. 9-308.

Chattel paper can be sold (assigned) by the creditor (the holder of the paper) in either of two ways:

1. It can be delivered by the creditor to the assignee, who then collects directly from the debtor. This arrangement is known as *notification* (or *direct collection*).

2. It can be sold to the assignee under an understanding that the secured creditor-seller will make collections from the debtor, with the secured creditor then remit-

ting the money to the assignee. In this kind of transaction, which is known as *nonnotification* (or *indirect collection*), the chattel paper may or may not be delivered to the assignee.

In either of the above cases, where perfection is made by filing only, if the paper is thereafter sold, a purchaser who gives *new value* and takes possession of the paper in the ordinary course of his or her business without knowledge that it is subject to a security interest usually *has priority over the secured creditor*—the seller of the paper. Additionally, what is said in Sec. 9-308 in regard to the purchasers of chattel paper is also generally applicable to purchasers of *instruments,* such as promissory notes and drafts. (Of course, the secured creditor will prevail against the purchaser if he or she retains possession of the paper.)

Priorities of Perfected Security Interests in the Same Collateral

In a variety of situations, two or more persons may claim interests in the same property. If this happens, there is obviously a conflict when the debtor defaults, and the claimants must consult their attorneys immediately in order to protect their interests. To help determine the general priorities, however, we will discuss some basic rules.

Under Secs. 9-312(5), (6), and (7), unless the collateral is under a purchase-money security interest or deals with a perfected security interest in crops, *conflicting security interests generally rank according to priority in time of filing or perfection, whichever is earlier.* To illustrate: A, a secured party, has a security agreement with X, a debtor, on X's inventory. A files a financing statement on March 1. On April 1, B, a third party, extends credit to X under a nonpurchase security agreement covering the same collateral as A's security interest. B also files a financing statement that same day. On May 1, A advances X additional credit on the same collateral, knowing at the time about B's security interest. On June 1, X defaults. Which security interest—A's or B's—will prevail, and to what extent? The answer is that A's will prevail, to the extent not only of the original security interest but also of the subsequent advance made on May 20, because he filed his security interest first. (This applies even though B's subsequent advance was made before A's subsequent advance and even though A knew of B's security interest at the time he made the May 20 advance.)

Since the time of perfection is so important in dealing with priority of claims, a brief outline of the moment perfection takes place is appropriate. As explained previously, there are three means of perfection—attachment, possession, and filing. The time of effectiveness of these means is explained below:

1. Where perfection is by attachment, it exists as soon as the secured party makes a security agreement and gives value and the debtor acquires an interest in the collateral.

2. Where perfection is by possession, it dates from the time possession is taken and continues as long as possession is retained.

3. Where perfection is by filing, it dates from the time of filing. Under Sec. 9-303, a secured party is allowed to file before the security interest attaches, but in such a case the security interest is perfected at the time of attachment rather than at the time of filing.

The *purchase-money security interest,* while normally invalid as to third parties, does have priority as against some conflicting claims, as indicated in the paragraph below. Such an interest is defined in Sec. 9-107 as an interest either taken or retained by the seller of the collateral to secure all or part of the purchase price, or one taken by a person who, through making advances or incurring an obligation, gives value to enable the debtor to acquire rights in or the use of collateral, if such value is in fact so used. To illustrate: B wants to purchase a washer from A but does not have sufficient cash to pay the purchase price. A sells the washer to B on credit, and when B makes a down payment, which gives A a purchase-money security interest in the washer for the balance. As another example: If X Bank had lent B the money to purchase the washer, taking a chattel mortgage on it, and if B had applied the funds to the purchase, then X Bank would have a purchase-money security interest.

Sec. 9-312(3) gives priority to a perfected purchase-money security interest *in inventory* over a conflicting security interest in the same inventory under limited conditions, designed primarily to be asserted as against after-acquired property clauses. As to purchase-money security interests in forms of collateral other than inventory, under Sec. 9-312(4), the purchase-money security interest takes priority over a conflicting security interest in the same collateral or its proceeds, provided that this interest is perfected when the debtor receives possession of the collateral or within ten days of receipt. Under Sec. 9-301(2), if the secured party files within this ten-day period or before, he or she takes priority over the transferee in bulk or the lien creditor whose interest arose between the time the security interest attached and the time of filing.

The following case illustrates not only certain previously discussed rules but also the priority of a purchase-money security interest in collateral other than inventory.

Kimbrell's Furniture Co., Inc. v. Friedman
Supreme Court of South Carolina, 198 S.E.2d 803 (1973)

This suit deals with two separate purchases made from the plaintiff, Kimbrell's Furniture Company—a new television set by Charlie O'Neal on July 11, 1972, and a tape player by his wife on July 15, 1972. Each purchase was on credit, and in each instance there was executed, as security, a conditional sale contract, designated a *purchase-money security agreement.* On the same day of each purchase, O'Neal took the item to defendant, Friedman, a pawnbroker doing business as Bonded Loan, and *pledged* it as security for a loan—the television for a loan of $30 and the tape player for a loan of $25.

Kimbrell's did not record any financing statement or notice of these security agreements.

Bonded Loan, which held possession of the television set and tape player as security for its loan, contended that its lien had priority over Kimbrell's unrecorded security interest. The lower court sustained this contention, and Kimbrell's appealed.

The question to be decided was the following: Is a conditional seller of consumer goods required to file a financing statement in order to perfect his or her security interest as against a pawnbroker who subsequently takes possession of such goods as security for a loan?

Lewis, Justice: ... Prior to the adoption of the Uniform Commercial Code (UCC), ... purchase money security interests, including conditional sales contracts for consumer goods, were required to be recorded in order to perfect such security interests against subsequent creditors, including pawnbrokers.

... However, insofar as it applied to the perfection of security interests in consumer goods, this rule has been repealed by the UCC and the provisions of the latter are controlling in the determination of the present question.

Goods are classified or defined for purposes of secured transactions under § 10.9-109. Subsection 1 defines "consumer goods" as those "used or bought for use primarily for personal, family or household purposes." The property here involved was a television set and tape player. They are normally used for personal, family or household purposes and the purchasers warranted that such was the intended use. It is undisputed in this case that the collateral involved was consumer goods within the meaning of the foregoing statutory definition.

Kimbrell clearly held a *purchase money security interest* in the consumer goods sold to the O'Neals and, by them, subsequently pledged to Bonded Loan. Section 10.9-107(a).

When filing is required to perfect a security interest, the UCC requires that a document designated as a financing statement (§ 10.9-402) must be filed. Section 10.9-302. Contrary to the prior provisions of § 60-101, supra, the UCC does not require filing in order to perfect a purchase money security interest in consumer goods. Pertinent here, § 10.9-302(1)(d) provides:

> "(1) A financing statement must be filed to perfect all security interests except the following: .... (d) a purchase money security interest in consumer goods; ...."

Since filing was not necessary, the security interest of Kimbrell attached and was perfected *when the debtors executed the purchase money security agreements and took possession of the property.* Sections 10.9-204, 10.9-303(1). [Emphasis added.] Therefore, Kimbrell's security interest has priority over the security interest of Bonded Loan by virtue of § 10.9-312(4), which provides:

> (4) A purchase money security interest in collateral other than inventory has priority over a conflicting security interest in the same collateral if the purchase money security interest is perfected at the time the debtor receives possession of the collateral or within ten days thereafter.

This result is consistent with and confirmed by the residual priority rule of 10.9-312(5)(b) providing for priority between conflicting security interests in the same collateral "... in the order of perfection unless both are perfected by filing...."

Bonded Loan, however, alleges that its interest takes priority over the security interest of Kimbrell by virtue of § 10.9-307(1), which is as follows:

(1) A buyer in ordinary course of business (subsection (9) of Section 10.1-201) other than a person buying farm products from a person engaged in farming operations takes free of a security interest created by his seller even though the security interest is perfected and even though a buyer knows of its existence.

The above section affords Bonded Loan no relief. It was not a buyer in the ordinary course of business so as to take free of the security interest of Kimbrell. A buyer in the ordinary course of business is defined in subsection (9) of § 10.1-201 as follows:

"Buyer in ordinary course of business" means a person who in good faith and without knowledge that the sale to him is in violation of the ownership rights or security interest of a third party in the goods buys in ordinary course from a person in the business of selling goods of that kind but does not include a pawnbroker.

In the Reporter's Comments to § 10.9-307(1), supra, Dean Robert W. Foster points out that, under the foregoing definition, a buyer in ordinary course of business "must be 'without knowledge that the sale to him is in violation of the ownership rights or security interest of a third party : . .' *and* the seller must be a 'person in the business of selling goods of that kind. . . .' Thus subsection (1) (of § 10.9-307) is limited to the *buyer out of inventory* who may know of the inventory financer's security interest but does not know that the sale to him is unauthorized." [Emphasis added.]

Therefore, Bonded Loan could not have been a buyer in the ordinary course of business when O'Neal pledged the property to it, because O'Neal was not "a person in the business of selling goods of that kind."

The judgment of the lower court is accordingly reversed and the cause remanded for entry of judgment in favor of plaintiff, Kimbrell's Furniture Company, Inc., in accordance with the views herein.

The security agreement determines most of the rights and duties of the debtor and secured party. However, other rights and duties are imposed by the UCC, some of which are applied in the absence of a security agreement.

Rights and Duties Prior to Termination

Release, Assignment, and Amendment

Under Sec. 9-406, the secured party of record can release all or part of any collateral described in the filed financing statement, thereby ending his or her security interest in the described collateral. Under Sec. 9-405, the secured party can also assign all or part of the security interest to an assignee, who, in order to become the secured party of record, must file either by a disclosure method provided for in the code (such as a notation on the front or back of the financing statement) or by a separate written statement of assignment.

If the debtor and secured party so agree, under Sec. 9-402, the financing statement can be amended (for example, to add new collateral to the security interest). But the filed amendment must be signed by both the debtor and the secured party. This amendment does not extend the time period of the perfection unless collateral is added; in such a case, the perfection for the new collateral applies from the date of filing the amendment.

The debtor's signature is needed for (1) the security agreement, (2) the original financing statement, and (3) amendments to the financing statements. All other documents can be filed with only the signature of the secured party.

Information Requests by Secured Parties

In most states the filing officer must furnish specified information on request to certain parties. For example, under Sec. 9-407(1), the person filing any of the above statements can furnish the filing officer with a duplicate and request that the officer note on such copy the file number, date, and hour of the original filing. The filing officer must send this copy to the person making the request, without charge.

Frequently, prospective secured parties request of the filing officer a certificate giving information on possible perfected financing statements with respect to a named debtor. Under Sec. 9-407(2), if so requested, the filing officer must furnish a copy of any filed financing statement or assignment. Given the priorities of secured interests and the attachment of security interest under the concept of the floating lien, business people ought to request such information before advancing credit to debtors.

Security Party in Possession of the Collateral

Sec. 9-207 provides that generally a secured party in possession of the collateral must use reasonable care in the custody and preservation of it and is subject to liability by the debtor for any failure to do so (although he or she does not lose the security interest thereby). The secured party can use or operate the collateral as permitted in the security agreement or to preserve its value. Should the collateral increase in value or profits be derived from it, the secured party can hold these increases as additional security unless they are in the form of money. Any increase in money must be either remitted to the debtor or applied to reduction of the secured obligation.

Under the same section, the secured party must keep the collateral identifiable (except that when the collateral is fungible, it can be commingled with like goods). He or she can repledge the collateral, but this must be done on terms that do not impair the debtor's right to redeem it upon paying the debt.

Again under the same section, unless the security agreement provides to the contrary, the debtor is responsible for all reasonable charges incurred in the custody, preservation, and operation of the collateral possessed by the secured party. These charges include insurance, taxes, storage, and the like.

Debtor's Right to Request Status of Debt

Under Sec. 9-208, the debtor can sign a statement indicating what he or she believes to be the aggregate amount of the unpaid indebtedness as of a specific date (and, under certain circumstances, including a list of collateral covered by the security agreement) with the request that the secured party approve or correct the statement. The secured party, unless he or she has a reasonable excuse, must comply with the request within two weeks of receipt or be liable for any loss caused to the debtor by such failure. Since the debtor could become a nuisance by making numerous and continuous requests to the secured party, he or she is entitled to make such a request without charge only once every six months. For each additional request made during this period, the secured party can require payment of a fee not exceeding $10.

In general, under Sec. 9-501, when the debtor is in default, the secured party can reduce his or her claim to judgment, foreclose, or otherwise enforce the security interest by any available judicial procedure. Under Sec. 9-503, unless otherwise agreed, the secured party also has the right to take possession of the collateral on default. This can be done without judicial process only if no breach of the peace occurs. Thus the creditor should not attempt to break into the debtor's home or take the collateral by force. If force is used, the debtor can file criminal charges against the secured party and can bring an action in tort for any damages he or she sustains. Sec. 9-503, the so-called "self-help" section on repossession, has come under attack in numerous cases where the debtor has contended that repossession without judicial process is a violation of the due process clauses of both the federal Constitution and the state constitutions (as discussed below).

Default of the Debtor

The following case deals with three issues:

1. Is Sec. 9-503 constitutional?

2. If repossession can be only by judicial process, does the replevin statute have to insure due process?

3. If the collateral is in the possession of a third party who himself or herself possesses a mechanic's lien, can the secured party pay off the lien holder to gain possession of the collateral?

Hunt, the plaintiff debtor, purchased a 1973 Lincoln Mark IV on April 24, 1973, from codefendant Heritage Lincoln Mercury, Inc., and financed the automobile through codefendant Marine Midland Bank-Central on a retail installment contract. Payment was to be made over a thirty-six month period beginning in June. Plaintiff made the June and July payments, but for a period of time she was in default for her August and September payments. On October 1, 1973, plaintiff made the August payment but did not pay the late charge and did not make the September payment.

On October 2, 1973, the bank learned that plaintiff had returned the car to the Heritage dealership in August for repairs and that Heritage still had possession, claiming a mechanic's lien on the car for nonpayment of the repair bill. The bank,

Hunt v. Marine Midland Bank-Central
Supreme Court, Onondoga County, 363 N.Y.S.2d 222 (1974)

determining that its security was in jeopardy, *paid off the lien and took possession of the car* pursuant to the terms of the security agreement and Sec. 9-503.

Although plaintiff did make the September payment, on October 4, she did not make any further payments during the month for her October obligation. Thus the bank, pursuant to the terms of the security agreement, sold the car in late October. From the proceeds of the sale it deducted costs and the balance due on the security agreement, including the repair charges by Heritage. A deficiency apparently existed, and plaintiff was asked to pay the balance. She refused and instead *sued the codefendants* on the alternate theories of conversion and violation of her constitutional right of due process, based on the manner of repossession.

Specifically, plaintiff contended that the self-help repossession procedures of Sec. 9-503 are unconstitutional, because they violate the due process clause of the federal Constitution and the state constitutions in that they do not require notice and an opportunity to be heard prior to taking the collateral in question. Marine Midland contended that under the terms of the installment contract it had the right to repossess the vehicle without judicial process as long as it was done peacefully. It further contended that under Sec. 9-503 it had the right to take possession in the event of default, especially where (as here) the security agreement provided for such procedure.

Aloi, Justice: ... Although plaintiff "owned" the goods which she had purchased under the installment sales contract, her title [as] vendee-debtor was encumbered [since] she had both title and possession of the goods *subject* to her contractual obligation to continue to make timely installment payments. Defendant, Marine Midland, as the vendor-creditor, also had an interest in the property in the form of a vendor's lien to secure the unpaid balance of the purchase price. This Court realizes that *both* the seller and buyer had current, real interests in the property. Resolution of the due process question must take account not only of the interests of the buyer of the property but those of the seller as well.

In striving for a constitutional accommodation of the respective rights and interests of both buyer and seller, this Court stands prepared to protect the buyer's possessory interest to use and enjoy her automobile and the seller's right in being timely paid in accordance with the contract or repossessing the goods for the purpose of foreclosing its lien and recovering the unpaid balance.

Plaintiff has asserted that the "self-help" remedy under Section 9-503 of the UCC is unconstitutional under the rationale of *Sniadach v. Family Finance Corp.,* 395 U.S. 337, and *Fuentes v. Shevin,* 407 U.S. 67. This Court acknowledges the distinction made by many commentators between "self-help repossession" when authorized by a private contract establishing a security interest, and replevin prior to a taking, even though both involve a "taking" of the debtor's property before any judicial determination of the validity of the taking.

In a recent case similar to the one at bar, the court held that "an agreement entered into in compliance with Section 9-503 of the Uniform Commercial Code must be held to be legal especially where the debtor has expressly authorized the 'self-help' provisions of the contract. Such an agreement cannot be held to be unconscionable when such terms are expressly authorized by statute." *Frost v. Mohawk National Bank,* 347 N.Y.S.2d 246 (1973). Plaintiff has contended that since Marine Midland accepted certain payments after the 7th of each month, it established a "course of conduct" which precluded it from demanding timely payment each month. This Court rejects this contention on the basis that a clear precedent for late payment was never clearly established nor did Marine Midland ever *intend* to waive its right to repossess despite accepting payment after the 7th of the month.

Heritage has asserted that under existing case and statutory law its lien was lawful and its transfer to marine Midland was a valid exercise of its rights and obligations pursuant to Section 184 of the Lien Law, which reads in part:

> A person keeping a garage, hangar or place for the storage, maintenance, keeping or repair of motor vehicles . . . and in connection therewith stores, maintains, keeps or repairs any motor vehicle . . . has a lien upon such motor vehicle . . . or the sum due for such . . . at any time it may be lawfully in his possession until such sum is paid.

Heritage therefore had a lawful lien on the automobile in question. Upon demand by Marine Midland of the automobile, because of the default in payment by the plaintiff, and upon the tender of a sum of money sufficient to satisfy the lien then in effect, Heritage had no choice but to transfer the automobile to a prior secured party who had the right to possession thereof. In *Kaufman v. Simons Motor Sales, Inc.,* 184 N.Y. 739 (1933), the court held that the assignee of a contract of sale has a right to take possession of the property upon the default of payment by the buyer.

Accordingly, it is the decision of this Court that defendants' motions for summary judgment dismissing plaintiff's complaint be granted in part and denied only as to the issues of plaintiff's alleged loss of personal property contained in the automobile and the determination of Heritage's counter claim for storage cost.[3]

Duty to Assemble Collateral

Under Sec. 9-503, if the security agreement so provides, the secured party can require the debtor to assemble the collateral upon default, and make it available at a location reasonably convenient to both. If it is impractical to move the collateral or it is too expensive to store, the secured party has the right to render the collateral unusable to the debtor and, following the proper procedure, to dispose of it on the debtor's premises.

Disposal of Collateral

Under Sec. 9-504(1), once the secured party obtains possession, he or she generally has the right to sell, lease, or otherwise dispose of the collateral in its then-existing condition or following any commercially reasonable preparation or process. Under 9-507(2), if the secured party sells the collateral, the sale must be handled in a "commercially reasonable manner." Although this is not expressly defined, the code does mention certain actions as being commercially reasonable. Sales made through such actions, or made otherwise and in good faith, are usually held to constitute compliance.

Under Sec. 9-504(3), the collateral can be disposed of at either a public or private

---

[3]Although most courts have upheld the constitutionality of Sec. 9-503 and its self-help provision, as here, at least one court has held to the contrary: *Watson v. Branch County Bank,* 380 F. Supp. 945 (1974).

sale if done in a commercially reasonable manner. Unless the collateral is perishable, threatens to decline quickly in value, or is of a type customarily sold in a recognized market, the secured party must give the debtor reasonable notice of the time and place of the sale (unless the debtor, after default, signed a statement renouncing or modifying this right to notification.) No additional notification need be sent in the case of consumer goods, but in other cases notice must also be sent to any other secured creditor from whom the secured party has received written notice of a claim of an interest in the collateral. (Failure of the secured party to give such notice makes him or her liable for any ensuing loss.) The secured party can buy at *any* public sale—and at a private sale if the collateral customarily is sold in a recognized market or is of a type that is the subject of a widely distributed standard price quotation. (Under Sec. 9-501(3)(b), these provisions cannot be waived or varied.)

Under Sec. 9-504(4), when collateral is disposed of by a secured party after default of the debtor, a purchaser for value receives all the debtor's rights in the collateral free from the security interest and subordinate interests and liens. This is true even if the secured party failed to comply with the requirements of disposal under the code or under judicial proceedings, so long as the purchaser bought in good faith, and, at a public sale, had no knowledge of such interests or rights.

Sec. 9-505 provides that, except where the defaulting debtor has paid 60 percent of an obligation involving consumer goods, the secured party, upon obtaining possession of the goods, can *retain the collateral* in satisfaction of the secured obligation. However, to do so, the secured party must send written notice of such intention to the debtor and (except in the case of consumer goods) to any other secured party from whom written notice of a claim of an interest in the collateral has been received before such notification is sent to the debtor. If no objection is received from such parties within twenty-one days after notice is sent, the secured party can retain the collateral. But if any timely objection is received, the collateral must be disposed of in compliance with Sec. 9-504.

Sec. 9-505(1) provides that in the case of consumer goods, where the debtor has paid 60 percent or more of the obligation prior to default, the secured party must *dispose of the collateral* as previously discussed (in Sec. 9-504) within ninety days after taking possession—unless the debtor has signed a statement renouncing all rights in the collateral. Under Sec. 9-507(1), should the secured party fail to do so within this period, the debtor can recover an amount "not less than the credit service charge plus 10 percent of the principal amount of the debt or the time price differential plus 10 percent of the cash price." It is thus obvious that the secured party may suffer a loss by waiting too long to dispose of the collateral in this situation.

Application of Proceeds

The proceeds of the sale are, under Sec. 9-504(1), applied first to the expenses incurred by the secured party in retaking, holding, and selling or leasing the collateral—including reasonable attorney's fees if the security agreement so provides. After these expenses are deducted, the remaining proceeds are applied to the indebtedness of the secured party. If any proceeds are then left, subordinate security interests, if any, are to be satisfied if the subordinate interest holders have made written demand for payment before the proceeds were distributed. (Of course, the secured party can demand that these holders give reasonable proof of their claims.) Thus, even if a business person's security interest is second in priority, it is still possible for that person to receive part of the proceeds in satisfaction of the claim by following the UCC procedure.

As a general rule, under Sec. 9-504(2), if any surplus is left after the expenses have been paid and the indebtedness and subordinate security interests have been satisfied, it goes to the debtor. Furthermore, under Sec. 9-501(3)(a), the duty to account to the debtor for this surplus cannot be waived or varied by agreement. Should the proceeds not cover the expenses and the indebtedness to the secured party, under Sec. 9-504(2), the debtor is liable for the deficiency unless otherwise agreed. If the collateral involves the sale of accounts or chattel paper, the rules regarding distribution of surplus and deficiency apply only if they are provided for in the security agreement.

Redemption of Collateral

Sec. 9-506 provides that the debtor (or any other subordinate secured party) can redeem the collateral at any time before the primary secured party has disposed of (or contracted to dispose of) it, unless he or she has waived the right of redemption in writing after the default. The redemption is accomplished by tendering payment of all obligations secured by the collateral as well as all reasonable costs incurred by the secured party. Under Sec. 9-501(3)(d), a sale of part of the collateral does not remove the right of redemption for any collateral left in the hands of the secured party, and this right can be waived only in the manner indicated here.

Termination

The ultimate goal of the parties is to have the debt paid and the security interest terminated, particularly where it has been perfected by a filing. To accomplish this, when the debt is paid, the secured party files a *termination statement* with the officers with whom the financing statement was filed.

Under Sec. 9-404, if the financing statement covers consumer goods, the secured party must file the termination statement within one month after the secured obligation is no longer outstanding; however, if the debtor demands the statement in writing, it must be filed within ten days after the obligation is no longer outstanding. Thus filing of a termination statement in the case of consumer goods is required even if no demand is made for it by the debtor. In all other cases the secured party must file or furnish the debtor with a termination statement within ten days after written demand is made by the debtor. If the secured party fails to file or furnish the statement to the debtor, he or she is liable to that person for $100 and for any loss caused to the debtor by such failure.

Questions and Problems

1. A, a furniture dealer, purchased a large number of sofas from W, a furniture wholesaler, signing a security agreement for the purchase price. A sold one of the sofas to B for $150, with B paying $100 down and signing a security agreement for the balance.

    a. How is an enforceable security interest created in this collateral?

    b. What is the classification of collateral as between A and W? Between A and B? Where would each security interest be properly perfected?

    c. Assuming W's interest is properly perfected, if A is in default to W, what rights does W have in the sofa purchased by B? Explain.

    d. Suppose B is in default. Discuss the rights of A as the secured party and B as the debtor.

2. S is a secured party, having signed a security agreement with D, the debtor. D is in default, and S has peacefully regained possession of the collateral. She wishes to keep the collateral as full satisfaction of the debt. Under what circumstances can she do so?

3. T borrowed money from P, putting up two of his milk cows as security for the loan and signing a security agreement to this effect. If the agreement is silent on the following matters, what are P's rights under the UCC? Discuss.

    a. P milks the cows daily. Is he allowed to milk them without T's consent? Assuming that he can, is he entitled to keep the milk? Explain.

    b. When one of the cows has a calf, T demands that P turn the calf over to him. Does P have to do so? Explain.

4. Referring to Question 3 above:

    a. Suppose that P wishes to mix these cows in with his own herd. Can he do so? Explain.

    b. If P incurs additional costs in keeping T's cows, can he charge these to T? Why or why not?

5. A secured party has the following problem: Four and a half years ago he properly created a security interest in the collateral of a debtor and filed a financing statement. The debtor is unable to fully repay the loan. The secured party feels that given more time the debtor will be able to pay the balance. However, another secured party whose filing came after his is in the same boat. The collateral is sufficient to satisfy the remaining balance of either loan but not both. What would you advise this secured party to do to protect his interest in the repayment of the loan?

6. Assume that a loan's collateral is a refrigerator. How would you as a secured party properly perfect your security interest in it under the following circumstances?

    a. You are a wholesaler and the refrigerator is part of a 250-appliance installment contract sale to a retailer.

    b. You are a retailer and sell the refrigerator, on an installment purchase plan, to a customer, for use in the customer's home.

    c. You are a retailer and sell the refrigerator, on an installment contract, to a farmer for use in storing eggs to be marketed.

7. You are a debtor who has a number of security agreements with a single secured party. You have put up numerous pieces of collateral as security for these loans, and you are no longer sure of the balance on any of them. You think some of the loans have been paid off, and you do not know which pieces of collateral are still subject to the remaining loans. You have called the secured party but have not received a satisfactory response. Is there anything you can legally do to get the information you want? Explain.

8. A customer purchased a dining room set on an installment contract, signing a security agreement and putting up the set as collateral. The secured party filed a financing statement properly. The debtor has now paid off the balance.

a. Is the secured party required to file a termination statement? Explain.

b. Suppose the collateral had been equipment. Would the secured party have been required to file a termination statement? Explain.

44   Bankruptcy

Overview of
Debtor-Creditor
Relations

The treatment of debtors has varied greatly over the years. During certain early periods, debtors were forced to become servants of their creditors, were thrown into prison, or even had body parts removed for failure to pay a debt. History finally demonstrated to both creditors and society that very little was accomplished by such methods. In seeking more humane solutions, the general problem has been how to balance the creditor's rights with the debtor's desire for relief from debts.

Numerous devices have been developed through the years for resolving debtor-creditor disputes. In this chapter we will deal primarily with one such procedure—bankruptcy under federal law. However, many of the other methods available under state common law principles, state statutes, and private agreements may actually be preferable to bankruptcy when it is possible to use them. Bankruptcy, therefore, is generally viewed as an avenue of last resort. Before we turn to a detailed examination of the federal bankruptcy law, we first will survey some of the alternatives.

Alternatives to Bankruptcy

Although time and space do not permit a detailed analysis of each method of debt resolution, the following methods are frequently used when a debtor cannot pay his or her obligation: (1) foreclosure on a real estate mortgage, (2) enforcement of a secured transaction (Article 9 of the UCC), (3) enforcement of an artisan's lien, (4) enforcement of a mechanic's lien, (5) writ of execution on a judgment, (6) garnishment, (7) attachment, (8) receivership, (9) cancelling a fraudulent conveyance, (10) composition of creditors, (11) assignment for benefit of creditors, and (12) creditors' committees.

Foreclosure on a Real Estate Mortgage: When a mortgagor (debtor) defaults under the terms of a mortgage agreement, the mortgagee (creditor) has the right to declare the entire mortgage debt due and enforce his or her rights through a remedy called *foreclosure*. In most states the mortgagee is required to sell the mortgaged real estate (even if it is the person's homestead) under the direction of the court, using the proceeds to pay the foreclosure costs and the balance of the debt. If any proceeds are left over, the surplus goes to the mortgagor. If the proceeds are insufficient to cover the costs of foreclosure and the remaining indebtedness, the mortgagor is liable to the mortgagee for the unpaid balance of the debt. However, before the actual foreclosure sale and for a certain period of time thereafter (set by state statute), the mortgagor can *redeem* the property by full payment of costs, indebtedness, and interest.

Enforcement of a Secured Transaction: As we saw in the last chapter, under Article 9 of the UCC, when a debtor defaults on the security agreement made with a secured party (the creditor), the collateral (personal property) that is the subject of the security agreement can be used to satisfy the debt. The secured party can retain possession of the collateral or take it from the debtor, either by court order or without court action if it can be accomplished peaceably. He or she can then either (1) *keep the collateral* in satisfaction of the debt by giving proper notice to the debtor of such intention (assuming the debtor does not object), or (2) *sell the collateral* through a "commercially reasonable" process. The secured party must always sell the collateral if proper objection is made by the debtor to the party keeping it or if the collateral is classified as "consumer goods" and the debtor has paid 60 percent or more of the debt.

   If the collateral is kept by the secured party, the debt is discharged. If the collateral is sold and the proceeds are insufficient to pay the debt and the costs of enforcing the security interest, the secured party is usually entitled to seek a deficiency judgment for the balance. The debtor can redeem the collateral at any time until its sale or disposal.

Enforcement of an Artisan's Lien: The *artisan's lien,* a possessory lien given to creditors who perform services on personal property or take care of goods entrusted to them, was developed at common law. If the debtor does not pay for the services, the creditor is permitted to obtain a judgment and/or foreclose and sell the property in satisfaction of the debt. Any proceeds remaining from the sale of the property after paying the debt and costs of sale must be returned to the debtor. In order to exercise this lien, the creditor must have retained possession of the property and must not have agreed to provide the services on credit. Many states have passed statutes governing the procedures to be followed in enforcing such a lien. If the creditor is a warehouseman, his claim arising from unpaid storage charges, the procedures he must follow are set forth in Article 7 of the Uniform Commercial Code.

Enforcement of a Mechanic's Lien: Certain other liens have been made available to creditors by state statutes. One of the most common is the *mechanic's lien*—a lien against real estate for labor, services, or material used in improving the realty. When the labor or materials are furnished, a debt is incurred. To make the real property itself security for the debt, the creditor must file a notice of lien in a manner provided by statute. To be effective, it usually must be filed within a specified period (usually 60 to 120 days) after the last materials or labor were furnished. If the notice is properly filed and the debt is not paid, the creditor can foreclose and sell the realty in satisfaction of the debt. (This is similar to a foreclosure of a real estate mortgage.)

Writ of Execution on a Judgment: Once a debt becomes overdue, a creditor can file suit for payment in a court of law and, if successful, be awarded a "judgment." If the judgment is not satisfied by the debtor, the creditor has the right to go back to court and obtain a *writ of execution.* The writ, issued by the clerk of the court, directs the sheriff or other officer to levy upon (seize) and sell any of the debtor's *nonexempt property* within the court's jurisdiction. The judgment is paid from the proceeds of the sale, and any balance is returned to the debtor. One limitation on the writ is that it can be levied only on nonexempt property. That is, exempt property, such as the debtor's homestead, cannot be taken to satisfy the judgment.

Garnishment: Another limitation of the writ of execution is that it usually cannot reach debts owed to the judgment debtor by third parties or the debtor's interests in personal property legally possessed by third parties. However, the law does permit the creditor (using the proper court procedure) to require these persons to turn over to the court or sheriff money owed or property belonging to the debtor. This method of satisfying a judgment is called *garnishment;* and the third party, called the *garnishee,* is legally bound by the court order. The most common types of "property" garnished are wages (usually limited to 25 percent of the debtor's weekly take-home pay) and bank accounts.

Attachment: The seizing of a debtor's property under a court order, known as *attachment,* is a statutory remedy and can be exercised only in strict accordance with the provisions of the particular state statutes. It is available to a creditor even *before* a judgment has been rendered, under some statutes. Statutory grounds for attachment prior to judgment are limited, usually including situations where the debtor is unavailable to be served with a summons or where there is a reasonable belief that the debtor may conceal or remove property from the jurisdiction of the court before the creditor can obtain a judgment.

To employ attachment as a remedy, the creditor must file with the court an affidavit attesting to the debtor's default and the legal reasons why attachment is sought. Additionally, the creditor must post a bond sufficient to cover at least the value of the debtor's property, the value of the loss of use of the goods suffered by the debtor (if any), and court costs in case the creditor loses the suit. The court then issues a *writ of attachment,* directing the sheriff or other officer to seize nonexempt property sufficient to satisfy the creditor's claim. If the creditor's suit against the debtor is successful, the property seized can then be sold to satisfy the judgment.

Receivership: Attachment may prove inadequate to protect creditors while they pursue their claims if the debtor's property requires care (such as crops, livestock, etc.). In such cases, on essentially the same grounds as for attachment, the court may appoint a "receiver" to care for and preserve the property pending the outcome of the lawsuit in which one or more creditors are seeking to collect unpaid debts. It is said that the debtor's property is placed "in receivership." The object of receivership is to prevent a debtor from "wasting" assets while being pursued by creditors. Receivership may also be the appropriate protective device where the debtor has a going business and where creditors can convince the court that it is being grossly mismanaged.

Cancelling a Fraudulent Conveyance: A debtor may transfer property to a third party by gift or contract under circumstances in which his or her creditors are defrauded. If such fraud can be established, any creditor can have the conveyance (transfer) set aside and the property made subject to his or her claim—even if the property is in the hands of a third party.

The fraud necessary to have a conveyance set aside can be either fraud in fact or fraud implied in law. *Fraud in fact* occurs when a debtor transfers property with the specific intent of defrauding his or her creditors. A creditor will usually encounter difficulty in having a conveyance voided on this ground, simply because of the inherent problems in proving fraudulent intent. The creditor's chances of proving this intent will, however, be somewhat greater if the transfer was to the debtor's spouse or other relative. In addition, it is often the case that the debtor actually had no such fraudulent intent, but the creditor is harmed nevertheless.

To assist the creditor, most states have enacted laws (such as the Uniform Fraudulent Conveyance Act) which create a *presumption* of fraud under certain circumstances. This means that, in some situations, the burden of proof shifts to the debtor. If the debtor fails to prove the absence of fraud, there is *fraud implied in law* and the transfer is voided. Generally speaking, these statutes create a presumption of fraud whenever a debtor transfers property without receiving "fair consideration" in return and the debtor has insufficient assets remaining to satisfy creditors.

Composition of Creditors: Sometimes a debtor and/or his or her creditors recognize early (before bankruptcy) that the debtor is in financial difficulty. Instead of pursuing remedies under bankruptcy, the debtor and creditors make a *contract* (agreement) to resolve the debts. The contract calls for the debtor's immediate payment of a sum less than that owed and for the creditor's immediate discharge of the debt. (This payment can be made from any of the debtor's assets, including exempt property.) Such contracts are held to be binding by the courts. The advantage of an immediate payment and minimum costs makes the composition attractive to creditors. Whether the composition agreement is binding on nonparticipating creditors depends on state law. At common law the agreement was not binding on these creditors.

Assignment for the Benefit of Creditors: Assignments for the benefit of creditors are possible under common law principles and, in some states, under statute. Under this device the debtor voluntarily transfers title to some or all assets to a "trustee" or "assignee" for the creditors' benefit. By such a transfer, the debtor irrevocably gives up any claim to or control over the property. The trustee or assignee liquidates (sells) the property and makes payment to the creditors on a pro rata basis.

Creditors can either accept or reject the partial payment. One accepting such a payment is in effect releasing the balance of his or her claim. In most states, creditors who do not participate in the assignment cannot reach the assets that have been so assigned. They do, however, have rights to any surplus remaining after participating creditors have been paid, any nonexempt property not assigned, and any nonexempt property acquired after the assignment. Nonparticipating creditors may also be able to force the debtor into bankruptcy.

Creditors' Committees: Sometimes creditors have reason to doubt the debtor's ability to manage his or her business affairs. Poor management often results in increased indebtedness and eventual failure of the debtor's business. In this situation, the debtor may agree to a payment plan satisfactory to the creditors. To be sure that the plan will not be altered, the debtor also agrees to submit his or her business and financial affairs to the control of a committee appointed by the creditors—called a *creditors' committee.* This committee will virtually control the debtor's business operations until the debts are paid.

History of Bankruptcy Statutes

Bankruptcy as a legal device was initially applied only to commercial business failures. The first Bankruptcy Act in England was adopted in 1542 and applied only to traders or merchants who were unable to pay their debts. It was not until 1861 that bankruptcy was extended to other types of debtors.

The founders of the United States were well acquainted with the problems of debtors. In drafting the U.S. Constitution they stated in Article I, Section 8, clause 4: "The Congress shall have the power . . . to establish . . . uniform laws on the subject of bankruptcies throughout the United States."

Despite the fact that some of the colonies were founded by debtors formerly imprisoned in England, U.S. bankruptcy laws had a shaky beginning. The first act was not passed until 1800, and it applied only to traders. This act was short-lived, being repealed three years later. The next act came in 1841, and although it extended beyond traders, it was repealed two years later. In 1867, Congress passed another bankruptcy act; this one was repealed in 1878. For the next twenty years Congress did not pass any bankruptcy acts, and various states took the opportunity to pass different types of insolvency laws. Finally, in 1898, Congress passed the Bankruptcy Act, which was substantially revised in 1938 and again in 1978.

Bankruptcy Proceedings Today

As we noted earlier, bankruptcy is a solution of last resort. Despite this fact, more cases are filed under the federal bankruptcy law than all other civil and criminal cases combined in the federal courts. The large number of cases is not, however, the only reason for the importance of modern bankruptcy law. Many people have their only direct exposure to our legal system in bankruptcy proceedings. In bankruptcy court debtors and creditors alike find final, if not totally satisfactory, conclusions to disputes that may have seemed endless. In bankruptcy court businesses of all sizes are liquidated or rehabilitated—often affecting the livelihoods of many employees, the security of suppliers and customers, and even the economies of local communities.

The overall objectives of the federal bankruptcy law are to treat creditors as fairly as possible under the circumstances and to give an honest but overextended debtor a fresh start. The most recent effort by Congress to achieve these objectives is the Bankruptcy Reform Act of 1978.[1] Prior to this new statute, the handling of bankruptcy cases was the responsibility of the Federal District Courts. In most cases, however, the judges of these courts delegated this responsibility to "referees," who were technically not federal judges but who performed the same functions. The 1978 Act recognizes the uniqueness of bankruptcy proceedings by creating a separate system of Federal Bankruptcy Courts. Each federal district within the United States contains such a court. (See Chapter 2 for an explanation of federal districts.) Bankruptcy judges are to be appointed by the President for fourteen-year terms.

The bankruptcy law provides for three different kinds of proceedings: (1) Liquidation; (2) Reorganization; and (3) Adjustment of the Debts of an Individual with Regular Income. Our discussion will focus primarily on the liquidation proceeding, often referred to as "straight bankruptcy," because it is the most common type.

---

[1] This Act became effective October 1, 1979.

We will, however, devote some attention to the other two types of proceedings at the end of this chapter. It should also be noted that the new bankruptcy law contains a special section dealing with the rehabilitation of bankrupt *municipalities,* which is beyond the scope of our discussion.

Liquidation Proceedings

Stated very generally, the object of a liquidation proceeding under Chapter 7 of the Bankruptcy Act is to sell the debtor's assets, pay off creditors insofar as it is possible to do so, and legally discharge the debtor from further responsibility.

Commencement of the Proceedings

A liquidation proceeding will be either a *voluntary case,* commenced by the debtor, or an *involuntary case,* commenced by creditors.

Voluntary Case: The filing of a voluntary case automatically subjects the debtor and its property to the jurisdiction and supervision of the Bankruptcy Court. Any debtor, whether an individual, a partnership, or a corporation, may file a petition for voluntary bankruptcy, with the following exceptions: (1) Banks; (2) Savings and loan associations; (3) Credit Unions; (4) Insurance companies; (5) Railroads; and (6) Governmental bodies. These exempted organizations are covered by special statutes and their liquidation is supervised by particular regulatory agencies.

A debtor does *not* have to be insolvent in order to file a petition for voluntary bankruptcy, but as a practical matter it is usually insolvency that prompts such a petition.[2] Under the new law, a husband and wife may file a joint case if both consent.

Involuntary Case: The types of organizations which are not permitted to file a voluntary liquidation case also cannot be subjected to an involuntary case. In addition to these exemptions, creditors also cannot file an involuntary case against *farmers*[3] or *nonprofit corporations.*

If the debtor has twelve or more creditors, at least three must join in filing the case. If there are fewer than twelve creditors, the involuntary case may be filed by one or more of them. Regardless of the number of creditors, those filing the petition must have noncontingent unsecured claims against the debtor totalling at least $5,000.

---

[2]Insolvency is defined in the federal bankruptcy law as the financial condition of a debtor whose debts exceed the fair market value of assets. The definition of insolvency under state law, as set forth in UCC Sec. 1-201(23), is broader. It states that a debtor is insolvent in the above situation *or* when the debtor "fails to pay his debts in the ordinary course of business or cannot pay his debts as they become due."

[3]Farmers are defined as persons (which includes individuals, partnerships, or corporations) who received more than eighty percent of their gross income during the preceding taxable year from farming operations owned and operated by them. "Farming operations" includes growing crops, dairy farming, and raising livestock or poultry.

The debtor and its property automatically become subject to the jurisdiction and supervision of the Bankruptcy Court if the involuntary petition is not challenged. However, if the debtor contests the creditors' petition, they must prove either (1) that the debtor has not been paying debts as they became due, or (2) that the debtor's property has been placed in a receivership or an assignment for the benefit of creditors within 120 days before the involuntary petition was filed. If the filing creditors prove either of the above, the debtor and its property are then under the supervision of the court. If no such proof is made, the petition is dismissed.

The Trustee

After the debtor becomes subject to the bankruptcy proceeding, the court must appoint an *interim trustee* to take over the debtor's property or business. Within a relatively short time thereafter, a *permanent trustee* will take over. This trustee is usually elected by the creditors, but if they do not do so, the interim trustee receives permanent status.

The trustee is an individual or corporation who, under the court's supervision, administers and represents the *debtor's estate*. (Which property is included within the debtor's estate will be discussed later.) The basic duties of the trustee are to: (1) Investigate the financial affairs of the debtor; (2) Collect assets and claims owned by the debtor; (3) Temporarily operate the debtor's business if necessary; (4) Reduce the debtor's assets to cash; (5) Receive and examine the claims of creditors, and challenge in Bankruptcy Court any claim which the trustee feels to be questionable; (6) Oppose the debtor's discharge from its obligations when the trustee feels there are legal reasons why the debtor should not be discharged; (7) Render a detailed accounting to the court of all assets received and the disposition made of them; and (8) Make a final report to the court when administration of the debtor's estate is completed. To fulfill these duties as representative of the debtor's estate, the trustee has the power to sue and be sued in that capacity and to employ accountants, attorneys, appraisers, auctioneers, and other professionals.

If they wish, unsecured creditors may elect a creditors' committee of three to eleven members for the purpose of consulting with the trustee. This committee may make recommendations to the trustee regarding the latter's duties and may submit questions to the court concerning administration of the debtor's estate.

Creditors' Meetings

Within a reasonable time after commencement of the case, the Bankruptcy Court must call a meeting of unsecured creditors. The debtor will have already supplied the court with a list of creditors, so that they may be notified of the meeting. The judge of the Bankruptcy Court is not permitted to attend a creditors' meeting.

At the first meeting, creditors will ordinarily elect the trustee. In order for such election to be possible, at least twenty percent of the total amount of unsecured claims which have been filed and allowed must be represented at the meeting. A trustee is elected by receiving the votes of creditors holding a majority, in amount, of unsecured claims represented at the meeting.

The other major item of business at the first creditors' meeting is an *examination of the debtor.* The debtor, under oath, will be questioned by the creditors and the trustee concerning: (1) the debtor's assets; and (2) matters relevant to whether the debtor will be entitled to a discharge.

If necessary, other creditors' meetings may be held. For instance, the trustee might resign or die and creditors would have to meet for the election of a successor trustee.

Duties of the Debtor

The bankruptcy law imposes the following duties on the debtor: (1) Within a reasonable time after commencement of the proceedings, file with the court a list of creditors, a schedule of assets and liabilities, and a statement of financial affairs; (2) Cooperate and respond truthfully during the examination conducted at the first creditors' meeting; (3) Surrender to the trustee all property to be included in the debtor's estate, as well as all documents, books, and records pertaining to this property; (4) Cooperate with the trustee in whatever way necessary to enable the trustee to perform his or her duties; and (5) Appear at the hearing conducted by the court concerning whether the debtor should be discharged.

A debtor who fails to fulfill any of these duties may be denied a discharge from liabilities.

The Debtor's Estate

Types of Property: The property owned by the debtor which becomes subject to the bankruptcy proceeding, ultimately to be sold by the trustee, is the *debtor's estate.* This includes all tangible and intangible property interests of any kind, unless specifically exempted. For example, the estate could consist of consumer goods, inventory, equipment, any of the various types of interests in real estate, patent rights, trademarks, copyrights, accounts receivable, and various contract rights.

After-Acquired Property: In addition to property owned at the time the bankruptcy petition (either voluntary or involuntary) was filed, the debtor's estate also includes after-acquired property under some circumstances. Specifically, the estate includes any type of property which the debtor acquires, or becomes entitled to acquire, within 180 days after the petition filing date (1) by inheritance, (2) as a beneficiary of a life insurance policy, or (3) as a result of a divorce decree or a property settlement agreement with the debtor's spouse. And, of course, if a particular item of property is part of the estate, any proceeds, income, production, or offspring from it will also be part of the estate. However, the debtor's earnings from his own labor or personal service after the filing date are *not* included in the estate.

Exemptions: A debtor who is an individual (rather than a partnership or corporation) may claim certain *exemptions*. This means that certain types of property are *exempt* and are not included in the debtor's estate. The debtor may keep such property and still receive a discharge from liabilities at the close of the proceedings. Every state has exemption statutes setting forth the types of property which are exempt from seizure under a writ of execution. Before passage of the new bankruptcy law, the debtor's exempt property in a federal bankruptcy case was determined solely by the exemption statutes of the state where he or she lived. The Bankruptcy Reform Act of 1978, however, includes for the first time a list of federal exemptions which are available to the debtor in bankruptcy regardless of the state of domicile.

Under the new bankruptcy law, the debtor may claim the following exemptions (and *each* spouse may claim them in a joint case): (1) The debtor's interest in a homestead used as a residence, up to a value of $7,500; (2) The debtor's interest in a motor vehicle, up to $1,200; (3) The debtor's interest, up to $200 *per item,* in household furnishings, appliances, wearing apparel, animals, crops, or musical instruments, which are owned primarily for personal, family, or household (*i.e.,* nonbusiness) uses; (4) The debtor's interest in jewelry, up to a total of $500, which is owned primarily for personal, family, or household uses; (5) The debtor's interest in any kind of property, up to a limit of $400 plus any unused portion of the $7,500 homestead exemption; (6) The debtor's interest in implements, tools, or professional books used in his or her trade; (7) Any unmatured life insurance policies owned by the debtor (except for credit life policies); (8) Professionally prescribed health aids; (9) The debtor's right to receive various government benefits, such as unemployment compensation, social security, veteran's benefits, etc.; and (10) The debtor's right to receive various private benefits, such as alimony, child support, pension payments, etc., to the extent reasonably necessary for support of the debtor or the debtor's dependents.

It is quite likely that the new law will achieve very little in the way of making debtors' exemptions more uniform in bankruptcy cases throughout the country. The reason is that this law also includes a provision permitting the debtor to choose either the federal exemptions or those of the state where the debtor lives.[4] Since some state exemption laws are more liberal than the federal, especially those placing no dollar limit on the homestead exemption, disparate state exemption laws will continue to be important in federal bankruptcy cases. This is made even more true by the fact that, for some reason, Congress also stated in the new law that any state legislature can prohibit debtors in that state from using the federal exemptions in a bankruptcy case.

Even though bankruptcy proceedings are governed by federal law, the ownership interests of a bankrupt debtor in particular items of property ordinarily are determined by *state* law. On the other hand, as we will see in the following case,

---

[4]The debtor must choose one or the other, as a whole; there cannot be a selection of some exemptions from the federal law and some from a state law.

if a principle of state law conflicts with the overall purposes of the Bankruptcy Act, the state rule will not be applied.

Mickelson v. Detlefsen

U.S. District Court, D. Minnesota, 466 F. Supp. 161 (1979)

In 1966 Gustav Detlefsen executed a will which would establish a trust to provide his wife with income during her life. Upon her death the principal of the trust was to be distributed to Gustav's living descendants. Gustav died in Chicago in 1974 and his will was probated in Illinois. His wife, Elsa, received income from the trust until her death in December 1976.

At the time of Elsa's death, Guy Detlefsen was Gustav's and Elsa's only living child and, therefore, was entitled to the trust principal. However, Guy Detlefsen had become subject to federal bankruptcy proceedings in Minnesota about six weeks before his mother died. After her death, Guy filed in an Illinois court a disclaimer of any interest in his father's will. The effect of this disclaimer, which complied with Illinois law, would be to make Guy's children entitled to the trust principal. At the time, the principal was in the form of cash and securities and was being held by a securities dealer.

Mickelson, the trustee in Guy's bankruptcy case, sued Guy and the securities dealer, asking the court to rule that the trust principal was part of the bankrupt debtor's estate. The Bankruptcy Court held for the trustee, and Guy appealed to a U.S. District Court.

MacLaughlin, Judge: . . . The law of the states plays an integral role in bankruptcy proceedings. In the Bankruptcy Act, for example, Congress grants the bankrupt the exemptions permitted by state law. More relevant, state law helps define the property of the bankrupt. . . . But although state law thus plays an important definitional part in bankruptcy proceedings, it remains subordinate to the federal policies that inhere in the Bankruptcy Act. . . . A principal purpose of the Bankruptcy Act is to marshal the bankrupt's assets and distribute them ratably to creditors.

Bequeathed property must "vest in the bankrupt within six months after bankruptcy" [to be included in the bankrupt debtor's estate.] [Note: Under the new Bankruptcy Act, this period has been changed from six months to 180 days.] The bankrupt's interest in the trust proceeds was defined at the time of his mother's death, which was within two months of the date he filed for bankruptcy. Under Illinois law, however, because of the disclaimer, the interest never vested in the bankrupt. . . .

The bankrupt contends that disclaimers as authorized by state law mesh with the policies of the Bankruptcy Act. He argues that no proof exists that his creditors in extending credit relied on his expectancy in the trust. . . . The absence of reliance, however, does not inexorably align Illinois and federal law. The bankrupt argues that no federal policy is frustrated because the disclaimer prevents him as well as his creditors from receiving the trust proceeds. But the argument ignores the exercise of choice by the bankrupt as to the proper recipient of his windfall: whether the windfall of bequest should devolve to the bankrupt's creditors or the beneficiaries of his disclaimer. Congress . . . has asserted its prerogative and taken the choice from the bankrupt. If the windfall occurs within six months [180 days] of bankruptcy, it is within reach of the trustee. If the windfall occurs more than six months [180 days] after bankruptcy, it is beyond the trustee's reach.

To permit the bankrupt to exercise the choice made available by state law would render [a portion of the federal bankruptcy law] largely nugatory. The common law recognized the right of a testamentary beneficiary [*i.e.,* a beneficiary under a will] to disclaim his inheritance, and some statutes grant an heir [*i.e.,* when there is no will] an equivalent right. . . . Thus, the law in a number of states would permit individuals who have filed for bankruptcy to divert legacies from creditors to persons with whom the bankrupt is usually on more amiable terms. The supremacy clause [of the U.S. Constitution] requires that such laws yield to apparent congressional intent.

In the instant case, the bankrupt's interest in the trust proceeds became fixed and determined at the time of his mother's death. . . . The bankrupt's disclaimer of the interest is [void]. [The principal of the trust, therefore, is part of the debtor's estate subject to the claims of his creditors.]

Affirmed.

Voidable Transfers

In a number of circumstances, the trustee has the power to sue and restore to the debtor's estate property or funds which the debtor (or someone acting in the debtor's behalf) had transferred to some third party. These situations are as follows:

1. The trustee generally may cancel any transfer of property of the debtor's estate which was made *after* the debtor became subject to the bankruptcy proceeding. The trustee must exercise this power within two years after the transfer was made, or before the bankruptcy case is concluded, whichever occurs first.

2. The trustee may cancel any *fraudulent transfer* made by the debtor within one year prior to the filing of the bankruptcy petition. This power of the trustee applies to both *fraud in fact* and *fraud implied in law,* as discussed earlier in the chapter. It will be remembered that insolvency is an element of fraud implied in law. In determining the fair value of assets for this purpose under the bankruptcy law, exempt property and the property transferred in the particular transaction being challenged are not included.

3. The trustee has the power to cancel a property transfer on any grounds that the debtor could have used, such as fraud, mistake, duress, undue influence, incapacity, failure of consideration, etc.

Voidable Preferences

One of the fundamental objectives of the bankruptcy law is to assure equal treatment of most types of unsecured creditors. The primary reason why we are so concerned with equal treatment of creditors, of course, is that a bankrupt debtor's assets are usually sufficient to pay only a fraction of creditors' total claims. As a result of this concern, the trustee has the power to cancel any transfer by the debtor to a creditor which amounted to a "preference." A preference is essentially a transfer of property or money, in payment of an existing debt, which causes that creditor to receive more of the debtor's estate than he or she would be entitled to receive in the bankruptcy proceeding.

General Rules for Cancelling Preferences: In the ordinary situation, a preferential transfer to a creditor can be cancelled by the trustee, and the property or funds returned to the debtor's estate, if (1) it occurred within *ninety days* prior to the filing of the bankruptcy petition, and (2) the debtor was *insolvent* at the time of the transfer. In this situation, however, insolvency is *presumed.* In other words, if a creditor has received a preferential transfer within the ninety-day period prior to the filing of the bankruptcy petition, that creditor must prove that the debtor was *not* insolvent.

Insiders: If the creditor receiving the preference was an "insider," the trustee's power of cancellation extends to any such transfer made within *one year* before the bankruptcy petition was filed. In general, an insider is an individual or business firm which had a close relationship with the debtor at the time of the transfer. Examples would include a relative or partner of the debtor, a corporation of which the debtor was a director or officer, or a director or officer of a corporate debtor. In such a case, however, the presumption of insolvency only applies to the ninety days prior to the petition filing. Therefore, if the preference being challenged by the trustee had taken place more than ninety days but less than a year before the petition filing, the trustee must prove that the debtor was insolvent. Furthermore, a preference received by an insider more than ninety days before the filing date can be cancelled only if the trustee proves that the recipient had reasonable cause to know that the debtor was insolvent at the time.

Exceptions: In certain circumstances, a payment or transfer to a creditor cannot be cancelled even though it meets the basic requirements of a voidable preference. Two of the most important exceptions are:

1. A transaction which involved a "contemporaneous" (that is, within a very short period of time) exchange between debtor and creditor cannot be cancelled by the trustee. For example, the debtor may have bought goods from the creditor and either paid for them immediately or within a few days. This type of transaction is treated differently than one in which the debtor was paying off a debt which had existed for some time. Such a contemporaneous exchange will be left standing even though it occurred during the ninety-day period prior to the filing date.

2. Even though there is no contemporaneous exchange, a payment or transfer to a creditor within the ninety-day period will not be cancelled if (1) the particular debt had been incurred by the debtor in the ordinary course of business, (2) the payment was made within forty-five days after creation of the debt, (3) the payment was made in the ordinary course of the debtor's business, and (4) the payment was made according to ordinary business terms. An example would be the debtor's payment, during the ninety-day period, of the previous month's utility bill.

Voidable preferences can occur in an almost infinite variety of circumstances. The following case illustrates one such situation.

In 1972 Samuel Block agreed to purchase a piece of real estate from Joel Kline for $100,000. At Kline's request, Block deposited a check for this amount in an escrow account at City Title and Escrow Company, Inc. (City Title). The funds were to be released to Kline only after Block's attorney approved certain documents relating to the real estate transaction. Although this approval never occurred, Kline obtained the funds from the account shortly after their deposit. Kline and Richard Sugarman, president of City Title, had a rather questionable arrangement by which Kline was permitted, upon request, to withdraw funds deposited by third parties at City Title.

Block discovered what had transpired and demanded his money from City Title. When City Title refused, Block sued both Kline and City Title. On September 7, 1973, Kline sold other real estate he owned (called the "Indianhead property") and used the proceeds to pay City Title $100,000. On September 11, 1973, City Title paid this $100,000 to Block. In return, Block agreed to drop his lawsuit and release Kline and City Title. Kline, whose real estate and securities transactions had gained him a measure of notoriety in the Baltimore-Washington D.C. area, became subject to involuntary bankruptcy proceedings on October 9, 1973.

Eugene Feinblatt, the trustee in Kline's bankruptcy case, sued Block in a U.S. District Court to recover the $100,000. The trustee claimed that Block had received a voidable preference and that the funds should be restored to the debtor's estate. Since the payment to Block had been made only a month before Kline went into bankruptcy, everyone agreed that it had occurred within the time period for voidable preferences. (This period was four months under the old bankruptcy law, which applied in this case, but is ninety days under the new bankruptcy law. Of course, that change would make no difference in this case.) The parties also agreed that Block received more of his claim than he would have received in the bankruptcy proceeding, and that Kline was insolvent at the time of the payment. Therefore, the issues remaining for the court to decide were (1) whether Kline and Block had a debtor-creditor relationship prior to the payment, and (2) whether there had been a "transfer" of Kline's assets to Block.

Feinblatt v. Block
U.S. District Court, D. Maryland, 456 F. Supp. 776 (1978)

Blair, Judge: . . . [I have already found] that the source of the $100,000 check drawn on the City Title account and ultimately paid to Block consisted of the proceeds of the sale of the Indianhead property. At the time, the proceeds belonged solely to Kline. Thus, the transfer was of property belonging to the bankrupt, and therefore depleted the bankrupt's estate. The fact that the payment to Block was made not directly by Kline but through City Title does not save the transfer from being a preference. Further, a transfer can constitute a voidable preference regardless of whether the transferee knew that the property transferred was part of the bankrupt's estate.

Quite clearly, no contractual or other formal debtor-creditor relationship existed between Kline and Block. Block's funds, deposited in a City Title escrow account, were misappropriated by Kline. The defendant contends that this appropriation did not serve to make Kline his debtor. Rather, he maintains, it was City Title, not Kline, which had an obligation to repay him the $100,000 deposit.

Defendant, however, misconceives the applicable law. "[A] willing extension of credit is not necessary in order to create an antecedent [i.e., preexisting] debt under the preference provision of the [Bankruptcy] Act." *Engelkes v. Farmers Co-operative Co.*, 194 F.Supp. 319 (N.D.Iowa 1961). To the contrary, it is a "well settled rule that property converted, embezzled, or otherwise taken by the bankrupt, or obtained by him by fraud, can be claimed from the bankrupt estate only so long as it can be definitely traced, with the consequence that an attempted repayment by the bankrupt prior to bankruptcy is a preference, except where made from the very property taken." *Morris Plan Industrial Bank of New York v. Schorn,* 135 F.2d 538 (2d Cir. 1943).

It is undisputed that the $100,000 deposited with City Title belonged to Block. The court has found that Kline, while withdrawing other funds from City Title, specifically misappropriated the money deposited by Block. In such a case, although Block may have had a cause of action against City Title for allowing Kline to withdraw his money, he certainly had a claim against Kline as well for conversion. [Note: Conversion is the name of the tort which is committed when someone takes another's property.] Kline's misappropriation of Block's money made him Block's debtor at the time of the misappropriation. Because Block was repaid with funds other than those taken by Kline, the payment constituted a voidable preference. . . .

. . . Judgment will be entered in favor of the plaintiff trustee against the defendant [Block] in the amount of $100,000.

Claims

As a general rule, any legal obligation of the debtor gives rise to a claim against the debtor's estate in the bankruptcy proceeding. There are, however, several special situations we should mention.

1. If the claim is *contingent* on the happening or nonhappening of some future event or, if its *amount is in dispute,* the bankruptcy court has the power to make an estimate of the claim's value.

2. If the claim against the debtor is for breach of contract, it will include any damages which accrued prior to the filing of the bankruptcy petition and also those damages attributable to the debtor's failure to perform any future obligations under the contract. Of course, this is no different from an ordinary breach of contract claim when bankruptcy is not involved. However, under the bankruptcy law, if the claim arises out of an *employment contract* or a *real estate lease,* damages for the debtor's future nonperformance are limited to a term of *one year* from the filing date or the date the contract was repudiated, whichever is earlier.

3. A creditor who has received a voidable transfer or preference may not assert a claim of any kind until the wrongfully received property or funds are returned to the debtor's estate.

Subject to the above limitations, any claim filed with the bankruptcy court is allowed unless it is contested by an interested party, such as the trustee, debtor, or another creditor. If challenged, the court will rule on the claim's validity after pertinent evidence is presented at a hearing held for that purpose. In this regard, claims against the debtor's estate will be subject to any defenses that the debtor could have asserted had there been no bankruptcy. The fact that a claim is allowed, of course, does not mean that the particular creditor will be paid in full; it just means that the creditor has the hope of receiving *something.*

Distribution of Debtor's Estate

A secured creditor—that is, one having a security interest or lien in a specific item of property—can proceed directly against that property for satisfaction of his or her claim. This is true even though the debtor is or is about to become subject to a bankruptcy proceeding. In a sense, then, secured creditors have priority over all classes of unsecured creditors. However, if a portion of a secured creditor's claim is not secured, that portion is treated like any other unsecured claim.

When the trustee has gathered all the assets of the debtor's estate and reduced them to cash, these proceeds will be distributed to unsecured creditors. There are certain unsecured claims which are given priority in this distribution. These claims are paid in full *in the order of their priority,* assuming there are sufficient proceeds available. The following six classes of debts are listed in order of priority. Each class must be fully paid before the next is entitled to anything. If the available funds are insufficient to satisfy all creditors within a class, payment to creditors in that class is made in proportion to the amounts of their claims.

1. First to be paid are all costs and expenses involved in the administration of the bankruptcy proceeding, such as an auctioneer's commission, the trustee's fee, and accountants' and attorneys' fees.

2. If the proceeding is an *involuntary* one, the second priority is any expense incurred in the ordinary course of the debtor's business or financial affairs *after* commencement of the case but *before* appointment of the trustee.

3. Next is any claim for wages, salaries, or commissions earned by an individual within ninety days before the filing of the petition or the cessation of the debtor's business, whichever occurs first. This priority, however, is limited to $2,000 per individual.

4. The fourth priority is any claim for contributions to an employee benefit plan arising from services performed within 180 days before filing or business cessation. Again the limit is $2,000 per individual. However, a particular individual cannot receive more than $2,000 under the third and fourth priorities combined.

5. Next are claims of individuals, up to $900 per person, for deposits made on consumer goods or services that were not received.

6. Claims of governmental units for various kinds of taxes, subject to time limits that differ depending on the type of tax, are the last priority.

If all priority claims are paid and funds still remain, other unsecured creditors (called "general" creditors) are paid in proportion to the amounts of their claims. Any portion of a priority claim that was beyond the limits of the priority is treated as a general claim. An example would be the amount by which an individual's wage claim exceeded $2,000.

Discharge

After the debtor's estate has been liquidated and distributed to creditors, the bankruptcy court will conduct a hearing to determine whether the debtor should be discharged from liability for remaining obligations.

Grounds for Refusal of Discharge: Under certain circumstances the court will refuse to grant the debtor a discharge. These are as follows:

1. Only an *individual,* not a corporation or partnership, can receive a discharge.

2. A debtor will be denied a discharge if he or she had previously received such a discharge within *six years* before the present bankruptcy petition was filed.

3. The debtor will be denied a discharge if he or she has committed any of the following acts: (a) Intentionally concealed or transferred assets for the purpose of evading creditors, within one year before the filing of the petition or during the bankruptcy proceedings; (b) Concealed, destroyed, falsified, or failed to keep business or financial records unless there was reasonable justification for such action or failure; (c) Failed to adequately explain any loss of assets; (d) Refused to obey a lawful court order or to answer a material court-approved question in connection with the bankruptcy case; or (e) Made any fraudulent statement or claim in connection with the bankruptcy case.

4. If a discharge has been granted, the court may revoke it within one year if it is discovered that the debtor had not acted honestly in connection with the bankruptcy proceeding.

Nondischargeable Claims: Even if the debtor is granted a general discharge from obligations, there nevertheless are a few types of claims for which he or she will continue to be liable. These "nondischargeable" debts are as follows:

1. Obligations for payment of taxes are not discharged if (a) the particular tax was entitled to a priority in the distribution of the debtor's estate, but was not paid; or (b) a tax return had been required but was not properly filed; or (c) the debtor had willfully attempted to evade the particular tax.

2. Claims arising out of the debtor's fraud, embezzlement, or larceny are not discharged.

3. The debtor is not excused from liability for a willful and malicious tort.

4. Claims for alimony and child support are not discharged.

5. The debtor is not discharged from a claim that he or she failed to list in the bankruptcy case if this failure caused the creditor to not assert the claim in time for it to be allowed.

6. An obligation for a student loan is not discharged if it became due and payable less than five years prior to the filing of the petition.

As we have just seen, a bankrupt debtor is not discharged from liability for fraud. The following case illustrates the approach of the courts in determining whether a creditor had been defrauded in its transaction with the debtor.

In March 1976, Danny Wood and his wife Sharon used their charge account to purchase approximately $700 worth of merchandise from Sears. In late April of the same year Wood filed a bankruptcy petition and subsequently was discharged from his debts. Sears then sued Wood for the amount of the debt, claiming that the merchandise had been obtained by "false pretenses or false representations," and that the debt was therefore not discharged. Both the Bankruptcy Court and the U.S. District Court ruled in favor of Wood, and Sears appealed.

Wood v. Sears, Roebuck, & Co.
U.S. Court of Appeals, Fifth Circuit, 571 F.2d 284 (1978)

Goldberg, Ainsworth, and Hill, Judges: . . . Despite Sears' allegations that Wood made materially false statements to obtain credit, Wood merely purchased goods through the ordinary use of his Sears account without referring to his ability to pay. The absence of explicit representations concerning financial condition by the bankrupt requires a holding that there have been no false pretenses or false representations. . . . [T]here is no evidence that Wood did not intend to pay for the merchandise or that he fraudulently concealed his financial condition.

This record reveals a creditor who simply overextended his credit. Until the filing of the bankruptcy petition, Wood had never missed a payment on his bills. Although the bankrupt's debts exceeded his assets by three thousand dollars, Wood had been able to meet his debts as they came due. Even at the time of bankruptcy the amount of his monthly expenses exceeded his net monthly income by a bare twenty-five dollars. There was evidence that the bankrupt had received some financial assistance from his family enabling him to bridge the gap between income and expenses. A factor in his current inability to meet his bills was additional medical expenses for his family. Finally, Wood testified that he had not contemplated bankruptcy until mid-April. Indeed, at the time he was advised to consider bankruptcy, he was attempting to consolidate his payments through his credit union. There is no support for a finding that Wood behaved fraudulently or that he did not intend to pay for the merchandise at the time he purchased it in March. Because we conclude that Wood's conduct was not fraudulent, [his debt to Sears was discharged in bankruptcy.]

Affirmed.

Reaffirmation

Prior to the 1978 Bankruptcy Act, a debtor could renew his or her obligation on a debt that had been discharged in bankruptcy simply by expressing a willingness to be bound. This "reaffirmation" required no new consideration by the creditor, but some states did require it to be in writing.

During the course of revising the bankruptcy law, Congress found that many of these reaffirmations were obtained by creditors through the use of coercion or deception. As a result, the new law places significant constraints on the making of a reaffirmation. Specifically, a reaffirmation is not valid unless (a) the bankruptcy court conducted a hearing at which the debtor was fully informed of the consequences of his or her action, and (b) the agreement to reaffirm was made *before* the debtor's discharge. In addition, the debtor can rescind the reaffirmation within thirty days after it was made.

**Business
Reorganization**

If it is felt that reorganization and continuance of a business is feasible and is preferable to liquidation, a petition for reorganization may be filed under Chapter 11 of the 1978 Bankruptcy Act. The reorganization procedure is intended for use by *businesses,* but it does not matter whether the owner of the business is an individual, partnership or corporation. A reorganization case can be either voluntary or involuntary, and the requirements for filing an involuntary case are the same as for a liquidation proceeding. In general, the types of debtors exempted from reorganization proceedings are the same as those exempted from liquidation proceedings. The major difference in coverage is that a railroad *can* be a debtor in a reorganization proceeding. The most important aspects of a reorganization case are summarized below.

1. After commencement of the case, the court must appoint a committee of unsecured creditors. If necessary, the court may appoint other creditors' committees to represent the special interests of particular types of creditors. A committee of shareholders may also be appointed to oversee the interests of that group, if the debtor is a corporation.

2. There may or may not be a trustee in a reorganization case. If not, the debtor remains in possession and control of the business. If a trustee is appointed, he or she will take over and will have basically the same duties and powers as in a liquidation case. Essentially, the court will appoint a trustee if requested by an interested party (such as a creditor) and if it appears that such an appointment would be in the best interests of all parties involved. Obviously a trustee will be appointed if the court feels there is a possibility of the debtor's business being mismanaged or assets being wasted or concealed.

3. The creditors' and shareholders' committees, and the trustee, if one was appointed, will investigate the business and financial affairs of the debtor. A *reorganization plan* will then be prepared and filed with the bankruptcy court. This plan must divide creditors' claims and shareholders' interests into classes according to their type. For instance, claims of employees, secured creditors, bondholders, real estate mortgage holders, and government units might be segregated into different classes. The plan must indicate how claims within each class are going to be handled and to what extent each class will receive less than full payment. Treatment of claims within each class must be equal.

4. The court will "confirm" (approve) the reorganization plan if (a) each class has approved the plan and (b) the court rules that the plan is "fair and equitable" to all classes. A plan is deemed to be accepted by a class of creditors if it received favorable votes from those representing at least two-thirds of the amount of claims and more than half of the number of creditors within that class. Acceptance by a class of shareholders requires an affirmative vote by those representing at least two-thirds of the shares in that class. If the parties are unable to produce an acceptable plan or if the plan subsequently does not work as expected, the court may either dismiss the case or convert it into a liquidation proceeding.

5. After the plan has been confirmed, the debtor is discharged from those claims

not provided for in the plan. However, the types of claims that are not discharged in a liquidation case are also not discharged in a reorganization case.

Chapter 13 of the 1978 Bankruptcy Act, entitled "Adjustment of Debts of an Individual with Regular Income," provides a method by which an individual can pay his or her debts from future income over an extended period of time. It is intended for use primarily by an individual whose primary income is from salary, wages, or commissions (that is, an employee). There is, however, nothing to prevent a self-employed individual, such as the owner of a business, from using this chapter of the bankruptcy law. But the debtor must be an individual; partnerships and corporations cannot file an adjustment case. The most important aspects of such a proceeding are summarized below.

Adjustment of Debts

1. There is no such thing as an involuntary adjustment case; only the debtor can file the petition. To be eligible to file an adjustment case, the debtor must have (a) "regular income," (b) less than $100,000 in noncontingent, undisputed debts which are *unsecured,* and (c) less than $350,000 in noncontingent, undisputed debts which are *secured.*

2. The Bankruptcy Court will always appoint a trustee in an adjustment case. The primary function of the trustee in this type of proceeding is to receive and distribute the debtor's income on a periodic basis.

3. The debtor prepares and files an *adjustment plan* with the court. Neither the trustee, creditors, or anyone else can file the plan. The essential functions of the plan are to designate the portion of the debtor's future income that will be turned over to the trustee for distribution to creditors, to describe how creditors are to be paid, and to indicate the period of time during which payment will be accomplished. If the plan segregates creditors into classes, each creditor within a class must be treated equally. As a general rule, the plan cannot extend the period for payment of debts more than three years. It can provide for less than full payment of many types of claims, but must call for full payment of the types of claims which are given priority in a liquidation case.

4. The court will confirm (approve) the plan if (a) the debtor proposed it in *good faith,* and (b) if all secured creditors have accepted it. It is not necessary for unsecured creditors to accept the plan; they are bound by it if the court confirms it, even if it modifies their claims. Furthermore, even if a secured creditor objects to the plan, the court may approve it if special provision is made to insure that the secured creditor is either fully paid or permitted to retain the lien or security interest protecting the claim.

5. At any time before or after confirmation of the plan, the debtor has the privilege of converting the adjustment proceeding to a liquidation case. The Bankruptcy Court may convert the adjustment proceeding to a liquidation case, or dismiss the case altogether, if the debtor fails to perform according to the plan. On the other

hand, if the debtor does perform, he or she will ordinarily be granted a discharge upon completion of the payments provided for in the plan. There is no discharge, however, from the types of claims that cannot be discharged in a liquidation case. A discharge may be revoked within one year if it is discovered that the discharge was obtained through fraud.

Questions and Problems

1. Monroe, owner of a stereo equipment dealership, was several months behind on his obligations to an office supply store, a janitorial service, an advertising agency, and an accountant. After being unable to work out settlements with Monroe, these creditors joined in filing a petition for involuntary bankruptcy. Their claims totalled $6,200, all of which were unsecured. Monroe contested the petition, claiming that he was merely having "cash flow problems" and that his business was actually solvent. He said that lately all his cash receipts had been required to pay his landlord and inventory suppliers. Audited financial statements showed Monroe's total liabilities to be $184,000 and the fair value of his assets $202,000. Can these creditors force Monroe into bankruptcy? Discuss.

2. Moore, a former law professor, filed a voluntary bankruptcy petition in June 1976. A few days later he filed a separate lawsuit against Slonim, president of the school at which Moore had been a faculty member. In this suit, Moore claimed that, as a result of Slonim's fraudulent misrepresentations, Moore had been induced to sign a contract deferring payment of certain back wages for a period of five years. Slonim sought to have the suit dismissed on the ground that only Moore's trustee in bankruptcy had authority to file such a lawsuit. *Moore v. Slonim,* 426 F. Supp. 524 (1977). Should Moore's suit have been dismissed? Explain.

3. Gay, an attorney, had performed legal services for Browy prior to Browy's bankruptcy. Because he had not been paid for these services, Gay exercised his legal right to keep those papers and records belonging to Browy which remained in Gay's possession. During Browy's bankruptcy proceeding, the trustee, Brannon, requested that the judge order Gay to turn over these records. These records contained information relevant to the trustee's investigation of Browy's financial affairs. Gay argued that, since he was merely asserting a lawful "retaining lien" which existed only if he retained possession, the trustee had no right to take the records from him. *Browy v. Brannon,* 527 F.2d 799 (1976). What resulted? Discuss.

4. Several affiliated companies, including Ron San Realty Co., Allvend Industries, Inc., and La Staiti Associates, Inc., were the subject of a single bankruptcy proceeding. Suval was employed by Allvend Industries as its bookkeeper. Although not officially employed by La Staiti, a subsidiary of Allvend, he performed most managerial functions at the subsidiary. In investigating the affairs of La Staiti, the Bankruptcy Court ordered Suval to appear at a hearing and be examined under oath. Suval claimed that he could not be required to testify for La Staiti since he had no formal relationship with that company. *In the Matter of Ron San Realty Co., Inc.,* 457 F. Supp. 994 (1978). Was Suval bound to perform the debtor's duties in the bankruptcy proceeding? Explain.

5. Which of the following items of property would *not* be part of a debtor's estate in a bankruptcy case? Explain. (a) A one-half interest in a patent on a machine the debtor had helped invent; (b) A fifty acre tract of ranch land, used by the debtor to pasture cattle; (c) An easement which permitted the debtor to drive his pickup and run his cattle over another person's land to get to the public road; (d) The debtor's residence in the city; (e) One

hundred head of cattle; (f) A diamond ring, as an inheritance from his father, which the debtor became entitled to receive thirty days after the petition filing date but which he actually received more than seven months later; (g) The debtor's salary earned within 180 days after the petition filing date; (h) Future payments under a veteran's pension, to which the debtor has a vested right; and (i) A claim by the debtor against a third party for breach of contract, whose claim could be worth anything from zero to $100,000.

6. In her bankruptcy case, Levin claimed a 1972 Volkswagen as exempt property under applicable Massachusetts law. The pertinent part of this statute provided an exemption for "an automobile necessary for personal transportation or to secure or maintain employment, not exceeding seven hundred dollars in value." The car had a fair market value of $1,000, subject to a $350 security interest, leaving Levin with an equity of $650. It was established that she needed the car for her job and for personal transportation. The trustee, Mauro, challenged the exemption. *Levin v. Mauro,* 425 F. Supp. 205 (1977). Was the automobile exempt? Discuss.

7. Ferris Enterprises, Inc. built and began operating a theater and restaurant on land leased from Atkinson for a twenty-five year term. Seven years later Ferris Enterprises had become insolvent and was approximately one year behind on rental payments to Atkinson. In accordance with the lease agreement and applicable state law, Atkinson terminated the lease and reclaimed the premises. One month after the termination, Ferris became subject to an involuntary bankruptcy proceeding. At this time, the value of the buildings and equipment which Ferris had added to the premises was at least $343,000. Ferris still owed $214,000 on the loan which had been taken out to construct the buildings and purchase the equipment. Thus, Ferris's interest was worth at least $129,000. By terminating the lease, Atkinson received this value, plus the right to income from the property. Atkinson lost about $6,000 in rent that Ferris had not paid, as well as the right to receive rental payments from Ferris for the remainder of the lease term. However, it was established that Atkinson could relet the premises to someone else for over twice the rental he was to get from Ferris. Ferris's trustee in bankruptcy sued to cancel the termination and reclaim the property for the unexpired portion of the lease, alleging that Atkinson had been the recipient of a fraudulent transfer. *In Re Ferris,* 415 F. Supp. 33 (1976). What was the result? Discuss.

8. Mr. and Mrs. Scanlon received a payment of $25,000 from Multipane, Inc., in settlement of the Scanlons' claim against Multipane for alleged securities law violations. Multipane was a subsidiary of Gluckin & Co. Two months after the payment, Gluckin & Co. went into bankruptcy. Gluckin's trustee, Mandel, sued the Scanlons, alleging that they had received a voidable preference. *Mandel v. Scanlon,* 426 F. Supp. 519 (1977). Was the trustee successful? Discuss.

9. During Martin's bankruptcy case, he sent his books and records to the trustee. When the trustee examined them, however, he discovered that check stubs covering a recent two-year period were missing. Martin claimed that he had sent the stubs and that they must have been lost in transit. He also asserted that the transactions covered by the missing check stubs could be documented by other records. The bankruptcy judge gave Martin no opportunity to prove these allegations, and denied his discharge on the basis of inadequate records. Martin appealed. *In the Matter of Martin,* 554 F.2d 55 (1977). What was the result on appeal? Discuss.

10. It is often said that the Bankruptcy Act aids the *honest* debtor. List and explain those provisions of the Act which indicate that this is true.

Part VIII

Introduction to Government Regulation

Government Regulation: An Overview 45

Today, for better or for worse, the major business activities that are carried on in this country are subject to an ever-increasing amount of federal and state regulation. This fact of life was mentioned in Chapter 6 (lawmaking by administrative agencies), because much of the regulation is, in fact, carried on by government boards and commissions.

In that chapter, however, our primary mission was to see how administrative agencies—whether regulatory or not—actually "make law." We did not attempt to cover the entire subject of government regulation itself. In these final chapters we will make several excursions into this highly complex area of law.

The subject of government regulation of business is so broad, far-reaching, and varied that a balanced treatment of it, in any degree of depth, would require a work of several volumes. Obviously, that cannot be undertaken here.

Instead, our goals will be more modest. In this chapter we will take a rather cursory look at the most important kinds of government regulation, identify the

Our Primary Goals

underlying factors that gave rise to such regulation, and characterize the two basic approaches to the study of the subject that are in vogue today. Then, in the following two chapters, we will focus on the so-called antitrust statutes, with particular attention to (1) the most common problems of interpretation that arise thereunder, and (2) consideration of the various factors—including questions of public policy—that affect the interpretive processes, as illustrated by selected "landmark" cases decided over the years by the U.S. Supreme Court.

The approach, then, is to be essentially environmental in nature, our primary purpose being a presentation of the *nature of the problems* that arise in this area of the law rather than a comprehensive examination of the statutes themselves.

A Historical Note

While this nation's founding fathers may not have been in complete agreement as to the structure and powers that the federal government ought to have, they did share several fundamental tenets. Chief among these, certainly, were the ideas that the right of private ownership of property should be fully protected, that the concept of free competition should be given the fullest possible recognition, and that government regulation of the individual should be kept to a minimum.

Accordingly, there were virtually no attempts by the federal government or the states to impose restrictions on business enterprises prior to the middle of the nineteenth century. The basic concept prevailing at that time (frequently referred to as the laissez-faire doctrine) was that free competition could best thrive—and the interests of the consumer best be served—by freeing economic enterprises from virtually all state direction and control.

In the early years of this country, the laissez-faire doctrine brought about generally satisfactory results. By about 1870, however, two factors caused both the federal and state governments to embark on a policy of limited regulation. The first of these was the recognition that the inherent nature of some industries "so affected the public interest" that the control of companies in such industries could not be left totally in the hands of private owners.[1] The banking, transportation and utility industries were prime examples of these.

Second, at about the same time, other companies engaged in more general types of commerce were taking advantage of the absence of regulation to engage in *non-competitive* practices that had serious consequences to their competitors and customers alike. For example, large firms—particularly those in the oil and sugar industries—increasingly entered price-fixing agreements and agreements not to compete with one another in specified areas. This second factor was the impetus for enactment of the federal antitrust laws over the next several decades, beginning with the Sherman Act in 1890.

---

[1]For simplicity, such companies will hereafter be referred to as the "regulated companies."

The area of government regulation of business has no precise boundaries. Many writers feel that the best approach for the beginning student is to present a broad overview of all types of regulation. Under this approach, a great deal of attention is given to the special problems of the regulated industries, with the antitrust laws being treated as just another segment of the "big picture." To others, the antitrust laws are the very heart of the subject.

Two Approaches to Regulation

In this chapter we will take the broader view, giving primary attention to the regulated industries, with only a cursory look at antitrust legislation. The last two chapters, by contrast, will deal with selected problems related to the antitrust laws alone. (Throughout, because of both time and space limitations, our major concern will be regulation at the federal, rather than state level.)

Railroads and Motor Carriers

The Regulated Industries

The railroad industry was the first industry subjected to specific regulatory statutes at both the state and federal levels—for two important reasons:

1. It had an obvious relationship to the public interest; literally thousands of business firms and millions of individuals relied upon the railroad companies' services in carrying on their daily activities.

2. The heavy financial investments that were inherently necessary to the construction and maintenance of railroad operations were such as to make it economically impossible for competing lines to be built in any but the most heavily populated areas. This condition (also true for the public utility industry) is what the economists refer to as a *natural monopoly*—a situation in which the expected revenues along given routes are sufficient to maintain profitable operation of one company but not two or more.

Some of the first railroads to be built took advantage of these conditions and began, soon after the Civil War, to fix shipping rates that many of their users felt were unreasonably high. Additionally, some lines engaged in rate discrimination that brought about widespread discontent. Early state laws, called "Granger laws" because the impetus for their enactment came from farm groups, were meant to eliminate these rate abuses; in general, however, they were ineffective.

Federal Legislation: In response to these problems and in recognition of the fact that unlimited regulation of the railroads simply could not, as a practical matter, be left to the states, Congress passed the Interstate Commerce Act in 1887. This statute expressly vested the primary control of interstate rail carriers in the federal government, required that the rates of such companies be "just and reasonable," and prohibited the charging of discriminatory rates. Additionally, it created the Interstate Commerce Commission for the purpose of enforcing the law's provisions.

Over the next few years, largely as the result of certain court decisions, various weaknesses in the law appeared. As a result of these inadequacies, Congress passed several more laws, beginning with the Elkins Act of 1903. This act expressly granted the commission power to fix maximum rates and gave the courts jurisdiction to set aside rates found to be in excess of those permitted. The Elkins Act was followed by the Hepburn Act in 1906, which broadened the authority of the Interstate Commerce Commission, allowing it to cover many railroad activities that had been outside its jurisdiction.

Rate-making: The general subject of rate-making is so complex as to preclude all but the most cursory mention in a text of this nature. Nonetheless, it is indisputable that one of the most vexing problems in the area of railroad regulation had to do with the factors upon which rate-fixing by the ICC could be lawfully based. The Valuation Act of 1913 prescribed certain standards by which the reasonableness of rates was to be judged, and the Transportation Act of 1920 provided, among other things, that rates were to give a "fair return on the fair value" of railroads' properties. Various difficulties in interpreting these laws, combined with the unusual economic conditions of the depression, resulted in the enactment of the Emergency Transportation Act of 1933. While this act provided more precise standards for the determination of rates, it too experienced difficulties in the courts.

These acts were followed by the Motor Carrier Act of 1935, which extended the jurisdiction of the Interstate Commerce Commission to motor carriers; the Transportation Act of 1940, which extended federal regulation to water carriers; and the Transportation Act of 1958. The latter provided, among other things, that the commission could not keep the rates of carriers in one industry artificially high for the purpose of "protecting the traffic of any other mode of transportation, giving due consideration to the objectives of the national transportation policy declared in this Act."

In general, these laws strengthened and clarified the authority of the ICC. Nonetheless, the interpretation of these laws by the commission—particularly the provisions quoted above—is often challenged in the courts today. Thus the precise effects of these acts are still being spelled out on a case-by-case basis.

Air Transportation

The regulation of air transport is essentially in the hands of two federal agencies. The Federal Aviation Administration (FAA), an agency within the U.S. Department of Transportation, is charged primarily with the safety aspects of air travel. Under its jurisdiction is the air control system, which regulates such matters as the establishment of the many airways (routes ten miles in width) across the country. It also has responsibility for the more than fifteen thousand traffic controllers at approximately three hundred airports.

The Civil Aeronautics Board (CAB) is the other independent agency possessing air regulatory powers. It controls the entry of airlines into the industry, approves airline schedules, sets subsidies, and regulates air fares. In the past, the CAB also was responsible for investigating air crashes in the U.S. In 1975, however, this responsibility was transferred to the National Transportation Safety Board (NTSB).

Public Utilities

The same general factors that gave rise to the regulation of railroads also existed in the area of public utilities. The economic considerations are much the same in the two industries, with public utility firms (such as light and power, natural gas, and telephone and telegraph companies) almost always existing as natural monopolies. The result is that particular companies in these fields are generally granted the exclusive right to operate in given areas. In return for this privilege the regulating government reserves the right to control rates and to prescribe the types of services that must be made available.

There is one major difference between the regulation of the two industries, however; whereas the transportation companies are essentially regulated by the federal government, the regulation of public utility companies is largely left in the hands of the states. Today all states have public utility or public service commissions with essentially similar regulatory authority over the various utility companies that operate within their jurisdictions.

The Electric Companies: State regulation of electric companies roughly parallels federal regulation of the railroads and other forms of transportation. That is, most of the work of the state commissions involves fixing rates and promulgating procedures designed to assure adequate availability of consumer services.

While the commissions of some states are strong, in the sense that they are well staffed by experts and exert impartial control, the commissions of other states frequently lack these qualities. In the latter states, the financial and political powers of the "regulated" companies are such that the protection afforded to consumers is often only nominal.

Other Utilities: In addition to regulating electric companies, most of the state commissions also have jurisdiction over gas and water companies, intrastate motor carriers, and telephone companies. The regulation of public utilities is not, however, entirely in the states' hands. The Federal Power Commission, for example, has regulatory authority—including rate-making powers—over the *interstate* transmission of natural gas and electricity; thus it is sometimes said that rate-fixing at the "wholesale" level is in the hands of the federal government, while at the consumer level it is left to the states. The Federal Power Commission also has jurisdiction of power company projects built on navigable rivers. Additionally, the Federal Communications Commission regulates interstate telephone and telegraph services, along with those of television and radio.

Banking

Banks are so inherently involved with the public interest that they have been subject to strict government regulation from the very beginning. In general, national banks are governed by the Comptroller of the Currency and the Federal Reserve System, while state banks are regulated by the banking department of the state governments. Additionally, all national banks are subject to the voluminous regulations of the Federal Deposit Insurance Corporation, as are the state banks that have elected to join that corporation.

Other Federal Regulations and Activities

Securities Exchange Act

In order to insure a degree of protection to the nation's investors, Congress passed the Securities Exchange Act of 1934, thereby creating the Securities and Exchange Commission. The act required organized stock exchanges, their dealers and brokers, and all securities listed on them to be registered with the commission and be subject to its rules and regulations. The commission has expressly outlawed certain manipulative practices by brokers, dealers, and firms whose securities are being sold—practices such as market pools and publication of false information about the financial position of such companies—and has severely limited other practices, such as short selling, that in the past had frequently been used for manipulative purposes.

Federal Trade Commission Act

In 1914 Congress passed the Federal Trade Commission Act for the purpose of creating the Federal Trade Commission and granting it the authority to enforce certain antitrust laws and to give some protection to the nation's consumers against "unfair methods of competition" by firms in interstate commerce. While this act is not an antitrust law, it is so closely related thereto that it will be considered separately in Chapter 47.

Trademark Laws

Trademarks used to be names or symbols that indicated the origin of particular goods. Beginning in 1888, Congress has enacted laws that permit the registration of trademarks and grant to their holders the exclusive right to their use.

The basic trademark statute today is the Trademark Act of 1946, commonly referred to as the Lanham Act. This statute permits the registration of any mark that has become "distinctive," regardless of whether it indicates the source or origin of particular goods. The act defines a trademark as "any word, name, symbol, or device, or any combination thereof adopted and used by a manufacturer or merchant to identify his goods and distinguish them from those manufactured or sold by others." Additionally, the law permits registration of "service marks"— distinctive marks adopted by firms in service businesses.

One of the most vexatious legal problems arising under the trademark laws has to do with the measure of protection that should be afforded the trademark owner and the extent to which that protection should depend on efforts of the owner to police the rights after acquiring them. The problem, essentially, is that once a mark is registered, if it is not adequately protected by the holder, it may become a generic term for the goods themselves rather than indicating the particular producer or distributor. The terms *cellophane, linoleum,* and *aspirin* were all registered trademarks at one time, but because of careless use (or their strong appeal to the public) they became accepted as the names of the goods themselves, and trademark rights were thereby lost.[2]

The Antitrust Laws

As noted earlier, certain statutes applicable to businesses were being enacted by Congress during the same period that control over the regulated industries was developing. Since these more general laws, which apply to virtually all businesses in interstate commerce, will be examined in some detail in the following chapters, only their basic import will be described here.

The Sherman Act

Passed in 1890, the Sherman Act was the first of the antitrust laws at the federal level. Prior to this time, a number of large firms were engaging in flagrant anticompetitive practices that had very serious consequences both to their smaller competitors and to the public at large. The increased use of the corporate form of organization, the concentration of industrial power in the hands of a few firms, and the development of markets on a national scale all provided a climate in which agreements to fix prices and to divide markets could be made with abandon.

While it is true that the common law outlawed monopolies, it proved to be completely inadequate in dealing with these practices. In the first place, the common-law principles usually prohibited only the end result—monopolies—rather than the *means* by which monopoly positions were attained. Secondly, even where monopolies did exist, action could be taken against them only when they were challenged by private parties in court. And thirdly, the common-law principles were only statewide in scope; thus the possibility of action by the federal government under such principles was virtually nil.

It was in this situation that Congress passed the Sherman Act. As we will see more fully in the next chapter, the act basically declared that contracts in restraint of trade in interstate commerce were illegal and, further, that whoever monopo-

---

[2]As one manifestation of this danger, the larger firms have people on their staffs whose sole duty, it seems, is to write letter to advertisers, newspapers, and writers who have used terms such as *Coca Cola* or *Kodak* in lower case form. Such letters politely point out that these terms are registered and should therefore always be capitalized in print.

lized (or attempted to monopolize) any part of such trade or commerce was guilty of a misdemeanor. Additionally, the act contained certain penalty provisions.[3]

Because the Sherman Act addressed only the twin evils of restraints of trade and monopolization, many other restrictive business practices remained perfectly lawful. For example, discriminatory pricing—the selling of goods to favored buyers at prices lower than those charged other buyers—did not, in and of itself, violate the act. For this reason Congress enacted the Clayton Act and the Robinson-Patman Act in subsequent years.

The Clayton Act

In 1914 Congress passed the Clayton Act to prohibit certain restrictive practices even if they did not result in the unreasonable restraint of trade, or in the creation of a monopoly. Since this act will be considered further in Chapter 47, suffice it to say that the statute generally forbade sellers of goods in interstate commerce "to discriminate in price between different purchasers of commodities" (with certain stated exceptions), prohibited the sale of products on condition that the buyer not handle the goods of a competitor, and generally forbade any corporation in interstate commerce to acquire the stock of a competitor.

The Robinson-Patman Act

The Robinson-Patman Act, a lengthy amendment to the Clayton Act, was enacted to prohibit certain practices used by sellers to escape the price discrimination provisions of the Clayton Act. Essentially, it further narrowed the situations in which price discrimination was permissible and forbade payment of commissions to brokers except where brokerage services were actually rendered. (This act will also be considered further in Chapter 47.)

The Problem of Interpretation

The precise meaning of a statute is never known until it is interpreted by the courts in settling actual controversies. Statutory interpretation of the antitrust laws is particularly difficult, because some of their provisions are deliberately imprecise and, even more importantly, because the fact-patterns presented by the cases are inherently complex. Be that as it may, in the remaining chapters certain representa-

---

[3]The use of the term *antitrust* to describe the Sherman Act and other related statutes grew out of the fact that many of the firms engaging in the noncompetitive practices described above used the "trust" device to attain their ends. Under this method, the owners of the controlling shares of stock in two or more competing corporations transferred title of these shares to a small number of specified individuals, called trustees. By virtue of such ownership, the trustees were able to control the policies of the affected companies with a single voice. In this sense, then, the Sherman Act is "antitrust." However, because the act prohibits monopolistic practices regardless of whether the trust device is used (and today it is used rarely), the term *antimonopoly* is a much more accurate label for this kind of legislation.

tive problems and cases that have arisen under the antitrust statutes will be examined, together with some of the policy considerations that have influenced the federal courts (especially the Supreme Court) in favoring one interpretation over another. Additionally, some other statutes, such as the Federal Trade Commission Act and the Miller-Tydings Amendment to the Sherman Act, will be given attention.

Exemptions from the Antitrust Laws

Three major types of organizations have full or partial statutory exemption from the antitrust laws: agricultural organizations, labor unions, and export associations. Additionally, companies in the regulated industries are subject to such extensive special regulation that the government has seldom seen fit to challenge the activities of these firms under the antitrust laws. However, such firms are not exempt from these laws; and recently, in special circumstances, successful antitrust actions have been brought against companies in the regulated industries. For example, in the case of *U.S. v. Philadelphia National Bank,* 374 U.S. 321 (1963), a proposed merger was found to be prohibited by Sec. 7 of the Clayton Act; and in *Otter Tail Power Company v. U.S.,* 410 U.S. 366 (1973), the utility was found to have monopolized its relevant market in violation of Sec. 2 of the Sherman Act.

Questions and Problems

1. Several problems during the laissez-faire era caused Congress to pass the Sherman Act. What kinds of problems were they?

2. What difficulties led Congress to pass the Interstate Commerce Act of 1887?

3. Is the Interstate Commerce Commission charged with the regulation of interstate commerce generally, or only with certain aspects of such commerce? Explain.

4. Companies that produce and transmit natural gas and electricity are subject to both state and federal regulation. As a rule of thumb, which of these companies' activities are governed by the state, and which by the federal government?

5. Some companies, because of their inherent nature, were regulated by the federal or state governments at a much earlier time than companies in more general types of commerce. Explain why this happened.

6. What factors are responsible for the fact that utility firms are characterized as "natural monopolies"?

7. What was a basic shortcoming in the Sherman Act that led to the passage of additional regulatory legislation by Congress?

8. Is it correct to say that companies in the regulated industries are exempt from operation of the antitrust laws? Why or why not?

The Sherman Act:
Selected Problems

The basic provisions of the Sherman Act are so short that they can be easily quoted almost in their entirety.

Section 1 reads as follows: "Every contract, combination in the form of trust or otherwise, or conspiracy, in restraint of trade or commerce among the several states, or with foreign nations is hereby declared to be illegal . . . ."

Section 2 provides: "Every person who shall monopolize, or attempt to monopolize, or combine or conspire with any other person or persons, to monopolize any part of the trade or commerce among the several states, or with foreign nations, shall be guilty of a misdemeanor . . . ."[1]

Because of their general nature these provisions have required a great deal of judicial interpretation in the complex cases that have arisen under them. In this

---

[1]The act contains six additional sections, some of which are procedural. The more important ones make the act's provisions applicable to commerce in any territory of the United States and in the District of Columbia, grant to the federal district courts jurisdiction of cases brought thereunder, and provide for the imposition of penalties against persons found guilty of violating its provisions. (Fines against corporations as high as $1 million are now authorized, and individuals are subject to fines up to $100,000 and/or three years imprisonment. Violations of this act are now felonies.)

chapter we will look at some of the most common problems presented by cases arising under Sections 1 and 2 of the Sherman Act. We will also discuss the somewhat narrower questions regarding the status of horizontal and vertical price-fixing agreements under these sections.

The cases appearing in this chapter are typical of those arising under the Sherman **General** Act. Before turning to their specific problems, however, we will make several **Observations** general observations about the act:

1. The language of Sections 1 and 2 is so general that it is obvious Congress meant to give the courts considerable latitude in interpreting the prohibitions that each contains. Thus it is left to the courts to decide whether a particular contract is "in restraint of trade" and what the criteria are for determining whether a company has "monopolized" part of the trade or commerce among the states.

2. While some specific types of conduct constitute violations of *both* Sections 1 and 2, these sections prohibit essentially *different kinds* of conduct. It is distinctly possible, for example, that two or more companies will enter into contracts which so restrain trade that they are guilty of violating Section 1—but not Section 2.

3. Since the federal antitrust laws are all based on the "commerce clause" of the Constitution, their provisions apply only to conduct that occurs in interstate commerce or in situations that "substantially affect" interstate commerce.

4. While many of the antitrust cases are criminal suits brought by the United States, civil actions are also possible. Section 4 of the Clayton Act provides that "any person who shall be injured in his business or property by reason of anything forbidden in the antitrust laws" can recover *treble damages* plus reasonable attorney fees. Thus enforcement of these laws is not entirely in the hands of the government. Additionally, an award of treble damages against a company found to have violated one of the acts can turn out to be a high penalty indeed.

Restraints of Trade

Selected Section 1 Problems

As noted earlier, Section 1 provides that contracts, combinations, and conspiracies in restraint of trade or commerce are illegal. Since each requires two or more parties, there will always be at least two defendants in any action. The plaintiff in such cases has the burden of proving that the defendants acted in concert—that is, as a result of some type of *agreement*—to bring about the restraint. If direct proof of agreement is weak or lacking, judgment will ordinarily be in favor of the defendants.

In some actions where direct proof is lacking, the plaintiff will fall back on the "doctrine of conscious parallelism." In such cases the plaintiff (usually the government) contends that evidence proving that the actions of each defendant closely parallelled those of the others should also be accepted as proof that such actions *resulted from prior agreement.* The usual view in this area is that parallel action in and of itself is not proof of agreement; however, proof of parallel action accompanied by almost any independent evidence tending to show agreement is usually enough to sustain a conviction.

The Rule of Reason

Section 1 provides that "every" contract and combination in restraint of trade is illegal. However, in the landmark case of *Standard Oil of New Jersey v. United States,* 221 U.S. 1 (1911), the U.S. Supreme Court ruled that it was the intent of Congress, in enacting Section 1, to prohibit only those contracts and combinations that *unreasonably* restrained trade.[2] Thus, beginning with this decision, the government not only had to prove that one or more restrictive agreements were entered into between the defendants but, additionally, that the agreements covered rather substantial quantities of goods or services. Thus if two small companies in the same industry entered into a restrictive contract (as for example, that neither would act in a particular way without the consent of the other), this agreement would not violate Section 1. On the other hand, the same agreement between two or major companies in the same industry *would* violate it.

"Per Se" Violations

Under the rule of reason, where the legality of a particular contract in restraint of trade is involved, an examination of the facts of the case is required to determine whether the effect of the restraint was actually unreasonable—that is, of such a magnitude as to adversely affect competition to a significant degree.

While this rule or test is still applied to some kinds of contracts in Section 1 cases, since the Standard Oil case the U.S. Supreme Court has taken the view in an increasing number of cases that certain kinds of restrictive contracts are so inherently anticompetitive that they restrain trade unreasonably *as a matter of law.* That is, they automatically violate Section 1, and there is no need to look at other facts to measure their impact or the scope of their use. Furthermore, in regard to such contracts, *no defenses* on the part of the defendant companies are accepted by the courts. Such contracts are called *per se violations* of Section 1.

Four major types of agreements or other joint actions in interstate commerce that are ordinarily held by the courts to constitute per se violations are (1) horizontal price fixing contracts, (2) vertical price fixing agreements, (3) horizontal market divisions, and (4) joint refusals to deal.

---

[2]In this case, the court found that the agreements in question clearly *did* restrain trade unreasonably, in view of the fact that they involved 34 of the nation's largest corporations in the oil and transportation industries. As a result of this violation of Section 1, the court ordered the Standard Oil of New Jersey holding company to be split up into a number of independent oil companies (such as Standard Oil of California, Standard Oil of Ohio, and Atlantic Richfield.)

Horizontal Price Fixing Contracts: A *horizontal price fixing contract* is one where competitors at the same level—such as two wholesalers—expressly or impliedly agree to charge the same prices for their competing products (or, perhaps, agree that their price changes will be made in parallel fashion). Since these agreements automatically remove the possibility of price competition between the two companies, they are inherently anticompetitive and thus a violation of Section 1 without resort to further facts.[2] Additionally, it is no defense to such an action that the prices actually fixed were reasonable—that is, no higher than those of their competitors—or that an insignificant amount of commerce was involved.

Vertical Price Fixing Contracts: As mentioned in Chapter 12, a *vertical price fixing agreement* (or resale price maintenance contract) is a contract in which a seller at one level—usually a manufacturer—sells goods to a buyer at a different level—usually a retailer—on condition that the buyer will, upon resale, not sell the goods below a certain price stated in the contract. Under U.S. Supreme Court decisions, such contracts today are per se violations of the Sherman Act. (Between 1937 and 1976 resale price maintenance contracts were lawful because another act of Congress, the Miller-Tydings Act, generally exempted them from the operation of the Sherman Act. This exemption ended in 1976, however, when Miller-Tydings was repealed.)

Presumably, the use of such contracts in interstate commerce since that date has been substantially abandoned, for such use would subject the seller to possible civil and criminal liability under that act.

Horizontal Market Divisions: When two competitors at the same level agree, expressly or impliedly, that one will not sell its products in a given geographical area and that the other, in return, will not sell its products in another area, a *market allocation contract* has been created. Because this type of agreement eliminates virtually all competition between the parties, it is considered essentially anticompetitive and therefore a per se violation of Section 1. The case of *U.S. v. Topco Associates, Inc.,* 405 U.S. 596 (1972) is one example of the strictness with which this view is applied. In that decision, the court held that such a contract violated Section 1 *as a matter of law* even though the defendant firms produced evidence tending to prove that their agreement actually *enhanced* competition, since it permitted them to compete more aggressively with other competitors.

Joint Refusals to Deal (Group Boycotts): As a general rule, any seller of goods or services has the right to select the customers with whom he or she will do business (subject to the qualification that a refusal to deal cannot be made on the basis of the customer's religious beliefs, color, or place of national origin). This principle is recognized under the antitrust laws, with the result that a refusal by a single manufacturer or a single wholesaler to sell goods to a potential buyer or

[2]Leading cases on this point are *U.S. v. Trenton Potteries,* 273 U.S. 392 (1927), and *U.S. v. Socony-Vacuum Oil Co.,* 310 U.S. 150 (1940).

group of buyers does not, in most circumstances, violate either the Sherman Act or the Clayton Act.

However, when two or more sellers *act in concert* in refusing to sell to a particular buyer or class of buyers, a much different situation is presented. Because the motive underlying the vast majority of such refusals is inherently anticompetitive in nature—i.e., the elimination of a competitor by the conspirators—such agreements are almost always found by the courts to violate one or more sections of either the Sherman or Clayton Acts.

The following case is described by the U.S. Supreme Court as a "classic example" of a group boycott.

United States v. General Motors Corp. et al.

U.S. Supreme Court, 384 U.S. 127 (1966)

In the 1950's, when automobile production was very high, twelve Chevrolet dealers in Southern California (referred to as the "participating dealers") frequently disposed of their excess inventory by selling new cars slightly above cost to "discounters" in the area. These discounters offered stiff competition to other local Chevrolet dealers, who complained to General Motors (and the Chevrolet Division) about the conduct of the participating dealers.

As a result, General Motors pressured all of its Southern California Chevrolet dealers and three dealers' associations to sign agreements promising never to sell cars to the discounters. Soon thereafter G.M. learned that several of the dealers had broken this agreement. When G.M. moved to punish these dealers for breach of contract, the dealers contended that all of the agreements violated Section 1 of the Sherman Act, and were thus illegal and unenforceable.

When the U.S. learned of the controversy it agreed with the dealers' position, and brought this action against G.M. and the dealers' associations asking that they be enjoined from enforcing the promises made by the dealers not to do business with the discounters. The trial court ruled that the agreements (the promises) did *not* violate the Sherman Act, on the ground that they were merely a valid implementation of the "location clause" that was contained in all of the dealers' basic franchise contracts with G.M. and dismissed the action. (The location clause essentially provided that a franchised dealer would not move to a new location, or establish a branch sales office at a new location, without approval of Chevrolet.) The government appealed to the U.S. Supreme Court.

Fortas, Justice: ... The appellee-defendants argue that ... [the trial court was correct in ruling that the participating dealers' arrangements with the discounters] constitute the establishment of additional sales outlets in violation of the location clause, and that the [conduct of General Motors in making all Chevrolet dealers promise not to deal with discounters was therefore lawful.]

[The court then conceded that the sale of the cars to discounters could be viewed as a breach of the location clause, in which case GM could proceed against any dealer violating the clause *if* the only agreements between GM and its dealers were the separate franchise agreements. In such a situation no antitrust violation would exist. But the court said that in this case the agreement between GM on the one hand and all of its Southern California dealers on the other was of a much different character. The court elaborated as follows]:

Here we have a classic conspiracy in restraint of trade [because of] *joint, collaborative action by dealers, dealers' associations, and General Motors to eliminate a class of competitors by terminating business dealings between them and a minority of Chevrolet dealers and to deprive franchised dealers of their freedom to deal through discounters if they so choose.* (Emphasis added.) Against this fact of unlawful combination [under the antitrust laws], the "location clause" is of no avail. . . .

Neither individual dealers nor the associations acted independently or separately. The dealers collaborated, through the associations and otherwise, among themselves and with General Motors, both to enlist the aid of General Motors and to enforce dealers' promises to forsake the discounters. The associations explicitly entered into a joint venture to assist General Motors in policing the dealers' promises, and their joint proffer of aid was accepted and utilized by General Motors. . . . What resulted was a fabric interwoven by many strands of joint action to eliminate the discounters from participation in the market, to inhibit the free choice of franchised dealers to select their own methods of trade . . . .

There can be no doubt that the effect of the combination or conspiracy here was to restrain trade and commerce within the meaning of the Sherman Act. *Elimination, by joint collaborative action, of discounters from access to the market is a per se violation of the act.* (Emphasis added.) . . .

Accordingly, we reverse [the judgment of the lower court] and remand the case to [it] in order that it may fashion appropriate equitable relief [in favor of the U.S. and those dealers wishing to continue to sell cars to the discounters.]

Vertical Customer and Territorial Limitations: Manufacturers often sell their products to wholesalers or retailers under contracts that prohibit such purchasers from reselling the products to certain classes of buyers, such as competing retailers, or to buyers whose businesses or residences are outside a designated geographical area. (The latter has been used especially when the wholesaler or retailer is an exclusive dealer—one who has been granted a certain territory within which the manufacturer/seller has promised not to install a competing dealer.) Restrictions of the first type are called *customer limitations* and those of the second type *territorial limitations*.

The U.S. Supreme Court once ruled that such provisions in sales contracts under which title passed directly to the purchaser (as distinguished from sales on consignment, where title was retained by the seller) violated Section 1 of the Sherman Act as a matter of law. *U.S. v. Arnold, Schwinn and Co.,* 388 U.S. 365 (1967). After the decision this restriction comprised a fifth type of *per se* violation. However, in a later case involving a closely-related issue, the Supreme Court expressly overruled that portion of *Schwinn* referred to above. *Continental T.V., Inc., et al. v. GTE Sylvania,* 433 U.S. 36, (1977). As a result of this case, which gives manufacturers substantially more control over how their products are to be distributed, customer and territorial limitation clauses are lawful—even when title passes to the buyer—unless it is shown, in a particular case, that their use actually restrains trade *unreasonably* under the circumstances.

Monopolization under Section 2

Having provided that it shall be unlawful to "monopolize" or to "attempt to monopolize" any part of trade or commerce, Congress left it up to the courts to interpret these terms on a case-by-case basis. As noted peripherally in the decision of the next case, *U.S. v. duPont,* the U.S. Supreme Court has adopted the general rule that a "monopolization" of commerce exists only when the evidence establishes that the defendant firm has reached such a size that it "has the power to control price" of the specified commodity or possesses the power "to exclude competitors from the market." (When either or both conditions are met, it is frequently said that the defendant possesses "overwhelming market power.")

Factors to Be Considered

To examine all the factors that the courts consider in determining whether or not monopoly power exists, it would be necessary to summarize the fact-patterns and decisions of the leading cases in this area of the law—an impossible task in a text of this sort. Nevertheless, we can say that the single most important factor is the *size of the market share* held by the defendant. Thus, if the market share of a manufacturer is shown to be only 20 or 30 percent of the total relevant market (as distinguished from, say, 75 percent), it is unlikely that additional facts would support a finding that the defendant-manufacturer possessed monopoly powers, and the action against it would probably fail. On the other hand, if the market share of a manufacturer approaches 75 percent or more of the relevant market, the courts are likely to rule that this fact alone would support a finding of monopoly power.

The great majority of cases, of course, present situations in which the market shares of the defendant companies fall within the extremes mentioned above. In these cases, then, the courts have to look to additional factors in order to determine whether or not the power to control prices or to exclude competitors really exists. These additional factors include the following: (1) the extent to which the defendant firm has achieved its size as a result of buying up competitors rather than through more natural growth, (2) the number of competitors in the relevant industry and their financial ability as compared to that of the defendant, (3) the extent to which the defendant has exerted unlawful pressures on competitors in gaining the market share that it presently enjoys, and (4) the extent to which the defendant has directly or indirectly prevented potential competitors from entering the market.

Determining the Relevant Market

In any action brought under Section 2 of the Sherman Act (and indeed in many actions brought under the other antitrust laws as well) one of the most critical questions likely to face the courts is that of determining the "relevant product market" within which the extent of the defendant company's production is to be measured. Obviously, a particular market has to be defined before one can go about the determination of market shares.

The landmark case brought against duPont, below, graphically illustrates this fact. Because duPont produced nearly 80 percent of the nation's cellophane, it probably would have possessed monopoly power if the relevant product market consisted of cellophane alone. On the other hand, if the relevant product market should properly be defined as consisting of all flexible wrapping materials, its market share would be much less significant.

The United States initiated this civil action against duPont in 1947, charging it with monopolizing, attempting to monopolize, and conspiring to monopolize interstate commerce in cellophane in violation of Section 2 of the Sherman Act. Relief by injunction was sought against the defendant company and its officers, forbidding "monopolizing or attempting to monopolize interstate trade in cellophane."

United States v. duPont de Nemours and Company
U.S. Supreme Court, 351 U.S. 377 (1956)

The government introduced evidence tending to show that the characteristics of cellophane were so different from other packaging materials that the relevant product market should be defined as consisting of cellophane alone. DuPont, by contrast introduced substantial evidence tending to prove that cellophane did, in fact, receive heavy competition from other flexible packaging materials, such as pliofilm and aluminum foil. The trial court, after making over 3000 findings of fact, agreed with duPont's position and ruled that the relevant product market consisted of *all flexible wrapping materials.* On this basis the court ruled that duPont's share of this larger market fell far short of constituting a monopoly, and dismissed the action. The government appealed to the U.S. Supreme Court.

Reed, Justice: . . . During the period that is relevant to this action duPont produced almost 75 percent of the cellophane sold in the United States, [but cellophane alone] constituted less than 20 percent of all "flexible packaging material" sales. . . .

If cellophane is the "market" that duPont is found to dominate, it may be assumed it does have monopoly power over that "market." Monopoly power is the power to control prices or exclude competition. . . . [It may be true that it is] practically impossible for anyone to commence manufacturing cellophane without full access to duPont's technique. However, duPont has no power to prevent competition from other wrapping materials. *The trial court consequently had to determine whether competition from the other wrappings prevented duPont from possessing monopoly power in violation of Section 2. . . .* (Emphasis added).

When a product is controlled by one interest, without substitutes available in the market, there is monopoly power. . . . But where there are market alternatives that buyers may readily use for their purposes, illegal monopoly does not exist merely because the product said to be monopolized differs from others. . . .

But despite cellophane's advantages, it has to meet competition from other materials in every one of its uses. [The court here summarized a number of the trial court's findings as follows]: Food products are the chief outlet, with cigarettes next. . . . [But] cellophane furnishes less than 7 percent of wrappings for bakery products, 25 percent for candy, 32 percent for snacks, 35 percent for meats and poultry, 27 percent for crackers and biscuits, 47 percent for fresh produce and 34 percent for frozen foods. . . . The result is that cellophane shares the packaging market with others, [and thus it can be said that] a very considerable degree of functional interchangeability exists between these products. . . .

An element for consideration . . . is the responsiveness of the sales of one product to price changes of the other. If a slight decrease in the price of cellophane causes a considerable number of customers of other flexible wrappings to switch to cellophane, it would be an indication that a high cross-elasticity of demand exists between them; that the products compete in the same market. The court below held that the "great sensitivity of customers in the flexible packaging markets to price or quality changes" prevented duPont from possessing monopoly control over price. The record sustains these findings [and also the finding that duPont never possessed power to exclude any other producers] from the rapidly expanding packaging market. . . .

It seems to us that duPont should not be found to monopolize cellophane when that product has the competition and interchangeability with other wrappings that this record shows. (Emphasis added.)

On the findings of the District Court, this judgment is affirmed.

The "Thrust Upon" Defense

Even if a company has been found to possess monopoly power, it is still possible that it does not violate Section 2 because it has achieved its overwhelming market power via *natural* rather than predatory means. Thus, if a company can show that its size is due entirely to superior production and marketing policies rather than to buying up competitors or using restrictive policies designed to exclude potential competitors, the company can successfully contend that the monopoly was "thrust upon" it—and it can thereby be found innocent of the charge of monopolization under Section 2.

One extreme situation in which the "thrust upon" defense would be accepted is that of the isolated country store; obviously the monopoly that results here is not brought about by any predatory of other anticompetitive conduct on the part of the store's owner. But in the real life monopolization cases brought to court the facts *very rarely* permit acceptance of the "thrust upon" defense.

A typical case is that of *U.S. v. Aluminum Company of America,* 148 F.2d 416 (1945), where Alcoa was found to be responsible for over 90 percent of the nation's production of virgin aluminum. Alcoa defended on the ground that its overwhelming size was due solely to an early headstart based on patent rights followed by superior business acumen. The appellate court acknowledged that there were some cases in which the thrust upon defense would be acceptable. It held, however, that in this particular case it did not apply, because evidence indicated that Alcoa's huge size was due at least in part to a "persistent determination [over the years] to maintain" its monopolistic position by "forestalling all competition" through doubling and tripling its productive capacity in advance of actual requirements in order to discourage potential competitors from entering the industry.

The Oligopolistic Industries

In general terms, an *oligopolistic industry* is one in which three or four companies are responsible for 75 percent or more of the industry's total output. (The automobile and cereal industries are two of the best examples.)

While oligopolistic situations are frequently referred to as "shared monopolies," companies in such industries do not violate Section 2 of the Sherman Act merely because of their size (assuming they have achieved such size through normal growth processes). Thus the mere fact that General Motors typically sells somewhat over 50 percent of all the new cars sold in the U.S. does not cause it to be in violation of Section 2.

On the other hand, if two or more companies in oligopolistic industries *act in concert* in any material way, their chance of having violated Section 2 is very high. An action brought by the U.S. against the American Tobacco Co., Liggett and Myers Tobacco Co., and R. J. Reynolds Tobacco Co. was a leading case of this kind. *American Tobacco Co. v. U.S.,* 328 U.S. 781 (1946). The defendant companies, which historically produced from 70 to 80 percent of the nation's cigarettes, were found guilty both of attempting to monopolize, and of monopolizing the cigarette industry. Substantial evidence was presented that the companies had, among other activities, systematically and concertedly purchased quantities of tobacco whenever this was necessary to keep it out of the hands of smaller competitors.

Questions and Problems

1. Certain types of business conduct might violate Section 1 of the Sherman Act without violating Section 2, and other kinds of conduct might violate Section 2 without violating Section 1. Give an example of each type of violation.

2. Members of the Chicago Board of Trade, consisting of 1600 grain traders, held daily "sessions" at which all offers to buy grain, and all sales of grain, were made public. All selling prices were thus known to members. After each session was over, which was usually 2 p.m., members were generally free to buy grain from country grain elevators at prices mutually agreed upon. To limit this activity, the Board of Trade adopted a rule that provided that such post-session purchases of grain could not be made at prices other than those in effect at the end of each regular session. Thus if the "to arrive" price of wheat at the end of the session was $1.50 per bushel, members could not buy wheat from grain elevators the rest of the day at prices higher or lower than that figure. This Board of Trade rule was promptly challenged in court as being a violation of Section 1 of the Sherman Act. If the legality of the rule were tested by the "rule of reason," do you think it might be found to be lawful under Sherman? Explain. (*Chicago Board of Trade* v. *United States,* 246 U.S. 231, 1918.)

3. Klor's, Inc., was a San Francisco retailer who sold radios, TVs and refrigerators in competition with a department store next door. (The store next-door was part of a large California retail chain.) Klors alleged that the chain, in order to injure Klor's business, pressured such manufacturers as General Electric, RCA and Zenith to agree amongst themselves not to sell any of their products to Klor's. When Klor's charged that this agreement between the chain and the manufacturers was a contract that unreasonably restrained trade in violation of Section 1 of Sherman, the chain's basic defense was that the agreement did *not* unreasonably restrain trade in view of the fact that there were a number of retailers in the immediate vicinity who continued to offer General Electric, RCA and Zenith products, and thus consumers who wished to buy these products from someone other than the chain could easily buy from these other retailers. Do you think the chain's argument is a valid one? Why or why not? (*Klor's, Inc.* v. *Broadway-Hale Stores, Inc.*, 359 U.S. 207, 1959.)

4. What is the "thrust upon" defense, and in what circumstances might it be accepted by the courts?

5. What is the explanation for the fact that some business practices are *per se* violations of the Sherman Act (i.e., violations even though the practices are not widespread, and affect only a small percentage of sales of goods within the relevant produce market)?

6. When a charge of "monopolization" under Section 2 of the Sherman Act is made against a company, why does the defendant's guilt or innocence sometimes turn upon the court's definition of the *relevant market?*

7. What is meant by the statement that in some situations there exists a "high degree of cross elasticity of demand" between two or more somewhat similar products?

8. What is an oligopolistic industry, and under what circumstances might firms in such an industry violate Section 2 of the Sherman Act?

The Clayton and Robinson-   47
Patman Acts: Selected Problems

As noted earlier, following the Sherman Act, Congress passed several statutes designed to prohibit certain practices in interstate commerce if their effect was substantially anticompetitive. In this chapter we will examine the salient provisions of such acts and the judicial interpretation given them by the courts, with particular emphasis on the Clayton Act and the Robinson-Patman Act (which amended the Clayton Act).

In the years following its enactment, the courts interpreted the Sherman Act rather strictly. While a number of cases were successfully prosecuted under it, others were dismissed, because the restrictive agreements complained of by the government were found not to have unreasonably restrained trade under Section 1 or not to have constituted monopolizations of or attempts to monopolize commerce under Section 2.

Thus, as a result of judicial interpretation, many anticompetitive agreements and practices continued to be lawful in particular situations. As one example, sellers

Original Provisions of the Clayton Act

remained free to discriminate in the prices they charged different customers as long as the discrimination did not restrain trade "unreasonably." In this situation Congress passed the Clayton Act in 1914, the primary purpose of which was to prohibit certain *specific* practices that were felt to be harmful to free competition. The act contained four particularly important sections, which we will summarize briefly below. Then we will consider selected problems arising under each section, as subsequently amended.

Section 2

Section 2 generally prohibited sellers of goods from discriminating in the prices charged different purchasers "where the effect of such discrimination may be to substantially lessen competition or tend to create a monopoly in any line of commerce." Certain exceptions were recognized, however. For example, quantity discounts could be granted under certain circumstances, as will be discussed in more detail later. Additionally, while sellers generally could not discriminate in prices charged to different buyers, they could refuse to make sales to any buyer at their discretion, as long as such refusal did not constitute an attempt to create a monopoly or unreasonably restrain trade. This right was guaranteed in a clause providing that "nothing herein contained shall prevent persons engaged in selling goods . . . from selecting their own customers in bona fide transactions and not in restraint of trade."

Section 3

Section 3 prohibited "exclusive dealing" contracts (and, by judicial interpretation, "tying" contracts) where the effect of these "may be to substantially lessen competition or tend to create a monopoly in any line of commerce." *Exclusive dealing contracts* are those in which the seller of goods, usually a manufacturer, requires the buyer to promise not to handle the products of a competitor of the seller. *Tying contracts* are those in which a seller of a commodity (or a lessor of equipment) agrees to sell or lease it only on condition that the buyer (or lessee) purchase other commodities or articles produced or distributed by the seller. (We will discuss both kinds of contracts later in the chapter.)

Section 7

Section 7 prohibited any corporation from acquiring "the whole or any part of the stock of another corporation where the effect . . . may be to substantially lessen competition between the corporation whose stock is so acquired and the corporation making the acquisition, or to restrain . . . commerce in any section or community, or tend to create a monopoly in any line of commerce . . . ." Acquisition of stock solely for investment purposes or for the purpose of forming lawful subsidiaries of the acquiring corporation was, however, expressly permitted. (This section, as amended by the Celler-Kefauver Act, is the primary law under which the legality of corporate mergers is tested today. It too will be discussed later in the chapter.)

The basic purpose of Section 2 of the Clayton Act was to prohibit those types of price discrimination that were being used by sellers as a means of achieving monopoly positions in their industries, especially the reduction of prices in certain areas for the purpose of keeping out competitors. While Section 2 was generally successful in this regard, it was found in practice to contain several shortcomings:

Price Discrimination under the Clayton Act

1. The clause that forbade price discrimination where the effect of such discrimination "may be to substantially lessen competition" was interpreted by the courts as meaning the lessening of competition only *between the seller and one or more competitors of the seller;* any other price discrimination continued to be lawful. Thus, if S sold goods to buyer A at lower prices than those charged buyer B, the mere fact that the discrimination lessened competition *between A and B* did not constitute a violation of this section.

2. Congress found by 1936 that many sellers were being pressured by large-scale buyers to grant them price reductions much larger than could be justified on economic grounds alone. That is, sellers were granting buyers discounts greatly in excess of the actual cost savings attributable to production and handling efficiencies resulting from the quantities being sold, and the courts were permitting this practice under the "quantity discount" exception.

3. It was also apparent by this time that many sellers were circumventing Section 2 by granting rebates to favored buyers and that some sellers were taking advantage of the exception permitting price reductions "to meet competition" by lowering their prices in certain areas far below those of their competitors for the purpose of driving them out of business.

The Robinson-Patman Act

To remedy these problems, Congress passed the Robinson-Patman Act in 1936. By this amendment to the Clayton Act, Section 2 was completely rewritten and considerably lengthened. The section now has six subsections, the first two of which merit particular attention.

Subsection A makes it unlawful for a seller "to discriminate in price between different purchasers 'of goods' of like grade and quality" where the effect of such discrimination "may be to substantially lessen competition or tend to create a monopoly in any line of commerce, or to injure, destroy or prevent competition *with any person who either grants or knowingly receives the benefit of such discrimination, or with customers of either of them . . . .*" (Emphasis added).

This section further provides, however, that price differences based on actual "differences in the cost of manufacture, sale or delivery resulting from the differing methods or quantities in which such commodities are ... sold or delivered" are lawful. In other words, if a manufacturer makes a large production run to fill a particular order with the result that his per-unit cost of production is less than what it normally would be, he may pass this saving along to the large-scale buyer. Additionally, Subsection A permits "price changes from time to time 'in' response to changing conditions affecting the market for or the marketability of the goods concerned . . . ." Subsection B contains an additional exception by providing that a seller may charge lower prices to some customers than it charges others if such reductions are made solely to meet prices of its competitors.

A Cautionary Note: While the Robinson-Patman Act brought about certain clarifications to the law, it can by no means be said that price discrimination problems have been eliminated. In the first place, considerable discriminatory pricing continues to exist in the real world of business because the act is enforced only sporadically (as the Federal Trade Commission occasionally admits). Secondly, as the following case indicates, difficult problems of statutory interpretation under Section 2 still arise—particularly on the question of whether proven price discrimination in a given case may result in a substantial lessening of competition.

Federal Trade Commission v. Morton Salt Company

U.S. Supreme Court, 334 U.S. 37 (1948)

The Morton Salt Company manufactured and sold different brands of table salt to wholesalers (jobbers) and to large retail grocery chains. Morton sold its finest brand of salt, Blue Label, on a "standard quantity discount system" which was purportedly available to all of its customers.

The Federal Trade Commission, after a hearing, concluded that Morton's sales of salt under system resulted in price discrimination in violation of Section 2 of the Robinson-Patman Act. Accordingly, the FTC issued a cease and desist order prohibiting further sales of salt under this system. A U.S. Court of Appeals set aside this order, finding no violation of Section 2. The FTC appealed this judgment to the U.S. Supreme Court.

In this appeal, there were two primary issues: (a) whether the discount system resulted in price discrimination within the meaning of Section 2; and (2) if so, whether the discrimination caused an injury to competition. (In the decision of the U.S. Supreme Court, Morton is referred to as "the respondent" throughout).

Black, Justice: . . . Under [respondent's] system the purchasers pay a delivered price, and the cost to both wholesale and retail purchasers of this brand differs according to the quantities bought. These prices are as follows, after making allowances for rebates and discounts:

	Per Case
Less-than-carload purchases	$1.60
Carload purchases	1.50
5,000-case purchases in any consecutive 12 months	1.40
50,000-case purchases in any consecutive 12 months	1.35

Only five companies have ever bought sufficient quantities of respondent's salt to obtain the $1.35 per case price. These companies could buy in such quantities because they operate large chains of retail stores in various parts of the country. As a result of this low price these five companies have been able to sell Blue Label salt at retail cheaper than wholesale purchasers from respondent could reasonably sell the same brand of salt to independently operated retail stores, many of whom competed with the local outlets of the five chain stores. . . .

In addition to these standard quantity discounts, special allowances were granted certain favored customers who competed with other customers to whom [the allowances] were denied.

Respondent's basic contention, which it argues this case hinges upon, is that its "standard quantity discounts, available to all on equal terms, as contrasted, for example, to hidden or special rebates, allowances, prices or discounts, are not discriminatory, within the meaning of the Robinson-Patman Act." Theoretically, these discounts are equally available to all, but functionally they are not. For as the record indicates (if reference to it on this point were necessary) no single independent retail grocery store, and probably no single wholesaler, bought as many as 50,000 cases or as much as $50,000 worth of table salt in one year. Furthermore, the record shows that, while certain purchasers were enjoying one or more of respondent's standard quantity discounts, some of their competitors made purchases in such small quantities that they could not qualify for any of respondent's discounts, even those based on carload shipments. The legislative history of the Robinson-Patman Act makes it abundantly clear that Congress considered it to be an evil that a large buyer could secure a competitive advantage over a small buyer solely because of the large buyer's quantity purchasing ability. The Robinson-Patman Act was passed to deprive a large buyer of such advantages except to the extent that a lower price *could be justified* by reason of a seller's diminished costs due to quantity manufacture, delivery, or sale, or by reason of the seller's good faith effort to meet a competitor's equally low price. [Emphasis added.] . . .

[The court then agreed with the FTC that Morton's evidence failed to justify its price differential—i.e., that Morton was unable to show that the discounts that it gave its very large customers were based on actual cost savings alone. The court then turned to the second question, the magnitude of the effect of the discrimination.]

It is argued [by respondent] that the findings fail to show that [its] discriminatory discounts had in fact caused injury to competition. There are specific findings that such injuries had resulted from respondent's discounts, although the statute does not require the Commission to find that injury has actually resulted. The statute requires no more than that the effect of the prohibited price discriminations "may be substantially to lessen competition . . . or to injure, destroy or prevent competition." After a careful consideration of this provision of the Robinson-Patman Act, we have said that "the statute does not require that the discriminations must in fact have harmed competition, *but only that there is a reasonable possibility that they 'may' have such an effect."* [Emphasis added.] *Corn Products Co. v. Federal Trade Comm'n,* 324 U.S. 726. Here the Commission found what would appear to be obvious, that the competitive opportunities of certain merchants were injured when they had to pay respondent substantially more for their goods than their competitors had to pay. The findings are adequate. . . . Judgment [of the Court of Appeals] reversed, [and order of the FTC reinstated.]

Exclusive Dealing and Tying Contracts under the Clayton Act

Exclusive Dealing Contracts

As noted earlier, exclusive dealing contracts are those under which a seller of goods requires the buyer (usually a retailer) to promise *not to handle the products of any competitor of the seller.* The controlling provision of the Clayton Act—Section 3—provides

> that it shall be unlawful for any person engaged in [interstate commerce] ... to lease or make a sale ... of goods, wares, merchandise, machinery, supplies or other commodities ... on the condition, agreement, or understanding that the lessee or purchaser thereof shall not use or deal in the goods, wares, merchandise, machinery, supplies, or other commodities of a competitor ... of the lessor or seller, where the effect of such lease, sale, or ... such condition, agreement, or understanding may be to substantially lessen competition or tend to create a monopoly in any line of commerce.

As one might expect, the typical case brought under Section 3 turns upon the question of whether the seller's contracts (within the particular fact-pattern presented) were likely to result in a substantial lessening of competition. In order to follow the thinking of the courts over the years on this point, we will refer briefly to several cases.

The "Dominant Seller" View: In several early cases, the Supreme Court ruled that exclusive dealing contracts substantially lessened competition (and thus were illegal) only when the seller "dominated" the relevant market. If such dominance was lacking, the seller's contracts were lawful even if such contracts were entered into with a number of buyers.

The "Substantial Share of Commerce" View: In somewhat more recent years, the U.S. Supreme Court has seemingly adopted a "harder" line in regard to exclusive dealing contracts. Beginning with the case of *Standard Oil of California v. United States,* 337 U.S. 293 (1949), the court has held that such contracts violate Section 3 if they affect a substantial portion of commerce, even if the seller does not occupy a dominant position in the industry. In that case, Standard Oil had exclusive dealing contracts with the operators of nearly 6,000 independent stations in the western states, (16 percent of the total independent gas stations in the area). Through these stations Standard sold $57 million worth of gasoline in 1947, which was about 7 percent of total retail gasoline sales in the western states. The U.S. Supreme Court ruled that such widespread use of exclusive dealing contracts constituted just such a "clog on competition" which Congress meant to eliminate by enacting Section 3. Thus the court found a violation of that section, even though it conceded that Standard was not the dominant seller of gasoline in the affected area.

Requirements Contracts: In most exclusive dealing contracts, such as those discussed so far, the buyer of goods is purchasing them for resale. Another form of exclusive dealing arrangement, however, arises out of *requirements contracts*—those in which the buyer of a commodity, such as coal or oil, agrees to purchase all of the commodity he or she will *need or use in his or her business* for a specified period from that seller and no one else.

As has been noted in Chapter 46, such contracts do restrain trade in that the buyer is prevented from buying his or her requirements from any other seller (and the seller is not able to sell this quantity of goods—whatever the buyer's requirements turn out to be—to any other buyer.) The contracts do not, however, necessarily violate Section 3; like others challenged under this section, their legality depends on whether they may result in a substantial lessening of competition. Under this test, there is little doubt that most requirements contracts *do not violate* the act, because the quantities of goods involved are normally rather small when compared to the quantities of similar goods produced by other sellers that remain available to other buyers in the affected market.

The leading case in point is *Tampa Electric Co. v. Nashville Coal Co. et al.,* 365 U.S. 320 (1961). There Tampa Electric had contracted to purchase all the coal that it would need over a twenty year period from Nashville Coal, at specified prices per ton. A dispute subsequently arose, and in resulting litigation the primary question was whether the contract violated Section 3 of the Clayton Act.

The trial court ruled that the contract *did* substantially lessen competition in violation of Section 3, in view of the fact that the quantities of coal that were involved greatly exceeded the total quantity of coal purchased by all other purchasers in southern Florida. The U.S. Supreme Court disagreed with this conclusion, noting that there were still 700 coal producers in addition to Nashville Coal who were able to fill these other buyers' needs, and that their total production was over 359 million tons of coal a year, of which 290 million tons were sold by them on the open market annually. Thus the contract was found to be lawful.

Tying Contracts

A contract in which a seller of a product makes the sale on condition that the buyer purchase other products or services from him or her usually is in violation of one or more of the antitrust laws. If it is shown that the contract unreasonably restrains trade or constitutes an attempt to create a monopoly, it is illegal under the Sherman Act. (There are a number of cases where such a showing has been made.) And even if the tying contract does not have this effect, it still violates Section 3 of the Clayton Act if its effect "may be to substantially lessen competition or tend to create a monopoly in any line of commerce." (Literally, Section 3 applies only to exclusive dealing contracts. However, it has been extended by judicial interpretation to cover tying contracts on the theory that in regard to the unwanted goods or services involved, the buyer is foreclosed from purchasing such goods or services from any competitor of the seller.)

The following case is one of the best known cases involving tying contracts that have reached the U.S. Supreme Court.

Northern Pacific Railway Co. v. United States

U.S. Supreme Court,
356 U.S. 1 (1958)

In the 1860s Congress granted the Northern Pacific Railway Company 40 million acres of land in several northwestern states and territories to facilitate its construction of a railroad line from Lake Superior to Puget Sound. This grant consisted of every alternate section of land in a belt 20 miles wide on each side of track through the states and 40 miles wide through the territories.

Some of the lands contained great stands of timber; some contained valuable minerals, and others were useful for agriculture, grazing, or industry. By 1949 the railroad had sold or leased almost all of these lands to farmers and corporations. Most of the sale and lease contracts contained "preferential routing" clauses, which compelled the buyer or lessee to ship over Northern Pacific lines all commodities produced or manufactured on the land (with minor exceptions).

In 1949 the government filed suit against the railroad, contending that the preferential clauses unreasonably restrained trade, and thus violated Section 1 of the Sherman Act. The trial court ruled that these contracts were *per se* violations of the act, and issued an order restraining the railroad from enforcing its preferential routing clauses. Northern Pacific appealed this order directly to the U.S. Supreme Court.

Black, Justice: ... Although [the Sherman Act's prohibition against restraints of trade] is literally all-encompassing, the courts have construed it as precluding only those contracts or combinations which "unreasonably" restrain competition. . . . However, there are certain agreements or practices which because of their pernicious effect on competition and lack of any redeeming virtue are conclusively presumed to be unreasonable, and therefore illegal, without elaborate inquiry as to the precise harm they have caused . . . . This is known as the principle of per se unreasonableness . . . .

For our purposes a tying arrangement may be defined as an agreement by a party to sell one product but only on condition that the buyer also purchases a different [or tied] product, or at least agrees that he will not purchase that product from any other supplier.

[The court then noted that, as a general rule, tying contracts were not illegal unless there was proof that their use actually restrained trade unreasonably. However, the court also noted that in some circumstances tying contracts had been held to be *per se* violations of the Sherman Act, as follows]: *Tying contracts are unreasonable in and of themselves whenever a party has sufficient economic power with respect to the tying product to appreciably restrain free competition in the market for the tied product and a "not insubstantial" amount of interstate commerce is affected.* [Emphasis added.] *International Salt Co. v. United States,* 332 U.S. 392. . . .

In this case, we believe the district judge was clearly correct in entering summary judgment declaring the defendant's "preferential routing" clauses unlawful restraints of trade. We wholly agree that the undisputed facts established beyond any genuine question that *the defendant possessed substantial economic power by virtue of its extensive landholdings which it used as leverage to induce large numbers of purchasers and lessees to give it preference, to the exclusion of its competitors, in carrying goods or produce from the land transferred to them. Nor can there by any real doubt that a "not insubstantial" amount of interstate commerce was and is affected by these restrictive provisions.* [Emphasis added.]

. . .

Judgment affirmed.

It is virtually impossible to summarize in a few pages the conditions under which corporate mergers may be unlawful under the antitrust acts today. One reason for this lies in the fact that mergers between companies in the regulated industries pose somewhat different problems than those in the nonregulated industries (the ordinary manufacturing and marketing enterprises). And, even if one limits his attention to mergers in the nonregulated fields—those of primary interest to most business persons—the fact-patterns are usually so complex that a great deal of analysis of prior cases is necessary in order discern the general principles of law that are applicable, and to understand the courts' attempts to harmonize these principles. Thus we will merely attempt here to examine the possible anticompetitive effects resulting from the most common types of mergers, and to get some familiarity with the courts' interpretations of the applicable federal statutes in selected cases.

Mergers under the Clayton Act (Amended by Celler-Kefauver)

The General Problem of Mergers

In a broad sense a merger occurs whenever two or more companies are brought under common direction and control. In many instances this occurs through formal merger proceedings in which, say, Company X makes an offer to absorb Company Y. If the shareholders of Company Y agree to the proposal, they normally are given stock in Company X in exchange for their stock in Company Y. When the merger is complete, Company Y disappears and only Corporation X remains. A similar result comes about when one company merely purchases the assets of another, in which event the purchasing corporation makes a cash payment to the acquired corporation, with the formal life of the latter again coming to an end. A third type of combination occurs when a new corporation—a holding company—is formed for the purpose of buying up controlling stock interests in two existing corporations.

Mergers may or may not have anticompetitive consequences, depending on such matters as the economic size of the merging companies, the extent to which strong competitors remain, and the extent to which the companies competed with one another before the merger took place. Hundreds of mergers take place every year that, based on these considerations, have little or no adverse effect on competition; and there is no reason why such combinations should be limited or prohibited by law. One example of such a merger is a small or medium-sized manufacturer in one industry acquiring a firm that produces entirely different products in an industry in which it is but one of many such manufacturers. Similarly, the acquisition by a medium-sized manufacturer of a small competitor—a firm engaged in producing the same kinds of products as the acquiring firm—will have little adverse effect if the remaining competitors in the industry are large in number and economically healthy.

On the other hand, many mergers do have very serious anticompetitive effects. In fact, the desire of one company to eliminate a serious competitor has undoubtedly been, over the years, one of the most powerful motivations underlying many corporate acquisitions. Where such an acquisition occurs, particularly in an industry having but few producers, the economic power the resulting firm is able to exert on both suppliers and retailers may be so great that it can virtually control the production and prices of goods offered for sale in a given market.

The Original Section 7

In an effort to prohibit undesirable mergers that fell short of violating the Sherman Act, Congress drew up Section 7 of the Clayton Act. The salient provision of this section prohibited one corporation from acquiring "the whole or part of the stock of another corporation where the effect may be to substantially lessen competition between the corporation whose stock is acquired and the corporation making the acquisition." In practice, the section proved to be quite ineffective for two major reasons:

1. It did not prevent one company from buying up the *assets* of another, and a good many firms were quick to take advantage of this loophole.

2. Even in the cases brought against corporations that *had* acquired stock of others, a violation of Section 7 required the government to show that competition between the merged firms was substantially lessened; a showing that the merger substantially injured competition between *customers* of the merged firms would not suffice. Additionally, the courts generally refused to find that a lessening of competition between the merged firms had occurred except in horizontal mergers (those involving firms operating at the same level)—and then only in the relatively rare case where the acquiring firm was a direct competitor of the firm whose stock was acquired. Putting it differently, *vertical mergers*—as where a manufacturer acquired a controlling stock interest in a supplier—were generally found to be lawful under Section 7.

The Celler-Kefauver Amendment

Aware of the basic shortcomings of Section 7, Congress amended it in 1950 by passing the Celler-Kefauver Act. This amendment expressly extended Section 7 to apply to asset acquisitions. It also substantially cured the second shortcoming of the original section 7 (noted above) by prohibiting mergers where the effect may be to substantially lessen competition or to tend to create a monopoly "in any line of commerce in any section of the country."

The amendment ushered in a new era in antitrust law, and the number of cases initiated under it against mergers increased greatly. However, there are still highly complex interpretations that must be made by the courts on a case-to-case basis. Ths most serious of these have to do with (1) determination of the "relevant product market" that is affected by a given merger, and (2) the degree of proof necessary to establish a reasonable probability of "substantial lessening of competition" within that market.

Types of Mergers

Before considering cases that present typical issues in this area of the law, we should be aware that mergers are commonly classified on a functional basis. Thus most mergers are said to be either horizontal, vertical, or conglomerate in nature.

Horizontal Mergers: This kind of merger results from the combination of two competing firms at the same level in the production and distribution network, such as two manufacturers or two retail chains handling similar products. Horizontal mergers are more likely to result in a substantial lessening of competition than are either of the other kinds of mergers for two reasons: (a) the number of competing firms is necessarily reduced, and (b) the courts are very quick to find a probable lessening "of competition in this kind of merger (as we will see in the *Brown Shoe case* later in the chapter.)

Vertical Mergers: This kind of merger results from the combination of two firms at different levels in the production and distribution network, like those occurring when a manufacturer acquires a retailer or a retail chain. Vertical mergers usually do not result in a substantial lessening of competition, because the combining firms did not compete with one another prior to the merger. (In other words, the number of competing manufacturers and the number of competing retailers remains unchanged.) However, if the acquiring firm is the "dominant" one in its industry and if the acquired firm is a very large purchaser of the acquiring firm's products, this may result in a substantial lessening of competition (and thus violate Section 7).[1] This results from the fact that the acquired firm is likely to buy all of its requirements from the acquiring firm (that is, competitors of the acquiring firm who used to sell to the acquired firm are now likely to be foreclosed from the acquired firm's market—i.e., purchases).

Conglomerate Mergers: This kind of merger, which achieved particular popularity in the 1960s and early 1970s, results when a firm in one industry acquires a firm in a generally unrelated industry—for example, the acquisition of the Hartford Insurance Company by International Telephone and Telegraph. Conglomerate mergers are least likely of all mergers to result in a substantial lessening of competition (but, as we will see later in the chapter, there are some circumstances in which this *may* come about).

With these general considerations in mind, we will now examine two significant cases involving the application of Section 7 to typical mergers. The first of these, the *Brown Shoe Company* case, is undoubtedly one of the most instructive cases yet decided under the amended section. There the court was required to assess *both* the vertical and horizontal aspects of a proposed merger between two major companies in the shoe industry, since each was involved in manufacturing and

---

[1] *United States v. E.I. duPont de Nemours et al.,* 353 U.S. 586 (1957).

retailing activities. (That part of the decision dealing only with the vertical aspects of the merger has been emphasized, because the second case—*Von's Grocery Company*—presents us with a purely horizontal merger.)

Brown Shoe Company v. United States

U.S. Supreme Court, 370 U.S. 294 (1962)

The government brought this action in 1955 to block a contemplated merger of the Brown Shoe Company with the Kinney Co. It contended that the effect of the merger of Brown—"the third largest seller of shoes by dollar volume in the United States, a leading manufacturer of men's, women's and children's shoes, and a retailer with over 1230 owned, operated or controlled retail outlets"—and Kinney—"the eighth largest company, by dollar volume, among those primarily engaged in selling shoes, itself a large manufacturer of shoes, and a retailer with over 350 outlets"—would violate Section 7 "by eliminating actual or potential competition in the production of shoes for the national wholesale shoe market and in the sale of shoes at retail in the Nation."

Many opposing contentions were made by the parties in the trial court (a U.S. district court), each supported by voluminous economic data. For our purposes, the major issues involved determination of the "relevant lines of commerce" and "sections of the country" within which the horizontal and vertical aspects of the merger should be considered.

The government contended that the relevant *product market* ("line of commerce") affected by the merger was footwear generally, or, in the alternative, men's, women's, and children's shoes, considered separately. Brown, on the other hand, argued that each of the latter classifications should be divided into submarkets, with each such submarket constituting a separate line of commerce—a contention which, if accepted, would result in a showing that the merger's effect on commerce was much less substantial than would otherwise be the case. In regard to determination of the relevant *geographic market,* the parties agreed that it was "the entire Nation" insofar as the vertical aspects of the merger were concerned. Regarding the horizontal aspects of the combination, however—particularly those related to retailing activities—there was again disagreement. The government urged a delineation that would result in the recognition of several larger market areas, in many of which the sales of suburban retail stores would be added to those attributable to stores located in the "central downtown areas" of the larger cities. Brown, on the other hand, urged a narrower definition more favorable to it.

In regard to these questions, the trial court found that the relevant product markets were those of men's, women's, and children's shoes, and that the geographic market —for measuring the effect at retail—was "every city with a population exceeding 10,000 and its immediate contiguous surrounding territory in which Brown and Kinney sold shoes at retail through stores they either owned or controlled." Both of these rulings were, essentially, consistent with the contentions of the government, the plaintiff.

On the basis of these and other findings and the relevant marketing data the court came to two final conclusions:

1. Viewing the *vertical aspects* of the combination alone, the proposed merger *would violate Section 7.* This ruling was based on the large number of retail stores that would be acquired by one manufacturer, Brown, which presumably would not

thereafter be free to sell shoes of other manufacturers as they had previously done. The other manufacturers would thus be foreclosed from a substantial share of the market.

2. Viewing only the *horizontal aspects* of the combination, the merger would also *violate Section 7* in that combining the Kinney retail stores with those already owned by Brown would result in Brown controlling an unlawful share of the relevant retail markets.

On the basis of these conclusions the court ordered Brown to divest itself of the stock it had already acquired in Kinney and to refrain from making additional purchases. Brown appealed to the U.S. Supreme Court.

That court affirmed the lower court's judgment. In doing so, it first enumerated the purposes of Congress in amending Section 7 and then examined both the vertical and horizontal aspects of the merger in detail. In that part of its decision entitled "The Vertical Aspects of the Merger," the court's major observations are set forth below; following these, the court's conclusion as to the horizontal aspects of the case is very briefly summarized.

Warren, Chief Justice: . . . 1. Economic arrangements between companies standing in a supplier-customer relationship are characterized as "vertical." The primary vice of a vertical merger or other arrangement tying a customer to a supplier is that, by foreclosing the competitors of either party from a segment of the market otherwise open to them, the arrangement may act as a "clog on competititon," *Standard Oil Company v. United States,* 337 U.S. 293, which "deprives . . . rivals of a fair opportunity to compete." Every extended vertical arrangement by its very nature, for at least a time, denies to competitors of the supplier the opportunity to compete for part or all of the trade of the customer-party to the vertical arrangement. However, the Clayton Act does not render unlawful all such vertical arrangements, but forbids only those whose effect "may be substantially to lessen competition, or to tend to create a monopoly in any line of commerce in any section of the country." Thus, as we have previously noted, "determination of the relevant market is a necessary predicate to a finding of a violation of the Clayton Act because the threatened monopoly must be one which will substantially lessen competition within the area of effective competition. Substantiality can be determined only in terms of the market affected." *United States v. E.I. duPont de Nemours & Co.,* 353 U.S. 586. The "area of effective competition" must be determined by reference to a product market (the "line of commerce") and a geographic market (the "section of the country").

2. The outer boundaries of a product market are determined by the reasonable interchangeability of use or the cross-elasticity of demand between the product itself and substitutes for it. However, within this broad market, well-defined submarkets may exist, which, in themselves, constitute product markets for antitrust purposes. The boundaries of such a submarket may be determined by examining such practical indicia as industry or public recognition of the submarket as a separate economic entity, the product's peculiar characteristics and uses, unique production facilities, distinct customers, distinct prices, sensitivity to price changes, and specialized vendors. Because Section 7 of the Clayton Act prohibits any merger which may substantially lessen competition "in *any* line of commerce," *it is necessary to examine the effects of a merger in each such economically significant submarket to determine if there is a reasonable probability that the merger will substantially lessen competition. If such a probability is found to exist, the merger is proscribed.* [Emphasis added.]

Applying these considerations to the present case, we conclude that the record supports the District Court's finding that the relevant lines of commerce are men's, women's, and children's shoes. These product lines are recognized by the public; each line is manufactured in separate plants; each has characteristics peculiar to itself rendering it generally noncompetitive with the others; and each is, of course, directed toward a distinct class of customers. . . .

4. We agree with the parties and the District Court that insofar as the vertical aspect of this merger is concerned, the relevant geographic market is the entire Nation. The relationships of product value, bulk, weight and consumer demand enable manufacturers to distribute their shoes on a nationwide basis, as Brown and Kinney, in fact, do. The anticompetitive effects of the merger are to be measured within this range of distribution.

5. Once the area of effective competition affected by a vertical arrangement has been defined, an analysis must be made to determine if the effect of the arrangement "may be substantially to lessen competition, or tend to create a monopoly in this market." [Stressing this point, the court noted that limited-term exclusive dealing contracts frequently do not have the effect of substantially lessening competition and, further, that a merger of two small companies or a merger designed to save a failing company does not violate Section 7. The court observed, however, that] the present merger involved neither small companies nor failing companies. In 1955, the date of this merger, Brown was the fourth largest manufacturer in the shoe industry with sales of approximately 25 million pairs of shoes and assets of over $72,000,000, while Kinney had sales of about 8 million pairs of shoes and assets of about $18,000,000. Not only was Brown one of the leading manufacturers of men's, women's, and children's shoes, but Kinney, with over 350 retail outlets, owned and operated the largest independent chain of family shoe stores in the Nation. *Thus, in this industry, no merger between a manufacturer and an independent retailer could involve a larger potential market foreclosure.* [Emphasis added. On the basis of these and other data, particularly those indicating a growing trend toward vertical integration in the shoe industry, the court affirmed the trial court's finding that the merger would probably result in a substantial lessening of competition in the relevant markets.]

[Turning to the horizontal aspects of the merger, the court first noted that prior to the merger many of Brown's 1230 retail stores competed in several geographical areas with a substantial number of Kinney's retail outlets. The court then concluded that Brown's post-merger share of these relevant markets—i.e., the share of the markets that Brown would control by selling shoes through its retail outlets *and* through the Kinney retailers—again was large enough to probably result in the lessening of competition in violation of Section 7].

Judgment affirmed.

Horizontal Mergers—Further Comments

In a part of the decision not appearing above, the U.S. Supreme Court indicated that a merger which resulted in the post-merger firm having as little as 5 percent of the relevant product market in a substantial number of cities might even justify a finding that the merger might substantially lessen competition in violation of Section 7, given the other circumstances of the case. The circumstance to which the court attached special significance was the fact that there had been a "history of tendency toward concentration in the industry." By this the court meant that a number of other mergers had occurred in recent years, resulting in fewer and fewer independent retailers and retail chains across the country. This tendency of the court to set aside horizontal mergers, even where the post-merger firm's market share is rather low, received added impetus in the case below.

The Von's Grocery Case:[2] Here, the government attacked a merger in which Von's Grocery, a large retail grocery chain in Los Angeles, had acquired another such chain in the area, Shopping Bag Food Stores. Prior to the merger, Von's retail sales ranked third in the Los Angeles area, and Shopping Bag's ranked sixth. Additionally, it was found that "the merger of these two highly successful, expanding and aggressive competitors created the second largest grocery chain in Los Angeles with sales of over $172 million annually."

Despite these statistics the trial court concluded as a matter of law that there was "not a reasonable probability that the merger would tend substantially to lessen competition" and, accordingly, entered judgment for the defendant companies. This conclusion was based on further statistics indicating that, despite the size of the two companies, the post-merger firm's share of the relevant market was only 7.5 percent, and that several thousand competing grocery stores remained in that market after the merger.

The U.S. Supreme Court reversed the trial court's judgment, concluding that the merger *did* threaten to substantially lessen competition under the total circumstances presented, and set the merger aside. First the court cited these additional facts that were established during the trial:

1. Prior to the merger the two companies "had enjoyed great success as rapidly growing companies. From 1948 to 1958 the number of Von's stores in the Los Angeles area practically doubled from 14 to 27, while at the same time the number of Shopping Bag's stores jumped from 15 to 34. During that same decade, Von's sales increased fourfold and its share of the market almost doubled while Shopping Bag's sales multiplied seven times and its share of the market tripled."

2. "The number of owners operating single stores in the Los Angeles retail grocery market decreased from 5,365 in 1950 to 3,818 in 1961. . . . Three years after the merger the number of single-store owners had dropped still further to 3,590."

3. During the period from 1953 to 1962, "the number of chains with two or more grocery stores increased from 96 to 150," and "in the period from 1949 to 1958 nine of the top 20 chains had acquired 126 stores from their smaller competitors . . . ."

Second, against this backdrop, the court made these observations:

---

[2]*U.S. v. Von's Grocery Co.,* 384 U.S. 279 (1966).

The facts of this case present exactly the threatening trend toward concentration which Congress wanted to halt. The number of small grocery companies in the Los Angeles retail grocery market had been declining rapidly before the merger and continued to decline rapidly afterwards. This rapid decline in the number of grocery store owners moved hand in hand with a large number of significant absorptions of the small companies by the larger ones. In the midst of this steadfast trend toward concentration, Von's and Shopping Bag, two of the most successful and largest companies in the area, jointly owning 66 grocery stores, merged to become the second largest chain in Los Angeles. This merger cannot be defended on the ground that one of the companies was about to fail or that the two had to merge to save themselves from destruction by some larger and more powerful competitor. What we have on the contrary is simply the case of two already powerful companies merging in a way which makes them even more powerful than they were before. If ever such a merger would not violate § 7, *certainly it does when it takes place in a market characterized by a long and continuous trend toward fewer and fewer owner-competitors, which is exactly the sort of trend which Congress, with power to do so, declared must be arrested.* [Emphasis added.]

The Conglomerate Problem

A merger between two firms whose products do not compete—because they are either unrelated products or products sold in separate geographical markets—will obviously have little or no adverse effect on competition in most circumstances. For this reason, conglomerate mergers in earlier years were seldom challenged under Section 7.

On the other hand, when one of the firms involved in such a merger is operating in a "highly concentrated" industry—one comprised almost entirely of a few major corporations—the merger increases the degree of concentration still further, the result being generally contrary to the philosophy underlying the antitrust laws. For this reason, especially when the pace of large-scale conglomerate mergers accelerated rapidly in the early 1960s, the government began to challenge a number of the largest of these mergers. The challenges required the government to formulate arguable contentions or theories establishing a reasonable possibility that even this type of merger might result in a substantial lessening of competition, at least in certain circumstances.

In a number of cases in which such challenges have been made in recent years, the Supreme Court has accepted one or more of these contentions in varying fact-patterns. The result, of course, is that the mergers are found to violate Section 7 and their dissolution is ordered. The decision in the case below (commonly referred to as the "Clorox case") was one of the first of this sort. In it, the court indicated that there were at least three grounds upon which the merger might violate Section 7. (Following the case is a more comprehensive listing of the possible anticompetitive effects of conglomerate mergers.)

In this action the Federal Trade Commission, after full hearings, ruled that Procter & Gamble's acquisition of the Clorox Chemical Company in 1957 "might substantially lessen competition" in the household liquid bleach industry and thus was in violation of Section 7. Accordingly, it ordered Procter to divest itself of the Clorox Company's assets acquired through the merger.

While recognizing that Procter did not, prior to the merger, produce a liquid bleach that would compete with the Clorox product, the commission based its finding of illegality on these facts:

1. Clorox was by far the dominant producer of liquid bleach in the United States, with annual sales of $40 million.

2. Procter had earlier considered entering the liquid bleach field, but as a consequence of the merger did not.

3. In the larger area of soaps, detergents, and general cleansers, Procter accounted for 54 percent of the sales.

4. The soaps, detergents, and cleansers industry was highly concentrated, with Procter and two competitors accounting for 80 percent of its sales.

5. Procter was the nation's largest advertiser ($80 million spent in 1957), and the success of liquid bleach sales depended more on heavy expenditures for advertising and promotional activities than on any other factor.

A U.S. court of appeals reversed the commission's finding of illegality, saying that it was based on "conjecture, mere possibility and suspicion." The government appealed this judgment to the U.S. Supreme Court.

After reviewing the economic position of the two companies, the Supreme Court found that the merger might indeed substantially lessen competition in several respects. It accordingly reversed the court of appeals and reinstated the commission's order.

Douglas, Justice: . . . 1. Section 7 of the Clayton Act was intended to arrest the anticompetitive effects of market power in their incipiency. The core question is whether a merger may substantially lessen competition, and necessarily requires a prediction of the merger's impact on competition, present and future. . . .

2. All mergers are within the reach of Section 7, and all must be tested by the same standard, whether they are classified as horizontal, vertical, conglomerate or other. As noted by the Commission, this merger is neither horizontal, vertical, nor (strictly speaking) conglomerate. Since the products of the acquired company are *complementary* to those of the acquiring company and may be produced with similar facilities, marketed through the same channels and in the same manner, and advertised by the same media, the Commission aptly called this acquisition a "product-extension merger." [Emphasis added.] . . .

3. The anticompetitive effects with which this product-extension merger is fraught can easily be seen: (1) the substitution of the powerful acquiring firm for the smaller, but already dominant, firm may substantially reduce the competitive structure of the industry by *raising entry barriers* and by *dissuading the smaller firms from aggressively competing;* (2) the acquisition *eliminates the potential competition of the acquiring firm.* [Emphasis added. Continuing, the court underscored its observation that the merger would raise "new entry barriers" by noting that:]

Federal Trade Commission v. Procter & Gamble Company
U.S. Supreme Court,
386 U.S. 568 (1967)

The major competitive weapon in the successful marketing of bleach is advertising. Clorox was limited in this area by its relatively small budget and its inability to obtain substantial discounts. By contrast Procter's budget was much larger; and, although it would not devote its entire budget to advertising Clorox, it could divert a large portion to meet the short-term threat of a new entrant. Procter would be able to use its volume discounts to advantage in advertising Clorox. Thus, a *new entrant would be much more reluctant to face the giant Procter than it would have been to face the smaller Clorox.* [Emphasis added.] . . .

[Further, in emphasizing its contention that the merger might dissuade the smaller firms from aggressively competing, the court noted that the interjection of a corporation the size of Procter into the liquid bleach market might considerably change these firms' role, saying:] there is every reason to assume that the smaller firms would become more cautious in competing, due to their fear of retaliation by Procter. It is probable that Procter would become the price leader and that oligopoly would become more rigid. . . .

Judgment reversed.

Conglomerate Mergers—Further Comments: Most conglomerate mergers, particularly those involving small and medium-sized companies, probably do not have significant anticompetitive effects, and most presumably are not even challenged by the government. Additionally, at least some of the mergers that have been challenged in court were found to be lawful on the ground that they actually enhanced competition rather than lessening it. (Such might be the case, for example, where two medium-sized firms merged in order to better compete with larger ones or where one of the two was a "failing company"—one that would drop out of the industry if unaided by the other.)

On the other hand, as already indicated, where the merging companies are large, the courts may indeed find that anticompetitive effects exist. Based on the *Clorox* case and others that have followed it, such mergers may substantially lessen competition (and thus violate Section 7 of the Clayton Act) where, in the particular circumstances presented, the merger may (1) "raise significant entry barriers," (2) "dissuade" existing companies in the industry from competing as aggressively as they did before, (3) eliminate the "potential competition" of the acquiring firm. A brief explanation of each of these factors follows.

Raising entry barriers. The term *entry barriers* refers to the degree of difficulty that confronts a company thinking of entering an industry new to it. Some industries have relatively low barriers, while in others the barriers are high (for example, the amount needed for initial investment is great, research and development costs are substantial, or the difficulties of establishing a marketing organization are formidable). Particularly in industries where the barriers are high to begin with, a conglomerate merger (as in the *Clorox* case) may raise them even higher by further discouraging potential entrants from entering into competition against a post-merger giant.

Dissuading competition. In some cases the courts decide on the basis of particular circumstances that the merger in question might result in the post-merger firm being so formidable as to cause smaller firms in the industry to become more cautious in their competitive tactics for fear of retaliation. Such a merger, said to "dissuade" existing firms from competing aggressively, produces another situation where competition may be substantially lessened in violation of Section 7 if the dissuasion is likely to be significant.

Eliminating potential competition. The possibility that a merger might substantially lessen competition "by eliminating the potential competition" of the acquiring firm is more difficult to see and can best be explained by an example. Suppose that a manufacturing industry has five major firms, A, B, C, D, and E. A sixth firm, F, has been actively considering entry into this industry for a substantial period of time. In some such situations economists can present an arguable case that the existence of the potential entrant by itself produces a beneficial competitive effect on the industry. That is, the five existing firms may refrain from raising prices too high for fear that the increased profits will be an added inducement for firm F to enter the industry. In such a situation, if firm F later merges with any of the existing companies, the beneficial effect produced by its "lurking in the background" is thereby removed; and freed of such indirect restraint the industry prices overall may increase markedly.

The Federal Trade Commission Act

In order to strengthen the enforcement of the Clayton Act and to provide a more continuous means of surveillance of business practices than that afforded by the federal courts, Congress passed the Federal Trade Commission Act in 1914. As noted earlier, this act created the Federal Trade Commission and granted it the power to enforce Sections 2, 3, 7, and 8 of the Clayton Act. Additionally, Section 5 of the FTC Act prohibited "unfair methods of competition" in interstate commerce and also delegated enforcement powers of the section to the FTC. (These twin responsibilities are actually unrelated—a fact that may explain why the FTC's activities over the years have been considerably less successful than originally hoped for.)

The Original Section 5

Section 5 simply prohibited "unfair methods of competition in commerce" and left it up to the FTC initially—and to the courts ultimately—to decide on a case-by-case basis the specific kinds of conduct that fell within that language. In many of the early actions brought under this section by the FTC, which had found the defendant corporations guilty of engaging in prohibited practices, the courts reversed the FTC's decisions. The primary reason for this reversal was that the courts interpreted Section 5 as prohibiting only those unfair methods of competition that *injured competitors of the defendant corporations;* a simple showing that customers of the defendant corporations had been injured by unfair or deceptive practices was not sufficient.

The Wheeler-Lea Amendment

As a result of this restrictive interpretation, in 1938 Congress passed the Wheeler-Lea Act, which amended Section 5 to read as follows: "Unfair methods of competition in commerce and unfair or deceptive acts or practices are hereby declared unlawful." The Wheeler-Lea Act also gave the FTC express powers to deal with certain deceptive advertising practices and made it a criminal offense for a firm to disobey a final cease-and-desist order of the commission.

The primary effect of this amendment, certainly, was to make it clear that unfair or deceptive acts or practices were flatly prohibited—and could be enjoined by the FTC—even if they did not result in injury to competitors of the firms engaging in them. Or, as it was put by the House committee reporting out the Wheeler-Lea bill, "This amendment makes *the consumer,* who may be injured by an unfair trade practice, of equal concern, before the law, with the merchant or manufacturer injured by the unfair methods of a dishonest competitor."

Unfair Methods of Competition

The various practices that have been ruled by the courts to constitute unfair methods of competition are too numerous and diverse to list in detail. The ones most likely to injure competitors, however, are certainly these: the use of false advertising; the making of unusually restrictive agreements, both horizontal and vertical; the entering of conspiracies to fix prices, allocate markets, or prevent others from procuring goods; the selling below cost to injure competitors; and the mislabeling of products. Other examples are the use of misleading names with respect to the identity of the seller or manufacturer, the inducement of breaches of competitor's contracts, and the offer of deceptive inducements to purchase goods.

Unfair or Deceptive Practices

Some of the acts listed above—particularly those of false advertising, mislabeling of products, and offering deceptive inducements to purchase—also clearly result in injuries to consumers. In fact, a substantial portion of the commission's time (too much, some critics say) is spent in investigating just these kinds of misconduct, particularly false advertising. As a result, many advertisers—especially those engaged in selling so-called health products—have been restrained from making unfounded claims in regard to the efficacy of their goods and from advertising "free" goods when, in fact, such goods can be obtained only by a consumer who first agrees to buy other products offered by the seller. Other practices likely to injure the consumer (and thus unlawful under this section) are the use of "bait" advertising and false endorsements, misrepresentation as to the provisions of purchase contracts, and, of course, the delivery of "short measures." (The case of *Jay Norris, Inc., v. FTC* in Chapter Six is illustrative of some of the kinds of unfair and deceptive practices with which the FTC is concerned).

1. Utah Pie had its bakery in Salt Lake City, and for some years had been the sole seller of frozen pies in the area. In 1960 another distributor of pies, Pet Milk, started selling pies in Salt Lake City in competition with Utah. A price war broke out, and continued for several years, with the result that (a) Pet sold its pies to groceries in Salt Lake City from time to time at prices lower than it was charging grocers located in other parts of the state in order to undercut Utah's prices, and (b) Utah suffered financial losses during the years that the war continued. Utah then sued Pet, charging Pet with price discrimination in violation of Section 2 of the Clayton Act. In regard to this charge, which of the facts stated above (if any) would support Utah's claim that Pet had engaged in discriminatory pricing at all? Discuss. (*Utah Pie Co. v. Continental Baking Co. et al.,* 386 U.S. 685, 1967.)

2. Referring to the Utah case, above, Utah had to prove—in addition to discriminatory pricing on Pet's part—an "injury" as a result of the pricing. On this aspect of the case, Utah proved not only that it had suffered occasional losses at specific times, but also introduced evidence of "predatory" pricing policies on the part of Pet—i.e., evidence that many of Pet's price cuts were so large as to be made only with the intent to drive Utah out of business. Do you think this kind of evidence is relevant in determining whether there was an injury, and, if so, the size of the injury? Explain.

3. Sun Oil sold gasoline to many independent retail dealers in Florida, including McLean's in Jacksonville. When a competitor of McLean's located just across the street started selling "Super Test" at prices lower than McLean was charging for Sunoco, Sun lowered its prices to McLean but did not lower them to other buyers of its gas in the area. The Federal Trade Commission then charged Sun with price discrimination in violation of the Clayton Act, and Sun defended on the ground that it had lowered its price simply to meet the price of a competitor as permitted by Clayton. The FTC replied that Sun had not lowered its price to meet that of a competitor, but rather to permit a customer to meet the price of one of *its* competitors (i.e., the FTC contended that this was not the case of Sun lowering its prices to meet those of Sun's competitors). Is the FTC argument valid? Why or why not? (*Federal Trade Commission v. Sun Oil,* 371 U.S. 505, 1963.)

4. On the subject of *requirements contracts,* (a) define such contracts, and (b) explain whether such contracts are usually lawful, or usually unlawful, under Section 3 of the Clayton Act.

5. Chicken Delight licensed several hundred franchisees to operate neighborhood fast food stores. It did not charge the franchisees any fees or royalties for use of its name, but it did require them to purchase certain packaging supplies and mixes exclusively from Chicken Delight, and also designated quantities of cookers and fryers. The prices charged the franchisees for these items were higher than those charged by competing suppliers. Several franchisees brought an action against Chicken Delight, claiming that the clauses in the franchises requiring them to buy these items from Chicken Delight alone were a form of tying contracts, and that these requirements therefore violated Sec. 1 of the Sherman Act. (a) Do you think these clauses do create tying contracts, and (b) if so, do you think that they unreasonably restrain trade in violation of the Sherman Act? Explain. (*Siegel v. Chicken Delight, Inc., 448 F.2d 43, 1971.*)

6. The Philadelphia National Bank (PNB) entered into a merger agreement with another Philadelphia bank, Girard Trust (GT). In Philadelphia and the surrounding four-county area, these banks were number 2 and 3 in size, respectively. If the proposed merger were to be consumated, the post-merger bank would be the biggest in the area. The government challenged the merger as a violation of Section 7 of the Clayton Act, contending that it would clearly substantially lessen competition in the Philadelphia area. The banks responded to this contention by showing that in past years each of them had competed with one another to some extent in other counties lying far outside the Philadelphia area—e.g., each had competed in making loans to borrowers outside the Philadelphia area, and each had tried to attract savings deposits from customers outside that area. Accordingly, the banks argued, the "relevant geographical market" against which the impact of the merger should be weighed was a much larger geographical area than just the Philadelphia one. The government attacked this defense by showing that most of the banks' activities, by far, was carried on only in the Philadelphia area, and that therefore the merger impact should be measured in that area alone. Do you agree with this contention of the government? Explain. (*United States* v. *Philadelphia National Bank,* 374 U.S. 321, 1963.)

7. It is probably true that conglomerate mergers are less likely to "substantially lessen competition" than are horizontal mergers. Why is this so?

Consumer Protection 48

A few years ago a manufacturer could feel reasonably secure designing, developing, producing, and marketing a product carefully. If a company provided understandable instructions for the product's assembly and use, and if it extended an appropriate warranty to the buyer, the company was under no obligation to make the product accident-proof or foolproof. Today, manufacturers do not find the going quite so easy. The old maxim *caveat emptor*—let the buyer beware—does not apply in the modern marketplace. Given the frailties of people and machines, manufacturers find it increasingly difficult to market liability-proof products so perfect in design and so free from defects that they can feel reasonably safe from lawsuits for injury or damage the product causes a consumer.

Similarly, the creditor/debtor relationship has undergone a significant shift in emphasis from protection of the creditor to protection of the debtor in the consumer transaction where credit is extended. This is not to say that the creditor in a consumer transaction—one in which someone borrows or buys for personal, family, or household use—is completely at the mercy of the customer. The bulk of consumer protection law *does* favor the buyer/debtor and is designed to protect the borrower from such things as usury (lending money at interest rates higher than

Caveat Emptor to Caveat Venditor

the law allows), excessive garnishments, and hidden costs in credit transactions. However, the seller/creditor has also had rights defined by the numerous laws on the subject. Therefore, a knowledge of the basic provisions of consumer protection statutes is essential to the business person of today if he or she is to operate a commercially successful venture and, at the same time, conduct consumer transactions within the law.

The law of consumer transactions is primarily statutory. Consumers derive their rights and incur their obligations from the many state and federal statutes available for their benefit. A number of statutes protect consumers in the financial dealings associated with borrowing or buying. Others afford protection in the purchasing process and set guidelines for the degree of performance and satisfaction it is reasonable to expect from a purchase.[1] Finally, some statutes and a large body of case law relate to product safety. They provide a measure of protection against unsafe products and allow recovery for damages or injury caused by such products. For purposes of identification and reference a table of some of the more important statutes is provided to assist in identifying and locating those which cover specific areas of general interest (see table).

Most of this chapter will address the first broad category, the consumer and financial transactions. Development of consumer protection law in credit transactions has been rapid and dramatic. To a large extent, it is a direct result of the government's expanding role in the regulation of business. There is nothing new in the idea that the consumer should be entitled to protection in dealing with business, big and small. The lending of money has long been regulated by state usury laws. Since 1914, the Federal Trade Commission has been authorized to investigate and stop unfair or deceptive trade practices. As big business has become bigger and the law of corporations has developed, federal and state legislation has been enacted to protect the investor from unscrupulous dealers in securities. In this century, the growth of big business has been phenomenal, and recent efforts to provide consumers with a statutory arsenal so they don't go defenseless into the marketplace have been equally so. This is especially evident in the field of credit transactions.

The Consumer Credit Protection Act (CCPA)

It is a fairly easy matter for the average householder to obtain and use any number of credit cards. The cash purchase of major appliances and automobiles is now a rare occurrence. Even the smallest supermarket purchases are paid for by check. The proliferation of credit has required legislation to define the rights and obligations of those who deal in it.

---

[1]The student should review Chapter 20, in which product liability, the Consumer Product Safety Act, warranties under the provisions of the Uniform Commercial Code, and the Magnuson-Moss Warranty Act are discussed.

Current Consumer Protection Statutes

Popular Name	Purpose	References
Child Protection	Requires special labeling and child-proof devices	15 U.S.C.A. §§ 1261 *et seq*
Cigarette Labeling and Ad	Surgeon general warning of possible health hazard	15 U.S.C.A. §§ 1331 *et seq*
Consumer Credit Protection	Comprehensive protection, all phases of credit transactions	15 U.S.C.A. §§ 1601 *et seq*
Consumer Product Safety	Protects consumer against defective or dangerous products	15 U.S.C.A. §§ 2051 *et seq*
Equal Credit Opportunity	Prohibits discrimination in extending credit	15 U.S.C.A. § 1691
Fair Credit Collection Practices	Prohibits abuses by debt collectors	15 U.S.C.A. § 1692
Fair Credit Reporting	Protects consumer's credit reputation	15 U.S.C.A. § 1681
Fair Packaging and Labeling	Requires accurate name, weights, quantities	15 U.S.C.A. §§ 1451 *et seq*
Federal Trade Commission	Prohibits unfair or deceptive trade practices	15 U.S.C.A. § 45
Flammable Fabrics	Eliminates or controls manufacture and marketing of dangerous fabrics	15 U.S.C.A. §§ 1191 *et seq*
Food, Drug, and Cosmetic	Prohibits marketing of impure, adulterated products	21 U.S.C.A. §§ 301 *et seq*
Fur Products Labeling	Prohibits misbranding of fur products	15 U.S.C.A. § 69
Magnuson-Moss Warranty	Rules governing content of warranties	15 U.S.C.A. §§ 2301 *et seq*
National Traffic and Motor Vehicle Safety	Promotes traffic and auto safety	15 U.S.C.A. §§ 1381 *et seq*
Real Estate Settlement Procedures	Requires disclosure of home buying costs	15 U.S.C.A. §§ 2601 *et seq*
Truth in Lending	Requires complete disclosure of credit terms	15 U.S.C.A. §§ 1601 *et seq*
Uniform Consumer Credit Code	Similar to federal Truth in Lending	8 states have adopted*
Uniform Commercial Code	Law of sales—unconscionable contracts	§ 2-302
Wholesome Meat	Controls meat processing	21 §§ 601 *et seq*
Wholesome Poultry Products	Controls processing of poultry and poultry products	21 U.S.C.A. §§ 451 *et seq*
Wool Products Labeling	Requires accurate labeling of wool products	15 U.S.C.A. § 68

*Colorado, Idaho, Indiana, Kansas, Maine, Oklahoma, Utah, Wyoming.

Congress enacted the Consumer Credit Protection Act (CCPA) in 1968 in response to unscrupulous and predatory practices on the part of creditors extending credit in consumer transactions. Congress was concerned with consumer credit disclosure methods, credit advertising, garnishment methods, questionable procedures used by some credit reporting agencies, and certain debt collection practices (a problem recognized in a 1977 amendment to the act). Since we are all concerned with credit, either as consumers or business people, it will be worthwhile to examine the important features of the CCPA.

Truth in Lending

The purpose of the truth in lending section of the CCPA is to strengthen competition among institutions that extend consumer credit by requiring them to disclose credit terms so that consumers can more readily compare the credit terms available to them and avoid the uninformed use of credit. To accomplish this, the consumer credit cost disclosure portion of the CCPA, known as the Truth in Lending Act, requires creditors to disclose both the finance charge and the annual percentage rate (APR) of the finance charge in a credit sale or loan to a consumer. The finance charge is that total of all charges payable for the extension of credit. It includes such items as interest, service or carrying charges, investigation or credit report fees, and premiums for any insurance the creditor requires as protection for the loan. The finance charge does not include certain items of expense to the debtor, primarily because they are paid to parties other than the creditor. Such items include taxes and, in the case of credit secured by an interest in real estate, fees for title examination, title insurance, and preparation of a deed or other necessary documents.

When the finance charge has been determined, it must then be expressed as the annual percentage rate (APR). The APR often is substantially higher than the annual interest rate. For example, if the finance charge, including 6 percent annual add-on interest, amounts to 1¼ percent per month, the APR is 15 percent, or 9 percent higher than the annual interest. These facts, together with information on delinquency or default charges, a description of any property used as security, and the total of the amount to be financed, must be revealed to the borrower in a disclosure statement before credit is extended. The information contained in the disclosure statement is supposed to permit the borrower to "shop around" for credit and select the creditor whose terms are the most favorable. The Truth in Lending Act does not put a ceiling on interest rates or limit finance charges. Its main requirement is that a creditor who regularly extends credit in the ordinary course of business make a full disclosure of the cost of credit to the consumer. It applies if the transaction between creditor and consumer involves a finance charge or if payment or repayment will be made in more than four installments. It does not, however, apply to personal loans between friends, loans to individuals for business purposes, or loans to corporations or partnerships.

Other features of the act require that the number of payments and the amount of each be disclosed and that complete disclosure be made when credit is advertised, when the loan is made or credit extended, and when periodic billing takes place. If the transaction involves a security interest in real property, the borrower is given three business days from the date of the transaction to rescind the transaction without penalty. This right to rescind must be brought to the attention of the borrower by means of a special notice to the customer on a prescribed form. Detailed procedures of the act are contained in regulation Z, issued by the Federal Reserve Board under the authority of the CCPA. Criminal penalties for willfully and knowingly failing to comply with the requirements of the act are a fine of up to $5,000 or imprisonment for one year, or both. Civil penalties can be recovered by the debtor in an amount equal to twice the finance charge but not less than $100 or more than $1,000, plus costs and attorney's fees in appropriate cases, such as the following:

Joseph v. Norman's Health Clubs, Inc.
U.S. Court of Appeals, Eighth Circuit, 532 F.2d 86 (1976)

A number of plaintiffs brought this action against Norman's Health Club and two finance companies, alleging that the activities of all three defendants violated the federal Truth in Lending Act.

Norman Saindon, one of the defendants, owned and operated a chain of health clubs in the St. Louis, Missouri area. "Lifetime memberships" were offered to the public for $360, payable in twenty-four equal installments of $15 each. Ninety-eight percent of club members chose to sign installment notes rather than pay cash for their memberships. The health club then "discounted" these notes to finance companies. That is, the club sold the notes to the finance companies for amounts considerably less than their face amounts, with the discounts ranging from $85 to $165 on the $360 notes.

The gist of the plaintiffs' complaint was that a number of patrons who paid cash for their memberships had been granted a 10 percent price reduction from the basic price charged installment members and that the failure of the health club and the finance companies to disclose this fact—and information about the discounts—to the installment members violated the Truth in Lending Act (TILA) of 1969. (A basic provision of TILA required persons "who extend credit" in consumer transactions to disclose the "true" cost of that credit to their installment purchasers.)

The trial court entered a judgment in favor of the plaintiffs against the health club but not against the two finance companies. That is, the court ruled that there was no violation of TILA by the finance companies, on the ground that they had "not extended credit" to the plaintiffs and the TILA therefore did not apply to them. The plaintiffs appealed.

Lay, Circuit Judge .... The fundamental purpose of the Truth in Lending Act, 15 U.S.C. § 1601 et seq., is to require creditors to disclose the "true" cost of consumer credit, so that consumers can make informed choices among available methods of payment. See 15 U.S.C. § 1601; *Mourning v. Family Publications Service, Inc.,* 411 U.S. 356, 364–65, 93 S.Ct. 1652, 1658, 36 L.Ed.2d 318, 326 (1973); Warren & Larmore, *Truth in Lending: Problems of Coverage,* 24 Stan. L.Rev. 793 (1972); W. Willier & F. Hart, Consumer Credit Handbook (1969). The Act is remedial in nature.

The Act was intended to change the practices of the consumer credit industry, and the statute reflects Congress' view that this should be done by imposing disclosure requirements on those who "regularly" extend or offer to extend consumer credit. In interpreting the Act, the Federal Reserve Board and the majority of courts have focused on the substance, rather than the form of credit transactions, and have looked to the practices of the trade, the course of dealing of the parties, and the intention of the parties in addition to specific contractual obligations. Thus, in *Mourning v. Family Publications Service, Inc., supra,* the Supreme Court said:

> The hearings held by Congress reflect the difficulty of the task it sought to accomplish. Whatever legislation was passed had to deal not only with the myriad forms in which credit transactions then occurred, but also with those which would be devised

in the future ... The language employed evinces the awareness of Congress that some creditors would attempt to characterize their transactions so as to fall one step outside whatever boundary Congress attempted to establish. 411 U.S. at 365, 93 S.CT. at 1658, 36 L.Ed.2d at 327.

The statute requires certain information, such as total finance charges and the applicable annual percentage rate, to be disclosed "to each person to whom consumer credit is extended and upon whom a finance charge is extended and upon whom a finance charge is or may be imposed." 15 U.S.C. § 1631(a). "Credit" includes "the right granted by a creditor to a customer to ... incur debt and defer its payment." Reg. Z, 12 C.F.R. § 226.2(1). The Act does not apply to loans or credit sales made "for business and commercial purposes" 15 U.S.C. § 1603(1); it covers only extensions of consumer credit, defined in the Act as credit "offered or extended [to] a natural person ... primarily for personal, family, household, or agricultural purposes." 15 U.S.C. § 1602(h). Failure to comply renders the creditor liable to the consumer in an amount equal to twice the finance charge, but not less than $100 or more than $1000. 15 U.S.C. § 1640(a). In the Act, Congress gave the Federal Reserve Board authority to promulgate regulations to ensure compliance. 15 U.S.C. § 1604; see *Mourning v. Family Publications Service,* supra at 365, 371–72, 93 S.Ct. at 1661, 36 L.Ed.2d at 330. Pursuant to that grant of authority, the Board promulgated Regulation Z, 12 C.F.R. § 226.1 et seq.

... In the instant case, the finance companies operated under a definite working arrangement with the Club. The evidence discloses that (1) the finance companies were alerted almost simultaneously with the customer's execution of a note; (2) an immediate credit check was then made by the finance companies; (3) if the customer's note was accepted, the finance companies paid the Club the amount of the note less the discount; (4) the finance companies accepted assignments without recourse to the Club, thus relying solely on the customer for payment; (5) the finance companies often contacted the customer the same day and upon approving him, the companies would send out their payment book describing the manner of payment and the notice of late charges (not mentioned in the note assigned); (6) the finance companies carried the note on their books as a "loan" and listed a "finance charge"; and (7) thereafter, the finance companies treated the club member in the same manner as they did their direct consumer loan customers. The situation was no different than if the finance companies had gone to the Club with the prospective member, paid the Club for the membership and then taken the customer's note just as they did take it.

We find, as have all but one of the courts faced with similar facts, that where the third-party financer becomes intimately involved in the relevant credit transactions it may become liable as an extender of credit. ...

The Discount as a Finance Charge.

Finding liability, the remaining issue is whether the discount constituted a finance charge under the Act.

The district court did not discuss whether the discount on the notes assigned to the finance companies was a finance charge which should have been disclosed by the Club. The district court did note, however, that unitary price schemes, under which the seller offers goods for the same price, whether paid in cash or on the installment plan, can hide a finance charge. 386 F.Supp. at 791.

The Act defines "finance charge" as:

the sum of *all* charges, payable directly or *indirectly by the person to whom the credit is extended,* and imposed directly or *indirectly* by the creditor as an incident to the extension of credit including ... any amount payable under a discount ... system. 15 U.S.C. § 1605(a) [Emphasis added].

The fact that a particular charge may not be included in the definitions of interest found in state usury laws is not controlling, for "finance charge" under TILA was intended to include not only "interest" but many other charges for credit. H.R. Rep. No. 1040, 90th Cong., 2d Sess., 2 U.S.Code Cong. & Admin. News pp.1962, 1977 (1968). The Federal Reserve Board has ruled that discounts paid by a seller (such as the Health Club) of consumer accounts receivable must be included in the stated finance charge if and to the extent that they are passed to the consumer. See 12 C.F.R. §§ 226.4(a), 226.406; FRB Letter No. 433 (Jan. 21, 1971) by Tynan Smith, CCH Consumer Credit Guide, para. 30, 627.

In the instant case, it is obvious that all of the discount originally agreed upon by the Club and the finance companies was passed along to the customers as a charge for use of credit. It may be, however, that some portion of the subsequent increases in the discount was not passed along to the customers and was rather absorbed by the Club as a reduction in its profit. On the other hand, adding more members may have permitted the seller so to reduce cost per member that it could provide the same services without increasing the face amount of the note. The district court should explore this matter on remand. See 12 C.F.R. § 226.406.

Since the amount of the discounts charged by the finance companies varied from time to time, it is necessary to remand to the district court for computation of the penalty to be assessed under the Act in favor of the plaintiffs and against the finance companies.

The judgment in favor of the finance companies is vacated and the cause reversed and remanded for further proceedings.

Restrictions on Garnishment

Garnishment can be defined as the legal proceedings of a judgment creditor to require a third person owing money to the debtor or holding property belonging to the debtor to turn over to the court or sheriff the property or money for the satisfaction of the judgment.[2] Congressional hearings leading to the enactment of the CCPA revealed that the unrestricted garnishment of wages encouraged predatory extension of credit, that employers were often quick to discharge an employee whose wages were garnished, and that the laws of the states on the subject were so different they effectively destroyed the uniformity of the bankruptcy laws and defeated their purpose. Consequently, the CCPA section on garnishment set limits on the extent to which the wages of an individual could be garnished. In general, wages cannot be garnished in any workweek in excess of 25 percent of the individual's disposable (after-tax) earnings or the amount by which the disposable earnings for that workweek exceed thirty times the federal minimum hourly wage, whichever is less. Such restrictions do not apply in the case of a court order for the support of any person (wife or child, for example), any order of a court of

---

[2]See the discussion on garnishment in Chapter 44.

bankruptcy under Chapter 13 (Adjustment of Debts of an Individual with Regular Income) of the Federal Bankruptcy Act, or any debt due for state or federal taxes.

The Fair Credit Reporting Act

The section of the CCPA known as the Fair Credit Reporting Act is directed at consumer reporting agencies. It is an effort by Congress to insure that the elaborate mechanism developed for investigating and evaluating the creditworthiness, credit standing, credit capacity, character, and general reputation of consumers is fair with respect to the confidentiality, accuracy, relevance, and proper utilization of the reported information. Too often in the past, the consumer was denied credit because of misleading or inaccurate information supplied to a prospective creditor by a consumer reporting agency.[3] The effect could be devastating, particularly as it affected the consumer's credit standing and general reputation in the business community.

The information on individual consumers is derived from many sources, including creditors, court and other official records, neighbors, and, in many cases, from facts consumers supply themselves. Information accumulated in a *consumer report* and disseminated to users can and often does include such items as judgments, liens, bankruptcies, arrest records, and employment history. In addition, the Fair Credit Reporting Act covers the *investigative reports* made by credit reporting agencies. Often used by prospective employers or by insurance companies, investigative reports are more personal in nature than consumer reports and can contain information on the subject's personal habits, marital status (past and present), education, political affiliation, and so on.

With regard to both consumer reports and investigative reports, the law requires that, upon request and proper identification, consumers are entitled to know the nature and substance of all information about them (except medical information) in the agency's file, the sources of the information, and the identity of those who have received the report from the credit reporting agency. Those entitled to receive consumer reports include businesses that may want to extend credit to the consumer, prospective employers or insurers, and government licensing agencies that may be concerned with the financial responsibility of the consumer. Access to the information can also be gained by court order. In addition, an investigative report cannot be prepared on an individual consumer unless that person is first notified and given the right to request information on the nature and scope of the pending investigation.

An important provision of the act requires that all information in consumer reports be current and that consumer reporting agencies maintain reasonable procedures designed to avoid violations of certain other provisions. This is an obvious effort to reduce the incidence of carelessly prepared reports having inaccurate information.

---

[3]This is not an agency of the government. Such agencies are persons or businesses that regularly assemble and evaluate credit information and provide it to others for a fee.

Finally, civil penalties for a *negligent* violation of the act include the actual damages to the consumer and, in a successful action, court costs and reasonable attorney's fees. In case of *willful* noncompliance, punitive damages may also be awarded to the successful plaintiff consumer. It is interesting to note that administrative enforcement of the act and compliance with its provisions is a function of the Federal Trade Commission because violations are considered unfair or deceptive acts or practices.

Credit Cards

The widespread use of credit cards, issued by all manner of companies, created much legal controversy when a card fell into the wrong hands through loss or theft. Many companies provided their credit cards indiscriminately to any person who might want one and to many who had not requested them. It became a major problem to determine who was to assume the liability for unauthorized credit card purchases: the person to whom the card was issued, the unauthorized user, the merchant who made the sale, or the credit card issuer.

Congress addressed the problem in CCPA provisions that prohibit the issuance of credit cards except in response to a request or application and that place limits on the liability of a cardholder for its unauthorized use. In general, if a cardholder loses a credit card and it is used by someone without authority to do so, the cardholder is liable if: (1) the liability does not exceed $50; (2) the card is an accepted card; (3) the issuer has given notice to the cardholder as to the potential liability; (4) the issuer has provided the cardholder with a self-addressed, pre-stamped notification to be mailed by the cardholder in the event of loss or theft; (5) the unauthorized use occurs before the cardholder has notified the issuer that an unauthorized use of the card has occurred; and (6) the card issuer has provided a method whereby the user of the card can be identified by the merchant, either by photograph or signature, as the authorized user.

The above provisions are obviously for the protection of a lawful cardholder. Unauthorized use of a credit card can result in severe penalties. If the unauthorized transaction involves goods or services, or both, having a retail value of $5,000 or more, the penalty can be a fine of up to $10,000 or imprisonment for up to five years, or both.

The Fair Debt Collection Practices Act

A 1977 amendment to the CCPA, the Fair Debt Collection Practices Act, became effective March 20, 1978. It has as its purpose the elimination of abusive debt collection practices by debt collectors and the protection of individual debtors against debt collection abuses. The act was brought about by the unscrupulous methods used by some debt collectors in pursuing debtors. Instances of harassment in the form of threats of violence, the use of obscene or profane language, publication of lists of consumers who allegedly refused to pay their debts, and annoyance by repeated use of the telephone were commonplace before the act was passed. The following excerpt, from *Duty v. General Finance Co.*, 273 S.W.2d 64 (Tex. 1954), illustrates some of the tactics employed by an overzealous debt collector. It is important to note that each and every tactic employed by the General Finance Company debt collector is now prohibited by the Fair Debt Collection Practices Act.

> The harassments alleged may be summarized as follows: Daily telephone calls to both Mr. & Mrs. Duty which extended to great length; threatening to blacklist them with the Merchants' Retail Credit Association; accusing them of being deadbeats; talking to them in a harsh, insinuating, loud voice; stating to their neighbors and employers that they were deadbeats; asking Mrs. Duty what she was doing with her money; accusing her of spending money in other ways than in payments on the loan transaction; threatening to cause both plaintiffs to lose their jobs unless they made the payments demanded; calling each of the plaintiffs at the respective places of their employment several times daily; threatening to garnishee their wages; berating plaintiffs to their fellow employees; requesting their employers to require them to pay; calling on them at their work; flooding them with a barrage of demand letters, dun cards, special delivery letters, and telegrams both at their homes and their places of work; sending them cards bearing this opening statement: "Dear Customer: We made you a loan because we thought that you were honest."; sending telegrams and special delivery letters to them at approximately midnight, causing them to be awakened from their sleep; calling a neighbor in the disguise of a sick brother of one of the plaintiffs, and on another occasion as a stepson; calling Mr. Duty's mother at her place of employment in Wichita Falls long distance, collect; leaving red cards in their door, with insulting notes on the back and thinly-veiled threats; calling Mr. Duty's brother long distance, collect, in Albuquerque, New Mexico, at his residence at a cost to him in excess of $11, and haranguing him about the alleged balance owed by plaintiffs.

The debt collector's communications with others and with the debtor in an effort to locate the debtor are governed by a provision of the act. The debt collector is prohibited from making false representations or misleading the debtor about the nature of the collection process. The collector cannot solicit or take from any person a check postdated by more than five days without notice of the intent to deposit the check. On occasion, debt collectors have encouraged the debtor to write a postdated check for the amount of the debt knowing that the debtor had insufficient funds to cover the check. A threat to deposit the postdated check was often enough to compel the debtor to seek the funds necessary to pay the collector and thereby avoid criminal prosecution for issuing a bad check. The act further provides that written notice of the amount of the debt and the name of the creditor be sent to the consumer together with a statement that, unless the consumer disputes the validity of the debt within thirty days, the debt collector can assume it is a valid obligation. If the consumer owes multiple debts and makes a single payment, the debt collector cannot apply the payment to any debt that is disputed by the consumer.[4]

The Fair Debt Collection Practices Act protects the consumer debtor and places significant burdens on the debt collector. Compliance with the act is enforced by the Federal Trade Commission, since violations are considered to be unfair or deceptive trade practices. A debt collector who fails to comply with the provisions of the act may incur civil liability to the extent of actual damages sustained by the plaintiff, additional punitive damages not to exceed $1,000, and court costs and reasonable attorney's fees.

Fair Credit Billing

Few of us have not disputed with a merchant or other creditor over a periodic statement of account. Prior to the Fair Credit Billing Act, the burden rested mainly on the customer-debtor to get things straightened out. This is no longer true. The Fair Credit Billing Act requires that creditors maintain procedures whereby consumers can complain about billing errors and obtain satisfaction within a specified period, not later than two billing cycles or ninety days. The consumer must give the creditor notice of the billing error with a statement explaining the reasons for questioning the item or items felt to be in error. The creditor must then either make appropriate corrections in the consumer's account or conduct an investigation into the matter. If, after the investigation, the creditor feels that the statement is accurate, it must so notify the debtor and explain why it believes the original statement of account to be correct. The act also requires that payments be credited promptly and that any overpayment be refunded (on request by the debtor) or credited to the debtor's account.

Equal Credit Opportunity

The Equal Credit Opportunity Act, as amended, quite simply prohibits discrimination based on race, color, religion, national origin, sex, marital status, or age in connection with extensions of credit. The applicant must, however, have contractual capacity; minors, for example, cannot insist on credit under the act. The enactment is the result of complaints by married persons that credit frequently was denied unless both parties to the marriage obligated themselves. Each party can now separately and voluntarily apply for and obtain credit accounts, and state laws prohibiting separate credit no longer apply. The act also directs the Board of Governors of the Federal Reserve System to establish a Consumer Advisory Council to provide advice and consultation on consumer credit and other matters.

---

[4]This provision may be contrary to a commonly accepted principle of contract law: Where a debtor owes multiple debts and fails to specify to which debt the payment is to be applied, the creditor can make the choice.

The Uniform Consumer Credit Code

Federal legislation does not necessarily preclude similar state legislation. For example, Sec. 1610 of the Consumer Credit Protection Act provides:

> This subchapter does not annul, alter, or affect, or exempt any creditor from complying with the laws of any State relating to the disclosure of information in connection with credit transactions, except to the extent that those laws are inconsistent with the provisions of this subchapter or regulations thereunder, and then only to the extent of the inconsistency.

Federal statutes frequently exempt state-regulated credit transactions if, for example, the state law is more stringent to creditors than it is to the credit consumer.[5] This principle—that state laws are enforceable even though they may regulate an area already covered by federal statutes—is illustrated by the Uniform Consumer Credit Code (UCCC), which has been adopted by eight states. The following case is illustrative.

United States v. Dumont

U.S. District Court, D. Montana 416 F. Supp. 632 (1976)

The United States obtained a judgment against Dumont. When the judgment was not paid, it sought in this action to "levy" on Dumont's wages. That is, the government brought a garnishment action to reach wages that were owed to Dumont by his employer. The U.S. contended that it could maintain this action under a federal statute, U.S.C. Sec. 1673. Dumont, however, claimed that Montana law was applicable. The Montana statute Dumont relied on provided that levy cannot be made where the debtor is the head of a family that depends upon him for support and where the wages sought to be levied upon are necessary for the use and support of his family. The decision below is that of the trial court.

Smith, Chief Judge .... These wages are totally exempt by virtue of R.C.M. 1947 § 93-5816 if the law of Montana is applicable. Fed.R.Civ.P. 69(a) provides in part:

> ... The procedure on execution, in proceedings supplementary to and in aid of a judgment, and in proceedings on and in aid of execution shall be in accordance with the practice and procedure of the state in which the district court is held, existing at the time the remedy is sought, except that any statute of the United States governs to the extent that it is applicable. (Footnote omitted)

The United States contends that 15 U.S.C. § 1673 is a statute of the United States which governs. This section, part of an act placing restrictions on garnishments, does not distinguish and was not enacted for the purpose of distinguishing between the United States and other creditors. It was enacted to protect debtors. In any event, that section cannot benefit the United States in this case. All that it does is specify the maximum amount of wages which may be subjected to garnishment. Were the section ambiguous in itself, the ambiguity is resolved by 15 U.S.C. § 1677 providing:

---

[5]For example, state laws that prohibit granishments or provide for more limited garnishments than are allowed under the federal statute are effective and enforceable despite the federal regulations on the same subject.

This subchapter does not annul, alter, or affect, or exempt any person from complying with, the laws of any State

(1) prohibiting garnishments or providing for more limited garnishments than are allowed under this subchapter . . . . See *Hodgson v. Hamilton Municipal Court,* 349 F.Supp. 1125 (S.D.Ohio 1972).

Defendants' objections to the levy are granted and the United States Marshal is directed to vacate any levies of execution or garnishment which are withholding from the defendant Dumont any wages due to him from his employer.

The Uniform Consumer Credit Code was promulgated in 1968 by the National Conference of Commissioners on Uniform State Laws. It is much like the Federal Consumer Credit Protection Act. It covers consumer credit sales, loans, garnishment, and insurance provided in relation to a consumer credit sale. Its truth-in-lending provisions require full disclosure to the consumer of all aspects of the credit transaction and further require that charges to the consumer be computed and disclosed as an annual percentage rate. The code does not prescribe any specific rates for credit service charges, but it sets maximums based on unpaid balances—36 percent per year on $300 or less, 21 percent per year for balances of $300 to $1,000, and 15 percent for unpaid balances in excess of $1,000. Since the law permits higher charges for smaller transactions, it forbids creditors from breaking large transactions down into smaller ones to take advantage of higher credit charges.

The UCCC covers door-to-door solicitation in some detail, since this is a troublesome area for consumers. Consumers tend to be more vulnerable to high-pressure selling tactics in their homes; and after signing an agreement to purchase, they often regret the decision. The UCCC therefore permits the rescission of a credit sale solicited and finalized in the customer's home if the customer gives written notice to the seller within seventy-two hours after signing the agreement to purchase.[6] The cancellation notice is effective when deposited in a mailbox and can take any form so long as it clearly expresses the buyer's intention to void the home solicitation sale. Sellers are required to provide a statement informing buyers of their right to cancel and including the mailing address for the written cancellation notice. The seller is permitted to retain a cancellation fee of 5 percent of the cash price of the sale, but the fee cannot exceed the amount of any cash down payment.

Generally, if debtors default on their payments, creditors can repossess the property that they purchased and sell it to satisfy the unpaid debt. If the sale earns too little to discharge the debt, the creditor can normally sue the debtor and obtain

---

[6]Many of the states that have not adopted the UCCC do have statutes governing door-to-door solicitation, and many municipalities have ordinances regulating solicitors, peddlers, and transient merchants. The latter regulations are known as Green River ordinances. See *Green River v. Fuller Brush Co.,* 65 F.2d 112 (1933).

a deficiency judgment. However, the UCCC distinguishes between debts incurred in the purchase of goods for $1,000 or less and debts exceeding $1,000. If the goods purchased were worth $1,000 or less, the creditor must *either* repossess the goods *or* sue the debtor for the unpaid balance. If the creditor chooses to repossess, the debtor is not personally liable for the unpaid balance. Only if the original sale exceeded $1,000 can the creditor repossess *and* seek a deficiency judgment if repossession fails to cover the unpaid balance.

With regard to garnishment, the UCCC prevents any prejudgment attachment of the debtor's unpaid earnings and limits the garnishment to 25 percent of net income or to that portion of the income in excess of forty times the federal minimum hourly wage. The UCCC also prohibits an employer from discharging an employee whose wages are garnished to pay a judgment arising from a consumer credit sale, lease, or loan.

Although the UCCC has been adopted by eight states, the law as adopted can vary considerably from state to state. It is generally true of the so-called uniform laws that a state can make significant changes so the law reflects local attitudes or conforms to local policy in the particular matter covered.

The Real Estate Settlement Procedures Act (RESPA)

The purchase of a residence is the largest single transaction most consumers ever make. It can be a traumatic experience for the novice who finds that, in addition to the down payment, substantial sums of money will be required on settlement, or closing day. Items to be paid for may include attorney's fees; title insurance; various inspections, surveys, and appraisals; agent's or broker's services; taxes and insurance; and many other miscellaneous items. Congress found that because of the variation in the kinds of items included in the settlement costs and the amount charged for each, significant reforms were needed in the real estate settlement process. The purpose of the Real Estate Settlement Procedures Act (RESPA), enacted in 1974 and amended in 1976, is to insure that buyers of residential property are given timely information on the nature and costs of the settlement process and that they are protected against obvious abuses. The act requires that effective advance disclosure be made to home buyers and sellers. It prohibits kickbacks or referral fees and, in general, affords considerable protection by letting the home buyer know what it is going to cost to buy a given home.

RESPA applies to all federally related mortgage loans and is administered and enforced by the Secretary of Housing and Urban Development.[7] The secretary has issued comprehensive regulations, known as Regulation X, to prescribe procedures for curbing questionable practices in real estate transactions. Various forms have been devised and are in use, and a special information booklet has been developed

---

[7]Most, if not all, mortgage loans on residential property are federally related. The deposits or accounts of the lending institution may be insured by an agency of the federal government, or the lender may be regulated by a federal agency.

for the lender to distribute to the borrower at the time a loan application is made. The lender is also required to provide the borrower with "good faith estimates" of the dollar amount or range of each settlement service charge that the borrower is likely to incur. Generally speaking, RESPA places the burden on the lender to provide the borrower good advance information about the costs of purchasing a home—the basic cost and the substantial sums needed on settlement day.

The Motor Vehicle Information and Cost Savings Act

With the increased emphasis on consumer product safety, cost disclosure requirements, the emerging energy crisis, and the quality of the environment, the automobile has been singled out for special treatment in the Motor Vehicle Information and Cost Savings Act, amended in 1975 and 1976. The legislation we discuss here does not directly affect credit, but it certainly affects consumers' pocketbooks. The purpose of the law is to help consumers make more reasoned judgments in their choice of automobiles, another large outlay for the average consumer. The act requires that the auto industry effect measures to reduce the cost of repairs, to provide consumers with the means to compare the safety and repairability of the many available models, to prevent tampering with the odometer readings of autos for sale, and to improve automobile fuel economy.

Congress has found that use of the so-called shock-absorbing or collapsible bumper will reduce economic loss from motor vehicle accidents. Consequently, the Secretary of Transportation, as administrator of the act, has developed and promulgated bumper standards that apply to most passenger vehicles. (A *passenger vehicle* is defined by the act as a motor vehicle designed for carrying twelve or fewer persons.) Bumper standards are developed in cooperation with the auto industry; manufacturers play a major role in the process. The Motor Vehicle Information and Cost Savings Act also provides that a comprehensive study be conducted by the Secretary of Transportation for the purpose of giving prospective auto buyers usable information about repair economy, damage susceptibility, and insurance rates for the many makes and models available to consumers.

Another provision of the act encourages the states to conduct diagnostic inspection demonstration projects consisting of periodic safety inspections of motor vehicles. Federal grants and technical assistance are available to those states that qualify and desire to participate. The purpose of this provision, strengthened by a 1974 amendment, is to promote the development of diagnostic equipment for use by inspection facilities designed to evaluate the safety, noise, emissions, and fuel efficiency of motor vehicles. It is also designed to encourage the development of equipment for use by smaller garages in conducting various tests on automobiles.

A major criterion in purchasing a "used" motor vehicle is its mileage. The purchaser should be able to rely on the odometer as an accurate reflection of the extent of prior use. The act forbids dealers and others from turning back odometers and from using devices that cause them to register fewer miles than the vehicle has actually traveled. Criminal and civil penalties are imposed for violations. The following case involves interpretation of the statute.

Grambo v. Loomis Cycle Sales, Inc.

U.S. District Court,
N.D. Indiana 404
F.Supp. 1073 (1975)

The plaintiff, Grambo, purchased a motorcycle from the defendant company. At the time of purchase the odometer read 875 miles. Later plaintiff learned that the actual mileage was over 14,000.

Grambo then brought this action to recover damages, alleging in the alternative (1) that defendant failed to disclose the actual mileage or that the true mileage was unknown; (2) that defendant altered the odometer with the intent to defraud; or (3) that defendant, while repairing the odometer, failed to adjust it to zero and failed to give notice of the repair of the odometer. Any of these allegations, if proven, would constitute a violation of the federal Motor Vehicle Information and Cost Savings Act.

The defendant filed a motion that the case be dismissed, contending (1) that the act did not apply to motorcycles; and (2) that if it did apply to motorcycles, the act was unconstitutionally vague. The latter argument was predicated on the provision of the statute that required a written notice of any alteration in mileage to be attached "to the left door frame of the vehicle" when the odometer was serviced and became incapable of showing the true mileage and on the fact that motorcycles do not have door frames. The decision below is that of the trial court.

Sharp, District Judge . . . . . Subchapter IV of the Motor Vehicle Information and Cost Savings Act, 15 U.S.C., Sections 1981-1991, was enacted by the United States Congress to prohibit tampering with odometers on motor vehicles and to establish certain safeguards for the protections (sic) of purchasers with respect to the sale of motor vehicles having altered or reset odometers. See 15 U.S.C., Section 1981.

(1) Whether Congress intended the term "motor vehicles" to cover motorcycles can be found in the legislative history of the Act where Congress described motor vehicles as including any vehicle driven or drawn by mechanical power for use in the public streets, roads, and highways. (1972 U.S. Code Congressional and Administrative News, page 3980.) This description clearly covers motorcycles and thus the act's prohibitions and requirements must be said to apply to such vehicles.

In devising safeguards against reset or altered odometers, the act and the regulations promulgated under it rely on disclosure. See 15 U.S.C., Sections 1987 and 1988, as well as the rules prescribed by the Secretary of Transportation in 49 C.F.R., part 580. The defendant, in his memorandum, attacks the disclosure requirement of Section 1987. His argument is based exclusively upon a statement in Section 1987 that requires a notice in writing to be attached to the left door frame of the vehicle when the odometer has been serviced, repaired or replaced and is incapable of registering the same mileage as before. Defendant argues that because motorcycles do not have door frames the act is vague and uncertain in its requirements and thus is unconstitutional as applied to motorcycle dealers.

(2) The basic principal which underlies the entire field of legal concepts pertaining to the validity of legislation is that by enactment of legislation a constitutional measure is presumed to be created. In a number of cases the courts have enunciated the fundamental rule that there is a presumption in favor of the constitutionality of a legislative enactment. *Davis Warehouse Co. v. Bowles,* 321 U.S. 144, 64 S.Ct. 474, 88 L.Ed. 635 (1943); *U.S. v. Carolene Products Co.,* 304 U.S. 144, 58 S.Ct. 778, 82 L.Ed. 1234 (1937); *Becker Steel Co. v. Cummings,* 296 U.S. 74, 56 S.Ct. 15,80 L.Ed. 54 (1935). The presumption in favor of constitutionality is especially strong in the case of statutes enacted to promote a public purpose. *McGowan v. State of Maryland,* 366 U.S. 420, 81 S.Ct. 1101, 6 L.Ed.2d 393 (1961); *U.S. v. Jacobs, Ill. and N.Y.,* 306 U.S. 363, 59 S.Ct. 551, 83 L.Ed. 763 (1938). The

Motor Vehicle Information and Cost Savings Act is just such a statute. It was enacted with the express public purpose of protecting purchasers when buying motor vehicles. See 15 U.S.C., Section 1981. Thus any interpretation of the Motor Vehicle Information and Cost Savings Act must begin with the presumption of its constitutionality.

(3,4) For a statute to fail to meet the requirements of due process it must be so vague and standardless as to leave the public uncertain as to its meaning. *Giaccio v. Pennsylvania,* 382 U.S. 399, 86 S.Ct. 518, 15 L.Ed.2d 447 (1966). The classic due process test is whether the statute either forbids or requires the doing of an act in terms so vague that men of common intelligence must necessarily guess at its meaning and differ as to its application. *United States v. Dellinger,* 472 F.2d 340 (7th Cir. 1972); *Livingston v. Garmire,* 437 F.2d 1050 (5th Cir. 1971). In applying this test to determine the constitutionality of the act as it applies to motorcycles this Court does not find the act to be so vague or uncertain as to leave reasonable [persons] without proper guidance. The purpose of the act, as outlined above, is twofold. First to prohibit alteration of odometers, and second, to disclose any change that service, repair, or replacement may have brought. Disclosure then becomes the key to Section 1987 and the requirement of disclosure is clear and unambiguous.

Being a relatively new statute, the courts have generally given the Motor Vehicle Information and Cost Savings Act a practical interpretation. *Stier v. Park Pontiac, Inc.,* 391 F.Supp. 397 (S.D.W.Va.1975); *Delay v. Hearn Ford,* 373 F.Supp. 791 (D.S.C.1974). Using such an approach it becomes clear that because an auto is large, the statute, in Section 1987, requires disclosure of any alteration in mileage to be on the left door frame where it can be looked for and noted. Thus, Section 1987 standardizes a place of attachment for such notice where a buyer can routinely look when contemplating the purchase of a used automobile. Such specific guidance is not needed for vehicles like motorcycles. Being relatively small vehicles motorcycles are easily subjected to inspection by purchasers, and reasonable men in the business of selling such vehicles would know that to satisfy the disclosure requirement of 15 U.S.C., Section 1987, they would only need to hang a tag on the cycle to place a potential purchaser on notice of an alteration in the mileage registered on the odometer.

Thus, in light of the presumption of constitutionality given to a statute enacted for a public purpose, and the clear satisfaction of the test developed in *Dillinger and Livingston,* supra, Section 1987 cannot be said to be unconstitutionally vague and uncertain.

Therefore, defendant's motion to dismiss pursuant to Federal Rules of Civil Procedure 12(b) (6) is denied.

Another section of the act deals with improving automotive efficiency and fuel economy. It prescribes the average fuel economy to be achieved by passenger automobiles, progressively improving from 1978 to 1985 and therafter. A direct response to the fuel shortage of the early 1970s, this portion of the act requires the auto industry to come up with products to conserve gasoline, a resource that some feel will be in short supply in years to come. The Secretary of Transportation will set fuel economy standards with the active involvement of the Environmental Protection Agency and the Department of Energy. This comprehensive program imposes considerable responsibility on auto manufacturers. The law imposes civil penalties on manufacturers for each tenth of a mile their products fall short of mileage standards and gives credit for each tenth of a mile their automobiles exceed standards. Large, powerful automobiles burn more fuel and emit more pollutants than do smaller vehicles. The auto industry is therefore trying to strike a balance between the "gas hog" and its comfort and the compact, more economical model, somewhat less luxurious and comfortable. At least for the immediate future, the answer lies somewhere in between with the mid-range models that can meet prescribed mileage standards.

Consumer Safety, Health, and Welfare

Thus far we have looked at some of the primarily federal legislation that insures fair treatment for consumers seeking credit, borrowing money, or contemplating the purchase of a residence or automobile. For the most part, the statutes we have examined in this chapter have been remedial in nature. Their purpose is to correct what Congress has determined to be persistent abuses. Many other statutes, however, are designed to protect the consumer's safety and well-being. These laws concern general health and welfare and alert the consumer to the possibility of harm from the use or misuse of certain products.

Packaging and Labeling

The controversial Public Health Cigarette Smoking Act of 1969, popularly known as the Cigarette Labeling and Advertising Act, establishes a comprehensive federal program to deal with labeling and advertising the ill effects of smoking on health. The act requires that the statement "Warning: The Surgeon General Has Determined That Cigarette Smoking Is Dangerous to Your Health" appear on cigarette and little cigar packages. Additionally, beginning in 1971, it became unlawful to advertise cigarettes and little cigars on any medium of electronic communication subject to the jurisdiction of the Federal Communications Commission.

The Wholesome Poultry Products Act and the Wholesome Meat Act are also examples of the protective statute. Each establishes procedures to insure that only wholesome products are distributed to consumers and that they are properly labeled and packaged.

The Federal Food, Drug, and Cosmetic Act establishes extensive controls over various products and regulates their development, premarketing testing, labeling, and packaging.

In the Fair Packaging and Labeling Act, effective July 1, 1967, Congress has stated that informed consumers are essential to the fair and efficient functioning of a free market economy and that packages and labels should enable consumers to obtain accurate information about the quantity of the contents and should facilitate value comparisons. The act therefore establishes comprehensive requirements for the identification of commodities and provides that net quantities must be conspicuously displayed in a uniform location on the principal panel of the product. The main purpose of the act, set forth in some detail, is the prevention of unfair or deceptive packaging and labeling and general misbranding of consumer commodities.

An important amendment, the Poison Prevention Packaging Act of 1970, resulted in the mandatory development and use of child-proof devices on household substances that could harm young children if mishandled or ingested. Other statutes for children are the Flammable Fabrics Act, the Child Protection Act, and the Child Protection and Toy Safety Act. The Consumer Product Safety Commission is responsible for administering many of the statutes relating to product safety.

Motor Vehicle Safety Standards

The purpose of the National Traffic Motor Vehicle Safety Act of 1966 is to reduce traffic accidents and deaths and injuries resulting from traffic accidents. To accomplish this purpose, the act focuses on automobile design and construction and directs the Secretary of Transportation to establish safety standards for motor vehicles and equipment. This cannot be done without the participation of the auto industry. Consequently, safety standards are developed and promulgated through a lengthy and complex process in which the auto makers play a meaningful role. There must be a balance between the cost involved in meeting safety standards and the degree of safety that is desirable. Much of the increase in the cost of automobiles comes from the added features required to meet safety standards.

Since the average adult spends so much time in automobiles, his or her preferences must be considered when safety standards are developed. The evolution of seat belts—from simple lap belt to shoulder and torso harness and from electronic interlock preventing starting to the current requirement for an eight-second buzzer —demonstrates the influence of public opinion on safety standards. Public dissatisfaction with a regulation can modify it. Motorists are generally safety conscious, but they dislike inconvenience intensely. To insure the participation of the general public, the Secretary of Transportation has established a National Motor Vehicle Safety Advisory Council. The majority of its members are representatives of the general public. Other members are representatives of state and local governments, motor vehicle and equipment manufacturers, and motor vehicle dealers. General public members of the council cannot be persons who have any connection with the auto industry, and the chairperson of the council must be a general public member.

Questions and Problems

1. Discuss a credit card holder's liability if the card has been lost and he or she is subsequently billed $350 for purchases someone else made.

2. A husband and wife signed an agreement to subscribe to several magazines with a door-to-door saleswoman who had called on them one evening during the dinner hour. What are the rights of both seller and buyer if the husband and wife decide the next morning that they have been high-pressured and want to void the transaction?

3. The main label on packages of crackers sold in a supermarket reads: "Diet-Thins Matzo Crackers." Would this label be false and misleading if the crackers were not lower in calories than other matzo crackers but did have other dietary benefits explained on a small side panel?

4. Discuss procedures to be used under the Fair Credit Billing Act if a consumer receives from a department store a statement of account he firmly believes contains an overcharge of $75.

5. In response to a request for information a consumer reporting agency reported to an insurance company that a specific applicant was an excessive drinker. Based on that information the insurance company refused to sell the applicant life insurance and his auto insurance was canceled. Applicant was in fact a nondrinker. Under what conditions may the applicant recover damages from the reporting agency for defamation?

6. John Smith is the sole proprietor of a small restaurant. Desiring to renovate and extend his premises he borrowed $30,000 from a local bank. Does the Truth in Lending Act have any applicability to this transaction?

7. Ms. Sarah Haynes was an unmarried dental technician who for years had maintained a charge account at a local department store. When she married the store closed her account and insisted that she reapply for credit in her husband's name. Is this procedure permissible under consumer protection laws?

8. In October 1974, Sheehan purchased a Ford automobile which was financed by Ford Credit on a retail installment contract. Later Sheehan moved to various locations and became delinquent on his account. When Ford Credit was unable to locate Sheehan it assigned the delinquent account to a central recovery office for collection or repossession. A short time later Sheehan's mother, who resided in Rhode Island, received a phone call from a woman who identified herself as an employee of the Mercy Hospital in San Francisco. (The call actually emanated from Ford Credit's office in Dearborn, Michigan.) She advised Sheehan's mother that one or both of Sheehan's children had been involved in a serious automobile accident and that she, the caller, was attempting to locate Sheehan. The mother supplied the caller with Sheehan's home and business addresses and phone numbers. The following day Sheehan's car was repossessed and subsequent inquiry revealed that the call referred to above was a ruse and that Sheehan's children had not been injured. *Ford Motor Credit Company v. Frances C. Sheehan,* 373 So.2d 956 (Fla. 1979). Are consumers protected against such practices?

9. A consumer who tried to obtain information from a credit reporting agency on the nature and substance of items in his file was denied such information and forced to return to the credit reporting agency's office several times. The consumer was finally given some of the information held by the agency, but several items were withheld. *Millstone v. O'Hanlon Reports, Inc.,* 383 F.Supp. 269 (1974). Discuss this situation with regard to the Fair Credit Reporting Act.

10. What are the economic implications of "consumerism?" In particular, how does it affect the purchase price of a new automobile?

Environmental Protection

49

Growing awareness of the environment in which we live and do business has led to an increased concern for its quality. We have finally realized that pollution poses a real threat to the health and general well-being of the world's inhabitants. Positive steps have been taken to reduce the ecological problems resulting from the tremendous rate at which science and technology have advanced. Unfortunately, however, the art of pollution control has not kept pace with material progress.

The early attitude toward the environmental consequences of *laissez-faire* was one of benign neglect, probably based on the assumptions that limitless resources were there for the taking and that the vastness of the earth made it unpollutable. The folly of such attitudes has forcefully and dramatically been brought to our attention daily in the news media. A thought-provoking study of the problem, *Limits to Growth,* suggests that such limits on the earth may be reached within the next hundred years if the current growth of world population, industrialization, pollution, and resource depletion continue unchecked. The study concludes that unless environmental damage is reversed, population and industrial capacity must inevitably decline.[1]

Others balance such pessimism with a degree of optimism. However, the rising incidence of carcinogens in the air we breathe and the products we use, the effect of excessive noise, the poor quality of the water we drink, and the mounting problem of waste disposal have led government and environmentalists to make concerted efforts to halt what are now considered to be real threats to the existence we enjoy today. This chapter examines some of the steps taken to alleviate specific problems—steps that, for the most part, consist of comprehensive and far-reaching federal legislation and, to a lesser extent, action at the state level.

The National Environmental Policy Act (NEPA)

Recognizing that a national policy was needed, Congress enacted the National Environmental Policy Act (NEPA) in 1969 to "encourage productive and enjoyable harmony between man and his environment and biosphere and stimulate the health and welfare of man; to enrich the understanding of the ecological systems and natural resources important to the Nation; and to establish a Council on Environmental Quality."[2] NEPA is a major step toward making each generation responsible to succeeding ones for the quality of the environment. Sec. 102(2)(c) of the act requires that an environmental impact statement be prepared whenever proposed major federal action will significantly affect the quality of the human environment. Responsible officials must provide a detailed statement describing the environmental impact of the proposed action, unavoidable adverse effects, acceptable alternatives to the proposed project, and any irreversible and irretrievable commitments of resources involved.

Environmental advocates, government agencies, and the courts have subjected NEPA to analysis and interpretation that emphasizes the great outdoors. However, urban development and the quality of life for the city dweller are within the scope of the act. The following case indicates its application to a specific project.

Hanly v. Kleindienst

U.S. Court of Appeals, Second Circuit, 471 F.2d 823 (1972)

The General Services Administration (a federal agency hereafter referred to as GSA) proposed to build an annex to the U.S. Courthouse in lower Manhattan to consist of two buildings: an office building for the staff of the U.S. Attorney, and a jail and detention center known as the Metropolitan Correction Center (MCC). The plaintiffs, Hanly and others, were residents or business people in the area who opposed the project.

In February 1972 plaintiffs asked for an injunction against construction of the MCC on the ground that GSA had failed to comply with the mandates of Sec. 102 of NEPA requiring a detailed environmental impact statement with respect to ma-

---

[1] D. H. Meadows et al., *The Limits to Growth,* 2d ed. (New York: Universe Books, 1972).
[2] 42 U.S.C.A. (United States Code Annotated, Title 42), Sec. 4321.

jor federal actions "significantly affecting the quality of the human environment." The district court denied the injunction on the ground that the annex would not have such an effect. On appeal, the U.S. Court of Appeals, Second Circuit, ruled that the district court was correct in permitting the construction of the office building. However, it further ruled that construction of the MCC should be delayed because GSA's "threshold determination" that the jail would not significantly affect the quality of the area's human environment was based on an environmental statement that was "too meager" to satisfy the NEPA requirements. In remanding the case, the higher court said that the statement gave insufficient consideraton to problems that could result from construction of the jail—the possibility of riots, noisy disturbances that might annoy area residents, and possible dangers to residents resulting from the MCC's outpatient center activities.

The GSA prepared a new twenty-five page assessment of the environmental impact that was more complete than the first statement. It examined in detail all design features, including the MCC's aesthetic relationship to neighboring buildings; its effect on the level of noise, smoke, and sewage; its energy demands; and the extent to which MCC occupants and their activities would be visible to area residents. All these effects were shown to be minimal.

The plaintiffs again asked for an injunction against the construction of MCC, and again the district court denied relief, ruling that GSA properly concluded from the new impact statement that the MCC would not significantly affect the human environment. Plaintiffs again appealed to the U.S. Court of Appeals, Second Circuit, the same court that heard the first appeal.

Mansfield, Circuit Judge. . . . At the outset we accept and agree with the decision of the *Hanly I* panel that the agency in charge of a proposed federal action . . . is the party authorized to make the threshold determination whether an action is one "significantly affecting the quality of the human environment." . . .

We are next confronted with a question that was deferred in *Hanly I*—the standard of review that must be applied by us in reviewing GSA's action. The action involves both a question of law—the meaning of the word "significantly" in the statutory phrase "significantly affecting the quality of the human environment"—and a question of fact—whether the MCC will have a "significantly" adverse environmental impact. Strictly speaking, our function as a reviewing court is to determine *de novo* "all relevant questions of law," . . . and, with respect to GSA's factual determinations, . . . whether its findings are "arbitrary, capricious, an abuse of discretion, or otherwise not in accordance with law" or "without observance of procedure required by law," APA § 10(e).

. . . Upon attempting, according to the foregoing standard, to interpret the amorphous term "significantly," as it is used in § 102(2) (c), we are faced with the fact that almost every major federal action, no matter how limited in scope, has some adverse effect on the human environment. . . .

. . . In the absence of any Congressional or administrative interpretation of the term, we are persuaded that in deciding whether a major federal action will "significantly" affect the quality of the human environment on the agency in charge, although vested with broad discretion, should normally be required to review the proposed action in the light of at least two relevant factors: (1) the extent to which the action will cause adverse environmental effects in excess of those created by existing uses in the area affected by it, and (2) the absolute quantitative adverse environmental effects of the action itself, including the cumulative harm that results from its contribution to existing adverse conditions or uses in the affected area. Where conduct conforms to existing uses, its adverse consequences will usually be less significant than when it represents a radical change. . . .

. . . Although this Court in *Hanly I* did not expressly articulate the standards we have used, its decision that the proposed office building portion of the Annex would not be environmentally significant conforms to the rationale. The office building would not differ substantially from the makeup of the surrounding area. Nor would it in absolute terms give rise to sizeable adverse environmental effects. Most of the employees occupying the building would merely be transferred from the existing Courthouse where the newly created space will be used primarily for courtrooms and desperately needed office space for court personnel. On the other hand, the proposed jail, for reasons set forth in detail in *Hanly I,* might have adverse effects differing both qualitatively and quantitatively from those associated with existing uses in the area. Moreover, there was insufficient evidence that the absolute environmental effect with respect to the jail had been analyzed and considered by the GSA. Thus the matter was remanded for reappraisal. Now that the GSA has made and submitted its redetermination in the form of a 25-page "Assessment," our task is to determine (1) whether it satisfies the foregoing tests as to environmental significance, and (2) whether GSA, in making its assessment and determination, has observed "procedure required by law" as that term is used in § 10 of the APA.

. . . Where a proposed major federal action may affect the sensibilities of a neighborhood, the prudent course would be for the agency in charge, before making a threshold decision, to give notice to the community of the contemplated action and to accept all pertinent information proffered by concerned citizens with respect to it. Furthermore, in line with the procedure usually followed in zoning disputes, particularly where emotions are likely to be aroused by fears, or rumors of misinformation, a public hearing serves the dual purpose of enabling the agency to obtain all relevant data and to satisfy the community that its views are being considered. However, neither NEPA nor any other federal statute mandates the specific type of procedure to be followed by federal agencies. There is no statutory requirement that a public hearing be held before a site for a house of detention is selected by the Attorney General or construction of the facility is undertaken by the GSA. . . . Although the Guidelines issued by the CEQ suggest that agencies "shall include, whenever appropriate, provision for public hearings, and shall provide the public with relevant information, including information on alternative course of action," . . . these provisions apply only to the procedure for preparation of detailed impact statements *after* the preliminary determination of significance has been made.

. . . The case is remanded for further proceedings not inconsistent with this opinion. . . .

The Environmental Protection Agency (EPA)

Until 1970, the responsibility for administering antipollution measures was divided among several government agencies. The Department of the Interior was concerned with water quality; the Department of Health, Education and Welfare administered air pollution control, solid waste, and water standards; and the Department of Agriculture was primarily responsible for pesticide registration and use. Recognizing that the environment is a single, interrelated system, the president, in his Reorganization Plan No. 3, established the Environmental Protection Agency to which the above, and other functions, were transferred for administration. The EPA establishes and enforces environmental protection standards, conducts research on pollution, provides assistance to state and local antipollution programs through grants and technical advice, and generally assists the Council on Environmental Quality (CEQ). The CEQ was established by executive order to facilitate implementation of NEPA by issuing guidelines for the preparation of impact statements and generally to assist and advise the president on environmental matters. In its guidelines, CEQ has required that environmental impact statements be prepared as early in the decision-making process as possible and that other agencies and the public be given a chance to comment and criticize before any final decision is made to go ahead with major federal action.[3]

Consolidation of diverse functions under one agency has provided a center of control for the continuing war on pollution. How it works can be illustrated by examining a few of the major areas of concern.

Water Pollution Control

As early as 1790 Congress was concerned with the nation's navigable rivers and harbors, primarily to ensure that they remained navigable and free of obstructions. In that year Congress approved Rhode Island, Maryland, and Georgia statutes that imposed duties on shipping to finance improvements of waterways. As commerce expanded, so also did the role of the federal government in fostering and regulating it. Early legislation was directed at keeping waterways navigable, but the pollution problem was finally addressed in 1886 when Congress enacted legislation prohibiting the dumping of refuse into New York City harbor. The Rivers and Harbors Act of 1890 made similar antidumping provisions applicable to *all* navigable waters. Responsibility for administration rested in the secretary of war, and considerable authority was given to the Army Corps of Engineers.

As part of an effort to remedy what had been ineffectual piecemeal legislation, the 1899 Rivers and Harbors Appropriation Act made it unlawful for ships and manufacturing establishments to discharge refuse into any navigable water of the United States or into any tributary of a navigable waterway. However, it was permissible under the act to discharge liquid wastes from streets and sewers into such waterways and tributaries. Legislation still emphasized obstructions to navigation, but it became increasingly useful as an antipollution device in the absence of statutes that could attack the problem more directly. Its use in a now-familiar problem area is illustrated by the following case.

United States v. Standard Oil Co.
U.S. Supreme Court, 384 U.S. 224 (1966)

The U.S. brought this criminal action against Standard Oil of Kentucky after one of its shutoff valves had accidentally been left open, causing a large quantity of aviation gasoline to be discharged into the St. Johns River in Florida. The government alleged that the discharge violated Sec. 13 of the Rivers and Harbors Act of

[3] 42 U.S.C.A., Sec. 4342.

1899, which provides that: "It shall not be lawful to throw, discharge, or deposit ... any refuse matter of any kind or description whatever other than that flowing from streets and sewers and passing therefrom in a liquid state, into any navigable water of the United States."

The trial court dismissed the indictment on the ground that the statutory phrase *refuse matter* did not include commercially valuable oil. The government appealed to the U.S. Supreme Court.

Mr. Justice Douglas delivered the opinion of the Court.

. . .This case comes to us at a time in the Nation's history when there is greater concern than ever over pollution—one of the main threats to our free-flowing rivers and to our lakes as well. The crisis that we face in this respect would not, of course, warrant us in manufacturing offenses where Congress has not acted nor in stretching statutory language in a criminal field to meet strange conditions. But whatever may be said of the rule of strict construction, it cannot provide a substitute for common sense, precedent, and legislative history. We cannot construe § 13 of the Rivers and Harbors Act in a vacuum. . . .

The statutory words are "any refuse matter of any kind or description." We said in *United States v. Republic Steel Corp.,* that the history of this provision and of related legislation dealing with our free-flowing rivers "forbids a narrow, cramped reading" of § 13. The District Court recognized that if this were waste oil it would be "refuse matter" within the meaning of § 13 but concluded that it was not within the statute because it was "valuable" oil. That is "a narrow, cramped reading" of § 13 in partial defeat of its purpose.

Oil is oil and whether useable or not by industrial standards it has the same deleterious effect on waterways. In either case, its presence in our rivers and harbors is both a menace to navigation and a pollutant. This seems to be the administrative construction of § 13, the Solicitor General advising us that it is the basis of prosecution in approximately one-third of the oil pollution cases reported to the Department of Justice by the Office of the Chief of Engineers.

. . . The Court of Appeals for the Second Circuit in *United States v. Ballard Oil Co.,* 195 F.2d 369 (1952) (L. Hand, Augustus Hand, and Harrie Chase, JJ.) held that causing good oil to spill into a watercourse violated § 13. The word "refuse" in that setting, said the court, "is satisfied by anything which has become waste, however useful it may earlier have been." There is nothing more deserving of the label "refuse" than oil spilled into a river.

That seems to us to be the common sense of the matter. The word "refuse" includes all foreign substances and pollutants apart from those "flowing from streets and sewers and passing therefrom in a liquid state" into the watercourse.

That reading of § 13 is in keeping with the teaching of Mr. Justice Holmes that a "river is more than an amenity, it is a treasure." . . .

Reversed.

Clean Water

Efforts to clean up the nation's waterways began in earnest with the passage of the Federal Water Pollution Control Act[4] in 1948 and continued piecemeal through

---

[4]33 U.S.C.A., Sec. 1151.

the amending process until the 1972 amendments provided a comprehensive plan to eliminate pollution. Since industry in this country uses a significant amount of water in its manufacturing and processing activities, the 1972 amendments set guidelines for controlling water pollution from industrial sources. In general, industry is expected to control and eliminate its discharge of pollutants through the "best available" technology by July 1, 1983.

The new law places primary responsibility in the states but provides for federal aid to local governments and small businesses to help them in their efforts to comply with the law's requirements. The new law also provides a licensing and permit system for discharging into waterways and a more workable enforcement program. Penalties for violations range from $25,000 per day and up to one year in prison for a first offense and from $50,000 per day and two years in prison for subsequent violations.[5]

The 1977 amendments to the Federal Water Pollution Control Act, the Clean Water Act of 1977,[6] address specific problems requiring either changes in procedure or particular emphasis. Congress reaffirmed its policy to assist state and local efforts to prevent, reduce, and eliminate pollution by supporting and aiding antipollution research with special attention to methods of handling sewage where conventional means may prove to be impractical or where, for traditional reasons, scientific sewage disposal is not practiced. For example, the 1977 amendments authorize the Alaska Village Demonstration Projects to develop a comprehensive program for achieving adequate sanitation services in Alaskan villages. The amendments also emphasize the construction of publicly owned waste water treatment works with provision for federal grants to state, municipality, or intermunicipal or interstate agencies for such construction. Funding for training facilities and the training of operating personnel of waste treatment works was included—$7 million for each year from 1978 through 1980.

In an area of special significance to coastal cities, the amendments require that the dumping of sewage sludge into the ocean end as soon as possible after 1977 and absolutely by 1981. Because this could pose a considerable problem for municipalities dumping waste into the ocean from waste water treatment plants, the 1977 amendments authorize some $6.5 million to be appropriated for research into the problem.

Finally, the Clean Water Act takes up the threat to coastal areas posed by the transport of petroleum products. All too frequently, vessels ranging from small coastal barges to huge supertankers discharge their cargoes into the sea near the coast. The ecological effect on fish, shellfish, and waterfowl and on public and private shorelines and beaches is immeasurable. Consequently, the Clean Water Act imposes severe sanctions on those responsible for such pollution. The owner or operator of a grounded oil-carrying vessel can be liable for up to $250,000 of the cost of cleaning up its spilled cargo; and if the oil spill is the result of willful

[5]33 U.S.C.A., Sec. 1319.
[6]33 U.S.C.A., Secs. 1251 to 1376.

negligence or misconduct, the owner or operator of the vessel can be held liable to the United States government for the full cost of cleaning up the shore.

Operators of onshore and offshore facilities are also held liable for spillage and pollution, under ordinary conditions, to the extent of $50 million and, where willful negligence and misconduct are involved, to the full extent of the cost of cleanup and removal, including the restoration or replacement of natural resources damaged or destroyed by the discharge of oil or hazardous substances.

Clean Air

The smog of Los Angeles, the brown pall over large industrial centers, the smoke and fumes from large incinerators and power generating plants, and, more recently, jet air traffic and aerosol propellants all contribute to air pollution and present a serious problem to the health and well-being of humans and animals, as well as to property, vegetation, and climate. The cost of such pollution in lives, dollars, and lost work hours is staggering. Its economic and social implications are far-reaching and, if unchecked, could contribute to the decline of population and industrial capacity alluded to earlier in this chapter. Fortunately, something is being done to clean up the air or at least to limit the extent to which it can continue to be polluted.

The Clean Air Act of 1970 (actually, sweeping amendments to the 1967 Air Quality Act) is the primary federal legislation directed at air pollution.[7] Under the administration of the Environmental Protection Agency it set a three-year deadline for attaining the primary ambient (outside) air quality standards Congress had designed to protect public health. Since achieving the standards is so costly, the EPA's role in balancing the economic, technological, and social factors that air polluters must consider has been contested in the courts. This is largely because the courts define and control the discretion of federal and state agencies in establishing goals and enforcing policies. Needless to say, if the courts are being called upon to establish the meaning of the various programs of the Clean Air Act, there is controversy. For example, it is estimated that 80 percent of the country's air is cleaner than the secondary (welfare) ambient standards set by the EPA. Should this air be permitted to deteriorate even though it could do so and remain at acceptable pollution levels? Consider the following case:

Sierra Club v. Ruckelshaus

U.S. District Court, District of Columbia, 344 F.Supp. 253 (1972)

Several States submitted air pollution control plans to the Environmental Protection Agency for its approval. The plans called for the implementation of controls and procedures to improve air quality in those parts of the states where it was below federal standards. Each of the states involved, however, had certain "clean air" regions where existing levels of pollution were much below those permitted by federal standards. The states' plans allowed future activities that would cause the

---

[7] U.S.C.A., Sec. 1857.

pollution level to rise in the clean air regions. As a result, the quality of their air would fall, though not below the minimum federal standards.

Plaintiffs, the Sierra Club and three other environmental groups, sought an injunction preventing EPA approval of the plans, contending that any plans permitting pollution levels to rise, even in clean air regions, violated the Clean Air Act of 1970. The trial court dismissed the action, and plaintiffs appealed.

Pratt, District Judge .... Previously, the Administrator had promulgated a regulation permitting states to submit plans which would allow clean air areas to be degraded, so long as the plans were merely "adequate to prevent such ambient pollution levels from exceeding such secondary standard." 40 C.F.R. § 51.12(b) (1972).

Plaintiffs' claim that the Administrator's interpretation of the extent of his authority is clearly erroneous and that his declination to assert his authority, evidenced in his remarks before Congress and his promulgation of a regulation that is contrary to the Clean Air Act, amounts to a failure to perform a nondiscretionary act or duty.

It would appear that such an allegation is precisely the type of claim which Congress, through 52 U.S.C. § 1857h-2(a), intended interested citizens to raise in the district courts. In view of this clear jurisdictional grant, the Administrator's assertion that plaintiffs should await his approval of the state plans (formulated, in part, pursuant to his allegedly illegal regulation) and then proceed to appeal his approval under 42 U.S.C. § 1857h-5, is in our opinion, untenable.

In discussing the merits of the present action—i.e., the extent of the Administrator's authority and the validity of the questioned regulation—we turn to the stated purpose of the Clean Air Act of 1970, the available legislative history of the Act and its predecessor, and the administrative interpretation of the Act.

Purpose of the Act

In Section 101(b) of the Clean Air Act, Congress states four basic purposes of the Act, the first of which is

"to protect and enhance the quality of the Nation's air resources so as to promote the public health and welfare and the productive capacity of its population." 42 U.S.C. § 1857(b) (1).

On its face, this language would appear to declare Congress' intent to improve the quality of the nation's air and to prevent deterioration of that air quality, no matter how presently pure that quality in some sections of the country happens to be.

Legislative History

The "protect and enhance" language of the Clean Air Act of 1970 stems directly from the predecessor Air Quality Act of 1967, 81 Stat. 485. The Senate Report underlying the 1967 Act makes it clear that all areas of the country were to come under the protection of the Act. S.Rep. No. 403, 90th Cong. 1st Sess. 2-3 (1967).

The administrative guidelines promulgated by the National Air Pollution Control Administration (NAPCA) of the Department of Health, Education and Welfare (HEW), which at that time had the responsibility of carrying out the directives of the Air Quality Act of 1967, point up the significance of the "protect and enhance" language as follows:

"[A]n explicit purpose of the Act is 'to *protect* and *enhance* the quality of the Nation's air resources' (emphasis added). Air quality standards which, even if fully implemented, would result in significant deterioration of air quality in any substantial portion of an air quality region clearly would conflict with this expressed purpose of the law." National Air Pollution Control Administration, U.S. Dept. of HEW, Guidelines for the Development of Air Quality Standards and Implementation Plans, Part I § 1.51, p. 7 (1969).

Turning now to the legislative history of the 1970 Act, we note at the outset that both Secretary Finch and Under Secretary Veneman of HEW testified before Congress that neither the 1967 Act nor the proposed Act would permit the quality of air to be degraded. Hearings on Air Pollution Before the Subcomm. on Air and Water Pollution of the Senate Public Works Comm., 91st Cong., 2d Sess., at 132-33, 143 (1970); Hearings on Air Pollution and Solid Waste Recycling Before the Subcomm. on Public Health and Welfare of the House Interstate and Foreign Commerce Comm., 91st Cong., 2d Sess., at 280, 287 (1970).

More important, of course, is the language of the Senate Report accompanying the bill which became the Clean Air Act of 1970. The Senate Report, in pertinent part, states:

"In areas where current air pollution levels are already equal to or better than the air quality goals, the Secretary shall not approve any implementation plan which does not provide, to the maximum extent practicable, for the continued maintenance of such ambient air quality." S.Rep.No. 1196, 91st Cong., 2d Sess., at 2 (1970). The House Report, although not as clear, does not appear to contradict the Senate Report. See H. Rep. No. 1146, 91st Cong., 2d Sess., at 1, 2 and 5 (1970), U.S.Code Cong. & Admin. News 1970, p. 5356.

Administrative Interpretation

As we noted under our discussion of the legislative history of the 1967 Act, the 1969 guidelines promulgated by HEW's NAPCA emphasized that significant deterioration of air quality in any region would subvert the "protect and enhance" language of the 1967 Act. We also pointed out that Secretary Finch and Under Secretary Veneman applied this same administrative interpretation to the very same language found in the proposed 1970 Act.

On the other hand, the present Administrator, in remarks made in January and February of 1972 before certain House and Senate Subcommittees, has taken the position that the 1970 Act allows degradation of clean air areas. Several Congressional leaders voiced their strong disagreement with the Administrator's interpretation. Unpublished transcript of Hearings Before the Subcomm. on Public Health and the Environment of the House Comm. on Interstate and Foreign Commerce, 92d Cong., 2d Sess., at 352 (remarks of Congressman Paul Rogers, Chairman of the Subcommittee); Unpublished transcript of Hearings Before the Subcomm. on Air and Water Pollution of the Senate Comm. on Public Works, 92d Cong., 2d Sess. at 33-34, 260 et seq. (remarks of Senator Thomas Eagleton, Vice-Chairman of the Subcommittee, presiding over the hearings at the time).

The Administrator's interpretation of the 1970 Act, as disclosed in his current regulations, appears to be self-contradictory. On the one hand, 40 C.F.R. § 50.2(c) (1970) provides:

"The promulgation of national primary and secondary air quality standards shall not be considered in any manner to allow significant deterioration of existing air quality in any portion of any State."

Yet, in 40 C.F.R. § 51.12(b), he states:

"In any region where measured or estimated ambient levels of a pollutant are below the levels specified by an applicable secondary standard, the State implementation plan shall set forth a control strategy which shall be adequate to prevent such ambient pollution levels from exceeding such secondary standard."

The former regulation appears to reflect a policy of nondegradation of clean air but the latter mirrors the Administrator's doubts as to his authority to impose such a policy upon the states in their implementation plans. In our view, these regulations are irreconcilable and they demonstrate the weakness of the Administrator's position in this case.

Initial Conclusions

Having considered the stated purpose of the Clean Air Act of 1970, the legislative history of the Act and its predecessor, and the past and present administrative interpretation of the Acts, it is our judgment that the Clean Air Act of 1970 is based in important part on a policy of nondegradation of existing clean air and that 40 C.F.R.s 51.2(b), in permitting the states to submit plans which allow pollution levels of clean air to rise to the secondary standard level of pollution, is contrary to the legislative policy of the Act and is, therefore, invalid. Accordingly, we hold that plaintiffs have made out a claim for relief.

Injunctive Relief

Whether this Court may properly grant injunctive relief depends on whether the plaintiffs have met the four criteria set forth in *Virginia Petroleum Jobbers Ass'n v. Federal Power Commission,* 104 U.S.App.D.C. 106, 259 F.2d 921 (1958) and such later authorities as *A Quaker Action Group, v. Hickel,* 137 U.S.App.D.C. 176, 421 F.2d 1111 (1969).

First, have the plaintiffs made a strong showing that they are likely to prevail on the merits? It appears to us, from our foregoing discussion, that the plaintiffs have made such a showing in this case.

Second, have the plaintiffs shown that without such relief they would suffer irreparable injury? In view of the nature and extent of the air pollution problem, once degradation is permitted the range of resulting damages could well have irreversible effects. Thus, we hold that plaintiffs have made the requisite showing of irreparable injury.

Third, will the issuance of a stay cause any significant harm or inconvenience to the Administrator or other parties interested in the proceedings? We are persuaded that no substantial harm or inconvenience will result from our order granting the preliminary injunction. The order is a very limited one. It was submitted by plaintiffs' counsel after consultation with counsel for the Administrator and, in our view, it provides the Administrator with sufficient time and flexibility so that he may exercise his expertise and carry out his duties under the Act with as little inconvenience as possible.

Fourth, and finally, where lies the public interest? It seems to us that the public interest in this case strongly supports the legislative policy of clean air and the nondegradation of areas in which clean air exists.

Conclusion

Having separately considered the four criteria for injunctive relief, and having found that plaintiffs have met each of these criteria, we conclude that we can and should grant the requested relief.

In addition to maintaining the quality of air when it is higher than primary and secondary standards, four other programs form the essential elements of the Clean Air Act. Foremost is the setting of primary (health) and secondary (welfare) ambient air quality standards. The standards have not been met because much valuable time has been lost in various attempts to balance the economic, technological, and social factors. However, there have been significant reductions in sulfur oxide concentrations, particulates, and carbon monoxide.

Another program of the act is the drafting, approving, and enforcing of state implementation plans (SIPs) for achieving ambient air quality standards. When approved by the EPA administrator, such plans permit the states to enforce air quality standards within their borders. Operators of air pollution sources may be required to monitor, sample, and keep appropriate records, all of which are subject to an on-premises inspection by the EPA.

Of particular concern to industry is the program for setting new source performance standards (NSPSs)—emission standards for various categories of large industrial facilities. The goal is for large industrial polluters to reduce emissions to meet primary and secondary standards in accordance with prescribed schedules. To do this, major polluters must use the best acceptable control devices, those with proven capabilities to reduce emissions and, ultimately, pollution.

The last program involves the automobile and the fuel it burns. In order to reduce pollution from the combustion engine, emission standards must be achieved and fuel additive regulations must be developed and followed. This program, of grave concern to the auto and fuel industries, has resulted in the catalytic converter and the extensive use of unleaded gasoline. However, there are indications that the catalytic converter, while controlling carbon monoxide and hydrocarbon emissions, may actually add to pollution in the form of sulfuric acid emissions. Further, due to the higher cost of unleaded fuel and mechanical problems (real or imagined) caused by the catalytic converter, motorists in increasing numbers have taken various measures to bypass the converter and burn the so-called "regular" gasoline. A recent federal statute now prohibits such procedures. Here economic, technological, and social factors all come into play. Standards and goals have been set, but meeting and enforcing them is an arduous process.

The penalties for continued pollution can be severe. Violators can be fined up to $25,000 per day or imprisoned for a year, and the fine and imprisonment can be doubled for subsequent convictions.

Common-law theory protects us from damage to our persons and property caused by excessive environmental noise,[8] but the Noise Control Act of 1972 represents the first major federal effort to eliminate the problem.[9] This act empowers the EPA to establish noise emission standards for specific products in cooperation with agencies otherwise concerned with them and to limit noise emissions from those products that can be categorized as noise producers. The act specifically lists transportation vehicles and equipment, machinery, appliances, and other commercial products. The act subjects federal facilities to state and local noise standards and expressly reserves the right to control environmental noise in the states through licensing and regulation or restriction of excessively noisy products.

Noise pollution law has not developed nearly so rapidly as water and air pollution law. Nevertheless, the problem has been identified, and something is being done about it. The thrust of the Noise Control Act is toward reducing environmental noise in an effort to prevent what are recognized as long-range effects (hearing problems) on public health and welfare. Violations of the prohibitions of the act are punishable by a fine of $25,000 per day or one year in prison or both.

Of recent interest was the noise problem posed by the British/French SST Concorde and the controversy over its landing rights in this country. While state and local authorities are given the right to control environmental noise, federal authority can be asserted in certain situations where, for example, uniformity is necessary or foreign policy considerations are compelling. The following case illustrates these principles and should be considered in light of the SST controversy.

Opinion of the Justices, 271 N.E.2d 354 (1971)

In early 1971 the Massachusetts House of Representatives considered an act prohibiting supersonic transport (SST) planes from landing or taking off within the state. Because the House was concerned with the legality of the proposed statute, it formally propounded and forwarded this question to the state's highest court: "Is it constitutionally competent for (this state) to enact (a bill) which in effect prohibits the landing of any commercial supersonic transport aircraft at any airport within the commonwealth notwithstanding that the operation of such aircraft in interstate and international commerce is regulated by the Congress?" (A copy of the bill was attached.)

After receiving the question, the Supreme Judicial Court requested that briefs be filed by the Attorney General and the Port Authority of Massachusetts, the U.S. Department of Transportation and the Federal Aviation Authority, several environmental groups, and the Societe Nationale Industrielle Aerospatiale. Upon consideration of the issues presented, the court rendered this opinion.

. . . Federal legislative action has been taken directly in the field which Senate Bill No. 1161, amended, purports to regulate. This has been done by the 1968 amendment to the Federal Aviation Act of 1958. See 49 U.S.C. § 1431 (Supp. V, 1965-1969). The amendment

---

[8]If, for example, a commercial enterprise or a neighbor is unreasonably noisy, such activity can be enjoined as interfering with property rights, and, in some cases, damages may be awarded.

[9]42 U.S.C.A., Secs. 4901–4918.

directs the FAA administrator to prescribe standards for the measurement of aircraft noise and sonic boom and rules and regulations for the control and abatement of aircraft noise and sonic boom. . . .

In issuing regulations pursuant to the 1968 amendment, the FAA has acted consistently with the legislative history in leaving some authority to airport proprietors in the regulation of noise. The amendment to the regulations is prefaced by the following statement: "*Relation to responsibility of airport proprietors.* Compliance with Part 36 is not to be construed as a Federal determination that the aircraft is 'acceptable,' from a noise standpoint, in particular airport environments. Responsibility for determining the permissible noise levels for aircraft using an airport remains with the proprietor of that airport. The noise limits specified in Part 36 are the technologically practicable and economically reasonable limits of aircraft noise reduction technology at the time of type certification and are not intended to substitute federally determined noise levels for those more restrictive limits determined to be necessary by individual airport proprietors in response to the locally determined desire for quiet and the locally determined need for the benefits of air commerce. . . ." The regulations themselves state, "No determination is made, under this part, that these noise levels are or should be acceptable or unacceptable for operaton at, into, or out of, any airport." 14 C.F.R § 3615. Also the regulations apply only to certain classes of subsonic aircraft. 14 C.F.R § 36.1.

American Airlines, Inc. v. Hempstead, 272 F.Supp. 226 (E.D.N.Y.), affd. 398 F.2d 369 (2d Cir.), cert. den. sub nom. *Hempstead v. American Airlines, Inc.,* 393 U.S. 1017, 89 S.Ct. 620, 21 L.Ed.2d 561, dealt with a town noise ordinance based upon decibel count which in effect required that aircraft deviate from FAA flight patterns. The Court of Appeals held that the ordinance was invalid since it was in direct conflict with FAA procedures for aircraft flying into Kennedy Airport. That court expressly did not reach the preemption or commerce issues stating, "it is this particular noise ordinance in this particular setting which is found to regulate flight paths and procedures; another noise ordinance might not have that effect."

. . . Even if the bill were framed in terms of "airport proprietors," there would still be serious doubt about its constitutional validity. Recently, the FAA issued notice of proposed noise control with respect to supersonic aircraft. See 35 Fed.Reg. 6189, 16980, 12555. Federal action in this field may well invalidate any State action in the area. Also, although the Justices have insufficient evidence to advise on this point, the extremely complex procedures established by the FAA for evaluating noise (14 C.F.R § 36.1581) may conflict with the simple and possibly imprecise "108 decibels" standard prescribed by the proposed legislation. Furthermore, if State regulation of noise in fact does have any effect on the operation of aircraft in the Commonwealth, there would remain the question whether the bill imposes an unreasonable or discriminatory burden on interstate commerce (footnote omitted) or conflicts with any treaty obligation of the United States Government. We need not, however, reach these difficult issues.

We answer the question, "No."

Solid Waste and Its Disposal

The disposal of the millions of tons of solid waste produced annually in this country presents a problem of staggering proportions. For most of us, periodic garbage pick-ups at our residences or small businesses or weekly trips to the county or municipal sanitary landfill solve the problem. However, less than 10 percent of solid waste is classified as residential, commercial, or institutional. The greater portion is classified as agricultural or mineral. Agriculture alone contributes over 50 percent. Undisposed of, the waste creates enormous health and pollution problems, but disposal operations often create greater hazards. If burned, solid waste pollutes the air. If dumped into waterways, lakes, or streams it can violate federal Water Pollution Control Act standards. Consequently, federal statutes have been enacted to combat the problem. Chief among these is the Solid Waste Disposal Act of 1976.[10] Its primary goal is more efficient management of waste and its disposal through financial and technical assistance to state and local agencies in the development and application of new methods of waste disposal. The act completely revises a 1965 enactment. Recognizing the seriousness of the waste disposal problem, it establishes an Office of Solid Waste within the Environmental Protection Agency. The act authorizes special attention to the disposal of discarded tires, the management of hazardous waste, the phasing out of open dumps, and the exclusive utilization of sanitary landfills.

In view of our present and extended energy needs, Congress's formal recognition that millions of tons of recoverable materials are needlessly buried each year and that technology now exists to produce usable energy from solid waste is of special interest.

States and localities have taken a variety of approaches to the solid waste problem, including extensive use of sanitary landfills, recycling of waste containers that lend themselves to such treatment, and encouraging industry to develop recyclable and biodegradable products. The following Oregon case arose out of that state's efforts to solve the litter problem created by the so-called "throw-away" container.

In 1971 the Oregon legislature enacted a so-called "bottle bill." The act had two basic provisions. The first required every retailer of beer and carbonated beverages to accept "empty beverage containers of the kind, common size and brand" sold by the retailer and to give refunds for such containers. The second provision prohibited the sale of all beverages in "pull top" cans. In essence, then, the law required that beer and soft drinks be sold only in returnable glass bottles. The stated purposes of the law were the reduction of litter and solid waste in the state and the reduction of injuries to people and animals due to discarded "pull tops."

The plaintiffs, a large number of persons, contended that the law was unconstitutional. Most of the plaintiffs were (a) manufacturers of cans, (b) companies that brewed and packaged beer in California and shipped it into Oregon, (c) soft drink companies that sold their products in Oregon, and (d) manufacturers of nonreturnable glass bottles. The plaintiffs' primary contentions were that the law violated the commerce clause, the due process clause, and the equal protection clause of the

American Can Co. v. Oregon Liquor Control Commission
Court of Appeals of Oregon, 517 P.2d 691 (1973).

---

[10]42 U.S.C.A., Secs. 6901–6987.

federal Constitution. The trial court ruled that the law was valid and dismissed the plaintiffs' requests for an injunction against its enforcement. Plaintiffs appealed.

Tanzer, Judge.

Commerce Clause Plaintiffs' most substantial challenge to the bottle bill is under the Commerce Clause of the United States Constitution.

The development of the one-way container provided a great technological opportunity for the beverage industry to turn logistical advantages into economic advantages. By obviating the expensive necessity of reshipping empty bottles back to the plant for refilling, the new containers enabled manufacturers to produce in a few centralized plants to serve more distant markets. The industry organized its manufacturing and distribution systems to capitalize maximally on the new technology.

The Oregon legislature was persuaded that the economic benefits to the beverage industry brought with it deleterious consequences to the environment and additional cost to the public. The aggravation of the problems of litter in public places and solid waste disposal and the attendant economic and esthetic burden to the public outweighed the narrower economic benefit to the industry. Thus the legislature enacted the bottle bill over the articulate opposition of the industries represented by plaintiffs.

As with every change of circumstance in the market place, there are gainers and there are losers. Just as there were gainers and losers, with plaintiffs apparently among the gainers, when the industry adapted to the development of nonreturnable containers, there will be new gainers and losers as they adapt to the ban. The economic losses complained of by plaintiffs in this case are essentially the consequences of readjustment of the beverage manufacturing and distribution systems to the older technology in order to compete in the Oregon market.

The purpose of the Commerce Clause, following the intolerable experience of the economic Balkanization of America which existed in the colonial period and under the Articles of Confederation, was to assure to the commercial enterprises in every state substantial equality of access to a free national market. It was not meant to usurp the police power of the states which was reserved under the Tenth Amendment. Therefore, although most exercises of the police power affect interstate commerce to some degree, not every such exercise is invalid under the Commerce Clause.

Plaintiffs acknowledge the authority of the state to act, but assert that the state exercise of its police power must yield to federal authority over interstate commerce because, they claim, the impact on interstate commerce in this case outweighs the putative benefit to the state and because alternative methods exist to achieve the state goal with a less deleterious impact on interstate commerce. They urge us to assume the role of a "super legislature," as they put it, and perform for ourselves the weighing process already performed by the Legislative Assembly, relying largely upon *Pike v. Bruce Church, Inc.,* 397 U.S. 137, 142, 90 S.Ct. 844, 25 L.Ed2d 174 (1970), which states:

Although the criteria for determining the validity of state statutes affecting interstate commerce have been variously stated, the general rule that emerges can be phrased as follows: Where the statute regulates evenhandedly to effectuate a legitimate local public interest, and its effects on interstate commerce are only incidental, it will be upheld unless the burden imposed on such commerce is clearly excessive in relation to the putative local benefits. *Huron Portland Cement Co. v. Detroit,* 362 U.S. 440, 443, 80 S.Ct. 813, 816, 4 L.Ed.2d 852. If a legitimate local purpose is found, then the question becomes one of degree. And the extent of the burden that will be tolerated will of course depend on the nature of the local interest involved, and on whether it could be promoted as well with a lesser impact on interstate commerce activities. . . .

The language of the United States Supreme Court is not always consistent in analyzing the application of the Commerce Clause to varying facts and it is difficult to rationalize it into one harmonious jurisprudential whole. On their facts, however, the cases cluster around certain basic concepts and the treatment accorded to state action is consistent within each grouping. The cases consistently hold that the Commerce Clause bars state police action only where:

(1) federal action has preempted regulation of the activity;
(2) the state action impedes the free physical flow of commerce from one state to another; or
(3) protectionist state action, even though under the guise of police power, discriminates against interstate commerce.

In this case there is no claim of federal preemption, so we are concerned only with the latter two concepts, interstate transportation and economic protectionism. No party cited and we were unable to find any case striking down state action under the Commerce Clause which did not come within one of these two categories.

The language of *Pike v. Bruce Church, Inc.*, supra, does not mechanically compel a weighing process in every case. The language is instructive in appropriate cases rather than mandatory in all cases. The blight of the landscape, the appropriation of lands for solid waste disposal, and the injury to children's feet caused by pull tops discarded in the sands of our ocean shores are concerns not divisible by the same units of measurement as is economic loss to elements of the beverage industry and we are unable to weigh them, one against the other. . . .

. . . The bottle bill is unquestionably a legitimate legislative exercise of the police power. The breadth of the police power was noted by the United States Supreme Court in *Berman v. Parker*, 348 U.S. 26, 33, 75 S.Ct. 98, 102, 99 L.Ed. 27 (1954):

. . . The values (public welfare) represents are spiritual as well as physical, aesthetic as well as monetary. It is within the power of the legislature to determine that the community should be beautiful as well as healthy, spacious as well as clean, well-balanced as well as carefully patrolled. . . .

. . . Because the bottle bill is a legitimate exercise of the police power, consistent with federal policy legislation, which does not impede the flow of interstate commerce and which does not discriminate against non-Oregon interests, we hold that it is valid legislation under the Commerce Clause. We turn now to plaintiffs' other constitutional challenges.

Due Process: Plaintiffs argue that the bottle bill is violative of the Due Process Clause of the Fourteenth Amendment and assert that this court must weigh the legislative purpose against the degree of oppression to individuals. We made such a general comparison above in the section dealing with cases of purported economic discrimination under the Commerce Clause and we saw no cause to disturb the legislative judgment. . . .

Equal Protection: Plaintiffs argue that the bottle bill is violative of the Equal Protection Clause as applied to them. . . . They argue that the bottle bill must fail because its goals do not justify its burdens upon the plaintiffs, and because it will not tend to accomplish its goals in that it applies only to beer and soft drink containers and not to other containers which are equally deleterious to the environment.

. . . We find that the bottle bill in all of its aspects is reasonably calculated to achieve legitimate state objectives under the police power as discussed above. The ban on pull tops is reasonably calculated to diminish the injuries to people who step on them and to animals who eat them at pasture as well as to reduce the litter which they create....

... Plaintiffs' right to equal protection has not been abridged.

... Plaintiffs' and intervenors' constitutional challenges having failed, we hold the bottle bill to be a valid exercise of Oregon's police power. In doing so, we acknowledge having had the benefit of an able analysis by the trial court.

Affirmed.

Questions and Problems

1. What is an Environmental Impact Statement? What purpose does it serve?

2. At the time the National Environmental Policy Act was passed, several nuclear power plants were in various stages of construction but had not yet been licensed to operate. The Atomic Energy Commission (AEC) maintained that it was not required to take independent action based upon material in environmental reports and environmental impact statements but could permit construction to continue on the original pre-NEPA plans with any alterations being deferred until the operating license proceedings were held.[11] *Calvert Cliffs' Coordinating Committee, Inc. v. United States Atomic Energy Commission,* 449 F.2d 1109 (1971). Are rules issued by the AEC to that effect likely to be upheld by a court?

3. The citizens of neighboring communities in Maryland and Delaware have repeatedly complained of a "horrible" and "nauseating" stench emanating from a nearby rendering and animal reduction plant. *United States v. Bishop Processing Co.,* 423 F.2d 469 (1970). If the operator of the plant refuses to abate the malodorous air pollution, can he be compelled to cease operations if the only evidence is personal observation and an odor log?

4. If you were planning to open a large commercial laundry on the banks of a navigable stream, what factors would you consider in making a decision regarding disposal of your waste wash and rinse water?

5. As part of its management function the U.S. Forestry Service sold timber, in the Boundary Waters Canoe Area, a wilderness area of some 1,000,000 acres, by executing contracts with logging firms. While this procedure, the logging, involved significant impact on the human environment, there was some question as to whether the role of the Forestry Service constituted "major federal action" requiring the filing of an environmental impact statement. *Minnesota Public Interest Research Group v. Butz,* 498 F.2d 1314 (1974). How would you decide this issue?

6. A cooperative creamery was charged with discharging refuse matter, consisting of milk wastes and wash water, into the Mississippi River without a permit. The creamery claimed in defense that its waste matter is sewerage in a liquid state and thus exempt and that, in any event, such discharge does not impede the navigability of the river. *United States v. Genoa Cooperative Creamery Co.,* 336 F.Supp. 539 (1972). Is there any merit to either of these defenses?

---

[11] The AEC was abolished in January 1975, and most of its functions were taken over by the Energy Research and Development Administration, which, in turn, was subsumed under the newly-formed Department of Energy in 1977.

7. A group of law students who use the nature facilities in the Washington, D.C. area challenged an ICC ruling allowing railroads to increase freight rates claiming that one effect would be to discourage the shipment and use of recyclable goods (cans, bottles, etc.). The students further alleged that there would be increased use of nonrecyclable commodities and thus a need to use more natural resources. Finally, the plaintiffs claimed that the use of nonrecyclable goods would adversely affect the environment. *U.S. v. Students Challenging Regulatory Agency Procedures (SCRAP)*, 412 U.S. 669 (1973). Are the students likely to succeed in their action?

8. The city of Rochester maintained the Emerson Street Landfill Area on which it continuously, night and day, engaged in open burning of items of trash too large to be disposed of by use of its incinerator. Certain homeowners, living within 800 yards of the site of open burning, filed an action to enjoin the city from further open burning and for damages to the exterior of their home and inside furnishings, caused by soot and smoke deposits. *Shearing v. City of Rochester*, 273 N.Y.S.2d 464. Are the homeowners justified in bringing the action?

9. The Army planned to relocate some missile maintenance and supply operations from Pueblo, Colorado to other installations. No construction was involved nor was there any commitment of natural resources. Noise, traffic and waste disposal problems would be lessened by the move. There would, however, be some diminution in police and fire protection in the community and some loss of jobs. *National Ass'n. of Government Employees v. Rumsfeld*, 413 F.Supp. 1224. In the absence of any negative impact on the area's ecosystems would some impact on the area's socioeconomic environment necessitate compliance with the procedural requirements of the NEPA?

10. A supertanker loaded with crude oil, en route from the Persian Gulf to Charleston, South Carolina, ran aground some five miles off the South Carolina coast. The grounding was caused by faulty navigation in a dense fog, and the ship's radar had been inoperative for more than six weeks. What is likely to be the cost to the owner of the tanker if damage to waterfowl, marine life, and public beaches is extensive and is attributable to the resulting oil spillage?

Appendix A

The Uniform Commercial Code*

1972 Official Text

Article 1

General Provisions

Part 1

Short Title, Construction, Application and Subject Matter of the Act

§1—101
Short Title

This Act shall be known and may be cited as Uniform Commercial Code.

§1—102
Purposes; Rules of Construction; Variation by Agreement

(1) This Act shall be liberally construed and applied to promote its underlying purposes and policies.

(2) Underlying purposes and policies of this Act are

    (a) to simplify, clarify and modernize the law governing commercial transactions;

    (b) to permit the continued expansion of commercial practices through custom, usage and agreement of the parties;

    (c) to make uniform the law among the various jurisdictions.

(3) The effect of provisions of this Act may be varied by agreement, except as otherwise provided in this Act and except that the obligations of good faith, diligence, reasonableness and care prescribed by this Act may not be disclaimed by agreement but the parties may by agreement determine the standards by which the performance of such obligations is to be measured if such standards are not manifestly unreasonable.

(4) The presence in certain provisions of this Act of the words "unless otherwise agreed" or words of similar import does not imply that the effect of other provisions may not be varied by agreement under subsection (3).

---

(5) In this Act unless the context otherwise requires

    (a) words in the singular number include the plural, and in the plural include the singular;

    (b) words of the masculine gender include the feminine and the neuter, and when the sense so indicates words of the neuter gender may refer to any gender.

§1—103
Supplementary General Principles of Law Applicable

Unless displaced by the particular provisions of this Act, the principles of law and equity, including the law merchant and the law relative to capacity to contract, principal and agent, estoppel, fraud, misrepresentation, duress, coercion, mistake, bankruptcy, or other validating or invalidating cause shall supplement its provisions.

§1—104
Construction Against Implicit Repeal

This Act being a general act intended as a unified coverage of its subject matter, no part of it shall be deemed to be impliedly repealed by subsequent legislation if such construction can reasonably be avoided.

§1—105
Territorial Application of the Act; Parties' Power to Choose Applicable Law

(1) Except as provided hereafter in this section, when a transaction bears a reasonable relation to this state and also to another state or nation the parties may agree that the law either of this state or of such other state or nation shall govern their rights and duties. Failing such agreement this Act applies to transactions bearing an appropriate relation to this state.

(2) Where one of the following provisions of this Act specifies the applicable law, that provision governs and a contrary agreement is effective only to the extent permitted by the law (including the conflict of laws rules) so specified:

    Rights of creditors against sold goods. Section 2—402.

    Applicability of the Article on Bank Deposits and Collections. Section 4—102.

    Bulk transfers subject to the Article on Bulk Transfers. Section 6—102.

    Applicability of the Article on Investment Securities. Section 8—106.

    Perfection provisions of the Article on Secured Transactions. Section 9—103.

As amended 1972.

§1—106
Remedies to Be Liberally Administered

(1) The remedies provided by this Act shall be liberally administered to the end that the aggrieved party may be put in as good a position as if the other party had fully performed but neither consequential or special nor penal damages may be had except as specifically provided in this Act or by other rule of law.

(2) Any right or obligation declared by this Act is enforceable by action unless the provision declaring it specifies a different and limited effect.

§1—107
Waiver or Renunciation of Claim or Right After Breach

Any claim or right arising out of an alleged breach can be discharged in whole or in part without consideration by a written waiver or renunciation signed and delivered by the aggrieved party.

§1—108
Severability

If any provision or clause of this Act or application thereof to any person or circumstances is held invalid, such invalidity shall not affect other provisions or applications of the Act which can be given effect without the invalid provision or application, and to this end the provisions of this Act are declared to be severable.

§1—109
Section Captions

Section captions are parts of this Act.

Part 2
General Definitions and Principles of Interpretation

§1—201
General Definitions

Subject to additional definitions contained in the subsequent Articles of this Act which are applicable to specific Articles or Parts thereof, and unless the context otherwise requires, in this Act:

(1) "Action" in the sense of a judicial proceeding includes recoupment, counterclaim, set-off, suit in equity and any other proceedings in which rights are determined.

(2) "Aggrieved party" means a party entitled to resort to a remedy.

(3) "Agreement" means the bargain of the parties in fact as found in their language or by implication from other circumstances including course of dealing or usage of trade or course of performance as provided in this Act (Sections 1—205 and 2—208). Whether an agreement has legal consequences is determined by the provisions of this Act, if applicable; otherwise by the law of contracts (Section 1—103). (Compare "Contract".)

(4) "Bank" means any person engaged in the business of banking.

(5) "Bearer" means the person in possession of an instrument, document of title, or security payable to bearer or indorsed in blank.

(6) "Bill of lading" means a document evidencing the receipt of goods for shipment issued by a person engaged in the

business of transporting or forwarding goods, and includes an airbill. "Airbill" means a document serving for air transportation as a bill of lading does for marine or rail transportation, and includes an air consignment note or airway bill.

(7) "Branch" includes a separately incorporated foreign branch of a bank.

(8) "Burden of establishing" a fact means the burden of persuading the triers of fact that the existence of the fact is more probable than its non-existence.

(9) "Buyer in ordinary course of business" means a person who in good faith and without knowledge that the sale to him is in violation of the ownership rights or security interest of a third party in the goods buys in ordinary course from a person in the business of selling goods of that kind but does not include a pawnbroker. All persons who sell minerals or the like (including oil and gas) at wellhead or minehead shall be deemed to be persons in the business of selling goods of that kind. "Buying" may be for cash or by exchange of other property or on secured or unsecured credit and includes receiving goods or documents of title under a pre-existing contract for sale but does not include a transfer in bulk or as security for or in total or partial satisfaction of a money debt.

(10) "Conspicuous": A term or clause is conspicuous when it is so written that a reasonable person against whom it is to operate ought to have noticed it. A printed heading in capitals (as: NON-NEGOTIABLE BILL OF LADING) is conspicuous. Language in the body of a form is "conspicuous" if it is in larger or other contrasting type or color. But in a telegram any stated term is "conspicuous". Whether a term or clause is "conspicuous" or not is for decision by the court.

(11) "Contract" means the total legal obligation which results from the parties' agreement as affected by this Act and any other applicable rules of law. (Compare "Agreement".)

(12) "Creditor" includes a general creditor, a secured creditor, a lien creditor and any representative of creditors, including an assignee for the benefit of creditors, a trustee in bankruptcy, a receiver in equity and an executor or administrator of an insolvent debtor's or assignor's estate.

(13) "Defendant" includes a person in the position of defendant in a cross-action or counterclaim.

(14) "Delivery" with respect to instruments, documents of title, chattel paper or securities means voluntary transfer of possession.

(15) "Document of title" includes bill of lading, dock warrant, dock receipt, warehouse receipt or order for the delivery of goods, and also any other document which in the regular course of business or financing is treated as adequately evidencing that the person in possession of it is entitled to receive, hold and dispose of the document and the goods it covers. To be a document of title a document must purport to be issued by or addressed to a bailee and purport to cover goods in the bailee's possession which are either identified or are fungible portions of an identified mass.

(16) "Fault" means wrongful act, omission or breach.

(17) "Fungible" with respect to goods or securities means goods or securities of which any unit is, by nature or usage of trade, the equivalent of any other like unit. Goods which are not fungible shall be deemed fungible for the purposes of this Act to the extent that under a particular agreement or document unlike units are treated as equivalents.

(18) "Genuine" means free of forgery or counterfeiting.

(19) "Good faith" means honesty in fact in the conduct or transaction concerned.

(20) "Holder" means a person who is in possession of a document of title or an instrument or an investment security drawn, issued or indorsed to him or to his order or to bearer or in blank.

(21) To "honor" is to pay or to accept and pay, or where a credit so engages to purchase or discount a draft complying with the terms of the credit.

(22) "Insolvency proceedings" includes any assignment for the benefit of creditors or other proceedings intended to liquidate or rehabilitate the estate of the person involved.

(23) A person is "insolvent" who either has ceased to pay his debts in the ordinary course of business or cannot pay his debts as they become due or is insolvent within the meaning of the federal bankruptcy law.

(24) "Money" means a medium of exchange authorized or adopted by a domestic or foreign government as a part of its currency.

(25) A person has "notice" of a fact when

    (a) he has actual knowledge of it; or

    (b) he has received a notice or notification of it; or

    (c) from all the facts and circumstances known to him at the time in question he has reason to know that it exists.

A person "knows" or has "knowledge" of a fact when he has actual knowledge of it. "Discover" or "learn" or a word or phrase of similar import refers to knowledge rather than to reason to know. The time and circumstances under which a notice or notification may cease to be effective are not determined by this Act.

(26) A person "notifies" or "gives" a notice or notification to another by taking such steps as may be reasonably required to inform the other in ordinary course whether or not such other actually comes to know of it. A person "receives" a notice or notification when

    (a) it comes to his attention; or

    (b) it is duly delivered at the place of business through which the contract was made or at any other place held out by him as the place for receipt of such communications.

(27) Notice, knowledge or a notice or notification received by an organization is effective for a particular transaction from the time when it is brought to the attention of the individual conducting that transaction, and in any event from the time when it would have been brought to his attention if the organization had exercised due diligence. An organization exercises due diligence if it maintains reasonable routines for communicating significant information to the person conducting the transaction and there is reasonable compliance with the routines. Due diligence does not require an individual acting for the organization to communicate information unless

such communication is part of his regular duties or unless he has reason to know of the transaction and that the transaction would be materially affected by the information.

(28) "Organization" includes a corporation, government or governmental subdivision or agency, business trust, estate, trust, partnership or association, two or more persons having a joint or common interest, or any other legal or commercial entity.

(29) "Party", as distinct from "third party", means a person who has engaged in a transaction or made an agreement within this Act.

(30) "Person" includes an individual or an organization (See Section 1—102).

(31) "Presumption" or "presumed" means that the trier of fact must find the existence of the fact presumed unless and until evidence is introduced which would support a finding of its non-existence.

(32) "Purchase" includes taking by sale, discount, negotiation, mortgage, pledge, lien, issue or re-issue, gift or any other voluntary transaction creating an interest in property.

(33) "Purchaser" means a person who takes by purchase.

(34) "Remedy" means any remedial right to which an aggrieved party is entitled with or without resort to a tribunal.

(35) "Representative" includes an agent, an officer of a corporation or association, and a trustee, executor or administrator of an estate, or any other person empowered to act for another.

(36) "Rights" includes remedies.

(37) "Security interest" means an interest in personal property or fixtures which secures payment or performance of an obligation. The retention or reservation of title by a seller of goods notwithstanding shipment or delivery to the buyer (Section 2—401) is limited in effect to a reservation of a "security interest". The term also includes any interest of a buyer of accounts or chattel paper which is subject to Article 9. The special property interest of a buyer of goods on identification of such goods to a contract for sale under Section 2—401 is not a "security interest", but a buyer may also acquire a "security interest" by complying with Article 9. Unless a lease or consignment is intended as security, reservation of title thereunder is not a "security interest" but a consignment is in any event subject to the provisions on consignment sales (Section 2—326). Whether a lease is intended as security is to be determined by the facts of each case; however, (a) the inclusion of an option to purchase does not of itself make the lease one intended for security, and (b) an agreement that upon compliance with the terms of the lease the lessee shall become or has the option to become the owner of the property for no additional consideration or for a nominal consideration does make the lease one intended for security.

(38) "Send" in connection with any writing or notice means to deposit in the mail or deliver for transmission by any other usual means of communication with postage or cost of transmission provided for and properly addressed and in the case of an instrument to an address specified thereon or otherwise agreed, or if there be none to any address reasonable under the circumstances. The receipt of any writing or notice with-

in the time at which it would have arrived if properly sent has the effect of a proper sending.

(39) "Signed" includes any symbol executed or adopted by a party with present intention to authenticate a writing.

(40) "Surety" includes guarantor.

(41) "Telegram" includes a message transmitted by radio, teletype, cable, any mechanical method of transmission, or the like.

(42) "Term" means that portion of an agreement which relates to a particular matter.

(43) "Unauthorized" signature or indorsement means one made without actual, implied or apparent authority and includes a forgery.

(44) "Value". Except as otherwise provided with respect to negotiable instruments and bank collections (Sections 3—303, 4—208 and 4—209) a person gives "value" for rights if he acquires them

   (a) in return for a binding commitment to extend credit or for the extension of immediately available credit whether or not drawn upon and whether or not a chargeback is provided for in the event of difficulties in collection; or

   (b) as security for or in total or partial satisfaction of a pre-existing claim; or

   (c) by accepting delivery pursuant to a pre-existing contract for purchase; or

   (d) generally, in return for any consideration sufficient to support a simple contract.

(45) "Warehouse receipt" means a receipt issued by a person engaged in the business of storing goods for hire.

(46) "Written" or "writing" includes printing, typewriting or any other intentional reduction to tangible form. As amended 1962 and 1972.

§1—202
Prima Facie Evidence by Third Party Documents

A document in due form purporting to be a bill of lading, policy or certificate of insurance, official weigher's or inspector's certificate, consular invoice, or any other document authorized or required by the contract to be issued by a third party shall be prima facie evidence of its own authenticity and genuineness and of the facts stated in the document by the third party.

§1—203
Obligation of Good Faith

Every contract or duty within this Act imposes an obligation of good faith in its performance or enforcement.

§1—204
Time; Reasonable Time; "Seasonably"

(1) Whenever this Act requires any action to be taken within a reasonable time, any time which is not manifestly unreasonable may be fixed by agreement.

(2) What is a reasonable time for taking any action depends on the nature, purpose and circumstances of such action.

(3) An action is taken "seasonably" when it is taken at or within the time agreed or if no time is agreed at or within a reasonable time.

§1—205
Course of Dealing and
Usage of Trade

(1) A course of dealing is a sequence of previous conduct between the parties to a particular transaction which is fairly to be regarded as establishing a common basis of understanding for interpreting their expressions and other conduct.

(2) A usage of trade is any practice or method of dealing having such regularity of observance in a place, vocation or trade as to justify an expectation that it will be observed with respect to the transaction in question. The existence and scope of such a usage are to be proved as facts. If it is established that such a usage is embodied in a written trade code or similar writing the interpretation of the writing is for the court.

(3) A course of dealing between parties and any usage of trade in the vocation or trade in which they are engaged or of which they are or should be aware give particular meaning to and supplement or qualify terms of an agreement.

(4) The express terms of an agreement and an applicable course of dealing or usage of trade shall be construed wherever reasonable as consistent with each other; but when such construction is unreasonable express terms control both course of dealing and usage of trade and course of dealing controls usage of trade.

(5) An applicable usage of trade in the place where any part of performance is to occur shall be used in interpreting the agreement as to that part of the performance.

(6) Evidence of a relevant usage of trade offered by one party is not admissible unless and until he has given the other party such notice as the court finds sufficient to prevent unfair surprise to the latter.

§1—206
Statute of Frauds for Kinds of
Personal Property Not Otherwise
Covered

(1) Except in the cases described in subsection (2) of this section a contract for the sale of personal property is not enforceable by way of action or defense beyond five thousand dollars in amount or value of remedy unless there is some writing which indicates that a contract for sale has been made between the parties at a defined or stated price, reasonably identifies the subject matter, and is signed by the party against whom enforcement is sought or by his authorized agent.

(2) Subsection (1) of this section does not apply to contracts for the sale of goods (Section 2—201) nor of securities (Section 8—319) nor to security agreements (Section 9—203).

§1—207
Performance or Acceptance Under
Reservation of Rights

A party who with explicit reservation of rights performs or promises performance or assents to performance in a manner demanded or offered by the other party does not thereby prejudice the rights reserved. Such words as "without prejudice", "under protest" or the like are sufficient.

§1—208
Option to Accelerate at Will

A term providing that one party or his successor in interest may accelerate payment or performance or require collateral or additional collateral "at will" or "when he deems himself insecure" or in words of similar import shall be construed to mean that he shall have power to do so only if he in good faith believes that the prospect of payment or performance is impaired. The burden of establishing lack of good faith is on the party against whom the power has been exercised.

§1—209
Subordinated Obligations

An obligation may be issued as subordinated to payment of another obligation of the person obligated, or a creditor may subordinate his right to payment of an obligation by agreement with either the person obligated or another creditor of the person obligated. Such a subordination does not create a security interest as against either the common debtor or a subordinated creditor. This section shall be construed as declaring the law as it existed prior to the enactment of this section and not as modifying it. Added 1966.

Note: This new section is proposed as an optional provision to make it clear that a subordination agreement does not create a security interest unless so intended.

Article 2
Sales

Part 1
Short Title, General Construction
and Subject Matter

§2—101
Short Title

This Article shall be known and may be cited as Uniform Commercial Code—Sales.

§2—102
Scope; Certain Security and Other
Transactions Excluded From This
Article

Unless the context otherwise requires, this Article applies to transactions in goods; it does not apply to any transaction which although in the form of an unconditional contract to sell or present sale is intended to operate only as a security transaction nor does this Article impair or repeal any statute regulating sales to consumers, farmers or other specified classes of buyers.

§2—103
Definitions and Index of Definitions

(1) In this Article unless the context otherwise requires

   (a) "Buyer" means a person who buys or contracts to buy goods.

   (b) "Good faith" in the case of a merchant means honesty in fact and the observance of reasonable commercial standards of fair dealing in the trade.

   (c) "Receipt" of goods means taking physical possession of them.

   (d) "Seller" means a person who sells or contracts to sell goods.

(2) Other definitions applying to this Article or to specified Parts thereof, and the sections in which they appear are:

"Acceptance".	Section 2—606.
"Banker's credit".	Section 2—325.
"Between merchants".	Section 2—104.
"Cancellation".	Section 2—106(4).
"Commercial unit".	Section 2—105.
"Confirmed credit".	Section 2—325.
"Conforming to contract".	Section 2—106.
"Contract for sale".	Section 2—106.
"Cover".	Section 2—712.
"Entrusting".	Section 2—403.
"Financing agency".	Section 2—104.
"Future goods".	Section 2—105.
"Goods".	Section 2—105.
"Identification".	Section 2—501.
"Installment contract".	Section 2—612.
"Letter of credit".	Section 2—325.
"Lot".	Section 2—105.
"Merchant".	Section 2—104.
"Overseas".	Section 2—323.
"Person in position of seller".	Section 2—707.
"Present sale".	Section 2—106.
"Sale".	Section 2—106.
"Sale on approval".	Section 2—326.
"Sale or return".	Section 2—326.
"Termination".	Section 2—106.

(3) The following definitions in other Articles apply to this Article:

"Check".	Section 3—104.
"Consignee".	Section 7—102.
"Consignor".	Section 7—102.
"Consumer goods".	Section 9—109.
"Dishonor".	Section 3—507.
"Draft".	Section 3—104.

(4) In addition Article 1 contains general definitions and principles of construction and interpretation applicable throughout this Article.

§2—104
Definitions: "Merchant"; "Between Merchants"; "Financing Agency"

(1) "Merchant" means a person who deals in goods of the kind or otherwise by his occupation holds himself out as hav-ing knowledge or skill peculiar to the practices or goods involved in the transaction or to whom such knowledge or skill may be attributed by his employment of an agent or broker or other intermediary who by his occupation holds himself out as having such knowledge or skill.

(2) "Financing agency" means a bank, finance company or other person who in the ordinary course of business makes advances against goods or documents of title or who by arrangement with either the seller or the buyer intervenes in ordinary course to make or collect payment due or claimed under the contract for sale, as by purchasing or paying the seller's draft or making advances against it or by merely taking it for collection whether or not documents of title accompany the draft. "Financing agency" includes also a bank or other person who similarly intervenes between persons who are in the position of seller and buyer in respect to the goods (Section 2—707).

(3) "Between merchants" means in any transaction with respect to which both parties are chargeable with the knowledge or skill of merchants.

§2—105
Definitions: Transferability; "Goods"; "Future" Goods; "Lot"; "Commercial Unit"

(1) "Goods" means all things (including specially manufactured goods) which are movable at the time of identification to the contract for sale other than the money in which the price is to be paid, investment securities (Article 8) and things in action. "Goods" also includes the unborn young of animals and growing crops and other identified things attached to realty as described in the section on goods to be severed from realty (Section 2—107).

(2) Goods must be both existing and identified before any interest in them can pass. Goods which are not both existing and identified are "future" goods. A purported present sale of future goods or of any interest therein operates as a contract to sell.

(3) There may be a sale of a part interest in existing identified goods.

(4) An undivided share in an identified bulk of fungible goods is sufficiently identified to be sold although the quantity of the bulk is not determined. Any agreed proportion of such a bulk or any quantity thereof agreed upon by number, weight or other measure may to the extent of the seller's interest in the bulk be sold to the buyer who then becomes an owner in common.

(5) "Lot" means a parcel or a single article which is the subject matter of a separate sale or delivery, whether or not it is sufficient to perform the contract.

(6) "Commercial unit" means such a unit of goods as by commercial usage is a single whole for purposes of sale and division of which materially impairs its character or value on the market or in use. A commercial unit may be a single article (as a machine) or a set of articles (as a suite of furniture or an assortment of sizes) or a quantity (as a bale, gross, or

carload) or any other unit treated in use or in the relevant market as a single whole.

§2—106
Definitions: "Contract"; "Agreement"; "Contract for Sale"; "Sale"; "Present Sale"; "Conforming to Contract"; "Termination"; "Cancellation"

(1) In this Article unless the context otherwise requires "contract" and "agreement" are limited to those relating to the present or future sale of goods. "Contract for sale" includes both a present sale of goods and a contract to sell goods at a future time. A "sale" consists in the passing of title from the seller to the buyer for a price (Section 2—401). A "present sale" means a sale which is accomplished by the making of the contract.

(2) Goods or conduct including any part of a performance are "conforming" or conform to the contract when they are in accordance with the obligations under the contract.

(3) "Termination" occurs when either party pursuant to a power created by agreement or law puts an end to the contract otherwise than for its breach. On "termination" all obligations which are still executory on both sides are discharged but any right based on prior breach or performance survives.

(4) "Cancellation" occurs when either party puts an end to the contract for breach by the other and its effect is the same as that of "termination" except that the cancelling party also retains any remedy for breach of the whole contract or any unperformed balance.

§2—107
Goods to Be Severed From Realty: Recording

(1) A contract for the sale of minerals or the like (including oil and gas) or a structure or its materials to be removed from realty is a contract for the sale of goods within this Article if they are to be severed by the seller but until severance a purported present sale thereof which is not effective as a transfer of an interest in land is effective only as a contract to sell.

(2) A contract for the sale apart from the land of growing crops or other things attached to realty and capable of severance without material harm thereto but not described in subsection (1) or of timber to be cut is a contract for the sale of goods within this Article whether the subject matter is to be severed by the buyer or by the seller even though it forms part of the realty at the time of contracting, and the parties can by identification effect a present sale before severance.

(3) The provisions of this section are subject to any third party rights provided by the law relating to realty records, and the contract for sale may be executed and recorded as a document transferring an interest in land and shall then constitute notice to third parties of the buyer's rights under the contract for sale. As amended 1972.

Part 2
Form, Formation and Readjustment of Contract

§2—201
Formal Requirements; Statute of Frauds

(1) Except as otherwise provided in this section a contract for the sale of goods for the price of $500 or more is not enforceable by way of action or defense unless there is some writing sufficient to indicate that a contract for sale has been made between the parties and signed by the party against whom enforcement is sought or by his authorized agent or broker. A writing is not insufficient because it omits or incorrectly states a term agreed upon but the contract is not enforceable under this paragraph beyond the quantity of goods shown in such writing.

(2) Between merchants if within a reasonable time a writing in confirmation of the contract and sufficient against the sender is received and the party receiving it has reason to know its contents, it satisfies the requirements of subsection (1) against such party unless written notice of objection to its contents is given within 10 days after it is received.

(3) A contract which does not satisfy the requirements of subsection (1) but which is valid in other respects is enforceable

   (a) if the goods are to be specially manufactured for the buyer and are not suitable for sale to others in the ordinary course of the seller's business and the seller, before notice of repudiation is received and under circumstances which reasonably indicate that the goods are for the buyer, has made either a substantial beginning of their manufacture or commitments for their procurement; or

   (b) if the party against whom enforcement is sought admits in his pleading, testimony or otherwise in court that a contract for sale was made, but the contract is not enforceable under this provision beyond the quantity of goods admitted; or

   (c) with respect to goods for which payment has been made and accepted or which have been received and accepted (Sec. 2—606).

§2—202
Final Written Expression: Parol or Extrinsic Evidence

Terms with respect to which the confirmatory memoranda of the parties agree or which are otherwise set forth in a writing intended by the parties as a final expression of their agreement with respect to such terms as are included therein may not be contradicted by evidence of any prior agreement or of a contemporaneous oral agreement but may be explained or supplemented

   (a) by course of dealing or usage of trade (Section 1—205) or by course of performance (Section 2—208); and

(b) by evidence of consistent additional terms unless the court finds the writing to have been intended also as a complete and exclusive statement of the terms of the agreement.

§2—203
Seals Inoperative

The affixing of a seal to a writing evidencing a contract for sale or an offer to buy or sell goods does not constitute the writing a sealed instrument and the law with respect to sealed instruments does not apply to such a contract or offer.

§2—204
Formation in General

(1) A contract for sale of goods may be made in any manner sufficient to show agreement, including conduct by both parties which recognizes the existence of such a contract.

(2) An agreement sufficient to constitute a contract for sale may be found even though the moment of its making is undetermined.

(3) Even though one or more terms are left open a contract for sale does not fail for indefiniteness if the parties have intended to make a contract and there is a reasonably certain basis for giving an appropriate remedy.

§2—205
Firm Offers

An offer by a merchant to buy or sell goods in a signed writing which by its terms gives assurance that it will be held open is not revocable, for lack of consideration, during the time stated or if no time is stated for a reasonable time, but in no event may such period of irrevocability exceed three months; but any such term of assurance on a form supplied by the offeree must be separately signed by the offeror.

§2—206
Offer and Acceptance in Formation of Contract

(1) Unless otherwise unambiguously indicated by the language or circumstances

(a) an offer to make a contract shall be construed as inviting acceptance in any manner and by any medium reasonable in the circumstances;

(b) an order or other offer to buy goods for prompt or current shipment shall be construed as inviting acceptance either by a prompt promise to ship or by the prompt or current shipment of conforming or non-conforming goods, but such a shipment of non-conforming goods does not constitute an acceptance if the seller seasonably notifies the buyer that the shipment is offered only as an accommodation to the buyer.

(2) Where the beginning of a requested performance is a reasonable mode of acceptance an offeror who is not notified of acceptance within a reasonable time may treat the offer as having lapsed before acceptance.

§2—207
Additional Terms in Acceptance or Confirmation

(1) A definite and seasonable expression of acceptance or a written confirmation which is sent within a reasonable time operates as an acceptance even though it states terms additional to or different from those offered or agreed upon, unless acceptance is expressly made conditional on assent to the additional or different terms.

(2) The additional terms are to be construed as proposals for addition to the contract. Between merchants such terms become part of the contract unless:

(a) the offer expressly limits acceptance to the terms of the offer;

(b) they materially alter it; or

(c) notification of objection to them has already been given or is given within a reasonable time after notice of them is received.

(3) Conduct by both parties which recognizes the existence of a contract is sufficient to establish a contract for sale although the writings of the parties do not otherwise establish a contract. In such case the terms of the particular contract consist of those terms on which the writings of the parties agree, together with any supplementary terms incorporated under any other provisions of this Act.

§2—208
Course of Performance or Practical Construction

(1) Where the contract for sale involves repeated occasions for performance by either party with knowledge of the nature of the performance and opportunity for objection to it by the other, any course of performance accepted or acquiesced in without objection shall be relevant to determine the meaning of the agreement.

(2) The express terms of the agreement and any such course of performance, as well as any course of dealing and usage of trade, shall be construed whenever reasonable as consistent with each other; but when such construction is unreasonable, express terms shall control course of performance and course of performance shall control both course of dealing and usage of trade (Section 1—205).

(3) Subject to the provisions of the next section on modification and waiver, such course of performance shall be relevant to show a waiver or modification of any term inconsistent with such course of performance.

§2—209
Modification, Rescission and Waiver

(1) An agreement modifying a contract within this Article needs no consideration to be binding.

(2) A signed agreement which excludes modification or rescission except by a signed writing cannot be otherwise modified or rescinded, but except as between merchants such a requirement on a form supplied by the merchant must be separately signed by the other party.

(3) The requirements of the statute of frauds section of this Article (Section 2—201) must be satisfied if the contract as modified is within its provisions.

(4) Although an attempt at modification or rescission does not satisfy the requirements of subsection (2) or (3) it can operate as a waiver.

(5) A party who has made a waiver affecting an executory portion of the contract may retract the waiver by reasonable notification received by the other party that strict performance will be required of any term waived, unless the retraction would be unjust in view of a material change of position in reliance on the waiver.

§2—210
Delegation of Performance; Assignment of Rights

(1) A party may perform his duty through a delegate unless otherwise agreed or unless the other party has a substantial interest in having his original promisor perform or control the acts required by the contract. No delegation of performance relieves the party delegating of any duty to perform or any liability for breach.

(2) Unless otherwise agreed all rights of either seller or buyer can be assigned except where the assignment would materially change the duty of the other party, or increase materially the burden or risk imposed on him by his contract, or impair materially his chance of obtaining return performance. A right to damages for breach of the whole contract or a right arising out of the assignor's due performance of his entire obligation can be assigned despite agreement otherwise.

(3) Unless the circumstances indicate the contrary a prohibition of assignment of "the contract" is to be construed as barring only the delegation to the assignee of the assignor's performance.

(4) An assignment of "the contract" or of "all my rights under the contract" or an assignment in similar general terms is an assignment of rights and and unless the language or the circumstances (as in an assignment for security) indicate the contrary, it is a delegation of performance of the duties of the assignor and its acceptance by the assignee constitutes a promise by him to perform those duties. This promise is enforceable by either the assignor or the other party to the original contract.

(5) The other party may treat any assignment which delegates performance as creating reasonable grounds for insecurity and may without prejudice to his rights against the assignor demand assurances from the assignee (Section 2—609).

Part 3

General Obligation and Construction of Contract

§2—301
General Obligations of Parties

The obligation of the seller is to transfer and deliver and that of the buyer is to accept and pay in accordance with the contract.

§2—302
Unconscionable Contract or Clause

(1) If the court as a matter of law finds the contract or any clause of the contract to have been unconscionable at the time it was made the court may refuse to enforce the contract, or it may enforce the remainder of the contract without the unconscionable clause, or it may so limit the application of any unconscionable clause as to avoid any unconscionable result.

(2) When it is claimed or appears to the court that the contract or any clause thereof may be unconscionable the parties shall be afforded a reasonable opportunity to present evidence as to its commercial setting, purpose and effect to aid the court in making the determination.

§2—303
Allocation or Division of Risks

Where this Article allocates a risk or a burden as between the parties "unless otherwise agreed", the agreement may not only shift the allocation but may also divide the risk or burden.

§2—304
Price Payable in Money, Goods, Realty, or Otherwise

(1) The price can be made payable in money or otherwise. If it is payable in whole or in part in goods each party is a seller of the goods which he is to transfer.

(2) Even though all or part of the price is payable in an interest in realty the transfer of the goods and the seller's obligations with reference to them are subject to this Article, but not the transfer of the interest in realty or the transferor's obligations in connection therewith.

§2—305
Open Price Term

(1) The parties if they so intend can conclude a contract for sale even though the price is not settled. In such a case the price is a reasonable price at the time for delivery if

   (a) nothing is said as to price; or

   (b) the price is left to be agreed by the parties and they fail to agree; or

   (c) the price is to be fixed in terms of some agreed market or other standard as set or recorded by a third person or agency and it is not so set or recorded.

(2) A price to be fixed by the seller or by the buyer means a price for him to fix in good faith.

(3) When a price left to be fixed otherwise than by agreement of the parties fails to be fixed through fault of one party the other may at his option treat the contract as cancelled or himself fix a reasonable price.

(4) Where, however, the parties intend not to be bound unless the price be fixed or agreed and it is not fixed or agreed there is no contract. In such a case the buyer must return any goods already received or if unable so to do must pay their reasonable value at the time of delivery and the seller must return any portion of the price paid on account.

§2—306
Output, Requirements and Exclusive Dealings

(1) A term which measures the quantity by the output of the seller or the requirements of the buyer means such actual output or requirements as may occur in good faith, except that no quantity unreasonably disproportionate to any stated estimate or in the absence of a stated estimate to any normal or otherwise comparable prior output or requirements may be tendered or demanded.

(2) A lawful agreement by either the seller or the buyer for exclusive dealing in the kind of goods concerned imposes unless otherwise agreed an obligation by the seller to use best efforts to supply the goods and by the buyer to use best efforts to promote their sale.

§2—307
Delivery in Single Lot or Several Lots

Unless otherwise agreed all goods called for by a contract for sale must be tendered in a single delivery and payment is due only on such tender but where the circumstances give either party the right to make or demand delivery in lots the price if it can be apportioned may be demanded for each lot.

§2—308
Absence of Specified Place for Delivery

Unless otherwise agreed

(a) the place for delivery of goods is the seller's place of business or if he has none his residence; but

(b) in a contract for sale of identified goods which to the knowledge of the parties at the time of contracting are in some other place, that place is the place for their delivery; and

(c) documents of title may be delivered through customary banking channels.

§2—309
Absence of Specific Time Provisions; Notice of Termination

(1) The time for shipment or delivery or any other action under a contract if not provided in this Article or agreed upon shall be a reasonable time.

(2) Where the contract provides for successive performances but is indefinite in duration it is valid for a reasonable time but unless otherwise agreed may be terminated at any time by either party.

(3) Termination of a contract by one party except on the happening of an agreed event requires that reasonable notification be received by the other party and an agreement dispensing with notification is invalid if its operation would be unconscionable.

§2—310
Open Time for Payment or Running of Credit; Authority to Ship Under Reservation

Unless otherwise agreed

(a) payment is due at the time and place at which the buyer is to receive the goods even though the place of shipment is the place of delivery; and

(b) if the seller is authorized to send the goods he may ship them under reservation, and may tender the documents of title, but the buyer may inspect the goods after their arrival before payment is due unless such inspection is inconsistent with the terms of the contract (Section 2—513); and

(c) if delivery is authorized and made by way of documents of title otherwise than by subsection (b) then payment is due at the time and place at which the buyer is to receive the documents regardless of where the goods are to be received; and

(d) where the seller is required or authorized to ship the goods on credit the credit period runs from the time of shipment but post-dating the invoice or delaying its dispatch will correspondingly delay the starting of the credit period.

§2—311
Options and Cooperation Respecting Performance

(1) An agreement for sale which is otherwise sufficiently definite (subsection (3) of Section 2—204) to be a contract is not made invalid by the fact that it leaves particulars of performance to be specified by one of the parties. Any such specification must be made in good faith and within limits set by commercial reasonableness.

(2) Unless otherwise agreed specifications relating to assortment of the goods are at the buyer's option and except as otherwise provided in subsections (1) (c) and (3) of Section 2—319 specifications or arrangements relating to shipment are at the seller's option.

(3) Where such specification would materially affect the other party's performance but is not seasonably made or where one party's cooperation is necessary to the agreed performance of the other but is not seasonably forthcoming, the other party in addition to all other remedies

(a) is excused for any resulting delay in his own performance; and

(b) may also either proceed to perform in any reasonable manner or after the time for a material part of his own performance treat the failure to specify or to cooperate as a breach by failure to deliver or accept the goods.

§2—312
Warranty of Title and Against Infringement; Buyer's Obligation Against Infringement

(1) Subject to subsection (2) there is in a contract for sale a warranty by the seller that

(a) the title conveyed shall be good, and its transfer rightful; and

(b) the goods shall be delivered free from any security interest or other lien or encumbrance of which the buyer at the time of contracting has no knowledge.

(2) A warranty under subsection (1) will be excluded or modified only by specific language or by circumstances which give the buyer reason to know that the person selling does not claim title in himself or that he is purporting to sell only such right or title as he or a third person may have.

(3) Unless otherwise agreed a seller who is a merchant regularly dealing in goods of the kind warrants that the goods shall be delivered free of the rightful claim of any third person by way of infringement or the like but a buyer who furnishes specifications to the seller must hold the seller harmless against any such claim which arises out of compliance with the specifications.

§2—313
Express Warranties by Affirmation, Promise, Description, Sample

(1) Express warranties by the seller are created as follows:

  (a) Any affirmation of fact or promise made by the seller to the buyer which relates to the goods and becomes part of the basis of the bargain creates an express warranty that the goods shall conform to the affirmation or promise.

  (b) Any description of the goods which is made part of the basis of the bargain creates an express warranty that the goods shall conform to the description.

  (c) Any sample or model which is made part of the basis of the bargain creates an express warranty that the whole of the goods shall conform to the sample or model.

(2) It is not necessary to the creation of an express warranty that the seller use formal words such as "warrant" or "guarantee" or that he have a specific intention to make a warranty, but an affirmation merely of the value of the goods or a statement purporting to be merely the seller's opinion or commendation of the goods does not create a warranty.

§2—314
Implied Warranty: Merchantability; Usage of Trade

(1) Unless excluded or modified (Section 2—316), a warranty that the goods shall be merchantable is implied in a contract for their sale if the seller is a merchant with respect to goods of that kind. Under this section the serving for value of food or drink to be consumed either on the premises or elsewhere is a sale.

(2) Goods to be merchantable must be at least such as

  (a) pass without objection in the trade under the contract description; and

  (b) in the case of fungible goods, are of fair average quality within the description; and

  (c) are fit for the ordinary purposes for which such goods are used; and

  (d) run, within the variations permitted by the agreement, of even kind, quality and quantity within each unit and among all units involved; and

  (e) are adequately contained, packaged, and labeled as the agreement may require; and

  (f) conform to the promises or affirmations of fact made on the container or label if any.

(3) Unless excluded or modified (Section 2—316) other implied warranties may arise from course of dealing or usage of trade.

§2—315
Implied Warranty: Fitness for Particular Purpose

Where the seller at the time of contracting has reason to know any particular purpose for which the goods are required and that the buyer is relying on the seller's skill or judgment to select or furnish suitable goods, there is unless excluded or modified under the next section an implied warranty that the goods shall be fit for such purpose.

§2—316
Exclusion or Modification of Warranties

(1) Words or conduct relevant to the creation of an express warranty and words or conduct tending to negate or limit warranty shall be construed wherever reasonable as consistent with each other; but subject to the provisions of this Article on parol or extrinsic evidence (Section 2—202) negation or limitation is inoperative to the extent that such construction is unreasonable.

(2) Subject to subsection (3), to exclude or modify the implied warranty of merchantability or any part of it the language must mention merchantability and in case of a writing must be conspicuous, and to exclude or modify any implied warranty of fitness the exclusion must be by a writing and conspicuous. Language to exclude all implied warranties of fitness is sufficient if it states, for example, that "There are no warranties which extend beyond the description on the face hereof."

(3) Notwithstanding subsection (2)

  (a) unless the circumstances indicate otherwise, all implied warranties are excluded by expressions like "as is", "with all faults" or other language which in common understanding calls the buyer's attention to the exclusion of warranties and makes plain that there is no implied warranty; and

  (b) when the buyer before entering into the contract has examined the goods or the sample or model as fully as he desired or has refused to examine the goods there is no implied warranty with regard to defects which an examination ought in the circumstances to have revealed to him; and

  (c) an implied warranty can also be excluded or modified by course of dealing or course of performance or usage of trade.

(4) Remedies for breach of warranty can be limited in accordance with the provisions of this Article on liquidation or limitation of damages and on contractual modification of remedy (Sections 2—718 and 2—719).

§2—317
Cumulation and Conflict of Warranties Express or Implied

Warranties whether express or implied shall be construed as consistent with each other and as cumulative, but if such construction is unreasonable the intention of the parties shall determine which warranty is dominant. In ascertaining that intention the following rules apply:

(a) Exact or technical specifications displace an inconsistent sample or model or general language of description.

(b) A sample from an existing bulk displaces inconsistent general language of description.

(c) Express warranties displace inconsistent implied warranties other than an implied warranty of fitness for a particular purpose.

§2—318
Third Party Beneficiaries of Warranties Express or Implied

Note: If this Act is introduced in the Congress of the United States this section should be omitted. (States to select one alternative.)

Alternative A

A seller's warranty whether express or implied extends to any natural person who is in the family or household of his buyer or who is a guest in his home if it is reasonable to expect that such person may use, consume or be affected by the goods and who is injured in person by breach of the warranty. A seller may not exclude or limit the operation of this section.

Alternative B

A seller's warranty whether express or implied extends to any natural person who may reasonably be expected to use, consume or be affected by the goods and who is injured in person by breach of the warranty. A seller may not exclude or limit the operation of this section.

Alternative C

A seller's warranty whether express or implied extends to any person who may reasonably be expected to use, consume or be affected by the goods and who is injured by breach of the warranty. A seller may not exclude or limit the operation of this section with respect to injury to the person of an individual to whom the warranty extends. As amended 1966.

§2—319
F.O.B. and F.A.S. Terms

(1) Unless otherwise agreed the term F.O.B. (which means "free on board") at a named place, even though used only in connection with the stated price, is a delivery term under which

(a) when the term is F.O.B. the place of shipment, the seller must at that place ship the goods in the manner provided in this Article (Section 2—504) and bear the

expense and risk of putting them into the possession of the carrier; or

(b) when the term is F.O.B. the place of destination, the seller must at his own expense and risk transport the goods to that place and there tender delivery of them in the manner provided in this Article (Section 2—503);

(c) when under either (a) or (b) the term is also F.O.B. vessel, car or other vehicle, the seller must in addition at his own expense and risk load the goods on board. If the term is F.O.B. vessel the buyer must name the vessel and in an appropriate case the seller must comply with the provisions of this Article on the form of bill of lading (Section 2—323).

(2) Unless otherwise agreed the term F.A.S. vessel (which means "free alongside") at a named port, even though used only in connection with the stated price, is a delivery term under which the seller must

(a) at his own expense and risk deliver the goods alongside the vessel in the manner usual in that port or on a dock designated and provided by the buyer; and

(b) obtain and tender a receipt for the goods in exchange for which the carrier is under a duty to issue a bill of lading.

(3) Unless otherwise agreed in any case falling within subsection (1) (a) or (c) or subsection (2) the buyer must seasonably give any needed instructions for making delivery, including when the term is F.A.S. or F.O.B. the loading berth of the vessel and in an appropriate case its name and sailing date. The seller may treat the failure of needed instructions as a failure of cooperation under this Article (Section 2—311). He may also at his option move the goods in any reasonable manner preparatory to delivery or shipment.

(4) Under the term F.O.B. vessel or F.A.S. unless otherwise agreed the buyer must make payment against tender of the required documents and the seller may not tender nor the buyer demand delivery of the goods in substitution for the documents.

§2—320
C.I.F. and C. & F. Terms

(1) The term C.I.F. means that the price includes in a lump sum the cost of the goods and the insurance and freight to the named destination. The term C. & F. or C.F. means that the price so includes cost and freight to the named destination.

(2) Unless otherwise agreed and even though used only in connection with the stated price and destination, the term C.I.F. destination or its equivalent requires the seller at his own expense and risk to

(a) put the goods into the possession of a carrier at the port for shipment and obtain a negotiable bill or bills of lading covering the entire transportation to the named destination; and

(b) load the goods and obtain a receipt from the carrier (which may be contained in the bill of lading) showing that the freight has been paid or provided for; and

(c) obtain a policy or certificate of insurance, including any war risk insurance, of a kind and on terms then current at the port of shipment in the usual amount, in the currency of the contract, shown to cover the same goods covered by the bill of lading and providing for payment of loss to the order of the buyer or for the account of whom it may concern; but the seller may add to the price the amount of the premium for any such war risk insurance; and

(d) prepare an invoice of the goods and procure any other documents required to effect shipment or to comply with the contract; and

(e) forward and tender with commercial promptness all the documents in due form and with any indorsement necessary to perfect the buyer's rights.

(3) Unless otherwise agreed the term C. & F. or its equivalent has the same effect and imposes upon the seller the same obligations and risks as a C.I.F. term except the obligation as to insurance.

(4) Under the term C.I.F. or C. & F. unless otherwise agreed the buyer must make payment against tender of the required documents and the seller may not tender nor the buyer demand delivery of the goods in substitution for the documents.

§2—321
C.I.F. or C. & F.: "Net Landed Weights"; "Payment on Arrival"; Warranty of Condition on Arrival

Under a contract containing a term C.I.F. or C. & F.

(1) Where the price is based on or is to be adjusted according to "net landed weights", "delivered weights", "out turn" quantity or quality or the like, unless otherwise agreed the seller must reasonably estimate the price. The payment due on tender of the documents called for by the contract is the amount so estimated, but after final adjustment of the price a settlement must be made with commercial promptness.

(2) An agreement described in subsection (1) or any warranty of quality or condition of the goods on arrival places upon the seller the risk of ordinary deterioration, shrinkage and the like in transportation but has no effect on the place or time of identification to the contract for sale or delivery or on the passing of the risk of loss.

(3) Unless otherwise agreed where the contract provides for payment on or after arrival of the goods the seller must before payment allow such preliminary inspection as is feasible; but if the goods are lost delivery of the documents and payment are due when the goods should have arrived.

§2—322
Delivery "Ex-Ship"

(1) Unless otherwise agreed a term for delivery of goods "ex-ship" (which means from the carrying vessel) or in equivalent language is not restricted to a particular ship and requires delivery from a ship which has reached a place at the named port of destination where goods of the kind are usually discharged.

(2) Under such a term unless otherwise agreed

(a) the seller must discharge all liens arising out of the carriage and furnish the buyer with a direction which puts the carrier under a duty to deliver the goods; and

(b) the risk of loss does not pass to the buyer until the goods leave the ship's tackle or are otherwise properly unloaded.

§2—323
Form of Bill of Lading Required in Overseas Shipment; "Overseas"

(1) Where the contract contemplates overseas shipment and contains a term C.I.F. or C. & F. or F.O.B. vessel, the seller unless otherwise agreed must obtain a negotiable bill of lading stating that the goods have been loaded on board or, in the case of a term C.I.F. or C. & F., received for shipment.

(2) Where in a case within subsection (1) a bill of lading has been issued in a set of parts, unless otherwise agreed if the documents are not to be sent from abroad the buyer may demand tender of the full set; otherwise only one part of the bill of lading need be tendered. Even if the agreement expressly requires a full set

(a) due tender of a single part is acceptable within the provisions of this Article on cure of improper delivery (subsection (1) of Section 2—508); and

(b) even though the full set is demanded, if the documents are sent from abroad the person tendering an incomplete set may nevertheless require payment upon furnishing an indemnity which the buyer in good faith deems adequate.

(3) A shipment by water or by air or a contract contemplating such shipment is "overseas" insofar as by usage of trade or agreement it is subject to the commercial, financing or shipping practices characteristic of international deep water commerce.

§2—324
"No Arrival, No Sale" Term

Under a term "no arrival, no sale" or terms of like meaning, unless otherwise agreed,

(a) the seller must properly ship conforming goods and if they arrive by any means he must tender them on arrival but he assumes no obligation that the goods will arrive unless he has caused the non-arrival; and

(b) where without fault of the seller the goods are in part lost or have so deteriorated as no longer to conform to the contract or arrive after the contract time, the buyer may proceed as if there had been casualty to identified goods (Section 2—613).

§2—325
"Letter of Credit" Term; "Confirmed Credit"

(1) Failure of the buyer seasonably to furnish an agreed letter of credit is a breach of the contract for sale.

(2) The delivery to seller of a proper letter of credit suspends the buyer's obligation to pay. If the letter of credit is dishonored, the seller may on seasonable notification to the buyer require payment directly from him.

(3) Unless otherwise agreed the term "letter of credit" or "banker's credit" in a contract for sale means an irrevocable credit issued by a financing agency of good repute and, where the shipment is overseas, of good international repute. The term "confirmed credit" means that the credit must also carry the direct obligation of such an agency which does business in the seller's financial market.

§2—326
Sale on Approval and Sale or Return; Consignment Sales and Rights of Creditors

(1) Unless otherwise agreed, if delivered goods may be returned by the buyer even though they conform to the contract, the transaction is

    (a) a "sale on approval" if the goods are delivered primarily for use, and

    (b) a "sale or return" if the goods are delivered primarily for resale.

(2) Except as provided in subsection (3), goods held on approval are not subject to the claims of the buyer's creditors until acceptance; goods held on sale or return are subject to such claims while in the buyer's possession.

(3) Where goods are delivered to a person for sale and such person maintains a place of business at which he deals in goods of the kind involved, under a name other than the name of the person making delivery, then with respect to claims of creditors of the person conducting the business the goods are deemed to be on sale or return. The provisions of this subsection are applicable even though an agreement purports to reserve title to the person making delivery until payment or resale or uses such words as "on consignment" or "on memorandum". However, this subsection is not applicable if the person making delivery

    (a) complies with an applicable law providing for a consignor's interest or the like to be evidenced by a sign, or

    (b) establishes that the person conducting the business is generally known by his creditors to be substantially engaged in selling the goods of others, or

    (c) complies with the filing provisions of the Article on Secured Transactions (Article 9).

(4) Any "or return" term of a contract for sale is to be treated as a separate contract for sale within the statute of frauds section of this Article (Section 2—201) and as contradicting the sale aspect of the contract within the provisions of this Article on parol or extrinsic evidence (Section 2—202).

§2—327
Special Incidents of Sale on Approval and Sale or Return

(1) Under a sale on approval unless otherwise agreed

    (a) although the goods are identified to the contract the risk of loss and the title do not pass to the buyer until acceptance; and

    (b) use of the goods consistent with the purpose of trial is not acceptance but failure seasonably to notify the seller of election to return the goods is acceptance,

and if the goods conform to the contract acceptance of any part is acceptance of the whole; and

    (c) after due notification of election to return, the return is at the seller's risk and expense but a merchant buyer must follow any reasonable instructions.

(2) Under a sale or return unless otherwise agreed

    (a) the option to return extends to the whole or any commercial unit of the goods while in substantially their original condition, but must be exercised seasonably; and

    (b) the return is at the buyer's risk and expense.

§2—328
Sale by Auction

(1) In a sale by auction if goods are put up in lots each lot is the subject of a separate sale.

(2) A sale by auction is complete when the auctioneer so announces by the fall of the hammer or in other customary manner. Where a bid is made while the hammer is falling in acceptance of a prior bid the auctioneer may in his discretion reopen the bidding or declare the goods sold under the bid on which the hammer was falling.

(3) Such a sale is with reserve unless the goods are in explicit terms put up without reserve. In an auction with reserve the auctioneer may withdraw the goods at any time until he announces completion of the sale. In an auction without reserve, after the auctioneer calls for bids on an article or lot, that article or lot cannot be withdrawn unless no bid is made within a reasonable time. In either case a bidder may retract his bid until the auctioneer's announcement of completion of the sale, but a bidder's retraction does not revive any previous bid.

(4) If the auctioneer knowingly receives a bid on the seller's behalf or the seller makes or procures such a bid, and notice has not been given that liberty for such bidding is reserved, the buyer may at his option avoid the sale or take the goods at the price of the last good faith bid prior to the completion of the sale. This subsection shall not apply to any bid at a forced sale.

Part 4

Title, Creditors and Good Faith Purchasers

§2—401
Passing of Title; Reservation for Security; Limited Application of This Section

Each provision of this Article with regard to the rights, obligations and remedies of the seller, the buyer, purchasers or other third parties applies irrespective of title to the goods except where the provision refers to such title. Insofar as situations are not covered by the other provisions of this Article and matters concerning title become material the following rules apply:

(1) Title to goods cannot pass under a contract for sale prior to their identification to the contract (Section 2—501), and

unless otherwise explicitly agreed the buyer acquires by their identification a special property as limited by this Act. Any retention or reservation by the seller of the title (property) in goods shipped or delivered to the buyer is limited in effect to a reservation of a security interest. Subject to these provisions and to the provisions of the Article on Secured Transactions (Article 9), title to goods passes from the seller to the buyer in any manner and on any conditions explicitly agreed on by the parties.

(2) Unless otherwise explicitly agreed title passes to the buyer at the time and place at which the seller completes his performance with reference to the physical delivery of the goods, despite any reservation of a security interest and even though a document of title is to be delivered at a different time or place; and in particular and despite any reservation of a security interest by the bill of lading

    (a) if the contract requires or authorizes the seller to send the goods to the buyer but does not require him to deliver them at destination, title passes to the buyer at the time and place of shipment; but

    (b) if the contract requires delivery at destination, title passes on tender there.

(3) Unless otherwise explicitly agreed where delivery is to be made without moving the goods,

    (a) if the seller is to deliver a document of title, title passes at the time when and the place where he delivers such documents; or

    (b) if the goods are at the time of contracting already identified and no documents are to be delivered, title passes at the time and place of contracting.

(4) A rejection or other refusal by the buyer to receive or retain the goods, whether or not justified, or a justified revocation of acceptance revests title to the goods in the seller. Such revesting occurs by operation of law and is not a "sale".

§2—402
Rights of Seller's Creditors Against Sold Goods

(1) Except as provided in subsections (2) and (3), rights of unsecured creditors of the seller with respect to goods which have been identified to a contract for sale are subject to the buyer's rights to recover the goods under this Article (Sections 2—502 and 2—716).

(2) A creditor of the seller may treat a sale or an identification of goods to a contract for sale as void if as against him a retention of possession by the seller is fraudulent under any rule of law of the state where the goods are situated, except that retention of possession in good faith and current course of trade by a merchant-seller for a commercially reasonable time after a sale or identification is not fraudulent.

(3) Nothing in this Article shall be deemed to impair the rights of creditors of the seller

    (a) under the provisions of the Article on Secured Transactions (Article 9); or

    (b) where identification to the contract or delivery is made not in current course of trade but in satisfaction of or as security for a pre-existing claim for money, security

or the like and is made under circumstances which under any rule of law of the state where the goods are situated would apart from this Article constitute the transaction a fraudulent transfer or voidable preference.

§2—403
Power to Transfer; Good Faith Purchase of Goods; "Entrusting"

(1) A purchaser of goods acquires all title which his transferor had or had power to transfer except that a purchaser of a limited interest acquires rights only to the extent of the interest purchased. A person with voidable title has power to transfer a good title to a good faith purchaser for value. When goods have been delivered under a transaction of purchase the purchaser has such power even though

    (a) the transferor was deceived as to the identity of the purchaser, or

    (b) the delivery was in exchange for a check which is later dishonored, or

    (c) it was agreed that the transaction was to be a "cash sale", or

    (d) the delivery was procured through fraud punishable as larcenous under the criminal law.

(2) Any entrusting of possession of goods to a merchant who deals in goods of that kind gives him power to transfer all rights of the entruster to a buyer in ordinary course of business.

(3) "Entrusting" includes any delivery and any acquiescence in retention of possession regardless of any condition expressed between the parties to the delivery or acquiescence and regardless of whether the procurement of the entrusting or the possessor's disposition of the goods have been such as to be larcenous under the criminal law.

(4) The rights of other purchasers of goods and of lien creditors are governed by the Articles on Secured Transactions (Article 9), Bulk Transfers (Article 6) and Documents of Title (Article 7).

Part 5
Performance

§2—501
Insurable Interest in Goods; Manner of Identification of Goods

(1) The buyer obtains a special property and an insurable interest in goods by identification of existing goods as goods to which the contract refers even though the goods so identified are non-conforming and he has an option to return or reject them. Such identification can be made at any time and in any manner explicitly agreed to by the parties. In the absence of explicit agreement identification occurs

    (a) when the contract is made if it is for the sale of goods already existing and identified;

(b) if the contract is for the sale of future goods other than those described in paragraph (c), when goods are shipped, marked or otherwise designated by the seller as goods to which the contract refers;

(c) when the crops are planted or otherwise become growing crops or the young are conceived if the contract is for the sale of unborn young to be born within twelve months after contracting or for the sale of crops to be harvested within twelve months or the next normal harvest season after contracting whichever is longer.

(2) The seller retains an insurable interest in goods so long as title to or any security interest in the goods remains in him and where the identification is by the seller alone he may until default or insolvency or notification to the buyer that the identification is final substitute other goods for those identified.

(3) Nothing in this section impairs any insurable interest recognized under any other statute or rule of law.

§2—502
Buyer's Right to Goods on Seller's Insolvency

(1) Subject to subsection (2) and even though the goods have not been shipped a buyer who has paid a part or all of the price of goods in which he has a special property under the provisions of the immediately preceding section may on making and keeping good a tender of any unpaid portion of their price recover them from the seller if the seller becomes insolvent within ten days after receipt of the first installment on their price.

(2) If the identification creating his special property has been made by the buyer he acquires the right to recover the goods only if they conform to the contract for sale.

§2—503
Manner of Seller's Tender of Delivery

(1) Tender of delivery requires that the seller put and hold conforming goods at the buyer's disposition and give the buyer any notification reasonably necessary to enable him to take delivery. The manner, time and place for tender are determined by the agreement and this Article, and in particular

(a) tender must be at a reasonable hour, and if it is of goods they must be kept available for the period reasonably necessary to enable the buyer to take possession; but

(b) unless otherwise agreed the buyer must furnish facilities reasonably suited to the receipt of the goods.

(2) Where the case is within the next section respecting shipment tender requires that the seller comply with its provisions.

(3) Where the seller is required to deliver at a particular destination tender requires that he comply with subsection (1) and also in any appropriate case tender documents as described in subsections (4) and (5) of this section.

(4) Where goods are in the possession of a bailee and are to be delivered without being moved

(a) tender requires that the seller either tender a negotiable document of title covering such goods or procure acknowledgment by the bailee of the buyer's right to possession of the goods; but

(b) tender to the buyer of a non-negotiable document of title or of a written direction to the bailee to deliver is sufficient tender unless the buyer seasonably objects, and receipt by the bailee of notification of the buyer's rights fixes those rights as against the bailee and all third persons; but risk of loss of the goods and of any failure by the bailee to honor the non-negotiable document of title or to obey the direction remains on the seller until the buyer has had a reasonable time to present the document or direction, and a refusal by the bailee to honor the document or to obey the direction defeats the tender.

(5) Where the contract requires the seller to deliver documents

(a) he must tender all such documents in correct form, except as provided in this Article with respect to bills of lading in a set (subsection (2) of Section 2—323); and

(b) tender through customary banking channels is sufficient and dishonor of a draft accompanying the documents constitutes non-acceptance or rejection.

§2—504
Shipment by Seller

Where the seller is required or authorized to send the goods to the buyer and the contract does not require him to deliver them at a particular destination, then unless otherwise agreed he must

(a) put the goods in the possession of such a carrier and make such a contract for their transportation as may be reasonable having regard to the nature of the goods and other circumstances of the case; and

(b) obtain and promptly deliver or tender in due form any document necessary to enable the buyer to obtain possession of the goods or otherwise required by the agreement or by usage of trade; and

(c) promptly notify the buyer of the shipment.

Failure to notify the buyer under paragraph (c) or to make a proper contract under paragraph (a) is a ground for rejection only if material delay or loss ensues.

§2—505
Seller's Shipment Under Reservation

(1) Where the seller has identified goods to the contract by or before shipment:

(a) his procurement of a negotiable bill of lading to his own order or otherwise reserves in him a security interest in the goods. His procurement of the bill to the order of a financing agency or of the buyer indicates in addition only the seller's expectation of transferring that interest to the person named.

(b) a non-negotiable bill of lading to himself or his nominee reserves possession of the goods as security but except in a case of conditional delivery (subsection (2) of Section 2—507) a non-negotiable bill of lading naming the buyer as consignee reserves no security interest even though the seller retains possession of the bill of lading.

(2) When shipment by the seller with reservation of a security interest is in violation of the contract for sale it constitutes an improper contract for transportation within the preceding section but impairs neither the rights given to the buyer by shipment and identification of the goods to the contract nor the seller's powers as a holder of a negotiable document.

§2—506
Rights of Financing Agency

(1) A financing agency by paying or purchasing for value a draft which relates to a shipment of goods acquires to the extent of the payment or purchase and in addition to its own rights under the draft and any document of title securing it any rights of the shipper in the goods including the right to stop delivery and the shipper's right to have the draft honored by the buyer.

(2) The right to reimbursement of a financing agency which has in good faith honored or purchased the draft under commitment to or authority from the buyer is not impaired by subsequent discovery of defects with reference to any relevant document which was apparently regular on its face.

§2—507
Effect of Seller's Tender; Delivery on Condition

(1) Tender of delivery is a condition to the buyer's duty to accept the goods and, unless otherwise agreed, to his duty to pay for them. Tender entitles the seller to acceptance of the goods and to payment according to the contract.

(2) Where payment is due and demanded on the delivery to the buyer of goods or documents of title, his right as against the seller to retain or dispose of them is conditional upon his making the payment due.

§2—508
Cure by Seller of Improper Tender or Delivery; Replacement

(1) Where any tender or delivery by the seller is rejected because non-conforming and the time for performance has not yet expired, the seller may seasonably notify the buyer of his intention to cure and may then within the contract time make a conforming delivery.

(2) Where the buyer rejects a non-conforming tender which the seller had reasonable grounds to believe would be acceptable with or without money allowance the seller may if he seasonably notifies the buyer have a further reasonable time to substitute a conforming tender.

§2—509
Risk of Loss in the Absence of Breach

(1) Where the contract requires or authorizes the seller to ship the goods by carrier

(a) if it does not require him to deliver them at a particular destination, the risk of loss passes to the buyer when the goods are duly delivered to the carrier even though the shipment is under reservation (Section 2—505); but

(b) if it does require him to deliver them at a particular destination and the goods are there duly tendered while in the possession of the carrier, the risk of loss passes to the buyer when the goods are there duly so tendered as to enable the buyer to take delivery.

(2) Where the goods are held by a bailee to be delivered without being moved, the risk of loss passes to the buyer

(a) on his receipt of a negotiable document of title covering the goods; or

(b) on acknowledgment by the bailee of the buyer's right to possession of the goods; or

(c) after his receipt of a non-negotiable document of title or other written direction to deliver, as provided in subsection (4) (b) of Section 2—503.

(3) In any case not within subsection (1) or (2), the risk of loss passes to the buyer on his receipt of the goods if the seller is a merchant; otherwise the risk passes to the buyer on tender of delivery.

(4) The provisions of this section are subject to contrary agreement of the parties and to the provisions of this Article on sale on approval (Section 2—327) and on effect of breach on risk of loss (Section 2—510).

§2—510
Effect of Breach on Risk of Loss

(1) Where a tender or delivery of goods so fails to conform to the contract as to give a right of rejection the risk of their loss remains on the seller until cure or acceptance.

(2) Where the buyer rightfully revokes acceptance he may to the extent of any deficiency in his effective insurance coverage treat the risk of loss as having rested on the seller from the beginning.

(3) Where the buyer as to conforming goods already identified to the contract for sale repudiates or is otherwise in breach before risk of their loss has passed to him, the seller may to the extent of any deficiency in his effective insurance coverage treat the risk of loss as resting on the buyer for a commercially reasonable time.

§2—511
Tender of Payment by Buyer; Payment by Check

(1) Unless otherwise agreed tender of payment is a condition to the seller's duty to tender and complete any delivery.

(2) Tender of payment is sufficient when made by any means or in any manner current in the ordinary course of business unless the seller demands payment in legal tender and gives any extension of time reasonably necessary to procure it.

(3) Subject to the provisions of this Act on the effect of an instrument on an obligation (Section 3—802), payment by check is conditional and is defeated as between the parties by dishonor of the check on due presentment.

§2—512
Payment by Buyer Before Inspection

(1) Where the contract requires payment before inspection non-conformity of the goods does not excuse the buyer from so making payment unless

    (a) the non-conformity appears without inspection; or

    (b) despite tender of the required documents the circumstances would justify injunction against honor under the provisions of this Act (Section 5—114).

(2) Payment pursuant to subsection (1) does not constitute an acceptance of goods or impair the buyer's right to inspect or any of his remedies.

§2—513
Buyer's Right to Inspection of Goods

(1) Unless otherwise agreed and subject to subsection (3), where goods are tendered or delivered or identified to the contract for sale, the buyer has a right before payment or acceptance to inspect them at any reasonable place and time and in any reasonable manner. When the seller is required or authorized to send the goods to the buyer, the inspection may be after their arrival.

(2) Expenses of inspection must be borne by the buyer but may be recovered from the seller if the goods do not conform and are rejected.

(3) Unless otherwise agreed and subject to the provisions of this Article on C.I.F. contracts (subsection (3) of Section 2—321), the buyer is not entitled to inspect the goods before payment of the price when the contract provides

    (a) for delivery "C.O.D." or on other like terms; or

    (b) for payment against documents of title, except where such payment is due only after the goods are to become available for inspection.

(4) A place or method of inspection fixed by the parties is presumed to be exclusive but unless otherwise expressly agreed it does not postpone identification or shift the place for delivery or for passing the risk of loss. If compliance becomes impossible, inspection shall be as provided in this section unless the place or method fixed was clearly intended as an indispensable condition failure of which avoids the contract.

§2—514
When Documents Deliverable on Acceptance; When on Payment

Unless otherwise agreed documents against which a draft is drawn are to be delivered to the drawee on acceptance of the draft if it is payable more than three days after presentment; otherwise, only on payment.

§2—515
Preserving Evidence of Goods in Dispute

In furtherance of the adjustment of any claim or dispute

    (a) either party on reasonable notification to the other and for the purpose of ascertaining the facts and preserv-

ing evidence has the right to inspect, test and sample the goods including such of them as may be in the possession or control of the other; and

    (b) the parties may agree to a third party inspection or survey to determine the conformity or condition of the goods and may agree that the findings shall be binding upon them in any subsequent litigation or adjustment.

Part 6
Breach, Repudiation and Excuse

§2—601
Buyer's Rights on Improper Delivery

Subject to the provisions of this Article on breach in installment contracts (Section 2—612) and unless otherwise agreed under the sections on contractual limitations of remedy (Sections 2—718 and 2—719), if the goods or the tender of delivery fail in any respect to conform to the contract, the buyer may

    (a) reject the whole; or

    (b) accept the whole; or

    (c) accept any commercial unit or units and reject the rest.

§2—602
Manner and Effect of Rightful Rejection

(1) Rejection of goods must be within a reasonable time after their delivery or tender. It is ineffective unless the buyer seasonably notifies the seller.

(2) Subject to the provisions of the two following sections on rejected goods (Sections 2—603 and 2—604),

    (a) after rejection any exercise of ownership by the buyer with respect to any commercial unit is wrongful as against the seller; and

    (b) if the buyer has before rejection taken physical possession of goods in which he does not have a security interest under the provisions of this Article (subsection (3) of Section 2—711), he is under a duty after rejection to hold them with reasonable care at the seller's disposition for a time sufficient to permit the seller to remove them; but

    (c) the buyer has no further obligations with regard to goods rightfully rejected.

(3) The seller's rights with respect to goods wrongfully rejected are governed by the provisions of this Article on Seller's remedies in general (Section 2—703).

§2—603
Merchant Buyer's Duties as to Rightfully Rejected Goods

(1) Subject to any security interest in the buyer (subsection (3) of Section 2—711), when the seller has no agent or place

of business at the market of rejection a merchant buyer is under a duty after rejection of goods in his possession or control to follow any reasonable instructions received from the seller with respect to the goods and in the absence of such instructions to make reasonable efforts to sell them for the seller's account if they are perishable or threaten to decline in value speedily. Instructions are not reasonable if on demand indemnity for expenses is not forthcoming.

(2) When the buyer sells goods under subsection (1), he is entitled to reimbursement from the seller or out of the proceeds for reasonable expenses of caring for and selling them, and if the expenses include no selling commission then to such commission as is usual in the trade or if there is none to a reasonable sum not exceeding ten per cent on the gross proceeds.

(3) In complying with this section the buyer is held only to good faith and good faith conduct hereunder is neither acceptance nor conversion nor the basis of an action for damages.

§2—604
Buyer's Options as to Salvage of Rightfully Rejected Goods

Subject to the provisions of the immediately preceding section on perishables if the seller gives no instructions within a reasonable time after notification of rejection the buyer may store the rejected goods for the seller's account or reship them to him or resell them for the seller's account with reimbursement as provided in the preceding section. Such action is not acceptance or conversion.

§2—605
Waiver of Buyer's Objections by Failure to Particularize

(1) The buyer's failure to state in connection with rejection a particular defect which is ascertainable by reasonable inspection precludes him from relying on the unstated defect to justify rejection or to establish breach

    (a) where the seller could have cured it if stated seasonably; or

    (b) between merchants when the seller has after rejection made a request in writing for a full and final written statement of all defects on which the buyer proposes to rely.

(2) Payment against documents made without reservation of rights precludes recovery of the payment for defects apparent on the face of the documents.

§2—606
What Constitutes Acceptance of Goods

(1) Acceptance of goods occurs when the buyer

    (a) after a reasonable opportunity to inspect the goods signifies to the seller that the goods are conforming or that he will take or retain them in spite of their non-conformity; or

    (b) fails to make an effective rejection (subsection (1) of Section 2—602), but such acceptance does not occur until the buyer has had a reasonable opportunity to inspect them; or

    (c) does any act inconsistent with the seller's ownership; but if such act is wrongful as against the seller it is an acceptance only if ratified by him.

(2) Acceptance of a part of any commercial unit is acceptance of that entire unit.

§2—607
Effect of Acceptance; Notice of Breach; Burden of Establishing Breach After Acceptance; Notice of Claim or Litigation to Person Answerable Over

(1) The buyer must pay at the contract rate for any goods accepted.

(2) Acceptance of goods by the buyer precludes rejection of the goods accepted and if made with knowledge of a non-conformity cannot be revoked because of it unless the acceptance was on the reasonable assumption that the non-conformity would be seasonably cured but acceptance does not of itself impair any other remedy provided by this Article for non-conformity.

(3) Where a tender has been accepted

    (a) the buyer must within a reasonable time after he discovers or should have discovered any breach notify the seller of breach or be barred from any remedy; and

    (b) if the claim is one for infringement or the like (subsection (3) of Section 2—312) and the buyer is sued as a result of such a breach he must so notify the seller within a reasonable time after he receives notice of the litigation or be barred from any remedy over for liability established by the litigation.

(4) The burden is on the buyer to establish any breach with respect to the goods accepted.

(5) Where the buyer is sued for breach of a warranty or other obligation for which his seller is answerable over

    (a) he may give his seller written notice of the litigation. If the notice states that the seller may come in and defend and that if the seller does not do so he will be bound in any action against him by his buyer by any determination of fact common to the two litigations, then unless the seller after seasonable receipt of the notice does come in and defend he is so bound.

    (b) if the claim is one for infringement or the like (subsection (3) of Section 2—312) the original seller may demand in writing that his buyer turn over to him control of the litigation including settlement or else be barred from any remedy over and if he also agrees to bear all expense and to satisfy any adverse judgment, then unless the buyer after seasonable receipt of the demand does turn over control the buyer is so barred.

(6) The provisions of subsections (3), (4) and (5) apply to any obligation of a buyer to hold the seller harmless against infringement or the like (subsection (3) of Section 2—312).

§2—608
Revocation of Acceptance in Whole or in Part

(1) The buyer may revoke his acceptance of a lot or commercial unit whose non-conformity substantially impairs its value to him if he has accepted it

(a) on the reasonable assumption that its non-conformity would be cured and it has not been seasonably cured; or

(b) without discovery of such non-conformity if his acceptance was reasonably induced either by the difficulty of discovery before acceptance or by the seller's assurances.

(2) Revocation of acceptance must occur within a reasonable time after the buyer discovers or should have discovered the ground for it and before any substantial change in condition of the goods which is not caused by their own defects. It is not effective until the buyer notifies the seller of it.

(3) A buyer who so revokes has the same rights and duties with regard to the goods involved as if he had rejected them.

§2—609
Right to Adequate Assurance of Performance

(1) A contract for sale imposes an obligation on each party that the other's expectation of receiving due performance will not be impaired. When reasonable grounds for insecurity arise with respect to the performance of either party the other may in writing demand adequate assurance of due performance and until he receives such assurance may if commercially reasonable suspend any performance for which he has not already received the agreed return.

(2) Between merchants the reasonableness of grounds for insecurity and the adequacy of any assurance offered shall be determined according to commercial standards.

(3) Acceptance of any improper delivery or payment does not prejudice the aggrieved party's right to demand adequate assurance of future performance.

(4) After receipt of a justified demand failure to provide within a reasonable time not exceeding thirty days such assurance of due performance as is adequate under the circumstances of the particular case is a repudiation of the contract.

§2—610
Anticipatory Repudiation

When either party repudiates the contract with respect to a performance not yet due the loss of which will substantially impair the value of the contract to the other, the aggrieved party may

(a) for a commercially reasonable time await performance by the repudiating party; or

(b) resort to any remedy for breach (Section 2—703 or Section 2—711), even though he has notified the repudiating party that he would await the latter's performance and has urged retraction; and

(c) in either case suspend his own performance or proceed in accordance with the provisions of this Article on

the seller's right to identify goods to the contract notwithstanding breach or to salvage unfinished goods (Section 2—704).

§2—611
Retraction of Anticipatory Repudiation

(1) Until the repudiating party's next performance is due he can retract his repudiation unless the aggrieved party has since the repudiation cancelled or materially changed his position or otherwise indicated that he considers the repudiation final.

(2) Retraction may be by any method which clearly indicates to the aggrieved party that the repudiating party intends to perform, but must include any assurance justifiably demanded under the provisions of this Article (Section 2—609).

(3) Retraction reinstates the repudiating party's rights under the contract with due excuse and allowance to the aggrieved party for any delay occasioned by the repudiation.

§2—612
"Installment Contract"; Breach

(1) An "installment contract" is one which requires or authorizes the delivery of goods in separate lots to be separately accepted, even though the contract contains a clause "each delivery is a separate contract" or its equivalent.

(2) The buyer may reject any installment which is non-conforming if the non-conformity substantially impairs the value of that installment and cannot be cured or if the non-conformity is a defect in the required documents; but if the non-conformity does not fall within subsection (3) and the seller gives adequate assurance of its cure the buyer must accept that installment.

(3) Whenever non-conformity or default with respect to one or more installments substantially impairs the value of the whole contract there is a breach of the whole. But the aggrieved party reinstates the contract if he accepts a non-conforming installment without seasonably notifying of cancellation or if he brings an action with respect only to past installments or demands performance as to future installments.

§2—613
Casualty to Identified Goods

Where the contract requires for its performance goods identified when the contract is made, and the goods suffer casualty without fault of either party before the risk of loss passes to the buyer, or in a proper case under a "no arrival, no sale" term (Section 2—324) then

(a) if the loss is total the contract is avoided; and

(b) if the loss is partial or the goods have so deteriorated as no longer to conform to the contract the buyer may nevertheless demand inspection and at his option either treat the contract as avoided or accept the goods with due allowance from the contract price for the deterioration or the deficiency in quantity but without further right against the seller.

§2—614
Substituted Performance

(1) Where without fault of either party the agreed berthing, loading, or unloading facilities fail or an agreed type of carrier becomes unavailable or the agreed manner of delivery otherwise becomes commercially impracticable but a commercially reasonable substitute is available, such substitute performance must be tendered and accepted.

(2) If the agreed means or manner of payment fails because of domestic or foreign governmental regulation, the seller may withhold or stop delivery unless the buyer provides a means or manner of payment which is commercially a substantial equivalent. If delivery has already been taken, payment by the means or in the manner provided by the regulation discharges the buyer's obligation unless the regulation is discriminatory, oppressive or predatory.

§2—615
Excuse by Failure of Presupposed Conditions

Except so far as a seller may have assumed a greater obligation and subject to the preceding section on substituted performance:

(a) Delay in delivery or non-delivery in whole or in part by a seller who complies with paragraphs (b) and (c) is not a breach of his duty under a contract for sale if performance as agreed has been made impracticable by the occurrence of a contingency the non-occurrence of which was a basic assumption on which the contract was made or by compliance in good faith with any applicable foreign or domestic governmental regulation or order whether or not it later proves to be invalid.

(b) Where the causes mentioned in paragraph (a) affect only a part of the seller's capacity to perform, he must allocate production and deliveries among his customers but may at his option include regular customers not then under contract as well as his own requirements for further manufacture. He may so allocate in any manner which is fair and reasonable.

(c) The seller must notify the buyer seasonably that there will be delay or non-delivery and, when allocation is required under paragraph (b), of the estimated quota thus made available for the buyer.

§2—616
Procedure on Notice Claiming Excuse

(1) Where the buyer receives notification of a material or indefinite delay or an allocation justified under the preceding section he may by written notification to the seller as to any delivery concerned, and where the prospective deficiency substantially impairs the value of the whole contract under the provisions of this Article relating to breach of installment contracts (Section 2—612), then also as to the whole,

(a) terminate and thereby discharge any unexecuted portion of the contract; or

(b) modify the contract by agreeing to take his available quota in substitution.

(2) If after receipt of such notification from the seller the buyer fails so to modify the contract within a reasonable time not exceeding thirty days the contract lapses with respect to any deliveries affected.

(3) The provisions of this section may not be negated by agreement except in so far as the seller has assumed a greater obligation under the preceding section.

Part 7
Remedies

§2—701
Remedies for Breach of Collateral Contracts Not Impaired

Remedies for breach of any obligation or promise collateral or ancillary to a contract for sale are not impaired by the provisions of this Article.

§2—702
Seller's Remedies on Discovery of Buyer's Insolvency

(1) Where the seller discovers the buyer to be insolvent he may refuse delivery except for cash including payment for all goods theretofore delivered under the contract, and stop delivery under this Article (Section 2—705).

(2) Where the seller discovers that the buyer has received goods on credit while insolvent he may reclaim the goods upon demand made within ten days after the receipt, but if misrepresentation of solvency has been made to the particular seller in writing within three months before delivery the ten day limitation does not apply. Except as provided in this subsection the seller may not base a right to reclaim goods on the buyer's fraudulent or innocent misrepresentation of solvency or of intent to pay.

(3) The seller's right to reclaim under subsection (2) is subject to the rights of a buyer in ordinary course or other good faith purchaser under this Article (Section 2—403). Successful reclamation of goods excludes all other remedies with respect to them. As amended 1966.

§2—703
Seller's Remedies in General

Where the buyer wrongfully rejects or revokes acceptance of goods or fails to make a payment due on or before delivery or repudiates with respect to a part or the whole, then with respect to any goods directly affected and, if the breach is of the whole contract (Section 2—612), then also with respect to the whole undelivered balance, the aggrieved seller may

(a) withhold delivery of such goods;

(b) stop delivery by any bailee as hereafter provided (Section 2—705);

(c) proceed under the next section respecting goods still unidentified to the contract;

(d) resell and recover damages as hereafter provided (Section 2—706);

(e) recover damages for non-acceptance (Section 2—708) or in a proper case the price (Section 2—709);

(f) cancel.

§2—704
Seller's Right to Identify Goods to the Contract Notwithstanding Breach or to Salvage Unfinished Goods

(1) An aggrieved seller under the preceding section may

(a) identify to the contract conforming goods not already identified if at the time he learned of the breach they are in his possession or control;

(b) treat as the subject of resale goods which have demonstrably been intended for the particular contract even though those goods are unfinished.

(2) Where the goods are unfinished an aggrieved seller may in the exercise of reasonable commercial judgment for the purposes of avoiding loss and of effective realization either complete the manufacture and wholly identify the goods to the contract or cease manufacture and resell for scrap or salvage value or proceed in any other reasonable manner.

§2—705
Seller's Stoppage of Delivery in Transit or Otherwise

(1) The seller may stop delivery of goods in the possession of a carrier or other bailee when he discovers the buyer to be insolvent (Section 2—702) and may stop delivery of carload, truckload, planeload or larger shipments of express or freight when the buyer repudiates or fails to make a payment due before delivery or if for any other reason the seller has a right to withhold or reclaim the goods.

(2) As against such buyer the seller may stop delivery until

(a) receipt of the goods by the buyer; or

(b) acknowledgment to the buyer by any bailee of the goods except a carrier that the bailee holds the goods for the buyer; or

(c) such acknowledgment to the buyer by a carrier by reshipment or as warehouseman; or

(d) negotiation to the buyer of any negotiable document of title covering the goods.

(3)

(a) To stop delivery the seller must so notify as to enable the bailee by reasonable diligence to prevent delivery of the goods.

(b) After such notification the bailee must hold and deliver the goods according to the directions of the seller but the seller is liable to the bailee for any ensuing charges or damages.

(c) If a negotiable document of title has been issued for goods the bailee is not obliged to obey a notification to stop until surrender of the document.

(d) A carrier who has issued a non-negotiable bill of lading is not obliged to obey a notification to stop received from a person other than the consignor.

§2—706
Seller's Resale Including Contract for Resale

(1) Under the conditions stated in Section 2—703 on seller's remedies, the seller may resell the goods concerned or the undelivered balance thereof. Where the resale is made in good faith and in a commercially reasonable manner the seller may recover the difference between the resale price and the contract price together with any incidental damages allowed under the provisions of this Article (Section 2—710), but less expenses saved in consequence of the buyer's breach.

(2) Except as otherwise provided in subsection (3) or unless otherwise agreed resale may be at public or private sale including sale by way of one or more contracts to sell or of identification to an existing contract of the seller. Sale may be as a unit or in parcels and at any time and place and on any terms but every aspect of the sale including the method, manner, time, place and terms must be commercially reasonable. The resale must be reasonably identified as referring to the broken contract, but it is not necessary that the goods be in existence or that any or all of them have been identified to the contract before the breach.

(3) Where the resale is at private sale the seller must give the buyer reasonable notification of his intention to resell.

(4) Where the resale is at public sale

(a) only identified goods can be sold except where there is a recognized market for a public sale of futures in goods of the kind; and

(b) it must be made at a usual place or market for public sale if one is reasonably available and except in the case of goods which are perishable or threaten to decline in value speedily the seller must give the buyer reasonable notice of the time and place of the resale; and

(c) if the goods are not to be within the view of those attending the sale the notification of sale must state the place where the goods are located and provide for their reasonable inspection by prospective bidders; and

(d) the seller may buy.

(5) A purchaser who buys in good faith at a resale takes the goods free of any rights of the original buyer even though the seller fails to comply with one or more of the requirements of this section.

(6) The seller is not accountable to the buyer for any profit made on any resale. A person in the position of a seller (Section 2—707) or a buyer who has rightfully rejected or justifiably revoked acceptance must account for any excess over the amount of his security interest, as hereinafter defined (subsection (3) of Section 2—711).

§2—707
"Person in the Position of a Seller"

(1) A "person in the position of a seller" includes as against a principal an agent who has paid or become responsible for the price of goods on behalf of his principal or anyone who otherwise holds a security interest or other right in goods similar to that of a seller.

(2) A person in the position of a seller may as provided in this Article withhold or stop delivery (Section 2—705) and resell (Section 2—706) and recover incidental damages (Section 2—710).

§2—708
Seller's Damages for Non-Acceptance or Repudiation

(1) Subject to subsection (2) and to the provisions of this Article with respect to proof of market price (Section 2—723), the measure of damages for non-acceptance or repudiation by the buyer is the difference between the market price at the time and place for tender and the unpaid contract price together with any incidental damages provided in this Article (Section 2—710), but less expenses saved in consequence of the buyer's breach.

(2) If the measure of damages provided in subsection (1) is inadequate to put the seller in as good a position as performance would have done then the measure of damages is the profit (including reasonable overhead) which the seller would have made from full performance by the buyer, together with any incidental damages provided in this Article (Section 2—710), due allowance for costs reasonably incurred and due credit for payments or proceeds of resale.

§2—709
Action for the Price

(1) When the buyer fails to pay the price as it becomes due the seller may recover, together with any incidental damages under the next section, the price

    (a) of goods accepted or of conforming goods lost or damaged within a commercially reasonable time after risk of their loss has passed to the buyer; and

    (b) of goods identified to the contract if the seller is unable after reasonable effort to resell them at a reasonable price or the circumstances reasonably indicate that such effort will be unavailing.

(2) Where the seller sues for the price he must hold for the buyer any goods which have been identified to the contract and are still in his control except that if resale becomes possible he may resell them at any time prior to the collection of the judgment. The net proceeds of any such resale must be credited to the buyer and payment of the judgment entitles him to any goods not resold.

(3) After the buyer has wrongfully rejected or revoked acceptance of the goods or has failed to make a payment due or has repudiated (Section 2—610), a seller who is held not entitled to the price under this section shall nevertheless be awarded damages for non-acceptance under the preceding section.

§2—710
Seller's Incidental Damages

Incidental damages to an aggrieved seller include any commercially reasonable charges, expenses or commissions incurred in stopping delivery, in the transportation, care and custody of goods after the buyer's breach, in connection with return or resale of the goods or otherwise resulting from the breach.

§2—711
Buyer's Remedies in General; Buyer's Security Interest in Rejected Goods

(1) Where the seller fails to make delivery or repudiates or the buyer rightfully rejects or justifiably revokes acceptance then with respect to any goods involved, and with respect to the whole if the breach goes to the whole contract (Section 2—612), the buyer may cancel and whether or not he has done so may in addition to recovering so much of the price as has been paid

    (a) "cover" and have damages under the next section as to all the goods affected whether or not they have been identified to the contract; or

    (b) recover damages for non-delivery as provided in this Article (Section 2—713).

(2) Where the seller fails to deliver or repudiates the buyer may also

    (a) if the goods have been identified recover them as provided in this Article (Section 2—502); or

    (b) in a proper case obtain specific performance or replevy the goods as provided in this Article (Section 2—716).

(3) On rightful rejection or justifiable revocation of acceptance a buyer has a security interest in goods in his possession or control for any payments made on their price and any expenses reasonably incurred in their inspection, receipt, transportation, care and custody and may hold such goods and resell them in like manner as an aggrieved seller (Section 2—706).

§2—712
"Cover"; Buyer's Procurement of Substitute Goods

(1) After a breach within the preceding section the buyer may "cover" by making in good faith and without unreasonable delay any reasonable purchase of or contract to purchase goods in substitution for those due from the seller.

(2) The buyer may recover from the seller as damages the difference between the cost of cover and the contract price together with any incidental or consequential damages as hereinafter defined (Section 2—715), but less expenses saved in consequence of the seller's breach.

(3) Failure of the buyer to effect cover within this section does not bar him from any other remedy.

§2—713
Buyer's Damages for Non-Delivery or Repudiation

(1) Subject to the provisions of this Article with respect to proof of market price (Section 2—723), the measure of damages for non-delivery or repudiation by the seller is the difference between the market price at the time when the buyer learned of the breach and the contract price together with any incidental and consequential damages provided in this Article (Section 2—715), but less expenses saved in consequence of the seller's breach.

(2) Market price is to be determined as of the place for tender or, in cases of rejection after arrival or revocation of acceptance, as of the place of arrival.

§2—714
Buyer's Damages for Breach in Regard to Accepted Goods

(1) Where the buyer has accepted goods and given notification (subsection (3) of Section 2—607) he may recover as damages for any non-conformity of tender the loss resulting in the ordinary course of events from the seller's breach as determined in any manner which is reasonable.

(2) The measure of damages for breach of warranty is the difference at the time and place of acceptance between the value of the goods accepted and the value they would have had if they had been as warranted, unless special circumstances show proximate damages of a different amount.

(3) In a proper case any incidental and consequential damages under the next section may also be recovered.

§2—715
Buyer's Incidental and Consequential Damages

(1) Incidental damages resulting from the seller's breach include expenses reasonably incurred in inspection, receipt, transportation and care and custody of goods rightfully rejected, any commercially reasonable charges, expenses or commissions in connection with effecting cover and any other reasonable expense incident to the delay or other breach.

(2) Consequential damages resulting from the seller's breach include

(a) any loss resulting from general or particular requirements and needs of which the seller at the time of contracting had reason to know and which could not reasonably be prevented by cover or otherwise; and

(b) injury to person or property proximately resulting from any breach of warranty.

§2—716
Buyer's Right to Specific Performance or Replevin

(1) Specific performance may be decreed where the goods are unique or in other proper circumstances.

(2) The decree for specific performance may include such terms and conditions as to payment of the price, damages, or other relief as the court may deem just.

(3) The buyer has a right of replevin for goods identified to the contract if after reasonable effort he is unable to effect cover for such goods or the circumstances reasonably indicate that such effort will be unavailing or if the goods have been shipped under reservation and satisfaction of the security interest in them has been made or tendered.

§2—717
Deduction of Damages From the Price

The buyer on notifying the seller of his intention to do so may deduct all or any part of the damages resulting from any breach of the contract from any part of the price still due under the same contract.

§2—718
Liquidation or Limitation of Damages; Deposits

(1) Damages for breach by either party may be liquidated in the agreement but only at an amount which is reasonable in the light of the anticipated or actual harm caused by the breach, the difficulties of proof of loss, and the inconvenience or nonfeasibility of otherwise obtaining an adequate remedy. A term fixing unreasonably large liquidated damages is void as a penalty.

(2) Where the seller justifiably withholds delivery of goods because of the buyer's breach, the buyer is entitled to restitution of any amount by which the sum of his payments exceeds

(a) the amount to which the seller is entitled by virtue of terms liquidating the seller's damages in accordance with subsection (1), or

(b) in the absence of such terms, twenty per cent of the value of the total performance for which the buyer is obligated under the contract or $500, whichever is smaller.

(3) The buyer's right to restitution under subsection (2) is subject to offset to the extent that the seller establishes

(a) a right to recover damages under the provisions of this Article other than subsection (1), and

(b) the amount or value of any benefits received by the buyer directly or indirectly by reason of the contract.

(4) Where a seller has received payment in goods their reasonable value or the proceeds of their resale shall be treated as payments for the purposes of subsection (2); but if the seller has notice of the buyer's breach before reselling goods received in part performance, his resale is subject to the conditions laid down in this Article on resale by an aggrieved seller (Section 2—706).

§2—719
Contractual Modification or Limitation of Remedy

(1) Subject to the provisions of subsections (2) and (3) of this section and of the preceding section on liquidation and limitation of damages,

(a) the agreement may provide for remedies in addition to or in substitution for those provided in this Article and may limit or alter the measure of damages recoverable under this Article, as by limiting the buyer's remedies to return of the goods and repayment of the price or to repair and replacement of non-conforming goods or parts; and

(b) resort to a remedy as provided is optional unless the remedy is expressly agreed to be exclusive, in which case it is the sole remedy.

(2) Where circumstances cause an exclusive or limited remedy to fail of its essential purpose, remedy may be had as provided in this Act.

(3) Consequential damages may be limited or excluded unless the limitation or exclusion is unconscionable. Limitation of consequential damages for injury to the person in the case of

consumer goods is prima facie unconscionable but limitation of damages where the loss is commercial is not.

§2—720
Effect of "Cancellation" or "Rescission" on Claims for Antecedent Breach

Unless the contrary intention clearly appears, expressions of "cancellation" or "rescission" of the contract or the like shall not be construed as a renunciation or discharge of any claim in damages for an antecedent breach.

§2—721
Remedies for Fraud

Remedies for material misrepresentation or fraud include all remedies available under this Article for non-fraudulent breach. Neither rescission or a claim for rescission of the contract for sale nor rejection or return of the goods shall bar or be deemed inconsistent with a claim for damages or other remedy.

§2—722
Who Can Sue Third Parties for Injury to Goods

Where a third party so deals with goods which have been identified to a contract for sale as to cause actionable injury to a party to that contract

(a) a right of action against the third party is in either party to the contract for sale who has title to or a security interest or a special property or an insurable interest in the goods; and if the goods have been destroyed or converted a right of action is also in the party who either bore the risk of loss under the contract for sale or has since the injury assumed that risk as against the other;

(b) if at the time of the injury the party plaintiff did not bear the risk of loss as against the other party to the contract for sale and there is no arrangement between them for disposition of the recovery, his suit or settlement is, subject to his own interest, as a fiduciary for the other party to the contract;

(c) either party may with the consent of the other sue for the benefit of whom it may concern.

§2—723
Proof of Market Price: Time and Place

(1) If an action based on anticipatory repudiation comes to trial before the time for performance with respect to some or all of the goods, any damages based on market price (Section 2—708 or Section 2—713) shall be determined according to the price of such goods prevailing at the time when the aggrieved party learned of the repudiation.

(2) If evidence of a price prevailing at the times or places described in this Article is not readily available the price prevailing within any reasonable time before or after the time described or at any other place which in commercial judgment or under usage of trade would serve as a reasonable substitute for the one described may be used, making any proper allowance for the cost of transporting the goods to or from such other place.

(3) Evidence of a relevant price prevailing at a time or place other than the one described in this Article offered by one party is not admissible unless and until he has given the other party such notice as the court finds sufficient to prevent unfair surprise.

§2—724
Admissibility of Market Quotations

Whenever the prevailing price or value of any goods regularly bought and sold in any established commodity market is in issue, reports in official publications or trade journals or in newspapers or periodicals of general circulation published as the reports of such market shall be admissible in evidence. The circumstances of the preparation of such a report may be shown to affect its weight but not its admissibility.

§2—725
Statute of Limitations in Contracts for Sale

(1) An action for breach of any contract for sale must be commenced within four years after the cause of action has accrued. By the original agreement the parties may reduce the period of limitation to not less than one year but may not extend it.

(2) A cause of action accrues when the breach occurs, regardless of the aggrieved party's lack of knowledge of the breach. A breach of warranty occurs when tender of delivery is made, except that where a warranty explicitly extends to future performance of the goods and discovery of the breach must await the time of such performance the cause of action accrues when the breach is or should have been discovered.

(3) Where an action commenced within the time limited by subsection (1) is so terminated as to leave available a remedy by another action for the same breach such other action may be commenced after the expiration of the time limited and within six months after the termination of the first action unless the termination resulted from voluntary discontinuance or from dismissal for failure or neglect to prosecute.

(4) This section does not alter the law on tolling of the statute of limitations nor does it apply to causes of action which have accrued before this Act becomes effective.

Article 3

Commercial Paper

Part 1

Short Title, Form and Interpretation

§3—101
Short Title

This Article shall be known and may be cited as Uniform Commercial Code—Commercial Paper.

§3—102
Definitions and Index of Definitions

(1) In this Article unless the context otherwise requires

    (a) "Issue" means the first delivery of an instrument to a holder or a remitter.

    (b) An "order" is a direction to pay and must be more than an authorization or request. It must identify the person to pay with reasonable certainty. It may be addressed to one or more such persons jointly or in the alternative but not in succession.

    (c) A "promise" is an undertaking to pay and must be more than an acknowledgment of an obligation.

    (d) "Secondary party" means a drawer or endorser.

    (e) "Instrument" means a negotiable instrument.

(2) Other definitions applying to this Article and the sections in which they appear are:

    "Acceptance". Section 3—410.
    "Accommodation party". Section 3—415.
    "Alteration". Section 3—407.
    "Certificate of deposit". Section 3—104.
    "Certification". Section 3—411.
    "Check". Section 3—104.
    "Definite time". Section 3—109.
    "Dishonor". Section 3—507.
    "Draft". Section 3—104.
    "Holder in due course". Section 3—302.
    "Negotiation". Section 3—202.
    "Note". Section 3—104.
    "Notice of dishonor". Section 3—508.
    "On demand". Section 3—108.
    "Presentment". Section 3—504.
    "Protest". Section 3—509.
    "Restrictive Indorsement". Section 3—205.
    "Signature". Section 3—401.

(3) The following definitions in other Articles apply to this Article:

    "Account". Section 4—104.
    "Banking Day". Section 4—104.
    "Clearing house". Section 4—104.
    "Collecting bank". Section 4—105.
    "Customer". Section 4—104.
    "Depositary Bank". Section 4—105.
    "Documentary Draft". Section 4—104.
    "Intermediary Bank". Section 4—105.
    "Item". Section 4—104.
    "Midnight deadline". Section 4—104.
    "Payor bank". Section 4—105.

(4) In addition Article 1 contains general definitions and principles of construction and interpretation applicable throughout this Article.

§3—103
Limitations on Scope of Article

(1) This Article does not apply to money, documents of title or investment securities.

(2) The provisions of this Article are subject to the provisions of the Article on Bank Deposits and Collections (Article 4) and Secured Transactions (Article 9).

§3—104
Form of Negotiable Instruments; "Draft"; "Check"; "Certificate of Deposit"; "Note"

(1) Any writing to be a negotiable instrument within this Article must

    (a) be signed by the maker or drawer; and

    (b) contain an unconditional promise or order to pay a sum certain in money and no other promise, order, obligation or power given by the maker or drawer except as authorized by this Article; and

    (c) be payable on demand or at a definite time; and

    (d) be payable to order or to bearer.

(2) A writing which complies with the requirements of this section is

    (a) a "draft" ("bill of exchange") if it is an order;

    (b) a "check" if it is a draft drawn on a bank and payable on demand;

    (c) a "certificate of deposit" if it is an acknowledgment by a bank of receipt of money with an engagement to repay it;

    (d) a "note" if it is a promise other than a certificate of deposit.

(3) As used in other Articles of this Act, and as the context may require, the terms "draft", "check", "certificate of deposit" and "note" may refer to instruments which are not negotiable within this Article as well as to instruments which are so negotiable.

§3—105
When Promise or Order Unconditional

(1) A promise or order otherwise unconditional is not made conditional by the fact that the instrument

    (a) is subject to implied or constructive conditions; or

    (b) states its consideration, whether performed or promised, or the transaction which gave rise to the instrument, or that the promise or order is made or the instrument matures in accordance with or "as per" such transaction; or

    (c) refers to or states that it arises out of a separate agreement or refers to a separate agreement for rights as to prepayment or acceleration; or

    (d) states that it is drawn under a letter of credit; or

    (e) states that it is secured, whether by mortgage, reservation of title or otherwise; or

(f) indicates a particular account to be debited or any other fund or source from which reimbursement is expected; or

(g) is limited to payment out of a particular fund or the proceeds of a particular source, if the instrument is issued by a government or governmental agency or unit; or

(h) is limited to payment out of the entire assets of a partnership, unincorporated association, trust or estate by or on behalf of which the instrument is issued.

(2) A promise or order is not unconditional if the instrument

(a) states that it is subject to or governed by any other agreement; or

(b) states that it is to be paid only out of a particular fund or source except as provided in this section. As amended 1962.

§3—106
Sum Certain

(1) The sum payable is a sum certain even though it is to be paid

(a) with stated interest or by stated installments; or

(b) with stated different rates of interest before and after default or a specified date; or

(c) with a stated discount or addition if paid before or after the date fixed for payment; or

(d) with exchange or less exchange, whether at a fixed rate or at the current rate; or

(e) with costs of collection or an attorney's fee or both upon default.

(2) Nothing in this section shall validate any term which is otherwise illegal.

§3—107
Money

(1) An instrument is payable in money if the medium of exchange in which it is payable is money at the time the instrument is made. An instrument payable in "currency" or "current funds" is payable in money.

(2) A promise or order to pay a sum stated in a foreign currency is for a sum certain in money and, unless a different medium of payment is specified in the instrument, may be satisfied by payment of that number of dollars which the stated foreign currency will purchase at the buying sight rate for that currency on the day on which the instrument is payable or, if payable on demand, on the day of demand. If such an instrument specifies a foreign currency as the medium of payment the instrument is payable in that currency.

§3—108
Payable on Demand

Instruments payable on demand include those payable at sight or on presentation and those in which no time for payment is stated.

§3—109
Definite Time

(1) An instrument is payable at a definite time if by its terms it is payable

(a) on or before a stated date or at a fixed period after a stated date; or

(b) at a fixed period after sight; or

(c) at a definite time subject to any acceleration; or

(d) at a definite time subject to extension at the option of the holder, or to extension to a further definite time at the option of the maker or acceptor or automatically upon or after a specified act or event.

(2) An instrument which by its terms is otherwise payable only upon an act or event uncertain as to time of occurrence is not payable at a definite time even though the act or event has occurred.

§3—110
Payable to Order

(1) An instrument is payable to order when by its terms it is payable to the order or assigns of any person therein specified with reasonable certainty, or to him or his order, or when it is conspicuously designated on its face as "exchange" or the like and names a payee. It may be payable to the order of

(a) the maker or drawer; or

(b) the drawee; or

(c) a payee who is not maker, drawer or drawee; or

(d) two or more payees together or in the alternative; or

(e) an estate, trust or fund, in which case it is payable to the order of the representative of such estate, trust or fund or his successors; or

(f) an office, or an officer by his title as such in which case it is payable to the principal but the incumbent of the office or his successors may act as if he or they were the holder; or

(g) a partnership or unincorporated association, in which case it is payable to the partnership or association and may be indorsed or transferred by any person thereto authorized.

(2) An instrument not payable to order is not made so payable by such words as "payable upon return of this instrument properly indorsed."

(3) An instrument made payable both to order and to bearer is payable to order unless the bearer words are handwritten or typewritten.

§3—111
Payable to Bearer

An instrument is payable to bearer when by its terms it is payable to

(a) bearer or the order of bearer; or

(b) a specified person or bearer; or

(c) "cash" or the order of "cash", or any other indication which does not purport to designate a specific payee.

§3—112
Terms and Omissions Not Affecting Negotiability

(1) The negotiability of an instrument is not affected by

(a) the omission of a statement of any consideration or of the place where the instrument is drawn or payable; or

(b) a statement that collateral has been given to secure obligations either on the instrument or otherwise of an obligor on the instrument or that in case of default on those obligations the holder may realize on or dispose of the collateral; or

(c) a promise or power to maintain or protect collateral or to give additional collateral; or

(d) a term authorizing a confession of judgment on the instrument if it is not paid when due; or

(e) a term purporting to waive the benefit of any law intended for the advantage or protection of any obligor; or

(f) a term in a draft providing that the payee by indorsing or cashing it acknowledges full satisfaction of an obligation of the drawer; or

(g) a statement in a draft drawn in a set of parts (Section 3—801) to the effect that the order is effective only if no other part has been honored.

(2) Nothing in this section shall validate any term which is otherwise illegal. As amended 1962.

§3—113
Seal

An instrument otherwise negotiable is within this Article even though it is under a seal.

§3—114
Date, Antedating, Postdating

(1) The negotiability of an instrument is not affected by the fact that it is undated, antedated or postdated.

(2) Where an instrument is antedated or postdated the time when it is payable is determined by the stated date if the instrument is payable on demand or at a fixed period after date.

(3) Where the instrument or any signature thereon is dated, the date is presumed to be correct.

§3—115
Incomplete Instruments

(1) When a paper whose contents at the time of signing show that it is intended to become an instrument is signed while still incomplete in any necessary respect it cannot be enforced until completed, but when it is completed in accordance with authority given it is effective as completed.

(2) If the completion is unauthorized the rules as to material alteration apply (Section 3—407), even though the paper was not delivered by the maker or drawer; but the burden of establishing that any completion is unauthorized is on the party so asserting.

§3—116
Instruments Payable to Two or More Persons

An instrument payable to the order of two or more persons

(a) if in the alternative is payable to any one of them and may be negotiated, discharged or enforced by any of them who has possession of it;

(b) if not in the alternative is payable to all of them and may be negotiated, discharged or enforced only by all of them.

§3—117
Instruments Payable With Words of Description

An instrument made payable to a named person with the addition of words describing him

(a) as agent or officer of a specified person is payable to his principal but the agent or officer may act as if he were the holder;

(b) as any other fiduciary for a specified person or purpose is payable to the payee and may be negotiated, discharged or enforced by him;

(c) in any other manner is payable to the payee unconditionally and the additional words are without effect on subsequent parties.

§3—118
Ambiguous Terms and Rules of Construction

The following rules apply to every instrument:

(a) Where there is doubt whether the instrument is a draft or a note the holder may treat it as either. A draft drawn on the drawer is effective as a note.

(b) Handwritten terms control typewritten and printed terms, and typewritten control printed.

(c) Words control figures except that if the words are ambiguous figures control.

(d) Unless otherwise specified a provision for interest means interest at the judgment rate at the place of payment from the date of the instrument, or if it is undated from the date of issue.

(e) Unless the instrument otherwise specifies two or more persons who sign as maker, acceptor or drawer or indorser and as a part of the same transaction are jointly and severally liable even though the instrument contains such words as "I promise to pay."

(f) Unless otherwise specified consent to extension authorizes a single extension for not longer than the original period. A consent to extension, expressed in the instrument, is binding on secondary parties and accommodation makers. A holder may not exercise his option to extend an instrument over the objection of a maker or acceptor or other party who in accordance with Section 3—604 tenders full payment when the instrument is due.

§3—119
Other Writings Affecting Instrument

(1) As between the obligor and his immediate obligee or any transferee the terms of an instrument may be modified or affected by any other written agreement executed as a part of the same transaction, except that a holder in due course is not affected by any limitation of his rights arising out of the separate written agreement if he had no notice of the limitation when he took the instrument.

(2) A separate agreement does not affect the negotiability of an instrument.

§3—120
Instruments "Payable Through" Bank

An instrument which states that it is "payable through" a bank or the like designates that bank as a collecting bank to make presentment but does not of itself authorize the bank to pay the instrument.

§3—121
Instruments Payable at Bank

Note: If this Act is introduced in the Congress of the United States this section should be omitted.

(States to select either alternative)

Alternative A

A note or acceptance which states that it is payable at a bank is the equivalent of a draft drawn on the bank payable when it falls due out of any funds of the maker or acceptor in current account or otherwise available for such payment.

Alternative B

A note or acceptance which states that it is payable at a bank is not of itself an order or authorization to the bank to pay it.

§3—122. Accrual of Cause of Action

(1) A cause of action against a maker or an acceptor accrues

    (a) in the case of a time instrument on the day after maturity;

    (b) in the case of a demand instrument upon its date or, if no date is stated, on the date of issue.

(2) A cause of action against the obligor of a demand or time certificate of deposit accrues upon demand, but demand on a time certificate may not be made until on or after the date of maturity.

(3) A cause of action against a drawer of a draft or an indorser of any instrument accrues upon demand following dishonor of the instrument. Notice of dishonor is a demand.

(4) Unless an instrument provides otherwise, interest runs at the rate provided by law for a judgment

    (a) in the case of a maker, acceptor or other primary obligor of a demand instrument, from the date of demand;

    (b) in all other cases from the date of accrual of the cause of action. As amended 1962.

Part 2
Transfer and Negotiation

§3—201
Transfer: Right to Indorsement

(1) Transfer of an instrument vests in the transferee such rights as the transferor has therein, except that a transferee who has himself been a party to any fraud or illegality affecting the instrument or who as a prior holder had notice of a defense or claim against it cannot improve his position by taking from a later holder in due course.

(2) A transfer of a security interest in an instrument vests the foregoing rights in the transferee to the extent of the interest transferred.

(3) Unless otherwise agreed any transfer for value of an instrument not then payable to bearer gives the transferee the specifically enforceable right to have the unqualified indorsement of the transferor. Negotiation takes effect only when the indorsement is made and until that time there is no presumption that the transferee is the owner.

§3—202
Negotiation

(1) Negotiation is the transfer of an instrument in such form that the transferee becomes a holder. If the instrument is payable to order it is negotiated by delivery with any necessary indorsement; if payable to bearer it is negotiated by delivery.

(2) An indorsement must be written by or on behalf of the holder and on the instrument or on a paper so firmly affixed thereto as to become a part thereof.

(3) An indorsement is effective for negotiation only when it conveys the entire instrument or any unpaid residue. If it purports to be of less it operates only as a partial assignment.

(4) Words of assignment, condition, waiver, guaranty, limitation or disclaimer of liability and the like accompanying an indorsement do not affect its character as an indorsement.

§3—203
Wrong or Misspelled Name

Where an instrument is made payable to a person under a misspelled name or one other than his own he may indorse in that name or his own or both; but signature in both names may be required by a person paying or giving value for the instrument.

§3—204
Special Indorsement; Blank Indorsement

(1) A special indorsement specifies the person to whom or to whose order it makes the instrument payable. Any instrument specially indorsed becomes payable to the order of the special indorsee and may be further negotiated only by his indorsement.

(2) An indorsement in blank specifies no particular indorsee and may consist of a mere signature. An instrument payable to order and indorsed in blank becomes payable to bearer and may be negotiated by delivery alone until specially indorsed.

(3) The holder may convert a blank indorsement into a special indorsement by writing over the signature of the indorser in blank any contract consistent with the character of the indorsement.

§3—205
Restrictive Indorsements

An indorsement is restrictive which either

(a) is conditional; or

(b) purports to prohibit further transfer of the instrument; or

(c) includes the words "for collection", "for deposit", "pay any bank", or like terms signifying a purpose of deposit or collection; or

(d) otherwise states that it is for the benefit or use of the indorser or of another person.

§3—206
Effect of Restrictive Indorsement

(1) No restrictive indorsement prevents further transfer or negotiation of the instrument.

(2) An intermediary bank, or a payor bank which is not the depositary bank, is neither given notice nor otherwise affected by a restrictive indorsement of any person except the bank's immediate transferor or the person presenting for payment.

(3) Except for an intermediary bank, any transferee under an indorsement which is conditional or includes the words "for collection", "for deposit", "pay any bank", or like terms (subparagraphs (a) and (c) of Section 3—205) must pay or apply any value given by him for or on the security of the instrument consistently with the indorsement and to the extent that he does so he becomes a holder for value. In addition such transferee is a holder in due course if he otherwise complies with the requirements of Section 3—302 on what constitutes a holder in due course.

(4) The first taker under an indorsement for the benefit of the indorser or another person (subparagraph (d) of Section 3—205) must pay or apply any value given by him for or on the security of the instrument consistently with the indorsement and to the extent that he does so he becomes a holder for value. In addition such taker is a holder in due course if he otherwise complies with the requirements of Section 3—302 on what constitutes a holder in due course. A later holder for value is neither given notice nor otherwise affected by such restrictive indorsement unless he has knowledge that a fiduciary or other person has negotiated the instrument in any transaction for his own benefit or otherwise in breach of duty (subsection (2) of Section 3—304).

§3—207
Negotiation Effective Although It May Be Rescinded

(1) Negotiation is effective to transfer the instrument although the negotiation is

(a) made by an infant, a corporation exceeding its powers, or any other person without capacity; or

(b) obtained by fraud, duress or mistake of any kind; or

(c) part of an illegal transaction; or

(d) made in breach of duty.

(2) Except as against a subsequent holder in due course such negotiation is in an appropriate case subject to rescission, the declaration of a constructive trust or any other remedy permitted by law.

§3—208
Reacquisition

Where an instrument is returned to or reacquired by a prior party he may cancel any indorsement which is not necessary to his title and reissue or further negotiate the instrument, but any intervening party is discharged as against the reacquiring party and subsequent holders not in due course and if his indorsement has been cancelled is discharged as against subsequent holders in due course as well.

Part 3
Rights of a Holder

§3—301
Rights of a Holder

The holder of an instrument whether or not he is the owner may transfer or negotiate it and, except as otherwise provided in Section 3—603 on payment or satisfaction, discharge it or enforce payment in his own name.

§3—302
Holder in Due Course

(1) A holder in due course is a holder who takes the instrument

(a) for value; and

(b) in good faith; and

(c) without notice that it is overdue or has been dishonored or of any defense against or claim to it on the part of any person.

(2) A payee may be a holder in due course.

(3) A holder does not become a holder in due course of an instrument:

(a) by purchase of it at judicial sale or by taking it under legal process; or

(b) by acquiring it in taking over an estate; or

(c) by purchasing it as part of a bulk transaction not in regular course of business of the transferor.

(4) A purchaser of a limited interest can be a holder in due course only to the extent of the interest purchased.

§3—303
Taking for Value

A holder takes the instrument for value

(a) to the extent that the agreed consideration has been performed or that he acquires a security interest in or a lien on the instrument otherwise than by legal process; or

(b) when he takes the instrument in payment of or as security for an antecedent claim against any person whether or not the claim is due; or

(c) when he gives a negotiable instrument for it or makes an irrevocable commitment to a third person.

§3—304
Notice to Purchaser

(1) The purchaser has notice of a claim or defense if

(a) the instrument is so incomplete, bears such visible evidence of forgery or alteration, or is otherwise so irregular as to call into question its validity, terms or ownership or to create an ambiguity as to the party to pay; or

(b) the purchaser has notice that the obligation of any party is voidable in whole or in part, or that all parties have been discharged.

(2) The purchaser has notice of a claim against the instrument when he has knowledge that a fiduciary has negotiated the instrument in payment of or as security for his own debt or in any transaction for his own benefit or otherwise in breach of duty.

(3) The purchaser has notice that an instrument is overdue if he has reason to know

(a) that any part of the principal amount is overdue or that there is an uncured default in payment of another instrument of the same series; or

(b) that acceleration of the instrument has been made; or

(c) that he is taking a demand instrument after demand has been made or more than a reasonable length of time after its issue. A reasonable time for a check drawn and payable within the states and territories of the United States and the District of Columbia is presumed to be thirty days.

(4) Knowledge of the following facts does not of itself give the purchaser notice of a defense or claim

(a) that the instrument is antedated or postdated;

(b) that it was issued or negotiated in return for an executory promise or accompanied by a separate agreement, unless the purchaser has notice that a defense or claim has arisen from the terms thereof;

(c) that any party has signed for accommodation;

(d) that an incomplete instrument has been completed, unless the purchaser has notice of any improper completion;

(e) that any person negotiating the instrument is or was a fiduciary;

(f) that there has been default in payment of interest on the instrument or in payment of any other instrument, except one of the same series.

(5) The filing or recording of a document does not of itself constitute notice within the provisions of this Article to a person who would otherwise be a holder in due course.

(6) To be effective notice must be received at such time and in such manner as to give a reasonable opportunity to act on it.

§3—305
Rights of a Holder in Due Course

To the extent that a holder is a holder in due course he takes the instrument free from

(1) all claims to it on the part of any person; and

(2) all defenses of any party to the instrument with whom the holder has not dealt except

(a) infancy, to the extent that it is a defense to a simple contract; and

(b) such other incapacity, or duress, or illegality of the transaction, as renders the obligation of the party a nullity; and

(c) such misrepresentation as has induced the party to sign the instrument with neither knowledge nor reasonable opportunity to obtain knowledge of its character or its essential terms; and

(d) discharge in insolvency proceedings; and

(e) any other discharge of which the holder has notice when he takes the instrument.

§3—306
Rights of One Not Holder in Due Course

Unless he has the rights of a holder in due course any person takes the instrument subject to

(a) all valid claims to it on the part of any person; and

(b) all defenses of any party which would be available in an action on a simple contract; and

(c) the defenses of want or failure of consideration, nonperformance of any condition precedent, non-delivery, or delivery for a special purpose (Section 3—408); and

(d) the defense that he or a person through whom he holds the instrument acquired it by theft, or that payment or satisfaction to such holder would be inconsistent with the terms of a restrictive indorsement. The claim of any third person to the instrument is not otherwise available as a defense to any party liable thereon unless the third person himself defends the action for such party.

§3—307
Burden of Establishing Signatures, Defenses and Due Course

(1) Unless specifically denied in the pleadings each signature on an instrument is admitted. When the effectiveness of a signature is put in issue

(a) the burden of establishing it is on the party claiming under the signature; but

(b) the signature is presumed to be genuine or authorized except where the action is to enforce the obligation of purported signer who has died or become incompetent before proof is required.

(2) When signatures are admitted or established, production of the instrument entitles a holder to recover on it unless the defendant establishes a defense.

(3) After it is shown that a defense exists a person claiming the rights of a holder in due course has the burden of establishing that he or some person under whom he claims is in all respects a holder in due course.

Part 4
Liability of Parties

§3—401
Signature

(1) No person is liable on an instrument unless his signature appears thereon.

(2) A signature is made by use of any name, including any trade or assumed name, upon an instrument, or by any word or mark used in lieu of a written signature.

§3—402
Signature in Ambiguous Capacity

Unless the instrument clearly indicates that a signature is made in some other capacity it is an indorsement.

§3—403
Signature by Authorized Representative

(1) A signature may be made by an agent or other representative, and his authority to make it may be established as in other cases of representation. No particular form of appointment is necessary to establish such authority.

(2) An authorized representative who signs his own name to an instrument

   (a) is personally obligated if the instrument neither names the person represented nor shows that the representative signed in a representative capacity;

   (b) except as otherwise established between the immediate parties, is personally obligated if the instrument names the person represented but does not show that the representative signed in a representative capacity, or if the instrument does not name the person represented but does show that the representative signed in a representative capacity.

(3) Except as otherwise established the name of an organization preceded or followed by the name and office of an authorized individual is a signature made in a representative capacity.

§3—404
Unauthorized Signatures

(1) Any unauthorized signature is wholly inoperative as that of the person whose name is signed unless he ratifies it or is precluded from denying it; but it operates as the signature of the unauthorized signer in favor of any person who in good faith pays the instrument or takes it for value.

(2) Any unauthorized signature may be ratified for all purposes of this Article. Such ratification does not of itself affect any rights of the person ratifying against the actual signer.

§3—405
Impostors; Signature in Name of Payee

(1) An indorsement by any person in the name of a named payee is effective if

   (a) an impostor by use of the mails or otherwise has induced the maker or drawer to issue the instrument to him or his confederate in the name of the payee; or

   (b) a person signing as or on behalf of a maker or drawer intends the payee to have no interest in the instrument; or

   (c) an agent or employee of the maker or drawer has supplied him with the name of the payee intending the latter to have no such interest.

(2) Nothing in this section shall affect the criminal or civil liability of the person so indorsing.

§3—406
Negligence Contributing to Alteration or Unauthorized Signature

Any person who by his negligence substantially contributes to a material alteration of the instrument or to the making of an unauthorized signature is precluded from asserting the alteration or lack of authority against a holder in due course or against a drawee or other payor who pays the instrument in good faith and in accordance with the reasonable commercial standards of the drawee's or payor's business.

§3—407
Alteration

(1) Any alteration of an instrument is material which changes the contract of any party thereto in any respect, including any such change in

   (a) the number or relations of the parties; or

   (b) an incomplete instrument, by completing it otherwise than as authorized; or

   (c) the writing as signed, by adding to it or by removing any part of it.

(2) As against any person other than a subsequent holder in due course

   (a) alteration by the holder which is both fraudulent and material discharges any party whose contract is thereby changed unless that party assents or is precluded from asserting the defense;

   (b) no other alteration discharges any party and the instrument may be enforced according to its original tenor, or as to incomplete instruments according to the authority given.

(3) A subsequent holder in due course may in all cases enforce the instrument according to its original tenor, and when an incomplete instrument has been completed, he may enforce it as completed.

§3—408
Consideration

Want or failure of consideration is a defense as against any person not having the rights of a holder in due course (Section 3—305), except that no consideration is necessary for an instrument or obligation thereon given in payment of or as security for an antecedent obligation of any kind. Nothing in this section shall be taken to displace any statute outside this Act under which a promise is enforceable notwithstanding lack or failure of consideration. Partial failure of consideration is a defense pro tanto whether or not the failure is in an ascertained or liquidated amount.

§3—409
Draft Not an Assignment

(1) A check or other draft does not of itself operate as an assignment of any funds in the hands of the drawee available for its payment, and the drawee is not liable on the instrument until he accepts it.

(2) Nothing in this section shall affect any liability in contract, tort, or otherwise arising from any letter of credit or other obligation or representation which is not an acceptance.

§3—410
Definition and Operation of Acceptance

(1) Acceptance is the drawee's signed engagement to honor the draft as presented. It must be written on the draft, and may consist of his signature alone. It becomes operative when completed by delivery or notification.

(2) A draft may be accepted although it has not been signed by the drawer or is otherwise incomplete or is overdue or has been dishonored.

(3) Where the draft is payable at a fixed period after sight and the acceptor fails to date his acceptance the holder may complete it by supplying a date in good faith.

§3—411
Certification of a Check

(1) Certification of a check is acceptance. Where a holder procures certification the drawer and all prior indorsers are discharged.

(2) Unless otherwise agreed a bank has no obligation to certify a check.

(3) A bank may certify a check before returning it for lack of proper indorsement. If it does so the drawer is discharged.

§3—412
Acceptance Varying Draft

(1) Where the drawee's proffered acceptance in any manner varies the draft as presented the holder may refuse the acceptance and treat the draft as dishonored in which case the drawee is entitled to have his acceptance cancelled.

(2) The terms of the draft are not varied by an acceptance to pay at any particular bank or place in the United States, unless the acceptance states that the draft is to be paid only at such bank or place.

(3) Where the holder assents to an acceptance varying the terms of the draft each drawer and indorser who does not affirmatively assent is discharged. As amended 1962.

§3—413
Contract of Maker, Drawer and Acceptor

(1) The maker or acceptor engages that he will pay the instrument according to its tenor at the time of his engagement or as completed pursuant to Section 3—115 on incomplete instruments.

(2) The drawer engages that upon dishonor of the draft and any necessary notice of dishonor or protest he will pay the amount of the draft to the holder or to any indorser who takes it up. The drawer may disclaim this liability by drawing without recourse.

(3) By making, drawing or accepting the party admits as against all subsequent parties including the drawee the existence of the payee and his then capacity to indorse.

§3—414
Contract of Indorser; Order of Liability

(1) Unless the indorsement otherwise specifies (as by such words as "without recourse") every indorser engages that upon dishonor and any necessary notice of dishonor and protest he will pay the instrument according to its tenor at the time of his indorsement to the holder or to any subsequent indorser who takes it up, even though the indorser who takes it up was not obligated to do so.

(2) Unless they otherwise agree indorsers are liable to one another in the order in which they indorse, which is presumed to be the order in which their signatures appear on the instrument.

§3—415
Contract of Accommodation Party

(1) An accommodation party is one who signs the instrument in any capacity for the purpose of lending his name to another party to it.

(2) When the instrument has been taken for value before it is due the accommodation party is liable in the capacity in which he has signed even though the taker knows of the accommodation.

(3) As against a holder in due course and without notice of the accommodation oral proof of the accommodation is not admissible to give the accommodation party the benefit of discharges dependent on his character as such. In other cases the accommodation character may be shown by oral proof.

(4) An indorsement which shows that it is not in the chain of title is notice of its accommodation character.

(5) An accommodation party is not liable to the party accommodated, and if he pays the instrument has a right of recourse on the instrument against such party.

§3—416
Contract of Guarantor

(1) "Payment guaranteed" or equivalent words added to a signature mean that the signer engages that if the instrument is not paid when due he will pay it according to its tenor without resort by the holder to any other party.

(2) "Collection guaranteed" or equivalent words added to a signature mean that the signer engages that if the instrument

is not paid when due he will pay it according to its tenor, but only after the holder has reduced his claim against the maker or acceptor to judgment and execution has been returned unsatisfied, or after the maker or acceptor has become insolvent or it is otherwise apparent that it is useless to proceed against him.

(3) Words of guaranty which do not otherwise specify guarantee payment.

(4) No words of guaranty added to the signature of a sole maker or acceptor affect his liability on the instrument. Such words added to the signature of one of two or more makers or acceptors create a presumption that the signature is for the accommodation of the others.

(5) When words of guaranty are used presentment, notice of dishonor and protest are not necessary to charge the user.

(6) Any guaranty written on the instrument is enforcible notwithstanding any statute of frauds.

§3—417
Warranties on Presentment and Transfer

(1) Any person who obtains payment or acceptance and any prior transferor warrants to a person who in good faith pays or accepts that

   (a) he has a good title to the instrument or is authorized to obtain payment or acceptance on behalf of one who has a good title; and

   (b) he has no knowledge that the signature of the maker or drawer is unauthorized, except that this warranty is not given by a holder in due course acting in good faith

      (i)   to a maker with respect to the maker's own signature; or

      (ii) to a drawer with respect to the drawer's own signature, whether or not the drawer is also the drawee; or

      (iii) to an acceptor of a draft if the holder in due course took the draft after the acceptance or obtained the acceptance without knowledge that the drawer's signature was unauthorized; and

   (c) the instrument has not been materially altered, except that this warranty is not given by a holder in due course acting in good faith

      (i)   to the maker of a note; or

      (ii) to the drawer of a draft whether or not the drawer is also the drawee; or

      (iii) to the acceptor of a draft with respect to an alteration made prior to the acceptance if the holder in due course took the draft after the acceptance, even though the acceptance provided "payable as originally drawn" or equivalent terms; or

      (iv) to the acceptor of a draft with respect to an alteration made after the acceptance.

(2) Any person who transfers an instrument and receives consideration warrants to his transferee and if the transfer is by indorsement to any subsequent holder who takes the instrument in good faith that

   (a) he has a good title to the instrument or is authorized to obtain payment or acceptance on behalf of one who has a good title and the transfer is otherwise rightful; and

   (b) all signatures are genuine or authorized; and

   (c) the instrument has not been materially altered; and

   (d) no defense of any party is good against him; and

   (e) he has no knowledge of any insolvency proceeding instituted with respect to the maker or acceptor or the drawer of an unaccepted instrument.

(3) By transferring "without recourse" the transferor limits the obligation stated in subsection (2) (d) to a warranty that he has no knowledge of such a defense.

(4) A selling agent or broker who does not disclose the fact that he is acting only as such gives the warranties provided in this section, but if he makes such disclosure warrants only his good faith and authority.

§3—418
Finality of Payment or Acceptance

Except for recovery of bank payments as provided in the Article on Bank Deposits and Collections (Article 4) and except for liability for breach of warranty on presentment under the preceding section, payment or acceptance of any instrument is final in favor of a holder in due course, or a person who has in good faith changed his position in reliance on the payment.

§3—419
Conversion of Instrument; Innocent Representative

(1) An instrument is converted when

   (a) a drawee to whom it is delivered for acceptance refuses to return it on demand; or

   (b) any person to whom it is delivered for payment refuses on demand either to pay or to return it; or

   (c) it is paid on a forged indorsement.

(2) In an action against a drawee under subsection (1) the measure of the drawee's liability is the face amount of the instrument. In any other action under subsection (1) the measure of liability is presumed to be the face amount of the instrument.

(3) Subject to the provisions of this Act concerning restrictive indorsements a representative, including a depositary or collecting bank, who has in good faith and in accordance with the reasonable commercial standards applicable to the business of such representative dealt with an instrument or its proceeds on behalf of one who was not the true owner is not liable in conversion or otherwise to the true owner beyond the amount of any proceeds remaining in his hands.

(4) An intermediary bank or payor bank which is not a depositary bank is not liable in conversion solely by reason of the fact that proceeds of an item indorsed restrictively (Sections 3—205 and 3—206) are not paid or applied consistently with the restrictive indorsement of an indorser other than its immediate transferor.

Part 5

Presentment, Notice of Dishonor and Protest

§3—501
When Presentment, Notice of Dishonor, and Protest Necessary or Permissible

(1) Unless excused (Section 3—511) presentment is necessary to charge secondary parties as follows:

    (a) presentment for acceptance is necessary to charge the drawer and indorsers of a draft where the draft so provides, or is payable elsewhere than at the residence or place of business of the drawee, or its date of payment depends upon such presentment. The holder may at his option present for acceptance any other draft payable at a stated date;

    (b) presentment for payment is necessary to charge any indorser;

    (c) in the case of any drawer, the acceptor of a draft payable at a bank or the maker of a note payable at a bank, presentment for payment is necessary, but failure to make presentment discharges such drawer, acceptor or maker only as stated in Section 3—502(1) (b).

(2) Unless excused (Section 3—511)

    (a) notice of any dishonor is necessary to charge any indorser;

    (b) in the case of any drawer, the acceptor of a draft payable at a bank or the maker of a note payable at a bank, notice of any dishonor is necessary, but failure to give such notice discharges such drawer, acceptor or maker only as stated in Section 3—502(1) (b)

(3) Unless excused (Section 3—511) protest of any dishonor is necessary to charge the drawer and indorsers of any draft which on its face appears to be drawn or payable outside of the states, territories, dependencies and possessions of the United States, the District of Columbia and the Commonwealth of Puerto Rico. The holder may at his option make protest of any dishonor of any other instrument and in the case of a foreign draft may on insolvency of the acceptor before maturity make protest for better security.

(4) Notwithstanding any provision of this section, neither presentment nor notice of dishonor nor protest is necessary to charge an indorser who has indorsed an instrument after maturity. As amended 1966.

§3—502
Unexcused Delay; Discharge

(1) Where without excuse any necessary presentment or notice of dishonor is delayed beyond the time when it is due

    (a) any indorser is discharged; and

    (b) any drawer or the acceptor of a draft payable at a bank or the maker of a note payable at a bank who because the drawee or payor bank becomes insolvent during the delay is deprived of funds maintained with the drawee or payor bank to cover the instrument may

discharge his liability by written assignment to the holder of his rights against the drawee or payor bank in respect of such funds, but such drawer, acceptor or maker is not otherwise discharged.

(2) Where without excuse a necessary protest is delayed beyond the time when it is due any drawer or indorser is discharged.

§3—503
Time of Presentment

(1) Unless a different time is expressed in the instrument the time for any presentment is determined as follows:

    (a) where an instrument is payable at or a fixed period after a stated date any presentment for acceptance must be made on or before the date it is payable;

    (b) where an instrument is payable after sight it must either be presented for acceptance or negotiated within a reasonable time after date or issue whichever is later;

    (c) where an instrument shows the date on which it is payable presentment for payment is due on that date;

    (d) where an instrument is accelerated presentment for payment is due within a reasonable time after the acceleration;

    (e) with respect to the liability of any secondary party presentment for acceptance or payment of any other instrument is due within a reasonable time after such party becomes liable thereon.

(2) A reasonable time for presentment is determined by the nature of the instrument, any usage of banking or trade and the facts of the particular case. In the case of an uncertified check which is drawn and payable within the United States and which is not a draft drawn by a bank the following are presumed to be reasonable periods within which to present for payment or to initiate bank collection:

    (a) with respect to the liability of the drawer, thirty days after date or issue whichever is later; and

    (b) with respect to the liability of an indorser, seven days after his indorsement.

(3) Where any presentment is due on a day which is not a full business day for either the person making presentment or the party to pay or accept, presentment is due on the next following day which is a full business day for both parties.

(4) Presentment to be sufficient must be made at a reasonable hour, and if at a bank during its banking day.

§3—504
How Presentment Made

(1) Presentment is a demand for acceptance or payment made upon the maker, acceptor, drawee or other payor by or on behalf of the holder.

(2) Presentment may be made

    (a) by mail, in which event the time of presentment is determined by the time of receipt of the mail; or

    (b) through a clearing house; or

    (c) at the place of acceptance or payment specified in the instrument or if there be none at the place of business or residence of the party to accept or pay. If neither the party to accept or pay nor anyone authorized to act for him is present or accessible at such place presentment is excused.

(3) It may be made

    (a) to any one of two or more makers, acceptors, drawees or other payors; or

    (b) to any person who has authority to make or refuse the acceptance or payment.

(4) A draft accepted or a note made payable at a bank in the United States must be presented at such bank.

(5) In the cases described in Section 4—210 presentment may be made in the manner and with the result stated in that section. As amended 1962.

§3—505
Rights of Party to Whom Presentment Is Made

(1) The party to whom presentment is made may without dishonor require

    (a) exhibition of the instrument; and

    (b) reasonable identification of the person making presentment and evidence of his authority to make it if made for another; and

    (c) that the instrument be produced for acceptance or payment at a place specified in it, or if there be none at any place reasonable in the circumstances; and

    (d) a signed receipt on the instrument for any partial or full payment and its surrender upon full payment.

(2) Failure to comply with any such requirement invalidates the presentment but the person presenting has a reasonable time in which to comply and the time for acceptance or payment runs from the time of compliance.

§3—506
Time Allowed for Acceptance or Payment

(1) Acceptance may be deferred without dishonor until the close of the next business day following presentment. The holder may also in a good faith effort to obtain acceptance and without either dishonor of the instrument or discharge of secondary parties allow postponement of acceptance for an additional business day.

(2) Except as a longer time is allowed in the case of documentary drafts drawn under a letter of credit, and unless an earlier time is agreed to by the party to pay, payment of an instrument may be deferred without dishonor pending reasonable examination to determine whether it is properly payable, but payment must be made in any event before the close of business on the day of presentment.

§3—507
Dishonor; Holder's Right of Recourse; Term Allowing Re-Presentment

(1) An instrument is dishonored when

    (a) a necessary or optional presentment is duly made and due acceptance or payment is refused or cannot be ob-

tained within the prescribed time or in case of bank collections the instrument is seasonably returned by the midnight deadline (Section 4—301); or

    (b) presentment is excused and the instrument is not duly accepted or paid.

(2) Subject to any necessary notice of dishonor and protest, the holder has upon dishonor an immediate right of recourse against the drawers and indorsers.

(3) Return of an instrument for lack of proper indorsement is not dishonor.

(4) A term in a draft or an indorsement thereof allowing a stated time for re-presentment in the event of any dishonor of the draft by nonacceptance if a time draft or by nonpayment if a sight draft gives the holder as against any secondary party bound by the term an option to waive the dishonor without affecting the liability of the secondary party and he may present again up to the end of the stated time.

§3—508
Notice of Dishonor

(1) Notice of dishonor may be given to any person who may be liable on the instrument by or on behalf of the holder or any party who has himself received notice, or any other party who can be compelled to pay the instrument. In addition an agent or bank in whose hands the instrument is dishonored may give notice to his principal or customer or to another agent or bank from which the instrument was received.

(2) Any necessary notice must be given by a bank before its midnight deadline and by any other person before midnight of the third business day after dishonor or receipt of notice of dishonor.

(3) Notice may be given in any reasonable manner. It may be oral or written and in any terms which identify the instrument and state that it has been dishonored. A misdescription which does not mislead the party notified does not vitiate the notice. Sending the instrument bearing a stamp, ticket or writing stating that acceptance or payment has been refused or sending a notice of debit with respect to the instrument is sufficient.

(4) Written notice is given when sent although it is not received.

(5) Notice to one partner is notice to each although the firm has been dissolved.

(6) When any party is in insolvency proceedings instituted after the issue of the instrument notice may be given either to the party or to the representative of his estate.

(7) When any party is dead or incompetent notice may be sent to his last known address or given to his personal representative.

(8) Notice operates for the benefit of all parties who have rights on the instrument against the party notified.

§3—509
Protest; Noting for Protest

(1) A protest is a certificate of dishonor made under the hand and seal of a United States consul or vice consul or a notary public or other person authorized to certify dishonor by the

law of the place where dishonor occurs. It may be made upon information satisfactory to such person.

(2) The protest must identify the instrument and certify either that due presentment has been made or the reason why it is excused and that the instrument has been dishonored by non-acceptance or nonpayment.

(3) The protest may also certify that notice of dishonor has been given to all parties or to specified parties.

(4) Subject to subsection (5) any necessary protest is due by the time that notice of dishonor is due.

(5) If, before protest is due, an instrument has been noted for protest by the officer to make protest, the protest may be made at any time thereafter as of the date of the noting.

§3—510
Evidence of Dishonor and Notice of Dishonor

The following are admissible as evidence and create a presumption of dishonor and of any notice of dishonor therein shown:

  (a) a document regular in form as provided in the preceding section which purports to be a protest;

  (b) the purported stamp or writing of the drawee, payor bank or presenting bank on the instrument or accompanying it stating that acceptance or payment has been refused for reasons consistent with dishonor;

  (c) any book or record of the drawee, payor bank, or any collecting bank kept in the usual course of business which shows dishonor, even though there is no evidence of who made the entry.

§3—511
Waived or Excused Presentment, Protest or Notice of Dishonor or Delay Therein

(1) Delay in presentment, protest or notice of dishonor is excused when the party is without notice that it is due or when the delay is caused by circumstances beyond his control and he exercises reasonable diligence after the cause of the delay ceases to operate.

(2) Presentment or notice or protest as the case may be is entirely excused when

  (a) the party to be charged has waived it expressly or by implication either before or after it is due; or

  (b) such party has himself dishonored the instrument or has countermanded payment or otherwise has no reason to expect or right to require that the instrument be accepted or paid; or

  (c) by reasonable diligence the presentment or protest cannot be made or the notice given.

(3) Presentment is also entirely excused when

  (a) the maker, acceptor or drawee of any instrument except a documentary draft is dead or in insolvency proceedings instituted after the issue of the instrument; or

  (b) acceptance or payment is refused but not for want of proper presentment.

(4) Where a draft has been dishonored by nonacceptance a later presentment for payment and any notice of dishonor and protest for nonpayment are excused unless in the meantime the instrument has been accepted.

(5) A waiver of protest is also a waiver of presentment and of notice of dishonor even though protest is not required.

(6) Where a waiver of presentment or notice or protest is embodied in the instrument itself it is binding upon all parties; but where it is written above the signature of an indorser it binds him only.

Part 6
Discharge

§3—601
Discharge of Parties

(1) The extent of the discharge of any party from liability on an instrument is governed by the sections on

  (a) payment or satisfaction (Section 3—603); or

  (b) tender of payment (Section 3—604); or

  (c) cancellation or renunciation (Section 3—605); or

  (d) impairment of right of recourse or of collateral (Section 3—606); or

  (e) reacquisition of the instrument by a prior party (Section 3—208); or

  (f) fraudulent and material alteration (Section 3—407); or

  (g) certification of a check (Section 3—411); or

  (h) acceptance varying a draft (Section 3—412); or

  (i) unexcused delay in presentment or notice of dishonor or protest (Section 3—502).

(2) Any party is also discharged from his liability on an instrument to another party by any other act or agreement with such party which would discharge his simple contract for the payment of money.

(3) The liability of all parties is discharged when any party who has himself no right of action or recourse on the instrument

  (a) reacquires the instrument in his own right; or

  (b) is discharged under any provision of this Article, except as otherwise provided with respect to discharge for impairment of recourse or of collateral (Section 3—606).

§3—602
Effect of Discharge Against Holder in Due Course

No discharge of any party provided by this Article is effective against a subsequent holder in due course unless he has notice thereof when he takes the instrument.

§3—603
Payment or Satisfaction

(1) The liability of any party is discharged to the extent of his payment or satisfaction to the holder even though it is

made with knowledge of a claim of another person to the instrument unless prior to such payment or satisfaction the person making the claim either supplies indemnity deemed adequate by the party seeking the discharge or enjoins payment or satisfaction by order of a court of competent jurisdiction in an action in which the adverse claimant and the holder are parties. This subsection does not, however, result in the discharge of the liability

    (a) of a party who in bad faith pays or satisfies a holder who acquired the instrument by theft or who (unless having the rights of a holder in due course) holds through one who so acquired it; or

    (b) of a party (other than an intermediary bank or a payor bank which is not a depositary bank) who pays or satisfies the holder of an instrument which has been restrictively indorsed in a manner not consistent with the terms of such restrictive indorsement.

(2) Payment or satisfaction may be made with the consent of the holder by any person including a stranger to the instrument. Surrender of the instrument to such a person gives him the rights of a transferee (Section 3—201).

§3—604
Tender of Payment

(1) Any party making tender of full payment to a holder when or after it is due is discharged to the extent of all subsequent liability for interest, costs and attorney's fees.

(2) The holder's refusal of such tender wholly discharges any party who has a right of recourse against the party making the tender.

(3) Where the maker or acceptor of an instrument payable otherwise than on demand is able and ready to pay at every place of payment specified in the instrument when it is due, it is equivalent to tender.

§3—605
Cancellation and Renunciation

(1) The holder of an instrument may even without consideration discharge any party

    (a) in any manner apparent on the face of the instrument or the indorsement, as by intentionally cancelling the instrument or the party's signature by destruction or mutilation, or by striking out the party's signature; or

    (b) by renouncing his rights by a writing signed and delivered or by surrender of the instrument to the party to be discharged.

(2) Neither cancellation nor renunciation without surrender of the instrument affects the title thereto.

§3—606
Impairment of Recourse or of Collateral

(1) The holder discharges any party to the instrument to the extent that without such party's consent the holder

    (a) without express reservation of rights releases or agrees not to sue any person against whom the party has to the knowledge of the holder a right of recourse or agrees to suspend the right to enforce against such

person the instrument or collateral or otherwise discharges such person, except that failure or delay in effecting any required presentment, protest or notice of dishonor with respect to any such person does not discharge any party as to whom presentment, protest or notice of dishonor is effective or unnecessary; or

    (b) unjustifiably impairs any collateral for the instrument given by or on behalf of the party or any person against whom he has a right of recourse.

(2) By express reservation of rights against a party with a right of recourse the holder preserves

    (a) all his rights against such party as of the time when the instrument was originally due; and

    (b) the right of the party to pay the instrument as of that time; and

    (c) all rights of such party to recourse against others.

Part 7

Advice of International Sight Draft

§3—701
Letter of Advice of International Sight Draft

(1) A "letter of advice" is a drawer's communication to the drawee that a described draft has been drawn.

(2) Unless otherwise agreed when a bank receives from another bank a letter of advice of an international sight draft the drawee bank may immediately debit the drawer's account and stop the running of interest pro tanto. Such a debit and any resulting credit to any account covering outstanding drafts leaves in the drawer full power to stop payment or otherwise dispose of the amount and creates no trust or interest in favor of the holder.

(3) Unless otherwise agreed and except where a draft is drawn under a credit issued by the drawee, the drawee of an international sight draft owes the drawer no duty to pay an unadvised draft but if it does so and the draft is genuine, may appropriately debit the drawer's account.

Part 8

Miscellaneous

§3—801
Drafts in a Set

(1) Where a draft is drawn in a set of parts, each of which is numbered and expressed to be an order only if no other part has been honored, the whole of the parts constitutes one draft but a taker of any part may become a holder in due course of the draft.

(2) Any person who negotiates, indorses or accepts a single part of a draft drawn in a set thereby becomes liable to any holder in due course of that part as if it were the whole set, but as between holders in due course to whom different parts have been negotiated the holder whose title first accrues has all rights to the draft and its proceeds.

(3) As against the drawee the first presented part of a draft drawn in a set is the part entitled to payment, or if a time draft to acceptance and payment. Acceptance of any subsequently presented part renders the drawee liable thereon under subsection (2). With respect both to a holder and to the drawer payment of a subsequently presented part of a draft payable at sight has the same effect as payment of a check notwithstanding an effective stop order (Section 4—407).

(4) Except as otherwise provided in this section, where any part of a draft in a set is discharged by payment or otherwise the whole draft is discharged.

§3—802
Effect of Instrument on Obligation for Which It Is Given

(1) Unless otherwise agreed where an instrument is taken for an underlying obligation

(a) the obligation is pro tanto discharged if a bank is drawer, maker or acceptor of the instrument and there is no recourse on the instrument against the underlying obligor; and

(b) in any other case the obligation is suspended pro tanto until the instrument is due or if it is payable on demand until its presentment. If the instrument is dishonored action may be maintained on either the instrument or the obligation; discharge of the underlying obligor on the instrument also discharges him on the obligation.

(2) The taking in good faith of a check which is not postdated does not of itself so extend the time on the original obligation as to discharge a surety.

§3—803
Notice to Third Party

Where a defendant is sued for breach of an obligation for which a third person is answerable over under this Article he may give the third person written notice of the litigation, and the person notified may then give similar notice to any other person who is answerable over to him under this Article. If the notice states that the person notified may come in and defend and that if the person notified does not do so he will in any action against him by the person giving the notice be bound by any determination of fact common to the two litigations, then unless after seasonable receipt of the notice the person notified does come in and defend he is so bound.

§3—804
Lost, Destroyed or Stolen Instruments

The owner of an instrument which is lost, whether by destruction, theft or otherwise, may maintain an action in his own name and recover from any party liable thereon upon due proof of his ownership, the facts which prevent his production of the instrument and its terms. The court may require security indemnifying the defendant against loss by reason of further claims on the instrument.

§3—805
Instruments Not Payable to Order or to Bearer

This Article applies to any instrument whose terms do not preclude transfer and which is otherwise negotiable within this Article but which is not payable to order or to bearer, except that there can be no holder in due course of such an instrument.

Article 4
Bank Deposits and Collections

Part 1
General Provisions and Definitions

§4—101
Short Title

This Article shall be known and may be cited as Uniform Commercial Code—Bank Deposits and Collections.

§4—102
Applicability

(1) To the extent that items within this Article are also within the scope of Articles 3 and 8, they are subject to the provisions of those Articles. In the event of conflict the provisions of this Article govern those of Article 3 but the provisions of Article 8 govern those of this Article.

(2) The liability of a bank for action or non-action with respect to any item handled by it for purposes of presentment, payment or collection is governed by the law of the place where the bank is located. In the case of action or non-action by or at a branch or separate office of a bank, its liability is governed by the law of the place where the branch or separate office is located.

§4—103
Variation by Agreement; Measure of Damages; Certain Action Constituting Ordinary Care

(1) The effect of the provisions of this Article may be varied by agreement except that no agreement can disclaim a bank's responsibility for its own lack of good faith or failure to exercise ordinary care or can limit the measure of damages for such lack or failure; but the parties may by agreement determine the standards by which such responsibility is to be measured if such standards are not manifestly unreasonable.

(2) Federal Reserve regulations and operating letters, clearing house rules, and the like, have the effect of agreements under subsection (1), whether or not specifically assented to by all parties interested in items handled.

(3) Action or non-action approved by this Article or pursuant to Federal Reserve regulations or operating letters constitutes the exercise of ordinary care and, in the absence of special instructions, action or non-action consistent with clearing house rules and the like or with a general banking usage not disapproved by this Article, prima facie constitutes the exercise of ordinary care.

(4) The specification or approval of certain procedures by this Article does not constitute disapproval of other procedures which may be reasonable under the circumstances.

(5) The measure of damages for failure to exercise ordinary care in handling an item is the amount of the item reduced by an amount which could not have been realized by the use of ordinary care, and where there is bad faith it includes other damages, if any, suffered by the party as a proximate consequence.

§4—104
Definitions and Index of Definitions

(1) In this Article unless the context otherwise requires

    (a) "Account" means any account with a bank and includes a checking, time, interest or savings account;

    (b) "Afternoon" means the period of a day between noon and midnight;

    (c) "Banking day" means that part of any day on which a bank is open to the public for carrying on substantially all of its banking functions;

    (d) "Clearing house" means any association of banks or other payors regularly clearing items;

    (e) "Customer" means any person having an account with a bank or for whom a bank has agreed to collect items and includes a bank carrying an account with another bank;

    (f) "Documentary draft" means any negotiable or non-negotiable draft with accompanying documents, securities or other papers to be delivered against honor of the draft;

    (g) "Item" means any instrument for the payment of money even though it is not negotiable but does not include money;

    (h) "Midnight deadline" with respect to a bank is midnight on its next banking day following the banking day on which it receives the relevant item or notice or from which the time for taking action commences to run, whichever is later;

    (i) "Properly payable" includes the availability of funds for payment at the time of decision to pay or dishonor;

    (j) "Settle" means to pay in cash, by clearing house settlement, in a charge or credit or by remittance, or otherwise as instructed. A settlement may be either provisional or final;

    (k) "Suspends payments" with respect to a bank means that it has been closed by order of the supervisory authorities, that a public officer has been appointed to take it over or that it ceases or refuses to make payments in the ordinary course of business.

(2) Other definitions applying to this Article and the sections in which they appear are:

"Collecting bank"	Section 4—105.
"Depositary bank"	Section 4—105.
"Intermediary bank"	Section 4—105.
"Payor bank"	Section 4—105.
"Presenting bank"	Section 4—105.
"Remitting bank"	Section 4—105.

(3) The following definitions in other Articles apply to this Article:

"Acceptance"	Section 3—410.
"Certificate of deposit"	Section 3—104.
"Certification"	Section 3—411.
"Check"	Section 3—104.
"Draft"	Section 3—104.
"Holder in due course"	Section 3—302.
"Notice of dishonor"	Section 3—508.
"Presentment"	Section 3—504.
"Protest"	Section 3—509.
"Secondary party"	Section 3—102.

(4) In addition Article 1 contains general definitions and principles of construction and interpretation applicable throughout this Article.

§4—105
"Depositary Bank"; "Intermediary Bank"; "Collecting Bank"; "Payor Bank"; "Presenting Bank"; "Remitting Bank"

In this Article unless the context otherwise requires:

    (a) "Depositary bank" means the first bank to which an item is transferred for collection even though it is also the payor bank;

    (b) "Payor bank" means a bank by which an item is payable as drawn or accepted;

    (c) "Intermediary bank" means any bank to which an item is transferred in course of collection except the depositary or payor bank;

    (d) "Collecting bank" means any bank handling the item for collection except the payor bank;

    (e) "Presenting bank" means any bank presenting an item except a payor bank;

    (f) "Remitting bank" means any payor or intermediary bank remitting for an item.

§4—106
Separate Office of a Bank

A branch or separate office of a bank [maintaining its own deposit ledgers] is a separate bank for the purpose of computing the time within which and determining the place at or to which action may be taken or notices or orders shall be given under this Article and under Article 3. As amended 1962.

Note: The brackets are to make it optional with the several states whether to require a branch to maintain its own deposit ledgers in order to be considered to be a separate bank for certain purposes under Article 4. In some states "maintaining its own deposit ledgers" is a satisfactory test. In others branch banking practices are such that this test would not be suitable.

§4—107
Time of Receipt of Items

(1) For the purpose of allowing time to process items, prove balances and make the necessary entries on its books to determine its position for the day, a bank may fix an afternoon hour of 2 P.M. or later as a cut-off hour for the handling of money and items and the making of entries on its books.

(2) Any item or deposit of money received on any day after a cut-off hour so fixed or after the close of the banking day may be treated as being received at the opening of the next banking day.

§4—108
Delays

(1) Unless otherwise instructed, a collecting bank in a good faith effort to secure payment may, in the case of specific items and with or without the approval of any person involved, waive, modify or extend time limits imposed or permitted by this Act for a period not in excess of an additional banking day without discharge of secondary parties and without liability to its transferor or any prior party.

(2) Delay by a collecting bank or payor bank beyond time limits prescribed or permitted by this Act or by instructions is excused if caused by interruption of communication facilities, suspension of payments by another bank, war, emergency conditions or other circumstances beyond the control of the bank provided it exercises such diligence as the circumstances require.

§4—109
Process of Posting

The "process of posting" means the usual procedure followed by a payor bank in determining to pay an item and in recording the payment including one or more of the following or other steps as determined by the bank:

    (a) verification of any signature;

    (b) ascertaining that sufficient funds are available;

    (c) affixing a "paid" or other stamp;

    (d) entering a charge or entry to a customer's account;

    (e) correcting or reversing an entry or erroneous action with respect to the item.

Added 1962.

Part 2

Collection of Items: Depositary and Collecting Banks

§4—201
Presumption and Duration of Agency Status of Collecting Banks and Provisional Status of Credits; Applicability of Article; Item Indorsed "Pay Any Bank"

(1) Unless a contrary intent clearly appears and prior to the time that a settlement given by a collecting bank for an item is or becomes final (subsection (3) of Section 4—211 and Sections 4—212 and 4—213) the bank is an agent or sub-agent of the owner of the item and any settlement given for the item is provisional. This provision applies regardless of the form of indorsement or lack of indorsement and even though credit given for the item is subject to immediate withdrawal as of right or is in fact withdrawn; but the continuance of ownership of an item by its owner and any rights of the owner to proceeds of the item are subject to rights of a collecting bank such as those resulting from outstanding advances on the item and valid rights of setoff. When an item is handled by banks for purposes of presentment, payment and collection, the relevant provisions of this Article apply even though action of parties clearly establishes that a particular bank has purchased the item and is the owner of it.

(2) After an item has been indorsed with the words "pay any bank" or the like, only a bank may acquire the rights of a holder

    (a) until the item has been returned to the customer initiating collection; or

    (b) until the item has been specially indorsed by a bank to a person who is not a bank.

§4—202
Responsibility for Collection; When Action Seasonable

(1) A collecting bank must use ordinary care in

    (a) presenting an item or sending it for presentment; and

    (b) sending notice of dishonor or non-payment or returning an item other than a documentary draft to the bank's transferor [or directly to the depositary bank under subsection (2) of Section 4—212] (*see note to Section 4—212*) after learning that the item has not been paid or accepted, as the case may be; and

    (c) settling for an item when the bank receives final settlement; and

    (d) making or providing for any necessary protest; and

    (e) notifying its transferor of any loss or delay in transit within a reasonable time after discovery thereof.

(2) A collecting bank taking proper action before its midnight deadline following receipt of an item, notice or payment acts seasonably; taking proper action within a reasonably longer time may be seasonable but the bank has the burden of so establishing.

(3) Subject to subsection (1) (a), a bank is not liable for the insolvency, neglect, misconduct, mistake or default of another bank or person or for loss or destruction of an item in transit or in the possession of others.

§4—203
Effect of Instructions

Subject to the provisions of Article 3 concerning conversion of instruments (Section 3—419) and the provisions of both Article 3 and this Article concerning restrictive indorsements only a collecting bank's transferor can give instructions which affect the bank or constitute notice to it and a collecting bank is not liable to prior parties for any action taken pursu-

ant to such instructions or in accordance with any agreement
with its transferor.

§4—204
Methods of Sending and Presenting; Sending Direct to Payor Bank

(1) A collecting bank must send items by reasonably prompt
method taking into consideration any relevant instructions,
the nature of the item, the number of such items on hand,
and the cost of collection involved and the method generally
used by it or others to present such items.

(2) A collecting bank may send

   (a) any item direct to the payor bank;

   (b) any item to any non-bank payor if authorized by its
      transferor; and

   (c) any item other than documentary drafts to any non-
      bank payor, if authorized by Federal Reserve regula-
      tion or operating letter, clearing house rule or the like.

(3) Presentment may be made by a presenting bank at a
place where the payor bank has requested that presentment
be made. As amended 1962.

§4—205
Supplying Missing Indorsement; No Notice from Prior Indorsement

(1) A depositary bank which has taken an item for collection
may supply any indorsement of the customer which is necessary to title unless the item contains the words "payee's indorsement required" or the like. In the absence of such a requirement a statement placed on the item by the depositary
bank to the effect that the item was deposited by a customer
or credited to his account is effective as the customer's indorsement.

(2) An intermediary bank, or payor bank which is not a
depositary bank, is neither given notice nor otherwise affected
by a restrictive indorsement of any person except the bank's
immediate transferor.

§4—206
Transfer Between Banks

Any agreed method which identifies the transferor bank is
sufficient for the item's further transfer to another bank.

§4—207
Warranties of Customer and Collecting Bank on Transfer or Presentment of Items; Time for Claims

(1) Each customer or collecting bank who obtains payment
or acceptance of an item and each prior customer and collecting bank warrants to the payor bank or other payor who in
good faith pays or accepts the item that

   (a) he has a good title to the item or is authorized to ob-
      tain payment or acceptance on behalf of one who has
      a good title; and

   (b) he has no knowledge that the signature of the maker
      or drawer is unauthorized, except that this warranty is

not given by any customer or collecting bank that is a
holder in due course and acts in good faith

   (i) to a maker with respect to the maker's own signa-
      ture; or

   (ii) to a drawer with respect to the drawer's own sig-
      nature, whether or not the drawer is also the
      drawee; or

   (iii) to an acceptor of an item if the holder in due
      course took the item after the acceptance or ob-
      tained the acceptance without knowledge that the
      drawer's signature was unauthorized; and

   (c) the item has not been materially altered, except that
      this warranty is not given by any customer or collect-
      ing bank that is a holder in due course and acts in
      good faith

   (i) to the maker of a note; or

   (ii) to the drawer of a draft whether or not the draw-
      er is also the drawee; or

   (iii) to the acceptor of an item with respect to an al-
      teration made prior to the acceptance if the hold-
      er in due course took the item after the accep-
      tance, even though the acceptance provided
      "payable as originally drawn" or equivalent terms;
      or

   (iv) to the acceptor of an item with respect to an al-
      teration made after the acceptance.

(2) Each customer and collecting bank who transfers an item
and receives a settlement or other consideration for it warrants to his transferee and to any subsequent collecting bank
who takes the item in good faith that

   (a) he has a good title to the item or is authorized to ob-
      tain payment or acceptance on behalf of one who has
      a good title and the transfer is otherwise rightful; and

   (b) all signatures are genuine or authorized; and

   (c) the item has not been materially altered; and

   (d) no defense of any party is good against him; and

   (e) he has no knowledge of any insolvency proceeding in-
      stituted with respect to the maker or acceptor or the
      drawer of an unaccepted item.

In addition each customer and collecting bank so transferring
an item and receiving a settlement or other consideration engages that upon dishonor and any necessary notice of dishon-
or and protest he will take up the item.

(3) The warranties and the engagement to honor set forth in
the two preceding subsections arise notwithstanding the absence of indorsement or words of guaranty or warranty in the
transfer or presentment and a collecting bank remains liable
for their breach despite remittance to its transferor. Damages
for breach of such warranties or engagement to honor shall
not exceed the consideration received by the customer or collecting bank responsible plus finance charges and expenses related to the item, if any.

(4) Unless a claim for breach of warranty under this section
is made within a reasonable time after the person claiming

learns of the breach, the person liable is discharged to the extent of any loss caused by the delay in making claim.

§4—208
Security Interest of Collecting Bank in Items. Accompanying Documents and Proceeds

(1) A bank has a security interest in an item and any accompanying documents or the proceeds of either

    (a) in case of an item deposited in an account to the extent to which credit given for the item has been withdrawn or applied;

    (b) in case of an item for which it has given credit available for withdrawal as of right, to the extent of the credit given whether or not the credit is drawn upon and whether or not there is a right of charge-back; or

    (c) if it makes an advance on or against the item.

(2) When credit which has been given for several items received at one time or pursuant to a single agreement is withdrawn or applied in part the security interest remains upon all the items, any accompanying documents or the proceeds of either. For the purpose of this section, credits first given are first withdrawn.

(3) Receipt by a collecting bank of a final settlement for an item is a realization on its security interest in the item, accompanying documents and proceeds. To the extent and so long as the bank does not receive final settlement for the item or give up possession of the item or accompanying documents for purposes other than collection, the security interest continues and is subject to the provisions of Article 9 except that

    (a) no security agreement is necessary to make the security interest enforceable (subsection (1) (b) of Section 9—203); and

    (b) no filing is required to perfect the security interest; and

    (c) the security interest has priority over conflicting perfected security interests in the item, accompanying documents or proceeds.

§4—209
When Bank Gives Value for Purposes of Holder in Due Course

For purposes of determining its status as a holder in due course, the bank has given value to the extent that it has a security interest in an item provided that the bank otherwise complies with the requirements of Section 3—302 on what constitutes a holder in due course.

§4—210
Presentment by Notice of Item Not Payable by, Through or at a Bank; Liability of Secondary Parties

(1) Unless otherwise instructed, a collecting bank may present an item not payable by, through or at a bank by sending to the party to accept or pay a written notice that the bank holds the item for acceptance or payment. The notice must be sent in time to be received on or before the day when presentment is due and the bank must meet any requirement of the party to accept or pay under Section 3—505 by the close of the bank's next banking day after it knows of the requirement.

(2) Where presentment is made by notice and neither honor nor request for compliance with a requirement under Section 3—505 is received by the close of business on the day after maturity or in the case of demand items by the close of business on the third banking day after notice was sent, the presenting bank may treat the item as dishonored and charge any secondary party by sending him notice of the facts.

§4—211
Media of Remittance; Provisional and Final Settlement in Remittance Cases

(1) A collecting bank may take in settlement of an item

    (a) a check of the remitting bank or of another bank on any bank except the remitting bank; or

    (b) a cashier's check or similar primary obligation of a remitting bank which is a member of or clears through a member of the same clearing house or group as the collecting bank; or

    (c) appropriate authority to charge an account of the remitting bank or of another bank with the collecting bank; or

    (d) if the item is drawn upon or payable by a person other than a bank, a cashier's check, certified check or other bank check or obligation.

(2) If before its midnight deadline the collecting bank properly dishonors a remittance check or authorization to charge on itself or presents or forwards for collection a remittance instrument of or on another bank which is of a kind approved by subsection (1) or has not been authorized by it, the collecting bank is not liable to prior parties in the event of the dishonor of such check, instrument or authorization.

(3) A settlement for an item by means of a remittance instrument or authorization to charge is or becomes a final settlement as to both the person making and the person receiving the settlement

    (a) if the remittance instrument or authorization to charge is of a kind approved by subsection (1) or has not been authorized by the person receiving the settlement and in either case the person receiving the settlement acts seasonably before its midnight deadline in presenting, forwarding for collection or paying the instrument or authorization,—at the time the remittance instrument or authorization is finally paid by the payor by which it is payable;

    (b) if the person receiving the settlement has authorized remittance by a non-bank check or obligation or by a cashier's check or similar primary obligation of or a check upon the payor or other remitting bank which is not of a kind approved by subsection (1) (b),—at the time of the receipt of such remittance check or obligation; or

(c) if in a case not covered by sub-paragraphs (a) or (b) the person receiving the settlement fails to seasonably present, forward for collection, pay or return a remittance instrument or authorization to it to charge before its midnight deadline,—at such midnight deadline.

§4—212
Right of Charge-Back or Refund

(1) If a collecting bank has made provisional settlement with its customer for an item and itself fails by reason of dishonor, suspension of payments by a bank or otherwise to receive a settlement for the item which is or becomes final, the bank may revoke the settlement given by it, charge back the amount of any credit given for the item to its customer's account or obtain refund from its customer whether or not it is able to return the items if by its midnight deadline or within a longer reasonable time after it learns the facts it returns the item or sends notification of the facts. These rights to revoke, charge-back and obtain refund terminate if and when a settlement for the item received by the bank is or becomes final (subsection (3) of Section 4—211 and subsections (2) and (3) of Section 4—213).

[(2) Within the time and manner prescribed by this section and Section 4—301, an intermediary or payor bank, as the case may be may return an unpaid item directly to the depositary bank and may send for collection a draft on the depositary bank and obtain reimbursement. In such case, if the depositary bank has received provisional settlement for the item, it must reimburse the bank drawing the draft and any provisional credits for the item between banks shall become and remain final.]

Note: Direct returns is recognized as an innovation that is not yet established bank practice, and therefore, Paragraph 2 has been bracketed. Some lawyers have doubts whether it should be included in legislation or left to development by agreement.

(3) A depositary bank which is also the payor may charge-back the amount of an item to its customer's account or obtain refund in accordance with the section governing return of an item received by a payor bank for credit on its books (Section 4—301).

(4) The right to charge-back is not affected by

(a) prior use of the credit given for the item; or

(b) failure by any bank to exercise ordinary care with respect to the item but any bank so failing remains liable.

(5) A failure to charge-back or claim refund does not affect other rights of the bank against the customer or any other party.

(6) If credit is given in dollars as the equivalent of the value of an item payable in a foreign currency the dollar amount of any charge-back or refund shall be calculated on the basis of the buying sight rate for the foreign currency prevailing on the day when the person entitled to the charge-back or refund learns that it will not receive payment in ordinary course.

§4—213
Final Payment of Item by Payor Bank; When Provisional Debits and Credits Become Final; When Certain Credits Become Available for Withdrawal

(1) An item is finally paid by a payor bank when the bank has done any of the following, whichever happens first:

(a) paid the item in cash; or

(b) settled for the item without reserving a right to revoke the settlement and without having such right under statute, clearing house rule or agreement; or

(c) completed the process of posting the item to the indicated account of the drawer, maker or other person to be charged therewith; or

(d) made a provisional settlement for the item and failed to revoke the settlement in the time and manner permitted by statute, clearing house rule or agreement.

Upon a final payment under subparagraphs (b), (c) or (d) the payor bank shall be accountable for the amount of the item.

(2) If provisional settlement for an item between the presenting and payor banks is made through a clearing house or by debits or credits in an account between them, then to the extent that provisional debits or credits for the item are entered in accounts between the presenting and payor banks or between the presenting and successive prior collecting banks seriatim, they become final upon final payment of the item by the payor bank.

(3) If a collecting bank receives a settlement for an item which is or becomes final (subsection (3) of Section 4—211, subsection (2) of Section 4—213) the bank is accountable to its customer for the amount of the item and any provisional credit given for the item in an account with its customer becomes final.

(4) Subject to any right of the bank to apply the credit to an obligation of the customer, credit given by a bank for an item in an account with its customer becomes available for withdrawal as of right

(a) in any case where the bank has received a provisional settlement for the item,—when such settlement becomes final and the bank has had a reasonable time to learn that the settlement is final;

(b) in any case where the bank is both a depositary bank and a payor bank and the item is finally paid,—at the opening of the bank's second banking day following receipt of the item.

(5) A deposit of money in a bank is final when made but, subject to any right of the bank to apply the deposit to an obligation of the customer, the deposit becomes available for withdrawal as of right at the opening of the bank's next banking day following receipt of the deposit.

§4—214
Insolvency and Preference

(1) Any item in or coming into the possession of a payor or

collecting bank which suspends payment and which item is not finally paid shall be returned by the receiver, trustee or agent in charge of the closed bank to the presenting bank or the closed bank's customer.

(2) If a payor bank finally pays an item and suspends payments without making a settlement for the item with its customer or the presenting bank which settlement is or becomes final, the owner of the item has a preferred claim against the payor bank.

(3) If a payor bank gives or a collecting bank gives or receives a provisional settlement for an item and thereafter suspends payments, the suspension does not prevent or interfere with the settlement becoming final if such finality occurs automatically upon the lapse of certain time or the happening of certain events (subsection (3) of Section 4—211, subsections (1) (d), (2) and (3) of Section 4—213).

(4) If a collecting bank receives from subsequent parties settlement for an item which settlement is or becomes final and suspends payments without making a settlement for the item with its customer which is or becomes final, the owner of the item has a preferred claim against such collecting bank.

Part 3

Collection of Items: Payor Banks

§4—301
Deferred Posting; Recovery of Payment by Return of Items; Time of Dishonor

(1) Where an authorized settlement for a demand item (other than a documentary draft) received by a payor bank otherwise than for immediate payment over the counter has been made before midnight of the banking day of receipt the payor bank may revoke the settlement and recover any payment if before it has made final payment (subsection (1) of Section 4—213) and before its midnight deadline it

    (a) returns the item; or

    (b) sends written notice of dishonor or nonpayment if the item is held for protest or is otherwise unavailable for return.

(2) If a demand item is received by a payor bank for credit on its books it may return such item or send notice of dishonor and may revoke any credit given or recover the amount thereof withdrawn by its customer, if it acts within the time limit and in the manner specified in the preceding subsection.

(3) Unless previous notice of dishonor has been sent an item is dishonored at the time when for purposes of dishonor it is returned or notice sent in accordance with this section.

(4) An item is returned:

    (a) as to an item received through a clearing house, when it is delivered to the presenting or last collecting bank or to the clearing house or is sent or delivered in accordance with its rules; or

    (b) in all other cases, when it is sent or delivered to the bank's customer or transferor or pursuant to his instructions.

§4—302
Payor Bank's Responsibility for Late Return of Item

In the absence of a valid defense such as breach of a presentment warranty (subsection (1) of Section 4—207), settlement effected or the like, if an item is presented on and received by a payor bank the bank is accountable for the amount of

    (a) a demand item other than a documentary draft whether properly payable or not if the bank, in any case where it is not also the depositary bank, retains the item beyond midnight of the banking day of receipt without settling for it or, regardless of whether it is also the depositary bank, does not pay or return the item or send notice of dishonor until after its midnight deadline; or

    (b) any other properly payable item unless within the time allowed for acceptance or payment of that item the bank either accepts or pays the item or returns it and accompanying documents.

§4—303
When Items Subject to Notice, Stop-Order, Legal Process or Setoff; Order in Which Items May Be Charged or Certified

(1) Any knowledge, notice or stop-order received by, legal process served upon or setoff exercised by a payor bank, whether or not effective under other rules of law to terminate, suspend or modify the bank's right or duty to pay an item or to charge its customer's account for the item, comes too late to so terminate, suspend or modify such right or duty if the knowledge, notice, stop-order or legal process is received or served and a reasonable time for the bank to act thereon expires or the setoff is exercised after the bank has done any of the following:

    (a) accepted or certified the item;

    (b) paid the item in cash;

    (c) settled for the item without reserving a right to revoke the settlement and without having such right under statute, clearing house rule or agreement;

    (d) completed the process of posting the item to the indicated account of the drawer, maker or other person to be charged therewith or otherwise has evidenced by examination of such indicated account and by action its decision to pay the item; or

    (e) become accountable for the amount of the item under subsection (1) (d) of Section 4—213 and Section 4—302 dealing with the payor bank's responsibility for late return of items.

(2) Subject to the provisions of subsection (1) items may be accepted, paid, certified or charged to the indicated account of its customer in any order convenient to the bank.

Part 4

Relationship Between Payor Bank and Its Customer

§4—401
When Bank May Charge Customer's Account

(1) As against its customer, a bank may charge against his account any item which is otherwise properly payable from that account even though the charge creates an overdraft.

(2) A bank which in good faith makes payment to a holder may charge the indicated account of its customer according to

    (a) the original tenor of his altered item; or

    (b) the tenor of his completed item, even though the bank knows the item has been completed unless the bank has notice that the completion was improper.

§4—402
Bank's Liability to Customer for Wrongful Dishonor

A payor bank is liable to its customer for damages proximately caused by the wrongful dishonor of an item. When the dishonor occurs through mistake liability is limited to actual damages proved. If so proximately caused and proved damages may include damages for an arrest or prosecution of the customer or other consequential damages. Whether any consequential damages are proximately caused by the wrongful dishonor is a question of fact to be determined in each case.

§4—403
Customer's Right to Stop Payment; Burden of Proof of Loss

(1) A customer may by order to his bank stop payment of any item payable for his account but the order must be received at such time and in such manner as to afford the bank a reasonable opportunity to act on it prior to any action by the bank with respect to the item described in Section 4—303.

(2) An oral order is binding upon the bank only for fourteen calendar days unless confirmed in writing within that period. A written order is effective for only six months unless renewed in writing.

(3) The burden of establishing the fact and amount of loss resulting from the payment of an item contrary to a binding stop payment order is on the customer.

§4—404
Bank Not Obligated to Pay Check More Than Six Months Old

A bank is under no obligation to a customer having a checking account to pay a check, other than a certified check, which is presented more than six months after its date, but it may charge its customer's account for a payment made thereafter in good faith.

§4—405
Death or Incompetence of Customer

(1) A payor or collecting bank's authority to accept, pay or collect an item or to account for proceeds of its collection if otherwise effective is not rendered ineffective by incompetence of a customer of either bank existing at the time the item is issued or its collection is undertaken if the bank does not know of an adjudication of incompetence. Neither death nor incompetence of a customer revokes such authority to accept, pay, collect or account until the bank knows of the fact of death or of an adjudication of incompetence and has reasonable opportunity to act on it.

(2) Even with knowledge a bank may for 10 days after the date of death pay or certify checks drawn on or prior to that date unless ordered to stop payment by a person claiming an interest in the account.

§4—406
Customer's Duty to Discover and Report Unauthorized Signature or Alteration

(1) When a bank sends to its customer a statement of account accompanied by items paid in good faith in support of the debit entries or holds the statement and items pursuant to a request or instructions of its customer or otherwise in a reasonable manner makes the statement and items available to the customer, the customer must exercise reasonable care and promptness to examine the statement and items to discover his unauthorized signature or any alteration on an item and must notify the bank promptly after discovery thereof.

(2) If the bank establishes that the customer failed with respect to an item to comply with the duties imposed on the customer by subsection (1) the customer is precluded from asserting against the bank

    (a) his unauthorized signature or any alteration on the item if the bank also establishes that it suffered a loss by reason of such failure; and

    (b) an unauthorized signature or alteration by the same wrongdoer on any other item paid in good faith by the bank after the first item and statement was available to the customer for a reasonable period not exceeding fourteen calendar days and before the bank receives notification from the customer of any such unauthorized signature or alteration.

(3) The preclusion under subsection (2) does not apply if the customer establishes lack of ordinary care on the part of the bank in paying the item(s).

(4) Without regard to care or lack of care of either the customer or the bank a customer who does not within one year from the time the statement and items are made available to the customer (subsection (1)) discover and report his unauthorized signature or any alteration on the face or back of the item or does not within 3 years from that time discover and report any unauthorized indorsement is precluded from asserting against the bank such unauthorized signature or indorsement or such alteration.

(5) If under this section a payor bank has a valid defense against a claim of a customer upon or resulting from pay-

ment of an item and waives or fails upon request to assert the defense the bank may not assert against any collecting bank or other prior party presenting or transferring the item a claim based upon the unauthorized signature or alteration giving rise to the customer's claim.

§4—407
Payor Bank's Right to Subrogation on Improper Payment

If a payor bank has paid an item over the stop payment order of the drawer or maker or otherwise under circumstances giving a basis for objection by the drawer or maker, to prevent unjust enrichment and only to the extent necessary to prevent loss to the bank by reason of its payment of the item, the payor bank shall be subrogated to the rights

(a) of any holder in due course on the item against the drawer or maker; and

(b) of the payee or any other holder of the item against the drawer or maker either on the item or under the transaction out of which the item arose; and

(c) of the drawer or maker against the payee or any other holder of the item with respect to the transaction out of which the item arose.

Part 5

Collection of Documentary Drafts

§4—501
Handling of Documentary Drafts; Duty to Send for Presentment and to Notify Customer of Dishonor

A bank which takes a documentary draft for collection must present or send the draft and accompanying documents for presentment and upon learning that the draft has not been paid or accepted in due course must seasonably notify its customer of such fact even though it may have discounted or bought the draft or extended credit available for withdrawal as of right.

§4—502
Presentment of "On Arrival" Drafts

When a draft or the relevant instructions require presentment "on arrival", "when goods arrive" or the like, the collecting bank need not present until in its judgment a reasonable time for arrival of the goods has expired. Refusal to pay or accept because the goods have not arrived is not dishonor; the bank must notify its transferor of such refusal but need not present the draft again until it is instructed to do so or learns of the arrival of the goods.

§4—503
Responsibility of Presenting Bank for Documents and Goods; Report of Reasons for Dishonor; Referee in Case of Need

Unless otherwise instructed and except as provided in Article 5 a bank presenting a documentary draft

(a) must deliver the documents to the drawee on acceptance of the draft if it is payable more than three days after presentment; otherwise, only on payment; and

(b) upon dishonor, either in the case of presentment for acceptance or presentment for payment, may seek and follow instructions from any referee in case of need designated in the draft or if the presenting bank does not choose to utilize his services it must use diligence and good faith to ascertain the reason for dishonor, must notify its transferor of the dishonor and of the results of its effort to ascertain the reasons therefor and must request instructions.

But the presenting bank is under no obligation with respect to goods represented by the documents except to follow any reasonable instructions seasonably received; it has a right to reimbursement for any expense incurred in following instructions and to prepayment of or indemnity for such expenses.

§4—504
Privilege of Presenting Bank to Deal With Goods; Security Interest for Expenses

(1) A presenting bank which, following the dishonor of a documentary draft, has seasonably requested instructions but does not receive them within a reasonable time may store, sell, or otherwise deal with the goods in any reasonable manner.

(2) For its reasonable expenses incurred by action under subsection (1) the presenting bank has a lien upon the goods or their proceeds, which may be foreclosed in the same manner as an unpaid seller's lien.

Article 5

Letters of Credit

§5—101
Short Title

This Article shall be known and may be cited as Uniform Commercial Code—Letters of Credit.

§5—102
Scope

(1) This Article applies

(a) to a credit issued by a bank if the credit requires a documentary draft or a documentary demand for payment; and

(b) to a credit issued by a person other than a bank if the credit requires that the draft or demand for payment be accompanied by a document of title; and

(c) to a credit issued by a bank or other person if the credit is not within subparagraphs (a) or (b) but conspicuously states that it is a letter of credit or is conspicuously so entitled.

(2) Unless the engagement meets the requirements of subsection (1), this Article does not apply to engagements to make

advances or to honor drafts or demands for payment, to authorities to pay or purchase, to guarantees or to general agreements.

(3) This Article deals with some but not all of the rules and concepts of letters of credit as such rules or concepts have developed prior to this act or may hereafter develop. The fact that this Article states a rule does not by itself require, imply or negate application of the same or a converse rule to a situation not provided for or to a person not specified by this Article.

§5—103
Definitions

(1) In this Article unless the context otherwise requires

   (a) "Credit" or "letter of credit" means an engagement by a bank or other person made at the request of a customer and of a kind within the scope of this Article (Section 5—102) that the issuer will honor drafts or other demands for payment upon compliance with the conditions specified in the credit. A credit may be either revocable or irrevocable. The engagement may be either an agreement to honor or a statement that the bank or other person is authorized to honor.

   (b) A "documentary draft" or a "documentary demand for payment" is one honor of which is conditioned upon the presentation of a document or documents. "Document" means any paper including document of title, security, invoice, certificate, notice of default and the like.

   (c) An "issuer" is a bank or other person issuing a credit.

   (d) A "beneficiary" of a credit is a person who is entitled under its terms to draw or demand payment.

   (e) An "advising bank" is a bank which gives notification of the issuance of a credit by another bank.

   (f) A "confirming bank" is a bank which engages either that it will itself honor a credit already issued by another bank or that such a credit will be honored by the issuer or a third bank.

   (g) A "customer" is a buyer or other person who causes an issuer to issue a credit. The term also includes a bank which procures issuance or confirmation on behalf of that bank's customer.

(2) Other definitions applying to this Article and the sections in which they appear are:

| "Notation of Credit". | Section 5—108. |
| "Presenter". | Section 5—112(3). |

(3) Definitions in other Articles applying to this Article and the sections in which they appear are:

"Accept" or "Acceptance".	Section 3—410.
"Contract for sale".	Section 2—106.
"Draft".	Section 3—104.
"Holder in due course".	Section 3—302.
"Midnight deadline".	Section 4—104.
"Security".	Section 8—102.

(4) In addition, Article 1 contains general definitions and principles of construction and interpretation applicable throughout this Article.

§5—104
Formal Requirements; Signing

(1) Except as otherwise required in subsection (1) (c) of Section 5—102 on scope, no particular form of phrasing is required for a credit. A credit must be in writing and signed by the issuer and a confirmation must be in writing and signed by the confirming bank. A modification of the terms of a credit or confirmation must be signed by the issuer or confirming bank.

(2) A telegram may be a sufficient signed writing if it identifies its sender by an authorized authentication. The authentication may be in code and the authorized naming of the issuer in an advice of credit is a sufficient signing.

§5—105. Consideration

No consideration is necessary to establish a credit or to enlarge or otherwise modify its terms.

§5—106
Time and Effect of Establishment
of Credit

(1) Unless otherwise agreed a credit is established

   (a) as regards the customer as soon as a letter of credit is sent to him or the letter of credit or an authorized written advice of its issuance is sent to the beneficiary; and

   (b) as regards the beneficiary when he receives a letter of credit or an authorized written advice of its issuance.

(2) Unless otherwise agreed once an irrevocable credit is established as regards the customer it can be modified or revoked only with the consent of the customer and once it is established as regards the beneficiary it can be modified or revoked only with his consent.

(3) Unless otherwise agreed after a revocable credit is established it may be modified or revoked by the issuer without notice to or consent from the customer or beneficiary.

(4) Notwithstanding any modification or revocation of a revocable credit any person authorized to honor or negotiate under the terms of the original credit is entitled to reimbursement for or honor of any draft or demand for payment duly honored or negotiated before receipt of notice of the modification or revocation and the issuer in turn is entitled to reimbursement from its customer.

§5—107
Advice of Credit; Confirmation; Error
in Statement of Terms

(1) Unless otherwise specified an advising bank by advising a credit issued by another bank does not assume any obligation to honor drafts drawn or demands for payment made under the credit but it does assume obligation for the accuracy of its own statement.

(2) A confirming bank by confirming a credit becomes directly obligated on the credit to the extent of its confirmation as though it were its issuer and acquires the rights of an issuer.

(3) Even though an advising bank incorrectly advises the terms of a credit it has been authorized to advise the credit is

established as against the issuer to the extent of its original terms.

(4) Unless otherwise specified the customer bears as against the issuer all risks of transmission and reasonable translation or interpretation of any message relating to a credit.

§5—108
"Notation Credit"; Exhaustion of Credit

(1) A credit which specifies that any person purchasing or paying drafts drawn or demands for payment made under it must note the amount of the draft or demand on the letter or advice of credit is a "notation credit".

(2) Under a notation credit

(a) a person paying the beneficiary or purchasing a draft or demand for payment from him acquires a right to honor only if the appropriate notation is made and by transferring or forwarding for honor the documents under the credit such a person warrants to the issuer that the notation has been made; and

(b) unless the credit or a signed statement that an appropriate notation has been made accompanies the draft or demand for payment the issuer may delay honor until evidence of notation has been procured which is satisfactory to it but its obligation and that of its customer continue for a reasonable time not exceeding thirty days to obtain such evidence.

(3) If the credit is not a notation credit

(a) the issuer may honor complying drafts or demands for payment presented to it in the order in which they are presented and is discharged pro tanto by honor of any such draft or demand;

(b) as between competing good faith purchasers of complying drafts or demands the person first purchasing has priority over a subsequent purchaser even though the later purchased draft or demand has been first honored.

§5—109
Issuer's Obligation to Its Customer

(1) An issuer's obligation to its customer includes good faith and observance of any general banking usage but unless otherwise agreed does not include liability or responsibility

(a) for performance of the underlying contract for sale or other transaction between the customer and the beneficiary; or

(b) for any act or omission of any person other than itself or its own branch or for loss or destruction of a draft, demand or document in transit or in the possession of others; or

(c) based on knowledge or lack of knowledge of any usage of any particular trade.

(2) An issuer must examine documents with care so as to ascertain that on their face they appear to comply with the terms of the credit but unless otherwise agreed assumes no liability or responsibility for the genuineness, falsification or effect of any document which appears on such examination to be regular on its surface.

(3) A non-bank issuer is not bound by any banking usage of which it has no knowledge.

§5—110
Availability of Credit in Portions; Presenter's Reservation of Lien or Claim

(1) Unless otherwise specified a credit may be used in portions in the discretion of the beneficiary.

(2) Unless otherwise specified a person by presenting a documentary draft or demand for payment under a credit relinquishes upon its honor all claims to the documents and a person by transferring such draft or demand or causing such presentment authorizes such relinquishment. An explicit reservation of claim makes the draft or demand non-complying.

§5—111
Warranties on Transfer and Presentment

(1) Unless otherwise agreed the beneficiary by transferring or presenting a documentary draft or demand for payment warrants to all interested parties that the necessary conditions of the credit have been complied with. This is in addition to any warranties arising under Articles 3, 4, 7 and 8.

(2) Unless otherwise agreed a negotiating, advising, confirming, collecting or issuing bank presenting or transferring a draft or demand for payment under a credit warrants only the matters warranted by a collecting bank under Article 4 and any such bank transferring a document warrants only the matters warranted by an intermediary under Articles 7 and 8.

§5—112
Time Allowed for Honor or Rejection; Withholding Honor or Rejection by Consent; "Presenter"

(1) A bank to which a documentary draft or demand for payment is presented under a credit may without dishonor of the draft, demand or credit

(a) defer honor until the close of the third banking day following receipt of the documents; and

(b) further defer honor if the presenter has expressly or impliedly consented thereto.

Failure to honor within the time here specified constitutes dishonor of the draft or demand and of the credit [except as otherwise provided in subsection (4) of Section 5—114 on conditional payment].

Note: The bracketed language in the last sentence of subsection (1) should be included only if the optional provisions of Section 5—114(4) and (5) are included.

(2) Upon dishonor the bank may unless otherwise instructed fulfill its duty to return the draft or demand and the documents by holding them at the disposal of the presenter and sending him an advice to that effect.

(3) "Presenter" means any person presenting a draft or demand for payment for honor under a credit even though that person is a confirming bank or other correspondent which is acting under an issuer's authorization.

§5—113
Indemnities

(1) A bank seeking to obtain (whether for itself or another) honor, negotiation or reimbursement under a credit may give an indemnity to induce such honor, negotiation or reimbursement.

(2) An indemnity agreement inducing honor, negotiation or reimbursement

    (a) unless otherwise explicitly agreed applies to defects in the documents but not in the goods; and

    (b) unless a longer time is explicitly agreed expires at the end of ten business days following receipt of the documents by the ultimate customer unless notice of objection is sent before such expiration date. The ultimate customer may send notice of objection to the person from whom he received the documents and any bank receiving such notice is under a duty to send notice to its transferor before its midnight deadline.

§5—114
Issuer's Duty and Privilege to Honor;
Right to Reimbursement

(1) An issuer must honor a draft or demand for payment which complies with the terms of the relevant credit regardless of whether the goods or documents conform to the underlying contract for sale or other contract between the customer and the beneficiary. The issuer is not excused from honor of such a draft or demand by reason of an additional general term that all documents must be satisfactory to the issuer, but an issuer may require that specified documents must be satisfactory to it.

(2) Unless otherwise agreed when documents appear on their face to comply with the terms of a credit but a required document does not in fact conform to the warranties made on negotiation or transfer of a document of title (Section 7—507) or of a security (Section 8—306) or is forged or fraudulent or there is fraud in the transaction

    (a) the issuer must honor the draft or demand for payment if honor is demanded by a negotiating bank or other holder of the draft or demand which has taken the draft or demand under the credit and under circumstances which would make it a holder in due course (Section 3—302) and in an appropriate case would make it a person to whom a document of title has been duly negotiated (Section 7—502) or a bona fide purchaser of a security (Section 8—302); and

    (b) in all other cases as against its customer, an issuer acting in good faith may honor the draft or demand for payment despite notification from the customer of fraud, forgery or other defect not apparent on the face of the documents but a court of appropriate jurisdiction may enjoin such honor.

(3) Unless otherwise agreed an issuer which has duly honored a draft or demand for payment is entitled to immediate reimbursement of any payment made under the credit and to be put in effectively available funds not later than the day before maturity of any acceptance made under the credit.

[(4) When a credit provides for payment by the issuer on receipt of notice that the required documents are in the possession of a correspondent or other agent of the issuer

    (a) any payment made on receipt of such notice is conditional; and

    (b) the issuer may reject documents which do not comply with the credit if it does so within three banking days following its receipt of the documents; and

    (c) in the event of such rejection, the issuer is entitled by charge back or otherwise to return of the payment made.]

[(5) In the case covered by subsection (4) failure to reject documents within the time specified in sub-paragraph (b) constitutes acceptance of the documents and makes the payment final in favor of the beneficiary.]

Note: Subsections (4) and (5) are bracketed as optional. If they are included the bracketed language in the last sentence of Section 5—112(1) should also be included.

§5—115
Remedy for Improper Dishonor or
Anticipatory Repudiation

(1) When an issuer wrongfully dishonors a draft or demand for payment presented under a credit the person entitled to honor has with respect to any documents the rights of a person in the position of a seller (Section 2—707) and may recover from the issuer the face amount of the draft or demand together with incidental damages under Section 2—710 on seller's incidental damages and interest but less any amount realized by resale or other use or disposition of the subject matter of the transaction. In the event no resale or other utilization is made the documents, goods or other subject matter involved in the transaction must be turned over to the issuer on payment of judgment.

(2) When an issuer wrongfully cancels or otherwise repudiates a credit before presentment of a draft or demand for payment drawn under it the beneficiary has the rights of a seller after anticipatory repudiation by the buyer under Section 2—610 if he learns of the repudiation in time reasonably to avoid procurement of the required documents. Otherwise the beneficiary has an immediate right of action for wrongful dishonor.

§5—116
Transfer and Assignment

(1) The right to draw under a credit can be transferred or assigned only when the credit is expressly designated as transferable or assignable.

(2) Even though the credit specifically states that it is nontransferable or nonassignable the beneficiary may before performance of the conditions of the credit assign his right to proceeds. Such an assignment is an assignment of a contract right under Article 9 on Secured Transactions and is governed by that Article except that

    (a) the assignment is ineffective until the letter of credit or advice of credit is delivered to the assignee which delivery constitutes perfection of the security interest under Article 9; and

(b) the issuer may honor drafts or demands for payment drawn under the credit until it receives a notification of the assignment signed by the beneficiary which reasonably identifies the credit involved in the assignment and contains a request to pay the assignee; and

(c) after what reasonably appears to be such a notification has been received the issuer may without dishonor refuse to accept or pay even to a person otherwise entitled to honor until the letter of credit or advice of credit is exhibited to the issuer.

(3) Except where the beneficiary has effectively assigned his right to draw or his right to proceeds, nothing in this section limits his right to transfer or negotiate drafts or demands drawn under the credit. Amended in 1972.

§5—117
Insolvency of Bank Holding Funds for Documentary Credit

(1) Where an issuer or an advising or confirming bank or a bank which has for a customer procured issuance of a credit by another bank becomes insolvent before final payment under the credit and the credit is one to which this Article is made applicable by paragraphs (a) or (b) of Section 5—102(1) on scope, the receipt or allocation of funds or collateral to secure or meet obligations under the credit shall have the following results:

(a) to the extent of any funds or collateral turned over after or before the insolvency as indemnity against or specifically for the purpose of payment of drafts or demands for payment drawn under the designated credit, the drafts or demands are entitled to payment in preference over depositors or other general creditors of the issuer or bank; and

(b) on expiration of the credit or surrender of the beneficiary's rights under it unused any person who has given such funds or collateral is similarly entitled to return thereof; and

(c) a charge to a general or current account with a bank if specifically consented to for the purpose of indemnity against or payment of drafts or demands for payment drawn under the designated credit falls under the same rules as if the funds had been drawn out in cash and then turned over with specific instructions.

(2) After honor or reimbursement under this section the customer or other person for whose account the insolvent bank has acted is entitled to receive the documents involved.

Article 6
Bulk Transfers

§6—101
Short Title

This Article shall be known and may be cited as Uniform Commercial Code—Bulk Transfers.

§6—102
"Bulk Transfers"; Transfers of Equipment; Enterprises Subject to This Article; Bulk Transfers Subject to This Article

(1) A "bulk transfer" is any transfer in bulk and not in the ordinary course of the transferor's business of a major part of the materials, supplies, merchandise or other inventory (Section 9—109) of an enterprise subject to this Article.

(2) A transfer of a substantial part of the equipment (Section 9—109) of such an enterprise is a bulk transfer if it is made in connection with a bulk transfer of inventory, but not otherwise.

(3) The enterprises subject to this Article are all those whose principal business is the sale of merchandise from stock, including those who manufacture what they sell.

(4) Except as limited by the following section all bulk transfers of goods located within this state are subject to this Article.

§6—103
Transfers Excepted From This Article

The following transfers are not subject to this Article:

(1) Those made to give security for the performance of an obligation;

(2) General assignments for the benefit of all the creditors of the transferor, and subsequent transfers by the assignee thereunder;

(3) Transfers in settlement or realization of a lien or other security interest;

(4) Sales by executors, administrators, receivers, trustees in bankruptcy, or any public officer under judicial process;

(5) Sales made in the course of judicial or administrative proceedings for the dissolution or reorganization of a corporation and of which notice is sent to the creditors of the corporation pursuant to order of the court or administrative agency;

(6) Transfers to a person maintaining a known place of business in this State who becomes bound to pay the debts of the transferor in full and gives public notice of that fact, and who is solvent after becoming so bound;

(7) A transfer to a new business enterprise organized to take over and continue the business, if public notice of the transaction is given and the new enterprise assumes the debts of the transferor and he receives nothing from the transaction except an interest in the new enterprise junior to the claims of creditors;

(8) Transfers of property which is exempt from execution.

Public notice under subsection (6) or subsection (7) may be given by publishing once a week for two consecutive weeks in a newspaper of general circulation where the transferor had its principal place of business in this state an advertisement including the names and addresses of the transferor and transferee and the effective date of the transfer.

§6—104
Schedule of Property; List of Creditors

(1) Except as provided with respect to auction sales (Section

6—108), a bulk transfer subject to this Article is ineffective against any creditor of the transferor unless:

(a) the transferee requires the transferor to furnish a list of his existing creditors prepared as stated in this section; and

(b) the parties prepare a schedule of the property transferred sufficient to identify it; and

(c) the transferee preserves the list and schedule for six months next following the transfer and permits inspection of either or both and copying therefrom at all reasonable hours by any creditor of the transferor, or files the list and schedule in (a public office to be here identified).

(2) The list of creditors must be signed and sworn to or affirmed by the transferor or his agent. It must contain the names and business addresses of all creditors of the transferor, with the amounts when known, and also the names of all persons who are known to the transferor to assert claims against him even though such claims are disputed. If the transferor is the obligor of an outstanding issue of bonds, debentures or the like as to which there is an indenture trustee, the list of creditors need include only the name and address of the indenture trustee and the aggregate outstanding principal amount of the issue.

(3) Responsibility for the completeness and accuracy of the list of creditors rests on the transferor, and the transfer is not rendered ineffective by errors or omissions therein unless the transferee is shown to have had knowledge.

§6—105
Notice to Creditors

In addition to the requirements of the preceding section, any bulk transfer subject to this Article except one made by auction sale (Section 6—108) is ineffective against any creditor of the transferor unless at least ten days before he takes possession of the goods or pays for them, whichever happens first, the transferee gives notice of the transfer in the manner and to the persons hereafter provided (Section 6—107).

[§6—106
Application of the Proceeds

In addition to the requirements of the two preceding sections:

(1) Upon every bulk transfer subject to this Article for which new consideration becomes payable except those made by sale at auction it is the duty of the transferee to assure that such consideration is applied so far as necessary to pay those debts of the transferor which are either shown on the list furnished by the transferor (Section 6–104) or filed in writing in the place stated in the notice (Section 6–107) within thirty days after the mailing of such notice. This duty of the transferee runs to all the holders of such debts, and may be enforced by any of them for the benefit of all.

(2) If any of said debts are in dispute the necessary sum may be withheld from distribution until the dispute is settled or adjudicated.

(3) If the consideration payable is not enough to pay all of the said debts in full distribution shall be made pro rata.]

Note: This section is bracketed to indicate division of opinion as to whether or not it is a wise provision, and to suggest that this is a point on which State enactments may differ without serious damage to the principle of uniformity.

In any State where this section is omitted, the following parts of sections, also bracketed in the text, should also be omitted, namely:

Section 6–107(2) (e).

6–108(3) (c).

6–109(2).

In any State where this section is enacted, these other provisions should be also.

Optional Subsection (4)

[(4) The transferee may within ten days after he takes possession of the goods pay the consideration into the (specify court) in the county where the transferor had its principal place of business in this state and thereafter may discharge his duty under this section by giving notice by registered or certified mail to all the persons to whom the duty runs that the consideration has been paid into that court and that they should file their claims there. On motion of any interested party, the court may order the distribution of the consideration to the persons entitled to it.]

Note: Optional subsection (4) is recommended for those states which do not have a general statute providing for payment of money into court.

§6–107
The Notice

(1) The notice to creditors (Section 6—105) shall state:

(a) that a bulk transfer is about to be made; and

(b) the names and business addresses of the transferor and transferee, and all other business names and addresses used by the transferor within three years last past so far as known to the transferee; and

(c) whether or not all the debts of the transferor are to be paid in full as they fall due as a result of the transaction, and if so, the address to which creditors should send their bills.

(2) If the debts of the transferor are not to be paid in full as they fall due or if the transferee is in doubt on that point then the notice shall state further:

(a) the location and general description of the property to be transferred and the estimated total of the transferor's debts;

(b) the address where the schedule of property and list of creditors (Section 6—104) may be inspected;

(c) whether the transfer is to pay existing debts and if so the amount of such debts and to whom owing;

(d) whether the transfer is for new consideration and if so the amount of such consideration and the time and place of payment; [and]

[(e) if for new consideration the time and place where creditors of the transferor are to file their claims.]

(3) The notice in any case shall be delivered personally or sent by registered or certified mail to all the persons shown

on the list of creditors furnished by the transferor (Section 6—104) and to all other persons who are known to the transferee to hold or assert claims against the transferor.

Note: The words in brackets are optional. See Note under §6—106.

§6—108
Auction Sales; "Auctioneer"

(1) A bulk transfer is subject to this Article even though it is by sale at auction, but only in the manner and with the results stated in this section.

(2) The transferor shall furnish a list of his creditors and assist in the preparation of a schedule of the property to be sold, both prepared as before stated (Section 6—104).

(3) The person or persons other than the transferor who direct, control or are responsible for the auction are collectively called the "auctioneer". The auctioneer shall:

    (a) receive and retain the list of creditors and prepare and retain the schedule of property for the period stated in this Article (Section 6—104);

    (b) give notice of the auction personally or by registered or certified mail at least ten days before it occurs to all persons shown on the list of creditors and to all other persons who are known to him to hold or assert claims against the transferor; [and]

    [(c) assure that the net proceeds of the auction are applied as provided in this Article (Section 6—106).]

(4) Failure of the auctioneer to perform any of these duties does not affect the validity of the sale or the title of the purchasers, but if the auctioneer knows that the auction constitutes a bulk transfer such failure renders the auctioneer liable to the creditors of the transferor as a class for the sums owing to them from the transferor up to but not exceeding the net proceeds of the auction. If the auctioneer consists of several persons their liability is joint and several.

Note: The words in brackets are optional. See Note under §6—106.

§6—109
What Creditors Protected; [Credit for Payment to Particular Creditors]

(1) The creditors of the transferor mentioned in this Article are those holding claims based on transactions or events occurring before the bulk transfer, but creditors who become such after notice to creditors is given (Sections 6—105 and 6—107) are not entitled to notice.

[(2) Against the aggregate obligation imposed by the provisions of this Article concerning the application of the proceeds (Section 6—106 and subsection (3) (c) of 6—108) the transferee or auctioneer is entitled to credit for sums paid to particular creditors of the transferor, not exceeding the sums believed in good faith at the time of the payment to be properly payable to such creditors.]

Note: The words in brackets are optional. See Note under §6—106.

§6—110
Subsequent Transfers

When the title of a transferee to property is subject to a de-fect by reason of his non-compliance with the requirements of this Article, then:

(1) a purchaser of any of such property from such transferee who pays no value or who takes with notice of such non-compliance takes subject to such defect, but

(2) a purchaser for value in good faith and without such notice takes free of such defect.

§6—111
Limitation of Actions and Levies

No action under this Article shall be brought nor levy made more than six months after the date on which the transferee took possession of the goods unless the transfer has been concealed. If the transfer has been concealed, actions may be brought or levies made within six months after its discovery.

Article 7

Warehouse Receipts, Bills of Lading and Other Documents of Title

Part 1

General

§7—101
Short Title

This Article shall be known and may be cited as Uniform Commercial Code—Documents of Title.

§7—102
Definitions and Index of Definitions

(1) In this Article, unless the context otherwise requires:

    (a) "Bailee" means the person who by a warehouse receipt, bill of lading or other document of title acknowledges possession of goods and contracts to deliver them.

    (b) "Consignee" means the person named in a bill to whom or to whose order the bill promises delivery.

    (c) "Consignor" means the person named in a bill as the person from whom the goods have been received for shipment.

    (d) "Delivery order" means a written order to deliver goods directed to a warehouseman, carrier or other person who in the ordinary course of business issues warehouse receipts or bills of lading.

    (e) "Document" means document of title as defined in the general definitions in Article 1 (Section 1—201).

    (f) "Goods" means all things which are treated as movable for the purposes of a contract of storage or transportation.

    (g) "Issuer" means a bailee who issues a document except that in relation to an unaccepted delivery order it means the person who orders the possessor of goods to deliver. Issuer includes any person for whom an agent or employee purports to act in issuing a document if the agent or employee has real or apparent authority to issue documents, notwithstanding that the issuer received no goods or that the goods were misdescribed or that in any other respect the agent or employee violated his instructions.

(h) "Warehouseman" is a person engaged in the business of storing goods for hire.

(2) Other definitions applying to this Article or to specified Parts thereof, and the sections in which they appear are:

"Duly negotiate".	Section 7—501.
"Person entitled under the document".	Section 7—403(4).

(3) Definitions in other Articles applying to this Article and the sections in which they appear are:

"Contract for sale".	Section 2—106.
"Overseas".	Section 2—323.
"Receipt" of goods.	Section 2—103.

(4) In addition Article 1 contains general definitions and principles of construction and interpretation applicable throughout this Article.

§7—103
Relation of Article to Treaty, Statute, Tariff, Classification or Regulation

To the extent that any treaty or statute of the United States, regulatory statute of this State or tariff, classification or regulation filed or issued pursuant thereto is applicable, the provisions of this Article are subject thereto.

§7—104
Negotiable and Non-Negotiable Warehouse Receipt, Bill of Lading or Other Document of Title

(1) A warehouse receipt, bill of lading or other document of title is negotiable

(a) if by its terms the goods are to be delivered to bearer or to the order of a named person; or

(b) where recognized in overseas trade, if it runs to a named person or assigns.

(2) Any other document is non-negotiable. A bill of lading in which it is stated that the goods are consigned to a named person is not made negotiable by a provision that the goods are to be delivered only against a written order signed by the same or another named person.

§7—105
Construction Against Negative Implication

The omission from either Part 2 or Part 3 of this Article of a provision corresponding to a provision made in the other Part does not imply that a corresponding rule of law is not applicable.

Part 2
Warehouse Receipts: Special Provisions

§7—201
Who May Issue a Warehouse Receipt; Storage Under Government Bond

(1) A warehouse receipt may be issued by any warehouseman.

(2) Where goods including distilled spirits and agricultural commodities are stored under a statute requiring a bond against withdrawal or a license for the issuance of receipts in the nature of warehouse receipts, a receipt issued for the goods has like effect as a warehouse receipt even though issued by a person who is the owner of the goods and is not a warehouseman.

§7—202
Form of Warehouse Receipt; Essential Terms; Optional Terms

(1) A warehouse receipt need not be in any particular form.

(2) Unless a warehouse receipt embodies within its written or printed terms each of the following, the warehouseman is liable for damages caused by the omission to a person injured thereby:

(a) the location of the warehouse where the goods are stored;

(b) the date of issue of the receipt;

(c) the consecutive number of the receipt;

(d) a statement whether the goods received will be delivered to the bearer, to a specified person, or to a specified person or his order;

(e) the rate of storage and handling charges, except that where goods are stored under a field warehousing arrangement a statement of that fact is sufficient on a non-negotiable receipt;

(f) a description of the goods or of the packages containing them;

(g) the signature of the warehouseman, which may be made by his authorized agent;

(h) if the receipt is issued for goods of which the warehouseman is owner, either solely or jointly or in common with others, the fact of such ownership; and

(i) a statement of the amount of advances made and of liabilities incurred for which the warehouseman claims a lien or security interest (Section 7—209). If the precise amount of such advances made or of such liabilities incurred is, at the time of the issue of the receipt, unknown to the warehouseman or to his agent who issues it, a statement of the fact that advances have been made or liabilities incurred and the purpose thereof is sufficient.

(3) A warehouseman may insert in his receipt any other terms which are not contrary to the provisions of this Act and do not impair his obligation of delivery (Section 7—403)

or his duty of care (Section 7—204). Any contrary provisions shall be ineffective.

§7—203
Liability for Non-Receipt or Misdescription

A party to or purchaser for value in good faith of a document of title other than a bill of lading relying in either case upon the description therein of the goods may recover from the issuer damages caused by the non-receipt or misdescription of the goods, except to the extent that the document conspicuously indicates that the issuer does not know whether any part or all of the goods in fact were received or conform to the description, as where the description is in terms of marks or labels or kind, quantity or condition, or the receipt or description is qualified by "contents, condition and quality unknown", "said to contain" or the like, if such indication be true, or the party or purchaser otherwise has notice.

§7—204
Duty of Care; Contractual Limitation of Warehouseman's Liability

(1) A warehouseman is liable for damages for loss of or injury to the goods caused by his failure to exercise such care in regard to them as a reasonably careful man would exercise under like circumstances but unless otherwise agreed he is not liable for damages which could not have been avoided by the exercise of such care.

(2) Damages may be limited by a term in the warehouse receipt or storage agreement limiting the amount of liability in case of loss or damage, and setting forth a specific liability per article or item, or value per unit of weight, beyond which the warehouseman shall not be liable; provided, however, that such liability may on written request of the bailor at the time of signing such storage agreement or within a reasonable time after receipt of the warehouse receipt be increased on part or all of the goods thereunder, in which event increased rates may be charged based on such increased valuation, but that no such increase shall be permitted contrary to a lawful limitation of liability contained in the warehouseman's tariff, if any. No such limitation is effective with respect to the warehouseman's liability for conversion to his own use.

(3) Reasonable provisions as to the time and manner of presenting claims and instituting actions based on the bailment may be included in the warehouse receipt or tariff.

(4) This section does not impair or repeal . . .

Note: Insert in subsection (4) a reference to any statute which imposes a higher responsibility upon the warehouseman or invalidates contractual limitations which would be permissible under this Article.

§7—205
Title Under Warehouse Receipt Defeated in Certain Cases

A buyer in the ordinary course of business of fungible goods sold and delivered by a warehouseman who is also in the business of buying and selling such goods takes free of any claim under a warehouse receipt even though it has been duly negotiated.

§7—206
Termination of Storage at Warehouseman's Option

(1) A warehouseman may on notifying the person on whose account the goods are held and any other person known to claim an interest in the goods require payment of any charges and removal of the goods from the warehouse at the termination of the period of storage fixed by the document, or, if no period is fixed, within a stated period not less than thirty days after the notification. If the goods are not removed before the date specified in the notification, the warehouseman may sell them in accordance with the provisions of the section on enforcement of a warehouseman's lien (Section 7—210).

(2) If a warehouseman in good faith believes that the goods are about to deteriorate or decline in value to less than the amount of his lien within the time prescribed in subsection (1) for notification, advertisement and sale, the warehouseman may specify in the notification any reasonable shorter time for removal of the goods and in case the goods are not removed, may sell them at public sale held not less than one week after a single advertisement or posting.

(3) If as a result of a quality or condition of the goods of which the warehouseman had no notice at the time of deposit the goods are a hazard to other property or to the warehouse or to persons, the warehouseman may sell the goods at public or private sale without advertisement on reasonable notification to all persons known to claim an interest in the goods. If the warehouseman after a reasonable effort is unable to sell the goods he may dispose of them in any lawful manner and shall incur no liability by reason of such disposition.

(4) The warehouseman must deliver the goods to any person entitled to them under this Article upon due demand made at any time prior to sale or other disposition under this section.

(5) The warehouseman may satisfy his lien from the proceeds of any sale or disposition under this section but must hold the balance for delivery on the demand of any person to whom he would have been bound to deliver the goods.

§7—207
Goods Must Be Kept Separate; Fungible Goods

(1) Unless the warehouse receipt otherwise provides, a warehouseman must keep separate the goods covered by each receipt so as to permit at all times identification and delivery of those goods except that different lots of fungible goods may be commingled.

(2) Fungible goods so commingled are owned in common by the persons entitled thereto and the warehouseman is severally liable to each owner for that owner's share. Where because of overissue a mass of fungible goods is insufficient to meet all the receipts which the warehouseman has issued against it, the persons entitled include all holders to whom overissued receipts have been duly negotiated.

§7—208
Altered Warehouse Receipts

Where a blank in a negotiable warehouse receipt has been

filled in without authority, a purchaser for value and without notice of the want of authority may treat the insertion as authorized. Any other unauthorized alteration leaves any receipt enforceable against the issuer according to its original tenor.

§7—209
Lien of Warehouseman

(1) A warehouseman has a lien against the bailor on the goods covered by a warehouse receipt or on the proceeds thereof in his possession for charges for storage or transportation (including demurrage and terminal charges), insurance, labor, or charges present or future in relation to the goods, and for expenses necessary for preservation of the goods or reasonably incurred in their sale pursuant to law. If the person on whose account the goods are held is liable for like charges or expenses in relation to other goods whenever deposited and it is stated in the receipt that a lien is claimed for charges and expenses in relation to other goods, the warehouseman also has a lien against him for such charges and expenses whether or not the other goods have been delivered by the warehouseman. But against a person to whom a negotiable warehouse receipt is duly negotiated a warehouseman's lien is limited to charges in an amount or at a rate specified on the receipt or if no charges are so specified then to a reasonable charge for storage of the goods covered by the receipt subsequent to the date of the receipt.

(2) The warehouseman may also reserve a security interest against the bailor for a maximum amount specified on the receipt for charges other than those specified in subsection (1), such as for money advanced and interest. Such a security interest is governed by the Article on Secured Transactions (Article 9).

(3)

(a) A warehouseman's lien for charges and expenses under subsection (1) or a security interest under subsection (2) is also effective against any person who so entrusted the bailor with possession of the goods that a pledge of them by him to a good faith purchaser for value would have been valid but is not effective against a person as to whom the document confers no right in the goods covered by it under Section 7—503.

(b) A warehouseman's lien on household goods for charges and expenses in relation to the goods under subsection (1) is also effective against all persons if the depositor was the legal possessor of the goods at the time of deposit. "Household goods" means furniture, furnishings and personal effects used by the depositor in a dwelling.

(4) A warehouseman loses his lien on any goods which he voluntarily delivers or which he unjustifiably refuses to deliver. (As amended in 1966.)

§7—210
Enforcement of Warehouseman's Lien

(1) Except as provided in subsection (2), a warehouseman's lien may be enforced by public or private sale of the goods in block or in parcels, at any time or place and on any terms which are commercially reasonable, after notifying all persons known to claim an interest in the goods. Such notification must include a statement of the amount due, the nature of the proposed sale and the time and place of any public sale. The fact that a better price could have been obtained by a sale at a different time or in a different method from that selected by the warehouseman is not of itself sufficient to establish that the sale was not made in a commercially reasonable manner. If the warehouseman either sells the goods in the usual manner in any recognized market therefor, or if he sells at the price current in such market at the time of his sale, or he has otherwise sold in conformity with commercially reasonable practices among dealers in the type of goods sold, he has sold in a commercially reasonable manner. A sale of more goods than apparently necessary to be offered to insure satisfaction of the obgliation is not commercially reasonable except in cases covered by the preceding sentence.

(2) A warehouseman's lien on goods other than goods stored by a merchant in the course of his business may be enforced only as follows:

(a) All persons known to claim an interest in the goods must be notified.

(b) The notification must be delivered in person or sent by registered or certified letter to the last known address of any person to be notified.

(c) The notification must include an itemized statement of the claim, a description of the goods subject to the lien, a demand for payment within a specified time not less than ten days after receipt of the notification, and a conspicuous statement that unless the claim is paid within that time the goods will be advertised for sale and sold by auction at a specified time and place.

(d) The sale must conform to the terms of the notification.

(e) The sale must be held at the nearest suitable place to that where the goods are held or stored.

(f) After the expiration of the time given in the notification, an advertisement of the sale must be published once a week for two weeks consecutively in a newspaper of general circulation where the sale is to be held. The advertisement must include a description of the goods, the name of the person on whose account they are being held, and the time and place of the sale. The sale must take place at least fifteen days after the first publication. If there is no newspaper of general circulation where the sale is to be held, the advertisement must be posted at least ten days before the sale in not less than six conspicuous places in the neighborhood of the proposed sale.

(3) Before any sale pursuant to this section any person claiming a right in the goods may pay the amount necessary to satisfy the lien and the reasonable expenses incurred under this section. In that event the goods must not be sold, but must be retained by the warehouseman subject to the terms of the receipt and this Article.

(4) The warehouseman may buy at any public sale pursuant to this section.

(5) A purchaser in good faith of goods sold to enforce a warehouseman's lien takes the goods free of any rights of per-

sons against whom the lien was valid, despite noncompliance by the warehouseman with the requirements of this section.

(6) The warehouseman may satisfy his lien from the proceeds of any sale pursuant to this section but must hold the balance, if any, for delivery on demand to any person to whom he would have been bound to deliver the goods.

(7) The rights provided by this section shall be in addition to all other rights allowed by law to a creditor against his debtor.

(8) Where a lien is on goods stored by a merchant in the course of his business the lien may be enforced in accordance with either subsection (1) or (2).

(9) The warehouseman is liable for damages caused by failure to comply with the requirements for sale under this section and in case of willful violation is liable for conversion. As amended in 1962.

Part 3

Bills of Lading: Special Provisions

§7—301
Liability for Non-Receipt or Misdescription; "Said to Contain"; "Shipper's Load and Count"; Improper Handling

(1) A consignee of a non-negotiable bill who has given value in good faith or a holder to whom a negotiable bill has been duly negotiated relying in either case upon the description therein of the goods, or upon the date therein shown, may recover from the issuer damages caused by the misdating of the bill or the non-receipt or misdescription of the goods, except to the extent that the document indicates that the issuer does not know whether any part or all of the goods in fact were received or conform to the description, as where the description is in terms of marks or labels or kind, quantity, or condition or the receipt or description is qualified by "contents or condition of contents of packages unknown", "said to contain", "shipper's weight, load and count" or the like, if such indication be true.

(2) When goods are loaded by an issuer who is a common carrier, the issuer must count the packages of goods if package freight and ascertain the kind and quantity if bulk freight. In such cases "shipper's weight, load and count" or other words indicating that the description was made by the shipper are ineffective except as to freight concealed by packages.

(3) When bulk freight is loaded by a shipper who makes available to the issuer adequate facilities for weighing such freight, an issuer who is a common carrier must ascertain the kind and quantity within a reasonable time after receiving the written request of the shipper to do so. In such cases "shipper's weight" or other words of like purport are ineffective.

(4) The issuer may by inserting in the bill the words "shipper's weight, load and count" or other words of like purport indicate that the goods were loaded by the shipper; and if such statement be true the issuer shall not be liable for dam-

ages caused by the improper loading. But their omission does not imply liability for such damages.

(5) The shipper shall be deemed to have guaranteed to the issuer the accuracy at the time of shipment of the description, marks, labels, number, kind, quantity, condition and weight, as furnished by him; and the shipper shall indemnify the issuer against damage caused by inaccuracies in such particulars. The right of the issuer to such indemnity shall in no way limit his responsibility and liability under the contract of carriage to any person other than the shipper.

§7—302
Through Bills of Lading and Similar Documents

(1) The issuer of a through bill of lading or other document embodying an undertaking to be performed in part by persons acting as its agents or by connecting carriers is liable to anyone entitled to recover on the document for any breach by such other persons or by a connecting carrier of its obligation under the document but to the extent that the bill covers an undertaking to be performed overseas or in territory not contiguous to the continental United States or an undertaking including matters other than transportation this liability may be varied by agreement of the parties.

(2) Where goods covered by a through bill of lading or other document embodying an undertaking to be performed in part by persons other than the issuer are received by any such person, he is subject with respect to his own performance while the goods are in his possession to the obligation of the issuer. His obligation is discharged by delivery of the goods to another such person pursuant to the document and does not include liability for breach by any other such persons or by the issuer.

(3) The issuer of such through bill of lading or other document shall be entitled to recover from the connecting carrier or such other person in possession of the goods when the breach of the obligation under the document occurred, the amount it may be required to pay to anyone entitled to recover on the document therefor, as may be evidenced by any receipt, judgment, or transcript thereof, and the amount of any expense reasonably incurred by it in defending any action brought by anyone entitled to recover on the document therefor.

§7—303
Diversion; Reconsignment; Change of Instructions

(1) Unless the bill of lading otherwise provides, the carrier may deliver the goods to a person or destination other than that stated in the bill or may otherwise dispose of the goods on instructions from

  (a) the holder of a negotiable bill; or

  (b) the consignor on a non-negotiable bill notwithstanding contrary instructions from the consignee; or

  (c) the consignee on a non-negotiable bill in the absence of contrary instructions from the consignor, if the goods have arrived at the billed destination or if the consignee is in possession of the bill; or

(d) the consignee on a non-negotiable bill if he is entitled as against the consignor to dispose of them.

(2) Unless such instructions are noted on a negotiable bill of lading, a person to whom the bill is duly negotiated can hold the bailee according to the original terms.

§7—304
Bills of Lading in a Set

(1) Except where customary in overseas transportation, a bill of lading must not be issued in a set of parts. The issuer is liable for damages caused by violation of this subsection.

(2) Where a bill of lading is lawfully drawn in a set of parts, each of which is numbered and expressed to be valid only if the goods have not been delivered against any other part, the whole of the parts constitute one bill.

(3) Where a bill of lading is lawfully issued in a set of parts and different parts are negotiated to different persons, the title of the holder to whom the first due negotiation is made prevails as to both the document and the goods even though any later holder may have received the goods from the carrier in good faith and discharged the carrier's obligation by surrender of his part.

(4) Any person who negotiates or transfers a single part of a bill of lading drawn in a set is liable to holders of that part as if it were the whole set.

(5) The bailee is obliged to deliver in accordance with Part 4 of this Article against the first presented part of a bill of lading lawfully drawn in a set. Such delivery discharges the bailee's obligation on the whole bill.

§7—305
Destination Bills

(1) Instead of issuing a bill of lading to the consignor at the place of shipment a carrier may at the request of the consignor procure the bill to be issued at destination or at any other place designated in the request.

(2) Upon request of anyone entitled as against the carrier to control the goods while in transit and on surrender of any outstanding bill of lading or other receipt covering such goods, the issuer may procure a substitute bill to be issued at any place designated in the request.

§7—306
Altered Bills of Lading

An unauthorized alteration or filling in of a blank in a bill of lading leaves the bill enforceable according to its original tenor.

§7—307
Lien of Carrier

(1) A carrier has a lien on the goods covered by a bill of lading for charges subsequent to the date of its receipt of the goods for storage or transportation (including demurrage and terminal charges) and for expenses necessary for preservation of the goods incident to their transportation or reasonably incurred in their sale pursuant to law. But against a purchaser for value of a negotiable bill of lading a carrier's lien is limited to charges stated in the bill or the applicable tariffs, or if no charges are stated then to a reasonable charge.

(2) A lien for charges and expenses under subsection (1) on goods which the carrier was required by law to receive for transportation is effective against the consignor or any person entitled to the goods unless the carrier had notice that the consignor lacked authority to subject the goods to such charges and expenses. Any other lien under subsection (1) is effective against the consignor and any person who permitted the bailor to have control or possession of the goods unless the carrier had notice that the bailor lacked such authority.

(3) A carrier loses his lien on any goods which he voluntarily delivers or which he unjustifiably refuses to deliver.

§7—308
Enforcement of Carrier's Lien

(1) A carrier's lien may be enforced by public or private sale of the goods, in block or in parcels, at any time or place and on any terms which are commercially reasonable, after notifying all persons known to claim an interest in the goods. Such notification must include a statement of the amount due, the nature of the proposed sale and the time and place of any public sale. The fact that a better price could have been obtained by a sale at a different time or in a different method from that selected by the carrier is not of itself sufficient to establish that the sale was not made in a commercially reasonable manner. If the carrier either sells the goods in the usual manner in any recognized market therefor or if he sells at the price current in such market at the time of his sale or if he has otherwise sold in conformity with commercially reasonable practices among dealers in the type of goods sold he has sold in a commercially reasonable manner. A sale of more goods than apparently necessary to be offered to ensure satisfaction of the obligation is not commercially reasonable except in cases covered by the preceding sentence.

(2) Before any sale pursuant to this section any person claiming a right in the goods may pay the amount necessary to satisfy the lien and the reasonable expenses incurred under this section. In that event the goods must not be sold, but must be retained by the carrier subject to the terms of the bill and this Article.

(3) The carrier may buy at any public sale pursuant to this section.

(4) A purchaser in good faith of goods sold to enforce a carrier's lien takes the goods free of any rights of persons against whom the lien was valid, despite noncompliance by the carrier with the requirements of this section.

(5) The carrier may satisfy his lien from the proceeds of any sale pursuant to this section but must hold the balance, if any, for delivery on demand to any person to whom he would have been bound to deliver the goods.

(6) The rights provided by this section shall be in addition to all other rights allowed by law to a creditor against his debtor.

(7) A carrier's lien may be enforced in accordance with either subsection (1) or the procedure set forth in subsection (2) of Section 7—210.

(8) The carrier is liable for damages caused by failure to comply with the requirements for sale under this section and in case of willful violation is liable for conversion.

§7—309
Duty of Care; Contractual Limitation of Carrier's Liability

(1) A carrier who issues a bill of lading whether negotiable or non-negotiable must exercise the degree of care in relation to the goods which a reasonably careful man would exercise under like circumstances. This subsection does not repeal or change any law or rule of law which imposes liability upon a common carrier for damages not caused by its negligence.

(2) Damages may be limited by a provision that the carrier's liability shall not exceed a value stated in the document if the carrier's rates are dependent upon value and the consignor by the carrier's tariff is afforded an opportunity to declare a higher value or a value as lawfully provided in the tariff, or where no tariff is filed he is otherwise advised of such opportunity; but no such limitation is effective with respect to the carrier's liability for conversion to its own use.

(3) Reasonable provisions as to the time and manner of presenting claims and instituting actions based on the shipment may be included in a bill of lading or tariff.

Part 4
Warehouse Receipts and Bills of Lading: General Obligations

§7—401
Irregularities in Issue of Receipt or Bill or Conduct of Issuer

The obligations imposed by this Article on an issuer apply to a document of title regardless of the fact that

   (a) the document may not comply with the requirements of this Article or of any other law or regulation regarding its issue, form or content; or

   (b) the issuer may have violated laws regulating the conduct of his business; or

   (c) the goods covered by the document were owned by the bailee at the time the document was issued; or

   (d) the person issuing the document does not come within the defintion of warehouseman if it purports to be a warehouse receipt.

§7—402
Duplicate Receipt or Bill; Overissue

Neither a duplicate nor any other document of title purporting to cover goods already represented by an outstanding document of the same issuer confers any right in the goods, except as provided in the case of bills in a set, overissue of documents for fungible goods and substitutes for lost, stolen or destroyed documents. But the issuer is liable for damages caused by this overissue or failure to identify a duplicate document as such by conspicuous notation on its face.

§7—403
Obligation of Warehouseman or Carrier to Deliver; Excuse

(1) The bailee must deliver the goods to a person entitled under the document who complies with subsection (2) and (3), unless and to the extent that the bailee establishes any of the following:

   (a) delivery of the goods to a person whose receipt was rightful as against the claimant;

   (b) damage to or to delay, loss or destruction of the goods for which the bailee is not liable [, but the burden of establishing negligence in such cases is on the person entitled under the document];

Note: The brackets in (1) (b) indicate that State enactments may differ on this point without serious damage to the principle of uniformity.

   (c) previous sale or other disposition of the goods in lawful enforcement of a lien or on warehouseman's lawful termination of storage;

   (d) the exercise by a seller of his right to stop delivery pursuant to the provisions of the Article on Sales (Section 2—705);

   (e) a diversion, reconsignment or other disposition pursuant to the provisions of this Article (Section 7—303) or tariff regulating such right;

   (f) release, satisfaction or any other fact affording a personal defense against the claimant;

   (g) any other lawful excuse.

(2) A person claiming goods covered by a document of title must satisfy the bailee's lien where the bailee so requests or where the bailee is prohibited by law from delivering the goods until the charges are paid.

(3) Unless the person claiming is one against whom the document confers no right under Section 7—503(1), he must surrender for cancellation or notation of partial deliveries any outstanding negotiable document covering the goods, and the bailee must cancel the document or conspicuously note the partial delivery thereon or be liable to any person to whom the document is duly negotiated.

(4) "Person entitled under the document" means holder in the case of a negotiable document, or the person to whom delivery is to be made by the terms of or pursuant to written instructions under a non-negotiable document.

§7—404
No Liability for Good Faith Delivery Pursuant to Receipt or Bill

A bailee who in good faith including observance of reasonable commercial standards has received goods and delivered or otherwise disposed of them according to the terms of the document of title or pursuant to this Article is not liable therefor. This rule applies even though the person from whom he received the goods had no authority to procure the document or to dispose of the goods and even though the person to whom he delivered the goods had no authority to receive them.

Part 5

Warehouse Receipts and Bills of Lading: Negotiation and Transfer

§7—501
Form of Negotiation and Requirements of "Due Negotiation"

(1) A negotiable document of title running to the order of a named person is negotiated by his indorsement and delivery. After his indorsement in blank or to bearer any person can negotiate it by delivery alone.

(2)

    (a) A negotiable document of title is also negotiated by delivery alone when by its original terms it runs to bearer.

    (b) When a document running to the order of a named person is delivered to him the effect is the same as if the document had been negotiated.

(3) Negotiation of a negotiable document of title after it has been indorsed to a specified person requires indorsement by the special indorsee as well as delivery.

(4) A negotiable document of title is "duly negotiated" when it is negotiated in the manner stated in this section to a holder who purchases it in good faith without notice of any defense against or claim to it on the part of any person and for value, unless it is established that the negotiation is not in the regular course of business or financing or involves receiving the document in settlement or payment of a money obligation.

(5) Indorsement of a non-negotiable document neither makes it negotiable nor adds to the transferee's rights.

(6) The naming in a negotiable bill of a person to be notified of the arrival of the goods does not limit the negotiability of the bill nor constitute notice to a purchaser thereof of any interest of such person in the goods.

§7—502
Rights Acquired by Due Negotiation

(1) Subject to the following section and to the provisions of Section 7—205 on fungible goods, a holder to whom a negotiable document of title has been duly negotiated acquires thereby:

    (a) title to the document;

    (b) title to the goods;

    (c) all rights accruing under the law of agency or estoppel, including rights to goods delivered to the bailee after the document was issued; and

    (d) the direct obligation of the issuer to hold or deliver the goods according to the terms of the documemt free of any defense or claim by him except those arising under the terms of the document or under this Article. In the case of a delivery order the bailee's obligation accrues only upon acceptance and the obligation acquired by the holder is that the issuer and any indorser will procure the acceptance of the bailee.

(2) Subject to the following section, title and rights so acquired are not defeated by any stoppage of the goods represented by the document or by surrender of such goods by the bailee, and are not impaired even though the negotiation or any prior negotiation constituted a breach of duty or even though any person has been deprived of possession of the document by misrepresentation, fraud, accident, mistake, duress, loss, theft, or conversion, or even though a previous sale or other transfer of the goods or document has been made to a third person.

§7—503
Document of Title to Goods Defeated in Certain Cases

(1) A document of title confers no right in goods against a person who before issuance of the document had a legal interest or a perfected security interest in them and who neither

    (a) delivered or entrusted them or any document of title covering them to the bailor or his nominee with actual or apparent authority to ship, store or sell or with power to obtain delivery under this Article (Section 7—403) or with power of disposition under this Act (Sections 2—403 and 9—307) or other statute or rule of law; nor

    (b) acquiesced in the procurement by the bailor or his nominee of any document of title.

(2) Title to goods based upon an unaccepted delivery order is subject to the rights of anyone to whom a negotiable warehouse receipt or bill of lading covering the goods has been duly negotiated. Such a title may be defeated under the next section to the same extent as the rights of the issuer or a transferee from the issuer.

(3) Title to goods based upon a bill of lading issued to a freight forwarder is subject to the rights of anyone to whom a bill issued by the freight forwarder is duly negotiated; but delivery by the carrier in accordance with Part 4 of this Article pursuant to its own bill of lading discharges the carrier's obligation to deliver.

§7—504
Rights Acquired in the Absence of Due Negotiation; Effect of Diverson; Seller's Stoppage of Delivery

(1) A transferee of a document, whether negotiable or non-negotiable, to whom the document has been delivered but not duly negotiated, acquires the title and rights which his transferor had or had actual authority to convey.

(2) In the case of a non-negotiable document, until but not after the bailee receives notification of the transfer, the rights of the transferee may be defeated

    (a) by those creditors of the transferor who could treat the sale as void under Section 2—402; or

    (b) by a buyer from the transferor in ordinary course of business if the bailee has delivered the goods to the buyer or received notification of his rights; or

(c) as against the bailee by good faith dealings of the bailee with the transferor.

(3) A diversion or other change of shipping instructions by the consignor in a non-negotiable bill of lading which causes the bailee not to deliver to the consignee defeats the consignee's title to the goods if they have been delivered to a buyer in ordinary course of business and in any event defeats the consignee's rights against the bailee.

(4) Delivery pursuant to a non-negotiable document may be stopped by a seller under Section 2—705, and subject to the requirement of due notification there provided. A bailee honoring the seller's instructions is entitled to be indemnified by the seller against any resulting loss or expense.

§7—505
Indorser Not a Guarantor for Other Parties

The indorsement of a document of title issued by a bailee does not make the indorser liable for any default by the bailee or by previous indorsers.

§7—506
Delivery Without Indorsement: Right to Compel Indorsement

The transferee of a negotiable document of title has a specifically enforceable right to have his transferor supply any necessary indorsement but the transfer becomes a negotiation only as of the time the indorsement is supplied.

§7—507
Warranties on Negotiation or Transfer of Receipt or Bill

Where a person negotiates or transfers a document of title for value otherwise than as a mere intermediary under the next following section, then unless otherwise agreed he warrants to his immediate purchaser only in addition to any warranty made in selling the goods

(a) that the document is genuine; and

(b) that he has no knowledge of any fact which would impair its validity or worth; and

(c) that his negotiation or transfer is rightful and fully effective with respect to the title to the document and the goods it represents.

§7—508
Warranties of Collecting Bank as to Documents

A collecting bank or other intermediary known to be entrusted with documents on behalf of another or with collection of a draft or other claim against delivery of documents warrants by such delivery of the documents only its own good faith and authority. This rule applies even though the intermediary has purchased or made advances against the claim or draft to be collected.

§7—509
Receipt or Bill: When Adequate Compliance With Commercial Contract

The question whether a document is adequate to fulfill the obligations of a contract for sale or the conditions of a credit is governed by the Articles on Sales (Article 2) and on Letters of Credit (Article 5).

Part 6
Warehouse Receipts and Bills of Lading: Miscellaneous Provisions

§7—601
Lost and Missing Documents

(1) If a document has been lost, stolen or destroyed, a court may order delivery of the goods or issuance of a substitute document and the bailee may without liability to any person comply with such order. If the document was negotiable the claimant must post security approved by the court to indemnify any person who may suffer loss as a result of non-surrender of the document. If the document was not negotiable, such security may be required at the discretion of the court. The court may also in its discretion order payment of the bailee's reasonable costs and counsel fees.

(2) A bailee who without court order delivers goods to a person claiming under a missing negotiable document is liable to any person injured thereby, and if the delivery is not in good faith becomes liable for conversion. Delivery in good faith is not conversion if made in accordance with a filed classification or tariff or, where no classification or tariff is filed, if the claimant posts security with the bailee in an amount at least double the value of the goods at the time of posting to indemnify any person injured by the delivery who files a notice of claim within one year after the delivery.

§7—602
Attachment of Goods Covered by a Negotiable Document

Except where the document was originally issued upon delivery of the goods by a person who had no power to dispose of them, no lien attaches by virtue of any judicial process to goods in the possession of a bailee for which a negotiable document of title is outstanding unless the document be first surrendered to the bailee or its negotiation enjoined, and the bailee shall not be compelled to deliver the goods pursuant to process until the document is surrendered to him or impounded by the court. One who purchases the document for value without notice of the process or injunction takes free of the lien imposed by judicial process.

§7—603
Conflicting Claims; Interpleader

If more than one person claims title or possession of the goods, the bailee is excused from delivery until he has had a reasonable time to ascertain the validity of the adverse claims or to bring an action to compel all claimants to interplead and may compel such interpleader, either in defending an action for non-delivery of the goods, or by original action, whichever is appropriate.

Article 8
Investment Securities

Part 1
Short Title and General Matters

§8—101
Short Title

This Article shall be known and may be cited as Uniform Commercial Code—Investment Securities.

§8—102
Definitions and Index of Definitions

(1) In this Article unless the context otherwise requires

  (a) A "security" is an instrument which

    (i) is issued in bearer or registered form; and

    (ii) is of a type commonly dealt in upon securities exchanges or markets or commonly recognized in any area in which it is issued or dealt in as a medium for investment; and

    (iii) is either one of a class or series or by its terms is divisible into a class or series of instruments; and

    (iv) evidences a share, participation or other interest in property or in an enterprise or evidences an obligation of the issuer.

  (b) A writing which is a security is governed by this Article and not by Uniform Commercial Code—Commercial Paper even though it also meets the requirements of that Article. This Article does not apply to money.

  (c) A security is in "registered form" when it specifies a person entitled to the security or to the rights it evidences and when its transfer may be registered upon books maintained for that purpose by or on behalf of an issuer or the security so states.

  (d) A security is in "bearer form" when it runs to bearer according to its terms and not by reason of any indorsement.

(2) A "subsequent purchaser" is a person who takes other than by original issue.

(3) A "clearing corporation" is a corporation all of the capital stock of which is held by or for a national securities exchange or association registered under a statute of the United States such as the Securities Exchange Act of 1934.

(4) A "custodian bank" is any bank or trust company which is supervised and examined by state or federal authority having supervision over banks and which is acting as custodian for a clearing corporation.

(5) Other definitions applying to this Article or to specified Parts thereof and the sections in which they appear are:

"Adverse claim".	Section 8—301.
"Bona fide purchaser".	Section 8—302.
"Broker".	Section 8—303.
"Guarantee of the signature".	Section 8—402.
"Intermediary Bank".	Section 4—105.
"Issuer".	Section 8—201.
"Overissue".	Section 8—104.

(6) In addition Article 1 contains general definitions and principles of construction and interpretation applicable throughout this Article.

§8—103
Issuer's Lien

A lien upon a security in favor of an issuer thereof is valid against a purchaser only if the right of the issuer to such lien is noted conspicuously on the security.

§8—104
Effect of Overissue; "Overissue"

(1) The provisions of this Article which validate a security or compel its issue or reissue do not apply to the extent that validation, issue or reissue would result in overissue; but

  (a) if an identical security which does not constitute an overissue is reasonably available for purchase, the person entitled to issue or validation may compel the issuer to purchase and deliver such a security to him against surrender of the security, if any, which he holds; or

  (b) if a security is not so available for purchase, the person entitled to issue or validation may recover from the issuer the price he or the last purchaser for value paid for it with interest from the date of his demand.

(2) "Overissue" means the issue of securities in excess of the amount which the issuer has corporate power to issue.

§8—105
Securities Negotiable; Presumptions

(1) Securities governed by this Article are negotiable instruments.

(2) In any action on a security

  (a) unless specifically denied in the pleadings, each signature on the security or in a necessary indorsement is admitted;

  (b) when the effectiveness of a signature is put in issue the burden of establishing it is on the party claiming under the signature but the signature is presumed to be genuine or authorized;

  (c) when signatures are admitted or established production of the instrument entitles a holder to recover on it unless the defendant establishes a defense or a defect going to the validity of the security; and

  (d) after it is shown that a defense or defect exists the plaintiff has the burden of establishing that he or some person under whom he claims is a person against whom the defense or defect is ineffective (Section 8—202).

§8—106
Applicability

The validity of a security and the rights and duties of the issuer with respect to registration of transfer are governed by the law (including the conflict of laws rules) of the jurisdiction of organization of the issuer.

§8—107
Securities Deliverable; Action for Price

(1) Unless otherwise agreed and subject to any applicable law or regulation respecting short sales, a person obligated to deliver securities may deliver any security of the specified issue in bearer form or registered in the name of the transferee or indorsed to him or in blank.

(2) When the buyer fails to pay the price as it comes due under a contract of sale the seller may recover the price

    (a) of securities accepted by the buyer; and

    (b) of other securities if efforts at their resale would be unduly burdensome or if there is no readily available market for their resale.

Part 2
Issue—Issuer

§8—201
"Issuer"

(1) With respect to obligations on or defenses to a security "issuer" includes a person who

    (a) places or authorizes the placing of his name on a security (otherwise than as authenticating trustee, registrar, transfer agent or the like) to evidence that it represents a share, participation or other interest in his property or in an enterprise or to evidence his duty to perform an obligation evidenced by the security; or

    (b) directly or indirectly creates fractional interests in his rights or property which fractional interests are evidenced by securities; or

    (c) becomes responsible for or in place of any other person described as an issuer in this section.

(2) With respect to obligations on or defenses to a security a guarantor is an issuer to the extent of his guaranty whether or not his obligation is noted on the security.

(3) With respect to registration of transfer (Part 4 of this Article) "issuer" means a person on whose behalf transfer books are maintained.

§8—202
Issuer's Responsibility and Defenses; Notice of Defect or Defense

(1) Even against a purchaser for value and without notice, the terms of a security include those stated on the security and those made part of the security by reference to another instrument, indenture or document or to a constitution, statute, ordinance, rule, regulation, order or the like to the extent that the terms so referred to do not conflict with the stated terms. Such a reference does not of itself charge a purchaser for value with notice of a defect going to the validity of the security even though the security expressly states that a person accepting it admits such notice.

(2)

    (a) A security other than one issued by a government or governmental agency or unit even though issued with a defect going to its validity is valid in the hands of a purchaser for value and without notice of the particular defect unless the defect involves a violation of constitutional provisions in which case the security is valid in the hands of a subsequent purchaser for value and without notice of the defect.

    (b) The rule of subparagraph (a) applies to an issuer which is a government or governmental agency or unit only if either there has been substantial compliance with the legal requirements governing the issue or the issuer has received a substantial consideration for the issue as a whole or for the particular security and a stated purpose of the issue is one for which the issuer has power to borrow money or issue the security.

(3) Except as otherwise provided in the case of certain unauthorized signatures on issue (Section 8—205), lack of genuineness of a security is a complete defense even against a purchaser for value and without notice.

(4) All other defenses of the issuer including nondelivery and conditional delivery of the security are ineffective against a purchaser for value who has taken without notice of the particular defense.

(5) Nothing in this section shall be construed to affect the right of a party to a "when, as and if issued" or a "when distributed" contract to cancel the contract in the event of a material change in the character of the security which is the subject of the contract or in the plan or arrangement pursuant to which such security is to be issued or distributed.

§8—203
Staleness as Notice of Defects or Defenses

(1) After an act or event which creates a right to immediate performance of the principal obligation evidenced by the security or which sets a date on or after which the security is to be presented or surrendered for redemption or exchange, a purchaser is charged with notice of any defect in its issue or defense of the issuer

    (a) if the act or event is one requiring the payment of money or the delivery of securities or both on presentation or surrender of the security and such funds or securities are available on the date set for payment or exchange and he takes the security more than one year after that date; and

    (b) if the act or event is not covered by paragraph (a) and he takes the security more than two years after the date set for surrender or presentation or the date on which such performance became due.

(2) A call which has been revoked is not within subsection (1).

§8—204
Effect of Issuer's Restrictions on Transfer

Unless noted conspicuously on the security a restriction on transfer imposed by the issuer even though otherwise lawful is ineffective except against a person with actual knowledge of it.

§8—205
Effect of Unauthorized Signature on Issue

An unauthorized signature placed on a security prior to or in the course of issue is ineffective except that the signature is effective in favor of a purchaser for value and without notice of the lack of authority if the signing has been done by

(a) an authenticating trustee, registrar, transfer agent or other person entrusted by the issuer with the signing of the security or of similar securities or their immediate preparation for signing; or

(b) an employee of the issuer or of any of the foregoing entrusted with responsible handling of the security.

§8—206
Completion or Alteration of Instrument

(1) Where a security contains the signatures necessary to its issue or transfer but is incomplete in any other respect

(a) any person may complete it by filling in the blanks as authorized; and

(b) even though the blanks are incorrectly filled in, the security as completed is enforceable by a purchaser who took it for value and without notice of such incorrectness.

(2) A complete security which has been improperly altered even though fraudulently remains enforceable but only according to its original terms.

§8—207
Rights of Issuer With Respect to Registered Owners

(1) Prior to due presentment for registration of transfer of a security in registered form the issuer or indenture trustee may treat the registered owner as the person exclusively entitled to vote, to receive notifications and otherwise to exercise all the rights and powers of an owner.

(2) Nothing in this Article shall be construed to affect the liability of the registered owner of a security for calls, assessments or the like.

§8—208
Effect of Signature of Authenticating Trustee, Registrar or Transfer Agent

(1) A person placing his signature upon a security as authenticating trustee, registrar, transfer agent or the like warrants

to a purchaser for value without notice of the particular defect that

(a) the security is genuine; and

(b) his own participation in the issue of the security is within his capacity and within the scope of the authorization received by him from the issuer; and

(c) he has reasonable grounds to believe that the security is in the form and within the amount the issuer is authorized to issue.

(2) Unless otherwise agreed, a person by so placing his signature does not assume responsibility for the validity of the security in other respects.

Part 3
Purchase

§8—301
Rights Acquired by Purchaser; "Adverse Claim"; Title Acquired by Bona Fide Purchaser

(1) Upon delivery of a security the purchaser acquires the rights in the security which his transferor had or had actual authority to convey except that a purchaser who has himself been a party to any fraud or illegality affecting the security or who as a prior holder had notice of an adverse claim cannot improve his position by taking from a later bona fide purchaser. "Adverse claim" includes a claim that a transfer was or would be wrongful or that a particular adverse person is the owner of or has an interest in the security.

(2) A bona fide purchaser in addition to acquiring the rights of a purchaser also acquires the security free of any adverse claim.

(3) A purchaser of a limited interest acquires rights only to the extent of the interest purchased.

§8—302
"Bona Fide Purchaser"

A "bona fide purchaser" is a purchaser for value in good faith and without notice of any adverse claim who takes delivery of a security in bearer form or of one in registered form issued to him or indorsed to him or in blank.

§8—303
"Broker"

"Broker" means a person engaged for all or part of his time in the business of buying and selling securities, who in the transaction concerned acts for, or buys a security from or sells a security to a customer. Nothing in this Article determines the capacity in which a person acts for purposes of any other statute or rule to which such person is subject.

§8—304
Notice to Purchaser of Adverse Claims

(1) A purchaser (including a broker for the seller or buyer but excluding an intermediary bank) of a security is charged with notice of adverse claims if

(a) the security whether in bearer or registered form has been indorsed "for collection" or "for surrender" or for some other purpose not involving transfer; or

(b) the security is in bearer form and has on it an unambiguous statement that it is the property of a person other than the transferor. The mere writing of a name on a security is not such a statement.

(2) The fact that the purchaser (including a broker for the seller or buyer) has notice that the security is held for a third person or is registered in the name of or indorsed by a fiduciary does not create a duty of inquiry into the rightfulness of the transfer or constitute notice of adverse claims. If, however, the purchaser (excluding an intermediary bank) has knowledge that the proceeds are being used or that the transaction is for the individual benefit of the fiduciary or otherwise in breach of duty, the purchaser is charged with notice of adverse claims.

§8—305
Staleness as Notice of Adverse Claims

An act or event which creates a right to immediate performance of the principal obligation evidenced by the security or which sets a date on or after which the security is to be presented or surrendered for redemption or exchange does not of itself constitute any notice of adverse claims except in the case of a purchase

(a) after one year from any date set for such presentment or surrender for redemption or exchange; or

(b) after six months from any date set for payment of money against presentation or surrender of the security if funds are available for payment on that date.

§8—306
Warranties on Presentment and Transfer

(1) A person who presents a security for registration of transfer or for payment or exchange warrants to the issuer that he is entitled to the registration, payment or exchange. But a purchaser for value without notice of adverse claims who receives a new, reissued or re-registered security on registration of transfer warrants only that he has no knowledge of any unauthorized signature (Section 8—311) in a necessary indorsement.

(2) A person by transferring a security to a purchaser for value warrants only that

(a) his transfer is effective and rightful; and

(b) the security is genuine and has not been materially altered; and

(c) he knows no fact which might impair the validity of the security.

(3) Where a security is delivered by an intermediary known to be entrusted with delivery of the security on behalf of another or with collection of a draft or other claim against such delivery, the intermediary by such delivery warrants only his own good faith and authority even though he has purchased or made advances against the claim to be collected against the delivery.

(4) A pledgee or other holder for security who redelivers the security received, or after payment and on order of the debtor delivers that security to a third person makes only the warranties of an intermediary under subsection (3).

(5) A broker gives to his customer and to the issuer and a purchaser the warranties provided in this section and has the rights and privileges of a purchaser under this section. The warranties of and in favor of the broker acting as an agent are in addition to applicable warranties given by and in favor of his customer.

§8—307
Effect of Delivery Without Indorsement; Right to Compel Indorsement

Where a security in registered form has been delivered to a purchaser without a necessary indorsement he may become a bona fide purchaser only as of the time the indorsement is supplied, but against the transferor the transfer is complete upon delivery and the purchaser has a specifically enforceable right to have any necessary indorsement supplied.

§8—308
Indorsement, How Made; Special Indorsement; Indorser Not a Guarantor; Partial Assignment

(1) An indorsement of a security in registered form is made when an appropriate person signs on it or on a separate document an assignment or transfer of the security or a power to assign or transfer it or when the signature of such person is written without more upon the back of the security.

(2) An indorsement may be in blank or special. An indorsement in blank includes an indorsement to bearer. A special indorsement specifies the person to whom the security is to be transferred, or who has power to transfer it. A holder may convert a blank indorsement into a special indorsement.

(3) "An appropriate person" in subsection (1) means

(a) the person specified by the security or by special indorsement to be entitled to the security; or

(b) where the person so specified is described as a fiduciary but is no longer serving in the described capacity, —either that person or his successor; or

(c) where the security or indorsement so specifies more than one person as fiduciaries and one or more are no longer serving in the described capacity,—the remaining fiduciary or fiduciaries, whether or not a successor has been appointed or qualified; or

(d) where the person so specified is an individual and is without capacity to act by virtue of death, incompetence, infancy or otherwise,—his executor, administrator, guardian or like fiduciary; or

(e) where the security or indorsement so specifies more than one person as tenants by the entirety or with right of survivorship and by reason of death all cannot sign,—the survivor or survivors; or

(f) a person having power to sign under applicable law or controlling instrument; or

(g) to the extent that any of the foregoing persons may act through an agent,—his authorized agent.

(4) Unless otherwise agreed the indorser by his indorsement assumes no obligation that the security will be honored by the issuer.

(5) An indorsement purporting to be only of part of a security representing units intended by the issuer to be separately transferable is effective to the extent of the indorsement.

(6) Whether the person signing is appropriate is determined as of the date of signing and an indorsement by such a person does not become unauthorized for the purposes of this Article by virtue of any subsequent change of circumstances.

(7) Failure of a fiduciary to comply with a controlling instrument or with the law of the state having jurisdiction of the fiduciary relationship, including any law requiring the fiduciary to obtain court approval of the transfer, does not render his indorsement unauthorized for the purposes of this Article.

§8—309
Effect of Indorsement Without Delivery

An indorsement of a security whether special or in blank does not constitute a transfer until delivery of the security on which it appears or if the indorsement is on a separate document until delivery of both the document and the security.

§8—310
Indorsement of Security in Bearer Form

An indorsement of a security in bearer form may give notice of adverse claims (Section 8—304) but does not otherwise affect any right to registration the holder may possess.

§8—311
Effect of Unauthorized Indorsement

Unless the owner has ratified an unauthorized indorsement or is otherwise precluded from asserting its ineffectiveness

(a) he may assert its ineffectiveness against the issuer or any purchaser other than a purchaser for value and without notice of adverse claims who has in good faith received a new, reissued or re-registered security on registration of transfer; and

(b) an issuer who registers the transfer of a security upon the unauthorized indorsement is subject to liability for improper registration (Section 8—404).

§8—312
Effect of Guaranteeing Signature or Indorsement

(1) Any person guaranteeing a signature of an indorser of a security warrants that at the time of signing

(a) the signature was genuine; and

(b) the signer was an appropriate person to indorse (Section 8—308); and

(c) the signer had legal capacity to sign.

But the guarantor does not otherwise warrant the rightfulness of the particular transfer.

(2) Any person may guarantee an indorsement of a security and by so doing warrants not only the signature (subsection 1) but also the rightfulness of the particular transfer in all respects. But no issuer may require a guarantee of indorsement as a condition to registration of transfer.

(3) The foregoing warranties are made to any person taking or dealing with the security in reliance on the guarantee and the guarantor is liable to such person for any loss resulting from breach of the warranties.

§8—313
When Delivery to the Purchaser Occurs; Purchaser's Broker as Holder

(1) Delivery to a purchaser occurs when

(a) he or a person designated by him acquires possession of a security; or

(b) his broker acquires possession of a security specially indorsed to or issued in the name of the purchaser; or

(c) his broker sends him confirmation of the purchase and also by book entry or otherwise identifies a specific security in the broker's possession as belonging to the purchaser; or

(d) with respect to an identified security to be delivered while still in the possession of a third person when that person acknowledges that he holds for the purchaser; or

(e) appropriate entries on the books of a clearing corporation are made under Section 8—320.

(2) The purchaser is the owner of a security held for him by his broker, but is not the holder except as specified in subparagraphs (b), (c) and (e) of subsection (1). Where a security is part of a fungible bulk the purchaser is the owner of a proportionate property interest in the fungible bulk.

(3) Notice of an adverse claim received by the broker or by the purchaser after the broker takes delivery as a holder for value is not effective either as to the broker or as to the purchaser. However, as between the broker and the purchaser the purchaser may demand delivery of an equivalent security as to which no notice of an adverse claim has been received.

§8—314
Duty to Deliver, When Completed

(1) Unless otherwise agreed where a sale of a security is made on an exchange or otherwise through brokers

(a) the selling customer fulfills his duty to deliver when he places such a security in the possession of the selling broker or of a person designated by the broker or if requested causes an acknowledgment to be made to the selling broker that it is held for him; and

(b) the selling broker including a correspondent broker acting for a selling customer fulfills his duty to deliver by placing the security or a like security in the possession of the buying broker or a person designated by him or by effecting clearance of the sale in accordance with the rules of the exchange on which the transaction took place.

(2) Except as otherwise provided in this section and unless otherwise agreed, a transferor's duty to deliver a security under a contract of purchase is not fulfilled until he places the security in form to be negotiated by the purchaser in the possession of the purchaser or of a person designated by him or at the purchaser's request causes an acknowledgment to be made to the purchaser that it is held for him. Unless made on an exchange a sale to a broker purchasing for his own account is within this subsection and not within subsection (1).

§8—315
Action Against Purchaser Based Upon Wrongful Transfer

(1) Any person against whom the transfer of a security is wrongful for any reason, including his incapacity, may against anyone except a bona fide purchaser reclaim possession of the security or obtain possession of any new security evidencing all or part of the same rights or have damages.

(2) If the transfer is wrongful because of an unauthorized indorsement, the owner may also reclaim or obtain possession of the security or new security even from a bona fide purchaser if the ineffectiveness of the purported indorsement can be asserted against him under the provisions of this Article on unauthorized indorsements (Section 8—311).

(3) The right to obtain or reclaim possession of a security may be specifically enforced and its transfer enjoined and the security impounded pending the litigation.

§8—316
Purchaser's Right to Requisites for Registration of Transfer on Books

Unless otherwise agreed the transferor must on due demand supply his purchaser with any proof of his authority to transfer or with any other requisite which may be necessary to obtain registration of the transfer of the security but if the transfer is not for value a transferor need not do so unless the purchaser furnishes the necessary expenses. Failure to comply with a demand made within a reasonable time gives the purchaser the right to reject or rescind the transfer.

§8—317
Attachment or Levy Upon Security

(1) No attachment or levy upon a security or any share or other interest evidenced thereby which is outstanding shall be valid until the security is actually seized by the officer making the attachment or levy but a security which has been surrendered to the issuer may be attached or levied upon at the source.

(2) A creditor whose debtor is the owner of a security shall be entitled to such aid from courts of appropriate jurisdiction, by injunction or otherwise, in reaching such security or in satisfying the claim by means thereof as is allowed at law or in equity in regard to property which cannot readily be attached or levied upon by ordinary legal process.

§8—318
No Conversion by Good Faith Delivery

An agent or bailee who in good faith (including observance of reasonable commercial standards if he is in the business of buying, selling or otherwise dealing with securities) has received securities and sold, pledged or delivered them according to the instructions of his principal is not liable for conversion or for participation in breach of fiduciary duty although the principal had no right to dispose of them.

§8—319
Statute of Frauds

A contract for the sale of securities is not enforceable by way of action or defense unless

(a) there is some writing signed by the party against whom enforcement is sought or by his authorized agent or broker sufficient to indicate that a contract has been made for sale of a stated quantity of described securities at a defined or stated price; or

(b) delivery of the security has been accepted or payment has been made but the contract is enforceable under this provision only to the extent of such delivery or payment; or

(c) within a reasonable time a writing in confirmation of the sale or purchase and sufficient against the sender under paragraph (a) has been received by the party against whom enforcement is sought and he has failed to send written objection to its contents within ten days after its receipt; or

(d) the party against whom enforcement is sought admits in his pleading, testimony or otherwise in court that a contract was made for sale of a stated quantity of described securities at a defined or stated price.

§8—320
Transfer or Pledge Within a Central Depository System

(1) If a security

(a) is in the custody of a clearing corporation or of a custodian bank or a nominee of either subject to the instructions of the clearing corporation; and

(b) is in bearer form or indorsed in blank by an appropriate person or registered in the name of the clearing corporation or custodian bank or a nominee of either; and

(c) is shown on the account of a transferor or pledgor on the books of the clearing corporation;

then, in addition to other methods, a transfer or pledge of the security or any interest therein may be effected by the making of appropriate entries on the books of the clearing corporation reducing the account of the transferor or pledgor and increasing the account of the transferee or pledgee by the amount of the obligation or the number of shares or rights transferred or pledged.

(2) Under this section entries may be with respect to like securities or interests therein as a part of a fungible bulk and may refer merely to a quantity of a particular security without reference to the name of the registered owner, certificate or bond number or the like and, in appropriate cases, may be on a net basis taking into account other transfers or pledges of the same security.

(3) A transfer or pledge under this section has the effect of a delivery of a security in bearer form or duly indorsed in blank

(Section 8—301) representing the amount of the obligation or the number of shares or rights transferred or pledged. If a pledge or the creation of a security interest is intended, the making of entries has the effect of a taking of delivery by the pledgee or a secured party (Sections 9—304 and 9—305). A transferee or pledgee under this section is a holder.

(4) A transfer or pledge under this section does not constitute a registration of transfer under Part 4 of this Article.

(5) That entries made on the books of the clearing corporation as provided in subsection (1) are not appropriate does not affect the validity or effect of the entries nor the liabilities or oigations of the clearing corporation to any person adversely affected thereby.

Part 4

Registration

§8—401
Duty of Issuer to Register Transfer

(1) Where a security in registered form is presented to the issuer with a request to register transfer, the issuer is under a duty to register the transfer as requested if

- (a) the security is indorsed by the appropriate person or persons (Section 8—308); and
- (b) reasonable assurance is given that those indorsements are genuine and effective (Section 8—402); and
- (c) the issuer has no duty to inquire into adverse claims or has discharged any such duty (Section 8—403); and
- (d) any applicable law relating to the collection of taxes has been complied with; and
- (e) the transfer is in fact rightful or is to a bona fide purchaser.

(2) Where an issuer is under a duty to register a transfer of a security the issuer is also liable to the person presenting it for registration or his principal for loss resulting from any unreasonable delay in registration or from failure or refusal to register the transfer.

§8—402
Assurance That Indorsements Are Effective

(1) The issuer may require the following assurance that each necessary indorsement (Section 8—308) is genuine and effective

- (a) in all cases, a guarantee of the signature (subsection (1) of Section 8—312) of the person indorsing; and
- (b) where the indorsement is by an agent, appropriate assurance of authority to sign;
- (c) where the indorsement is by a fiduciary, appropriate evidence of appointment or incumbency;
- (d) where there is more than one fiduciary, reasonable assurance that all who are required to sign have done so;
- (e) where the indorsement is by a person not covered by any of the foregoing, assurance appropriate to the case corresponding as nearly as may be to the foregoing.

(2) A "guarantee of the signature" in subsection (1) means a guarantee signed by or on behalf of a person reasonably believed by the issuer to be responsible. The issuer may adopt standards with respect to responsibility provided such standards are not manifestly unreasonable.

(3) "Appropriate evidence of appointment or incumbency" in subsection (1) means

- (a) in the case of a fiduciary appointed or qualified by a court, a certificate issued by or under the direction or supervision of that court or an officer thereof and dated within sixty days before the date of presentation for transfer; or
- (b) in any other case, a copy of a document showing the appointment or a certificate issued by or on behalf of a person reasonably believed by the issuer to be responsible or, in the absence of such a document or certificate, other evidence reasonably deemed by the issuer to be appropriate. The issuer may adopt standards with respect to such evidence provided such standards are not manifestly unreasonable. The issuer is not charged with notice of the contents of any document obtained pursuant to this paragraph (b) except to the extent that the contents relate directly to the appointment or incumbency.

(4) The issuer may elect to require reasonable assurance beyond that specified in this section but if it does so and for a purpose other than that specified in subsection 3(b) both requires and obtains a copy of a will, trust, indenture, articles of co-partnership, by-laws or other controlling instrument it is charged with notice of all matters contained therein affecting the transfer.

§8—403
Limited Duty of Inquiry

(1) An issuer to whom a security is presented for registration is under a duty to inquire into adverse claims if

- (a) a written notification of an adverse claim is received at a time and in a manner which affords the issuer a reasonable opportunity to act on it prior to the issuance of a new, reissued or re-registered security and the notification identifies the claimant, the registered owner and the issue of which the security is a part and provides an address for communications directed to the claimant; or
- (b) the issuer is charged with notice of an adverse claim from a controlling instrument which it has elected to require under subsection (4) of Section 8—402.

(2) The issuer may discharge any duty of inquiry by any reasonable means, including notifying an adverse claimant by registered or certified mail at the address furnished by him or if there be no such address at his residence or regular place of business that the security has been presented for registration of transfer by a named person, and that the transfer will be registered unless within thirty days from the date of mailing the notification, either

- (a) an appropriate restraining order, injunction or other process issues from a court of competent jurisdiction; or

(b) an indemnity bond sufficient in the issuer's judgment to protect the issuer and any transfer agent, registrar or other agent of the issuer involved, from any loss which it or they may suffer by complying with the adverse claim is filed with the issuer.

(3) Unless an issuer is charged with notice of an adverse claim from a controlling instrument which it has elected to require under subsection (4) of Section 8—402 or receives notification of an adverse claim under subsection (1) of this section, where a security presented for registration is indorsed by the appropriate person or persons the issuer is under no duty to inquire into adverse claims. In particular

(a) an issuer registering a security in the name of a person who is a fiduciary or who is described as a fiduciary is not bound to inquire into the existence, extent, or correct description of the fiduciary relationship and thereafter the issuer may assume without inquiry that the newly registered owner continues to be the fiduciary until the issuer receives written notice that the fiduciary is no longer acting as such with respect to the particular security;

(b) an issuer registering transfer on an indorsement by a fiduciary is not bound to inquire whether the transfer is made in compliance with a controlling instrument or with the law of the state having jurisdiction of the fiduciary relationship, including any law requiring the fiduciary to obtain court approval of the transfer; and

(c) the issuer is not charged with notice of the contents of any court record or file or other recorded or unrecorded document even though the document is in its possession and even though the transfer is made on the indorsement of a fiduciary to the fiduciary himself or to his nominee.

§8—404
Liability and Non-Liability for Registration

(1) Except as otherwise provided in any law relating to the collection of taxes, the issuer is not liable to the owner or any other person suffering loss as a result of the registration of a transfer of a security if

(a) there were on or with the security the necessary indorsements (Section 8—308); and

(b) the issuer had no duty to inquire into adverse claims or has discharged any such duty (Section 8—403).

(2) Where an issuer has registered a transfer of a security to a person not entitled to it the issuer on demand must deliver a like security to the true owner unless

(a) the registration was pursuant to subsection (1); or

(b) the owner is precluded from asserting any claim for registering the transfer under subsection (1) of the following section; or

(c) such delivery would result in overissue, in which case the issuer's liability is governed by Section 8—104.

§8—405
Lost, Destroyed and Stolen Securities

(1) Where a security has been lost, apparently destroyed or

wrongfully taken and the owner fails to notify the issuer of that fact within a reasonable time after he has notice of it and the issuer registers a transfer of the security before receiving such a notification, the owner is precluded from asserting against the issuer any claim for registering the transfer under the preceding section or any claim to a new security under this section.

(2) Where the owner of a security claims that the security has been lost, destroyed or wrongfully taken, the issuer must issue a new security in place of the original security if the owner

(a) so requests before the issuer has notice that the security has been acquired by a bona fide purchaser; and

(b) files with the issuer a sufficient indemnity bond; and

(c) satisfies any other reasonable requirements imposed by the issuer.

(3) If, after the issue of the new security, a bona fide purchaser of the original security presents it for registration of transfer, the issuer must register the transfer unless registration would result in overissue, in which event the issuer's liability is governed by Section 8—104. In addition to any rights on the indemnity bond, the issuer may recover the new security from the person to whom it was issued or any person taking under him except a bona fide purchaser.

§8—406
Duty of Authenticating Trustee, Transfer Agent or Registrar

(1) Where a person acts as authenticating trustee, transfer agent, registrar, or other agent for an issuer in the registration of transfers of its securities or in the issue of new securities or in the cancellation of surrendered securities

(a) he is under a duty to the issuer to exercise good faith and due diligence in performing his functions; and

(b) he has with regard to the particular functions he performs the same obligation to the holder or owner of the security and has the same rights and privileges as the issuer has in regard to those functions.

(2) Notice to an authenticating trustee, transfer agent, registrar or other such agent is notice to the issuer with respect to the functions performed by the agent.

Article 9
Secured Transactions; Sales of Accounts and Chattel Paper

Part 1
Short Title, Applicability and Definitions

§9—101
Short Title
This Article shall be known and may be cited as Uniform Commercial Code—Secured Transactions.

§9—102
Policy and Subject Matter of Article

(1) Except as otherwise provided in Section 9—104 on excluded transactions, this Article applies

(a) to any transaction (regardless of its form) which is intended to create a security interest in personal property or fixtures including goods, documents, instruments, general intangibles, chattel paper or accounts; and also

(b) to any sale of accounts or chattel paper.

(2) This Article applies to security interests created by contract including pledge, assignment, chattel mortgage, chattel trust, trust deed, factor's lien, equipment trust, conditional sale, trust receipt, other lien or title retention contract and lease or consignment intended as security. This Article does not apply to statutory liens except as provided in Section 9—310.

(3) The application of this Article to a security interest in a secured obligation is not affected by the fact that the obligation is itself secured by a transaction or interest to which this Article does not apply. Amended in 1972.

Note: The adoption of this Article should be accompanied by the repeal of existing statutes dealing with conditional sales, trust receipts, factor's liens where the factor is given a non-possessory lien, chattel mortgages, crop mortgages, mortgages on railroad equipment, assignment of accounts and generally statutes regulating security interests in personal property.

Where the state has a retail installment selling act or small loan act, that legislation should be carefully examined to determine what changes in those acts are needed to conform them to this Article. This Article primarily sets out rules defining rights of a secured party against persons dealing with the debtor; it does not prescribe regulations and controls which may be necessary to curb abuses arising in the small loan business or in the financing of consumer purchases on credit. Accordingly there is no intention to repeal existing regulatory acts in those fields by enactment or re-enactment of Article 9. See Section 9—203(4) and the Note thereto.

§9—103
Perfection of Security Interests in Multiple State Transactions

(1) Documents, instruments and ordinary goods.

(a) This subsection applies to documents and instruments and to goods other than those covered by a certificate of title described in subsection (2), mobile goods described in subsection (3), and minerals described in subsection (5).

(b) Except as otherwise provided in this subsection, perfection and the effect of perfection or non-perfection of a security interest in collateral are governed by the law of the jurisdiction where the collateral is when the last event occurs on which is based the assertion that the security interest is perfected or unperfected.

(c) If the parties to a transaction creating a purchase money security interest in goods in one jurisdiction understand at the time that the security interest attaches that the goods will be kept in another jurisdiction, then the law of the other jurisdiction governs the perfection and the effect of perfection or non-perfection of the security interest from the time it attaches until thirty days after the debtor receives possession of the goods and thereafter if the goods are taken to the other jurisdiction before the end of the thirty-day period.

(d) When collateral is brought into and kept in this state while subject to a security interest perfected under the law of the jurisdiction from which the collateral was removed, the security interest remains perfected, but if action is required by Part 3 of this Article to perfect the security interest,

(i) if the action is not taken before the expiration of the period of perfection in the other jurisdiction or the end of four months after the collateral is brought into this state, whichever period first expires, the security interest becomes unperfected at the end of that period and is thereafter deemed to have been unperfected as against a person who became a purchaser after removal;

(ii) if the action is taken before the expiration of the period specified in subparagraph (i), the security interest continues perfected thereafter;

(iii) for the purpose of priority over a buyer of consumer goods (subsection (2) of Section 9—307), the period of the effectiveness of a filing in the jurisdiction from which the collateral is removed is governed by the rules with respect to perfection in subparagraphs (i) and (ii).

(2) Certificate of title.

(a) This subsection applies to goods covered by a certificate of title issued under a statute of this state or of another jurisdiction under the law of which indication of a security interest on the certificate is required as a condition of perfection.

(b) Except as otherwise provided in this subsection, perfection and the effect of perfection or non-perfection of the security interest are governed by the law (including the conflict of laws rules) of the jurisdiction issuing the certificate until four months after the goods are removed from that jurisdiction and thereafter until the goods are registered in another jurisdiction, but in any event not beyond surrender of the certificate. After the expiration of that period, the goods are not covered by the certificate of title within the meaning of this section.

(c) Except with respect to the rights of a buyer described in the next paragraph, a security interest, perfected in another jurisdiction otherwise than by notation on a certificate of title, in goods brought into this state and thereafter covered by a certificate of title issued by this state is subject to the rules stated in paragraph (d) of subsection (1).

(d) If goods are brought into this state while a security interest therein is perfected in any manner under the law of the jurisdiction from which the goods are removed and a certificate of title is issued by this state and the certificate does not show that the goods are subject to the security interest or that they may be subject to security interests not shown on the certificate, the security interest is subordinate to the rights of a buyer of the goods who is not in the business of selling goods of that kind to the extent that he gives value and receives delivery of the goods after issuance of the certificate and without knowledge of the security interest.

(3) Accounts, general intangibles and mobile goods.

(a) This subsection applies to accounts (other than an account described in subsection (5) on minerals) and general intangibles and to goods which are mobile and which are of a type normally used in more than one jurisdiction, such as motor vehicles, trailers, rolling stock, airplanes, shipping containers, road building and construction machinery and commercial harvesting machinery and the like, if the goods are equipment or are inventory leased or held for lease by the debtor to others, and are not covered by a certificate of title described in subsection (2).

(b) The law (including the conflict of laws rules) of the jurisdiction in which the debtor is located governs the perfection and the effect of perfection or non-perfection of the security interest.

(c) If, however, the debtor is located in a jurisdiction which is not a part of the United States, and which does not provide for perfection of the security interest by filing or recording in that jurisdiction, the law of the jurisdiction in the United States in which the debtor has its major executive office in the United States governs the perfection and the effect of perfection or non-perfection of the security interest through filing. In the alternative, if the debtor is located in a jurisdiction which is not a part of the United States or Canada and the collateral is accounts or general intangibles for money due or to become due, the security interest may be perfected by notification to the account debtor. As used in this paragraph, "United States" includes its territories and possessions and the Commonwealth of Puerto Rico.

(d) A debtor shall be deemed located at his place of business if he has one, at his chief executive office if he has more than one place of business, otherwise at his residence. If, however, the debtor is a foreign air carrier under the Federal Aviation Act of 1958, as amended, it shall be deemed located at the designated office of the agent upon whom service of process may be made on behalf of the foreign air carrier.

(e) A security interest perfected under the law of the jurisdiction of the location of the debtor is perfected until the expiration of four months after a change of the debtor's location to another jurisdiction, or until perfection would have ceased by the law of the first jurisdiction, whichever period first expires. Unless perfected in the new jurisdiction before the end of that period, it becomes unperfected thereafter and is deemed to have been unperfected as against a person who became a purchaser after the change.

(4) Chattel paper.

The rules stated for goods in subsection (1) apply to a possessory security interest in chattel paper. The rules stated for accounts in subsection (3) apply to a non-possessory security interest in chattel paper, but the security interest may not be perfected by notification to the account debtor.

(5) Minerals.

Perfection and the effect of perfection or non-perfection of a security interest which is created by a debtor who has an interest in minerals or the like (including oil and gas) before extraction and which attaches thereto as extracted, or which attaches to an account resulting from the sale thereof at the wellhead or minehead are governed by the law (including the conflict of laws rules) of the jurisdiction wherein the wellhead or minehead is located. Amended in 1972.

§9—104
Transactions Excluded From Article

This Article does not apply

(a) to a security interest subject to any statute of the United States, to the extent that such statute governs the rights of parties to and third parties affected by transactions in particular types of property; or

(b) to a landlord's lien; or

(c) to a lien given by statute or other rule of law for services or materials except as provided in Section 9—310 on priority of such liens; or

(d) to a transfer of a claim for wages, salary or other compensation of an employee; or

(e) to a transfer by a government or governmental subdivision or agency; or

(f) to a sale of accounts or chattel paper as part of a sale of the business out of which they arose, or an assignment of accounts or chattel paper which is for the purpose of collection only, or a transfer of a right to payment under a contract to an assignee who is also to do the performance under the contract or a transfer of a single account to an assignee in whole or partial satisfaction of a preexisting indebtedness; or

(g) to a transfer of an interest in or claim in or under any policy of insurance, except as provided with respect to proceeds (Section 9—306) and priorities in proceeds (Section 9—312); or

(h) to a right represented by a judgment (other than a judgment taken on a right to payment which was collateral); or

(i) to any right of set-off; or

(j) except to the extent that provision is made for fixtures in Section 9—313, to the creation or transfer of an interest in or lien on real estate, including a lease or rents thereunder; or

(k) to a transfer in whole or in part of any claim arising out of tort; or

(l) to a transfer of an interest in any deposit account (subsection (1) of Section 9—105), except as provided with respect to proceeds (Section 9—306) and priorities in proceeds (Section 9—312).

Amended in 1972.

§9—105
Definitions and Index of Definitions

(1) In this Article unless the context otherwise requires:

(a) "Account debtor" means the person who is obligated on an account, chattel paper or general intangible;

(b) "Chattel paper" means a writing or writings which evidence both a monetary obligation and a security interest in or a lease of specific goods, but a charter or other contract involving the use or hire of a vessel is not chattel paper. When a transaction is evidenced both by such a security agreement or a lease and by an instrument or a series of instruments, the group of writings taken together constitutes chattel paper;

(c) "Collateral" means the property subject to a security interest, and includes accounts and chattel paper which have been sold;

(d) "Debtor" means the person who owes payment or other performance of the obligation secured, whether or not he owns or has rights in the collateral, and includes the seller of accounts or chattel paper. Where the debtor and the owner of the collateral are not the same person, the term "debtor" means the owner of the collateral in any provision of the Article dealing with the collateral, the obligor in any provision dealing with the obligation, and may include both where the context so requires;

(e) "Deposit account" means a demand, time, savings, passbook or like account maintained with a bank, savings and loan association, credit union or like organization, other than an account evidenced by a certificate of deposit;

(f) "Document" means document of title as defined in the general definitions of Article 1 (Section 1—201), and a receipt of the kind described in subsection (2) of Section 7—201;

(g) "Encumbrance" includes real estate mortgages and other liens on real estate and all other rights in real estate that are not ownership interests;

(h) "Goods" includes all things which are movable at the time the security interest attaches or which are fixtures (Section 9—313), but does not include money, documents, instruments, accounts, chattel paper, general intangibles, or minerals or the like (including oil and gas) before extraction. "Goods" also includes standing timber which is to be cut and removed under a conveyance or contract for sale, the unborn young of animals, and growing crops;

(i) "Instrument" means a negotiable instrument (defined in Section 3—104), or a security (defined in Section 8—102) or any other writing which evidences a right to the payment of money and is not itself a security agreement or lease and is of a type which is in ordinary course of business transferred by delivery with any necessary indorsement or assignment;

(j) "Mortgage" means a consensual interest created by a real estate mortgage, a trust deed on real estate, or the like;

(k) An advance is made "pursuant to commitment" if the secured party has bound himself to make it, whether or not a subsequent event of default or other event

not within his control has relieved or may relieve him from his obligation;

(l) "Security agreement" means an agreement which creates or provides for a security interest;

(m) "Secured party" means a lender, seller or other person in whose favor there is a security interest, including a person to whom accounts or chattel paper have been sold. When the holders of obligations issued under an indenture of trust, equipment trust agreement or the like are represented by a trustee or other person, the representative is the secured party;

(n) "Transmitting utility" means any person primarily engaged in the railroad, street railway or trolley bus business, the electric or electronics communications transmission business, the transmission of goods by pipeline, or the transmission or the production and transmission of electricity, steam, gas or water, or the provision of sewer service.

(2) Other definitions applying to this Article and the sections in which they appear are:

"Account".	Section 9—106.
"Attach".	Section 9—203.
"Construction mortgage".	Section 9—313(1).
"Consumer goods".	Section 9—109(1).
"Equipment".	Section 9—109(2).
"Farm products".	Section 9—109(3).
"Fixture".	Section 9—313(1).
"Fixture filing".	Section 9—313(1).
"General intangibles".	Section 9—106.
"Inventory".	Section 9—109(4).
"Lien creditor".	Section 9—301(3).
"Proceeds".	Section 9—306(1).
"Purchase money security interest".	Section 9—107.
"United States".	Section 9—103.

(3) The following definitions in other Articles apply to this Article:

"Check".	Section 3—104.
"Contract for sale".	Section 2—106.
"Holder in due course".	Section 3—302.
"Note".	Section 3—104.
"Sale".	Section 2—106.

(4) In addition Article 1 contains general definitions and principles of construction and interpretation applicable throughout this Article. Amended in 1966, 1972.

§9—106
Definitions: "Account"; "General Intangibles"

"Account" means any right to payment for goods sold or leased or for services rendered which is not evidenced by an instrument or chattel paper, whether or not it has been earned by performance. "General intangibles" means any personal property (including things in action) other than goods, accounts, chattel paper, documents, instruments, and money. All rights to payment earned or unearned under a charter or other contract involving the use or hire of a vessel and all rights incident to the charter or contract are accounts. Amended in 1966, 1972.

§9—107
Definitions: "Purchase Money Security Interest"

A security interest is a "purchase money security interest" to the extent that it is

(a) taken or retained by the seller of the collateral to secure all or part of its price; or

(b) taken by a person who by making advances or incurring an obligation gives value to enable the debtor to acquire rights in or the use of collateral if such value is in fact so used.

§9—108
When After-Acquired Collateral Not Security for Antecedent Debt

Where a secured party makes an advance, incurs an obligation, releases a perfected security interest, or otherwise gives new value which is to be secured in whole or in part by after-acquired property his security interest in the after-acquired collateral shall be deemed to be taken for new value and not as security for an antecedent debt if the debtor acquires his rights in such collateral either in the ordinary course of his business or under a contract of purchase made pursuant to the security agreement within a reasonable time after new value is given.

§9—109
Classification of Goods; "Consumer Goods"; "Equipment"; "Farm Products"; "Inventory"

Goods are

(1) "consumer goods" if they are used or bought for use primarily for personal, family or household purposes;

(2) "equipment" if they are used or bought for use primarily in business (including farming or a profession) or by a debtor who is a non-profit organization or a governmental subdivision or agency or if the goods are not included in the definitions of inventory, farm products or consumer goods;

(3) "farm products" if they are crops or livestock or supplies used or produced in farming operations or if they are products of crops or livestock in their unmanufactured states (such as ginned cotton, wool-clip, maple syrup, milk and eggs), and if they are in the possession of a debtor engaged in raising, fattening, grazing or other farming operations. If goods are farm products they are neither equipment nor inventory;

(4) "inventory" if they are held by a person who holds them for sale or lease or to be furnished under contracts of service or if he has so furnished them, or if they are raw materials, work in process or materials used or consumed in a business. Inventory of a person is not to be classified as his equipment.

§9—110
Sufficiency of Description

For the purposes of this Article any description of personal property or real estate is sufficient whether or not it is specific if it reasonably identifies what is described.

§9—111
Applicability of Bulk Transfer Laws

The creation of a security interest is not a bulk transfer under Article 6 (see Section 6—103).

§9—112
Where Collateral Is Not Owned by Debtor

Unless otherwise agreed, when a secured party knows that collateral is owned by a person who is not the debtor, the owner of the collateral is entitled to receive from the secured party any surplus under Section 9—502(2) or under Section 9—504(1), and is not liable for the debt or for any deficiency after resale, and he has the same right as the debtor

(a) to receive statements under Section 9—208;

(b) to receive notice of and to object to a secured party's proposal to retain the collateral in satisfaction of the indebtedness under Section 9—505;

(c) to redeem the collateral under Section 9—506;

(d) to obtain injunctive or other relief under Section 9—507(1); and

(e) to recover losses caused to him under Section 9—208(2).

§9—113
Security Interests Arising Under Article on Sales

A security interest arising solely under the Article on Sales (Article 2) is subject to the provisions of this Article except that to the extent that and so long as the debtor does not have or does not lawfully obtain possession of the goods

(a) no security agreement is necessary to make the security interest enforceable; and

(b) no filing is required to perfect the security interest; and

(c) the rights of the secured party on default by the debtor are governed by the Article on Sales (Article 2).

§9—114
Consignment

(1) A person who delivers goods under a consignment which is not a security interest and who would be required to file under this Article by paragraph (3) (c) of Section 2—326 has priority over a secured party who is or becomes a creditor of the consignee and who would have a perfected security interest in the goods if they were the property of the consignee, and also has priority with respect to identifiable cash proceeds received on or before delivery of the goods to a buyer, if

(a) the consignor complies with the filing provision of the Article on Sales with respect to consignments (paragraph (3) (c) of Section 2—326) before the consignee receives possession of the goods; and

(b) the consignor gives notification in writing to the holder of the security interest if the holder has filed a financing statement covering the same types of goods before the date of the filing made by the consignor; and

(c) the holder of the security interest receives the notification within five years before the consignee receives possession of the goods; and

(d) the notification states that the consignor expects to deliver goods on consignment to the consignee, describing the goods by item or type.

(2) In the case of a consignment which is not a security interest and in which the requirements of the preceding subsection have not been met, a person who delivers goods to another is subordinate to a person who would have a perfected security interest in the goods if they were the property of the debtor. Added in 1972.

Part 2
Validity of Security Agreement and Rights of Parties Thereto

§9—201
General Validity of Security Agreement

Except as otherwise provided by this Act a security agreement is effective according to its terms between the parties, against purchasers of the collateral and against creditors. Nothing in this Article validates any charge or practice illegal under any statute or regulation thereunder governing usury, small loans, retail installment sales, or the like, or extends the application of any such statute or regulation to any transaction not otherwise subject thereto.

§9—202
Title to Collateral Immaterial

Each provision of this Article with regard to rights, obligations and remedies applies whether title to collateral is in the secured party or in the debtor.

§9—203
Attachment and Enforceability of Security Interest; Proceeds; Formal Requisites

(1) Subject to the provisions of Section 4—208 on the security interest of a collecting bank and Section 9—113 on a security interest arising under the Article on Sales, a security interest is not enforceable against the debtor or third parties with respect to the collateral and does not attach unless

(a) the collateral is in the possession of the secured party pursuant to agreement, or the debtor has signed a security agreement which contains a description of the collateral and in addition, when the security interest covers crops growing or to be grown or timber to be cut, a description of the land concerned; and

(b) value has been given; and

(c) the debtor has rights in the collateral.

(2) A security interest attaches when it becomes enforceable against the debtor with respect to the collateral. Attachment occurs as soon as all of the events specified in subsection (1) have taken place unless explicit agreement postpones the time of attaching.

(3) Unless otherwise agreed a security agreement gives the secured party the rights to proceeds provided by Section 9—306.

(4) A transaction, although subject to this Article, is also subject to .... *, and in the case of conflict between the provisions of this Article and any such statute, the provisions of such statute control. Failure to comply with any applicable statute has only the effect which is specified therein. Amended in 1972.

Note: At * in subsection (4) insert reference to any local statute regulating small loans, retail installment sales and the like.

The foregoing subsection (4) is designed to make it clear that certain transactions, although subject to this Article, must also comply with other applicable legislation.

This Article is designed to regulate all the "security" aspects of transactions within its scope. There is, however, much regulatory legislation, particularly in the consumer field, which supplements this Article and should not be repealed by its enactment. Examples are small loan acts, retail installment selling acts and the like. Such acts may provide for licensing and rate regulation and may prescribe particular forms of contract. Such provisions should remain in force despite the enactment of this Article. On the other hand if a retail installment selling act contains provisions on filing, rights on default, etc., such provisions should be repealed as inconsistent with this Article except that inconsistent provisions as to deficiencies, penalties, etc., in the Uniform Consumer Credit Code and other recent related legislation should remain because those statutes were drafted after the substantial enactment of the Article and with the intention of modifying certain provisions of this Article as to consumer credit.

§9—204
After-Acquired Property; Future Advances

(1) Except as provided in subsection (2), a security agreement may provide that any or all obligations covered by the security agreement are to be secured by after-acquired collateral.

(2) No security interest attaches under an after-acquired property clause to consumer goods other than accessions (Section 9—314) when given as additional security unless the debtor acquires rights in them within ten days after the secured party gives value.

(3) Obligations covered by a security agreement may include future advances or other value whether or not the advances or value are given pursuant to commitment (subsection (1) of Section 9—105). Amended in 1972.

§9—205
Use or Disposition of Collateral Without Accounting Permissible

A security interest is not invalid or fraudulent against creditors by reason of liberty in the debtor to use, commingle or dispose of all or part of the collateral (including returned or repossessed goods) or to collect or compromise accounts or chattel paper, or to accept the return of goods or make repossessions, or to use, commingle or dispose of proceeds, or by reason of the failure of the secured party to require the debtor to account for proceeds or replace collateral. This section does not relax the requirements of possession where perfection of a security interest depends upon possession of the collateral by the secured party or by a bailee. Amended in 1972.

§9—206
Agreement Not to Assert Defenses Against Assignee; Modification of Sales Warranties Where Security Agreement Exists

(1) Subject to any statute or decision which establishes a different rule for buyers or lessees of consumer goods, an agreement by a buyer or lessee that he will not assert against an assignee any claim or defense which he may have against the seller or lessor is enforceable by an assignee who takes his assignment for value, in good faith and without notice of a claim or defense, except as to defenses of a type which may be asserted against a holder in due course of a negotiable instrument under the Article on Commercial Paper (Article 3). A buyer who as part of one transaction signs both a negotiable instrument and a security agreement makes such an agreement.

(2) When a seller retains a purchase money security interest in goods the Article on Sales (Article 2) governs the sale and any disclaimer, limitation or modification of the seller's warranties. Amended in 1962.

§9—207
Rights and Duties When Collateral Is in Secured Party's Possession

(1) A secured party must use reasonable care in the custody and preservation of collateral in his possession. In the case of an instrument or chattel paper reasonable care includes taking necessary steps to preserve rights against prior parties unless otherwise agreed.

(2) Unless otherwise agreed, when collateral is in the secured party's possession

    (a) reasonable expenses (including the cost of any insurance and payment of taxes or other charges) incurred in the custody, preservation, use or operation of the collateral are chargeable to the debtor and are secured by the collateral;

    (b) the risk of accidental loss or damage is on the debtor to the extent of any deficiency in any effective insurance coverage;

    (c) the secured party may hold as additional security any increase or profits (except money) received from the collateral, but money so received, unless remitted to the debtor, shall be applied in reduction of the secured obligation;

    (d) the secured party must keep the collateral identifiable but fungible collateral may be commingled;

    (e) the secured party may repledge the collateral upon terms which do not impair the debtor's right to redeem it.

(3) A secured party is liable for any loss caused by his failure to meet any obligation imposed by the preceding subsections but does not lose his security interest.

(4) A secured party may use or operate the collateral for the purpose of preserving the collateral or its value or pursuant to the order of a court of appropriate jurisdiction or, except in the case of consumer goods, in the manner and to the extent provided in the security agreement.

§9—208
Request for Statement of Account or List of Collateral

(1) A debtor may sign a statement indicating what he believes to be the aggregate amount of unpaid indebtedness as of a specified date and may send it to the secured party with a request that the statement be approved or corrected and returned to the debtor. When the security agreement or any other record kept by the secured party identifies the collateral a debtor may similarly request the secured party to approve or correct a list of the collateral.

(2) The secured party must comply with such a request within two weeks after receipt by sending a written correction or approval. If the secured party claims a security interest in all of a particular type of collateral owned by the debtor he may indicate that fact in his reply and need not approve or correct an itemized list of such collateral. If the secured party without reasonable excuse fails to comply he is liable for any loss caused to the debtor thereby; and if the debtor has properly included in his request a good faith statement of the obligation or a list of the collateral or both the secured party may claim a security interest only as shown in the statement against persons misled by his failure to comply. If he no longer has an interest in the obligation or collateral at the time the request is received he must disclose the name and address of any successor in interest known to him and he is liable for any loss caused to the debtor as a result of failure to disclose. A successor in interest is not subject to this section until a request is received by him.

(3) A debtor is entitled to such a statement once every six months without charge. The secured party may require payment of a charge not exceeding $10 for each additional statement furnished.

Part 3
Rights of Third Parties; Perfected and Unperfected Security Interests; Rules of Priority

§9—301
Persons Who Take Priority Over Unperfected Security Interests; Rights of "Lien Creditor"

(1) Except as otherwise provided in subsection (2), an unperfected security interest is subordinate to the rights of

    (a) persons entitled to priority under Section 9—312;

(b) a person who becomes a lien creditor before the security interest is perfected;

(c) in the case of goods, instruments, documents, and chattel paper, a person who is not a secured party and who is a transferee in bulk or other buyer not in ordinary course of business or is a buyer of farm products in ordinary course of business, to the extent that he gives value and receives delivery of the collateral without knowledge of the security interest and before it is perfected;

(d) in the case of accounts and general intangibles, a person who is not a secured party and who is a transferee to the extent that he gives value without knowledge of the security interest and before it is perfected.

(2) If the secured party files with respect to a purchase money security interest before or within ten days after the debtor receives possession of the collateral, he takes priority over the rights of a transferee in bulk or of a lien creditor which arise between the time the security interest attaches and the time of filing.

(3) A "lien creditor" means a creditor who has acquired a lien on the property involved by attachment, levy or the like and includes an assignee for benefit of creditors from the time of assignment, and a trustee in bankruptcy from the date of the filing of the petition or a receiver in equity from the time of appointment.

(4) A person who becomes a lien creditor while a security interest is perfected takes subject to the security interest only to the extent that it secures advances made before he becomes a lien creditor or within 45 days thereafter or made without knowledge of the lien or pursuant to a commitment entered into without knowledge of the lien. Amended in 1972.

§9—302
When Filing Is Required to Perfect Security Interest; Security Interests to Which Filing Provisions of This Article Do Not Apply

(1) A financing statement must be filed to perfect all security interests except the following:

(a) a security interest in collateral in possession of the secured party under Section 9—305;

(b) a security interest temporarily perfected in instruments or documents without delivery under Section 9—304 or in proceeds for a 10 day period under Section 9—306;

(c) a security interest created by an assignment of a beneficial interest in a trust or a decedent's estate;

(d) a purchase money security interest in consumer goods; but filing is required for a motor vehicle required to be registered; and fixture filing is required for priority over conflicting interests in fixtures to the extent provided in Section 9—313;

(e) an assignment of accounts which does not alone or in conjunction with other assignments to the same assignee transfer a significant part of the outstanding accounts of the assignor;

(f) a security interest of a collecting bank (Section 4—208) or arising under the Article on Sales (see Section 9—113) or covered in subsection (3) of this section;

(g) an assignment for the benefit of all the creditors of the transferor, and subsequent transfers by the assignee thereunder.

(2) If a secured party assigns a perfected security interest, no filing under this Article is required in order to continue the perfected status of the security interest against creditors of and transferees from the original debtor.

(3) The filing of a financing statement otherwise required by this Article is not necessary or effective to perfect a security interest in property subject to

(a) a statute or treaty of the United States which provides for a national or international registration or a national or international certificate of title or which specifies a place of filing different from that specified in this Article for filing of the security interest; or

(b) the following statutes of this state; [list any certificate of title statute covering automobiles, trailers, mobile homes, boats, farm tractors, or the like, and any central filing statute*]; but during any period in which collateral is inventory held for sale by a person who is in the business of selling goods of that kind, the filing provisions of this Article (Part 4) apply to a security interest in that collateral created by him as debtor; or

(c) a certificate of title statute of another jurisdiction under the law of which indication of a security interest on the certificate is required as a condition of perfection (subsection (2) of Section 9—103).

(4) Compliance with a statute or treaty described in subsection (3) is equivalent to the filing of a financing statement under this Article, and a security interest in property subject to the statute or treaty can be perfected only by compliance therewith except as provided in Section 9—103 on multiple state transactions. Duration and renewal of perfection of a security interest perfected by compliance with the statute or treaty are governed by the provisions of the statute or treaty; in other respects the security interest is subject to this Article. Amended in 1972.

* **Note:** It is recommended that the provisions of certificate of title acts for perfection of security interests by notation on the certificates should be amended to exclude coverage of inventory held for sale.

§9—303
When Security Interest Is Perfected; Continuity of Perfection

(1) A security interest is perfected when it has attached and when all of the applicable steps required for perfection have been taken. Such steps are specified in Sections 9—302, 9—304, 9—305 and 9—306. If such steps are taken before the security interest attaches, it is perfected at the time when it attaches.

(2) If a security interest is originally perfected in any way permitted under this Article and is subsequently perfected in some other way under this Article, without an intermediate period when it was unperfected, the security interest shall be

deemed to be perfected continuously for the purposes of this Article.

§9—304
Perfection of Security Interest in Instruments, Documents, and Goods Covered by Documents; Perfection by Permissive Filing; Temporary Perfection Without Filing or Transfer of Possession

(1) A security interest in chattel paper or negotiable documents may be perfected by filing. A security interest in money or instruments (other than instruments which constitute part of chattel paper) can be perfected only by the secured party's taking possession, except as provided in subsections (4) and (5) of this section and subsections (2) and (3) of Section 9—306 on proceeds.

(2) During the period that goods are in the possession of the issuer of a negotiable document therefor, a security interest in the goods is perfected by perfecting a security interest in the document, and any security interest in the goods otherwise perfected during such period is subject thereto.

(3) A security interest in goods in the possession of a bailee other than one who has issued a negotiable document therefor is perfected by issuance of a document in the name of the secured party or by the bailee's receipt of notification of the secured party's interest or by filing as to the goods.

(4) A security interest in instruments or negotiable documents is perfected without filing or the taking of possession for a period of 21 days from the time it attaches to the extent that it arises for new value given under a written security agreement.

(5) A security interest remains perfected for a period of 21 days without filing where a secured party having a perfected security interest in an instrument, a negotiable document or goods in possession of a bailee other than one who has issued a negotiable document therefor

(a) makes available to the debtor the goods or documents representing the goods for the purpose of ultimate sale or exchange or for the purpose of loading, unloading, storing, shipping, transshipping, manufacturing, processing or otherwise dealing with them in a manner preliminary to their sale or exchange, but priority between conflicting security interests in the goods is subject to subsection (3) of Section 9—312; or

(b) delivers the instrument to the debtor for the purpose of ultimate sale or exchange or of presentation, collection, renewal or registration of transfer.

(6) After the 21 day period in subsections (4) and (5) perfection depends upon compliance with applicable provisions of this Article. Amended in 1972.

§9—305
When Possession by Secured Party Perfects Security Interest Without Filing

A security interest in letters of credit and advices of credit (subsection (2)(a) of Section 5—116), goods, instruments, money, negotiable documents or chattel paper may be perfected by the secured party's taking possession of the collateral. If such collateral other than goods covered by a negotiable document is held by a bailee, the secured party is deemed to have possession from the time the bailee receives notification of the secured party's interest. A security interest is perfected by possession from the time possession is taken without relation back and continues only so long as possession is retained, unless otherwise specified in this Article. The security interest may be otherwise perfected as provided in this Article before or after the period of possession by the secured party. Amended in 1972.

§9—306
"Proceeds"; Secured Party's Rights on Disposition of Collateral

(1) "Proceeds" includes whatever is received upon the sale, exchange, collection or other disposition of collateral or proceeds. Insurance payable by reason of loss or damage to the collateral is proceeds, except to the extent that it is payable to a person other than a party to the security agreement. Money, checks, deposit accounts, and the like are "cash proceeds". All other proceeds are "non-cash proceeds".

(2) Except where this Article otherwise provides, a security interest continues in collateral notwithstanding sale, exchange or other disposition thereof unless the disposition was authorized by the secured party in the security agreement or otherwise, and also continues in any identifiable proceeds including collections received by the debtor.

(3) The security interest in proceeds is a continuously perfected security interest if the interest in the original collateral was perfected but it ceases to be a perfected security interest and becomes unperfected ten days after receipt of the proceeds by the debtor unless

(a) a filed financing statement covers the original collateral and the proceeds are collateral in which a security interest may be perfected by filing in the office or offices where the financing statement has been filed and, if the proceeds are acquired with cash proceeds, the description of collateral in the financing statement indicates the types of property constituting the proceeds; or

(b) a filed financing statement covers the original collateral and the proceeds are identifiable cash proceeds; or

(c) the security interest in the proceeds is perfected before the expiration of the ten day period.

Except as provided in this section, a security interest in proceeds can be perfected only by the methods or under the circumstances permitted in this Article for original collateral of the same type.

(4) In the event of insolvency proceedings instituted by or against a debtor, a secured party with a perfected security interest in proceeds has a perfected security interest only in the following proceeds:

(a) in identifiable non-cash proceeds and in separate deposit accounts containing only proceeds;

(b) in identifiable cash proceeds in the form of money which is neither commingled with other money nor deposited in a deposit account prior to the insolvency proceedings;

(c) in identifiable cash proceeds in the form of checks and the like which are not deposited in a deposit account prior to the insolvency proceedings; and

(d) in all cash and deposit accounts of the debtor in which proceeds have been commingled with other funds, but the perfected security interest under this paragraph (d) is

    (i) subject to any right to set-off; and

    (ii) limited to an amount not greater than the amount of any cash proceeds received by the debtor within ten days before the institution of the insolvency proceedings less the sum of (I) the payments to the secured party on account of cash proceeds received by the debtor during such period and (II) the cash proceeds received by the debtor during such period to which the secured party is entitled under paragraphs (a) through (c) of this subsection (4).

(5) If a sale of goods results in an account or chattel paper which is transferred by the seller to a secured party, and if the goods are returned to or are repossessed by the seller or the secured party, the following rules determine priorities:

(a) If the goods were collateral at the time of sale, for an indebtedness of the seller which is still unpaid, the original security interest attaches again to the goods and continues as a perfected security interest if it was perfected at the time when the goods were sold. If the security interest was originally perfected by a filing which is still effective, nothing further is required to continue the perfected status; in any other case, the secured party must take possession of the returned or repossessed goods or must file.

(b) An unpaid transferee of the chattel paper has a security interest in the goods against the transferor. Such security interest is prior to a security interest asserted under paragraph (a) to the extent that the transferee of the chattel paper was entitled to priority under Section 9—308.

(c) An unpaid transferee of the account has a security interest in the goods against the transferor. Such security interest is subordinate to a security interest asserted under paragraph (a).

(d) A security interest of an unpaid transferee asserted under paragraph (b) or (c) must be perfected for protection against creditors of the transferor and purchasers of the returned or repossessed goods.

Amended in 1972.

§9—307
Protection of Buyers of Goods

(1) A buyer in ordinary course of business (subsection (9) of Section 1—201) other than a person buying farm products from a person engaged in farming operations takes free of a security interest created by his seller even though the security interest is perfected and even though the buyer knows of its existence.

(2) In the case of consumer goods, a buyer takes free of a security interest even though perfected if he buys without knowledge of the security interest, for value and for his own personal, family or household purposes unless prior to the purchase the secured party has filed a financing statement covering such goods.

(3) A buyer other than a buyer in ordinary course of business (subsection (1) of this section) takes free of a security interest to the extent that it secures future advances made after the secured party acquires knowledge of the purchase, or more than 45 days after the purchase, whichever first occurs, unless made pursuant to a commitment entered into without knowledge of the purchase and before the expiration of the 45 day period. Amended in 1972.

§9—308
Purchase of Chattel Paper and Instruments

A purchaser of chattel paper or an instrument who gives new value and takes possession of it in the ordinary course of his business has priority over a security interest in the chattel paper or instrument

    (a) which is perfected under Section 9—304 (permissive filing and temporary perfection) or under Section 9—306 (perfection as to proceeds) if he acts without knowledge that the specific paper or instrument is subject to a security interest; or

    (b) which is claimed merely as proceeds of inventory subject to a security interest (Section 9—306) even though he knows that the specific paper or instrument is subject to the security interest.

Amended in 1972.

§9—309
Protection of Purchasers of Instruments and Documents

Nothing in this Article limits the rights of a holder in due course of a negotiable instrument (Section 3—302) or a holder to whom a negotiable document of title has been duly negotiated (Section 7—501) or a bona fide purchaser of a security (Section 8—301) and such holders or purchasers take priority over an earlier security interest even though perfected. Filing under this Article does not constitute notice of the security interest to such holders or purchasers.

§9—310
Priority of Certain Liens Arising by Operation of Law

When a person in the ordinary course of his business furnishes services or materials with respect to goods subject to a security interest, a lien upon goods in the possession of such person given by statute or rule of law for such materials or services takes priority over a perfected security interest unless the lien is statutory and the statute expressly provides otherwise.

§9—311
Alienability of Debtor's Rights: Judicial Process

The debtor's rights in collateral may be voluntarily or involuntarily transferred (by way of sale, creation of a security interest, attachment, levy, garnishment or other judicial process) notwithstanding a provision in the security agreement prohibiting any transfer or making the transfer constitute a default.

§9—312
Priorities Among Conflicting Security Interests in the Same Collateral

(1) The rules of priority stated in other sections of this Part and in the following sections shall govern when applicable: Section 4—208 with respect to the security interests of collecting banks in items being collected, accompanying documents and proceeds; Section 9—103 on security interests related to other jurisdictions; Section 9—114 on consignments.

(2) A perfected security interest in crops for new value given to enable the debtor to produce the crops during the production season and given not more than three months before the crops become growing crops by planting or otherwise takes priority over an earlier perfected security interest to the extent that such earlier interest secures obligations due more than six months before the crops become growing crops by planting or otherwise, even though the person giving new value had knowledge of the earlier security interest.

(3) A perfected purchase money security interest in inventory has priority over a conflicting security interest in the same inventory and also has priority in identifiable cash proceeds received on or before the delivery of the inventory to a buyer if

(a) the purchase money security interest is perfected at the time the debtor receives possession of the inventory; and

(b) the purchase money secured party gives notification in writing to the holder of the conflicting security interest if the holder had filed a financing statement covering the same types of inventory (i) before the date of the filing made by the purchase money secured party, or (ii) before the beginning of the 21 day period where the purchase money security interest is temporarily perfected without filing or possession (subsection (5) of Section 9—304); and

(c) the holder of the conflicting security interest receives the notification within five years before the debtor receives possession of the inventory; and

(d) the notification states that the person giving the notice has or expects to acquire a purchase money security interest in inventory of the debtor, describing such inventory by item or type.

(4) A purchase money security interest in collateral other than inventory has priority over a conflicting security interest in the same collateral or its proceeds if the purchase money security interest is perfected at the time the debtor receives possession of the collateral or within ten days thereafter.

(5) In all cases not governed by other rules stated in this section (including cases of purchase money security interests which do not qualify for the special priorities set forth in subsections (3) and (4) of this section), priority between conflicting security interests in the same collateral shall be determined according to the following rules:

(a) Conflicting security interests rank according to priority in time of filing or perfection. Priority dates from the time a filing is first made covering the collateral or the time the security interest is first perfected, whichever is earlier, provided that there is no period thereafter when there is neither filing nor perfection.

(b) So long as conflicting security interests are unperfected, the first to attach has priority.

(6) For the purposes of subsection (5) a date of filing or perfection as to collateral is also a date of filing or perfection as to proceeds.

(7) If future advances are made while a security interest is perfected by filing or the taking of possession, the security interest has the same priority for the purposes of subsection (5) with respect to the future advances as it does with respect to the first advance. If a commitment is made before or while the security interest is so perfected, the security interest has the same priority with respect to advances made pursuant thereto. In other cases a perfected security interest has priority from the date the advance is made. Amended in 1972.

§9—313
Priority of Security Interests in Fixtures

(1) In this section and in the provisions of Part 4 of this Article referring to fixture filing, unless the context otherwise requires

(a) goods are "fixtures" when they become so related to particular real estate that an interest in them arises under real estate law;

(b) a "fixture filing" is the filing in the office where a mortgage on the real estate would be filed or recorded of a financing statement covering goods which are or are to become fixtures and conforming to the requirements of subsection (5) of Section 9—402;

(c) a mortgage is a "construction mortgage" to the extent that it secures an obligation incurred for the construction of an improvement on land including the acquisition cost of the land, if the recorded writing so indicates.

(2) A security interest under this Article may be created in goods which are fixtures or may continue in goods which become fixtures, but no security interest exists under this Article in ordinary building materials incorporated into an improvement on land.

(3) This Article does not prevent creation of an encumbrance upon fixtures pursuant to real estate law.

(4) A perfected security interest in fixtures has priority over the conflicting interest of an encumbrancer or owner of the real estate where

(a) the security interest is a purchase money security interest, the interest of the encumbrancer or owner arises before the goods become fixtures, the security interest is perfected by a fixture filing before the goods become fixtures or within ten days thereafter, and the debtor has an interest of record in the real estate or is in possession of the real estate; or

(b) the security interest is perfected by a fixture filing before the interest of the encumbrancer or owner is of record, the security interest has priority over any conflicting interest of a predecessor in title of the encumbrancer or owner, and the debtor has an interest of record in the real estate or is in possession of the real estate; or

(c) the fixtures are readily removable factory or office machines or readily removable replacements of domestic appliances which are consumer goods, and before the goods become fixtures the security interest is perfected by any method permitted by this Article; or

(d) the conflicting interest is a lien on the real estate obtained by legal or equitable proceedings after the security interest was perfected by any method permitted by this Article.

(5) A security interest in fixtures, whether or not perfected, has priority over the conflicting interest of an encumbrancer or owner of the real estate where

(a) the encumbrancer or owner has consented in writing to the security interest or has disclaimed an interest in the goods as fixtures; or

(b) the debtor has a right to remove the goods as against the encumbrancer or owner. If the debtor's right terminates, the priority of the security interest continues for a reasonable time.

(6) Notwithstanding paragraph (a) of subsection (4) but otherwise subject to subsections (4) and (5), a security interest in fixtures is subordinate to a construction mortgage recorded before the goods become fixtures if the goods become fixtures before the completion of the construction. To the extent that it is given to refinance a construction mortgage, a mortgage has this priority to the same extent as the construction mortgage.

(7) In cases not within the preceding subsections, a security interest in fixtures is subordinate to the conflicting interest of an encumbrancer or owner of the related real estate who is not the debtor.

(8) When the secured party has priority over all owners and encumbrancers of the real estate, he may, on default, subject to the provisions of Part 5, remove his collateral from the real estate but he must reimburse any encumbrancer or owner of the real estate who is not the debtor and who has not otherwise agreed for the cost of repair of any physical injury, but not for any diminution in value of the real estate caused by the absence of the goods removed or by any necessity of replacing them. A person entitled to reimbursement may refuse permission to remove until the secured party gives adequate security for the performance of this obligation. Amended in 1972.

§9—314
Accessions

(1) A security interest in goods which attaches before they are installed in or affixed to other goods takes priority as to the goods installed or affixed (called in this section "accessions") over the claims of all persons to the whole except as stated in subsection (3) and subject to Section 9—315(1).

(2) A security interest which attaches to goods after they become part of a whole is valid against all persons subsequently acquiring interests in the whole except as stated in subsection (3) but is invalid against any person with an interest in the whole at the time the security interest attaches to the goods who has not in writing consented to the security interest or disclaimed an interest in the goods as part of the whole.

(3) The security interests described in subsections (1) and (2) do not take priority over

(a) a subsequent purchaser for value of any interest in the whole; or

(b) a creditor with a lien on the whole subsequently obtained by judicial proceedings; or

(c) a creditor with a prior perfected security interest in the whole to the extent that he makes subsequent advances

if the subsequent purchase is made, the lien by judicial proceedings obtained or the subsequent advance under the prior perfected security interest is made or contracted for without knowledge of the security interest and before it is perfected. A purchaser of the whole at a foreclosure sale other than the holder of a perfected security interest purchasing at his own foreclosure sale is a subsequent purchaser within this section.

(4) When under subsections (1) or (2) and (3) a secured party has an interest in accessions which has priority over the claims of all persons who have interests in the whole, he may on default subject to the provisions of Part 5 remove his collateral from the whole but he must reimburse any encumbrancer or owner of the whole who is not the debtor and who has not otherwise agreed for the cost of repair of any physical injury but not for any diminution in value of the whole caused by the absence of the goods removed or by any necessity for replacing them. A person entitled to reimbursement may refuse permission to remove until the secured party gives adequate security for the performance of this obligation.

§9—315
Priority When Goods Are Commingled or Processed

(1) If a security interest in goods was perfected and subsequently the goods or a part thereof have become part of a product or mass, the security interest continues in the product or mass if

(a) the goods are so manufactured, processed, assembled or commingled that their identity is lost in the product or mass; or

(b) a financing statement covering the original goods also covers the product into which the goods have been manufactured, processed or assembled.

In a case to which paragraph (b) applies, no separate security interest in that part of the original goods which has been manufactured, processed or assembled into the product may be claimed under Section 9—314.

(2) When under subsection (1) more than one security inter-

est attaches to the product or mass, they rank equally according to the ratio that the cost of the goods to which each interest originally attached bears to the cost of the total product or mass.

§9—316
Priority Subject to Subordination
Nothing in this Article prevents subordination by agreement by any person entitled to priority.

§9—317
Secured Party Not Obligated on Contract of Debtor
The mere existence of a security interest or authority given to the debtor to dispose of or use collateral does not impose contract or tort liability upon the secured party for the debtor's acts or omissions.

§9—318
Defenses Against Assignee; Modification of Contract After Notification of Assignment; Term Prohibiting Assignment Ineffective; Identification and Proof of Assignment
(1) Unless an account debtor has made an enforceable agreement not to assert defenses or claims arising out of a sale as provided in Section 9—206 the rights of an assignee are subject to

(a) all the terms of the contract between the account debtor and assignor and any defense or claim arising therefrom; and

(b) any other defense or claim of the account debtor against the assignor which accrues before the account debtor receives notification of the assignment.

(2) So far as the right to payment or a part thereof under an assigned contract has not been fully earned by performance, and notwithstanding notification of the assignment, any modification of or substitution for the contract made in good faith and in accordance with reasonable commercial standards is effective against an assignee unless the account debtor has otherwise agreed but the assignee acquires corresponding rights under the modified or substituted contract. The assignment may provide that such modification or substitution is a breach by the assignor.

(3) The account debtor is authorized to pay the assignor until the account debtor receives notification that the amount due or to become due has been assigned and that payment is to be made to the assignee. A notification which does not reasonably identify the rights assigned is ineffective. If requested by the account debtor, the assignee must seasonably furnish reasonable proof that the assignment has been made and unless he does so the account debtor may pay the assignor.

(4) A term in any contract between an account debtor and an assignor is ineffective if it prohibits assignment of an account or prohibits creation of a security interest in a general intangible for money due or to become due or requires the account debtor's consent to such assignment or security interest. Amended in 1972.

Part 4
Filing

§9—401
Place of Filing; Erroneous Filing; Removal of Collateral
First Alternative Subsection (1)

(1) The proper place to file in order to perfect a security interest is as follows:

(a) when the collateral is timber to be cut or is minerals or the like (including oil and gas) or accounts subject to subsection (5) of Section 9—103, or when the financing statement is filed as a fixture filing (Section 9—313) and the collateral is goods which are or are to become fixtures, then in the office where a mortgage on the real estate would be filed or recorded;

(b) in all other cases, in the office of the [Secretary of State].

Second Alternative Subsection (1)

(1) The proper place to file in order to perfect a security interest is as follows:

(a) when the collateral is equipment used in farming operations, or farm products, or accounts or general intangibles arising from or relating to the sale of farm products by a farmer, or consumer goods, then in the office of the .... in the county of the debtor's residence or if the debtor is not a resident of this state then in the office of the .... in the county where the goods are kept, and in addition when the collateral is crops growing or to be grown in the office of the .... in the county where the land is located;

(b) when the collateral is timber to be cut or is minerals or the like (including oil and gas) or accounts subject to subsection (5) of Section 9—103, or when the financing statement is filed as a fixture filing (Section 9—313) and the collateral is goods which are or are to become fixtures, then in the office where a mortgage on the real estate would be filed or recorded;

(c) in all other cases, in the office of the [Secretary of State].

Third Alternative Subsection (1)

(1) The proper place to file in order to perfect a security interest is as follows:

(a) when the collateral is equipment used in farming operations, or farm products, or accounts or general intangibles arising from or relating to the sale of farm products by a farmer, or consumer goods, then in the office of the .... in the county of the debtor's residence or if the debtor is not a resident of this state then in the office of the .... in the county where the goods are kept, and in addition when the collateral is crops growing or to be grown in the office of the .... in the county where the land is located;

(b) when the collateral is timber to be cut or is minerals or the like (including oil and gas) or accounts subject to subsection (5) of Section 9—103, or when the financing statement is filed as a fixture filing (Section 9—313) and the collateral is goods which are or are to become fixtures, then in the office where a mortgage on the real estate would be filed or recorded;

(c) in all other cases, in the office of the [Secretary of State] and in addition, if the debtor has a place of business in only one county of this state, also in the office of .... of such county, or, if the debtor has no place of business in this state, but resides in the state, also in the office of .... of the county in which he resides.

Note: One of the three alternatives should be selected as subsection (1).

(2) A filing which is made in good faith in an improper place or not in all of the places required by this section is nevertheless effective with regard to any collateral as to which the filing complied with the requirements of this Article and is also effective with regard to collateral covered by the financing statement against any person who has knowledge of the contents of such financing statement.

(3) A filing which is made in the proper place in this state continues effective even though the debtor's residence or place of business or the location of the collateral or its use, whichever controlled the original filing, is thereafter changed.

Alternative Subsection (3)

[(3) A filing which is made in the proper county continues effective for four months after a change to another county of the debtor's residence or place of business or the location of the collateral, whichever controlled the original filing. It becomes ineffective thereafter unless a copy of the financing statement signed by the secured party is filed in the new county within said period. The security interest may also be perfected in the new county after the expiration of the four-month period; in such case perfection dates from the time of perfection in the new county. A change in the use of the collateral does not impair the effectiveness of the original filing.]

(4) The rules stated in Section 9—103 determine whether filing is necessary in this state.

(5) Notwithstanding the preceding subsections, and subject to subsection (3) of Section 9—302, the proper place to file in order to perfect a security interest in collateral, including fixtures, of a transmitting utility is the office of the [Secretary of State]. This filing constitutes a fixture filing (Section 9—313) as to the collateral described therein which is or is to become fixtures.

(6) For the purposes of this section, the residence of an organization is its place of business if it has one or its chief executive office if it has more than one place of business. Amended in 1962 and 1972.

Note: Subsection (6) should be used only if the state chooses the Second or Third Alternative Subsection (1).

§9—402
Formal Requisites of Financing Statement; Amendments; Mortgage as Financing Statement

(1) A financing statement is sufficient if it gives the names of the debtor and the secured party, is signed by the debtor, gives an address of the secured party from which information concerning the security interest may be obtained, gives a mailing address of the debtor and contains a statement indicating the types, or describing the items, of collateral. A financing statement may be filed before a security agreement is made or a security interest otherwise attaches. When the financing statement covers crops growing or to be grown, the statement must also contain a description of the real estate concerned. When the financing statement covers timber to be cut or covers minerals or the like (including oil and gas) or accounts subject to subsection (5) of Section 9—103, or when the financing statement is filed as a fixture filing (Section 9—313) and the collateral is goods which are or are to become fixtures, the statement must also comply with subsection (5). A copy of the security agreement is sufficient as a financing statement if it contains the above information and is signed by the debtor. A carbon, photographic or other reproduction of a security agreement or a financing statement is sufficient as a financing statement if the security agreement so provides or if the original has been filed in this state.

(2) A financing statement which otherwise complies with subsection (1) is sufficient when it is signed by the secured party instead of the debtor if it is filed to perfect a security interest in

(a) collateral already subject to a security interest in another jurisdiction when it is brought into this state, or when the debtor's location is changed to this state. Such a financing statement must state that the collateral was brought into this state or that the debtor's location was changed to this state under such circumstances; or

(b) proceeds under Section 9—306 if the security interest in the original collateral was perfected. Such a financing statement must describe the original collateral; or

(c) collateral as to which the filing has lapsed; or

(d) collateral acquired after a change of name, identity or corporate structure of the debtor (subsection [7]).

(3) A form substantially as follows is sufficient to comply with subsection (1):

Name of debtor (or assignor) ....
Address ....
Name of secured party (or assignee) ....
Address ....

1. This financing statement covers the following types (or items) of property:
   (Describe)

2. (If collateral is crops) The above described crops are growing or are to be grown on:
   (Describe Real Estate) ....

3. (If applicable) The above goods are to become fixtures on*
(Describe Real Estate) .... and this financing statement is to be filed [for record] in the real estate records. (If the debtor does not have an interest of record) The name of a record owner is ....

4. (If products of collateral are claimed) Products of the collateral are also covered.
      (use whichever signature is applicable)

....
Signature of Debtor (or Assignor)

....
Signature of Secured Party (or Assignee)

(4) A financing statement may be amended by filing a writing signed by both the debtor and the secured party. An amendment does not extend the period of effectiveness of a financing statement. If any amendment adds collateral, it is effective as to the added collateral only from the filing date of the amendment. In this Article, unless the context otherwise requires, the term "financing statement" means the original financing statement and any amendments.

(5) A financing statement covering timber to be cut or covering minerals or the like (including oil and gas) or accounts subject to subsection (5) of Section 9—103, or a financing statement filed as a fixture filing (Section 9—313) where the debtor is not a transmitting utility, must show that it covers this type of collateral, must recite that it is to be filed [for record] in the real estate records, and the financing statement must contain a description of the real estate [sufficient if it were contained in a mortgage of the real estate to give constructive notice of the mortgage under the law of this state]. If the debtor does not have an interest of record in the real estate, the financing statement must show the name of a record owner.

(6) A mortgage is effective as a financing statement filed as a fixture filing from the date of its recording if

(a) the goods are described in the mortgage by item or type; and

(b) the goods are or are to become fixtures related to the real estate described in the mortgage; and

(c) the mortgage complies with the requirements for a financing statement in this section other than a recital that it is to be filed in the real estate records; and

(d) the mortgage is duly recorded.

No fee with reference to the financing statement is required other than the regular recording and satisfaction fees with respect to the mortgage.

(7) A financing statement sufficiently shows the name of the debtor if it gives the individual, partnership or corporate name of the debtor, whether or not it adds other trade names or names of partners. Where the debtor so changes his name or in the case of an organization its name, identity or corporate structure that a filed financing statement becomes seri-

ously misleading, the filing is not effective to perfect a security interest in collateral acquired by the debtor more than four months after the change, unless a new appropriate financing statement is filed before the expiration of that time. A filed financing statement remains effective with respect to collateral transferred by the debtor even though the secured party knows of or consents to the transfer.

(8) A financing statement substantially complying with the requirements of this section is effective even though it contains minor errors which are not seriously misleading. Amended in 1972.

Note: Language in brackets is optional.

Note: Where the state has any special recording system for real estate other than the usual grantor-grantee index (as, for instance, a tract system or a title registration or Torrens system) local adaptations of subsection (5) and Section 9—403(7) may be necessary. See Mass. Gen. Laws Chapter 106, Section 9—409.

§9—403
What Constitutes Filing; Duration of Filing; Effect of Lapsed Filing; Duties of Filing Officer

(1) Presentation for filing of a financing statement and tender of the filing fee or acceptance of the statement by the filing officer constitutes filing under this Article.

(2) Except as provided in subsection (6) a filed financing statement is effective for a period of five years from the date of filing. The effectiveness of a filed financing statement lapses on the expiration of the five year period unless a continuation statement is filed prior to the lapse. If a security interest perfected by filing exists at the time insolvency proceedings are commenced by or against the debtor, the security interest remains perfected until termination of the insolvency proceedings and thereafter for a period of sixty days or until expiration of the five year period, whichever occurs later. Upon lapse the security interest becomes unperfected, unless it is perfected without filing. If the security interest becomes unperfected upon lapse, it is deemed to have been unperfected as against a person who became a purchaser or lien creditor before lapse.

(3) A continuation statement may be filed by the secured party within six months prior to the expiration of the five year period specified in subsection (2). Any such continuation statement must be signed by the secured party, identify the original statement by file number and state that the original statement is still effective. A continuation statement signed by a person other than the secured party of record must be accompanied by a separate written statement of assignment signed by the secured party of record and complying with subsection (2) of Section 9—405, including payment of the required fee. Upon timely filing of the continuation statement, the effectiveness of the original statement is continued for five years after the last date to which the filing was effective whereupon it lapses in the same manner as provided in subsection (2) unless another continuation statement is filed prior to such lapse. Succeeding continuation statements may be filed in the same manner to continue the effectiveness of the original statement. Unless a statute on disposition of public records provides otherwise, the filing officer may remove a

---

*Where appropriate substitute either "The above timber is standing on ...." or "The above minerals or the like (including oil and gas) or accounts will be financed at the wellhead or minehead of the well or mine located on ...."

lapsed statement from the files and destroy it immediately if he has retained a microfilm or other photographic record, or in other cases after one year after the lapse. The filing officer shall so arrange matters by physical annexation of financing statements to continuation statements or other related filings, or by other means, that if he physically destroys the financing statements of a period more than five years past, those which have been continued by a continuation statement or which are still effective under subsection (6) shall be retained.

(4) Except as provided in subsection (7) a filing officer shall mark each statement with a file number and with the date and hour of filing and shall hold the statement or a microfilm or other photographic copy thereof for public inspection. In addition the filing officer shall index the statement according to the name of the debtor and shall note in the index the file number and the address of the debtor given in the statement.

(5) The uniform fee for filing and indexing and for stamping a copy furnished by the secured party to show the date and place of filing for an original financing statement or for a continuation statement shall be $ . . . . if the statement is in the standard form prescribed by the [Secretary of State] and otherwise shall be $ . . . . , plus in each case, if the financing statement is subject to subsection (5) of Section 9—402, $ . . . . The uniform fee for each name more than one required to be indexed shall be $ . . . . The secured party may at his option show a trade name for any person and an extra uniform indexing fee of $ . . . . shall be paid with respect thereto.

(6) If the debtor is a transmitting utility (subsection (5) of Section 9—401) and a filed financing statement so states, it is effective until a termination statement is filed. A real estate mortgage which is effective as a fixture filing under subsection (6) of Section 9—402 remains effective as a fixture filing until the mortgage is released or satisfied of record or its effectiveness otherwise terminates as to the real estate.

(7) When a financing statement covers timber to be cut or covers minerals or the like (including oil and gas) or accounts subject to subsection (5) of Section 9—103, or is filed as a fixture filing, [it shall be filed for record and] the filing officer shall index it under the names of the debtor and any owner of record shown on the financing statement in the same fashion as if they were the mortgagors in a mortgage of the real estate described, and, to the extent that the law of this state provides for indexing of mortgages under the name of the mortgagee, under the name of the secured party as if he were the mortgagee thereunder, or where indexing is by description in the same fashion as if the financing statement were a mortgage of the real estate described. Amended in 1972.

Note: In states in which writings will not appear in the real estate records and indices unless actually recorded the bracketed language in subsection (7) should be used.

§9—404
Termination Statement

(1) If a financing statement covering consumer goods is filed on or after . . . . , then within one month or within ten days following written demand by the debtor after there is no outstanding secured obligation and no commitment to make advances, incur obligations or otherwise give value, the secured party must file with each filing officer with whom the financing statement was filed, a termination statement to the effect that he no longer claims a security interest under the financing statement, which shall be identified by file number. In other cases whenever there is no outstanding secured obligation and no commitment to make advances, incur obligations or otherwise give value, the secured party must on written demand by the debtor send the debtor, for each filing officer with whom the financing statement was filed, a termination statement to the effect that he no longer claims a security interest under the financing statement, which shall be identified by file number. A termination statement signed by a person other than the secured party of record must be accompanied by a separate written statement of assignment signed by the secured party of record complying with subsection (2) of Section 9—405, including payment of the required fee. If the affected secured party fails to file such a termination statement as required by this subsection, or to send such a termination statement within ten days after proper demand therefor, he shall be liable to the debtor for one hundred dollars, and in addition for any loss caused to the debtor by such failure.

(2) On presentation to the filing officer of such a termination statement he must note it in the index. If he has received the termination statement in duplicate, he shall return one copy of the termination statement to the secured party stamped to show the time of receipt thereof. If the filing officer has a microfilm or other photographic record of the financing statement, and of any related continuation statement, statement of assignment and statement of release, he may remove the originals from the files at any time after receipt of the termination statement, or if he has no such record, he may remove them from the files at any time after one year after receipt of the termination statement.

(3) If the termination statement is in the standard form prescribed by the [Secretary of State], the uniform fee for filing and indexing the termination statement shall be $ . . . . , and otherwise shall be $ . . . . , plus in each case an additional fee of $ . . . . for each name more than one against which the termination statement is required to be indexed. Amended in 1972.

Note: The date to be inserted should be the effective date of the revised Article 9.

§9—405
Assignment of Security Interest; Duties of Filing Officer; Fees

(1) A financing statement may disclose an assignment of a security interest in the collateral described in the financing statement by indication in the financing statement of the name and address of the assignee or by an assignment itself or a copy thereof on the face or back of the statement. On presentation to the filing officer of such a financing statement the filing officer shall mark the same as provided in Section 9—403(4). The uniform fee for filing, indexing and furnishing filing data for a financing statement so indicating an assignment shall be $ . . . . if the statement is in the standard form prescribed by the [Secretary of State] and oth-

erwise shall be $ . . . ., plus in each case an additional fee of $ . . . . for each name more than one against which the financing statement is required to be indexed.

(2) A secured party may assign of record all or part of his rights under a financing statement by the filing in the place where the original financing statement was filed of a separate written statement of assignment signed by the secured party of record and setting forth the name of the secured party of record and the debtor, the file number and the date of filing of the financing statement and the name and address of the assignee and containing a description of the collateral assigned. A copy of the assignment is sufficient as a separate statement if it complies with the preceding sentence. On presentation to the filing officer of such a separate statement, the filing officer shall mark such separate statement with the date and hour of the filing. He shall note the assignment on the index of the financing statement, or in the case of a fixture filing, or a filing covering timber to be cut, or covering minerals or the like (including oil and gas) or accounts subject to subsection (5) of Section 9—103, he shall index the assignment under the name of the assignor as grantor and, to the extent that the law of this state provides for indexing the assignment of a mortgage under the name of the assignee, he shall index the assignment of the financing statement under the name of the assignee. The uniform fee for filing, indexing and furnishing filing data about such a separate statement of assignment shall be $ . . . . if the statement is in the standard form prescribed by the [Secretary of State] and otherwise shall be $ . . . ., plus in each case an additional fee of $ . . . . for each name more than one against which the statement of assignment is required to be indexed. Notwithstanding the provisions of this subsection, an assignment of record of a security interest in a fixture contained in a mortgage effective as a fixture filing (subsection (6) of Section 9—402) may be made only by an assignment of the mortgage in the manner provided by the law of this state other than this Act.

(3) After the disclosure or filing of an assignment under this section, the assignee is the secured party of record. Amended in 1972.

§9—406
Release of Collateral; Duties of Filing Officer; Fees

A secured party of record may by his signed statement release all or a part of any collateral described in a filed financing statement. The statement of release is sufficient if it contains a description of the collateral being released, the name and address of the debtor, the name and address of the secured party, and the file number of the financing statement. A statement of release signed by a person other than the secured party of record must be accompanied by a separate written statement of assignment signed by the secured party of record and complying with subsection (2) of Section 9—405, including payment of the required fee. Upon presentation of such a statement of release to the filing officer he shall mark the statement with the hour and date of filing and shall note the same upon the margin of the index of the

filing of the financing statement. The uniform fee for filing and noting such a statement of release shall be $ . . . . if the statement is in the standard form prescribed by the [Secretary of State] and otherwise shall be $ . . . ., plus in each case an additional fee of $ . . . . for each name more than one against which the statement of release is required to be indexed. Amended in 1972.

§9—407.
Information From Filing Officer]

[(1) If the person filing any financing statement, termination statement, statement of assignment, or statement of release, furnishes the filing officer a copy thereof, the filing officer shall upon request note upon the copy the file number and date and hour of the filing of the original and deliver or send the copy to such person.]

[(2) Upon request of any person, the filing officer shall issue his certificate showing whether there is on file on the date and hour stated therein, any presently effective financing statement naming a particular debtor and any statement of assignment thereof and if there is, giving the date and hour of filing of each such statement and the names and addresses of each secured party therein. The uniform fee for such a certificate shall be $ . . . . if the request for the certificate is in the standard form prescribed by the [Secretary of State] and otherwise shall be $ . . . . Upon request the filing officer shall furnish a copy of any filed financing statement or statement of assignment for a uniform fee of $ . . . . per page.] Amended in 1972.

Note: This section is proposed as an optional provision to require filing officers to furnish certificates. Local law and practices should be consulted with regard to the advisability of adoption.

§9—408.
Financing Statements Covering Consigned or Leased Goods

A consignor or lessor of goods may file a financing statement using the terms "consignor," "consignee," "lessor," "lessee" or the like instead of the terms specified in Section 9—402. The provisions of this Part shall apply as appropriate to such a financing statement but its filing shall not of itself be a factor in determining whether or not the consignment or lease is intended as security (Section 1—201[37]). However, if it is determined for other reasons that the consignment or lease is so intended, a security interest of the consignor or lessor which attaches to the consigned or leased goods is perfected by such filing. Added in 1972.

Part 5

Default

§9—501
Default; Procedure When Security Agreement Covers Both Real and Personal Property

(1) When a debtor is in default under a security agreement, a secured party has the rights and remedies provided in this

Part and except as limited by subsection (3) those provided in the security agreement. He may reduce his claim to judgment, foreclose or otherwise enforce the security interest by any available judicial procedure. If the collateral is documents the secured party may proceed either as to the documents or as to the goods covered thereby. A secured party in possession has the rights, remedies and duties provided in Section 9—207. The rights and remedies referred to in this subsection are cumulative.

(2) After default, the debtor has the rights and remedies provided in this Part, those provided in the security agreement and those provided in Section 9—207.

(3) To the extent that they give rights to the debtor and impose duties on the secured party, the rules stated in the subsections referred to below may not be waived or varied except as provided with respect to compulsory disposition of collateral (subsection (3) of Section 9—504 and Section 9—505) and with respect to redemption of collateral (Section 9—506) but the parties may by agreement determine the standards by which the fulfillment of these rights and duties is to be measured if such standards are not manifestly unreasonable:

  (a) subsection (2) of Section 9—502 and subsection (2) of Section 9—504 insofar as they require accounting for surplus proceeds of collateral;

  (b) subsection (3) of Section 9—504 and subsection (1) of Section 9—505 which deal with disposition of collateral;

  (c) subsection (2) of Section 9—505 which deals with acceptance of collateral as discharge of obligation;

  (d) Section 9—506 which deals with redemption of collateral; and

  (e) subsection (1) of Section 9—507 which deals with the secured party's liability for failure to comply with this Part.

(4) If the security agreement covers both real and personal property, the secured party may proceed under this Part as to the personal property or he may proceed as to both the real and the personal property in accordance with his rights and remedies in respect of the real property in which case the provisions of this Part do not apply.

(5) When a secured party has reduced his claim to judgment the lien of any levy which may be made upon his collateral by virtue of any execution based upon the judgment shall relate back to the date of the perfection of the security interest in such collateral. A judicial sale, pursuant to such execution, is a foreclosure of the security interest by judicial procedure within the meaning of this section, and the secured party may purchase at the sale and thereafter hold the collateral free of any other requirements of this Article. Amended in 1972.

§9—502
Collection Rights of Secured Party

(1) When so agreed and in any event on default the secured party is entitled to notify an account debtor or the obligor on an instrument to make payment to him whether or not the assignor was theretofore making collections on the collateral,

and also to take control of any proceeds to which he is entitled under Section 9—306.

(2) A secured party who by agreement is entitled to charge back uncollected collateral or otherwise to full or limited recourse against the debtor and who undertakes to collect from the account debtors or obligors must proceed in a commercially reasonable manner and may deduct his reasonable expenses of realization from the collections. If the security agreement secures an indebtedness, the secured party must account to the debtor for any surplus, and unless otherwise agreed, the debtor is liable for any deficiency. But, if the underlying transaction was a sale of accounts or chattel paper, the debtor is entitled to any surplus or is liable for any deficiency only if the security agreement so provides. Amended in 1972.

§9—503
Secured Party's Right to Take Possession After Default

Unless otherwise agreed a secured party has on default the right to take possession of the collateral. In taking possession a secured party may proceed without judicial process if this can be done without breach of the peace or may proceed by action. If the security agreement so provides the secured party may require the debtor to assemble the collateral and make it available to the secured party at a place to be designated by the secured party which is reasonably convenient to both parties. Without removal a secured party may render equipment unusable, and may dispose of collateral on the debtor's premises under Section 9—504.

§9—504
Secured Party's Right to Dispose of Collateral After Default; Effect of Disposition

(1) A secured party after default may sell, lease or otherwise dispose of any or all of the collateral in its then condition or following any commercially reasonable preparation or processing. Any sale of goods is subject to the Article on Sales (Article 2). The proceeds of disposition shall be applied in the order following to

  (a) the reasonable expenses of retaking, holding, preparing for sale or lease, selling, leasing and the like and, to the extent provided for in the agreement and not prohibited by law, the reasonable attorneys' fees and legal expenses incurred by the secured party;

  (b) the satisfaction of indebtedness secured by the security interest under which the disposition is made;

  (c) the satisfaction of indebtedness secured by any subordinate security interest in the collateral if written notification of demand therefor is received before distribution of the proceeds is completed. If requested by the secured party, the holder of a subordinate security interest must seasonably furnish reasonable proof of his interest, and unless he does so, the secured party need not comply with his demand.

(2) If the security interest secures an indebtedness, the secured party must account to the debtor for any surplus,

and, unless otherwise agreed, the debtor is liable for any deficiency. But if the underlying transaction was a sale of accounts or chattel paper, the debtor is entitled to any surplus or is liable for any deficiency only if the security agreement so provides.

(3) Disposition of the collateral may be by public or private proceedings and may be made by way of one or more contracts. Sale or other disposition may be as a unit or in parcels and at any time and place and on any terms but every aspect of the disposition including the method, manner, time, place and terms must be commercially reasonable. Unless collateral is perishable or threatens to decline speedily in value or is of a type customarily sold on a recognized market, reasonable notification of the time and place of any public sale or reasonable notification of the time after which any private sale or other intended disposition is to be made shall be sent by the secured party to the debtor, if he has not signed after default a statement renouncing or modifying his right to notification of sale. In the case of consumer goods no other notification need be sent. In other cases notification shall be sent to any other secured party from whom the secured party has received (before sending his notification to the debtor or before the debtor's renunciation of his rights) written notice of a claim of an interest in the collateral. The secured party may buy at any public sale and if the collateral is of a type customarily sold in a recognized market or is of a type which is the subject of widely distributed standard price quotations he may buy at private sale.

(4) When collateral is disposed of by a secured party after default, the disposition transfers to a purchaser for value all of the debtor's rights therein, discharges the security interest under which it is made and any security interest or lien subordinate thereto. The purchaser takes free of all such rights and interests even though the secured party fails to comply with the requirements of this Part or of any judicial proceedings

    (a) in the case of a public sale, if the purchaser has no knowledge of any defects in the sale and if he does not buy in collusion with the secured party, other bidders or the person conducting the sale; or

    (b) in any other case, if the purchaser acts in good faith.

(5) A person who is liable to a secured party under a guaranty, indorsement, repurchase agreement or the like and who receives a transfer of collateral from the secured party or is subrogated to his rights has thereafter the rights and duties of the secured party. Such a transfer of collateral is not a sale or disposition of the collateral under this Article. Amended in 1972.

§9—505
Compulsory Disposition of Collateral; Acceptance of the Collateral as Discharge of Obligation

(1) If the debtor has paid sixty per cent of the cash price in the case of a purchase money security interest in consumer goods or sixty per cent of the loan in the case of another security interest in consumer goods, and has not signed after default a statement renouncing or modifying his rights under this Part a secured party who has taken possession of collateral must dispose of it under Section 9—504 and if he fails to do so within ninety days after he takes possession the debtor at his option may recover in conversion or under Section 9—507(1) on secured party's liability.

(2) In any other case involving consumer goods or any other collateral a secured party in possession may, after default, propose to retain the collateral in satisfaction of the obligation. Written notice of such proposal shall be sent to the debtor if he has not signed after default a statement renouncing or modifying his rights under this subsection. In the case of consumer goods no other notice need be given. In other cases notice shall be sent to any other secured party from whom the secured party has received (before sending his notice to the debtor or before the debtor's renunciation of his rights) written notice of a claim of an interest in the collateral. If the secured party receives objection in writing from a person entitled to receive notification within twenty-one days after the notice was sent, the secured party must dispose of the collateral under Section 9—504. In the absence of such written objection the secured party may retain the collateral in satisfaction of the debtor's obligation. Amended in 1972.

§9—506
Debtor's Right to Redeem Collateral

At any time before the secured party has disposed of collateral or entered into a contract for its disposition under Section 9—504 or before the obligation has been discharged under Section 9—505(2) the debtor or any other secured party may unless otherwise agreed in writing after default redeem the collateral by tendering fulfillment of all obligations secured by the collateral as well as the expenses reasonably incurred by the secured party in retaking, holding and preparing the collateral for disposition, in arranging for the sale, and to the extent provided in the agreement and not prohibited by law, his reasonable attorneys' fees and legal expenses.

§9—507
Secured Party's Liability for Failure to Comply With This Part

(1) If it is established that the secured party is not proceeding in accordance with the provisions of this Part disposition may be ordered or restrained on appropriate terms and conditions. If the disposition has occurred the debtor or any person entitled to notification or whose security interest has been made known to the secured party prior to the disposition has a right to recover from the secured party any loss caused by a failure to comply with the provisions of this Part. If the collateral is consumer goods, the debtor has a right to recover in any event an amount not less than the credit service charge plus ten per cent of the principal amount of the debt or the time price differential plus 10 per cent of the cash price.

(2) The fact that a better price could have been obtained by a sale at a different time or in a different method from that selected by the secured party is not of itself sufficient to establish that the sale was not made in a commercially reasonable manner. If the secured party either sells the collateral in the usual manner in any recognized market therefor or if he sells at the price current in such market at the time of his sale or if he has otherwise sold in conformity with reasonable commercial practices among dealers in the type of property

sold he has sold in a commercially reasonable manner. The principles stated in the two preceding sentences with respect to sales also apply as may be appropriate to other types of disposition. A disposition which has been approved in any judicial proceeding or by any bona fide creditors' committee or representative of creditors shall conclusively be deemed to be commercially reasonable, but this sentence does not indicate that any such approval must be obtained in any case nor does it indicate that any disposition not so approved is not commercially reasonable.

Appendix B

The Uniform Partnership Act

Part I

Preliminary Provisions

§1
Name of Act

This act may be cited as Uniform Partnership Act.

§2
Definition of Terms

In this act, "Court" includes every court and judge having jurisdiction in the case.

"Business" includes every trade, occupation, or profession.

"Person" includes individuals, partnerships, corporations, and other associations.

"Bankrupt" includes bankrupt under the Federal Bankruptcy Act or insolvent under any state insolvent act.

"Conveyance" includes every assignment, lease, mortgage, or encumbrance.

"Real property" includes land and any interest or estate in land.

§3
Interpretation of Knowledge and Notice

(1) A person has "knowledge" of a fact within the meaning of this act not only when he has actual knowledge thereof, but also when he has knowledge of such other facts as in the circumstances shows bad faith.

(2) A person has "notice" of a fact within the meaning of this act when the person who claims the benefit of the notice:

(a) States the fact to such person, or

(b) Delivers through the mail, or by other means of communication, a written statement of the fact to such person or to a proper person at his place of business or residence.

§4
Rules of Construction

(1) The rule that statutes in derogation of the common law are to be strictly construed shall have no application to this act.

(2) The law of estoppel shall apply under this act.

(3) The law of agency shall apply under this act.

(4) This act shall be so interpreted and construed as to effect its general purpose to make uniform the law of those states which enact it.

(5) This act shall not be construed so as to impair the obligations of any contract existing when the act goes into effect, nor to affect any action or proceedings begun or right accrued before this act takes effect.

§5
Rules for Cases Not Provided for in This Act

In any case not provided for in this act the rules of law and equity, including the law merchant, shall govern.

Part II
Nature of Partnership

§6
Partnership Defined

(1) A partnership is an association of two or more persons to carry on as co-owners a business for profit.

(2) But any association formed under any other statute of this state, or any statute adopted by authority, other than the authority of this state, is not a partnership under this act, unless such association would have been a partnership in this state prior to the adoption of this act; but this act shall apply to limited partnerships except in so far as the statutes relating to such partnerships are inconsistent herewith.

§7
Rules for Determining the Existence of a Partnership

In determining whether a partnership exists, these rules shall apply:

(1) Except as provided by section 16 persons who are not partners as to each other are not partners as to third persons.

(2) Joint tenancy, tenancy in common, tenancy by the entireties, joint property, common property, or part ownership does not of itself establish a partnership, whether such co-owners do or do not share any profits made by the use of the property.

(3) The sharing of gross returns does not of itself establish a partnership, whether or not the persons sharing them have a joint or common right or interest in any property from which the returns are derived.

(4) The receipt by a person of a share of the profits of a business is prima facie evidence that he is a partner in the business, but no such inference shall be drawn if such profits were received in payment:

(a) As a debt by installments or otherwise,

(b) As wages of an employee or rent to a landlord,

(c) As an annuity to a widow or representative of a deceased partner,

(d) As interest on a loan, though the amount of payment vary with the profits of the business,

(e) As the consideration for the sale of a good-will of a business or other property by installments or otherwise.

§8
Partnership Property

(1) All property originally brought into the partnership stock or subsequently acquired by purchase or otherwise, on account of the partnership, is partnership property.

(2) Unless the contrary intention appears, property acquired with partnership funds is partnership property.

(3) Any estate in real property may be acquired in the partnership name. Title so acquired can be conveyed only in the partnership name.

(4) A conveyance to a partnership in the partnership name, though without words of inheritance, passes the entire estate of the grantor unless a contrary intent appears.

Part III
Relations of Partners to Persons Dealing with the Partnership

§9
Partner Agent of Partnership as to Partnership Business

(1) Every partner is an agent of the partnership for the purpose of its business, and the act of every partner, including the execution in the partnership name of any instrument, for apparently carrying on in the usual way the business of the partnership of which he is a member binds the partnership, unless the partner so acting has in fact no authority to act for the partnership in the particular matter, and the person with whom he is dealing has knowledge of the fact that he has no such authority.

(2) An act of a partner which is not apparently for the carrying on of the business of the partnership in the usual way does not bind the partnership unless authorized by the other partners.

(3) Unless authorized by the other partners or unless they have abandoned the business, one or more but less than all the partners have no authority to:

(a) Assign the partnership property in trust for creditors or on the assignee's promise to pay the debts of the partnership,

(b) Dispose of the good-will of the business,

(c) Do any other act which would make it impossible to carry on the ordinary business of a partnership,

(d) Confess a judgment,

(e) Submit a partnership claim or liability to arbitration or reference.

(4) No act of a partner in contravention of a restriction on authority shall bind the partnership to persons having knowledge of the restriction.

§10
Conveyance of Real Property of the Partnership

(1) Where title to real property is in the partnership name, any partner may convey title to such property by a conveyance executed in the partnership name; but the partnership may recover such property unless the partner's act binds the partnership under the provisions of paragraph (1) of section 9, or unless such property has been conveyed by the grantee or a person claiming through such grantee to a holder for value without knowledge that the partner, in making the conveyance, has exceeded his authority.

(2) Where title to real property is in the name of the partnership, a conveyance executed by a partner, in his own name, passes the equitable interest of the partnership, provided the act is one within the authority of the partner under the provisions of paragraph (1) of section 9.

(3) Where title to real property is in the name of one or more but not all the partners, and the record does not disclose the right of the partnership, the partners in whose name the title stands may convey title to such property, but the partnership may recover such property if the partners' act does not bind the partnership under the provisions of paragraph (1) of section 9, unless the purchaser or his assignee, is a holder for value, without knowledge.

(4) Where the title to real property is in the name of one or more or all the partners, or in a third person in trust for the partnership, a conveyance executed by a partner in the partnership name, or in his own name, passes the equitable interest of the partnership, provided the act is one within the authority of the partner under the provisions of paragraph (1) of section 9.

(5) Where the title to real property is in the names of all the partners a conveyance executed by all the partners passes all their rights in such property.

§11
Partnership Bound by Admission of Partner

An admission or representation made by any partner concerning partnership affairs within the scope of his authority as conferred by this act is evidence against the partnership.

§12
Partnership Charged with Knowledge of or Notice to Partner

Notice to any partner of any matter relating to partnership affairs, and the knowledge of the partner acting in the particular matter, acquired while a partner or then present to his mind, and the knowledge of any other partner who reasonably could and should have communicated it to the acting partner, operate as notice to or knowledge of the partnership, except in the case of a fraud on the partnership committed by or with the consent of that partner.

§13
Partnership Bound by Partner's Wrongful Act

Where, by any wrongful act or omission of any partner acting in the ordinary course of the business of the partnership or with the authority of his co-partners, loss or injury is caused to any person, not being a partner in the partnership, or any penalty is incurred, the partnership is liable therefor to the same extent as the partner so acting or omitting to act.

§14
Partnership Bound by Partner's Breach of Trust

The partnership is bound to make good the loss:

(a) Where one partner acting within the scope of his apparent authority receives money or property of a third person and misapplies it; and

(b) Where the partnership in the course of its business receives money or property of a third person and the money or property so received is misapplied by any partner while it is in the custody of the partnership.

§15
Nature of Partner's Liability

All partners are liable

(a) Jointly and severally for everything chargeable to the partnership under sections 13 and 14.

(b) Jointly for all other debts and obligations of the partnership; but any partner may enter into a separate obligation to perform a partnership contract.

§16
Partner by Estoppel

(1) When a person, by words spoken or written or by conduct, represents himself, or consents to another representing him to any one, as a partner in an existing partnership or with one or more persons not actual partners, he is liable to any such person to whom such representation has been made, who has, on the faith of such representation, given credit to the actual or apparent partnership, and if he has made such representation or consented to its being made in a public manner he is liable to such person, whether the representation has or has not been made or communicated to such person so giving credit by or with the knowledge of the apparent partner making the representation or consenting to its being made.

(a) When a partnership liability results, he is liable as though he were an actual member of the partnership.

(b) When no partnership liability results, he is liable jointly with the other persons, if any, so consenting to the contract or representation as to incur liability, otherwise separately.

(2) When a person has been thus represented to be a partner in an existing partnership, or with one or more persons not actual partners, he is an agent of the persons consenting to such representation to bind them to the same extent and in the same manner as though he were a partner in fact, with respect to persons who rely upon the representation. Where all the members of the existing partnership consent to the representation, a partnership act or obligation results; but in all other cases it is the joint act or obligation of the person acting and the persons consenting to the representation.

§17
Liability of Incoming Partner

A person admitted as a partner into an existing partnership is liable for all the obligations of the partnership arising before his admission as though he had been a partner when such obligations were incurred, except that this liability shall be satisfied only out of partnership property.

Part IV

Relations of Partners to One Another

§18
Rules Determining Rights and Duties of Partners

The rights and duties of the partners in relation to the partnership shall be determined, subject to any agreement between them, by the following rules:

(a) Each partner shall be repaid his contributions, whether by way of capital or advances to the partnership property and share equally in the profits and surplus remaining after all liabilities, including those to partners, are satisfied; and must contribute towards the losses, whether of capital or otherwise, sustained by the partnership according to his share in the profits.

(b) The partnership must indemnify every partner in respect of payments made and personal liabilities reasonably incurred by him in the ordinary and proper conduct of its business, or for the preservation of its business or property.

(c) A partner, who in aid of the partnership makes any payment or advance beyond the amount of capital which he agreed to contribute, shall be paid interest from the date of the payment or advance.

(d) A partner shall receive interest on the capital contributed by him only from the date when repayment should be made.

(e) All partners have equal rights in the management and conduct of the partnership business.

(f) No partner is entitled to remuneration for acting in the partnership business, except that a surviving partner is entitled to reasonable compensation for his services in winding up the partnership affairs.

(g) No person can become a member of a partnership without the consent of all the partners.

(h) Any difference arising as to ordinary matters connected with the partnership business may be decided by a majority of the partners; but no act in contravention of any agreement between the partners may be done rightfully without the consent of all the partners.

§19
Partnership Books

The partnership books shall be kept, subject to any agreement between the partners, at the principal place of business of the partnership, and every partner shall at all times have access to and may inspect and copy any of them.

§20
Duty of Partners to Render Information

Partners shall render on demand true and full information of all things affecting the partnership to any partner or the legal representative of any deceased partner or partner under legal disability.

§21
Partner Accountable as a Fiduciary

(1) Every partner must account to the partnership for any benefit, and hold as trustee for it any profits derived by him without the consent of the other partners from any transaction connected with the formation, conduct, or liquidation of the partnership or from any use by him of its property.

(2) This section applies also to the representatives of a deceased partner engaged in the liquidation of the affairs of the partnership as the personal representatives of the last surviving partner.

§22
Right to an Account

Any partner shall have the right to a formal account as to partnership affairs:

(a) If he is wrongfully excluded from the partnership business or possession of its property by his co-partners,

(b) If the right exists under the terms of any agreement,

(c) As provided by section 21,

(d) Whenever other circumstances render it just and reasonable.

§23
Continuation of Partnership Beyond Fixed Term

(1) When a partnership for a fixed term or particular undertaking is continued after the termination of such term or particular undertaking without any express agreement, the rights and duties of the partners remain the same as they were at such termination, so far as is consistent with a partnership at will.

(2) A continuation of the business by the partners or such of them as habitually acted therein during the term, without any settlement or liquidation of the partnership affairs, is prima facie evidence of a continuation of the partnership.

Part V

Property Rights of a Partner

§24
Extent of Property Rights of a Partner

The property rights of a partner are (1) his rights in specific partnership property, (2) his interest in the partnership, and (3) his right to participate in the management.

§25
Nature of a Partner's Right in Specific Partnership Property

(1) A partner is co-owner with his partners of specific part-

nership property holding as a tenant in partnership.

(2) The incidents of this tenancy are such that:

(a) A partner, subject to the provisions of this act and to any agreement between the partners, has an equal right with his partners to possess specific partnership property for partnership purposes; but he has no right to possess such property for any other purpose without the consent of his partners.

(b) A partner's right in specific partnership property is not assignable except in connection with the assignment of rights of all the partners in the same property.

(c) A partner's right in specific partnership property is not subject to attachment or execution, except on a claim against the partnership. When partnership property is attached for a partnership debt the partners, or any of them, or the representatives of a deceased partner, cannot claim any right under the homestead or exemption laws.

(d) On the death of a partner his right in specific partnership property vests in the surviving partner or partners, except where the deceased was the last surviving partner, when his right in such property vests in his legal representative. Such surviving partner or partners, or the legal representative of the last surviving partner, has no right to possess the partnership property for any but a partnership purpose.

(e) A partner's right in specific partnership property is not subject to dower, curtesy, or allowances to widows, heirs, or next of kin.

§26
Nature of Partner's Interest in the Partnership

A partner's interest in the partnership is his share of the profits and surplus, and the same is personal property.

§27
Assignment of Partner's Interest

(1) A conveyance by a partner of his interest in the partnership does not of itself dissolve the partnership, nor, as against the other partners in the absence of agreement, entitle the assignee, during the continuance of the partnership, to interfere in the management or administration of the partnership business or affairs, or to require any information or account of partnership transactions, or to inspect the partnership books; but it merely entitles the assignee to receive in accordance with his contract the profits to which the assigning partner would otherwise be entitled.

(2) In case of a dissolution of the partnership, the assignee is entitled to receive his assignor's interest and may require an account from the date only of the last account agreed to by all the partners.

§28
Partner's Interest Subject to Charging Order

(1) On due application to a competent court by any judgment creditor of a partner, the court which entered the judgment, order, or decree, or any other court, may charge the interest of the debtor partner with payment of the unsatisfied amount of such judgment debt with interest thereon; and

may then or later appoint a receiver of his share of the profits, and of any other money due or to fall due to him in respect of the partnership, and make all other orders, directions, accounts and inquiries which the debtor partner might have made, or which the circumstances of the case may require.

(2) The interest charged may be redeemed at any time before foreclosure, or in case of a sale being directed by the court may be purchased without thereby causing a dissolution:

(a) With separate property, by any one or more of the partners, or

(b) With partnership property, by any one or more of the partners with the consent of all the partners whose interests are not so charged or sold.

(3) Nothing in this act shall be held to deprive a partner of his right, if any, under the exemption laws, as regards his interest in the partnership.

Part VI
Dissolution and Winding Up

§29
Dissolution Defined

The dissolution of a partnership is the change in the relation of the partners caused by any partner ceasing to be associated in the carrying on as distinguished from the winding up of the business.

§30
Partnership not Terminated by Dissolution

On dissolution the partnership is not terminated, but continues until the winding up of partnership affairs is completed.

§31
Causes of Dissolution

Dissolution is caused:

(1) Without violation of the agreement between the partners,

(a) By the termination of the definite term or particular undertaking specified in the agreement,

(b) By the express will of any partner when no definite term or particular undertaking is specified,

(c) By the express will of all the partners who have not assigned their interests or suffered them to be charged for their separate debts, either before or after the termination of any specified term or particular undertaking,

(d) By the expulsion of any partner from the business bona fide in accordance with such a power conferred by the agreement between the partners;

(2) In contravention of the agreement between the partners, where the circumstances do not permit a dissolution under any other provision of this section, by the express will of any partner at any time;

(3) By any event which makes it unlawful for the business of the partnership to be carried on or for the members to carry it on in partnership;

(4) By the death of any partner;

(5) By the bankruptcy of any partner or the partnership;

(6) By decree of court under section 32.

§32
Dissolution by Decree of Court

(1) On application by or for a partner the court shall decree a dissolution whenever:

(a) A partner has been declared a lunatic in any judicial proceeding or is shown to be of unsound mind,

(b) A partner becomes in any other way incapable of performing his part of the partnership contract,

(c) A partner has been guilty of such conduct as tends to affect prejudicially the carrying on of the business,

(d) A partner wilfully or persistently commits a breach of the partnership agreement, or otherwise so conducts himself in matters relating to the partnership business that it is not reasonably practicable to carry on the business in partnership with him,

(e) The business of the partnership can only be carried on at a loss,

(f) Other circumstances render a dissolution equitable.

(2) On the application of the purchaser of a partner's interest under sections 28 or 29:

(a) After the termination of the specified term or particular undertaking,

(b) At any time if the partnership was a partnership at will when the interest was assigned or when the charging order was issued.

§33
General Effect of Dissolution on Authority of Partner

Except so far as may be necessary to wind up partnership affairs or to complete transactions begun but not then finished, dissolution terminates all authority of any partner to act for the partnership,

(1) With respect to the partners,

(a) When the dissolution is not by the act, bankruptcy or death of a partner; or

(b) When the dissolution is by such act, bankruptcy or death of a partner, in cases where section 34 so requires.

(2) With respect to persons not partners, as declared in section 35.

§34
Right of Partner to Contribution from Co-partners after Dissolution

Where the dissolution is caused by the act, death or bankruptcy of a partner, each partner is liable to his co-partners for his share of any liability created by any partner acting for the partnership as if the partnership had not been dissolved unless

(a) The dissolution being by act of any partner, the partner acting for the partnership had knowledge of the dissolution, or

(b) The dissolution being by the death or bankruptcy of a partner, the partner acting for the partnership had knowledge or notice of the death or bankruptcy.

§35
Power of Partner to Bind Partnership to Third Persons after Dissolution

(1) After dissolution a partner can bind the partnership except as provided in Paragraph (3)

(a) By any act appropriate for winding up partnership affairs or completing transactions unfinished at dissolution;

(b) By any transaction which would bind the partnership if dissolution had not taken place, provided the other party to the transaction

(I) Had extended credit to the partnership prior to dissolution and had no knowledge or notice of the dissolution; or

(II) Though he had not so extended credit, had nevertheless known of the partnership prior to dissolution, and, having no knowledge or notice of dissolution, the fact of dissolution had not been advertised in a newspaper of general circulation in the place (or in each place if more than one) at which the partnership business was regularly carried on.

(2) The liability of a partner under Paragraph (1b) shall be satisfied out of partnership assets alone when such partner had been prior to dissolution

(a) Unknown as a partner to the person with whom the contract is made; and

(b) So far unknown and inactive in partnership affairs that the business reputation of the partnership could not be said to have been in any degree due to his connection with it.

(3) The partnership is in no case bound by any act of a partner after dissolution

(a) Where the partnership is dissolved because it is unlawful to carry on the business, unless the act is appropriate for winding up partnership affairs; or

(b) Where the partner has become bankrupt; or

(c) Where the partner has no authority to wind up partnership affairs; except by a transaction with one who

(I) Had extended credit to the partnership prior to dissolution and had no knowledge or notice of his want of authority; or

(II) Had not extended credit to the partnership prior to dissolution, and, having no knowledge or notice of his want of authority, the fact of his want of authority has not been advertised in the manner provided for advertising the fact of dissolution in Paragraph (1bII).

(4) Nothing in this section shall affect the liability under Section 16 of any person who after dissolution represents himself or consents to another representing him as a partner in a partnership engaged in carrying on business.

§36
Effect of Dissolution on Partner's Existing Liability

(1) The dissolution of the partnership does not of itself discharge the existing liability of any partner.

(2) A partner is discharged from any existing liability upon dissolution of the partnership by an agreement to that effect between himself, the partnership creditor and the person or partnership continuing the business; and such agreement may be inferred from the course of dealing between the creditor having knowledge of the dissolution and the person or partnership continuing the business.

(3) Where a person agrees to assume the existing obligations of a dissolved partnership, the partners whose obligations have been assumed shall be discharged from any liability to any creditor of the partnership who, knowing of the agreement, consents to a material alteration in the nature or time of payment of such obligations.

(4) The individual property of a deceased partner shall be liable for all obligations of the partnership incurred while he was a partner but subject to the prior payment of his separate debts.

§37
Right to Wind Up

Unless otherwise agreed the partners who have not wrongfully dissolved the partnership or the legal representative of the last surviving partner, not bankrupt, has the right to wind up the partnership affairs; provided, however, that any partner, his legal representative or his assignee, upon cause shown, may obtain winding up by the court.

§38
Rights of Partners to Application of Partnership Property

(1) When dissolution is caused in any way, except in contravention of the partnership agreement, each partner, as against his co-partners and all persons claiming through them in respect of their interests in the partnership, unless otherwise agreed, may have the partnership property applied to discharge its liabilities, and the surplus applied to pay in cash the net amount owing to the respective partners. But if dissolution is caused by expulsion of a partner, bona fide under the partnership agreement and if the expelled partner is discharged from all partnership liabilities, either by payment or agreement under section 36(2), he shall receive in cash only the net amount due him from the partnership.

(2) When dissolution is caused in contravention of the partnership agreement the rights of the partners shall be as follows:

(a) Each partner who has not caused dissolution wrongfully shall have,

I. All the rights specified in paragraph (1) of this section, and

II. The right, as against each partner who has caused the dissolution wrongfully, to damages for breach of the agreement.

(b) The partners who have not caused the dissolution wrongfully, if they all desire to continue the business in the same name, either by themselves or jointly with others, may do so, during the agreed term for the partnership and for that purpose may possess the partnership property, provided they secure the payment by bond approved by the court, or pay to any partner who has caused the dissolution wrongfully, the value of his interest in the partnership at the dissolution, less any damages recoverable under clause (2aII) of this section, and in like manner indemnify him against all present or future partnership liabilities.

(c) A partner who has caused the dissolution wrongfully shall have:

I. If the business is not continued under the provisions of paragraph (2b) all the rights of a partner under paragraph (1), subject to clause (2aII), of this section,

II. If the business is continued under paragraph (2b) of this section the right as against his co-partners and all claiming through them in respect of their interests in the partnership, to have the value of his interest in the partnership, less any damages caused to his co-partners by the dissolution, ascertained and paid to him in cash, or the payment secured by bond approved by the court, and to be released from all existing liabilities of the partnership; but in ascertaining the value of the partner's interest the value of the good-will of the business shall not be considered.

§39
Rights Where Partnership Is Dissolved for Fraud or Misrepresentation

Where a partnership contract is rescinded on the ground of the fraud or misrepresentation of one of the parties thereto, the party entitled to rescind is, without prejudice to any other right, entitled,

(a) To a lien on, or a right of retention of, the surplus of the partnership property after satisfying the partnership liabilities to third persons for any sum of money paid by him for the purchase of an interest in the partnership and for any capital or advances contributed by him; and

(b) To stand, after all liabilities to third persons have been satisfied, in the place of the creditors of the partnership for any payments made by him in respect of the partnership liabilities; and

(c) To be indemnified by the person guilty of the fraud or making the representation against all debts and liabilities of the partnership.

§40
Rules for Distribution

In settling accounts between the partners after dissolution, the following rules shall be observed, subject to any agreement to the contrary:

(a) The assets of the partnership are:

I. The partnership property,

II. The contributions of the partners necessary for the payment of all the liabilities specified in clause (b) of this paragraph.

(b) The liabilities of the partnership shall rank in order of payment, as follows:

I. Those owing to creditors other than partners,

II. Those owing to partners other than for capital and profits,

III. Those owing to partners in respect of capital,

IV. Those owing to partners in respect of profits.

(c) The assets shall be applied in order of their declaration in clause (a) of this paragraph to the satisfaction of the liabilities.

(d) The partners shall contribute, as provided by section 18(a) the amount necessary to satisfy the liabilities; but if any, but not all, of the partners are insolvent, or, not being subject to process, refuse to contribute, the other partners shall contribute their share of the liabilities, and, in the relative proportions in which they share the profits, the additional amount necessary to pay the liabilities.

(e) An assignee for the benefit of creditors or any person appointed by the court shall have the right to enforce the contributions specified in clause (d) of this paragraph.

(f) Any partner or his legal representative shall have the right to enforce the contributions specified in clause (d) of this paragraph, to the extent of the amount which he has paid in excess of his share of the liability.

(g) The individual property of a deceased partner shall be liable for the contributions specified in clause (d) of this paragraph.

(h) When partnership property and the individual properties of the partners are in possession of a court for distribution, partnership creditors shall have priority on partnership property and separate creditors on individual property, saving the rights of lien or secured creditors as heretofore.

(i) Where a partner has become bankrupt or his estate is insolvent the claims against his separate property shall rank in the following order:

I. Those owing to separate creditors,

II. Those owing to partnership creditors,

III. Those owing to partners by way of contribution.

§41
Liability of Persons Continuing the Business in Certain Cases

(1) When any new partner is admitted into an existing partnership, or when any partner retires and assigns (or the representative of the deceased partner assigns) his rights in partnership property to two or more of the partners, or to one or more of the partners and one or more third persons, if the business is continued without liquidation of the partnership affairs, creditors of the first or dissolved partnership are also creditors of the partnership so continuing the business.

(2) When all but one partner retire and assign (or the representative of a deceased partner assigns) their rights in partnership property to the remaining partner, who continues the business without liquidation of partnership affairs, either alone or with others, creditors of the dissolved partnership are also creditors of the person or partnership so continuing the business.

(3) When any partner retires or dies and the business of the

dissolved partnership is continued as set forth in paragraphs (1) and (2) of this section, with the consent of the retired partners or the representative of the deceased partner, but without any assignment of his right in partnership property, rights of creditors of the dissolved partnership and of the creditors of the person or partnership continuing the business shall be as if such assignment had been made.

(4) When all the partners or their representatives assign their rights in partnership property to one or more third persons who promise to pay the debts and who continue the business of the dissolved partnership, creditors of the dissolved partnership are also creditors of the person or partnership continuing the business.

(5) When any partner wrongfully causes a dissolution and the remaining partners continue the business under the provisions of section 38(2b), either alone or with others, and without liquidation of the partnership affairs, creditors of the dissolved partnership are also creditors of the person or partnership continuing the business.

(6) When a partner is expelled and the remaining partners continue the business either alone or with others, without liquidation of the partnership affairs, creditors of the dissolved partnership are also creditors of the person or partnership continuing the business.

(7) The liability of a third person becoming a partner in the partnership continuing the business, under this section, to the creditors of the dissolved partnership shall be satisfied out of partnership property only.

(8) When the business of a partnership after dissolution is continued under any conditions set forth in this section the creditors of the dissolved partnership, as against the separate creditors of the retiring or deceased partner or the representative of the deceased partner, have a prior right to any claim of the retired partner or the representative of the deceased partner against the person or partnership continuing the business, on account of the retired or deceased partner's interest in the dissolved partnership or on account of any consideration promised for such interest or for his right in partnership property.

(9) Nothing in this section shall be held to modify any right of creditors to set aside any assignment on the ground of fraud.

(10) The use by the person or partnership continuing the business of the partnership name, or the name of a deceased partner as part thereof, shall not of itself make the individual property of the deceased partner liable for any debts contracted by such person or partnership.

§42
Rights of Retiring or Estate of Deceased Partner When the Business Is Continued

When any partner retires or dies, and the business is continued under any of the conditions set forth in section 41(1, 2, 3, 5, 6), or section 38(2b) without any settlement of accounts as between him or his estate and the person or partnership continuing the business, unless otherwise agreed, he or his legal representative as against such persons or partnership may have the value of his interest at the date of dissolution ascertained, and shall receive as an ordinary creditor an amount equal to the value of his interest in the dissolved partnership with interest, or, at his option or at the option of his legal representative, in lieu of interest, the profits attributable to the use of his right in the property of the dissolved partnership; provided that the creditors of the dissolved partnership as against the separate creditors, or the representative of the retired or deceased partner, shall have priority on any claim arising under this section, as provided by section 41(8) of this act.

§43
Accrual of Actions

The right to an account of his interest shall accrue to any partner, or his legal representative, as against the winding up partners or the surviving partners or the person or partnership continuing the business, at the date of dissolution, in the absence of any agreement to the contrary.

Part VII
Miscellaneous Provisions

§44.
When Act Takes Effect

This act shall take effect on the . . . . day of . . . . one thousand nine hundred and . . . .

§45
Legislation Repealed

All acts or parts of acts inconsistent with this act are hereby repealed.

Glossary

abandoned property Property that is unowned because the owner has given up dominion and control with the intent to relinquish all claim or rights to it.

ab initio From the very beginning (Latin).

abstract In real property law, a summary compilation of the official records relating to a particular parcel of land.

abuse of discretion The failure of a judge or administrator to use sound or reasonable judgment in arriving at a decision.

acceleration clause In commercial paper, a statement in a time instrument (where payment is to be made at a prescribed time or times) that permits the entire debt to become due immediately upon the occurrence of some event, such as failure to pay one installment when due.

acceptance (1) In commercial paper, the drawee's signed engagement to honor the draft as presented. (2) In contract law, the agreement of the offeree to the proposal or offer of the offeror.

acceptor In commercial paper, a drawee who agrees by his or her signature to honor a draft as presented.

accession An addition to, product of, or change in personal property; depending on the circumstances, either the owner of the original property or another person responsible for the accession might be the owner of the altered property.

accommodated party The person who benefits by having another party lend his or her name (credit) on an instrument.

accommodation party A person who signs an instrument for the purpose of lending his or her name (credit) to another party on that instrument.

accord and satisfaction A form of discharge in contract law by which an agreement between the parties of a contract permits a substituted performance in lieu of the required obligation under the existing contract. The contract can be effectively terminated (satisfied) by perfor-

1009

mance as originally agreed upon or by the substitute performance.

account receivable A record of a debt owed to a person but not yet paid.

accretion The gradual adding of land by natural causes, such as a deposit of soil by the action of a river.

acknowledgment A formal declaration or admission before a designated public official, such as a notary public, that something is genuine or that a particular act has taken place.

action at law A suit initiated in a court of law, as distinguished from a suit in equity. The usual remedy sought in such a suit is a judgment for monetary damages.

action in equity A civil suit in which the plaintiff is seeking an equitable remedy, such as an injunction or decree of specific performance.

action *in personam* A suit to hold a defendant personally liable for a wrong committed.

action *in rem* A suit to enforce a right against property of the defendant.

act of bankruptcy Any action of a debtor, as specified in the federal Bankruptcy Act, committed within four months preceding the filing of a petition in bankruptcy that is a sufficient ground for declaring the debtor bankrupt.

actual authority The express and implied authority of an agent.

adjudication The legal process of resolving a dispute.

adjudicatory power In administrative agency law, the right of an administrative agency to initiate actions as both prosecutor and judge against those thought to be in violation of the law (including agency rules and regulations) under the jurisdiction of the administrative agency —referred to as the quasi-judicial function of an agency.

administrative agency A board, commission, agency, or service authorized by a legislative enactment to implement specific laws on either the local, state, or national level.

administrative law Public law administered and/or formulated by a government unit such as a board, agency, or commission to govern the conduct of an individual, association, or corporation.

administrator In probate law, a person appointed by a probate court to supervise the distribution of a deceased person's property. This title is usually given when there is no will or when the person named as executor or executrix in the will cannot serve.

adverse possession The acquisition of title to real property by actually taking possession of the land without the

owner's consent and retaining such possession openly for a prescribed statutory period.

affidavit A written sworn statement made before a person officially authorized to administer an oath.

affirmative defense A defendant's claim to dissolve himself or herself of liability even if the plaintiff's claim is true.

after-acquired property Property received or added after a specific event has taken place. For example, in secured transactions law, an after-acquired property clause in a security agreement means that property received by the debtor after the security agreement is made will be subject to the same security interest as the existing property referred to therein.

agency A relationship created by contract, agreement, or law between a principal and an agent whereby the principal is bound by the authorized actions of the agent.

agency coupled with an interest A relationship in which an agent, with consideration, has the right to exercise authority or is given an interest in the property of the principal subject to the agency.

agent One who is authorized to act for another, called a principal, whose acts bind the principal to his or her actions.

aggregate theory An approach under which associations or organizations are treated as a collection of persons, each with individual rights and liabilities.

agreement A meeting of the minds between two or more parties, which may or may not constitute a contract.

air rights A landowner's rights to the air space above his or her real property.

alien corporation A corporation chartered or incorporated in another country but doing business in the United States.

alteration (material) In commercial paper, the modification of the terms of an instrument that results in a change of the contract of any party on that instrument.

amendment The changing of a law, right, or interest that usually becomes binding upon fulfillment of a required act or action.

annual percentage rate The total of the items making up the finance charge, or cost of borrowing money or buying on credit, expressed as a yearly percentage rate that the consumer can use to "shop around" for the best credit terms.

answer In pleadings, the defendant's response to the plaintiff's complaint or petition.

anticipatory breach The repudiation of a contract by a party before the time of performance has arrived, allowing the nonbreaching party the opportunity to seek a remedy.

apparent authority Authority created by the words or conduct of the principal that leads a third person to believe the agent has such authority.

apparent intent The establishment of a person's motive from his or her actions and/or words as interpreted by a reasonable person.

appellant The party who appeals a decision of a lower court, usually that of a trial court.

appellee The party against whom an appeal is made (sometimes referred to as a respondent—a person who defends on an appeal).

appraisal right The right of a dissenting shareholder to sell back his or her shares to the corporation for cash.

arbitration The submission of a dispute to a third party or parties for settlement.

articles of incorporation A legal document, meeting the legal requirements of a given state, filed with a designated state official as an application for a certificate of incorporation.

articles of partnership The agreement of the partners that forms and governs the operation of the partnership.

artisan's lien A possessory lien held by one who has expended labor upon or added value to another's personal property as security for the work performed (labor and/or value added).

ascendants The heirs of a decedent in the ascending line—parents or grandparents.

assault The intentional movement or exhibition of force that would place a reasonable person in fear of physical attack or harm.

assault and battery Any intentional physical contact by a person on another without consent or privilege.

assignee The one to whom an assignment has been made.

assignment The transfer of rights or a property interest to a third person, who can receive no greater rights than those possessed by the transferor.

assignment for the benefit of creditors The voluntary transfer by a debtor of some or all of his or her property to an assignee or trustee, who sells or liquidates the debtor's assets and tenders to the creditors (on a pro rata basis) payment in satisfaction of the debt.

assignor The one who makes an assignment.

association The voluntary act or agreement by which two or more persons unite together for some special purpose or business.

attachment (1) A legal proceeding provided by statute that permits a plaintiff in an existing court action to have nonexempt property of the defendant seized and a lien placed on the property as security of a judgment that may be rendered in the plaintiff's favor (this action being independent of plaintiff's suit and exercisable only on grounds provided by statute). (2) In secured transactions law, a method of perfecting a security interest without the secured party taking possession of the collateral or making a proper filing (which in most states applies only to a purchase-money security interest in consumer goods).

attestation The act of witnessing a document, such as a will, and signing to that effect.

attorney-at-law A lawyer.

attorney-in-fact An agent.

auction with reserve An auction in which the auctioneer, as agent for the owner of the goods, has the right to withdraw the goods from sale at any time prior to accepting a particular bid (such acceptance usually being signified by the fall of the hammer).

auction without reserve An auction where once the goods are placed on the auction block (for sale) they must be sold to the highest bidder.

bailee The person to whom a bailor has entrusted or transferred personal property without transferring title.

bailee's lien Usually a possessory lien held by a bailee on bailed property for which the bailee is entitled to compensation or reimbursement.

bailment The creation of a legal relationship through delivery or transfer of personal property (but not title) by one person, called the bailor, to another person, called the bailee, usually for a specific purpose as directed by the bailor.

bailor A person who entrusts or transfers personal property (but not title) to another, called the bailee, usually for the accomplishment of a specific purpose.

bank draft A draft by one bank on funds held by another bank.

bankruptcy A court procedure by which a person who is unable to pay his or her debts may be declared bankrupt, have nonexempt assets distributed to his or her creditors, and thereupon be given a release from any further payment of the balance due on most of these debts.

battery The wrongful intentional physical contact by a person (or object under control of that person) on another.

bearer In commercial paper, the person possessing an instrument either payable to anyone without specific designation, or one indorsed in blank.

bearer instrument An instrument either payable to anyone without specific designation, or one indorsed in blank.

beneficiary A person for whose benefit a will, trust, insurance policy, or contract is made.

benefit test A test through which the law determines whether a promise has consideration by seeing if the promisor has received an advantage, profit, or privilege from his or her promise. (In the majority of situations, if the promisee has suffered a legal detriment, the promisor has received a corresponding benefit. Thus the detriment test is stressed in determining whether the agreement is supported by consideration.)

bequest In a will a gift by the testator of specific personal property other than money.

bilateral contract A contract formed by the mutual exchange of promises of the offeror and the offeree.

bilateral mistake A mistake in which both parties to a contract are in error as to the terms of or performance expected under the contract.

bill of lading A negotiable or nonnegotiable document of title evidencing the receipt of goods for shipment, with shipping instructions to the carrier. A negotiable bill of lading is both a receipt and evidence of title to the goods shipped.

blank indorsement An indorsement that specifies no particular indorsee and that usually consists of a mere signature of the indorser.

blue sky laws State laws regulating the issuance, transfer, and sale of securities—designed primarily to prevent fraud.

board of directors A body composed of persons elected by the corporation's shareholders and entrusted with the responsibility of managing the corporation.

bonds In corporate financing, secured or unsecured debt obligations of a corporation in the form of securities (instruments).

breach of duty Failure to fulfill a legal obligation.

broker In real property law, an agent employed by a landowner to find an acceptable buyer for his or her real property or employed by a prospective buyer to find a landowner willing to sell such property.

bulk transfer A transfer of goods—such as materials, supplies, merchandise, or inventory (including equipment)—in such quantity or under such circumstances that the transfer is considered not to be in the ordinary course of the transferor's business.

burden of proof The duty of a party to prove or disprove to the triers of fact a stated cause of action.

business trust A business association created by agreement in which legal ownership and management of property is transferred, in return for trust certificates, to trustees who have the power to operate the business for the benefit of the original owners or certificate holders. It is usually treated in the same manner as a corporation if certificate holders do not control the management activities of the trustees.

bylaws The internal rules made to regulate and govern the actions and affairs of a corporation.

capacity The legal ability to perform an act—especially an act from which legal consequences flow, such as the making of a contract.

cashier's check A check drawn by a bank on itself.

cause of action A person's right to seek a remedy when his or her rights have been breached or violated.

caveat emptor In sales law, "let the buyer beware."

certificate of authority A foreign corporation's permission to do business in the state of issuance.

certificate of deposit An instrument (essentially a note) that is an acknowledgment by a bank that it has received money and promises to repay the amount upon presentment when due.

certificate of incorporation A document of a state that grants permission to do business in that state in the corporate form—sometimes called a charter.

certificate of title A written opinion by an attorney as to the validity of a title.

certified check A bank's guaranty (acceptance) by an appropriate signature that it will pay the check upon presentment.

challenge for cause In jury selection, an objection to a prospective juror hearing a particular case, stating a reason that questions the impartiality of the juror to render a fair verdict.

chattel Any property or interest therein other than real property.

chattel mortgage A security document whereby the owner of personal property either transfers title to the lender or gives the lender a lien on the property as security for the performance of an obligation owed by the owner. Called a security interest under the UCC.

chattel paper Any writing or writings that evidence both a monetary obligation for and a security interest in (or a lease of) specific goods.

check A draft drawn on a bank (drawee) payable on demand.

CIF Cost, insurance, and freight; that is, the price

charged by the seller includes not only the cost of the goods but also the cost of freight and insurance charges on the goods to the named destination.

circumstantial context A court's interpretation of a given statute, dependent upon an examination of the problem or problems that caused the enactment of the statute.

civil law As compared to criminal law, rules for establishing rights and duties between individuals whereby an individual can seek personal redress for a wrong committed by another individual. As compared to common law, codified rules reduced to formal written propositions as the law of a state or country. The written code serves as the basis of all decisions.

Clayton Act A 1914 congressional enactment to generally prohibit in commerce discrimination in pricing by a seller to competitive buyers, to generally prohibit exclusive dealing of a seller's products, to prohibit mergers and consolidations of corporations that result in a substantial lessening of competition or tend to create a monopoly, and to prohibit certain interlocking directorates.

close corporation A corporation that has a limited number of outstanding shares of stock, usually held by a single person or small group of persons, with restrictions on the right to transfer those shares to others.

closing In real property law, a meeting between the seller and buyer and any other interested parties at which passage of title and matters relating thereto are executed.

COD Collect on delivery; that is, the buyer must pay for the goods before he or she can inspect or receive possession of them.

codicil An addition to or change in a will executed with the same formalities as the will itself.

collateral In secured transactions law, the property subject to a security interest.

collateral note A note secured by personal property.

co-makers Two or more persons who create or execute a note or certificate of deposit.

commerce clause Article I, Section 8, of the U.S. Constitution, which permits Congress to control trade among the several states (and with foreign nations).

commercial contract A contract between two or more persons (merchants) engaged in trade or commerce.

commercial paper Instruments that are written promises or obligations to pay sums of money (called drafts, checks, certificates of deposit, or notes). When used in Article 3 of the UCC, the term refers only to negotiable instruments; when used elsewhere, to negotiable and non-negotiable instruments.

commingle To blend or mix together.

common carrier A carrier that holds itself out for hire to the general public to transport goods.

common law Rules that have been developed from custom or judicial decisions without the aid of written legislation, and subsequently used as a basis for later decisions by a court—also referred to as judge-made or case law.

common stock A class of stock that carries no rights or priorities over other classes of stock as to payment of dividends or distribution of corporate assets upon dissolution.

community property A system of marital property ownership recognized in eight states under which property acquired after marriage (except by gift or inheritance) is co-owned by the husband and wife, regardless of which person acquired it.

comparative negligence The rule used in negligence cases in many states that provides for computing both the plaintiff's and the defendant's negligence, with the plaintiff's damages being reduced by a percentage representing the degree of his or her contributing fault. If the plaintiff's negligence is found to be greater than the defendant's, the plaintiff will receive nothing and will be subject to a counterclaim by the defendant.

compensatory damages A monetary sum awarded for the actual loss a person has sustained for a wrong committed by another person.

complaint In an action at law, the initial pleading filed by the plaintiff in a court with proper jurisdiction. In an action in equity, it is frequently referred to as a petition.

composition of creditors An agreement between a debtor and his or her creditors that each creditor will accept a lesser amount than the debt owed as full satisfaction of that debt.

conclusions of law Answers derived by applying law to facts.

concurrent jurisdiction Where more than one court of a different name or classification has the right to hear a particular controversy.

condemnation The process by which the government either exercises its power of eminent domain to take private property, or officially declares property unfit for use.

condition In contract law, a provision or clause in a contract which, upon the occurrence or nonoccurrence of a specified event, either creates, suspends, or terminates the rights and duties of the contracting parties.

condition concurrent A condition in a contract that both parties' performances are to take place at the same time.

condition precedent A condition that must take place before the parties are bound to their contractual obligations.

condition subsequent A condition that terminates the rights and obligations of the parties under an existing contract.

conditional indorsement An indorsement whereby the indorser agrees to be liable on the instrument only if a specified event takes place.

conditional sale contract Usually a contract for the sale of goods wherein the seller reserves title (though possession is with the buyer) until the purchase price is paid in full (used as a security device). Called a security interest under the UCC.

confession of judgment An agreement whereby a debtor allows a creditor to obtain a court judgment without legal proceedings in the event of nonpayment or other breach by the debtor.

confusion In personal property law, property of two or more persons intermingled so that the property of each can no longer be distinguished.

conglomerate merger A merger between two companies whose products or services are unrelated, as distinguished from horizontal and vertical mergers.

consensual actions or agreements Actions or agreements made with mutual consent.

consideration In contract law, a detriment to the promisee or benefit to the promisor, bargained for and given in exchange for a promise. To be consideration, the law requires that the thing promised or done have a legal value, be legally sufficient, and be a bargain for something to be done or not to be done.

consolidation A transaction in which two corporations combine to form an entirely new corporation, thereby losing their former identities.

constructive annexation The situation existing when personal property not physically attached to real property is adapted to the use to which the realty is designed so that the law considers it a fixture.

constructive bailment A bailment created when a bailee comes into possession of personal property without the consent of the owner. (An example is lost property found by a person—a bailee.)

constructive trust A trust imposed by law to correct or rectify a fraud or to prevent one party from being unjustly enriched at the expense of another.

consumer goods Goods that are used or bought primarily for personal, family, or household purposes.

consumerism The movement that has led to increased protection for the consumer and substantial burdens on the manufacturer and merchant.

Consumer Product Safety Act A congressional enact-ment that created the Consumer Product Safety Commission, which has the responsibility of establishing and enforcing rules and standards to insure that products covered under the Act are safe for consumers' use.

continuation statement In secured transactions law, a document filed with a proper public official to continue public notice of the priority of an existing security interest in collateral upon the expiration of a previous filing.

contract An agreement that establishes enforceable legal relationships between two or more persons.

contract carrier A carrier who transports goods only for those under individual contract.

contributory negligence The fault (negligence) of a plaintiff, the result of which contributed to or added to his or her injury (used as a defense by a defendant against whom the plaintiff has filed a negligence action).

controlling shareholders Usually the majority shareholders or those with sufficient voting power to elect a majority of the directors, pass motions, or make binding decisions.

conveyance A transfer of an interest in property.

corporate opportunity A doctrine that prohibits directors, officers, or any other corporate managers from personally taking advantage of business situations that belong solely to or should be given to the corporation.

corporate stock Shares of stock, each representing an ownership interest in the business, issued by a corporation for the purpose of raising capital.

corporation An association of persons created by statute as a legal entity (artificial person) with authority to act and to have liability separate and apart from its owners.

counterclaim A pleading by the defendant in a civil suit against the plaintiff, the purpose being to defeat or sue the plaintiff so as to gain a judgment favorable to the defendant.

counter-offer A proposal made by an offeree in response to the offer extended him or her, the terms varying appreciably from the terms of the offer. Such a proposal by the offeree constitutes a rejection of the offer.

course of dealing The situation in which past conduct between two parties in performing a prior contract is used as a basis for interpreting their present conduct or agreement.

course of performance When a contract for the sale of goods involves repeated occasions for performance known by both parties and not objected to by either, the performance is considered interpretive of the remaining obligations of the contract.

covenant against encumbrances A guaranty by a grantor that there are no outstanding liens, easements, or liabilities held by a third party on the real property he or she is conveying, except as stated in the deed.

covenant for quiet enjoyment A guaranty by a grantor of real property that the grantee or those who hold the property in the future will not be evicted or disturbed by a person having a better title or a right of foreclosure of a lien.

covenant not to compete A clause within a contract legally permitting a restraint of trade where such is a legitimate protection of a property interest and the restraint as to area and time is reasonable under the circumstances. An example is a clause in a sale of business contract where the seller agrees not to start up a competing business within a reasonable time and within the area where the said business has been operating.

covenant of seisin A guaranty by a grantor that he or she has good title to the real property being conveyed.

covenants of title The guarantees given by the grantor in a warranty deed.

creditor beneficiary A creditor who has rights in a contract (of which he or she is not a party) made by the debtor and a third person, where the terms of said contract expressly benefit the creditor.

creditors' committee A committee composed of a debtor's creditors, which manages the debtor's business and financial affairs until his or her debts are paid off. The committee's formation is by agreement between the debtor and creditors and is usually part of an agreed-upon payment plan of the debtor.

crime Any wrongful action by an individual or persons for which a statute prescribes redress in the form of a death penalty, imprisonment, fine, or removal from an office of public trust.

criminal law The law of crimes.

cumulative preferred stock A type of preferred stock on which dividends not paid in any given year are accumulated to the next succeeding year. The total amount accumulated must be paid before common shareholders can receive a dividend.

cumulative voting Where permitted, the procedure by which a shareholder is entitled to take his or her total number of shares, multiply that total by the number of directors to be elected, and cast the multiplied total for any director or directors to be elected.

curtesy The common-law right of a surviving husband to a life estate in a portion of his deceased wife's real property.

cy pres So near or as near. The doctrine by which the courts will find a substitute purpose when the stated purpose of a charitable trust is not possible to accomplish.

damages The monetary loss suffered by a party as a result of a wrong.

deadlock A situation in a corporation where two equally divided factions exist in opposition to each other, thus bringing the affairs of the corporation to a virtual standstill.

debit A charge of indebtedness to an account (for example, a charge against a bank deposit account).

debt securities Instruments representing the bonded indebtedness of a corporation; (they may be secured by corporate property or simply by a general obligation debt of the corporation).

debtor A person who owes payment of a debt and/or performance on an obligation.

decedent A person who has died.

deceit A false statement, usually intentional, that causes another person harm.

deed The document representing ownership of real property.

deed of bargain and sale A deed without warranties.

de facto corporation A corporation not formed in substantial compliance with the laws of a given state but which has sufficiently complied to be a corporation in fact, not right. Only the state can challenge the corporation's existence.

defamation Injury of a person's character or reputation, usually by publication of a false statement about that person.

default The failure to perform a legal obligation.

defendant The party who defends the initial action brought against him or her by the plaintiff.

defense Any matter which is advanced or put forth by a defendant as a reason in law or fact why the plaintiff is not entitled to recover the relief he seeks.

deficiency judgment A personal judgment given by a court against a debtor in default where the value of the property placed as security for the debt is less than the debt owed.

de jure corporation A corporation formed in substantial compliance with the laws of a given state; a corporation by right.

delegated powers The constitutional right of the federal government to pass laws concerning certain subjects and fields, thereby keeping the states from passing laws in these areas (sometimes referred to as enumerated powers).

delegation In contract law, the transfer of the power or right to represent or act for another; usually referred to as the delegation of duties to a third party, as compared to the assignment of rights to a third party.

demurrer A pleading by a defendant in the form of a motion denying that plaintiff's complaint or petition states a cause of action.

de novo To start completely new. A trial *de novo* is a completely new trial requiring the same degree of proof as if the case were being heard for the first time.

depositary bank The first bank to which an instrument is transferred for collection.

descendants The lineal heirs of a decedent in a descending line—children and grandchildren.

destination contract In sales law, a contract whereby the seller is required to tender goods to the buyer at a place designated by the buyer.

detriment test A test to determine whether a promise is supported by consideration. The law requires the promisee to have done something not otherwise legally required or to have refrained from doing something he or she had a right to do.

devise A term of conveyance in real estate transactions. In a will, a gift of real estate by the testator is a devise.

direct collection The collection by the assignee (of an assignor-creditor) of a debt originally owed the creditor.

directed verdict A verdict that the jury is instructed (or directed) by the court to return in accordance with a motion by one of the parties that reasonable persons could not differ as to the result.

disaffirmance The legal avoidance, or setting aside, of an obligation.

discharge in bankruptcy A release granted by a bankruptcy court to a debtor who has gone through proper bankruptcy proceedings; the release frees the person from any further liability on provable claims filed during the proceedings.

disclaimer A provision in a sales contract which attempts to prevent the creation of a warranty.

discretionary powers The right of an administrative agency to exercise judgment and discretion in carrying out the law, as opposed to ministerial powers (the routine day-to-day duty to enforce the law).

dishonor In commercial paper, a refusal to pay or accept an instrument upon proper presentment.

disparagement of goods Making malicious and false statements of fact as to the quality or performance of another's goods.

dissolution The actual termination of a partnership's or corporation's right to exist as a going concern.

diversity of citizenship An action in which the plaintiff and defendant are citizens of different states.

dividend A payment made by a corporation in cash or property from the income or profit of the corporation to a shareholder on the basis of his or her investment.

documents of title Bills of lading, dock warrants, dock receipts, warehouse receipts, and any other paper that, in the regular course of business or financing, is evidence of the holder's right to obtain possession of the goods covered.

domestic corporation A corporation chartered or incorporated in the state in which the corporation is doing business.

dominant estate The land that benefits from an easement appurtenant.

donee The person to whom a gift is made or a power is given.

donee beneficiary A person who has rights in a contract (to which he or she is not a party) made between two or more parties for his or her express benefit.

donor The person making a gift or giving another the power to do something.

dower The common-law right of a widow to a life estate in a specific portion of her deceased husband's real property.

draft An instrument created by a party (the drawer) that orders another (the drawee) to pay the instrument to a third party (the payee); also called a bill of exchange.

drawee The person on whom a draft or check is drawn and who is requested (ordered) to pay the instrument.

drawee bank A bank on which a draft or check is drawn, such bank being ordered to pay the instrument when it is duly presented.

drawer The person creating (drafting) a draft or check.

due process The right of every person not to be deprived of life, liberty, or property without a fair hearing and/or just compensation.

duress The overcoming of a person's free will through the use of threat, force, or actions whereby the person is forced to do something he or she otherwise would not do.

duty to speak A legal obligation of one party to divulge information to another party.

earnest money A deposit paid by a buyer to hold a seller to a contractual obligation. Frequently this amount also serves as liquidated damages in the event of the buyer's breach. Historically, the deposit was said to show the buyer's good faith in entering into the contract with the seller.

easement A nonpossessory interest in real property that gives the holder the right to use another's land in a particular way.

easement appurtenant An easement created specifically for use in connection with an adjoining tract of land.

easement in gross An easement that is not used in connection with another tract of land.

economic duress The overcoming of a person's free will by means of a threat or other action involving the wrongful use of economic pressure, whereby the person is forced to do something he or she otherwise would not do.

election A principle of law whereby a third person who learns of the identify of the undisclosed principal prior to receiving a judgment must choose to receive the judgment against either the agent or the undisclosed principal. Election of one releases the other from liability to the third party.

eminent domain The power of the government to take private property for public use by paying just compensation.

entity theory An approach under which associations or organizations are treated as a single legal person.

environmental impact statement The statement required by federal law that describes the effect of proposed major federal action on the quality of the human environment.

Environmental Protection Agency The federal agency charged with the responsibility for establishing and enforcing environmental standards and for continuing research on pollution and measures to eliminate or control it.

equal protection of the laws A constitutional guaranty that no state government shall enact a law that is not uniform in its operation, that treats persons unfairly, or that gives persons unequal treatment by reason of race, religion, national origin, or sex.

equipment Goods that are used or bought for use primarily in business.

equitable action An action brought in a court seeking an equitable remedy, such as an injunction or decree of specific performance.

equity securities Shares of capital stock representing an ownership interest in the corporation.

escrow agent An agent who, by agreement, holds property, documents, or money of one party with the author-ity to transfer such property to a designated person upon the occurrence of a specified event.

exclusive agency In real property law, the arrangement by a seller of real property with a broker that only that broker is entitled to a commission if a sale of the real property is made through the efforts of anyone other than the seller.

exclusive dealing contract In antitrust law, a contract by a seller to sell his or her product to a buyer on condition that the buyer will not handle the product of the seller's competitor(s).

exclusive right to sell In real property law, the arrangement by a seller of real property with a broker that the broker is entitled to his or her commission if a sale of the real property is made through the effort of anyone, including the seller.

executed contract A contract wholly performed by both parties to the contract, as opposed to an executory contract, which is wholly unperformed by both parties.

execution of a judgment The process by which a judgment creditor obtains a writ directing the sheriff or other officer to seize nonexempt property of the debtor and sell it to satisfy the judgment.

executive committee In a corporation, a certain number of the members of the board of directors appointed by the board as a committee with the delegated authority to make decisions concerning ordinary business matters that come up during intervals between regular board meetings.

executive order An order by the president of the United States or governor of a state that has the force of law.

executor (female, executrix) The personal representative in a testator's will to dispose of an estate as the will has directed.

executory contract A contract wholly unperformed by both parties to the contract, as opposed to an executed contract, where both parties have fully performed their obligations under the contract.

executory interest A future interest held by a third party.

executrix A woman selected by a testator or testatrix (the deceased) in a will to administer the will (estate) of the deceased.

exempt property Real or personal property of a debtor that cannot by law be seized to satisfy a debt owed to an unsecured creditor.

ex parte On one side only. For example, an *ex parte* proceeding is held on the application of one party only, without notice to the other party; and an *ex parte* order is made at the request of one party when the other party fails to show up in court, when the other party's presence is not needed, or when there is no other party.

express authority Authority specifically given by the principal to the agent.

express contract A contract formed wholly from the words (oral and/or in writing) of the parties, as opposed to an implied contract, which is formed from the conduct of the parties.

express warranty In sales law, a guarantee or assurance as to the quality or performance of goods that arises from the words or conduct of the seller.

ex-ship From the carrying vessel; a delivery term indicating that the seller's risk and expense for shipment of goods by vessel extends until the goods are unloaded at the port of destination.

extension clause A clause in a time instrument providing that under certain circumstances the maturity date can be extended.

extraordinary bailment A bailment in which the bailee is given by law greater duties and liabilities than an ordinary bailee. Common carriers and innkeepers are the most common examples of extraordinary bailees.

fair courts Courts established by early merchants to settle disputes and obligations among themselves. These were not recognized as law courts.

false imprisonment The wrongful detention or restraint of one person by another.

family purpose doctrine The doctrine under which, in a few states, the head of a household is liable for the negligent acts of any members of his or her family that occur while they are driving the family car.

farm products Goods that are crops, livestock, or supplies used or produced in farming operations, or goods that are products or livestock in their unmanufactured state (such as ginned cotton, maple syrup, milk, and eggs). For secured transactions law these goods must be in the possession of a debtor engaged in raising, fattening, grazing, or other farm operations.

FAS Free alongside ship; a delivery term indicating that the seller must deliver goods to the designated dock alongside the vessel on which the goods are to be loaded and must bear the expenses of delivery to the dock site.

fault Breach of a legal duty, sometimes used in lieu of the term *negligence*. The UCC definition is "wrongful act, omission, or breach."

Federal Communications Commission (FCC) A seven-member commission established in 1934 by congressional enactment of the Federal Communications Act.

The commission is empowered to regulate all interstate communication by telephone, telegraph, radio, and television.

Federal Power Commission (FPC) A five-member commission established in 1920 by congressional enactment of the Federal Water Power Act. The commission regulates interstate transporation, production, and use of electric power and natural gas.

Federal Trade Commission (FTC) A five-member commission established in 1914 by congressional enactment of the Federal Trade Commission Act. The commission enforces prohibitions against unfair methods of competition and unfair or deceptive acts or practices in commerce; it also enforces numerous federal laws (particularly federal consumer protection acts, such as "Truth in Lending" and "Fair Packing and Labeling").

fee simple The absolute ownership of real property.

fee simple defeasible An ownership interest in real property subject to termination by the occurrence of a specific event.

felony A serious crime resulting in either punishment by death or imprisonment in a state or federal penitentiary, or where a given statute declares a wrong to be a felony without regard to a specific punishment.

fictitious payee A payee on an instrument who is either nonexistent or an actual person not entitled to payment. (Usually the fraud is perpetrated by a dishonest employee in charge of payroll or payment of accounts who drafts an instrument with intent to defraud his or her employer.)

fiduciary A position of trust in relation to another person or his or her property.

financing statement An instrument filed with a proper public official that gives notice of an outstanding security interest in collateral.

finding of fact The process whereby from testimony and evidence a judge, agency, or examiner determines that certain matters, events, or acts took place upon which conclusions of law can be based.

firm offer In sales law, an irrevocable offer dealing with the sale of goods made by a merchant offeror in a signed writing and giving assurance to the offeree that the offer will remain open. This offer is irrevocable without consideration for the stated period of time or, if no period is stated, for a reasonable period, neither period to exceed three months.

fixture A piece of personal property that is attached to real property in such a manner that the law deems the item to be part of the real property.

floating lien concept In secured transactions law, the concept whereby a security interest is permitted to be retained in collateral even though the collateral changes in character and classification. For example, a security interest in raw materials is retained even if the raw materials change character in the manufacturing process and end up as inventory.

FOB Free on board; a delivery term indicating that the seller must ship the goods and bear the expenses of shipment to the F.O.B. point of designation (which can be either the seller's or the buyer's place of business).

forebearance The refraining from doing something that a person has a legal right to do.

foreclosure The procedure or action taken by a mortgagee, upon default of the mortgagor, whereby the mortgagee satisfies his or her claim by some action (usually by selling off the mortgaged property).

foreign corporation A corporation chartered or incorporated in one state but doing business in a different state.

forgery A fraudulent, fake instrument or document, or a signature of another without authorization.

formal contract A contract that derives its validity only from compliance with a specific form or format required by law. Examples are contracts under seal (where a seal is required), negotiable instruments, and recognizances (formal acknowledgments of indebtedness made in a court of law).

franchise (1) A business conducted under someone else's trademark or tradename. The owner of the business, which may be a sole proprietorship, partnership, corporation, or other form of organization, is usually referred to as the *franchisee*. The owner of the trademark or tradename, who contractually permits use of the mark or name, in return for a fee and usually subject to various restrictions, is ordinarily referred to as the *franchisor*. The permission to use the mark or name, which is part of the franchising agreement, is called a *trademark license*. (2) The term can also be used to refer to a privilege granted by a governmental body, such as the exclusive right granted to someone by a city to provide cable TV service in that city.

fraud An intentional or reckless misrepresentation of a material fact that causes anyone relying on it injury or damage.

fraud in execution In commercial paper, inducing a person to sign an instrument, the party signing being deceived as to the nature or essential terms of the instrument.

fraud in inducement In commercial paper, the use of deceit in inducing a person to sign an instrument, although the deceived party knows what he or she is signing and the essential terms of the instrument. This knowledge

is what distinguishes fraud in inducement from fraud in execution.

fraudulent conveyance The transfer of property in such a manner that the conveyance is deemed either in fact or by law to defraud creditors.

fungible In sales or securities law, goods or securities of which any unit is, by nature or usage of trade, the equivalent of any other like unit.

future advance In secured transactions law, the concept whereby an outstanding security interest applies to future loans made by the secured party. If the security interest is properly perfected, the future loan, for priority purposes, dates back to the time the original security interest was created.

future interest An interest in real property, the use or enjoyment of which is postponed until a later date or the occurrence of a designated event.

futures contract A contract to buy or sell standard commodities (such as rice, coffee, or wheat) at a future date and a specified price. (The seller is agreeing to sell goods he or she does not own at the time of making the contract.)

garnishee A person who holds money owed to or property of a debtor subject to a garnishment action.

garnishment The legal proceeding of a judgment creditor to require a third person owing money to the debtor or holding property belonging to the debtor to turn over to the court or sheriff the property or money owed for the satisfaction of the judgment. State and federal laws generally permit only a limited amount of a debtor's wages to be garnished.

gift A voluntary transfer of property to another without consideration.

gift *causa mortis* A gift made by a donor in contemplation of his or her death from some existing affliction or impending peril.

gift *inter vivos* A gift made during the lifetime of a donor and not in contemplation of his or her death.

good faith Honesty in fact on the part of a person in negotiating a contract, or in the carrying on of some other transactions.

goods Tangible and movable personal property except for money used as medium of exchange.

grantee The person to whom an interest in real property is conveyed by deed.

grantor The person conveying an interest in real property by deed.

Green River ordinances State and municipal laws that regulate door-to-door sales on private premises. So called after the Green River, Wyoming, case in which such laws were held to be valid and enforceable.

group boycott In antitrust law, the express or implied agreement of two or more persons or firms to refuse to deal (buy, sell, etc.) with a third party. Such an agreement is usually illegal.

guaranty A promise to pay an obligation of a debtor if the debtor is in default.

holder Any person in possession of a document, security, or instrument that is drawn, issued, or indorsed to him or her.

holder in due course (HDC) A holder who takes an instrument for value, in good faith, and without notice that the instrument is overdue or has been dishonored or that any defense or claim by any person exists against it.

holder through a holder in due course A holder who fails to qualify as a holder in due course but has the rights of one (by law of assignment) if he or she can show that a prior holder of the instrument qualified as a holder in due course. This is referred to as the "shelter provision."

holographic will A will entirely in the handwriting of the testator. Witnesses are not required for its execution but are necessary at probate to prove the handwriting of the testator.

horizontal merger A merger between two competitors.

horizontal price fixing An illegal agreement, express or implied, by competitors to set prices.

illusory contract An agreement of the parties that, on examination, lacks mutuality of obligation—i.e., one in which consideration is found to be lacking on the part of one party. The result is that neither party is bound by the agreement.

implied agency rule In contract law, the rule that the method of communication used by an offeror in transmitting his or her offer to the offeree is, by implication, the proper method of communication (the proper agency) to be used by the offeree in transmitting his or her acceptance to the offeror. Under this rule, a contract is formed the moment the offeree deposits his or her acceptance with that agency.

implied authority Authority inferred for an agent to carry out his or her express authority and/or authority inferred from the position held by the agent to fulfill his or her agency duties.

implied contract A contract in which the parties' manifestation of assent or agreement is inferred, in whole or in part, from their conduct, as opposed to an express contract formed by the parties' words.

implied warranties Assurances or guarantees of certain standards or actions imposed by law.

incorporated partnership A close corporation with more than one shareholder.

incorporation The act or process of forming or creating a corporation.

indemnification Where allowed, the right to reimbursement for expenses, losses, or costs incurred.

independent contractor One who is hired by another to perform a given task in a manner and method independent from the control of employer.

indirect collection The creditor's collection of payment(s) of a debt, even though the debt has been assigned by the creditor to an assignee.

indorsee The person who receives an indorsed instrument.

indorsement The signature of the indorser (usually on the back of an instrument) for the purpose of transferring an instrument and establishing the limits of his or her liability.

indorsement for deposit A type of restrictive indorsement that requires the depositary bank to place into the account of the restrictive indorser the amount of the instrument.

indorsement in trust A type of restrictive indorsement whereby the amount on the instrument is to be paid to the indorsee, who in turn is to use or hold the funds for the benefit of the indorser or a third party.

indorser The person who indorses an instrument, usually for the purpose of transferring it to a third person.

informal contract Any contract that does not depend on a specified form or formality for its validity.

injunction A decree issued by a court of equity either prohibiting a person from performing a certain act or acts or requiring the person to perform a certain act or acts.

innkeeper An operator of a hotel, motel, or any place of business offering living accommodations for transient guests.

innocent misrepresentation A false statement of fact, not known to be false, that causes another harm or damage.

insolvency In bankruptcy law, the financial condition of a debtor when his or her assets at fair market value are less than his or her debts and liabilities.

installment contract In sales law, a contract that authorizes or requires the delivery and acceptance of goods in separate lots.

installment note An instrument (note) in which the principal (plus interest usually) is payable in specified partial amounts at specified times until the full amount is paid.

insurable interest The rights of a person who will be directly or financially affected by the death of a person or the loss of property. Only these rights can be protected by an insurance policy.

intermediary bank Any bank to which an instrument is transferred in the course of collection and which is not the depositary or payor bank.

Interstate Commerce Commission (ICC) An eleven-member commission established in 1887 by congressional enactment of the Interstate Commerce Act regulating the licensing and rates of common carriers in interstate commerce.

inter vivos "Between the living," as an *inter vivos* gift (one made during the life of the donor) or an *inter vivos* trust.

intestate The situation in which a person dies without leaving a valid will.

inventory Goods held by a person or firm for sale or lease in the ordinary course of business; also refers to raw materials (and work in process on them) where held by a manufacturing company.

investigative power In administrative agency law, the right of an administrative agency by statute to hold hearings, subpoena witnesses, examine persons under oath, and require that records be submitted to it in order to determine violations and to do research for future rule making.

investment company Any corporation organized for the purpose of owning and holding the stock of other corporations.

involuntary bankruptcy Bankruptcy of a person upon petition of a certain number of creditors whose claims are statutorily sufficient in amount and who properly allege that the person committed an act of bankruptcy.

irrevocable offer An offer or proposal that by law cannot be withdrawn by an offeror without liability.

issue The first delivery of an instrument to a holder.

joint stock company An unincorporated association of persons with certain characteristics of a corporation but generally treated as a partnership.

joint tenancy A co-ownership of property by two or more parties in which each owns an undivided interest that passes to the other co-owners on his or her death (known as the "right of survivorship").

joint tortfeasors Two or more persons who in concert commit a tort; also two or more persons whose independent torts are so linked to an injury that a court will hold either or both liable.

joint venture An undertaking by two or more persons or firms to pursue some endeavor (usually a business), limited in scope and/or time, for their mutual benefit. If the venture has a business purpose, the participants are often treated as partners in a partnership.

judgment note An instrument (note) in which the maker authorizes, on default, immediate confession and entry of judgment against him or her by a court without due process of service or trial. Most states have abolished or restricted confession of judgment notes.

judicial self-restraint The philosophy that controversies must be settled, insofar as possible, in conformity with previously established principles and decisions.

junior security interest A security interest or right that is subordinate to another security interest or right.

jurisdiction of a court The right, by law, of a specific court to hear designated controversies.

justice The application of rules to arrive at what is recognized as a fair and reasonable result; also a title given to a judge.

laissez-faire doctrine The doctrine whereby business is permitted to operate without interference by government.

latent defect In sales law, an imperfection in a good that cannot be discovered by ordinary observation or inspection.

law Enforceable rules governing the relationship of individuals and persons, their relationship to each other, and their relationship to an organized society.

law merchant Rules and regulations developed by merchants and traders that governed their transactions before being absorbed by common law. These rules and regulations were developed and enforced by "fair courts" established by the merchants themselves.

lease A conveyance to another of the right to possess property in return for a payment called rent.

leasehold The interest acquired by the lessee under a lease.

legacy In a will, a specific gift of money.

legal entity An association recognized by law as having the legal rights and duties of a person.

legal impossibility of performance An event that takes place after a contract is made, rendering performance under the contract, in the eyes of the law, something that cannot be done. Also referred to as objective impossibility, it legally discharges a party's obligation; it can be compared to subjective impossibility, which makes the contractual obligation more difficult to perform but does not discharge it.

legally sufficient consideration The type of detriment to the promisee or benefit to the promisor that in the eyes of the law binds the offeror and offeree to an enforceable contract, as opposed to adequacy of consideration, which measures the value of the detriment or benefit.

legal rate of interest The rate of interest applied by statute where there is an agreement for interest to be paid but none is stated, or where the law implies a duty to pay interest irrespective of agreement. In the latter case, this may be referred to as a judgment rate, a rate of interest applied to judgments until paid by the defendant.

legal tender Any currency recognized by law as the medium of exchange that must be accepted by a creditor in satisfaction of a debtor's debt.

legal title That which represents ownership of property.

legislative history The history of the legislative enactment used by the court as a means of interpreting the terms of a statute.

lessee The person who leases or rents property from a lessor. If the lease involves an interest in real property, the lessee is frequently referred to as the tenant.

lessor The person who leases property to the lessee. If the lease involves an interest in real property, the lessor is frequently referred to as the landlord.

libel Written defamation of one's character or reputation.

license In real property law, the landowner's permission for another to come upon his or her land.

lien An interest held by a creditor in property of the debtor for the purpose of securing payment of the debt.

lien creditor In secured transactions law, any creditor who is able to legally attach the property of the debtor. This includes an assignee for the benefit of creditors, a trustee in bankruptcy, or an appointed receiver in equity.

life estate An interest in real property for the duration of the life of some designated person, who may be the life tenant or a third person.

life tenant The person holding (owning) a life estate in designated property.

limitation of remedies A provision in a sales contract which attempts to limit the remedies available to a party; usually employed by a seller to limit a buyer's remedies for breach of warranty.

limited defense See *personal defense.*

limited partnership A partnership created under statute with at least one limited and one general partner. The limited partner's liability to third persons is restricted to his or her capital contributions.

liquidated damages A specific sum of money contained in a provision of a contract that one of the parties is entitled to recover from the other in the event of the latter's breach of contract. This amount can be enforced in a court of law, provided that at the time the contract was made, the designated amount was a reasonable estimate of the probable loss.

liquidated debt An undisputed debt; that is, a debt about which there is no reasonable basis for dispute as to its existence or amount.

liquidating partner After an act of dissolution of the partnership, any partner who has authority to wind up the partnership, thereby terminating it.

liquidation preference Preferred shareholder's priority over common shareholders to the distribution of corporate assets upon the corporation's dissolution.

liquidation Conversion of the assets of a corporation to cash and the subsequent distribution of the cash to creditors and shareholders.

lobbying contract A contract made by one person with another under the terms of which the former agrees to represent the latter's interest before legislative or administrative bodies by attempting to influence their votes or decisions on legislative, quasi-legislative, or related proceedings.

long-arm statutes Laws that permit a plaintiff to bring a certain action and recover a judgment in a court in his or her home state against a defendant who resides in another state. This judgment can be filed by the plaintiff and enforced by the courts in the defendant's home state.

lost property Property located at a place where it was not put by its owner, which place is unknown by the owner.

Magnuson-Moss Warranty Act A congressional enactment designed to prevent deceptive warranty practices, make warranties easier to understand, and create procedures for consumer enforcement of warranties. The act applies only to written warrantees given in a consumer sales transaction and can be enforced by the Federal Trade Commission, Attorney General, or an aggrieved party.

maker The person who creates or executes a promissory note or certificate of deposit.

marital deduction An estate planning device that can be used by the surviving husband or wife to effect substantial estate tax savings.

master In employment law, one who appoints or designates another to perform physical tasks or activities for him or her and under his or her control as to the manner of performance (sometimes designated employer).

maturity In commercial paper, the time when a debt or obligation is due.

maximum rate of interest A statutory limit on the amount of interest that can be charged on a given transaction.

mechanic's lien A statutory lien against real property for labor, services, or materials used in improving the real property.

merchant In sales law, a person who customarily deals in goods of the kind that are involved in a transactiion, or who otherwise by occupation holds himself or herself out as having knowledge of or skill peculiar to the goods involved in the transaction.

merger In the strictest sense, a transaction in which one corporation absorbs another corporation; the former retains its identity, and the latter loses its identity.

metes and bounds A method of describing real property by measuring the boundary distances at fixed points and angles. Sometimes these fixed points are natural or artificial landmarks ("monuments") such as rivers, trees, or roads.

ministerial power In administrative agency law, the routine day-to-day administration of the law, as opposed to discretionary powers, which involve the power to exercise judgment in the rendering of decisions.

minor An infant; any person under the age of majority. In most states the age of majority is eighteen years; in some it is twenty-one.

minority shareholders Those shareholders whose voting power is not sufficient to elect a majority of the directors, pass motions, or make binding decisions.

misdemeanor Any crime less serious than a felony, resulting in a fine and/or confinement in a jail other than a state or federal penitentiary.

mislaid property Property located at a place where it was put by the owner, who has now forgotten the location.

mistake An unintentional error.

Model Business Corporation Act Uniform rules governing the incorporation and operation of corporations for profit recommended by the American Bar Association for enactment by the various states.

money In commercial paper, any medium of exchange authorized or adopted by a domestic or foreign government as part of its currency.

monopoly The exclusive or virtually exclusive ownership of the source of a commodity or product, or the equiva-

lent control of that commodity or product's distribution; sometimes created by governmental authority.

morals Rules of conduct established by a given community and enforced by voluntary compliance of those within the community. If the rule is a law, it is also enforceable by judicial process.

mortgage The agreement by which a lien on a debtor's property is conveyed to a creditor.

mortgagee The creditor in a mortgage agreement.

mortgagor The debtor in a mortgage agreement.

mutual-benefit bailment A nongratuitous bailment frequently formed by contract through which both parties benefit.

necessaries In contract law, items contracted for which the law deems essential to a person's life or health (usually such items as food, clothing, shelter, medical services, and primary and secondary education).

negligence The failure to exercise reasonable care required under the circumstances, which failure is the proximate or direct cause of damage or injury to another.

negotiability The status of an instrument that meets the requirements under the UCC for an instrument to be negotiable.

negotiable instrument A signed written document that contains an unconditional promise or order to pay a sum certain in money on demand or at a definite time to the order of a specific person or to bearer. The document can be either a draft, a check, a certificate of deposit, or a note.

negotiation The transfer of an instrument in such form that the transferee becomes a holder.

nominal damages A monetary award by a court where there is a breach of duty or contract but where no financial loss has occurred or been proven.

nonexempt property The property of a debtor subject to the claims of unsecured creditors.

nonexistent principal A principal not recognized by law.

nonnegotiable instrument An instrument that does not meet the requirements of negotiability under the UCC.

nonprofit corporation A private corporation formed to perform a religious, charitable, educational, or benevolent purpose without a profit-oriented goal.

nonstock corporation A corporation in which capital stock is not issued; usually occurs only in the case of a nonprofit corporation.

nontrading partnership A partnership formed primarily for the production (but not sale) of commodities or for the providing of services.

no-par value stock Stock issued by a corporation with no amount stated in the certificate. The amount a subscriber pays is determined by the board of directors.

note In commercial paper, an instrument whereby one party (the maker) promises to pay another (the payee or bearer) a sum of money on demand or at a stated date.

notice A fact that a person actually knows, or one he or she should know exists based on all facts and circumstances.

novation The substitution, by agreement, of a new contract for an existing one, thereby terminating the old contract. This is usually accomplished by a three-sided agreement of the parties that a third person's performance be substituted for that of one of the original parties to the contract.

nuncupative will An oral will permitted by some states but on which significant restrictions and conditions are imposed by statute.

obligee The person to whom a duty is owed.

obligor A person who owes a duty to another.

occupation In personal property law, the acquisition of unowned property by the first person to take possession with an intent to become the owner.

offer In contract law, a proposal made by an offeror, usually for an offeree's acceptance or rejection.

offeree The person to whom a promise or proposal is made (usually for acceptance).

offeror A person who makes a proposal to another, with the view in mind that if it is accepted, it will create a legally enforceable agreement between the parties.

open listing The arrangement by a seller of real property whereby the seller's obligation to pay a commission to a broker arises only if he or she is the first broker to procure an acceptable buyer (a buyer who is ready, willing, and able to buy at the stated price).

option An irrevocable offer formed by contract and supported by consideration.

order instrument An instrument payable to a designated payee or payees, or whomever they so direct, and requiring for its negotiation the indorsement of those persons.

ordinary bailment Any bailment not classified as an extraordinary bailment.

output contract An enforceable agreement for the sale of all the goods produced by a seller (the exact amount of which is not set or known at the time of the agreement) or all those produced at a given plant of the seller during the term of the contract; a contract in which the seller agrees to sell and the buyer agrees to buy all or up to a stated amount that the seller produces.

owner-consent statute A legislative enactment in a few states whereby the owner is liable for the negligence of any person driving the owner's car with his or her permission.

ownership in place The rights to oil, gas, and other minerals while they are still in the ground.

pari delicto Parties equally at fault.

par value stock Stock that has been assigned a specific value by the board of directors; the amount is stated in the certificate, and the subscriber to the corporation must pay at least this amount.

parol evidence rule A rule that in some instances prohibits the introduction of evidence, oral or written, that would, if admitted, vary, change, alter, or modify any terms or provisions of a complete and unambiguous written contract.

partially-disclosed principal In agency law, a principal who is known to exist but whose identity is unknown by third persons dealing with the agent.

participating preferred stock A type of preferred stock giving its holders the right to share with common shareholders in any dividends remaining after the preferred shareholders have received their preferred dividend and common shareholders have received their specified dividend.

partition The dividing of land co-owned by several persons into specific designated pieces (sections) of property.

partnership An association of two or more persons who by agreement as co-owners carry on a business for profit.

payee The person to whom an instrument is made payable.

payment against documents A term in a contract that requires payment for goods upon receipt of their documents of title, even though the goods have not as yet arrived.

payor bank The bank (drawee) on which an instrument is drawn (payable).

per capita "By heads," in descent and distribution of a decedent's estate where the heirs are of one class (such as children) and take equal shares.

peremptory challenge The right to prohibit a prospective juror from hearing a particular case without having to state a reason or cause.

perfect tender rule In sales law, a rule of law providing that it is a seller's obligation to deliver or tender delivery of goods that are in strict conformance with the terms of the sales contract.

perfection In secured transactions law, the concept whereby a secured party obtains a priority claim on the collateral of his or her debtor as against other interested parties by giving some form of notice of his or her outstanding security interest.

performance Carrying out of an obligation or promise according to the terms agreed to or specified. In contract law, complete performance by both parties discharges the contract.

periodic tenancy The interest created by a lease for an indefinite duration where rent is paid at specified intervals and a prescribed time for giving notice of termination is required.

personal defense In commercial paper, any defense by a party that cannot be asserted against a holder in due course or against a holder through a holder in due course. A personal defense (often referred to as a limited defense) is effective only against ordinary holders.

personal property All property not classified as real property.

per stirpes "By roots or stocks," in descent and distribution of a decedent's estate, where a class of heirs take the share their predeceased ancestor would have taken.

piercing the corporate veil The action of a court in disregarding the separate legal entity (identity) of the corporation, thereby subjecting the owners to possible personal liability.

plain meaning rule The rule under which a court applies a particular statute literally, where it feels the wording of the statute is so clear as to require no interpretation (that is, no resort to outside factors).

plaintiff The party who initiates an action at law and who seeks a specified remedy.

plat A map showing how pieces of real property are subdivided.

pledge In secured transactions law, a transfer of personal property from the debtor to the creditor, as security for a debt owed.

pledgee A person to whom personal property is pledged by a pledgor.

pledgor A person who makes a pledge of personal property to a pledgee.

possibility of reverter A future interest retained by the grantor when he or she conveys real property subject to a condition that upon the occurrence of a designated event the title will automatically be returned to the grantor or his or her heirs.

power of attorney An instrument or document authorizing one person to act as an agent for another (the principal), who is issuing the instrument or document. The agent does not have to be an attorney-at-law.

practical merger A merger by which one corporation acquires another corporation through the purchase of its assets and/or stock (also known as a de facto merger).

precatory Expressive of a wish or desire, as in a devise by a testator of real estate expressing the "hope" that the devisee will pass it on to another named party. Such language may not be legally binding.

precedent A rule of a previously decided case that serves as authority for a decision in a current controversy—the basis of the principle of *stare decisis.*

preemptive right The right of a shareholder to purchase shares of new stock issues of a corporation equal in number to enable the shareholder to maintain his or her proportionate interest in the corporation.

preexisting obligation A legal duty for performance previously contracted or imposed by statute. A later promise to perform an existing contractual obligation or a promise to perform a duty imposed by law is a promise without consideration and therefore unenforceable.

preference The transfer of property or payment of money by a debtor to one or more creditors in a manner that results in favoring those creditors over others. This is an act of bankruptcy, and the trustee can set aside the transfer if the creditors knew or had reason to know that the debtor was insolvent and if the transfer took place within four months of filing the petition in bankruptcy.

preferred stock A class of stock that has a priority or right over common stock as to payment of dividends and/or distribution of corporate assets upon dissolution.

preliminary negotiations In contract law, usually an invitation to a party to make an offer—not the offer itself but only an inquiry.

preponderance of the evidence The degree or weight of evidence sufficient in the eyes of the triers of fact to render a proper verdict.

prescriptive easement An easement acquired without consent of the owner by continuous and open use for a prescribed statutory period.

presentment In commercial paper, the demand by a holder for payment or acceptance of an instrument.

presumption Upon introduction of certain proof, a fact that is assumed even though direct proof is lacking. Presumptions of fact usually are rebuttable while presumptions of law usually are not.

prima facie At first sight (Latin); on the face of it; a fact that will be considered as true unless disproved.

primary party The maker of a note or the acceptor of a draft or check.

principal One who agrees with another (called an agent) that that person will act on his or her behalf.

private corporation A corporation formed by individuals, as compared to one formed by the government.

private law Rules that govern the rights and duties of an individual, association, or corporation to another.

privilege An advantage or right granted by law. Using it as a defense, a person is permitted to perform an act that is not ordinarily permitted to others without liability. In some cases the defense of privilege is absolute, resulting in complete immunity from liability, while in other cases it is qualified, resulting in immunity only if certain factors are proven.

privity of contract Relationship of contract; a relationship that exists between two parties by virtue of their having entered into a contract.

probate The legal procedure by which a deceased person's property is inventoried and appraised, claims against the estate are paid, and remaining property is distributed to the heirs under the will or according to state law if there is no will.

procedural law The rules for carrying on a lawsuit (pleading, evidence, jurisdiction), as opposed to substantive law.

proceeds The money or property received from a sale.

professional corporation Where permitted, the formation of a corporation by persons engaged in a particular profession, such as medicine, law, or architecture.

profit Under real property law, a nonpossessory right to go upon the land of another and take something from it—sometimes referred to as "profit à prendre" (French), particularly when the interest involves the right to take growing crops from another's land.

promise In commercial paper, an undertaking to pay an instrument. The promise must be more than a mere acknowledgment of an obligation, such as an IOU.

promisee The person who has the legal right to demand performance of the promisor's obligation. In a bilateral contract both the offeror and the offeree are promisees. In a unilateral contract only the offeree is the promisee.

promisor The person who obligates himself or herself to do something. In a bilateral contract both offeror and offeree are promisors. In a unilateral contract only the offeror is the promisor.

promissory estoppel A doctrine whereby a promise made by a promisor will be enforced, although not supported by consideration, if such promise would reasonably induce the promisee to rely on that promise and thereby so change his or her position that injustice can be avoided only by enforcement of the promise.

promissory note A note containing the promise of the maker to pay the instrument upon presentment when due.

promoter A person who makes necessary arrangements and/or contracts for the formation of a corporation. Promoters are the planners for the creation of a corporation.

protest A formal certification of an instrument's notice of dishonor, under the seal of an authorized person or a notary public (required only for notice of dishonor of foreign drafts).

proximate cause The foreseeable or direct connection between the breach of duty and an injury resulting from that breach.

proxy Where permitted, an authorization by one person to act for another (used primarily by an individual who wants another to vote in his or her place at a meeting because he or she cannot attend).

public corporation A corporation formed by the government, as compared to one formed by private parties.

public law Rules that deal with either the operation of government or the relationship between a government and its people.

public policy Any conduct, act, or objective that the law recognizes as being in the best interest of society at a given time. Any act or conduct contrary to the recognized standard is illegal, even if there is no statute expressly governing such act or conduct.

punitive damages A monetary sum awarded as a punishment for certain wrongs committed by one person against another. The plaintiff must prove his or her actual out-of-pocket losses directly flowing from the wrong before punitive damages will be awarded. In the past, punitive damages were limited to "triple damages."

purchase-money security interest A security interest taken or retained by a seller to secure all or part of the price of the collateral; also a security interest taken by a secured party who lends money specifically to allow the debtor to acquire the collateral (where the acquisition does subsequently take place).

qualified indorsement An indorsement whereby the indorser does not guarantee payment but does extend warranties to subsequent holders; usually a blank or special indorsement accompanied by the words *without recourse*.

quasi-contract A contract imposed upon the parties by law to prevent unjust enrichment, even though the parties did not intend to enter into a contract (sometimes referred to as an implied-in-law contract).

quasi-judicial The case-hearing function of an administrative agency.

quasi-legislative The rule-making power of an administrative agency.

quitclaim deed A deed by a grantor that passes to the grantee only those rights and interests (if any) the grantor has in the real property. This deed does not purport to convey any particular interest.

quorum The number of qualified persons whose presence is required at a meeting for any action taken at the meeting to be valid. Unless otherwise specified, a majority.

ratification The affirmance of a previous act.

real defenses In commercial paper, certain defenses listed in the UCC that can be asserted against any holder, including a holder in due course (sometimes referred to as universal defenses).

real estate mortgage note A note secured by a parcel or parcels of the maker's real property.

real property Land and most things attached to the land, such as buildings and vegetation.

reasonable definiteness In contract law, the requirement that a contract possess sufficient certainty to enable a court to determine the rights and obligations of the parties (especially to determine whether a breach has occurred).

receiver A person appointed and supervised by the court to temporarily manage a business or other assets for the benefit of creditors or others who ultimately may be entitled to the assets. The business or other property is said to be placed in *receivership*.

recording The filing of a document with a proper public official, which serves as notice to the public of a person's interest.

redemption The exercise of the right to buy back or reclaim property upon the performance of a specified act.

rejection In contract law, a refusal by the offeree of proposal or offer of the offeror, such refusal being known to the offeror.

release The voluntary relinquishing of a right, lien, interest, or any other obligation.

relevant market In antitrust law, the geographic market area and/or product or products of a defendant established by a court or government unit to measure whether an antitrust violation has taken place.

remand To send back a case from an appellate court to the lower court with instructions (usually to hold a new trial).

renunciation In commercial paper, the action of a holder who gives up his or her rights against a party to an instrument by either giving a signed writing or by surrendering the instrument to that party.

replevin A legal remedy that permits recovery of possession of chattels (personal property).

repossession The taking back or regaining of possession of property, usually on the default of a debtor. Repossession can take place peaceably (without breach of the peace) or by judicial process.

requirement contract An enforceable agreement for a supply of goods, the exact amount of which is not set or known at the time of the agreement but which are intended to satisfy the needs of a buyer during the term of the contract; a contract in which the seller agrees to sell and the buyer agrees to buy all (or up to a stated amount) of the goods that the buyer needs.

res In law a thing or things; property (corpus) made subject to a trust.

rescission In contract law, the cancellation of a contract by a court, the effect being as if the contract had never been made.

reserved powers The constitutional rights of states to pass laws under powers that are not specifically delegated to the federal government.

respondeat superior The doctrine under which a master or employer can be held liable for the actions of his or her subordinate.

restraint of trade Any contract, agreement, or combination which eliminates or restricts competition (usually held to be against public policy and therefore illegal).

restrictive indorsement An indorsement that either is conditional or purports to prohibit the further transfer of an instrument, or an indorsement that states a particular purpose to be fulfilled before the restrictive indorser can be held liable on the instrument.

resulting trust A trust created by law, when none was intended, to carry out the intentions of the parties to a transaction where one of the parties is guilty of wrongdoing.

revocation In contract law, the withdrawing of an offer by the offeror.

risk of loss The financial burden for damage or destruction of property.

Robinson-Patman Act A 1936 congressional enactment that substantially amended Section 2 of the Clayton Act, basically making it illegal for a seller in interstate commerce to so discriminate in price that the result would be competitive injury among his or her buyers (with limited exceptions) and prohibiting illegal brokerage fees, allowances, and discounts.

rule-making power The statutory right of an administrative agency to issue rules and regulations governing both the conduct and the activities of those within the agency's

jurisdiction (referred to as an agency's quasi-legislative function).

sale Passage of a title from a seller to a buyer for a price.

sale of control A transfer by sale of a sufficient number of a corporation's shares of stock to allow the purchaser to control the corporation.

sale on approval A bailment of goods coupled with an offer to sell the goods to the bailee.

sale or return A sale of goods with possession and title passing to the buyer but with the buyer given the right, by agreement, to retransfer both possession and title to the seller without liability for doing so.

scope of employment The range of activities of a servant for which the master is liable to third persons. These actions may be expressly directed by the master or incidental to or foreseeable in the performance of employment duties.

secondary party The drawer or indorser of an instrument.

secured party The lender, seller, or other person in whose favor there is a security interest.

Securities Act of 1933 A federal statute establishing requirements for the registration of securities sold in interstate commerce or through the mails (prior to sale). The statute basically requires that pertinent financial information be disclosed to both the Securities and Exchange Commission and to the prospective purchaser. A misleading failure to make such disclosure renders directors, officers, accountants, and underwriters severally and jointly liable.

Securities and Exchange Commission A federal agency given the responsibility to administer and enforce federal securities laws.

Securities Exchange Act of 1934 A federal statute designed to strengthen the Securities Act of 1933 and expand regulation in the securities business. This Act deals with regulation of national stock exchanges and over-the-counter markets. Numerous provisions were enacted to prevent unfair practices in trading of stock, to control bank credit used for speculation, to compel publicity as to the affairs of corporations listed on these exchanges, and to prohibit the use of inside information. This act created the Securities and Exchange Commission (SEC).

security A type of instrument (bond or share of stock) that is issued in a bearer or registered form and that is most often bought, sold, or traded on recognized exchanges or markets. Securities are used in corporate financing by a corporation to acquire capital and by purchasers as investments.

security agreement The contractual arrangement made between a debtor and a secured party.

security interest The right or interest in property held by a secured party to guarantee the payment or performance of an obligation.

separation of powers The result of the U.S. Constitution, which created and balanced the powers of three branches of government (executive, legislative, and judicial) by giving each separate duties and jurisdictions.

servant In employment law, one who performs physical tasks or activities for and under the control of a master (sometimes designated an employee of the master).

servient estate The land that gives up or is subject to an easement.

settlor The party who establishes a trust by transferring property to a trustee to be managed for the benefit of another.

severable In contract law, the portion of a contract that, in the eyes of the law, is capable of possessing an independent legal existence separate from other parts of the same contract. Thus certain obligations of a severable contract may be construed as legally valid even though a clause or part of the contract purporting to create other obligations is declared illegal.

shareholder The owner of one or more shares of capital stock in a corporation.

shareholder agreement A binding agreement made prior to a meeting by a group of shareholders as to the manner in which they will cast their votes on certain issues.

shares of capital stock Instruments in the form of equity securities representing an ownership interest in a corporation.

Sherman Antitrust Act An 1890 congressional enactment that (1) made illegal every contract, combination in the form of trust or otherwise, or conspiracy in restraint of trade or commerce among the several states, and (2) made it illegal for any person to monopolize, or attempt to monopolize, or combine or conspire with any other person or persons to monopolize any part of the trade or commerce among the several states.

shipment contract In sales law, a contract whereby the seller is authorized or required to ship goods to the buyer by delivery to a carrier.

short-swing profits In securities law, any profits made on a sale and purchase or purchase and sale of securities where both took place within a six-month period.

sight draft A draft payable on demand; that is, upon presentment to the drawee.

slander Oral defamation of one's character or reputation.

sole proprietorship A person engaged in business for himself or herself without creating any form of business organization.

special indorsement An indorsement that specifies the person to whom or to whose order the instrument is payable and that requires a proper indorsement of the indorsee for further negotiation.

special warranty deed A deed containing a warranty by the grantor that the title being conveyed has not been impaired by the grantor's own act; in other words, the grantor's liability is limited to his or her own actions.

specific performance A decree issued by a court of equity that compels a person to perform his or her part of the contract where damages are inadequate as a remedy and the subject matter of the contract is unique.

spendthrift trust A provision in a private, express trust to prevent the beneficiary from squandering the principal or income of the trust.

stale check A check outstanding more than six months from its date of issue.

stare decisis Literally "stand by the decision"—a principle by which once a decision has been made by a court, it serves as a precedent or a basis for future decisions of similar cases.

station in life The standard of living that a certain person is accustomed to (used frequently in deciding whether an item contracted for by a minor is a necessity and in determining the amount of alimony awards).

Statute of Frauds The requirement that certain types of contracts be in writing (or that there be written evidence of the existence of the oral contract) in order for the contract to be enforceable in a lawsuit.

statute of limitations A law that sets forth a maximum time period, from the happening of an event, for a legal action to be properly filed in or taken to court. The statute bars the use of the courts for recovery if such action is not filed during the specified time.

statutes of descent and distribution State laws that specify to whom and in what proportions the estate of an intestate decedent will be distributed.

statutory law Enforceable rules enacted by a legislative body.

stock subscription An offer by a prospective investor to buy shares in a corporation.

stop payment order A bank customer's direction (order) to his or her bank to refuse to honor (pay) a check drawn by him or her upon presentment.

strict liability A legal theory under which a person can be held liable for damage or injury even if not at fault or

negligent. Basically, any seller of a defective product that is unreasonably dangerous is liable for any damage or injury caused by the product, provided that the seller is a merchant and the product has not been modified or substantially changed since leaving the seller's possession. This rule applies even if there is no sale of the product and even if the seller exercised due care.

Subchapter S corporation A corporation with only one class of stock held by fifteen or fewer individual stockholders who all agree in writing that the corporation will be taxed in the same manner as a partnership.

sublease The transfer by the lessee (tenant) of a portion of the leasehold to a third party, as compared to an assignment of a lease, where the lessee transfers the entire unexpired term of the leasehold to a third party.

subrogation The substitution of one person in another's place, allowing the party substituted the same rights and claims as the party being substituted.

subsidiary corporation A corporation that is controlled by another corporation (called a parent corporation) through the ownership of a controlling amount of voting stock.

substantial performance The doctrine that a person who performs his or her contract in all major respects and in good faith, with only slight deviation, has adequately performed the contract and can therefore recover the contract price less any damages resulting from the slight deviation.

substantive law. The basic rights and duties of parties as provided for in any field of law, as opposed to procedural law, under which these rights and duties are determined in a lawsuit.

subsurface rights The right of a landowner to use or own minerals, oil, gas, and the like beneath the land's surface.

summary judgment A court's judgment for one party in a lawsuit, before trial, on the ground that there are no disputed issues of fact which would necessitate a trial. The court's conclusion is based upon the motion of that party, the pleadings, affidavits, and depositions of other documentary evidence.

summons A writ by a court that is served on the defendant, notifying that person of the cause of action claimed by the plaintiff and of the requirement to answer.

surety A person or business entity that insures or guarantees the debt of another by becoming legally liable for the debt upon default.

symbolic delivery The delivery of something that represents ownership of or control over an item of property in a case where actual physical delivery of the property itself is not feasible because of its bulk or because it is intangible (often referred to as constructive delivery).

syndicate An association or combination of individual investors formed primarily for a particular financial transaction.

tellers Impartial individuals used to supervise an election (sometimes referred to as judges or inspectors).

tenancy at sufferance The interest held by a tenant who remains on the land beyond the period of his or her rightful tenancy and without permission of the landlord.

tenancy at will The interest created by a lease for an indefinite duration that either party can terminate at any time.

tenancy by the entirety A joint tenancy between husband and wife. In some states neither of the spouses can convey their interest without the consent of the other.

tenancy for years The interest created by a lease for a specific period of time.

tenancy in common A co-ownership of property by two or more parties in which each owns an undivided interest that passes to his or her heirs at death.

tenants in partnership The legal interest of partners in partnership property.

tender An offer by a contracting party to pay money, or deliver goods, or perform any other act required of him or her under the contract.

tender of delivery In sales law, where the seller places or holds conforming goods at the buyer's disposition and gives the buyer notification sufficient to enable that person to take possession of the goods.

tenor In commercial paper, the exact copy of an instrument. If the amount of an instrument has been altered, the holder in due course can recover only the original amount on the instrument, called the original tenor.

termination The ending of an offer, contract, or legal relationship (usually an ending without liability).

testamentary capacity The state of mind of a testator in knowing what property is owned and how he or she wants to dispose of it.

testate The situation in which a person dies leaving a valid will.

testator (female, testatrix) A person who makes a will.

textual content The court's interpretation of the meaning of a given statute, which comes from reading the statute in its entirety rather than a single section or part.

time is of the essence In contract law, a phrase in a contract that requires performance within a specified time as a condition precedent to liability.

title A person's right of ownership in property. The extent of this right is dependent on the type of title held.

title examination The buyer's investigation of a seller's title to real property.

title insurance A policy issued by an insurance company to compensate a buyer of real property for any loss he or she will suffer if the title proves to be defective.

title warranty In sales law, an assurance or guarantee given by the seller, expressly or impliedly, to the buyer that he or she has good title and the right to transfer that title, and that the goods are free from undisclosed security interests.

tort A noncontractual wrong committed by one against another. To be considered a tort, the wrong must be a breach of a legal duty directly resulting in harm.

tortfeasor A person who commits a noncontractual wrong (sometimes referred to as a wrongdoer).

tort of conversion One's unlawful interference with the right of another to possess or use his or her personal property.

trade acceptance A draft or bill of exchange drawn by a seller of goods on the purchaser and obligating the purchaser to pay the instrument upon acceptance.

trade fixture A piece of personal property affixed by a tenant to the real property that is necessary for carrying on the tenant's business.

trademark A distinctive mark, sign, or motto that a business can reserve by law for its exclusive use in identifying itself or its product.

trading partnership A partnership formed primarily for the purpose of buying and selling commodities.

transferee A person to whom a transfer is made.

transferor A person who makes a transfer.

treasury stock Shares of stock that were originally issued by a corporation and that subsequently were reacquired by it.

trespass In realty and personalty, the wrongful invasion of the property rights of another.

trust Two or more companies that have a monopoly. In the law of property, a relationship whereby a settlor transfers legal ownership of property to a trustee to be held and managed for a beneficiary who has equitable title to the property.

trustee A person, natural or artificial, who administers a trust.

trustee in bankruptcy A person elected or appointed to administer the estate of the bankrupt person.

tying contract In antitrust law, a contract by a seller to sell a product to a buyer on condition that the buyer purchase additional products or services.

ultra vires Any acts or actions of a corporation that are held to be unauthorized and beyond the scope of the corporate business as determined by law or by the articles of incorporation.

unconscionable contract A contract or a clause within a contract which is so grossly unfair that a court will refuse to enforce it.

undisclosed principal In agency law, a principal whose identity and existence are unknown by third parties, leading them to believe that the agent is acting solely for himself or herself.

undue influence The overcoming of a person's free will by misusing a position of confidence or relationship, thereby taking advantage of that person to affect his or her decisions or actions.

unenforceable contract Generally a valid contract that cannot be enforced in a court of law because of a special rule of law or a failure to meet an additional legal requirement (such as a writing).

Uniform Commercial Code (UCC) Uniform rules dealing with the sales of goods, commercial paper, secured transactions in personal property, and certain aspects of banking, documents of title, and investment securities. Recommended by the National Conference of Commissioners on Uniform State Laws for enactment by the various states, it has been adopted by forty-nine states (and Louisiana has adopted parts of it).

Uniform Limited Partnership Act (ULPA) Uniform rules governing the organization and operation of limited partnerships recommended by the National Conference of Commissioners on Uniform State Laws for enactment by the various states. All the states except for Delaware and Louisiana have adopted the ULPA.

Uniform Partnership Act (UPA) Uniform rules governing the partnership operation, particularly in the absence of an agreement, recommended by the National Conference of Commissioners on Uniform State Laws for enactment by the various states. All the states except Georgia, Louisiana, and Mississippi have adopted the UPA.

unilateral contract An offer or promise of the offeror which can become binding only by the completed performance of the offeree; an act for a promise, whereby the offeree's act is not only his or her acceptance but also the completed performance under the contract.

unilateral mistake A mistake in which only one party to a contract is in error as to the terms or performance expected under the contract.

universal defenses See *real defenses.*

unliquidated debt A disputed debt; a debt about which there is a reasonable basis for dispute as to its existence or amount.

unqualified indorsement A special or blank indorsement that guarantees payment upon proper presentment, dishonor, and notice of dishonor.

usage of trade Any practice or method repeated with such regularity in a vocation or business that it becomes the legal basis for expected performance in future events within that vocation or business.

usury An interest charge exceeding the maximum amount permitted by statute.

valid contract A contract that meets the four basic requirements for enforceability by the parties to it.

venue A designation of the right of the defendant to be tried in a proper court within a specific geographic area.

vertical merger A merger between a supplier and a customer. If the supplier acquires the customer, it is referred to as a forward vertical merger. If the customer acquires the supplier, it is referred to as a backward vertical merger.

vertical price fixing An illegal agreement, express or implied, where a seller sells a product to a buyer, obligating the buyer to resell the product at a set price (sometimes referred to as resale price maintenance contracts).

vicarious liability The liability of a person, not himself or herself at fault, for the actions of others.

voidable contract A contract from which one or both parties can, if they choose, legally withdraw without liability.

voidable transfer In bankruptcy law, a transfer by a bankrupt debtor that can be set aside by a trustee in bankruptcy.

void contract A contract without legal effect.

voluntary bankruptcy Bankruptcy based upon petition of the debtor.

voting trust A trust whereby shareholders transfer their shares of stock to a trustee for the sole purpose of voting those shares. The shareholders, through trust certificates, retain all other rights as they pertain to the transferred shares.

wagering agreement Any agreement, bet, or lottery arrangement the performance of which is dependent primarily upon chance, such agreement usually being prohibited by statute. These agreements are in contrast to risk-shifting (insurance) contracts and speculative bargaining (commodity market) transactions, which are usually legal by statute.

waiver The voluntary giving up of a legal right.

warehouseman A person engaged in the business of storing the property of others for compensation.

warehouse receipt A document of title issued by a person engaged in the business of storing goods for hire and containing the terms of the storage agreement. A negotiable warehouse receipt acts as both receipt and evidence of title to the goods stored.

warranty An assurance or guaranty, expressly or impliedly made, that certain actions or rights can take place, that information given is correct, or that performance of a product will conform to certain standards.

warranty deed A deed with covenants, express or implied, that the title to real property is good and complete.

warranty of fitness for a particular purpose In sales law, an implied warranty imposed by law on a seller who has reason to know of the buyer's use of the goods (where the buyer relies on the seller's skill and judgment) that the goods are suitable for the buyer's intended use.

warranty of merchantability In sales law, an implied warranty imposed by law upon a merchant seller of goods that the goods are fit for the ordinary purposes for which goods of that kind are used.

watered stock Shares of stock issued by a corporation for a consideration less than the par value or stated value of the stock.

will A document by which a person directs the disposition of his or her property (estate) upon his or her death.

writ of certiorari What the appellant seeks by application to a higher court. An order issued by an appellate court directing a lower court to remit to it the record and proceedings of a particular case so that the actions of the lower court may be reviewed.

Case Index*

---

*Cases appearing in bold face are summarized in the text.

Subject Index

A